THE
INDEPENDENT
BOOK OF
ANNIVERSARIES

THE *INDEPENDENT* BOOK OF ANNIVERSARIES

George Beal

HEADLINE

Copyright © 1992 Newspaper Publishing plc

The right of George Beal to be identified as the author of
the work has been asserted by him in accordance with the
Copyright, Designs and Patents Act 1988

First published in 1992
by HEADLINE BOOK PUBLISHING PLC

10 9 8 7 6 5 4 3 2 1

British Library Cataloguing in Publication Data

Beal, George
"Independent" Book of Anniversaries
I. Title
909

ISBN 0–7472–0684–8

Typeset by Keyboard Services, Luton

Printed and bound in Great Britain by
Clays Ltd, St Ives PLC

HEADLINE BOOK PUBLISHING PLC
Headline House
79 Great Titchfield Street
London W1P 7FN

For Jayne, with love

INTRODUCTION

The contents of this book are based on the information which has, for many years, been published daily in the *Independent*. It is, of necessity, an edited version, to produce a text to fit within the confines of a single book. It follows the style of the column which appears in the newspaper, items being arranged according to each day of the year. However, entries which appear under the daily dates have been indexed, so it is possible to trace these when only names or events are known.

The Independent Book of Anniversaries falls into that category of publications known as 'books of days', of which many have been published during the last two centuries or so.

Probably the best known of these is *The Book of Days*, edited and collated by Robert Chambers, the publisher and author. He described this as 'a miscellany of popular antiquities in connection with the calendar, including anecdotes, biographies, curiosities of literature, and oddities of human life and character'. The two-volume work appeared between the years 1862 and 1864.

The work was not, of course, confined to listing anniversaries and events, but contained much other matter, not entirely connected with the particular day under which it was listed. It was a large undertaking, and Chambers left Edinburgh for London for a time, so that he could concentrate his efforts on the work, and particularly in order to use the resources of the British Museum.

It was not a happy time for him, and his health suffered as a result of his efforts and in working long hours. He said, in fact: 'That book was my death-blow'. He died seven years later at the age of sixty-nine.

Forty years or so before Chambers's *The Book of Days* was published, the author and bookseller William Hone had produced a number of volumes in similar vein. The first of these was *The Every Day Book*, which appeared between 1826 and 1827. It was issued in two volumes, the contents arranged on a daily basis, and he described the work as 'an Everlasting Calendar of Popular Amusements, Sports, Pastimes, Ceremonies, Manners, Customs, and Events, incident to each of the Three Hundred and Sixty-Five Days, in Past and Present Times, forming a complete History of the Year, Months and Seasons, and a perpetual

Key to the Almanack'. Although he did not achieve the success he hoped, the book was well received, and he was acclaimed by Sir Walter Scott, John Wilson, Horace Smith and Robert Southey.

He was encouraged to continue, and in 1827–28 he published two further volumes of similar material under the title *The Table Book*. This was followed in 1828 by *The Year Book*, 'of Daily Recreation and Information, concerning Remarkable Men, Manners, Times, Seasons, Solemnities, &c'.

Charles Lamb went so far as to write verses in the *London Magazine* about Hone and his books: 'I like you and your book, ingenuous Hone'.

Other books of days were *The Clavis Calendaria* (1805), by John Brady, and *Perennial Kalendar and Companion to the Almanack* (1824), by T. Forster.

In more recent times there have been *A Book of Days* (1951), by Sir William Darling, and *The Book of Days* (1979) by Anthony Frewin. Both these works follow a similar plan to that adopted in the present one: a page to each day of the year, listing births, deaths and events.

There have, of course, been a number of books of chronology, the best, and most thorough, being the series of four: *Chronology of the Ancient World* by H. E. L. Mellersh (1976), *Chronology of the Medieval World* (1973), by R. L. Storey, *Chronology of the Expanding World* (1969) by Neville Williams, and *Chronology of the Modern World* (1966) by Neville Williams. These are arranged by years, rather than days, but are all indexed in detail.

I am grateful to all those who have helped in supplying information, particularly on the more obscure dates and subjects, and further information or, indeed, corrections, are always welcome.

Finally, I would like to thank James Fergusson, editor of the 'Gazette' page of the *Independent*, for his support and patience over the years. It was, indeed, he who originally conceived the idea that the *Independent* should publish the material in book form. I would also like to thank the other members of the 'Gazette' page staff, who have been so co-operative, and offer my gratitude to Celia Kent and other staff members at Headline.

GEORGE BEAL

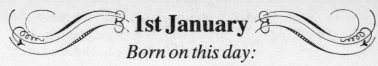

1st January

Born on this day:

Joe Orton [John Kingsley Orton], playwright, 1933;
Zena Marshall, actress, 1927;
Valentina Cortese, Italian film actress, 1924;
J. D. Salinger, US author, 1919;
Colonel Patrick Porteous VC, 1918;
Harold Adrian Russell 'Kim' Philby, former Foreign Office official and defector, 1912;
Dana Andrews, US film actor, 1909;
John Edgar Hoover, director of the FBI, 1895;
Martin Niemöller, anti-Nazi German priest, 1892;
Charles Bickford, US film actor, 1889;
William Fox [Wilhelm Fried], US movie mogul, 1879;
Edward Morgan Forster, novelist, 1879;
Baron Pierre de Coubertin, French educator and sportsman, 1863;
Sir James George Frazer, anthropologist, 1854;
Ouida [Marie Louise de la Ramée], novelist, 1839;
Sándor Petöfi, Hungarian poet, 1823;
Arthur Hugh Clough, poet, 1819;
Francis Egerton, Earl of Ellesmere, statesman and poet, 1800;
Maria Edgeworth, novelist, 1767;
Paul Revere, silversmith and American hero, 1735;
Lorenzo de'Medici ['The Magnificent'], statesman, 1449.

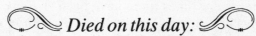

Died on this day:

Lord David Cecil, author, 1986;
Lafayette Ronald Hubbard [L. Ron Hubbard], US science-fiction writer and propounder of Scientology, 1986;
Hephzibah Menuhin, pianist, 1981;
Frank Soskice [Lord Stow Hill], statesman, 1979;
Maurice Chevalier, French entertainer and actor, 1972;
Sir Edwin Landseer Lutyens, architect, 1944;
'Rita' [Mrs Eliza Margaret (Desmond) Humphreys], novelist, 1938;
Jakob Wasserman, German novelist, 1934;
Heinrich Rudolph Hertz, German physicist, 1894;
Johann Christian Bach, German composer, 1782;
James Francis Edward Stuart, the Old Pretender, 1766;
Johann Bernoulli, Swiss mathematician, 1748;
William Wycherley, playwright, 1716;
Pope Innocent X, 1655;
Louis XII, King of France, 1515.

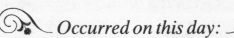

Occurred on this day:

UK fishing limits were extended to 200 miles around the British coast, 1977;
Great Britain, the Irish Republic and Denmark joined the EEC, 1973;
The Foreign and Commonwealth offices were amalgamated to form the Diplomatic Service, 1965;
The European Economic Community came into being, 1958;
The British telephone service passed into the control of the Post Office, 1912;
The Commonwealth of Australia was set up, 1901;
The Manchester Ship Canal opened, 1894;
The electric chair was adopted in New York for capital punishment, 1889;
The first postal orders were issued in Great Britain, 1881;
Queen Victoria was proclaimed Empress of India, 1877;
Britain proclaimed sovereignty over the Falkland Islands, 1833;
The Act of Union between Great Britain and Ireland came into being, 1801;
The first issue of *The Daily Universal Register* [later *The Times*] appeared, 1785.

TODAY IS NEW YEAR'S DAY AND THE FEAST DAY OF St Almachius, St Eugendus or Oyend, St Felix of Bourges, St Fulgentius of Ruspe, St Mochua or Cuan, St Odilo, St Peter of Atroa and St William of Dijon.

# 2nd January

Born on this day:

David Bailey, photographer and film director, 1938;

Christopher Campbell, chairman, British Shipbuilders, 1936;

Roger Miller, US singer and composer, 1936;

Sir Keith Thomas, president, Corpus Christi College, Oxford, 1933;

Sir Charles Reece, former research and technology director, ICI, 1927;

Dame Rachel Waterhouse, former chairman, Consumers' Association, 1922;

The Duke of Devonshire, 1920;

Prof. Isaac Asimov, US biochemist and science-fiction author, 1920;

Lord Nelson of Stafford, former chairman, GEC, 1917;

Edmund de Rothschild, director, N.M. Rothschild and Sons, 1916;

Air Marshal Sir Ernest Sidey, 1913;

Sir Michael Tippett OM, CH, composer, 1905;

Jimmy Nervo [James Holloway], comedian, 1897;

George Gilbert Aimé Murray, classical scholar, 1866;

Karl Wilhelm Dindorf, German classical scholar, 1802;

Philip Morin Freneau, US sailor and 'poet of the Revolution', 1752;

James Wolfe, British general, 1727;

John Manners, Marquis of Granby, military commander, 1721;

Nathaniel Bacon, American colonial leader, 1647.

 ## Died on this day:

Dick Emery, comedian, 1983;

Princess Alice, Countess of Athlone, 1981;

Edna May, actress, 1948;

Eleanor Rathbone, social reformer, 1946;

Sabine Baring-Gould, clergyman and author, 1924;

Léon-Philippe Teisserence de Bort, French meteorologist, 1913;

Sir George Biddell Airy, Astronomer Royal, 1892;

Alexander William Kinglake, author, 1891;

General Tom Thumb [Charles Sherwood Stratton], dwarf, 1883;

Friedrich Wilhelm IV, King of Prussia, 1861;

Fabian Gottlieb Bellingshausen, Russian polar explorer, 1852;

Philip V, King of France, 1322;

Ovid [Publius Ovidius Naso], Roman poet, 17.

 ## Occurred on this day: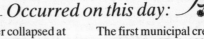

66 people died after a barrier collapsed at Ibrox Park football ground, Glasgow, 1971;

The first rocket to pass near the moon – the unmanned Russian *Luna I* – was launched, 1959;

Cupro-nickel coins were issued in the United Kingdom to replace silver, 1947;

King Zog of Albania, absent from his country, was deposed, 1946;

The present building of the Theatre Royal, Haymarket, London, opened, 1905;

The first municipal crematorium was opened at Hull, 1901;

Wagner's opera *The Flying Dutchman* was first produced, Dresden, 1843;

Louis Daguerre took the first photograph of the moon, 1839;

Georgia became the fourth of the United States, 1788;

The Académie Française was established by Cardinal Richelieu, 1635;

The Spanish army recaptured Granada from the Moors, 1492.

TODAY IS THE FEAST DAY OF St Adalhard or Adelard, St Basil, St Caspar del Bufalo, St Gregory Nazianzen, St Macarius of Alexandria, St Munchin, St Seraphim of Sarov, St Vincentian and the Holy Name of Jesus.

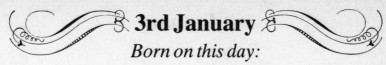

3rd January

Born on this day:

Fran Cotton, former rugby international, 1948;

John Paul Jones, rock musician and producer, 1946;

John Thaw, actor, 1942;

Sir Robin Butler, Secretary of the Cabinet and Head of the Civil Service, 1938;

David Vine, sports commentator, 1936;

Michael Barratt, TV presenter, 1928;

Sir Roy Harding, educationist, 1924;

Maxene Andrews, singer [of the Andrews Sisters], 1918;

Victor Borge, Danish musician and comedian, 1909;

Pamela Frankau, novelist, 1908;

Ray Milland [Reginald Truscott-Jones], film actor, 1907;

John Ronald Reuel Tolkien, academic and novelist, 1892;

James Bridie [Osborne Henry Mavor], playwright and physician, 1888;

Herbert Stanley Morrison, Baron Morrison of Lambeth, statesman, 1888;

Clement Richard Attlee, 1st Earl, statesman, 1883;

Henry Handel Richardson [Ethel Florence Richardson], novelist, 1870;

Father Damien [Joseph de Veuster], missionary, 1840;

Douglas William Jerrold, playwright and humorist, 1803;

Pietro Antonio Metastasio, Italian poet, 1698;

Marcus Tullius Cicero, Roman orator and statesman, 106 BC.

Died on this day:

Conrad Nicholson Hilton, US hotel magnate, 1979;

Dick Powell [Richard Ewing Powell], US film actor and singer, 1963;

William Joyce ['Lord Haw-Haw'], British traitor, executed, 1946;

Marshal Joseph-Jacques-Césaire Joffre, French soldier, 1931;

Jaroslav Hašek, Czech novelist, 1923;

James Elroy Flecker, poet, 1915;

William Harrison Ainsworth, novelist, 1882;

Pierre-Athanase Larousse, French editor and encyclopaedist, 1875;

Rachel [Élisa Félix], French actress, 1858;

Josiah Wedgwood, potter, 1795;

Beatrice d'Este, Duchess of Milan, Italian diplomat and arts patron, 1497.

Occurred on this day:

Alaska became the 49th of the United States, 1959;

The Federation of the West Indies was formed, 1958;

Sir Edmund Hillary reached the South Pole, 1958;

General Theodoros Pangalos was declared dictator of Greece, 1926;

Howard Carter discovered the sarcophagus in the tomb of Tutankhamun, 1924;

The price of bread in London was raised to 9d [old pence] for a 4lb loaf, 1916;

The Siege of Sidney Street took place, when anarchists led by 'Peter the Painter' were besieged by the police in the East End of London, 1911;

Wilhelm II, King of Germany, sent a congratulatory telegram to Paul Kruger on suppressing the Jameson Raid, 1896;

Marshal Francisco Serrano became dictator of Spain, 1874;

Work on the Brooklyn bridge began, 1870;

George Washington defeated the British army at the Battle of Princeton, 1777.

TODAY IS THE FEAST DAY OF St Antherus, pope, St Bertilia of Mareuil, St Genevieve or Genovefa and St Peter Balsam.

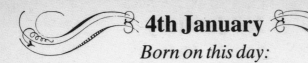

4th January

Born on this day:

Mick Mills, footballer, 1949;

Margaret Marshall, concert singer, 1949;

John McLaughlin, blues and jazz guitarist, 1943;

Prof. Brian Josephson, physicist, 1940;

Dyan Cannon, US actress, 1939;

Grace Bumbry, US opera and concert singer, 1937;

Floyd Patterson, US boxing champion, 1935;

Iain Cuthbertson, actor, 1930;

Barbara Rush, US film actress, 1930;

Rosalie Crutchley, actress, 1922;

Jane Wyman, US film actress, 1914;

William Bendix, US film actor, 1906;

Sterling Holloway, US film actor and comedian, 1905;

Augustus Edwin John, painter, 1878;

Alfred Edgar Coppard, poet and short-story writer, 1878;

Sir Isaac Pitman, publisher and inventor of Pitman's shorthand, 1813;

Louis Braille, French deviser of an alphabet for the blind, 1809;

Henry George Bohn, publisher and bookseller, 1796;

Jakob Ludwig Karl Grimm, philologist and folklorist, 1785;

Giovanni Battista Pergolesi, Italian composer, 1710.

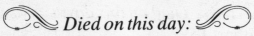

Died on this day:

Christopher William Bradshaw Isherwood, novelist and playwright, 1986;

Lieut.-Gen. Sir Brian Gwynne Horrocks, military strategist and historian, 1985;

Joy Friederike Victoria Adamson, naturalist and writer, 1980;

Donald Malcolm Campbell, land and water speedster, killed, 1967;

Thomas Stearns Eliot OM, poet and critic, 1965;

Albert Camus, French novelist and playwright, killed, 1960;

Ralph Vaughan Williams, composer, 1958;

Henri Bergson, French philosopher, 1941;

Benito Pérez Galdós, Spanish author and poet, 1920;

Charles Samuel Keene, humorous artist and illustrator, 1891;

Charlotte Lennox [née Ramsay], novelist and poet, 1804.

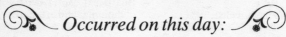

Occurred on this day:

Rose Heilbron became the first woman to sit as a judge at the Old Bailey, London, 1972;

Pope Paul VI began a tour of the Holy Land, 1964;

Burma became an independent republic, 1948;

The British Fifth Army in Italy attacked Monte Cassino, 1944;

The French liner *Atlantique* caught fire off Cherbourg, and 18 members of the crew lost their lives, 1933;

Utah became the 45th of the United States, 1896;

The first appendicitis operation was performed, 1885;

The Fabian Society was founded, 1884;

Donizetti's opera *Don Pasquale* was first performed, Paris, 1843;

Columbus sailed from America back to Spain in the *Niña*, 1493.

TODAY IS THE FEAST DAY OF St Elizabeth Bayley Seton, St Gregory of Langres, St Pharaïldis, St Rigobert of Reims and St Roger of Ellant.

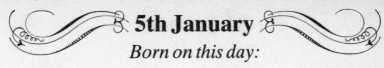

5th January

Born on this day:

Diane Keaton, US film actress, 1946;
Ferreira da Silva Eusebio, Portuguese footballer, 1943;
Mansur Ali Khan, Nawab of Pataudi, former Indian cricketer, 1941;
Juan Carlos, King of Spain, 1938;
Robert Duvall, US film actor, 1931;
Alfred Brendel, Austrian concert pianist, 1931;
Robin Leigh-Pemberton, governor of the Bank of England, 1927;
Jean, Grand Duke of Luxembourg, 1921;
Jean-Pierre Aumont, French film actor, 1911;

Stella Dorothea Gibbons [Mrs Allan Bourne Webb], poet and novelist, 1902;
Clifford Grey, actor, author and lyricist, 1887;
Humbert Wolfe, poet, 1885;
Konrad Adenauer, German statesman, 1876;
King Camp Gillette, US safety-razor inventor, 1855;
John Burke, Irish genealogist, founder of *Burke's Peerage*, 1787;
Jean-Baptiste Say, French political economist, 1767;
Dr Benjamin Rush, US politician, 1745.

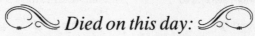

Died on this day:

George Washington Carver, US scientist, 1943;
Amy Johnson [Mollison], aviator, 1941;
Humbert Wolfe, poet, 1940;
John Calvin Coolidge, 30th president of the USA, 1933;
Sir Ernest Henry Shackleton, explorer, 1922;
Anton Mauve, Dutch landscape painter, 1888;

Joseph Gillott, steel pen manufacturer, 1873;
Johann Josef Wenzel, Count Radetzky, Austrian soldier, 1858;
Elizabeth Petrovna Empress of Russia, 1762;
Catherine de'Medici, Queen of France, 1589;
Giambattista Moroni, Italian portrait painter, 1578;
St Edward the Confessor, 1066.

Occurred on this day:

Pope Paul VI and Patriarch Athenagoras I met in Jerusalem, the first meeting of leaders of the RC and Orthodox Churches for over 500 years, 1964;
FM radio was first demonstrated in the USA by Major Edwin H. Armstrong, 1940;
King Alexander of Yugoslavia established himself as a dictator, 1929;
The first US woman governor, Mrs Nellie Tayloe Ross, was elected, 1925;
The National Socialist Party was formed in Munich by Anton Drexler, 1919;

The Kingdom of Serbs, Croats and Slovenes [Yugoslavia] was established, 1919;
The first demonstration of X-rays was given by Röntgen, 1896;
Gilbert and Sullivan's opera *Princess Ida* was first performed, London, 1884;
An attempt was made on the life of Louis XV of France by Robert-François Damiens, 1757;
Charles the Bold, King of France, was killed by the Swiss at the Battle of Nancy, 1477.

TODAY IS WASSAIL EVE AND THE FEAST DAY OF St Apollinaris, St Convoyon, St Dorotheus the Younger, St Gerlac, St John Nepomucene Neumann, St Simeon Stylites and St Syncletica.

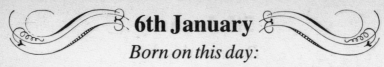

6th January

Born on this day:

Kapil Dev, Indian cricketer, 1959;
Nancy Lopez-Melton, US golfer, 1957;
Rowan Atkinson, actor and comedian, 1955;
Barry John, former Welsh rugby international, 1945;
Terry Venables, football manager, 1944;
Sylvia Syms, actress, 1934;
Sacha Distel, French singer, 1932;
P.J. Kavanagh, poet and novelist, 1931;
Loretta Young, US film actress, 1913;
Khalil Gibran, Syrian/US writer, 1883;
Tom Mix [Thomas Edwin Mix], US Western film actor, 1880;
Carl Sandburg, US poet, 1878;
Fred Niblo [Federico Nobile], US film director, 1874;
Alexander Nikolaievich Scriabin, Russian composer, 1872;
Max Karl August Bruch, German composer, 1838;
Gustave-Paul Doré, illustrator and engraver, 1833;
Heinrich Schliemann, German archaeologist, 1822;
Jacques-Étienne Montgolfier, French balloonist, 1745;
Giuseppe Sammartini, Italian composer, 1695;
St Joan of Arc, 'Maid of Orléans', 1412;
King Richard II, 1367.

Died on this day:

Archibald Joseph Cronin, novelist, 1981;
Victor Fleming, US film director, 1949;
André-René-Louis Maginot, French politician, 1932;
Theodore Roosevelt, 26th president of the USA, 1919;
Philip Danforth Armour, US food manufacturer, 1901;
Gregor Johann Mendel, Austrian monk and geneticist, 1884;
Richard Henry Dana, US novelist and lawyer, 1882;
Louis Braille, French deviser of an alphabet for the blind, 1852;
Fanny [Frances] Wright, Scottish/US social reformer, 1852;
Hartley Coleridge, author and poet, 1849;
Fanny Burney [Madame d'Arblay], novelist and diarist, 1840;
Rodolphe Kreutzer, French violinist and composer, 1831;
Jean-Étienne Guettard, French naturalist and geologist, 1786;
Seth Ward, bishop, mathematician and astronomer, 1689;
Baldassare Peruzzi, Italian architect and painter, 1536.

Occurred on this day:

Britain recognised the Communist regime in China, 1950;
The Battle of the Bulge ended, 1945;
The new Sadler's Wells Theatre opened in London, 1931;
The first opera [*The Magic Flute*] was broadcast in Britain, 1923;
The Allies began to evacuate Gallipoli, 1916;
New Mexico became the 47th of the United States, 1912;
Samuel Morse gave the first public demonstration of his electric telegraph, 1838;
King Henry VIII was married to Anne of Cleves, 'the Flanders Mare', 1540;
Harold was crowned King of England in succession to Edward the Confessor, 1066;
King Alfred defeated the Danes at the Battle of Ashdown, 871.

TODAY IS EPIPHANY, AND THE FEAST DAY OF St Erminold, St Guarinus or Guerin of Sion, St John de Ribera, St Raphaela Porras and St Wiltrudis.

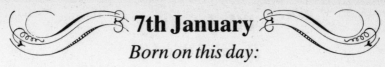

7th January

Born on this day:

Helen Worth, TV actress, 1951;
Tom Kiernan, rugby player, 1939;
Ian La Frenais, screenwriter and producer, 1937;
Hunter Davies, author and broadcaster, 1937;
The Viscount of Oxfuird, 1934;
Gerald Durrell, author and naturalist, 1925;
Geoffrey Bayldon, actor, 1924;
Air Comdre. the Hon. Sir Peter Vanneck, former MEP, 1922;
Prof. Keble Sykes, Emeritus professor of physical chemistry, Queen Mary's College, London, 1921;
Sir Alastair Pilkington, president of Pilkington plc, 1920;
Lord Taylor of Hadfield, founder of the Taylor Woodrow Group, 1905;
Francis-Jean-Marcel Poulenc, French composer, 1899;
Albert Alick [Al] Bowlly, singer, 1899;
Charles-Pierre Péguy, French poet and socialist, 1873;
Adolph Zukor, US film magnate, 1873;
Carl Laemmle, US film producer, founder of Universal Pictures, 1867;
St Bernadette of Lourdes [Marie-Bernarde Soubirous], 1844;
Heinrich von Stephan, German politician and pioneer of the UPU, 1831;
Millard Fillmore, 13th president of the USA, 1800;
Joseph Bonaparte, King of Naples, 1768;
James Harrington, political theorist, 1611;
Pope Gregory XIII, 1502.

Died on this day:

Trevor Wallace Howard, actor, 1988;
Dr Alfred Kastler, physicist, 1984;
Alvar Lidell, broadcaster, 1981;
Nikola Tesla, Croatian/US inventor, 1943;
Andrei Bely [Boris Nikolayevich Bugaev], Russian novelist and poet, 1934;
Henry Arthur Jones, playwright, 1929;
Sophia Louisa Jex-Blake, physician and women's rights champion, 1912;
John Hookham Frere, author and poet, 1846;
Sir Thomas Lawrence, painter, 1830;
Allan Ramsay, Scottish poet, 1758;
François de Salignac de La Mothe Fénelon, French priest and author, 1715;
Nicholas Hillyarde, first English miniaturist painter, 1619;
Catherine of Aragon, first wife of Henry VIII, 1536.

Occurred on this day:

The Forsyte Saga television serialisation began on BBC1, 1967;
Princess Juliana of the Netherlands married Prince Bernhard at The Hague, 1937;
A picture-by-wire service was established between Britain and Germany, 1930;
The first woman was elected as foreman of a jury in Britain, 1921;
The London General Omnibus Company started operating, 1857;
The first national election in the USA was held, 1789;
Jean-Pierre Blanchard, with Dr John Jeffries, crossed the Channel by balloon from England to France, 1785;
Galileo discovered the four satellites of Jupiter, 1610;
Calais, held by the British, was recaptured by France, 1558;
The University of Glasgow was founded, 1450.

TODAY IS CHRISTMAS DAY IN THE ORTHODOX CHURCH AND THE FEAST DAY OF St Aldric, St Canute Lavard, St Lucian of Antioch, St Raymund of Peñafort, St Reinold, St Tillo and St Valentine.

7

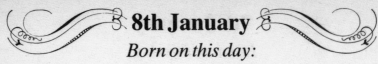

8th January

Born on this day:

David Bowie, rock singer and actor, 1947;

Prof. Stephen Hawking, mathematician, 1942;

Shirley Bassey, singer, 1937;

Elvis Presley, US rock singer, 1935;

Prof. Charles Tomlinson, professor of English, University of Bristol, 1927;

Ron Moody, actor, 1924;

Prof. Brian Reddaway, economic consultant to the World Bank, 1913;

José Vicente Ferrer Otero y Cintron [José Ferrer], US actor, 1912;

Galina Ulanova, Russian former prima ballerina, 1910;

Solomon West Ridgeway Dias Bandaranaike, Sri Lankan prime minister, 1899;

Dennis Yates Wheatley, novelist, 1897;

Jaromir Weinberger, US/Czech composer, 1896;

John Joseph Curtin, Australian prime minister, 1885;

Viscount Craigavon [James Craig], Ulster statesman, 1871;

Frank Nelson Doubleday, US publisher and editor, 1862;

Hans Guido von Bülow, German pianist and conductor, 1830;

William Wilkie Collins, novelist, 1824;

Alfred Russel Wallace, naturalist, 1823.

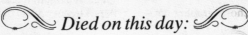

Died on this day:

Georgi Maksimilianovich Malenkov, former Soviet leader, 1988;

André-François Poncet, French politician, 1978;

Zhou Enlai, Chinese leader, 1976;

Richard Tauber [Ernst Seiffert (Denemy)], tenor, 1948;

Robert Stephenson Smyth Baden-Powell, 1st Baron, founder of the Boy Scouts, 1941;

Paul Verlaine, French poet, 1895;

Eli Whitney, US inventor and perfector of the cotton gin, 1825;

Jean-Marie Collot d'Herbois, French revolutionary, 1796;

John Baskerville, printer and typographer, 1775;

Arcangelo Corelli, Italian composer and violinist, 1713;

Sir John Dalrymple, 1st Earl of Stair, politician and lawyer, 1707;

Galileo Galilei, Italian astronomer, 1642;

Ambroglio Giotto di Bondone, Italian painter, 1337;

Pope Celestine III, 1198.

Occurred on this day:

Pan American World Airways filed for bankruptcy in the United States, 1991;

The first London production of the musical show *Company* took place, 1972;

In Uruguay, the British ambassador, Geoffrey Jackson, was kidnapped by guerillas, 1971;

In New York, seven floors of the Empire State Building caught fire, 1963;

General Charles de Gaulle became President of the French Fifth Republic, 1959;

Sugar, bacon and butter were rationed in Britain, 1940;

Ibn Saud became King of the Hejaz, a name which he changed to Saudi Arabia, 1926;

Chequers Court was occupied by its first prime minister tenant, David Lloyd George, 1921;

The British evacuated Gallipoli, 1916;

The Severn Railway Tunnel was opened, 1886;

The Americans defeated the British at the Battle of New Orleans, 1815;

Britain occupied the Cape of Good Hope, 1806;

The French explorer La Salle reached Niagara Falls, 1679.

TODAY IS THE FEAST DAY OF St Severinus of Noricum, St Severinus of Septempeda and St Wulsin.

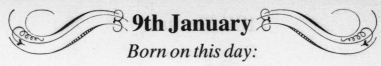

9th January

Born on this day:

Graham Fletcher, show jumper, 1951;
Susannah York, actress, 1942;
Joan Baez, US singer, 1941;
Terry Hands, chief executive, Royal Shakespeare Company, 1942;
Geoffrey Wragg, racehorse trainer, 1931;
David Holbrook, author, 1923;
Clive Dunn, actor and comedian, 1922;
Herbert Lom, actor, 1917;
Gypsy Rose Lee [Rose Louise Hovick], US actress and strip-tease artist, 1914;
Richard Nixon, 37th US president, 1913;
Gilbert Abbot à Beckett, humorous writer, 1811;
Simone de Beauvoir, French novelist and critic, 1908;
George Balanchine, choreographer, 1904;

Sir Rudolf Bing, founder of the Edinburgh Festival, 1902;
Dame Gracie Fields [Grace Stansfield], singer and actress, 1898;
Dr Karel Čapek, Czech playwright, 1890;
Charles Kortright, cricketer, 1871;
Carrie Chapman Catt [Lane], US suffragette, 1859;
Lady Randolph Churchill, wife of Lord Randolph Churchill, 1854;
William Powell Frith, painter, 1819;
John Jervis, Earl of St Vincent, admiral, 1735;
Simon Vouet, French painter, 1590;
Georg Draud [Draudius], German pastor and bibliographer, 1573;
Pope Gregory XV, 1554.

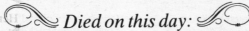

Died on this day:

Sir Robert Mayer, musical philanthropist, 1985;
Sir Frederick Gibberd, architect, 1984;
Pierre Fresnay [Pierre Laudenbach], French actor, 1975;
Waldo David Frank, US novelist, 1967;
Karl Mannheim, German sociologist, 1947;
Katherine Mansfield [Beauchamp] [Kathleen Middleton Murry], author, 1923;

Wilhelm Busch, German cartoonist, 1908;
Napoleon III [Louis-Napoleon], French emperor, in exile, 1873;
Caroline Lucretia Herschel, astronomer, 1848;
Bernard Le Bovier, Sieur de Fontenelle, French writer and philosopher, 1757.

Occurred on this day:

Swan and Edgar, the Piccadilly department store, closed permanently, 1982;
In Hong Kong harbour, the liner *Queen Elizabeth* was destroyed by fire, 1972;
The first trial flight of Concorde took place, Bristol, 1969;
The De Havilland Trident aircraft made its maiden flight, 1962;
Anthony Eden resigned as prime minister, 1957;
After the Union Castle liner *Dunbar Castle* hit a mine, 152 people died, 1940;
Hitler re-opened the Reichstage, 1939;
The last of Admiral Koltchak's White Russian troops surrendered to the Bolsheviks, 1920;

Edith Thompson and Frederick Bywaters were hanged for murder, 1923;
On the death of Victor Emmanuel, Umberto I became King of Italy, 1878;
Sir Humphry Davy's safety lamp was first used in a coal mine, 1816;
Income tax was introduced by the Younger Pitt, the rate being two shillings in the pound, 1799;
Jean-Pierre Blanchard, French aeronaut, made the first balloon ascent in America, near Woodbury, New Jersey, 1793.

TODAY IS THE FEAST DAY OF St Berhtwald of Canterbury, Saints Julian and Basilissa, St Marciana of Rusuccur, St Peter of Sebastea and St Waningus or Vaneng.

10th January

Born on this day:

Rod Stewart, rock singer, 1945;
Freddie Starr, comedian, 1944;
Anton Rodgers, actor, 1933;
Dr Peter Mathias, Master of Downing
  College, Cambridge, 1928;
Derek Hammond-Stroud, baritone, 1926;
Dorothy Malone, US film actress, 1925;
Terence Kilmartin, author, 1923;
Sidney Griller, leader of the Griller String
  Quartet, 1911;
Paul Henreid [Paul George Julius von
  Hernreid], actor, 1908;
Dame Barbara Hepworth, sculptor, 1903;

John Robinson Jeffers, US poet, 1887;
Francis Xavier Bushman, US film actor,
  1883;
Alexei Nikolayevich Tolstoy, Russian
  novelist and playwright, 1883;
Grock [Adrien Wettach], Swiss-born
  international clown, 1880;
John Emerich Edward Dalberg, 1st Baron
  Acton, historian, 1834;
Dr George Birkbeck, educationist,
  1776;
Michel Ney, marshal of France, 1769;
Niels Stensen, Danish anatomist, 1638.

Died on this day:

Anton Karas, Austrian composer and
  zither-player, 1985;
Binnie Hale [Beatrice Mary Hale-Monro],
  musical comedy actress, 1984;
Chester Burnett ['Howling Wolf'], US
  blues singer, 1976;
Nubar Sarkis Gulbenkian, millionaire,
  1972;
Gabrielle [Coco] Chanel, 1971;
Samuel Dashiell Hammett, US detective-
  story writer, 1961;
Harry Sinclair Lewis, US novelist, 1951;
Harry Von Tilzer, US songwriter, 1946;
Gabriela Mistral, Chilean poet, 1945;

Frank Bridge, composer, 1941;
Sir John Lavery, painter, 1941;
William Frederick Cody ['Buffalo Bill'],
  1917;
Samuel Colt, US gunsmith, 1862;
Mary Russell Mitford, author, 1855;
Adrien-Marie Legendre, French
  mathematician, 1833;
Edward Cave, printer, 1778;
Carolus Linnaeus, Swedish botanist,
  1778;
William Laud, Archbishop of Canterbury,
  beheaded, 1645;
Pope Gregory X, 1276.

Occurred on this day:

In Zaïre, the Niragong volcano erupted,
  causing over 2,000 deaths, 1977;
The New London Theatre, Drury Lane,
  opened, 1973;
The European Coal and Steel Community
  met for the first time, 1953;
The first assembly of the United Nations
  was held in London, 1946;
HMS *Southampton* and HMS
  Illustrious, while on convoy, were
  crippled by German dive bombers, 1941;
The cartoon character 'Tintin' appeared for
  the first time, 1929;
The film *Metropolis*, by Fritz Lang, was
  first shown, Berlin, 1926;

Memel, under Allied occupation, was
  seized by Lithuania, 1923;
Juan de la Cierva demonstrated the first
  autogiro, Spain, 1923;
The League of Nations was inaugurated,
  1920;
The tomb of Cleopatra was discovered,
  1890;
The London Underground [Metropolitan
  Railway] system was started, 1863;
The penny post was begun, when
  112,000 letters were posted in London,
  1840;
The Royal Exchange, designed by Sir
  Christopher Wren, burned down, 1838.

TODAY IS THE FEAST DAY OF St Agatho, pope, St Dermot or Diarmaid, St John the
Good, St Marcian of Constantinople, St Peter Orseolo and St William of Bourges.

11th January

Born on this day:

John Sessions, actor and comedian, 1953;
Anna Calder-Marshall, actress, 1947;
Bryan Robson, former England football captain, 1947;
David Cecil, racehorse breeder, 1944;
Henry Cecil, racehorse trainer, 1944;
Barry Flanagan, sculptor, 1942;
Arthur Scargill, president of the National Union of Mineworkers, 1938;
Ann Firbank, actress, 1934;
Rod Taylor, Australian film actor, 1929;
Kathleen Byron, actress, 1923;
Neville Duke, test pilot, 1922;
Pierre Mendès-France, French politician, 1907;
Manfred Bennington Lee [Lepovsky], author, of the 'Ellery Queen' partnership, 1905;

Maurice Duruflé, French organist and composer, 1902;
Henry Gordon Selfridge, founder of the London store, 1864;
George Nathaniel Curzon, 1st Marquess Curzon of Kedleston, Viceroy of India, 1859;
Fred Archer, jockey, 1857;
Ezra Cornell, founder of Cornell University, New York, 1807;
Alexander Hamilton, US statesman, 1755;
Adam Frans van der Meulen, Flemish painter, 1632;
Parmigianino [Girolamo Francesco Maria Mazzola], Italian painter, 1503.

Died on this day:

Barbara Mary Pym, novelist, 1980;
Padraic Colum, poet and founder of the Irish National Theatre, 1972;
Richmal Crompton [Lamburn], author and creator of 'William', 1969;
Alberto Giacometti, Swiss sculptor and painter, 1966;
Oscar Straus, Austrian composer, 1954;
Jean-Marie-Gabriel de Lattre de Tassigny, French general, 1952;
Caradoc Evans, novelist, 1945;
Galeazzo Ciano, conte di Cortellazzo, Italian diplomat, shot by pro-Mussolini partisans, 1944;

Thomas Hardy, poet and novelist, 1928;
Baron Georges-Eugène Haussmann, rebuilder of Paris, 1891;
Francis Scott Key, US attorney and poet, author of *The Star-Spangled Banner*, 1843;
Domenico Cimarosa, Italian composer, 1801;
Louis-François Roubillac [Roubiliac], French sculptor, 1762;
Sir Hans Sloane, physician and naturalist, 1753;
Domenico [de Tommaso Bigordi] Ghirlandaio, Florentine painter, 1494.

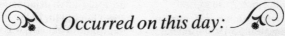

Occurred on this day:

The Open University awarded its first degrees, 1973;
After a landslide down Huascaran, Peru, 3,000 people were killed, 1962;
The Ruhr was occupied by French and Belgian troops, following the failure of Germany to pay reparations, 1923;
The first women jurors were sworn in at the Old Bailey, 1921;
The Representation of the People Bill was passed, giving votes to women, 1918;

Major Esterhazy, on trial for forgery in the Dreyfus case, was acquitted, 1898;
Charing Cross station, London, was formally opened, 1864;
Benito Juárez returned to Mexico City, 1861;
Joachim Murat deserted Napoleon and joined the Allies, 1814;
Matthew Flinders and George Bass returned to Port Jackson, having proved that Tasmania was an island, 1799;
The Dutch surrendered Trincomalee, Ceylon, to the British, 1782.

TODAY IS THE FEAST DAY OF St Salvius or Sauve of Amiens and St Theodosius the Cenobiarch.

12th January

Born on this day:

Anthony Andrews, actor, 1948;

Brendan Foster, former Olympic athlete, 1948;

Joe Frazier, heavyweight boxer, 1944;

Anne Howells, opera and concert singer, 1941;

Michael Aspel, TV presenter, 1933;

Des O'Connor, comedian and singer, 1932;

Pieter Willem Botha, former president of South Africa, 1916;

Luise Rainer, film actress, 1910;

Tex Ritter [Woodward Maurice Ritter], US film star of Westerns, 1907;

Paul Müller, Swiss chemist, producer of DDT, 1899;

Hermann Goering, German Nazi leader, 1893;

Ferenc Molnár, Hungarian playwright, 1878;

John Griffith [Jack] London, novelist, 1876;

Joseph-Jacques-Césaire Joffre, French marshal, 1852;

Johann Heinrich Pestalozzi, Swiss educational reformer, 1746;

Edmund Burke, statesman, 1729;

Lazzaro Spallanzani, Italian physiologist and chemist, 1729;

José Ribera ['Lo Spagnoletto'], Spanish painter, 1588;

Jean Baptiste van Helmont, chemist, 1580.

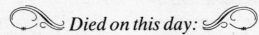

Died on this day:

Dame Agatha Mary Clarissa Christie, detective-story writer, 1976;

Nevil Shute [Norway], novelist, 1960;

Jean-Léon Gérôme, French painter, 1904;

Sir Isaac Pitman, printer and publisher, 1897;

Stafford Henry Northcote, 1st Earl of Iddesleigh, 1887;

John Singer Sargent, US portrait painter, 1856;

George William Frederick Villiers, 4th Earl of Clarendon, 1800;

Johann Georg Adam Forster, German explorer and scientist, 1794;

Pierre de Fermat, French mathematician, 1665;

Jan Brueghel the Elder, Flemish painter, 1625;

Fernando Alvarez de Toledo, 3rd Duke of Alba, Spanish military commander, 1582;

Lorenzo di Credi, Italian painter, 1537;

Maximilian I, Holy Roman Emperor, 1519.

 ## Occurred on this day:

After the Biafran army surrendered, the civil war in Nigeria ended, 1970;

The Boeing 747 touched down at Heathrow after its first transatlantic flight from New York, 1970;

Following a rebellion in Zanzibar, the Sultan was banished and a republic declared, 1964;

More than 200 people were killed during an avalanche in Austria, 1954;

The New Zealand parliament was opened by Queen Elizabeth II, 1954;

In the General Election, there was a Liberal landslide, 1906;

The Zulu War began, 1879;

The Royal Aeronautical Society was founded, 1866;

Protestants in Switzerland introduced the Gregorian calendar, 1701.

TODAY IS THE FEAST DAY OF St Arcadius, St Benedict or Benet Biscop, St Caesaria, St Eutropius, St Margaret Bourgeoys, St Tatiana and St Victorian.

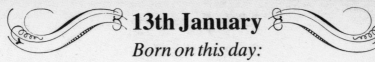

13th January

Born on this day:

Stephen Hendry, snooker player, 1969;
Tim Flavin, actor, dancer and singer, 1959;
Dr Sydney Brenner CH, biologist, 1927;
Craigie Aitchison, painter, 1926;
Michael Bond, creator of 'Paddington Bear', 1926;
Albert Lamorisse, French film director, 1922;
Robert Stack, US film actor, 1919;
Lord Willis, playwright, 1918;
Sir Johannes Bjelke-Petersen, former prime minister of Queensland, 1911;
Oliver Hilary Samborne Messel, designer, 1905;
Louis de Rochemont, US film producer and director, 1899;
Prince Arthur Frederick Patrick, Duke of Connaught, 1883;
Horatio Alger, US clergyman and author of boys' books, 1834;
Jacques-Alfred-Félix Clément, French musicologist, 1822;
Charles Perrault, French collector and publisher of fairy tales, 1628;
Jan Josephzoon van Goyen, Dutch landscape painter, 1596.

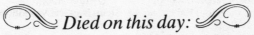

Died on this day:

Hubert Horatio Humphrey, vice-president of the USA, 1978;
Robert Still, composer, 1971;
Alfred Edgar Coppard, writer, 1957;
James Joyce, Irish novelist, 1941;
Sebastian Ziani de Ferranti, electrical engineer, 1930;
William Frend De Morgan, artist and author, 1917;
Louis-Pierre Baltard, French architect and engineer, 1874;
Stephen Collins Foster, US songwriter, 1864;
Maria Sibylla [Graff] Merian, painter and engraver, 1717;
George Fox, founder of the Society of Friends, 1691.

Occurred on this day:

The world's largest airport was opened in Dallas, Texas, USA, 1974;
Britain appointed her first ambassador to communist China, 1972;
A plebiscite in the Saar voted for incorporation into Germany, 1935;
A 388-carat diamond was found in a mine at Kimberley, South Africa, 1919;
Sir Satyendra Prassano Sinha was the first Indian to become a peer, 1919;
29,000 people died after a massive earthquake in Central Italy, 1915;
Lee De Forest broadcast an opera from the stage of the Metropolitan, New York, 1910;
Following the acquittal of Major Esterhazy, Émile Zola published his open letter *J'accuse* to the French president, 1898;
The Independent Labour Party was formed under Keir Hardie, 1893;
The Vaudeville Theatre, London, second building, opened, 1891;
The Hudson's Bay Company acquired Vancouver Island, British Columbia, 1848;
William Lyon Mackenzie, Canadian rebel, was arrested in the USA, 1838.

TODAY IS THE FEAST DAY OF St Agrecius, St Berno and St Hilary of Poitiers.

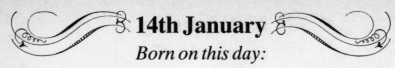

14th January

Born on this day:

Bill Werberniuk, Canadian snooker player, 1947;

Maina Gielgud, ballerina, 1945;

Faye Dunaway, US actress, 1941;

Trevor Nunn, theatre director, 1940;

Jack Jones, US singer, 1938;

The Earl of Drogheda, 1937;

Richard Briers, actor, 1934;

Caterina Valente, French/Italian guitarist and singer, 1932;

Peter Barkworth, actor, 1929;

Prof. Sir Hans Kornberg, Master of Christ's College, Cambridge, 1928;

Warren Mitchell, actor, 1926;

Joseph Losey, US film director, 1909;

Sir Cecil Walter Hardy Beaton, photographer and stage designer, 1904;

John Roderigo Dos Passos, US novelist, 1896;

Hal Roach, US film producer and director, 1892;

Hugh Lofting, author, 1886;

Dr Albert Schweitzer, French missionary surgeon, 1875;

Pierre Loti [Louis-Marie-Julien-Viaud], French novelist, 1850;

Jean de Reszke [Jan Mieczyslaw], Polish tenor, 1850;

Ignace-Henri-Jean-Théodore Fantin-Latour, French painter, 1836;

Benedict Arnold, US soldier and spy, 1741;

Jean-Baptiste Vanloo, French painter, 1684.

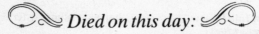

Died on this day:

Gilbert Spencer, artist, 1979;

Sir Robert Anthony Eden, 1st Earl of Avon, statesman, 1977;

Anaïs Nin, French/US writer and poetess, 1977;

Peter Finch [William Mitchell], actor, 1977;

Frederick IX, King of Denmark, 1972;

Humphrey DeForest Bogart, US film actor, 1957;

Harry Furniss, caricaturist and illustrator, 1925;

Lewis Carroll [Charles Lutwidge Dodgson], author, 1898;

Henry Edward Manning, Cardinal, 1892;

Lord Napier of Magdala, soldier, 1890;

Jean-Auguste-Dominique Ingres, French painter, 1867;

Edmond Halley, astronomer, 1742;

Pietro Francesco Cavalli, Italian composer, 1676;

Odoric of Pordenone, Italian Franciscan and traveller, 1331.

Occurred on this day:

The musical show *The Boy Friend* was first produced, London, 1954;

Marshal Tito was elected first president of the Yugoslav republic, 1953;

The Players' Theatre, London, opened, 1946;

Winston Churchill and Franklin Roosevelt met at Casablanca, 1943;

In the Italian general election, 29 Fascists were returned, 1921;

German warships bombarded Yarmouth, 1918;

An earthquake in Jamaica destroyed Kingston, killing over 1,000, 1907;

Puccini's opera *Tosca* was first performed, Rome, 1900;

Queen Victoria heard a concert relayed to her by telephone, 1878;

An attempt was made on the life of Napoleon III by Felice Orsini, an Italian revolutionary, 1858;

Norway was ceded to the King of Sweden by the King of Denmark, 1814;

A Frost Fair was held on the Thames, 1814;

A Frost Fair began on the Thames, 1205.

TODAY IS THE FEAST DAY OF St Antony Pucci, St Barbasymas or Barbascemin, St Datius, St Felix of Nola, St Kentigern or Mungo, St Macrina the Elder, The Martyrs of Mount Sinai and St Sava.

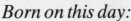

15th January

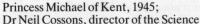

Born on this day:

Princess Michael of Kent, 1945;
Dr Neil Cossons, director of the Science
  Museum, 1939;
Margaret O'Brien, US film actress, 1937;
Frank Bough, TV presenter, 1933;
Martin Luther King, black civil rights
  leader, 1929;
Maria Schell, Austrian film actress, 1926;
John Terraine, author, 1921;
Frank Thornton, actor and comedian, 1921;
Sir John Junor, former editor of the *Sunday
  Express*, 1920;
Melvin J. Lasky, editor and publisher of
  Encounter, 1921;
Gamal Abdel Nasser, Egyptian leader,
  1918;

Lord Dacre of Glanton, historian, 1914;
Lloyd Bridges, US film actor, 1913;
Aristotle Onassis, Greek shipowner, 1906;
David Ivor Novello [Davies], actor,
  composer and director, 1893;
Mazo de la Roche, Canadian novelist, 1885;
Jean-Baptiste Faure, French baritone,
  1830;
Pierre-Joseph Proudhon, French social
  reformer, 1809;
Franz Grillparzer, Austrian playwright,
  1791;
Louis de Rouvroy, Duc de Saint-Simon,
  French writer, 1675;
Molière [Jean-Baptiste Poquelin], French
  playwright, baptised, 1622.

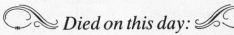 Died on this day:

Daisy [Margaret Mary Julia] Ashford,
  author of *The Young Visiters*,
  1972;
Jack [Weldon Leo] Teagarden, US jazz
  musician, vocalist and bandleader,
  1964;
Rosa Luxemburg, German socialist,
  murdered, 1919;

Mathew B. Brady, US Civil War
  photographer, 1896;
Frances Anne [Fanny] Kemble, actress,
  1893;
Emma, Lady Hamilton [Lyon], mistress to
  Lord Nelson, 1815;
Servius Sulpicius Galba, Roman emperor,
  assassinated, 69.

Occurred on this day:

Golda Meir was the first Israeli head of state
  to be received by the Pope, 1973.
Queen Margrethe II acceded to the throne
  of Denmark, 1972;
The Aswan High Dam in Egypt was
  officially opened, 1971;
In the USSR, Grigori Zinoviev and other
  leaders were convicted of treason and
  imprisoned, 1935;
In Berlin, Rosa Luxemburg and Karl
  Liebknecht, Spartacist revolutionaries,
  were assassinated, 1919;
The British National Health Insurance Act
  came into effect, 1912;

The first aerial propaganda leaflets
  were dropped by the Italians over Libya,
  1912;
The London Hippodrome theatre opened,
  1900;
Women were able to take degrees at
  London University for the first time,
  1878;
The British Museum opened in London,
  1759;
The Act of Supremacy was passed in
  England, 1535.

TODAY IS THE FEAST DAY OF St Bonitus or Bonet, St Ceolwulf, St Isidore of
Alexandria, St Ita, St John Calybites and St Macarius the Elder.

 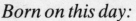

16th January

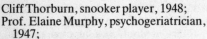

Born on this day:

Cliff Thorburn, snooker player, 1948;
Prof. Elaine Murphy, psychogeriatrician, 1947;
Christine Truman, tennis player, 1941;
Lady Marina Vaizey, art critic, 1938;
Michael White, theatre and film producer, 1936;
Prof. John Enderby, physicist, 1932;
Prof. Sir Peter Hirsch, metallurgist, 1926;
Keith Shackleton, artist and naturalist, 1923;
Prof. Sir Frederick Stewart, geologist, 1916;
Ethel Merman [Zimmerman], US singer and actress, 1909;
Alexander Knox, Canadian film actor, 1907;
Prof. Archibald Hunter, New Testament scholar, 1906;

Fulgencio Batista y Zaldivar, Cuban dictator, 1901;
Joan Rosita Forbes, traveller and writer, 1890;
Karl Freund, Austrian cinema photographer, 1890;
Robert William Service, Canadian writer and poet, 1874;
Edward Gordon Craig, theatre designer, 1872;
Sir Johnston Forbes-Robertson, actor-manager, 1853;
André Michelin, French tyre-maker, 1853;
Franz Brentano, German philosopher, 1838;
François-Joseph Talma, French actor-manager, 1763;
Niccolò Piccinni, opera composer, 1728;
Richard Savage, poet, 1697.

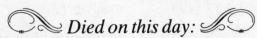

Died on this day:

Robert Jemison Van de Graaff, US nuclear physicist, 1967;
Arturo Toscanini, conductor, 1957;
Carole Lombard [Jane Alice Peters], US film actress, killed in an air crash, 1942;
Marshall Field, US department store owner, 1906;
Arnold Böcklin, Swiss painter, 1901;

Clément-Philibert-Léo Delibes, French composer, 1891;
Amilcare Ponchielli, Italian composer, 1886;
General Sir John Moore, died of wounds at Corunna, 1809;
Edward Gibbon, historian, 1794;
Edmund Spenser, poet, 1599.

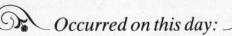

Occurred on this day:

The Gulf War started with the launch of Operation Desert Storm, when allied air attacks were made on Iraq and occupied Kuwait, 1991;
Colonel Gaddafi became the prime minister of Libya, 1970;
Vincent Auriol was elected as President of France, 1947;
The BBC publication *The Listener* was first published, 1929;
In the USA, the 18th Amendment was ratified, prohibiting the sale of alcoholic beverages, 1920;

The first meeting of the Council of the League of Nations was held in Paris, 1920;
The US Senate voted against joining the League of Nations, 1920;
The Battle of Corunna was fought, 1809;
The Spanish were defeated at Cape St Vincent by Admiral George Rodney, 1780;
Charles V, Holy Roman Emperor, abdicated, 1556;
Ivan the Terrible, first Russian Tsar, crowned, 1547.

TODAY IS THE FEAST DAY OF St Berard and Others, St Fursey, St Henry of Cocket, St Honoratus of Arles, St Marcellus I, pope and St Priscilla.

17th January

Born on this day:

Paul Young, singer, 1956;
Gillian Weir, concert organist, 1942;
Françoise Hardy, French singer and song-writer, 1944;
Muhammad Ali, US former boxing champion, 1942;
Prince Sadruddin Aga Khan, 1933;
Monica Furlong, writer, 1930;
Vidal Sassoon, hair stylist, 1928;
Moira Shearer, former ballerina, 1926;
Clyde Walcott, West Indies cricket administrator, 1926;
Lord Joseph, CH, former MP and government minister, 1918;
Lottie Berk, German former dancer and fitness expert, 1914;
Sir Edward Fennessy, pioneer of radar, 1913;
Al [Alphonse] Capone, US gangster, 1899;
Nevil Shute [Norway], novelist, 1899;

Ronald Arthur Annesley Firbank, novelist, 1886;
Sir Edward Montague Compton Mackenzie, novelist, 1883;
Mack Sennett [Michael Sinnott], US film producer, 1880;
David Lloyd George, 1st Earl, statesman, 1863;
Konstantin Stanislavsky [Konstantin Sergeyevich Alekseyev], Russian actor-manager, 1863;
Douglas Hyde, poet, historian and first president of the Irish Republic, 1860;
George Lyttelton, 1st Baron, statesman and poet, 1709;
Benjamin Franklin, US printer and diplomat, 1706;
Thomas Fairfax, 3rd Baron, Parliamentary army commander, 1612.

Died on this day:

Neil Miller Gunn, Scottish novelist, 1973;
Terence Hanbury White, author, 1964;
Sir Francis Galton, explorer and anthropologist, 1911;
Quintin Hogg, merchant and founder of the Polytechnic, 1903;
Charles-Marie-René Leconte de Lisle, French poet, 1894;

George Bancroft, US diplomat and historian, 1891;
Émile-Jean-Horace Vernet, French painter, 1863;
Juan Crisóstomo Arriaga, Spanish composer, 1826;
Tomaso Giovanni Albinoni, Italian composer, 1751;
John Ray, naturalist, 1705;
Carlo Dolci, Italian painter, 1686.

Occurred on this day:

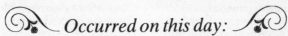

Gary Gilmore, a double murderer, was executed by firing squad at Utah State prison, 1977;
Senegal and the French Sudan united to form the Federal State of Mali, 1959;
Hawaii was proclaimed a republic, 1893;
The Star, London evening newspaper, was first published, 1888;

Captain Cook's ship, the *Resolution*, was the first to cross the Antarctic Circle, 1773;
The Papal See was removed from Avignon to Rome, 1377;
The city of Baghdad was captured and destroyed by the Mongols, 1258.

TODAY IS THE FEAST DAY OF St Antony the Abbot, St Genulf or Genou, St Julian Sabas, St Richimir, St Sabinus of Piacenza, Saints Speusippus, Eleusippus and Meleusippus and St Sulpicius II or Sulpice of Bourges.

18th January

Born on this day:

Richard Dunwoody, jockey, 1965;
Rocco Forte, member of the House of Forte, 1946;
Paul Freeman, actor, 1943;
Raymond Briggs, author and illustrator, 1934;
Dr David Bellamy, botanist, 1933;
John Boorman, film director, 1933;
Terence Higgins, parliamentarian and former Olympic athlete, 1928;
Constance Moore, US film actress, 1922;
Dame Jennifer Jenkins, chairman, the National Trust, 1921;
William Sansom, author, 1912;
Cary Grant [Archibald Alexander Leach], film actor, 1904;
Oliver Norvell Hardy, US comedian, 1892;
Antoine Pevsner, French sculptor, 1886;
Arthur Mitchell Ransome, critic and writer of children's books, 1884;
Alan Alexander Milne, author, 1882;
Félix Rubén García Sarmiento [Rubén Darío], Nicaraguan poet, 1867;
Alexis-Emmanuel Chabrier, French composer, 1841;
Sir Edward Frankland, chemist, 1825;
Charles John Kean, actor, 1811;
Daniel Webster, US statesman, 1782;
Peter Mark Roget, lexicographer, 1779;
Charles-Louis de Secondat, Baron de Montesquieu, French philosopher, 1689.

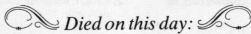

Died on this day:

Sir Cecil Walter Hardy Beaton, designer and photographer, 1980;
Hugh Todd Naylor Gaitskell, statesman, 1963;
George Morrow, illustrator, 1955;
Sydney Greenstreet, film actor, 1954;
Joseph Rudyard Kipling, author, 1936;
Edward George Earle Lytton Bulwer-Lytton, 1st Baron Lytton, author, 1873;
Sir George Hayter, painter, 1871;
John Tyler, 10th president of the USA, 1862;
Joseph Haydn, compiler of the *Dictionary of Dates*, 1856;
Sir John Pringle, physician, 1782;
Jan van Riebeck, founder of Cape Town, 1677.

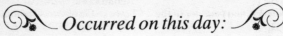

Occurred on this day:

Leningrad, under siege by the Germans, was relieved, 1944;
The Peace Conference opened at Versailles, 1919;
Captain Robert Falcon Scott reached the South Pole, 1912;
The first building of the Prince of Wales's Theatre opened as the Prince's Theatre, London, 1884;
The German Reich or Empire was proclaimed in the Hall of Mirrors, Versailles, 1871;
Wilhelm of Prussia was proclaimed the first German Emperor, 1871;
Captain Cook discovered the Sandwich Islands [Hawaii], 1778;
The first English tragedy, *Gordobuc*, by Sackville and Norton, first performed, 1561;
Lima, capital of Peru, founded by Pizarro, 1535;
Henry VII of Lancaster and Elizabeth of York were married, 1486.

TODAY IS THE FEAST DAY OF St Desle or Deicolus, St Peter's Chair, Rome, St Prisca and St Volusian.

19th January

Born on this day:

Stefan Edberg, tennis player, 1966;
Simon Rattle, orchestral conductor, 1955;
Robert Palmer, rock singer and guitarist, 1950;
Dolly Parton, US country music singer, 1946;
Rod Evans, rock singer, 1945;
Michael Crawford, actor and singer, 1942;
Patsy Rowlands, actress, 1940;
Phil Everly, US rock singer, 1939;
Richard Lester, film director, 1932;
Joan Regan, singer, 1929;
Nina Bawden, novelist, 1925;
Patricia Highsmith, US thriller writer, 1921;
Bernard Dunstan, painter, 1920;
Nigel Nicolson, former MP and author, 1918;

Hans Hotter, German bass baritone, 1909;
Iris Guiver Wilkinson [Robin Hyde], novelist and journalist, 1906;
Paul Cézanne, French painter, 1839;
Sir Henry Bessemer, engineer, 1813;
Edgar Allan Poe, US author and poet, 1809;
Robert Edward Lee, Confederate general, 1807;
Isidore-Auguste-Marie-François Comte, French philosopher, 1798;
Jacques-Henri Bernardin de Saint-Pierre, French author, 1737;
James Watt, inventor and perfector of the steam engine, 1736;
Francis II, King of France, 1544.

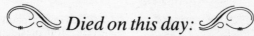 Died on this day:

George Henry Boughton, painter, 1905;
Auguste-Ferdinand-François Mariette, French Egyptologist, 1881;
Henri-Victor Regnault, French physicist and chemist, 1878;
Henri Regnault, French painter, 1871;
Pierre-Joseph Proudhon, French journalist and socialist, 1865;
Jean-Baptiste Paulin, French painter, 1855;

Louis-Joseph-Ferdinand Hérold, French composer, 1833;
William Congreve, playwright, 1729;
Hans Sachs, German poet and song composer, 1576;
Paris Bordone, Venetian painter, 1571;
Henry Howard, Earl of Surrey, courtier, poet and soldier, executed, 1547.

Occurred on this day:

Indira Gandhi became prime minister of India, 1966;
Burma was invaded by the Japanese, 1942;
An explosion occurred in an East London munitions factory, with 450 casualties, including 69 killed, 1917;
The first raid on England by German Zeppelins took place, when bombs were dropped on Great Yarmouth and King's Lynn, 1915;
President Theodore Roosevelt sent greetings to King Edward VII from Washington to London by wireless telegraphy, 1903;

Britain and Egypt established a Condominium over the Sudan, 1899;
Massenet's opera *Manon* was first performed, Paris, 1884;
Verdi's opera *Il Trovatore* was performed for the first time, Rome, 1853;
The coast of Antarctica was discovered by the American sailor, Captain Charles Wilkes, 1840;
Louis XVI, King of France, was tried at the French Convention, 1793;
The Heidelberg Catechism was published, 1563;
King Edward III established the Order of the Garter, 1348.

TODAY IS THE FEAST DAY OF Saints Abachum and Audifax, St Albert of Cashel, St Canute IV of Denmark, St Charles of Sezze, St Fillan or Foelan, St Germanicus, St Henry of Uppsala, Saints Marius and Martha, St Messalina, St Nathalan and St Wulfstan.

20th January

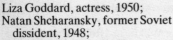

Born on this day:

Liza Goddard, actress, 1950;
Natan Shcharansky, former Soviet dissident, 1948;
Malcolm McLaren, rock impressario, 1947;
Eric Stewart, rock guitarist, 1945;
Prof. Nalin Chandra Wickramasinghe, astronomer, 1939;
Tom Baker, actor, 1936;
Dr Edwin [Buzz] Aldrin, US astronaut, 1930;
Patricia Neal, US actress, 1926;
Lord Hanson, industrialist, 1922;
Federico Fellini, Italian film director, 1920;
Major Dick Hern, racehorse trainer, 1921;
Royalton Kisch, conductor, 1919;

Joy Friederike Victoria [Gessner] Adamson, companion of wild animals and author, 1910;
George Burns, US comedian and actor, 1896;
Huddie Ledbetter ['Leadbelly'], US blues artist, 1889;
Johannes Jensen, Danish poet and novelist, 1873;
Richard Le Gallienne, writer, 1866;
André-Marie Ampère, French physicist, 1775;
Theobald Wolfe Tone, Irish nationalist, 1763;
Jean-Jacques Barthélemy, French abbé and scholar, 1716;
Francesco Bartolommeo Conti, Italian lutenist and composer, 1681.

Died on this day: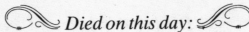

[Peter John] Johnny Weissmuller, US actor and swimmer, 1984;
Derick Heathcoat Amory, 1st Viscount Amory, statesman, 1981;
Edmund Charles Blunden, poet and critic, 1974;
King George V, 1936;
Richard Doddridge Blackmore, novelist, 1900;
John Ruskin, social reformer, art critic and writer, 1900;

Jean-François Millet, French painter, 1875;
Sir John Soane, architect, 1837;
John Howard, prison reformer, 1790;
David Garrick, actor, 1779;
Charles Yorke, Lord Chancellor, 1770;
Charles VII [Charles of Bavaria], Holy Roman Emperor, 1745;
Charles Montagu, 1st Duke of Manchester, 1722;
Rudolf II, Holy Roman Emperor, 1612.

Occurred on this day: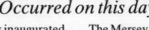

John Fitzgerald Kennedy was inaugurated as the 35th president of the USA, 1961;
Sir Vivian Fuchs, leading the Commonwealth Trans-Antarctic Expedition, arrived at the South Pole, 1958;
The RAF dropped 2,300 tons of bombs on Berlin, 1944;
Britain and China signed the Treaty of Peking, 1925;
The first game of basketball was played at Springfield, Mass., USA, 1892;

The Mersey Tunnel was opened by the Prince of Wales, 1886;
Hong Kong was ceded to Britain by China, 1841;
London Docks were first opened, 1805;
The First Fleet sent to Botany Bay arrived in New South Wales, 1788;
The trial of King Charles I began, 1649;
The first English parliament met in Westminster Hall, 1265.

TODAY IS THE FEAST DAY OF St Euthymius the Great, St Fabian, pope, St Fechin and St Sebastian.

 # 21st January

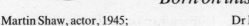

Born on this day:

Martin Shaw, actor, 1945;
Dr Alan Borg, director-general, Imperial War Museum, 1942;
Placido Domingo, Spanish operatic tenor, 1941;
Jack Nicklaus, golfer, 1940;
The Marquess of Tavistock, 1940;
Sir Nicholas Phillips, High Court judge, 1938;
Norman Willis, general secretary of the TUC, 1933;
Dr John Hayes, director, National Portrait Gallery, 1929;
Benny Hill [Alfred Hawthorn Hill], comedian, 1924;
Telly Savalas, TV actor, 1924;
Paul Scofield, actor, 1922;
Rear-Admiral Sir Richard Trowbridge, 1920;
Dr Rohan Butler, historian, 1917;
Laurence Whistler, glass-engraver and writer, 1912;
Maj.-Gen. Adrian Hope, 1911;
Christian Dior, exponent of *haute couture*, 1905;
Charles Langbridge Morgan, author, 1894;
Amédée-Ernest Chausson, composer, 1855;
Sophia Louisa Jex-Blake, physician and women's liberation pioneer, 1840;
Oscar II, King of Sweden and Norway, 1829;
Thomas Jonathan ['Stonewall'] Jackson, Confederate general, 1824;
John Charles Frémont, explorer, 1813.

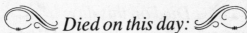

Died on this day:

Marie Löhr, actress, 1975;
Cecil Blount De Mille, US film director, 1959;
George Orwell [Eric Arthur Blair], novelist, 1950;
Ermanno Wolf-Ferrari, composer, 1948;
Will [William Henry] Dyson, cartoonist and etcher, 1938;
Georges Méliès, cinema pioneer, 1938;
Lytton Giles Strachey, biographer and critic, 1932;
Lenin [Vladimir Ilyich Ulyanov], Russian leader, 1924;
Elisha Gray, inventor, 1901;
Franz Grillparzer, playwright, 1872;
Henry Hallam, historian, 1859;
Moritz von Schwind, German painter, 1804;
Louis XVI, King of France, executed, 1793;
Peter De Wint, painter, 1784;
Anthony Ashley Cooper, 1st Earl of Shaftesbury, statesman, 1683;
Adriaen Vandevelde, painter, 1672;
Pope Paschal II, 1118.

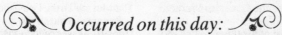

Occurred on this day:

The inaugural flight to Bahrain was made by Concorde, 1976;
The USS *Nautilus*, world's first nuclear-powered submarine, was launched, 1954;
Edward VIII was proclaimed king, 1936;
Taxi-cabs were first officially recognised in Britain, 1907;
The *Daily News*, the newspaper edited by Charles Dickens, was first issued, 1846;
The 'Letters of Junius' ceased on the same day and month, 1772;
The 'Letters of Junius' began being published, 1769.

TODAY IS THE FEAST DAY OF St Agnes, St Alban or Bartholomew Roe, St Epiphanius of Pavia, St Fructuosus of Tarragona, St Meinrad and St Patroclus of Troyes.

22nd January

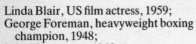

Born on this day:

Linda Blair, US film actress, 1959;
George Foreman, heavyweight boxing champion, 1948;
John Hurt, actor, 1940;
Gillian Shepherd, MP, 1940;
Margaret Hall, head of design, British Museum, 1936;
Nyree Dawn Porter, actress, 1936;
Piper Laurie, US film actress, 1932;
Claire Rayner, journalist and broadcaster, 1931;
Baroness Lockwood, former president, Birkbeck College, 1924;
Sir Alfred Ramsey, former soccer manager, 1920;
Mary Hayley Bell, playwright, 1911;
Ann Sothern, US film actress, 1909;

U Thant, Secretary-General of the United Nations, 1909;
Horace Greeley Hjalmar Schacht, German minister of economics, 1877;
David Wark Griffith, silent film producer and director, 1875;
Maurice Henry Hewlett, novelist and poet, 1861;
Beatrice Potter Webb, social reformer, 1858;
August Strindberg, Swedish playwright, 1849;
George Gordon Byron, 6th Baron, poet, 1788;
Sir Francis Bacon, Viscount St Albans, statesman and lawyer, 1561;
Ivan III [the Great], Grand Duke of Muscovy, 1440.

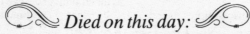

Died on this day:

Sir Arthur Bryant, historian, 1985;
Herbert Sutcliffe, cricketer, 1978;
Lyndon Baines Johnson, US statesman, 1973;
Walter Richard Sickert, painter, 1942;
James Bryce, 1st Viscount, politician, 1922;
Pope Benedict XV, 1922;
Queen Victoria, 1901;

David Edward Hughes, inventor of the teleprinter and microphone, 1900;
Sir Joseph Whitworth, mechanical engineer, 1887;
Sir George Harvey, Scottish painter, 1876;
Charles Kean, actor-manager, 1868;
William Paterson, Scottish financier and founder of the Bank of England, 1719;

 ## Occurred on this day:

The United Kingdom, Irish Republic and Denmark joined the Common Market, 1972;
The first broadcast of a football match took place [Arsenal v. Sheffield United] at Highbury, London, 1927;
Ramsay MacDonald, the first Labour prime minister, took office, 1924;
This was Bloody Sunday in St Petersburg, when 120,000 citizens marched on the Winter Palace, only to be fired upon, 1905;

The Hay-Herran Pact was concluded, under which the USA acquired the Panama Canal, 1903;
Edward VII acceded to the throne, 1901;
British troops were massacred by the Zulus at Isandhlwana, 1879;
Gilbert and Sullivan's opera *Ruddigore* was first performed, London, 1887;
The Falkland Islands were ceded to Britain by Spain, 1771;
The South Sea Bubble speculation fever started, 1720.

TODAY IS THE FEAST DAY OF St Anastasius the Persian, St Berhtwald of Ramsbury, St Blesilla, St Dominic of Sora, St Vincent Pallotti and St Vincent of Saragossa.

23rd January

Born on this day:

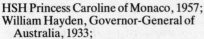

HSH Princess Caroline of Monaco, 1957;
William Hayden, Governor-General of Australia, 1933;
Jeanne Moreau, French actress, 1928;
Lord Strathcarron, motorist and author, 1924;
Bob Paisley, football manager, 1919;
Lord Denning, former Master of the Rolls, 1899;
Sergei Mikhailovich Eisenstein, Russian film director, 1898;
Subhas Chandra Bose, Indian politician, 1897;
Gilbert Ledward, sculptor, 1888;

Rutland Boughton, composer, 1878;
Antoinette Sterling, US contralto, 1850;
Benoît-Constant Coquelin, French actor, 1841;
Ernst Abbe, German physicist and industrialist, 1840;
Édouard Manet, French impressionistic painter, 1832;
Stendhal [Marie-Henri Beyle], French novelist, 1783;
Muzio Clementi, Italian composer, 1752;
Philipp Jakob Spener, German protestant theologian, 1635.

Died on this day:

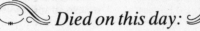

Freddie Bartholomew, former child film actor, 1992;
Sir Emile Littler, theatrical impresario, 1985;
Samuel Barber, US composer, 1981;
Frank Owen, editor and journalist, 1979;
Paul Bustill Robeson, US actor and singer, 1976;
Edward 'Kid' Ory, US jazz musician, 1973;
Sir Alexander Korda [Sandor Laszlo Korda], film producer, 1956;
Pierre Bonnard, French impressionistic painter and designer, 1947;
Edvard Munch, Norwegian painter, 1944;
Dame Clara Ellen Butt, contralto, 1936;

Anna Pavlova, Russian ballerina, 1931;
William Whiteley, 'The Universal Provider', department store owner, shot dead, 1907;
Gustave-Paul Doré, French artist, 1883;
Charles Kingsley, poet and novelist, 1875;
Thomas Love Peacock, novelist and poet, 1866;
John Hoppner, portrait painter, 1810;
William Pitt the Younger, statesman, 1806;
John Cleland, author of *Fanny Hill*, 1789;
William Caslon, typefounder, 1766;
Giambattista Vico, Italian philosopher and jurist, 1744;
William Baffin, explorer, 1622.

Occurred on this day:

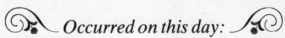

The proceedings of the House of Lords were televised for the first time, 1985;
The USS *Pueblo* was seized by the North Koreans, 1968;
The bathyscaphe *Trieste* designed by Prof. Piccard descended to a depth of 35,800 feet in the Pacific Ocean, 1960;
Tripoli was captured by the British, 1943;
The show trial of Karl Radek and other alleged Trotskyists was held in Moscow, 1937;

The first Labour Government was formed, under Ramsay McDonald, 1924;
The musical show *Our Miss Gibbs* was first performed, London, 1909;
The Battle of Spion Kop was fought during the Boer War, 1900;
Fletcher Christian and the *Bounty* mutineers landed on Pitcairn Island, 1790;
The Principality of Liechtenstein was constituted, 1719;
The Royal Exchange, London, was opened by Queen Elizabeth I, 1571.

TODAY IS THE FEAST DAY OF St Asclas, St Bernard of Vienne, Saints Clement and Agathangelus, St Emerentiana, St Ildephonsus, St John the Almsgiver, St Lufthildis and St Maimbod.

24th January

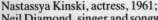

Born on this day:

Nastassya Kinski, actress, 1961;
Neil Diamond, singer and songwriter, 1941;
Bamber Gascoigne, author and quizmaster, 1937;
Dr Desmond Morris, zoologist, 1928;
Sir Donald Murray, a Lord Justice of Appeal, Supreme Court of Northern Ireland, 1923;
Nora Beloff, author, 1919;
Ernest Borgnine, US film actor, 1917;
Ann Todd, actress, 1909;
Field Marshal Sir Thomas Albert Blamey, Australian soldier, 1884;
Beatrice Harraden, novelist, 1864;
Edith Newbold [Jones] Wharton, US novelist, 1862;
Harry Quilter, barrister, artist and author, 1851;

Sir Edwin Chadwick, sanitary pioneer, 1800;
Charles James Fox, politician, 1749;
Gustavus III, King of Sweden, 1746;
Pierre-Augustin Caron de Beaumarchais, French playwright, 1732;
Frederick the Great, King of Prussia, 1712;
Farinelli [Carlo Broschi], Italian castrato singer, 1705;
William Congreve, playwright, 1670;
Sir John Vanbrugh, playwright, baptised, 1664;
Charles Sackville, Earl of Dorset, courtier and poet, 1638;
Hadrian, Roman emperor, 76.

Died on this day:

George Cukor, US film director, 1983;
St John Greer Ervine, playwright and dramatic critic, 1971;
Sir Winston Leonard Spencer Churchill, statesman, 1965;
Otto Harbach [Otto Abels Hauerbach], US librettist and lyricist, 1963;
Amedeo Modigliani, painter and sculptor, 1920;
Lord Randolph Henry Spencer Churchill, politician, 1895;

Baron Friedrich von Flotow, German composer, 1883;
Adam Black, politician and publisher, 1874;
Gasparo Spontini, Italian composer, 1851;
Franciabigio [Francesco de Cristofano], Italian painter, 1525;
Caligula, Roman emperor, assassinated, 41.

Occurred on this day:

Mae West made a London stage debut in her own play, *Diamond Lil*, 1948;
The Casablanca Conference ended, 1943;
The Central Statistical Office was founded, 1941;
Clarence Hatry, financier, was found guilty of fraud and sentenced to 14 years, 1930;
The first Conscription Bill was passed by the House of Commons, 1916;
The Battle of the Dogger Bank was fought, when the German armoured cruiser *Blücher* was sunk, 1915;

The first troop of Boy Scouts was formed in Britain, 1908;
The first train passed over the Forth Bridge, 1890;
Mussorgsky's opera *Boris Godunov* was first performed, Petrograd, 1874;
Gold was first discovered by James Marshall at Sutter's sawmill in California, 1848;
Cape Horn was rounded by Willem Corneliszoon Schouten, 1616;
Henry III, King of England, married Eleanor of Provence, 1236.

TODAY IS THE FEAST DAY OF St Babylas of Antioch, St Felician of Foligno, St Francis of Sales and St Macedonius the Barley-eater.

25th January

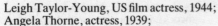

Born on this day:

Leigh Taylor-Young, US film actress, 1944;

Angela Thorne, actress, 1939;

Sir David Nicholas, chairman and chief executive, ITN, 1930;

Raymond Baxter, broadcaster and writer, 1922;

Russell Braddon, Australian author, 1921;

Prof. Edward Ullendorff, Semitic languages authority, 1920;

Witold Lutoslawski, Polish composer and conductor, 1913;

Howard Levett, cricketer, 1908;

Paul-Henri Spaak, Belgian statesman, 1899;

Sir John Moores, founder of the Littlewoods Organisation, 1896;

Dame Gwen Ffrangcon-Davies, actress, 1891;

Wilhelm Furtwängler, German conductor, 1886;

Adeline Virginia Woolf, author, 1882;

William Somerset Maugham, author, 1874;

Hugh Cecil Lowther, 5th Earl of Lonsdale, 1857;

John Arbuthnot Fisher, 1st Baron, admiral, 1841;

Daniel Maclise, Irish painter, 1806;

Robert Burns, poet, 1759;

Stephanie-Félicité, Comtesse de Genlis, French author, 1746;

Comte Joseph-Louis Lagrange, French mathematician and physicist, 1736;

Pompeo Girolamo Batoni, Italian painter, 1708;

Robert Boyle, physicist and chemist, 1627;

Govaert Flinck, Dutch painter, 1615;

Hendrik van Avercamp, Dutch painter, 1585;

St Edmund Campion, Jesuit martyr, 1540.

Died on this day:

Robertson Hare, actor, 1979;

Rutland Boughton, composer, 1960;

Al [Alphonse] Capone, US gangster, 1947;

Ouida [Marie Louise de la Ramée], author, 1908;

Frederick Leighton, 1st Baron, painter and sculptor, 1896;

Dorothy Wordsworth, writer and sister of the poet, 1855;

George Augustus Selwyn, MP and wit, 1791;

Rev. Robert Burton, author of *The Anatomy of Melancholy*, 1640;

Lucas Cranach the Younger, German painter, 1586;

Marcus Cocceius Nerva, Roman emperor, 98.

Occurred on this day:

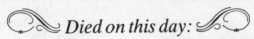

General Idi Amin deposed Milton Obote, president of Uganda, 1971;

In the USA, Charles Manson and others were found guilty of multiple murder, 1971;

The first Canadian-born Governor-General, Vincent Massey, was appointed in Canada, 1952;

The Pentagon building in Washington was completed, 1943;

John Dillinger, US bank-robber and 'Public Enemy No. 1', was captured at Tucson, Arizona, 1934;

The USA purchased the Danish West Indies for $25 million, 1917;

Nelly Bly, US journalist, ended a round-the-world trip in just over 73 days, 1890;

William Henry Fox Talbot published a description of his invention, the photographic negative, 1839;

Rossini's opera *La Cenerentola* was first performed, Rome, 1817;

Henry VIII married Anne Boleyn, 1533;

Edward III acceded to the English throne, 1327.

TODAY IS BURNS NIGHT AND THE FEAST DAY OF St Apollo, St Artemas, the Conversion of St Paul, St Dwynwen, Saints Juventinus and Maximimus, St Poppo, St Praejectus or Prix and St Publius.

26th January

Born on this day:

Christopher Hampton, playwright, 1946;
Marti Caine, singer and comedienne, 1945;
Jules Feiffer, US playwright and cartoonist, 1929;
Dr John Sykes, lexicographer, 1929;
Eartha Kitt, US singer, 1928;
Admiral Sir Desmond Cassidi, former C.-in-C. Naval Home Command, 1925;
The Rt. Rev. David Jenkins, Bishop of Durham, 1925;
Joan Leslie, US film actress, 1925;
Paul Newman, US actor, 1925;
Michael Bentine, humorist and writer, 1922;
Kaye Webb, founder of Puffin Books, 1914;
Jimmy Van Heusen [Edward Chester Babcock], US popular composer, 1913;
Stephane Grappelli, jazz violinist, 1908;
The Marquess of Bath, 1905;
Edward Sapir, US linguist and anthropologist, 1884;
Douglas MacArthur, US general, 1880;
Frederick Corder, conductor and composer, 1852;
Ugo Foscolo, Italian poet, 1778;
Charles XIV, King of Sweden, 1763;
Lord George Sackville [George Sackville Germain, 1st Viscount Sackville], soldier and politician, 1716;
Claude Adrien Helvetius, French philosopher and encyclopaedist, 1715.

 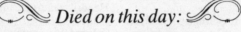 ## Died on this day:

José Vicente Ferrer Otero y Cintron [José Ferrer], US actor, 1992;
Mark James Walter Cameron, journalist, 1985;
Georges Bidault, French statesman, 1983;
Nelson Aldrich Rockefeller, US statesman, 1979;
Edward G. Robinson [Emanuel Goldenberg], US film actor, 1973;
Grace Moore [Mary Willie Grace Moore], US singer and actress, killed in KLM air crash, Copenhagen, 1947;
Nikolaus August Otto, German internal combustion engine inventor, 1891;
Charles George Gordon, general, killed at Khartoum, 1885;
Léon-Michel Gambetta, French lawyer and statesman, 1882;
William Marsden, surgeon and founder of hospitals, 1867;
Jean-Louis-André-Théodore Géricault, French painter, 1824;
Edward Jenner, physician, discoverer of vaccination, 1823;
Jean-François de Troy, French painter, 1752.

 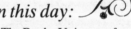 ## Occurred on this day:

The first London production of the musical *Godspell* was presented, 1972;
Hindi was made the official language of India, 1965;
India became a republic within the Commonwealth, 1950;
Strauss's opera *Der Rosenkavalier* was first performed, Dresden, 1911;
The Cullinan Diamond was found by Captain Wells near Pretoria, South Africa, 1905;
Khartoum was captured by the Mahdi, 1885;
The Rugby Union was founded, 1871;
Hong Kong became a British sovereign territory, 1841;
Michigan became the 26th of the United States, 1837;
Mozart's opera *Cosí Fan Tutte* was first performed, Vienna, 1790;
Sydney, Australia, was founded by Governor Arthur Phillip, 1788;
Brazil was discovered by Vicente Yáñes Pinzón, 1500.

TODAY IS AUSTRALIA DAY, REPUBLIC DAY, INDIA AND THE FEAST DAY OF St Alberic, St Conan of Man, St Eystein, St Margaret of Hungary, St Paula, St Thordgith or Theorigitha of Barking, St Timothy and St Titus.

27th January

Born on this day:

Federico Mayor Zaragoza, director-general, UNESCO, 1934;
John Hopkins, playwright, 1931;
Mordecai Richler, Canadian novelist and playwright, 1931;
Michael Craig, actor and playwright, 1929;
John Bury, theatre, opera and film designer, 1925;
Dr Robert Burchfield, former editor of the *Oxford English Dictionary* Supplement, 1924;
Lord Rix, actor and former secretary-general of Mencap, 1924;
Nina Milkina, concert pianist, 1919;
William Randolph Hearst, Jr., US newspaper editor-in-chief, 1908;
Sir John Eccles, physiologist, 1903;
Hyman George Rickover, US admiral, 1900;
Buddy DeSylva [George Gard DeSylva], US lyricist and director, 1895;

Ilya Grigoryevich Ehrenburg, Russian poet and novelist, 1891;
Jerome David Kern, US composer, 1885;
Wilhelm II, former Emperor of Germany, 1859;
Lewis Carroll [Charles Lutwidge Dodgson], author, 1832;
Jozef Israëls, Dutch painter, 1824;
Victor-Antoine-Édouard Lalo, French composer, 1823;
Eugène-Emmanuel Viollet-le-Duc, French architect, 1814;
Samuel Palmer, landscape painter, 1805;
Wolfgang Amadeus Mozart, Austrian composer, 1756;
Samuel Foote, actor and playwright, baptised, 1720;
Jean-François de Troy, French painter, 1679.

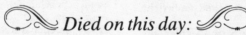

Died on this day:

Dame Gwen Ffrangcon-Davies, actress, 1992;
Charles Arthur Bertram Marshall, author, broadcaster and wit, 1989;
Mahalia Jackson, US gospel singer, 1972;
Carl Gustav Emil von Mannerheim, Finnish soldier and statesman, 1951;
Bert Lee, popular composer, 1947;
Emile Cohl [Courtet], French film animator, 1938;
Giovanni Verga, Italian novelist and playwright, 1922;

Giuseppe Fortunino Francesco Verdi, Italian composer, 1901;
Sir Edward Shepherd Creasy, historian, 1878;
John Gibson, sculptor, 1866;
John James Audubon, US artist and naturalist, 1851;
Samuel Hood, 1st Viscount, admiral, 1816;
Willem van Mieris, Dutch painter, 1747;
Sir William Temple, diplomat and statesman, 1669.

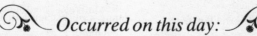

Occurred on this day:

A cease-fire began in Vietnam, 1973;
Three US astronauts lost their lives during tests in the *Apollo* capsule at Cape Kennedy, 1967;
The US made their first bombing raid on Germany, 1943;
Television was first demonstrated publicly by John Logie Baird, 1926;

In Berlin, the communist party 'Spartacus' was formed, 1916;
A patent for the electric lamp was taken out by Thomas A. Edison, 1879;
The independence of Greece was proclaimed, 1822;
The University of Georgia, USA, was founded, 1785.

TODAY IS THE FEAST DAY OF St Angela Merici, St Julian of Le Mans, St Marius or May and St Vitalian, pope.

# 28th January

Born on this day:

Mikhail Baryshnikov, dancer, 1948;

Robert Wyatt, rock musician, 1945;

Prof. John Tavener, composer, 1944;

Alan Alda, US TV and film actor, 1936;

Enid Castle, principal, the Cheltenham Ladies' College, 1936;

Prof. David Lodge, author and professor of literature, 1935;

Lord Windlesham, principal, Brasenose College, Oxford, 1932;

Acker Bilk, jazz clarinettist, 1930;

Claes Oldenburg, pop artist, 1929;

Ronnie Scott, jazz musician, 1927;

Alfred Marks, actor and comedian, 1921;

Paul Jackson Pollock, US abstract artist, 1912;

Ernst Lubitsch, US film director, 1892;

Artur Rubinstein, pianist, 1889;

Auguste Piccard, Swiss balloonist and deep sea explorer, 1884;

Ruby Mildred Ayres, novelist, 1883;

Colette [Sidonie-Gabrielle Colette], French author, 1873;

William Seward Burroughs, US adding-machine inventor, 1855;

Sir Henry Morton Stanley, journalist and explorer, 1841;

Sabine Baring-Gould, clergyman and author, 1834;

Charles George Gordon, general and hero of Khartoum, 1833;

John Baskerville, typographer and printer, 1706;

King Henry VII, 1457.

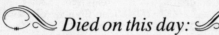## Died on this day:

Herbert Ernest Bates, novelist, 1974;

William Butler Yeats, poet and playwright, 1939;

Vicente Blasco Ibáñez, Spanish writer and politician, 1928;

Adalbert Stifter, Austrian novelist, 1868;

William Hickling Prescott, US historian, 1859;

William Burke, body-snatcher, hanged, 1829;

Sir Thomas Bodley, scholar and founder of the Bodleian, 1613;

Sir Francis Drake, sailor, at sea, 1596;

King Henry VIII, 1547;

Charlemagne, King of the Franks and Emperor of the West, 814.

 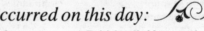## Occurred on this day:

The Independent on Sunday was first published, 1990;

The US space shuttle *Challenger* exploded moments after take-off, killing six astronauts and a woman teacher, 1986;

The British Eighth Army retreated to El Alamein, 1942;

Shanghai was occupied by the Japanese, 1932;

The Carnegie Institute was established in Washington, DC, USA, 1902;

A British relief force arrived at Khartoum, but General Gordon had died two days earlier, 1885;

Paris surrendered to the German army, 1871;

The penal colony at Botany Bay, New South Wales, was founded, 1788;

Edward VI acceded to the throne of England, 1547;

The Diet of Worms began, 1521.

TODAY IS THE FEAST DAY OF St Amadeus of Lausanne, St Paulinus of Aquileia, St Peter Nolasco, St Peter Thomas and St Thomas Aquinas.

29th January

Born on this day:

Raymond Keene, chess champion, 1949;
Tom Selleck, US TV and film actor, 1945;
Katharine Ross, US film actress, 1943;
Germaine Greer, feminist and author, 1939;
Leslie Bricusse, composer, 1931;
John Junkin, actor and scriptwriter, 1930;
Peter Byrne, actor and director, 1928;
Brian Trubshaw, former test pilot, 1924;
Paddy Sidney Chayefsky, US playwright and scriptwriter, 1923;
John Forsythe, US film and TV actor, 1917;
Victor Mature, US film actor, 1915;
Maj.-Gen. Sir George Burns, 1911;
Viscount Tonypandy, former Speaker of the House of Commons, 1909;
Maj.-Gen. Kenneth Mackay Lewis, 1897;
W. C. Fields [William Claude Dukenfield], US film comedian, 1880;
Havergal Brian, composer, 1876;
Sir William Rothenstein, artist, 1872;
Vicente Blasco Ibáñez, Spanish novelist, 1867;
Frederick Delius, composer, 1862;
Anton Pavlovich Chekhov, Russian author and playwright, 1860;
William McKinley, 25th president of the USA, 1843;
Thomas Paine, writer and reformer, 1737;
Emanuel Swedenborg, Swedish scientist and philosopher, 1688.

Died on this day:

Jimmy [James Francis] Durante, US comedian, 1980;
Robert Lee Frost, US poet, 1963;
Fritz Kreisler, US violinist, 1962;
Angela Margaret Thirkell, novelist, 1961;
Henry Louis Mencken, US writer, author of *The American Language*, 1956;
James Bridie [Osborne Henry Mavor], playwright and physician, 1951;
Ioannis Metaxas, Greek statesman and general, 1941;
William Butler Yeats, Irish poet and playwright, 1939;
Douglas, 1st Earl Haig, field marshal, 1928;
Evelyn Baring, 1st Earl of Cromer, diplomat, 1917;
Alfred Sisley, landscape painter, 1899;
Edward Lear, landscape painter and writer, 1888;
King George III, 1820.

Occurred on this day:

'Desert Island Discs' was first broadcast, 1942;
The first bombing of Paris by Zeppelins took place, 1916;
Kansas became the 34th of the United States, 1861;
The Victoria Cross was founded, 1856;
The marriage of Napoleon III and Eugénie de Montijo took place at the Tuileries, Paris, 1853;
George IV acceded to the British throne, 1820;
The Good-Natured Man by Oliver Goldsmith, was first performed, Covent Garden, London, 1768;
The Beggar's Opera by John Gay was first performed, Lincoln's Inn Fields Theatre, London, 1728;
The Académie Française was incorporated, 1635.

TODAY IS THE FEAST DAY OF St Gildas the Wise, St Sabinian of Troyes and St Sulpicius 'Severus'.

30th January

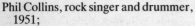
Born on this day:

Phil Collins, rock singer and drummer, 1951;

Victoria Principal, US actress and writer, 1950;

Derek Ricketts, show jumper, 1950;

Mitch Murray, pop song composer and producer, 1940;

Boris Spassky, chess champion, 1938;

Vanessa Redgrave, actress, 1937;

Gene Hackman, US film actor, 1932;

Hal Prince, US theatrical director and producer, 1928;

Sven Olof Joachim Palme, prime minister of Sweden, 1927;

Sir Robert Gatehouse, High Court judge, 1924;

Patrick Heron, abstract painter, 1920;

Lord Lowry, former Lord Chief Justice of Northern Ireland, 1919;

John Profumo, president, Toynbee Hall, 1915;

John Ireland, US film actor, 1914;

Louis Osman, architect and goldsmith, 1914;

Christina Foyle, bookshop proprietor, 1911;

Angela Margaret Thirkell, novelist, 1891;

Franklin Delano Roosevelt, 32nd president of the USA, 1882;

Sir Edward Seymour George Hicks, actor-manager and author, 1871;

Francis Herbert Bradley, philosopher, 1846;

Walter Savage Landor, author, 1775.

Died on this day:

Stanley Holloway, actor and vocalist, 1982;

Francis-Jean-Marcel Poulenc, French composer and pianist, 1963;

Mohandas Karamchand Gandhi, Indian leader, assassinated, 1948;

Orville Wright, US aviation pioneer, 1948;

Frank Nelson Doubleday, US publisher and editor, 1934;

Peter II, Tsar of Russia, 1730;

King Charles I, executed, 1649;

Sir Everard Digby, Thomas Winter, John Grant and Thomas Bates, Gunpowder Plot conspirators, executed, 1606.

Occurred on this day:

During riots following an illegal march, 13 civilians were shot by British troops in Londonderry, 1972;

Pakistan left the British Commonwealth, 1972;

The US Embassy in Saigon was captured by the Vietcong, 1968;

The state funeral of Sir Winston Churchill took place, 1965;

General Paulus and 16 generals of the remaining German forces were captured at Stalingrad, 1943;

Adolf Hitler was appointed Chancellor of Germany, 1933;

Crown Prince Franz Karl Josef Rudolf and Marie Vetsera committed suicide at Mayerling, Austria, 1889;

The first regular concert was given by the Hallé Orchestra, 1858;

All trade with Great Britain was forbidden by the Emperor of China, 1840;

The Menai Suspension Bridge, built by Telford, was opened, 1826;

The Commonwealth of England was established, 1649.

TODAY IS THE FEAST DAY OF St Adelelmus or Aleaume, St Aldegundis, St Barsimaeus, St Bathildis, St Hyacintha Mariscotti and St Martina.

 # 31st January

Born on this day:

HM Queen Beatrix of the Netherlands, 1938;

Christopher Chataway, former athlete and government minister, 1931;

Jean Simmons, actress, 1929;

Robert Clatworthy, sculptor, 1928;

Joanne Dru, US film actress, 1923;

Norman Mailer, US novelist, 1923;

Carol Channing, US actress and singer, 1921;

William Crosbie, artist, 1916;

Miron Grindea, editor, *ADAM International Review*, 1909;

John Henry O'Hara, US novelist, 1905;

The Rev. Lord Soper, Methodist leader and broadcaster, 1903;

Tallulah Brockman Bankhead, US film actress, 1903;

Dame Freya Stark, traveller and writer, 1893;

Eddie Cantor [Edward Israel Itzkowitz], US actor and entertainer, 1892;

Peter Dawson, Australian bass-baritone, 1882;

Anna Pavlova, Russian dancer, 1882;

Zane Grey, US novelist, 1872;

Franz Peter Schubert, Austrian composer, 1797;

André-Jacques Garnerin, French aeronaut, 1769;

Michel-Guillaume-Jean de Crèvecoeur, French/US writer, 1735.

Died on this day:

Winifred Atwell, pianist, 1983;

Samuel Goldwyn [Samuel Goldfish], US film producer, 1974;

Alan Alexander Milne, author, 1956;

Sir Charles Blake Cochran, theatrical producer, 1951;

Hippolyte-Jean Giraudoux, French novelist, playwright and diplomat, 1944;

John Galsworthy, novelist, 1933;

Charles Haddon Spurgeon, nonconformist preacher, 1892;

Jean-Louis-Ernest Meissonier, French painter, 1891;

Charles Edward Stuart, the Young Pretender, 1788;

William Chamberlayne, poet and physician, 1689;

Guy Fawkes, Gunpowder Plot conspirator, executed, 1606;

Gaudenzio Ferrari, Italian painter, 1546.

Occurred on this day:

Apollo 14 was launched on the moon mission from Cape Kennedy, 1971;

Explorer I, the US satellite, was successfully launched, 1958;

Arthur Alfred Rouse was found guilty of the 'blazing car' murder, 1931;

Leon Trotsky [Lev Davidovich Bronstein], Russian revolutionary, was expelled from the USSR, 1929;

The *Westminster Gazette* newspaper was last issued, 1928;

The Allied Military control of Germany was abolished, 1927;

The *Westminster Gazette* newspaper was first issued, 1893;

The Palace Theatre, London, opened as the Royal Opera House, 1891;

Offenbach's operetta *La Belle Hélène* was first performed, Paris, 1864;

The steamship *Great Eastern* was launched, 1858;

Sir Robert Peel repealed the Corn Laws, 1846.

TODAY IS THE FEAST DAY OF St Adamnan of Coldingham, St Aidan or Maedoc of Ferns, Saints Cyrus and John of Alexandria, St Eusebius of St Gall, St Francis Xavier Bianchi, St John Bosco, St Marcella of Rome and St Ulphia.

1st February

Born on this day:

Princess Stephanie of Monaco, 1966;
Don Everly, US rock singer, 1937;
Sir John Nott, former MP, 1932;
Prof. Sir Sam Edwards, physicist, 1928;
The Very Rev. Eric Evans, dean of St Paul's, 1928;
Renata Tebaldi, Italian operatic soprano, 1922;
Peter Sallis, actor, 1921;
Muriel Spark, novelist, 1918;
Sir Stanley Matthews, former footballer, 1915;
Robert Gittings, poet and playwright, 1911;
George Pal, US film director, 1908;
Hildegarde, US singer and actress, 1906;
Sidney Joseph Perelman, US humorous writer, 1904;
William Clark Gable, US film actor, 1901;

Stephen Meredith Potter, author and 'gamesman', 1900;
John Ford [Sean O'Fearn], US film director, 1895;
Louis Stephen St Laurent, Canadian prime minister, 1882;
Hugo von Hofmannsthal, Austrian playwright and poet, 1874;
Dame Clara Ellen Butt, contralto singer, 1872;
Victor Herbert, US composer, 1859;
Maximilien-Paul-Émile Littré, French lexicographer and scholar, 1801;
John Philip Kemble, actor, 1757;
Francesco Maria Veracini, Italian violinist and composer, 1690;
Sir Edward Coke, Lord Chief Justice and author, 1552.

Died on this day:

Buster [Joseph Francis] Keaton, silent film comedian, 1966;
Piet Mondrian, Dutch abstract painter, 1944;
Prince Aritomo Yamagata, Japanese military commander and prime minister, 1922;
Carlos I, King of Portugal, assassinated, 1908;
Sir George Gabriel Stokes, mathematician, 1903;

George Cruikshank, caricaturist and illustrator, 1878;
Mary Wollstonecraft Shelley [Godwin], author of *Frankenstein*, 1851;
John Lemprière, classical scholar, 1824;
Pope Alexander VIII, 1691;
René Descartes, French scientist and philosopher, 1650.

Occurred on this day:

Some 1,200 people were killed after an earthquake in Afghanistan and Pakistan, 1991;
Over 100 deaths resulted from blizzards which raged throughout the North East of the United States, 1977;
Clothes rationing ended in Britain, 1949;
Vidkun Quisling became prime minister of Norway, 1942;
The Austrian chancellor, Engelbert Dollfuss, dissolved all political parties except his own 'Fatherland Front', 1934;
The first British labour exchanges opened, 1910;

La Bohème, the opera by Puccini, was first staged in Turin, 1896;
Manon Lescaut, the opera by Puccini, was first staged in Turin, 1893;
The first volume of the *Oxford English Dictionary* was published, 1884;
Bell Rock lighthouse began operating, 1811;
The first meeting of the US Supreme Court took place, 1790;
Alexander Selkirk, the castaway, was discovered by Captain Thomas Dover on the island of Juan Fernandez, 1709.

TODAY IS THE FEAST DAY OF St Bride or Brigid of Kildare, St Henry Morse, St John of the Grating, St Pionius, St Seiriol and St Sigebert III of Austria.

2nd February

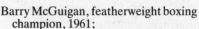

Born on this day:

Barry McGuigan, featherweight boxing champion, 1961;
Libby Purves, TV presenter, 1950;
Farrah Fawcett, US TV actress, 1946;
Andrew Davis, musical director, Glyndebourne Opera, 1944;
David Jason, actor, 1940;
Norman Fowler, politician, 1938;
Les Dawson, comedian, 1933;
Glynn Edwards, actor, 1931;
Elaine Stritch, US actress and singer, 1927;
Valéry Giscard d'Estaing, former French president, 1926;
Hughie Green, quizmaster, 1920;
Abba Eban, former Israeli foreign minister, 1914;
Jussi Björling, Swedish singer, 1911;

James Augustine Joyce, Irish author, 1882;
James Stephens, Irish poet and novelist, 1882;
Fritz Kreisler, US violinist and composer, 1875;
Henry Havelock Ellis, sex psychologist, 1859;
Daniel Maclise, Irish historical painter, 1806;
Girolamo Crescentini, Italian male soprano singer, 1766;
Charles-Maurice de Talleyrand-Périgord, French statesman and diplomat, 1754;
[Eleanor] Nell Gwyn, actress and mistress of Charles II, 1650;
Lodovico Ferrari, Italian mathematician, 1522.

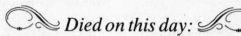

Died on this day:

Alistair Maclean, novelist, 1987;
Bertrand Russell, 3rd Earl, philosopher, 1970;
Sir Owen Seaman, editor of *Punch*, 1936;
Alexander Vasilievich Koltchak, Russian admiral, shot by Bolsheviks, 1920;
John Lawrence Sullivan, US bare-knuckle fighter, 1918;
Dmitri Ivanovich Mendeleyev, Russian chemist, 1907;

Francis Hayman, painter, 1776;
Pope Clement XIII, 1769;
Giovanni Pierluigi da Palestrina, Italian composer, 1594;
Baldassare Castiglione, Italian writer and courtier, 1529;
Martin Schongauer [or Schön], German engraver and painter, 1491.

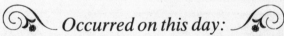

Occurred on this day:

A mob in Dublin burned down the British Embassy, 1972;
In Uganda, Maj.-Gen. Idi Amin declared himself to be absolute ruler, 1971;
The remaining German army at Stalingrad surrendered to the Russians, 1943;
Following a Russian-Estonian peace treaty, Estonia was declared independent, 1920;
Bread rationing introduced in Britain, 1917;
Greece declared war on Turkey, 1878;

The war between the United States and Mexico was ended after the signing of the Treaty of Guadalupe Hidalgo, 1848;
The first parliament assembled of Great Britain and Ireland, 1801;
Buenos Aires was founded by Pedro de Mendoza, 1535;
At the Battle of Mortimer's Cross, the Yorkists defeated the Lancastrians, 1461;
King Stephen was defeated and captured at the Battle of Lincoln, 1141.

TODAY IS CANDLEMAS [WIVES' FEAST DAY] AND THE FEAST DAY OF St Adalbald of Ostrevant, St Joan de Lestonnac, The Martyrs of Ebsdorf and The Purification.

# 3rd February

Born on this day:

Michael Dickinson, racehorse trainer, 1950;

Maev Alexander, actress, 1948;

Robert Simpson, Australian cricketer and manager, 1936;

Viscount Dunluce [the Earl of Antrim], Keeper of Conservation, Tate Gallery, 1935;

Jeremy Kemp, actor, 1935;

Gillian Ayres, painter, 1930;

Val Doonican, singer, 1929;

Frankie Vaughan, singer, 1928;

Shelley Berman, US comedian, 1926;

Glen Tetley, US ballet choreographer, 1926;

Air Chief Marshal Sir John Gingell, Gentleman Usher of the Black Rod, 1925;

Sir Anthony Alment, obstetrician and gynaecologist, 1922;

Doris Speed, TV actress, 1914;

James Michener, US novelist, 1907;

Lord Sherfield, chancellor, Reading University, 1904;

Alvar Aalto, Finnish architect, 1898;

Gertrude Stein, US author and critic, 1874;

Robert Arthur Talbot Gascoyne Cecil, 3rd Marquess of Salisbury, 1830;

Walter Bagehot, economist, author and journalist, 1826;

Elizabeth Blackwell, first woman medical practitioner, 1821;

Horace Greeley, US newspaper editor, 1811;

Jakob Ludwig Felix Mendelssohn-Bartholdy, German composer, 1809.

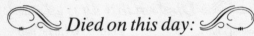## Died on this day:

John Cassavetes, US actor, director and screenwriter, 1989;

Boris Karloff [William Henry Pratt], film actor, 1969;

Edward Phillips Oppenheim, author of thrillers, 1946;

Oliver Heaviside, physicist, 1925;

John Lane, publisher, 1925;

Edward Charles Pickering, US astronomer, 1919;

George Crabbe, poet, 1832;

Nicholas-Edme Restif de la Bretonne, French novelist, 1806;

Richard 'Beau' Nash, gambler and dandy, 1762;

Germain Pilon, French sculptor, 1590;

John of Gaunt, Duke of Lancaster, 1399.

 ## Occurred on this day:

The Soviet spacecraft *Luna 9* reached the moon, sending back TV pictures, 1966;

Harold Macmillan made his 'Wind of Change' speech in Cape Town, South Africa, 1960;

Berlin was bombed in daylight by the Allies using over 1,000 aircraft, 1945;

In New Zealand, the cities of Napier and Hastings were almost destroyed in an earthquake when 256 people were killed, 1931;

The first London performance of the musical show *The Student Prince in Heidelberg* was staged, 1926;

The first meeting of the League of Nations was held in Paris, with Woodrow Wilson presiding, 1919;

Kiev, in the Ukraine, was captured by the Bolsheviks, 1919;

The United States and Germany broke off diplomatic relations, 1917;

Illinois was organised as a Territory of the United States, 1809;

Montevideo was taken by British forces under Sir Samuel Auchmuty, 1807;

Bartholomew Diaz landed at Mossal Bay, Cape of Good Hope, 1488.

TODAY IS THE FEAST DAY OF St Anskar, St Blaise, St Ia the Virgin, St Laurence of Canterbury, St Laurence of Spoleto, Saint Margaret 'of England' and St Werburga.

4th February

Born on this day:

Sir James Nicholson, a judge of the High Court of Northern Ireland, 1933;
Russell Hoban, author, 1925;
Norman Wisdom, comedian, 1920;
The Most Rev. Derek Worlock, RC Archbishop of Liverpool, 1920;
The Hon. Sir Clive Bossom, Bt., former MP, 1918;
Ida Lupino, film actress, 1918;
Erich Leinsdorf, US conductor, 1912;
Dr James McIntosh Patrick, painter and etcher, 1907;
Dietrich Bonhoeffer, German theologian, 1906;
Lord Shawcross QC, 1902;
Charles Augustus Lindbergh, US aviator, 1902;

Jacques Prévert, French poet and novelist, 1900;
Ugo Betti, Italian playwright, 1892;
Walter Catlett, US film actor, 1889;
Edwin John Pratt, Canadian poet, 1883;
Fernand Léger, French cubist painter, 1881;
William Harrison Ainsworth, novelist, 1805;
Tadeusz Andrzej Bonawentura Kościuszko, Polish patriot, 1746;
Karl Michael Bellmann, Swedish songwriter, 1740;
George Lillo, playwright, 1693;
Pierre Carlet de Chamblain de Marivaux, French playwright and novelist, 1688.

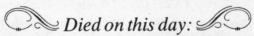

Died on this day:

Karen Carpenter, US singer, 1983;
Sir William Darling, Lord Provost of Edinburgh, 1962;
Lord [Montagu Collet] Norman, banker, 1950;
Edward Sapir, US linguist and anthropologist, 1939;
Pompeo Girolamo Batoni, Italian painter, 1787;

John Hamilton Mortimer, historical painter, 1779;
Robert Blair, Scottish poet, 1746;
Louis Elzevier, Dutch printer, 1617;
Giambattista della Porta, Italian natural philosopher, 1615;
Antonio Pollaiuolo [de Jacobo Benci], Florentine sculptor, 1498;
Lucius Septimius Severus, Roman emperor, 211.

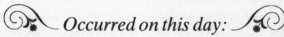

Occurred on this day:

The world's largest hovercraft [165 tonnes] was launched at Cowes, 1968;
The Sunday Times issued the first colour supplement in Britain, 1962;
Ceylon [later known as Sri Lanka] became an independent state, 1948;
The Yalta Conference opened, when Churchill, Roosevelt and Stalin met, 1945;
Submarine warfare was declared by Germany, 1915;

A naval blockade of Germany was announced by Britain, 1915;
The Russo-Japanese war began, when Port Arthur was besieged, 1904;
Charles Peace was found guilty of murder, 1879;
The Ashanti War ended following the Battle of Kumasi, 1874;

TODAY IS THE FEAST DAY OF St Andrew Corsini, bishop, St Isidore of Pelusium, St Joan of Valois, St John de Britto, St Joseph of Leonessa, St Modan, St Nicholas Studites, St Phileas, St Rembert and St Theophilus the Penitent.

5th February

Born on this day:

Charlotte Rampling, actress, 1946;
Susan Hill, novelist and playwright, 1942;
John Nettleton, actor, 1929;
Arthur Sulzberger, chairman and publisher of the *New York Times*, 1926;
Frank Muir, writer and broadcaster, 1920;
Red Buttons, US actor and comedian, 1919;
Prof. Sir Alan Hodgkin OM, former Master, Trinity College, Cambridge, 1914;
William S. Burroughs, US novelist, 1914;
Wing Comdr. Roderick Learoyd VC, 1913;
Adlai Ewing Stevenson, US statesman and ambassador, 1900;
'Patsy' Elias H. Hendren, cricketer, 1889;
Sir William Newzam Prior Nicholson, painter and engraver, 1872;
Sir Arthur Keith, Scottish anthropologist, 1866;
Joris Karl Huysmans, French writer, 1848;
Sir Hiram Stevens Maxim, inventor, 1840;
John Boyd Dunlop, inventor of the pneumatic tyre, 1840;
Thomas Creswick, painter, 1811;
Sir Robert Peel, statesman, 1788;
John Lingard, historian, 1771;
Marie de Rabutin-Chantal, Marquise de Sévigné, French writer, 1626.

Died on this day:

Emeric Pressburger, film producer, 1988;
Marianne Craig Moore, US poet, 1972;
Jacques Ibert, French composer, 1962;
Henry Major Tomlinson, novelist and essayist, 1958;
George Arliss [George Augustus Andrews], actor, 1946;
Andrew Barton ['Banjo'] Paterson, Australian journalist and poet, 1941;
William Morris Davis, US founder of geomorphology, 1934;
Anton Mauve, Dutch landscape painter, 1888;
Thomas Carlyle, author and historian, 1881;
Henry Crabb Robinson, diarist and lawyer, 1867;
Philipp Jakob Spener, German protestant theologian, 1705;
Joost van den Vondel, Dutch poet and playwright, 1679;
Giambattista Moroni, Italian portrait painter, 1578.

Occurred on this day:

The British airline Laker Airways collapsed with debts of £270 million, 1982;
The *Sunday Telegraph* was first published, 1961;
US troops under General MacArthur entered Manila, in the Philippines, 1945;
The first London performance of the musical show *On Your Toes* was staged, 1937;
The 'Corporative State' was established in Italy, 1934;
The Globe newspaper was last issued, 1921;
The first London performance of the comic opera *Maid Marian* was staged, 1891;
Verdi's opera *Otello* was first performed, Milan, 1887;
Charles XIV was proclaimed King of Sweden, 1818;
Rossini's opera *The Barber of Seville* was first performed, Rome, 1816;
The Prince of Wales ['Prinny'] was declared Prince Regent, 1811;
The Spanish captured Minorca from the British, 1782.

TODAY IS THE FEAST DAY OF St Adelaide of Bellich, St Agatha, St Avitus of Vienne, St Bertulph or Bertoul of Renty, Saints Indractus and Dominica and St Vodalus or Voel.

6th February

Born on this day:

Manuel Orantes, Spanish tennis player, 1949;

Gayle Hunnicutt, US actress, 1943;

Jimmy Tarbuck, comedian, 1940;

Leslie Crowther, comedian and quizmaster, 1933;

François Truffaut, French film director, 1932;

Fred Trueman, former England cricketer, 1931;

Rip Torn, US film actor and director, 1931;

Keith Waterhouse, writer, 1929;

Billy Wright, former England football captain, 1924;

Patrick MacNee, actor, 1922;

Denis Norden, writer and broadcaster, 1922;

Zsa Zsa Gabor, actress, 1920;

Eva Braun, Hitler's mistress, 1912;

Ronald Reagan, former president of the USA, 1911;

Lord Roskill, former Lord of Appeal in Ordinary, 1911;

Ramón Novarro [Samaniegos], Mexican/ US film actor, 1899;

Alberto Cavalcanti, documentary film maker, 1897;

George Herman ['Babe'] Ruth, US baseball player, 1895;

Sir Henry Irving [John Henry Brodribb], actor, 1838;

Sir Charles Wheatstone, inventor and physicist, 1802;

Queen Anne, 1665;

Christopher Marlowe, playwright, 1564.

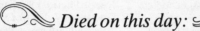

Died on this day:

Marghanita Laski, author, 1988;

Turner Layton, US singer and composer, 1978;

Charles Langbridge Morgan, author, 1958;

King George VI, 1952;

Elihu Root, US statesman and lawyer, 1937;

Gustav Klimt, Austrian painter, 1918;

The Rev. Ebenezer Cobham Brewer, author of the *Dictionary of Phrase and Fable*, 1897;

James Hadley Chase, novelist, 1985;

Isabella Mary Beeton [Mayson], author of household and cookery books, 1865;

Joseph Priestley, cleric and chemist, 1804;

Carlo Goldoni, Italian playwright, 1793;

Lancelot 'Capability' Brown, landscape gardener, 1783;

King Charles II, 1685;

Jacques Amyot, French scholar, 1593;

Aldus Manutius [Teobaldo Mannucci], Venetian printer, 1515.

Occurred on this day:

Agreement was reached between Britain and France on a Channel Tunnel, 1964;

Seven members of the Manchester United football team were among 21 killed in an air crash at Munich, 1958;

H.M. Queen Elizabeth II succeeded to the throne, 1952;

Sarawak was ceded to Great Britain, 1946;

Cardinal Achille Ratti was elected as Pope Pius XI, 1922;

The German airline Deutsche Luft-Reederei was established, flying between Berlin and Weimar, 1919;

An Act of Parliament granted votes for women over 30, 1918;

The Boy Scouts of America were chartered, 1910;

General Robert E. Lee became commander-in-chief of the Confederate armies, 1865;

Great Britain and Maori chiefs signed the Treaty of Waitangi in New Zealand, 1840;

Massachusetts became the 6th of the United States, 1788;

James II acceded to the throne of Great Britain, 1685.

TODAY IS THE FEAST DAY OF St Amand, St Guarinus of Palestrina, St Hildegund, Saints Mel and Melchu, St Paul Miki and his Companions and St Vedast or Vaast.

7th February

Born on this day:

Sammy Lee, footballer, 1959;
Gerald Davies, rugby footballer, 1945;
Gareth Hunt, actor, 1943;
Caroline Bingham, author, 1938 ;
Peter Jay, writer and broadcaster, 1937;
Dr Barbara McGibbon, pathologist, 1928;
Dora Bryan, actress, 1924;
The Earl of Harewood, 1923;
Eddie Bracken, US film actor, 1920;
Lord Bottomley, former government minister, 1907;
Harry Sinclair Lewis, US novelist, 1885;
Alfred Adler, Austrian psychoanalyst, 1870;

Ernst Frank, German conductor and composer, 1847;
Sir James Augustus Henry Murray, editor of the Oxford *New English Dictionary*, 1837;
Sir William Huggins, astronomer, 1824;
Charles John Huffam Dickens, novelist, 1812;
Henry Fuseli [Johann Heinrich Füssli], painter and writer on art, 1741;
Philippe Buache, French geographer and cartographer, 1700;
Thomas Killigrew, playwright, 1612;
St Thomas More, 1478.

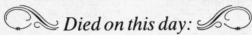

Died on this day:

Igor Vasilevich Kuchatov, Russian nuclear physicist, 1960;
Daniel François Malan, South African prime minister, 1959;
Maxwell Bodenheim, US novelist, poet and playwright, 1954;
Adolphe Sax, Belgian inventor of the saxophone, 1894;
Pope Pius IX, 1878;

Joseph Sheridan Le Fanu, novelist, 1873;
Gustavus IV, King of Sweden, 1837;
Ann Radcliffe [Ann Ward], romantic novelist, 1823;
William Boyce, organist and composer, 1779;
Jan van Huysum, Dutch painter, 1749;
James Stewart, 2nd Earl of Moray, murdered, 1591.

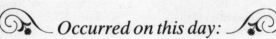

Occurred on this day:

Grenada became independent, 1974;
The main group of the Dead Sea Scrolls was discovered, 1947;
Benghazi was captured by the British, 1941;
The Tivoli Theatre, London, closed, 1914;
The *Pall Mall Gazette* was first published, 1865;
HMS *Orpheus* was wrecked off the coast of New Zealand, with the loss of 185 lives, 1863;

While visiting the British Museum, William Lloyd smashed the 1st-century Portland Vase, 1845;
The London, Chatham and Dover railway was opened, 1844;
Austria and Prussia formed an alliance against France, 1792;
Edward of Caernarvon [later King Edward II] was created Prince of Wales, 1301.

TODAY IS THE FEAST DAY OF St Adaucus, St Luke the Younger, St Moses, St Richard, 'king', St Silvin and St Theodore of Heraclea.

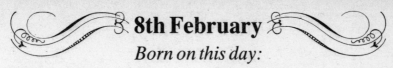

8th February

Born on this day:

Prof. Averil Cameron, historian, 1940;
John Williams, US composer and
  conductor, 1932;
James Dean, US film actor, 1931;
Osian Ellis, harpist, 1928;
Jack Lemmon, US film actor, 1925;
Lord Jakobovits, former Chief Rabbi,
  1921;
Lana Turner, US film actress, 1920;
Admiral of the Fleet Lord Hill-Norton,
  1915;
Marshal of the RAF Sir John Grandy,
  1913;
Prof. Ann Lambton, scholar of the Persian
  language, 1912;
Lord O'Brien of Lothbury, former
  Governor of the Bank of England, 1908;

Chester Floyd Carlson, US inventor of
  Xerox copying, 1906;
King Wallis Vidor, US film director, 1894;
Dame Edith Mary Evans, actress, 1888;
Martin Buber, Austrian Jewish religious
  philosopher, 1878;
Jules Verne, French novelist, 1828;
Henry Walter Bates, naturalist and
  explorer, 1825;
William Tecumseh Sherman, US general,
  1820;
John Ruskin, writer, artist and art critic,
  1819;
Samuel Butler, satirist, 1612;
Guercino [Giovanni Francesco Barbieri],
  Italian painter, 1590;
Robert Burton, author and scholar, 1577.

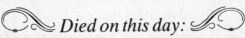

Died on this day:

Sir Victor Gollancz, publisher and writer,
  1967;
Prince Nicholas of Greece, 1938;
Max Liebermann, German painter and
  etcher, 1935;
William Bateson, biologist and geneticist,
  1926;
Prince Peter Alekseivich Kropotkin,
  Russian anarchist and geographer, 1921;

Gustaf Fröding, Swedish poet, 1911;
Jean-François Portaels, Belgian painter,
  1895;
Robert Michael Ballantyne, author of
  books for boys, 1894;
Peter the Great, Tsar of Russia, 1725;
Giuseppe Torelli, Italian composer,
  1709;
Mary, Queen of Scots, beheaded, 1587.

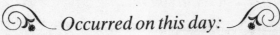

Occurred on this day:

In Angola, 14 British mercenaries were
  executed by firing squad, 1976;
In the USSR, Malenkov resigned and was
  succeeded by N. A. Bulganin, 1955;
374 lives were lost after the French cruiser
  Admiral Charner was torpedoed off the
  Syrian coast, 1916;
The film *Birth of a Nation*, by D. W.
  Griffiths, was first shown, 1915;

Looting and riots broke out after a
  peaceable demonstration in Trafalgar
  Square by the unemployed, 1886;
The Confederate States of America were
  formed, 1861;
The Great Frost of London ended, 1740;
Catherine I became Empress of Russia
  in succession to Peter the Great,
  1725.

TODAY IS THE FEAST OF St Cuthman, St Elfleda, St Jerome Emiliani, St John of
Matha, St Meingold, St Nicetius or Nizier of Besançon and St Stephen of Muret.

# 9th February

Born on this day:

Sandy Lyle, golfer, 1958;
Bernard Gallacher, golfer, 1949;
Mia Farrow, US acress, 1945;
Ryland Davies, operatic tenor, 1943;
Janet Suzman, actress, 1939;
Clive Swift, actor, 1936;
Dr Garret FitzGerald, former prime minister, Irish Republic, 1926;
Brendan Behan, Irish playwright, 1923;
Dr George Guest, organist, 1924;
Kathryn Grayson, US actress and singer, 1922;
Dean Rusk, former US Secretary of State, 1909;
Gwen Catley, soprano, 1906;
Ronald Colman, film actor, 1891;

Alban Maria Johannes Berg, Austrian composer, 1885;
Amy Lowell, US poet, 1874;
Mrs Patrick Campbell [Beatrice Stella Tanner], actress, 1865;
Anthony Hope [Sir Anthony Hope Hawkins], novelist, 1863;
John St Loe Strachey, editor, 1860;
Edward Henry Carson, 1st Baron, Ulster politician, 1854;
Captain Adrian Jones, sculptor, 1845;
Sir Evelyn Henry Wood, Field Marshal, 1838;
Daniel Bernoulli, Swiss mathematician, 1700.

Died on this day:

Bill Haley [William John Clifton Haley], US rock musician, 1981;
Sergei Vladimirovich Ilyushin, Russian aircraft designer, 1977;
Alexandre Nikolayevich Benois, Russian painter and theatre designer, 1960;
Miklós Horthy de Nagybánya, Hungarian admiral and former Regent, 1957;
George Norman Douglas, novelist and essayist, 1952;

Fyodor Mikhailovich Dostoevsky, Russian novelist, 1881;
Jules Michelet, French historian, 1874;
Nevil Maskelyne, astronomer royal, 1811;
John Hooper, bishop of Gloucester and Worcester, burnt at the stake, 1555;
Dr Rowland Taylor, English protestant martyr, 1555;
Agnes Sorel, mistress of Charles VII of France, 1450.

Occurred on this day:

Lithuania voted to secede from the Soviet Union, 1991;
Spain and the USSR re-established diplomatic relations after 38 years, 1977;
An earthquake in southern California claimed 64 lives in and around Los Angeles, 1971;
The Threepenny Opera had its first London performance, 1956;
Guadalcanal Island was evacuated by the Japanese, 1943;

Soap rationing began in Britain, 1942;
The French liner *Normandie* burned at a pier in New York and sank, 1942;
Sybil Thorndike made her London debut in *The Marquis*, 1908;
Verdi's opera *Falstaff* was first performed, Milan, 1893;
Charles Sturt reached the mouth of the Murray River at Lake Alexandrina, Australia, 1830.

TODAY IS THE FEAST DAY OF St Alto, St Ansbert, St Apollonia, St Nicephorus of Antioch, St Sabinus of Canosa and St Teilo.

10th February

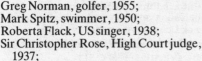

Born on this day:

Greg Norman, golfer, 1955;

Mark Spitz, swimmer, 1950;

Roberta Flack, US singer, 1938;

Sir Christopher Rose, High Court judge, 1937;

Air Marshal Sir William Richardson, former Chief Engineer, RAF, 1932;

Robert Wagner, US actor, 1930;

Field Marshal Sir Nigel Bagnall, former Chief of the General Staff, 1927;

Danny Blanchflower, footballer, 1926;

Leontyne Price, US soprano, 1927;

Dr Alexander Comfort, physician, poet and novelist, 1920;

Larry Adler, US mouth organist, 1914;

Joyce Irene Grenfell, actress, writer and entertainer, 1910;

Field Marshal Lord Milne, 1909;

Lon Chaney Jr. [Creighton Chaney], US actor, 1906;

Bertolt Brecht [Eugen Berthold Friedrich], German playwright and poet, 1898;

Maurice Harold Macmillan, 1st Earl of Stockton, statesman and publisher, 1894;

Jimmy [James Francis] Durante, US comedian, 1893;

William Tatem Tilden, US tennis champion, 1893;

Elisabeth Carson, lieder singer, 1892;

Boris Leonidovich Pasternak, Russian novelist, 1890;

Howard Spring, novelist, 1889;

Samuel Plimsoll, social reformer, 1824;

Henry Hart Milman, poet and dean of St Paul's, London, 1791;

Charles Lamb, essayist and poet, 1775.

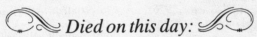

Died on this day:

Brian Aherne, film actor, 1986;

Sophie Tucker [Sophia Abuza], US singer, 1966;

Billy Rose [William Samuel Rosenberg], US producer and lyricist, 1966;

Marshal of the RAF Hugh Montague Trenchard, 1st Viscount, administrator, 1956;

Pope Pius XI [Achille Ratti], 1939;

Edgar Richard Horatio Wallace, thriller writer, 1932;

Wilhelm Konrad von Röntgen, German physicist, 1923;

Joseph Lister, 1st Baron, surgeon, 1912;

Alexander Sergeyevich Pushkin, Russian author, 1837;

Pope Leo XII, 1829;

Charles-Louis de Secondat, Baron de Montesquieu, French lawyer and philosopher, 1755;

Henry Stuart, Lord Darnley, consort of Mary, Queen of Scots, murdered 1567.

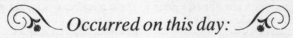

Occurred on this day:

Hundreds of people died and many made homeless after floods in Bolivia, 1979;

'Pay As You Earn' income tax was introduced, 1944;

New Delhi was inaugurated as capital of India, 1931;

The musical show *Maid of the Mountains* was first produced, London, 1917;

The British battleship *Dreadnought* was launched at Portsmouth, 1906;

Offenbach's opera *The Tales of Hoffman* was first performed, Paris, 1881;

Queen Victoria married Prince Albert of Saxe-Coburg-Gotha, 1840;

The Treaty of Paris, ceding Canada and other territories to Britain, was signed, 1763.

TODAY IS THE FEAST DAY OF St Austreberta, St Scholastica, St Soteris, St Trumwin and St William of Maleval.

11th February

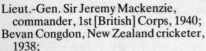

Born on this day:

Lieut.-Gen. Sir Jeremy Mackenzie, commander, 1st [British] Corps, 1940;

Bevan Congdon, New Zealand cricketer, 1938;

Prof. Marilyn Butler, professor of English literature, 1937;

Burt Reynolds, US film actor, 1936;

Mary Quant, fashion creator, 1934;

John Surtees, motor and motor-cycle racing champion, 1934;

Mr Dennis Skinner, MP, 1932;

Sir Alexander Gibson, conductor, 1926;

Leslie Nielsen, US film actor, 1926;

Vice-Admiral Sir Peter Berger, 1925;

Kim Stanley, US film actress, 1925;

Farouk I, King of Egypt, 1920.

Mabel Allan, mystery writer, 1915;

Patrick Leigh Fermor, author, 1915;

Sir Alexander Cairncross, chancellor of Glasgow University, 1911;

Joseph L. Mankiewicz, US film writer and director, 1909;

Sir Vivian Fuchs, Antarctic explorer, 1908;

Ernest [E.W.] Swanton, sporting author and BBC commentator, 1907;

Air Chief Marshal Sir Denis Barnett, 1906;

Thomas Alva Edison, US inventor, 1847;

William Henry Fox Talbot, photographic pioneer, 1800;

Pope Gregory XIV, 1535.

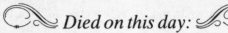

Died on this day:

David Garnett, novelist, 1981;

Lee J. Cobb [Leo Jacob], US actor, 1976;

Johannes Hans Daniel Jensen, German physicist, 1973;

Henry Mayo Bateman, cartoonist, 1970;

Ernö von Dohnányi, Hungarian composer, 1960;

Axel Martin Fredrik Munthe, Swedish physician and writer, 1949;

Sergei Mikhailovich Eisenstein, Russian film director, 1948;

Al Dubin, US popular lyricist, 1945;

Sir John Buchan, 1st Baron Tweedsmuir, governor-general of Canada and novelist, 1940;

Franz Schmidt, Austrian composer, 1939;

Sir Charles Algernon Parsons, inventor of the multi-stage steam turbine, 1931;

James Augustus Grant, African explorer and travel writer, 1892;

Honoré Daumier, French caricaturist, 1879;

William Shenstone, poet and gardener, 1763.

Occurred on this day:

In South Africa, the black nationalist leader Nelson Mandela was released from prison after 27 years, 1990;

Margaret Thatcher became the first woman leader of a British political party, 1975;

The musical show Fings Ain't Wot They Used t' Be was first produced, London, 1960;

The first London performance of the musical show Paint Your Wagon was staged, 1953;

The Lateran Treaty established an independent Vatican State in Rome, covering 108 acres, 1929;

The musical show Cinders was first produced, London, 1929;

Friedrich Ebert was elected President of the German republic, 1919;

The Welsh Guards [fifth regiment of Guards] was founded, 1915;

The first weekly weather report was issued by the Meteorological Office, 1878;

The Miracle of Lourdes occurred, when St Bernadette had her vision of the Virgin, 1858;

London University received its deed of settlement, 1826.

TODAY IS THE FEAST DAY OF St Benedict of Aniane, St Caedmon, St Gregory II, pope, St Lazarus of Milan, St Lucius of Adrianople, St Pascal I, pope, Saints Saturninus, Dativus, and Others and St Severinus of Agaunum.

12th February

Born on this day:

Simon MacCorkindale, actor, 1952;
Gundappa Visvanath, Indian cricketer, 1949;
Annette Crosbie, actress, 1934;
Anthony Howard, political journalist, 1934;
Paul Hamlyn, publisher, 1926;
Franco Zeffirelli, Italian film director, 1923;
Lord Wigoder QC, 1921;
Marie Lloyd [Matilda Alice Victoria Wood], music-hall artiste, 1870;
George Meredith, novelist, 1828;
Edward Forbes, naturalist, 1815;
Charles Darwin, naturalist, 1809;

Abraham Lincoln, 16th president of the USA, 1809;
Ferdinand de Braekeleer, Belgian painter, 1792;
Francis II, Emperor of Austria and last Holy Roman Emperor, 1768;
Cotton Mather, American colonist and writer, 1663;
Jacques Courtois [Giacomo Cortese], French painter, 1621;
John Winthrop, lawyer and first governor of the Massachusetts Bay Colony, 1588;
Thomas Campion, composer and poet, 1567.

Died on this day:

Henry Hathaway, US film-maker, 1985;
Tom Keating, art faker, 1984;
Benjamin Frankel, composer, 1973;
George Antheil, US composer, 1959;
Charles Francis Annesley Voysey, architect, 1941;
Marie-Eugène-Henri Fouques Duparc, French composer, 1933;
Lillie Langtry [Emilie Charlotte Le Breton], actress, 1929;
Hans Guido von Bülow, pianist and conductor, 1894;

Randolph Caldecott, artist and illustrator, 1886;
Immanuel Kant, German philosopher, 1804;
Pierre Carlet de Chamblain de Marivaux, French novelist, 1763;
Charles Le Brun, French painter, 1690;
Giambattista Marini, Neapolitan poet, 1625;
George Heriot, Scottish jeweller and philanthropist, 1624;
Lady Jane Grey, Queen for nine days, executed 1553.

Occurred on this day:

In the USA, it was announced that Borazon, a material harder than diamonds, had been made, 1957;
The European Broadcasting Union was formed, 1950;
George Gershwin's *Rhapsody in Blue* was first performed in New York, 1924;
The Manchu dynasty was overthrown, and China became a republic, 1912;
The Pacific islands Marianas, Caroline and Pelew were bought from Spain by Germany, 1899;

The London County Council was formed, 1889;
The independence of Chile was proclaimed in Santiago, 1818;
Over 1,000 French troops made an unsuccessful invasion attempt on the coast of Pembrokeshire, 1797;
Alexander Selkirk was taken off the island of Juan Fernandez by Captain Woodes Rogers, 1709;
The French were defeated by the English at the Battle of the Herrings [Rouvray], 1429.

TODAY IS THE FEAST DAY OF St Antony Kauleas, St Ethelwald of Lindisfarne, St Julian the Hospitaller, St Ludan, St Marina or Pelagia and St Meletius.

13th February

Born on this day:

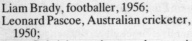

Liam Brady, footballer, 1956;
Leonard Pascoe, Australian cricketer, 1950;
Peter Gabriel, pop singer and songwriter, 1950;
Jacqueline Clarke, actress, 1942;
Oliver Reed, actor, 1938;
John Harris, cricket umpire, 1936;
George Segal, US film actor, 1934;
Caroline Blakiston, actress, 1933;
Kim Novak, US film actress, 1933;
Dr David Hessayon, horticultural author, 1928;
Jean-Jacques Servan-Schreiber, French author and politician, 1924;
Lord Pym, former government minister, 1922;

Eileen Farrell, US soprano, 1920;
Margaretta Scott, actress, 1912;
Georges Simenon, Belgian novelist, 1901;
Sir Neville Pearson, publisher, 1898;
Eleanor Farjeon, writer, 1881;
Feodor Ivanovich Chaliapin, Russian operatic bass singer, 1873;
William Strang, Scottish painter and engraver, 1859;
Lord Randolph Henry Spencer Churchill, politician, 1849;
David Allan, Scottish painter, 1744;
John Hunter, Scottish surgeon and anatomist, 1728;
Robert Dodsley, poet and bookseller, 1703.

Died on this day:

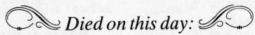

Jean Renoir, French film-maker, 1979;
Lily [Alice Josephine] Pons, US singer, 1976;
Georges-Henri Rouault, French expressionist painter, 1958;
Dame Christabel Harriette Pankhurst, suffragette, 1958;
Lloyd Cassel Douglas, US novelist, 1951;
Rafael Sabatini, Italian novelist, 1950;
Alphonse Bertillon, French criminologist, 1914;

Wilhelm Richard Wagner, German composer, 1883;
Cotton Mather, American colonist and writer, 1728;
Jacopo Bassano, Venetian painter, 1592;
Benvenuto Cellini, Italian sculptor and goldsmith, 1571;
Catherine Howard, 5th wife of Henry VIII, executed 1542.

Occurred on this day:

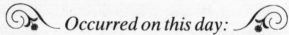

Alexander Solzhenitsyn was expelled from the USSR, 1974;
The Nuffield Foundation was set up, 1943;
Strauss's waltz *The Blue Danube* was first played in Vienna, 1867;
The Corps of Commissionaires was founded, 1859;
Asiatic cholera first appeared in Limehouse and Rotherhithe, London, 1832;

The trial of Warren Hastings began in Westminster Hall, 1788;
The Glencoe Massacre took place, when the Campbells murdered the Macdonalds, 1692;
William and Mary ascended the throne, 1689.

TODAY IS THE FEAST DAY OF St Catherine dei Ricci, St Ermenilda or Ermengild, St Licinius or Lesin, St Martinian the Hermit, St Modomnoc, St Polyeuctes of Melitene and St Stephen of Rieti.

 # 14th February

Born on this day:

Manuela Maleeva, tennis player, 1967;

Kevin Keegan, footballer, 1951;

Christopher Lillicrap, actor and musician, 1949;

Prince Hans Adam II of Liechtenstein, 1945;

Michael Rudman, theatre director and producer, 1939;

Lord Wilson, Governor of Hong Kong, 1935;

Sir Jack Hibbert, director, Central Statistical Office, 1932;

Jocelyn Stevens, Rector and vice-Provost, Royal College of Art, 1932;

Duncan Stewart, principal, Lady Margaret Hall, Oxford, 1930;

Lois Maxwell, actress, 1927;

Countess Mountbatten of Burma, 1924;

Dr Sir Albert Sloman, former vice-Chancellor, Essex University, 1921;

Jack Benny [Benjamin Kubelsky], US comedian and actor, 1894;

Israel Zangwill, novelist, playwright and Zionist leader, 1864;

Frank [James Thomas] Harris, Irish journalist and author, 1856;

Quintin Hogg, founder of the Polytechnic, 1845;

Hans Seeling, Czech pianist and conductor, 1828;

Christopher Latham Sholes, US inventor of an early typewriter, 1819;

Thomas Robert Malthus, economist, 1766;

Pietro Francesco [Caletti di Bruni] Cavalli, Italian composer, 1602.

Died on this day:

Frederick [Fritz] Loewe, US composer, 1988;

Sir Pelham Grenville [P.G.] Wodehouse, 1975;

Sir Julian Sorell Huxley, biologist and philosopher, 1975;

Sir William Rothenstein, artist, 1945;

Maj.-Gen. Henry Edward Manning Douglas, VC, 1939;

William Tecumseh Sherman, US general, 1891;

William Dyce, Scottish painter, 1864;

Henry Maudslay, engineer and inventor, 1831;

Sir William Blackstone, jurist, 1780;

Captain James Cook, sea-captain and explorer, murdered, 1779;

John Hadley, mathematician and inventor, 1744;

Fiorenzo di Lorenzo, Italian painter, 1525;

King Richard II, 1400.

Occurred on this day:

Harold Wilson became leader of the British Labour Party, 1963;

Nikita Khrushchev, at the 20th Soviet Communist Party Conference, denounced the policies of Josef Stalin, 1956;

The Bank of England was nationalised, 1946;

The German 42,345-ton battleship *Bismarck* was launched, 1939;

The St Valentine's Day Massacre took place in Chicago, 1929;

Marconi began the first regular broadcasting transmissions in England, 1922;

Yuan Shi-kai became the first president of the Chinese republic, 1912;

Arizona became the 48th of the United States, 1912;

Hawaii was annexed by treaty to the USA [withdrawn on 9th March by the President], 1893;

Oregon became the 33rd of the United States, 1859;

The Spanish Fleet was defeated off Cape St Vincent by John Jervis and Horatio Nelson, 1797.

TODAY IS THE FEAST DAY OF St Abraham of Carrhae, St Adolf of Osnabrück, St Antoninus of Sorrento, St Auxentius, St Conran, Saints Cyril and Methodius, St John Baptist of the Conception, St Maro and St Valentine.

15th February

Born on this day:

Jane Seymour, actress, 1951;

Diana Jones, jockey, 1950;

Paddy McMahon, Irish former show-jumper, 1933;

Claire Bloom, actress, 1931;

Gerald Harper, actor, 1929;

Graham Hill, racing driver, 1929;

Frank Dunlop, former director of the Edinburgh Festival, 1926;

Cesar Romero, US film actor, 1907;

Harold Arlen [Hyman Arluck], US composer and singer, 1905;

Mary Adshead, mural painter, 1904;

Sir George Taylor, botanist and horticulturalist, 1904;

Walter Donaldson, US composer and pianist, 1893;

Horatio Nicholls [Lawrence Wright], composer and publisher, 1888;

Henry Mayo Bateman, cartoonist, 1887;

John Barrymore [Blythe], US actor, 1882;

Sir Ernest Henry Shackleton, Antarctic explorer, 1874;

Alfred North Whitehead, philosopher and mathematician, 1861;

Elihu Root, US lawyer and statesman, 1845;

Jeremy Bentham, philospher and writer, 1748;

Jean-Nicolas Buache, French geographer and cartographer, 1741;

Louis XV, King of France, 1710;

Charles Andrew Vanloo, French painter, 1705;

Galileo Galilei, astronomer and mathematician, 1564;

Pedro Menendez de Avilés, Spanish navigator, 1519;

Philip Melanchthon [Schwarzerd], reformer and theologian, 1497.

Died on this day:

Ethel Merman [Zimmerman], US singer and actress, 1984;

Nat 'King' Cole [Nathaniel Adams Coles], US singer and musician, 1965;

Herbert Henry, Earl of Oxford and Asquith, statesman, 1928;

Lionel Monckton, composer, 1924;

Lew [Lewis] Wallace, US soldier, lawyer, diplomat and author, 1905;

Mikhail Ivanovich Glinka, Russian composer, 1857;

Gotthold Ephraim Lessing, German author, 1781;

Michael Praetorius [Schultheiss], German composer and musical historian, 1621;

Il Sodoma [Giovanni Antonio Bazzi], Italian painter, 1549.

Occurred on this day:

Britain changed over to decimal currency, 1971;

British troops reached the Rhine, 1945;

The Monte Cassino monastery in Italy was bombed by Allied aircraft, 1944;

Singapore surrendered to the Japanese, 1942;

The Balkan Entente Conference was held in Athens, 1937;

Kimberley was relieved, 1900;

The first cargo of frozen meat left New Zealand for Britain, 1882.

TODAY IS THE FEAST DAY OF St Agape of Terni, St Sigfrid of Växjö, St Tanco or Tatto and St Walfrid or Galfrid.

 # 16th February

Born on this day:

John McEnroe, US tennis player, 1959;
Ian Lavender, actor, 1946;
Jeremy Bullock, actor, 1945;
Anthony Dowell, director of the Royal Ballet, 1943;
Paul Bailey, novelist, 1937;
Peter Hobday, radio presenter, 1937;
Frederick Cuming, painter, 1930;
Peter Porter, author and poet, 1929;
John Schlesinger, film director, 1926;
Sir Geraint Evans, operatic baritone, 1922;
Patti Andrews, US singer [of the Andrews Sisters], 1920;
Jeffrey Lynn, US film actor, 1909;
Lord Franks OM, former ambassador to the USA, 1905;
Katherine Cornell, US actress, 1898;
Louis Calhern [Carl Henry Vogt], US film actor, 1895;
Robert Joseph Flaherty, US film-maker, 1884;
George Macaulay Trevelyan, historian, 1876;
Sir William Gurney Benham, editor and newspaper proprietor, 1859;
Hugo Marie de Vries, Dutch botanist, 1848;
Ernst Heinrich Haeckel, German naturalist, 1834;
Sir Francis Galton, anthropologist and geneticist, 1822;
Heinrich Barth, German explorer, 1821;
Giambattista Bodoni, Italian printer and typographer, 1740.

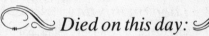 ## Died on this day:

Henry Cabot Lodge, US statesman, 1985;
Sir Isaac Leslie Hore-Belisha, 1st Baron, statesman, 1957;
James Harvey Robinson, US historian, 1936;
Giosuè Carducci, Italian poet, 1907;
Henry Walter Bates, explorer and naturalist, 1892;
Elisha Kent Kane, US explorer, 1857;
Lionel Lukin, lifeboat inventor, 1834;
François-Joseph Gossec, French composer, 1829;
Pierre-Paul Prud'hon, French painter, 1823;
Richard Mead, royal physician, 1754;
Henry Deane, Archbishop of Canterbury, 1503;
Alfonso III, King of Portugal, 1279.

 ## Occurred on this day:

The first London production of the musical show *Fiddler on the Roof* took place, 1967;
The US nuclear submarine *Triton* set off on an underwater round-the-world trip, 1960;
Fidel Castro became prime minister of Cuba, 1959;
US forces took Bataan, in the Philippines, 1945;
HMS *Cossack* rescued British prisoners from the *Altmark* in Norwegian waters, 1940;
In Spain, the 'Popular Front' won the general election, 1936;
The musical show *Conversation Piece* was first produced, London, 1934;
The Fianna Fáil party, led by Éamon de Valera, won the Irish general election, 1932;
The Confederate forces surrendered Fort Grant to General Ulysses S. Grant, 1862;
The Athenaeum Club, London, was founded, 1824;
Spain was invaded by France, 1808.

TODAY IS THE FEAST DAY OF Saints Elias, Jeremy and their Companions, St Gilbert of Sempringham, St Juliana of Cumae and St Onesimus the Slave.

 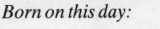

17th February

Born on this day:

Princess Marie-Astrid of Luxembourg, 1954;
Prunella Gee, actress, 1950;
Julia McKenzie, actress and singer, 1941;
Gene Pitney, US country and western singer and composer, 1941;
Jim Brown, US film actor, 1935;
Alan Bates, actor, 1934;
Barry Humphries, Australian entertainer, 1934;
Ruth Rendell, crime novelist, 1930;
Yasser Arafat, Arab leader, 1929;
Patricia Routledge, actress, 1929;
Lord Ridley of Liddesdale [Nicholas Ridley] former MP, 1929;
Elleston Trevor, author, 1920;

Lord Kearton, chancellor, University of Bath, 1911;
Lord Foot, solicitor, 1909;
Marian Anderson, US contralto, 1901;
Ronald Arbuthnott Knox, theologian and essayist, 1888;
Andrew Barton ['Banjo'] Paterson, Australian poet and journalist, 1864;
Sir Edward German [Edward German Jones], composer, 1862;
Frederick Eugene Ives, US half-tone process inventor, 1856;
René Laënnec, French army doctor, inventor of the stethoscope, 1781;
John Pinkerton, Scottish historian, 1758;
Arcangelo Corelli, Italian composer, 1653.

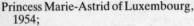 Died on this day:

Lee Strasberg, US actor and founder of the Actors' Studio, 1982;
Graham Vivian Sutherland, painter, 1980;
Sir Donald Wolfit, actor, 1968;
Gus Elen [Ernest Augustus Elen], music hall artiste, 1940;
Albert I, King of the Belgians, 1934;
Geronimo [Goyathlay – 'One Who Yawns'] Apache chief, 1909;
Henry Steel Olcott, a US founder of the Theosophical Society, 1907;
Christopher Latham Sholes, US inventor of a typewriter, 1890;
Harry [Heinrich] Heine, German poet, 1856;

William Collins, painter, 1847;
Johann Heinrich Pestalozzi, Swiss educationist, 1827;
Antoine Galland, French orientalist and translator of *The Thousand and One Nights*, 1715;
James Renwick, Scottish Covenanter, executed, 1688;
Molière [Jean-Baptiste Poquelin], French playwright, 1673;
Giordano Bruno, Italian philosopher, burnt at the stake, 1600;
Tamerlane the Great, Mongol leader, 1405.

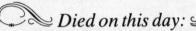 Occurred on this day:

A majority in the House of Commons decided that Britain should join the Common Market, 1972;
The British National Health Service White Paper was issued, 1944;
The inner tomb of Tutankhamun was opened at Luxor by the team led by Lord Carnarvon, 1923;
Puccini's opera, *Madame Butterfly*, was first produced, Milan, 1904;
An attempt to assassinate Tsar Alexander II of Russia was made by an explosion at the Winter Palace, St Petersburg, 1880;

The USS *Housatonic* was sunk by the Confederate submarine *Hunley*, 1864;
Verdi's opera, *Un Ballo in Maschera*, was first produced, Rome, 1859;
The 'draisine', forerunner of the bicycle, was patented by Baron Karl von Drais de Sauerbrun, 1818;
The Yorkists were defeated by the Lancastrians at the Battle of St Albans, 1461.

TODAY IS THE FEAST DAY OF St Evermod, St Finan of Lindisfarne, St Fintan of Cloeenagh, St Loman, The Seven Servite Founders and Saints Theodulus and Julian.

# 18th February

Born on this day:

Greta Scacchi, film actress, 1960;
John Travolta, US actor, 1954;
Sinead Cusack, actress, 1948;
José-Maria Canizares, golfer, 1947;
Graeme Garden, actor and scriptwriter, 1943;
Prue Leith, cookery editor and restaurateur, 1940;
Lieut.-Gen. Sir John Wilsey, G.O.C., Northern Ireland, 1939;
Yoko Ono Lennon, widow of John Lennon, 1934;
Milos Forman, film director, 1932;
Bobby Robson, football manager, 1933;
Ned Sherrin, TV presenter and producer, 1931;
Len Deighton, novelist, 1929;

Helen Gurley Brown, US author and magazine editor, 1922;
Jack Palance, US film actor, 1920;
Phyllis Calvert, actress, 1915;
Dane Clark, US film actor, 1913;
Andrés Segovia, Spanish guitarist, 1894;
Wendell Louis Wilkie, US politician, 1892;
Edward Arnold [Gunther Schneider], US film actor, 1890;
Sholem Aleichem [Solomon J. Rabinowitz], Yiddish writer, 1859;
Ernst Mach, Austrian physicist, 1838;
Niccolò Paganini, Italian violinist and composer, 1784;
Count Alessandro Volta, Italian physicist, 1745;
Mary I, Queen of England, 1516.

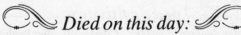## Died on this day:

Hans Richter, US painter and film-maker, 1976;
Jacob Robert Oppenheimer, US physicist, 1967;
Gustave Charpentier, French composer, 1956;
James John Corbett ['Gentleman Jim'], US pugilist, 1933;
Carolus-Duran [Charles-Auguste-Émile Durand], French painter, 1917;

Maurice Quentin de La Tour, French pastel artist, 1788;
Michelangelo Buonarroti, Italian artist, 1564;
Martin Luther, Protestant reformer, 1546;
Fra Angelico [Giovanni da Fiesole], Italian painter, 1455.

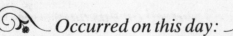## Occurred on this day:

The Gambia became an independent state within the Commonwealth, 1965;
A constitutional monarchy was proclaimed in Nepal by the King, 1951;
After the French submarine Le Surcouf was rammed by a merchant ship in the Caribbean, 30 men lost their lives, 1942;
The Golden Gate International Exposition opened in San Francisco, 1939;
Germany's blockade of Britain by submarine began, 1915;

In South Africa, Piet Cronje surrendered to the British at Paardeberg, 1900;
Charleston was taken by the Union fleet, 1865;
The first Congress of the Confederate States met in Richmond, Virginia, 1862;
The first Italian parliament met, and proclaimed Victor Emmanuel as king, 1861;
The Order of the Bath was revived, 1725;
Pilgrim's Progress, by John Bunyan, was published, 1678

TODAY IS THE FEAST DAY OF St Angilbert, St Colman of Lindisfarne, St Flavian of Constantinople, St Helladius of Toledo, St Leo and Paregorius, St Simeon of Jerusalem and St Theotonius.

 # 19th February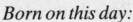

Born on this day:

Andrew Jameson, swimmer, 1965;
Hana Mandlikova, Australian tennis
  champion, 1962;
HRH The Duke of York, 1960;
Erin Pizzey, founder of battered wives'
  homes, 1939;
Gwen Taylor, actress, 1939;
Lord Forbes, premier Lord of Scotland,
  1918;
Lula Carson McCullers [Smith], US
  novelist, 1917;
John Freeman, international relations
  consultant and former diplomat, 1915;
Prof. Bernard Meadows, sculptor, 1915;
Stan Kenton [Stanley Newcomb], US jazz
  bandleader, 1912;

Merle Oberon [Estelle Merle O'Brien
  Thompson], film actress, 1911;
Frances Perry, horticulturist, 1907;
Sven Anders Hedin, Swedish explorer,
  1865;
Adelina Patti, soprano, 1843;
Sir Roderick Impey Murchison, geologist,
  1792;
Luigi Boccherini, Italian cellist and
  composer, 1743;
Richard Cumberland, playwright, 1732;
George Brydges Rodney, 1st Baron,
  admiral, 1718;
David Garrick, actor, 1717;
Nicolaus Copernicus Polish astronomer,
  1473.

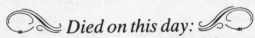 ## Died on this day:

Luigi Dallapiccola, Italian composer, 1975;
John Grierson, documentary film-maker,
  1972;
Knut Hamsun [Pedersen], Norwegian
  novelist and poet, 1952;
André-Paul-Guillaume Gide, French
  novelist, 1951;
Sir Herbert Hamilton Harty, conductor,
  1941;
Ernst Mach, Austrian physicist, 1916;

Charles Blondin [Jean-François Gravelet],
  French tight-rope walker, 1897;
Charles-François Daubigny, French
  landscape painter, 1878;
Bernard Barton, poet, 1849;
Georg Büchner, German playwright, 1837;
Elizabeth Carter, poet, translator and
  scholar, 1806;
Sir Henry Savile, scholar and
  philanthropist, 1622.

 ## Occurred on this day:

The USSR agreed to withdraw its forces
  from Cuba. 1963;
An agreement for the independence of
  Cyprus was signed in London by the
  prime ministers of Britain, Turkey and
  Greece, 1959;
US troops landed on Iwo Jima, 1945;
Darwin, Australia, was bombed by
  Japanese aircraft, 1942;
British troops from Kenya invaded Italian
  Somaliland, 1941;
The International Drug Convention was
  signed in Geneva, 1924;

The phonograph was patented by Thomas
  A. Edison, 1878;
Bread riots took place in Liverpool,
  1855;
Napoleon Bonaparte established himself as
  First Consul, 1800;
The Peace of Westminster was signed,
  under which New Netherlands [New
  York] became British, 1674;
The rebels were defeated by King Henry IV
  at Bramham Moor, 1408.

TODAY IS THE FEAST DAY OF St Barbatus, St Beatus of Liebana, St Boniface of
Lausanne, St Conrad of Piacenza and St Mesrop.

20th February

Born on this day:

Phil Neal, former England footballer, 1951;
Eddie Hemmings, cricketer, 1949;
Mike Leigh, playwright and theatre director, 1943;
Jimmy Greaves, TV commentator and ex-footballer, 1940;
Sidney Poitier, US film actor, 1927;
George Waring, actor and director, 1927;
Robert Altman, US film director, 1925;
Dr Ruth Gipps, composer and conductor, 1921;
The Rt. Rev. George Appleton, religious writer and missionary, 1902;
Georges Bernanos, French novelist, 1888;

Dame Marie Rambert [Cyvia Rambam], founder of the Ballet Rambert, 1888;
Charles Vincent Massey, Canadian statesman and diplomat, 1887;
Béla Kun, Hungarian communist, 1885;
William Terriss [William Charles James Lewin], actor and matinee idol, 1847;
Honoré Daumier, French caricaturist and painter, 1808;
Charles-Auguste de Bériot, Belgian violinist and composer, 1802;
Adam Black, Scottish politician and publisher, 1784.

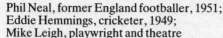

Died on this day:

Mikhail Aleksandrovich Sholokhov, Russian author, 1984;
Chester William Nimitz, US admiral, 1966;
Percy Aldridge Grainger, composer, 1961;
Sir Charles Leonard Woolley, archaeologist, 1960;
Laurence Housman, playwright, novelist and illustrator, 1959;
Robert Edwin Peary, US Arctic explorer, 1920;
George Paul Chalmers, Scottish painter, 1878;

Augustin-Eugène Scribe, French playwright, 1861;
Andreas Hofer, Tyrolean patriot, executed, 1810;
Aurangzeb, last Mogul emperor of India, 1707;
Gentile Bellini, Italian painter, 1507;
Luca della Robbia, Italian sculptor, 1482;
James I, King of Scotland, assassinated, 1437;
Pope Martin V, 1431.

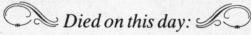

Occurred on this day:

The first London production of the musical show *Mame* took place, 1969;
John Glenn, US astronaut [now a senator], was launched into space in the Mercury capsule, *Friendship 7*, 1962;
Anthony Eden resigned as British Foreign Secretary, 1938;
The Netherlands West Indies were purchased by the USA, 1917;
The Panama-Pacific International Exposition opened in San Francisco, 1915;

A great storm raged in England, with much damage to the Crystal Palace, while the steeple of Chichester Cathedral was blown away, 1861;
Austria declared herself to be bankrupt, 1811;
The French defeated the Spanish at the Battle of Saragossa, 1809;
Admiral Blake defeated the Dutch fleet under Van Tromp off Portsmouth, 1653.

TODAY IS THE FEAST DAY OF St Eleutherius of Tournai, St Eucherius of Orléans, St Sadoth, Saints Tyrannio, Zenobius and their Companions and St Wulfric.

21st February

Born on this day:

Jacqueline Tong, actress, 1950;

David Wood, actor and playwright, 1944;

Peter McEnery, actor, 1940;

Harald V, King of Norway, 1937;

Jilly Cooper, author and journalist, 1937;

Nina Simone, US singer, 1934;

Hubert de Givenchy, French fashion designer, 1927;

Richard Turner-Warwick, surgeon and urologist, 1925;

Robert Mugabe, president of Zimbabwe, 1924;

Douglas Bader, WWII pilot, 1910;

Wystan Hugh Auden, poet, 1907;

Madeleine Renaud, French actress, 1903;

Anaïs Nin, French author, 1903;

Sacha Guitry, French actor, playwright and director, 1885;

Gertie Millar, Countess of Dudley, musical comedy actress, 1879;

Constantin Brancusi, Romanian sculptor, 1876;

August von Wasserman, German bacteriologist, 1866;

George Lansbury, statesman, 1859;

Clément-Philibert-Léo Delibes, French composer, 1836;

Jean-Louis-Ernest Meissonier, French painter, 1815;

John Henry Newman, Cardinal, 1801;

Antonio López de Santa Anna, Mexican revolutionary and president, 1794;

Anne Grant, poet and essayist, 1755.

Died on this day:

Victor Canning, author, 1986;

Shigechiyo Izumi, a Japanese, at the age of 120 years, 237 days, 1986;

Louis Hayward [Seafield Grant], film actor, 1985;

Howard Walter Florey, Baron Florey, pathologist, 1968;

Malcolm X [Little], US black leader, murdered, 1965;

Jacques Becker, French film director, 1960;

Sir Frederick Banting, Canadian scientist, killed in air crash, 1941;

George Ellery Hale, US astronomer, 1938;

Lewis Grassic Gibbon [James Leslie Mitchell], Scottish novelist, 1935;

Jethro Tull, agricultural writer, 1741;

Baruch [Benedict] Spinoza, Dutch philosopher, 1677;

Robert Southwell, poet, Jesuit and martyr, hanged, 1595;

Pope Julius II, 1513.

Occurred on this day:

Identity cards were abolished in Britain, 1952;

A mutiny in the Indian navy occurred at Bombay, 1946;

General Eisenhower became supreme commander of Allied forces in North Africa, 1943;

The New Statesman was founded, 1931;

The Battle of Verdun commenced, 1916;

The first republic of Cuba was founded, 1901;

The Apollo Theatre, London, opened, 1901;

The British Post Office inaugurated a mailbag service operated by pneumatic conveyors below streets, 1863;

Richard Trevithick demonstrated a self-powered railway locomotive in Glamorgan, 1804;

John Wilkes, MP, expelled from the House of Commons after being found guilty of publishing an 'impious libel', the Essay on Woman, 1764.

TODAY IS THE FEAST DAY OF St George of Amastris, St Germanus of Granfel, St Peter Damian, St Robert Southwell and St Severian of Scythopolis.

22nd February

Born on this day:

Ian Stark, show-jumper, 1954;
Julie Walters, actress, 1950;
Niki Lauda, motor-racing champion, 1949;
Judy Cornwell, actress, 1942;
Noel Murphy, rugby footballer, 1937;
Joseph Ettedgui, fashion designer, 1936;
The Duchess of Kent, 1933;
Sheila Hancock, actress, 1933;
Senator Edward Kennedy, 1932;
Bruce Forsyth, entertainer, 1928;
Warren Stanley Tute, novelist, sailor and playwright, 1914;
Sir John Mills, actor, director and producer, 1908;
Robert Young, US film actor, 1907;
Luis Buñuel, Spanish film director, 1900;
Nacio Herb Brown, US popular composer and publisher, 1896;
Lady Olave St Clair Baden-Powell, World Chief Guide from 1930, 1889;
Lew Cody [Louis Joseph Cote], US actor, 1884;
Arthur Eric Rowton Gill, artist, sculptor and typographer, 1882;
Norman Alfred William Lindsay, Australian cartoonist, illustrator and novelist, 1879;
Sir Robert Stephenson Smyth Baden-Powell, 1st Baron, founder of the Boy Scouts, 1857;
Arthur Schopenhauer, German philosopher, 1788;
George Washington, 1st president of the USA, 1732.

Died on this day:

Oskar Kokoschka, Austrian painter and playwright, 1980;
Elizabeth Dorothea Cole Bowen, novelist, 1973;
Sir Max Pemberton, author, 1950;
Stefan Zweig, writer, 1942;
Francisco Indalecio Madero, Mexican politician, 1913;
Sir Leslie Stephen, biographer, author and editor, 1904;
Jean-Baptiste-Camille Corot, French painter, 1875;
Sir Charles Lyell, geologist, 1875;
Sydney Smith, social reformer, 1845;
James Barry, Irish historical painter, 1806;
Nicolaes Berchem, Dutch painter, 1683;
Govaert Flinck, Dutch painter, 1660;
Amerigo Vespucci, Italian navigator, 1512.

 ## Occurred on this day:

Pakistan recognised the independence of Bangladesh, 1974;
An IRA bomb attack at Aldershot killed seven people, 1972;
Dr Selman Abraham Waksman announced his discovery of streptomycin, 1946;
Frank Winfield Woolworth opened his first 'five-and-ten-cent-store', at Utica, New York, 1879;
Jefferson Davis was inaugurated as president of the Confederate States of America, 1862;
The Mexicans were defeated by US forces under General Taylor at the Battle of Buena Vista, 1847;
Florida was ceded to the USA by Spain, 1819;
The last invasion of Britain took place when the French landed at Fishguard, and were made prisoners, 1797;
Robert II acceded to the throne of Scotland, 1370.

TODAY IS THE FEAST DAY OF St Baradates, St Margaret of Cortona and Saints Thalassius and Limnaeus.

23rd February

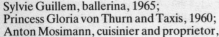

Born on this day:

Sylvie Guillem, ballerina, 1965;
Princess Gloria von Thurn and Taxis, 1960;
Anton Mosimann, cuisinier and proprietor, Mosimann's, 1947;
Peter Fonda, US actor, 1940;
Lord Ezra, former Coal Board chief, 1919;
The Rt. Rev. Dom Aelred Watkin, former Abbot of Glastonbury, 1918;
Erich Kästner, German poet and writer for children, 1899;
Kathleen Harrison, actress, 1892;
John Gilbert Winant, US diplomat, 1889;
Victor Fleming, US film director, 1883;
Karl Jaspers, German philosopher, 1883;
William Edward Burghardt Du Bois, Ghanaian novelist, 1868;
Franz von Stuck, German painter and sculptor, 1863;
Sir George Frederick Watts, sculptor and painter, 1817;
Gertrud Elisabeth Mara [Schmeling], German soprano, 1749;
Meyer Amschel Rothschild, banker, 1743;
George Frederick Handel, composer, 1685;
Samuel Pepys, naval official and diarist, 1633.

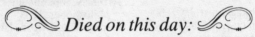

Died on this day:

Sir Adrian Boult, conductor, 1983;
Laurence Stephen Lowry, painter, 1976;
Fannie Hurst, US novelist, 1968;
Stan Laurel [Arthur Stanley Jefferson], film comedian, 1965;
Paul-Louis-Charles Claudel, French poet, playwright and diplomat, 1955;
Leo Hendrik Baekeland, Belgian/US inventor of Bakelite, 1944;
Sir Edward William Elgar, composer, 1934;
Dame Nellie Melba [Helen Porter Mitchell], Australian operatic singer, 1931;
Thomas Woodrow Wilson, 28th president of the USA, 1924;
Samuel Rawson Gardiner, historian, 1902;
William Butterfield, architect, 1900;
Ernest Christopher Dowson, poet, 1900;
Auguste Bonheur, French painter, 1884;
Karl Friedrich Gauss, mathematician and astronomer, 1855;
John Quincy Adams, 6th president of the USA, 1848;
John Keats, poet, 1821;
Sir Joshua Reynolds, painter, 1792;
Agostino Carracci, Italian painter, 1602;
Pope Eugene IV, 1447.

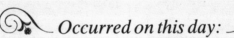

Occurred on this day:

Guyana became a republic within the Commonwealth, 1970;
The present building of the Vaudeville Theatre, London, opened, 1926;
Benito Mussolini founded the Fascist Party in Italy, 1919;
In Russia, the February Revolution began [Old Style date], 1917;
The United States Steel Corporation was founded by J.P. Morgan, 1901;
In France, Émile Zola was imprisoned for writing the open letter *J'accuse*, 1898;
Lawn tennis, then called 'Sphairistike', was patented, 1874;
The Cato Street Conspiracy to murder Cabinet ministers was discovered, 1820.

TODAY IS THE FEAST DAY OF St Alexander Akimetes, St Boisil or Boswell, St Dositheus, St Milburga or Mildgytha, St Polycarp of Smyrna, St Serenus of Cerneuf the Gardener and St Willigis.

24th February

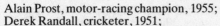
Alain Prost, motor-racing champion, 1955;
Derek Randall, cricketer, 1951;
Dennis Waterman, actor, 1948;
Paul Jones, actor and singer, 1942;
Denis Law, footballer, 1940;
James Farentino, US film actor, 1938;
Michel Legrand, French composer and conductor, 1932;
Brian Close, former England cricket captain, 1931;
Richard Hamilton, pop-art painter, 1922;
Betty Marsden, actress, 1919;
David Langdon, cartoonist and illustrator, 1914;
Prof. Eric Boyland, biochemist, 1905;
Chester William Nimitz, US admiral, 1885;
Sir Cyril Arthur Pearson, newspaper proprietor, 1866;

Eugene Arnold Dolmetsch, early music enthusiast, 1858;
George Augustus Moore, Irish novelist, 1852;
Grant Allen [Charles Grant Blairfindie Allen], Canadian writer and man of letters, 1848;
Winslow Homer, US painter and illustrator, 1836;
Wilhelm Karl Grimm, German philologist and folklorist, 1786;
Charles Le Brun, French historical painter, 1619;
Don John of Austria, Spanish soldier, 1547;
Charles V [Charles I of Spain], Holy Roman Emperor, 1500.

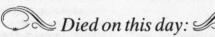
Died on this day:

Marcel Grandjany, French/US composer, 1975;
Grant Franklin Thomas Richards, publisher, 1948;
Pierre-Marie-Félix Janet, French psychologist and neurologist, 1947;
Ahmed Pasha, Egyptian prime minister, assassinated, 1945;
Sir Edward Marshall Hall, lawyer, 1927;
Edmund John Armstrong, Irish poet, 1865;
Thomas Bowdler, editor and prudish censor, 1825;

Thomas Coutts, banker, 1822;
Robert Fulton, US steamboat pioneer, 1815;
Henry Cavendish, physicist, 1810;
Sir James Radcliffe Bt., 3rd Earl of Derwentwater, statesman, 1716;
Sir Edmund Andros, governor of Virginia, 1714;
Marc-Antoine Charpentier, French composer, 1704;
Francis, Duc de Guise, French military commander, assassinated, 1563.

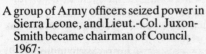
Occurred on this day:

A group of Army officers seized power in Sierra Leone, and Lieut.-Col. Juxon-Smith became chairman of Council, 1967;
The government of Dr Kwame Nkrumah in Ghana was overthrown by a military coup, 1966;
Juan Domingo Perón was elected president of Argentina, 1946;
The first commercial nylon product – toothbrush bristles – was produced in the USA, 1938;
A world land-speed record of 253.96 mph was set up by Sir Malcolm Campbell, 1932;

The Arnold Dolmetsch Foundation was set up, 1928;
The 'Flying Scotsman' went into service, 1923;
The Simplon Tunnel, Switzerland/Italy, was completed, 1905;
Louis-Philippe, King of France, abdicated, 1848;
The Battle of the Alamo began, 1836;
Pope Gregory XIII issued a Bull announcing the Gregorian Calendar, 1582;
Francis I of France was defeated at the Battle of Pavia, 1525.

TODAY IS THE FEAST DAY OF Saints Montanus, Lucius, and their Companions and St Praetextatus or Prix.

25th February

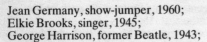

Born on this day:

Jean Germany, show-jumper, 1960;
Elkie Brooks, singer, 1945;
George Harrison, former Beatle, 1943;
David Puttnam, film producer, 1941;
Prof. Stewart Sutherland, vice-Chancellor, University of London, 1941;
Farokh Engineer, Indian cricketer, 1938;
Tom Courtenay, actor, 1937;
Bernard Bresslaw, comedy actor, 1934;
Marshal of the RAF Sir Keith Williamson, former Chief of Air Staff, 1928;
Anthony Burgess, novelist, 1917;
Herbert ['Zeppo'] Marx, comedian and actor, 1901;
Dame Myra Hess, pianist, 1890;
John Foster Dulles, US statesman, 1888;
Benedetto Croce, Italian philosopher, 1866;
Karl May, German author of Western-style juvenile books, 1842;
Pierre-Firmin-Auguste Renoir, French painter, 1841;
José Francisco de San Martín, Argentinian leader, 1778;
Carlo Goldoni, Italian playwright, 1707.

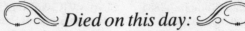

Died on this day:

Tennessee [Thomas Lanier] Williams, US playwright, 1983;
Mark Rothko, US painter, 1970;
Alexander Archipenko, US sculptor, 1965;
George Richards Minot, US physician, 1950;
James Boyd, US novelist, 1944;
Henri-Desiré Landru, French multi-murderer, executed, 1922;
Sir John Tenniel, artist and illustrator, 1914;
Paul Julius, Baron von Reuter, founder of the news agency, 1899;
George Don, botanist, 1856;
Thomas Moore, poet and musician, 1852;
Eliza Hayward [Fowler], novelist, playwright and actress, 1756;
Sir Christopher Wren, architect, 1723;
Frederick I, King of Prussia, 1713;
Albrecht von Wallenstein, Austrian general, assassinated, 1634;
Robert Devereux, 2nd Earl of Essex, executed, 1601.

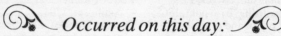

Occurred on this day:

The US spacecraft *Pioneer 10* was launched, its destination being Jupiter, 1972;
A Communist coup took place in Czechoslovakia and a People's Republic was proclaimed, 1948;
The Gaiety Theatre, Strand, London, closed, 1939;
Meat and butter were rationed in Southern England, 1918;
Paper currency, called 'greenbacks', was first issued in the USA by Abraham Lincoln, 1862;
Edward John Eyre set out to explore the Great Australian Bight, 1841;
The rules of cricket were formulated in the 'Star and Garter', Pall Mall, 1774;
Queen Elizabeth I was excommunicated by Pope Pius V, 1570.

TODAY IS THE FEAST DAY OF St Caesarius of Nazianzen, St Calixto Caravario, St Ethelbert of Kent, St Gerland, St Louis Versiglia, St Tarasius, St Victorinus of Corinth and his Companions and St Walburga.

26th February

Born on this day:

Emma Kirkby, soprano, 1949;
David Edgar, playwright, 1948;
Sandie Shaw, singer, 1947;
Tony Selby, actor, 1938;
Sir James Goldsmith, financier and entrepreneur, 1933;
Johnny Cash, singer, 1932;
Fats Domino, US singer, 1928;
Sir Donald Farquharson, a Lord Justice of Appeal, 1928;
Everton Weekes, West Indian cricketer, 1925;
Margaret Leighton, actress, 1922;
Betty Hutton, US film actress, 1921;
Dr Basil Greenhill, author and nautical authority, 1920;
Frank Bridge, conductor and composer, 1879;

Leonard Borwick, pianist, 1868;
Émile Coué, French psychotherapist, 1857;
William Frederick Cody ['Buffalo Bill'], showman, 1846;
Evelyn Baring, 1st Earl of Cromer, statesman and diplomat, 1841;
Alexis Holländer, German pianist and conductor, 1840;
Elihu Vedder, US painter and illustrator, 1836;
Victor-Marie Hugo, French author, 1802;
Antonin Reicha, Bohemian/French composer, 1770;
Anthony Ashley Cooper, 3rd Earl of Shaftesbury, philosopher and writer, 1671.

Died on this day:

Fernandel [Fernand Contandin], French actor and comedian, 1971;
Karl Jaspers, German philosopher, 1969;
Levi Eshkol, Israeli prime minister, 1969;
Sir Patrick Gardiner Hastings, lawyer and politician, 1952;
Sir Harry Lauder [MacLennan], Scottish comedian, 1950;
Lady Anne Isabella Ritchie [Thackeray], author, 1919;
Caran d'Ache [Emmanuel Poiré], French illustrator, 1909;

Richard Jordan Gatling, US inventor of the Gatling gun, 1903;
Frederick Tennyson, poet, 1898;
Alois Senefelder, German inventor of lithography, 1834;
John Philip Kemble, actor-manager, 1823;
Alexander Geddes, biblical critic and poet, 1802;
Thomas d'Urfey, satirist, 1723;
Manfred, King of Naples and Sicily, died in battle, 1266;
Roger II, King of Sicily, 1154.

Occurred on this day:

Diplomatic relations between Israel and Egypt were established, 1980;
Winston Churchill announced that Britain had produced its own atomic bomb, 1952;
The French transport ship *Provence II* was sunk in the Mediterranean, with the loss of 930 lives, 1916;
The troop ship *Birkenhead* sank off Simon's Bay, South Africa, with the loss of 485 lives, 1852;
The Second French Republic was proclaimed, 1848;

The Grand National steeplechase was first run, Aintree, 1839;
Russia annexed Poland, 1832;
Napoleon Bonaparte escaped from Elba, 1815;
The Bank of England issued the first one-pound note, 1797;
20,000 people were killed after an earthquake in Lisbon, 1531;
Manfred was defeated by a French army under Charles I of Anjou at the Battle of Benevento, 1266.

TODAY IS THE FEAST DAY OF St Alexander of Alexandria, St Nestor of Magydus, St Porphyry of Gaza and St Victor or Vittre the Hermit.

27th February

Born on this day:

Rabbi Julia Neuberger, 1950;
Tom Chadbon, actor, 1946;
Paddy Ashdown, politician, leader, Liberal Democrats, 1941;
Air Marshal Sir Sandy Wilson, C.-in-C., RAF Germany, 1941;
Antoinette Sibley, prima ballerina, 1939;
Kenzo Takada, Japanese fashion designer, 1939;
Alberto Remedios, operatic singer, 1935;
Ralph Nader, US author and consumer activist, 1934;
Elizabeth Taylor, actress, 1932;
Joanne Woodward, US film actress, 1930;
Mervyn Jones, author, 1922;
Viscount Cowdray, president, Pearson plc, 1910;

Gene Sarazen, US golfer, 1902;
John Ernst Steinbeck, US author, 1902;
Marino Marini, Italian sculptor, 1901;
Charles Herbert Best, Canadian co-discoverer of insulin as a diabetes treatment, 1899;
Enrico Caruso, Italian operatic tenor, 1873;
Rudolf Steiner, Austrian social philosopher, 1861;
Sir Charles Hubert Hastings Parry, composer, 1848;
Dame Ellen Alicia Terry, actress, 1847;
Henry Wadsworth Longfellow, US poet, 1807;
Constantine the Great, Roman emperor, 280.

Died on this day:

Edward Dahlberg, US author, 1977;
John Dickson Carr [Carter Dickson], US writer of detective stories, 1976;
Peter Behrens, German architect, 1940;
Ivan Petrovich Pavlov, Russian physiologist, 1936;
Sir Samuel Luke Fildes, painter, 1927;
Adam Sedgwick, zoologist, 1913;
Samuel Pierpont Langley, US astronomer and aeronaut, 1906;
Alexander Porfirievich Borodin, Russian composer, 1887;

George Manson, Scottish water-colour painter, 1876;
Hugues-Félicité-Robert de Lamennais, French church reformer, 1854;
Francis Marion [the 'Swamp Fox'], American revolutionary commander, 1795;
John Arbuthnot, Scottish satirist and creator of the character 'John Bull', 1735;
John Evelyn, diarist, 1706.

Occurred on this day:

The Gulf War ended after Iraqi troops retreated and Kuwait was liberated, 1991;
The Japanese attacked Java, starting the two-day battle, 1942;
General Franco's government in Spain was recognised by Britain and France, 1939;
Borley Rectory, England's most haunted house, burned down, 1939;

The Reichstag in Berlin burned following what was called a 'Communist plot' by Hitler, 1933;
The British Labour Party was founded, with Ramsay MacDonald as secretary, 1900;
The Boers defeated the British at Majuba Hill, South Africa, 1881;
The first trade mission from Russia reached London, 1558.

TODAY IS THE FEAST DAY OF St Alnoth, St Anne Line, St Baldomerius or Galmier, St Gabriel Possenti, St Herefrith of Louth, St John of Gorze, Saints Julian, Cronion, Besas and Eunus, St Leander of Seville and St Thalelaeus the Hermit.

28th February
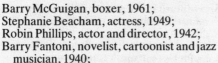

Born on this day:

Barry McGuigan, boxer, 1961;

Stephanie Beacham, actress, 1949;

Robin Phillips, actor and director, 1942;

Barry Fantoni, novelist, cartoonist and jazz musician, 1940;

Maj.-Gen. Michael Hobbs, director, Duke of Edinburgh's Award Scheme, 1937;

Brian Moore, football commentator, 1932;

Peter Alliss, golfer and TV commentator, 1931;

John Carson, actor, 1927;

George Malcolm, musician, 1917;

Sir Peter Brian Medawar, immunologist, 1915;

Vicente Minelli, US film director, 1913;

Prof. Sir Stephen Spender, poet and critic, 1909;

Field Marshal Sir James Cassels, 1907;

Sir Anthony Havelock-Allan, film producer, 1904;

Prof. Linus Pauling, US chemist, 1901;

Douglas McGarel Hogg, 1st Viscount Hailsham, Lord Chancellor, 1872;

Charles Blondin [Jean-François Gravelet], French tight-rope walker, 1824;

Joseph-Ernest Renan, French historian and philosopher, 1823;

Sir John Tenniel, artist and illustrator, 1820;

William Henry Giles Kingston, author of books for boys, 1814;

Louis-Joseph de Montcalm-Gozon, Marquis de Montcalm de Saint-Véran, French commander in Canada, 1712;

René-Antoine-Ferchault de Réaumur, French inventor of a thermometer scale, 1683;

Michel Eyquem de Montaigne, French essayist, 1533.

Died on this day:

Henry Robinson Luce, US magazine publisher, 1967;

Rajendra Prasad, first president of the Republic of India, 1963;

Maxwell Anderson, US playwright, 1959;

Alfonso XIII, ex-King of Spain, 1941;

Eugene Arnold Dolmetsch, early music enthusiast, 1940;

Friedrich Ebert, president of Germany, 1925;

Henry James, novelist, 1916;

Alphonse-Marie-Louis-de Prat de Lamartine, French poet and writer, 1869;

Jacques-Raymond Brascassat, French painter, 1867;

Manuel John Johnson, astronomer, 1859;

Francisco de Zurbarán, Spanish painter, 1664;

Christian IV, King of Denmark, 1648;

Robert Fabyan, chronicler, 1513.

Occurred on this day:

Spain withdrew from the Spanish Sahara territory, 1976;

Peter Lorenz, West German Opposition leader, was kidnapped by anarchists, 1975;

After a London underground train crashed into a siding at Moorgate, 42 people were killed, 1975;

A General Election in Britain resulted in no overall majority, 1974;

The first London production of the musical show *Cabaret* was presented, 1968;

The last British troops left India, 1948;

Forces of the USA landed in Honduras, 1924;

The British protectorate on Egypt ended, 1922;

Ladysmith, South Africa, was relieved by General Buller, 1900;

The Tichborne claimant, Arthur Orton, was found guilty of perjury, 1874;

John Wesley signed the 'deed of declaration' of the Wesleyan faith, 1784.

TODAY IS THE FEAST DAY OF The Martyrs of the Plague at Alexandria, St Hilarus, pope, St Lupicinus, St Oswald of Worcester, St Proterius and St Romanus.

# 29th February

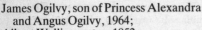
Born on this day:

James Ogilvy, son of Princess Alexandra and Angus Ogilvy, 1964;
Albert Welling, actor, 1952;
Mario Andretti, US Grand Prix driver, 1940;
Gretchen Christopher, rock singer, 1940;
Baroness Dunn, chairman, Hong Kong Trade Development Council, 1940;
Joss Ackland, actor, 1928;
Alan Loveday, violinist, 1928;
Sir David Beattie, former Governor General of New Zealand, 1924;
Michèle Morgan, French film actress, 1920;
Anthony Lingard, former director-general of St John Ambulance Association, 1916;
Major the Hon. John Bingham, 1904;
Jimmy Dorsey [James Francis Dorsey], US bandleader, 1904;

Shri Morarji Desai, former Indian prime minister, 1896;
William Augustus Wellman, US film director, 1896;
John Philip Holland, US modern submarine pioneer, 1840;
Hermann Hirschbach, German composer, 1812;
Gioacchino Antonio Rossini, Italian operatic composer, 1792;
Karl Ernst von Baer, Russian embryologist, 1792;
Ann Lee [Mother Ann], founder of the American Society of Shakers, 1736;
John Byrom, poet and inventor of a shorthand system, 1692;
Pope Paul III, 1468.

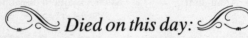
Died on this day:

Sir Theobald Mathew, Director of Public Prosecutions, 1964;
Edward Frederic Benson, novelist, 1940;
Adolphe Appia, Swiss theatrical designer, 1928;
John Landseer, painter, engraver and author, 1852;

John Whitgift, Archbishop of Canterbury, 1604;
Patrick Hamilton, Scottish martyr, burnt at the stake, 1528;
St Oswald, Bishop of Worcester and Archbishop of York, 992.

Occurred on this day:

The discovery of the first 'pulsar' [pulsating radio source] was announced by Dr Jocelyn Burnell, 1968.
Agadir, a large city in Morocco, was almost totally destroyed in an earthquake, followed by a tidal wave, resulting in a loss of life totalling more than 12,000, 1960;
Pakistan became an Islamic republic, 1956;
27 British soldiers were killed and 35 injured after the Cairo-to-Haifa train was mined north of Rehoboth by the Stern Gang, 1948;

The constitution of Czechoslovakia was adopted, 1920;
An order was issued to the German navy to sink armed merchantmen on sight, 1916;
The Behring Sea Arbitration Treaty was signed, 1892;
The St Gothard Tunnel was completed, 1880.

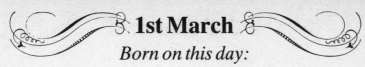

1st March

Born on this day:

Lady Rose Windsor, 1980;
Mike Read, pop music presenter, 1951;
Roger Daltrey, actor and singer, 1944;
David Scott Cowper, solo yachtsman, 1942;
David Broome, show-jumper, 1940;
Brian Waites, golfer, 1940;
Harry Belafonte, actor and entertainer, 1927;
Douglas Bunn, founder, all-England Jumping Course, Hickstead, 1928;
Andrew Faulds, actor and politician, 1923;
Dinah Shore, US singer, 1917;
Robert Traill Spence Lowell, US poet, 1917;
James David Graham Niven, film actor, 1910;

Alton Glenn Miller, US bandleader, 1904;
Sir Keith Falkner, vice-president, Royal College of Music, 1900;
Oskar Kokoschka, Austrian expressionist painter, 1886;
Roger Martin du Gard, French playwright and novelist, 1881;
Lytton Giles Strachey, author and biographer, 1880;
Ebenezer Prout, composer, 1835;
Augustus Welby Northmore Pugin, architect, 1812;
Frédéric-François [Fryderyk Franciszek] Chopin, Polish composer, 1810;
Gottfried Weber, German composer, 1779;
Sir Samuel Romilly, law reformer, 1757.

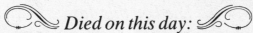

Died on this day:

Tommy Farr, heavyweight boxer, 1986;
Jackie [Jack Leslie] Coogan, US film actor, 1984;
Mack Gordon [Morris Gittler], US lyricist, 1959;
Gabriele D'Annunzio, poet, Italian politician and playwright, 1938;
George Grossmith, comedian and singer, 1912;
Prince Alexander Mikhailovich Gorchakov, Russian statesman, 1883;

Leopold II, Holy Roman Emperor, 1792;
Edward Moore, playwright and writer of fables, 1757;
Thomas Ellwood, poet, 1713;
Girolamo Frescobaldi, Italian organist and composer, 1643;
George Herbert, clergyman and poet, 1633;
Thomas Campion, poet and composer, 1620;
Dom Francisco d'Almeida, Portuguese viceroy, killed at Table Bay, 1510.

Occurred on this day:

The Soviet spacecraft *Venus 3* touched down on Venus, 1966;
The 19-month-old son of Charles Lindbergh, US aviator, was kidnapped, 1932;
Admiral Horthy was elected Regent of Hungary, 1920;
St Dunstan's in Regent's Park, London, was opened as a hostel for the blind, 1915;
The Abyssinians defeated the Italian invading army at Adowa, 1896;
Nebraska became the 37th of the United States, 1867;
Texas was annexed by the United States, 1845;

Mehemet Ali of Egypt massacred the Mamelukes and obtained total power, 1811;
Ohio became the 17th of the United States, 1803;
Slavery was abolished by Pennsylvania, the first US state to do so, 1780;
Charles I of Spain expelled the Jesuits from the country, 1767;
The Spectator was first published, 1711;
1,200 French Huguenots were massacred at Vassy, 1562;
Mozambique was discovered by Vasco da Gama, 1498.

TODAY IS THE FEAST DAY OF St Aubin or Albinus of Angers, St David or Dewi, St Felix III, pope, St Rudesind or Rosendo and St Swithbert.

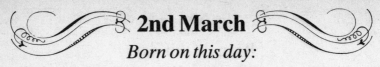

2nd March

Born on this day:

Ian Woosnam, golfer, 1958;

John Peter Rhys Williams, rugby player and surgeon, 1949;

Dame Naomi James, yachtswoman, 1948;

Margaret Barbieri, ballet dancer, 1947;

Robert Lloyd, operatic bass, 1941;

Jon Finch, actor, 1940;

Mikhail Gorbachev, Russian statesman, 1931;

Pat Arrowsmith, pacifist and socialist, 1930;

Sir John Manduell, composer, 1928;

Cardinal Basil Hume, Archbishop of Westminster, 1923;

Robert Simpson, composer, 1921;

Jennifer Jones, US film actress, 1919;

John Linton Gardner, composer, 1917;

Harry Blech, founder of the London Mozart Players, 1910;

Geoffrey Edward Harvey Grigson, poet and critic, 1905;

Kurt Julian Weill, German/US composer, 1900;

Ivar Kreuger, Swedish industrialist and swindler, 1880;

Pope Pius XII [Eugenio Pacelli], 1876;

Bedřich Smetana, Czech composer, 1824;

Pope Leo XIII, 1810;

Samuel Houston, Texas statesman, 1793;

Sir Thomas Bodley, diplomat and bibliophile, 1545.

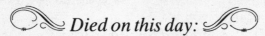 Died on this day:

Randolph Scott [Crane], US film actor, 1987;

Joan Greenwood, actress, 1987;

Lloyd Logan Pearsall Smith, US essayist, 1946;

Howard Carter, painter and Egyptologist, 1939;

David Herbert Lawrence, novelist, 1930;

Queen Elizabeth of Romania [Carmen Silva, novelist], 1916;

Ismail Pasha, Khedive of Egypt, 1895;

Hugh Gough, 1st Viscount, field marshal, 1869;

Nicholas I, Tsar of Russia, 1855;

Heinrich Wilhelm Matthias Olbers, German astronomer, 1840;

Francis II, Emperor of Austria and last Holy Roman Emperor, 1835;

Horace Walpole, 4th Earl of Orford, novelist and historian, 1797;

John Wesley, founder of Methodism, 1791.

Occurred on this day:

Rhodesia was proclaimed a republic, 1970;

The French prototype *Concorde* made its first test flight, 1969;

Morocco once more became independent, 1956;

Captain James Gallagher and a crew of 13 USAF men completed the first round-the-world flight in 94 hours, 1949;

In Burma, the British 14th Army entered Mandalay, 1945;

The Battle of the Bismarck Sea began, 1943;

Turkey closed the strait of the Dardanelles to all ships except those having special permits, 1941;

Cardinal Eugenio Pacelli was elected as Pope Pius XII, 1939;

A mutiny of sailors aboard Russian battleships at Kronstadt led to a general revolt, 1921;

The *Morning Chronicle* newspaper was first published, 1865;

59 citizens proclaimed Texas a republic, independent of Mexico, 1836;

Work began on the Thames Tunnel, 1825;

The 'War of Oranges' started between Spain and Portugal, 1801.

TODAY IS THE FEAST DAY OF St Chad or Caedda, St Joavan of Brittany and The Martyrs under the Lombards.

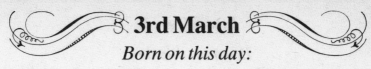

3rd March

Born on this day:

Miranda Richardson, actress, 1958;

Ronald Searle, artist and cartoonist, 1920;

Peter O'Sullevan, racing commentator, 1918;

Lord Mellish, former government minister, 1913;

Jean Harlow [Harlean Carpenter], US film actress, 1911;

Philip Edward Thomas, poet and critic, 1878;

Sir Henry Joseph Wood, founder of Promenade Concerts, 1869;

Émile-Auguste Chartier ['Alain'], French philosopher, 1868;

Arthur Llewellyn Jones Machen, novelist, actor and journalist, 1863;

Lilian Adelaide Neilson [Elizabeth Ann Brown], actress, 1848;

Alexander Graham Bell, inventor of the telephone, 1847;

George Mortimer Pullman, US industrialist and inventor, 1831;

Alexandre-Gabriel Decamps, French painter, 1803;

William Charles Macready, actor and manager, 1793;

William Godwin, novelist and political writer, 1756;

Thomas Otway, playwright, 1652;

Edmund Waller, poet, 1606;

Sir William D'Avenant, poet, baptised, 1606;

Sir Edward Herbert, 1st Baron Herbert of Cherbury, poet, 1583.

Died on this day:

Danny Kaye [Daniel Kaminsky], US actor and entertainer, 1987;

Arthur Koestler, author, 1983;

Lou Costello [Louis Francis Cristillo], US actor and comedian, 1959;

Noel Gay [Richard Moxon Armitage], composer and pianist, 1954;

Sir Sidney Lee, editor, scholar and biographer, 1926;

The Rev. John George Wood, writer on natural history, 1889;

Joseph Bonomi [the Younger], sculptor and draughtsman, 1878;

Giovanni Domenico Tiepolo, Italian painter and engraver, 1804;

Francis Egerton, 3rd Duke of Bridgewater, canal engineer, 1803;

Robert Adam, architect, 1792;

Niccola Antonio Porpora, Italian composer, 1768;

William Stukeley, antiquary and physician, 1765;

Robert Hooke, physicist, 1703;

Sir Nicholas Carew, courtier and diplomat, executed, 1539.

Occurred on this day:

Estonia and Latvia voted to secede from the Soviet Union, 1991;

One of the world's worst air disasters occurred when a Turkish DC-10 crashed after take-off from Paris, with the loss of 346 lives, 1974;

The *Apollo 9* spacecraft was launched from Cape Kennedy, 1969;

Italian Somaliland fell to the British army, and Italians fled to Ethiopia, 1941;

The US Congress adopted the *Star-Spangled Banner* as the national anthem, 1931;

The Turkish National Assembly abolished the Caliphate, and disestablished the Islamic religion, 1924;

The Treaty of Brest-Litovsk was signed between Germany and Russia, 1918;

Bizet's opera *Carmen* was first performed at the Opéra Comique, Paris, 1875;

Serfdom was abolished in Russia, 1861;

Florida became the 27th of the United States, 1845.

TODAY IS THE FEAST DAY OF St Aelred of Rievaulx, St Anselm of Nonantola, St Arthelais, St Chef, St Cunegund, empress, St Emeterius, St Gervinus, Saints Marinus and Astyrius, St Non or Nonnita and St Winwaloe or Guénolé.

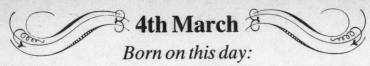

4th March

Born on this day:

Kenny Dalglish, football player and manager, 1951;

Michael Barrett ['Shakin' Stevens'], rock singer, 1948;

Peter Skellern, composer and singer, 1947;

Harvey Goldsmith, pop music presenter, 1946;

Ralph Kirshbaum, cellist, 1946;

Paula Prentiss, US film and TV actress, 1939;

Graham Dowling, New Zealand cricketer, 1937;

Miriam Makeba, South African singer, 1931;

Bernard Haitink, violinist and conductor, 1929;

Alan Sillitoe, playwright and novelist, 1928;

Francis King, author and drama critic, 1923;

Patrick Moore, astronomer, 1923;

Prof. Hans Eysenck, psychologist, 1916;

Fritz Graebner, German ethnologist, 1877;

Thomas Sturge Moore, poet and wood-engraver, 1870;

Charles Oberthür, German harpist and composer, 1819;

Robert Lindley, cellist and composer, 1776;

Sir Henry Raeburn, portrait painter, 1756;

Count Casimir Pulaski, Polish soldier, 1748;

Charles Dibdin, playwright and songwriter, 1745;

Antonio Lucio Vivaldi, Venetian composer and violinist, 1678;

Prince Henry the Navigator, sponsor of voyages, 1394.

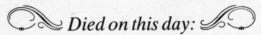

Died on this day:

Richard Thomas Church, poet and novelist, 1972;

William Carlos Williams, US physician and poet, 1963;

[Cuthbert] Dale Collins, Australian journalist and novelist, 1956;

Antonin Artaud, French actor, playwright and stage director, 1948;

William Willett, builder, and promoter of 'daylight saving time', 1915;

Nikolai Vasilyevich Gogol, Russian playwright and novelist, 1852;

Jean-François Champollion, French Egyptologist, 1832;

Bernard Gilpin, clergyman, known as the 'Apostle of the North', 1583;

Sir Thomas Malory, writer of *La Morte d'Arthur*, 1470;

Saladin, Sultan of Egypt and Syria, 1193.

Occurred on this day:

Edward Heath resigned, and Harold Wilson became prime minister, forming a Labour government, 1974;

The French submarine *Eurydice* sank off the coast of Toulon, when all the crew of 57 were lost, 1970;

North Sea gas was first piped ashore near Durham, 1967;

German radio declared that Dresden had been 'wiped off the map of Europe' by Allied bombing, 1945;

British commandos raided the Lofoten Islands off Norway, then German-occupied, 1941;

The Comintern [Communist International] was formed, 1919;

Woodrow Wilson was inaugurated as 28th president of the USA, 1913;

The Forth Bridge was officially opened, 1890;

The New York *Daily Graphic*, first illustrated daily newspaper, appeared, 1873;

The Royal National Lifeboat Institution was founded, 1824;

Vermont became the 14th of the United States, 1791;

The first meeting of Congress was held in New York, 1789;

Pennsylvania was granted by charter to William Penn, 1681.

TODAY IS THE FEAST DAY OF St Adrian and his Companions, St Casimir of Poland and St Peter of Cava.

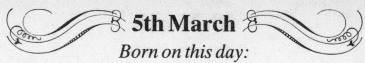

5th March

Born on this day:

Richard Hickox, conductor, 1948;
Samantha Eggar, film actress, 1939;
Dean Stockwell, US film actor, 1936;
Air Marshal Sir Thomas Stonor, 1936;
Anthony Hedges, composer, 1931;
Barry Tuckwell, horn player and
    conductor, 1931;
Sir Jack Rumbold, former president,
    Industrial Tribunals, 1920;
Elspeth March, actress, 1911;
Sir Rex Carey Harrison, actor, 1908;
Herbert Farjeon, critic and playwright,
    1887;
Heitor Villa-Lobos, Brazilian composer,
    1887;
William Henry, 1st Baron Beveridge,
    author of the Beveridge Report on social
    insurance, 1879;

Rosa Luxemburg, German Spartacist
    [socialist] agitator, 1871;
Sir Henry Hughes Wilson, field marshal,
    1864;
Howard Pyle, US artist and illustrator,
    1853;
Sir Austen Henry Layard, archaeologist,
    1817;
James Madison, 4th president of the USA,
    1751;
Giovanni Battista Tiepolo, Venetian
    painter, 1696;
Antoine de la Mothe Cadillac, French
    soldier, 1658;
Gerardus Mercator [Gerhard Kremer],
    Flemish cartographer, 1512.

Died on this day:

Tito Gobbi, Italian baritone, 1984;
William Powell, US film actor, 1984;
E.Y. 'Yip' Harburg [Isidore Hochberg], US
    composer, killed in a car crash, 1981;
William Cameron Menzies, US film
    director, 1957;
Sergei Sergeyevich Prokofiev, Russian
    composer, 1953;
Joseph Stalin [Iosif Vissarionovich
    Dzhugashvili], Russian leader, 1953;
Edward Lee Masters, US novelist and poet,
    1950;

Count Leopoldo Cicognara, Italian
    archaeologist and writer, 1834;
Count Alessandro Giuseppe Volta, Italian
    physicist, 1827;
Franz Anton Mesmer, physician and
    founder of 'animal magnetism', 1815;
Flora Macdonald, Jacobite heroine, 1790;
Thomas Augustine Arne, composer [Rule,
    Britannia], 1778;
Michael Coxcie, Flemish painter, 1592;
Antonio Allegri da Correggio, Italian
    painter, 1534.

Occurred on this day:

In West Germany, Dr Gustav Heinemann
    became president in succession to Dr
    Heinrich Lübke, 1969;
Winston Churchill made a speech
    at Fulton, USA, referring to an
    'Iron Curtain' across Europe,
    1946;
The Battle of the Bismarck Sea ended,
    1943;
The Nazis made large gains in the German
    general election, 1933;
Civil disobedience in India ended, 1931;

The Spanish steamer Principe de Asturias
    struck a rock and sank off Brazil, with the
    loss of over 400 lives, 1916;
Lee De Forest demonstrated an
    experimental radio broadcast from New
    York, 1907;
Covent Garden Theatre, London, was
    destroyed by fire, 1856;
Soldiers fought civilians at Boston, Mass.,
    in the Boston Massacre, 1770;
The foundation stone of New College,
    Oxford, was laid, 1397.

TODAY IS THE FEAST DAY OF Saints Adrian and Eubulus, St Eusebius of Cremona,
St Gerasimus, St John Joseph of the Cross, St Kieran of Saighir, St Phocas of Antioch, St
Piran and St Virgil of Arles.

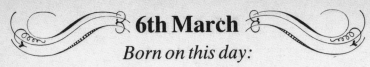

6th March

Born on this day:

Dame Kiri Te Kanawa, New Zealand operatic soprano, 1944;

Mary Wilson, US singer, 1944;

Valentina Vladimirovna Tereshkova, Russian astronaut, 1937;

Jean Boht, actress, 1936;

William Davis, editor and publisher, 1933;

Lorin Maazel, US violinist and conductor, 1930;

The Rt. Rev. David Sheppard, Bishop of Liverpool and former cricketer, 1929;

Frankie Howerd [Francis Alex Howard], comedian, 1922;

Dr Madge Adam, astronomer, 1912;

Lou Costello [Louis Francis Cristillo], US actor and comedian, 1906;

Adolfo Salazar, Spanish musicologist and composer, 1890;

Ringgold Wilmer Lardner, US humorous writer, 1885;

Bronson James Albery, theatrical manager, 1881;

Oskar Straus, Austrian/French composer, 1870;

George Louis Palmella Busson du Maurier, caricaturist and novelist, 1834;

Elizabeth Barrett Browning, poet, 1806;

Savinien Cyrano de Bergerac, French novelist and playwright, 1619;

Francesco Guicciardini, Florentine statesman and historian, 1483;

Michelangelo Buonarroti, Italian painter, sculptor and poet, 1475.

Died on this day:

Henry [Harry] Wilcoxon, film actor, 1984;

Donald Maclean, former diplomat and Soviet agent, 1983;

Pearl Sydenstricker Buck, US novelist, 1971;

Zoltán Kodály, Hungarian composer, 1967;

Herbert Stanley Morrison [Baron], statesman, 1965;

King Paul I of the Hellenes, 1964;

George Formby [William Hoy Booth], singer and comedian, 1961;

David Ivor Novello [Davies], composer and playwright, 1951;

John Philip Sousa, US bandmaster and composer, 1932;

Alfred von Tirpitz, German naval commander and statesman, 1930;

Gottlieb Daimler, German mechanical engineer, 1900;

Louisa May Alcott, US novelist, 1888;

Artemus Ward [Charles Farrar Browne], US humorous writer, 1867;

Peter von Cornelius, German painter, 1867;

Davy Crockett, US frontiersman, killed at the Alamo, 1836;

Francis Beaumont, playwright, 1616.

Occurred on this day:

Constantine II succeeded Paul I as King of the Hellenes, 1964;

Ghana [formerly the Gold Coast and Togoland] became independent, 1957;

The US Air Force began daylight bombing raids on Berlin, 1944;

Stalin was granted the title of Marshal of the Soviet Union, 1943;

Frozen food was first put on sale by the Birdseye company, 1930;

The Shakespeare Memorial Theatre at Stratford-upon-Avon was destroyed by fire, 1926;

British soldiers were granted the right to wear spectacles on or off duty, 1902;

Serbia was proclaimed a kingdom, 1882;

Verdi's opera La Traviata was first performed, Venice, 1853;

The Battle and Siege of the Alamo, Texas, ended, when there were only six survivors left of 155 Texans, 1836.

TODAY IS THE FEAST DAY OF Saints Balred and Bilfrid, St Cadroe, St Chrodegang of Metz, St Colette, Saints Cyneburga, Cyneswide and Tibba, St Cyril of Constantinople, St Fridolin, St Ollegarius or Oldegar and Saints Perpetua and Felicity.

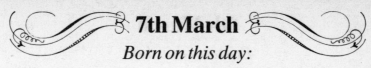

7th March

Born on this day:

Ivan Lendl, tennis player, 1960;
William Boyd, author, 1952;
Viv Richards, West Indian cricketer, 1952;
Michael Finnissy, composer and pianist, 1946;
Sir Ranulph Twistleton-Wykeham-Fiennes, explorer, 1944;
Piers Paul Read, novelist and author, 1941;
Martin Tickner, theatrical producer, 1941;
Zena Walker, actress, 1934;
The Earl of Snowdon, photographer, 1930;
Dan Jacobson, South African novelist, 1929;
Richard Vernon, actor, 1925;
Prof. Sir Eduardo Paolozzi, sculptor, 1924;

Joseph-Maurice Ravel, French composer, 1875;
Piet [Pieter Cornelis] Mondrian, Dutch abstract painter, 1872;
Tomáš Garrigue Masaryk, 1st president of Czechoslovakia, 1850;
Ludwig Mond, chemist and industrialist, 1839;
Henry Draper, US astronomer, 1837;
Henry Moore, painter, 1831;
Sir Edwin Henry Landseer, painter, 1802;
Sir John Frederick William Herschel, astronomer, 1792;
Alessandro Francesco Manzoni, Italian poet and novelist, 1785;
Joseph Nicéphore Niepce, French photographic inventor, 1765.

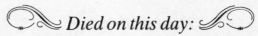

Died on this day:

Florence Margaret [Stevie] Smith, poet, 1971;
Percy Wyndham Lewis, writer and artist, 1957;
Herman J. Mankiewicz, US screenwriter, 1953;
Bertrand Edward, 1st Viscount Dawson, physician, 1945;
Aristide Briand, French premier, 1932;
Antonio Fogazzaro, Italian novelist, 1911;
John Richard Green, cleric and historian, 1883;

Louis Boulanger, French painter and lithographer, 1867;
Francesco Bartolozzi, Italian engraver, 1815;
Cuthbert, 1st Baron Collingwood, admiral, 1810;
Jean-Pierre-François Blanchard, French balloonist, 1809;
Pope Innocent XIII, 1724;
St Thomas Aquinas, Christian philosopher, 1274;
Antoninus Pius, Roman emperor, 161.

Occurred on this day:

At Heathrow Airport, London, armed raiders stole £850,000 worth of diamonds and currency, 1977;
In London, the Victoria underground line was opened by the Queen, 1969;
British forces withdrew from Rangoon, 1942;
British troops invaded Italian-held Ethiopia, 1941;
Parliamentary government in Austria was suspended, 1933;

The transatlantic radio-telephone was established between New York and London, 1926;
The first jazz record, *The Dixie Jazz Band One-step*, went on sale in the USA, 1917;
The first telephone was patented by Alexander Graham Bell, 1876;
Jenny Lind, the 'Swedish Nightingale', made her debut, 1838;
The Neapolitans were overwhelmed by the Austrians at the Battle of Rieti, 1821;
Napoleon defeated Blücher at the Battle of Craonne, 1814.

TODAY IS THE FEAST DAY OF St Ardo, St Drausius or Drausin, St Esterwine, St Paul the Simple and St Theophylact.

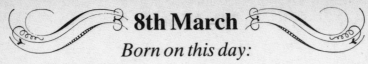

8th March

Born on this day:

Gary Numan, rock musician, 1958;
Gyles Brandreth, MP and broadcaster, 1948;
Dr Jonathan Sacks, chief rabbi, 1948;
Ann Jenner, Australian ballerina, 1944;
Lynn Redgrave, actress, 1943;
Prof. Norman Stone, historian, 1941;
Lynn Seymour, ballerina, 1939;
Robert Tear, operatic tenor, 1939;
Douglas Hurd, statesman, 1930;
Sir Anthony Caro, sculptor, 1924;
Cyd Charisse, US film actress and dancer, 1921;
Eileen Herlie, actress, 1920;
Claire Trevor, US film actress, 1909;
Leonard Alfred George Strong, novelist, poet and playwright, 1896;

Otto Hahn, German physicist and chemist, 1879;
Frederic William Goudy, US printer and typographer, 1865;
Kenneth Grahame, author, 1859;
Ruggiero Leoncavallo, Italian composer, 1858;
Franco Faccio, Italian conductor and composer, 1840;
Jean Delphin Alard, French violinist and composer, 1815;
Richard Howe, 1st Earl, admiral, 1726;
Carl Philipp Emanuel Bach, German composer, 1714;
John Fothergill, physician, 1712.

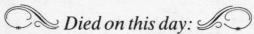

Died on this day:

Ralph Mcallister Ingersoll, US publisher, author and journalist, 1985;
Sir William Turner Walton, composer, 1983;
Richard Austen Butler, Baron Butler of Saffron Walden, statesman, 1982;
Sir Thomas Beecham Bt., conductor, 1961;
Sherwood Anderson, US author, 1941;
William Howard Taft, 27th president of the USA, 1930;

Count Ferdinand Adolf August Heinrich von Zeppelin, German soldier and inventor, 1917;
John Ericsson, US engineer and inventor, 1889;
Millard Fillmore, 13th president of the USA, 1874;
Louis-Hector Berlioz, French composer, 1869;
Charles XIV, King of Sweden, 1844;
Sawrey Gilpin, animal painter, 1807;
Abraham Darby, ironfounder, 1717;
King William III, 1702.

Occurred on this day:

In Dublin, the Nelson Column was destroyed by an IRA bomb, 1966;
The USA landed 3,500 marines in South Vietnam, 1965;
The USSR claimed to be the possessor of the atomic bomb, 1950;
The first London production of the musical show *Kiss Me Kate* was presented, 1945;
A coal strike began in Britain, 1944;
Mahatma Gandhi started a civil disobedience campaign in India, 1930;

French troops occupied the Ruhr after Germany failed to pay reparations, 1921;
The 'February' Revolution [Old Style date, see 23rd February] began in Russia at Petrograd, 1917;
The Confederate ironclad *Virginia* [formerly the *Merrimac*] sank the USS *Cumberland* during the Battle of Hampton Roads, 1862;
The British Army captured Aboukir, 1801;
Queen Anne acceded to the throne, 1702.

TODAY IS THE FEAST DAY OF St Duthac, St Felix of Dunwich, St Humphrey or Hunfrid, St John of God, St Julian of Toledo, Saints Philemon and Apollonius, St Pontius of Carthage, St Senan of Scattery, St Stephen of Obazine and St Veremund.

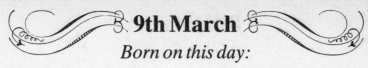

9th March

Born on this day:

Bill Beaumont, rugby player and sports commentator, 1952;
Bobby Fischer, US chess champion, 1943;
Sir Donald Rattee, High Court judge, 1937;
Yuri Alekseyevich Gagarin, Russian astronaut, 1934;
Prof. Sir David Weatherall, haematologist, 1933;
André Courrèges, French couturier, 1923;
Mickey Spillane, US novelist, 1918;
Samuel Barber, US composer, 1910;
David Smith, US sculptor, 1906;
Peter Quennell, author, 1905;
Rex Ernest Warner, novelist, historian and translator, 1905;
David Garnett, novelist, 1892;

Vita Mary Sackville-West, novelist, 1892;
Vyacheslav Mikhailovich Molotov [Skriabin], Russian politician, 1890;
Ernest Bevin, statesman, 1881;
Bertrand Edward, 1st Viscount Dawson, physician, 1864;
Ernest Goodrich Acheson, US chemist, 1856;
Sir William Hamo Thornycroft, sculptor, 1850;
Jean Joseph Bott, German violinist and composer, 1826;
William Cobbett, politician and author, 1763;
Honoré-Gabriel-Riqueti, Comte de Mirabeau, French statesman, 1749;
Amerigo Vespucci, Italian explorer, 1454.

Died on this day:

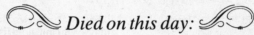

Imogen Holst, musician, 1984;
Barbara Mullen, US-born actress, 1979;
Frank Wedekind, German poet and playwright, 1918;
Wilhelm I, former Emperor of Germany, 1888;
Charles Knight, author and publisher, 1873;
John Gully, MP, prize-fighter and horse-racer, 1863;

Anna Letitia Barbauld [Aikin], poetess, teacher and hymn-writer, 1825;
Ozias Humphry, painter, 1810;
Samuel Jebb, physician and scholar, 1772;
Simon Fraser, 12th Baron Lovat, Scottish Jacobite, executed for treason, 1747;
Jules Mazarin [Giulio Mazarini], French cardinal and statesman, 1661;
David Rizzio, musician and secretary to Mary, Queen of Scots, murdered, 1566.

Occurred on this day:

The USSR sent Laika, the first dog into space, in *Sputnik 9*, 1961;
Archbishop Makarios was deported from Cyprus to the Seychelles, 1956;
Eamon de Valera became president of the Irish Republic, 1932;
Fiume was annexed by Italy, 1924;
The capital of Russia was moved from Petrograd [Leningrad] to Moscow, 1918;
The Defence of the Realm Act was passed, 1915;
King George V laid the foundation stone of London County Hall, 1912;
The Russians were defeated by the Japanese at Mukden, 1905;

Southern England was swept by great snowstorms, causing shipwrecks and great loss of life, 1891;
The Battle of Hampton Roads continued between the Confederate battleship *Virginia* and the USS *Monitor*, the result being a stalemate, 1862;
Louis-Philippe of France founded the French Foreign Legion in Algeria, 1831;
Napoleon Bonaparte married Josephine de Beauharnais, 1796;
Pope Gregory VII declared all married RC priests to be excommunicated, 1074.

TODAY IS THE FEAST DAY OF St Bosa, St Catharine of Bologna, St Dominic Savio, St Frances of Rome, St Gregory of Nyssa and St Pacianus.

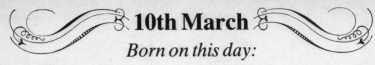

10th March

Born on this day:

HRH Prince Edward, 1964;
Terry Holmes, Welsh rugby player, 1957;
Hugh Johnson, wine connoisseur, 1939;
Fou Ts'ong, pianist, 1934;
Lady Falkender, 1932;
Sir Charles Groves, conductor, 1915;
Air Chief Marshal Sir Brian Burnett, 1913;
Bix [Leon Bismarck] Beidebecke, US jazz cornet-player and composer, 1903;
Arthur Honegger, French composer, 1892;
Tamara Platonovna Karsavina, Russian ballerina, 1885;
Leonard Raven-Hill, cartoonist, artist and illustrator, 1867;

Henry Watson Fowler, author of *English Usage*, 1858;
Pablo Martin Melitón de Sarasate y Navascuéz, Spanish violinist, 1844;
Joseph Bernard Coninck, Belgian teacher and composer, 1827;
Sir Samuel Ferguson, Irish poet, 1810;
Thomas Gordon Hake, physician and poet, 1809;
William Etty, painter, 1787;
Carl Wilhelm Friedrich von Schlegel, German poet and critic, 1772;
John Playfair, mathematician and geologist, 1748;
Marcello Malpighi, Italian anatomist, 1628;
Ferdinand I, Holy Roman Emperor, 1503.

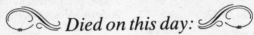

Died on this day:

Ray Milland [Reginald Truscott-Jones], film actor, 1986;
Frank O'Connor [Michael O'Donovan], Irish short-story writer, 1966;
Sir Philip Armand Hamilton Gibbs, author, 1962;
Jan Garrigue Masaryk, Czechoslovak statesman, committed suicide, 1948;
Irvin Shrewsbury Cobb, US short-story writer and journalist, 1944;
Charles John Cutcliffe Wright Hyne, novelist, 1944;
Robert Laurence Binyon, poet, 1943;

Mikhail Afanasyevich Bulgakov, Russian playwright and novelist, 1940;
Admiral of the Fleet David Beatty, 1st Earl, 1936;
F. Anstey [Thomas Anstey Guthrie], humorist and playwright, 1934;
Charles Frederick Worth, fashion designer, 1895;
Giuseppe Mazzini, Italian nationalist, 1872;
Muzio Clementi, pianist and composer, 1832;
Sir John Denham, poet, 1669.

Occurred on this day:

Crown Princess Beatrix of the Netherlands married Claus von Amsberg, 1966;
Peter Twiss, test pilot, was the first man to fly at more than 1,000 mph, 1956;
Rangoon, Burma, fell to the Japanese, 1942;
Sir Oswald Mosley was expelled from the Labour Party, 1931;
The Battle of Neuve-Chapelle [World War I] began, 1915;

The 'Rokeby Venus' painting by Velazquez in the National Gallery was damaged by suffragettes, 1914;
The Bakerloo Line on London's underground opened, 1906;
Edward [later King Edward VII] married Princess Alexandra of Denmark, 1863;
Napoleon was defeated by Blücher at the Battle of Laon, 1814;
The first British Census began, 1801.

TODAY IS THE FEAST DAY OF St Anastasia Patricia, St Attalas, St Codratus and Others, St Droctoveus or Drotte, St Hymelin, St John Ogilvie, St Kessog, St Macarius of Jerusalem and St Simplicius, pope.

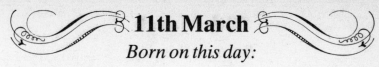

11th March

Born on this day:

Lord Lawson of Blaby [Nigel Lawson], former Chancellor of the Exchequer, 1932;

Rupert Murdoch, newspaper proprietor, 1931;

David Gentleman, designer and painter, 1930;

Raymond Jackson [Jak], cartoonist, 1927;

Ron Todd, general secretary, TGWU, 1927;

Air Marshal Sir Alec Morris, consulting engineer, 1926;

Patricia Tindale, architect, 1926;

Terence Alexander, actor, 1923;

Louise Brough, tennis champion, 1923;

Lord Wilson of Rievaulx, former prime minister, 1916;

Sir Fitzroy Maclean Bt., diplomat, soldier and politician, 1911;

Margaret Herbison, former government minister, 1907;

Jessie Matthews, actress and dancer, 1907;

Dorothy Gish [de Guiche], silent screen actress, 1898;

Raoul Walsh, US film director, 1892;

Sir Malcolm Campbell, speed record holder, 1885;

Marius Petipa, French director of the ballet, 1819;

Sir Henry Tate, sugar refiner and art collector, 1819;

Louis Boulanger, French painter and lithographer, 1807;

Prince Paul Anton von Galanthea Esterhazy, Austrian diplomat, 1786;

Torquato Tasso, Italian poet and playwright, 1544.

Died on this day:

Erle Stanley Gardner, US lawyer, author and creator of 'Perry Mason', 1970;

Admiral Richard Evelyn Byrd, US aviator and explorer, 1957;

Sir Alexander Fleming, bacteriologist, 1955;

Christian Victor Hely-Hutchinson, pianist and composer, 1947;

Sir Henry Walford Davies, composer and organist, 1941;

Rolf Boldrewood [Thomas Alexander Browne], Australian author, 1915;

Edmondo De Amicis, Italian author, 1908;

General Sir James Outram, 1863;

Sir Alexander Mackenzie, explorer, 1820;

Benjamin West, US painter, 1820;

Philip James de Loutherbourg, painter, 1812;

Hannah Cowley [Parkhouse], playwright and poet, 1809;

Paul I, Tsar of Russia, assassinated, 1801.

Occurred on this day:

Mount Etna, Sicily, erupted, 1974;

During a thousand-bomber raid on Germany, the Krupps factory was destroyed, 1945;

Meat rationing began in Britain, 1940;

The German Army marched into Austria, 1938;

Following a proclamation by Hermann Goering, the Luftwaffe was created, 1935;

The first London performance of the musical show *No, No, Nanette* was presented, London, 1925;

The first telephone call was made by Alexander Graham Bell, 1876;

The Bradfield reservoir, near Sheffield, burst its banks, and 250 people lost their lives, 1864;

The first performance of *Rigoletto* by Verdi was given in Venice, 1851;

The first successful English daily newspaper, the single-sheet *Daily Courant*, was published near Fleet Street, London, 1702;

Chelsea Hospital for old soldiers was founded, 1682.

TODAY IS THE FEAST DAY OF St Aurea, St Benedict of Milan, St Constantine of Cornwall, St Eulogius of Cordova, St Oengus or Aengus the Culdee, St Sophronius of Jerusalem, St Teresa Margaret Redi and St Vindician.

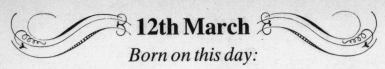

12th March

Born on this day:

Willie Duggan, rugby footballer, 1950;
Liza Minnelli, US actress and singer, 1946;
Elizabeth Vaughan, operatic soprano, 1937;
Edward Albee, US playwright, 1928;
Gudrun Ure, actress, 1926;
Norbert Brainin, violinist, 1923;
Jack [Jean-Louis] Kerouac, US novelist, 1922;
Dr Giovanni Agnelli, chairman Fiat SpA, 1921;
Ralph Shapey, US composer and conductor, 1921;
Googie Withers, actress, 1917;
Kylie [Kathleen] Tennant, Australian novelist, 1912;
Vaslav Fomich Nijinsky, Russian dancer, 1890;

Philip Guedalla, historian, 1889;
Kemal Atatürk [Mustapha Kemal], Turkish soldier and statesman, 1881;
Gabriele D'Annunzio, Italian poet and politician, 1863;
Adolph Simon Ochs, US newspaper proprietor, 1858;
Sir William Henry Perkin, chemist, 1838;
Capt. Charles Cunningham Boycott, land agent, from whose name the word 'boycott' is taken, 1832;
Thomas Augustine Arne, composer, *Rule, Britannia*, 1710;
John Aubrey, antiquarian, 1626;
André de Lenôtre, French landscape architect, 1613.

Died on this day:

Arnold Ridley, playwright and actor, 1984;
Tolchard Evans, popular composer and conductor, 1978;
Sir William Bragg, scientist, 1942;
Charles-Marie-Jean-Albert Widor, French organist and composer, 1937;
Ivar Kreuger, Swedish industralist and swindler, 1932;
Sun Yat-sen, Chinese leader, 1925;
Hilaire, Comte de Chardonnet, inventor of rayon, 1924;

George Westinghouse, US inventor, 1914;
Gaetano Milanesi, Italian scholar and painter, 1895;
Frans van Mieris the Elder, Dutch painter, 1681;
Cesare Borgia, Italian cardinal, soldier and politician, killed, 1507;
Ranulf Higden, author of the *Polychronicon* history, 1364;
St Gregory I, pope, 604.

Occurred on this day:

Mauritius became independent, 1968;
Finland signed a peace treaty which made territorial concessions to the USSR, 1940;
In Britain a 30 mph speed limit was imposed for cars in built-up areas, 1935;
The foundation stone of the Australian capital Canberra was laid, 1913;
The Girl Guides [later Scouts] movement was started in the United States by Juliette Gordon Low, 1912;

The French battleship *Iena* exploded at Toulon, killing 118 men, 1907;
The first main line electric train in the UK ran from Liverpool to Southport, 1904;
The Albery Theatre, London, opened as the New Theatre, 1903;
Britain annexed Basutoland, 1868;
The Theatre Royal, Drury Lane, London, [third theatre] opened, 1794;
The Bermudas became an English colony, 1609.

TODAY IS THE FEAST DAY OF St Alphege of Winchester, St Bernard of Capua, St Maximilian of Theveste, St Paul Aurelian or of Leon, Saints Peter, Gorgonius and Dorotheus, St Seraphina or Fina and St Theophanes the Chronicler.

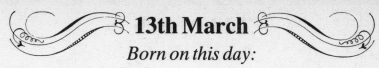

Born on this day:

Joe Bugner, heavyweight boxing champion, 1950;

Lesley Collier, ballet dancer, 1947;

Christopher Gable, actor and ballet dancer, 1940;

Terence Brady, playwright, novelist and actor, 1939;

Neil Sedaka, songwriter and singer, 1939;

Sir Michael Checkland, director-general of the BBC, 1936;

Tessie O'Shea, actress and entertainer, 1918;

Sir Robert Mark, former Commissioner of the Metropolitan Police, 1917;

Walter Annenberg, US publisher and former ambassador to Britain, 1908;

George Seferis [Giorgos Stylianou Seferiades], Greek poet and diplomat, 1900;

Henry Hathaway, US film director, 1898;

Sir Hugh Seymour Walpole, novelist, 1884;

Ramón Menéndez Pidal, Spanish philologist and historian, 1869;

Hugo Wolf, Austrian composer, 1860;

Percival Lowell, US astronomer, 1855;

Thomas Henry Tizard, oceanographer, 1839;

Karl Friedrich Schinkel, German architect and painter, 1781;

Daniel Lambert, fat man who weighed over 52 stones [728 lb. or 330 kg.], 1770;

Charles Grey, 2nd Earl, former prime minister, 1764;

Joseph II, Holy Roman Emperor, 1741;

Dr Joseph Priestley, scientist and clergyman, 1733;

James Kent, organist and composer, 1700.

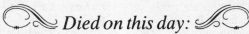

Robert Cecil Romer Maugham, 2nd Viscount [Robin Maugham], novelist, 1981;

John Middleton Murry, author, 1957;

Angela Brazil, girls' school-story writer, 1947;

Winston Churchill, US novelist, 1947;

Stephen Vincent Benét, US novelist and poet, 1943;

Thomas [Tom] Mann, trade union leader, 1941;

Lucien Lévy-Bruhl, French philosopher, 1939;

Clarence Seward Darrow, US lawyer, 1938;

Benjamin Harrison, 23rd president of the USA, 1901;

Felice Orsini, Italian politician and assassin, executed, 1858;

Sophia Lee, novelist and playwright, 1824;

Nicolas Boileau-Despréaux, French poet and critic, 1711;

Richard Burbage, actor, 1619;

John Barbour, poet, 1395.

Occurred on this day:

In the USSR, the Soviet Congress voted to abolish the political monopoly of the Communist party, 1990;

The Battle of Dien Bien Phu began in Indo-China, 1954;

Austria was declared to be part of the German Reich [the Anschluss], and was renamed 'Ostmark', 1938;

The St Francis dam near Los Angeles burst, flooding the countryside, and drowning 450 people, 1928;

General Roberts captured Bloemfontein, South Africa, 1900;

Standard time was established in the USA, 1884;

The planet Uranus was discovered by Sir William Herschel, 1781;

As predicted by Halley in 1682, Halley's Comet came to its perihelion, 1758;

The French Huguenots were defeated at the Battle of Jarnac, 1569;

The Yorkists defeated the Lancastrians at the Battle of Stamford, 1470.

TODAY IS THE FEAST DAY OF St Ansovinus, St Euphrasia or Eupraxia, St Gerald of Mayo, St Heldrad, St Mochoemoc, St Nicephorus of Constantinople and Saints Roderic and Salomon.

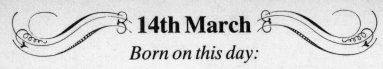

14th March

Born on this day:

Tessa Sanderson, javelin thrower, 1956;
Pam Ayres, poet, 1947;
Jasper Carrott, comedian, 1945;
Rita Tushingham, actress, 1942;
Michael Caine, actor, 1933;
Quincy Jones, US bandleader, 1933;
Lord Marsh, former chairman, Newspaper Publishers' Association, 1928;
John Wain, novelist, 1925;
Air Chief Marshal Sir Douglas Lowe, 1922;
John McCallum, actor and producer, 1918;
Bill Owen, actor, 1915;

Richard Eurich, painter, 1903;
James Laver, writer and editor, 1899;
Albert Einstein, physicist, 1879;
Norman Houston O'Neill, composer, 1875;
Paul Ehrlich, German bacteriologist, 1854;
John Lane, publisher, 1854;
Isabella Mary Beeton [Mayson], author of household and cookery books, 1836;
Giovanni Virginio Schiaparelli, Italian astronomer, 1835;
Victor Emmanuel II, King of Italy, 1820;
Johann Strauss the Elder, composer, 1804.

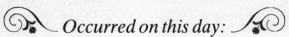

Died on this day:

Sir Huw Pyrs Wheldon, TV broadcaster and administrator, 1986;
Busby Berkeley [William Berkeley Enos], US choreographer, 1976;
Klement Gottwald, Czech leader, 1953;
Nikolai Ivanovich Bukharin, Russian journalist and politician, executed, 1938;
George Eastman, US photographic inventor, 1932;
Walter Crane, painter and illustrator, 1915;
William Hale White ['Mark Rutherford'], novelist, 1913;

Karl Marx, German political philosopher, 1883;
Louis-Antoine Jullien [Julien], French conductor and composer, 1860;
John Jervis, Earl of St Vincent, admiral of the fleet, 1823;
Friedrich Gottlieb Klopstock, German poet, 1803;
Admiral John Byng, executed for neglect of duty, 1757;
Field Marshal George Wade, 1748;
Jakob van Ruysdael, Dutch painter, 1682.

Occurred on this day:

The New English Bible [New Testament], a new translation, was published in London, 1961;
The first transatlantic radio broadcast was made, 1925;
A provisional government was set up in Russia, 1917;
The German army began a retreat to the Hindenburg Line, 1917;
The German cruiser *Dresden* was sunk, 1915;
The first submarine telephone line was laid by the *Monarch* across the English Channel, 1891;

The first production of *The Mikado*, by Gilbert and Sullivan, was staged at the Savoy Theatre, London, 1885;
Lake Albert, Africa, was discovered and named by Sir Samuel Baker, 1864;
Asiatic cholera first appeared in Ireland at Belfast, 1832;
Henry IV defeated the League at the Battle of Ivry-la-Bataille, 1590.

TODAY IS THE FEAST DAY OF St Eutychius or Eustathius of Carrhae, St Leobinus or Lubin and St Matilda.

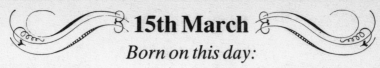

15th March

Born on this day:

John Duttine, actor, 1949;
Ry Cooder, US folk and blues guitarist, 1947;
Robert Nye, novelist and poet, 1939;
Admiral Sir Raymond Lygo, former chief executive, British Aerospace, 1924;
Sir Philip Powell CH, architect, 1921;
Earl Haig, painter, 1918;
Macdonald Carey, US film actor, 1913;
Enid Wilson, golfer, 1910;
George Brent [George Brendan Nolan], US film actor, 1904;
Leslie Stuart [Thomas Augustine Barrett], popular composer, *Lily of Laguna*, 1864;

Emil von Behring, German bacteriologist, 1854;
Lady Isabella Augusta Gregory [Persse], playwright and a founder of the Abbey Theatre, Dublin, 1852;
Dame Madge Kendall, actress, 1849;
Toby Edward Rosenthal, US painter, 1848;
Nicola Vaccai, Italian composer, 1790;
William Lamb, 2nd Viscount Melbourne, statesman, 1779;
Andrew Jackson, 7th president of the United States, 1767.

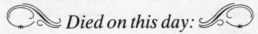

Died on this day:

Dame Rebecca West [Cicily Isabel Fairfield], author, 1983;
Aristotle Onassis, Greek ship-owner, 1975;
Mario Castelnuovo-Tedesco, Italian composer, 1968;
Arthur Holly Compton, US physicist, 1962;
Nevil Vincent Sidgwick, chemist, 1952;
Howard Phillips Lovecraft, US author, 1937;
Sir Henry Bessemer, engineer, 1898;

James Joseph Sylvester, mathematician, 1897;
Sir Joseph William Bazalgette, engineer, 1891;
Henri Scheffer, French painter, 1862;
Luigi Cherubini, Italian composer, 1842;
Salvator Rosa [Salvatoriello], Italian painter, 1673;
Gaius Julius Caesar, Roman emperor, assassinated, 44 BC.

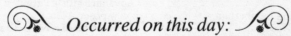

Occurred on this day:

The German army invaded Bohemia and Moravia [Czechoslovakia], 1939;
The American Legion for servicemen and women was founded, 1919;
Nicholas II, Tsar of Russia, abdicated, 1917;
The London department store, Selfridges, opened, 1909;
The British conquest of Northern Nigeria was completed, 1903;
An attempt was made by Irish-Americans to blow up the offices of *The Times*, 1883;

The first 11-a-side cricket test match was played, Australia v. England, at Sydney, 1876;
Maine became the 23rd of the United States, 1820;
The American colonists were defeated by Cornwallis at the Battle of Guilford Court House, North Carolina, 1781;
Columbus returned to Spain after his first voyage to America, 1493.

TODODAY IS THE FEAST DAY OF St Clement Mary Hofbauer, St Longinus, St Louise de Marillac, St Lucretia or Leocritia, St Matrona and St Zachary, pope.

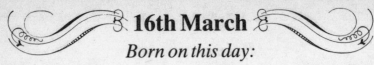

16th March

Born on this day:

Kate Nelligan, actress, 1951;
Bernardo Bertolucci, Italian film director, 1941;
Teresa Berganza, Spanish mezzo-soprano, 1935;
Roger Norrington, conductor, 1934;
Leo McKern, actor, 1920;
Air Chief Marshal Sir Christopher Foxley-Norris, 1917;
Sybille Bedford, author, 1911;
Robert Rossen [Rosen], US film director, 1908;
Dame Lucie Rie, potter, 1902;
Émile Cammaerts, Belgian poet and writer, 1878;
Sir John Lavery, painter, 1856;

René-François-Armand Sully Prudhomme, French poet, 1839;
Marie-Rosalie [Rosa] Bonheur, French painter, 1822;
Georg Simon Ohm, German physicist, 1787;
Matthew Flinders, circumnavigator of Tasmania, 1774;
James Madison, 4th president of the USA, 1751;
Caroline Lucretia Herschel, astronomer, 1750;
Giuseppe Maria Crespi, Italian painter and etcher, 1665;
Pieter Corneliszoon Hooft, Dutch historian and poet, 1581.

Died on this day:

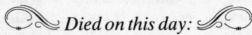

Jean-Omer-Marie-Gabriel Monnet, French political economist, 1979;
Léonide Massine, Russian choreographer, 1979;
William Henry Beveridge, 1st Baron Beveridge of Tuggal, social security pioneer, 1963;
Selma Ottiliana Lovisa Lagerlöf, Swedish novelist, 1940;
Sir Joseph Austen Chamberlain, statesman, 1937;
Miguel Primo de Rivera y Orbaneja, Marqués de Estella, Spanish general and dictator, 1930;

Aubrey Vincent Beardsley, artist and illustrator, 1898;
William Banting, obese undertaker and slimming pioneer, 1878;
Robert Smith Surtees, novelist, 1864;
John Hoadly, poet and playwright, 1776;
Giovanni Battista Pergolesi, Italian composer, 1736;
Tiberius Claudius Nero, Roman emperor, 37.

Occurred on this day:

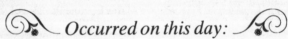

Soviet cosmonauts completed an orbit of 35 million miles, 1978;
The new London Bridge was opened, 1973;
The New English Bible [Old Testament], a new translation, was published in London, 1961;
Slovakia was placed under German 'protection', while Hungary annexed Ruthenia, both part of Czechoslovakia, 1939;
Hitler renounced the Treaty of Versailles, and reintroduced compulsory military service, 1935;

In the USA, Dr Robert H. Goddard demonstrated the practicality of rockets, 1926;
The first Football Association Cup Final was played at Kennington Oval, when the Wanderers beat the Royal Engineers 1–0, 1872;
The United States Military Academy was established at West Point, 1802;
Gustavus III, King of Sweden, shot by Jakob Johan Anckarström, 1792;
The Long Parliament of England, which sat for 20 years, was dissolved, 1660.

TODAY IS THE FEAST DAY OF St Abraham Kidunaia, St Eusebia of Hamage, St Finian Lobhair [The Leper], St Gregory Makar, St Heribert of Cologne and St Julian of Antioch.

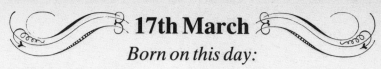

17th March

Born on this day:

Lesley-Anne Down, actress, 1954;
Patrick Duffy, US TV actor, 1949;
Prof. John Lill, concert pianist, 1944;
Robin Knox-Johnston, yachtsman, 1939;
Rudolf Nureyev, ballet star and director, 1938;
Galina Samsova, ballet dancer, 1937;
Penelope Lively, author, 1933;
Patrick Allen, actor, 1927;
Mercedes McCambridge, US film actress, 1918;
Nat 'King' Cole [Nathaniel Adams Coles], US singer and pianist, 1919;
Dr David Stafford-Clark, psychiatrist, 1916;
Robert Tyre [Bobby] Jones, US golfer, 1902;

Sydney Chaplin, US actor, 1885;
Sir Patrick Gardiner Hastings, lawyer and politician, 1880;
Margaret Grace Bondfield, first woman Cabinet Minister, 1873;
Kate Greenaway, artist and children's book illustrator, 1846;
Gottlieb Daimler, German automobile pioneer, 1834;
Jean Ingelow, poet, 1820;
Edmund Kean, actor, 1789;
Dirck Hals, Dutch painter, 1591;
Francesco Albani [Albano], Italian painter, 1578;
James IV, King of Scotland, 1473.

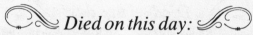

Died on this day:

Lieut.-Gen. Sir John Bagot Glubb [Glubb Pasha], commander of the Arab Legion, 1986;
Sir George Hubert Wilkins, Australian explorer and aviator, 1958;
Isaak Emmanuilovich Babel, Russian author, 1941;
Jules-François-Camille Ferry, French statesman, 1893;
Robert Chambers, publisher and author, 1871;
Christian Johann Doppler, Austrian physicist, 1853;
Jean-Ignace-Isidore Gérard ['Grandville'], French caricaturist, 1847;

Daniel Benouilli, Swiss mathematician, 1782;
Jean-Baptiste Rousseau, French playwright and poet, 1741;
Jan van Mieris, Dutch painter, 1690;
François Duc de La Rochefoucauld-Liancourt, French author, 1680;
Denys Calvaert [Dionisio Fiammingo], Flemish/Italian painter, 1619;
Harold Harefoot, King of England, 1040;
Marcus Aurelius, Roman emperor, 180.

Occurred on this day:

The *Amoco Cadiz* oil tanker ran aground on the Brittany coast, 1978;
Vanguard I spacecraft was launched at Cape Canaveral, 1958;
The US army defeated the Japanese at the Battle of Iwo Jima, 1945;
Vienna was bombed by US aircraft, 1944;
A mutiny aboard a Russian battleship at Kronstadt was finally put down after 16 days, 1921;
Captain Lawrence Oates, with Scott's expedition, walked out into the Antarctic wastes, never to return, 1912;

Bob Fitzsimmons of Cornwall beat the American heavyweight champion 'Gentleman Jim' Corbett, at Carson, Nevada, 1897;
George Washington forced British troops to withdraw from Boston, 1776;
Oliver Cromwell declared England to be a Commonwealth, abolishing the position of King, 1649;
The Duchy of Cornwall was created, 1337.

TODAY IS THE FEAST DAY OF The Martyrs of the Serapeum, St Gertrude of Nivelles, St Joseph of Arimathea, St Patrick and St Paul of Cyprus.

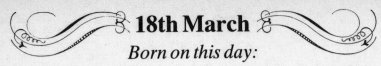

18th March

Born on this day:

Ingemar Stenmark, ski champion, 1956;
Pat Eddery, jockey, 1952;
James Conlon, conductor, 1950;
Alex Higgins, snooker player, 1949;
Wilson Pickett, singer, 1941;
Kenny Lynch, singer and actor, 1939;
John Updike, novelist, 1932;
John Fraser, actor, 1931;
René Clement, French film director, 1913;
Prof. John Young, zoologist, 1907;
Friederich Robert Donat, film actor, 1905;
Lavrenti Pavlovich Beria, Russian chief of the secret police, 1899;
Betty Compson [Eleanor Luicime Compson], US film actress, 1897;
Wilfred Owen, poet, 1893;

Kurt Koffka, German psychologist, 1886;
Gian Francesco Malipiero, Italian composer, 1882;
Arthur Neville Chamberlain, statesman, 1869;
Rudolf Diesel, German engineer and inventor, 1858;
Nikolai Andreyevich Rimsky-Korsakov, Russian composer, 1844;
Stéphane Mallarmé, French poet, 1842;
Stephen Grover Cleveland, 22nd and 24th president of the USA, 1837;
Marie-Madeleine Pioche de la Vergne, Comtesse de La Fayette, French novelist, baptised, 1634.

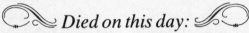

Died on this day:

Lauritz Melchior, Danish/US tenor, 1973;
Farouk I, ex-King of Egypt, 1965;
Louis Bromfield, US novelist, 1956;
William De Mille, US film and theatrical producer, 1955;
Eleutherios Venizelos, Greek statesman, 1936;
George I, King of the Hellenes, assassinated, 1913;
Pierre-Eugène-Marcelin Berthelot, French organic chemist, 1907;
Laurence Sterne, clergyman and author, 1768;

Sir Robert Walpole, 1st Earl of Orford, statesman, 1745;
Jenny Diver [Mary Young], 'Queen of the Pickpockets', hanged, 1741;
Philip Massinger, playwright, 1640;
Ivan IV ['The Terrible'], Tsar of Russia, 1584;
Jacques-Bernard de Boweg Molay, Grand Master of the Knights Templars, burnt at the stake, 1314;
St Edward the Martyr, King of the English, murdered, 978.

Occurred on this day:

700,000 barrels of oil were spilled into the sea when the *Torrey Canyon* oil tanker grounded off the Cornish coast, 1967;
The first 'walk in space' from the Soviet spaceship *Voskhod 2* was made by Alexei Leonov, 1965;
The planet Pluto was discovered by the US astronomer Clyde Tombaugh, 1930;
The telephone link between London and Paris was opened, 1891;
The rising of the Communards began in Paris, 1871;

The Alhambra Theatre, London, opened as the Royal Panopticon of Science and Art, 1854;
The American Express Company was organised at Buffalo, New York, 1850;
A five-day revolution broke out in Milan against Austrian rule, 1848;
In Tolpuddle, Dorset, six farm labourers were sentenced to be transported for forming a trade union, 1834;
The Austrians defeated the French at the Battle of Neerwinden, 1793.

TODAY IS THE FEAST DAY OF St Alexander of Jerusalem, St Anselm of Lucca, St Cyril of Jerusalem, St Edward the Martyr, St Frigidian or Frediano and St Salvator of Horta.

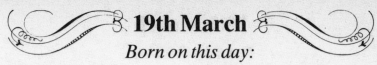

19th March

Born on this day:

Glenn Close, US actress, 1947;
Maurice Roëves, actor and director, 1937;
Ursula Andress, film actress, 1936;
Philip Roth, US novelist, 1933;
Patrick McGoohan, actor, 1928;
Sir Peter Masefield, aviation authority, 1914;
Michael Rothenstein, painter, 1908;
Dame Elizabeth Maconchy, composer, 1907;
Philip Mason, novelist, 1906;
Joseph Albers, US abstract painter and poet, 1888;
Sir John Hubert Marshall, archaeologist, 1876;
Sergei Pavlovich Diaghilev, Russian founder of the ballet company, 1872;
William Jennings Bryan, US politician and speaker, 1860;
William Allingham, Irish poet, 1824;
Sir Richard Francis Burton, scholar and explorer, 1821;
Dr David Livingstone, explorer and missionary, 1813;
Tobias George Smollett, physician and author, 1721;
Alonso Cano, Spanish painter, 1601;
Georges de la Tour, French painter, 1593.

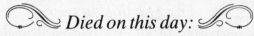

Died on this day:

Alan Badel, actor, 1982;
Faith Cuthrell Baldwin, US romantic novelist, 1978;
Stephen Graham, travel writer, 1975;
Edgar Rice Burroughs, novelist and creator of 'Tarzan', 1950;
Arthur James Balfour, 1st Earl, statesman, 1930;
Antoine-Thomson d'Abbadie, French explorer and scientist, 1897;
George Richmond, painter, 1896;
Friedrich Wilhelm Schadow-Godenhaus, German painter, 1862;
William Henry Playfair, architect, 1857;
Mary Anning, finder of Ichthyosaurus fossil, 1847;
Thomas William Daniell, landscape painter, 1840;
René Robert Cavelier, Sieur de la Salle, French explorer, murdered by his own men in Texas, 1687;
Thomas Killigrew, playwright, 1683.

Occurred on this day:

Willy Brandt and Willi Stoph, heads of West and East Germany, met for the first time at Erfurt, 1970;
During a severe gale, the 1,260-foot TV mast at Emley Moor, Yorks, crashed to the ground, 1970;
Following an internal dispute, British parachute troops took over the Caribbean island of Anguilla, 1969;
Sydney Harbour bridge was officially opened, 1932;
The US Senate refused to ratify the Versailles Treaty and the League of Nations Covenant, 1920;
The opera *Faust* by Gounod was performed in Paris for the first time, 1859;
The Rev. John White formed the New England Company in Massachusetts Bay, 1628.

TODAY IS THE FEAST DAY OF St Alcmund, prince of Northumbria, St John of Panaca, St Joseph [husband of the Virgin] and St Landoald.

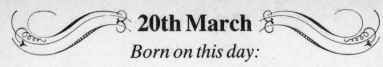

20th March

Born on this day:

Madan Lal, Indian cricketer, 1951;
Brian Mulroney, prime minister of Canada, 1939;
Sir Mark Saville QC, High Court judge, 1936;
Anthony Blond, publisher, 1928;
John Joubert, composer, 1927;
Dame Vera Lynn, singer, 1917;
Sviatoslav Richter, Russian pianist, 1915;
Wendell Corey, US actor, 1914;
Sir Michael Scudamore Redgrave, actor, 1908;
Max Brand [Frederick Schiller Faust], US novelist and screenwriter, 1892;
Beniamino Gigli, Italian operatic tenor, 1890;
Lauritz Melchior, Danish/US operatic tenor, 1890;
Henrik Ibsen, Norwegian playwright, 1828;
Ned Buntline [Edward Zane Carroll Judson], US sensational novelist, 1823;
William Barnes, Dorset dialect poet, 1801;
Thomas Webster, figure painter, 1800;
Jean-Antoine Houdon, French sculptor, 1741;
Ovid [Publius Ovidius Naso], Roman poet, 43 BC.

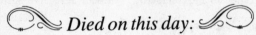

Died on this day:

Brendan Behan, Irish writer, 1964;
Henry Handel Richardson [Ethel Florence Richardson], novelist, 1946;
Lord Alfred Bruce Douglas, editor and poet, 1945;
Lieut.-Comdr. Percy Thomson Dean, VC, 1939;
Robert Bontine Cunninghame Graham, author, 1936;
Ferdinand Foch, Marshal of France, 1929;
George Nathaniel Curzon, 1st Marquess, Viceroy of India, 1925;
Lajos Kossuth, Hungarian patriot, 1894;
Henry David Inglis, traveller and writer, 1835;
Louis-Léopold Robert, French painter, 1835;
Sir Isaac Newton, scientist, 1727;
Sir Thomas Seymour, Baron, Lord High Admiral of England, executed, 1549;
Sir Thomas Elyot, diplomat, doctor and writer, 1546;
King Henry IV, 1413.

Occurred on this day:

Isabel Perón, former president of Argentina, was jailed for eight years for corruption, 1981;
Mandalay was recaptured from the Japanese by the British, 1945;
The British Council was established, 1935;
The Nazis opened their first concentration camp at Dachau, near Munich, 1933;
The first London production of the musical show *Rose-Marie* was presented, 1925;
Uncle Tom's Cabin, by Harriet Beecher Stowe, was first published in book form, 1852;
Marble Arch, formerly at Buckingham Palace, was unveiled at its present site in London, 1851;
The Burlington Arcade, London, was opened, 1819;
Napoleon arrived at Fontainebleau and the 'Hundred Days' began, 1815;
The Battle between the Allies and Napoleon at Arcis-sur-Aube began, 1814;
The foundation stone of Dartmoor Prison, Devon, was laid, 1806;
The New England *Weekly Journal* was first published, 1727;
The Dutch East India Company was founded, 1602.

TODAY IS THE FEAST DAY OF St Cuthbert, St Herbert, St Martin of Braga, St Photina and her Companions, St Wulfram and The Martyrs of Mar Saba.

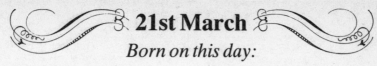

21st March

Born on this day:

Ayrton Senna, Brazilian racing driver, 1960;

Alvin Kallicharran, cricketer, 1949;

Michael Foreman, author and illustrator, 1938;

Roger Whittaker, singer and songwriter, 1936;

Brian Clough, football manager, 1935;

Ved Mehta, blind Indian author and journalist, 1934;

Michael Heseltine, politician, 1933;

Lord Oaksey, racing journalist and commentator, 1929;

Peter Brook, theatrical producer, 1925;

Antony Hopkins, composer and conductor, 1921;

Lord Wilson of Langside QC, former Lord Advocate, 1916;

Nikolaos Skalkottas, Greek composer, 1904;

Florenz Ziegfeld, US stage producer, 1869;

Herbert Albert Laurens Fisher, historian, 1865;

Albert Chevalier, actor, music-hall entertainer and singer, 1861;

Modest Petrovich Mussorgsky, Russian composer, 1839;

Dorothea Beale, educationalist, 1831;

Thomas John Dibdin, songwriter, 1771;

Claude-Nicolas Ledoux, French architect, 1736;

Johann Sebastian Bach, German composer, 1685.

Died on this day:

Robert Preston [Meservey], US film actor, 1987;

Sir Michael Scudamore Redgrave, actor, 1985;

Harry H. Corbett, actor, 1982;

Philip Wilson Steer, painter, 1942;

Alexander Konstantinovich Glazunov, Russian composer, 1936;

Franz Schreker, German composer, 1934;

Fernand-Anne Piestre [Cormon], French painter, 1924;

Jean-Hippolyte Flandrin, French painter, 1864;

Robert Southey, poet, 1843;

George Engleheart, miniature painter, 1839;

Jean-Baptiste Greuze, French painter, 1805;

James Ussher, Archbishop of Armagh, scholar and theologian, 1656;

Hans Asper, Swiss painter, 1571;

Thomas Cranmer, Archbishop of Canterbury, burned at the stake, 1556.

Occurred on this day:

Namibia, formerly known as South West Africa, became independent, 1990;

Martin Luther King led a civil rights march, starting at Selma, Alabama, 1965;

The musical show *Half a Sixpence* was first produced, London, 1963;

In South Africa, many African demonstrators at Sharpeville were shot, 1960;

The London Planetarium opened, 1958;

The Sudan became independent, 1953;

Dr Kwame Nkrumah became the first African prime minister south of the Sahara, 1952;

Hitler seized the city of Memel from Lithuania, 1939;

The rebuilt Waterloo Station, London, was opened, 1922;

The last offensive by the Germans began on the Western front; second Battle of the Somme, 1918;

The Tsar and Tsarina of Russia were arrested by the revolutionary forces, 1917;

The Scottish National Gallery in Edinburgh was opened, 1859;

General Sir Ralph Abercromby defeated the French at the Battle of Alexandria [Aboukir], 1801.

TODAY IS THE FEAST DAY OF St Enda, St Fanchea and St Serapion of Thmuis.

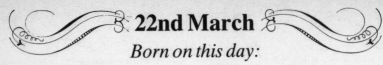

22nd March

Born on this day:

Peter McEvoy, golfer, 1953;
Mary Tamm, actress, 1950;
Brian Hanrahan, broadcaster, 1949;
Sir Andrew Lloyd Webber, composer, 1948;
Paul Schockemöhle, show-jumper, 1945;
George Benson, jazz guitarist, 1943;
William Shatner, US TV and film actor, 1931;
Leslie Thomas, author, 1931;
Stephen Sondheim, US composer and lyricist, 1930;
Marcel Marceau, French mime artist, 1923;
Air Marshal Sir Denis Crowley-Milling, 1919;
Werner Klemperer, US actor, 1919;

Paul Rogers, actor, 1917;
Karl Malden, US film actor, 1913;
Robert Andrews Millikan, US physicist, 1868;
Randolph Caldecott, artist and illustrator, 1846;
Carl August Nicolas Rosa, German violinist and composer, and founder of the Carl Rosa opera company, 1842;
Wilhelm I, King of Prussia and Emperor of Germany, 1797;
Adam Sedgwick, geologist, 1785;
Sir Anthony van Dyck, Flemish painter, 1599;
Maximilian I, Holy Roman Emperor, 1459.

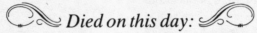

Died on this day:

Ben Lyon, US actor, entertainer and producer, 1979;
Sir Richard Sykes, ambassador to the Netherlands, shot dead, 1979;
Michael Todd [Avram Goldenbogen], US film producer, killed, 1958;
Benjamin Williams Leader, landscape painter, 1923;
Ernest William Hornung, novelist, 1921;

Frederic William Farrar, author and cleric, 1903;
Thomas Hughes, jurist, reformer and author, 1896;
Johann Wolfgang von Goethe, German author, 1832;
John Canton, physicist, 1772;
Jean-Baptiste Lully, French composer, 1687;
Thomas Carew, poet, 1639.

Occurred on this day:

Jordan became independent, 1946;
The Arab League was founded in Cairo, 1945;
The world's first high-definition TV service was inaugurated in Berlin, 1935;
The musical show *This Year of Grace!* was first produced, London, 1928;
The first international airline service began, flying between Paris and Brussels weekly, 1919;
Colour pictures were printed in the *New York Illustrated Mirror*, the first in any newspaper, 1904;

Auguste and Louis Lumière made the first demonstration of motion pictures using celluloid film, Paris, 1895;
The English Football League was founded, 1888;
The National Gallery in London was founded by the purchase of 38 pictures from J. J. Angerstein, 1824;
In the American Colonies, the Stamp Act came into force, 1765;
The English were defeated by the Scots at Anjou, 1421;
The Order of the Templars was abolished by the Pope, 1312.

TODAY IS THE FEAST DAY OF St Basil of Ancyra, St Benvenuto of Osimo, St Deogratias, St Nicholas Owen, St Nicholas von Flüe and St Paul of Narbonne.

23rd March

Born on this day:

Barry Cryer, writer and comedian, 1935;

Norman Bailey, baritone, 1933;

Sir Roger Bannister, neurologist and Master of Pembroke College, Oxford, 1929;

Michael Manser, architect, 1929;

Donald Malcolm Campbell, land and water speedster, 1921;

Geoffrey Bush, composer, 1920;

Wernher Magnus Maximilian von Braun, German/US rocket engineer, 1912;

Marshal of the RAF Lord Elworthy, 1911;

Akira Kurosawa, Japanese film director, 1910;

Lale Andersen, Danish singer of *Lilli Marlene*, 1910;

Lord Jay, journalist and former MP, 1907;

Joan Crawford [Lucille Le Sueur], US film actress, 1904;

Robert Gibbings, wood engraver and author, 1889;

Juan Gris, Spanish cubist painter, 1887;

Roger Martin du Gard, French novelist and playwright, 1881;

Horatio William Bottomley, journalist and swindler, 1860;

Alfred, Viscount Milner, statesman, 1854;

Jean-Hippolyte Flandrin, French painter, 1809;

Pierre Simon, Marquis de Laplace, French astronomer and mathematician, 1749;

Margaret of Anjou, wife of King Henry VI, 1430.

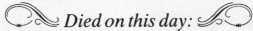

Died on this day:

Friedrich August von Hayek, Austrian-born economist, 1991;

Richard, Baron Beeching, reorganiser of British Rail, 1985;

Robert Louis Constantine Lee-Dillon FitzGibbon, author, 1983;

Field Marshal Sir Claude John Auchinleck, 1981;

Mike Hailwood, motor-cycle champion, 1981;

Peter Lorre [Laszlo Löwenstein], Hungarian-born US actor, 1964;

Raoul Dufy, French painter and designer, 1953;

Richard Halliburton, US writer and traveller, drowned in the Pacific, 1939;

Stendhal [Marie-Henri Beyle], French novelist, 1842;

August Friedrich Ferdinand von Kotzebue, German playwright, murdered, 1819;

Thomas Holcroft, playwright, novelist and translator, 1809;

Paul I, Tsar of Russia, assassinated, 1801;

Pedro the Cruel, King of Castile and Leon, killed, 1369.

Occurred on this day:

Bangladesh, formerly East Pakistan, proclaimed her independence, 1971;

The Archbishop of Canterbury visited Rome and met the Pope, the first official meeting between the two churches for 400 years, 1966;

The musical show *The Dancing Years* was first produced, London, 1939;

Adolf Hitler became dictator of Germany, 1933;

In the USA, the governor of Tennessee signed an Act, forbidding the teaching of evolution in state schools, 1925;

The German gun 'Big Bertha' shelled Paris from a distance of 75 miles, 1918;

Lithuania proclaimed her independence, 1918;

The first trams in London began operating in Bayswater, 1861;

The Austrians, under General Radetzky, were defeated by the Piedmontese at the Battle of Novara, 1849;

The Stamp Act, intended for taxing colonists in America, was passed by Parliament, 1765;

The marriage of Catherine of Aragon to King Henry VIII was declared valid by the Pope, although in 1533 Henry had 'married' Anne Boleyn, 1534.

TODAY IS THE FEAST DAY OF St Benedict the Hermit, St Ethelwald the Hermit, St Joseph Oriol, St Turibius of Lima and St Victorian.

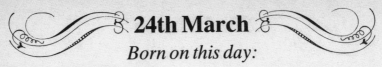

24th March

Born on this day:

Robert Fox, theatrical producer, 1952;
Peter Powell, disc jockey, 1951;
Archie Gemmill, footballer, 1947;
Alan Sugar, chairman of Amstrad, 1947;
Barbara Daly, make-up artist, 1945;
Patrick Malahide, actor, 1945;
Benjamin Luxon, baritone, 1937;
Terrence Steven [Steve] McQueen, US film actor, 1930;
Wilson Harris, Guyanese novelist, 1921;
Gene Nelson, US dancer, actor and director, 1920;
Prof. Harry Whittington, geologist, 1916;
Richard Conte [Nicolas Peter Conte], US film actor, 1914;
Christopher Vernon Hassall, author, actor and poet, 1912;

Jane Drew, architect, 1911;
Thomas Edmund Dewey, US politician, 1902;
U. B. Iwerks, US film animator, co-creator with Disney of 'Mickey Mouse', 1901;
Frank Weston Benson, US painter, 1862;
Olive Emilie Albertina Schreiner, South African author, 1855;
Silas Kitto Hocking, novelist, 1850;
William Morris, socialist, artist, poet and typographer, 1834;
John Passmore Edwards, newspaper proprietor and philanthropist, 1823;
Michiel Adrianszoon de Ruyter, Dutch naval commander, 1607;
Georg Agricola [Bauer], German mineralogist, 1490.

Died on this day:

Yvonne Mitchell, actress and novelist, 1979;
Field Marshal Bernard Law Montgomery, 1st Viscount Montgomery of Alamein, 1976;
Ernest Howard Shepard, artist and illustrator [*Winnie the Pooh*], 1976;
Auguste Piccard, Swiss deep-sea explorer and balloonist, 1962;
Queen Mary, wife of King George V, 1953;
General Orde Charles Wingate, killed in an air crash, 1944;
Marcus Stone, painter, 1921;
Enrique Granados, Spanish composer, at sea, 1916;

John Millington Synge, Irish playwright, 1909;
Jules Verne, French novelist, 1905;
Charlotte Mary Yonge, author, 1901;
Henry Wadsworth Longfellow, US poet, 1882;
John Harrison, horologist and inventor of the marine chronometer, 1776;
Philip Dormer Stanhope, 4th Earl of Chesterfield, author and statesman, 1773;
Jacques Callot, French painter and engraver, 1635;
Queen Elizabeth I, 1603;
The Caliph Haroun-al-Raschid, 809.

Occurred on this day:

President Isabel Perón of Argentina was deposed after a bloodless military coup, 1976;
The unique British Guiana 1-cent black-on-magenta postage stamp was sold for £116,600, 1970;
The national loaf was introduced into Britain, 1942;
A Royal Commission on decimal coinage reported against changing the existing system, 1920;

The University Boat Race between Oxford and Cambridge ended in a dead heat, 1877;
After King James [James I of England, James VI of Scotland], ascended the throne of England, the English and Scottish crowns were united, 1603;
The city of Damascus was captured by Tamerlane, 1401.

TODAY IS THE FEAST DAY OF St Aldemar, St Catharine of Vadstena, St Irenaeus of Sirmium, St Simon of Trent and St William of Norwich.

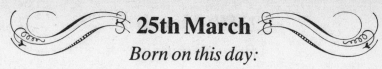

25th March

Born on this day:

Nick Lowe, guitarist, singer and songwriter, 1949;

Elton John, singer, songwriter and pianist, 1947;

Paul Michael Glaser, US TV actor, 1944;

Aretha Franklin, US soul singer, 1942;

Lord Walker of Worcester [Peter Walker], former MP, 1932;

Penelope Gilliatt, author, 1932;

Humphrey Burton, TV producer, 1931;

David Hicks, interior designer, 1929;

Prof. Sir Patrick Forrest, surgeon, 1923;

Queen Alexandra of Yugoslavia, 1921;

Prof. Mary Douglas, anthropologist, 1921;

Dorothy Squires, singer, 1915;

Jerry Livingston [Jerome Levinson], US composer and lyricist, 1909;

Sir David Lean, film director, 1908;

Prof. Sir Raymond Firth, anthropologist, 1901;

Andy Clyde, Scottish film actor and comedian, 1892;

Béla Bartók, Hungarian composer, 1881;

Arturo Toscanini, Italian conductor, 1867;

Anne Brontë ['Acton Bell'], novelist, 1820;

Giovanni Battista Amici, Italian astronomer and optician, 1786;

King Henry II, 1133.

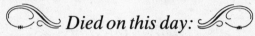

Died on this day:

Alan John Percivale Taylor, historian, 1990;

Walter Susskind, conductor and pianist, 1980;

King Faisal of Saudi Arabia, assassinated by Prince Museid, his 'mentally deranged' nephew, 1975;

John Drinkwater, poet and playwright, 1937;

Achille-Claude Debussy, French composer, 1918;

Frédéric Mistral, Provençal poet, 1914;

Garnet Joseph, Viscount Wolseley, soldier and army reformer, 1913;

James Payn, novelist, 1898;

Nicholas Hawksmoor, architect, 1836;

Anna Seward, poet and novelist, 1809;

'Novalis' [Friedrich Leopold, Baron von Hardenberg], German poet, 1801;

William Hamilton [of Bangour], poet, 1754.

Occurred on this day:

The European Community was established when the Treaty of Rome was signed by the 'Six', 1957;

King George of Greece was deposed, and a republic was proclaimed, 1924;

The first gold medal of the modern Olympic Games was presented, 1896;

The Italians invaded Abyssinia [Ethiopia], 1895;

Gilbert and Sullivan's opera *Trial by Jury* was first produced, London, 1875;

Rotherhithe pedestrian tunnel beneath the Thames was opened, 1843;

The British parliament abolished the slave trade, 1807;

Henry Hudson sailed from Amsterdam on behalf of the Dutch East India Company in an effort to find the North West Passage, 1609;

Sir Walter Raleigh was granted a patent to exploit Virginia, 1584;

The Council of Pisa met, 1409;

Robert [I] Bruce was crowned King of Scots at Scone, Perthshire, 1306.

TODAY IS THE FEAST DAY OF St Alfwold, St Barontius, St Dismas, the Good Thief, St Hermenland, St Lucy Filippini and St Margaret Clitherow.

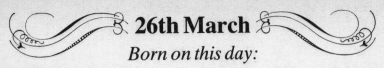

26th March

Born on this day:

Kyung-wha Chung, Korean concert violinist, 1948;

Diana Ross, US singer, 1944;

James Caan, US film actor, 1939;

Alan Arkin, US actor, 1934;

Leonard Nimoy, US screen actor, 1931;

Carole Carr, singer, 1928;

Pierre Boulez, conductor and composer, 1925;

Elizabeth Jane Howard, novelist, 1923;

Air Marshal Sir Peter Horsley, chairman, ML Holdings, 1921;

Harry Rabinowitz, conductor and composer, 1916;

Tennessee [Thomas Lanier] Williams, US playwright, 1911;

Richard Thomas Church, poet and novelist, 1893;

Leonard ['Chico'] Marx, US comedian, 1887;

Robert Lee Frost, US poet, 1874;

Sir Gerald Hubert Edward Busson du Maurier, actor-manager, 1873;

Alfred Edward Housman, poet, 1859;

Harry Furniss, caricaturist and illustrator, 1854;

George Smith, Assyriologist, 1840;

William Edward Hartpole Lecky, historian, 1838;

Konrad von Gesner, Swiss physicist and naturalist, 1516.

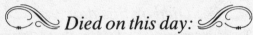

Died on this day:

Walter Abel, US film actor, 1987;

Sir Noël Pierce Coward, writer, composer and performer, 1973;

Raymond Thornton Chandler, US novelist and scriptwriter, 1959;

Édouard Herriot, French statesman, 1957;

Max Ophüls [Maximilian Oppenheimer], German film director, 1957;

David Lloyd George, 1st Earl Lloyd George of Dwyfor, statesman, 1945;

Sarah Bernhardt [Rosine Bernard], French actress, 1923;

Cecil John Rhodes, financier and statesman, 1902;

Walt Whitman, US poet and essayist, 1892;

Ludwig van Beethoven, German composer, 1827;

Sir John Vanbrugh, playwright and architect, 1726;

John Winthrop, first governor of the Massachusetts Bay Colony, 1649.

Occurred on this day:

For the first time, women were allowed on the floor of the London Stock Exchange, 1973;

The Battle of Iwo Jima ended, 1945;

Driving tests in Britain were introduced, 1934;

The Gaumont-British Film Corporation was founded, 1927;

The Allies decided to appoint Marshal Foch as Allied commander-in-chief, 1918;

The first cremation in England took place at Woking, 1886;

The Paris Commune was established, 1871;

The second theatre of Her Majesty's, London, opened as the King's Theatre, 1791;

The *British Gazette and Sunday Monitor*, first British Sunday newspaper, published, 1780;

The Theatre Royal, Drury Lane, London [second theatre] opened, 1674.

TODAY IS THE FEAST DAY OF St Basil the Younger, St Braulio, St Castulus of Rome, St Felix of Trier, St Ludger and St Macartan.

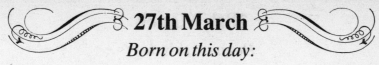

27th March

Born on this day:

Maria Ewing, opera singer, 1950;
Michael York, actor, 1942;
Julian Glover, actor, 1935;
Mstislav Rostropovich, Russian cellist and conductor, 1927;
Sir Louis Blom-Cooper QC, barrister and author, 1926;
Victor Hochhauser, impresario, 1923;
Cyrus Vance, former US Secretary of State, 1917;
Richard Denning, US film actor, 1914;
Budd Schulberg, US novelist and screenwriter, 1914;
Lord Callaghan of Cardiff, former prime minister, 1912;
Gloria May Josephine Swanson, US film actress, 1899;

Karl Mannheim, German sociologist, 1893;
Ferde Grofé [Ferdinand Rudolf von Grofé], US composer, 1892;
Margaret Irwin, novelist, 1889;
Ludwig Mies van der Rohe, German architect, 1886;
Sir Frederick Henry Royce, motor-car designer, 1863;
Paul-Marie-Théodore-Vincent d'Indy, French composer, 1851;
Wilhelm Konrad von Röntgen, German physicist, 1845;
Baron Georges-Eugène Haussmann, replanner of Paris, 1809;
Louis XVII, King of France, 1785.

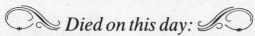 Died on this day:

Yuri Alekseyevich Gagarin, Russian cosmonaut, killed in an aircraft accident, 1968;
Enoch Arnold Bennett, novelist, 1931;
Leslie Stuart [Thomas Augustine Barrett], popular composer, *Lily of Laguna*, 1928;
Sir James Dewar, physicist and inventor of the vacuum flask, 1923;
Henry Brooks Adams, US historian, 1918;

John Bright, statesman, 1889;
Sir George Gilbert Scott, architect, 1878;
Giovanni Battista Tiepolo, Venetian painter, 1770;
James VI of Scotland/James I of Great Britain, 1625;
Marguerite de Valois, Queen of Navarre, 1615;
Pope Gregory XI, 1378.

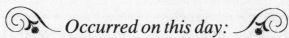 Occurred on this day:

At Tenerife, Canary Islands, a Pan Am jumbo jet collided on take-off with a KLM jumbo on the runway, killing 583, 1977;
A United Nations Peace Force took over in Cyprus, 1964;
Severe earthquakes and tidal waves were experienced on the US Pacific coast, 1964;

Nikita Khrushchev became chairman of the Council of Ministers in the USSR, 1958;
The Treaty of Amiens was concluded between France and Britain, 1802;
The United States Navy was formed, 1794;
Oliver Goldsmith's *Vicar of Wakefield* was published, 1766.

TODAY IS THE FEAST DAY OF St Alkeld or Athilda and St John of Egypt.

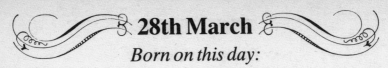

28th March

Born on this day:

Richard Stilgoe, entertainer and musician, 1943;

Neil Kinnock, politician, 1942;

Michael Parkinson, TV and radio presenter, 1935;

Freddie Bartholomew, former child film actor, 1924;

Dirk Bogarde, actor and author, 1921;

Raymond Lister, artist and author, 1919;

HM Queen Ingrid of Denmark, 1910;

Dame Flora Robson, actress, 1902;

Robert Harris, actor, 1900;

Corneille Heymans, Belgian physiologist, 1892;

Paul Samuel Whiteman, US bandleader, 1891;

Maxim Gorki [Alexei Maximovich Peshkov], Russian novelist, 1868;

Aristide Briand, French statesman, 1862;

Sir Joseph William Bazalgette, engineer, 1819;

Thomas Clarkson, abolitionist, 1760;

King George I, 1660;

Johann Amos Comenius [Jan Amos Komensky] Moravian reformer, 1592;

St Teresa of Avila, Carmelite nun, 1515;

Raphael Sanzio, Italian painter, 1483;

Fra Bartolommeo di Pagholo [Baccio della Porta], Italian painter, 1472.

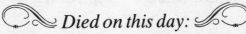

Died on this day:

Marc Chagall, Russian/French painter, 1985;

Dorothy Fields, US lyricist, 1974;

Dwight David Eisenhower, US general and former president, 1969;

William Christopher Handy, US blues composer, 1958;

Christopher Darlington Morley, US novelist and playwright, 1957;

Stephen Butler Leacock, Canadian humorist and author, 1944;

Sergei Vasilievich Rachmaninov, Russian composer, 1943;

Virginia Woolf [Adeline Virginia Stephen], author and critic, 1941;

Modest Petrovich Mussorgsky, Russian composer, 1881;

Peg [Margaret] Woffington, Irish actress, 1760;

Juan Fernández de Navarrete ['El Mudo'], Spanish painter, 1579;

Publius Helvius Pertinax, Roman emperor, murdered, 193.

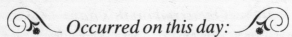

Occurred on this day:

The pirate radio station 'Radio Caroline' began to transmit from a ship in the North Sea, 1964;

The last German V2 rocket fell on Britain, 1945;

British commandos raided the French naval port of St Nazaire, 1942;

After Madrid surrendered to General Franco, the Spanish Civil War ended, 1939;

The name of Constantinople was changed to Istanbul, and Angora to Ankara, 1930;

The marriage took place in Hollywood of Douglas Fairbanks and Mary Pickford, 1920;

After the dissolution of the Hungarian parliament, Admiral Miklós Horthy became dictator, 1920;

Electric lighting was installed in the Houses of Parliament, 1878;

Britain declared war on Russia [the Crimean War], 1854;

The Act of Union with England was passed by the Irish Parliament, 1800.

TODAY IS THE FEAST DAY OF St Guntramnus or Gontran and St Tutilo.

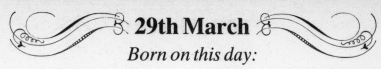

29th March

Born on this day:

John Suchet, TV reporter and newscaster, 1944;
John Major MP, prime minister, 1943;
Richard Rodney Bennett, composer, 1936;
Ruby Murray, singer, 1935;
Lord Tebbit [Norman Tebbit], CH, politician, 1931;
Frederick Treves, actor, 1925;
George Chisholm, trombonist, 1915;
Chapman Pincher, journalist and investigator, 1914;
Jack Jones, CH, former trade union leader, 1913;
Sir William Turner Walton, composer, 1902;

Sir Edwin Landseer Lutyens, architect, 1869;
Elihu Thomson, US inventor and electrician, 1853;
Wilhelmina [Wilma] Maria Francisca Norman-Neruda [Lady Hallé], violinist, 1839;
Edward George Stanley, 14th Earl of Derby, statesman, 1799;
John Tyler, 10th president of the USA, 1790;
Nicolas-Jean de Dieu Soult, Duke of Dalmatia, French soldier, 1769.

Died on this day:

Paul Henreid [Paul George Julius von Hernreid], actor, 1992;
Annunzio Paolo Mantovani, musician, 1980;
Joseph Arthur, 1st Baron Rank, cinema magnate, 1972;
Raymond William Postgate, historian and novelist, 1971;
Vera Mary Brittain, author, 1970;
Joyce [Arthur Joyce Lunel] Cary, novelist, 1957;
Sir Charles Villiers Stanford, composer, 1924;

Robert Falcon Scott, Arctic explorer, 1912;
Georges-Pierre Seurat, French impressionist painter, 1891;
John Keble, theologian, 1866;
John Jacob Astor [John Jakob Ashdour], fur trader, 1848;
Maria Anne Fitzherbert, mistress [and 'illegal' wife] of George IV, 1837;
Charles Wesley, writer of hymns, 1788;
Emanuel Swedenborg, Swedish scientist and philosopher, 1772.

Occurred on this day:

The first close-up pictures of Mercury were taken by the US spacecraft *Mariner 10*, 1974.
The last US troops left Vietnam, 1973;
In Georgia, USA, Lieut. William Calley was found guilty of murdering 22 civilians at My Lai, Vietnam, and received a life sentence, 1971;
The last flying bomb fell in England, 1945;
In Germany, it was claimed that in the general election, 99 per cent of voters had voted for the National Socialist [Nazi] party, 1936;
Richmond Park, near London, was opened to the public, 1904;

Tchaikovsky's opera *Eugène Onegin* first performed, Moscow, 1879;
The Royal Albert Hall was opened by Queen Victoria, 1871;
Jean-Jacques Dessalines was declared 'governor for life' of Haiti following his massacre of white people, 1804;
Ten cantons of Switzerland formed the Helvetic republic, 1798;
At the Battle of Towton, Yorks, King Henry VI of Lancaster was defeated, 1461.

TODAY IS THE FEAST DAY OF Saints Armogastes, Masculas, Achinimus and Saturus, St Berthold, St Cyril of Heliopolis, St Gundleus or Woolo, St Gwladys, Saints Jonas, Barachisius and Others, St Mark of Arethusa and St Rupert of Salzburg.

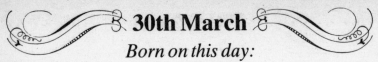

30th March

Born on this day:

Eric Clapton, rock guitarist, 1945;
Sarah Badel, actress, 1943;
Warren Beatty, US actor, 1937;
Sir Ian MacLaurin, chairman, Tesco, 1937;
John Astin, US TV and film actor, 1930;
Rolf Harris, Australian entertainer, 1930;
Tom Sharpe, novelist and historian, 1928;
Lord Rayner, chairman and chief
    executive, Marks and Spencer, 1926;
Alan Davidson, culinary author, publisher
    and former diplomat, 1924;
Frankie Laine, US singer, 1913;
Prof. Sir Ernst Gombrich, art historian,
    1909;
Joyce Carey, actress, 1898;
Jo Davidson, US sculptor, 1883;
Melanie Klein [Reizes], Austrian/British
    child psychologist, 1882;
Sean O'Casey, Irish playwright and writer,
    1880;
Vincent Van Gogh, Dutch painter,
    1853;
Paul Verlaine, French poet, 1844;
Charles Booth, shipowner and sociologist,
    1840;
Friedrich Wilhelm Raiffeisen, German
    economist, 1818;
Angelo Catelani, Italian conductor and
    composer, 1811;
Francisco José de Goya y Lucientes,
    Spanish painter, 1746;
Sir John Hawkins, publisher, editor and
    historian, 1719;
Maimonides [Moses ben Maimon], Jewish
    philosopher, 1135.

Died on this day:

James Cagney, US film actor, 1986;
Airey Middleton Sheffield Neave, MP,
    barrister and author, killed, 1979;
Léon Blum, French statesman, 1950;
Friedrich Bergius, German inventor, 1949;
Rudolf Steiner, Austrian social philospher,
    1925;
Tito Mattei, Italian pianist, composer and
    conductor, 1914;
Thomas Couture, French painter, 1879;
Marie-Louise-Anne-Elisabeth Vigée-
    Lebrun, French painter, 1842;
George Bryan 'Beau' Brummel, dandy and
    leader of fashion, 1840;
Rudolph Ackermann, German printseller
    and publisher, 1834;
William Hunter, anatomist, obstetrician
    and medical writer, 1783;
Sébastien Le Prestre de Vauban, French
    military engineer, 1707.

Occurred on this day:

In Washington, D.C., President Reagan
    was shot in the chest by would-be assassin
    John W. Hinckley Jr, 1981;
The US Embassy in Saigon, Vietnam was
    blown up by the Vietcong, killing 13
    people, 1966;
Thomas Francis Bayard, first US
    ambassador to Great Britain, arrived at
    his post, 1893;
A treaty for the purchase of Alaska from
    Russia for the sum of $7,200,000 was
    submitted to the US Senate, 1867;
The Treaty of Paris was signed, ending the
    Crimean War between Russia on one side
    and England, France, Turkey and
    Sardinia on the other, 1856;
Britain and the Allies against Napoleon
    marched triumphantly into Paris, 1814;
Joseph Bonaparte was made King of
    Naples, 1806;
The English parliament enacted the New
    England Restriction Act, which forbade
    the colonies of New England to trade
    with anyone except England, 1775.

TODAY IS THE FEAST DAY OF St John Climacus, St Leonard Murialdo, St Ludolf, St
Rieul or Regulus and St Zosimus of Syracuse.

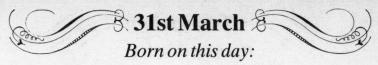

31st March

Born on this day:

Sir David Steel, politician, 1939;
Herb Alpert, US musician, 1936;
Richard Chamberlain, US actor, 1936;
Shirley Jones, US film actress, 1935;
Sydney Chaplin, US actor, 1927;
John Fowles, novelist, 1927;
Henry Morgan, US comedian and entertainer, 1916;
Robert Hamer, film director, 1911;
Andrew Lang, scholar, poet and editor, 1844;
John La Farge, US landscape and figure painter, 1835;
Robert Wilhelm von Bunsen, German physicist and chemist, 1811;
Nikolai Vasilyevich Gogol, Russian novelist and playwright, 1809;
Edward FitzGerald, English translator of the *Rubáiyát of Omar Khayyám*, 1809;
Franz Joseph Haydn, Austrian composer, 1732;
Sir Charles Sedley, Bt., playwright, 1639;
Andrew Marvell, English poet, pamphleteer and politician, 1621;
René Descartes, French philospher, 1596;
Pope Pius IV, 1499.

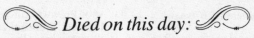

Died on this day:

Enid Bagnold [Lady Roderick Jones], British novelist, 1981;
Jesse Owens [James Cleveland], US athlete, 1980;
Leonard Raven-Hill, artist and illustrator, 1942;
Sir Hubert von Herkomer, painter, 1914;
John Pierpont Morgan, US financier and philanthropist, 1913;
Karl Friedrich May, German novelist for juveniles, 1912;
Sir John Stainer, organist and composer, 1901;
Charlotte Brontë ['Currer Bell'], novelist, 1855;
John Constable, painter, 1837;
John Donne, poet, 1631;
Philip III, King of Spain, 1621;
Francis I, King of France, 1547.

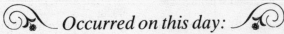

Occurred on this day:

The USSR offered to join NATO, 1954;
The first London performance of the musical show *Pal Joey* was staged, 1954;
Germany began a counter-offensive against the British in North Africa, 1941;
Britain and France agreed to support Poland if that country was invaded by Hitler, 1939;
The United States took possession of the Danish West Indies, renaming them the Virgin Islands, 1917;
A Zeppelin raid took place in eastern and north-eastern England; 43 people were killed, but the Zeppelin *L15* was destroyed, 1916;
In Switzerland, the Lötschberg Tunnel between Kandersteg and the Rhône Valley was completed, 1911;
Whitcomb Judson, US inventor, patented the first zip fastener, 1896;
In Paris, the Eiffel Tower was inaugurated, 1889;
The Treaty of Kanagawa was concluded, which opened up Japanese ports to US trade, 1854;
The first instalment of Charles Dickens' *Pickwick Papers* appeared as a monthly number, 1836.

TODAY IS THE FEAST DAY OF St Acacius or Achatius, St Balbina, St Benjamin and St Guy of Pomposa.

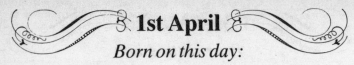

1st April

Born on this day:

Gaie Johnson Houghton, jockey, 1941;
Ali MacGraw, US film actress, 1938;
Dr Richard Repp, Master of St Cross
College, Oxford, 1934;
Debbie Reynolds, US actress, 1932;
George Baker, actor and writer, 1931;
Jane Powell, US singer and film actress,
1929;
Sir William Macpherson of Cluny, High
Court judge, 1926;
William Manchester, US author and history
professor, 1922;
Steve Race, musician and broadcaster,
1921;
Prof. Sir Dimitri Obolensky, Russian
historian, 1918;
Dame Cicely Courtneidge, actress, 1893;
Leonard Bloomfield, US linguist, 1887;
Wallace Beery, US film actor, 1885;
Baroness Clementine Ogilvy Spencer-
Churchill [Hozier], 1885;
Lon [Alonso] Chaney, US actor, 1883;
Edgar Richard Horatio Wallace, journalist
and thriller writer, 1875;
Sergei Vasilievich Rachmaninov, Russian
composer, 1873;
Edmond-Eugène-Alexis Rostand, French
playwright, 1868;
Sir Frederic Truby King, mothercraft
pioneer, 1858;
Prince Otto Eduard Leopold von Bismarck-
Schönhausen, German statesman,
1815;
L'Abbé Prévost [Antoine-François Prévost
d'Exiles], French writer, 1697;
William Harvey, physician, discoverer
of the circulation of the blood,
1578.

Died on this day:

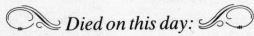

René Cutforth, journalist and broadcaster,
1984;
Elizabeth de Beauchamp Goudge, author,
1984;
Max Ernst, German Surrealist painter and
sculptor, 1976;
Lev Davidovich Landau, Russian physicist,
1968;
Ferenc Molnár, Hungarian playwright,
1952;
John Atkinson Hobson, economist,
1940;
Mortimer Menpes, painter and etcher,
1938;
Karl Franz Josef, Emperor of Austria,
1922;
Sigismund I, King of Poland, 1548;
Robert III, King of Scotland, 1406;
Eleanor of Aquitaine, Queen of France and
of England, 1204.

Occurred on this day:

The military side of the Warsaw Pact was
disbanded, 1991;
In Britain, Purchase Tax and Selective
Employment Tax were abolished, and
Value Added Tax [VAT] took their
place, 1973;
The world's first meteorological satellite,
Tiros 1, was launched by the USA, 1960;
Newfoundland, up to this date a separate
Dominion, became the 10th province of
Canada, 1949;
The USSR began a land blockade of Berlin,
1948;
Electricity undertakings in Britain, both
private and municipal, were nationalised
as the British Electricity Authority,
1947;
The Battle of Okinawa began when
US troops landed there, 1945;
Persecution of the Jews in Germany
began, 1933;
The Royal Air Force came into being as a
separate arm, 1918;
The Territorial Army was founded, 1908;
The title 'Commonwealth of Australia' was
adopted, 1891.

TODAY IS THE FEAST DAY OF St Catharine of Palma, St Gilbert of Caithness, St
Hugh of Bonnevaux, St Hugh of Grenoble, St Macarius the Wonderworker, St Melito and
St Valery or Walaricus.

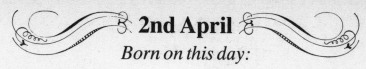

2nd April

Born on this day:

Linford Christie, athlete, 1960;
Penelope Keith, actress, 1939;
Brian Glover, actor, 1934;
Catherine Gaskin, romantic novelist, 1929;
Sir Jack Brabham, racing driver, 1926;
Michael Rizzello, sculptor and coin designer, 1926;
George MacDonald Fraser, author and journalist, 1925;
Sir Ian Hunter, impresario, 1919;
Air Marshal Sir Geoffrey Dhenin, 1918;
Sir Alec Guinness, actor, 1914;
Buddy Ebsen, US dancer and film actor, 1908;
Serge Lifar, Russian choreographer, 1905;
Maj.-Gen. Sir Stuart Greeves, former Adjutant-General, India, 1897;

Jack Buchanan, actor and singer, 1891;
Max Ernst, German surrealist painter and sculptor, 1891;
Sir Neville Cardus, cricket and music writer, 1889;
Émile-Édouard-Charles-Antoine Zola, French novelist, 1840;
Léon-Michel Gambetta, French statesman, 1838;
William Holman Hunt, Pre-Raphaelite painter, 1827;
Hans Christian Andersen, Danish author, 1805;
Charlemagne, King of the Franks and Emperor of the West, 742.

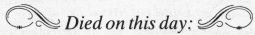

Died on this day:

Georges-Jean-Raymond Pompidou, president of France, 1974;
Cecil Scott Forester, novelist, 1966;
Wallingford Riegger, US composer, 1961;
Jean Epstein, French film director, 1953;
Vibhaji Ranjitsinghi, Maharaja of Nawanagar, cricketer, 1933;

Edward O'Connor Terry, actor and theatrical manager, 1912;
Samuel Finley Breese Morse, US inventor, 1872;
Richard Cobden, politician, 1865;
Honoré-Gabriel-Riqueti, Comte de Mirabeau, French politician and writer, 1791;
Gerard Edelinck, Flemish engraver, 1707.

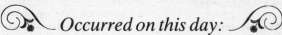

Occurred on this day:

Argentina invaded and captured the Falkland Islands, 1982;
NATO Allied Command, Europe, was set up, 1951;
The United Nations Security Council voted to place former Japanese-held Pacific Islands under United States trusteeship, 1947;
Sandhurst and Woolwich were combined to form the Royal Military Academy at Sandhurst, 1946;
The Oxford and Cambridge Boat Race was first broadcast, 1927;

The operetta *Merrie England* by Sir Edward German was first performed, London, 1902;
Zazel, an acrobatic lady, was fired from a cannon at a London circus, 1877;
The first parliament of Italy met at Turin, 1860;
The naval Battle of Copenhagen was fought, 1801;
The Mint of the United States was established, 1792.

TODAY IS THE FEAST DAY OF Saints Apphian and Theodosia, St Francis of Paola, St John Payne, St Mary of Egypt, St Nicetius or Nizier of Lyons and St Zosimus.

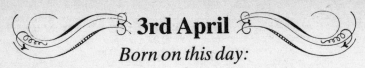

3rd April

Born on this day:

Richard Thompson, guitarist and songwriter, 1949;

John Virgo, snooker player, 1946;

Jonathan Lynn, director, actor and author, 1943;

Sir Martin Nourse, Lord Justice of Appeal, 1932;

Herr Helmut Kohl, German chancellor, 1930;

Timothy Bateson, actor, 1926;

Anthony Wedgwood Benn, politician, 1925;

Marlon Brando, US actor, 1924;

Doris Day, US film actress and singer, 1924;

Jan Sterling, US film and stage actress, 1923;

Hugh Burden, actor, 1913;

Prof. Kathleen Tillotson, scholar and author, 1906;

Henry Robinson Luce, US publisher and founder of *Time* and *Fortune* magazines, 1898;

Dooley [Arthur] Wilson, US singer, 1894;

Joseph Aloysius [Allan] Dwan, Canadian film director, 1885;

James Barry Munnik Hertzog, South African statesman, 1866;

Edward Everett Hale, US writer, 1822;

Washington Irving, US essayist and historian, 1783;

King Henry IV, 1367;

Philip III, King of France, 1245.

Died on this day:

Henry Graham Greene, novelist, 1991;

Ray [Stanley Raymond] Noble, bandleader and composer, 1978;

Ferde Grofé [Ferdinand Rudolf von Grofé], US composer, 1972;

Kurt Julian Weill, German/US composer, 1950;

Conrad Veidt, German film actor, 1943;

Bruno Richard Hauptmann, executed for the murder of the Lindbergh baby, 1936;

Madame Albani [Marie-Louise Lejeunesse], French singer, 1930;

Jean de Reszke [Jan Mieczyslaw], Polish singer, 1925;

Richard D'Oyly Carte, operatic impresario, 1901;

Johannes Brahms, German pianist and composer, 1897;

Jesse Woodson James, US outlaw, shot in the back, 1882;

Sir James Clark Ross, explorer, 1862;

Melchior D'Hondecoeter, Dutch painter, 1695;

Bartolomé Esteban Murillo, Spanish painter, 1682.

Occurred on this day:

In Korea, a Japanese Boeing 727 was hijacked by nine Japanese and flown to Pyongyang, 1970;

The Arab nations concluded an armistice with Israel, 1949;

The German Afrika Korps captured Benghazi in Libya, 1941;

Haile Selassie [Ras Tafari] was proclaimed Emperor of Ethiopia, 1930;

The first London performance of the musical show *Rio Rita* was staged, 1930;

Emily Pankhurst was sentenced to three years' penal servitude for inciting others to place explosives at the house of David Lloyd George, 1913;

The first Pony Express began at St Joseph, Missouri across the United States, to Sacramento, California, 1860;

The Peace of Cateau-Cambresis, ending the Hapsburg-Valois wars, was signed, 1559.

TODAY IS THE FEAST DAY OF Saints Agape, Chionia, and Irene, St Burgundofara or Fare, St Nicetas, St Pancras of Taormina, St Richard of Chichester and St Sixtus I, pope.

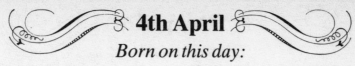

4th April

Born on this day:

Trevor Griffiths, playwright, 1935;
Anthony Perkins, US actor, 1932;
Margaret Dupont, former tennis champion, 1918;
Muddy Waters [McKinley Morganfield], US rhythm and blues singer, 1915;
Marguerite Duras, French author and playwright, 1914;
Frances Langford, US singer and actress, 1935;
Viscount Leathers, politician, 1908;
Robert Emmet Sherwood, US playwright, 1896;
Maurice de Vlaminck, French painter, 1876;
Rémy de Gourmont, French critic, 1858;

Dr Hans Richter, Austrian conductor, 1843;
José Echegaray y Eizaguirre, Spanish playwright, writer and scientist, 1832;
Margaret Oliphant, novelist and historian, 1828;
Sir Charles William [Karl Wilhelm] Siemens, metallurgist and inventor, 1823;
John Hoppner, portrait painter, 1758;
Pierre-Paul Prud'hon, French painter, 1758;
Nicolo Antonio Zingarelli, Italian composer, 1752;
Grinling Gibbons, sculptor and woodcarver, 1648.

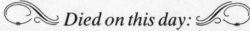 Died on this day:

Gloria Swanson [Gloria Josephine Mae Swenson], US film actress, 1983;
Zulfikar Ali Bhutto, former Pakistani prime minister, executed, 1979;
Martin Luther King, black clergyman and civil rights leader, assassinated, 1968;
Ex-King Carol II of Romania, 1953;
Ghazi, King of Iraq, 1939;
Wilhelm Ostwald, German physical chemist, 1932;
André Michelin, French tyre manufacturer, 1931;
Karl Friedrich Benz, German automobile engineer, 1929;

Sir William Crookes, physicist and chemist, 1919;
William Henry Harrison, 9th president of the USA, 1841;
Joseph-Jérôme de Lalande [Le Français], French astronomer, 1807;
Oliver Goldsmith, playwright, 1774;
John Napier, mathematician and inventor of logarithms, 1617;
Thomas Churchyard, poet and pamphleteer, 1604;
Frederick II, King of Denmark, 1588;
Alfonso X, King of Castile and Leon, 1284.

Occurred on this day:

A US Air Force transport aircraft carrying orphans from Saigon crashed on take-off from Vietnam, killing 155, 1975;
The North Atlantic Treaty [NATO] was signed in Washington, D.C., 1949;
British troops captured Addis Ababa, 1941;
Faisal II acceded to the throne of Iraq, 1939;
The US dirigible airship *Akron* crashed off the New Jersey coast, with the loss of 73 lives, 1933;
The first London performance of the musical show *The New Moon* was staged, 1929;

The second Battle of the Somme ended, 1918;
A Chinese republic was proclaimed in Tibet, 1912;
During the American Civil War, the Battle of Yorktown started, 1862;
Francis Drake completed his circumnavigation of the world and was knighted by Queen Elizabeth I, 1581;
Ignatius of Loyola became the first Superior-General of the Jesuits, 1541;
The University of Basle, Switzerland, was founded, 1460.

TODAY IS THE FEAST DAY OF Saints Agathopus and Theodulus, St Benedict the Black, St Isidore of Seville, St Plato and St Tigernach.

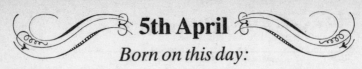

5th April

Born on this day:

Agnetha Fältskog, singer with the pop group Abba, 1950;

Jane Asher, actress, 1946;

Jennifer Penney, ballerina, 1946;

Prof. John Albery, Master of University College, Oxford, 1936;

Prof. Donald Lynden-Bell, astronomer, 1935;

Nigel Hawthorne, actor, 1929;

Michael Bryant, actor, 1928;

Roger Corman, US film director and producer, 1926;

Stanley Orme, politician, 1923;

Tom Finney, footballer, 1922;

Arthur Hailey, author, 1920;

Gregory Peck, US film actor, 1916;

Bette [Ruth Elizabeth] Davis, US film actress, 1908;

Spencer Tracy, US film actor, 1900;

Algernon Charles Swinburne, poet, 1837;

Jules-François-Camille Ferry, French statesman, 1832;

Joseph Lister, 1st Baron, surgeon and pioneer of antiseptics in surgery, 1827;

Sébastien Érard, French piano and harp maker, 1752;

Jean-Honoré Fragonard, French painter, 1732;

Giovanni Jacopo Casanova de Seingalt, Italian lover and adventurer, 1724;

Elihu Yale, merchant, administrator and founder of the College, 1649;

Thomas Hobbes, philosopher, 1588.

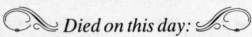

Died on this day:

Molly Picon, US actress and comedienne, 1992;

Marshal of the RAF Sir Arthur Travers Harris Bt., former chief of Bomber Command, 1984;

Howard Robard Hughes, US aviator, industrialist and film producer, 1976;

Chiang Kai-shek, Chinese statesman and soldier, 1975;

Douglas MacArthur, US general, 1964;

Vincent Millet Youmans, US composer, 1946;

Jane Ellen Harrison, scholar and archaeologist, 1928;

George Edward Stanhope Molyneux Herbert, 5th Earl of Carnarvon, Egyptologist, 1923;

Robert Raikes, founder of Sunday Schools, 1811;

Edward Young, poet, 1765;

William Brouncker, 2nd Viscount, first president of the Royal Society, 1684.

Occurred on this day:

Sir Harold Wilson resigned as prime minister, 1976;

In Sicily, Mount Etna erupted, followed by violent flows of lava, 1971;

In Guatemala, the West German ambassador was found murdered after having been kidnapped by left-wing rebels five days earlier, 1970;

The Cunard liner *Queen Elizabeth* was sold to an American syndicate for £3,230,000, 1968;

The first driverless automatic trains ran on London's Underground, 1964;

Sir Winston Churchill resigned as prime minister, 1955;

The Dail Eireann chose a Sinn Fein Executive, with Eamon de Valera as president, 1919;

The *Observer* newspaper was acquired by W.W. [later Lord] Astor, 1911;

Strauss's opera *Die Fledermaus* was first performed, Vienna, 1874;

The Addled Parliament [which made no enactments] began sitting, 1614.

TODAY IS THE FEAST DAY OF St Albert of Montecorvino, St Derfel-Gadarn, St Ethelburga of Lyminge, St Gerald of Sauve-Majeure and St Vincent Ferrer.

6th April

Born on this day:

Felicity Palmer, mezzo-soprano, 1944;
Paul Daniels, stage magician, 1938;
Dudley Sutton, actor, 1933;
Joan Carlyle, soprano, 1931;
Willis Hall, writer, 1929;
André Previn, US composer and
　conductor, 1929;
Gerry Mulligan, saxophonist and
　bandleader, 1927;
The Rev. Ian Paisley, politician, 1926;
Sir John Knox, High Court judge, 1925;
Franta Belsky, sculptor, 1921;
Bernard Carter, painter and etcher,
　1920;

Admiral Sir Desmond Dreyer, 1910;
Sir John Betjeman, poet, 1906;
Leo Robin, US lyricist and writer of *Thanks
　for the Memory*, 1900;
Anthony Herman Gerard Fokker, Dutch
　aircraft designer, 1890;
Harry Houdini [Erich Weiss], US stage
　magician and escapologist, 1874;
Louis Raemaekers, Dutch artist and
　cartoonist, 1869;
René Lalique, designer of jewellery, 1860;
Gustave Moreau, French painter, 1826;
Jean-Baptiste Rousseau, French playwright
　and poet, 1671.

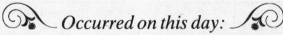

Died on this day:

Jimmy Kennedy, songwriter [*South of the
　Border*], 1984;
Milton Ager, US popular composer, 1979;
Igor Fyodorovich Stravinsky, Russian
　composer, 1971;
Jules-Jean-Baptiste-Vincent Bordet,
　Belgian bacteriologist, 1961;
Robert Courtneidge, theatrical producer,
　1939;

Edward Arlington Robinson, US poet,
　1935;
John Stow, historian and antiquary, 1605;
Sir Francis Walsingham, statesman, 1590;
Albrecht Dürer, German artist, 1528;
Raphael Sanzio, Italian painter, 1520;
Matthias Corvinus, King of Hungary, 1490;
King Richard I [Coeur de Lion], killed in
　battle, 1199.

Occurred on this day:

Early Bird, the first commercial
　communications satellite, was launched
　in the USA, 1965;
In Britain, Sir Anthony Eden became prime
　minister, 1955;
The *Yamato*, and five other Japanese
　warships were sunk by US carrier aircraft
　near Kyushu, 1945;
After Rommel's retreat in North Africa,
　the British and US armies linked up,
　1943;
Having invaded the two countries,
　Germany issued an ultimatum calling for
　the surrender of Greece and Yugoslavia,
　1941;
The United States declared war on
　Germany, 1917;

The first modern Olympic Games were
　inaugurated at Athens, 1896;
Vancouver, British Columbia, was
　founded, 1886;
The Mormon Church was organised by
　Joseph Smith at Fayette, New York,
　1830;
George Washington was elected as 1st
　president of the USA, 1789;
Jan van Riebeeck landed at the Cape,
　South Africa, to establish a trading
　station for the Dutch East India
　Company, 1652;
St Paul's Cathedral and other churches
　were badly damaged following
　an earthquake tremor in London,
　1580.

TODAY IS THE FEAST DAY OF St Celestine I, pope, St Eutychius of Constantinople,
St Marcellinus of Carthage, St Prudentius of Troyes and St William of Eskilsoë.

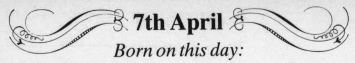

7th April

Born on this day:

Martyn Lewis, TV newsreader, 1945;
Dennis Amiss, cricketer, 1943;
Gorden Kaye, actor, 1941;
Francis Ford Coppola, US film director and screenwriter, 1939;
David Frost, TV presenter, 1939;
Angela Bonallack, golfer, 1937;
Ian Richardson, actor, 1934;
Cliff Morgan, former head of Outside Broadcasting, BBC TV, 1930;
Andrew Sachs, actor, 1930;
James Garner, US film and TV actor, 1928;
Sir Anthony Lincoln, High Court judge, 1920;
Ravi Shankar, sitar player, 1920;

Billie Holiday [Eleanora Fagan], US jazz singer, 1915;
Fredda Brilliant, sculptor, 1908;
[Cuthbert] Dale Collins, Australian journalist and novelist, 1897;
Sir David Alexander Cecil Low, cartoonist and caricaturist, 1891;
Daisy [Margaret Mary Julia] Ashford, author, at 9 years old, of *The Young Visiters*, 1881;
Edward Knoblock, playwright, 1874;
Gilbert Arthur A Beckett, playwright and author, 1837;
William Wordsworth, poet, 1770;
Gerhard Douw, Dutch painter, 1613;
St Francis Xavier, Jesuit missionary, 1506.

Died on this day:

Sheik Abeid Karume, dictator of Zanzibar, assassinated, 1972;
James [Jim] Clark, car-racing champion, killed, 1968;
Theda Bara [Theodosia Goodman], US silent film actress, 1955;
Henry Ford, US motor manufacturer, 1947;
Joseph Aloysius Lyons, Australian statesman, 1939;
Albert Venn Dicey, jurist, 1922;
Phineas Taylor Barnum, US showman, 1891;

Anton Diabelli, Austrian music publisher and composer, 1858;
Richard [Dick] Turpin, highwayman, hanged, 1739;
Jean-Baptiste, Abbé de La Salle, founder of the Christian Brothers, 1719;
Sir William D'Avenant, poet and playwright, 1668;
El Greco [Domenikos Theotokopoulos], Cretan painter, 1614.

Occurred on this day:

The Cominform was dissolved, 1956;
Spain relinquished its protectorate over Morrocco, 1956;
Dag Hammarskjöld of Sweden was elected Secretary-General of the United Nations, 1953;
The World Health Organization was formed as a specialised UN agency, 1948;
Itàly invaded Albania, 1939;

The first London production of the musical show *The Desert Song* was staged, 1927;
The first London production of the musical show *Irene* was staged, 1920;
The Canadian Grand Trunk Railway was completed, 1914;
The Conference of Algeciras, considering the ownership of Morocco, ended, 1906;
In France, the metre was made the official measuring unit of length, 1795.

TODAY IS THE FEAST DAY OF St Aphraates, St Celsus or Ceallach of Armagh, St George the Younger, St Hegesippus, St Henry Walpole, St Herman Joseph and St John Baptist de la Salle.

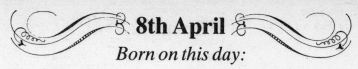

8th April

Born on this day:

Julian Lennon, rock musician, 1963;
Hywel Bennett, actor, 1944;
Dorothy Tutin, actress, 1931;
Eric Porter, actor, 1928;
General Sir Anthony Farrar-Hockley, 1924;
Carmen McRae, jazz singer, 1922;
Virginia O'Brien, US actress and singer, 1921;
Sonja Henie, Norwegian skater and film actress, 1912;
Sir Neil Lawson, former High Court judge, 1908;
Ilka Chase, US novelist, playwright and actress, 1903;
E. Y. 'Yip' Harburg [Isidore Hochberg], US lyricist and librettist, 1898;
Mary Pickford [Gladys Smith], US film actress, 1893;
Sir Adrian Boult, conductor, 1889;
Walter Connolly, US actor, 1887;
Victor Schertzinger, US film director, composer and lyricist, 1880;
Albert I, King of the Belgians, 1875;
John Claudius Loudon, Scottish horticulturist, 1783;
Giuseppe Tartini, Italian composer, 1692;
Cornelis de Heem, Dutch still-life painter, 1631;
Philip IV, King of Spain, 1605;
Claudio Merulo [Claudio da Correggio or Merlotti], Italian organist and composer, 1533.

Died on this day:

Omar Nelson Bradley, US general, 1981;
Pablo Ruiz y Picasso, Spanish painter and sculptor, 1973;
Vaslav Fomich Nijinsky, Russian dancer and choreographer, 1950;
Eugène-Marcel Prévost, French novelist, 1941;
Sir William Henry Hadow, author and musicologist, 1937;
Adolph Simon Ochs, US newspaper proprietor, 1935;
Eric Axel Karlfeldt, Swedish poet, 1931;
Heinrich von Stephan, German politician and promoter of the Universal Postal Union, 1897;
Elisha Graves Otis, US inventor of the safety lift, 1861;
Domenico Gaetano Maria Donizetti, Italian composer, 1848;
Wilhelm, Baron von Humboldt, German philologist, 1835;
Marie-Jean-Antoine-Nicolas de Caritat, Marquis de Condorcet, French mathematician and revolutionary, 1794;
Caracalla [Marcus Aurelius Antoninus], Roman emperor, 217.

Occurred on this day:

In Kenya, Jomo Kenyatta and five others were convicted of being involved with Mau Mau, 1953;
The final assembly of the League of Nations was held, 1946;
King Zog of Albania abdicated, 1939;
The first London production of the musical play White Horse Inn was staged, 1931;
A treaty was signed between Colombia and the United States agreeing control of the Panama Canal Zone, 1914;
Herbert Henry Asquith became prime minister, 1908;
The Anglo-French agreement called the Entente Cordiale was signed, 1904;
Ponchielli's opera La Gioconda was first performed, Milan, 1876;
The steamship Great Western began her maiden voyage to New York from Bristol, 1838;
Florida was discovered by Juan Ponce de León, 1513.

TODAY IS THE FEAST DAY OF St Dionysius of Corinth, St Julia Billiart, St Perpetuus of Tours and St Walter of Pontoise.

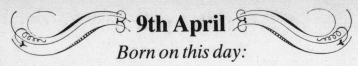

9th April

Born on this day:

Tony Sibson, middleweight boxer, 1958;

Severiano Ballesteros, Spanish golfer, 1957;

Hannah Gordon, actress, 1941;

Jean-Paul Belmondo, French film actor, 1933;

Carl Perkins, US modern jazz pianist, 1932;

Tom Lehrer, US songwriter and lecturer, 1928;

Sir Robert Murray Helpmann, Australian dancer, 1909;

Hugh Todd Naylor Gaitskell, statesman, 1906;

Ward Bond, US film actor, 1903;

Paul Bustill Robeson, US actor and singer, 1898;

Efrem Zimbalist, Russian violinist, 1889;

Sol Hurok, US theatrical impresario, 1888;

Sir Gerald Festus Kelly, artist, 1879;

Léon Blum, French statesman, 1872;

Erich Friedrich Wilhelm von Ludendorff, German general and politician, 1865;

Sir Francesco Paolo Tosti, composer, 1847;

Leopold II, King of the Belgians, 1835;

Eadweard Muybridge [Edward James Muggeridge], photographer and inventor, 1830;

Charles-Pierre Baudelaire, French poet, 1821;

Isambard Kingdom Brunel, engineer, 1806;

James Scott, Duke of Monmouth, 1649.

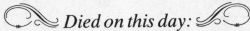

Died on this day:

Sir Basil Henry Blackwell, bookseller and publisher, 1984;

Frank Lloyd Wright, US architect, 1959;

Dietrich Bonhoeffer, German theologian, 1945;

Mrs Patrick Campbell [Beatrice Stella Tanner], actress, 1940;

Edward Thomas, poet, killed in action, 1917;

Charles Conder, artist, 1909;

Isabella II, Queen of Spain, 1904;

Dante Gabriel Rossetti, poet and Pre-Raphaelite painter, 1882;

William Prout, physician and chemist, 1850;

John Opie, infant prodigy, painter and illustrator, 1807;

Francis Bacon, Viscount St Albans, statesman, 1626;

François Rabelais, French author, 1553;

Lorenzo de' Medici ['The Magnificent'], Florentine statesman, 1492;

King Edward IV, 1483.

Occurred on this day:

Georgia voted to secede from the Soviet Union, 1991;

The Suez Canal was cleared for all shipping, 1957;

The USS Liberty exploded in Bari harbour, Italy, killing 360 people, 1945;

Bataan surrendered to the Japanese, 1942;

Germany invaded Norway and Denmark, 1940;

Latvia proclaimed her independence, 1918;

Vimy Ridge, France, was stormed by Canadian troops, 1917;

The Battle of Arras began, 1917;

General Robert E. Lee surrendered to General Ulysees S. Grant at Appomattox, ending the American Civil War, 1865;

The National Gallery, London, was opened, 1838;

Botany Bay, Australia, was discovered by Captain James Cook, 1770;

The Mongol armies defeated the Poles and Germans at the Battle of Liegnitz [Wahlstatt], 1241.

TODAY IS THE FEAST DAY OF St Gaucherius, St Hugh of Rouen, St Mary Cleophas, St Uramar and St Waldetrudis or Waudru.

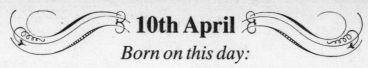

10th April

Born on this day:

David Moorcroft, athlete, 1953;
Paul Theroux, US author, 1941;
Gloria Hunniford, radio presenter, 1940;
Patrick Garland, theatre and film director, 1935;
Robert Rhodes James, MP and historian, 1933;
Omar Sharif, actor, 1932;
Max von Sydow, Swedish actor, 1929;
Lyndon Brook, actor, 1926;
Chuck Connors, US film actor, 1921;
Maurice Schumann, French author and former government minister, 1911;
Aidan Crawley, former chairman, London Weekend Television, 1908;
Kathleen Major, former principal, St Hilda's College, Oxford, 1906;

Claire Booth Luce, US playwright, 1903;
Harry Mortimer, musician, 1902;
George Arliss [George Augustus Andrews], actor, 1868;
Joseph Pulitzer, US newspaper proprietor and founder of the Prizes, 1847;
William Booth, founder of the Salvation Army, 1829;
Lew [Lewis] Wallace, US novelist, author of *Ben Hur*, 1827;
Commodore Matthew Calbraith Perry, US naval officer, 1794;
William Hazlitt, essayist and critic, 1778;
Christian Friedrich Samuel Hahnemann, German founder of homeopathy, 1755;
James V, King of Scotland, 1512.

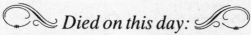

Died on this day:

Antonia White, journalist and novelist, 1980;
Evelyn Arthur St John Waugh, novelist, 1966;
Michael Curtiz [Mihaly Kertesz], US film director, 1962;
Arthur Benjamin, composer, 1960;
Auguste-Marie-Louis Lumière, French cine pioneer, 1954;

Edgar Middleton, journalist and playwright, 1939;
Stanley John Weyman, novelist, 1928;
Algernon Charles Swinburne, poet, 1909;
Joseph-Louis Lagrange, French astronomer, mathematician and physicist, 1813;
Agostino Agazzari, Italian composer, 1640.

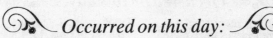

Occurred on this day:

The first London performance of the musical show *Chicago* was staged, 1979;
Over 3,000 people were killed after severe earthquakes occurred in Iran, 1972;
The US submarine *Thresher* was lost off Cape Cod, with all the crew of 125, 1963;
The US Senate passed the Civil Rights Bill, 1960;
The German battleships *Blücher* and *Karlsruhe* were sunk, 1940;
Vimy Ridge was finally taken by the Canadian troops, 1917;

The Archduke Maximilian of Austria became Emperor of Mexico, 1864;
The Chartists met on Kennington Common, London, and presented their petition to Parliament, 1848;
The first British settlers arrived at Algoa Bay, in the Eastern Cape, South Africa, 1820;
Napoleon's army under General Soult was defeated by the Allies in the Battle of Toulouse, 1814;
Bananas were displayed in a London shop window, 1633.

TODAY IS THE FEAST DAY OF St Bademus, St Fulbert of Chartres, St Macarius or Macaire of Ghent, St Michael de Sanctis, St Paternus of Abdinghof and The Martyrs under the Danes.

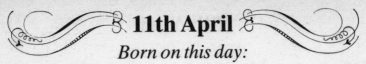

11th April

Born on this day:

Jill Gascoine, actress, 1938;

Joel Grey, US actor and singer, 1933;

Clive Exton, scriptwriter, 1931;

Ronald Fraser, actor, 1931;

Gervase de Peyer, clarinettist, 1927;

Richard Wainwright, former MP, 1919;

Norman McLaren, film aninator, 1914;

Leo C. Rosten, US author and political scientist, 1908;

Glenway Wescott, US novelist and poet, 1901;

Dean Gooderham Acheson, US lawyer and statesman, 1893;

Walter James Macqueen-Pope, theatrical historian, 1888;

Sir Charles Hallé [Carl Halle], pianist and conductor, 1819;

Jean-Baptiste Isabey, French miniature painter, 1767;

James Parkinson, physician and palaeontologist, discoverer of Parkinson's disease, 1755;

Sir John Eliot, parliamentarian, 1592;

Marguerite d'Angoulême, Queen of Navarre, 1492.

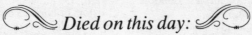

Died on this day:

Erskine Caldwell, US novelist, 1987;

Marie Ney [Menzies], actress, 1981;

John Henry O'Hara, US novelist, 1970;

Freeman Wills Crofts, detective story writer, 1957;

Edgar Jepson, novelist, 1938;

Sir Gerald Hubert Edward Busson du Maurier, actor and manager, 1934;

Luther Burbank, US 'plant wizard', 1926;

James Anthony Bailey, US circus proprietor, 1906;

Charles Reade, novelist and playwright, 1884;

Antoine Coypel, French painter, 1661;

Sir Thomas Wyatt, conspirator, executed, 1554;

Donato Bramante [d'Agnolo], Italian architect, 1514;

Llywelyn ap Iorwerth, Prince of Wales, 1240.

Occurred on this day:

The first London performance of the musical *Blood Brothers* was staged, 1983;

A skeleton discovered in Berlin was stated to be definitely that of Martin Bormann, Hitler's deputy, 1974;

President Truman relieved General Douglas MacArthur of his command in the Far East, 1951;

A major 'blitz' air raid was made over Coventry by German aircraft, 1941;

The musical show *New Faces* was first produced, London, 1940;

The International Labour Organisation was founded, 1919;

Uganda was declared a British Protectorate, 1894;

The Treaty of Fontainebleau was signed, 1814;

Napoleon abdicated, and was banished to the Isle of Elba, 1814;

Louis XVIII acceded to the throne of France, 1814;

The Treaty of Utrecht was signed by France and England, ceding Gibraltar and Newfoundland to England, 1713;

William III and Mary II were crowned joint monarchs, 1689;

Sir Thomas Fairfax was victorious at the Battle of Selby during the English Civil War, 1644;

The French were victorious at the Battle of Ravenna, Italy, but their leader, Gaston de Foix, was killed, 1512.

TODAY IS THE FEAST DAY OF St Barsanuphius, St Gemma Galgani, St Godeberta, St Guthlac, St Isaac of Spoleto and St Stanislaus of Cracow.

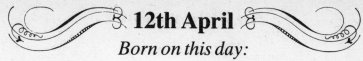

12th April

Born on this day:

David Cassidy, singer, 1949;
Paul Cook, jockey, 1946;
Bobby Moore, footballer, 1941;
Alan Ayckbourn, playwright, 1939;
Edward Hide, jockey, 1937;
Montserrat Caballé, operatic singer, 1933;
Hardy Kruger, German actor, 1928;
Jane Withers, US film actress, 1926;
Raymond Barre, French economist and politician, 1924;
Ann Miller, US film actress and singer, 1923;
Lionel Hampton, US bandleader, 1913;
James Louis Garvin, newspaper editor, 1868;
Edmond Audran, French composer, 1840;
Henry Hugh Pierson [Pearson], composer, 1815;
Henry Clay, US statesman, 1777;
Edward Bird, painter, 1772.

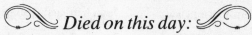

Died on this day:

Alan Stewart Paton, South African politician and author, 1988;
Desmond Bagley, novelist, 1983;
Joe Louis [Joseph Louis Barrow], US heavyweight boxer, 1981;
Charles McMoran Wilson Moran, 1st Baron, physician, 1977;
Josephine Baker, US/French singer, 1975;
Antoine Pevsner, French sculptor and painter, 1962;
Sir Archibald Hector McIndoe, New Zealand plastic surgeon, 1960;
Franklin Delano Roosevelt, 32nd president of the USA, 1945;
Feodor Ivanovich Chaliapin, Russian bass singer, 1938;
Flora Annie Steel [Webster], novelist, 1929;
William Strang, artist, 1921;
Charles-Joseph Messier, French astronomer, 1817;
Dr Charles Burney, organist and music historian, 1814;
Pietro Antonio Metastasio, Italian poet and playwright, 1782;
William Kent, landscape gardener and architect, 1748;
Kaspar Merian, German engraver, 1686;
Niccolo Amati, violin-maker, 1684.

Occurred on this day:

The *Columbia* space shuttle went into space, completing its mission two days later, 1981;
The first manned space flight was made by the Russian cosmonaut Yuri Gagarin, 1961;
The first London production of *The Belle of New York* was presented, 1898;
The American Civil War began at the siege of Fort Sumter, South Carolina, 1861;
The British settlers defeated the Zulus under Dingaan at the Battle of Tugela, 1838;
Napoleon Bonaparte defeated the Austrians and Sardinians at the Battle of Montenotte, 1796;
The Battle of the Saints was fought, when Admiral Rodney defeated the French and Spanish fleets in the West Indies, 1782;
The *Tatler* was first published, 1709;
The Union Jack [Union flag] was first adopted in England, 1606;
The armies of the Fourth Crusade captured Constantinople [Istanbul], 1204.

TODAY IS THE FEAST DAY OF St Alferius, St Julius I, pope, St Sabas the Goth and Others and St Zeno of Verona.

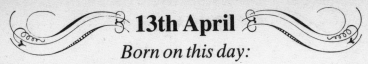

13th April

Born on this day:

Gary Kasparov, chess champion, 1963;
Alan Devonshire, footballer, 1956;
Peter Davison, actor, 1951;
Christopher Strauli, actor, 1946;
Margaret Price, operatic singer, 1941;
Marjorie Yates, actress, 1941;
Seamus Heaney, poet, 1939;
Edward Fox, actor, 1937;
Beverley Cross, playwright, 1931;
Sir Jeremiah Harman, High Court judge, 1930;
Stanley Donen, US film director and producer, 1924;
John Gerard Braine, novelist, 1922;
Howard Keel, US singer and actor, 1917;
Godfrey Kenton, actor, 1902;
Marshal of the RAF Sir Arthur Harris, wartime chief of Bomber Command, 1892;
Frank Winfield Woolworth, chain-store pioneer, 1852;
William Sterndale Bennett, pianist and composer, 1816;
Félicien-César David, French composer, 1810;
Richard Trevithick, engineer and railway pioneer, 1771;
Joseph Bramah, locksmith and inventor, 1748;
Thomas Jefferson, 3rd president of the USA, 1743;

Died on this day:

Travers Christmas Humphreys, judge, 1983;
Abdul Salam Arif, president of Iraq, killed in a helicopter crash, 1966;
Hugh Cecil Lowther, 5th Earl of Lonsdale, sportsman, 1944;
James Buchanan Brady ['Diamond Jim'], US financier, 1917;
Sir William Quiller Orchardson, painter, 1910;
Richard Garnett, librarian, 1906;
Vasili Vasilievich Vereshchagin, Russian artist and traveller, 1904;
Hugh Clapperton, Scottish explorer in Africa, 1827;
Jean de La Fontaine, French writer of fables, 1695;
Boris Feodorovich Godunov, Tsar of Russia, 1605.

Occurred on this day:

The first London production of *Funny Girl* was presented, 1966;
In Beirut, Lebanon, fighting broke out between Moslems and Christians, 1975;
The Royal Flying Corps was constituted by Royal Warrant, 1912;
The Anti-Semitic League was founded in Prussia, 1882;
Magdala, Abyssinia [Ethiopia] was taken by the British under Sir Robert Napier, 1868;
The Catholic Emancipation Act was passed in Britain, 1829;
Napoleon defeated the Austrians at the Battle of Millesimo, 1796;
Warren Hastings was appointed governor of Bengal, 1772;
The Messiah by George Frederick Handel, was first performed, Dublin, 1742;
The Royal Military Academy was established at Woolwich, 1741;
The Edict of Nantes, giving Huguenots equal rights with Catholics, was issued by Henry IV of France, 1598.

TODAY IS THE FEAST DAY OF Saints Agathonice, Carpus, and Papylus, St Guinoch, St Hermenegild, St Martin I, pope and St Martius or Mars.

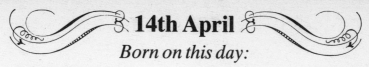

14th April

Born on this day:

Julian Lloyd Webber, cellist, 1951;

Julie Christie, actress, 1940;

Loretta Lynn, US country singer, 1935;

Vice-Admiral Sir Geoffrey Dalton, former deputy Supreme Allied Commander, Atlantic, 1931;

Bradford Dillman, US film and TV actor, 1930;

Prof. John Roberts, warden, Merton College, Oxford, 1928;

Rod Steiger, US actor, 1925;

Baroness Warnock, Mistress of Girton College, Cambridge, 1924;

Valerie Hobson [Mrs John Profumo], former actress, 1917;

François Duvalier, ['Papa Doc'], Haitian dictator, 1907;

Sir John Gielgud CH, actor, 1904;

Vere Gordon Childe, Australian archaeologist, 1892;

Arnold Joseph Toynbee, historian, 1889;

James Branch Cabell, US novelist, 1879;

Peter Behrens, German architect and industrial designer, 1868;

William Henry Bentinck, 3rd Duke of Portland, prime minister, 1738;

Christiaan Huygens, Dutch astronomer and physicist, 1629;

Philip III, King of Spain, 1578;

Abraham Ortelius [Oertel], Flemish cartographer, 1527.

Died on this day:

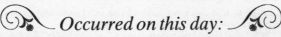

Simone de Beauvoir, French writer and feminist, 1986;

Fredric March [Ernest Frederick McIntyre Bickel], US actor, 1975;

Ernest Bevin, statesman and trade union leader, 1951;

Louis Henri Sullivan, US architect, 1924;

Dr Ludovik Lazarus Zamenhof, creator of Esperanto, 1917;

George Frederick Handel, composer, violinist and organist, 1759;

Thomas Otway, playwright, 1685;

James Hepburn, 4th Earl of Bothwell, husband of Mary, Queen of Scots, 1578;

Richard Neville, Earl of Warwick ['the Kingmaker'], killed in battle, 1471;

Godwin, Earl of the West Saxons, 1053;

Pope Sergius III, 911.

Occurred on this day:

The first London production of the musical show *Brigadoon* was presented, 1949;

The first London production of the operetta *The Dubarry* was presented, 1932;

After Alfonso XIII, King of Spain, abdicated and fled the country, a revolutionary provisional republican government was set up, 1931;

The first London production of the musical show *Lady Be Good* was presented, 1926;

The Pan American Union was established, 1890;

Abraham Lincoln, 16th president of the USA, was shot by the assassin, John Wilkes Booth, 1865;

The Battle of Fort Sumter ended when it was captured by Confederate troops, 1861;

Noah Webster's *American Dictionary of the English Language* was published, 1828;

The Battle of Millesimo ended when Napoleon defeated the Austrians, 1796;

The Yorkists defeated the Lancastrians at the Battle of Barnet, 1471.

TODAY IS THE FEAST DAY OF Saints Antony, John and Eustace, St Ardalion, St Benezet, St Bernard of Tiron or Abbeville, St Caradoc, St John of Vilna, St Lambert of Lyons, Saints Tiburtius, Valerius and Maximus and The Martyrs of Lithuania.

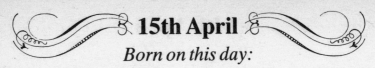

15th April

Born on this day:

Samantha Fox, dancer and model, 1966;

Emma Thompson, actress, 1959;

Lord Archer of Weston-super-Mare [Jeffrey Archer], novelist, 1940;

Marty Wilde, rock singer, 1939;

Claudia Cardinale, Italian actress, 1938;

Prof. Charles Marsden, neurologist, 1938;

Elizabeth Montgomery, US film actress, 1933;

Sir Neville Marriner, conductor, 1924;

Dr Richard von Weizsäcker, president of the Federal Republic of Germany, 1920;

Meriol Trevor, novelist and biographer, 1919;

Bessie Smith, US blues singer, 1894;

William Bliss Carman, Canadian poet, 1861;

Henry James, US novelist, 1843;

Wilhelm Busch, German cartoonist and poet, 1832;

John Lothrop Motley, US diplomat and historian, 1814;

Pierre-Étienne-Théodore Rousseau, French painter, 1812;

Sir James Clark Ross, polar explorer, 1800;

Étienne Geoffroy Saint-Hilaire, French naturalist, 1772;

Jan van Huysum, Dutch painter, 1682;

Nanak, founder of the Sikhs, 1469.

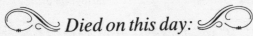

Died on this day:

Tommy Cooper, comedian, 1984;

Arthur Lowe, TV actor, 1982;

Jean-Paul Sartre, French philosopher and writer, 1980;

Richard Conte [Nicolas Peter Conte], US film actor, 1975;

Wallace Beery, US film actor, 1949;

John Singer Sargent, US portrait painter, 1925;

William Thomas Stead, editor, lost on the *Titanic*, 1912;

Father Damien [Joseph de Veuster], Belgian missionary, 1889;

Matthew Arnold, educationalist and poet, 1888;

Abraham Lincoln, 16th president of the USA, from shot wound, 1865;

Oliver Evans, US inventor, 1819;

Hubert Robert, French landscape painter, 1808;

Mikhail Vasilievich Lomonosov, Russian writer, 1765;

Jeanne-Antoinette, Marquise de Pompadour, mistress of King Louis XV, 1764;

Lorenzo Lippi, Italian poet and painter, 1664;

Domenichino [Domenico Zampieri], Bolognese painter, 1641.

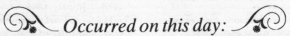

Occurred on this day:

The first London production of the musical show *A Little Night Music* was presented, 1975;

The Battle of Berlin began, 1945;

The Ulster Parliament was opened by the Governor of Northern Ireland, 1925;

The first public sound-on-film performance was shown at the Rialto Theatre, New York, 1923;

Insulin was discovered by Sir Frederick Banting with J.R.R. Macleod and Charles H. Best, 1922;

The White Star liner *Titanic* sank on her maiden voyage after colliding with an iceberg, and 1,513 lives were lost, 1912;

The *Daily Herald* newspaper was first published, 1912;

Thomas Edison publicly demonstrated the kinetoscope moving picture machine, New York, 1891;

Andrew Johnson was sworn in as 17th president of the USA, 1865;

A naval mutiny occurred at Spithead, 1797;

The Bank of England issued the first five-pound note, 1793;

Dr Samuel Johnson published his *Dictionary*, 1755;

The *Passion According to St Matthew* by Johann Sebastian Bach, was first performed, St Thomas's, Leipzig, 1729.

TODAY IS THE FEAST DAY OF Saints Anastasia and Basilissa, St Hunna or Huva, St Patern or Padarn of Wales and St Ruadhan.

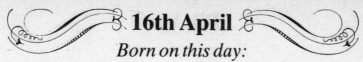

16th April

Born on this day:

Gabriella Sabatini, tennis player, 1970;
Ruth Madoc, actress, 1943;
Queen Margrethe II of Denmark, 1940;
Dusty Springfield, singer, 1940;
Donald MacCormick, TV presenter, 1939;
Joan Bakewell, TV presenter, 1933;
Vince Hill, singer, 1932;
Sir John Harvey-Jones, former chairman, ICI, 1924;
Henry Mancini, US composer, 1924;
Sir Kingsley Amis, novelist, 1922;
Sir Peter Ustinov, actor and writer, 1921;
Spike Milligan, comedian and writer, 1918;
Constance Shacklock, operatic singer, 1913;

Sir Charles Spencer Chaplin, comedian, 1889;
John Millington Synge, Irish poet and playwright, 1871;
Wilbur Wright, US aviation pioneer, 1867;
Anatole France [Jacques-Anatole Thibault], French novelist, 1844;
Ford Madox Brown, painter, 1821;
William Chambers, author and publisher, 1800;
Sir John Franklin, Arctic explorer, 1786;
Sir Hans Sloane, physician and naturalist, 1660.

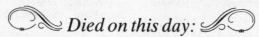

Died on this day:

Alfreda Rose Hodson, concert singer, 1992;
Sir David Lean, film director, 1991:
Fay Bainter, US actress, 1968;
Edna Ferber, US author, 1968;
Albert Alick [Al] Bowlly, singer, 1941;
Josiah Charles Stamp, 1st Baron, statistician and administrator, 1941;
Bertram Wagstaff Mills, circus proprietor, 1938;

Samuel Smiles, writer and social reformer, 1904;
Bernadette Soubirous, St Bernadette of Lourdes, 1879;
Marie [Gresholtz] Tussaud, Swiss-born waxworks show proprietor, 1850;
Georges-Louis Leclerc, Comte de Buffon, French naturalist, 1788;
Aphra Behn, playwright and novelist, the first woman professional writer, 1689.

Occurred on this day:

The submarine *Affray* sank in the English Channel, with the loss of 75 lives, 1951;
The Organisation for European Economic Co-operation [EEC] was set up, 1948;
The island of Malta was awarded the George Cross by King George VI, 1942;
The Little Theatre, Adelphi, Strand, London, closed, 1941;
The second Battle of the Aisne River began, 1917;
The English Channel was flown by a woman, Harriet Quimby, 1912;

Paul Kruger became president of the South African Republic, 1883;
The Vaudeville Theatre, Strand, London, first building, opened, 1870;
The Declaration of Paris was signed, abolishing privateering, 1856;
Charles Edward Stuart, the Young Pretender, was decisively defeated at Culloden by Cumberland, 1746;
Martin Luther arrived at the Diet of Worms, 1521.

TODAY IS THE FEAST DAY OF St Bernadette, St Drogo or Druon, St Encratis, St Fructuosus Braga, St Joseph Benedict Labre, St Magnus of Orkney, St Optatus and the Martyrs of Saragossa, St Paternus or Pair of Avranches and St Turibius of Astorga.

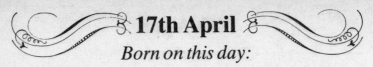

17th April

Born on this day:

Olivia Hussey, film actress, 1951;

Clare Francis, novelist and yachtswoman, 1946;

Chris Barber, jazz musician, 1930;

James Last, bandleader, 1929;

Lindsay Anderson, film and theatre director, 1923;

Ann Shirley, US film actress, 1918;

Sirimavo Bandaranaike, former prime minister of Sri Lanka, 1916;

Sir Vincent Wigglesworth, entomologist, 1899;

Thornton Niven Wilder, US novelist and playwright, 1897;

Nikita Sergeyevich Khruschchev, Russian leader, 1894;

Dame Margaret Teyte [Maggie Tate], soprano, 1888;

Sir [Charles] Leonard Woolley, archaeologist, 1880;

Ian Hay [John Hay Beith], novelist, 1876;

Konstantinos Petrou Kavafis [Constantine Cavafy], Greek poet, 1863;

John Pierpont Morgan, US financier, 1837;

Vicat Cole, painter, 1833;

James Thom, self-taught sculptor, 1802 [see also Deaths];

Vaclav Jan [Wenzel Johann] Tomasek, Bohemian organist, pianist and composer, 1774;

Johann Gottlieb Naumann, German composer, 1741;

John Ford, playwright, 1586.

Died on this day:

Scott Brady [Gerald Tierney], US actor, 1985;

General Mark Wayne Clark, US soldier, 1984;

Kawabata Yasunari, Japanese novelist, 1972;

Theodore Komisarjevsky, theatre director, 1954;

James Thom, self-taught sculptor, 1850 [see also Births];

William Henry Ireland, forger of Shakespearean manuscripts, 1835;

Catherine Maria Fanshawe, painter and poet, 1834;

Benjamin Franklin, US author, diplomat and scientist, 1790;

Joseph I, Holy Roman Emperor, 1711;

Marie de Rabutin-Chantal, Marquise de Sévigné, French writer, 1696.

Occurred on this day:

In Cambodia, the civil war ended after the capital, Phnom Penh, surrendered to the Khmer Rouge forces, 1975;

The attempted invasion of Cuba took place at the Bay of Pigs, 1961;

Premium Savings Bonds were introduced in Britain, 1956;

Yugoslavia surrendered to the Germans, 1940;

The comic opera *Tom Jones* was first produced, London, 1907;

The Empire Theatre, London, opened as the Royal London Panorama, 1870;

The Republic of Guatemala was founded, 1839;

The *Georgia Gazette* newspaper was first issued in Savannah, 1763;

Martin Luther was excommunicated by the Diet of Worms, 1521;

Ferdinand and Isabella of Castile signed their grant to Columbus, 1492;

At Dordrecht [Dort], Holland, the sea broke through the dykes, and over 100,000 people were drowned, 1421.

TODAY IS THE FEAST DAY OF St Aybert, St Donnan and Others, St Innocent of Tortona, St Mappalicus and Others, St Robert of Chaise-Dieu and St Stephen Harding.

18th April

Born on this day:

Hayley Mills, actress, 1946;

Peter Jeffrey, actor, 1929;

Lord Mason of Barnsley, former MP, 1924;

Avril Angers, actress, 1922;

Barbara Hale, US film actress, 1922;

Roger de Grey, president of the Royal Academy, 1918;

Sylvia Fisher, soprano, 1910;

Miklos Rozsa, film and TV composer, 1907;

Sir Arnold Henry Moore Lunn, skier, 1888;

Leopold Antoni Stanislaw Stokowski, conductor and composer, 1882;

Richard Harding Davis, US journalist and novelist, 1864;

Sir George Clausen, painter, 1852;

Antero Tarquinio de Quental, Portuguese poet, 1842;

Henry Clarence Kendall, Australian poet, 1839;

Franz von Suppé [Francesco Suppé Demelli], Austrian composer, 1820;

George Henry Lewes, journalist and critic, 1817;

Louis-Adolphe Thiers, French statesman, 1797;

Bernhard Anselm Weber, German pianist, conductor and composer, 1764;

Sir Francis Baring, banker and merchant, 1740;

George Colman [the Elder], playwright, baptised, 1732;

Lucrezia Borgia, Duchess of Ferrara, daughter of Pope Alexander VI, 1480.

Died on this day:

Benny Hill [Alfred Hawthorn Hill], comedian, 1992;

Albert Einstein, physicist, 1955;

Leonard Bloomfield, US linguist and philologist, 1949;

Sir John Ambrose Fleming, electrical engineer, 1945;

Cécile Chaminade, French composer, 1944;

Herbert Albert Laurens Fisher, historian, 1940;

Florrie Forde, music-hall artiste, 1940;

Sir Richard Runciman Terry, musicologist, 1938;

Ottorino Respighi, Italian composer, 1936;

Erasmus Darwin, physician and writer, 1802;

George Jeffreys, 1st Baron Jeffreys of Wem, infamous judge, 1689;

Gonzales Cocx [or Coques], Flemish painter, 1684;

John Foxe, author of *The Book of Martyrs*, 1587;

John Leland, antiquary, 1552;

Filippino Lippi, Italian painter, 1504.

Occurred on this day:

London Bridge was sold to a US oil company; the bridge was later re-erected in Arizona, 1968;

France, West Germany, Italy, Belgium, Luxembourg and the Netherlands set up the Coal and Steel Community, 1951;

The Republic of Ireland Act came into force when Eire became a republic, 1949;

The International Court of Justice was opened at The Hague, 1946;

The League of Nations was formally dissolved, and its assets handed over to the United Nations, 1946;

San Francisco, USA, was devastated by a great earthquake, 1906;

The Natural History Museum in South Kensington was opened, 1881;

The 2,000 Guineas horse-race was first run at Newmarket, 1809;

Paul Revere, American silversmith and patriot, made his dramatic ride from Boston to Lexington, 1775.

TODAY IS THE FEAST DAY OF St Apollonius the Apologist, Saints Eleutherius and Anthia, St Galdinus, St Idesbald and St Laserian or Molaisse.

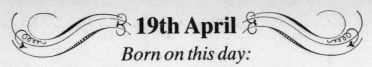

19th April

Born on this day:

Sue Barker, tennis player, 1956;
Trevor Francis, footballer, 1954;
Murray Perahia, pianist, 1947;
Alan Price, singer, 1942;
Michel Roux, chef de cuisine, 1941;
Dudley Moore, actor, 1935;
Jayne Mansfield [Vera Jayne Palmer], US film actress, 1933;
Garfield Morgan, actor, 1931;
Sydney Harpley, sculptor, 1927;
Hugh O'Brian, US film and TV actor, 1925;
Roland Michener QC, former Governor-General of Canada, 1900;
Richard Arthur Warren Hughes, novelist, 1900;

Getulio Dornelles Vargas, Brazilian president, 1883;
Lucien Lévy-Bruhl, French philosopher, 1857;
Edward John Gregory, painter and engraver, 1850;
John Phillip, Scottish painter, 1817;
Charles-Édmond-Henri Coussemaker, French musicologist, 1805;
Heinrich Maria von Hess, German historical painter, 1798;
Christian Gottfried Ehrenburg, German zoologist, 1795;
David Ricardo, economist, 1772;
Giuseppe Catrufo, Italian composer, 1771.

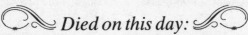

Died on this day:

Frankie Howerd [Francis Alex Howard], comedian, 1992;
Konrad Adenauer, German statesman, 1967;
Sir Henry John Newbolt, poet and author, 1938;
Sir Squire Bancroft, actor-manager, 1926;
Charles Pierce, US philosopher and scientist, 1914;
Pierre Curie, French chemist and physicist, 1906;
John Addington Symonds, critic and poet, 1893;

Charles Robert Darwin, biologist, 1882;
Benjamin Disraeli, Earl of Beaconsfield, statesman and novelist, 1881;
Owen Jones, architect, 1874;
Sir Robert Smirke, architect, 1867;
George Gordon Byron, 6th Baron, poet, 1824;
Queen Christina of Sweden, 1689;
Anton van Diemen, Dutch colonial administrator, 1645;
Paolo Veronese [Cagliari], Italian painter, 1588;
Robert II, King of Scotland, 1390;
Pope Leo IX, 1054.

Occurred on this day:

Bangladesh was admitted to the Commonwealth, 1972;
Prince Rainier III of Monaco married Grace Kelly, US film actress, 1956;
The first London production of the musical show *The Vagabond King* was presented, 1927;
The opera *Monsieur Beaucaire* was first produced, London, 1919;
The first London production of the musical show *The Bing Boys are Here* was presented, 1916;
The San Francisco earthquake and fire ended, with 452 people dead, 1906;

Planquette's opera *Les Cloches de Corneville* was first produced in Paris, 1877;
The British General Gage fired on a small crowd at Lexington, Massachusetts, thus opening the American War of Independence, 1775;
Sir Francis Drake sailed into the harbour of Cadiz and sank the Spanish fleet at harbour; this he called 'singeing the King of Spain's beard', 1587.

TODAY IS THE FEAST DAY OF St Alphege or Elphege of Canterbury, St Expeditus, St Geroldus and St Leo IX, pope.

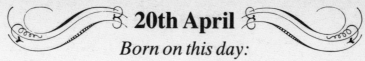

20th April

Born on this day:

Mauricio Gugelmin, racing driver, 1963;
Nicholas Lyndhurst, actor, 1961;
Paul Heiney, writer and broadcaster, 1949;
John Eliot Gardiner, conductor, 1943;
Ryan O'Neal, US actor, 1941;
Ray Brooks, actor, 1939;
Peter Snow, TV presenter and newscaster, 1938;
Eddie Kulukundis, theatrical producer, 1932;
Sir Antony Jay, author and scriptwriter, 1930;
Nina Foch, US film actress, 1924;
Leslie Phillips, actor, 1924;
William Baillie, painter, 1923;

Bruce Cabot [Jacques-Etienne de Bujac], US film actor, 1904;
Sir Donald Wolfit, actor-manager, 1902;
Harold Lloyd, US film comedian, 1893;
Joan Miró, Catalan abstract painter, 1893;
Adolf Hitler, German dictator, 1889;
Charles Maurras, French writer and philosopher, 1868;
Dinah Maria Mulock Craik, novelist, 1826;
Napoleon III [Charles-Louis-Napoleon Bonaparte], Emperor of France, 1808;
Johannes Agricola [Schneider], German Lutheran reformer, 1494;
Pietro Aretino, Italian satirist, 1492.

Died on this day:

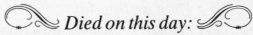

William Sansom, author, 1976;
Christian X, King of Denmark, 1947;
Briton Riviere, artist, 1920;
Abraham [Bram] Stoker, theatre manager and author of *Dracula*, 1912;
Joseph Wolf, Anglo-German artist, 1899;
Pontiac, Ottawa Indian chief, 1769;

Canaletto [Giovanni Antonio Canale] Venetian painter, 1768;
Jean-Louis Petit, French surgeon, 1750;
Claudio Coello, Spanish painter, 1693;
Eliza Barton, the Nun or 'Holy Maid of Kent', executed at Tyburn, 1534.

Occurred on this day:

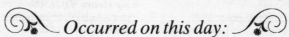

The first London production of the musical show *Kismet* was presented, 1955;
Soviet troops entered Berlin, 1945;
In the USA, the electron microscope was first demonstrated, 1940;
The second Battle of the Aisne River ended, 1917;
The Bimetallist Conference met in Brussels, 1896;
Captain James Cook discovered New South Wales, Australia, 1770;

The Siege of Londonderry began when the city was attacked by the supporters of King James II, 1689;
The Battle of Santa Cruz was fought, when Admiral Blake defeated the Spanish fleet off the Canary Islands, 1657;
Jacques Cartier, French navigator, reached the coast of Labrador, 1534;
The Moguls totally defeated the Afghans at the Battle of Panipat, 1526.

TODAY IS THE FEAST DAY OF St Agnes of Montepulciano, St Caedwalla, St Hildegund, St Marcellinus of Embrun, St Marcian or Marian of Auxerre and St Peter of Verona.

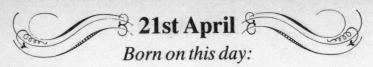

21st April

Born on this day:

HM the Queen, 1926;

Srinivas Venkataraghavan, Indian cricketer, 1946;

John McCabe, composer and pianist, 1939;

Angela Mortimer, tennis player, 1932;

Prof. Gerald Benney, goldsmith, 1930;

John Mortimer QC, author and playwright, 1923;

Ronald Magill, actor, 1920;

Anthony Quinn, US actor, 1915;

Randall Thompson, US composer, 1899;

Henri-Marie-Joseph Millon de Montherlant, French novelist and playwright, 1896;

Gilbert Frankau, novelist, 1884;

Sir Herbert Atkinson Barker, surgeon, 1869;

Hippolyte-Adolphe Taine, French historian, 1828;

Charlotte Brontë novelist [Currer Bell], 1816;

Reginald Heber, hymn-writer and bishop, 1783;

Friedrich Wilhelm August Froebel, German educationist, 1782;

Jan van Riebeeck, Dutch naval surgeon and founder of Cape Town, 1634;

Lodovico Carracci, Italian painter, 1555.

Died on this day:

François Duvalier ['Papa Doc'], president of Haiti, 1971;

Sir Edward Victor Appleton, physicist, 1965;

Sara Margery Fry, social reformer, 1958;

Sir Richard Stafford Cripps, lawyer, diplomat and statesman, 1952;

John Maynard Keynes, 1st Baron, economist, 1946;

Robert Seymour Bridges, poet, 1930;

Marie Corelli [Mary Mackay], author, 1924;

Eleonora Duse, Italian actress, 1924;

Baron Manfred von Richthofen, German aviator, killed in action, 1918;

Mark Twain [Samuel Langhorne Clemens], US novelist, 1910;

Jean-Baptiste-Léon Say, French statesman, 1896;

Jean-Baptiste Racine, French playwright, 1699;

King Henry VII, 1509;

Peter Abelard, French philosopher and theologian, 1142;

St Anselm, Archbishop of Canterbury, 1109.

Occurred on this day:

A French army revolt led by General Challe began in Algeria, 1961;

The first London production of the musical show *The Most Happy Fella* was presented, 1960;

The world's first jet-liner service was begun by BOAC flying Comets between London and Rome, 1952;

The first performance of the musical show *Perchance to Dream* was presented, London, 1945;

The Canadian North-West Mounted Police were established, 1873;

Mexico was defeated at the Battle of San Jacinto by Texas, 1836;

Napoleon's army overtook the Austrians and defeated them at the Battle of Landshut, 1809;

Baber founded the Mogul Empire in India, 1526;

The City of Rome was founded [traditional date], 753 BC.

TODAY IS THE FEAST DAY OF St Anastasius I of Antioch, St Anselm of Canterbury, St Beuno, St Conrad of Parzham, St Malrubius or Maelrubha and St Simeon Barsabas and Others.

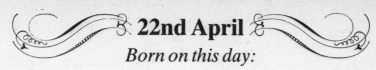

22nd April

Born on this day:

Lloyd Honeyghan, welterweight boxing champion, 1960;

Peter Frampton, rock guitarist, 1950;

Carole Drinkwater, actress, 1948;

Glen Campbell, country singer, 1938;

Jack Nicholson, US actor, 1937;

George Cole, actor, 1925;

Yvette Chauviré, French ballerina assoluta, 1917;

Sir Sidney Nolan OM, Australian painter, 1917;

Sir Yehudi Menuhin OM, violinist, 1916;

Charles Sisson, author and poet, 1914;

Kathleen Mary Ferrier, contralto, 1912;

Eddie Albert, US film actor, 1908;

Vladimir Vladimirovich Nabokov, Russian novelist, poet and lepidopterist, 1899;

Sergei Sergeyevich Prokofiev, Russian composer, 1891;

Lenin [Vladimir Ilyich Ulyanov], Russian Communist leader, 1870;

Phil [Philip William] May, caricaturist, 1864;

Madame de Staël [Anne-Louise-Germaine Necker, Baronne de Staël-Holstein], French writer, 1766;

Immanuel Kant, German philosopher, 1724;

Henry Fielding, novelist, 1707;

Giuseppe Torelli, Italian composer, 1658;

Isabella I, Queen of Castile and Aragon, 1451.

Died on this day:

Basil Dean, actor, manager and playwright, 1978;

Ignatius Roy Dunnachie Campbell, South African poet, 1957;

Frederick Henry Royce, motor-car pioneer, 1933;

John Passmore Edwards, newspaper proprietor and philanthropist, 1911;

Sir Henry Campbell-Bannerman, statesman, 1908;

William Stubbs, historian and bishop, 1901;

Victor-Antoine-Édouard Lalo, French composer, 1892;

Richard Trevithick, steam engineer, 1833;

Thomas Rowlandson, cartoonist, 1827;

John Crome, landscape painter, 1821;

James Hargreaves, inventor of the spinning jenny, 1778;

John Tradescant the Younger, gardener, 1662.

Occurred on this day:

Robin Knox-Johnston sailed into Falmouth after a 312-day non-stop voyage, 1969;

The army in Greece effected a coup, and martial law was declared, 1967;

The New York World's Fair re-opened, 1964;

Allied forces landed in New Guinea, 1944;

British forces made a raid on Zeebrugge, 1918;

The second Battle of Ypres began, when poison gas was used for the first time by Germany, 1915;

The first parliament in South Australia opened, 1857;

St Helena became a Crown Colony, 1834;

The Baltic Exchange, London was founded [as the Baltic Club], 1823;

The Royal Society was incorporated, 1662;

Pedro Alvarez de Cabral reached Brazil and claimed it for Portugal, 1500.

TODAY IS THE FEAST DAY OF St Agipatus I, pope, Saints Epipodius and Alexander, St Leonides of Alexandria, St Opportuna and St Theodore of Sykeon.

23rd April

Born on this day:

Tessa Wyatt, actress, 1948;

Lee Majors, US actor, 1940;

The Hon. Victoria Glendinning, author, 1937;

Prof. George Steiner, professor of English, 1929;

Shirley Temple Black, former child actress and US ambassador, 1928;

Bill Cotton, chairman, Noel Gay Television, 1928;

James Donleavy, Irish author, 1926;

James Kirkup, author and playwright, 1923;

Ronald Neame, film producer and director, 1911;

Harold French, actor, theatre and film director, 1897;

Leslie French, actor, singer and director, 1904;

Dame Edith Ngaio Marsh, New Zealand novelist, 1899;

Margaret Kennedy, novelist, 1896;

Frank Borzage, US film director, 1893;

Max Ludwig Planck, German physicist, 1858;

Dame Ethel Mary Smyth, composer, 1858;

James Anthony Froude, historian, 1818;

Maria Taglioni [Countess de Voisins] Italian ballerina, 1804 [see also Deaths];

James Buchanan, 15th president of the USA, 1791;

Joseph Mallord William Turner, painter, 1775;

George, Baron Anson, admiral and explorer, 1697;

Maarten Harpertszoon Tromp, Dutch naval commander, 1598;

William Shakespeare, playwright and poet, 1564 [see also Deaths].

Died on this day:

Satyajit Ray, Bengali film director, 1992;

Arthur Michael, Lord Ramsey, former Archbishop of Canterbury, 1988;

Harold Arlen [Hyman Arluck], US composer, 1986;

Otto Preminger, US film director, 1986;

Kent Smith, US film actor, 1985;

Elisabeth Schumann, US singer, 1952;

Joseph Pennell, US artist and author, 1926;

Rupert Chawner Brooke, poet, 1915;

Larry 'Buster' Crabbe [Clarence Lindon Crabbe], US swimmer and film actor, 1983;

Maria Taglioni [Countess de Voisins] Italian ballerina, 1884 [see also Births];

William Wordsworth, poet, 1850;

William Shakespeare, playwright and poet, 1616 [see also Births];

Miguel de Cervantes Saavedra, Spanish author, 1616.

Occurred on this day:

The first decimal coins were issued in Britain [5p and 10p], but were used as 1-shilling and 2-shilling pieces until decimalisation, 1968;

The first performance of the musical show Expresso Bongo was presented, London, 1958;

The Shakespeare Memorial Theatre was opened at Stratford-upon-Avon, 1932;

The first London performance of the operetta Frasquita was staged, 1925;

The British Empire Exhibition was opened at Wembley, 1924;

The Battle of Zeebrugge ended, 1918;

Gilbert and Sullivan's opera Patience was first produced, London, 1881;

Warren Hastings was acquitted of high treason, 1795;

Connecticut was chartered as an English colony, 1662;

The Order of the Garter was founded by King Edward III, 1349.

TODAY IS THE FEAST DAY OF St Adalbert of Prague, Saints Felix, Fortunatus and Achilleus, St George the Martyr, St Gerard of Toul and St Ibar.

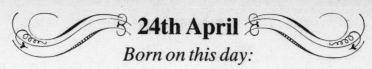

24th April

Born on this day:

Barbra Streisand, US actress and singer, 1942;
John Williams, Australian guitarist, 1941;
Shirley Maclaine, US film actress, 1934;
Bridget Riley, painter, 1931;
Ralph Brown, sculptor, 1928;
Martin Seymour-Smith, writer, 1928;
Sir Clement Freud, writer and former MP, 1924;
Admiral Sir Rae McKaig, former UK military representative to NATO, 1922;
Field Marshal Lord Carver, former Chief of the Defence Staff, 1915;
William Joyce ['Lord Haw-Haw'], collaborator with the Nazis, 1906;
Sir Richard Stafford Cripps, lawyer, diplomat and statesman, 1889;
Air Chief Marshal Hugh Caswall Tremenheere Dowding, 1st Baron, 1882;
Arthur Christopher Benson, scholar and author, 1862;
Henri-Philippe Pétain, French soldier and leader, 1856;
Marcus Andrew Hislop Clarke, author, 1846;
Anthony Trollope, author and inventor of the pillar box, 1815;
Edmund Cartwright, inventor of the power loom, 1743;
Giambattista Martini, Italian historian of music, 1706;
William the Silent, Prince of Orange, 1533.

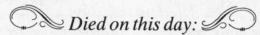

Died on this day:

Bill [William John] Edrich, cricketer, 1986;
The Duchess of Windsor [Wallis Warfield], 1986;
Gerhard Domagk, German bacteriologist, 1964;
Manuel Ponce, Mexican composer, 1948;
Willa Cather, US novelist, 1947;
George de Forest Brush, US painter, 1941;
Justin M'Carthy, Irish politician, historian and novelist, 1912;
Maria Faglioni, ballerina, 1884;
Louisa Stuart Costello, Irish artist and poet, 1870;
Daniel Defoe, author, 1731;
Jacopo Sannazaro, Neapolitan poet, 1530.

Occurred on this day:

The Gambia was proclaimed a republic, 1970;
The first performance of the musical show *Man of La Mancha* was presented, London, 1968;
The first Bandoeng Conference ended, 1955;
In the German general election, Nazis won many seats in large cities, 1932;
The Republican insurrection in Ireland known as the Easter Rising occurred on Easter Monday, 1916;
Founded by Sir Arthur Pearson, the first issue of the *Daily Express* appeared, 1900;
Spain declared war on the United States, 1898;
Joshua Slocum set sail from Boston, Massachusetts, USA, on the first solo round-the-world voyage, 1895;
The Garrick Theatre, London, opened, 1889;
The Alhambra Theatre, London, reopened as the Royal Alhambra Palace of Varieties, 1871;
The Library of Congress, Washington, D.C., USA, was established, 1800;
In America, the *Boston News-Letter* was first issued, 1704;
Mary, Queen of Scots, aged 16, married the Dauphin of France, 1558;
The Holy Roman Emperor, Charles V, defeated the Protestants at Mühlberg, 1547.

TODAY IS THE FEAST DAY OF St Egbert, St Fidelis of Sigmaringen, St Ives or Ivo, St Mary Euphrasia Pelletier, St Mellitus of Canterbury and St William Firmatus.

25th April

Born on this day:

Eric Bristow, darts champion, 1957;
Dr John Nunn, chess player, 1955;
Al Pacino, US film actor, 1940;
The Earl of Lichfield, photographer, 1939;
William Roache, actor, 1932;
David Shepherd, artist, 1931;
Sir Francis Graham-Smith, Astronomer Royal, 1923;
Ella Fitzgerald, US singer, 1918;
Ross Lockridge, US novelist, 1914;
Edward [Egbert] Roscoe Murrow, US broadcaster and journalist, 1908;
Lord Gladwyn, 1900;
Wolfgang Pauli, Austrian physicist, 1900;
Guglielmo Marconi, Italian radio pioneer, 1874;

Walter de la Mare, poet and novelist, 1873;
Charles Burgess Fry, cricketer and writer, 1872;
Emerich de Vattel, Swiss diplomat and jurist, 1714;
John Keble, Anglican priest and founder-member of the Oxford Movement, 1792.
Sir Mark Isambard Brunel, engineer and inventor, 1769;
James Ferguson, astronomer, 1710;
Oliver Cromwell, Lord Protector of England, 1559;
King Edward II, 1284.

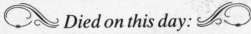

Died on this day:

Dame Celia Johnson, actress, 1982;
Sir Carol Reed, film director, 1976;
Constance Collier [Laura Constance Hardie], actress, 1955;
Joseph Hergesheimer, US novelist, 1954;
Gertie Millar [Countess of Dudley], musical comedy actress, 1952;
Kawanabe Kyosai, Japanese painter, 1889;
Louis-Gabriel-Eugène Isabey, French painter and lithographer, 1886;

Daniel Maclise, painter, 1870;
William Cowper, poet, 1800;
Anders Celsius, Swedish inventor of the centigrade thermometer, 1744;
David Teniers the Younger, Flemish painter, 1690;
Torquato Tasso, Italian poet, 1595;
Leon Battista degli Alberti, Italian architect, sculptor, writer and musician, 1472.

Occurred on this day:

Portugal held its first free elections for 50 years; three main non-Communist parties winning a large majority, 1975;
The BBC radio serial *The Dales* ended after 21 years and over 5,400 episodes, 1969;
In North America, the St Lawrence Seaway, 89 miles long, was opened, 1959;
The San Francisco Conference of Allied Nations opened, 1945;
Puccini's opera *Turandot* was first performed, Milan, 1926;
Field Marshal Paul von Hindenburg became president of Germany, 1925;

British, French, Australian and New Zealand forces landed at the Gallipoli peninsula, Turkey, 1915;
The musical show *The Geisha* was first produced, London, 1896;
Arthur Daly opened Daly's Theatre in London, 1896;
The Confederate forces surrendered to Admiral Farragut at the Battle of New Orleans, 1862;
Construction of the Suez Canal began, 1859;
The guillotine was first erected in Paris, 1792.

TODAY IS THE FEAST DAY OF St Anianus of Alexandria, St Heribald and St Mark the Evangelist.

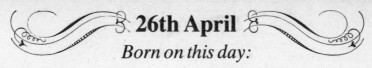

26th April

Born on this day:

Peter Schaufuss, director of ballet, Deutsche Oper, Berlin, 1950;

Carol Burnett, US comedienne, 1936;

Derek Waring, actor, 1930;

Dr Anne McLaren, zoologist, 1927;

David Coleman, sports commentator, 1926;

Sir James Holt, mediaeval historian, 1922;

Prof. Jack Morpurgo, Emeritus professor of American literature, 1918;

Morris West, novelist, 1916;

Prof. Wilfrid Mellers, composer, 1914;

Maj.-Gen. Sir Leslie Tyler, former Colonel Commandant, REME, 1903;

John Grierson, documentary film-maker, 1898;

Rudolf Hess, Nazi leader, 1894;

Anita Loos, US screenwriter, novelist and playwright, 1893;

Ludwig Wittgenstein, Austrian philosopher, 1889;

Michel [Mikhail Mikhailovich] Fokine, choreographer, 1880;

Harold Sidney Harmsworth, 1st Viscount Rothermere, newspaper publisher, 1868;

Alfred Krupp, German ironfounder and armaments manufacturer, 1812;

Ferdinand-Victor-Eugène Delacroix, French painter, 1798;

John James Audubon, US naturalist and artist, 1785;

Leonardo da Vinci, Italian painter, sculptor and architect, 1452;

Marcus Aurelius, Roman emperor, 121.

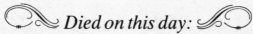

Died on this day:

Broderick Crawford, US film actor, 1986;

William 'Count' Basie, US jazz pianist and bandleader, 1984;

Dame Cicely Courtneidge, actress, 1980;

Edwin John Pratt, Canadian poet and professor of literature, 1964;

Edward Arnold [Gunther Schneider], US film actor, 1956;

Karl Bosch, German chemist, 1940;

Nelson Keys, stage and film comedian, 1939;

Björnstjerne Björnson, Norwegian poet and playwright, 1910;

John Wilkes Booth, US actor and assassin, shot while trying to escape, 1865;

Jeremy Collier, historian and opponent of the theatre, 1726.

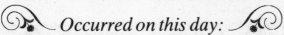

Occurred on this day:

An accident at the Soviet nuclear power station at Chernobyl resulted in a massive nuclear leak, 1986;

President Reagan began a visit to China, 1984;

The musical show *Two Gentlemen of Verona* was first produced, London, 1973;

Tanganyika and Zanzibar united to form Tanzania, 1964;

The first Anglo-American satellite, *Ariel*, was launched, 1962;

A revolt in the French army failed, and the leaders were arrested, 1961;

The musical show *Bless the Bride* was first produced, London, 1947;

German planes bombed Guernica in Spain during the Civil War, 1937;

The Duke of York [later King George VI] married Elizabeth Bowes-Lyon [later Queen Elizabeth], 1923;

The Pact of London was signed between the Allies and Italy, 1915;

At the Convention of Bartenstein, Russia and Prussia formed an alliance to drive France out of the German states, 1807.

TODAY IS THE FEAST DAY OF St Franca of Piacenza, St Paschasius Radbertus, St Peter of Braga, St Richarius or Riquier and St Stephen of Perm.

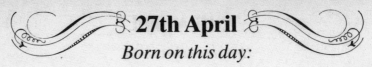

27th April

Born on this day:

Sheena Easton, singer, 1959;
Michael Fish, weatherman, 1944;
Sir Peter Imbert, Commissioner of the Metropolitan Police, 1933;
Anouk Aimée, French film actress, 1932;
Pik Botha, South African Minister of Foreign Affairs, 1932;
Igor Oistrakh, violinist, 1931;
Alan Reynolds, painter and printmaker, 1926;
Jack Klugman, US film actor, 1922;
Cecil Day Lewis, poet and novelist, 1904;
Ludwig Bemelmans, US juvenile author and illustrator, 1898;
Wallace Carothers, US chemist and developer of nylon, 1896;

Maurice Baring, novelist, playwright and poet, 1874;
Edward Whymper, mountaineer and artist, 1840;
Ulysses Simpson Grant, general and 18th president of the USA, 1822;
Herbert Spencer, philosopher, 1820;
Friedrich, Baron von Flotow, German composer, 1812;
Samuel Finley Breese Morse, US inventor of the Morse Code, 1791;
Mary Wollstonecraft Godwin, author and champion of women's rights, 1759;
Edward Gibbon, historian, author of *Decline and Fall of the Roman Empire*, 1737;
Jean-François Millet, Dutch painter, 1642.

Died on this day:

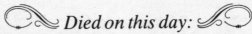

Kwame Nkrumah, former president of Ghana, 1972;
Harold Hart Crane, US poet, committed suicide, 1932;
Alexander Nikolaievich Scriabin, Russian composer and pianist, 1915;
Henry Hobson Richardson, US architect, 1886;
Ralph Waldo Emerson, US author, 1882;

William Charles Macready, actor-manager, 1873;
James Bruce, explorer, 1794;
Sir William Jones, orientalist, 1794;
Gerrit van Honthorst, Dutch painter, 1656;
Jan Josephszoon van Goyen, Dutch landscape painter, 1656;
Ferdinand Magellan, Portuguese navigator, killed by Philippine natives, 1521.

Occurred on this day:

Sierra Leone became independent, 1961;
Togo became independent, 1960;
Britain recognised the state of Israel, 1950;
German troops occupied Athens, 1941;
In Britain, it was announced that men aged 20–21 would be conscripted, 1939;
The Piccadilly Theatre, London, opened, 1928;

The Carlton Theatre, London [now a cinema] opened, 1927;
Gounod's opera *Romeo and Juliet* was first performed, Paris, 1867;
The London Zoological Gardens in Regent's Park opened, 1828;
The Order of St Michael and St George was founded, 1817;
The English defeated the Scots at the Battle of Dunbar, 1296.

TODAY IS THE FEAST DAY OF St Anthimus of Nicomedia, St Asicus or Tassach, Saints Castor and Stephen, St Floribert of Liège, St Maughold or Maccul, St Zita.

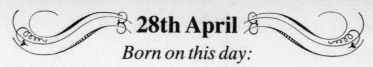

28th April

Born on this day:

Nicola Le Fanu, composer, 1947;

Dr Jeffrey Tate, conductor, 1943;

Ann-Margret, Swedish actress, 1941;

Garfield Weston, chairman, Associated British Foods, 1927;

Dr Kenneth Kaunda, former president of Zambia, 1924;

Odette Hallowes GC, wartime secret agent, 1912;

Antonio de Oliveira Salazar, prime minister and dictator of Portugal, 1889;

Lionel Barrymore [Blythe], US actor, 1878;

Frances Mary Hodgkins, New Zealand painter, 1869;

Anthony Ashley Cooper, 7th Earl of Shaftesbury, statesman and philanthropist, 1801;

Charles Sturt, explorer of Australia, 1795;

James Monroe, 5th president of the USA, 1758;

Jean Audran, French artist and engraver, 1667;

King Edward IV, 1442.

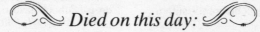

Died on this day:

Francis Bacon, painter, 1992;

Richard Arthur Warren Hughes, novelist, 1976;

Ed [Edward James] Begley, US actor, 1970;

Benito Amilcare Andrea Mussolini, executed by Italian partisans, 1945;

Luisa Tetrazzini, Italian soprano, 1940;

Fuad I, King of Egypt, 1936;

Gavrilo Princip, Bosnian revolutionary and assassin, 1918;

Arthur Fitzwilliam Tait, US artist, 1905;

Sir Charles Bell, anatomist, 1842;

John Abernethy, surgeon, 1831;

Thomas Betterton, actor, 1710.

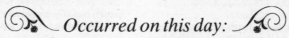

Occurred on this day:

Anwar El-Sadat was appointed acting president of Egypt, 1970;

General de Gaulle resigned as president of France, 1969;

US forces were sent to the Dominican Republic to protect US citizens and prevent a Communist revolution, 1965;

Japan regained its sovereignty, 1952;

Thor Heyerdahl and companions set off from Peru on the Kon-Tiki expedition, 1947;

Farouk became King of Egypt, 1936;

The League of Nations was founded, 1919;

The musical show *The Arcadians* was first produced, London, 1909;

Her Majesty's Theatre, London [present building], opened, 1897;

The crew of HMS *Bounty*, led by Fletcher Christian, mutinied, 1789;

Captain Cook landed at, and named, Botany Bay and New South Wales, 1770;

Pope Clement XII issued a Bull condemning freemasonry, 1738;

The Spaniards defeated a French fleet and won a decisive victory at the Battle of Cerignola, 1503;

The foundation stone of Salisbury Cathedral was laid, 1220.

TODAY IS THE FEAST DAY OF St Cronan of Roscrea, St Cyril of Turov, St Louis Grignion of Montfort, St Pamphilus of Sulmona, St Peter Mary Chanel, St Pollio, Saints Theodora and Didymus, St Valeria and St Vitalis.

29th April

Born on this day:

Cheryl Kennedy, actress, 1947;
Richard Warwick, actor, 1945;
Baroness Chalker of Wallasey [Lynda Chalker], former MP, 1942;
Ann Bell, actress, 1940;
Saddam Hussein, president of Iraq, 1937;
Zubin Mehta, conductor, 1936;
Lieut.-Gen. Sir Peter de la Billière, 1934;
Rod McKuen, composer and poet, 1933;
Lieut.-Gen. Sir Patrick Palmer, C.-in-C., Allied Forces, Northern Europe, 1933;
Lonnie Donegan, skiffle musician, 1931;
Jeremy Thorpe, former MP, 1929;
Prof. Heinz Wolff, bioengineer, 1928;
Sir Anthony Laughton, oceanographer, 1927;

Celeste Holm, US film actress, 1919;
Deryck Guyler, actor and comedian, 1914;
Fred Zinnemann, US film director, 1907;
Rudolf Schwarz, conductor, 1905;
Edward Kennedy 'Duke' Ellington, US jazz composer and bandleader, 1899;
Sir Malcolm Sargent, conductor, 1895;
Sir Thomas Beecham, conductor, 1879;
Rafael Sabatini, Italian author, 1875;
William Randolph Hearst, US newspaper proprietor, 1863;
Sir James Brooke, Rajah of Sarawak, 1803.

Died on this day:

Barbara Goolden, novelist, 1990;
Sir Alfred Joseph Hitchcock, film director, 1980;
Wallace Carothers, US chemist and developer of nylon, 1937;
Konstantinos Petrou Kavafis [Constantine Cavafy], Greek poet, 1933;

Charles Bell, anatomist, 1842;
George Farquhar, playwright, 1707;
Michiel Adrianszoon de Ruyter, Dutch naval commander, 1676;
John Cleveland, poet, 1658.

Occurred on this day:

The first London performance of the musical show *She Loves Me* was staged, 1964;
The first London performance of the musical show *Oklahoma!* was staged, 1947;
In Italy, the German army surrendered unconditionally to Field Marshal Alexander, 1945;

General Pétain was appointed Chief of the French General Staff, 1917;
The Dublin Post Office was burnt by Sinn Fein rebels, 1916;
At Oxford University a statute was passed, admitting women to examinations, 1884;
The Siege of Orléans was relieved, 1429.

TODAY IS THE FEAST DAY OF St Catherine of Siena, St Hugh of Cluny, St Joseph Cottolengo, St Robert of Molesmes and St Wilfrid the Younger.

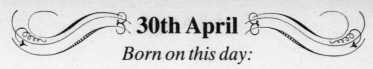

30th April

Born on this day:

HM King Carl XVI Gustav of Sweden, 1946;

Leslie Grantham, actor, 1946;

Jill Clayburgh, US film actress, 1944;

Sir William Adams, ambassador to Egypt, 1932;

Dr Gerald Aylmer, Master of St Peter's College, Oxford, 1926;

Cloris Leachman, US film actress, 1926;

Princess Juliana of the Netherlands, 1909;

Edward McWilliam, sculptor, 1909;

Joachim von Ribbentrop, German politician, 1893;

Jaroslav Hašek, Czech novelist, 1883;

Franz Lehár, Hungarian composer, 1870;

Karl Piutti, German organist and composer, 1846;

Sir John Lubbock, 1st Baron Avebury, banker, writer and entomologist, 1834;

Karl Kammerlander, German songwriter and composer, 1828;

Richard Redgrave, painter, 1804;

William Mulready, painter, 1786;

David Thompson, explorer, 1770;

Queen Mary II, 1662;

William Lilly, astrologer and fortune-teller, 1602;

Casimir III, King of Poland, 1310.

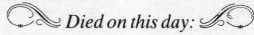

Died on this day:

George Balanchine, choreographer, 1983;

Sir Almroth Wright, bacteriologist, 1947;

Adolf Hitler, committed suicide, 1945;

Eva Braun, mistress of Adolf Hitler, committed suicide, 1945;

Beatrice [Potter] Webb, writer and socialist, 1943;

Otto Jespersen, Danish philologist, 1943;

Alfred Edward Housman, poet and scholar, 1936;

Carl August Nicolas Rosa, German operatic impresario, 1889;

Édouard Manet, French impressionist painter, 1883;

Robert Fitzroy, admiral and hydrographer, 1865;

Sir Henry Rowley Bishop, composer, 1855.

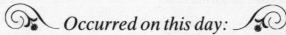

Occurred on this day:

The first London production of the comic operetta *Candide* was staged, 1959;

The first London performance of the musical show *My Fair Lady* was staged, 1958;

The New York World's Fair opened, 1939;

Debussy's opera *Pelléas et Mélisande* was first performed, Paris, 1902;

Hawaii became a US territory, 1900;

Louisiana became the 18th of the United States, 1812;

The US purchased the Louisiana Territory from France, 1803;

General George Washington was inaugurated as 1st president of the USA, 1789;

Under an Edict issued by Galerius Valerius Maximianus, Christians were legally recognised in the Roman Empire, 311.

TODAY IS THE FEAST DAY OF St Eutropius of Saintes, St Forannan, St Gualfardus or Wolfhard, Saints Marianus, James and Others, St Maximus of Ephesus and St Pius V, pope.

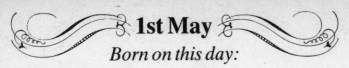

1st May

Born on this day:

Lady Sarah Armstrong-Jones, 1964;
Gordon Greenidge, West Indies cricketer, 1951;
Joanna Lumley, actress, 1946;
Bo Nilsson, Swedish composer, 1937;
Una Stubbs, actress, 1937;
Ian Curteis, playwright, 1935;
Julian Mitchell, writer and playwright, 1935;
Prof. Philip King, sculptor, 1934;
Sir Bob Reid, chairman, British Rail, 1934;
Sir Peter Taylor, a Lord Justice of Appeal, 1930;
Ralf Dahrendorf, Warden, St Antony's College, Oxford, 1929;
Sonny Ramadhin, West Indies cricketer, 1929;

Gary Bertini, Israeli conductor, 1927;
Joseph Heller, US novelist, 1923;
Dan O'Herlihy, film actor, 1919;
Wendy Toye, theatrical producer, 1917;
Glenn Ford, US film actor, 1916;
Air Comdre. Dame Felicity Peake, first director, WRAF, 1913;
Sir Philip Armand Hamilton Gibbs, author, 1877;
Marie Corelli [Mary Mackay], novelist, 1855;
Arthur Wellesley [Wesley], 1st Duke of Wellington, field marshal and politician, 1769;
Joseph Addison, diarist and essayist, 1672;
Michiel Janszoon van Mierevelt, Dutch painter, 1567.

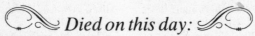

Died on this day:

Sylvia Townsend Warner, novelist, 1978;
Sir Harold George Nicolson, diplomat and biographer, 1968;
William Fox [Wilhelm Fried], US film producer, 1952;
Joseph Goebbels, Nazi leader and propaganda chief, committed suicide, 1945;
Antonín Leopold Dvořák, Czech composer, 1904;

Mihaly von Munkácsy [Michael Lieb], Hungarian painter, 1900;
David Livingstone, missionary and explorer, 1873;
Dr John Walker, inventor of the friction match, 1859;
Jean-François de Troy, French painter, 1730;
John Dryden, poet, 1700.

Occurred on this day:

The musical show *Billy* was first produced, London, 1974;
The USSR shot down a US U-2 aircraft piloted by Francis Gary Powers, 1960;
The London Library was officially opened, 1841;
Professor Auguste Piccard made the first ascent into the stratosphere, a distance of just over 10 miles, 1931;
In New York, the Empire State Building was opened, 1931;
Cyprus became a British Crown Colony, 1925;

The British naval raid on Ostend started, 1918;
German submarines sank the US ship *Gulflight*, 1915;
Queen Victoria was proclaimed Empress of India, 1876;
The Great Exhibition was opened by Queen Victoria in Hyde Park, London, 1851;
Mozart's opera *The Marriage of Figaro* was first performed, Vienna, 1786;
The Union of Scotland and England was proclaimed, 1707.

TODAY IS MAY DAY AND THE FEAST DAY OF St Amator or Amatre, St Briocus or Brieuc, St Joseph the Worker, St Peregrine Laziosi, St Sigismund of Burgundy and St Theodard of Narbonne.

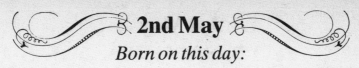

2nd May

Born on this day:

David Suchet, actor, 1946;
Engelbert Humperdinck, pop singer, 1936;
Dr Malcolm Lipkin, composer, 1932;
Maj.-Gen. David Alexander-Sinclair, 1927;
Clive Jenkins, trade union leader, 1926;
Air Marshal Sir Ian Pedder, chairman, Dan-Air Services, 1926;
Theodore Bikel, Austrian actor, 1924;
John Neville, actor, 1924;
Satyajit Ray, Indian film-maker, 1921;
Peter Foster, architect, 1919;
Air Chief Marshal Sir John Barraclough, 1918;
Alastair Forbes, journalist and writer, 1918;
Peggy Mount, actress, 1916;
Bing [Harry Lillis] Crosby, US singer, 1904;

Dr Benjamin Spock, US child care specialist, 1903;
Brian Aherne, film actor, 1902;
Lorenz Milton Hart, US songwriter and composer, 1895;
Baron Manfred von Richthofen, German aviator, 1892;
Theodor Herzl, Hungarian-born founder of Zionism, 1860;
Jerome Klapka Jerome, novelist and playwright, 1859;
Rev. Ebenezer Cobham Brewer, author of the *Dictionary of Phrase and Fable*, 1810;
Catherine II [the Great], Empress of Russia, 1729;
Pietro Alessandro Gaspare Scarlatti, Italian composer, 1660;
William Camden, antiquarian and historian, 1551.

Died on this day:
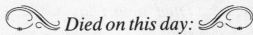

Milton Stover Eisenhower, US diplomat, 1985;
John Edgar Hoover, US director of the FBI, 1972;
Nancy, Viscountess Astor, first woman to sit in Parliament, 1964;
Joseph Raymond McCarthy, US judge and senator, 1957;

Giacomo Meyerbeer [Jakob Liebmann Beer], German/French composer, 1864;
Louis-Charles-Alfred de Musset, French playwright, 1857;
Leonardo da Vinci, Florentine painter, sculptor and scientist, 1519.

Occurred on this day:

Queen Elizabeth II sailed from Southampton on her maiden voyage, 1969;
Early Bird, the first communications satellite for regular TV relay, began operating, 1965;
Public VHF broadcasting was first introduced to Britain, 1955;
The first jet-aircraft passenger service between London and Johannesburg began, 1952;
The Battle for Berlin ended, and the Germans surrendered, 1945;

During the American Civil War, the Battle of Chancellorsville started, 1863;
Despite losses, the French were victorious at the Battle of Lützen, 1813;
The British navy mutinied at the Nore, 1797;
The Hudson's Bay Company was chartered, 1670;
The Authorised Version [King James] of the Bible was published, 1611.

TODAY IS THE FEAST DAY OF St Athanasius, Saints Exuperius or Hesperius and Zoe, St Mefalda, St Ultan of Fosses, St Waldebert and St Wiborada.

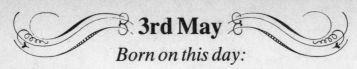

3rd May

Born on this day:

Kathy Cook, athlete, 1960;
Alan Wells, athlete, 1952;
Peter Oosterhuis, golfer, 1949;
Henry Cooper, heavyweight boxing champion, 1934;
James Brown, US singer, songwriter and musician, 1933;
Norman Thelwell, illustrator and cartoonist, 1923;
Betty Comden, US playwright and screenwriter, 1919;
Pete Seeger, US folk singer, 1919;
Randle Manwaring, poet and author, former insurance broker, 1912;
Prof. Anne Robertson, Roman numismatist, 1910;
Sir William Glock, music lecturer and critic, 1908;

Mary Astor [Lucille Vasconcellos Langhanke], US film actress, 1906;
Golda Meir [Goldie Meyerson, née Mabovitch], Israeli prime minister, 1898;
François Coty [Francesco Giuseppe Spoturno], French perfume manufacturer, 1874;
Prince Bernhard von Bülow, German statesman, 1849;
Richard D'Oyly Carte, operatic impresario, 1844;
August Friedrich Ferdinand von Kotzebue, German playwright, 1761;
Alessandro Allori, Italian painter, 1535;
Niccolò di Bernardo dei Machiavelli, Italian author and statesman, 1469.

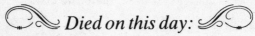

Died on this day:

George Lloyd Murphy, US film actor, dancer, singer and politician, 1992;
Bruce Cabot [Jacques-Etienne de Bujac], US film actor, 1972;
Karl Freund, Czech-born film cameraman and director, 1969;
Henry Cornelius, South African-born film director, 1958;

Herbert Farjeon, critic and playwright, 1945;
Alfred William Hunt, painter, 1896;
Thomas Barry Sullivan, actor, 1891;
Thomas Hood, poet, 1845;
Eglon van der Neer, Dutch painter, 1703;
Lorenzo Costa, Italian painter, 1535.

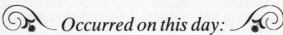

Occurred on this day:

The first London production of the musical show *Annie* was staged, 1978;
In the Antarctic, a new range of mountains was discovered with two peaks of over 13,000 feet, 1956;
The Festival of Britain opened, 1951;
The first London production of the musical show *Show Boat* was staged, 1928;
New Zealand was proclaimed a British colony, 1841;

The first daily evening newspaper, *The Star and Evening Advertiser*, was issued in London, 1788;
The British defeated the French at the Battle of Cape Finisterre, 1747;
Pedro Alvares Cabral, Portuguese navigator, landed in Brazil, 1500;
Jamaica was discovered by Columbus, 1494.

TODAY IS THE FEAST DAY OF Saints Alexander, Eventius and Theodulus, St James the Less, St Juvenal of Narni, St Philip the Apostle, St Philip of Zell and Saints Timothy and Maura.

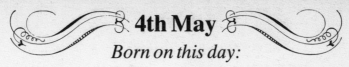

4th May

Born on this day:

Liz Robertson, actress and singer, 1954;
Edwin Russell, sculptor, 1939;
Prof. Marisa Robles, harpist, 1937;
Gennadi Rozhdestvensky, conductor, 1931;
Audrey Hepburn, film actress, 1929;
Brian Innes, jazz musician, 1929;
Muhammad Hosni Mubarak, president of Egypt, 1928;
Terry Scott, actor, 1927;
Eric Sykes, comedian and writer, 1923;
Mátyás Seiber, Hungarian composer, 1905;
Sir Archibald Hector McIndoe, New Zealand plastic surgeon, 1900;
Cardinal Francis Joseph Spellman, RC Archbishop of New York, 1889;
Israel Moses Sieff, Baron Sieff, president of Marks and Spencer, 1889;

Estelle Sylvia Pankhurst, artist and feminist, 1882;
Alexandre Nikolaievich Benois, Russian painter and theatrical designer, 1870;
Alice Liddell, the original of *Alice in Wonderland*, 1852;
John Hanning Speke, discoverer of the source of the Nile, 1827;
Thomas Henry Huxley, biologist and natural historian, 1825;
William Hickling Prescott, US historian, 1796;
Sir Thomas Lawrence, portrait painter, 1769;
Bartolommeo di Francesco Cristofori, harpsichord maker, 1655.

Died on this day:

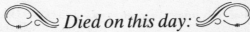

Diana Dors [Fluck], film actress, 1984;
Josip Broz Tito, president of Yugoslavia, 1980;
Sir Francis Osbert Sacheverell Sitwell, author, 1969;
Georges Enesco [Gheorghe Enescu], Romanian violinist and composer, 1955;

William Rose Benét, US author, 1950;
Carl von Ossietzky, German pacifist journalist and Nobel prizewinner, in a Nazi concentration camp, 1938;
William Froude, engineer and naval architect, 1879;
Sir James Thornhill, historical painter, 1734.

Occurred on this day:

Margaret Thatcher became Britain's first woman prime minister, 1979;
Waltzing Matilda became the national anthem of Australia, 1976;
The Battle of the Coral Sea began, 1942;
The first president of the Irish Republic was elected, Douglas Hyde, a Protestant, 1938;
The first London production of the musical show *Watch Your Step* was staged, 1928;
The General Strike in Britain began, 1926;

Work on excavating the Panama Canal began, 1904;
The *Daily Mail* was first published, price one halfpenny, 1896;
The Cunard shipping line was founded by Sir Samuel Cunard, of Halifax, Nova Scotia, 1839;
The first Derby was run at Epsom and won by Diomed, 1780;
The Lancastrians were defeated by the Yorkists at the Battle of Tewkesbury, 1471.

TODAY IS THE FEAST DAY OF St Augustine Webster, St Cyriacus or Judas Quiriacus, St Florian of Lorch, St Gothard or Godehard, St John Houghton, St Pelagia of Tarsus, St Robert Lawrence and St Venerius of Milan.

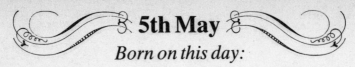

5th May

Born on this day:

Dilys Watling, actress, 1946;
Roger Rees, actor and playwright, 1944;
Michael Palin, comedian and actor, 1943;
Tammy Wynette, singer, 1942;
Prof. Monica Cole, geographer, 1922;
Glanmor Williams, historian, 1920;
Alice Faye, US film actress and singer, 1915;
General Sir Charles Harington, 1910;
Lady Plowden, former chairman, IBA, 1910;
Sir Gordon Richards, jockey, 1904;
Christopher Darlington Morley, US novelist and playwright, 1890;
Archibald Percival Wavell, 1st Earl, soldier, 1883;
Sir Douglas Mawson, Antarctic explorer, 1882;
Henryk Sienkiewicz, Polish novelist, author of *Quo Vadis?*, 1846;
The Empress Eugénie of France [Eugénie Marie de Montijo de Guzman], 1826;
Karl Marx, German author and socialist, 1818;
Eugene-Martin Labiche, French playwright and farceur, 1815;
Sören Aabye Kierkegaard, Danish philosopher, 1813;
Louis-Christophe-François Hachette, French bookseller and publisher, 1800;
Leopold II, Holy Roman Emperor, 1747;
Rupert, King of Germany, 1352.

Died on this day:

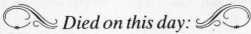

Sir Donald Coleman Bailey, wartime bridge designer, 1985;
Ludwig Erhard, former West German chancellor, 1977;
James Branch Cabell, US novelist, 1958;
Beatrice Harraden, novelist, 1936;
William Friese-Greene [William Green], cinematograph pioneer, 1921;
Francis Bret Harte, US author, 1902;
Joseph-Nicolas Robert Fleury, French painter, 1890;
Napoleon I [Napoleon Bonaparte], Emperor of France, 1821;
Samuel Cooper, miniature painter, 1672.

Occurred on this day:

US Commander Alan B. Shepard went into space in a *Mercury* capsule, 1961;
Major Yuri Gagarin, cosmonaut of the USSR, orbited the earth, 1961;
The Federal Republic of Germany became a sovereign state, 1955;
The Council of Europe was set up in London, 1949;
British forces invaded Madagascar, 1942;
Italian forces captured Addis Ababa, 1936;
Amy Johnson began a solo flight to Australia, 1930;
Excavation of the Corinth Canal in Greece began, 1882;
The first train robbery in the USA took place near North Bend, Ohio, 1865;
The Battle of the Wilderness began during the American Civil War, 1864;
The Confederates were victorious at the Battle of Williamsburg, 1862;
The British defeated the French at the Battle of Fuentes de Oñoro, 1811;
St Helena was occupied by Captain John Dutton of the East India Company, 1659.

TODAY IS THE FEAST DAY OF St Angelo, St Avertinus, St Hilary of Arles, St Hilary of Galeata, St Jutta and St Mauruntius.

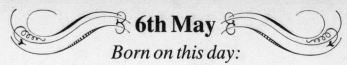

6th May

Born on this day:

Alessandra Ferri, ballerina, 1963;
Susan Brown, actress, 1946;
Joanna Dunham, actress, 1936;
Rosemary Cramp, archaeologist, 1929;
Alan Ross, author and publisher, 1922;
Freddy Randall, jazz trumpeter, 1921;
Vice-Admiral Sir Hugh Martell, 1920;
George Orson Welles, US actor, director and writer, 1915;
Stewart Granger, film actor, 1913;
Air Chief Marshal Sir Walter Dawson, 1902;
Max Ophüls [Maximilian Oppenheimer], German film director, 1902;
Rudolph Valentino [Rodolfo Alfonzo Raffaele Pierre Philibert Guglielmi], Italian-born film actor, 1895;
Stanley Arthur Morison, typographer, 1889;
William Edmund, 1st Baron Ironside, soldier, 1880;
Sigmund Freud, Austrian neurologist and psychoanalyst, 1856;
Robert Edwin Peary, US Arctic explorer, 1856;
Maximilien-François-Marie-Isidore de Robespierre, French revolutionary, 1758;
André Massena, Duc de Rivoli, Prince d'Essling, French marshal and soldier, 1756;
Lorenzo Lippi [Perlone Zipoli], Florentine poet and painter, 1606;
Frans Francken the Younger, Flemish painter, 1581 [see also Deaths].

Died on this day:

Marlene Dietrich, German-born actress, 1992;
Wilfrid Hyde White, actor, 1991;
Edgar Mittelholzer, Guyanan novelist, 1965;
Maria Montessori, Italian physician and educationist, 1952;
Count Maurice-Polydore-Marie-Bernard Maeterlinck, Belgian poet and playwright, 1949;
Lyman Frank Baum, US author of *The Wizard of Oz*, 1919;
King Edward VII, 1910;
Franz von Lenbach, German portrait painter, 1904;
Henry David Thoreau, US poet and essayist, 1862;
Friedrich Heinrich Alexander, Baron von Humboldt, German explorer and scientist, 1859;
Frans Francken the Younger, Flemish painter, 1642 [see also Births];
Cornelius Jansen, Dutch theologian, 1638.

Occurred on this day:

Princess Margaret married Antony Armstrong-Jones in Westminster Abbey, 1960;
Roger Bannister was first to run a mile in under four minutes, 1954;
Corregidor surrendered to the Japanese, 1942;
The German Zeppelin *Hindenburg* crashed and was destroyed by fire at Lakehurst, New Jersey, USA, 1937;
King George V acceded to the throne, 1910;
General Lee defeated the Union army at the Battle of the Wilderness, 1864;
The Union army was routed by the Confederates under General Robert E. Lee at the Battle of Chancellorsville, Virginia, 1863;
The first postage stamp, the Penny Black, was issued, 1840;
The Austrians were victorious at the Battle of Prague during the Seven Years' War, 1757;
The island of Manhattan was bought from the Indians by the Dutch settler, Peter Minuit, for trinkets worth about $25, 1626.

TODAY IS THE FEAST DAY OF St Edbert, St Evodius of Antioch, St John Before the Latin Gate and St Petronax.

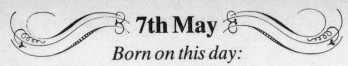

7th May

Born on this day:

Richard O'Sullivan, actor, 1944;
Peter Carey, author, 1943;
Robin Hanbury-Tennison, explorer and author, 1936;
Dr Tony O'Reilly, chairman and chief executive, H. J. Heinz, and rugby player, 1936;
Teresa Brewer, US film actress and singer, 1931;
Ruth Prawer Jhabvala, author, 1927;
Elizabeth Söderström, soprano, 1927;
Maj.-Gen. Henry Woods, 1924;
Anne Baxter, US film actress, 1923;
Lord Briggs, historian, 1921;
Maria Eva Duarte Perón [Ibarguren], Argentinian leader, 1919;
David Tomlinson, actor, 1917;
Scobie Breasley, jockey, 1915;
David Leach, potter, 1911;
Gary [Frank James] Cooper, US film actor, 1901;
Kitty Godfree, tennis player, 1896;
Josip Broz Tito, president of Yugoslavia, 1892;
Alfred Edward Woodley Mason, novelist, 1865;
Rabindranath Tagore, Indian poet, 1861;
Peter Ilyich Tchaikovsky, Russian composer, 1840;
Johannes Brahms, German composer, 1833;
Robert Browning, poet, 1812;
David Hume, philosopher and historian, 1711.

Died on this day:

Dawn Addams, actress, 1985;
John Masters, novelist, 1983;
Paul Felix Weingartner, Austrian composer and conductor, 1942;
Sir James George Frazer, anthropologist, author of *The Golden Bough*, 1941;
George Lansbury, leader of the Labour party, 1940;
Paul Doumer, French president, assassinated by the Russian Paul Gorgoulov, 1932;
William Hesketh Lever, 1st Viscount Leverhulme, soap millionaire, 1925;
James Nasmyth, engineer and inventor of the steam hammer, 1890.

Occurred on this day:

The first London performance of the musical *La Cage aux Folles* was presented, 1986;
The Vietminh captured Dien Bien Phu from the French, 1954;
Germany surrendered unconditionally to the Allies, 1945;
The qualifying age of women voters was reduced from 30 to 21 [the 'Flappers' Vote'], 1928;
The Cunard liner *Lusitania* was sunk by a German submarine, with a total of 1,198 lives lost, 1915;
The Battle of Spotsylvania began during the American Civil War, 1864;
The Battle of Vicksburg began during the American Civil War, 1863;
Greece was proclaimed an independent kingdom, 1832;
HMS *Victory*, Nelson's flagship, was launched at Chatham, 1765;
The first Theatre Royal, Drury Lane, opened in London, 1663.

TODAY IS THE FEAST DAY OF St Domitian of Maestricht, St John of Beverley, St Letard or Liudhard and Saints Serenicus and Serenus.

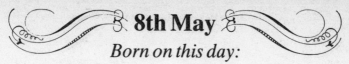

8th May

Born on this day:

Gary Wilmot, entertainer, 1956;

Felicity Lott, soprano, 1947;

Gary Glitter, rock performer, 1944;

Norman Lamont, MP, government minister, 1942;

Peter Benchley, author, 1940;

Air Marshal Sir Michael Simmons, deputy Controller Aircraft, Ministry of Defence, 1937;

Jack Charlton, football manager, 1935;

Heather Harper, soprano, 1930;

Sir David Attenborough, broadcaster and naturalist, 1926;

Lord Jauncey of Tullichettle, a Lord of Appeal in Ordinary, 1925;

The Rt. Rev. Graham Leonard, Bishop of London, 1921;

John Snagge, BBC commentator, 1904;

Friedrich August von Hayek CH, economist, 1899;

Edmund Wilson, US novelist, playwright and poet, 1895;

Harry S. Truman, 33rd president of the USA, 1884;

Nevil Vincent Sidgwick, chemist, 1873;

John Meade Falkner, novelist, 1858;

Jean-Henri Dunant, Swiss founder of the Red Cross, 1828.

Died on this day:

Emanuel, Baron Shinwell, statesman, 1986;

Harry Gordon Selfridge, founder of the store, 1947;

Dame Ethel Mary Smyth, composer and suffragist, 1944;

Oswald Spengler, German philosopher, 1936;

Eadweard Muybridge [Edward James Muggeridge], photographer and inventor, 1904;

Eugène-Henri-Paul Gauguin, French post-impressionist painter, 1903;

Gustave Flaubert, French novelist, 1880;

John Stuart Mill, political economist, 1873;

José de Madrazo y Kuntz, Spanish painter, 1859;

Antoine-Laurent Lavoisier, French chemist, guillotined, 1794.

Occurred on this day:

John Osborne's play *Look Back in Anger* was first performed, Royal Court Theatre, London, 1956;

The Battle of Cassino, Italy, ended, 1944;

The Battle of the Coral Sea ended, 1942;

The first London performance of the operetta *The Land of Smiles* was presented, 1931;

Mount Pelée on Martinique erupted, destroying the city of St Pierre and killing 30,000 people, 1902;

The US forces defeated the Mexicans at the Battle of Palo Alto, 1846;

The British monarchy was restored, 1660;

The Act of Uniformity was signed by Queen Elizabeth I, 1559.

TODAY IS THE FEAST DAY OF St Acacius or Agathus, St Benedict II, pope, St Boniface IV, pope, St Desideratus or Désiré of Bourges, St Gibrian, St Otger, St Peter of Tarentaise, St Plechelm, St Victor Maurus and St Wiro.

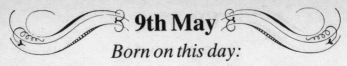

9th May

Born on this day:

Patrick Ryecart, actor, 1952;
Matthew Kelly, actor and TV presenter, 1950;
Billy Joel, singer, 1949;
Candice Bergen, US actress, 1946;
Terry Downes, boxer, 1936;
Albert Finney, actor and director, 1936;
Glenda Jackson, MP and actress, 1936;
Alan Bennett, actor and playwright, 1934;
Gavin Lyall, author, 1932;
Geraldine McEwan, actress, 1932;
Joan Sims, actress, 1930;
Pancho Gonzales, tennis player, 1928;
Sheila Burrell, actress, 1922;
Richard Adams, author, 1920;
Arthur English, actor and comedian, 1919;

John Arnatt, actor, 1917;
Dr Douglas Guest, organist, 1916;
Dr Bernard Rose, organist, 1916;
Frank Chacksfield, arranger and orchestra leader, 1914;
Carlo Maria Giulini, conductor, 1914;
Lilian Mary Baylis, manager of the Old Vic and Sadlers Wells theatres, 1874;
Howard Carter, painter and Egyptologist, 1873;
Sir James Matthew Barrie, novelist and playwright, 1860;
John Brown, US abolitionist, 1800;
Abraham van Diepenbeeck, Dutch painter, 1596.

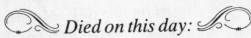

Died on this day:

Edmond O'Brien, US actor, 1985;
James Jones, US author, 1977;
Louis II, Prince of Monaco, 1949;
Joseph Mallaby Dent, publisher, 1926;
Helena Petrovna Blavatsky, Russian occultist and a founder of the Theosophical Society, 1891;

Louis-Joseph Gay-Lussac, French chemist and physicist, 1850;
Johann Christoph Friedrich von Schiller, German poet and playwright, 1805;
William Bradford, governor of Plymouth Colony, Massachusetts, 1657.

Occurred on this day:

Impeachment proceedings against President Nixon were opened in the USA, 1974;
Britain's first launderette opened in Queensway, London, 1949;
Prince Rainier III became chief of state of Monaco, 1949;
Victor Emmanuel III, King of Italy, abdicated, 1946;
Piccadilly Circus was first lit by electricity, 1932;

The North Pole was flown over for the first time by Richard E. Byrd and Floyd Bennett, 1926;
Colonel Thomas Blood, Irish adventurer, attempted to steal the Crown Jewels, 1671;
Christopher Columbus began his fourth voyage, 1502;
Lincoln Cathedral was consecrated, 1092.

TODAY IS THE FEAST DAY OF St Beatus of Lungern, St Beatus of Vendôme, St Gerontius of Cervia and St Pachomius.

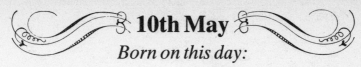

10th May

Born on this day:

Maureen Lipman, actress, 1946;
Sir Michael Mustill, a Lord Justice of Appeal, 1931;
June Knox-Mawer, radio presenter, 1930;
Monica Dickens, author, 1915;
Sir Denis Thatcher, 1915;
Sir Edward Gardner QC, 1912;
Brigadier Dame Margot Turner, former matron-in-chief, Army Nursing Service, 1910;
David Oliver Selznick, US film producer, 1902;
Fred Astaire [Frederick Austerlitz], US dancer and actor, 1899;
Dimitri Tiomkin, US composer, 1894;
Maximilian [Max] Raoul Steiner, Austrian/US film composer, 1888;

Karl Barth, Swiss theologian and author, 1886;
Sir Thomas Johnstone Lipton, millionaire grocer and sportsman, 1850;
Benito Pérez Galdós, Spanish novelist and playwright, 1843;
James, 1st Viscount Bryce, historian and statesman, 1838;
John Wilkes Booth, US actor and assassin of Abraham Lincoln, 1838;
Augustin-Jean Fresnel, French physicist, 1788;
Claude-Joseph Rouget de Lisle, French soldier, author and musician, composer of the *Marseillaise*, 1760;
Jean-Marie Leclair, French composer, 1697.

Died on this day:

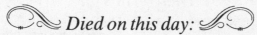

John Cameron Andrieu Bingham Morton ['Beachcomber'], humorous writer, 1979;
Joan Crawford [Lucille Le Sueur], US film actress, 1977;
Sir Henry Morton Stanley, journalist and explorer, 1904;
Thomas Jonathan 'Stonewall' Jackson, Confederate general, 1863;
Katsushuka Hokusai, Japanese artist, 1849;

Thomas Young, physicist and decipherer of Egyptian hieroglyphics, 1829;
Paul Revere, American hero, 1818;
George Vancouver, navigator, 1798;
Louis XV, King of France, 1774;
Leonhard Fuchs, German physician and botanist, 1566;
Gaius Julius Verus Maximinus the Thracian, Roman emperor, murdered, 238.

Occurred on this day:

The House of Commons was destroyed during the heaviest air raid on London, 1941;
Rudolf Hess, Hitler's deputy, flew to Scotland and made a parachute landing near Glasgow, 1941;
Germany invaded the Netherlands, Luxembourg and Belgium, starting the Battle of Flanders, 1940;
The Local Defence Volunteers [LDV], later called the Home Guard, was formed, 1940;
Nearly a hundred bombs were dropped on Southend-on-Sea by a Zeppelin, 1915;

Mother's Day was first celebrated in Philadelphia, in the United States, by the suffragist and temperance worker Anna May Jarvis, 1908;
The first US transcontinental railway was completed when the Central Pacific and Union Pacific railways linked up, 1869;
The Indian Mutiny began with a revolt of Sepoys at Meerut, 1857;
Warren Hastings was impeached in Parliament by Edmund Burke, 1787.

TODAY IS THE FEAST DAY OF St Alphius, St Antoninus of Florence, St Calepodius, St Cataldus or Cathal, St Conleth or Conlaed, St Epimarchus, St Gordian, St John of Avila and St Solange.

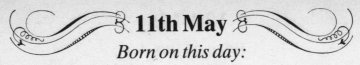

11th May

Born on this day:

Natasha Richardson, actress, 1963;

Mike Sleman, rugby player, 1951;

Jeremy Paxman, TV presenter and reporter, 1950;

Lady Rachel Billington, writer, 1942;

Eric Burdon, rock musician, 1941;

Ian Redpath, Australian cricketer, 1941;

Doug McClure, US film actor, 1935;

Mort Sahl, US comedian, 1927;

Prof. Antony Hewish, radio astronomer, 1926;

Dr Rhodes Boyson, MP, 1925;

The Hon. Montague Woodhouse, historian, 1917;

Mikhail Alexandrovich Sholokhov, Russian novelist, 1905;

Dame Margaret Rutherford, actress, 1892;

Paul Nash, painter, 1889;

Irving Berlin [Israel Isadore Baline], 1888;

George Grossmith the Younger, actor, 1874;

Charles John Cutcliffe Wright Hyne, novelist, 1865;

Ottmar Mergenthaler, German inventor of the Linotype machine, 1854;

The original Siamese twins [of Chinese parentage], Chang and Eng, 1811;

Reginald Pole, Archbishop of Canterbury, 1500.

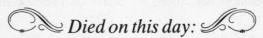

Died on this day:

Harold Adrian Russell 'Kim' Philby, spy for the USSR, 1988;

Chester Gould, US cartoonist, 1985;

Barbara Hutton, US heiress, 1979;

Frederic William Goudy, US typographer and printer, 1947;

Sir John Frederick Herschel, astronomer, 1871;

François-Eugène Vidocq, French adventurer and detective, 1857;

Tom Cribb, pugilist, 1848;

Spencer Perceval, prime minister, assassinated in the House of Commons by John Bellingham, 1812;

William Pitt, 1st Earl of Chatham, statesman, 1778;

Catharine Cockburn, playwright and author, 1749;

Otto von Guericke, German physicist, 1686;

Matteo Ricci, Jesuit missionary in China, 1610;

Sir Edward Dyer, poet, buried, 1607.

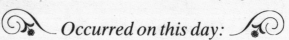

Occurred on this day:

The musical show *Cats* was first produced, London, 1981;

The *Daily Sketch* newspaper appeared for the last time, 1971;

The liner *France* was launched at St Nazaire, 1960;

Siam changed its name to Thailand, 1949;

The Kingsway Theatre, London, closed, 1941;

The New York World's Fair re-opened, 1940;

The first London performance of the operetta *Princess Caprice* was presented, 1912;

The musical play *Box and Cox* was first performed, London, 1867;

Minnesota became the 32nd of the United States, 1858;

The French army was victorious against the Allies [Austria, England and Holland] at the Battle of Fontenoy, 1745;

Constantinople was dedicated as the new capital of the Roman Empire, 330.

TODAY IS THE FEAST DAY OF St Ansfrid, St Asaph, St Comgall, St Francis di Girolamo, St Gengulf or Gengoul, St Ignatius of Laconi, St Mayeul or Majolus, St Mamertus, St Richard Reynolds, St Tudy or Tudec of Brittany and St Walter of L'Esterp.

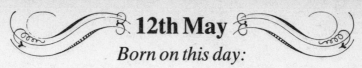

12th May

Born on this day:

Colin Dowdeswell, tennis player, 1955;
Steve Winwood, singer and songwriter, 1948;
Alan Ball, football manager, 1945;
Nicky Henson, actor, 1945;
Chris Patten, Governor of Hong Kong, 1944;
Susan Hampshire, actress, 1942;
Dr Miriam Stoppard, writer and broadcaster, 1937;
Burt Bacharach, US composer, 1929;
The Rt. Rev. Hugh Montefiore, former Bishop of Birmingham, 1920;
Thorley Walters, actor, 1913;
Dorothy Hodgkin OM, chemist, 1910;
Leslie Charteris, novelist and creator of 'The Saint', 1907;
Wilfrid Hyde White, actor, 1903;
Sir Francis Meynell, book designer, publisher and poet, 1891;
Lincoln Ellsworth, US aviator and polar explorer, 1880;
Lord Aberconway [Charles Benjamin Bright McLaren], politician, 1850;
Gabriel-Urbain Fauré, French composer, 1845;
Jules-Émile-Frédéric Massenet, French composer, 1842;
Dante Gabriel Rossetti, poet and and Pre-Raphaelite painter, 1828;
Florence Nightingale, pioneer of nursing, 1820;
Edward Lear, artist, humorist and versifier, 1812;
Justus, Baron von Liebig, German chemist, discoverer of chloroform, 1803;
Emma [Lyon], Lady Hamilton, mistress of Lord Nelson, 1765.

Died on this day:

Elisabeth Bergner, film actress, 1986;
John Edward Masefield, poet, 1967;
Erich von Stroheim [Erich Oswald Stroheim], film actor and director, 1957;
Louis Calhern [Carl Henry Vogt], US actor, 1956;
Sir John Alexander Hammerton, editor and critic, 1949;
Józef Clemens Piłsudski, Polish statesman, 1935;
Amy Lowell, US poet, 1925;
Joris Karl Huysmans, French writer, 1907;
Bedřich Smetana, Czech composer, 1884;
Sir Charles Barry, architect, 1860;
Thomas Wentworth, 1st Earl of Strafford, statesman, executed, 1641;
Pope Silvester II, 1003.

Occurred on this day:

The blockade of Berlin by the USSR was lifted, although other disputes caused the airlift to continue, 1949;
The complete surrender of the Germans in Tunisia was effected, 1943;
The coronation of King George VI and Queen Elizabeth took place, 1937;
The Lindbergh baby, kidnapped on 1st March, was found dead, 1932;
The General Strike in Britain collapsed, 1926;
Captain Amundsen crossed the North Pole in the airship Norge, 1926;
Horatio Bottomley began publishing John Bull, 1906;
The French were defeated at Oporto by General Sir Arthur Wellesley [later Duke of Wellington], 1809;
During the American War of Independence, Charleston fell to the British, 1780.

TODAY IS THE FEAST DAY OF St Dominic of the Causeway, St Epiphanius of Salamis, St Ethelhard, St Germanus of Constantinople, St John Stone, St Modoaldus, Saints Nereus and Achilleus, St Pancras of Rome and St Rictrudis.

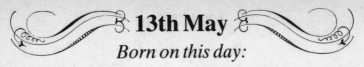

13th May

Born on this day:

Selina Scott, TV presenter, 1951;
Stevie Wonder, singer, 1950;
Dr Jane Glover, conductor, 1949;
Zoë Wanamaker, actress, 1949;
David Hughes, cricketer, 1947;
Tim Pigott-Smith, actor, 1946;
Joe Brown, actor and singer, 1941;
Eileen Diss, theatrical designer, 1931;
Clive Barnes, drama critic, *New York Post*, 1927;
Beatrice Arthur, US film actress, 1926;
Sir John Habakkuk, former principal, Jesus College, Oxford, 1915;
Joe Louis [Joseph Louis Barrow], US heavyweight boxing champion, 1914;
Sir Laurence Kirwan, archaeologist, 1907;

Dame Daphne du Maurier [Lady Browning], author, 1907;
Georges Braque, French cubist painter, 1882;
Sir Frank [François Guillaume] Brangwyn, artist, 1867;
Sir Ronald Ross, physician and bacteriologist, 1857;
Sir Arthur Seymour Sullivan, composer, 1842;
Alphonse Daudet, French novelist, 1840;
Josephine Elizabeth Butler, social reformer, 1828;
Maria Theresa, Queen of Hungary and Bohemia, 1717;
Dante [Durante] Alighieri, Italian poet, 1265.

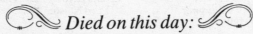

Died on this day:

Gary [Frank James] Cooper, US film actor, 1961;
Frances Mary Hodgkins, New Zealand painter, 1947;
Sir William Gurney Benham, editor and newspaper proprietor, 1944;
Fridtjof Nansen, Norwegian Arctic explorer, 1930;
Alfred, 1st Viscount Milner, statesman, 1925;

Sholem Aleichem [Solomon J. Rabinowitz], US Yiddish writer, 1916;
Alexander Buchan, Scottish meteorologist, 1907;
Juliana Horatia Ewing, writer of children's books, 1885;
Cyrus Hall McCormick, US inventor, 1884;
John Nash, architect, planner of Regent's Park and Regent Street, 1835;
Georges, Baron Cuvier, French zoologist and statesman, 1832.

Occurred on this day:

In Algeria, rioting by French settlers led to the French Army seizing power, 1958;
German and Italian forces in Africa surrendered, 1943;
Igor Sikorsky test-flew a very large airliner, 1931;
An aboriginal team of Australian cricketers arrived in England and played 47 matches, 1868;
The United States declared war on Mexico, 1846;

The Presidency of Quito became the Republic of Ecuador, 1830;
After Captain John Smith and his party landed, the first permanent English settlement was made at Jamestown, Virginia, 1607;
Mary Queen of Scots was defeated during the rebellion at the Battle of Langside [Glasgow], 1568.

TODAY IS THE FEAST DAY OF St Andrew Hubert Fournet, St Erconwald, St Euthymius the Enlightener, St Glyceria of Heraclea, St John the Silent, St Mucius or Mocius, St Peter Regalatus, St Servatius or Servais and St Solomon.

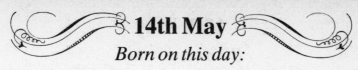

14th May

Born on this day:

Peter Kirsten, South African cricketer, 1955;
Bob Woolmer, cricketer, 1949;
Francesca Annis, actress, 1945;
Chay Blyth, yachtsman, 1940;
Siân Phillips, actress, 1934;
Patricia Turner, trade union leader, 1927;
Denis Cannan, playwright, 1919;
Phil Drabble, TV commentator, 1914;
Dr Hastings Kamuzu Banda, president of Malawi, 1905;
Otto Klemperer, German conductor, 1885;
Sir Thomas Henry Hall Caine, novelist, 1853;
Sir Squire Bancroft, actor and manager, 1841;
Johann Peter Emilius Hartmann, Danish composer and organist, 1805;
Robert Owen, social reformer, 1771;
Timothy Dwight, US scholar and poet, 1752;
Thomas Gainsborough, painter, baptised, 1727;
Johann Philipp Förtsch, German physician, composer and singer, 1652;
Marguerite de Valois, Queen of Navarre, 1553;
Charles IV, Holy Roman Emperor, 1316.

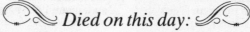

Died on this day:

Jean Rhys [Williams], novelist, 1979;
Sir William Dobell, Australian painter, 1970;
Billie Burke [Mary William Ethelbert Appleton Burke], US actress, 1970;
Edmund Henry Hynman Allenby, 1st Viscount Allenby of Megiddo, field marshal, 1936;
David Belasco, US playwright and producer, 1931;
Sir Henry Rider Haggard, novelist, 1925;
Henry John Heinz, US food manufacturer, 1919;
James Gordon Bennett, US newspaper proprietor, 1918;
August Strindberg, Swedish playwright, 1912;
Matthew Gregory Lewis ['Monk Lewis'], novelist and playwright, 1818;
Louis XIII, King of France, 1643;
Henry IV, King of France, assassinated by the religious fanatic François Ravaillac, 1610.

Occurred on this day:

The first performance of the musical *Chess* was presented, London, 1986;
The Warsaw Pact was signed by the USSR, Albania, Bulgaria, Czechoslovakia, Hungary, Poland, Romania and East Germany, 1955;
The first British-made Cinemascope film, *Knights of the Round Table*, was shown at the Empire cinema, Leicester Square, London, 1954;
In Palestine, the British mandate ended and Israel was proclaimed an independent state, 1948;
The centre of Rotterdam was destroyed by German bombing, 1940;
The BBC's last programme from the Savoy Hill Studio in London was broadcast, 1932;
In Italy, 29 members of the Fascist Party were elected, 1921;
The first London production of the musical comedy *The Prince of Pilsen* was staged, 1904;
The *Illustrated London News* was first issued, 1842;
Paraguay proclaimed her independence, 1811;
Edward Jenner was successful in his first public vaccination experiment, 1796;
Louis XIV became King of France at the age of four, 1643;
The English barons were victorious against Henry III at the Battle of Lewes, 1264.

TODAY IS THE FEAST DAY OF St Carthage the Younger, St Erembert, St Mary Mazzarello, St Matthias, St Michael Garicoïts and St Pontius of Cimiez.

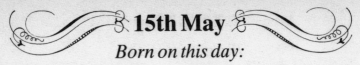

15th May

Born on this day:

Mike Oldfield, composer and guitarist, 1953;

Brian Eno, rock musician, 1948;

Neil Stacey, actor, 1941;

Ralph Steadman, cartoonist, 1936;

Ted Dexter, chairman, England Cricket Selectors Committee, 1935;

Michael Browning, actor, 1930;

Anthony Shaffer, playwright, 1926;

Peter Shaffer, playwright, 1926;

Richard Hough, author, 1922;

Barbara Lott, actress, 1920;

Constance Cummings, actress, 1910;

James Mason, actor, 1909;

Joseph Cotten, US actor, 1905;

Mikhail Afanasyevich Bulgakov, Russian playwright and novelist, 1891;

Katherine Anne Porter, US author, 1890;

Edwin Muir, Scottish poet and translator, 1887;

Arthur Schnitzler, Austrian playwright and novelist, 1862;

Pierre Curie, French physicist, 1859;

Lyman Frank Baum, US author of *The Wizard of Oz*, 1856;

Clarence Edward Dutton, US geologist, 1841;

Michael William Balfe, composer, 1808;

Klemens Weazel Lothar, Prince Metternich-Winneburg, Austrian statesman, 1773;

Carlo Cignani, Italian painter, 1628.

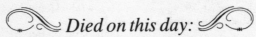

Died on this day:

Rita Hayworth [Margarita Carmen Cansino], US film actress, 1987;

Sir Robert Menzies, former prime minister of Australia, 1978;

Herbert Wilcox, film producer, 1977;

Philip, Viscount Snowden, statesman, 1937;

William John Locke, novelist, 1930;

Étienne-Jules Marey, French motion-picture pioneer, 1904;

Joseph Whitaker, publisher and founder of *Whitaker's Almanack*, 1895;

Emily Elizabeth Dickinson, US poet, 1886;

Daniel O'Connell, Irish leader, 1847;

Edmund Kean, actor, 1833;

Ephraim Chambers, encyclopaedist, 1740.

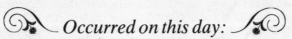

Occurred on this day:

Edith Cresson became the first woman prime minister of France, 1991;

A British nuclear bomb was exploded at Christmas Island, in the central Pacific, 1957;

The Vienna Treaty was signed by Britain, France, the USA and the USSR, restoring Austria as an independent nation, 1955;

The Gloster-Whittle E.28/39 turbojet flew for the first time, 1941;

The first London production of the musical show *Music Box Revue* was presented, 1923;

General Henri Pétain became French commander-in-chief, 1917;

Giuseppe Garibaldi defeated the Neapolitan army at the Battle of Calatafimi, 1860;

The Theatre Royal Covent Garden [Royal Opera House] third theatre was opened, 1858;

The Ashmolean Museum, Oxford [named after Elias Ashmole], was founded, 1679.

TODAY IS THE FEAST DAY OF Saints Bertha and Rupert, St Dymphna, St Gerebernus, St Hallvard, St Hilary of Galeata, St Isaias of Rostov, St Isidore of Chios, St Isidore the Farmer, St Peter of Lampsacus and St Torquatus and his Companions.

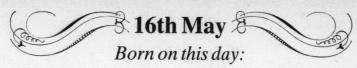

16th May

Born on this day:

Janet Maw, actress, 1954;

Pierce Brosnan, Irish film actor, 1951;

Roy Hudd, comedian, 1936;

Prof. Peter Levi, poet and archaeologist, 1931;

Maj.-Gen. Sir Desmond Langley, Governor of Bermuda, 1930;

Martine Carol [Maryse Mourer], French actress, 1922;

Richard Mason, author, 1919;

Liberace [Wladsiu Valentino], US pianist and entertainer, 1919;

Geraint Jones, conductor and organist, 1917;

Bernard Braden, broadcaster, 1916;

Woody [Woodrow Charles] Herman, US jazz clarinettist and bandleader, 1913;

Studs Terkel, US writer and interviewer, 1912;

Herbert Ernest Bates, novelist, 1905;

Henry Fonda, US film actor, 1905;

Richard Tauber [Ernst Seiffert], Austrian tenor and conductor, 1892;

Philip Danforth Armour, US food industrialist, 1832;

David Edward Hughes, inventor of the microphone and teleprinter, 1831;

Elizabeth Palmer Peabody, US educationist, 1804;

John Sell Cotman, water-colour artist, 1782;

John Opie, artist, 1761.

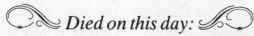

Died on this day:

Irwin Shaw, US author, 1984;

Randolph Turpin, boxer, shot dead in his home, 1966;

James Agee, US author and screenwriter, 1955;

Max Brand [Frederick Schiller Faust], US Western author, 1944;

Bronislaw Kasper Malinowski, anthropologist, 1942;

Stephen Fairbairn, Australian oarsman and coach, 1938;

Lilli Lehmann, German soprano, 1929;

Sir Edmund William Gosse, poet and author, 1928;

Edward Augustus Freeman, historian, 1892;

Felicia Dorothea Hemans, poet and hymn-writer, 1835;

Daniel Charles Solander, botanist, 1782;

Charles Perrault, French author and fairy-tale writer, 1703;

Pietro da Cortona, Florentine painter and architect, 1669.

Occurred on this day:

Queen Elizabeth become the first British monarch to address the US Congress, 1991;

The Soviet spacecraft *Venus 5* touched down on Venus, 1969;

An earthquake in Northern Japan killed 47 and injured 217, 1968;

A 'bouncing bomb' invented by Dr Barnes Wallis was dropped on the large Möhne and Eder dams in the Ruhr, Germany, 1943;

The first Academy Awards for films ceremony was held in Hollywood, best actor and actress being Emil Jannings and Janet Gaynor, 1929;

The German Zeppelin *Deutschland* was wrecked at Düsseldorf, 1911;

The world's first electric tram went into public service, Lichterfelde, near Berlin, 1881;

The Kentucky Derby was first run at Louisville, Kentucky, 1875;

During the Peninsular War, the French were defeated by the Allies at Albuera, 1811.

TODAY IS THE FEAST DAY OF St Brendan, St Carantoc or Carannog, St Domnolus of Le Mans, St Germerius or Germier, St Honoratus of Amiens, St John Nepomucen, St Peregrinus of Auxerre, St Possidius, St Simon Stock and St Ubaldus of Gubbio.

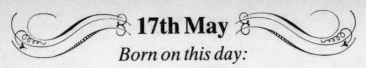

17th May

Born on this day:

Sue Carpenter, TV presenter and journalist, 1956;

Sugar Ray Leonard, US boxing champion, 1956;

John Iles, actor, 1954;

Bhagwat Chandrasekhar, Indian cricketer, 1945;

Dennis Potter, playwright, 1935;

Prof. Donald Cameron Watt, historian, 1928;

Marshal of the RAF Sir Michael Beetham, chairman, GEC Avionics, 1923;

Peter Mennin, US composer, 1923;

Birgit Nilsson, Swedish operatic soprano, 1918;

Lieut.-Gen. Sir Douglas Packard, 1903;

Henri Barbusse, French editor and novelist, 1873;

Dorothy Miller Richardson, novelist, 1873;

Erik Alfred Leslie Satie, French composer, 1866;

Sir Joseph Norman Lockyer, astronomer, 1836;

Charlotte Helen Sainton-Dolby, contralto and composer, 1821;

Robert Smith Surtees, novelist, 1803;

Anna Brownell Jameson, author, 1794;

Johann Friedrich Hugo, Reichsfreiherr von Dalberg, German composer and pianist, 1752;

Edward Jenner, surgeon and discoverer of vaccination, 1749.

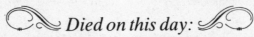

Died on this day:

Margaret Hamilton, US actress, 1985;

John Selwyn Brooke Selwyn-Lloyd, Baron, former Speaker of the House of Commons, 1978;

Nigel Marlin Balchin, novelist, 1970;

Paul Abraham Dukas, French composer, 1935;

Lydia Estes Pinkham, US patent-medicine manufacturer, 1883;

Charles-Maurice de Talleyrand-Périgord, French statesman, 1838;

Catherine I, Empress of Russia, 1727;

Cornelis de Heem, Dutch painter, 1695;

Matthew Parker, Archbishop of Canterbury, 1575;

Sandro Botticelli [Alessandro di Mariano dei Filipepi], Italian painter, 1510.

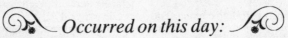

Occurred on this day:

Germany invaded France, 1940;

The first London production of the operetta *The Marriage Market* was presented, 1913;

Mafeking, under siege by the Boers, was relieved by Colonel Plumer, 1900;

The foundation stone of the Victoria and Albert Museum was laid by Queen Victoria, 1899;

The first regular weekly comic paper, *Comic Cuts*, was issued by Alfred Harmsworth [later Lord Northcliffe], 1890;

Mascagni's opera *Cavalleria Rusticana* was first performed, Rome, 1890;

The Revised Version of the New Testament was issued, 1881;

Frederick the Great, Emperor of Prussia, was victorious against the Austrians at the Battles of Czaslau and Chotusitz, 1742;

Louis Joliet and Jacques Marquette set out to explore the Mississippi, 1673.

TODAY IS THE FEAST DAY OF St Bruno of Würzburg, St Madron or Madern and St Paschal Baylon.

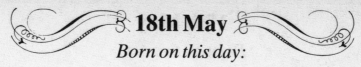

18th May

Born on this day:

Toyah Willcox, singer and actress, 1958;
Rodger Davis, golfer, 1951;
Rick Wakeman, rock keyboard player and composer, 1949;
Brian Fletcher, former jockey, 1947;
Miriam Charles, fashion designer, 1942;
Norbert 'Nobby' Stiles, footballer, 1942;
Prof. Malcolm Longair, Astronomer Royal for Scotland, 1941;
Miriam Margolyes, actress, 1941;
Ray Lonen, actor, 1939;
Lord St John of Fawsley, author, barrister and former MP, 1929;
His Holiness the Pope, John Paul II, 1920;
Boris Christoff, bass opera singer, 1914;
Richard Brooks, US film director, 1912;
Perry Como, US singer, 1912;
Fred Perry, tennis champion, 1909;
Rodney Ackland [Bernstein], playwright, 1908;
Norman Hepple, painter, 1908;
Frank Capra, writer and film director, 1897;
Walter Adolph Gropius, US architect, 1883;
Bertrand Arthur William Russell, 3rd Earl, philosopher, 1872;
Nicholas II, Tsar of Russia, 1868;
William Heinemann, publisher, 1863;
Oliver Heaviside, physicist, 1850;
Kawanabe Kyosai, Japanese painter, 1831.

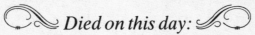

Died on this day:

William Saroyan, US author, 1981;
James Truslow Adams, US historian, 1949;
John Nevil Maskelyne, stage magician, 1917;
Gustav Mahler, Austrian composer, 1911;
George Meredith, novelist, 1909;
Isaac Manuel Francisco Albéniz, Spanish pianist and composer, 1909;
Pierre-Augustin Caron de Beaumarchais, French playwright, 1799;
Elias Ashmole, antiquarian, 1692;
Rupert, King of Germany, 1410.

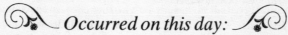

Occurred on this day:

In Washington State, USA, Mount St Helens erupted in a blast 500 times more powerful than the Hiroshima atom bomb, 1980;
The first London production of the musical show *The Sound of Music* was presented, 1961;
The European Convention of Human Rights came into force, 1954;
Monte Cassino, Italy, was captured by the Allies, 1944;
The first Mount Everest reconnaissance party started, led by Colonel Howard Bury, 1921;
Tonga was proclaimed a British protectorate, 1900;
The present Eddystone Lighthouse was opened, 1882;
Don Carlos abdicated his rights to the Spanish crown in favour of his son, 1845;
Napoleon was proclaimed Emperor of France, 1804;
Montreal [Ville Marie] in Canada was founded, 1642;
King Henry II, married Eleanor of Aquitaine, 1152.

TODAY IS THE FEAST DAY OF St Elgiva, St Eric, King of Sweden, St Felix of Cantalicio, St John I, pope, St Potamon and Saints Theodotus and Thecusa.

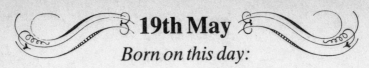

19th May

Born on this day:

Victoria Wood, writer and comedienne, 1953;

Paul Moriarty, actor, 1946;

Pete Townshend, guitarist and singer, 1945;

Robert Kilroy-Silk, TV presenter, 1942;

James Fox, actor, 1939;

Dr Edward de Bono, lateral thinker, 1933;

Mel Calman, cartoonist, artist and writer, 1931;

Air Chief Marshal Sir Thomas Kennedy, 1928;

David Jacobs, radio and TV presenter, 1926;

Sandy Wilson, composer and playwright, 1924;

Leslie Sands, actor and playwright, 1921;

Dr Max Perutz OM CH, molecular biologist, 1914;

Noel Mander, organ maker, 1912;

Bruce Bennett [Herman Brix], US film actor, 1909;

Ho Chi Minh, Vietnamese leader, 1890;

William Waldorf Astor, 2nd Viscount, 1879;

Viscountess Astor [Nancy Witcher], 1879;

Dame Nellie Melba [Helen Porter Mitchell], Australian singer, 1861;

Jacob Jordaens, Belgian painter, 1593.

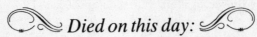

Died on this day:

Sir John Betjeman, Poet Laureate, 1984;

Frederic Ogden Nash, US writer and humorist, 1971;

Horatio Nicholls [Lawrence Wright], composer and publisher, 1964;

Ronald Colman, film actor, 1958;

Charles Edward Ives, US composer, 1954;

Newton Booth Tarkington, US novelist, 1946;

Thomas Edward Lawrence, explorer and author, accidentally killed, 1935;

William Ewart Gladstone, statesman, 1898;

José Julián Martí y Pérez, Cuban poet and patriot, 1895;

Nathaniel Hawthorne, US novelist, 1864;

James Boswell, biographer of Dr Johnson, 1795;

Karl Wilhelm Scheele, Swedish chemist, 1786;

Ann Boleyn, 2nd wife of Henry VIII, executed, 1536;

Alcuin, Anglo-Latin poet and scholar, 804.

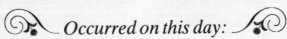

Occurred on this day:

The first London production of the musical show *Music in the Air* was presented, 1933;

The Simplon Tunnel was officially opened, 1906;

The Tonga Islands were annexed by Britain, 1900;

William Hamilton, an Irish bricklayer, fired a pistol charged with powder at Queen Victoria, 1849;

The Légion d'Honneur was instituted by Napoleon, 1802;

The Spaniards were defeated by the French at the Battle of Rocroi, 1643;

The Spanish Armada set sail from Lisbon, 1588.

TODAY IS THE FEAST DAY OF Saints Calocerus and Parthenius, St Crispin of Viterbo, St Dunstan, St Ivo of Kermartin, St Peter Morrone and St Pudens.

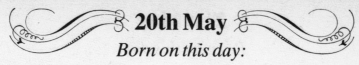

20th May

Born on this day:

Keith Fletcher, cricketer, 1944;
Deryck Murray, former West Indies cricketer, 1943;
Lynn Davies, long jump athlete, 1942;
Peter Shore, MP, 1924;
General Sir Hugh Beach, 1923;
Flight Lieut. John Cruickshank VC, banker, 1920;
Prof. Richard Cobb, historian, 1917;
The Rev. Prof. Owen Chadwick OM, chancellor, University of East Anglia, 1916;
Peter Copley, actor, 1915;
Moshe Dayan, Israeli military commander, 1915;
Prof. Henry Cadbury-Brown, architect, 1913;

James Stewart, US film actor, 1908;
Margery Allingham, detective story writer, 1904;
Sigrid Undset, Norwegian novelist, 1882;
Wladyslaw Sikorski, Polish statesman, 1881;
William George Fargo, a founder of Wells Fargo, 1818;
John Stuart Mill, political economist, 1806;
Honoré de Balzac, French novelist, 1799;
Pietro Bembo, Venetian cardinal and theologian, 1470;
Sir Henry Percy [Harry Hotspur], soldier and politician, 1364.

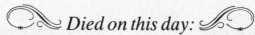

Died on this day:

Dame Jocelyn Barbara Hepworth, sculptor, 1975;
Sir Max [Henry Maximilian] Beerbohm, caricaturist and writer, 1956;
André Eugene Maurice Charlot, theatrical manager and actor, 1956;
Clara Josephine Schumann, German pianist, 1896;
William Chambers, author and publisher, 1883;

John Clare, farmer and poet, 1864;
Mary Lamb, writer, 1847;
The Rev. Joseph [José Maria] Blanco White, theological writer, 1841;
Marie-Joseph-Paul-Yves-Roch-Gilbert du Motier, Marquis de Lafayette, French nobleman and soldier, 1834;
Christopher Columbus, Genoese explorer and navigator, 1506.

Occurred on this day:

The first US hydrogen bomb was dropped over Bikini Atoll, 1956;
Germany launched an aerial invasion of Crete, landing 7,000 parachute troops from gliders, 1941;
Pan American Airways began regular flights between the USA and Europe, 1939;
Amelia Earhart was the first woman to make a solo crossing of the Atlantic, 1932;
Charles A. Lindbergh began his first non-stop solo transatlantic flight, New York to Paris in 37 hours, 1927;
The P & O liner *Egypt* sank after a collision off Ushant with the loss of 87 lives, 1922;

The foundation stone of the Royal Albert Hall was laid, 1867;
York Minster was badly damaged following a fire, 1840;
Napoleon defeated the Allies at the Battle of Bautzen, 1813;
The Mecklenburg declaration of independence was adopted at Charlotte, North Carolina, 1775;
Ascension Island was discovered by the Portuguese navigator, João da Nova Castell, 1501;
Vasco da Gama, Portuguese navigator, arrived at Calicut, India, 1498;
The Earl of Pembroke defeated the French at the Battle [or Fair] of Lincoln, 1217.

TODAY IS THE FEAST DAY OF St Austregisilus or Outrill, St Basilla or Basilissa, St Baudelius, St Bernardino of Siena, St Ethelbert and Saints Thalelaeus, Asterius, Alexander and Others.

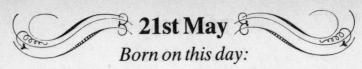

21st May

Born on this day:

Andrew Neil, editor of the *Sunday Times*, 1949;

Rosalind Plowright, soprano, 1949;

Leo Sayer, pop singer and songwriter, 1948;

David Hunt, MP, Secretary of State for Wales, 1942;

Terry Lightfoot, bandleader and jazz musician, 1935;

Desmond Wilcox, radio and TV presenter, 1931;

Malcolm Fraser CH, former prime minister of Australia, 1930;

Prof. Stanley Wells, Shakespearean scholar, 1930;

Raymond Burr, US film actor, 1917;

Leonard Manasseh, architect, 1916;

Harold Robbins, US novelist, 1916;

Thomas Wright [Fats] Waller, US songwriter and pianist, 1904;

Glenn Hammond Curtiss, US aviation pioneer, 1878;

Émile Verhaeren, Belgian poet, 1855;

Henri Rousseau, French primitive painter, 1844;

Elizabeth Fry [Gurney], prison reformer, 1780;

Francis Egerton, 3rd Duke of Bridgewater, canal pioneer, 1736;

Alexander Pope, poet and satirist, 1688;

Philip II, King of Spain, 1527;

Albrecht Dürer, German painter and engraver, 1471.

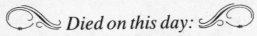

Died on this day:

Joan Sanderson, actress, 1992;

Dino Grandi, Conte de Mordano, Italian politician, 1988;

Kenneth Mackenzie Clark, Baron, art historian, 1983;

Jane Addams, US sociologist, 1935;

Hugo de Vries, Dutch geneticist, 1935;

Ronald Arthur Annesley Firbank, novelist, 1926;

Franz von Suppé [Francesco Suppé Demelli], Austrian composer, 1895;

Prince Paul Anton von Galanthea Esterhazy, Austrian diplomat, 1866;

Robert Harley, 1st Earl of Oxford, statesman, 1724;

Hieronymus Fabricius, Italian physician, 1619;

Hernando de Soto, soldier and explorer, 1542;

King Henry VI, murdered, 1471.

Occurred on this day:

Charles A. Lindbergh reached Paris at the end of his flight across the Atlantic, 1927;

Summer Time [daylight saving] was begun in Britain, 1916;

The Manchester Ship Canal was officially opened, 1894;

Leoncavallo's opera *I Pagliacci* was first performed, Milan, 1892;

During the American Civil War, the Battle of Spotsylvania ended, 1864;

Gold was discovered in Australia, 1851;

Captain William Hobson proclaimed British sovereignty over the whole of New Zealand, 1840;

The Standard newspaper was first published, 1827;

Napoleon was defeated by the Austrians at the Battle of Aspern-Essling, 1809;

St Helena was discovered by the Portuguese navigator, João da Nova Castell, 1502.

TODAY IS THE FEAST DAY OF St Andrew Bobola, St Godfric and St Theophilus of Corte.

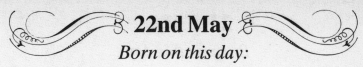

22nd May

Born on this day:

Paul Mariner, footballer, 1953;
Cheryl Campbell, actress, 1949;
Anthony Holden, journalist and
broadcaster, 1947;
George Best, former footballer, 1946;
Richard Benjamin, US film and TV actor,
1938;
Jean Challis, radio presenter, 1934;
Kenny Ball, jazz trumpeter, 1930;
Charles Aznavour, French singer, 1924;
Sir Edwin Leather, writer and broadcaster,
former governor of Bermuda, 1919;
Hew Lorimer, sculptor, 1907;
Laurence Kerr Olivier, Baron, actor and
director, 1907;
Thomas Edward Neil Driberg, 1st Baron,
politician and journalist, 1905;

Giacomo Matteotti, Italian politician,
1885;
Sir Ernest Oppenheimer, South African
mining magnate, 1880;
Daniel François Malan, South African
politician, 1874;
Sir Arthur Conan Doyle, novelist, 1859;
Félix-Joseph-Auguste Bracquemond,
French painter and engraver,
1833;
Wilhelm Richard Wagner, German
composer, 1813;
Gérard de Nerval [Gérard Labrunie],
French poet and writer, 1808;
William Sturgeon, electrical engineer,
1783;
Hubert Robert, French painter, 1733.

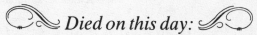

Died on this day:

Rajiv Gandhi, former Indian prime
minister, assassinated, 1991;
Cecil Day Lewis, poet and author, 1972;
James Langston Hughes, US poet, 1967;
Augusta, Lady Gregory, poet, playwright
and theatre director, 1932;
Sir John Denton Pinkstone French, 1st Earl
of Ypres, soldier, 1925;
Victor-Marie Hugo, French author, 1885;

Alessandro Francesco Manzoni, Italian
poet, 1873;
Jacques-Nicolas-Augustin Thierry, French
historian, 1856;
Maria Edgeworth, Irish novelist, 1849;
Francesco Guicciardini, Florentine
historian and diplomat, 1540;
Constantine the Great, Roman emperor,
337.

Occurred on this day:

Ceylon changed its named to Sri Lanka and
became a republic, 1972;
An earthquake lasting 20 seconds destroyed
the small town of Bingol, in Turkey,
where over 1,000 people died,
1972;
The Battle of Anzio started, 1944;
The first London production of the musical
show *Going Up* was presented,
1918;
The Strand Theatre, London, opened,
1905;

The Blackwall Tunnel under the Thames
was officially opened, 1897;
The US vessel *Savannah*, powered by steam
and sail, crossed the Atlantic from West
to East, 1819;
The title 'baronet' was created when James I
ennobled 18 men, 1611;
The Lancastrians defeated the Yorkists at
the Battle of St Albans, 1455;
Louis VIII, King of France, invaded
England, landing at Stonor, 1216.

TODAY IS THE FEAST DAY OF St Aigulf of Ayoul or Bourges, Saints Castus and
Aemilius, St Helen of Caernarvon, St Humility, St Joachima de Mas, St Julia of Corsica, St
Quiteria, St Rita [Margarita] of Cascia and St Romanus.

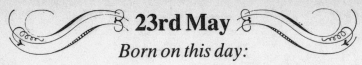

23rd May

Born on this day:

Anatoly Karpov, chess player, 1951;
Peter Preston, editor of the *Guardian*, 1938;
Joan Collins, actress, 1933;
Rosemary Clooney, US singer, 1928;
Nigel Davenport, actor and trade unionist, 1928;
Desmond Carrington, actor and radio presenter, 1926;
Humphrey Lyttelton, jazz musician, 1921;
Betty Garrett, US film actress, 1919;
Denis Compton, author and former cricketer, 1918;
Jean Françaix, French composer, 1912;
Marius Goring, actor, 1912;
Sir Hugh Casson CH, architect, 1910;
Artie Shaw, US clarinettist and bandleader, 1909;

Air Chief Marshal Sir Hugh Constantine, 1908;
Edmund Rubbra, composer, 1901.
Pär Fabian Lagerkvist, Sweden novelist and poet, 1891;
Herbert Marshall, film actor, 1890;
Douglas Fairbanks [Douglas Elton Thomas Ulman], US film actor, 1883;
Otto Lilienthal, German pioneer aviator, 1848;
Thomas Hood, poet and humorist, 1799;
Sir Charles Barry, architect, 1795;
Franz Anton Mesmer, German physician, 1734;
William Hunter, obstetrician and medical writer, 1718;
Carolus Linnaeus, Swedish botanist, 1707;
Elias Ashmole, antiquarian, 1617.

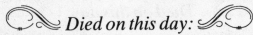

Died on this day:

Jimmy [James Francis] McHugh, US popular composer [*I Can't Give You Anything But Love*], 1969;
Heinrich Himmler, Nazi leader, committed suicide, 1945;
Lord Austin [Herbert Austin], motor manufacturer, 1941;
John Davison Rockefeller, US industrialist and philanthropist, 1937;
Bonnie Parker and Clyde Barrow, US outlaws, killed in ambush, 1934;

Henrik Johan Ibsen, playwright, 1906;
Kit Carson, US frontiersman, 1881;
Leopold von Ranke, German historian, 1881;
Captain William Kidd, naval officer, pirate and murderer, hanged in London, 1701;
Girolamo Savonarola, Florentine priest and reformer, strangled and burnt at the stake, 1498.

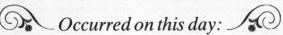

Occurred on this day:

The George Cross decoration was inaugurated, 1939;
Whipsnade Zoo was opened at Whipsnade, Beds, 1931;
Marlborough defeated the French at the Battle of Ramillies, 1706;

King Henry VIII was divorced from Catherine of Aragon, 1533;
Joan of Arc was taken prisoner by the English, 1430.

TODAY IS THE FEAST DAY OF St Aldhelm, St Desiderius of Vienne, St Euphrosyne of Polotsk, St Guibert, St Ivo of Chartres, St John Baptist dei Rossi, St Leontius of Rostov and St William of Rochester.

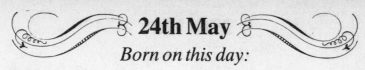

24th May

Born on this day:

Bob Dylan, US singer, 1941;

Sir Christopher Staughton, a Lord Justice of Appeal, 1933;

Sir James Anderton, chief constable of Greater Manchester, 1932;

Arnold Wesker, playwright, 1932;

Stanley Baxter, comedian, 1928;

William Trevor, writer, 1928;

Mai Zetterling, Swedish film actress and director, 1925;

The Duke of Bedford, 1917;

Sir Roden Cutler VC, diplomat, 1916;

Dame Joan Hammond, soprano, 1912;

George Formby [William Hoy Booth], singer and comedian, 1904.

Suzanne Lenglen, French tennis player, 1899;

Kathleen Hale, children's author and illustrator, 1898;

Jan Christiaan Smuts, South African soldier and statesman, 1870;

Sir Arthur Wing Pinero, playwright, 1855;

Admiral Prince Louis Mountbatten, 1854;

Robert Bontine Cunninghame Graham, author and politician, 1852;

Sir Ernest Albert Waterlow, water-colour painter, 1850;

Queen Victoria, Empress of India, 1819;

Gabriel Daniel Fahrenheit, German inventor of the mercury thermometer, 1686;

Philip Wouwerman, Dutch painter, 1619.

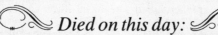

Died on this day:

Hamish Hamilton, publisher, 1988;

Hermione Ferdinanda Gingold, actress, 1987;

Jack Warner [Waters], film actor and variety artiste, 1981;

Edward Kennedy ['Duke'] Ellington, US musician, 1974;

Bernard Rogers, US composer, 1968;

John Foster Dulles, US statesman, 1959;

Robert Cecil, 1st Earl of Salisbury, statesman, 1612;

Nicolaus Copernicus, Polish astronomer, 1543;

David I, King of Scots, 1153.

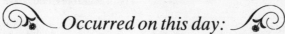

Occurred on this day:

The battleship HMS *Hood* was sunk by the *Bismarck* off Greenland, 1941;

The first London performance of the operetta *Casanova* was staged, 1932;

Amy Johnson landed at Port Darwin after flying from London, 1930;

Conscription began in Britain, 1916;

Empire Day was first celebrated in Britain, 1902;

Henry Irving became the first theatrical knight, 1895;

Brooklyn Bridge, New York, was opened, 1883;

Westminster Bridge across the Thames was opened, 1862;

Dartmoor Prison was opened to house French prisoners of war, 1809;

Malcolm IV became King of Scotland, 1153.

TODAY IS THE FEAST DAY OF St David I of Scotland, Saints Donatian and Rogatian, St Nicetas of Pereaslav and St Vincent of Lerins.

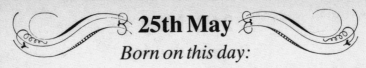

25th May

Born on this day:

David Jenkins, athlete, 1952;
Baroness Hooper, 1939;
Sir Ian McKellen, actor, 1939;
Margaret Forster, novelist and biographer, 1938;
Beverley Sills, operatic soprano, 1929;
Miles Davis, US jazz trumpeter, 1926;
David Wynne, sculptor, 1926;
Jeanne Crain, US film actress, 1925;
Livia Gollancz, publisher, 1920;
Claude Akins, US film actor, 1918;
Dillwyn Miles, the Herald Bard, 1916;

Igor Ivan Sikorsky, pioneer Russian/US aircraft designer, and inventor of the helicopter, 1889;
Miles Malleson, actor and director, 1888;
William Maxwell Aitken, 1st Baron Beaverbrook, newspaper proprietor, 1879;
Tom Sayers, bare-knuckle pugilist, 1826;
Ralph Waldo Emerson, US poet and essayist, 1803;
Edward George Earle Lytton Bulwer-Lytton, 1st Baron Lytton, novelist, 1803;
Carlo Dolci, Italian painter, 1616.

Died on this day:

Sydney Box, film producer, 1983;
Robert Capa, US war photographer, killed in Vietnam, 1954;
Jacques Feyder, French film director, 1948;
Joseph, 1st Baron Duveen of Millbank, art dealer, 1939;
Gustav Theodore Holst, composer, 1934;
Marie-Rosalie Bonheur, French artist, 1899;
Thomas Duncan, Scottish painter, 1845;

John Joseph William Molesworth Oxley, naval officer and explorer of Australia, 1828;
Marie-Madeleine Pioche de la Vergne, Comtesse de La Fayette, French author, 1693;
Pedro Calderón de la Barca, Spanish playwright and poet, 1681;
Gaspard [Doughet] Poussin, French painter, 1675;
Pope Gregory VII, 1085;
The Venerable Bede, 735.

Occurred on this day:

The new Coventry Cathedral, designed by Sir Basil Spence, was consecrated, 1962;
The Battle of Anzio ended, 1944;
Jesse Owens, US black athlete, broke five world records at the Olympic Games in Berlin, 1936;
Transjordan [now the Kingdom of Jordan] became independent, 1923;
The second Battle of Ypres ended, 1915;
The British House of Commons passed the Irish Home Rule Act, 1914;

Oscar Slater [who later proved to be innocent] was sentenced to life imprisonment for murder, 1909;
Gilbert and Sullivan's opera *HMS Pinafore* was first produced in London, 1878;
Lloyd's insurance society received a Royal Charter, 1871;
Kelly's Theatre [later the Royalty] opened in London, 1840;
Captain Cook sailed on his first voyage, 1768.

TODAY IS THE FEAST DAY OF St Bede, St Dionysius of Milan, St Gennadius of Astorga, St Gregory VII, pope, St Leo or Lye of Mantenay, St Madeleine Sophie Barat, St Mary Magdalen dei Pazzi and St Zenobius.

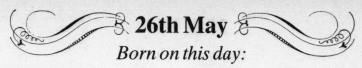

26th May

Born on this day:

Helena Bonham-Carter, actress, 1966;
Zola Budd, athlete, 1966;
Michael Portillo, MP, government minister, 1953;
Sir David English, editor of the *Daily Mail*, 1931;
Jacques Bergerac, French film actor, 1927;
Roy Dotrice, actor, 1925;
Alec McCowen, actor, 1925;
James Arness, US film actor, 1923;
Stan Mortensen, former footballer, 1921;
Peggy Lee, US singer, 1920;
Peter Cushing, actor, 1913;
Sir Matt Busby, football manager and president, 1909;
Robert Morley, actor, 1908;
John Wayne [Marion Michael Morrison], US film actor, 1907;
Sir Eugene Aynesley Goossens, composer, 1893;
Al Jolson [Asa Yoelson], US singer and entertainer, 1886;
Henry Farman, French aircraft designer, 1874;
Princess Mary of Teck [Queen Mary, consort of King George V], 1867;
Edmond-Louis-Antoine Huot de Goncourt, French novelist, 1822;
John Churchill, 1st Duke of Marlborough, military commander, 1650;
Charles, Duc d'Orléans, French poet, 1391.

Died on this day:

George Brent [George Brendan Nolan], US film actor, 1979;
Jacques Lipchitz, French sculptor and poet, 1973;
Victor Herbert, US composer, 1924;
Ernest Solvay, Belgian industrial chemist, 1922;
Charles Horace Mayo, US surgeon, 1922;
Jean-Joseph-Benjamin Constant, French painter, 1902;
John Curwen, music educator, 1880;
Samuel Pepys, diarist, 1703;
St Augustine, 1st Archbishop of Canterbury, 604.

Occurred on this day:

An Icelandic gunboat shelled and holed a British trawler, 1973;
Guyana became independent, 1966;
In South Africa, a Nationalist government was elected with apartheid policies, 1948;
Emily Duncan, the first woman magistrate in Britain, was appointed, 1913;
Vauxhall Bridge, London, was opened, 1906;
Mount Etna in Sicily started a series of violent eruptions, 1870;
Michael Barrett, Fenian terrorist, was hanged for causing an explosion and 13 deaths, this being Britain's last public execution, 1868;
The Confederate Army surrendered in Texas, so ending the American Civil War, 1865;
Napoleon Bonaparte was crowned King of Italy in Milan Cathedral, 1805;
The Battle of Tara was fought, 1798.

TODAY IS THE FEAST DAY OF St Lambert of Venice, St Mariana of Quito, St Philip Neri, St Priscus or Prix of Auxerre and St Quadratus of Athens.

27th May

Born on this day:

Pat Cash, tennis player, 1965;
Duncan Goodhew, swimmer, 1957;
John Conteh, boxer, 1951;
Cilla Black, singer, 1943;
Admiral Sir Benjamin Bathurst, Vice Chief
of the Defence Staff, 1936;
Jeffrey Bernard, writer, 1932;
Gen. Sir John Chapple, Chief of the
General Staff, 1931;
Thea Musgrave, composer, 1928;
Dr Henry Kissinger, US statesman, 1923;
Christopher Lee, actor, 1922;
Herman Wouk, US novelist, 1915;
The Rt. Rev. Mervyn Stockwood, former
Bishop of Southwark, 1913;
Sam Snead, golfer, 1912;

Vincent Price, US film actor, 1911;
Sir John Douglas Cockcroft, physicist,
1897;
Samuel Dashiell Hammett, US detective
story writer, 1894;
Isadora Duncan, US dancer, 1878;
Enoch Arnold Bennett, novelist,
1867;
James Butler 'Wild Bill' Hickok, US
frontier scout, 1837;
Amelia Jenks Bloomer, US women's rights
campaigner, 1818;
Jacques-François-Fromental-Élie Halévy
[Élie Lévy], French composer, 1799;
Sir Francis Beaufort, admiral and
hydrographer, 1774.

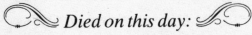 Died on this day:

Jawalharlal Nehru, Indian statesman, 1964;
Field Marshal Sir Thomas Blamey,
Australian soldier, 1951;
Sir Joseph Wilson Swan, physicist and
chemist, 1914;

Robert Koch, German bacteriologist, 1910;
Joseph Bosworth, lexicographer and
scholar, 1876;
Niccolò Paganini, Italian violinist, 1840;
John Calvin, Swiss theologian, 1564.

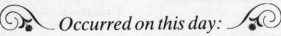 Occurred on this day:

The European Defence Community was set
up, 1952;
The German battleship *Bismarck* was sunk,
1941;
The Golden Gate Bridge, San Francisco,
opened, 1937;
The Cunard liner *Queen Mary* sailed on her
maiden voyage from Southampton to
New York, 1936;

The third Battle of Aisne started, 1918;
The trial of William Palmer, doctor and
poisoner, ended with a verdict of guilty,
1856;
St Petersburg [Leningrad] was founded by
Peter the Great, 1703;
The Habeas Corpus Act was passed,
1679.

TODAY IS THE FEAST DAY OF St Augustine of Canterbury, St Eutropius of Orange,
St Julius of Durostorum, St Melangel or Monacella and St Restituta of Sora.

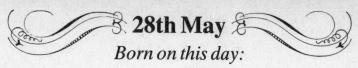

28th May

Born on this day:

Sue Holderness, actress, 1949;
Liz Edgar, showjumper, 1943;
The Dionne Quintuplets, Cecilie, Yvonne, Annette, Émilie and Marie, 1934;
Carroll Baker, US film actress, 1932;
Julian Slade, composer, 1930;
Dietrich Fischer-Dieskau, German baritone, 1925;
Sir Edward du Cann, chairman of Lonrho, 1924;
Lord Rippon QC, former government minister, 1924;
Prof. György Ligeti, composer, 1923;
Frank Middlemass, actor, 1919;
Thora Hird, actress, 1916;
Wolfgang Schneiderhan, German violinist, 1915;

Rachel Kempson, actress, 1910;
Prof. Stuart Piggott, archaeologist, 1910;
Ian Lancaster Fleming, author and creator of 'James Bond', 1908;
Brigadier Dame Mary Railton, former director, WRAC, 1906;
Eduard Beneš, Czech statesman, 1884;
Jean-Louis-Rodolphe Agassiz, Swiss/US naturalist, 1807;
Thomas Moore, Irish poet and musician, 1779;
William Pitt the Younger, statesman, 1759;
Joseph-Ignace Guillotin, French physician and politician, 1738.

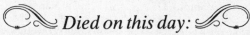

Died on this day:

Eric Morecambe [Eric Bartholomew], comedian, 1984;
Edward, Duke of Windsor, 1972;
Alfred Adler, Austrian psychiatrist, 1937;
Sir John Lubbock, 1st Baron Avebury, banker and author, 1913;
Sir George Grove, engineer and first director of the Royal College of Music, 1900;

John Russell, 1st Earl Russell, statesman, 1878;
Anne Brontë ['Acton Bell'], novelist, 1849;
Noah Webster, US lexicographer, 1843;
Jan van der Meer [Jan Vermeer van Haarlem the Younger], Dutch painter, buried, 1705;
Lanfranc, Archbishop of Canterbury, 1089.

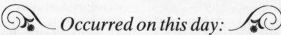

Occurred on this day:

The first London production of the musical show *Lock Up Your Daughters* was presented, 1959;
The first London production of the musical show *Guys and Dolls* was presented, 1953;
The Belgian Army surrendered to the Germans, 1940;
The Battle of Narvik started, 1940;

Neville Chamberlain became prime minister, 1937;
The Zuider Zee became an inland lake [as the Ijsselmeer] after the dyke was built connecting North Holland with Friesland, 1932;
Hernando de Soto landed in Florida, 1539.

TODAY IS THE FEAST DAY OF St Germanus of Paris, St Ignatius of Rostov, St Justus of Urgel, St Senator of Milan and St William of Gellone.

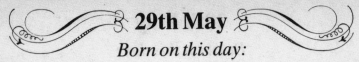

29th May

Born on this day:

Rupert Everett, actor, 1959;
Michael Berkeley, composer and broadcaster, 1948;
Linda Esther Gray, opera singer, 1948;
Douglas Scott, mountaineer, 1941;
Nanette Newman, actress and writer, 1939;
Alwin Schockemöhle, showjumper, 1935;
Iannis Xenakis, Greek/French composer, architect and engineer, 1922;
John Fitzgerald Kennedy, 35th president of the USA, 1917;
Carl Toms, stage designer, 1928;
Sir Bernard Waley-Cohen, former Lord Mayor of London, 1914;
Terence Hanbury White, novelist, 1906;
Prof. Robert Knox, bacteriologist, 1905;
Sebastian Shaw, actor, 1905;
Bob Hope, US actor and comedian, 1903;
Joseph von Sternberg, US film director, 1894;
Oswald Spengler, German philosopher, 1880;
Gilbert Keith Chesterton, author, 1874;
Isaac Manuel Francisco Albéniz, Spanish composer, 1860;
Patrick Henry, US orator and statesman, 1736;
King Charles II, 1630.

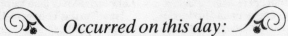

Died on this day:

Mary Pickford [Gladys Mary Smith], US film actress, 1979;
Juan Ramón Jiménez, Spanish poet, 1956;
Fanny Brice [Fannie Borach], US comedienne, 1951;
John Barrymore [Blythe], US actor, 1942;
Sir William Schwenck Gilbert, librettist and playwright, 1911;
John Lothrop Motley, diplomat and historian, 1877;
Sir Humphry Davy, scientist and inventor of the miner's safety lamp, 1829;
Henry Dundas, 1st Viscount Melville, statesman, 1811.

Occurred on this day:

The first London production of the musical show *Gypsy* was presented, 1973;
Charles de Gaulle formed a government of national safety in France, 1959;
Sir Edmund Hillary and Sherpa Tenzing reached the summit of Mount Everest, 1953;
The evacuation from Dunkirk began, 1940;
The French liner *Normandie* left Le Havre on her maiden voyage to New York, via Southampton, 1935;
Wisconsin became the 30th of the United States, 1848;
Rhode Island became the 13th of the United States, 1790;
Constantinople fell to the Turks, 1453.

TODAY IS THE FEAST DAY OF St Bernard of Montjoux or Menthon, St Cyril of Caesarea, St Maximinus of Trier, Saints Sisinnius, Martyrius and Alexander, St Theodosia of Constantinople and Saints William, Stephen, Raymund and their Companions.

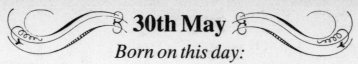

30th May

Born on this day:

Bob Willis, cricketer, 1949;
Norman Eshley, actor, 1945;
Peter Ellis, actor, 1936;
Ray Cooney, theatrical producer, 1932;
Clint Walker, US film actor, 1927;
Mikhail Alexandrovich Bakunin, Russian anarchist, 1814;
Julian Symons, author, 1912;
Benny [Benjamin David] Goodman, US bandleader and clarinettist, 1909;
Lord Zuckerman OM, chairman, British Industrial Biological Research Association, 1904;
Prof. Seton Lloyd, archaeologist, 1902;
Howard Hawks, US film director, 1896;
Alexander Porfirevich Archipenko, US sculptor and painter, 1887;
Pierre-Marie-Félix Janet, French psychologist, 1859;
Peter Carl [Karl Gustavovich] Fabergé, Russian goldsmith, 1846;
Alfred Austin, poet, 1835.

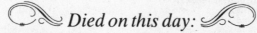

Died on this day:

Marcel Dupré, French organist and composer, 1971;
Claude Rains, film actor, 1967;
Boris Leonidovich Pasternak, Russian poet and author, 1960;
Hermann Broch, Austrian poet and novelist, 1951;
Wilbur Wright, US pioneer aviator, 1912;
Voltaire [François-Marie Arouet], French philosopher and writer, 1778;
François Boucher, French painter, 1770;
Alexander Pope, poet and satirist, 1744;
Pierre Mignard le Romain, French painter, 1695;
Sir Peter Paul Rubens, Flemish painter, 1640;
Christopher Marlowe, playwright, killed in a brawl, 1593;
Joan of Arc, burnt at the stake at Rouen, 1431.

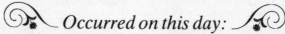

Occurred on this day:

The first London production of the musical show *Little Me* was presented, 1984;
The first London production of the musical show *On the Town* was presented, 1963;
The first hovercraft flight took place at Cowes, Isle of Wight, 1959;
The Balkan War was ended by the Treaty of London, which created the new state of Albania, 1913;
Smetana's opera *The Bartered Bride* was first performed in Prague, 1866;
Napoleon annexed Tuscany, 1808;
The Grenadier Guards were formed, 1656;
King Henry VIII was married to Jane Seymour, 1536;
Christopher Columbus set sail on his third voyage, 1498.

TODAY IS THE FEAST DAY OF St Exuperantius of Ravenna, St Ferdinand of Castile, St Isaac of Constantinople, St Joan of Arc, St Luke Kirby, St Madelgisilus or Maugeille and St Walstan.

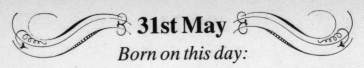

31st May

Born on this day:

Lynda Bellingham, actress, 1948;

Terry Waite, Anglican emissary, 1939;

John Prescott, MP, 1938;

Sir Michael Turner, High Court judge, 1931;

Clint Eastwood, US film actor, 1930;

Derek Birley, vice-chancellor, University of Ulster, 1926;

HSH Prince Rainier III of Monaco, 1923;

Denholm Elliott, actor, 1922;

Judith Wright, Australian author and poet, 1915;

Don Ameche, US film actor, 1908;

Air Marshal Sir Valston Hancock, 1907;

Florence Desmond, actress, 1905;

Helen Waddell, poet and scholar, 1889;

William Heath Robinson, illustrator, 1872;

Sir Francis Edward Younghusband, explorer, 1863;

Walter Richard Sickert, painter, 1860;

Pope Pius XI [Achille Ratti], 1857;

William Worrall Mayo, US physician, 1819;

Walt Whitman, US author and poet, 1819;

Alexander Cruden, compiler of the *Concordance of the Holy Scriptures*, 1701.

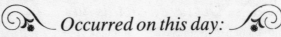

Died on this day:

Jack Dempsey, US heavyweight boxer, 1983;

Adolf Eichmann, Nazi war criminal, hanged, 1962;

Reinhard Heydrich, Nazi 'protector' of Bohemia and Moravia, assassinated, 1942;

John White Alexander, US painter, 1915;

Elizabeth Blackwell, US physician [the first woman doctor], 1910;

George Green, mathematician and physicist, 1841;

Joseph Grimaldi, comic actor and clown, 1837;

William Smith, abolitionist and emancipator, 1835;

Franz Joseph Haydn, Austrian composer, 1809;

Tintoretto [Jacopo Robusti], Italian painter, 1594.

Occurred on this day:

The Union of South Africa became a republic, 1961;

The Volga-Don Canal was opened, 1952;

In Germany, the Gothic, or Black Letter printing type, was officially abandoned in favour of the Roman character, 1941;

The Daily Chronicle and the *Daily News* ceased separate publication and became the *News Chronicle*, 1930;

The naval Battle of Jutland began, 1916;

The White Star liner *Titanic* was launched at Belfast, 1911;

The Peace of Vereeniging brought the end of the Boer War, 1902;

Rossini's opera *The Thieving Magpie* was first performed, Milan, 1817.

TODAY IS DAY OF THE VISITATION AND THE FEAST DAY OF Saints Cantius, Cantianus, Cantianella and Protus, St Mechtildis of Edelstetten and St Petronilla.

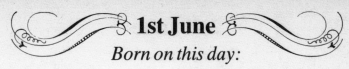

1st June

Born on this day:

Gemma Craven, actress, 1950;
Jonathan Pryce, actor, 1947;
Robert Powell, actor, 1944;
Gerald Scarfe, artist and cartoonist, 1936;
Pat Boone, US film actor, 1934;
Edward Woodward, actor, 1930;
Bob Monkhouse, comedian, 1928;
Marilyn Monroe [Norma Jean Mortenson], US film actress, 1926;
[Beatrice] Joan Caulfield, US film actress, 1922;
Lord Deedes, former editor, the *Daily Telegraph*, 1913;
Air Comdr. Sir Frank Whittle OM, inventor of the jet engine, 1907;
Molly Picon, US actress and comedienne, 1898;
Charles Kay Ogden, linguist and originator of Basic English, 1889;
John Drinkwater, author and playwright, 1882;
John Edward Masefield, poet and novelist, 1878;
William James Stillman, US painter and journalist, 1828;
Otto I, King of Greece, 1815;
Mikhail Ivanovich Glinka, Russian composer, 1803;
Brigham Young, US Mormon leader, 1801;
Nicolas-Léonard-Sadi Carnot, French physicist, 1796;
Henry Francis Lyte, hymn-writer, 1793;
Robert Cecil, 1st Earl of Salisbury, statesman, 1563.

Died on this day:

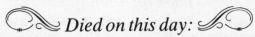

Richard Greene, film actor, 1985;
Eric Honeywood Partridge, lexicographer, 1979;
John Gunther, US journalist, 1970;
Helen Adams Keller, US blind, deaf and mute scholar, 1968;
Ion Antonescu, Romanian dictator, executed for war crimes, 1946;
Sir Hugh Seymour Walpole, novelist, 1941;
Lizzie Borden, alleged US axe murderess, 1927;
Lucien-Germain Guitry, French actor, 1925;
Charles Lever, novelist, 1872;
James Buchanan, 15th president of the USA, 1868;
James Gillray, caricaturist, 1815;
Cornelius Huysmans, Dutch painter, 1727;
Honoré d'Urfe, French author, 1625.

Occurred on this day:

General Charles de Gaulle became prime minister of France, 1958;
The first Premium Savings Bonds were drawn, 1957;
The submarine HMS *Thetis* sank in Liverpool Bay with the loss of 99 lives, 1939;
The Battle of Jutland ended, 1916;
The first Zeppelin air raid took place over Britain, 1915;
The first London performance of the operetta *Gipsy Love* was staged, 1912;
Lunch was served on the first Pullman train on a British railway which ran from St Pancras to Bedford, 1874;
Tennessee became the 16th of the United States, 1796;
Kentucky became the 15th of the United States, 1792.

TODAY IS THE FEAST DAY OF St Candida or Wite, St Caprasius of Lérins, St Inigo or Eneco, St Justin, St Pamphilus of Caesarea, St Proculus the Bishop, St Proculus the Soldier, St Simeon of Syracuse, St Theobald of Alba and St Wistan.

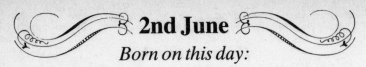

2nd June

Born on this day:

Dave 'Boy' Green, boxer, 1953;
Heather Couper, astronomer and broadcaster, 1949;
Marvin Hamlisch, US composer, 1944;
Stacy Keach, US actor, 1941;
Constantine, King of the Hellenes, 1940;
Sally Kellerman, US film actress, 1937;
The Rt Rev. Richard Harries, Bishop of Oxford, 1936;
Admiral Sir Richard Fitch, 1929;
Leonard Parkin, broadcaster, 1929;
Sir Christopher Slade, a Lord of Appeal, 1927;
Air Marshal Sir Ivor Broom, aerospace consultant, 1920;

Johnny Speight, scriptwriter, 1920;
Prof. Robin Orr, composer, 1909;
[Peter John] Johnny Weissmuller, US swimmer and film 'Tarzan', 1903;
Nubar Sarkis Gulbenkian, millionaire, 1896;
Arthur Stuart Menteth Hutchinson, novelist, 1879;
Sir Edward William Elgar, composer, 1857;
Thomas Hardy, novelist, 1840;
Pope Pius X [Giuseppe Melchiorre Sarto], 1835;
Grace Aguilar, novelist and historian, 1816;
Donatien-Alphonse-François, Marquis de Sade, French writer and libertine, 1740.

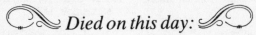

Died on this day:

Sir Rex Carey Harrison, actor, 1990;
Andrés Segovia, Spanish guitarist, 1987;
George Alfred, Baron George-Brown, statesman, 1985;
Vita Mary Sackville-West, writer, 1962;
George Simon Kaufman, US playwright, 1961;
Émile-Auguste Chartier ['Alain'], French philosopher, 1951;
Herman Darewski, composer, 1947;

Sir Redvers Henry Buller VC, general, 1908;
Alexander Nikolaevich Ostrovsky, Russian playwright, 1886;
Giuseppe Garibaldi, Italian nationalist leader, 1882;
Maximilien-Paul-Émile Littré, French lexicographer, 1881;
Madeleine de Scudéry, French poet and novelist, 1701.

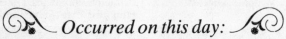

Occurred on this day:

The Coronation of Queen Elizabeth II took place in Westminster Abbey, 1953;
Clothes rationing began, 1941;
Under the terms of the Snyder Act, US-born American Indians became US citizens, 1924;
The world's first patent for wireless telegraphy was granted to Guglielmo Marconi, 1896;

Japan took possession of Formosa [Taiwan] from China, 1895;
President Grover Cleveland of the USA married Frances Folsom at the White House, 1886;
Corfu was occupied by Greek troops, 1864; ·
Lord George Gordon led 'No Popery Riots' in London, 1780.

TODAY IS THE FEAST DAY OF St Attalus, St Erasmus or Elmo, St Eugenius I, pope, Saints Marcellinus and Peter, St Nicholas the Pigrim, St Pothinus and his Companions and St Stephen of Sweden.

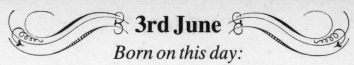

3rd June

Born on this day:

Suzi Quatro, rock singer and actress, 1950;
Penelope Wilton, actress, 1947;
Hale Irwin, US golfer, 1945;
Anita Harris, singer and actress, 1942;
Colin Meads, rugby player, 1936;
Allen Ginsberg, US poet, 1926;
Tony Curtis, US film actor, 1925;
Alain Resnais, French film director, 1922;
Patrick Cargill, actor, 1918;
The Hon. William Douglas-Home, playwright, 1912;
Paulette Goddard [Marion Levy], US film actress, 1911;
Wilfred Thesiger, explorer and writer, 1910;

Adele [Adela Helena] Dixon, actress, 1908;
Paul Rotha, film director and author, 1907;
Josephine Baker, US/French singer, 1906;
Raoul Dufy, French painter, 1877;
King George V, 1865;
Sir William Matthew Flinders Petrie, archaeologist, 1853;
Jefferson Davis, president of the Confederate States of America, 1808;
Richard Cobden, political reformer, 1804;
William Hone, writer and satirist, 1780;
Willem van Mieris, Dutch painter, 1662.

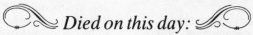

Died on this day:

Robert Morley, actor, 1992;
Dame Anna Neagle [Marjorie Robertson], actress and dancer, 1986;
James Laver, man of letters, 1975;
Arthur Mitchell Ransome, critic and writer of children's books, 1967;
Pope John XXIII [Angelo Giuseppe Roncalli], 1963;
Franz Kafka, Austrian writer, 1924;
Johann Strauss the Younger, Austrian composer and conductor, 1899;

Samuel Plimsoll, politician and social reformer, 1898;
Lionel de Rothschild, banker, 1879;
Georges [Alexandre-César-Léopold] Bizet, French composer, 1875;
Jean-François Millet, Dutch painter, buried, 1679;
William Harvey, exponent of the theory of the circulation of the blood, 1657.

Occurred on this day:

At a French air show, a Russian Tupolev-144 supersonic airliner crashed six miles from Le Bourget, killing 13 people, 1973;
Ed White, the first US astronaut to walk in space, spent 21 minutes outside *Gemini 4*, 1965;
Third-class travel on British Railways was abolished, 1956;
In the United States, the Mount Palomar telescope was dedicated, 1948;

The Battle of Midway Island began, 1942;
The British army was evacuated from Dunkirk, 1940;
The Duke of Windsor married Mrs Wallis Warfield Simpson, 1937;
A great fire at Constantinople [Istanbul] rendered 15,000 people homeless, 1912;
The Dutch were defeated by the English fleet at the Battle of Lowestoft, 1665.

TODAY IS THE FEAST DAY OF St Cecilius, St Charles Lwanga, St Clothilde, St Genesius of Clermont, St Isaac of Cordova, St Joseph Mkasa, St Kevin or Coemgen, St Liphardus and Urbicius, St Lucillian and his Companions, St Morand and Saints Pergentinus and Laurentinus.

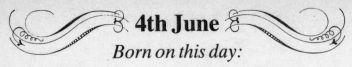

4th June

Born on this day:

Andrea Jaeger, tennis player, 1965;

Tony Pigott, cricketer, 1958;

Bob Champion, trainer and former jockey, 1948;

Daniel Topolski, writer, photographer and coach, 1945;

Geoffrey Palmer, actor, 1927;

Dennis Weaver, US film actor, 1924;

Gene Barry, US film actor, 1922;

Sir Christopher Cockerell, inventor of the hovercraft, 1910;

The Earl of Halsbury, Chancellor, Brunel University, 1908;

Carl Gustav Emil von Mannerheim, Finnish soldier and statesman, 1867;

Nassau William Senior, economist, 1864;

Garnet Joseph, 1st Viscount Wolseley, soldier, 1833;

Sir James Pennethorne, architect, 1801;

John Scott, 1st Earl of Eldon, Lord High Chancellor of England, 1751;

King George III, 1738.

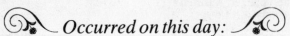

Died on this day:

György Lukacs, Hungarian philosopher, 1971;

Horace Greeley [Hjalmar Schacht], German minister of Economics, 1970;

Dorothy Gish [de Guiche], US film actress, 1968;

Serge Koussevitsky, US conductor, 1951;

Georg Kaiser, German playwright, 1945;

Wilhelm II, former Emperor of Germany, 1941;

Frederick Robert Spofforth, Australian cricketer and 'demon bowler', 1926;

William Halse Rivers Rivers, psychologist and anthropologist, 1922;

Emily Wilding Davidson, suffragette, trampled to death by a horse at the Derby, 1913;

Eugen Adam, German painter, 1880;

William Edward Frost, painter, 1877;

Marguerite, Countess Blessington, Irish woman of letters, 1849;

Nicolai Abraham Abildgaard, Danish painter, 1809;

Giovanni Jacopo Casanova de Seingalt, Italian adventurer and writer, 1798.

Occurred on this day:

Tonga became independent, 1970;

Rome was liberated by the Allies, 1944;

The Order of the British Empire was instituted, 1917;

The French defeated the Austrians at the Battle of Magenta, 1859;

War broke out between Mexico and the USA, 1845;

Leopold, Duke of Kendal [Georges Chrétien Frédéric], was proclaimed first King of the Belgians, 1831;

Mme Thible, a French opera singer, was the first woman to fly in a hot-air balloon, 1784;

Frederick the Great defeated the Austrians and Saxons in the Battle of Hohenfriedberg, Silesia, 1745.

TODAY IS THE FEAST DAY OF St Francis Caracciolo, St Metrophanes, St Optatus of Milevis, St Petroc, St Quirinus of Siscia and St Vincentia Gerosa.

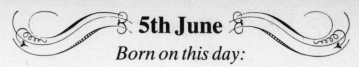

5th June

Born on this day:

David Hare, playwright, 1947;
Chris Finnegan, Olympic boxing champion, 1944;
Nigel Rees, author, 1944;
Moira Anderson, singer, 1940;
Margaret Drabble, novelist, 1939;
A. R. Dawson, Irish rugby player, 1932;
Tony Richardson, film and theatre director, 1928;
Beatrice de Cardi, archaeologist, 1914;
Rose Hill, actress and singer, 1914;
Gilbert Charles Harding, TV personality, 1907;
Margaret Rawlings, actress, 1906;

Prof. Christopher Hawkes, archaeologist, 1905;
Barbara Goolden, novelist, 1900;
Federico García Lorca, Spanish poet and playwright, 1898;
William [Bill] Boyd, US film actor, 1898;
Dame Ivy Compton-Burnett, novelist, 1884;
John Maynard Keynes, 1st Baron, 1883;
Sir Robert Mayer, musical philanthropist, 1879;
Pancho [Francisco] Villa, Mexican revolutionary leader, 1878;
John Couch Adams, astronomer, 1819;
Adam Smith, political economist, 1723.

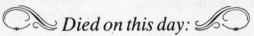

Died on this day:

Harry James, US bandleader, 1983;
Georges-Léon-Jules-Marie Feydeau, French playwright, 1921;
Horatio Herbert, 1st Earl Kitchener of Khartoum, field marshal, lost at sea in HMS *Hampshire*, 1916;
Henri Gaudier-Brzeska, French sculptor, 1915;

O. Henry [William Sydney Porter], US short-story writer, 1910;
Stephen Crane, US novelist and poet, 1900;
John McDonall Stuart, explorer of Australia, 1866;
Orlando Gibbons, composer and organist, 1625;
Louis X, King of France, 1316.

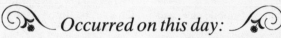

Occurred on this day:

Mikhail Gorbachev received the 1990 Nobel Peace Prize, 1991;
Britain's first referendum was held; it resulted in a two-to-one majority in favour of staying in the Common Market, 1975;
Robert Francis Kennedy, US senator, was shot by an assassin, dying 25 hours later, 1968;
The Six Day War between the Arab states and Israel broke out, 1967;
Ramsay MacDonald formed a minority Labour Government in Britain, 1929;

An Arab revolt against the Turks broke out, 1916;
The cruiser HMS *Hampshire* struck a mine off the Orkneys and sank, 1916;
The Ambassadors Theatre, London, opened, 1913;
Louis Bonaparte became King of Holland, 1806;
The hot-air balloon was first demonstrated by the Montgolfier brothers, 1783.

TODAY IS THE FEAST DAY OF St Boniface of Mainz or Crediton, St Dorotheus of Tyre, St Sanctius or Sancho and St Tudno.

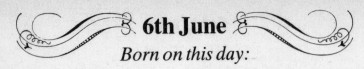

6th June

Born on this day:

Mike Gatting, cricketer, 1958;
Björn Borg, tennis player, 1956;
Marion Mould, show jumper, 1947;
Asif Iqbal, former Pakistan cricket captain, 1943;
Willie-John McBride, rugby player, 1940;
Billie Whitelaw, actress, 1932;
Frank Tyson, former England cricketer, 1930;
Klaus Tennstedt, German conductor, 1926;
Iain Hamilton, composer, 1922;
Lord Carrington CH, chairman, Christie's International, 1919;
Air Marshal Sir Charles Pringle, 1919;
Sir Isaiah Berlin OM, former president, the British Academy, 1909;

Prof. Robert Humphreys, historian, 1907;
Aram Ilich Khatchaturian, Russian composer, 1903;
Dame Ninette de Valois CH, founder of the Royal Ballet, 1898;
Walter Abel, US film actor, 1898;
Robert Cedric Sherriff, playwright and novelist, 1896;
Thomas Mann, German novelist, 1875;
Captain Robert Falcon Scott, Antarctic explorer, 1868;
Sir Henry John Newbolt, poet, 1862;
Aleksander Sergeyevich Pushkin, Russian poet, novelist and playwright, 1799;
Diego Rodríguez de Silva y Velázquez, Spanish painter, baptised, 1599.

Died on this day:

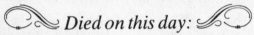

William [Bill] Voce, cricketer, 1984;
Jean Paul Getty, US oil magnate, 1976;
Robert Francis Kennedy, US statesman, assassinated, 1968;
Carl Gustav Jung, Swiss psychiatrist, 1961;
James Evershed Agate, author and journalist, 1947;
Louis Chevrolet, US automobile racer and designer, 1941;

George Grossmith, the Younger, actor and author, 1935;
Count Camillo Benso di Cavour, Italian statesman, 1861;
Jeremy Bentham, philosopher and jurist, 1832;
Patrick Henry, US statesman, 1799;
George, 1st Baron Anson, sailor and explorer, 1762.

Occurred on this day:

Croatia and Slovenia declared themselves to be 'independent and sovereign' republics, 1991;
Eurovision began with a relay networked directly from Montreux, 1954;
The Allied invasion of Normandy took place – D-Day, 1944;
The Battle of Midway Island ended with the defeat of the Japanese, 1942;

The Nazis burned the village of Lidice in Bohemia as a reprisal for the killing of Heydrich, 1942;
Finland declared war on the USSR, 1919;
The Treaty of Badajoz was signed between Spain and Portugal, 1801;
In Oxford, the Ashmolean Museum, founded by Elias Ashmole, was opened, 1683.

TODAY IS THE FEAST DAY OF St Ceratius or Cerase, St Claud of Besançon, St Eustorgius II of Milan, St Gudwal or Gurval, St Jarlath, St Norbert and St Philip the Deacon.

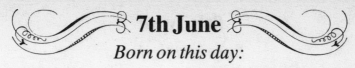

7th June

Born on this day:

Michael Pennington, actor and writer, 1943;
Elizabeth Counsell, actress, 1942;
Jaime Laredo, violinist, 1941;
Alfreda Rose Hodgson, concert singer, 1940;
Tom Jones, singer, 1940;
Ronald Pickup, actor, 1940;
Ann Beach, actress and singer, 1938;
The Very Rev. John A. Simpson, Dean of Canterbury, 1933;
Virginia McKenna, actress, 1931;
James Ivory, US film director, 1928;
Norman Strouse, US popular composer, 1928;

Sir Robert Lusty, publisher, 1909;
Jessica Tandy, film actress, 1909;
Elizabeth Bowen [Elizabeth Dorothea Cole], novelist, 1899;
Sir Landon Ronald, conductor, pianist and composer, 1873;
Ernest William Hornung, novelist, 1866;
Eugène-Henri-Paul Gauguin, French painter, 1848;
Richard Doddridge Blackmore, novelist, 1825;
George Bryan ['Beau'] Brummel, English dandy, 1778;
John Rennie, civil engineer, 1761.

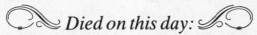

Died on this day:

Elizabeth Josephine Craig, cookery writer, 1980;
Henry Valentine Miller, US novelist, 1980;
Edward Morgan Forster, novelist, 1970;
Dorothy Parker [Rothschild], US poet and journalist, 1967;
Hans Arp, French painter, engraver, sculptor and poet, 1966;
Jean Harlow [Harlean Carpenter], US film actress, 1937;

Theodore Walter Watts-Dunton, poet, literary critic, novelist and solicitor, 1914;
Richard March Hoe, US inventor of the rotary printing press, 1886;
David Cox, landscape painter and water-colourist, 1859;
Robert I [the Bruce], King of Scotland, 1329.

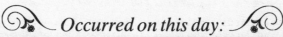

Occurred on this day:

The first London production of the musical show *Carousel* was presented, 1950;
The musical show *Annie Get Your Gun* opened in London, 1947;
Britten's opera *Peter Grimes* was first produced, London, 1945;
The Vatican City was set up in Rome, 1929;
The Battle of Messines was fought, 1917;

The Cunard liner *Lusitania* was launched, 1906;
The French forces occupied Mexico City, 1863;
King Henry VIII and Francis I, King of France, met near Calais at the Field of the Cloth of Gold, 1520;
David II became King of Scotland, 1329.

TODAY IS THE FEAST DAY OF St Antony Gianelli, St Colman of Dromore, St Gottschalk, St Meriadoc or Meriasek, St Paul I of Constantinople, St Robert of Newminster, St Vulflagius or Wulphy and St Willibald.

8th June

Born on this day:

Derek Underwood, cricketer, 1945;
Colin Baker, actor, 1943;
Doug Mountjoy, snooker player, 1942;
Nancy Sinatra, US singer, 1940;
Millicent Martin, actress and singer, 1934;
Ray Illingworth, cricketer, 1932;
Sir Iain Glidewell, a Lord Justice of Appeal, 1924;
Alexis Smith, US film actress, 1921;
Gwen Harwood, Australian poet, 1920;
Tony Mottram, tennis player, 1920;
Robert Preston [Meservey], US film actor, 1918;
Alaric Jacob, author, 1909;

Frank Lloyd Wright, US architect, 1869;
Mary Cholmondeley, novelist, 1859;
Sir John Everett Millais, Pre-Raphaelite painter, 1829;
Sir Samuel White Baker, explorer, 1821;
Charles Reade, novelist, 1814;
Robert Alexander Schumann, German composer, 1810;
Robert Stevenson, civil engineer, 1772;
John Smeaton, civil engineer, 1724;
William Dampier, buccaneer and navigator, baptised, 1652;
Giovanni Domenico Cassini, Italian astronomer, 1625.

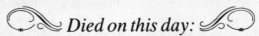

Died on this day:

Sir Norman Hartnell, Royal dressmaker, 1979;
Katharine Cornell, US actress, 1974;
Pamela Frankau, novelist, 1967;
Sir Godfrey Seymour Tearle, actor, 1953;
Gerard Manley Hopkins, poet, 1889;
George Sand [Amandine-Aurore-Lucile Dupin], French writer, 1876;
Sir Joseph Paxton, architect, 1865;

Douglas William Jerrold, playwright and humorist, 1857;
Andrew Jackson, 7th president of the USA, 1845;
Sarah Siddons [Sarah Kemble], actress, 1831;
Thomas Paine, radical author, 1809;
Edward, the Black Prince, 1376;
The Prophet Mohammed, 632.

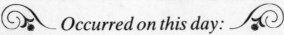

Occurred on this day:

James Earl Ray was arrested in London and charged with the murder of Martin Luther King, 1968;
In Romania, King Carol resumed the throne, 1930;

The second Labour Government, with Ramsay MacDonald as prime minister, took office, 1929;
The first London production of the operetta *The Merry Widow* was presented, 1907.

TODAY IS THE FEAST DAY OF St Cloud of Metz, St Maximinus of Aix, St Medard and St William of York or Thwayt.

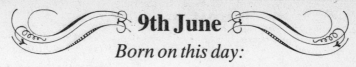

9th June

Born on this day:

David Troughton, actor, 1950;
Charles Saatchi, advertising executive, 1943;
Sir Nicholas Lloyd, editor of the *Daily Express*, 1942;
Michael Mates, MP, Minister of State, Northern Ireland, 1934;
Vice-Admiral Sir Patrick Symons, Supreme Allied Commander Atlantic's Representative in Europe, 1933;
Geraint Gruffydd, Welsh and Celtic language authority, 1928;
Tony Britton, actor, 1924;
Sheila Keith, actress, 1920;
Edgar Evans, tenor, 1912;
Charles Clarence Robert Orville Main Cummings, US film actor, 1910;
Cole Albert Porter, US composer and lyricist, 1893;
E.M. Delafield [Edmée Elizabeth Monica de la Pasture], novelist, 1890;
Elizabeth Garrett Anderson, physician, 1836;
George Stephenson, locomotive designer, 1781;
Georg Friedrich Grotefend, German classical and cuneiform scholar, 1775;
Andrew Ramsay, Scottish writer, 1686;
Peter the Great, Tsar of Russia, 1672;
Leopold I, Holy Roman Emperor, 1640.

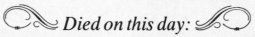

Died on this day:

Dame Sybil Thorndike, actress, 1976;
William Maxwell Aitken, 1st Baron Beaverbrook, 1964;
Ugo Betti, Italian playwright and judge, 1953;
Sir Walter Besant, author and philanthropist, 1901;
Edward Moran, US artist, 1901;
Charles John Huffam Dickens, novelist, 1870;
George Payne Rainsford James, novelist, 1860;
Pope Gregory XVI, 1846;
William Lilly, astrologer and publisher of almanacs, 1681.

Occurred on this day:

In Britain, the proceedings of the House of Commons were broadcast live for the first time, 1975;
The USS *George Washington*, the first ballistic-missile submarine, was launched, 1959;
Charles Kingsford-Smith and Charles Ulm became the first to pilot an aircraft across the Pacific [California to Brisbane, Australia], 1928;
The London Symphony Orchestra gave its first concert, 1904;
Heavyweight boxer James J. Jeffries of the USA beat Bob Fitzsimmons of Great Britain in New York, 1899;
Alsace-Lorraine was annexed to Germany, 1871;
The French defeated the Austrians at the Battle of Montebello Casteggio, 1800;
The first Book of Common Prayer was issued to all dioceses in the Church of England, 1549.

TODAY IS THE FEAST DAY OF St Columba of Iona, St Ephraem, St Pelagia of Antioch, Saints Primus and Felician, St Richard of Andria and St Vincent of Agen.

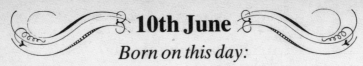

10th June

Born on this day:

Simon Jenkins, journalist and author, 1943;
Guy Harwood, racehorse trainer, 1939;
Graham Carleton Greene, publisher, 1936;
Maurice Sendak, US writer and illustrator, 1928;
June Haver, US film actress, 1927;
Lionel Jeffries, actor, 1926;
Ian Robert Maxwell [Jan Ludvik Hoch], late chairman of the Mirror Group, 1923;
Judy Garland [Frances Ethel Gumm], US singer and actress, 1922;
HRH Prince Philip, Duke of Edinburgh, 1921;
Bill Waddington, actor and comedian, 1916;
Saul Bellow, US author, 1915;
Dr Polly Hill, anthropologist, 1914;
Sir Terence Mervyn Rattigan, playwright, 1911;
Robert Still, composer, 1910;
Robert Eddison, actor, 1908;
Frederick Loewe, US composer, 1901;
Al Dubin, US lyricist, 1891;
Sir Edwin Arnold, poet, 1832;
Nikolaus August Otto, inventor of the four-stroke internal combustion engine, 1832;
Gustave Courbet, French painter, 1819;
James Francis Edward Stuart, the Old Pretender, 1688.

Died on this day:

Henry, Duke of Gloucester, 1974;
Spencer Tracy, US film actor, 1967;
Frederick Theodore Albert Delius, composer, 1934;
Giacomo Matteotti, Italian socialist leader, assassinated, 1924;
Pierre Loti [Louis-Marie-Julien Viaud], French novelist and naval officer, 1923;
Richard John Seddon, New Zealand statesman, at sea, 1906;
André-Marie Ampère, French physicist, 1836;
King George I, 1727;
Luis Vaz de Camões, Portuguese poet, 1580;
Frederick I, Barbarossa, Holy Roman Emperor, 1190.

Occurred on this day:

The Battle of Narvik ended, 1940;
Alcoholics Anonymous was founded in the USA by William Wilson, a broker, and Dr Robert Smith, a physician, 1938;
The Battle of Belleau Wood ended, 1918;
Wagner's opera *Tristan und Isolde* was first produced, Munich, 1865;
The Crystal Palace at Sydenham near London was officially opened, 1854;
The first Oxford and Cambridge Boat Race was rowed, and was won by Oxford, 1829;
The first of the witches of Salem was hanged in Massachusetts, USA, 1692.

TODAY IS THE FEAST DAY OF St Bogumilus, St Getulius and his Companions, St Ithamar and St Landericus or Landry of Paris.

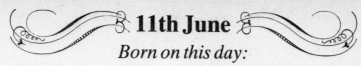

11th June

Born on this day:

John Dyson, Australian cricketer, 1954;
Lindsey de Paul, singer and composer, 1950;
Jenny Pitman, racehorse trainer, 1946;
Lieut.-Gen. Sir Michael Wilkes, Commander, UK Field Army, 1946;
Rachael Heyhoe Flint, journalist, broadcaster and cricketer, 1940;
Jackie Stewart, champion racing driver, 1939;
Gene Wilder, US film actor, 1935;
Athol Fugard, actor, director and playwright, 1932;
The Hon. Timothy Sainsbury MP, government minister, 1932;
Lord Cameron of Lochbroom, Lord Advocate, 1931;
Dame Beryl Grey, former prima ballerina, 1927;
Michael Cacoyannis, film and stage director, 1922;
Richard Todd, actor, 1919;
James Bostock, painter and engraver, 917;
Jacques Cousteau, undersea explorer, 1910;
Bert Lee, popular composer, 1880;
Azorín [José Martínez Ruiz], Spanish novelist, 1874;
Richard Strauss, German composer, 1864;
Mrs Humphry Ward [Mary Augusta Arnold], novelist, 1851;
Hablot Knight Browne ['Phiz'], artist and illustrator, 1815;
John Constable, painter, 1776;
Ben Jonson, playwright, 1572.

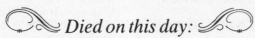 Died on this day:

John Wayne [Marion Michael Morrison], US film actor, 1979;
Alexander Feodorevich Kerensky, Russian social democratic leader, 1970;
John Llewellyn Lewis, US labour leader, 1969;
Sir Frank [François Guillaume] Brangwyn, artist, 1956;
Stephen Lucius Gwynn, Irish novelist, poet and MP, 1950;
King Alexander and Queen Draga of Serbia, assassinated at Belgrade, 1903;
Sir James Brooke, Rajah of Sarawak, 1868;
Sir John Franklin, explorer, 1847;
James III, King of Scotland, assassinated, 1488.

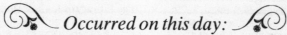 Occurred on this day:

The London production of the musical show *Barnum* opened, 1981;
The first oil from the British North Sea oilfields was pumped ashore, 1975;
The liner *Empress of Britain* was launched at Clydebank, 1930;
The *Evening Standard* newspaper was first published, 1860;
George II was proclaimed King of Great Britain, 1727;
Michiel de Ruyter, Dutch naval commander, defeated the English Admiral George Monck at the Battle of Dover Strait, 1666;
King Henry VIII was married to Catherine of Aragon, 1509;
James IV became King of Scotland, 1488.

TODAY IS THE FEAST DAY OF St Barnabas, Saints Felix and Fortunatus and St Parisio.

12th June

Born on this day:

Robert Smith, show-jumper, 1961;

Mark Calcavecchia, golfer, 1960;

Oliver Knussen, composer and conductor, 1952;

Pat Jennings, footballer, 1945;

Roy Harper, rock singer and songwriter, 1941;

Lady Herries of Terregles, racehorse trainer, 1938;

Sir Paul Kennedy, High Court judge, 1935;

Brigid Brophy, novelist, 1929;

Anne Frank, Dutch/Jewish diarist, 1929;

Vic Damone, US singer, 1928;

Jackie Pallo, wrestler, 1926;

George Bush, 41st president of the United States, 1924;

Peter Jones, actor, 1920;

Sir Kenneth Hollings, High Court judge, 1918;

Priscilla Lane, US film actress, 1917;

Lord Mayhew, former government minister, 1915;

Robert Anthony Eden, 1st Earl of Avon, statesman, 1897;

Sir Oliver Joseph Lodge, physicist, 1851;

Charles Kingsley, novelist, 1819;

Harriet Martineau, novelist and historian, 1802.

Died on this day:

Dame Marie Rambert [Cyvia Rambam], ballet producer, director and teacher, 1982;

Edmund Wilson, US novelist, playwright and poet, 1972;

Sir Herbert Read, poet and critic, 1968;

John Nicholson Ireland, composer, 1962;

Montague Rhodes James, author and editor, 1936;

Dr Thomas Arnold, educationist, 1842;

Edward Troughton, scientific instrument maker, 1835;

Jean Etienne Liotard, Swiss painter, 1789;

William Collins, poet, 1759.

Occurred on this day:

Boris Yeltsin was elected president of the Russian Republic, 1991;

The London production of the musical show *Hold Everything!* opened, 1929;

In Greece, King Constantine abdicated in favour of his second son, Alexander, 1917;

The Rotherhithe-Stepney Tunnel beneath the Thames was opened, 1908;

The first electric telegraph was patented by Sir William Cooke and Sir Charles Wheatstone, 1837;

The Library of John Cotton was presented to the nation and now forms part of the British Library, 1700;

Magdalen College, Oxford, was founded, 1458.

TODAY IS THE FEAST DAY OF St Antonina or Antonia, St Eskil, St John of Sahagun, St Leo III, pope, St Odulf, St Onuphrius, St Paula Frassinetti, St Peter of Mount Athos and St Ternan.

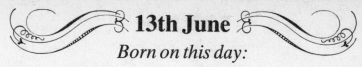

13th June

Born on this day:

Peter Scudamore, jockey, 1958;
David Curry, MP, government minister, 1944;
Malcolm McDowell, actor, 1943;
Gwynne Howell, opera bass singer, 1938;
Andreas Whittam Smith, editor and chief executive, the *Independent*, 1937;
Dr Barbara Reynolds, lexicographer, 1914;
Carlos Antonio de Padua Chávez, Mexican conductor and composer, 1899;
Dorothy Leigh Sayers, thriller writer and playwright, 1893;
Basil Rathbone [Philip St John Basil Rathbone], film actor, 1892;
Elisabeth Schumann, German/US operatic soprano, 1885;
Jules Bordet, Belgian bacteriologist, 1870;

William Butler Yeats, Irish poet, 1865;
Sir Charles Algernon Parsons, inventor of the steam turbine, 1854;
James Clerk Maxwell, physicist, 1831;
Dr Thomas Arnold, Head of Rugby School, 1795;
Thomas Young, linguist and physicist, translator of the demotic inscriptions of the Rosetta Stone, 1773;
Anton Eberl, Austrian composer and pianist, 1765;
Nicolas Dalayrac [d'Alayrac], French operetta composer, 1753;
[Frances] Fanny Burney [Madame D'Arblay], novelist and diarist, 1752;
Wenzel Hollar, Bohemian etcher, 1607.

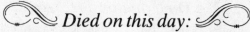 Died on this day:

Benjamin David [Benny] Goodman, US clarinettist and bandleader, 1986;
Georg von Békésy, US physiologist, 1972;
Martin Buber, German/Jewish philosopher, 1965;
Sir Eugene Aynesley Goossens, conductor and composer, 1962;
Gaston-Pierre-Étienne Flandin, French statesman, 1958;

Charles Butterworth, US actor, 1946;
Sir Henry [O'Neal de Hane] Segrave, racing motorist, killed, 1930;
Ludwig II [Otto Friedrich Wilhelm II], King of Bavaria, committed suicide by drowning, 1886;
Mikhail Alexandrovich Bakunin, Russian anarchist, 1876;
Alexander the Great, 323 BC.

Occurred on this day:

The Queen bestowed the title 'Princess Royal' on Princess Anne, 1987;
Six shots from a blank cartridge pistol were fired at the Queen in the Mall by a 17-year-old youth, 1981;
Geraldine Brodrick of Sydney, Australia, gave birth to nonuplets [nine children, of whom two boys and four girls survived], 1971;
The last British troops left the base of Suez, 1956;

The first V-1 flying-bombs fell on London, 1944;
162 people were killed and 432 injured in a German daylight air raid on London, 1917;
In Paris, the ballet *Petrushka*, by Igor Stravinsky, was performed for the first time, 1911;
In China, the Boxer Rebellion started when rebels besieged foreign legations, 1900.

TODAY IS THE FEAST DAY OF St Antony of Padua, St Aquilina, St Felicula and St Triphyllius.

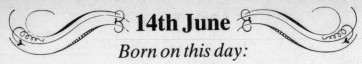

14th June

Born on this day:

Steffi Graf, German tennis player, 1969;
Nigel Short, chess player, 1965;
Jeremy Sinden, actor, 1950;
Jonathan Raban, novelist and travel writer, 1942;
Mike Yarwood, entertainer and impressionist, 1941;
Che [Ernesto] Guevara, Argentinian revolutionary, 1928;
Pierre Salinger, US politician and journalist, 1925;
Dorothy McGuire, US film actress, 1919;
Sam Wanamaker, US actor, director and producer, 1919;
Lord Rootes, former chairman, Chrysler UK, 1917;
Burl Ives, actor and singer, 1909;
Air Marshal Sir Arthur McDonald, 1903;
Count John McCormack, Irish/US tenor, 1884;
Karl Landsteiner, Austrian/US pathologist, 1868;
Robert Marion La Follette, US political leader, 1855;
Bernard Bosanquet, philosopher, 1848;
Harriet Beecher Stowe, US novelist, 1811;
Charles Augustin de Coulomb, French physicist, 1736;
Tomaso Giovanni Albinoni, Italian composer, 1671.

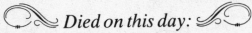

Died on this day:

Jorge Luis Borges, Argentine author, 1986;
Alan Jay Lerner, US lyricist and playwright, 1986;
John Logie Baird, TV pioneer, 1946;
Gilbert Keith Chesterton, author, 1936;
Maxim Gorky [Alexei Maximovich Pyeshkov], Russian author, 1936;
Emmeline Pankhurst [née Goulden], women's rights champion, 1928;
Jerome Klapka Jerome, writer, 1927;
Edward FitzGerald, poet and translator of *The Rubáiyát of Omar Khayyám*, 1883;
Benedict Arnold, US soldier and traitor, 1801;
Sir Henry Vane, parliamentarian, executed, 1662.

Occurred on this day:

A cease-fire was agreed in the Falklands, 1982;
The world's first nuclear-powered submarine, the USS *Nautilus*, was launched in the USA, 1952;
The German army entered and occupied Paris, 1940;
The first London performance of the musical show *Anything Goes* was staged, 1935;
Henley Regatta was held for the first time, 1839;
The Austrians were defeated by Napoleon's forces at the Battle of Marengo, 1800;
The Stars and Stripes flag was adopted by the Continental Congress in America, 1777;
King William III landed at Carrickfergus in Ireland, 1690;
King Charles I's troops were defeated by Cromwell's army at the Battle of Naseby, 1645.

TODAY IS THE FEAST DAY OF St Dogmael, St Methodius I of Constantinople and Saints Valerius and Rufinus.

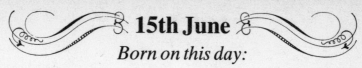

15th June

Born on this day:

John Redwood, MP, government minister, 1950;
Simon Callow, actor and director, 1949;
Nicola Pagett, actress, 1945;
Ken Fletcher, Australian tennis player, 1940;
Air Chief Marshal Sir Joseph Gilbert, 1931;
Richard Baker, broadcaster, 1925;
The Most Rev. Trevor Huddleston, human rights campaigner, 1913;
Maj.-Gen. Sir John Nelson, 1912;
Admiral Sir Charles Madden, former C.-in-C. Home Fleet, 1906;
James Norval Harald Robertson-Justice, film actor, 1905;

Mary Ellis, singer and actress, 1900;
Harry Langdon, US silent film comedian, 1884;
Edvard Grieg, Norwegian composer, 1843;
Charles de Lafosse, French historical painter, 1636;
Thomas Randolph, poet and playwright, 1605;
Nicolas Poussin, French painter, 1594;
George Heriot, jeweller and goldsmith, 1563;
Edward, the Black Prince, 1330.

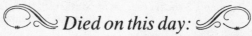 Died on this day:

Evelyn Underhill, poet and writer, 1941;
Charles Francis Bush, inventor of the arc lamp, 1929;
Maurice Henry Hewlett, novelist and poet, 1923;
Mihail Eminescu, Romanian poet, 1889;
Frederick III, Emperor of Germany, 1888;
Ary Scheffer, French painter, 1858;
James Knox Polk, 11th president of the USA, 1849;

Thomas Campbell, poet, 1844;
Guillaume Courtois [Guglielmo Cortese], French painter, 1679;
Philip the Good, Duke of Burgundy, 1467;
Wat Tyler, rebel, beheaded at Smithfield, 1381;
Robert I, King of the Franks, killed in battle, 923.

Occurred on this day:

Major-General Jeremy Moore accepted the surrender of all Argentine forces on East and West Falkland, 1982;
The first general election in Spain for more than 40 years resulted in a victory for the Democratic Centre party, 1977;
The first London performance of the musical show *Bye Bye Birdie* was staged, 1961;
The first non-stop transatlantic flight was completed by Alcock and Brown, 1919;
The Boy Scouts of America were incorporated, 1916;

The Battle of Givenchy was fought, 1915;
The Stamp Duty on newspapers in Britain was abolished, 1855;
Arkansas became the 25th of the United States, 1836;
The first stone of the new London Bridge was laid by the Duke of York, 1825;
Harrow School was founded, 1571;
The Magna Carta was sealed by King John at Runnymede, near Windsor, 1215.

TODAY IS THE OFFICIAL BIRTHDAY OF HM THE QUEEN AND THE FEAST DAY OF St Aleydia or Alice, St Bardo, St Edburga of Winchester, St Germaine Cousin of Pibrac, St Hesychius of Durostorum, St Landelinus, St Orsiesus, St Tatian Dulas and St Vitus.

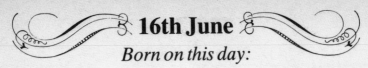

16th June

Born on this day:

John Salthouse, actor, 1951;
Simon Williams, actor, 1946;
James Bolam, actor, 1938;
Michael Culver, actor, 1938;
Helen Ryan, actress, 1938;
Eileen Atkins, actress, 1934;
Lord Patrick Beresford, bloodstock agent, 1934;
The Rt. Rev. David Konstant, RC Bishop of Leeds, 1930;
Tom Graveney, cricketer, 1927;
Enoch Powell, former MP, 1912;

John Hadfield, author and publisher, 1907;
Maj.-Gen. Richard Jelf, 1904;
Lupino Lane [Henry Lupino], singer and entertainer, 1892;
Stan Laurel [Arthur Stanley Jefferson], film comedian, 1890;
Arthur Meighen, Canadian statesman, 1874;
Gustav V, King of Sweden, 1858;
Otto Jahn, German philologist and archaeologist, 1813;
Sir John Cheke, classical scholar, 1514.

Died on this day:

Wernher von Braun, German/US rocket engineer, 1977;
Sir John Charles Walsham Reith, 1st Baron Reith of Stonehaven, first director-general of the BBC, 1971;
Harold Rupert Leofric George, 1st Earl Alexander of Tunis, field marshal, 1969;
Imre Nagy, Hungarian prime minister, executed, 1958;

Margaret Grace Bondfield, trade union leader and 1st woman cabinet minister, 1953;
DuBose Heyward, US novelist and playwright, 1940;
Charles Sturt, explorer of Australia, 1869;
John Churchill, 1st Duke of Marlborough, 1722.

Occurred on this day:

Burglars were arrested at the Democratic Party headquarters, Watergate Building, Washington, D.C., USA, 1972;
The first London performance of the musical show *1776* was staged, 1970;
The first woman cosmonaut, Valentina Tereshkova, blasted off in *Vostok 6*, 1963;
Marshal Pétain took over the French government and asked Germany for an armistice, 1940;
Mixed bathing in the Serpentine in Hyde Park, London, was first permitted, 1930;

The first public meeting of the League of Nations council was held in London, 1920;
The Automobile Association was founded, 1905;
King George II defeated the French at the Battle of Dettingen, 1743;
The English and Dutch squadrons under Admiral Rooke were defeated by the French at the Battle of Cape St Vincent, 1693.

TODAY IS THE FEAST DAY OF St Aurelian, St Benno of Meissen, Saints Cyr and Julitta, Saints Ferreolus and Ferrutio, St John Francis Regis, St Lutgarde and St Tychon of Amathus.

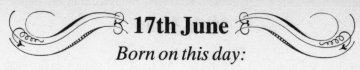

17th June

Born on this day:

Barry Manilow, singer and composer, 1946;
Ken Livingstone, MP, 1945;
Kenneth Loach, TV and film director, 1936;
Derek Ibbotson, athlete, 1932;
Brian Statham, cricketer, 1930;
Air Chief Marshal Sir Peter Le Cheminant, former lieutenant governor of Guernsey, 1920;
Beryl Reid, actress, 1920;
Dean Martin, singer, 1917;
John Hersey, US writer and journalist, 1914;
Ralph Rex Bellamy, US film actor, 1904;
Igor Fyodorovich Stravinsky, Russian/US composer, 1882;
Henry Hertzberg Lawson [Larsen], Australian author and poet, 1867;
Sir William Crookes, physicist, 1832;
Charles-François Gounod, French composer, 1818;
John Wesley, evangelist, 1703;
Charles XII, King of Sweden, 1682;
Jan van Mieris, Dutch painter, 1660;
Pedro Calderón de la Barca, Spanish playwright, 1600;
King Edward I, 1239.

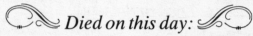

Died on this day:

John Cowper Powys, novelist and poet, 1963;
Dorothy Miller Richardson, novelist, 1957;
Arthur Christopher Benson, scholar and author, 1925;
Sir Edward Coley Burne-Jones, painter, 1898;
William Hart, US landscape and cattle painter, 1894;
Richard Harris Barham, poet and author of the *Ingoldsby Legends*, 1845;
Jean Audran, French artist and engraver, 1756;
Joseph Addison, essayist, 1719;
John III Sobieski, King of Poland, 1696;
Giacomo Torelli, theatrical designer, 1678.

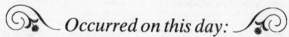

Occurred on this day:

The South African Parliament repealed a law, by which apartheid was ended, 1991;
The May Fair Theatre opened in London, 1963;
Latvia was occupied by the USSR, 1940;
The British troop ship HMS *Lancastria* was bombed and sunk off St Nazaire, with the loss of 2,500 lives, 1940;
The British Expeditionary Force from France was finally evacuated, 1940;
A steamboat service on the Thames started, 1905;
The *Great Eastern* left the Needles, Isle of Wight, on her first transatlantic voyage, 1860;
The Opera House, London, burned down, 1789;
The Battle of Bunker Hill, beginning the American War of Independence, was fought, 1775;
Francis Drake proclaimed English sovereignty over New Albion [now California], 1579.

TODAY IS THE FEAST DAY OF St Adulf, St Avitus, St Bessarion, St Botulph, St Emily de Vialai, St Hervé or Harvet, St Hypatius, St Moling, St Nectan, Saints Nicander and Marcian, St Rainerius of Pisa and Saints Teresa and Sanchia of Portugal.

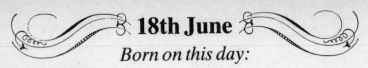

18th June

Born on this day:

Alison Moyet, singer, 1961;
Linda Thorsen, actress, 1947;
Barry Evans, actor, 1943;
Paul McCartney, songwriter and former Beatle, 1942;
Delia Smith, TV cookery expert, 1940;
Lieut.-Gen. Sir Brian Kenny, Deputy Supreme Allied Commander, Europe, 1934;
Eva Bartok, US film actress, 1929;
Michael Blakemore, freelance theatre director, 1928;
Paul Eddington, actor, 1927;
Ian Carmichael, actor, 1920;
John Young, actor, 1916;

Richard Allen Boone, US film actor, 1916;
Sammy Cahn, US lyricist, 1913;
Llewellyn Rees, actor and theatre administrator, 1900;
Édouard Daladier, French statesman, 1884;
Miklós Horthy de Nagybánya, Hungarian statesman, 1868;
Edward Wyllis Scripps, US publisher and journalist, 1854;
Cyrus Hermann Kotzschmar Curtis, US publisher and editor, 1850;
Sir Thomas Overbury, poet, baptised, 1581.

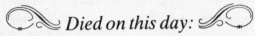

Died on this day:

[Beatrice] Joan Caulfield, US film actress, 1991;
Bruce Marshall, novelist, 1987;
Ethel Barrymore [Blythe], US actress, 1959;
Roald Amundsen, Norwegian explorer, lost in the Arctic, 1928;
Robert Marion La Follette, US political leader, 1925;

Samuel Butler, author, 1902;
George Grote, historian, 1871;
William Cobbett, writer and politician, 1835;
William Combe, adventurer and poet, creator of 'Dr Syntax', 1823;
Rogier van der Weyden, Flemish painter, 1464.

Occurred on this day:

A watercolour by Joseph William Turner was sold at auction for £340,000, 1976;
The *Sunday Citizen* newspaper was published for the last time, 1967;
Egypt was proclaimed a republic, and General Neguib became president, 1953;
The first London performance of the musical show *Cage Me a Peacock* was staged, 1948;
Amelia Earhart, US aviator, became the first woman to fly the Atlantic, 1928;
Weber's opera *Der Freischütz* was first performed, Berlin, 1821;

Waterloo Bridge over the Thames in London opened, 1817;
The Duke of Wellington, allied with von Blücher, defeated the French under Napoleon at the Battle of Waterloo, 1815;
War broke out between Britain and the USA, 1812;
The English were defeated by the French under Joan of Arc at the Battle of Patay, 1429.

TODAY IS THE FEAST DAY OF St Amandus of Bordeaux, St Elisabeth of Schönau, St Gregory Barbarigo, Saints Marcellian and Mark.

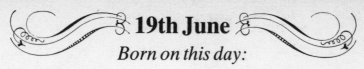

19th June

Born on this day:

Salman Rushdie, novelist, 1947;
Bryan Kneale, sculptor, 1930;
Charlie Drake, comedian, 1925;
Brigadier Eileen Nolan, former director, WRAC, 1920;
Louis Jourdan, French film actor, 1919;
Sir Francis Purchas, a Lord Justice of Appeal, 1919;
Surgeon Vice-Admiral Sir Derek Steele-Perkins, 1908;
Sir Ernst Boris Chain, bacteriologist and pioneer of penicillin, 1906;
Walter Reginald Hammond, cricketer, 1903;
Guy Lombardo, Canadian bandleader, 1902;
Bessie Wallis Warfield Simpson, Duchess of Windsor, 1896;

Charles Coburn, US actor, 1877;
Sir Max Pemberton, author and editor, 1863;
Douglas, 1st Earl Haig, soldier, 1861;
Sir George Alexander [George Samson], actor-manager, 1858;
Charles Haddon Spurgeon, Baptist minister, 1834;
Richard Monckton Milnes, 1st Baron, poet, 1809;
John Gibson, sculptor, 1790;
Blaise Pascal, French mathematician and philosopher, 1623;
James VI, King of Scotland/James I, King of England, 1566.

Died on this day:

Jean Arthur [Gladys Georgianna Greene], US film actress, 1991;
Julius and Ethel Rosenberg, US spies for the USSR, executed, 1953;
Sir James Matthew Barrie, author and playwright, 1937;
John Emerich Edward Dalberg, 1st Baron Acton, historian and philosopher, 1902;
Étienne Geoffroy Saint-Hilaire, French naturalist, 1884;
Maximilian, Archduke of Austria and Emperor of Mexico, executed, 1867;

Sir Joseph Banks, naturalist and explorer, 1820;
John Brown, Scottish scholar and theologian, 1787;
Nicholas Lémery, French physician and chemist, 1715;
Matthew Merian the Elder, Swiss engraver and bookseller, 1650;
Piers Gaveston, Earl of Cornwall, court favourite, beheaded, 1312.

Occurred on this day:

Kuwait became independent, 1961;
The Battle of the Philippine Sea began, 1944;
All German titles and names were renounced by the British Royal Family, who adopted the name Windsor, 1917;
King George V conferred peerages on members of the Teck and Battenberg families, 1917;

A republic was proclaimed in Portugal, 1911;
The first Zeppelin dirigible airship, the *Deutschland*, was launched, 1910;
An Act was passed founding the Metropolitan Police, 1829.

TODAY IS THE FEAST DAY OF St Boniface or Bruno of Querfurt, St Deodatus or Die of Nevers, Saints Gervase and Protase, St Juliana Falconieri, St Odo of Cambrai and St Romuald.

20th June

Born on this day:

Alan Lamb, cricketer, 1954;
Paul Ramirez, tennis player, 1953;
Lionel Richie, singer and songwriter, 1949;
HRH the Duchess of Gloucester, 1946;
Stephen Frears, film director, 1941;
Budge Rogers, rugby player, 1939;
Wendy Craig, actress, 1934;
Claire Tomalin, writer and editor, 1933;
Ronald Hines, actor, 1929;
Sir Haydn Tudor Evans, High Court judge, 1920;
Johnny Morris, broadcaster, 1916;
Errol Flynn, film actor, 1909;
Catherine Cookson, novelist, 1906;
Kurt Schwitters, German artist and poet, 1887;
Medardo Rosso, Italian sculptor, 1858;
Jacques Offenbach [Jakob Levy Eberst], German/French composer, 1819;
Anna Letitia Barbauld [Aikin], poetess, teacher and hymn-writer, 1743;
Salvatore Rosa, Italian painter, poet and musician, 1615.

Died on this day:

Gustaf Allan Petterssen, Swedish composer, 1980;
Bernard Mannes Baruch, financier, 1965;
Pancho [Francisco] Villa, Mexican revolutionary, assassinated, 1923;
Jules-Alfred Huot de Goncourt, French writer, 1870;
King William IV, 1837;
Emmanuel-Joseph Sieyès, French revolutionary leader, 1836;
Karl Friedrich Abel, viola player and composer, 1787;
Willem Barents, Dutch explorer, in the Arctic, 1597.

Occurred on this day:

Sheila Scott arrived at London Airport after being the first Briton to make a round-the-world solo flight, 1966;
The Battle of the Philippine Sea ended, 1944;
The first trolley-bus service in Britain was opened in Leeds, 1911;
The Kiel Canal was formally opened, 1895;
A new Tay Railway Bridge was opened for public traffic, 1887;
West Virginia became the 35th of the United States, 1863;
On the death of her uncle, William IV, Queen Victoria ascended the throne, 1837;
The paddle-wheel steamer *Savannah* arrived at Liverpool under sail, the first steamship to cross the Atlantic, 1819;
147 people were confined in the cell later called the Black Hole of Calcutta, from which only 23 came out alive, 1756.

TODAY IS THE FEAST DAY OF St Adalbert of Magdeburg, St Bain or Bagnus, St Goban, St John of Matera or Pulsano and St Silverius, pope.

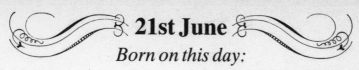

21st June

Born on this day:

Prince William, 1982;

Jeremy Coney, New Zealand cricketer, 1952;

Malcolm Rifkind QC, MP, government minister, 1946;

Maurice Saatchi, chairman, Saatchi & Saatchi, 1946;

Prof. Anna Davies, philologist, 1937;

John Edrich, cricketer, 1937;

Françoise Sagan, French author, 1935;

Sir Bernard Ingham, former chief secretary to prime minister, 1932;

Gerald Kaufman, MP, 1930;

Wally Fawkes, cartoonist and jazz musician, 1924;

Jane Russell, US film actress, 1920;

Maj.-Gen. Robert Goldsmith, 1907;

Jean-Paul Sartre, French Existentialist, writer and philosopher, 1905;

Mack Gordon [Morris Gittler], US lyricist, 1904;

Pier Luigi Nervi, Italian architect, 1891;

Field Marshal Sir Claude Auchinleck, WWII commander, 1884;

Henry Major Tomlinson, novelist and essayist, 1873;

William Edmonstoune Aytoun, poet and critic, 1813;

Abraham Mignon, Dutch painter, 1640;

Increase Mather, President of Harvard, 1639;

Pope Leo IX, 1002.

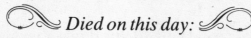

Died on this day:

Sukarno [Kusnasosro], president of Indonesia, 1970;

Rex Ingram [Reginald Ingram Montgomery Hitchcock], US actor and film director, 1950;

Jean-Édouard Vuillard, French painter, 1940;

Nikolai Andreyevich Rimsky-Korsakov, 1908;

John Hatchard, publisher and bookseller, 1849;

Inigo Jones, architect, 1652;

John Smith, Virginian colonist, 1631;

John Skelton, poet, 1529;

Niccolò di Bernardo dei Machiavelli, diplomat and author, 1527;

King Edward III, 1377.

Occurred on this day:

The musical show *Evita* was first produced, London, 1978;

In the USA, Dr Peter Goldmark demonstrated the first successful Long Playing record, 1948;

The German Fleet was scuttled at Scapa Flow, 1919;

Wagner's opera *Die Meistersinger* was first performed, Munich, 1868;

The Royal College of Surgeons was founded, 1843;

The French were defeated by the Duke of Wellington at the Battle of Vitoria in Spain, 1813;

New Hampshire became the 9th of the United States, 1788;

The foundation stone of the new St Paul's Cathedral, London, was laid, 1675;

Dulwich College was founded by Edward Alleyn, 1619.

TODAY IS THE FEAST DAY OF St Alban or Albinus of Mainz, St Aloysius Gonzaga, St Engelmund, St Eusebius of Samosata, St John Rigby, St Leutfridus or Leufroy and St Meen or Mewan.

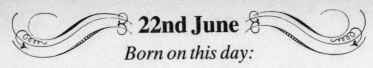

22nd June

Born on this day:

Diana Young, jockey, 1956;
Alastair Stewart, newscaster and reporter, 1952;
Alan Osmond, US singer, 1949;
Meryl Streep, US actress, 1949;
Esther Rantzen, TV presenter, 1940;
Kris Kristofferson, US singer, songwriter and actor, 1936;
Prunella Scales, actress, 1932;
Lord Wakeham, government minister, 1932;
Bruce Kent, nuclear disarmament activist, 1929;
Field Marshal Sir Roland Gibbs, Lord Lieutenant for Wiltshire, 1921;
Katherine Dunham, US choreographer, 1910;

Lord Hunt, mountaineer, 1910;
Sir Peter Pears, tenor, 1910;
Michael Todd [Avram Goldenbogen], US film producer, 1907;
Billy Wilder, US film director and screenwriter, 1906;
Erich Maria Remarque, German novelist, 1898;
Sir Julian Sorell Huxley, biologist, 1887;
Sir Henry Rider Haggard, novelist, 1856;
Giuseppe Mazzini, Italian leader, 1805;
Karl Wilhelm von Humboldt, German philologist, 1767;
George Vancouver, navigator and explorer, 1757;
Thomas Day, philanthropist and author, 1748.

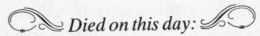

Died on this day:

Fred Astaire [Frederick Austerlitz], US actor and dancer, 1987;
Joseph Losey, US film director, 1984;
Darius Milhaud, French composer, 1974;
Judy Garland [Frances Gumm], US actress and singer, 1969;
Walter John de la Mare, poet and author, 1956;

Clarence Michael James Dennis, Australian poet and journalist, 1936;
Sir Henry Hughes Wilson, field marshal, assassinated, 1922;
Katherine Philips [Fowler], verse-writer, 1664;
Pope Innocent V, 1276;
Roger I, King of Sicily, 1101.

Occurred on this day:

The Battle of Okinawa ended, 1945;
German armies launched an invasion of the USSR on three wide fronts stretching from the Baltic to the Black Sea, 1941;
France and Germany signed an armistice at Compiègne, 1940;
The Northern Underground Line, London, was opened, 1907;
The Wallace Collection, London, was opened, 1900;

Queen Victoria celebrated her Diamond Jubilee, 1897;
The St George's Channel was crossed by a balloon, 1817;
The first cricket match was played at Lord's Cricket Ground [present site], 1814;
Richard II ascended the English throne, 1377.

TODAY IS THE FEAST DAY OF St Eberhard of Salzburg, St John Fisher, St Nicetas of Remesiana, St Paulinus of Nola and St Thomas More.

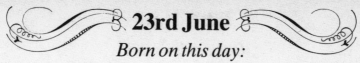

23rd June

Born on this day:

Julian Hipwood, polo player, 1946;
Prof. Martin Rees, astronomer, 1942;
Adam Faith, singer and actor, 1940;
Sir Peter Millett, High Court judge, 1932;
Anthony Thwaite, poet, 1931;
The Most Rev. Dr John Habgood,
    Archbishop of York, 1927;
Miriam Karlin, actress, 1925;
Irene Worth, actress, 1916;
John Prebble, novelist, historian and
    playwright, 1915;
Admiral Sir Francis Turner, 1912;
Admiral Sir Horace Law, 1911;
Margaret Lane, novelist, 1907;

Prof. Isaac Schapera, anthropologist, 1905;
Winifred Holtby, novelist, 1898;
Edward, Duke of Windsor, 1894;
Dr Alfred Charles Kinsey, US sex
    investigator and author, 1894;
Anna Akhmatova [Anna Andreyevna
    Gorenko], Russian poet, 1889;
William Ewart Berry, 1st Viscount
    Camrose, 1879;
Irvin Shrewsbury Cobb, US playwright
    novelist and actor, 1876;
Joséphine de Beauharnais [Marie-Josèphe-
    Rose Tascher de la Pagerie], wife of
    Napoleon, 1763.

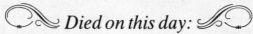

Died on this day:

Kay Kyser [James Kern Kyser], US
    bandleader and quizmaster, 1985;
Olivia Manning, novelist, 1980;
Michael Arlen [Dikran Kouyoumdjian],
    novelist, 1956;
Mark Gertler, painter, 1939;
Cecil James Sharp, founder of the English
    Folk Society, 1924;

Lady Hester Lucy Stanhope, traveller and
    eccentric, 1839;
Mark Akenside, poet and physician,
    1770;
Pedro de Mendoza, Spanish soldier and
    explorer, at sea, 1537;
Vespasian [Titus Flavius Sabinus
    Vespasianus], Roman emperor, 79.

Occurred on this day:

The Royalty Theatre opened in London,
    1960;
Gamal Abdel Nasser was elected as
    president of the Republic of Egypt,
    1956;
The British diplomats Guy Burgess and
    Donald Maclean fled to the USSR, 1951;

Keble College, Oxford, opened, 1870;
The Battle of Plassey was fought by British
    troops under Robert Clive against the
    Bengalis, 1757;
Henry Hudson, navigator and explorer,
    was cast adrift to die with his son and a
    few sick men, 1611.

TODAY IS THE FEAST DAY OF St Agrippina, St Etheldreda or Audrey, St Joseph
Cafasso, St Lietbertus or Libert and St Thomas Garnet.

24th June

Born on this day:

Betty Stove, Dutch tennis player, 1945;
Jeff Beck, blues and rock guitarist, 1944;
Mick Fleetwood, rock musician, 1942;
Claude Chabrol, French film director, 1930;
Sir Fred Hoyle, astronomer and writer of
science fiction, 1915;
Brian Johnston, broadcaster, 1912;
Juan Fangio, Argentinian motor racing
champion, 1911;
Lieut.-Gen. Sir William Pike, former chief
commander, St John's Ambulance,
1905;

Phil Harris, US actor and entertainer, 1904;
Jack Dempsey, US heavyweight boxer,
1895;
Horatio Herbert, Earl Kitchener, soldier,
1850;
Ambrose Gwinnett Bierce, US writer and
satirist, 1842;
William Henry [W.H.] Smith, bookseller
and politician, 1825;
Henry Ward Beecher, US clergyman, 1813;
Sir John Ross, Arctic explorer, 1777;
St John of the Cross, Spanish mystic, 1542.

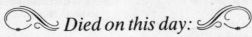

Died on this day:

Rex Ernest Warner, author, 1986;
Valentine Dyall, actor, 1985;
Stuart Davis, US abstract artist, 1964;
Walter Rathenau, German statesman,
assassinated, 1922;
Stephen Grover Cleveland, 22nd and 24th
president of the USA, 1908;
Adam Lindsay Gordon, Australian poet,
committed suicide, 1870;

Marie Leszczynska, Queen and wife of
Louis XV of France, 1768;
John Hampden, Parliamentary general,
from wounds, 1643;
Lucrezia Borgia, Duchess of Ferrara,
1519;
Ferdinand I [the Great], King of Castile and
Leon, 1065;

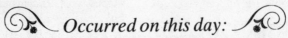

Occurred on this day:

The Mersey Tunnel was opened, 1971;
The blockade of Berlin by the USSR began,
1948;
The Russian fleet in the Black Sea mutinied
at Sebastopol, 1917;
The Archduke Albert of Austria defeated
the Italians at the Battle of Custoza,
1866;
The French defeated the Austrians at the
Battle of Solferino, 1859;

Napoleon's armies invaded Russia,
1812;
John Cabot reached the shores of North
America, 1497;
The English fleet defeated the French at the
Battle of Sluys, 1340;
Robert the Bruce and his army defeated the
forces of Edward II at Bannockburn,
1314.

TODAY IS THE FEAST DAY OF St Bartholomew of Farne, St John the Baptist, St
Ralph or Raoul of Bourges and St Simplicius of Autun.

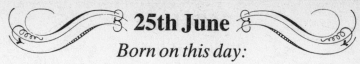

25th June

Born on this day:

Victor Marks, cricketer, 1955;
Patrick Tambay, French racing driver, 1949;
John Hilton, table-tennis champion, 1947;
Carly Simon, US singer and songwriter, 1945;
Eddie Large, comedian, 1942;
Roy Marsden, actor, 1941;
Doreen Wells, ballerina, 1937;
Moray Watson, actor, 1928;
Peter Clayton, radio presenter, 1927;
Sidney Lumet, US film director, 1924;
Lord Ravensdale, author, 1923;
Howard Newby, novelist, 1918;
Cyril Fletcher, comedian and broadcaster, 1913;
Arthur Tracy, US singer, 1903;
George Orwell [Eric Blair], author and essayist, 1903;
Louis, 1st Earl Mountbatten of Burma, 1900;
Hermann Julius Oberth, German rocket pioneer, 1894;
George Abbott, US theatre director, 1887;
William De Mille, film and theatre producer and writer, 1878;
Robert Erskine Childers, author and Irish nationalist, 1870;
John Horne Tooke, politician and philologist, 1736.

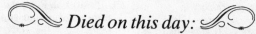

Died on this day:

Johnny [John Herndon] Mercer, US composer, lyricist and singer, 1976;
Leon Quartermaine, actor, 1967;
Colin Clive [Clive Greig], actor, 1937;
Sir Laurence Alma-Tadema, painter, 1912;
Margaret Oliphant, author, 1897;
George Armstrong Custer, US cavalry officer, killed in battle, 1876;
William Smellie, printer and antiquary, 1795;
John Marston, playwright and satirist, 1634;
Anthony Woodville, 2nd Earl Rivers, statesman, executed, 1483.

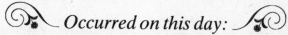

Occurred on this day:

Erskine Childers became president of the Irish Republic, succeeding Eamon de Valera, 1973;
The Battle of Caen began, 1944;
The RAF made a 1,000-bomber raid on Bremen, Germany, 1942;
General Sir Claude Auchinleck became commander of the Eighth Army, 1942;
Dr Douglas Hyde, a Gaelic scholar and Protestant, was inaugurated as the first president of the Irish Republic, 1938;
The Strand Magazine published the first 'Sherlock Holmes' story by Arthur Conan Doyle, 1891;
The Battle of the Little Big Horn River was fought – Custer's Last Stand, 1876;
Virginia become the 10th of the United States, 1788;
Samuel de Champlain hoisted the French flag in Nova Scotia at France's first settlement in North America, 1604.

TODAY IS THE FEAST DAY OF St Adalbert of Egmond, St Eurosia, St Febronia, St Gallicanus, St Gohard, St Maximus of Turin, St Moloc or Luan, St Prosper of Aquitaine, St Prosper of Reggio, St Thea and St William of Vercelli or Monte Vergine.

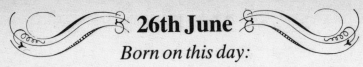

26th June

Born on this day:

The Earl of St Andrews, son of the Duke and Duchess of Kent, 1962;

Gordon McQueen, footballer, 1952;

Georgie Fame, singer and songwriter, 1943;

Claudio Abbado, conductor, 1933;

Colin Wilson, author, 1931;

Ian Prestt, ornithologist, 1929;

Syd Lawrence, bandleader, 1924;

Eleanor Parker, US film actress, 1922;

William Hamilton, former MP, 1917;

Laurie Lee, poet and author, 1914;

The Hon. Betty Askwith, author, 1909;

Peter Lorre [Laszlo Löwenstein], US film actor, 1904;

Willy Messerschmitt, German aircraft designer, 1898;

Pearl Sydenstricker Buck, US novelist, 1892;

Sir Robert Laird Borden, Canadian statesman, 1854;

William Thomson, 1st Baron Kelvin, physicist and inventor, 1824;

George Morland, painter, 1763;

Charles-Joseph Messier, French astronomer, 1730.

Died on this day:

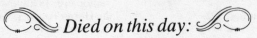

Carl Foreman, US film producer, 1984;

George Horace Gallup, poll organiser, 1984;

Sandy Powell, comedian, 1982;

André Tchaikowsky, pianist and composer, 1982;

Inia Te Wiata, New Zealand opera singer, 1971;

Ford Madox Ford, novelist and poet, 1939;

Edward Verrall Lucas, essayist, 1938;

Claude-Joseph Rouget de Lisle, French author and composer of the *Marseillaise*, 1836;

King George IV, 1830;

Samuel Crompton, spinning mule inventor, 1827;

Joseph-Michel Montgolfier, French balloonist, 1810;

The Rev. Gilbert White, naturalist and cleric, 1793;

Francisco Pizarro, Spanish conqueror of Peru, assassinated, 1541.

Occurred on this day:

The first London production of the musical show *Grease* was presented, 1973;

Madagascar proclaimed its independence as the Malagasy Republic, 1960;

The St Lawrence Seaway was opened by Queen Elizabeth II and President Eisenhower, 1959;

The United Nations Charter was signed by 50 nations in San Francisco, 1945;

The new Victoria and Albert Museum was opened, 1909;

The Order of Merit was instituted by King Edward VII, 1902;

Wagner's opera *The Valkyries* was first performed, Munich, 1870;

William IV ascended the British throne, 1830;

Christ's Hospital [the Bluecoat School] was granted its charter, 1553.

TODAY IS THE FEAST DAY OF St Anthelmus, bishop, St John of the Goths, St Maxentius, St Pelagius of Cordova, Saints Salvius or Sauvé and Superius and St Vigilius of Trent.

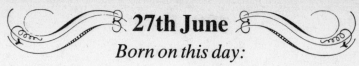

27th June

Born on this day:

Ian Lang MP, government minister, 1940;
Eric Richard, actor, 1940;
Tommy Cannon, comedian, 1938;
Alan Coren, author, journalist and broadcaster, 1938;
Shirley Ann Field, actress, 1938;
Lord Hope, Lord Justice-General of Scotland, 1938;
Hugh Wood, composer, 1932;
Michael Dummett, former Wykeham Professor of Logic, Oxford University, 1925;
Dr Thurstan Shaw, archaeologist, 1914;

Rika Markus [Erika Scharfstein], bridge journalist and author, 1910;
Sir Lewis Bernstein Namier, Polish/British historian, 1888;
Helen Adams Keller, US blind, deaf and mute scholar and teacher, 1880;
Paul Lawrence Dunbar, poet, 1872;
Sir John Monash, Australian engineer and general, 1865;
Charles Stewart Parnell, Irish nationalist leader, 1846;
Charles IX, King of France, 1550;
Louis XII, King of France, 1462.

Died on this day:

Allan Jones, US actor and singer, 1992;
Mohammed Reza Pahlavi, former Shah of Iran, 1980;
Sir Arthur David Waley, orientalist, 1966;
Clarence Malcolm Lowry, novelist, 1957;
Sir John Logan Campbell, New Zealand statesman, 1912;
Harriet Martineau, novelist and economist, 1876;

Joseph Smith, founder of the Mormons [Church of Jesus Christ of Latter-Day Saints], murdered in prison, 1844;
James Lewis Macie Smithson, scientist and founder of the Smithsonian Institution, 1829;
Michiel Janszoon van Mierevelt, Dutch painter, 1641;
Giorgio Vasari, Italian painter and art historian, 1574.

Occurred on this day:

President Truman ordered the United States Air Force and Navy to Korea, 1950;
Cherbourg was taken by the Allies, 1944;
The musical show *The Co-Optimists* was first produced, London, 1921;
The Battle of Château Thierry was fought, 1918;
The Central London Electric Railway was opened, running between Shepherd's Bush and the Bank, 1900;

Joshua Slocum completed the first solo voyage around the world, 1898;
British forces defeated the French, and Cairo was entered, 1801;
The Battle of Quebec began, 1759;
The Ladies' Mercury, the first woman's magazine, was issued, 1693;
Jack Cade defeated Henry VI's forces under Stafford at Sevenoaks, 1450.

TODAY IS THE FEAST DAY OF St Cyril of Alexandria, St George Mtasmindeli, St John of Chinon, St Ladislas, King of Hungary, St Samson of Constantinople, The Martyrs of Arras and St Zoilus of Cordova.

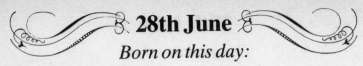

28th June

Born on this day:

David Duckham, rugby player, 1947;
John Inman, actor, 1937;
Jack Gold, film director, 1931;
Stan Barstow, writer, 1929;
Harold Evans, newspaper and publishing editor, 1929;
Sir Cyril Smith, former MP, 1929;
Correlli Barnett, author, 1928;
Mel Brooks, US author, actor and director, 1927;
Viscount Whitelaw CH, 1919;
Eric Ambler, novelist and screenwriter, 1910;
Rowland Hilder, painter and illustrator, 1906;
Richard Charles Rodgers, US composer and lyricist, 1902;
James Mallahan Cain, US novelist, 1892;
Pierre Laval, French politician, 1883;
Luisa Tetrazzini, Italian operatic singer, 1871;
Luigi Pirandello, Italian playwright, 1867;
Jean-Jacques Rousseau, French writer and philosopher, 1712;
Sir Peter Paul Rubens, painter, 1577;
King Henry VIII, 1491;
Pope Paul IV, 1476.

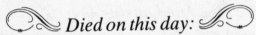

Died on this day:

William Wyler, US film director, 1981;
Rod Serling, US author and screenwriter, 1975;
Alfred Noyes, poet, 1958;
Victor Thomas Trumper, Australian cricketer, 1915;
Robert O'Hara Burke, explorer of Australia, 1861;
Fitzroy James Henry Somerset, 1st Baron Raglan, soldier, 1855;
James Madison, 4th president of the USA, 1836;
Gerhard Johann David von Scharnhorst, Prussian general, 1813;
Pope Paul I, 767.

Occurred on this day:

The Seychelles became an independent republic within the Commonwealth, 1976;
The Treaty of Versailles was signed, 1919;
The Archduke Francis Ferdinand of Austria and his wife were shot by Gavrilo Princip, a Bosnian revolutionary, at Sarajevo, 1914;
The Lötschberg Tunnel, Switzerland, was formally opened, 1913;
Westminster Cathedral was consecrated, 1910;
A mutiny of Russian sailors took place on the battleship *Potemkin*, 1905;
Queen Victoria was crowned, 1838;
The British were defeated by Washington's army at the Battle of Monmouth, New Jersey, 1778;
The British were repulsed at Charleston, 1776;
The *Morning Chronicle* newspaper was first issued, 1769.

TODAY IS THE FEAST DAY OF St Heimrad, St Irenaeus of Lyons, St John Southworth, St Paul I, pope, Saints Plutarch, Potamiaena and Companions and Saints Sergius and Germanus of Valaam.

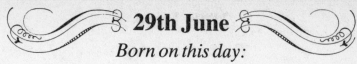

29th June

Born on this day:

Michael McIntyre, yachtsman, 1956;
The Hon. Charlotte Bingham, author, 1942;
Sir Brian Hutton, Lord Chief Justice of Northern Ireland, 1931;
Ian Bannen, actor, 1928;
David Donaldson, painter, 1916;
Geoffrey Woolley, journalist, 1915;
Rafael Kubelik, conductor, 1914;
HRH Prince Bernhard of the Netherlands, 1911;
Frank Loesser, US composer and lyricist, 1910;
Ellen Pollock, actress, 1902;

Nelson Eddy, US film actor and singer, 1901;
Antoine-Marie-Roger de Saint-Exupéry, French aviator and author, 1900;
Robert Schuman, French statesman, 1886;
George Ellery Hale, US astronomer, 1868;
James Harvey Robinson, US historian, 1863;
William James Mayo, US surgeon and co-founder of the Mayo Clinic, 1861;
George Washington Goethals, builder of the Panama Canal, 1858;
Conte Giacomo Leopardi, Italian poet and classicist, 1798.

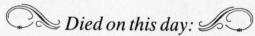

Died on this day:

Pierre-Alexandre Balmain, French fashion designer, 1982;
Maj.-Gen. Sir Francis Wilfred de Guingand, soldier, 1979;
Jayne Mansfield [Vera Jayne Palmer], US actress, killed in a car crash, 1967;
Ignaz Jan Paderewski, Polish pianist and statesman, 1941;
Paul Klee, Swiss modernist painter, 1940;
Sir Henry Stuart Jones, scholar and lexicographer, 1939;

Lady Randolph Churchill [Jennie Jerome], 1921;
Karl Brugmann, philologist, 1919;
Thomas Henry Huxley, biologist, 1895;
Adolphe-Joseph-Thomas Monticelli, French painter, 1886;
Joseph Aloysius Hansom, architect and inventor of the hansom cab, 1882;
Elizabeth Barrett Browning, poet, 1861.

Occurred on this day:

US planes bombed Hanoi, North Vietnam, 1966;
The US forces landed in New Guinea, and raided the Solomon Islands, 1943;
Sir Roger Casement, Irish revolutionary, was condemned to death for treason, 1916;
Tahiti was annexed by France, 1880;

The Press Association news agency was founded, London, 1868;
The Great Comet was seen over France and England, 1861;
The Daily Telegraph was first published, 1855;
Shakespeare's Globe Theatre burned down, 1613.

TODAY IS THE FEAST DAY OF St Cassius of Narni, St Paul the Apostle, St Peter the Apostle and Saints Salome and Judith.

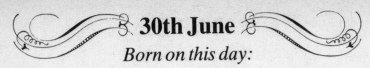

30th June

Born on this day:

Mike Tyson, US heavyweight boxer, 1966;
Tony Hatch, songwriter and lyricist, 1939;
Mike J.K. Smith, cricketer and rugby player, 1933;
James Loughran, conductor, 1931;
Susan Hayward [Edythe Marrener], US film actress, 1918;
Lena Horne, US singer, 1917;
Lieut.-Gen. Sir Henry Leask, former GOC Scotland, 1913;
Anthony Mann [Emil Anton Bundmann], US film director, 1906;
Harold Joseph Laski, politician and economist, 1893;

Walter Ulbricht, East German leader, 1893;
Sir Stanley Spencer, painter, 1891;
Hervé [Florimond Ronger], French composer, 1825;
Sir Joseph Dalton Hooker, surgeon and botanist, 1817;
Tom Oliver, prize-fighter, 1789;
Émile-Jean-Horace Vernet, French painter, 1789;
Vicomte Paul-François-Jean-Nicolas de Barras, French statesman, 1755;
John Gay, poet and playwright, 1685.

Died on this day:

Lillian Hellman, US playwright, 1984;
Nancy Freeman Mitford, author, 1973;
Joan Rosita Forbes, traveller and writer, 1967;
Margery Allingham, novelist, 1966;
Robert Chester Ruark, US novelist, 1965;
Dr Lee De Forest, US radio and sound engineer, 1961;
John William Strutt, 3rd Baron Rayleigh, physicist, 1919;

Abraham Gottlob Werner, German geologist, 1817;
Alexander Brome, poet, 1666;
William Oughtred, mathematician and inventor of the slide rule, 1660;
Simon Vouet, French painter, 1649;
Pieter van Laer [Laar], Dutch painter, 1642;
Montezuma II, Aztec emperor, killed, 1520.

Occurred on this day:

The musical show *Singin' in the Rain* was first produced, London, 1983;
Cardinal Montini was elected as Pope Paul VI, 1963;
The musical show *Oliver!* was first produced, London, 1960;
Zaïre became independent, 1960;
Guernsey was occupied by German forces, 1940;
The novel *Gone with the Wind*, by Margaret Mitchell, was first published, 1936;
The 'Night of the Long Knives' – Hitler's purge of the Nazis – took place, when Von Schleicher, Roehm and others were killed, 1934;

Tower Bridge in London was officially opened, 1894;
The comic opera *The Nautch Girl* was first produced, London, 1891;
The use of the pillory was abolished by Parliament, 1837;
The naval Mutiny at the Nore was suppressed, 1797;
The English and Dutch fleets were defeated by the French under Tourville at the Battle of Beachy Head, 1690;
The Royalists were victorious at the Battle of Atherton Moor, 1643.

TODAY IS THE FEAST DAY OF St Bertrand of Le Mans, St Emma, St Erentrude, St Martial of Limoges, St Theobald or Thibaud of Provins and The First Martyrs of the Church of Rome.

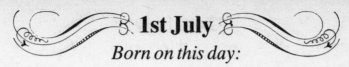

1st July

Born on this day:

HRH the Princess of Wales, 1961;
Trevor Eve, actor, 1951;
Genevieve Bujold, French-Canadian film actress, 1942;
John Gould, composer and musical comedian, 1941;
Kenneth Clarke, government minister, 1940;
Jean Marsh, actress, 1934;
Sydney Pollack, US film director, 1934;
Peter Walwyn, racing trainer, 1933;
Leslie Caron, French film actress, 1931;
Hans Werner Henze, German composer, 1926;
Farley Granger, US film actor, 1925;
Olivia de Havilland, film actress, 1916;
Amy Johnson, aviator, 1903;
William Wyler, US film director and producer, 1902;
Charles Laughton, film actor, 1899;
Isaak Emmanuilovich Babel, Russian short-story writer, 1894;
Sir Bernard Thomas Heinze, Australian musician and conductor, 1894;
Maundy Gregory, infamous 'honours broker', 1877;
Sir Nigel Ross Playfair, actor and manager, 1874;
Louis Blériot, French aviator, 1872;
Sir Robert Stawell Ball, astronomer and mathematician, 1840;
George Sand [Amandine-Aurore-Lucile Dupin], French novelist, 1804;
Baron Gottfried Wilhelm von Leibniz, German philosopher and mathematician, 1646.

Died on this day:

Juan Domingo Perón, Argentine president, 1974;
Alphonse-Marie-Léon Daudet, French novelist, 1942;
Erik Alfred Leslie Satie, French composer, 1925;
George Frederick Watts, painter and sculptor, 1904;
Harriet Beecher Stowe, US author of *Uncle Tom's Cabin*, 1896;
Allan Pinkerton, Scottish/US founder of the Detective Agency, 1884;
Charles Goodyear, US inventor, 1860;
Christophe Plantin, French typographer and printer, 1589;
John Bradford, Protestant martyr, burnt at the stake, 1555.

Occurred on this day:

The Warsaw Pact was finally abolished, 1991;
The first tests of nuclear bombs began over Bikini Atoll, 1946;
Jersey was occupied by German forces, 1940;
The first conscripts in Britain were called up, 1939;
The first Battle of the Somme began, 1916;
The Union of South Africa was formed, with Dominion status, 1910;
Bernard Shaw's play *Candida* was first performed, 1900;
The Dominion of Canada was established, 1867;
The Battle of Gettysburg [American Civil War] began, 1863;
King William III defeated the Jacobites under James II at the Battle of the Boyne, 1690.

TODAY IS THE FEAST DAY OF Saints Aaron and Julius, St Carilephus or Calais, St Eparchius or Cybard, St Gall of Clermont, St Oliver Plunket, St Servanus or Serf, St Shenute, St Simeon Salus and St Thierry or Theodoric of Mont d'Or.

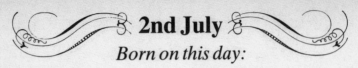

2nd July

Born on this day:

Kenneth Clarke, MP, 1940;

Lord Owen [Dr David Owen], former MP, 1938;

John Timpson, broadcaster, 1928;

Lord Mackay of Clashfern, Lord Chancellor, 1927;

Dennis Flanders, artist, 1915;

Lord Beloff, historian, 1913;

René Lacoste, former tennis champion, 1905;

Lord Home of the Hirsel, former prime minister, 1903;

Jack Hylton, bandleader, 1892;

Hermann Hesse, German poet and novelist, 1877;

Sir William Henry Bragg, physicist, 1862;

Theodor Hildebrand, German painter, 1804;

Friedrich Gottfried Klopstock, German poet, 1724;

Christoph Willibald Glück, German composer, 1714;

Thomas Cranmer, Archbishop of Canterbury, 1489;

Jacopo Tatti Sansovino, Florentine sculptor, 1486.

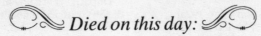

Died on this day:

Vladimir Vladimirovich Nabokov, Russian novelist and lepidopterist, 1977;

Betty Grable [Elizabeth Ruth Grable], US film actress, 1973;

Ernest Miller Hemingway, US novelist, committed suicide, 1961;

Amelia Earhart, US aviator, disappeared over the Pacific, 1937;

Manoel II, ex-King of Portugal, 1932;

Émile Coué, French psychotherapist, 1926;

Sir Herbert Beerbohm Tree, actor-manager, 1917;

José de la Cruz Porfirio Díaz, Mexican military leader and dictator, 1915;

Joseph Chamberlain, statesman, 1914;

Sir Robert Peel, statesman, 1850;

Christian Friedrich Samuel Hahnemann, German physician and founder of homeopathy, 1843;

Jean-Jacques Rousseau, French philosopher and writer, 1778;

Nostradamus [Michel de Nostre-Dame], astrologer, 1566;

Henry the Fowler, King of Germany, 936.

Occurred on this day:

The Erskine Bridge over the River Clyde in Scotland was opened, 1971;

In the USA, President Johnson signed the Civil Rights Act, 1964;

A German submarine sank the British prison ship *Arandora Star*, carrying 1,640 interned Germans and Italians to Canada; of whom more than 1,000 were drowned, 1940;

The Vichy government was set up in France, 1940;

James Abram Garfield, 20th president of the USA, was shot by Charles Jules Guiteau, 1881;

Oliver Cromwell defeated the Royalist troops at the Battle of Marston Moor, 1644.

TODAY IS THE FEAST DAY OF St Monegundis, St Otto of Bamberg and Saints Processus and Martinian.

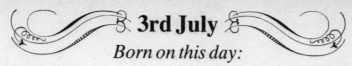

3rd July

Born on this day:

Sir Richard Hadlee, New Zealand cricketer, 1951;
Susan Penhaligon, actress, 1950;
Iain Macdonald-Smith, yachtsman, 1945;
Paul Young, actor, 1944;
Judith Durham, singer, 1943;
Tom Stoppard, playwright, 1937;
Carlos Kleiber, conductor, 1930;
Evelyn Anthony, author, 1928;
Ken Russell, film director, 1927;
Baroness Ryder of Warsaw, founder of homes for the disabled, 1923;
Elizabeth Taylor [Coles], novelist, 1912;
Stavros Niarchos, Greek shipping magnate, 1909;
Francis Steegmuller, US author, 1906;
Franz Kafka, Czech writer, 1883;
George Michael Cohan, US entertainer and songwriter, 1878;
William Henry Davies, poet, 1871;
Richard Bedford Bennett, 1st Viscount, Canadian statesman, 1870;
Leoš Janáček, Czech composer, 1854;
Henry Grattan, Irish patriot, 1746;
John Singleton Copley, US portrait and historical painter, 1737;
Robert Adam, architect and designer, 1728;
Louis XI, King of France, 1423.

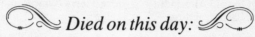

Died on this day:

Deems Taylor, US composer, 1966;
David Alfred Thomas, 1st Viscount Rhondda, statesman, 1918;
Joel Chandler Harris, US author and creator of 'Uncle Remus', 1908;
Theodor Herzl, Zionist leader, 1904;
Karl Adolf Heinrich Hess, German painter, 1849;
Dorothea Jordan [Phillips], actress and royal mistress, 1816;
Marie de' Medici, Queen of France, 1642;
Giuseppe Cesari [Cavaliere d'Arpino], Italian painter, 1640.

Occurred on this day:

An Israeli commando force made an airborne raid on Entebbe airport, Uganda, to free 105 hostages from a hijacked aircraft, 1976;
France proclaimed the independence of Algeria after a referendum, 1962;
Food rationing in Britain ended, 1954;
The Four-Power occupation of Berlin began, 1945;
The Royal Navy sank the French fleets at Oran and other ports in North Africa, 1940;
John Logie Baird transmitted the first colour television, London, 1928;
Idaho became the 43rd of the United States, 1890;
The Austrians were defeated by the Prussians at the Battle of Sadowa [Königgratz], 1866;
General Meade, leading the Union forces, defeated the Confederates at the Battle of Gettysburg, 1863;
King Louis XVIII entered Paris, ending the 'Hundred Days', 1815;
George Washington became commander-in-chief of American forces, 1775.

TODAY IS THE FEAST DAY OF St Anatolius of Constantinople, St Anatolius of Laodicea, St Bernardino Realino, St Helidorus of Altino, Saints Irenaeus and Mustiola, St Leo II, pope, St Rumold or Rombaut and St Thomas the Apostle.

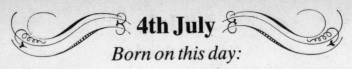

4th July

Born on this day:

Alastair Goodlad, MP, 1943;
HRH Prince Michael of Kent, 1942;
Colin Welland, actor and playwright, 1934;
Gina Lollobrigida, Italian film actress, 1927;
Neil Simon, US playwright, 1927;
Alec Bedser, cricketer, 1918;
Eric Bedser, cricketer, 1918;
Lord Wyatt of Weeford [Woodrow Wyatt], 1918;
Virginia Graham, US film actress, 1912;
George Lloyd Murphy, US film actor, dancer, singer and politician, 1902;
Daniel Louis Armstrong, US jazz trumpeter and singer, 1900;
Gertrude Lawrence [Gertrud Alexandra Dagmar Lawrence Klasen], actress, 1898;

Louis Burt Mayer, Hollywood 'movie mogul', 1885;
John Calvin Coolidge, 30th president of the USA, 1872;
Hugo Winckler, German Assyriologist, 1863;
Joseph Pennell, US etcher and author, 1860;
Dr Thomas John Barnardo, philanthropist, 1845;
Stephen Collins Foster, US songwriter, 1826;
Giuseppe Garibaldi, Italian leader, 1807;
Nathaniel Hawthorne, US author, 1804;
Jean-Pierre Blanchard, French balloonist, 1753.

Died on this day:

Louis Wain, illustrator of cats, 1939;
Suzanne Lenglen, French tennis player, 1938;
Marie Curie [Marja Sklodowska], Polish/French chemist, 1934;
James Monroe, 5th president of the USA, 1831;
François-René Viscomte de Chateaubriand, French politician and writer, 1848;

John Adams, 2nd president of the USA, 1826;
Thomas Jefferson, 3rd president of the USA, 1826;
Samuel Richardson, novelist and author of *Pamela*, 1761;
Ortelius [Abraham Oertel], Flemish cartographer, 1598;
Bencivieni di Pepo [Giovanni Cimabue], Italian painter, 1302.

Occurred on this day:

Hanna Reitsch made the first successful flight in a helicopter, Germany, 1937;
The construction of the Panama Canal began, 1904;
The Statue of Liberty was presented by the people of France to the USA, 1883;
The Union army defeated the Confederates at the Battle of Vicksburg, 1863;
Karl Heinrich Marx and Friedrich Engels published the *Communist Manifesto*, 1848;

The first London bus ran from Marylebone Road to the Bank of England, 1829;
The US Military Academy was opened at West Point with 10 cadets, 1802;
The American Declaration of Independence was adopted, 1776;
Providence, Rhode Island, was founded by the English Puritan, Roger Williams, 1636;
Saladin defeated the Crusaders at the Battle of Tiberias, 1187.

TODAY IS THE FEAST DAY OF St Andrew of Crete, St Bertha of Blangy, St Elizabeth of Portugal, St Odo of Canterbury, St Ulric of Augsburg and The Martyrs of Dorchester.

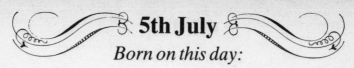

5th July

Born on this day:

John Wright, New Zealand cricketer, 1954;
Elizabeth Emanuel, royal dressmaker, 1953;
Mark Cox, tennis player, 1943;
Philip Madoc, actor, 1934;
Tony Lock, cricketer, 1929;
Maj.-Gen. Sir Jeremy Moore, former commander, Land Forces, Falkland Islands, 1928;
Lord Gormley, former trade union leader, 1917;
Georges Pompidou, president of France, 1911;
Sir Harold Acton, author, 1904;
Gordon Jacob, composer, 1895;
Jean Cocteau, French poet, novelist and artist, 1889;

Jan Kubelik, Czech violinist, 1880;
Dwight Filley Davis, US statesman and founder of the Davis Tennis Cup, 1879;
Édouard Herriot, French statesman and writer, 1872;
Cecil John Rhodes, colonial developer and politician, 1853;
William Thomas Stead, journalist and social reformer, 1849;
Phineas Taylor Barnum, US showman, 1810;
George Henry Borrow, author and linguist, 1803;
William Crotch, composer and musical prodigy, 1775;
Sarah Siddons [Kemble], actress, 1755;
Luke Hansard, printer of *Hansard*, 1752.

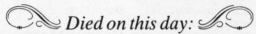

Died on this day:

Georgette Heyer, novelist, 1974;
Wilhelm Backhaus, Austrian pianist, 1969;
Walter Adolph Gropius, US architect, 1969;
Thomas Joseph Mboya, Kenyan statesman, assassinated, 1969;
Georges Bernanos, French novelist and writer, 1948;

Sir Austen Henry Layard, archaeologist, 1894;
Joseph-Nicéphore Niepce, French pioneer in photography, 1833;
Sir Thomas Stamford Raffles, founder of Singapore, 1826;
Ernst Theodor Wilhelm Amadeus Hoffmann, German author, artist and composer, 1822.

Occurred on this day:

The first Assembly opened of the Western European Union at Strasbourg, 1955;
The National Health Service came into operation, 1948;
After the General Election, the Labour Party received its first absolute majority, 1945;
Oliveira Salazar became virtual dictator of Portugal at the head of a fascist regime, 1932;
The Salvation Army was founded, when William Booth held the first open-air Christian Mission at Mile End, London, 1865;

The travel agents, Thomas Cook and Son, were founded, 1841;
The gold sovereign coin was first issued, 1817;
George Hammond, the first British ambassador to the USA, was appointed, 1791;
In London, the Star Chamber was abolished, 1641.

TODAY IS THE FEAST DAY OF St Antony-Mary Zaccaria and St Athanasius the Athonite.

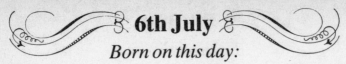

6th July

Born on this day:

Geraldine James, actress, 1950;
The Hon. Jonathon Porritt, ecologist, 1950;
Sylvester Stallone, US film actor and director, 1946;
Jeff King, jockey, 1941;
Mary Peters, athlete, 1939;
Vladimir Ashkenazy, Russian pianist, 1937;
Dave Allen, comedian, 1936;
Peter Glossop, operatic baritone, 1928;
Janet Leigh, US film actress, 1927;
Elisabeth Lutyens, composer, 1906;
Walter Runciman, 1st Baron Runciman, shipowner, 1847;

Maximilian, Emperor of Mexico, 1832;
Karl Engel, German musicologist, 1818;
Nicholas I, Tsar of Russia, 1796;
Sir William Jackson Hooker, botanist, 1785;
Sir Thomas Stamford Raffles, founder of Singapore, at sea, off Port Morant, Jamaica, 1781;
Catherine Maria Fanshawe, painter and poet, 1765;
John Flaxman, sculptor, 1755;
John Paul Jones, US naval hero, 1747.

Died on this day:

Otto Klemperer, German conductor, 1973;
Daniel Louis Armstrong, US jazz musician, 1971;
William Harrison Faulkner, US novelist, 1962;
Aneurin Bevan, statesman, 1960;
Kenneth Grahame, children's author, 1932;
Odilon Redon, French painter and engraver, 1916;
Henri-René-Albert-Guy de Maupassant, French writer, 1893;

Baron Pierre-Narcisse Guérin, French painter, 1833;
Sigismund II Augustus, King of Poland, 1572;
King Edward VI, 1553;
St Thomas More, executed, 1535;
Ludovico Ariosto, Italian poet, 1533;
Jan Huss, Bohemian religious reformer, burnt at the stake, 1415;
King Henry II, 1189.

Occurred on this day:

Civil war erupted in Nigeria, when fighting broke out between federal troops and men from the province of Biafra, 1967;
Nyasaland, renamed Malawi, became independent, 1964;
The Saar became part of West Germany, 1959;
London's last tram ran, 1952;
The first all-talking feature film, *The Lights of New York*, was shown in New York, 1928;
The first airship to cross the Atlantic, the British *R34*, reached New York, having crossed in 108 hours, 1919;

Brooklands motor racing circuit was opened, 1907;
The Duke of York [later King George V] married Princess Victoria Mary of Teck, 1893;
Louis Pasteur successfully treated a subject with his anti-rabies vaccine, 1885;
Queensland, Australia, was separated from New South Wales as a colony in its own right, 1859;
At the Battle of Sedgemoor, the last to be fought on English soil, the troops of James II defeated the Duke of Monmouth, 1685.

TODAY IS THE FEAST DAY OF St Dominica, St Goar, St Godeleva, St Mary Goretti, St Modwenna, St Romulus of Fiesole, St Sexburga and St Sisoes.

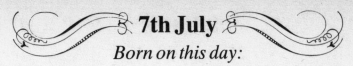

7th July

Born on this day:

Alessandro Nannini, Italian racing driver, 1959;

Tony Jacklin, golfer, 1944;

Michael Howard, MP, 1941;

Bill Oddie, actor, comedian and ornithologist, 1941;

Ringo Starr, former Beatle, 1940;

Hamish MacInnes, mountaineer, 1930;

Charles Dyer, playwright, novelist and actor, 1928;

Brenda Bruce, actress, 1922;

Pierre Cardin, French fashion designer, 1922;

Jon Pertwee, actor, 1919;

Gretchen Franklin, actress, 1911;

Gian Carlo Menotti, Italian composer, 1911;

Lieut.-Gen. Sir Ian Harris, racehorse breeder, 1910;

The Hon. Sir Steven Runciman CH, historian, 1903;

Vittorio de Sica, Italian film director, 1901;

George Cukor, US film director, 1899;

Marc Chagall, Russian painter and designer, 1887;

Lion Feuchtwanger, German novelist and playwright, 1884;

Gustav Mahler, Austrian composer, 1860;

Félicien Rops, Belgian painter and engraver, 1833;

Joseph-Marie Jacquard, French silk-weaver and inventor, 1752;

Thomas Hooker, clergyman and Puritan, 1586 [see also Deaths].

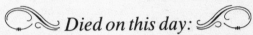

Died on this day:

Dame Flora Robson, actress, 1984;

Sir Allen Lane, publisher and founder of Penguin Books, 1970;

Sir Arthur Conan Doyle, author, 1930;

Leo Sowerby, US composer, 1895;

Georg Simon Ohm, German physicist, 1854;

Richard Brinsley Butler Sheridan, playwright, 1816;

Thomas Blacklock, poet, 1791;

Thomas Hooker, clergyman and Puritan, 1647 [see also Births];

Giacomo da Vignola, Italian architect, 1573;

King Edward I, 1307.

Occurred on this day:

The musical show *Mutiny* was first produced, London, 1985;

The 53,300-ton liner *United States* captured the Blue Riband of the Atlantic from the *Queen Mary* on her maiden voyage from New York to Southampton, 1952;

The musical show *The Ace of Clubs* was first produced, London, 1950;

The Vatican City became a sovereign state, 1929;

The BBC broadcast the first gramophone record programme, presented by Christopher Stone, 1927;

Kelvin Hall exhibition building in Glasgow was destroyed by fire, 1925;

Captain Matthew Calbraith Perry arrived in Japan, opening contacts with the West, 1853.

TODAY IS THE FEAST DAY OF Saints Cyril and Methodius, Saints Ethelburga, Ercongota and Sethrida, St Felix of Nantes, St Hedda of Winchester, St Palladius and St Pantaenus.

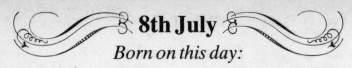

8th July

Born on this day:

Keith Fielding, rugby player, 1949;

Brian Walden, journalist and broadcaster, 1932;

Bruce Gyngell, managing director, TV-am, 1929;

Sir Roy Shaw, former secretary-general, the Arts Council, 1918;

Billy Eckstine, US singer, 1915;

Nelson Aldrich Rockefeller, US politician, 1908;

Alec [Alexander Raban] Waugh, writer, 1898;

Richard Aldington, novelist and critic, 1892;

Stanton Macdonald-Wright, US abstract painter, 1890;

Mary Agnes Hamilton, novelist, 1884;

Percy Aldridge Grainger [George Percy], Australian composer and pianist, 1882;

Harry Von Tilzer [Harry Gumm], US composer, 1872;

Ferguson Wright Hume [Fergus Hume], novelist, 1859;

Sir Arthur John Evans, archaeologist, 1851;

John Davison Rockefeller, US millionaire, 1839;

Ferdinand Adolf August Heinrich, Count von Zeppelin, German soldier and inventor, 1838;

Joseph Chamberlain, statesman, 1836;

Tom Cribb, pugilist, 1781;

Jean de la Fontaine, French poet and writer of fables, 1621.

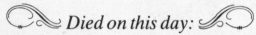

Died on this day:

Frank Hampson, creator of 'Dan Dare', 1985;

Michael Wilding, film actor, 1979;

Vivien Leigh [Vivian Mary Hartley], film actress, 1967;

Henry Havelock Ellis, physician and author, 1939;

Anthony Hope [Sir Anthony Hope Hawkins], novelist, 1933;

Hablot Knight Browne ['Phiz'], artist, 1882;

Sir William Edward Parry, Arctic explorer, 1855;

Sir Henry Raeburn, portrait painter, 1823;

Percy Bysshe Shelley, poet, at sea at La Spezia, Italy, 1822;

Christiaan Huygens, Dutch physicist, 1695;

Pope Gregory XV, 1623.

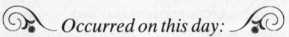

Occurred on this day:

General Douglas MacArthur was appointed commander of United Nations forces in Korea, 1950;

Britain took over the East African Protectorate as Kenya Colony, 1920;

The Ziegfeld Follies opened for the first time, New York, 1907;

French victory at Fort Ticonderoga stemmed the advance of the British upon Quebec, 1758;

The Battle of Poltava was fought, when Peter the Great of Russia soundly defeated the invading Swedish army of Charles XII, 1709;

Vasco da Gama, Portuguese navigator, set sail from Lisbon with four ships on a voyage to India, 1497.

TODAY IS THE FEAST DAY OF St Adrian III, pope, Saints Aquila and Prisca or Priscilla [husband and wife], St Grimbald, St Kilian and his Companions, St Procopius of Caesarea, St Raymund of Toulouse, St Sunniva and her Companions and St Withburga.

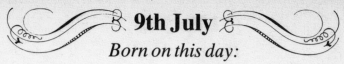

9th July

Born on this day:

Steve Coppell, footballer, 1955;
David Hockney, painter, 1937;
Richard Wilson, actor and director, 1936;
Michael Williams, actor, 1935;
Richard Demarco, water-colour artist, 1930;
John Heath-Stubbs, poet and lecturer, 1918;
General Jarl Wahlström, of the Salvation Army, 1918;
Edward Heath, MP and former prime minister, 1916;
Sir George Edwards OM, former chairman, BAC, 1908;
Dame Barbara Cartland, romantic novelist, 1901;

Charles Bruce Bairnsfather, cartoonist, 1888;
Simon Marks, 1st Baron Marks of Broughton, a founder of Marks and Spencer, 1888;
Ottorino Respighi, Italian composer, 1879;
Franz Boas, Germany anthropologist, 1858;
Robert Frederick Blum, US artist, 1857;
Nikola Tesla, US electrician and inventor, 1856;
Elias Howe, US inventor of the sewing-machine, 1819;
Rudolf Schadow, German sculptor, 1786;
Henry Hallam, historian, 1777;
Ann Radcliffe [Ann Ward], novelist, 1764.

Died on this day:

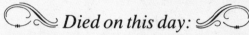

Randall Thompson, US composer, 1984;
Sir Francis Meredith Wilfrid Meynell, book designer and typographer, 1975;
King Camp Gillette, US safety-razor inventor and manufacturer, 1932;
Alexander Keith Johnston the Elder, geographer, 1871;

Zachary Taylor, 12th president of the USA, 1850;
Edmund Burke, statesman, 1797;
Philip V, King of Spain, 1746;
Sir William Berkeley, governor of Virginia, 1677;
Jan van Eyck, Flemish painter, 1440;
Stephen Langton, Archbishop of Canterbury, 1228.

Occurred on this day:

The Bahamas became independent, 1973;
The Bank of England issued £20 banknotes [previous £20 notes had been withdrawn in 1945], 1970;
The Allies captured Caen in Normandy, 1944;
The Treaty of Versailles was ratified by Germany, 1919;
German South-West Africa surrendered to General Smuts, 1915;
In Edinburgh, Madeleine Hamilton Smith was acquitted of murder, the verdict being 'not proven', 1857;

The Congress of Tucuman was held, at which Argentina declared its independence from Spain, 1816;
Holland was joined to France under Napoleon, 1810;
French troops and Indians attacked General Braddock's forces near Fort Duquesne, 1755;
King Henry VIII divorced Anne of Cleves, 1540.

TODAY IS THE FEAST DAY OF St Everild, St Nicholas Pieck and his Companions, The Martyrs of Gorcum [Holland] and St Veronica de Julianis.

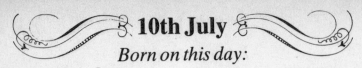

10th July

Born on this day:

Tommy Carmody, jockey, 1956;
Virginia Wade, tennis player, 1945;
Arthur Ashe, tennis player, 1943;
Keith Stackpole, Australian cricketer, 1940;
John Dunlop, racehorse trainer, 1939;
Sir Wyn Roberts, MP, 1930;
Josephine Veasey, mezzo-soprano opera singer, 1930;
Ian Wallace, actor, broadcaster and concert singer, 1919;
James Aldridge, author, 1918;
Reg Smythe, cartoonist, 1917;
Evelyn Laye, actress and singer, 1900;
Carl Orff, German composer, 1895;
Jimmy McHugh, US composer, 1892;

John Standish Surtees Prendergast Vereker, 6th Viscount Gort, soldier, 1886;
Marcel Proust, French author, 1871;
Will Bradley, US artist, author and film director, 1868;
Camille Pissarro, French painter, 1830;
Robert Chambers, publisher and author, 1802;
Captain Frederick Marryat, novelist, 1792;
Sir William Blackstone, jurist, 1723;
Aphra Behn, playwright and novelist, baptised, 1640;
John Calvin, French religious reformer, 1509.

Died on this day:

Giorgio de Chirico, Italian painter, 1978;
Sholem Asch, US novelist, 1957;
[Ferdinand] Jelly Roll Morton, US ragtime composer and pianist, 1941;
Albert Chevalier, music-hall artiste, 1923;
Pedro Antonio de Alarcón y Ariza, Spanish writer and journalist, 1891;
Karl Richard Lepsius, German Egyptologist, 1884;

Louis-Jacques-Mandé Daguerre, French photographic pioneer, 1851;
George Stubbs, animal painter, 1806;
William I, the Silent, Prince of Orange, assassinated, 1584;
Henry II, King of France, killed, 1559;
El Cid [Rodrigo Díaz de Vivar], Spanish hero, 1099;
Hadrian [Publius Aelius Hadrianus], Roman emperor, 138.

Occurred on this day:

The communications satellite, *Telstar*, was launched, 1962;
The first parking meters were installed in London, 1958;
The Allied invasion of Sicily began, 1943;
The Battle of Britain began, 1940;
Mongolia was proclaimed an independent state, 1921;

Wyoming became the 44th of the United States, 1890;
Lady Jane Grey was proclaimed Queen of England, 1553;
King Henry VI of Lancaster was captured by the Yorkists at the Battle of Northampton, 1460.

TODAY IS THE FEAST DAY OF St Amelberga, Saints Rufina and Secunda, The Seven Brothers and St Felicity.

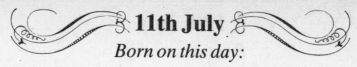

11th July

Born on this day:

Peter de Savary, entrepreneur and yachtsman, 1944;
John Stride, actor, 1936;
Julia Trevelyan Oman, TV, film and theatre designer, 1930;
Hermann Prey, German baritone, 1929;
Greville Janner, MP, 1928;
Theodore Maiman, US physicist and inventor of the laser, 1927;
Bill Crozier, radio producer, 1924;
Gough Whitlam QC, former Australian prime minister, 1916;
Sir John Rothenstein, former director, the Tate Gallery, 1901;
Arthur William Tedder, 1st Baron, marshal of the RAF, 1890;

Celestin-François Nanteuil, French painter and engraver, 1813;
John Quincy Adams, 6th president of the USA, 1767;
Thomas Bowdler, editor and self-appointed censor of Shakespeare, 1754;
Joseph-Jérôme de Lalande [Le Français], French astronomer, 1732;
Charles-Antoine Coypel, French painter, 1694;
Frederick I, King of Prussia, 1657;
Sir Kenelm Digby, diplomat and writer, 1603;
Luis de Góngora y Argote, Spanish poet and writer, 1561;
Robert the Bruce, King of Scotland, 1274.

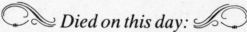

Died on this day:

Laurence Kerr Olivier, Baron, actor, 1989;
Buddy DeSylva [George Gard DeSylva], US lyricist and film director, 1950;
Paul Nash, painter, printmaker and photographer, 1946;
Lucien Pissarro, French landscape painter and book designer, 1944;
Sir Arthur John Evans, archaeologist, 1941;
George Gershwin [Jacob Gershvin], US composer, 1937;

Alfred Dreyfus, French soldier, 1935;
William Ernest Henley, poet and critic, 1903;
Charles Macklin, Irish actor and playwright, 1797;
William Robertson, Scottish historian, 1793;
Girolamo Genga, Italian painter and architect, 1551.

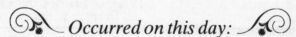

Occurred on this day:

The Britannia Road Bridge across the Menai Strait was opened by the Prince of Wales, 1980.
The first TV transmissions via *Telstar* began from Maine, USA, to France, 1962;
The province of Katanga in Zaïre was proclaimed independent by its prime minister, Moise Tshombe, 1960;
Following a plebiscite, Allenstein and Marienwerder in Poland voted for union with Germany, 1920;

The bombardment of Alexandria by the British Fleet began, 1882;
Waterloo Station, London, was officially opened, 1848;
Captain James Cook sailed from Plymouth on his last voyage, 1776;
The Duke of Marlborough was victorious over the French at the Battle of Oudenarde, 1708.

TODAY IS THE FEAST DAY OF St Benedict, St Drostan, St Hidulf, St John of Bergamo and St Olga.

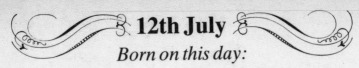

12th July

Born on this day:

Jennifer Saunders, comedienne and actress, 1958;

Gareth Edwards, rugby player, 1947;

Bill Cosby, US comedian and actor, 1937;

Michael Gough Matthews, director, Royal College of Music, 1931;

Sir Alastair Burnet, broadcaster, 1928;

Frank Windsor, actor, 1927;

Prof. Sir Randolph Quirk, linguistics authority, 1920;

Yul Brynner [Youl Bryner], US film actor, 1915;

Viscount Camrose, former chairman, the *Daily Telegraph*, 1909;

Milton Berle, US comedian, 1908;

Oscar Hammerstein II, US lyricist and author, 1895;

Kirsten Flagstad, Norwegian operatic singer, 1895;

Amedeo Modigliani, Italian painter and sculptor, 1884;

Frederick Edwin Smith, 1st Earl of Birkenhead, statesman, 1872;

Charles Cottet, French landscape painter, 1863;

George Eastman, US photographic pioneer, 1854;

Eugène-Louis Boudin, French painter, 1825;

Ludwig Molitor, German composer, 1817;

Henry David Thoreau, US author and naturalist, 1817;

Josiah Wedgwood, potter, 1730;

Jean Petitot, French-Swiss enamel painter, 1607;

Gaius Julius Caesar, Roman emperor, 100 BC.

Died on this day:

Kenneth More, actor, 1982;

Mazo de la Roche, Canadian novelist, 1961;

Joseph Jongen, Belgian composer, 1953;

Douglas Hyde, poet, historian and first president of the Irish Republic, 1949;

Ferguson Wright Hume [Fergus Hume], novelist, 1932;

Gertrude Margaret Lowthian Bell, traveller and archaeologist, 1926;

The Hon. Charles Stewart Rolls, aviator and automobile manufacturer, killed, 1910;

Robert Stevenson, Scottish lighthouse engineer, 1850;

Alexander Hamilton, US statesman, 1804;

Titus Oates, impostor and conspirator, 1705;

Jean Picard, astronomer, 1682;

Desiderius Erasmus, Dutch scholar, 1536;

Jack [John] Cade, English rebel leader, 1450.

Occurred on this day:

Reed International agreed to sell the Mirror Group newspapers to Robert Maxwell's Pergamon Press, 1984;

Thor Heyerdahl and a crew of seven crossed the Atlantic from Morocco to Barbados in 57 days, using a papyrus boat, 1970;

The musical show *Bitter Sweet* was first performed, London, 1929;

Alfred Dreyfus was pardoned, his sentence quashed and he was restored to his regiment, 1906;

Britain took possession of Cyprus, 1878;

Victoria Embankment, London, was opened by the Prince of Wales, 1870;

The Battle of Aughrim was fought in Ireland by William of Orange, 1691;

The Armada set sail from Spain, 1588;

King Henry VIII married Catherine Parr at Hampton Court Palace, 1543;

The Crusaders took Acre, 1191.

TODAY IS THE FEAST DAY OF St Felix, Saints Hermagoras and Fortunatus, St Jason, St John Gualbert, St John Jones, St John the Iberian and St Veronica.

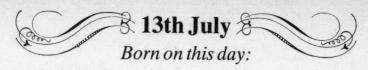

13th July

Born on this day:

Larry Gomes, West Indies cricketer, 1953;
Bryan Murray, actor, 1949;
Chris Serle, TV presenter, 1943;
Harrison Ford, US actor, 1942;
Patrick Stewart, actor, 1940;
David Storey, playwright, 1933;
Sir James Craig, Arabic scholar, 1924;
Kenneth MacKenzie Clark, 1st Baron, art historian, 1903;
Sidney Blackmer, US film actor, 1895;
Clifford Bax, playwright, 1886;
Sidney James Webb, 1st Baron Passfield, social reformer, 1859;
Sir George Gilbert Scott, architect, 1811;
Marshal Marie-Edmé-Patrice-Maurice MacMahon, Marshal of France and president, 1808;
John Clare, peasant poet and farm labourer, 1793;
John Dee, scholar, mathematician and astrologer, 1527.

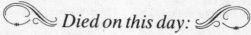 Died on this day:

Sir Seretse Khama, president of Botswana, 1980.
Oliver Hilary Sambourne Messel, designer, 1978;
Arnold Schoenberg, Austrian/US composer, 1951;
Walter Donaldson, US composer, 1947;
John Charles Frémont, US explorer, 1890;
James Northcote, painter, 1831;
Jean-Paul Marat, French revolutionary leader, murdered, 1793;
James Bradley, astronomer, 1762;
Richard Cromwell, Lord Protector of England, 1712;
Bertrand du Guesclin, Constable of France, 1380.

Occurred on this day:

In Germany, all political parties but the Nazis were banned, 1933;
The *France II* [5,806 tons], the world's largest sailing vessel, was wrecked off the coast of New Caledonia, 1922;
The airship *R34* landed in Norfolk after returning from the USA, 1919;
The British bombardment of Alexandria ended, 1882;
The Treaty of Berlin was signed, granting Bosnia and Herzegovina to Austria, 1878;
The independence of Romania from Turkey was proclaimed, 1878;
The Scottish Reform Act was passed, 1868;
Queen Victoria went to live in Buckingham Palace, 1837;
Charlotte Corday murdered Jean-Paul Marat in his bath, 1793;
The Parliamentarians were defeated at the Battle of Devizes, 1643;
The Spanish and English armies defeated the French at Gravelines, 1558;
Christ Church, Oxford, was founded as Cardinal College by Cardinal Wolsey, 1525.

TODAY IS THE FEAST DAY OF Saints Bridget and Maura, St Eugenius of Carthage, St Francis Solano, St Henry the Emperor, St Mildred and St Silas or Silvanus.

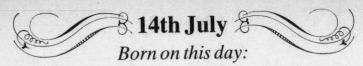

14th July

Born on this day:

Bruce Oldfield, fashion designer, 1950;
Sue Lawley, TV presenter, 1946;
Robert Stephens, actor, 1931;
Polly Bergen, US film actress, singer and cosmetics executive, 1930;
Lord Rees-Mogg, chairman, Broadcasting Standards Council, 1928;
Air Chief Marshal Sir David Evans, military adviser to British Aerospace, 1924;
James Otis Purdy, US novelist, 1923;
Leon Garfield, author, 1921;
Ingmar Bergman, Swedish film-maker, 1918;
Woody Guthrie, US folk singer, 1912;
Isaac Bashevis Singer, Polish author, 1904;

Gerald Finzi, composer, 1901;
Gertrude Margaret Lowthian Bell, traveller and archaeologist, 1868;
Gustav Klimt, Austrian art nouveau painter, 1862;
Owen Wister, US novelist, 1860;
Emmeline Pankhurst, social reformer and suffragist, 1858;
James Abbott McNeill Whistler, painter and writer, 1834;
Joseph Arthur, Comte de Gobineau, French diplomat and author, 1816;
Jakob Stainer [Steiner], German violin-maker, 1621;
Jules Mazarin [Giulio Mazarini], French cardinal and statesman, 1602.

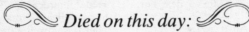

Died on this day:

Adlai Ewing Stevenson, US statesman, 1965;
Grock [Karl Adrien Wettach], Swiss clown, 1959;
Jacinto Benavente y Martínez, Spanish playwright and poet, 1954;
Sir William Henry Perkin, chemist and inventor of aniline dyes, 1907;

Stephanus Johannes Paulus Kruger, Boer leader, 1904;
Alfred Krupp, German industrialist, 1887;
Madame de Staël [Anne-Louise-Germaine Necker], Baronne de Staël-Holstein, French writer, 1817;
Pelham Humfrey, composer, 1674;
Philip II Augustus, King of France, 1223.

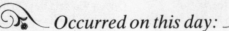 ## Occurred on this day: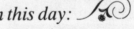

The first BBC television play, *The Man With a Flower in His Mouth*, was transmitted, 1930;
442 lives were lost after the Messageries Maritime SS *Djemnah* was torpedoed in the Mediterranean, 1918;
Dynamite was first demonstrated by Alfred Nobel, 1867;
The first ascent of the Matterhorn was made by Edward Whymper, 1865;

The Battle of Waitzen, between Russians and Hungarians, started, 1849;
The Oxford Movement was launched after a sermon by John Keble, 1833;
During the French Revolution, the Bastille in Paris was stormed, 1789;
The Grand Council of Nîmes ended, 1096.

TODAY IS BASTILLE DAY IN FRANCE AND THE FEAST DAY OF St Camillus de Lellis, St Deusdedit of Canterbury, St Marcellinus or Marchelm and St Ulric of Zell.

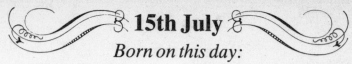

15th July

Born on this day:

Trevor Horn, popular songwriter, 1949;
Linda Ronstadt, US singer, 1946;
Carmen Callil, publisher, 1938;
Sir Harrison Birtwistle, composer, 1934;
Julian Bream, guitarist, 1933;
Ann Jellicoe, playwright and theatre director, 1927;
Dame Iris Murdoch, novelist and philosopher, 1919;
Robert Conquest, author, 1917;
Ralph Hammond Innes, novelist, 1913;
Juliet Pannett, portrait painter, 1911;
Dorothy Fields, US lyricist, 1905;
Noel Gay [Richard Moxon Armitage], composer, 1898;
Alfred Charles William Harmsworth, 1st Viscount Northcliffe, newspaper proprietor, 1865;

Dame Marie Tempest [Marie Susan Etherington] actress, 1864;
Reinhold Begas, German sculptor, 1831;
Heinrich Esser, German conductor and composer, 1818;
Arnaud-Michel d'Abbadie, French explorer, 1815;
Benno Adam, German animal painter, 1812;
Henry Edward Manning, Cardinal Archbishop of Westminster, 1808;
John Barnett [Beer], composer, 1802;
Rembrandt Harmenszoon van Rijn, Dutch painter, 1606;
Inigo Jones, architect, 1573.

Died on this day:

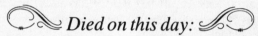

Margaret Mary Lockwood, film actress, 1990;
Paul William Gallico, US writer, 1976;
John Joseph Pershing, US soldier, 1948;
Hugo von Hofmannsthal, Austrian playwright and poet, 1929;
Anton Pavlovich Chekhov, Russian playwright and author, 1904;
Carl Czerny, Austrian pianist and composer, 1857;

Jean-Antoine Houdon, French sculptor, 1828;
James Scott, Duke of Monmouth, illegitimate son of Charles II, executed, 1685;
Annibale Carracci, Italian painter, 1609;
Rudolf I, King of Germany and Holy Roman Emperor, 1291.

Occurred on this day:

Close-up pictures of Mars were transmitted by TV from the US *Mariner IV* satellite, 1965;
Alcoholics Anonymous was founded in Britain, 1948;
Clara Adams of New York was the first woman to complete a round-the-world flight [19 hours, 4 minutes], 1939;
Social insurance came into effect in Britain, 1912;
Margarine was patented by Hippolyte Mège-Mouriès of Paris, 1869;

The *Marseillaise* was adopted as the French national anthem, 1795;
The Royal Society was granted a royal charter, 1662;
The Battle of Tannenburg was fought between the Teutonic Knights and King Ladislas II of Poland, 1410;
Jerusalem was captured by the Crusaders, 1099.

TODAY IS THE FEAST DAY OF St Athanasius of Naples, St Barhadbesaba, St Bonaventure, St David of Munktorp, St Donald, St Edith of Polesworth, St Pompilio Pirrotti, St Swithin and St Vladimir of Kiev.

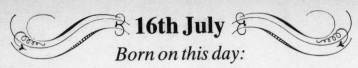

16th July

Born on this day:

Pinchas Zukerman, violinist, 1948;
Margaret Court, tennis player, 1942;
Prof. Anita Brookner, art historian and novelist, 1938;
Tom Rosenthal, publisher, 1935;
Shirley Hughes, author and illustrator, 1927;
Ginger Rogers, US film actress and dancer, 1911;
Trygve Halvdan Lie, Norwegian statesman, 1896;
Roald Amundsen, Norwegian polar explorer, 1872;
George A. Birmingham [Rev. James Owen Hannay], novelist, 1865;
Jens Otto Harry Jespersen, Danish linguist and philologist, 1860;

Eugène Auguste Ysaye, Belgian composer and violinist, 1858;
Henri Viotta, Dutch conductor and composer, 1848;
Luigi Arditi, Italian violinist and composer, 1822;
Mary Baker Eddy, US founder of the Church of Christ, Scientist, 1821;
Jean-Baptiste-Camille Corot, French painter, 1796;
Sir Joshua Reynolds, painter, 1723;
Joseph Wilton, sculptor, 1722;
Andrea del Sarto, Florentine painter, 1486.

Died on this day:

John Phillips Marquand, US novelist, 1960;
Joseph Hilaire Belloc, author, 1953;
Nicholas II, last Tsar of Russia, 1918;
Edmond-Louis-Antoine Huot de Goncourt, French novelist, 1896;
William Hamilton Gibson, US illustrator, author and naturalist, 1896;
Gottfried Keller, Swiss novelist and poet, 1890;
Ned Buntline [Edward Zane Carroll Judson], US Western author, 1886;

Pierre-Jean de Béranger, French poet, 1857;
Josiah Spode, potter, 1827;
Giuseppe Maria Crespi, Italian painter and etcher, 1747;
François-Michel Le Tellier, Marquis de Louvois, French statesman, 1691;
Anne of Cleves, 4th wife of King Henry VIII, 1557;
Pope Innocent III, 1216.

Occurred on this day:

The Bill to abolish the Greater London Council received Royal Assent, 1985;
The Mont Blanc road tunnel, between France and Italy, was opened, 1965;
Leopold III, King of the Belgians, abdicated, 1951;
The first atomic test bomb was exploded at Los Alamos, New Mexico, 1945;
The world's first parking meters were installed in Oklahoma City, USA, 1935;
The Tsar of Russia [Nicholas II] and all his family were murdered by Bolsheviks at Ekaterinburg [Sverdlovsk], 1918;

The District of Columbia was established in the USA, 1790;
Mozart's opera *Il Seraglio* was first performed, Vienna, 1782;
The first banknotes in Europe were issued by the Bank of Stockholm, 1661;
The Spanish defeated the Moors at the Battle of Tolosa, 1212;
The Islamic Era began when Mohammed began his flight from Mecca to Medina [the Hejira], 622.

TODAY IS THE FEAST DAY OF St Athenogenes, St Eustathius of Antioch, St Fulrad, St Helier, St Mary Magdalen Postel and St Reineldis.

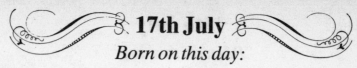

17th July

Born on this day:

Elizabeth Quinn, US deaf actress, 1948;

Wayne Sleep, dancer and choreographer, 1948;

John Patten, MP, 1945;

Mark Burgess, New Zealand cricketer, 1944;

Peter Sissons, TV presenter and newscaster, 1942;

Tim Brooke-Taylor, actor, 1940;

Diahann Carroll, US actress and singer, 1935;

Donald Sutherland, US film actor, 1935;

Ray Galton, scriptwriter, 1930;

Lord Lane, Lord Chief Justice of England, 1918;

Phyllis Diller, US comedienne and concert pianist, 1917;

Sir Hardy Amies, royal dressmaker, 1909;

Christina Ellen Stead, Australian novelist, 1902;

James Cagney, US film actor, 1899;

Mary Clare, stage and film actress, 1894;

Erle Stanley Gardner, US novelist and creator of 'Perry Mason', 1889;

Maxim Maximovich Litvinov [Wallach], Soviet leader, 1876;

Sir Donald Francis Tovey, musicologist, 1875;

Johan August Södermann, composer, 1832;

Hippolyte-Paul Delaroche, French painter, 1797;

John Jacob Astor, US fur trader and merchant, 1763;

Isaac Watts, hymn writer and author of *O God, Our Help in Ages Past*, 1674.

Died on this day:

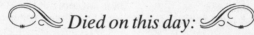

Billie Holiday [Eleanora Fagan], US jazz singer, 1959;

Dragolub [Draza] Mihajlovic, Serbian nationalist, executed, 1946;

George William Russell ['AE'], poet, 1935;

James Abbott McNeill Whistler, painter, 1903;

John Lingard, historian, 1851;

Charles Grey, 2nd Earl, statesman, 1845;

Charlotte Corday, murderess of Marat, executed, 1793;

Adam Smith, political economist and writer, 1790;

William Somerville, poet, 1742.

Occurred on this day:

The Humber Estuary Bridge was opened, 1981;

The US *Apollo* spacecraft and the Russian *Soyuz* ship docked successfully while in orbit, 1975;

Donald Campbell reached a speed of 429.3 mph in his Bluebird car at Lake Eyre, South Australia, 1964;

The musical show *Irma La Douce* was first performed, London, 1958;

Disneyland opened in California, 1955;

The Potsdam Conference was held to consider the occupation of Germany, 1945;

The humorous magazine *Punch* was first published, 1841;

Thomas Saint patented the first sewing machine, 1790;

The Hundred Years' War ended after the defeat of the English at Castillon, 1453.

TODAY IS THE FEAST DAY OF St Clement of Okhrida and his Companions, St Ennodius, St Kenelm, St Leo IV, pope, St Marcellina, St Nerses Lampronazi, The Seven Apostles of Bulgaria and St Speratus and his Companions.

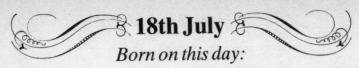

18th July

Born on this day:

Nick Faldo, golfer, 1947;

Richard Branson, founder and chairman, Virgin Group, 1950;

Dennis Lillee, Australian cricketer, 1949;

David Hemery, athlete, 1944;

James Brolin, US actor, 1940;

Edward Bond, playwright and stage director, 1934;

Yevgeny Yevtushenko, Russian poet, 1933;

Michael Medwin, actor, 1929;

Richard Pasco, actor, 1926;

Senator John Glenn, former US astronaut, 1921;

Nelson Mandela, South African politician and lawyer, 1918;

Kenneth Armitage, sculptor, 1916;

Sir Anthony Cox, architect, 1915;

Clifford Odets, US playwright, 1906;

Sydney Horler, thriller writer, 1888;

Vidkun Quisling, Norwegian traitor, 1887;

Laurence Housman, playwright, novelist and illustrator, 1865;

Dr William Gilbert Grace, cricketer, 1848;

William Makepeace Thackeray, novelist and poet, 1811;

The Rev. Gilbert White, naturalist and author, 1720;

Robert Hooke, physicist, 1635.

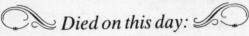

Died on this day:

Jack Hawkins, film actor, 1973;

Vitezslav Novák, Czech pianist and composer, 1949;

Thomas Sturge Moore, poet and engraver, 1944;

Horatio Alger, US clergyman and author of boys' books, 1899;

Charles-Marie Leconte de Lisle, French poet, 1894;

Jane Austen, novelist, 1817;

John Paul Jones, American naval officer, 1792;

Peter III, Tsar of Russia, murdered, 1762;

Jean-Antoine Watteau, French painter, 1721;

Michelangelo Merisi da Caravaggio, Italian painter, 1610.

Occurred on this day:

Vietnam became a member of the United Nations, 1977;

The Spanish Civil War began after a revolt under Emilio Mola and Francisco Franco, 1936;

The Mersey Tunnel was formally opened, 1934;

The first volume of *Mein Kampf* by Adolf Hitler was published, 1925;

The Matrimonial Causes Bill, which gave women equal divorce rights with men, received Royal Assent, 1923;

The Second Battle of the Marne was fought, 1918;

The Dogma of Papal Infallibility in matters of faith and morals was proclaimed by the Vatican Council, 1870.

TODAY IS THE FEAST DAY OF St Arnoul or Arnulf of Metz, St Bruno of Segni, St Frederick of Utrecht and St Pambo.

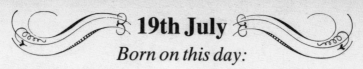

19th July

Born on this day:

Dominic Muldowney, composer and music director, National Theatre, 1952;
Simon Cadell, actor, 1950;
Adrian Noble, artistic director, Royal Shakespeare Company, 1950;
Ilie Nastase, Romanian tennis player, 1946;
George Hamilton IV, US country singer, 1937;
Nicholas Danby, organist, 1935;
John Bratby, painter, 1928;
Ivor Roberts, actor, 1925;
Rear-Admiral Godfrey Place VC, 1921;
Herbert Marcuse, political theorist, 1898;
Dr Archibald Joseph Cronin, novelist, 1896;

Vladimir Vladimirovich Mayakovsky, Russian poet, 1894;
Charles Horace Mayo, US surgeon and co-founder of the Mayo Clinic, 1865;
Lizzie Andrew Borden, alleged US axe murderess, 1860;
Hilaire-Germaine-Edgar Degas, French impressionist painter, 1834;
Gottfried Keller, Swiss poet and novelist, 1819;
Samuel Colt, US inventor of the revolver, 1814;
John Martin, historical painter, 1789.

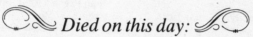

Died on this day:

Edward Knoblock, playwright, 1945;
Thomas ['Tom'] Walter Hayward, cricketer, 1939;
Thomas Cook, travel agent, 1892;
Georges-Maurice de Guérin du Cayla, French poet, 1839;

Matthew Flinders, explorer of Australia, 1814;
Dr John Caius [Keys], physician, founder of the Cambridge college, 1573;
Petrarch [Francesco Petrarca], Italian scholar, poet and humanist, 1374.

Occurred on this day:

The Sandinista forces of Nicaragua entered Managua, 1979;
Laos became independent, 1949;
Liverpool Cathedral was consecrated, 1924;
The Metro in Paris was opened, 1900;
The first Wimbledon Men's Singles Tennis final was played at Wimbledon, 1877;
The Franco-German conflict began after France declared war, 1870;
The *Great Western* steamship was launched at Bristol, 1837;

Queen Caroline was forcibly prevented from appearing at the coronation of King George IV, 1821;
King William III was defeated at Landen [Neerwinden] by the French Marshal Luxembourg, 1693;
The Spanish Armada was sighted off the coast of England, 1588;
The *Mary Rose*, flagship of King Henry VIII, sank in the Solent with the loss of 700 lives, 1545;
King Edward III defeated the Scots at the Battle of Halidon Hill, 1333.

TODAY IS THE FEAST DAY OF St Ambrose Autpert, St Arsenius the Great, St James of Nisibia, St John Plesington, Saints Justa and Rufina, St Macrina the Younger and St Symmachus, pope.

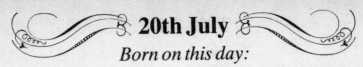

20th July

Born on this day:

Jonathon Morris, actor, 1960;

Desmond Douglas, table tennis player, 1955;

Michael Quinn, chef de cuisine, 1946;

Roger Hunt, footballer, 1938;

Diana Rigg, actress, 1938;

Ted Rogers, comedian, 1935;

Sally Ann Howes, actress, 1930;

Jacques Delors, president, Commission of the EEC, 1925;

Sir Edmund Hillary, New Zealand mountaineer, 1919;

Dame Veronica Wedgwood OM, historian, 1910;

Molly Keane [M. J. Farrell], playwright and author, 1905;

James [Jimmy] Kennedy, popular music composer, 1902;

Dilys Powell, film critic, 1901;

Theda Bara [Theodosia Goodman], US film actress, 1890;

Sir John Charles Walsham Reith, 1st Baron, 1st director-general of the BBC, 1889;

Joseph-Marie Deodat de Severac, French composer, 1873;

Alberto Santos-Dumont, Brazilian aviator, 1873;

Max Liebermann, German painter and etcher, 1847;

John Augustin Daly, US playwright and theatrical manager, 1838;

Sir Richard Owen, palaeontologist and biologist, 1804;

Hyacinthe Rigaud [Hyacinthe-François-Honoré-Mathias-Pierre-Martyr-André-Jean Rigau y Ros], French portrait painter, 1659;

Petrarch [Francesco Petrarca], Italian scholar, lyric poet and humanist, 1304.

Died on this day:

Iain Norman Macleod, statesman, 1970;

Ambroise-Paul-Toussaint-Jules Valéry, French poet and philosopher, 1945;

Guglielmo Marconi, Italian inventor, 1937;

Andrew Lang, scholar, author and fairy-tale editor, 1912;

Pope Leo XIII, 1903;

Jean Ingelow, poet, 1897;

Sir Richard Wallace, founder of the Wallace Collection, 1890;

Prof. John Playfair, mathematician and geologist, 1819;

Hugh O'Neill, 2nd Earl of Tyrone, Irish nationalist, 1616;

Robert II, King of France, 1031.

Occurred on this day:

The space probe *Viking 1* separated its lander which made a soft landing on Mars, 1975;

Turkish forces invaded northern Cyprus, 1974;

The musical show *Stop the World – I Want to Get Off* was first produced, London, 1961;

In Indo-China, an armistice was signed under which Vietnam was divided into North and South, 1954;

The Peace Conference began in Paris, 1946;

At a meeting in Rastenburg, Germany, Colonel von Stauffenburg attempted to assassinate Hitler by planting a bomb, 1944;

The XIth Olympic Games opened in Berlin, 1936;

Oscar Slater's conviction [due to mistaken identity] was quashed, 1928;

Charles Sturt, Australian explorer, entered Simpson's Desert, 1845;

Euston Station, London, opened, 1837.

TODAY IS THE FEAST DAY OF St Ansegisus, St Aurelius of Carthage, St Elias of Jerusalem, St Flavian of Antioch, St Gregory Lopez, St Joseph Barsabas the Just, St Margaret of Antioch, St Wilgefortis or Liberata and St Wulmar.

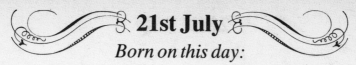

21st July

Born on this day:

Cat Stevens, rock singer and songwriter, 1948;

Barry Richards, South African cricketer, 1945;

Leigh Lawrence, actor, 1943;

Julian Pettifer, broadcaster, 1935;

Dr Jonathan Miller, TV, film and theatre director, 1934;

Norman Jewison, Canadian film director, 1926;

Bill Pertwee, actor, 1926;

Karel Reisz, film director, 1926;

Kay Starr, US singer, 1922;

Isaac Stern, violinist, 1920;

Harold Hart Crane, US poet, 1899;

Ernest Miller Hemingway, US novelist, 1899;

Eugen Schüfftan [Eugene Shuftan], German/US cameraman, sculptor and painter, 1893;

Jacques Feyder [Frederix], Belgian film director, 1888;

Frances Parkinson Keyes, US novelist, 1885;

John George Wood, clergyman and writer on natural history, 1827;

Paul Julius, Baron von Reuter [Israel Beer Josaphat], news agency founder, 1816;

Elizabeth Hamilton, writer, 1758;

Matthew Prior, poet, 1664;

Jean Picard, French astronomer, 1620.

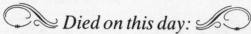

Died on this day:

Philip St John Basil Rathbone, actor, 1967;

Albert John Luthuli, president of the African National Congress, 1967;

George Macaulay Trevelyan, historian, 1962;

Kenneth Lewis Roberts, US novelist, 1957;

Owen Wister, US novelist, 1938;

Louis-Hubert Gonzalve Lyautey, Marshal of France and statesman, 1934;

Dame Ellen Alicia Terry, actress, 1928;

Colvin Smith, Scottish portrait painter, 1875;

Robert Burns, Scottish poet, 1796.

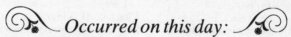

Occurred on this day:

Commander Neil Armstrong became the first man to set foot on the moon, 1969;

Runcorn Bridge across the Mersey opened, 1961;

In the USA, the first nuclear merchant ship, the NS *Savannah* was launched, 1959;

The Tate Gallery, presented to the nation by Sir Henry Tate, was opened, 1897;

Battersea Bridge, London, opened, 1890;

The Confederates were victorious in the first Battle of Bull Run, 1861;

George Christian Frederick Leopold of Saxe-Coburg-Gotha was proclaimed Leopold I, King of the Belgians after the country became a separate kingdom, 1831;

Napoleon defeated the Mamelukes in Egypt in the Battle of the Pyramids, 1798;

The Society of Jesus was dissolved by Pope Clement XIV, 1773.

TODAY IS THE FEAST DAY OF St Arbogastes, St Laurence of Brindisi, St Praxedes and St Victor of Marseilles.

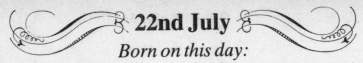

22nd July

Born on this day:

Bonnie Langford, actress, 1964;

Terence Stamp, actor, 1938;

Jimmy Hill, TV soccer presenter, 1928;

Bryan Forbes, novelist and film producer, 1926;

Stephen Vincent Benét, US poet and novelist, 1898;

Alexander Calder, US bent-wire and metal sculptor, 1898;

James Whale, film director, 1896;

Artur von Seyss-Inquart, Nazi High Commissioner of Bohemia, 1892;

Rose Kennedy, matriarch of the US Kennedy family, 1890;

Selman Abraham Waksman, US biochemist, 1888;

Gus Elen [Ernest Augustus Elen], music-hall artiste, 1862;

Frederick William Rolfe ['Baron Corvo'], writer, 1860;

William Poel [Pole], actor-manager, 1852;

The Rev. William Archibald Spooner, originator of 'spoonerisms', 1844;

Sir Herbert Stanley Oakeley, composer and organist, 1830;

Gregor Johann Mendel, Austrian Augustinian monk and botanist, 1822;

Eugène-Louis-Gabriel Isabey, French painter and lithographer, 1803;

Friedrich Wilhelm Bessel, German astronomer and mathematician, 1784;

Anthony Ashley Cooper, 1st Earl of Shaftesbury, statesman, 1621;

Philip I, King of Spain, 1478.

Died on this day:

Sir Robert Eric Mortimer Wheeler, archaeologist, 1976;

Carl Sandburg, US poet, 1967;

William Lyon Mackenzie King, Canadian statesman, 1950;

John Dillinger, US 'Public Enemy No. 1', shot dead in ambush, 1934;

John Meade Falkner, novelist, 1932;

Florenz Ziegfeld, US theatrical producer, 1932;

James Whitcombe Riley, US poet, 1916;

Wilson Barrett [William Henry], actor and playwright, 1904;

Marie-François-Xavier Bichat, French anatomist, 1802;

John Dalton, poet, 1763;

Henry III, King of France, assassinated, 1589;

Charles VII, King of France, 1461;

Simon Langham, Archbishop of Canterbury, 1376.

Occurred on this day:

The first London performance of the musical show *A Chorus Line* was staged, 1976;

The Russian unmanned spacecraft *Venera 8* made a soft landing on Venus, 1972;

In Britain, bread rationing started, 1946;

Wiley Post completed the first round-the-world solo air flight in 7 days, 18 hours, 49 minutes, 1933;

In Russia, Alexander Kerensky became prime minister, 1917;

The Mormons, moving westwards, reached the site of Salt Lake City, 1847;

In Spain, the Duke of Wellington defeated the French in the Battle of Salamanca, 1812;

The English fleet drove off the French at the Battle of Cape Finisterre, 1805;

Belgrade was besieged by the Ottoman Turks, 1456;

The English defeated the Scots, led by Wallace, at the Battle of Falkirk, 1298;

The French defeated the English at the Battle of Saintes, 1242.

TODAY IS THE FEAST DAY OF St John Lloyd, St Joseph of Palestine, St Mary Magdalen, St Philip Evans and St Vandrille or Wandregesilus.

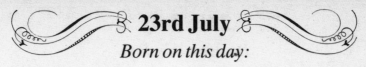

23rd July

Born on this day:

Graham Gooch, cricketer, 1953;
David Essex, entertainer, 1947;
Sir Richard Rogers, architect, 1933;
Viktor Korchnoi, Russian chess champion, 1931;
Gloria DeHaven, US film actress, 1924;
Peter Twiss, former test pilot, 1921;
Michael Foot, former MP, 1913;
Michael Wilding, actor, 1912;
Elspeth Huxley, author, 1907;
Raymond Thornton Chandler, US novelist, 1888;
Salvador de Madariaga y Rojo, Spanish writer and diplomat, 1886;

Sir Arthur Whitten Brown, aviator, 1886;
Alan Francis Brooke, 1st Viscount Alanbrooke, field marshal, 1883;
Coventry Kersey Dighton Patmore, poet, 1823;
Franz Adolf Berwald, Swedish composer, 1796;
George Catlin, US artist and author, 1796;
François-Eugène Vidocq, French police detective, 1775;
Antonio Maria Gasparo Sacchini, Italian opera composer, 1734;
Francesco Sforza, soldier, 1401.

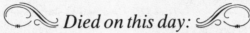

Died on this day:

Eddie Rickenbacker [Edward Vernon Rickenbacher], US WWI fighter pilot, 1973;
Edward Montgomery Clift, US film actor, 1966;
Cordell Hull, US statesman, 1955;
Robert Joseph Flaherty, US documentary film-maker, 1951;
Henri-Philippe Pétain, French soldier and Vichy leader, 1951;
David Wark Griffith, US film director, 1948;
Glenn Hammond Curtiss, US aviator, 1930;

Sir William Ramsay, chemist, 1916;
Ulysses Simpson Grant, general and 18th president of the USA, 1885;
Isaac Merritt Singer, US sewing-machine inventor, 1875;
Elizabeth Hamilton, novelist, 1816;
Domenico Scarlatti, Italian composer and harpsichordist, 1757;
Richard Gibson, miniature-painter, 1690;
Sir Henry Percy [Harry Hotspur], killed in battle, 1403.

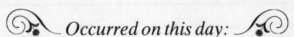

Occurred on this day:

King Farouk of Egypt was deposed by General Neguib, 1952;
John Boyd Dunlop applied to patent a pneumatic tyre, 1888;
The Jewish Disabilities Removal Act was passed by Parliament, 1858;

Charles Stuart, the Young Pretender, landed at Eriskay Island in the Hebrides, 1745;
The Battle of Shrewsbury was fought by the Percys against King Henry IV, 1403.

TODAY IS THE FEAST DAY OF St Anne or Susanna, St Apollinaris of Ravenna, St Bridget of Sweden, St John Cassian, St Liborius, St Romula and her Companions and The Three Wise Men.

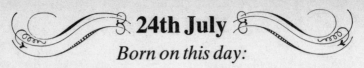

24th July

Born on this day:

Lynda Carter, US actress and singer, 1951;
Jacques Fouroux, French rugby player, 1947;
Les Reed, songwriter, 1935;
Peter Yates, film director and producer, 1929;
Wilfred Josephs, composer, 1927;
Ruggiero Ricci, US violinist, 1918;
Robert Farnon, Canadian composer, 1916;
Edwin Mirvish, proprietor, the Old Vic, 1914;
Nora Swinburne, actress, 1902;
Amelia Earhart, US aviator, 1898;

Ernst Bloch, US/Swiss composer, 1880;
Edward John Moreton Drax Plunkett, 18th Baron Dunsany, author, 1878;
Edward Frederic Benson, novelist, 1867;
Frank Wedekind, German playwright, 1864;
Adolphe Charles Adam, French composer, 1803;
Alexandre Dumas *père* [Davy de la Pailleterie], French author, 1802;
Simón Bolívar, South American liberator, 1783.

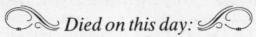

Died on this day:

Peter Richard Henry Sellers, actor, 1980;
Sir James Chadwick, physicist, 1974;
Alan Rawsthorne, composer, 1971;
Constance Bennett, US film actress, 1965;
Sacha [Alexander] Guitry, French actor and playwright, 1957;
Captain Matthew Webb, cross-Channel swimmer, 1883;

Martin van Buren, 8th president of the USA, 1862;
John Sell Cotman, landscape painter, 1842;
John Dyer, poet, 1758;
Benedetto Marcello, Italian composer, 1739;
Jacob van Artevelde, Flemish statesman, murdered, 1345.

Occurred on this day:

14 people were named as the first life peers, 1958.
The Treaty of Lausanne was signed between Turkey and the Allied Powers, 1923;
The window tax was abolished in Britain, 1851;
Gibraltar was won from Spain by Admiral Sir George Rooke, 1704;

The city of Detroit, USA, was founded by the Frenchman Antoine de la Mothe Cadillac, 1701;
King William III was defeated at Steinkirk [Enghein] by the French, 1692;
James VI acceded to the Scottish throne, 1567;
Jacques Cartier landed in Canada, claiming the area for France, 1534.

TODAY IS THE FEAST DAY OF St Boris or Romanus, St Christina of Bolsena, St Christina the Astonishing, St Declan, St Gleb or David and St Lewinna.

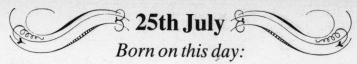

25th July

Born on this day:

Lynne Frederick, actress, 1954;
Prof. Colin Renfrew, archaeologist, 1937;
James Butler, sculptor, 1931;
Annie Ross, singer, 1930;
Sir David Napley, solicitor, 1915;
Walter Brennan, US film actor, 1894;
Alfredo Casella, Italian composer, 1883;
Elizabeth, Queen of the Belgians, 1876;

David Belasco, US playwright and producer, 1859;
Arthur James Balfour, 1st Earl, statesman, 1848;
Thomas Eakins, US sculptor, portrait and figure painter, 1844;
Karl Liebig, German clarinettist and conductor, 1808;
Giacomo Cordella, Italian opera composer, 1786;
William Burkitt, theologian, 1650.

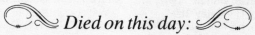

Died on this day:

Louis Stephen St Laurent, Canadian statesman, 1973;
Douglas Stuart Moore, US composer, 1969;
Engelbert Dollfuss, Austrian statesman, assassinated, 1934;
Nathaniel ['Nat'] Gould, racing novelist, 1919;
Henry Mayhew, a founder of *Punch* and social investigator, 1887;
Charles Macintosh, waterproof clothing inventor, 1843;

Jean-Charles-Léonard Simonde de Sismondi, Swiss historian, 1842;
Samuel Taylor Coleridge, poet, 1834;
Charles Dibdin, composer, playwright, actor and manager, 1814;
André-Marie de Chénier, French poet, executed, 1794;
Pope Innocent VIII, 1492;
Flavius Valerius Constantius, Roman emperor, 306.

Occurred on this day:

The first test-tube baby was born in Oldham, Lancs, 1978;
Hovercraft SR-N1 made its first Channel crossing in less than two hours, 1959;
The European Coal and Steel Community came into being, 1952;
In Britain, bread rationing ended, 1948;
The Brussels Treaty on Western Union came into force, 1948;
Mussolini was forced to resign in Italy, 1943;
Louis Blériot made the first Channel crossing by aircraft, 1909;

The Turks were defeated near Aboukir by Napoleon, 1799;
The Dutch fleet was totally routed by English at the second naval Battle of the North Foreland, 1666;
The seven northern provinces of the Netherlands proclaimed their independence from Spain, 1581;
Queen Mary I was married to Philip of Spain at Winchester, 1554;
The Moors were defeated at Ourique by Alfonso I of Portugal, 1139.

TODAY IS THE FEAST DAY OF St Christopher, St James the Greater, St Magnericus and Saints Thea, Valentina and Paul.

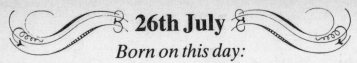

26th July

Born on this day:

Susan George, actress, 1950;
Steve Oldham, cricketer, 1948;
Helen Mirren, actress, 1946;
Mick Jagger, rock singer, 1943;
Lance Percival, entertainer, 1933;
Barbara Jefford, actress, 1930;
Stanley Kubrick, US film producer and director, 1928;
Danny La Rue, entertainer, 1927;
Jason Robards, US film actor, 1922;
Lord Thorneycroft CH, 1909;
Prof. Gioconda De Vito, violinist, 1907;
Paul William Gallico, US writer, 1897;
Charles Butterworth, US film actor, 1896;
Robert Ranke Graves, poet, 1895;

Aldous Leonard Huxley, novelist, 1894;
Georg Grosz, US/German expressionist artist, 1893;
André Maurois [Emile Salomon Wilhelm Herzog], French author, 1885;
André Eugene Maurice Charlot, theatrical manager and actor, 1882;
Carl Gustav Jung, Swiss psychologist, 1875;
Francesco Cilea, Italian composer, 1866;
George Bernard Shaw, Irish playwright, 1856;
Sir Richard Wallace, founder of the Wallace Collection, 1818;
John Field, Irish pianist and composer, 1782.

Died on this day:

Sir James Augustus Henry Murray, lexicographer, 1915;
George Borrow, writer, 1881;
Samuel Houston, Texan soldier and president of the Republic of Texas, 1863;

Gérard Audran, French artist and engraver, 1703;
Pablo de Cespedes, Spanish poet, painter, sculptor and architect, 1608;
Pope Paul II, 1471.

Occurred on this day:

Prince Charles was created Prince of Wales by the Queen, 1958;
The Labour Party came to power after the General Election, 1945;
The Federal Bureau of Investigation was inaugurated, 1908;
Wagner's opera *Parsifal* was first performed, Bayreuth, 1882;
The London *Evening News* was first published, 1881;

Lionel Rothschild [elected 1847] was the first Jewish MP to take his seat in Parliament, 1858;
Liberia was proclaimed an independent republic, 1847;
A violent earthquake erupted in Naples, with the loss of over 6,000 lives, 1805;
New York became the 11th of the United States, 1788.

TODAY IS THE FEAST DAY OF St Anne, St Bartholomea Capitanio, St Joachim and St Simeon the Armenian.

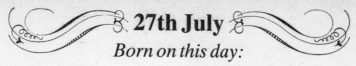

27th July

Born on this day:

Jo Durie, tennis player, 1960;
Christopher Dean, skater, 1958;
Bobbie Gentry, US singer, 1942;
Anna Dawson, actress and comedienne, 1937;
John Pardoe, former MP, 1934;
Shirley Williams, former president, Social Democratic Party, 1930;
Jack Higgins [Harry Patterson], novelist, 1929;
Peter Coker, artist, 1926;
Group Capt. John Cunningham, former test pilot, 1917;
Anton Dolin [Patrick Healey-Kay], dancer and choreographer, 1904;
Ernö von Dohnányi, Hungarian composer, 1877;
Joseph Hilaire Pierre Belloc, poet and author, 1870;
Enrique Granados, Spanish pianist and composer, 1867;
Sir Ernest Alfred Thompson Wallis Budge, orientalist and museum curator, 1857;
Giosuè Carducci, Italian poet, 1835;
Alexandre Dumas *fils*, French playwright, 1824;
Sir George Biddell Airy, Astronomer Royal, 1801;
André-Georges-Louis Onslow, French composer, 1784;
Mauro Giuliani, Italian composer, 1781;
Thomas Campbell, poet, 1777;
Jean Bernoulli, Swiss mathematician, 1667.

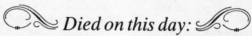

Died on this day:

James Mason, actor, 1984;
Antonio de Oliveira Salazar, Portuguese prime minister and dictator, 1970;
Richard Aldington, novelist and biographer, 1962;
Gertrude Stein, US novelist and poet, 1946;
Sir William Matthew Flinders Petrie, Egyptologist, 1942;
Ferruccio Benvenuto Busoni, Italian pianist and composer, 1924;
John Dalton, physicist and chemist, 1844;
Mikhail Yuryevich Lermontov, Russian poet and novelist, 1841;
Gilbert Charles Stuart, US painter, 1828.

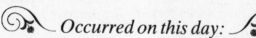

Occurred on this day:

The St James's Theatre, London, closed, 1957;
Austria once more became independent, 1955;
The *Comet* – first jet-propelled airliner – flew for the first time, 1949;
The German army entered the Ukraine, 1941;
Insulin was isolated in Canada by Sir Frederick Banting and Charles Best at the University of Toronto, 1921;
A radio compass was used for the first time to direct navigation of aircraft, 1920;
The Atlantic telegraph cable, laid by the *Great Eastern*, was completed, 1866;
Chartist riots broke out in Birmingham and other towns, 1839;
Adelaide, South Australia, was founded, 1836;
The Bank of England was granted a 12 year charter by Act of Parliament, 1694;
Cromwell defeated the Royalists at the Battle of Gainsborough, 1643.

TODAY IS THE FEAST DAY OF St Aurelia, Natalia and their Companions, St Pantaleon, The Martyrs of Salsette, The Seven Sleepers of Ephesus and St Theobald of Marly.

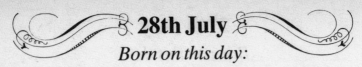

28th July

Born on this day:

Riccardo Muti, conductor, 1941;
Sir Garfield Sobers, cricketer, 1936;
Sir Russell Johnston, MP, 1932;
Jacqueline Onassis, 1929;
Prunella Stack, president, Women's
  League of Health and Beauty, 1914;
Clarence Malcolm Boden Lowry, novelist,
  1909;
Prof. Sir Karl Popper CH, philosopher,
  1902;
Rudy [Hubert Prior] Vallee, US singer,
  1901;

Marie Löhr, actress, 1890;
Marcel Duchamp, French Surrealist
  painter, 1887;
Helen Beatrix Potter, author and
  illustrator, 1866;
Gerard Manley Hopkins, poet, 1844;
Henri-Joseph Harpignies, French
  landscape painter, 1819;
Jacopo Sannazaro, Neapolitan poet,
  1456.

Died on this day:

Margot [Emma Alice Margaret] Asquith,
  writer, 1945;
Otto Hahn, German nuclear physicist,
  1944;
William James Mayo, surgeon and co-
  founder of the Mayo Clinic, 1939;
Sir Moses Haim Montefiore, philanthropist
  and centenarian, 1885;
Nathan Mayer Rothschild, banker,
  1836;
Giuseppe Sarti, Italian composer,
  1802;
Maximilien-François-Marie-Isidore de
  Robespierre, French revolutionary
  leader, executed, 1794;

Louis-Antoine-Léon-Florelle de
  Richebourg de St Just, French
  revolutionary leader, executed, 1794;
Johann Sebastian Bach, German
  composer, 1750;
Antonio Lucio Vivaldi, Italian priest,
  composer and violinist, 1741;
Abraham Cowley, poet, 1667;
Savinien de Cyrano de Bergerac, French
  poet and soldier, 1655;
John Speed, historian and cartographer,
  1629;
Thomas Cromwell, Earl of Essex,
  Chancellor to King Henry VIII,
  executed, 1540.

Occurred on this day:

An earthquake took place in the Tangshan
  area of China, with more than 800,000
  deaths, 1976;
The 34,000-ton Cunard-White Star liner
  Mauretania was launched at Cammell-
  Laird's yard at Birkenhead, 1938;
Austria-Hungary declared war on Serbia,
  1914;
In the USA, the 14th Amendment to the
  Constitution was ratified, 1868;
Peru declared its independence from Spain,
  1821;

The British under Arthur Wellesley
  defeated the French at the Battle of
  Talavera, 1809;
The Forth and Clyde Canal was opened,
  1790;
The Battle of Warsaw began, when Charles
  V Gustav of Sweden invaded Poland,
  1656;
Potatoes were first brought to England from
  Colombia, 1586.

TODAY IS THE FEAST DAY OF St Botvid, Saints Nazarius and Celsus and St Samson
of Dol.

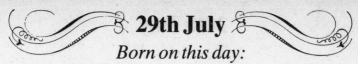

29th July

Born on this day:

Joe Johnson, snooker player, 1952;
Nigel Aspinall, croquet player, 1946;
Diane Keen, actress, 1946;
Wendy Taylor, sculptor, 1945;
Mikis Theodorakis, Greek composer, 1925;
Max Faulkner, golfer, 1916;
Kay Dick, author, 1915;
Lord Grimond, Liberal leader, 1913;
Lt.-Col. Harold Ervine-Andrews VC, 1911;
Lord Scarman, former Lord of Appeal, 1911;
Hjalmar Hammarskjöld, Secretary-General of the United Nations, 1905;

William Cameron Menzies, US film director and designer, 1896;
Sigmund Romberg, US/Hungarian composer, 1887;
Benito Amilcare Andrea Mussolini, Italian leader, 1883;
Donald Robert Perry Marquis, US author, 1878;
Newton Booth Tarkington, US author, 1869;
George Bradshaw, publisher and originator of railway guides, 1801;
Jan Kollar, Slavonic scholar and poet, 1793;
Peter von Hess, German painter, 1792.

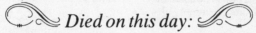

Died on this day:

Luis Buñuel, Spanish film director, 1983;
James David Graham Niven, film actor, 1983;
Raymond Massey, film actor, 1983;
Herbert Marcuse, German/US philosopher, 1979;
Erich Kästner, German author, 1974;
Sir John [Giovanni Battista] Barbirolli, conductor, 1970;
Edward Gordon Craig, actor, designer and director, 1966;

Umberto I, King of Italy, assassinated, 1900;
Vincent Van Gogh, painter, committed suicide, 1890;
Robert Alexander Schumann, German composer, 1856;
William Wilberforce, campaigner for the abolition of slavery, 1833;
David Teniers the Elder, Flemish painter, 1649;
Philip I, King of France, 1108.

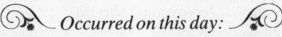

Occurred on this day:

The Prince of Wales was married to Lady Diana Spencer, 1981;
A military coup took place in Nigeria when President Gowon was deposed while he was out of the country, 1975;
The airship *R100* set off on a trip across the Atlantic, 1930;

The Good Companions, a novel by J. B. Priestley, was published, 1929;
The Permanent Court of Arbitration was set up at The Hague, 1899;
The Spanish Armada was defeated, 1588;
Mary, Queen of Scots married Henry Stuart, Lord Darnley, 1565.

TODAY IS THE FEAST DAY OF Saints Beatrice and Simplicius, St Felix II, antipope, Saints Faustinus and Beatrice, St Lupus of Troyes, St Martha, St Olav, King of Norway and St William of Saint-Brieuc.

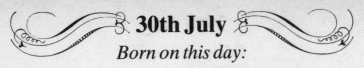

30th July

Born on this day:

Kate Bush, singer and songwriter, 1958;
Daley Thompson, athlete, 1958;
Christopher Warren-Green, violinist, 1955;
Harriet Harman, MP, 1950;
Teresa Cahill, opera singer, 1944;
Frances de la Tour, actress, 1944;
Paul Anka, Canadian songwriter and
    singer, 1941;
Peter Bogdanovich, US film director, 1939;
Donald Fraser, artist, 1929;
Richard Johnson, actor, producer and
    restaurateur, 1927;
Stan Stennett, actor, 1927;
Meredith Davies, conductor, 1922;
Lord Killanin, author, film producer and
    Olympics honorary life president, 1914;

Anne Ridler, author, 1912;
Prof. Cyril Northcote Parkinson, inventor
    of 'The Law', 1909;
Henry Moore, sculptor, 1898;
Jean-Jacques Bernard, French playwright
    and novelist, 1888;
Henry Ford, US motor-car manufacturer,
    1863;
Richard Burdon Haldane, 1st Viscount,
    statesman and founder of the Territorial
    Army, 1856;
Emily Brontë ['Ellis Bell'], novelist, 1818;
Samuel Rogers, poet, 1763;
Giorgio Vasari, Italian painter, architect
    and writer, 1511.

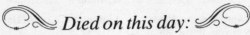

Died on this day:

Howard Dietz, US lyricist, 1983;
Lynn Fontanne, actress, 1983;
John Lawrence Toole, actor and theatrical
    manager, 1906;
Prince Otto Eduard Leopold von Bismarck-
    Schönhausen, German chancellor,
    1898;
Walter Horatio Pater, writer, 1894;

Sir Charles Hastings, physician, founder of
    the British Medical Association, 1866;
Denis Diderot, French encyclopaedist,
    1784;
Thomas Gray, poet, 1771;
William Penn, Quaker leader, 1718;
Jacopo Palma [Negreti], Italian painter,
    1528.

Occurred on this day:

TV transmission of pictures from Mars were
    sent back to Earth by the US *Mariner 6*
    spacecraft, 1969;
England won the Football World Cup,
    beating West Germany 4–2 at Wembley,
    1966;
The world's first port radar station opened
    at Liverpool, 1948;
The first Penguin books were published,
    1935;

Kurt von Schuschnigg became Chancellor
    of Austria, 1934;
Toronto [then called York] was founded by
    General John Simcoe, 1793;
The Jacobites were defeated at Newton
    Butler, 1689;
The Battle of Warsaw ended, with the
    defeat of the Poles, 1656.

TODAY IS THE FEAST DAY OF Saints Abdon and Sennen, St Julitta of Caesarea, St
Peter Chrysologus and St Tatwin, Archbishop of Canterbury.

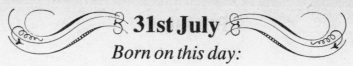

31st July

Born on this day:

Evonne Cawley, tennis player, 1951;
Geraldine Chaplin, US film actress, 1944;
Jonathan Dimbleby, TV and radio presenter, 1944;
Steuart Bedford, conductor, 1939;
Lynne Reid Banks, author, 1929;
Peter Nichols, playwright, 1927;
Ralph Koltai, stage designer, 1924;
Norman Del Mar, conductor, 1919;
Brian Inglis, author and editor, 1916;
Henri Decaë, French director of cinema photography, 1915;
Prof. Milton Friedman, US monetarist authority, 1912;

Theobald Smith, US pathologist, 1859;
Leon Adolphe Willette, French painter, 1857;
Oskar Begas, German painter, 1828;
François-Auguste Gevaert, Belgian composer, 1828;
John Ericsson, US/Swedish naval engineer, 1803;
Friedrich Wöhler, German chemist, 1800;
Amelie-Julie Candeille, French actress, singer and composer, 1767;
John Canton, physicist, 1718;
Maximilian II, Holy Roman Emperor, 1527.

Died on this day:

Lord Cheshire VC, OM, founder of homes for the disabled, 1992;
Gian Francesco Malipiero, Italian composer, 1973;
Margaret Kennedy, novelist, 1967;
Jim Reeves, US country singer, killed, 1964;
Guilhermina Suggia, cellist, 1950;
Owen Ramsay Nares, actor-manager, 1943;
Captain Hedley Verity, cricketer, on active service, 1943;
Sir Francis Younghusband, soldier, diplomat and explorer, 1942;
Sir Harry Hamilton Johnston, explorer, 1927;
Frank Holl, painter, 1888;
Franz Liszt, Hungarian composer, 1886;

Andrew Johnson, 17th president of the USA, 1875;
Benoît Fourneyron, French inventor of the water turbine, 1867;
Louis-Christophe-François Hachette, French publisher and bookseller, 1864;
Sándor Petöfi [Alexander Petrovics], Hungarian poet, killed in battle, 1849;
Juste-Aurèle Meissonier, French goldsmith, painter and sculptor, 1750;
Jacobus Gallus [Jakob Händl], Slovenian composer, 1591;
St Ignatius of Loyola, founder of the Jesuits, 1556.

Occurred on this day:

Pope Paul VI visited Uganda – the first time that a pope had visited Africa, 1969;
The cross-Channel hovercraft service was inaugurated, 1968;
Mount Godwin-Austin [K2] was climbed by an Italian expedition, 1954;
The third Battle of Ypres [Passchendaele] began, 1917;
Dr Crippen was arrested on board the SS Montrose for the murder of his wife, 1910;

The Boy Scout movement was inaugurated by Sir Robert Baden-Powell, 1908;
The London Echo newspaper was last issued, 1905;
The US yacht America, first winner of the America's Cup, reached Cowes, Isle of Wight, 1851;
Trinidad was discovered by Christopher Columbus on his third voyage, 1498;
William Caxton published Le Morte D'Arthur by Sir Thomas Mallory, 1485.

TODAY IS THE FEAST DAY OF St Helen of Skövde, St Ignatius of Loyola, St Justin de Jacobis and St Neot.

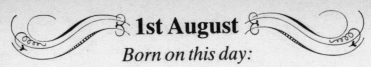

1st August

Born on this day:

Andy Roxburgh, manager, Scotland soccer team, 1943;

Yves Saint Laurent, French haute couturier, 1936;

Prof. Laurie Taylor, sociologist and broadcaster, 1936;

Lionel Bart, composer, 1930;

Frank Hauser, theatrical director, 1922;

Jack Kramer, tennis champion, 1921;

Jeffrey Segal, actor and playwright, 1920;

Stanley Middleton, novelist, 1919;

Sir William Hayter, former diplomat, 1906;

Ivan Mestrovic, US sculptor, 1883;

Dame Emilie Rose Macaulay, author, 1881;

Montague Rhodes James, scholar, author and editor, 1862;

Herman Melville, US sailor, novelist and poet, 1819;

Richard Henry Dana, US novelist and lawyer, 1815;

Francis Scott Key, US poet and attorney; author of *The Star-Spangled Banner*, 1779;

William Clark, US soldier and explorer, 1770;

Jean-Baptiste-Pierre-Antoine Monnet, Chevalier de Lamarck, French zoologist, 1744;

Richard Wilson, Welsh landscape painter, 1714;

Benedetto Marcello, Italian composer and author, 1686;

Sigismund II Augustus, King of Poland, 1520;

Claudius, Roman emperor, 10 BC.

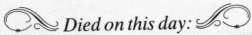

Died on this day:

Theodore Roethke, US poet, 1963;

Edwin Austin Abbey, US painter, 1911;

Sir William Robert Grove, scientist and lawyer, 1896;

Henry Clarence Kendall, Australian poet, 1882;

Charles Turner, engraver, 1857;

Walter Geikie, Scottish painter, 1837;

Elizabeth Inchbald [Simpson], actress and author, 1821;

Richard Savage, poet, 1743;

Queen Anne, last of the Stuart sovereigns, 1714;

Louis VI, King of France, 1137;

Justin I, Byzantine emperor, 527.

Occurred on this day:

Dahomey became independent, 1960;

Colorado became the 38th of the United States, 1876;

The Rotherhithe Thames Tunnel was opened, 1842;

Slavery was abolished throughout the British Empire, 1834;

The new London Bridge was opened, 1831;

The French Fleet was destroyed by the English under Lord Nelson at the Battle of the Nile, 1798;

Sir Joseph Priestley discovered oxygen, 1774;

The French were defeated by the British and Hanoverians at the Battle of Minden, 1759;

The foundation stone of the Bank of England was laid, 1732;

The watermen's race on the Thames for Doggett's Coat and Badge was first rowed, 1716;

George Louis, Elector of Hanover, was proclaimed King George I, 1714;

Christopher Columbus landed on mainland America, and believing it to be an island, named it Isla Santa, 1498.

TODAY IS THE FEAST DAY OF St Almedha or Aled, St Alphonse Liguori, St Ethelwold of Winchester, The Holy Machabees, St Peter Julian Eymard and Saints Pistis, Elpis and Agape [Faith, Hope and Charity].

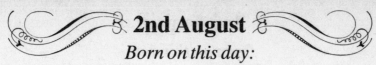

2nd August

Born on this day:

Sammy McIlroy, footballer, 1954;
Anne Leuchars, TV journalist, 1953;
Rose Tremain, novelist and playwright, 1943;
Peter O'Toole, actor, 1932;
Alan Whicker, TV broadcaster, 1925;
Myrna Loy, US film actress, 1905;
Sir Arthur Edward Drummond Bliss, composer, 1891;
Leslie Lincoln Henson, actor-manager, 1891;
Ethel Mary Dell [Mrs G.T. Savage], novelist, 1881;
Ernest Christopher Dowson, poet, 1867;

Francis Marion Crawford, novelist, 1854;
Elisha Gray, a US inventor of the telephone, 1835;
Henry Steel Olcott, US co-founder of the Theosophical Society, 1832;
Edward Augustus Freeman, historian, 1823;
Nicholas Patrick Stephen Wiseman, Cardinal, 1st Archbishop of Westminster, 1802;
Gerard Audran, French artist and engraver, 1640;
Samuel Dircksz van Hoogstraten, Dutch painter, 1627.

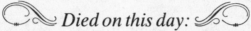

Died on this day:

Carlos Chávez, Mexican composer, 1978;
Fritz Lang, Austrian film director, 1976;
Oliver Hazard Perry La Farge, US author, 1963;
Wallace Stevens, US poet, 1955;
Pietro Mascagni, Italian composer, 1945;
Louis Blériot, French aviator, 1936;
Paul Ludwig Hans Anton von Beneckendorf und von Hindenburg, German soldier and statesman, 1934;
Warren Gamaliel Harding, 29th president of the United States, 1923;

Alexander Graham Bell, inventor of the telephone, 1922;
Enrico Caruso, Italian operatic tenor, 1921;
Marcus Andrew Hislop Clarke, author, 1881;
'Wild Bill' Hickok [James Butler], US western Marshal, shot dead, 1876;
Jacques-Étienne Montgolfier, French balloonist, 1799;
Thomas Gainsborough, painter, 1788;
King William II [William Rufus], shot in the New Forest, 1100.

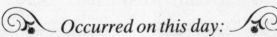

Occurred on this day:

Iraqi tanks and infantry invaded and occupied Kuwait, 1990;
The Potsdam Conference ended, 1945;
Death duties first introduced, 1894;
The transatlantic cable, which was being laid by the *Great Eastern*, snapped and was lost, 1865;
The government of India was transferred from the East India Company to the Crown, 1858;

British Columbia became a Crown Colony, 1858;
Napoleon was declared 'Consul for life', 1802;
The Quadruple Alliance between Britain, France, Austria and Holland against Spain was concluded in London, 1718.

TODAY IS THE FEAST DAY OF St Eusebius of Vercelli, St Plegmund, archbishop of Canterbury, St Sidwell or Sativola, St Stephen I, pope, St Syagrius of Autun and St Theodota and her Three Sons.

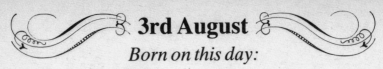

3rd August

Born on this day:

Osvaldo Ardiles, Argentine footballer, 1953;

Josh Gifford, racehorse trainer, 1941;

Martin Sheen, US actor, 1940;

Terry Wogan, radio and TV broadcaster, 1938;

Steven Berkoff, actor and director, 1937;

Peter Easterby, racehorse trainer, 1929;

Tony Bennett, US singer, 1926;

Anthony Sampson, author and journalist, 1926;

Richard Adler, US composer, 1921;

Baroness James of Holland Park [P. D. James] author, 1920;

Walter Van Tilburg Clark, US Western author, 1909;

Rupert Chawner Brooke, poet, 1887;

Louis Gruenberg, US composer, 1884;

King Haakon VII of Norway, 1872;

Stanley Baldwin, 1st Earl Baldwin of Bewdley, statesman, 1867;

Juliana Horatia Ewing, writer of children's books, 1841;

Frederic Clay, composer, 1840;

Elisha Graves Otis, US inventor of the safety lift, 1811;

Sir Joseph Paxton, architect and landscape gardener, 1801.

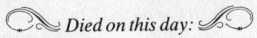

Died on this day:

Archbishop Makarios III, president of Cyprus, 1977;

Colette [Sidonie-Gabrielle Colette], French novelist, 1954;

Joseph Conrad [Jósef Teodor Konrad Naleçz Korzeniowski], novelist, 1924;

Sir Roger David Casement, Irish nationalist, executed for treason, 1916;

Reinhold Begas, German sculptor, 1911;

Augustus Saint-Gaudens, US sculptor, 1907;

Jean-Louis-Charles Garnier, French architect, 1898;

Sir Richard Arkwright, inventor of the spinning frame, 1792;

Grinling Gibbons, sculptor and wood carver, 1721;

James II, King of Scotland, killed, 1460.

Occurred on this day:

The US nuclear-powered submarine *Nautilus* made its first undersea crossing of the North Pole, 1958;

The first VTOL aircraft – 'The Flying Bedstead' – was flown in Britain, 1954;

The Council of Europe was inaugurated, 1949;

Latvia became part of the Soviet Union, 1940;

The London Pavilion, previously a music hall, opened as a theatre, 1918;

The first ship passed through the Panama Canal, 1914;

Germany declared war on France, 1914;

British troops under Colonel Younghusband and General Macdonald entered the forbidden city of Lhasa, Tibet, 1904;

John Hanning Speke discovered the source of the river Nile to be Lake Victoria, 1858;

La Scala opera house in Milan was opened, 1778;

Hudson's Bay was discovered by Henry Hudson, 1610;

Christopher Columbus left Palos in Andalusia, Spain on his first voyage to America, 1492;

Hannibal won a victory over Rome at Cannae, 216 BC.

TODAY IS THE FEAST DAY OF St Germanus of Auxerre, St Thomas of Hales or Dover and St Walthen or Waltheof.

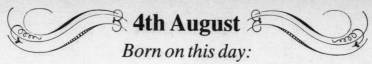

4th August

Born on this day:

Peter Squires, rugby player, 1951;
Georgina Hale, actress, 1943;
Martin Jarvis, actor, 1941;
Simon Preston, organist, 1938;
David Bedford, composer, 1937;
William Cooper, novelist, 1910;
Sir Osbert Lancaster, artist and writer, 1908;
Sir Harold Hobson, drama critic, 1904;
HM Queen Elizabeth, the Queen Mother, 1900;
Sir Harry Lauder [MacLennan], Scottish comedian, 1870;
Knut Hamsun [Pedersen], Norwegian writer, 1859;
William Henry Hudson, writer and naturalist, 1841;
Walter Horatio Pater, essayist and critic, 1839;
Georges-Maurice de Guérin de Cayla, French poet, 1810;
Percy Bysshe Shelley, poet, 1792;
The Rev. Edward Irving, founder of the Irvingites, 1792;
John Tradescant the Younger, horticulturist, 1608.

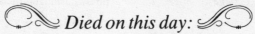

Died on this day:

Edgar Douglas Adrian, 1st Baron, physiologist, 1977;
Roy Herbert Thomson, 1st Baron Thomson of Fleet, Canadian newspaper publisher, 1976;
James Cruze, US film director, 1942;
William Babington Maxwell, novelist, 1938;
Pearl White, US silent-movie serial queen, 1938;
Baron Carl Auer von Welsbach, Austrian chemist, inventor of the gas mantle, 1929;
Hans Christian Andersen, Danish writer of fairy tales, 1875;
John Burgoyne, military commander and playwright, 1792;
William Cecil, 1st Baron Burghley, statesman, 1598;
Sebastian, King of Portugal, killed in battle, 1578;
Simon de Montfort, Earl of Leicester, killed in battle at Evesham, 1265;
Henry I, King of France, 1060.

Occurred on this day:

President Idi Amin of Uganda ordered the expulsion of about 40,000 Asians, 1972;
Kenya, the Sudan and British Somaliland were invaded by Italy, 1940;
The second battle of the Marne ended, 1918;
Belgium was invaded by Germany, 1914;
Britain declared war on Germany, 1914;
President Wilson proclaimed the neutrality of the USA, 1914;
Lord Wantage founded the British Red Cross Society, 1870;
The duty on newspaper advertisements was repealed in Britain, 1853;
The Portuguese were defeated by the Moors at the Battle of Al Kasr al Kebir [Alcazarquivir], 1578;
Malacca was captured by Affonso de Albuquerque, 1511;
The Barons were defeated by Prince Edward at the Battle of Evesham, 1265.

TODAY IS THE FEAST DAY OF St Ia, St John-Baptist Vianney, St Molua or Lughaidh and St Sezni.

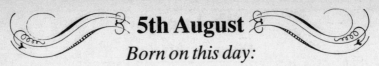

5th August

Born on this day:

John Whitaker, showjumper, 1956;
Ray Clemence, footballer, 1948;
Rodney Pattison, yachtsman, 1943;
Alan Howard, actor, 1937;
John Saxon, US film actor, 1935;
Nicholas Scott, MP, 1933;
Neil Armstrong, first man on the moon, 1930;
Robert Taylor [Spangler Arlington Brugh], US film actor, 1911;
Jacquetta Hawkes, archaeologist and author, 1910;
Joan Hickson, actress, 1906;
Conrad Potter Aiken, US novelist and poet, 1889;
Henri-René-Albert-Guy de Maupassant, French author, 1850;
Edward John Eyre, administrator and explorer of Australia, 1815;
Charles-Louis-Ambroise Thomas, French composer, 1811;
Alexander William Kinglake, historian and traveller, 1809;
Niels Henrik Abel, Norwegian mathematician, 1802;
Count Johann von Struensee, German physician and politician, 1737.

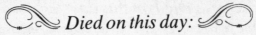

Died on this day:

Richard Burton [Richard Walter Jenkins], actor, 1984;
Marilyn Monroe [Norma Jean Mortenson], US film actress, 1962;
Joseph Holbrooke, composer, 1958;
George Butterworth, composer, 1916;
'Phil' [Philip William] May, caricaturist, 1903;
Friedrich Engels, German political writer, 1895;
Henry Charles Litolff, Anglo-Alsatian composer, 1891;
William Henry Giles Kingston, author of boys' books, 1880;
Alexis-Benoît Soyer, French master cook and writer, 1858;
Earl Richard Howe ['Black Dick'], naval officer, 1799;
Lord Frederick North, 2nd Earl of Guilford, statesman, 1792;
Thomas Newcomen, inventor and engineer, 1729;
Louis III, King of France, 882.

Occurred on this day:

A nuclear test ban treaty was signed by Britain, the USA and the USSR, 1963;
The French colony of Upper Volta became independent, 1960;
The French Southern and Antarctic Territories were created, 1955;
The musical show *Salad Days* was first produced, London, 1954;
The British transatlantic airmail service was started, 1939;
Polygamy was abolished in Turkey, 1924;
German forces entered Warsaw, 1915;
The first electrical traffic signals were installed, Cleveland, Ohio, USA, 1914;
Sir Humphrey Gilbert took possession of Newfoundland for England, 1583;
Sir William Wallace, leader of the Scots, was captured by the English, 1305.

TODAY IS THE FEAST DAY OF Saints Addai and Mari, St Afra and St Nonna.

6th August

Born on this day:

David O'Brien, racehorse trainer, 1956;
John Reid, jockey, 1955;
Barbara Windsor, actress, 1937;
Chris Bonington, mountaineer, 1934;
Michael Deeley, film producer, 1933;
Sir Howard Hodgkin, painter, 1932;
Charles Wood, TV and film writer, 1932;
Frank Finlay, actor, 1926;
Moira Lister, actress, 1923;
Sir Freddie Laker, air travel pioneer, 1922;
Robert Mitchum, US film actor, 1917;
William Joseph Slim, 1st Viscount, British field marshal, 1891;
John Middleton Murry, author and editor, 1889;
Sir Alexander Fleming, bacteriologist and discoverer of penicillin, 1881;

Leo Carrillo, US film actor, 1880;
Paul-Louis-Charles-Marie Claudel, French poet, 1868;
Rolf Boldrewood [Thomas Alexander Browne], novelist and author of *Robbery Under Arms*, 1826;
Alfred, 1st Baron Tennyson, poet, 1809;
Daniel O'Connell, Irish leader and lawyer, 1775;
William Hyde Wollaston, chemist and physicist, 1766;
François de Salignac de La Mothe Fénelon, French playwright, priest and author, 1651;
Matthew Parker ['Nosey Parker'], Archbishop of Canterbury, 1504.

Died on this day:

Pope Paul VI [Giovanni Battista Montini], 1978;
Fulgencio Batista y Zaldivar, Cuban dictator, 1973;
Nancy Carroll [Ann Veronica La Hiff], US film actress, 1965;
Preston Sturges, US film director, 1959;
John George Haigh, 'acid bath' murderer, executed, 1949;
Wilhelm Liebknecht, German journalist and socialist, 1900;

David Allan, Scottish historical painter, 1796;
Eugene Aram, schoolmaster, philologist and murderer, hanged, 1759;
Diego Rodríguez de Silva y Velázquez, Spanish painter, 1660;
Ben Jonson, playwright, 1637;
Anne Hathaway, wife of William Shakespeare, 1623.

Occurred on this day:

Jamaica became independent, 1962;
The first atomic bomb was dropped on Hiroshima, 1945;
Gertrude Ederle, US swimmer, became the first woman to swim the English Channel, 1926;
Don Juan, the first feature-length sound film, was publicly shown in the USA, 1926;
The Allies landed at Suvla Bay, Gallipoli, 1915;
The Corinth Canal, Greece, was opened, 1893;
In the USA, the electric chair was used for the first time to execute a murderer [William Kemmler] in New York, 1890;

The Savoy Hotel, London, was opened, 1889;
Bolivia declared its independence from Peru, 1825;
The Holy Roman Empire ended after the crown was renounced by Francis II, who became Francis I, Emperor of Austria, 1806;
The Virginia Gazette was first issued in Williamsburg, Virginia, 1736;
The Moors were defeated by the Spanish at the Battle of Simancas, 939.

TODAY IS THE FEAST DAY OF St Hormisdas, pope, and Saints Justus and Pastor.

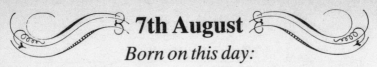

7th August

Born on this day:

Walter Swinburn, jockey, 1961;
Alexei Sayle, comedian, 1952;
Matthew Parrish, journalist and
  broadcaster, 1949;
Greg Chappell, Australian cricketer, 1948;
Nick Ross, journalist and broadcaster,
  1947;
Sue Lloyd, actress, 1939;
Owen Luder, architect, 1928;
Stan Freberg, US TV satirist, 1926;
Kenneth Kendall, broadcaster, 1924;
Philip Snow, author, 1915;
Baroness Seear, deputy leader, Social and
  Liberal Democrats in the House of
  Lords, 1913;
Ralph Johnson Bunche, US diplomat and
  Nobel prizewinner, 1904;
Dame Ella Macknight, gynaecologist, 1904;

Louis Seymour Bazett Leakey,
  archaeologist and anthropologist,
  1903;
Major Sir Guy Lloyd, former MP, 1890;
Sydney Howard, comedian, 1885;
Billie Burke [Mary William Ethelbert
  Appleton Burke], US actress, 1885;
Mata Hari [Margaretha Geertruide Zelle],
  Dutch-born German spy, 1876;
Sir Granville Bantock, composer and
  conductor, 1868;
Dean Frederic William Farrar, theologian
  and author of *Eric, or Little by Little*,
  1831;
Henry Charles Litolff, Anglo-Alsatian
  composer, 1818;
Abbé Maximilian Stadler, Austrian priest
  and composer, 1748.

Died on this day:

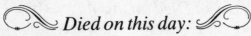

Oliver Norvell Hardy, US film comedian,
  1957;
Rabindranath Tagore, Indian writer, 1941;
Konstantin Stanislavsky [Konstantin
  Sergeyevich Alekseyev], Russian theatre
  director, 1938;
Bix [Leon Bismarck] Beiderbecke, US jazz
  cornet-player and composer, 1931;
Curbastro Gregorio Ricci, Italian
  mathematician, 1925;

Aleksandr Aleksandrovich Blok, Russian
  poet, 1921;
Jacob Maris, Dutch painter, 1899;
James Hall, US geologist and
  palaeontologist, 1898;
Joseph-Marie Jacquard, French weaver and
  inventor, 1834;
Caroline, Queen of George IV, 1821;
Robert Blake, British admiral, 1657.

Occurred on this day:

The French colony of the Ivory Coast
  became independent, 1960;
US forces landed on Guadalcanal, 1942;
The first motor racing Grand Prix in Britain
  was held at Brooklands, 1926;
The Daylight Saving Act, which
  permanently established British Summer
  Time, was passed, 1925;
Britain issued £1 and 10-shilling notes,
  1914;
Florence Maybrick was found guilty of
  murdering her husband, 1889;
Ottawa [formerly Bytown] became the
  capital of Canada, 1858;

An Act of Parliament was passed
  prohibiting the employment of climbing
  boys as chimney-sweeps, 1840;
Louis-Philippe was proclaimed 'Citizen
  King' of France, 1830;
The newspaper *New England Courant* was
  first published in Boston, 1721;
The first race meeting at Ascot
  was instituted by Queen Anne,
  1711;
Henry Tudor [later King Henry VII] landed
  at Milford Haven in a bid for the crown,
  1485.

TODAY IS THE FEAST DAY OF Saints Agapitus, Sixtus II and Felicissimus, St Albert
of Trapani, St Cajetan or Gaetano, St Claudia, St Dogmetius the Persian, St Donatus of
Arezzo and St Victricius.

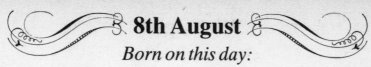

8th August

Born on this day:

Nigel Mansell, racing driver, 1953;

Keith Carradine, US actor, singer and songwriter, 1950;

Connie Stevens, US film actress and singer, 1938;

Dustin Hoffman, US film actor, 1937;

Keith Barron, actor, 1934;

Richard Anderson, US film actor, 1926;

Esther Williams, US swimmer and film actress, 1923;

Rory Calhoun, US film actor, 1922;

Lord Chapple, former trade union leader, 1921;

Sylvia Sidney, US film actress, 1910;

John Yudkin, nutritionist, 1910;

Paul Adrien Maurice Dirac, physicist, 1902;

Victor Young, US composer and conductor, 1900;

Marjorie Kinnan Rawlings, US novelist, 1896;

Frank Richards [Charles Harold St John Hamilton], author and creator of 'Billy Bunter', 1876;

Cécile-Louise-Stéphanie Chaminade, French composer and pianist, 1861;

F. Anstey [Thomas Anstey Guthrie], author, 1856;

Theodule Augustin Ribot, French painter, 1823;

George Cattermole, water-colour painter, 1800;

Sir Godfrey Kneller [Gottfried Kniller], German-born painter, 1646.

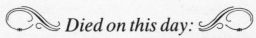

Died on this day:

Louise Brooks, US film actress, 1985;

Nicholas John Turney Montsarrat, novelist, 1979;

James Gould Cozzens, US novelist, 1978;

Jaromir Weinberger, Czech/US composer, 1967;

Shirley Jackson, US author, 1965;

Anton Ivanovich Denikin, anti-Bolshevik Russian general, 1947;

Frank Winfield Woolworth, US chainstore founder, 1919;

James-Joseph-Jacques Tissot, French painter and illustrator, 1902;

Eugène-Louis Boudin, French painter, 1898;

Alonso Sanchez Coello, Spanish painter, 1588;

Girolamo Fracastoro, Italian astronomer, poet and physician, 1553;

Thomas à Kempis [Thomas Hammerken von Kempen], Dutch Augustinian monk and writer, 1471.

Occurred on this day:

John McCarthy, the journalist held hostage by Islamic Jihad in the Lebanon since 1986, was freed, 1991;

The London production of the musical show *42nd Street* was first presented, 1984;

President Richard Nixon resigned, the first US president to do so, 1974;

The Great Train Robbery occurred when £2,500,000 was stolen from a train at Cheddington, near Bletchley, Bucks, 1963;

The Battle of Britain began, 1940;

The Treaty of Rawalpindi was signed, 1919;

The Battle of Amiens began, 1918;

The first British troops arrived in France, 1914;

The British Academy was granted a Royal Charter, 1902;

The Red Cross League, founded by Jean-Henri Dunant, was granted immunity in time of war at the Geneva Convention, 1864;

The first mail coach ran in Britain – from London to Bristol, 1784.

TODAY IS THE FEAST DAY OF St Altman, Saints Cyriacus, Largus and Smaragdus, St Dominic, The Fourteen Holy Helpers and St Hormisdas the Martyr.

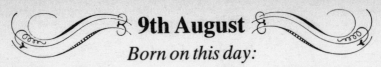

9th August

Born on this day:

Rod Laver, tennis player, 1938;

Philip Arthur Larkin, poet, 1922;

Robert Aldrich, US film director, 1918;

Giles Stannus Cooper, Irish playwright, 1918;

Léonide Massine, Russian dancer and choreographer, 1896;

Jean Piaget, Swiss child psychologist, 1896;

Albert William Ketèlbey, composer, 1875;

Reynaldo Hahn, Venezuelan composer, 1874;

Leonid Nikolayevich Andreyev, Russian novelist and playwright, 1871;

George Payne Rainsford James, novelist, 1799;

Robert Nicolas Charles Bochsa, French harpist and composer, 1789;

Michael Umlauf, Austrian violinist and composer, 1781;

Fabian Gottlieb Bellingshausen [Faddei Faddeyevich Bellingsgauzen], Russian polar explorer, 1778;

Thomas Telford, civil engineer, 1757;

Izaak Walton, author of *The Compleat Angler*, 1593.

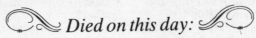

Died on this day:

Dmitri Dmitryevich Shostakovich, Russian composer, 1975;

Hermann Hesse, German poet and novelist, 1962;

John Jeffrey Farnol, novelist, 1952;

Nikolai Miaskovsky, Russian composer, 1950;

Sir John Bernard Partridge, artist and cartoonist, 1945;

Ernst Heinrich Haeckel, German biologist, 1919;

Ruggiero Leoncavallo, Italian composer, 1919;

Sir Edward Frankland, chemist, 1899;

Sir Samuel Ferguson, Irish poet, 1886;

Captain Frederick Marryat, novelist, 1848;

Maarten Harpertszoon Tromp, Dutch admiral, 1653;

Trajan, Roman emperor, 117.

Occurred on this day:

Gerald Ford succeeded Richard Nixon as 38th president of the USA, 1974;

The London production of the musical show *Jesus Christ Superstar* was first presented, 1972;

Singapore became independent, 1965;

An atomic bomb was dropped on Nagasaki, 1945;

Following an earthquake in the area of Constantinople [Istanbul], 6,000 people were killed and 40,000 rendered homeless, 1912;

The island of Heligoland was transferred to Germany, 1890;

The Elementary Education Act was passed, 1870;

The Married Women's Property Act was passed, improving the situation of British wives, 1870;

The first Atlantic cable was completed by Cyrus Field, 1858;

The border between Canada and the United States was established, 1842;

Revolutionaries established the Commune in Paris, 1792;

The Siege of Limerick started, 1690;

The Battle of Adrianople was fought between the Goths and the Roman emperor Valens, 378.

TODAY IS THE FEAST DAY OF St Emygius, Saints Nathy and Felim, St Oswald of Northumbria and St Romanus.

10th August

Born on this day:

Anita Lonsborough Porter, Olympic swimmer, 1941;

Barbara Mills, QC, Director of Public Prosecutions, 1940;

Kate O'Mara, actress, 1939;

Dame Elizabeth Butler-Sloss, a Lord Justice of Appeal, 1933;

Alexander Goehr, composer, 1932;

John Alldis, conductor, 1929;

Eddie Fisher, US singer, 1928;

General Sir George Cooper, Chief Royal Engineer, 1925;

Rhonda Fleming, US film actress, 1923;

Noah Beery, US film actor, 1916;

Jane Wyatt, US film actress, 1911;

Cardinal Gordon Gray, former Archbishop of St Andrews and Edinburgh, 1910;

Douglas Stuart Moore, US composer, 1893;

Herbert Clark Hoover, 31st president of the USA, 1874;

Laurence Robert Binyon, poet and playwright, 1869;

Hugo Eckener, Prussian aeronautical engineer, 1868;

Charles Samuel Keene, artist and illustrator, 1823;

Camillo Benso, Conte di Cavour, Italian statesman, 1810;

Sir Charles James Napier, military commander, 1782;

Samuel Arnold, organist and composer, 1740;

Bernhard Nieuwentijt, Dutch mathematician, 1654.

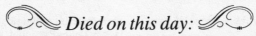

Died on this day:

Oswald Veblen, mathematician, 1960;

Otto Lilienthal, German aviator, 1896;

George Long, scholar and editor, 1879;

Edward William Lane, translator of *The Thousand and One Nights*, 1876;

Charles Wentworth Dilke, antiquarian, critic and journalist, 1864;

Henri Ethelbert Louis Victor Hebert, Comte de Richemont, French pretender, 1853;

Karl Wilhelm Naundorff, French pretender, 1845;

Allan Ramsay, Scottish portrait painter, 1784;

Ferdinand VI ['the Wise'], King of Spain, 1759.

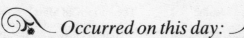

Occurred on this day:

France declared war on Austria-Hungary, 1914;

The Parliament Act was passed, reducing the power of the House of Lords, 1911;

British Members of Parliament voted to receive salaries for the first time [£400 p.a.], 1911;

Heavy losses were inflicted by the Japanese on the Russian Fleet off Port Arthur during the Battle of the Yellow Sea, 1904;

The Automobile Club of Great Britain and Ireland was founded [later 'Royal'], 1897;

The first Promenade Concert was given by Henry Wood [later Sir] at the Queen's Hall, London, 1895;

The Smithsonian Institution in Washington was established, 1846;

The Mines Act prohibited women and young children from working underground, 1842;

Missouri became the 24th of the United States, 1821;

The foundation stone of the Royal Greenwich Observatory was laid by King Charles II, 1675;

The Spanish and the English defeated the French at the Battle of St Quentin, 1557;

The Scots defeated the English at the Battle of Otterburn, 1388.

TODAY IS THE FEAST DAY OF St Laurence of Rome.

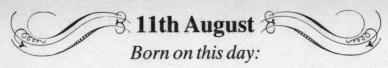

11th August

Born on this day:

Anna Massey, actress, 1937;
Admiral Sir Julian Oswald, First Sea Lord and Chief of Naval Staff, 1933;
Dame Angela Rumbold, MP, 1932;
Alun Hoddinott, composer, 1929;
Raymond Leppard, conductor, 1927;
Sir Aaron Klug, molecular biologist, 1926;
Arlene Dahl, US film actress, 1924;
Jean Parker, US film actress, 1912;
Enid Mary Blyton, children's author, 1897;
Marie Goossens, harpist, 1894;
Hugh MacDiarmid [Christopher Murray Grieve], Scottish poet, 1892;

Helen Broderick, US film actress and Broadway comedienne, 1891;
Christiaan Eijkman, Dutch physician, 1858;
Charlotte Mary Yonge, novelist, 1823;
John Christian Schetky, Scottish marine painter, 1778;
Rowland Hill, 1st Viscount, general, 1772;
Jean-Victor-Marie Moreau, French general, 1763;
Joseph Nollekens, sculptor, 1737;
Richard Mead, physician, 1673.

Died on this day:

Paul Jackson Pollock, US abstract painter, 1956;
Edith Newbold [Jones] Wharton, US novelist, 1937;
Joaquin Sorolla y Bastida, Spanish painter, 1923;
Andrew Carnegie, US industrialist and philanthropist, 1919;
John Henry Newman, Cardinal, 1890;

James Wilson, founder of *The Economist*, 1860;
Marshall Hall, physiologist, 1857;
Henry James Pye, poet, 1813;
Richard Monckton Milnes, 1st Baron, poet, 1809;
Hans Memling, Flemish painter, 1495;
János Corvinus Hunyadi, Hungarian leader, 1456;
John I, King of Portugal, 1433.

Occurred on this day:

The French colony of Chad became independent, 1960;
King Talal of Jordan was deposed because of his mental illness, 1952;
King Hussein succeeded to the throne of Jordan, 1952;
The new Waterloo Bridge, London, was opened to traffic, 1942;
The Atlantic Charter was signed by Winston Churchill and President Roosevelt, 1941;

The 'moons' of Mars, Phobos and Deimos, were discovered by Professor Asaph Hall, US astronomer, 1877;
During severe earthquakes in the Azores, the village of São Miguel sank, 1810;
The Battle of Passero Cape was fought when Admiral Byng attacked the Spanish fleet, 1718;
Sir Martin Frobisher entered the bay now named after him, 1576.

TODAY IS THE FEAST DAY OF St Alexander of Comana, St Attracta or Araght, St Blane, St Clare of Assisi, St Equitius, St Gerard of Gallinaro, St Gery or Gaugericus, St Lelia, St Susanna and St Tiburtius.

12th August

Born on this day:

Simon Groom, TV presenter, 1950;

Mark Knopfler, rock guitarist, 1949;

Michael Brunson, TV reporter and newscaster, 1940;

George Hamilton, US film actor, 1939;

Norris McWhirter, a founder of the *Guinness Book of Records*, 1925;

Peter West, sports commentator, 1920;

Erwin Schrödinger, Austrian physicist, 1887;

Frank Swinnerton, novelist, 1884;

Cecil Blount De Mille, US film producer and director, 1881;

Marguerite ['John'] Radclyffe-Hall, author, 1880;

Mary Roberts Rinehart, US novelist and playwright, 1876;

Jacinto Benavente y Martínez, Spanish playwright, 1866;

Sir Alfred Gilbert, sculptor and goldsmith, 1854;

Sir Joseph Barnby, conductor and academic principal, 1838;

Sir Frederick Arthur Gore Ouseley, composer, 1825;

Robert Southey, poet, 1774;

Thomas Bewick, wood engraver, artist and naturalist, 1753;

King George IV, 1762.

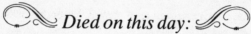

Died on this day:

Henry Fonda, US film actor, 1982;

Ian Lancaster Fleming, novelist, creator of 'James Bond', 1964;

Thomas Mann, German novelist, 1955;

Leoš Janáček, Czech composer, 1928;

John Philip Holland, US designer of the submarine, 1914;

Nils Adolf Erik, Baron Nordenskjöld, Swedish geologist and explorer, 1901;

James Russell Lowell, US poet, critic and diplomat, 1891;

Sir William Jackson Hooker, botanist, 1865;

William Daniel Conybeare, geologist, 1857;

George Stephenson, locomotive engineer, 1848;

William Blake, poet and painter, 1827;

Nahum Tate, Irish playwright, 1715;

Philippe de Champaigne, Belgian painter, 1674;

Giovanni Gabrieli, Venetian composer, 1612.

Occurred on this day:

Echo I, the first communications satellite, 100 feet in diameter, was launched, 1960;

During World War II, the 'pipe line under the ocean' [PLUTO] began operating beneath the English Channel, 1944;

The USA and Spain concluded an armistice over Cuba and other possessions, 1898;

In a contest, the schooner *America* beat the British yacht *Aurora*, thus giving rise later to the America's Cup, 1851;

The Duke of Wellington's troops entered Madrid, 1812;

The Russian-Austrian army overpowered the Prussians at the Battle of Kunersdorf, 1759;

Ottoman invaders of Hungary were routed at the Battle of Mohacs, 1687.

TODAY IS THE FEAST DAY OF St Euplus, St Jambert, Archbishop of Canterbury, St Murtagh or Muredach and St Porcarius and his Companions.

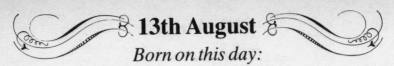

13th August

Born on this day:

Robin Jackman, cricketer, 1945;
Susan Jameson, actress, 1943;
Madhur Jaffrey, actress and cookery writer, 1933;
Dr Fidel Castro, president of Cuba, 1927;
Neville Brand, US film actor, 1921;
George Shearing, pianist, 1920;
Dr Frederick Sanger OM CH, biochemist, 1918;
Archbishop Makarios III [Michael Christodolou Mouskos], Cypriot priest and president, 1913;
Ben Hogan, US golfer, 1912;
John Beal, US film actor, 1909;
Gene Raymond, US film actor, 1908;
Sir Basil Urwin Spence, architect, 1907;

Lord Sainsbury, joint-president of the grocery chain, 1902;
Felix Wankel, German engineer, 1902;
Alfred Joseph Hitchcock, film director, 1899;
Jean Borotra, French tennis player, 1898;
Christopher Richard Wynne Nevinson, painter, 1889;
John Logie Baird, television pioneer, 1888;
John Nicholson Ireland, composer, 1879;
Sir William Alexander Craigie, lexicographer, 1867;
Sir George Grove, engineer and editor, *Dictionary of Music and Musicians*, 1820;
Queen Adelaide, consort of William IV, 1792;
James Gillray, caricaturist, 1756.

Died on this day:

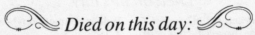

Henry Williamson, novelist, 1977;
Herbert George Wells, novelist, 1946;
Walter Runciman, 1st Baron, shipowner, 1937;
Jules-Émile-Frédéric Massenet, French composer, 1912;
Florence Nightingale, nursing pioneer, 1910;
Sir John Everett Millais, Pre-Raphaelite painter, 1896;
Edward John Trelawny, traveller and author, 1881;

Ferdinand-Victor-Eugène Delacroix, French painter, 1863;
René Laënnec, French physician and inventor of the stethoscope, 1826;
Acisclo Antonio Palomino de Castro y Velasco, Spanish painter and art historian, 1726;
Gerard David [Gheeraert Davit], Flemish painter, 1523.

Occurred on this day:

The last US troops left Vietnam, 1972;
The last hangings in Britain took place when two men were executed for murder at Liverpool and Manchester, 1964;
The frontier between East and West Germany was closed, 1961;
The Central African Republic became independent, 1960;
Mustapha Kemal [Atatürk] was elected president of Turkey, 1923;

Earthquakes in Peru and Ecuador destroyed four cities and killed over 25,000 people, 1868;
Cape of Good Hope Province was ceded to Britain by the Dutch, and it became a British colony, 1814;
The French armies were defeated at Blenheim by the Austrians and English, 1704;
Cortés, leading his Spanish troops, took Tenochtitlán [Mexico City], 1521.

TODAY IS THE FEAST DAY OF St Benildus, St Cassian of Imola, St Hippolytus of Rome, St Maximus the Confessor, St Narses Klaietus, St Pontian, pope, St Radegund, queen of Thuringia, St Simplician of Milan and St Wigbert.

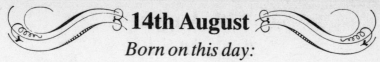

14th August

Born on this day:

Sarah Brightman, soprano, 1961;
Tony Scannell, actor, 1945;
Frederic Raphael, novelist, 1931;
Dr Oliver Neville, principal, Royal Academy of Dramatic Art, 1929;
Buddy Greco, jazz pianist and singer, 1926;
Lord Mishcon, solicitor, 1915;
Sydney Wooderson, athlete, 1914;
Fred Davis, snooker player, 1913;
John Galsworthy, novelist and playwright, 1867;
Baron Richard von Krafft-Ebing, German physician, 1840;

Briton Riviere, artist, 1840;
Sir Walter Besant, novelist and philanthropist, 1836;
Samuel Sebastian Wesley, organist and composer, 1810;
Letitia Elizabeth Landon, author, 1802;
Friedrich Ludwig Dulon, blind German flautist and composer, 1769;
Claude-Joseph Vernet, French painter, 1714;
Fra Paolo Sarpi [Paulus Venetus], Italian scholar and philosopher, 1552.

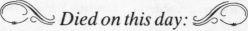

Died on this day:

John Boynton Priestley, novelist and playwright, 1984;
Jules Romains [Louis Farigoule], French novelist, playwright and poet, 1972;
Oscar Levant, US composer and pianist, 1972;
Leonard Sidney Woolf, publisher, 1969;
Clifford Odets, US playwright, 1963;
Henri-Édouard-Prosper Breuil, priest and archaeologist, 1961;
Bertolt Brecht, German writer, 1956;
William Randolph Hearst, US newspaper proprietor, 1951;
Sir Landon Ronald, composer and pianist, 1938;

Alfred Charles William Harmsworth, 1st Viscount Northcliffe, newspaper proprietor, 1922;
Richard Jefferies, naturalist and essayist, 1887;
Admiral David [James] Glasgow Farragut, US naval officer, 1870;
George Combe, phrenologist, 1858;
William Buckland, Dean of Westminster and geologist, 1856;
George Colman [the Elder], playwright, 1794;
Augustus Montague Toplady, hymn-writer and author of *Rock of Ages*, 1778.

Occurred on this day:

Japan surrendered to the Allies unconditionally, 1945;
The British transport *Royal Edward* was sunk by a German U-boat in the Aegean, with the loss of 1,000 lives, 1915;
The landing of 2,000 US Marines helped to capture Peking, thus ending the Boxer uprising, 1900;
Cetewayo, the Zulu chief, was received by Queen Victoria at Osborne, 1882;

Cologne Cathedral, started in 1248, was completed, 1880;
Tristan da Cunha was annexed to Great Britain, 1816;
The French repulsed William of Orange at the Battle of Mons, 1678;
The Portuguese defeated the Castilians at the Battle of Aljubarotta, 1385.

TODAY IS THE FEAST DAY OF St Athanasia of Aegina, St Eusebius of Rome, St Fachanan, St Marcellus of Apamea and St Maximilian Kolbe.

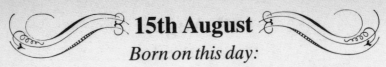

15th August

Born on this day:

HRH the Princess Royal, 1950;
Jenny Hanley, actress, 1947;
William Waldegrave, MP, government
  minister, 1946;
Jimmy Webb, songwriter, 1946;
Jim Dale, actor, 1935;
Oscar Peterson, jazz pianist, 1925;
Robert Bolt, playwright, 1924;
Lukas Foss, US composer, 1922;
Dame Wendy Hiller, actress, 1912;
Hans Feibusch, mural painter and sculptor,
  1898;
Jacques-François-Antoine Ibert,
  composer, 1890;
Thomas Edward Lawrence, soldier and
  writer, 1888;
Edna Ferber, US novelist and playwright,
  1887;

Ethel Barrymore [Ethel Mae Blythe], US
  actress, 1879;
Samuel Coleridge-Taylor, composer, 1875;
James Keir Hardie, Labour Party veteran,
  1856;
Walter Crane, painter and illustrator,
  1845;
Thomas De Quincey, essayist and critic,
  1785;
Edouard de Hartog, Dutch composer,
  1828;
Sir Walter Scott, Scottish novelist, 1771;
Napoleon Bonaparte, French emperor,
  1769;
Frederick William I, King of Prussia, 1688;
Robert Blake, admiral, 1599;
Agostino Carracci, Italian painter, 1557;
Luigi Pulci, Florentine poet, 1432.

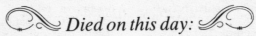 *Died on this day:*

René-François-Ghislain Magritte, Belgian
  surrealist painter, 1967;
Paul Signac, French painter, 1935;
Wiley Post, US aviator, killed in an air
  crash, 1935;
William Penn ['Will'] Rogers, US humorist,
  killed in an air crash, 1935;

Joseph Joachim, Hungarian violinist,
  1907;
Lilian Adelaide Neilson [Elizabeth Ann
  Brown], actress, 1880;
Pope Pius II, 1464;
Macbeth, King of Scotland, killed in battle,
  1057.

Occurred on this day:

Bahrain became independent, 1971;
The French Congo became independent,
  1960;
The republic of [South] Korea was
  proclaimed, 1948;
India became independent, 1947;
Pakistan, having separated from India,
  became independent, 1947;
The first London performance of the
  musical show *Good News* was presented,
  1928;

The Panama Canal was officially opened,
  1914;
The Jesuits [Society of Jesus] were
  founded in Paris by Ignatius de Loyola,
  1534;
Nearly 500 French ships were destroyed
  by the Duke of Bedford at Harfleur,
  1416.

TODAY IS THE FEAST DAY OF The Assumption of the Virgin Mary, St Arnulph of
Soissons and St Tarsicius.

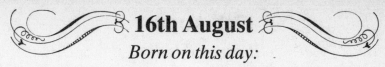

16th August

Born on this day:

Madonna [Louise Vernon Ciccione], US rock singer, 1958;

Jeff Thomson, Australian cricketer, 1950;

Katharine Hamnett, fashion designer, 1947;

Trevor McDonald, TV news presenter, 1939;

John Standing [Sir John Leon Bt.], actor, 1934;

Eydie Gormé, US singer, 1932;

Ted Hughes, Poet Laureate, 1930;

Ann Blyth, US film actress, 1928;

The Rt. Rev. Ronald Bowlby, Bishop of Southwark, 1926;

Menachem Begin, former Israeli prime minister, 1913;

Ted Drake, footballer, 1912;

Prof. Brian Woledge, authority on the French language, 1904;

Georgette Heyer, novelist, 1902;

Dame Mary Gilmore, Australian poet, 1865;

Jules Laforgue, French poet and critic, 1860;

Johan Siegwald Dahl, Norwegian/German painter, 1827;

Arthur Cayley, mathematician, 1821;

Moritz Wilhelm Drobisch, German mathematician and philosopher, 1802;

Heinrich August Marschner, German operatic composer, 1795;

Catharine Cockburn, playwright and philosopher, 1679.

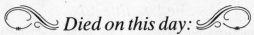

Died on this day:

Elvis Presley, US rock singer, 1977;

Selman Waksman, microbiologist and discoverer of streptomycin, 1973;

Wanda Louis Landowska, French harpsichordist, 1959;

Bela Lugosi [Bela Blasko], US film actor, 1956;

George Herman ['Babe'] Ruth, US baseball player, 1948;

Umberto Boccioni, Italian futurist sculptor, 1916;

Robert Wilhelm Bunsen, German chemist and inventor, 1899;

Ramakrishna [Gadadhur Chatterji], Hindu mystic, 1886;

Joe Miller, comedian, 1738;

Jacques Bernoulli, Swiss mathematician, 1705;

Andrew Marvell, poet, 1678.

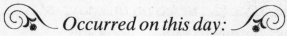

Occurred on this day:

Cyprus became an independent republic, 1960;

The US explorer William Beebe descended 3,028 feet [1,922 metres] in his bathysphere into the ocean near Bermuda, 1934;

The Tate Gallery, London, was opened, 1897;

The Republic of Bolivia was proclaimed, 1825;

The Peterloo Massacre took place at St Peter's Field, Manchester, 1819;

During Napoleon's invasion of Russia, the Battle of Smolensk began, 1812;

King Henry VIII and his army defeated the French at Guinegatte in the Battle of the Spurs, 1513.

TODAY IS THE FEAST DAY OF St Armel, St Arsacius and St Stephen of Hungary.

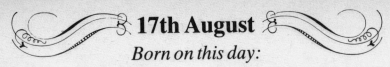

17th August

Born on this day:

Robin Cousins, ice-skater, 1957;

Nelson Piquet, racing driver, 1952;

Guillermo Vilas, Argentinian tennis player, 1952;

Alan Minter, middleweight boxer, 1951;

Jean-Bernard Pommier, French pianist, 1944;

Edward Cowie, lecturer and composer, 1943;

Robert De Niro, US film actor, 1943;

Richard Stott, editor, the *People*, 1943;

Anthony Valentine, actor, 1939;

Sir Vidiadhar Naipaul, novelist, 1932;

George Melly, jazz singer, 1926;

Maureen O'Hara, US film actress, 1921;

Mae West, US film actress, 1892;

Wilfrid Scawen Blunt, diplomat, poet and traveller, 1840;

Pierre-Léonard-Léopold Benoît, Belgian composer, 1834;

Richard Lalor Sheil, Irish playwright and politician, 1791;

Davy Crockett, US frontiersman, 1786;

John Varley, water-colour painter, 1778;

William Carey, orientalist and missionary, 1761;

Thomas Stothard, illustrator, 1755;

Niccola Antonio Porpora, Italian composer, 1686;

Pierre de Fermat, French mathematician, 1601.

Died on this day:

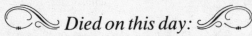

Walter Richard Rudolf Hess, Hitler's former deputy, 1987;

Ira Gershwin [Israel Gershvin], US lyricist, 1983;

Conrad Potter Aiken, US novelist and poet, 1973;

Ludwig Mies van der Rohe, US architect, 1969;

Leonard Alfred George Strong, novelist, 1958;

Fernand Léger, French Cubist painter, 1955;

Thomas Faed, Scottish painter, 1900;

Honoré de Balzac, French novelist, 1850;

José Francisco de San Martín, Argentinian revolutionary, 1850;

Frederick II [the Great], King of Prussia, 1786.

Occurred on this day:

Indonesia was proclaimed an independent republic, 1945;

The RAF raided the German rocket base at Peenemünde, Rostock, 1943;

The first London performance of the musical play *Waltzes from Vienna* was staged, 1931;

Gold was discovered in the Klondyke, Canada, 1896;

Wagner's opera *Götterdämmerung* was first performed, Bayreuth, 1876;

On the point of starvation, the Sioux Indian nation rebelled in Minnesota, killing over 800 soldiers and settlers, 1862;

The registration of births, deaths and marriages was introduced in Britain under the Registration Act, 1836;

Robert Fulton began operating his *Clermont* steamboat from New York to Albany, 1807;

Cromwell's army was victorious at the Battle of Preston, 1648;

The English defeated the Scots and French at the Battle of Verneuil, 1424.

TODAY IS THE FEAST DAY OF St Clare of Montefalco, St Eusebius, pope, St Hyacinth, St Joan Delanoue, St Liberatus of Capua, St Mamas and St Rock or Roch.

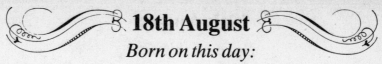

18th August

Born on this day:

Robert Redford, US film actor, 1937;
Willie Rushton, broadcaster, 1937;
Roman Polanski, film director, 1933;
Brian Aldiss, science-fiction author, 1925;
Alain Robbe-Grillet, French novelist and film director, 1922;
Shelley Winters, US film actress, 1922;
Godfrey Evans, cricketer, 1920;
Caspar Weinberger, former US Secretary of Defence, 1917;
Dame Moura Lympany, concert pianist, 1916;
Marcel Carné, French film director, 1909;

Otto Harbach [Otto Abels Hauerbach], US librettist and lyricist, 1873;
Benjamin-Louis-Paul Godard, French composer, 1849;
Franz Josef I, Emperor of Austria-Hungary, 1830;
John Russell, 1st Earl Russell, statesman, 1792;
Meriwether Lewis, US explorer, 1774;
Antonio Salieri, Italian composer, 1750;
Virginia Dare, first child of English parents to be born in America, 1587.

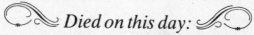 Died on this day:

Sir Nikolaus Pevsner, architectural historian, 1983;
William Henry Hudson, naturalist and writer, 1922;
Sir Henry Thompson, surgeon, 1904;
Frederick Nicholls Crouch, musician and composer, 1896;
George J. S. Miller, sculptor, 1876;

Sir William Fairbairn, Scottish engineer and inventor, 1874;
André-Jacques Garnerin, French balloonist, 1823;
Matthew Boulton, engineer, 1809;
James Beattie, Scottish poet, 1803;
Guido Reni, Italian painter, 1642;
Pope Paul IV, 1559;
Genghis Khan, 1227.

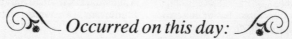 Occurred on this day:

The liner *Queen Mary* was sold to the town of Long Beach, California, 1967;
The Tay Road Bridge was opened, 1966;
The National Fire Service in Britain was established, 1941;
The Prussians were victorious over the French at the Battle of Gravelotte, 1870;

The Treaty of Alliance forming the North German Confederation was signed, 1866;
US forces captured Santa Fé, 1846;
The Russians were defeated by Napoleon at Smolensk, 1812;
The French under De la Clue were defeated in the Battle of Lagos by Admiral Boscawen, 1759.

TODAY IS THE FEAST DAY OF St Agapitus, St Alipius, St Beatrice or Brites da Silva, Saints Florus and Laurus and St Helena.

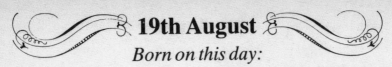

19th August

Born on this day:

Ian Gould, cricketer, 1957;
Billy J. Kramer, rock singer, 1943;
Jill St John, US film actress, 1940;
Richard Ingrams, journalist, 1937;
Willie Shoemaker, US jockey, 1931;
Bernard Levin, journalist and author, 1928;
Rose Heilbron, former High Court judge, 1914;
Arthur Calder-Marshall, author, 1908;
Frederic Ogden Nash, US humorist, 1902;
Sir Arthur David Waley, scholar, 1889;
Gabrielle [Coco] Chanel, French fashion designer, 1883;

Georges Enesco [Gheorghe Enescu], Romanian composer and violinist, 1881;
Orville Wright, US pioneer aviator, 1871;
James Nasmyth, inventor of the steam hammer, 1808;
Samuel Richardson, novelist, baptised, 1689;
John Flamsteed, first Astronomer Royal, 1646;
John Dryden, poet, 1631;
Gerbrand van den Eeckhout, Dutch painter, 1621;
James Crichton ['The Admirable Crichton'], scholar, 1560.

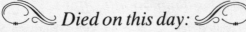

Died on this day:

Sir Frederick Ashton, choreographer, 1988;
Hermione Baddeley, actress, 1986;
Julius ['Groucho'] Marx, US comedian, 1977;
Alastair Sim, comedy actor, 1976;
Sir Henry Joseph Wood, conductor, 1944;
Federico García Lorca, Spanish poet and playwright, 1936;
Sergei Pavlovich Diaghilev, ballet director and choreographer, 1929;

Richard Burdon Haldane, 1st Viscount, statesman, 1928;
George Smith, Assyriologist, decipherer of cuneiform scripts, 1876;
Sir Martin Archer Shee, portrait painter, 1850;
Blaise Pascal, French theologian and mathematician, 1662;
Augustus [Gaius Octavianus], 1st Roman emperor, 14.

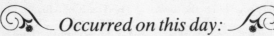

Occurred on this day:

The first London performance of the musical show *Camelot* was presented, 1964;
The raid on Dieppe by British and Canadian commandos took place, 1942;
General Alexander replaced General Auchinleck as Commander-in-Chief, Middle East, 1942;
Lieutenant-General Bernard Montgomery became commander of the British Eighth Army in North Africa, 1942;

British forces were driven out of Somaliland, 1940;
A plebiscite held in Germany gave sole power to the Führer, Adolf Hitler, 1934;
James Mollison completed the first westbound transatlantic solo flight, 1932.

TODAY IS THE FEAST DAY OF Saints Agapius and Timothy, St Andrew the Tribune, St Bertulf of Bobbio, St Credan of Evesham, St John Eudes, St Louis of Anjou, St Mocha, St Sebald, St Sixtus III and St Thecla.

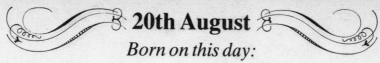

20th August

Born on this day:

Mike Garnham, cricketer, 1960;
John Emburey, cricketer, 1952;
Robert Plant, rock singer, 1948;
Jim Reeves, US country singer, 1924;
Anatole Fistoulari, conductor, 1907;
'Bunny' [H.W.] Austin, former tennis player, 1906;
Christian Bérard, French painter and sculptor, 1902;
Howard Phillips Lovecraft, novelist, 1890;
Shaul Tchernichowski, Hebrew poet, 1875;
Raymond-Nicolas-Landry Poincaré, French statesman, 1860;

Kristina Nilsson, Swedish soprano, 1843;
Benjamin Harrison, 23rd president of the USA, 1833;
Jöns Jakob, Baron Berzelius, Swedish chemist, 1779;
Bernardo O'Higgins, Chilean patriot, 1778;
Thomas Corneille, French playwright, 1625;
George Villiers, 1st Duke of Buckingham, courtier, 1592.

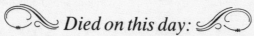

Died on this day:

Jessie Matthews, singer, dancer and actress, 1981;
Leon Trotsky [Lev Davidovich Bronstein], Russian politician, murdered, 1940;
Vilfredo Pareto, Italian economist and sociologist, 1923;
Paul Ehrlich, German biochemist, 1915;
William Booth, founder of the Salvation Army, 1912;
William-Adolphe Bouguereau, French painter, 1905;

Mrs Charles Kean [Ellen Tree], actress, 1880;
William Miller, Scottish 'nursery' poet, 1872;
Friedrich Wilhelm Joseph von Schelling, German philosopher, 1854;
Pope Pius VII, 1823;
Sir Charles Sedley, playwright, 1701;
Lord Herbert of Cherbury, philosopher and poet, 1648;
Martin Opitz von Boberfeld, German poet, 1639.

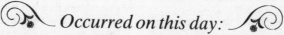

Occurred on this day:

Russian troops invaded Czechoslovakia, and fighting broke out in Prague, 1968;
The first London performance of the musical show *Gentlemen Prefer Blondes* was presented, 1962;
The French colony of Senegal became independent, 1960;

Calder Hall nuclear-power station began operating, 1956;
The German army occupied Brussels, 1914;
The Austrians defeated the French at the Battle of Saragossa, 1710.

TODAY IS THE FEAST DAY OF St Amator or Amadour, St Bernard of Clairvaux, St Oswin, St Rognwald or Ronald and St Philibert.

233

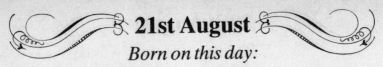

21st August

Born on this day:

Anne Hobbs, tennis player, 1959;
Kenny Rogers, US country and western singer, 1941;
Dame Janet Baker, mezzo-soprano, 1933;
Barry Norman, broadcaster, 1933;
HRH Princess Margaret, 1930;
Christopher Brasher, athlete and newspaper columnist, 1928;
Anthony Abbott, stage designer, 1923;
Diana Churchill, actress, 1913;
Lord Goodman CH, 1913;
William 'Count' Basie, US jazz pianist and bandleader, 1904;

Henry Hinchliffe Ainley, actor, 1879;
Charles Gerhardt, French chemist, 1816;
Jules Michelet, French historian, 1798;
King William IV, 1765;
William Murdock, inventor, 1754;
Jean-Baptiste Greuze, French painter, 1725;
St Francis de Sales, French bishop, 1567;
Philip II [Philip-Augustus], King of France, 1165.

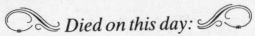

Died on this day:

Benigno Aquino, Philippine politician, assassinated, 1983;
Norman Shelley, actor, 1980;
Sir Jacob Epstein, sculptor, 1959;
Leonard Constant Lambert, composer, 1951;
Sir Aston Webb, architect, 1930;

Conrad Martens, Australian painter, 1878;
William Maginn, poet and journalist, 1842;
Sir Benjamin Thompson, Count von Rumford, physicist, 1814;
Lady Mary Wortley Montagu, author, 1762;
Richard Crashaw, poet, 1649.

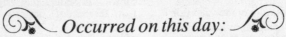

Occurred on this day:

It was announced in the USSR that a coup had failed and that President Gorbachev had been reinstated, 1991;
Hawaii became the 50th of the United States, 1959;
The Dumbarton Oaks conference started, 1944;
Civil Defence was started in Britain, 1939;
The Battle of Bapaume-Péronne started, 1918;

The 'Mona Lisa' by da Vinci painting was stolen from the Louvre, 1911;
Marshal Jean-Baptiste Bernadotte was selected as Crown Prince of Sweden, 1810;
Wellington defeated the French forces under General Junot at the Battle of Vimiero, 1808.

TODAY IS THE FEAST DAY OF St Abraham of Smolensk, Saints Bonosus and Maximian, Saints Luxorius, Cisellus and Camerinus, St Pius X, pope and St Sidonius Apollinaris.

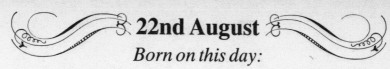

22nd August

Born on this day:

Mats Wilander, tennis player, 1964;

Steve Davis, snooker player, 1957;

John Banham, director-general, CBI, 1940;

Karlheinz Stockhausen, composer and conductor, 1928;

Marc Bohan, dress designer, 1926;

Ray Bradbury, author, 1920;

Henri Cartier-Bresson, French photographer, 1908;

Leni [Helene Bertha Amalie] Riefenstahl, German actress, film producer and photographer, 1902;

Dorothy Parker [Rothschild], US humorist and writer, 1893;

Jacques Lipchitz, Latvian/French painter and sculptor, 1891;

Claude-Achille Debussy, French composer, 1862;

Gustaf Fröding, Swedish poet, 1860;

Alexander Campbell Mackenzie, Scottish composer, 1847;

Dr John Hill Burton, Scottish historian and jurist, 1809;

Pope Leo XII, 1760;

Denis Papin, French physicist and inventor, 1647.

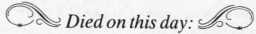

Died on this day:

Jomo Kenyatta [Kamau], Kenyan leader, 1978;

William Richard Morris, 1st Viscount Nuffield, motor manufacturer, 1963;

Roger Martin du Gard, French novelist and playwright, 1958;

Michael [Mikhail Mikhailovich] Fokine, US dancer and choreographer, 1942;

Sir Oliver Joseph Lodge, physicist, 1940;

Michael Collins, Irish nationalist leader, killed in ambush, 1922;

Robert Arthur Talbot Gascoyne Cecil, 3rd Marquess of Salisbury, statesman, 1903;

Henry George Bohn, bookseller and publisher, 1884;

Sydney Thompson Dobell, poet, 1874;

George Shillibeer, pioneer of London's first bus service, 1866;

Alexandre-Gabriel Decamps, French painter, 1860;

Franz Joseph Gall, German neurophysiologist and founder of phrenology, 1828;

Warren Hastings, 1st governor-general of India, 1818;

Jean-Honoré Fragonard, French painter, 1806;

William Whiston, translator of Josephus, 1752;

Luca Marenzio, Italian organist and composer, 1599;

Jan Kochanowski, Polish poet, 1584;

King Richard III, killed at Bosworth Field, 1485;

Philip VI, King of France, 1350;

Pope Gregory IX, 1241.

Occurred on this day:

The first regular BBC television service began, 1932;

Korea was annexed by Japan, 1910;

The International Red Cross organisation was founded, 1864;

New Mexico was annexed by the USA, 1846;

The Civil War began in England, 1642;

Richard III was defeated by Henry VII's men at the Battle of Bosworth Field, 1485;

The Scots were defeated by the English at the Battle of the Standard [Northallerton], 1138.

TODAY IS THE FEAST DAY OF St Andrew of Fiesole, St John Kemble, St Sigfrid of Wearmouth, St Symphorian and St Timothy.

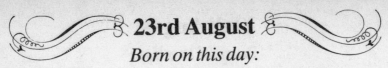

23rd August

Born on this day:

Christopher Blake, actor, 1949;
David Robb, actor, 1947;
Willy Russell, author and playwright, 1947;
Peter Lilley, MP, 1943;
Roger Greenaway, popular song composer, 1938;
Sir Roy Strong, writer and historian, 1935;
Gen. Sir Richard Vincent, Chief of the Defence Staff, 1931;
Peter Thomson, Australian golfer, 1929;
James Quinn, film producer and exhibitor, 1919;
Gene Kelly, US dancer and singer, 1912;
Dr Carl Dolmetsch, director, Haslemere Festival, 1911;
Leonard Constant Lambert, composer and critic, 1905;

C. H. Rolph [Cecil Rolph Hewitt], author, 1901;
Sir Henry Thomas Tizard, scientist, 1885;
Edgar Lee Masters, US poet and novelist, 1869;
Eleutherios Venizelos, Greek statesman, 1864;
Moritz Moszkowski, Polish/German composer, 1854;
William Ernest Henley, poet and critic, 1849;
Georges, Baron Cuvier, French zoologist and statesman, 1769;
Sir Astley Paston Cooper, surgeon, 1768;
Louis XVI, King of France, 1754.

Died on this day:
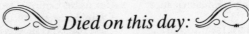

Lancelot Thomas Hogben, scientific writer, 1975;
Oscar Hammerstein II, US lyricist, 1960;
Sidney Coe Howard, US playwright, in an accident, 1939;
Albert Roussel, French composer, 1937;
Félicien Rops, Belgian painter and engraver, 1898;
Philip Henry Gosse, naturalist, 1888;
Rudolph Valentino [Rodolfo Alfonzo Raffaele Pierre Philibert Guglielmi], Italian-born film actor, 1926;

Alexander Wilson, US ornithologist, 1813;
Charles-Augustin de Coulomb, French physicist, 1806;
Guillaume Budé [Guglielmus Budaeus], French classical scholar, 1540;
Sir Thomas Littleton [Lyttelton], legal author and jurist, 1481;
Sir William Wallace, Scottish patriot, executed, 1305.

Occurred on this day:
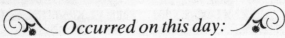

The Battle of Stalingrad began, 1942;
The London Blitz started, 1940;
Feisal I was crowned as King of Iraq, 1921;
Japan declared war on Germany, 1914;
The Battle of Mons began, 1914;
The Albert Bridge across the Thames at Chelsea was opened, 1873;

Hong Kong was taken by the British, 1839;
Mexico was declared to be independent, 1821;
The Prussians under von Bülow drove back the French at the Battle of Grossbeeren, 1813.

TODAY IS THE FEAST DAY OF Saints Asterius and Claudius, St Eugene or Eoghan of Ardstraw, St Philip Benizi, St Rose of Lima and St Tydfil.

24th August

Born on this day:

Stephen Fry, actor and writer, 1957;
Sam Torrance, golfer, 1953;
Carlo Curley, organist, 1952;
Antonia Byatt, writer, 1936;
Paul Barker, writer and broadcaster, 1935;
Richard Meale, Australian composer, 1932;
Charles Causley, poet and broadcaster, 1917;
Graham Vivian Sutherland, artist, 1903;

Jorge Luis Borges, Argentinian writer, 1899;
Jean Rhys, novelist, 1894;
Sir Max [Henry Maximilian] Beerbohm, author and caricaturist, 1872;
James Weddell, Antarctic explorer, 1787;
William Wilberforce, philanthropist, 1759;
George Stubbs, animal and portrait painter, 1724;
Robert Herrick, poet, baptised, 1591.

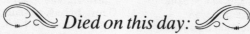

Died on this day:

Getulio Dornelles Vargas, Brazilian president, committed suicide, 1954;
John William Dunne, philosopher, 1949;
Margaret Fairless Barber [Michael Fairless], essayist, 1901;
Theodore Edward Hook, playwright and author, 1841;
Nicolas-Léonard-Sadi Carnot, French physicist, 1832;
Thomas Chatterton, poet and forger, committed suicide, 1770;

Colonel Thomas Blood, Irish adventurer, 1680;
Jean-François-Paul de Gondi, Cardinal de Retz, French politician, 1679;
Gaspard II de Coligny, French admiral and Huguenot leader, killed, 1572;
Francesco Parmigianino [Girolamo Francesco Maria Mazzola], Italian artist, 1540;
Alaric I, King of the Visigoths, 410;
Pliny the Elder, Roman naturalist and writer, 79.

Occurred on this day:

Mustafa Kemal, leading the Turkish army, drove back the Greeks at the Battle of the Sakkaria River, 1921;
The outskirts of London were raided by Zeppelins, killing eight people, 1916;
The Allies retreated from Mons, 1914;
Matthew Webb was the first man to swim the English Channel, 1875;
Washington, D.C., was captured by British troops, who burned down the White House, 1814;
The English-Dutch fleets defeated the French at the Battle of Malaga, 1704;

The Massacre of St Bartholomew occurred in France when thousands of Huguenots were killed in Paris, 1572;
England achieved her first naval victory in the Battle of the Key, when Hubert de Burgh defeated the French fleet under Eustace the Monk, 1217;
Rome was captured by the Visigoths, 410;
The cities of Pompeii and Herculaneum were buried under volcanic ash after the eruption of Vesuvius, 79.

TODAY IS THE FEAST DAY OF St Audenoeus or Ouen, St Bartholomew and The Martyrs of Utica.

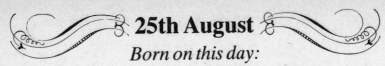

25th August

Born on this day:

Pamela Armstrong, TV newsreader, 1951;
Martin Amis, novelist, 1949;
Ross Davidson, actor, 1949;
Conrad Black, chairman, the *Daily Telegraph*, 1944;
Frederick Forsyth, novelist, 1938;
Sean Connery, film actor, 1930;
Karl Korte, US composer, 1928;
Brian Moore, novelist, 1921;
Leonard Bernstein, US conductor and composer, 1918;
Richard Greene, film actor, 1918;
Mel Ferrer, US film actor and director, 1917;
Van Johnson, US film actor, 1917;
Bob Crosby, US dance bandleader, 1913;
Ruby Keeler, US film actress and dancer, 1909;

Dr Desmond Flower, author and former chairman, Cassell & Co., 1907;
Clara Bow, US film actress, 1905;
Ludwig II, King of Bavaria, 1845;
Jacob Maris, Dutch painter, 1837;
Francis Bret Harte, US novelist, 1836;
Narcisse Virgilio Diaz, French painter, 1808;
Ludwig I, King of Bavaria, 1786;
Louis-Antoine-Léon de Richebourg de St Just, French revolutionary leader, 1767;
Johann Gottfried von Herder, German writer and critic, 1744;
Ivan IV ['The Terrible'], Tsar of Russia, 1530.

Died on this day:

Truman Capote, US author, 1984;
Paul Muni [Muni Weisenfreund], US film actor, 1967;
Henri-Joseph Harpignies, French landscape painter, 1916;
Antoine-Henri Becquerel, French physicist, 1908;
Ignace-Henri-Joseph-Théodore Fantin-Latour, French painter, 1904;
Friedrich Wilhelm Nietzsche, German philosopher, 1900;
Michael Faraday, chemist and physicist, 1867;

Sir William [Friedrich Wilhelm] Herschel, astronomer, 1822;
James Watt, engineer and inventor, 1819;
David Hume, Scottish philosopher and historian, 1776;
Jan van der Meer [Jan Vermeer van Haarlem], Dutch painter, buried, 1691;
Sir Henry Morgan, buccaneer, 1688;
St Louis IX, King of France, a victim of the plague, 1270.

Occurred on this day:

Paris was liberated by the Allies, 1944;
The RAF made the first air raid on Berlin, 1940;
Ramsay MacDonald formed a National Government, 1931;

The first daily scheduled airline flights started between London and Paris, 1919;
The independence of Uruguay [the Banda Oriental] was declared, 1825.

TODAY IS THE FEAST DAY OF St Ebba, St Genesius of Arles, St Genesius the Comedian, St Gregory of Utrecht, St Joan Antide-Thouret, St Joseph Calasanctius, St Louis IX, King of France, St Mennas of Constantinople and St Patricia.

26th August

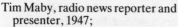

Born on this day:

Tim Maby, radio news reporter and presenter, 1947;

Alison Steadman, actress, 1946;

HRH the Duke of Gloucester, 1944;

Malcolm Pyrah, show jumper, 1941;

Michael Cockerell, TV reporter, 1940;

Gordon Clough, radio presenter, 1934;

Christopher William Bradshaw Isherwood, novelist, 1904;

Jules Romains [Louis-Henri-Jean Farigoule], French novelist, playwright and poet, 1885;

Guillaume Apollinaire [Wilhelm Apollinaris de Kostrowitsky], French poet, 1880;

Sir John Buchan, 1st Baron Tweedsmuir, Governor-General of Canada and novelist, 1875;

Lee De Forest, US radio and TV inventor, 1873;

Stephen Joseph Perry, astronomer and Jesuit, 1833;

Prince Albert, Consort to Queen Victoria, 1819;

Antoine-Laurent Lavoisier, French chemist, 1743;

Joseph-Michel Montgolfier, French balloonist, 1740;

Johann Heinrich Lambert, German mathematician, 1728;

Sir Robert Walpole, Earl of Orford, statesman, 1676.

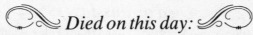

Died on this day:

Charles Boyer, French film actor, 1978;

Charles Augustus Lindbergh, US pioneer aviator, 1974;

Sir Francis Charles Chichester, aviator and yachtsman, 1972;

Naomi Ellington Jacob, novelist, 1964;

Ralph Vaughan Williams, composer, 1958;

Frank [James Thomas] Harris, Irish editor and author, 1931;

Lon [Alonso] Chaney, US film actor, 1930;

William James, US psychologist and philosopher, 1910;

George Manville Fenn, novelist, 1909;

Louis-Philippe, 'Citizen King' of France, 1850;

Count Alessandro de Cagliostro [Giuseppe Balsamo], Italian impostor, 1795;

Antoni van Leeuwenhoek, Dutch naturalist and microscopist, 1723;

Frans Hals, Dutch painter, 1666;

Ottakar II, King of Bohemia, killed in battle, 1278.

Occurred on this day:

Under the 19th Amendment women in the USA were granted the right to vote, 1920;

The Battle of Tannenberg began when the Russians were opposed by German forces, 1914;

Krakatoa, the island volcano, began erupting, killing over 36,000 people, 1883;

Mendelssohn's oratorio *Elijah* was first performed, Birmingham Festival, 1846;

General Blücher routed the French army at the Battle of Katzbach, 1813;

King Edward III, aided by the Black Prince, his son, defeated the French at the Battle of Crécy, 1346;

Julius Caesar landed in Britain, 55 BC.

TODAY IS THE FEAST DAY OF St Bregwine, St Elizabeth Bichier des Ages, St Herluin, St John Wall, St Mary Desmaisières, St Pandonia and St Teresa Jornet Ihars.

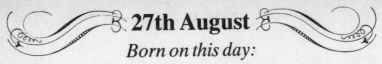

27th August

Born on this day:

Gerhard Berger, motor racing driver, 1959;
Bernhard Langer, golfer, 1957;
John Lloyd, tennis player, 1954;
Andy Turnell, jockey, 1948;
Michael Holroyd, author, 1935;
Lady Antonia Fraser, author, 1932;
Viscount Rothermere, newspaper proprietor, 1925;
Lord Winstanley, 1918;
Martha Raye, US actress and comedienne, 1916;
Mother Teresa, missionary, 1910;
Sir Donald Bradman, Australian cricketer, 1908;
Lyndon Baines Johnson, 36th president of the USA, 1908;

Cecil Scott Forester, novelist, 1899;
Eric Coates, viola player and composer, 1886;
Samuel Goldwyn [Samuel Goldfish], US film magnate, 1882;
Lloyd Cassel Douglas, US novelist, 1877;
The Hon. Charles Stewart Rolls, motor manufacturer, 1877;
Theodore Herman Albert Dreiser, US novelist, 1871;
Georg Wilhelm Friedrich Hegel, German philosopher, 1770;
Alessandro Farnese, Duke of Parma, Italian general and diplomat, 1545;
Confucius, Chinese philosopher, 551 BC.

Died on this day:

Earl Mountbatten of Burma, murdered by the IRA, 1979;
Dame Ivy Compton-Burnett, novelist, 1969;
Le Corbusier [Charles-Édouard Jeanneret], Swiss architect, 1965;
Louis Botha, South African soldier and statesman, 1919;
Sir Rowland Hill, founder of penny postage, 1879;
Eugène-Samuel-Auguste Fromentin, French novelist and painter, 1876;

John Henry Foley, sculptor, 1874;
James Thomson, poet, 1748;
Lope Felix de Vega Carpio, Spanish playwright and poet, 1635;
Tomás Luis de Victoria, Spanish composer, 1611;
Titian [Tiziano Vecelli], Italian painter, a victim of the plague, 1576;
Josquin Desprez, French composer, 1521.

Occurred on this day:

The USSR launched *Sputnik 3*, carrying two dogs, 1958;
The Heinkel 178, first jet-propelled aircraft, made its first flight, 1939;
The interior of the Metropolitan Opera House, New York, was destroyed by fire, 1892;

Napoleon defeated the Austrians at the Battle of Dresden, 1813;
The Declaration of the Rights of Man was adopted by the French National Assembly, 1789;
The first balloon ascent was made in Britain by James Tytler at Edinburgh, 1784.

TODAY IS THE FEAST DAY OF St Caesarius of Arles, St David Lewis, Little St Hugh, St Marcellus of Tomi, St Margaret the Barefooted, St Monica and St Poemen.

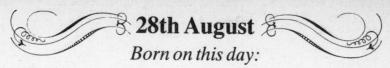

28th August

Born on this day:

Imogen Cooper, pianist, 1949;

Emlyn Hughes, footballer and broadcaster, 1947;

David Soul, US film actor, 1944;

Elain Mellor, jockey, 1943;

John Shirley-Quirk, bass-baritone, 1931;

Windsor Davies, actor, 1930;

Ben Gazzara, US film actor, 1930;

Donald O'Connor, US film actor and dancer, 1925;

Janet Frame, New Zealand novelist, 1924;

Sir Godfrey Hounsfield, inventor of the EMI-scanner, 1919;

Max Robertson, radio commentator and broadcaster, 1915;

Lord Cudlipp, former newspaper chairman, 1913;

Arthur Lindsay Hassett, Australian cricketer, 1913;

Sir Rupert Hart-Davis, author, editor and former publisher, 1907;

Charles Boyer, French film actor, 1897;

Liam O'Flaherty, Irish novelist, 1896;

Ira David Sankey, US hymn-writer and revivalist, 1840;

Sir Edward Coley Burne-Jones, painter, 1833;

Joseph Sheridan Le Fanu, novelist, 1814;

Constant Troyon, French painter, 1810;

Johann Wolfgang von Goethe, German poet, playwright and author, 1749.

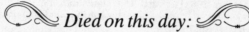

Died on this day:

Prince William of Gloucester, killed in an air crash, 1972;

Bohuslav Martinů, Czech composer, 1959;

Ernest Orlando Lawrence, US physicist, 1958;

Anatol Konstantinovich Liadov, Russian composer, 1914;

James Henry Leigh Hunt, critic and poet, 1859;

William Smith, geologist, 1839;

Karl Theodor Körner, German poet, playwright and patriot, 1813;

John Leyden, Scottish physician and poet, 1811;

Hugo Grotius, jurist and lawyer, 1645.

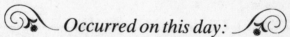

Occurred on this day:

200,000 black Americans demonstrated in Washington, D.C., for civil rights, 1963;

US forces under General George Marshall landed in Japan, 1945;

The Battle of the Heligoland Bight was fought, 1914;

Montenegro was proclaimed an independent kingdom under Nicholas I, 1910;

Cetewayo, the Zulu chief, was captured by the British, 1879;

Wagner's opera *Lohengrin* was first performed in Weimar, 1850;

The Scots routed the Royalist army at the Battle of Newburn, 1640.

TODAY IS THE FEAST DAY OF St Alexander of Constantinople, St Augustine of Hippo, St Edmund Arrowsmith, St Hermes of Rome, St John of Constantinople, St Julian of Brioude, St Moses of Abyssinia and St Paul IV of Constantinople.

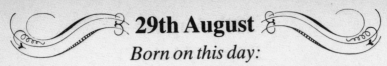

29th August

Born on this day:

Lenny Henry, comedian, 1958;
Michael Jackson, US pop singer, 1958;
Richard Gere, actor, 1949;
James Hunt, racing driver, 1947;
Elliott Gould, US film actor, 1938;
Antony Newton, MP, 1937;
Thom Gunn, poet, 1929;
Sir Richard Attenborough, actor, producer and director, 1923;
Marmaduke Hussey, BBC chairman, 1923;
Dame Mary Donaldson, first woman [former] Lord Mayor of London, 1921;
Ingrid Bergman, film actress, 1915 [see also Deaths];

Jack [Weldon Leo] Teagarden, US jazz musician, vocalist and bandleader, 1905;
Maurice-Polydore-Marie-Bernard Maeterlinck, Belgian poet and playwright, 1862;
John Leech, caricaturist and illustrator, 1817;
Oliver Wendell Holmes, US physician and writer, 1809;
Jean-Auguste-Dominique Ingres, French painter, 1780;
John Locke, philosopher, 1632;
Jean-Baptiste Colbert, French statesman and founder of the French navy, 1619.

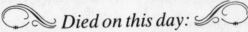

Died on this day:

Lee Marvin, US film actor, 1987;
Ingrid Bergman, film actress, 1982 [see also Births];
Éamon de Valera, Irish statesman, 1975;
Vicki [Hedwig] Baum, US novelist, 1960;
The Rev. William Archibald Spooner, perpetrator of 'spoonerisms', 1930;
Brigham Young, US Mormon leader, 1877;
Félicien-César David, French composer, 1876;
Christian Friedrich Schönbein, German chemist, 1868;

Sir Charles James Napier, soldier and statesman, 1853;
Joseph Wright [of Derby], painter, 1797;
Edmond Hoyle, writer on card-playing, 1769;
Louis Couperin, French composer, 1661;
John Fletcher, playwright, 1625;
Alessio Baldovinetti, Florentine painter, 1499.

Occurred on this day:

The USSR exploded a hydrogen bomb, 1953;
The Rugby League [originally 'Northern Union'], was formed from 21 clubs in the North of England, 1895;
The *Sporting Times* published an 'obituary' for English cricket, and first mentioned 'the Ashes', 1882;
The Treaty of Nanking was signed, ending the Anglo-Chinese War, and agreeing the lease of the Hong Kong territories to Britain, 1842;

The city of Melbourne, Australia, was founded, 1835;
Michael Faraday discovered the induction of electric currents, 1831;
HMS *Royal George* sank off Spithead while at anchor, with the loss of over 900 lives, 1782;
The Turks defeated the Hungarians at the Battle of Mohacs, 1526;
The Spanish fleet was defeated by King Edward III at Winchelsea, 1350.

TODAY IS THE FEAST DAY OF St Edwold of Cerne, St Medericus or Merry and St Sabina of Rome.

30th August

Born on this day:

Sue MacGregor, BBC radio presenter, 1941;

Elizabeth Ashley, US actress, 1939;

Air Marshal Sir Frank Holroyd, Chief Engineer, RAF, 1935;

Sir Peter Parker, company chairman, 1924;

Lord Healey [Denis Healey], CH, former MP, 1917;

Allan Davis, actor, director and producer, 1913;

Joan Blondell, US film actress, 1909;

Fred MacMurray, US film actor, 1908;

Shirley Booth, US actress, 1907;

The Countess of Longford, 1906;

John Gunther, US author and journalist, 1901;

Raymond Massey, Canadian film actor, 1896;

Ernest, 1st Baron Rutherford of Nelson, physicist, 1871;

Joseph Mallaby Dent, publisher, 1849;

Mary Wollstonecraft Shelley, novelist and creator of Frankenstein's monster, 1797;

Jacques-Louis David, French painter, 1748;

Pedro the Cruel, King of Castile and Leon, 1334.

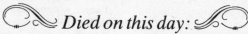

Died on this day:

Sir Joseph John Thomson, physicist, 1940;

Henri Barbusse, French novelist and editor, 1935;

Wilhelm Wien, German physicist, 1928;

Georges-Eugène Sorel, French socialist thinker, 1922;

Thomas Thornycroft, sculptor, 1885;

Dr James Collis Browne, inventor of 'Chlorodyne', 1884;

Gilbert Abbott à Beckett, comic writer and playwright, 1856;

Admiral Sir John Ross, explorer, 1856;

Feargus Edward O'Connor, Irish Chartist leader, 1855;

Francis Baily, astronomer, 1844;

Louis XI, King of France, 1483;

Cleopatra, Queen of Egypt, committed suicide, 30 BC.

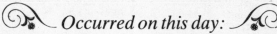

Occurred on this day:

The siege of Leningrad began, 1941;

Paul von Hindenburg became Chief of the General Staff of Germany, 1916;

The Battle of Tannenberg ended when the Russians were defeated by German forces, 1914;

Alberta became a province of Canada, 1905;

The vacuum cleaner was patented by Hubert Cecil Booth, 1901;

The first British tram service began, Birkenhead, 1860;

The Battle of Chesapeake Capes [American War of Independence] began, 1781;

Frederick II, King of Prussia, was defeated by the French at Johannisberg, 1762.

TODAY IS THE FEAST DAY OF St Fantinus, Saints Felix and Adauctus, St Margaret Ward, St Pammachius and St Ruan or Rumon.

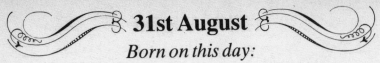

31st August

Born on this day:

Edwin Moses, athlete, 1955;
Van Morrison, rock vocalist, 1945;
Itzhak Perlman, violinist, 1945;
Clive Lloyd, cricketer, 1944;
Bryan Organ, painter, 1935;
Roy Castle, entertainer, 1932;
Larry Grayson, entertainer, 1930;
Charles Kay, actor, 1930;
James Coburn, US film actor, 1928;
Buddy Hackett, US film actor and comedian, 1924;
Alan Jay Lerner, US author and lyricist, 1918;
Prof. Robert Hanbury Brown, astronomer, 1916;
Richard Basehart, US film actor, 1914;

Prof. Sir Bernard Lovell, former director, Jodrell Bank Station, 1913;
William Saroyan, US author, 1908;
Roland Culver, actor, 1900;
Fredric March [Ernest Frederick McIntyre Bickel], US film actor, 1897;
Edwin DuBose Heyward, US novelist and playwright, 1885;
Wilhelmina, Queen of the Netherlands, 1880;
Maria Montessori, Italian educationist, 1870;
Pierre-Jules-Théophile Gautier, French novelist and poet, 1811;
Charles James Lever, Irish novelist, 1806;
Jahangir, Mogul emperor, 1569;
Caligula, Roman emperor, 12.

Died on this day:

Henry Moore, sculptor, 1986;
John Ford [Sean O'Fearn], US film director, 1973;
Rocky Marciano [Rocco Marchegiano], US heavyweight boxer, killed in an air crash, 1969;
Georges Braque, French cubist painter, 1963;
Harley Granville Barker, actor, playwright and critic, 1946;

Sir Thomas Henry Hall Caine, novelist, 1931;
Charles-Pierre Baudelaire, French poet, 1867;
Sir Arthur Phillip, 1st governor of New South Wales, 1814;
John Bunyan, author, 1688;
King Henry V, 1422.

Occurred on this day:

A South Korean airliner was shot down by the USSR, killing 269 people aboard, 1983;
Trinidad and Tobago became independent, 1962;
Malaya became independent, 1957;
Kurt Weill's opera *Die Dreigroschenoper* was first performed, Berlin, 1928;
The first London production of the musical show *Tip-Toes* was presented, 1926;

The musical show *Chu Chin Chow* was first performed, London, 1916;
Mary Anne 'Polly' Nichols, a prostitute, was found dead in Whitechapel, London, the first victim of Jack the Ripper, 1888;
At the Battle of Flores, Sir Richard Grenville engaged the whole Spanish Fleet in the *Revenge*, but was captured and later died, 1591;
Henry VI acceded as King at the age of nine months, 1422.

TODAY IS THE FEAST DAY OF St Aidan of Lindisfarne, St Paulinus of Trier, St Raymond Nonnatus and The Servite Martyrs of Prague.

1st September

Born on this day:

Leonard Slatkin, US conductor, 1954;

Manuel Pinero, golfer, 1952;

David Bairstow, cricketer, 1951;

Barry Gibb, singer, 1946;

Lily Tomlin, US TV entertainer, 1939;

Allen Jones, artist, 1937;

Lord Parkinson [Cecil Parkinson], former MP, 1931;

Rocky Marciano [Rocco Marchegiano], US heavyweight boxer, 1923;

Yvonne de Carlo, US film actress, 1922;

Milton Shulman, film and theatre critic, 1918;

Gwynfor Evans, honorary president, Plaid Cymru, 1912;

Komei Abe, Japanese composer, 1911;

Francis William Aston, physicist, 1877;

Rex Ellingwood Beach, US novelist, 1877;

Edgar Rice Burroughs, US novelist and creator of 'Tarzan', 1875;

'Gentleman Jim' James John Corbett, US heavyweight boxer, 1866;

Sir Roger David Casement, conspirator for Irish nationalism, 1864;

Baron Carl Auer von Welsbach, Austrian chemist, inventor of the gas mantle, 1858;

Engelbert Humperdinck, German composer, 1854;

Amilcare Ponchielli, Italian composer, 1834;

The Rev. John Thomson, Scottish landscape painter, 1778;

Giacomo Torelli, Italian theatrical designer, 1608;

Edward Alleyn, actor and founder of Dulwich College, 1566;

Taddeo Zuccaro [Zucchero], Italian painter, 1529.

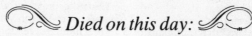

Died on this day:

François Mauriac, French poet and novelist, 1970;

Ilya Grigoriyevich Ehrenburg, Russian novelist and poet, 1967;

Siegfried Lorraine Sassoon, writer, 1967;

William Wymark Jacobs, short-story writer, 1943;

Samuel Coleridge-Taylor, composer, 1912;

Sir Richard Westmacott, sculptor, 1856;

William Clark, US explorer of the American Northwest, 1838;

Sir Richard Steele, essayist and playwright, 1729;

Louis XIV, the 'Sun King' of France, 1715;

Jacques Cartier, French explorer, 1557;

Pope Hadrian IV [Nicholas Breakspear, the only Englishman to be pope], 1159.

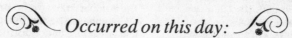

Occurred on this day:

After overthrowing King Idris I, Colonel Gaddafi seized power in Libya, 1969;

Poland was invaded by Germany, and Danzig Free City was seized, 1939;

The Alhambra Theatre, London, was demolished, 1936;

Albania was declared a kingdom, and Zogu I became king, 1928;

Nearly 200,000 people were killed in earthquakes in Tokyo and Yokohama, 1923;

In Russia, St Petersburg was renamed Petrograd, 1914;

The Severn Tunnel was opened for goods traffic, 1886;

The Prussians defeated the French at the Battle of Sedan, 1870;

The world's first triangular postage stamps were issued by the Cape of Good Hope, 1853.

TODAY IS THE FEAST DAY OF St Drithelm, St Fiacre, St Giles or Aegidius, St Lupus or Leu of Sens, St Priscus of Capua, St Sebbe and St Verena.

2nd September

Born on this day:

Jimmy Connors, tennis player, 1952;
Michael Hastings, playwright, 1938;
Derek Fowlds, actor, 1937;
Victor Spinetti, actor and director, 1933;
Francis Matthews, actor, 1931;
Ronnie Stevens, actor and director, 1930;
Russ Conway, pianist and entertainer, 1925;
Lord George-Brown, statesman, 1914;
Sir Robert Bruce Lockhart, diplomat and author, 1887;

Frederick Soddy, chemist and physicist, 1877;
Friedrich Wilhelm Ostwald, German chemist, 1853;
Giovanni Verga, Italian novelist and playwright, 1840;
Karl Friedrich August Hering, German violinist and composer, 1819;
Peter Nikolaus Petersen, German flautist and composer, 1761;
John Howard, prison reformer, 1726.

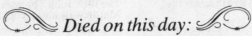

Died on this day:

Sir Felix Aylmer [Felix Edward Aylmer-Jones], actor, 1979;
John Ronald Reuel Tolkien, South African-born philologist and novelist, 1973;
Sir William Alexander Craigie, lexicogapher, 1957;
Baron Pierre de Coubertin, French advocate of the modern Olympic Games, 1937;
Henry Hertzberg Lawson, Australian author, 1922;
Henri Rousseau, French primitive painter, 1910;
Johann Franz Encke, astronomer, 1865;

Sir William Rowan Hamilton, astronomer, 1865;
Thomas Telford, civil engineer, 1834;
Russ Columbo [Ruggiero Eugenio de Rudolpho], US singer and composer, 1934;
General Jean-Victor-Marie Moreau, French soldier, 1813;
José Ribera ['Lo Spagnoletto'], Spanish painter, 1652;
Karel van Mander, Dutch painter and poet, 1606;
Taddeo Zuccaro [Zucchero], Italian painter, 1566.

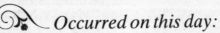

Occurred on this day:

The first television station in China was opened in Peking, 1958;
Men between the ages of 19 and 41 were conscripted in Britain under the National Service Bill, 1939;
The Battle of Omdurman was won against the Mahdists by an army led by Lord Kitchener, 1898;

The bombardment by the British of Copenhagen began, 1807;
The Great Fire of London began, 1666;
Augustus Octavian defeated Antony at the Battle of Actium, 31 BC.

TODAY IS THE FEAST DAY OF St Agricolus, St Antoninus of Pamiers, St Brocard, St Castor of Apt, St William of Roskilde and The Martyrs of September 1792.

3rd September

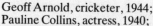

Born on this day:

Geoff Arnold, cricketer, 1944;

Pauline Collins, actress, 1940;

Brian Lochore, New Zealand rugby player, 1940;

Alan Ladd, US film actor, 1913;

James Hanley, novelist and playwright, 1901;

Urho Kaleva Kekkonen, Finnish prime minister and president, 1900;

Sir Frank Macfarlane Burnet, Australian immunologist, 1899;

Cecil Parker [Cecil Schwabe], actor, 1897;

Marcel Grandjany, French/US composer, 1891;

Jean-Joseph-Marie-Auguste Jaurès, French socialist writer and speaker, 1859;

Louis Henry Sullivan, US architect, 1856;

James Hannington, bishop in Africa, 1847;

Ernst Pasque, German baritone, composer and novelist, 1821;

James Joseph Sylvester, mathematician, 1814;

John Francis, sculptor, 1780;

Joseph Wright, painter, 1734;

Matthew Boulton, engineer, 1728.

Died on this day:

Frank Capra, writer and film director, 1991;

Arthur Schwartz, US popular composer, 1984;

Frederic Dannay, US novelist [one-half of the team called 'Ellery Queen'], 1982;

Ho Chi Minh, president of North Vietnam, 1969;

Frederick Louis MacNiece, Irish-born poet and playwright, 1963;

e.e. cummings [Edward Estlin Cummings], US poet, 1962;

Eduard Beneš, president of Czechoslovakia, 1948;

Ivan Sergeyevich Turgenev, Russian playwright, 1883;

Louis-Adolphe Thiers, former president of France, 1877;

George Lillo, playwright, 1739;

Oliver Cromwell, Lord Protector, 1658;

Sir Edward Coke, lawyer, 1634;

Robert Greene, playwright, 1592.

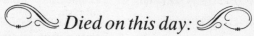

Occurred on this day:

The Allies landed at Salerno, on the mainland of Italy, and the Italian government surrendered, 1943;

Under the Lend-Lease agreement, the USA sent destroyers to Britain, 1940;

Great Britain and France declared war on Germany, 1939;

Sir Malcolm Campbell set up a land speed record of 301.13 mph, 1935;

Santo Domingo, in the Dominican Republic, was destroyed and 5,000 killed when a hurricane hit the city, 1930;

The first Zeppelin was shot down by Flt.-Lieutenant W. Leefe Robinson in an air raid over England, 1916;

Cardinal Giacomo Della Chiesa was elected pope as Benedict XV, 1914;

Bartholomew Fair, dating from 1123, was proclaimed at Smithfield, London, for the last time, 1855;

The American War of Independence came to an end after Britain and the USA signed the Treaty of Paris, 1783;

The Gregorian Calendar was introduced in Britain, replacing the Julian, when 3rd September became 14th September, 1752;

Richard Cromwell became Lord Protector of England, 1658;

Oliver Cromwell defeated the Royalist troops at the Battle of Worcester, 1651;

The Battle of Dunbar was fought, when Cromwell defeated the Scots, 1650.

TODAY IS THE FEAST DAY OF St Aigulf or Ayoul of Lerins, St Cuthburga, St Gregory the Great, St Hildelitha, St Macanisius, St Phoebe, St Remacius and St Simeon Stylites the Younger.

4th September

Born on this day:

Tom Watson, golfer, 1949;

Bill Kenwright, theatrical impresario, 1945;

Sir Nicholas Jackson, organist, harpsichordist and composer, 1934;

Dinsdale Landen, actor, 1932;

Ann Dummett, consultant on racial equality, 1930;

Mitzi Gaynor, US film actress and dancer, 1930;

Joan Aiken, author of novels, plays and poetry for children, 1924;

Lord Howell [Denis Howell], former MP, 1923;

Richard Nathaniel Wright, US novelist and essayist, 1908;

Mary Renault [Mary Challens], novelist, 1905;

Antonin Artaud, French playwright and director, 1896;

Harry Joel, racehorse owner, 1894;

Darius Milhaud, French composer, 1892;

Albert Joseph Moore, decorative painter, 1841;

Daniel Godfrey, composer and bandmaster for the Grenadier Guards, 1831;

Dadabhai Naoroji, first Asian member of parliament, 1825;

Anton Bruckner, Austrian composer and organist, 1824;

François-René, Vicomte de Chateaubriand, French author and politician, 1768;

Robert Raikes, publisher and founder of Sunday Schools, 1736.

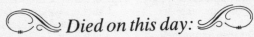 Died on this day:

Albert Schweitzer, organist, doctor and missionary, 1965;

Robert Schuman, French statesman, 1963;

Walford Graham Robertson, playwright and artist, 1948;

Edvard Hagerup Grieg, Norwegian composer, 1907;

Celestin-François Nanteuil, French painter and engraver, 1873;

James Wyatt, architect, 1813;

Charles Townshend, Chancellor of the Exchequer, 1767;

Robert Dudley, Earl of Leicester, favourite of Queen Elizabeth I, 1588.

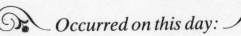 Occurred on this day:

The Forth Road bridge was opened by HM the Queen, 1964;

Queen Wilhelmina of the Netherlands abdicated in favour of her daughter, Juliana, 1948;

Antwerp was liberated by the Allies, 1944;

A demonstration of colour TV was given on station W2XAB by the Columbia Broadcasting System, USA, 1940;

The British liner *Athenia* sank after being torpedoed by a German U-boat the previous day, with the loss of 93 lives, 1939;

The Cambridge Theatre, London, opened, 1930;

The Germans retreated to the Siegfried Line, 1918;

The world's first rally of Boy Scouts was held at the Crystal Palace, near London, 1909;

The Apache chief Geronimo surrendered to the US army, 1886;

In France, Emperor Napoleon III was deposed, and the Third Republic proclaimed, 1870;

The Battle of Montaperti was fought between the Guelphs and Ghibellines, 1260.

TODAY IS THE FEAST DAY OF St Boniface I, pope, St Ida of Herzfeld, Saints Marcellus and Valerian, St Marinus of San Marino, St Rosalia, St Rose of Viterbo and St Ultan of Ardbraccan.

5th September

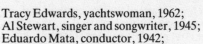

Born on this day:

Tracy Edwards, yachtswoman, 1962;
Al Stewart, singer and songwriter, 1945;
Eduardo Mata, conductor, 1942;
Raquel Welch, US actress, 1940;
George Tremlett, author, journalist and
  bookseller, 1939;
Dick Clement, director and scriptwriter,
  1937;
Johnny Briggs, actor, 1935;
Bob Newhart, US actor and comedian,
  1929;
Malcolm Allison, football manager, 1927;
Michael Lees, actor, 1927;
Frank Yerby, novelist, 1916;
John Cage, US composer, 1912;
Lord Delfont, 1909;
Arthur Koestler, author, 1905;

Darryl Francis Zanuck, US film producer,
  1902;
Jesse Woodson James, US outlaw, 1847;
Victorien Sardou, French playwright,
  1831;
John Wisden, cricketer and cricket records
  compiler, 1826;
Giacomo Meyerbeer [Jakob Liebmann
  Beer], German composer, 1791;
Robert Fergusson, Scottish vernacular
  poet, 1750;
Johann Christian Bach, German composer,
  1735;
Maurice-Quentin de La Tour, French
  pastellist, 1704;
Louis XIV, the 'Sun King' of France, 1638;
Louis VIII, King of France, 1187.

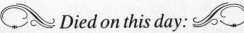

Died on this day:

Group Captain Sir Douglas Robert Steuart
  Bader, WWII pilot, 1982;
Josh White, US blues singer, 1969;
Charles-Pierre Péguy, French poet, killed
  in action, 1914;
Jules-Élie Delaunay, French painter, 1891;
John Christian Schetky, Scottish marine
  painter, 1874;
Isidore-Auguste-Marie-François-Xavier
  Comte, French philosopher and founder
  of Positivism, 1857;

John Home, clergyman and playwright,
  1808;
Jean-François Regnard, French poet and
  playwright, 1709;
Richard Tarlton, actor and fencer,
  1588;
Pieter Brueghel the Elder, Flemish painter,
  1569.

Occurred on this day:

Terrorists of the Arab Black September
  group killed 11 Israelis at the Olympic
  Games in Germany, 1972;
Brussels was liberated by the Allies, 1944;
The first Battle of the Marne began, 1914;
The operetta *The Girl in the Taxi* was
  produced on the London stage for the
  first time, 1912;
The Russo-Japanese War ended following
  the signing of the Treaty of Portsmouth,
  USA, 1905;

The island of Heligoland was seized from
  Denmark by the British, 1807;
Malta was surrendered to the British by the
  French after Nelson's fleet had blockaded
  them, 1800;
The first Continental Congress in America
  opened at Philadelphia, 1774.

TODAY IS THE FEAST DAY OF St Bertinus, St Genebald of Laon, St Laurence
Giustiniani and Saints Urban and Theodore and their Companions.

6th September

Born on this day:

Britt Ekland, film actress, 1943;
Roger Law, puppeteer, 1941;
Monica Mason, ballerina, 1941;
Jackie Trent, singer and lyricist, 1940;
King Peter of Yugoslavia, 1923;
George Mann, cricketer, 1917;
Stephen Murray, actor, 1912;
Sir James Stubblefield, geologist, 1901;
Billy Rose [William Samuel Rosenberg], US producer and lyricist, 1899;
Sir Edward Victor Appleton, physicist, 1892;
Joseph Patrick Kennedy, US financier and diplomat, 1888;
John James Rickard Macleod, one of the discoverers of insulin, 1876;
Sir Henry Walford Davies, organist and composer, 1869;
Jane Addams, US sociologist, 1860;
Friedrich Wilhelm Schadow-Godenhaus, German painter, 1789;
Anton Diabelli, Austrian composer and publisher, 1781;
Vincent Novello, organist, composer and founder of the music publishers, 1781;
John Dalton, chemist and physicist, 1766;
Marie-Joseph-Paul-Yves-Roch-Gilbert du Motier, Marquis de Lafayette, French statesman and soldier, 1757;
Sebastiano Serlio, Italian architect, 1475.

Died on this day:

Hendrik Frensch Verwoerd, South African prime minister, assassinated, 1966;
Arthur Rackham, illustrator, 1939;
Sir Horatio Gilbert George Parker, author and politician, 1932;
Sir James Guthrie, Scottish painter, 1930;
George Alexander Stevens, writer and humorist, 1784;
Carlo Cignani, Italian painter, 1719;
Jean-Baptiste Colbert, French statesman, 1683;
Suleiman I [the Magnificent; the Lawgiver], Sultan of Turkey, 1566;
Benvenuto Tisio [Il Garofalo], Italian painter, 1559.

Occurred on this day:

In Turkey, a massive earthquake centred on Lice resulted in nearly 3,000 deaths, 1975;
Swaziland became an independent kingdom, 1968;
India invaded West Pakistan, 1965;
Juliana became Queen of the Netherlands, 1948;
In Romania, King Carol II abdicated in favour of his son Michael, 1940;
William McKinley, 25th president of the USA, was fatally wounded by an anarchist, 1901;
The first cricket test match in England was played at the Oval between England and Australia, 1880;
The first telephone exchange in Britain opened in Lombard Street, London, 1879;
The Great Fire of London came to an end, 1666;
Del Cano, commanding the *Vittoria*, Magellan's ship, completed the first circumnavigation of the world, 1522;
King Richard I defeated the Saracens at the Battle of Arsouf, 1191.

TODAY IS THE FEAST DAY OF St Cagnoald or Chainoaldus, Saints Donatian, Laetus and Others and St Eleutherius of Spoleto.

7th September

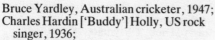

Born on this day:

Bruce Yardley, Australian cricketer, 1947;

Charles Hardin ['Buddy'] Holly, US rock singer, 1936;

Prof. Malcolm Bradbury, academic and novelist, 1932;

J. Paul Getty II, US philanthropist, 1932;

HM King Baudouin of the Belgians, 1930;

Lord Jenkin of Roding, former MP, 1926;

Peter Lawford, actor, 1923;

Lord Cheshire VC, OM, founder of homes for the disabled, 1917;

Sir John Anthony Quayle, actor, 1913;

Elia Kazan, US author and film director, 1909;

Joan Cross, operatic soprano, 1900;

Dame Edith Sitwell, writer, 1887;

Anna Mary ['Grandma'] Moses, US primitive painter, 1860;

William Friese-Greene, pioneer of the cinema, 1855;

Sir Henry Campbell-Bannerman, statesman, 1836;

John McDouall Stuart, explorer of Australia, 1815;

William Butterfield, church architect, 1814;

Thomas Coutts, banker, 1735;

Georges-Louis Leclerc, Comte de Buffon, French naturalist, 1707;

Stephen Hales, botanist and inventor, 1677;

Queen Elizabeth I, 1533;

Thomas Lüber [Thomas Erastus], Swiss theologian and physician, 1524.

Died on this day:

Liam O'Flaherty, Irish novelist, 1984;

Patrick Gordon Campbell, 3rd Baron Glenavy, writer and broadcaster, 1981;

Spring Byington, US film actress, 1971;

Charles Burgess Fry, cricketer, footballer and journalist, 1956;

William Holman Hunt, Pre-Raphaelite painter, 1910;

René-François-Armand Sully Prudhomme, French poet, 1907;

John Greenleaf Whittier, US poet and naturalist, 1892;

Sidney Lanier, US poet, 1881;

Hannah More, author and evangelist, 1833;

Catherine Parr, 6th wife of King Henry VIII, 1548;

Ferdinand IV ['El Emplazado'], King of Castile and Leon, 1312.

 ## Occurred on this day:

The British explorer Sir Francis Younghusband led an expedition to Tibet, where a treaty was signed with the Dalai Lama, 1904;

The Peace of Peking ended the Boxer Rising in China, 1901;

Grace Horsley Darling and her father William rescued the crew of the *Forfarshire* steamship at the Farne Islands, 1838;

The independence of Brazil from Portugal was declared, 1822;

The first known reference to 'Uncle Sam' was in an editorial in the *Troy Post* [New York], 1813;

The French army under Napoleon defeated the Russians at the Battle of Borodino, 1812;

The French were defeated by Prince Eugene at Turin, 1706.

TODAY IS THE FEAST DAY OF Saints Alcmund and Tilbert, St Anastasius the Fuller, St Cloud or Clodoald, St Grimonia, St John of Nicomedia, St Regina or Reine of Alise and St Sozon.

8th September

Born on this day:

Stefan Johansson, motor racing driver, 1956;

Anne Diamond, TV presenter, 1954;

Geoff Miller, cricketer, 1952;

Yves St Martin, French jockey, 1941;

Frankie Avalon, US singer, 1940;

Sir Peter Maxwell Davies, composer, 1934;

Michael Frayn, author and playwright, 1933;

Alan Oliver, showjumper, 1932;

Jack Rosenthal, playwright, 1931;

Jeannette Altwegg, Olympic skater, 1930;

Peter Richard Henry Sellers, actor and comedian, 1925;

Sir Harry Secombe, comedian and singer, 1921;

Jean-Louis Barrault, French actor, 1910;

Hendrik Frensch Verwoerd, South African politician, 1901;

Howard Dietz, US lyricist, 1896;

Siegfried Lorraine Sassoon, poet and critic, 1886;

William Wymark Jacobs, short-story writer, 1863;

Antonín Leopold Dvořák, Czech composer, 1841;

Joseph-Étienne-Frédéric Mistral, Provençal poet, 1830;

Eduard Friedrich Mörike, German poet, 1804;

William Collins, landscape painter, 1788;

August Wilhelm von Schlegel, German poet and author, 1767;

Ludovico Ariosto, Italian poet, 1474;

King Richard I [Coeur de Lion], 1157.

Died on this day:

Sir Leonard George Holden Huxley, physicist, 1988;

André Derain, French painter, 1954;

Richard Georg Strauss, German composer, 1949;

Léon-Joseph-Florentin Bonnat, French painter, 1922;

George Bradshaw, printer and publisher of railway guides, 1853;

William James Müller, landscape and figure painter, 1845;

Francisco Gomez de Quevedo y Villegas, Spanish poet and satirist, 1645;

Francis Quarles, poet, 1644.

Occurred on this day:

President Ford granted a full pardon to Richard Nixon for 'any offences he might have committed while in office', 1974;

The Severn Road Bridge was officially opened, 1966;

The Manila Conference ended, and the South East Asia Defence Treaty was signed, 1954;

The Treaty of Peace with Japan was signed by 49 powers in San Francisco, 1951;

The first V2 flying bombs landed in London, 1944;

Germany was admitted to the League of Nations, 1926;

Johannesburg, South Africa, was founded, 1886;

William IV was crowned King of Great Britain, 1831;

New Amsterdam in North America was surrendered by the Dutch to the English and renamed New York, 1664.

TODAY IS THE FEAST DAY OF Saints Adrian and Natalia, St Corbinian, St Disibod, St Eusebius, St Kingsmark or Cynfarch Oer, St Nestabus, St Nestor, St Sergius I, pope and St Zeno.

9th September

Born on this day:

John Curry, figure skating champion, 1949;
Richard Sharpe, rugby footballer, 1938;
Chaim Topol, Israeli actor, 1935;
Dr the Hon. Shirley Summerskill, former Labour MP, 1931;
Margaret Tyzack, actress, 1931;
Countess Spencer, stepmother of the Princess of Wales, 1929;
Cliff Robertson, US film actor, 1925;
Pauline Baynes, designer and book illustrator, 1922;
Michael Aldridge, actor, 1920;
Sir John Gorton CH, Australian statesman, 1911;
James Hilton, novelist, 1900;
Arthur Freed, US popular composer, 1894;

James Evershed Agate, theatre critic, 1877;
Max Reinhardt [Goldmann], Austrian theatre director, 1873;
Ralph Hodgson, poet, 1871;
Houston Stewart Chamberlain, renegade English writer, 1855;
Jane Ellen Harrison, scholar and archaeologist, 1850;
Count Leo Nikolayevich Tolstoy, Russian author, 1828;
Alexander Nasmyth, Scottish painter, 1758;
William Bligh, captain of the *Bounty*, 1754;
Luigi Galvani, Italian physicist, 1737;
Armand-Jean-du Plessis de Richelieu, cardinal and French statesman, 1585.

Died on this day:

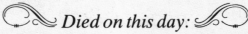

Hugh MacDiarmid [Christopher Murray Grieve], poet and critic, 1978;
Mao Tse-tung, Chinese leader, 1976;
Roger Eliot Fry, artist, 1934;
Henri-Marie-Raymond de Toulouse-Lautrec, French painter, 1901;
Stéphane Mallarmé, French poet, 1898;
William Theed the Younger, sculptor, 1891;
John Singleton Copley, historical painter, 1815;

Giambattista Piranesi, Italian architect, painter and engraver, 1778;
Tobias George Smollett, physician and author, 1771;
Sir Humphrey Gilbert, explorer, drowned off the Azores, 1583;
James IV, King of Scotland, killed in battle at Flodden, 1513;
King William I [the Conqueror], 1087.

Occurred on this day:

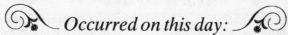

North Korea was proclaimed a separate independent state, 1948;
General Douglas MacArthur took over supervision of Japan, 1945;
The operetta *Frederica* by Franz Lehar had its first London production, 1930;
California became the 31st of the United States, 1850;

San Sebastian, held by the French, surrendered to the Duke of Wellington, 1813;
The *Squirrel* frigate was lost off the Azores, with the loss of all on board, 1583;
The English defeated the Scots at the Battle of Flodden Field, 1513.

TODAY IS THE FEAST DAY OF St Bettelin, St Ciaran or Kieran of Clonmacnois, St Gorgonius, St Isaac or Sahak the Great, St Joseph of Volokolamsk, St Omer or Audomarus and St Peter Claver.

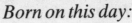

10th September

Born on this day:

Bill Rogers, US golfer, 1951;

Judy Geeson, actress, 1948;

José Feliciano, US singer, 1945;

David Hamilton, disc jockey, 1939;

Arnold Palmer, US golfer, 1929;

Gwen Watford, actress, 1927;

Beryl Cook, painter, 1926;

Robert Wise, US film director and producer, 1914;

Fay Wray, US film actress, 1908;

Cyril Vernon Connolly, author, journalist and critic, 1903;

Bessie Love [Juanita Horton], US film actress, 1898;

Franz Werfel, German novelist and poet, 1890;

Vibhaji Ranjitsinghi, Maharaja of Nawanagar, cricketer, 1872;

Robert Koldewey, German archaeologist, 1855;

Philip Gilbert Hamerton, artist and author, 1834;

Sir John Robert Seeley, historian and essayist, 1834;

Mungo Park, explorer of Africa, 1771;

Sir John Soane, architect, 1753;

Giovanni Domenico Tiepolo, Italian painter and engraver, 1727;

Niccoló Jommelli, Italian composer, 1714;

Thomas Sydenham, physician, 1624;

Quentin Massys, Flemish painter, 1466.

Died on this day:

Balthazar Johannes Vorster, former prime minister and president of South Africa, 1983;

Charles Cruft, founder of the dog show, 1938;

Huey Pierce Long, US senator from Louisiana, assassinated, 1935;

Arthur Reed Ropes ['Adrian Ross'], lyricist and librettist, 1933;

Wilfrid Scawen Blunt, traveller, politician and poet, 1922;

George Bentham, botanist, 1884;

Ugo Foscolo, Italian poet, 1827;

Mary Wollstonecraft Godwin, feminist, 1797;

Dr Edward Pococke, scholar and orientalist, 1691;

Louis IV, King of France, 954.

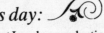 Occurred on this day:

The people of Gibraltar voted overwhelmingly to stay under British rule, 1967;

Sir Seretse Khama became the first president of the Republic of Botswana, 1966;

In Norway, Lauritz Vidkun Quisling was sentenced to death for treason, 1945;

British forces arrived in France, 1939;

The first motorway [autobahn] was completed in Germany, 1921;

The first London production of the musical show *Sally* was presented, 1921;

The first London production of the operetta *The Chocolate Soldier* was presented, 1910;

The Duke of York's Theatre, London, opened [as the 'Trafalgar Square'], 1892;

Simón Bolívar became the dictator of Peru, 1823;

The English defeated the Scots at the Battle of Pinkie, 1547.

TODAY IS THE FEAST DAY OF St Ambrose Barlow, St Aubert of Avranches, St Finnian of Moville, Saints Menodora, Metrodora and Nymphodora, St Nemesian, St Nicholas of Tolentino, St Pulcheria, St Salvius or Salvy of Albi and St Theodard of Maestricht.

11th September

Born on this day:

Richard Linley, jockey, 1954;

Barry Sheene, racing motor cyclist, 1950;

Roger Uttley, rugby football player, 1949;

Michael Lambert, racehorse trainer, 1944;

Paul Cole, racehorse trainer, 1941;

Sir Patrick Mayhew QC, MP, 1929;

Sir Bernard Feilden, architect, 1919;

Jessica Mitford, author, 1917;

David Herbert Lawrence, novelist, 1885;

Sir James Hopwood Jeans, mathematician and astrophysicist, 1877;

O. Henry [William Sydney Porter], US short-story writer, 1862;

Eduard Hanslick, Austrian music critic, 1825;

Thomas Barnes, editor of *The Times*, 1785;

James Thomson, poet, author of *Rule, Britannia*, 1700;

Henri de La Tour d'Auvergne, Vicomte de Turenne, Marshal-General of France, 1611;

Pierre de Ronsard, French poet, 1524.

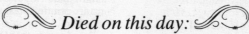

Died on this day:

Salvador Allende Gossens, president of Chile, allegedly committed suicide, 1973;

Nikita Sergeyevich Khrushchev, Russian leader, 1971;

Robert William Service, Canadian novelist and poet, 1958;

Field-Marshal Jan Christian Smuts, South African statesman, 1950;

Mohammed Ali Jinnah, first governor-general of Pakistan, 1948;

Prince Louis Mountbatten [1st Marquess of Milford Haven], admiral, 1921;

Antero Tarquinio de Quental, Portuguese poet, 1891;

Théodule Ribot, French painter, 1891;

Thomas Graham, Scottish chemist, 1869;

David Ricardo, economist, 1823;

John Brand, antiquary and topographer, 1806;

Giovanni Domenico Cassini, Italian astronomer, 1712;

James Harrington, political theorist, 1677.

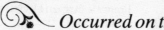

Occurred on this day:

In Chile, the government was ousted by a military coup, and government was taken over by a junta, 1973;

A British mandate was declared in Palestine, 1922;

The Allies took Sebastopol after the city was abandoned by the Russians, 1855;

The USA was victorious against the British at Lake Champlain, 1814;

The British, commanded by General Howe, defeated the Americans under General George Washington at the Battle of Brandywine Creek, 1777;

The Duke of Marlborough defeated the French at the battle of Malplaquet, the bloodiest war of the century, 1709;

The English, under Warenne and Cressingham, were defeated by the Scots under William Wallace at Stirling Bridge, 1297.

TODAY IS THE FEAST DAY OF St Deiniol, St Paphnutius, St Patiens of Lyons, St Peter of Chavanon, Saints Protus and Hyacinth and St Theodora of Alexandria.

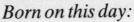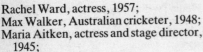

12th September

Born on this day:

Rachel Ward, actress, 1957;

Max Walker, Australian cricketer, 1948;

Maria Aitken, actress and stage director, 1945;

Linda Gray, US actress, 1941;

Patrick Mower, actor, 1941;

Wesley Hall, West Indies cricketer and politician, 1937;

Ian Holm, actor, 1931;

Freddie Jones, actor, 1927;

Han Suyin, doctor and author, 1917;

Kenneth Lo, tennis player and Chinese gourmet, 1913;

John Cleveland [Jesse] Owens, US athlete, 1913;

Chili Bouchier, actress, 1909;

Frederick Louis MacNeice, poet and broadcaster, 1907;

Maurice Chevalier, French entertainer and actor, 1888;

Henry Louis Mencken, journalist and author of *The American Language*, 1880;

Herbert Henry Asquith, 1st Earl of Oxford and Asquith, statesman, 1852;

Anselm Feuerbach, German painter, 1829;

Richard Jordan Gatling, US inventor [the Gatling gun], 1818;

Sir Edward Shepherd Creasy, historian, 1812;

Richard Marsh Hoe, US inventor of the rotary printing press, 1812;

James Hall, US geologist and palaeontologist, 1811;

Sir William Dugdale, herald and antiquary, 1605;

Lodovico Cardi da Cigoli, Italian painter and architect, 1559.

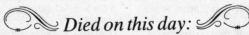

Died on this day:

Robert Traill Spence Lowell, US poet, 1977;

William [Bill] Boyd, US film actor, 1972;

Rupert D'Oyly Carte, operatic impresario, 1948;

Dr Peter Mark Roget, lexicographer, 1869;

Field Marshal Gebhard Leberecht von Blücher, Prussian commander, 1819;

Jean-Philippe Rameau, French composer, 1764;

François Couperin ['Le Grand'], French composer, 1733.

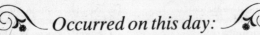

Occurred on this day:

A military coup deposed the Emperor Haile Selassie in Ethiopia, 1974;

Benito Mussolini, imprisoned by the Allies, was rescued by the Germans, 1943;

The Lascaux Caves, France, containing examples of Cro-Magnon man's art, were discovered, 1940;

Gabriele D'Annunzio led an unofficial Italian army and seized Fiume from Yugoslavia, 1919;

The Allies were victorious at the Battle of the Marne, 1914;

The obelisk of Thothmes III ['Cleopatra's Needle'] was erected on the Thames Embankment, London, 1878;

The Hudson River was discovered by Henry Hudson, 1609;

Eton College received its first charter, 1440.

TODAY IS THE FEAST DAY OF St Ailbhe, St Eanswida and St Guy of Anderlecht.

# 13th September

Born on this day:

Carol Barnes, TV newsreader, 1944;
Jacqueline Bissett, actress, 1944;
John Smith, MP, 1938;
Mel Tormé, US singer, 1925;
The Most Rev. George Noakes, Archbishop of Wales, 1924;
Lord Weidenfeld, publisher, 1919;
Claudette Colbert, US film actress, 1903;
John Boynton Priestley, author, 1894;
Sherwood Anderson, US story-writer, 1876;
Arnold Schoenberg, Austrian composer, 1874;
Arthur Henderson, politician and Nobel prizewinner, 1863;

Charles William Gordon [Ralph Connor], clergyman and novelist, 1860;
John Joseph Pershing, US expeditionary force commander during WW1, 1860;
Milton Snavely Hershey, US chocolate company founder, 1857;
Dr Walter Reed, US bacteriologist, 1851;
Clara Josephine Schumann [Wieck], pianist, 1819;
William Henry West Betty [the 'Young Roscius'], actor, 1791;
Oliver Evans, US inventor, 1755;
William Cecil, 1st Baron Burghley, statesman, 1520.

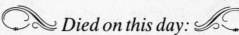 Died on this day:

Leopold Antoni Stanislaw Stokowski, conductor, 1977;
Schack August Steenberg Krogh, Danish physiologist, 1949;
William Heath Robinson, artist and illustrator, 1944;
Alexis-Emmanuel Chabrier, French composer, 1894;
Alexandre Herculano de Carvalho e Araujo, Portuguese poet, historian and politician, 1877;

Ludwig Feuerbach, philosopher and economist, 1872;
Charles James Fox, statesman, 1806;
General James Wolfe, British soldier, killed in action, 1759;
Philip II, King of Spain, 1598;
Michel Eyquem de Montaigne, French essayist, 1592;
Sir John Cheke, classical scholar, 1557;
Andrea Mantegna, Italian painter, 1506.

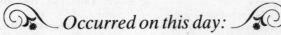 Occurred on this day:

General Chiang Kai-shek was re-elected president of the Republic of China, 1943;
The German attack on Stalingrad began, 1942;
The first Battle of the Aisne began, 1914;
Wolseley was victorious at the Battle of Tel el Kebir, Egypt, 1882;

New York became the capital of the new United States of America, 1788;
The Battle of Quebec was fought, when the British defeated the French, 1759;
Montrose was defeated by the Covenanters at Philiphaugh, 1645;
The Battle of Marignano between the French and Swiss started, 1515.

TODAY IS THE FEAST DAY OF St Amatus or Amé, abbot, St Amatus or Amé, bishop, St Eulogius of Alexandria, St John Chrysostom and St Maurilius of Angers.

14th September

Born on this day:

Kepler Wessels, Australian cricketer, 1957;
Paul Allott, cricketer, 1956;
Ray Wilkins, footballer, 1956;
Amanda Barrie, actress, 1939;
Nicol Williamson, actor, 1938;
Terence Donovan, photographer, 1936;
The Hon. Angus Ogilvy, husband of Princess Alexandra, 1928;
Sandra Blow, painter, 1925;
Lordy Cledwyn of Penrhos CH, former Labour minister, 1916;
Jack Hawkins, film actor, 1910;
Jan Garrigue Masaryk, Czech statesman, 1886;

Charles Dana Gibson, US artist, creator of the 'Gibson Girls', 1867;
Theodor Woldsen Storm, German poet and novelist, 1817;
Friedrich Heinrich Alexander, Baron von Humboldt, German traveller and naturalist, 1769;
Luigi Cherubini, Italian composer, 1760;
Sir Peter Lely [Van der Faes], painter, 1617;
Cornelius Agrippa, scholar and astrologer, 1486.

Died on this day:

Janet Gaynor [Laura Gainor], US film actress, 1984;
Princess Grace of Monaco [Grace Kelly], after a car crash, 1982;
Richard Thomas Le Gallienne, poet and essayist, 1947;
Tomás Garrigue Masaryk, first president of Czechoslovakia, 1937;
Dame Madge Kendall, actress, 1935;
Isadora Duncan, US dancer, killed in car crash, 1927;
William McKinley, 25th president of the USA, after being shot, 1901;
Georges Leclanché, French inventor and engineer, 1882;
Sir James Stephen, colonial administrator and historian, 1859;

Arthur Wellesley, 1st Duke of Wellington, soldier and statesman, 1852;
Augustus Welby Northmore Pugin, architect, 1852;
James Fenimore Cooper, US novelist, 1851;
Louis-Joseph de Montcalm-Gozon, Marquis de Montcalm de Saint-Véran, French general, killed in action, 1759;
Nicolas Lancret, French painter, 1743;
Robert Devereux, 3rd Earl of Sussex, soldier, 1646;
Dante [Durante] Alighieri, Italian poet, 1321.

Occurred on this day:

The first space machine landed on the moon: the Soviet *Lunik II*, 1959;
US forces captured Mexico City, 1847;
Francis Scott Key composed the poem *The Star-Spangled Banner*, 1814;
Napoleon and his army entered Moscow, 1812;

The Gregorian Calendar was adopted in Britain, when 3rd September became 14th September, 1752;
The English defeated the Scots at the Battle of Homildon-hill, 1402.

TODAY IS THE FEAST DAY OF St Maternus of Cologne and St Notburga.

15th September

Born on this day:

Freddie Mercury, rock singer, 1946;
Mike Procter, cricketer, 1946;
Jessye Norman, US soprano, 1945;
Graham Taylor, manager, England soccer team, 1944;
Rafael Frühbeck de Burgos, conductor, 1933;
Charles Bone, painter and lecturer, 1926;
Jackie Cooper, US film actor, 1922;
Dr Richard Gordon, novelist, 1921;
Richard Arnell, composer, conductor and film-maker, 1917;
Margaret Mary Lockwood, actress, 1916;
Jean Batten, aviator, 1909;
Tom Conway [Thomas Charles Sanders], film actor, 1904;
Dame Sylvia Crowe, landscape architect, 1901;
Jean Renoir, French film director, 1894;
Dame Agatha Mary Clarissa Christie, detective-story writer, 1890;

Frank Martin, Swiss composer, 1890;
Robert Charles Benchley, US humorist, 1889;
Hans Arp, French painter, engraver, sculptor and poet, 1887;
Bruno Walter [Schlesinger], German conductor, 1876;
William Howard Taft, 27th president of the USA, 1857;
Henry Sweet, philologist and phonetician, 1845;
James Fenimore Cooper, US novelist, 1789;
Titus Oates, impostor and fabricator of the 'Popish Plot', 1649;
François, Duc de La Rochefoucauld-Liancourt, French writer, 1613;
Albrecht Wenzel Eusebius von Wallenstein, German soldier and statesman, 1583;
Trajan, Roman emperor, 53.

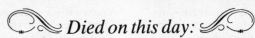

Died on this day:

Gustaf VI Adolf, King of Sweden, 1973;
Geoffrey Francis Fisher, Lord Fisher of Canterbury, former Archbishop of Canterbury, 1972;
Anton Friedrich Wilhelm von Webern, Austrian composer, 1945;
José Echegaray y Eizaguirre, Spanish writer and scientist, 1916;
William Seward Burroughs, US adding-machine pioneer, 1898;

John Hanning Speke, explorer, shot by accident, 1864;
Isambard Kingdom Brunel, engineer, 1859;
Arthur Henry Hallam, historian, 1833;
Richard Boyle, 1st Earl of Cork, 1643;
Sir Thomas Overbury, poet, poisoned while in the Tower of London, 1613.

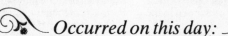

Occurred on this day:

The *Sun* newspaper was first published, 1964;
The first traffic wardens went on duty in London, 1960;
The musical show *King's Rhapsody* was first produced, London, 1949;
In Germany, the Nuremburg laws were passed, outlawing Jews and making the swastika the official flag of the country, 1935;
Russia was proclaimed a republic by Alexander Kerensky, 1917;

Tanks were first used in battle by the British army at the Somme, 1916;
The Manchester and Liverpool railway opened, during which ceremony, William Huskisson, MP, was killed, 1830;
Guatemala was declared independent, 1821;
To halt the French occupation, the Russians set fire to Moscow, 1812.

TODAY IS THE FEAST DAY OF St Aachard or Aichardus, St Catherine of Genoa, St Mirin, St Nicetas the Goth and St Nicomedes.

16th September

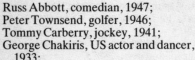

Born on this day:

Russ Abbott, comedian, 1947;
Peter Townsend, golfer, 1946;
Tommy Carberry, jockey, 1941;
George Chakiris, US actor and dancer, 1933;
Anne Francis, US actress, 1932;
Mickey Stewart, cricketer, 1932;
Peter Falk, US TV actor, 1927;
Jack Kelly, US actor, 1927;
B. B. King, US singer, 1926;
Charles Haughey, former Irish prime minister, 1925;
Lauren Bacall, US actress, 1924;
Lee Kuan Yew, prime minister of Singapore, 1923;
Janis Paige, US actress, 1922;
Sir Alexander Korda [Sandor Laszlo Korda], film director and producer, 1893;

Grand Admiral Karl Doenitz, German sailor, 1891;
Alfred Noyes, poet, 1880;
Sir Edward Marshall Hall, criminal law advocate, 1858;
Andrew Bonar Law, statesman, 1858;
Francis Parkman, US historian, 1823;
Sir Anthony Panizzi [Antonio Genesio Maria Panizzi], bibliophile and scholar, 1797;
Nathan Mayer Rothschild, banker, 1777;
Mikhail Illarionovich Kutuzov, Russian soldier and diplomat, 1745;
King Henry V, 1387.

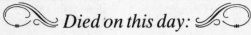

Died on this day:

Maria Callas [Cecilia Sophia Anna Maria Kalogeropoulos], opera singer, 1977;
Walter Greenwood, novelist and playwright, 1974;
Michael Carr [Maurice Cohen], composer, 1968;
Leopold Charles Maurice Stennett Amery, statesman and journalist, 1955;
Grace Aguilar, novelist and historian, 1847;

Sir James Hopkins Jeans, physicist, 1946;
[Count] John Francis McCormack, US/ Irish tenor, 1945;
Edward Bouverie Pusey, theologian, 1882;
Louis XVIII, King of France, 1824;
Gabriel Daniel Fahrenheit, physicist, 1736;
John Colet, scholar and theologian, 1519;
Tomás de Torquemada, Dominican monk and Spanish Inquisitor-General, 1498.

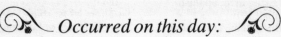

Occurred on this day:

In the United States, the Episcopal Church approved the ordination of women to the priesthood, 1976;
Papua New Guinea became independent, 1975;
Resolution, Britain's first Polaris submarine, was launched, 1966;

Malaysia became independent, 1963;
Reza Khan Pahlavi, Shah of Iran, abdicated, 1941;
David Livingstone discovered Lake Nyasa, 1859.

TODAY IS THE FEAST DAY OF Saints Abundius and Abundantius, St Cornelius, pope, St Cyprian, St Edith of Wilton, St Euphemia, St Ludmila and St Ninian.

17th September

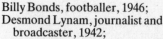

Born on this day:

Billy Bonds, footballer, 1946;
Desmond Lynam, journalist and broadcaster, 1942;
Jennifer Dickson, artist and photographer, 1936;
Anne Bancroft, US actress, 1931;
Stirling Moss, racing driver, 1929;
Roddy McDowell, US film actor, 1928;
Brian Matthew, radio presenter, 1928;
Reginald Marsh, actor, 1926;
Dinah Sheridan, actress, 1920;
Chaim Herzog, Israeli president, 1918;
Mary Stewart [Lady Stewart], historical novelist, 1916;
Helen Vinson, US actress, 1907;
Sir Frederick Ashton, choreographer, 1906;
Dolores Costello, US film actress, 1906;
Sir Francis Charles Chichester, yachtsman and aviator, 1901;
Edward William Lane, translator of *The Thousand and One Nights*, 1801;
Samuel Prout, water-colour painter, 1783;
Marie-Jean-Antoine-Nicolas de Caritat, Marquis de Condorcet, French mathematician and philosopher, 1743;
Francisco Gomez de Quevado y Villegas, Spanish poet and satirist, 1580;
Pope Paul V, 1552.

Died on this day:

Richard Basehart, US film actor, 1984;
Katherine Anne Porter, US novelist, 1980;
Count Folke Bernadotte, Swedish diplomat, assassinated, 1948;
Dame Lilian Braithwaite, actress, 1948;
Ethel Mary Dell [Mrs G. T. Savage], romantic novelist, 1939;
Eugène-Emmanuel Viollet-le-Duc, French Gothic architect, 1879;
William Henry Fox Talbot, photographic pioneer, 1877;
Walter Savage Landor, author, 1864;
Alfred Victor, Comte de Vigny, French poet, 1863;
Tobias George Smollett, novelist, 1771;
Philip IV, King of Spain, 1665;
Pedro Menendez de Avilés, Spanish soldier and navigator, 1574.

Occurred on this day:

Estonia, Latvia, Lithuania, North and South Korea, the Marshall Islands and Micronesia were admitted to the United Nations, 1991;
The 1st British Airborne Division landed at Arnhem, Netherlands, 1944;
Poland was invaded by the USSR, 1939;
The operetta *Viktoria and Her Hussar* was performed in London for the first time, 1931;
The first long-playing records were demonstrated in New York, but the venture failed, 1931;
The Commonwealth of Australia was proclaimed as a federal union of six colonies, 1900;
The Mont Cenis railway tunnel, Switzerland, opened, 1871.

TODAY IS THE FEAST DAY OF St Columba of Cordova, St Francis of Camporosso, St Hildegard, St Lambert of Maastricht, St Peter Arbues, St Robert Bellarmine, St Satyrus of Milan, Saints Socrates and Stephen and St Theodora.

# 18th September

Born on this day:

Geoff Baxter, jockey, 1946;
John Spencer, snooker player, 1935;
Robert Blake, US actor, 1933;
Ray Alan, ventriloquist, 1930;
Baroness Hart, former MP, 1924;
Jack Warden, US film actor, 1920;
Rossano Brazzi, Italian film actor, 1916;
Kwame Nkrumah, Ghanaian prime minister, 1909;
Greta Garbo [Greta Lovisa Gustafsson], Swedish film actress, 1905;
Viscount Eccles CH, former MP, 1904;
John George Diefenbaker, Canadian statesman, 1895;

Fay Compton [Virginia Lilian Emeline Compton], actress, 1894;
Arthur Benjamin, composer, 1893;
Gerald Hugh Tyrwhitt-Wilson Berners, 14th Baron, composer, 1883;
Anton Mauve, Dutch landscape painter, 1838;
Jean-Bernard-Léon Foucault, French physicist, 1819;
Pope Gregory XVI, 1765;
Dr Samuel Johnson, lexicographer and writer, 1709;
Gilbert Burnet, Bishop of Salisbury and author, 1643.

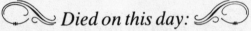# *Died on this day:*

Franchot Tone [Stanislas Pascal Franchot Tone], US film actor, 1968;
Sean O'Casey, Irish playwright, 1964;
Dr Dag Hammarskjöld, secretary-general of the UN, 1961;
Sir John Douglas Cockcroft, physicist, 1951;
Francis Herbert Bradley, philosopher, 1924;
George MacDonald, poet and novelist, 1905;
Armand-Hippolyte-Louis Fizeau, French physicist, 1896;

Dion Boucicault [Dionysius Lardner Boursiquot], Irish/US playwright and actor, 1890;
William Hazlitt, critic and essayist, 1830;
Robert Pollok, poet, 1827;
Leonhard Euler, Swiss mathematician, 1783;
Andrew Foulis, Scottish bookseller and printer, 1775;
Matthew Prior, poet and diplomat, 1721;
Hubert [Huybrecht] van Eyck, Flemish painter, 1426.

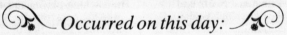# *Occurred on this day:*

The USSR was admitted to the League of Nations, 1934;
Manchuria was taken by the Japanese, who set up the puppet state of Manchukuo, 1931;
In the United States, the Columbia Broadcasting System was inaugurated, 1927;
The Battle of Megiddo [Palestine] started, 1918;

The *New York Times* was first published, 1851;
Chile revolted and became independent of Spain, 1810;
The Theatre Royal, Covent Garden, London [Royal Opera House] second theatre opened, 1809.

TODAY IS THE FEAST DAY OF St Ferreolus of Limoges, St Ferreolus of Vienne, St John Massias, St Joseph of Cupertino, St Methodius of Olympus and St Richardis.

19th September

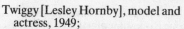
Born on this day:

Twiggy [Lesley Hornby], model and actress, 1949;
Rosemary Casals, tennis player, 1948;
Jeremy Irons, actor, 1948;
Michael Elphick, actor, 1946;
Kate Adie, TV journalist, 1945;
Capt. Jim Fox, pentathlon winner, 1941;
Zandra Rhodes, fashion designer, 1940;
Paul Williams, US composer and lyricist, 1940;
David McCallum, actor, 1933;
Derek Nimmo, actor, 1932;
Rosemary Harris, actress, 1930;
Pete Murray, broadcaster, 1928;
Dr Arthur Wills, composer and organist, 1926;
Penelope Mortimer, novelist, 1918;
Sir William Golding, novelist, 1911;
William Gordon [Billy] Reid, popular composer, 1902;
Joe Pasternak, US film producer, 1901;
Sidonie Goossens, harpist, 1900;
Ricardo Cortez [Jacob Krantz], US actor and director, 1899;
Arthur Rackham, illustrator, 1867;
William Hesketh Lever, 1st Viscount Leverhulme, soap manufacturer and philanthropist, 1851;
George Cadbury, chocolate manufacturer and social reformer, 1839;
William Dyce, Scottish painter, 1806;
Lajos Kossuth, Hungarian statesman, 1802;
Rev. William Kirby, entomologist, 1759.

Died on this day:

Roy Kinnear, actor and comedian, 1988;
Sir David Alexander Cecil Low, cartoonist, 1963;
Raimu [Jules Muraire], French actor, 1946;
Pauline Frederick [Beatrice Pauline Libbey], US stage and film actress, 1938;
Thomas John Barnardo, physician and philanthropist, 1905;
James Abram Garfield, 20th president of the USA, after being shot, 1881;
Giovanni Battista Donati, Italian astronomer, 1873;
Meyer Amschel Rothschild, banker, 1812.

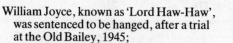
Occurred on this day:

William Joyce, known as 'Lord Haw-Haw', was sentenced to be hanged, after a trial at the Old Bailey, 1945;
The Germans took Kiev, 1941;
Melville Reuben Bissell, US inventor, patented the first carpet-sweeper, 1876;
Auckland, New Zealand, was founded, 1840;
The English defeated the French at the Battle of Poitiers, 1356.

TODAY IS THE FEAST DAY OF St Emily de Rodat, St Goericus or Abbo, St Januarius of Benevento, St Mary of Cerevellon, St Peleus and his Companions, St Sequanus or Seine, St Susanna of Eleutheropolis and St Theodore of Canterbury.

20th September

Born on this day:

José Rivero, golfer, 1955;
Sir Jeremy Child, actor, 1944;
Jane Manning, soprano, 1938;
Sophia Loren, Italian film actress, 1934;
John Dankworth, bandleader and jazzman, 1927;
Fred Winter, National Hunt trainer, 1926;
Kenneth More, film actor, 1914;
Charles Walter Stansby Williams, author and playwright, 1886;
Ildebrando Pizzetti, Italian composer, 1880;

Upton Beall Sinclair, US novelist, 1878;
Sir George Robey [George Edward Wade], comedian, 1869;
Henry Arthur Jones, playwright, 1851;
Sir James Dewar, chemist and physicist, inventor of the vacuum flask, 1842;
Charles Voss, German pianist and composer, 1815;
Friedrich Gauermann, Austrian painter, 1807;
Sir Titus Salt, MP, manufacturer and philanthropist, 1803 [see also Deaths];
Alexander the Great, 356 BC.

Died on this day:

George Seferis [Giorgos Stylianou Seferiades], Greek poet and diplomat, 1971;
Jean Julius Christian Sibelius, Finnish composer, 1957;
Fiorello Henry La Guardia, mayor of New York, 1947;
Annie Besant, social reformer and theosophist, 1933;
Pablo Martin Melitón de Sarasate y Navascuéz, Spanish violinist and composer, 1908;

Theodor Fontane, German poet and novelist, 1898;
Sir Titus Salt, MP, manufacturer and philanthropist, 1876 [see also Births];
Jakob Ludwig Karl Grimm, philologist and folklorist, 1863;
Admiral Sir Thomas Masterman Hardy Bt., 1839;
Utamaro Kitagawa, Japanese painter, 1806;
Robert Emmet, Irish nationalist, executed, 1803.

Occurred on this day:

The liner *Queen Elizabeth II* was launched at Clydebank, 1966;
The first London production of the musical comedy *Once Upon a Mattress* was presented, 1960;
The Methodist Church of Great Britain and Ireland was established, 1932;
The liner *Mauretania* was launched, 1906;
During the Crimean War, the Russian army was defeated by the Allied [Britain, France and Turkey] armies at the Battle of Alma, 1854;
Six Victoria Crosses were awarded for gallantry at the Battle of Alma, 1854;
The French defeated the Prussians at the Battle of Valmy, 1792;

The Treaty of Ryswick was signed by France, England, Spain and Holland, 1697;
The Treaty of Hampton Court was signed between Queen Elizabeth I and Louis I de Bourbon, 1562;
Ferdinand Magellan and a fleet of five ships set off from Seville on a circumnavigation of the world, 1519;
Salisbury Cathedral was consecrated, 1258;
Richard I defeated the French at Gisors, 1198;
Aëtius, Roman general, defeated the Huns under Attila at Châlons-sur-Marne, 451.

TODAY IS THE FEAST DAY OF St Candida of Carthage, Saints Fausta and Evilasius, Saints Theodore, Philippa and their Companions and St Vincent Madelgarius.

21st September

Born on this day:

Richard Ellison, cricketer, 1959;
Stephen King, novelist, 1948;
Susan Fleetwood, actress, 1944;
Ian Albery, impresario, 1936;
Shirley Conran, novelist, 1932;
Larry Hagman, US actor, 1931;
Donald McCain, horse trainer, 1930;
Dawn Addams, film actress, 1930;
Jimmy Young, radio presenter, 1923;
Nigel Stock, actor, 1919;
Baron Constantine [Sir Learie Nicholas Constantine], West Indies cricketer and diplomat, 1902;
Sir Allen Lane [Allen Lane Williams], publisher and founder of Penguin Books, 1902;

Gustav Holst [Gustavus Theodore von Holst], composer, 1874;
Herbert George Wells, novelist, 1866;
Sir Edmund William Gosse, writer and critic, 1849;
John Loudon McAdam, roadmaking engineer and inventor, 1756;
Francesco Bartolozzi, Italian engraver, 1727;
John Home, Scottish cleric and playwright, 1722;
Louis Joliet, French explorer, 1645;
Girolamo Savonarola, Italian martyr and church reformer, 1452.

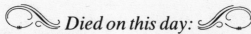

Died on this day:

Walter Brennan, US film actor, 1974;
William Charles Franklyn Plomer, South African author, 1973;
Henri-Marie-Joseph Millon de Montherlant, French novelist and playwright, 1972;
Haakon VII, King of Norway, 1957;
Roger Cuthbert Quilter, composer, 1953;
Arthur Schopenhauer, German philosopher, 1860;

Lord William George Frederic Cavendish Bentinck, MP and sportsman, 1848;
Sir Walter Scott, novelist, 1832;
Marguerite d'Angoulême, Queen of Navarre, 1549;
King Edward II, murdered, 1327;
Virgil [Publius Vergilius Maro], Roman poet, 19 BC.

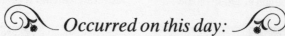

Occurred on this day:

In Honduras, floods caused by hurricanes resulted in the deaths of over 8,000 people, 1974;
Malta became independent, 1964;
The Federal Republic of Germany [West Germany] was inaugurated, 1949;
The Czech cabinet accepted the Anglo-French plan to cede Sudeten territories to Germany, 1938;
The Reichstag fire trial opened in Leipzig, 1933;
Britain abandoned the Gold Standard, and the pound fell from $4.86 to $3.49, 1931;

The first London performance of the musical show *Oh, Kay!* was presented, 1927;
The independence of Latvia was proclaimed, 1917;
Stonehenge was sold by auction for £6,600, 1915;
Charles Edward Stuart defeated the English under General Cope at the Battle of Prestonpans, 1745;
The Turkish army of Suleiman the Magnificent was repulsed at Vienna, 1529.

TODAY IS THE FEAST DAY OF St Matthew, St Maura of Troyes, St Michael of Chernigov, St Theodore of Chernigov and The Martyrs of Korea.

22nd September

Born on this day:

Catherine Oxenberg, US film actress, 1961;
John Caird, theatre director, 1948;
Captain Mark Phillips, horseman, 1948;
Gina Fratini, fashion designer, 1931;
Colin Graham, musical director, 1931;
Fay Weldon, author, 1931;
Maria Charles, actress, 1929;
William Franklyn, actor, 1926;
Dr Dannie Abse, physician, surgeon and poet, 1923;
Paul Muni [Muni Weisenfreund], US film actor, 1895;
Erich von Stroheim [Erich Oswald Stroheim], actor and film director, 1885;

Dame Christabel Harriette Pankhurst, suffragette, 1880;
Shigeru Yoshida [Takeuchi], Japanese statesman, 1878;
George Bentham, botanist, 1800;
Michael Faraday, physicist and chemist, 1791;
Theodore Edward Hook, popular song writer and playwright, 1788;
Jean-Étienne Guettard, French botanist and geologist, 1715;
Philip Dormer Stanhope, 4th Earl of Chesterfield, literary patron and statesman, 1694;
Anne of Cleves, 4th wife of King Henry VIII, 1515.

Died on this day:

Irving Berlin, US composer, 1989;
Axel Springer, German publisher, 1985;
Harry Warren [Salvatore Guaragna], US composer, 1981;
Mary Roberts Rinehart, US novelist, 1958;
Frederick Soddy, physicist and chemist, 1956;
Thomas Burke, novelist and author, 1945;
Sir Charles Santley, bass-baritone, 1922;
Alain-Fournier [Henri-Alban Fournier], French writer, killed in action on the Marne, 1914;

Mary Martha Sherwood [Butt], author of children's books, 1851;
Nathan Hale, American revolutionary patriot, hanged, 1776;
Alessandro Allori, Italian painter, 1607;
Johann Agricola [Schneider or Schnitter], German Protestant reformer, 1566;
Sturluson Snorri, Icelandic poet and historian, killed, 1241.

Occurred on this day:

Mali became independent, 1960;
Independent TV began operating in Britain, 1955;
Juan Perón, Argentinian leader, was deposed, 1955;
Gene Tunney beat Jack Dempsey for the world heavyweight boxing title, 1927;
The British cruisers *Aboukir*, *Hogue* and *Cressy* were torpedoed by German U-boats, 1914;
Wagner's opera *Das Rheingold* was first performed, Munich, 1869;
Abraham Lincoln issued the Emancipation Proclamation, ordering the freeing of slaves, 1862;

Joseph Smith announced the discovery of the *Book of Mormon*, 1827;
France was declared to be a Republic, 1792;
In France, the Revolutionary Calendar came into use, 1792;
Sir Robert Walpole became the first prime minister to move into No. 10, Downing Street, 1735;
Sir Philip Sidney was mortally wounded at the relief of the Spanish colony of Zutphen in the Netherlands, 1586.

TODAY IS THE FEAST DAY OF St Bodo, St Emmeramus, St Felix III [IV], pope, St Laudus or Lô, St Maurice of Agaunum, St Phocas the Gardener, St Salaberga, St Thomas of Villanova and The Theban Legion.

23rd September

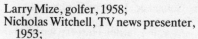

Born on this day:

Larry Mize, golfer, 1958;

Nicholas Witchell, TV news presenter, 1953;

Jeff Squire, rugby footballer, 1951;

Bruce Springsteen, US rock singer and songwriter, 1949;

Julio Iglesias, musician, 1943;

Toby Balding, racehorse trainer, 1936;

Ray Charles, rhythm and blues singer, 1930;

Mickey Rooney, US film actor, 1920;

Paul Delraux, Belgian painter, 1897;

Walter Lippman, US journalist and author, 1889;

Emma Magdalena Rosalia Marie Josepha Barbara, Baroness Orczy, novelist, 1865;

Mary Elizabeth Coleridge, novelist and poet, 1861;

William Archer, dramatic critic and playwright, 1856;

Armand-Hippolyte-Louis Fizeau, French physicist, 1819;

Karl Theodor Körner, German poet, playwright and patriot, 1791;

Peter von Cornelius, German painter, 1783;

Ferdinand VI, King of Spain, 1713;

Jeremy Collier, clergyman and historian, 1650;

Augustus [Gaius Octavianus] 1st Roman emperor, 63 BC;

Euripides, Greek playwright, 480 BC.

Died on this day:

Pablo Neruda [Neftalí Ricardo Reyes], Chilean poet, 1973;

Elinor Glyn, novelist, 1943;

Sigmund Freud, Austrian psychoanalyst, 1939;

John Morley, 1st Viscount Morley, statesman, 1923;

William Wilkie Collins, novelist, 1889;

Eliza Cook, poet, 1889;

Urbain-Jean-Joseph Leverrier, French astronomer, 1877;

Prosper Merimée, French novelist, 1870;

Richard Parkes Bonington, landscape painter, 1828;

Robert Dodsley, poet, publisher and bookseller, founder of the *Annual Register*, 1764;

Hermann Boerhaave, Dutch physician and teacher, 1738;

Nicholas-François Mansart, French architect, 1666.

Occurred on this day:

Two awards for gallantry: the George Cross and the George Medal, were instituted, 1940;

Johann Gottfried Galle discovered the planet Neptune, 1846;

The New York *Daily Sun* newspaper appeared for the first time, 1833;

The British under Wellesley defeated Scindia and the Rajah of Berar at Assaye, 1803;

The naval battle between the *Bonhomme Richard* and the *Serapis* was fought off Flamborough Head, 1779;

The Battle of Worcester was won by Prince Rupert, 1642;

The Lancastrians were defeated by the Yorkists at Bloreheath, 1459;

The Greeks defeated the Persians at the Battle of Salamis, 480 BC.

TODAY IS THE FEAST DAY OF St Adamnan or Eunan of Iona and Saints Andrew, John, Peter and Antony.

24th September

Born on this day:

Richard Northcott, film producer, 1947;
Gerry Marsden, rock musician, 1942;
Linda McCartney, photographer, 1941;
Robert Lang, actor and director, 1934;
Svetlana Beriozova, former ballerina, 1932;
Brian Glanville, author and journalist, 1931;
Anthony Newley, actor and composer, 1931;
Prof. Richard Hoggart, author, 1918;
Andrzej Panufnik, composer and conductor, 1914;
Howard Walter Florey, Baron Florey, pathologist, 1898;
Francis Scott Key Fitzgerald, US novelist, 1896;

André Cournand, French/US physician, 1895;
Sir Alan [A. P.] Patrick Herbert, writer and MP, 1890;
Georges Claude, French engineer and inventor of the neon light, 1870;
Samuel Rutherford Crockett, novelist, 1860;
Antoine-Louis Barye, French sculptor, 1795;
John Marshall, US Secretary of State, 1755;
Horace Walpole, 4th Earl of Orford, writer, 1717;
Johan de Witt, Dutch statesman, 1625;
Geronimo Cardano, Italian physician and mathematician, 1501.

Died on this day:

Dame Isobel Baillie, oratorio singer, 1983;
Mátyás Seiber, composer, 1960;
Carl Laemmle, US film producer, 1939;
Niels Ryberg Finsen, Danish physician, 1904;
Henry Hart Milman, cleric, poetic professor and historian, 1868;

Henry, 1st Viscount Hardinge of Lahore, governor-general of India, 1856;
Paracelsus [Theophrastus Bombastus von Hohenheim], Swiss physician, 1541;
Pope Innocent II, 1143;
Pépin III [the Short], King of the Franks, 768.

Occurred on this day:

The USS *Enterprise*, first nuclear-powered aircraft-carrier, was launched at Newport, Virginia, 1960;
The first Cinemascope film, *The Robe*, had its world première in Hollywood, 1953;
The Phoenix Theatre, London, opened, 1930;
The first provincial daily newspaper in England was founded in Liverpool: *The Northern Daily Times*, 1853;
New Caledonia was annexed by France, 1853;

Henri Giffard, a French mechanic, flew from Paris to Trappe in the first dirigible balloon, 1852;
A Papal Bull was issued, establishing a Roman Catholic hierarchy in England, 1850;
Sir James Brooke was appointed Rajah of Sarawak, 1841;
In the United States, the Supreme Court was created by the Federal Judiciary Act, 1789;
The St Leger horse race was run for the first time, 1776.

TODAY IS THE FEAST DAY OF St Gerard of Csanad, St Geremarus or Germer, St Pacifico of San Severino and St Robert Flower of Knaresborough.

25th September

Born on this day:

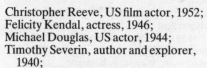

Christopher Reeve, US film actor, 1952;
Felicity Kendal, actress, 1946;
Michael Douglas, US actor, 1944;
Timothy Severin, author and explorer, 1940;
Leon Brittan QC, vice-president, Commission of the European Communities, 1939;
Juliet Prowse, US singer and actress, 1937;
Andrew Gardner, TV newsreader, 1932;
Ronnie Barker, comedian, 1929;
Sir Colin Davis, conductor, 1927;
Norman Ayrton, theatre and opera director, 1924;
Robert Bresson, French film director, 1907;
Dmitri Dmitriyevich Shostakovich, Russian composer, 1906;

Mark Rothko [Marcus Rothkovich], US painter, 1903;
William Harrison Faulkner, US novelist, 1897;
Sir Charles Blake Cochran, impresario, 1872;
Léon Boëllmann, French composer, 1862;
Henri Scheffer, French painter, 1798;
Felicia Dorothea Hemans, poet, 1793;
Abraham Gottlob Werner, German geologist, 1750;
Jean-Philippe Rameau, French composer, 1683;
Jacques-Bénigne Bossuet, French theologian, 1627;
Matthew Merian the Elder, Swiss engraver and bookseller, 1593.

Died on this day:

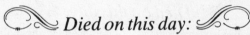

Walter Pidgeon, US film actor, 1984;
Leopold III, former King of the Belgians, 1983;
Erich Maria Remarque, German novelist, 1970;
Emily Post [Price], US writer and columnist, 1960;
Helen Broderick, US comedienne and actress, 1959;
Johann Baptist Strauss the Elder, Austrian composer, 1849;

Jacques-Étienne-Joseph-Alexandre Macdonald, Duc de Tarente, French soldier, 1840;
Richard Porson, scholar, 1808;
Johann Heinrich Lambert, German mathematician, 1777;
Samuel Butler, poet, writer and satirist, 1680;
Philip I [the Handsome] King of Spain, 1506.

Occurred on this day:

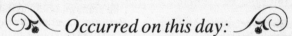

In a referendum, Norway voted against joining the Common Market, 1972;
The German High Commissioner in Norway set up a government with Vidkun Quisling at its head, 1940;
The Battle of Loos began, 1915;
The French battleship *Liberté* exploded, causing 226 deaths in Toulon Harbour, 1911;
The first London performance of the musical show *The Dollar Princess* was presented, 1909;

The Royal Court Theatre, Sloane Square, London, opened, 1888;
The comedy opera *Dorothy* was first produced in London, 1886;
The relief of Lucknow by Havelock and Outram began, 1857;
The Pacific Ocean was discovered by Vasco Nuñez de Balboa, 1513;
King Harold II defeated his brother the Earl Tostig and King Harold Hardrada of Norway at the Battle of Stamford Bridge, 1066.

TODAY IS THE FEAST DAY OF St Albert of Jerusalem, St Aunacharius or Aunaire, St Ceolfrith, St Finbar or Bairre, St Firminus of Amiens, St Sergius of Radonezh and St Vincent Strambi.

26th September

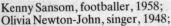

Born on this day:

Kenny Sansom, footballer, 1958;

Olivia Newton-John, singer, 1948;

Ian Chappell, Australian cricketer, 1943;

Lucette Aldous, Australian prima
ballerina, 1938;

Lennie Bennett, comedian, 1938;

Neil Coles, golfer, 1934;

Philip Bosco, US actor, 1930;

Peter Dews, theatre director, 1929;

Margaret Thomas, artist, 1916;

George Gershwin [Jacob Gershvin], US
composer, 1898;

Pope Paul VI [Giovanni Battista Montini],
1897;

Martin Heidegger, German philosopher,
1889;

Thomas Stearns Eliot OM, poet and
playwright, 1888;

Sir Barnes Wallis, airship and bomb
designer, 1887;

Ivan Petrovich Pavlov, Russian
physiologist, 1849;

Charles Bradlaugh, politician and social
reformer, 1833;

John Sims Reeves, tenor, 1818;

Thomas Sidney Cooper, painter,
1803;

Jean-Louis-André-Théodore Géricault,
French painter, 1791;

Cuthbert Collingwood, 1st Baron,
Admiral, 1750.

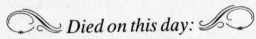

Died on this day:

Peter Dawson, Australian bass-baritone,
1961;

Hugh John Lofting, author and creator of
'Dr Dolittle', 1947;

Béla Bartók, Hungarian composer,
1945;

William Henry Davies, poet, 1940;

Adelina Patti, singer, 1919;

James Keir Hardie, Labour Party pioneer,
1915;

Lafcadio Hearn [Koizumi Yakumo], writer
on Japan, 1904;

Robert Anderson, poet, 1833;

Daniel Boone, US frontiersman, 1820;

Bishop Lancelot Andrewes, theologian,
1626.

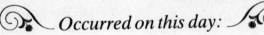

Occurred on this day:

In Britain, sugar rationing was ended,
1953;

The liner *Queen Mary* was launched by
Queen Mary herself, 1934;

The Battle of the Meuse-Argonne began,
1918;

New Zealand became a Dominion, 1907;

The first talking machine for playing discs
[the gramophone] was patented by Emile
Berliner, a German immigrant in the
USA, 1887;

The Parthenon and the Propyleiea were
destroyed when the Venetians
bombarded Athens, 1687.

TODAY IS THE FEAST DAY OF St Colman of Lann Elo, Saints Cosmas and Damian,
St John of Meda, St Nilus of Rossano and St Teresa Couderc.

# 27th September

Born on this day:

Philip Blacker, jockey, 1949;
Barbara Dickson, singer, 1948;
Michele Dotrice, actress, 1948;
Denis Lawson, actor, 1947;
Robin Nedwell, actor, 1946;
Alvin Stardust, rock singer, 1942;
Josephine Barstow, soprano, 1940;
Gordon Honeycombe, author and
    broadcaster, 1936;
Barbara Murray, actress, 1929;
Sir Martin Ryle, astronomer, 1918;
Giles Playfair, author, 1910;
Sir William Empson, poet and critic,
    1906;
Vincent Miller Youmans, US composer,
    1898;
George Raft, US film actor, 1895;
Cyril Meir Scott, composer, 1879;
Thomas Nast, US cartoonist and illustrator,
    1840;
Henri Frédéric Amiel, Swiss poet and
    philosopher, 1821;
Paul-Henri-Corentin Féval, French
    novelist, 1817;
George Cruikshank, illustrator and
    caricaturist, 1792;
Samuel Adams, American revolutionary
    leader, 1722.

 ## *Died on this day:*

Lloyd Nolan, US film actor, 1985;
Dame Gracie Fields, singer and
    entertainer, 1979;
Clara Bow, US film actress – the 'It' girl,
    1965;
Gerald Finzi, composer, 1956;
Aristide-Joseph-Bonaventure Maillol,
    French painter and sculptor, 1944;
Engelbert Humperdinck, German
    composer, 1921;
Hilaire-Germain-Edgar Degas, French
    painter, 1917;
Rémy de Gourmont, French writer,
    1915;
Ivan Aleksandrovich Goncharov, Russian
    novelist and travel writer, 1891;
Laurence Eusden, poet, 1730;
Marco Girolamo Vida, Italian bishop,
    humanist and poet, 1566;
William of Wykeham, bishop and founder
    of Winchester College and New College,
    Oxford, 1404.

 ## *Occurred on this day:*

The first London performance of the
    musical *Hair* was presented, 1968;
Hitler announced his intention to annex the
    Sudetenland, 1939;
Warsaw surrendered to the German forces,
    1939;
The liner *Queen Elizabeth* was launched by
    Queen Elizabeth, now the Queen
    Mother, 1938;
The first passenger railway opened between
    Stockton and Darlington, 1826;
The Society of Jesus was founded, 1540.

TODAY IS THE FEAST DAY OF St Barrog or Barnoch, St Elzear of Sabran and St
Vincent de Paul.

28th September

Born on this day:

Sylvia Kristal, actress, 1952;
Peter Egan, actor, 1946;
Fiona Lewis, actress, 1946;
Helen Shapiro, singer, 1946;
Brigitte Bardot, French film actress, 1934;
Jeremy Isaacs, general director, Royal Opera House, Covent Garden, 1932;
Marcello Mastroianni, Italian actor, 1924;
Ellen Malcolm, painter, 1923;
Michael Somes, dancer, 1917;
Peter Finch, actor, 1916;
Stanley Jackson, author, 1910;
Herman Cyril McNeile ['Sapper'], novelist, 1888;
Wilhelm Kühnert, German animal painter, 1865;

Field Marshal John Denton Pinkstone French, 1st Earl of Ypres, 1852;
Georges Clemenceau, French statesman, 1841;
Francis Turner Palgrave, poet and editor, 1824;
Prosper Merimée, French playwright and novelist, 1803;
William Julius Mickle, Scottish poet, 1735;
Pierre de Maupertius, French astronomer and mathematician, 1698;
Johann Mattheson, German composer and writer, 1681;
Michelangelo Merisi da Caravaggio, Italian painter, 1573.

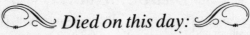

Died on this day:

Sir Robert Helpmann, dancer and actor, 1986;
Wystan Hugh Auden, poet, 1973;
John Dos Passos, US novelist, 1970;
André Breton, French poet and pioneer of surrealism, 1966;
Arthur ['Harpo'] Marx, US comedian, 1964;
Estelle Sylvia Pankhurst, artist and feminist, 1960;

Sir Alfred East, painter and etcher, 1913;
Émile-Édouard-Charles-Antoine Zola, French novelist, 1902;
Louis Pasteur, French chemist, 1895;
Herman Melville, US novelist, 1891;
Étienne-Émile Gaboriau, French novelist, 1873;
Thomas Day, writer, 1789;
Andrea del Sarto, Italian painter, 1530.

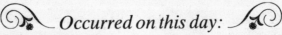

Occurred on this day:

German forces reached Warsaw, 1939;
The *Radio Times* was first published, 1923;
Marks and Spencer's first shop opened in Manchester, 1894;
Elizabeth Garrett Anderson was admitted to the register as the first qualified woman physician and surgeon in Britain, 1865;

God Save the King, the national anthem, was sung for the first time, at the Drury Lane Theatre, London, 1745;
Judge Jeffreys was appointed Lord Chancellor of England, 1685;
Admiral Blake defeated the Dutch Admiral Van Tromp off Dover, 1652;
The Persians were defeated by the Greeks at the Battle of Marathon, 490 BC.

TODAY IS THE FEAST DAY OF St Annemund or Chamond, St Eustochium of Bethlehem, St Exuperius or Soupire of Toulouse, St Faustus of Riez, St Ferreolus of Vienne, St Lioba and St Wenceslaus of Bohemia.

# 29th September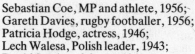

Born on this day:

Sebastian Coe, MP and athlete, 1956;
Gareth Davies, rugby footballer, 1956;
Patricia Hodge, actress, 1946;
Lech Walesa, Polish leader, 1943;
David Steele, cricketer, 1941;
John Dawes, rugby player and coach, 1940;
Jerry Lee Lewis, rock and roll singer and pianist, 1935;
Lance Gibbs, West Indies cricketer, 1934;
James Villiers, actor, 1933;
Anita Ekberg, Swedish actress, 1931;
Richard Bonynge, Australian conductor, 1930;
Lizabeth Scott, US film actress, 1922;
Carl Giles, cartoonist, 1916;
Stanley Kramer, US film producer, 1913;

Michelangelo Antonioni, Italian film director, 1912;
Gene Autry, US western film actor, 1911;
Greer Garson, film actress, 1908;
Enrico Fermi, US physicist, 1901;
Sir Billy Butlin, holiday camp pioneer, 1899;
Elizabeth Cleghorn Gaskell, novelist, 1810;
Horatio, Viscount Nelson, 1758;
Robert Clive, Baron Clive of Plassey, 1725;
François Boucher, French painter, 1703;
Miguel de Cervantes Saavedra, Spanish playwright and novelist, 1547;
Tintoretto [Jacopo Robusti], Italian painter, 1518.

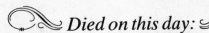 Died on this day:

Pope John Paul I [Albino Luciani], reigned only 33 days, 1978;
Bruce Bairnsfather, cartoonist, 1959;
Winifred Holtby, novelist, 1935;
Sir William Orpen, painter, 1931;

Willem Einthoven, physician, 1927;
Rudolf Diesel, German engineer, at sea, 1913;
Winslow Homer, US painter, 1910;
André Grétry, French composer, 1813.

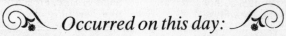 Occurred on this day:

Soviet troops invaded Yugoslavia, 1944;
The agreement between Germany and Italy, France and Britain was signed at Munich by Hitler, Mussolini, Daladier and Neville Chamberlain, 1938;
The Whitehall Theatre, London, opened, 1930;
The Allies broke through the German Hindenburg Line, 1918;
Italy declared war on Turkey over Tripoli, 1911;

The first London performance of the musical show *A Trip to Chinatown* was presented, 1894;
The police force inaugurated by Sir Robert Peel started duty in London, 1829;
The Congress of Aix-la-Chapelle started, 1818;
The New River, bringing water supplies to London, was opened, 1613;
Richard II abdicated the throne, and was deposed by Parliament, 1399.

TODAY IS THE FEAST DAY OF St Gabriel, St Michael and St Raphael, archangels, Saints Rhipsime, Gaiana and Companions and St Theodota of Philippolis.

 # 30th September

Born on this day:

Rula Lenska, actress, 1947;
Ian Ogilvy, film actor, 1943;
Anthony Green, painter, 1939;
Alan Hacker, US clarinettist, 1938;
Stewart Steven, editor, the *Mail on Sunday*, 1938;
Johnny Mathis, US ballad singer, 1937;
Angie Dickinson, US actress, 1931;
Truman Capote, US author, 1924;
Donald Swann, pianist and entertainer, 1923;
Deborah Kerr, actress, 1921;
David Fyodorovich Oistrakh, Russian violinist, 1908;
Michael Innes [J. I. M. Stewart], Oxford don and author, 1906;
Lewis Milestone, US film director, 1895;

Hermann Sudermann, German playwright, 1857;
William Willett, promoter of Daylight Saving, 1856;
Sir Charles Villiers Stanford, composer, 1852;
Johan Severin Svendsen, Norwegian composer, 1840;
Frederick Sleigh Roberts, 1st Earl, field marshal, 1832;
Karl Begas, German painter, 1794;
Fitzroy James Henry Somerset, 1st Baron Raglan, field marshal, 1788;
Jacques Necker, Swiss financier, 1732;
Étienne de Condillac, French philosopher, 1715.

Died on this day:

Simone Signoret [Simone Kaminker], French film actress, 1985;
James Dean, US film actor, killed, 1955;
Richard Austin Freeman, author and creator of 'Dr John Thorndyke', 1943;
Sir Robert Hadfield, metallurgist, 1940;
Frederick Edwin Smith, 1st Earl of Birkenhead, Lord Chancellor, 1930;

Georges-Ernest-Jean-Marie Boulanger, French general and politician, committed suicide, 1891;
Augustin-François-César Prouvençal de Saint-Hilaire, French botanist and traveller, 1853;
James Brindley, canal engineer, 1772;
George Whitefield, US religious leader, 1770;
Sir Fulke Greville, Lord Brooke, poet, murdered, 1628.

Occurred on this day:

Cinerama was first exhibited by the inventor, Fred Waller, in New York, 1952;
After 277,264 flights, the Berlin airlift ended, 1949;
Germany and the USSR signed a pact agreeing on the partition of Poland, 1939;
Identity cards were issued in Britain, 1939;
A British Expeditionary Force of 158,000 men was sent to France, 1939;
The *Morning Post* newspaper was last issued, 1937;
Gershwin's opera *Porgy and Bess* was first performed, Boston, 1935;

The first experimental TV broadcast by the BBC took place, 1929;
The discovery of penicillin was first announced, 1928;
Benito Mussolini formed the first Fascist government in Italy, 1922;
Artificial silk [rayon] was first patented, 1902;
Bizet's opera *The Pearl Fishers* was first performed, Paris, 1863;
Mozart's opera *The Magic Flute* was first performed, Vienna, 1791.

TODAY IS THE FEAST DAY OF St Gregory the Enlightener, St Honorius of Canterbury, St Jerome and St Simon of Crépy.

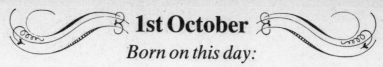

1st October

Born on this day:

Graham Leach, radio news foreign correspondent, 1948;
Geoffrey Whitehead, actor, 1939;
Julie Andrews, actress and singer, 1935;
Richard Harris, actor, 1933;
Laurence Harvey [Laruska Mischa Skikne], actor, 1928;
Sandy Gall, TV news presenter, 1927;
Jimmy Carter, 39th US president, 1924;
James Whitmore, US film actor, 1921;
Major David Jamieson, VC, 1920;
Walter Matthau, US film actor, 1920;
Stanley Holloway, actor and entertainer, 1890;
Paul Dukas, French composer, 1865;

Annie Besant, social reformer and theosophist, 1847;
Karl von Piloty, German painter, 1826;
Sir Robert Smirke, architect, 1781;
William Thomas Beckford, author and millionaire, 1759;
Paul I, Tsar of Russia, 1754;
Alessandro Stradella, Italian singer and composer, 1644;
Giovanni Matteo Asola, Italian priest and composer, 1609;
Giacomo da Vignola [Giacomo Barozzi], Italian architect, 1507;
King Henry III, 1207.

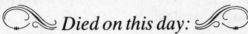

Died on this day:

Roy Harris, US composer, 1979;
Louis Seymour Bazett Leakey, anthropologist, 1972;
Ludwig Bemelmans, US author and illustrator for children, 1962;
Albert Von Tilzer, US composer and publisher, 1956;
Gregorio Martinez Sierra, Spanish poet and playwright, 1947;
Conway Tearle [Frederick Levy], US stage and film actor, 1938;

Wilhelm Dilthey, philosopher, 1911;
Benjamin Jowett, classical scholar, 1893;
Anthony Ashley Cooper, 7th Earl of Shaftesbury, social reformer, 1885;
Sir Edwin Henry Landseer, painter, 1873;
John Blow, organist and composer, 1708;
Pierre Corneille, French playwright, 1684;
Don John of Austria, soldier, 1578;
Marsilio Ficino, scholar and philosopher, 1499.

Occurred on this day:

In the USA, the Watergate trial started, 1974;
Nigeria became independent, 1960;
The People's Republic of China was proclaimed, 1949;
German forces entered the Sudetenland, 1938;
The Model T was introduced by Henry Ford, 1908;
Austria issued the first postcards, 1869;

The Midland Railway opened St Pancras Station, 1868;
The *News of the World* was first published, 1843;
Louisiana was ceded to France by Spain, 1800;
Belgium became part of the French Republic, 1795;
Money orders were first issued in Britain, 1792.

TODAY IS THE FEAST DAY OF St Bavo or Allowin, St Melorus or Mylor, St Remigius or Remi, St Romanus the Melodist and St Thérèse of Lisieux.

2nd October

Born on this day:

Sting [Gordon Sumner], rock singer, 1951;
Trevor Brooking, footballer, 1948;
Don McLean, US folk singer, 1945;
Anna Ford, broadcaster, 1943;
Peter Frankl, pianist, 1935;
Jan Morris, author, 1926;
The Most Rev. Lord Runcie, former
  Archbishop of Canterbury, 1921;
Lieut.-Col. Eric Wilson VC, 1912;
Lord Todd, OM, chemist, 1907;
Henry Graham Greene, novelist, 1904;
Ignatius Roy Dunnachie Campbell, South
  African poet, 1901;
Budd Abbot, US comedian, 1895;
Joseph-Ernest Renan, French historian and
  philosopher, 1892;
Julius ['Groucho'] Marx, US comedian,
  1890;

Wallace Stevens, US poet, 1879;
Cordell Hull, US statesman, 1871;
Mohandas Karamchand Gandhi, Indian
  leader, 1869;
Sir William Ramsay, chemist, 1852;
Ferdinand Foch, Marshal of France,
  1851;
Paul Ludwig Hans von Beneckendorf und
  von Hindenburg, German field marshal
  and president, 1847;
Hans Thoma, German painter, 1839;
Julius von Sachs, botanist and naturalist,
  1832;
Sir Edward Burnett Tylor, anthropologist,
  1832;
Mikhail Yuryevich Lermontov, Russian
  poet, 1814;
King Richard III, 1452.

Died on this day:

Rock Hudson [Roy Fitzgerald Scherer], US
  film actor, 1985;
Paavo Nurmi, Finnish athlete, 1973;
Marcel Duchamp [Henri-Pierre Roche],
  French surrealist painter, 1968;
Marie Stopes, birth control pioneer, 1958;
Sir Thomas Johnstone Lipton, sportsman
  and merchant, 1931;

Svante August Arrhenius, Swedish
  chemist, 1927;
Max Bruch, composer, 1920;
Samuel Adams, US statesman, 1803;
John André, English army officer,
  executed by George Washington for
  spying, 1780;
Isaac Oliver, miniature painter, 1617.

Occurred on this day:

Guinea became an independent republic,
  1958;
The musical show *Valmouth* was first
  produced in London, 1958;
The liner *Empress of Britain*, bound for
  Canada with refugees, was sunk, 1940;
The British Council received a Royal
  Charter, 1940;
Abyssinia [Ethiopia] was invaded by Italy,
  1935;

The first rugby football match was played at
  Twickenham, 1909;
The first Royal Naval submarine was
  launched at Barrow, 1901;
Rome became the capital city of Italy,
  1870;
Alkmaar in the Netherlands was captured
  by the Duke of York, 1799.

TODAY IS THE FEAST DAY OF St Eleutherius of Nicomedia, The Guardian Angels
and St Leger or Leodegarius.

3rd October

Born on this day:

John Suthern, jockey, 1951;
Christopher Bruce, dancer and choreographer, 1945;
Chubby Checker, rock singer, 1941;
Ruggero Raimondi, Italian operatic bass, 1941;
Steve Michael Reich, US composer, 1936;
Neale Fraser, tennis player, 1933;
Gore Vidal, US author, 1925;
Ray Lindwall, Australian cricketer, 1921;
James Herriot [James Wight], author, 1916;
Sir Michael Hordern, actor, 1911;
Leo McCarey, US film director, 1898;
Louis Aragon, French poet and novelist, 1897;
Alain Fournier [Henri-Alban Fournier], French writer, 1886;
Pierre Bonnard, French painter, 1867;
Eleanora Duse, Italian actress, 1858;
Sir Patrick Manson, physician and parasitologist, 1844;
Heinrich Panofka, German violinist and composer, 1807;
George Bancroft, US diplomat and historian, 1800.

Died on this day:

Jean Anouilh, French playwright, 1987;
Sir Henry Malcolm Watts Sargent, conductor, 1967;
Woody [Woodrow Wilson] Guthrie, US singer and composer, 1967;
Sir Arnold Edward Trevor Bax, composer, 1953;
Carl Nielsen, Danish composer, 1931;
Gustav Stresemann, German statesman, 1929;
William Morris, writer, artist and printer, 1896;
Hans Makart, Austrian painter, 1884;
Elias Howe, US sewing machine inventor, 1867;
Myles Standish, Pilgrim Fathers leader, 1656;
Vincenzo Campi, Italian painter, 1591.

Occurred on this day:

East and West Germany were reunited as the Federal Republic of Germany, 1990;
The first London production of the musical show *A Funny Thing Happened on the Way to the Forum* was presented, 1963;
The Bolshoi Ballet appeared at Covent Garden for the first time, 1956;
The first British atomic device was exploded in the Monte Bello islands, in the Pacific, 1952;
The Dominion Theatre, London, opened, 1929;
The name of the Kingdom of Serbs, Croats and Slovenes was changed to Yugoslavia, 1929;
The first London production of the musical show *Follow Through* was presented, 1929;
Tsar Ferdinand of Bulgaria abdicated, 1918;
Gilbert and Sullivan's *Yeomen of the Guard* was first performed at the Savoy Theatre, London, 1888.

TODAY IS THE FEAST DAY OF St Attilanus, St Froilan, St Gerard of Brogne, St Ewald the Dark, St Ewald the Fair, St Hesychius and St Thomas Cantelupe of Hereford.

 # 4th October

Born on this day:

Yvonne Murray, athlete, 1964;

Tony Meo, snooker champion, 1959;

Anneka Rice, TV presenter, 1958;

John Rutherford, rugby footballer, 1955;

Ann Widdecombe, MP, 1947;

Gavin Pritchard-Gordon, racehorse trainer, 1945;

Jackie Collins, author, 1937;

Basil D'Oliveira, cricketer, 1931;

Charlton Heston, US film actor, 1924;

Buster Keaton [Joseph Francis Keaton], US film comedian, 1895;

Engelbert Dollfuss, Austrian statesman, 1892;

Henri Gaudier-Brzeska, French sculptor, 1891;

Alfred Damon Runyon, US writer and journalist, 1884;

Admiral of the Fleet Sir Roger John Brownlow Keyes, 1st Baron, naval officer, 1862;

Frederic Remington, US painter, illustrator and sculptor, 1861;

Rutherford Birchard Hayes, 19th president of the USA, 1822;

Jean-François Millet, French painter, 1814;

François-Pierre-Guillaume Guizot, French historian and statesman, 1787;

Auguste-François-César Prouvençal de Saint Hilaire, French botanist and traveller, 1799;

Edmund Malone, Shakespearean scholar, 1741;

Giambattista Piranesi, Italian engraver, 1720;

Richard Cromwell, Lord Protector, 1626;

Lucas Cranach the Younger, German painter, 1515;

Lucas Cranach the Elder, German painter, 1472.

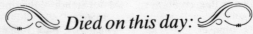 ## Died on this day:

Sir Arthur Whitten Brown, pioneer aviator, 1948;

Max Ludwig Planck, German physicist, 1947;

John Rennie, civil engineer, 1821;

Henry Carey, poet and musician, committed suicide, 1743;

Rembrandt Harmenszoon van Rijn, Dutch painter, 1669;

Alonso Cano, Spanish painter, architect and sculptor, 1667;

Francesco Albani [Albano], Italian painter, 1660;

Benozzo Gozzoli [Benozzo di Lese], Italian painter, 1497.

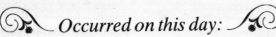 ## Occurred on this day:

The first close-up pictures of the moon were made from the Soviet *Lunik III*, 1959;

The first transatlantic passenger jet service started operating, 1958;

The world's first artificial satellite, *Sputnik I*, was launched by the USSR, 1957;

The first public escalator was opened at Earl's Court underground station, 1911;

The Boys Brigade was founded in Glasgow by Sir William Smith, 1883;

The independence of Belgium was proclaimed, 1830;

George Washington was defeated at Germantown, 1777;

Miles Coverdale's translation of the Bible was published, 1535.

TODAY IS THE FEAST DAY OF St Ammon, St Francis of Assisi and St Petronius of Bologna.

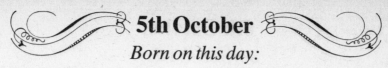

5th October

Born on this day:

Bob Geldof, Hon. KBE, Irish rock singer
and philanthropist, 1954;
Dave Watson, footballer, 1946;
Diane Cilento, actress, 1933;
David Mellor, silversmith and designer,
1930;
Herbert Kretzmer, journalist and lyricist,
1925;
Barbara Kelly, actress and broadcaster,
1924;
Glynis Johns, actress, 1923;
Robin Bailey, actor, 1919;
Robert Kee, author and broadcaster, 1919;
Donald Pleasance, actor, 1919;
Joshua Lockwood Logan, US film and stage
director, 1908;

Jean-Baptiste-Édouard Detaille, French
painter, 1848;
John Addington Symonds, poet, critic and
historian, 1840;
Chester Alan Arthur, 21st president of the
USA, 1830;
William Scoresby, Arctic explorer,
1789;
Charles-Geneviève-Louis-Auguste-André-
Timothé d'Éon de Beaumont [Chevalier
d'Éon], French spy and transvestite,
1728;
Denis Diderot, French scholar and
encyclopaedist, 1713;
Francesco Guardi, Venetian painter,
1712.

Died on this day:

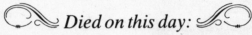

Nelson Smock Riddle, US composer and
arranger, 1985;
Jean Vigo, French film director, 1934;
William Heinemann, publisher and
playwright, 1920;
Hans von Bartels, German painter, 1913;
Jacques Offenbach [Jakob Levy Eberst],
French composer, 1880;
Sir Francis Grant, Scottish portrait painter,
1878;

'Barry Cornwall' [Bryan Waller Procter],
poet, 1874;
Charles, 1st Marquess Cornwallis,
statesman and soldier, 1805;
Lodovico Ferrari, mathematician,
1565;
Joachim de Patenier [Patinir], Dutch
painter, 1524;
Philip III ['the Bold'], King of France,
1285.

Occurred on this day:

Tea rationing ended in Britain, 1952;
The march of unemployed shipyard
workers from Jarrow to London started,
1936;
The British airship *R101* crashed near
Beauvais, France, with the loss of 48
lives, 1930;
The Allies landed at Salonika, 1915;
The first air battle took place between
German and French aircraft, 1914;
Tripoli was occupied by Italian troops,
1911;

In Portugal, King Manoel, having fled the
country, was deposed and a republic
declared, 1910;
Bulgaria declared its independence from
Turkey, and Ferdinand I became Tsar,
1908;
The first production of the musical show *A
Chinese Honeymoon* was presented,
London, 1901;
The United States was victorious at the
Battle of the Thames, Ontario, 1813;
Spain declared war on Britain, 1796.

TODAY IS THE FEAST DAY OF St Apollinaris of Valence, St Flora of Beaulieu, St
Galla, St Magenulf or Meinulf and St Maurus.

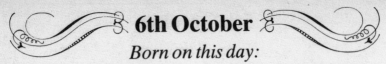

6th October

Born on this day:

Clive Rees, rugby international, 1951;

Tony Greig, cricketer, 1946;

Melvyn Bragg, writer and TV presenter, 1939;

Anna Quayle, actress, 1937;

Richie Benaud, Australian cricket commentator, 1930;

Tommy Lawton, footballer, 1919;

Dr Thor Heyerdahl, Norwegian explorer and anthropologist, 1914;

Baroness Castle, former MP and MEP, 1910;

Helen Wills Moody [Roark], US former tennis player, 1905;

Milton Ager, US popular composer, 1893;

Le Corbusier [Charles-Édouard Jeanneret], Swiss architect and town planner, 1887;

Karol Maciej Szymanowski, Polish composer, 1883;

George Westinghouse, US inventor of the airbrake, 1846;

Jenny [Johanna Maria] Lind, Swedish operatic soprano, 1820;

Thomas Keightley, author, 1789;

Louis-Philippe, 'Citizen King' of France, 1773;

Nevil Maskelyne, Astronomer Royal, 1732;

Matteo Ricci, Italian Jesuit missionary, 1552.

Died on this day:

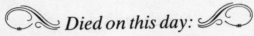

Anwar Sadat, president of Egypt, assassinated, 1981;

Sir John Gilbert, painter and illustrator, 1897;

George Louis Palmella du Maurier, novelist and artist, 1896;

Ford Madox Brown, painter, 1893;

Alfred, 1st Baron Tennyson, poet, 1892;

Charles Stewart Parnell, Irish political leader, 1891;

William Henry Smith, newsagent, bookseller and statesman, 1891;

Jules Dupré, French painter, 1889;

William Tyndale, Bible translator, strangled and burnt at the stake, 1536;

Charles II [the Bald], Holy Roman Emperor, 877.

Occurred on this day:

The first production of the musical show *Nymph Errant* was presented, London, 1933;

Chiang Kai-shek became president of China, 1928;

The Jazz Singer, the first feature-length talking film, began showing in New York, 1927;

Austria annexed Bosnia and Herzegovina, 1908;

Manchester University was opened, 1903;

In the USA, the Mormons in Utah renounced bigamy, 1890;

The Rainhill trials of railway locomotives began, 1829;

Captain Cook landed in New Zealand, 1769.

TODAY IS THE FEAST DAY OF St Bruno, St Faith of Agen, St Mary Frances of Naples and St Nicetas of Constantinople.

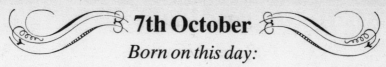

7th October

Born on this day:

Jayne Torvill, ice dance champion, 1957;
Yo Yo Ma, cellist, 1955;
Graham Yallop, Australian cricketer, 1952;
Clive James, Australian critic and TV
  presenter, 1939;
Christopher Booker, journalist and author,
  1937;
Thomas Keneally, author, 1935;
Dr Mark Girouard, architectural historian,
  1931;
The Most Rev. Desmond Tutu, Archbishop
  of Cape Town, 1931;
Yaltah Menuhin, pianist, 1921;
June Allyson, US film actress, 1917;

Joseph Cooper, pianist and broadcaster,
  1912;
Shura Cherkassky, pianist, 1911;
Richard Caldicot, actor, 1908;
Heinrich Himmler, Nazi head of the SS,
  1900;
Niels Henrik David Bohr, Danish physicist,
  1885;
James Whitcomb Riley, US poet, 1849;
Maj.-Gen. Sir Ralph Abercromby, soldier,
  1734;
William Laud, Archbishop of Canterbury,
  1573.

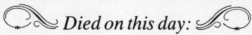

Died on this day:

Sir Norman Angell [Ralph Norman Angell
  Lane], author and journalist, 1967;
Clarence Birdseye, US inventor of quick-
  freezing, 1956;
Christopher Richard Wynne Nevinson,
  painter, 1946;
Marguerite Radclyffe Hall, author, 1943;
Charles de Souzy Ricketts, artist, 1931;
Marie Lloyd [Matilda Alice Victoria
  Wood], music hall comedienne, 1922;
Sir Charles Hubert Hastings Parry,
  composer, 1918;

Oliver Wendell Holmes, US physician and
  writer, 1894;
Thomas Woolner, sculptor and poet,
  1892;
William Barnes, Dorset dialect poet,
  1886;
Edgar Allan Poe, US novelist, 1849;
Paul Bril, Flemish painter, 1626;
Giovanni Battista Guarini, Italian poet,
  1612;
George Gascoigne, poet and playwright,
  1577.

Occurred on this day:

The *Independent* was first published, 1986;
The first pictures of the far side of the moon
  were taken by the Soviet spacecraft
  Lunik III, 1959;
The London Philharmonic Orchestra gave
  its first performance at Queen's Hall,
  1932;
The Westminster Theatre, London,
  opened, 1931;

The Dutch airline KLM [Koninklijke
  Luchtvaart Maatschappij] was founded,
  1919;
The Great Chicago Fire began, when over
  250 people were killed and 95,000 made
  homeless, 1871;
The Battle of Lepanto was fought, when
  Don John defeated the Turks in a naval
  engagement, 1571.

TODAY IS THE FEAST DAY OF St Artaldus or Arthaud, St Helanus, St Justina of
Padua, St Mark, pope and St Osyth.

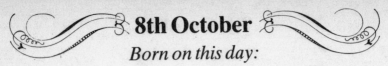

8th October

Born on this day:

Dame Merle Park, director of the Royal Ballet School, 1937;
David Carradine, US actor, 1936;
Albert Roux, chef de cuisine, 1935;
Ray Reardon, snooker champion, 1932;
Toru Takemitsu, Japanese composer, 1930;
Betty Boothroyd, MP, the Speaker, 1929;
Neil Harvey, Australian cricketer, 1928;
Bill Maynard, TV actor and comedian, 1928;
Peter Wood, theatre and TV director, 1928;
Godfrey Talbot, author, broadcaster and former BBC Court correspondent, 1908;
Milner Gray, artist and designer, 1899;
Rouben Mamoulian, US film director, 1898;
Juan Perón, president of Argentina, 1895;

Eddie Rickenbacker [Edward Vernon Rickenbacher], US fighter pilot in WWI, 1890;
Ernst Kretschmer, German psychologist, 1888;
Sir Alfred John Munnings, artist, 1878;
John Cowper Powys, novelist, 1872;
Henri-Louis Le Châtelier, French chemist, 1850;
Montagu William Lowry-Corry, 1st Baron Rowton, founder of Rowton Houses for working men, 1838;
Alicia [Alison] Cockburn [Rutherford], poet, 1713;
Heinrich Schütz [Sagittarius], German composer, 1585.

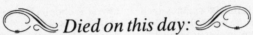

Died on this day:

Clement Richard Attlee, 1st Earl, statesman, 1967;
Kathleen Mary Ferrier, contralto, 1953;
Gus Kahn, US lyricist, 1941;
Sir John Monash, commander of the Australian Army Corps in France in WWI, 1931;
Franklin Pierce, 14th president of the USA, 1869;

Richard Earlom, mezzotint engraver, 1822;
Count Vittorio Alfieri, Italian poet, 1803;
Pierre Fournier, French typographer and engraver, 1768;
Henry Fielding, novelist, 1754;
Jan Massys, Flemish painter, 1575;
Cola di Rienzi, Italian reformer, murdered, 1354.

Occurred on this day:

Britain's first legal commercial radio station, LBC, started transmitting, 1973;
The Post Office Tower, London, opened, 1965;
The first London production of the musical show *The King and I* was presented, 1953;
At Harrow and Wealdstone, London, 112 people were killed and 340 injured in a collision between a local and an express train, 1952;

Western Poland was made part of the German Reich, 1939;
The Saville Theatre, London, opened, 1931;
The Battle of Loos ended, 1915;
Charles Nessler first used a permanent waving machine on a woman's hair, 1905;
Bechuanaland was proclaimed British territory, 1885;
King's College, London, was opened, 1831.

TODAY IS THE FEAST DAY OF St Demetrius, St Simeon Senex, St Keyne, St Marcellus, St Pelagia [or Margaret] the Penitent, St Reparata of Caesarea and St Thaïs.

9th October

Born on this day:

Steve Ovett, athlete, 1955;
Geoff Cook, cricketer, 1951;
John Winston Lennon, former Beatle, 1940;
Denzil Davies, MP, 1938;
Brian Blessed, actor, 1937;
HRH the Duke of Kent, 1935;
Paul Channon, MP, 1935;
Don McCullin, war photographer, 1935;
Bill Tidy, cartoonist, 1933;
Donald Sinden, actor, 1923;
Irmgard Seefried, German soprano, 1919;
Earl St Aldwyn, politician, 1912;
The Rt. Rev. Lord Coggan, former Archbishop of Canterbury, 1909;

Jacques Tati [Tatischeff], French actor and film director, 1908;
Lord Hailsham of St Marylebone CH, 1907;
Alastair Sim, actor, 1900;
Nikolai Ivanovich Bukharin, Russian leader, 1888;
Max Theodor Felix von Laue, German physicist, 1879;
Charles-Camille Saint-Saëns, French composer, 1835;
Giuseppi Bonomi [The Younger], sculptor and draughtsman, 1796;
Charles X, King of France, 1757;
Robert de Sorbon, founder of the Paris college of the Sorbonne, 1201.

Died on this day:

Che [Ernesto] Guevara, South American Marxist revolutionary, captured and shot, 1967;
André Maurois [Emile Salomon Wilhelm Herzog], French writer, 1967;
Pope Pius XII [Eugenio Pacelli], 1958;

Karl Friedrich Schinkel, German architect and painter, 1841;
Barbara Villiers, Duchess of Cleveland, mistress of King Charles II, 1709;
Gabriel Fallopius, Italian anatomist, 1562;
Robert Grosseteste, theologian, 1253.

Occurred on this day:

Uganda became independent, 1962;
The first London production of the musical show *Porgy and Bess* was presented, 1952;
King Alexander of Yugoslavia and Louis Barthou, French foreign minister, were assassinated in Marseilles by a Croatian terrorist, 1934;
The first petrol-driven motor bus began operating in London, 1899;

The Universal Postal Union was founded in Rome, 1875;
Hobart, Tasmania, was founded, 1804;
The first Luddite riots began in Manchester against the introduction of machinery for spinning cotton, 1779;
Yale College, in the United States, received its charter, 1701.

TODAY IS THE FEAST DAY OF Saints Andronicus and Athanasia, St Demetrius of Alexandria, St Denis or Dionysius of Paris, St Dionysius the Areopagite, Saints Eleutherius and Rusticus, St Ghislain or Gislenus, St Louis Bertrán, St John Leonardi, St Publia and St Savin.

10th October

Born on this day:

Laura Davies, golfer, 1963;
Fiona Fullerton, actress, 1956;
Charles Dance, actor, 1946;
Ben Vereen, US actor, 1946;
Winston S. Churchill, MP, 1940;
Ted Edgar, show jumper, 1935;
Daniel Massey, actor, 1933;
Harold Pinter, playwright, 1930;
Nicholas Parsons, broadcaster, 1928;
James Clavell, novelist and screenwriter, 1926;
Thelonius Sphere Monk, US pianist and pioneer of 'bop', 1918;
Alberto Giacometti, Swiss sculptor, 1901;
Helen Hayes, US actress, 1900;
William Richard Morris, 1st Viscount Nuffield, 1877;
Charles Conder, artist, 1868;

Fridtjof Nansen, Norwegian explorer and statesman, 1861;
Rufus Daniel Isaacs, 1st Marquess of Reading, 1860;
Isabella II, Queen of Spain, 1830;
Stephanus Johannes Paulus Kruger, farmer and Boer statesman, 1825;
Giuseppe Fortunino Francesco Verdi, Italian composer, 1813;
Hugh Miller, geologist and writer, 1802;
Benjamin West, painter, 1738;
Henry Cavendish, physicist and chemist, 1731;
Jean-Antoine Watteau, French painter, 1684;
Jacobus Arminius [Hermansen], Dutch theologian, 1560.

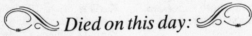 Died on this day:

Yul Brynner [Youl Bryner], US film actor, 1985;
George Orson Welles, US actor and producer, 1985;
Sir Ralph David Richardson, actor, 1983;
Sir Cyril Lodowic Burt, psychologist, 1971;
Édouard Daladier, French statesman, 1970;

Eddie Cantor [Edward Israel Iskowitz], US entertainer and actor, 1964;
Edith Piaf [Edith Giovanna Gassion], French singer, 1963;
King Carol [Karl Eitel Friedrich] of Romania, 1914;
François-Marie-Charles Fourier, French social theorist, 1837;
Fra Filippo Lippi, Italian painter, 1469.

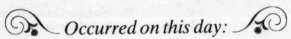 Occurred on this day:

After being fined $10,000 for income tax evasion, Spiro Agnew resigned as US vice-president, 1973;
Sir John Betjeman became Poet Laureate, 1972;
Fiji became independent, 1970;
Gershwin's *Porgy and Bess* opened in New York City, 1935;
The Savoy Theatre, London, opened with a performance of *Patience* by Gilbert and Sullivan, 1881;

The fourth and present building of the Theatre Royal, Drury Lane, opened, 1812;
The Saracens were defeated by the Franks under Charles Martel at the Battle of Tours, 732.

TODAY IS THE FEAST DAY OF St Cerbonius, St Daniel, Saints Eulampius and Eulampia, St Francis Borgia, St Gereon, St Maharsapor and St Paulinus of York.

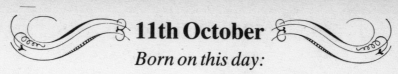

11th October

Born on this day:

Dawn French, actress and comedienne, 1957;

David Rendall, tenor, 1948;

Alan Pascoe, former Olympic hurdler, 1947;

Maria Bueno, tennis player, 1939;

Bobby Charlton, footballer, 1937;

Richard Burton [Richard Walter Jenkins], actor, 1925;

Jerome Robbins, US choreographer, 1918;

Ethel Edith Mannin, novelist and travel writer, 1900;

François Mauriac, French author, 1885;

Friedrich Bergius, German chemist, 1884;

Anna Eleanor Roosevelt, US writer and lecturer, 1884;

Sir John Bernard Partridge, artist and cartoonist, 1861;

Henry John Heinz, US food-products magnate, 1844;

Sir George Williams, merchant and founder of the YMCA, 1821;

Joseph Gillott, pen manufacturer, 1799;

Heinrich Wilhelm Matthäus Olbers, German astronomer, 1758;

James Barry, Irish historical painter, 1741;

Arthur Phillip, admiral and 1st governor of New South Wales, 1738.

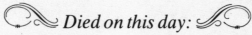

Died on this day:

Jean Cocteau, French poet, playwright and film-director, 1963;

Leonard ['Chico'] Marx, US comedian, 1961;

Maurice de Vlaminck, French painter, 1958;

Jean-Henri Fabre, French entomologist, 1915;

Léon Boëllmann, French composer, 1897;

Josef Anton Bruckner, Austrian composer, 1896;

James Prescott Joule, physicist, 1889;

Samuel Wesley, composer and organist, 1837;

Meriwether Lewis, US explorer, 1809;

Huldrych Zwingli, Swiss religious reformer, killed in battle, 1531.

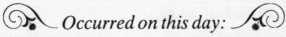

Occurred on this day:

The *Apollo 7* spacecraft, with a crew of three, was launched from Cape Kennedy, 1968;

Enormous inflation overtook German currency, with the mark dropping to an exchange rate of 10,000,000,000 to the pound, 1923;

The Anglo-Boer War started, 1899;

The Chicago Fire ended, having almost completely destroyed the city at a cost of $196 million, 1871;

During the Irish Rebellion, a Dutch fleet aiding the rebels was defeated off Camperdown [Kamperduin] by Admiral Adam Duncan, 1797;

Peter the Great became Tsar of Russia, 1669;

The title 'Defender of the Faith' was conferred on Henry VIII by Pope Leo X, 1521;

The Order of the Bath was constituted, 1399.

TODAY IS THE FEAST DAY OF St Agilbert, St Alexander Sauli, Saints Andronicus, Tarachus, and Probus, St Bruno the Great of Cologne, St Canice or Kenneth, St Gummarus or Gomaire, St Mary Soledad and St Nectarius of Constantinople.

12th October

Born on this day:

David Threlfall, actor, 1953;
Angela Rippon, TV presenter, 1944;
Luciano Pavarotti, operatic tenor, 1935;
Magnus Magnusson, TV quizmaster and writer, 1929;
Jaroslav Drobny, former tennis player, 1921;
Kenneth Griffith, actor, writer and documentary film maker, 1921;
Luís de Freitas Branco, Portuguese composer, 1890;
Sir Godfrey Seymour Tearle, actor, 1884;
Aleister Edward Alexander Crowley, author and occultist, 1875;

Ralph Vaughan Williams, composer, 1872;
James Ramsay MacDonald, statesman, 1866;
Elmer Ambrose Sperry, US inventor, 1860;
Helen Modjeska [Helena Modrzejewska, formerly Jadwiga Opid], Polish actress, 1844;
Theodore Walter Watts-Dunton, poet, critic and novelist, 1832;
John Liptrott Hatton, composer, 1809;
Pedro I [Antonio Pedro de Alcantara Bourbon], emperor of Brazil, 1798;
King Edward VI, 1537.

Died on this day:

Sonja Henie, Norwegian skater and film actress, 1969;
Tom Mix [Thomas Edwin Mix], US western film actor, 1940;
Anatole France [Jacques-Anatole Thibault], French author, 1924;
Edith Louisa Cavell, nurse, executed by the Germans, 1915;
François-Pierre Guizot, French statesman and historian, 1874;
Robert Edward Lee, Confederate general, 1870;

Robert Stephenson, civil engineer, 1859;
Ando Tokitaro Hiroshige, Japanese artist, 1858;
Elizabeth Fry [Gurney], Quaker prison reformer, 1845;
Carel Fabritius [Pieterz], Dutch painter, killed, 1654;
Piero della Francesca, Italian painter and writer, 1492.

Occurred on this day:

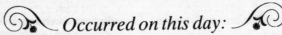

In the USA, Gerald Ford was nominated vice-president by Richard Nixon, 1973;
Equatorial Guinea became independent, 1968;
The first Morris Minor car designed by Alec Issigonis was produced at Cowley, Oxon, 1948;

An iron lung was used for the first time, at Boston, Mass., USA, 1928;
The German Zeppelin Z3 flew from Friedrichshafen to Lakehurst, New Jersey, 1924;
The French fleet was defeated off Vigo by Admiral Sir George Rooke, 1702.

TODAY IS THE FEAST DAY OF St Edwin, St Ethelburga of Barking, Saints Felix and Cyprian, St Maximilian of Lorch and St Wilfrid of York.

13th October

Born on this day:

Marie Osmond, US singer, 1959;

Edwina Currie, MP, 1946;

John Shaw, cricketer, 1941;

Paul Simon, US singer and songwriter, 1941;

Baroness Thatcher [Margaret Thatcher], former prime minister, 1925;

Rosemary Anne Sisson, author and scriptwriter, 1923;

Yves Montand [Ivo Livi], French singer and actor, 1921;

Laraine Day, US film actress, 1920;

Harry Bentley, golfer, 1907;

Conrad Michael Richter, US novelist, 1890;

Walter James Redfern Turner, poet, music critic and playwright, 1889;

Mary Henrietta Kingsley, writer and explorer, 1862;

Lillie Langtry [Emilie Charlotte Le Breton], actress, 1853;

Sir James Thomas Knowles, editor and architect, 1831;

Rudolf Ludwig Karl Virchow, pathologist, 1821;

Allan Ramsay, Scottish portrait painter, 1713.

Died on this day:

Sidney James Webb, 1st Baron Passfield, social reformer, 1947;

Saul Gutmanovich Tchernichowsky, Hebrew poet, 1943;

David Devant, illusionist, 1941;

Willie Clarkson, theatrical costumier and wigmaker, 1934;

Sir Henry Irving [John Henry Brodribb], actor, 1905;

Maximilian I Joseph, King of Bavaria, 1825;

Antonio Canova, Italian sculptor, 1822;

Joachim Murat, King of the Two Sicilies, executed, 1815;

Robert Nugent, 1st Earl, politician and poet, 1788;

Nicolas de Malebranche, French philosopher, 1715;

Pope Gregory XII, 1417;

Claudius I, Roman emperor, poisoned by his wife Agrippina, 54.

Occurred on this day:

The first London production of the musical show *The Pajama Game* was presented, 1955;

Athens was liberated by the Allies, 1944;

Italy declared war on Germany, 1943;

Ankara became the new capital of Turkey, 1923;

41 people were killed during a German air raid on London, 1915;

Greenwich was adopted as the universal meridian at the Washington Conference, 1884;

British forces defeated the Americans at the Battle of Queenston Heights, 1812;

The foundation stone of the White House, Washington, was laid by President George Washington, 1792;

Benedict Arnold was defeated at Lake Champlain, 1776;

The arrest of the Templars for heresy took place in Paris, on the orders of Philip IV, 1307.

TODAY IS THE FEAST DAY OF St Coloman, St Comgan, St Edward the Confessor, St Faustus of Cordova, St Gerald of Aurillac, Saints Januarius and Martial and St Maurice of Carnoët.

14th October

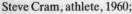

Born on this day:

Steve Cram, athlete, 1960;
William Jarvis, racehorse trainer, 1960;
Thomas Dolby, rock band keyboard player, 1958;
Roland Butcher, West Indies cricketer, 1953;
Françoise Pascal, French actress, 1949;
Roger Taylor, tennis player, 1941;
Cliff Richard, singer, 1940;
Christopher Timothy, actor, 1940;
Roger Moore, film actor, 1927;
Allan Jones, US film actor and singer, 1907;
Lillian Gish, US film actress, 1899;
e.e. cummings [Edward Estlin Cummings], US poet and painter, 1894.
Dwight David Eisenhower, 34th president of the USA, 1890;

Katherine Mansfield [Beauchamp] [Kathleen Middleton Murry], writer, 1888;
Éamon de Valera, Irish statesman, 1882;
Masaoka Shiki, Japanese poet, 1867;
Adolphe-Joseph-Thomas Monticelli, French painter, 1824;
Sir Edward Sabine, astronomer, 1788;
Ferdinand VII, King of Spain, 1784;
William Penn, Quaker founder of Pennsylvania, 1644;
James II, King of Great Britain and Ireland, 1633;
Cornelis Janssen [van Ceulen], Flemish painter, 1593;
Alessio Baldovinetti, Florentine painter, 1427.

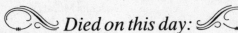

Died on this day:

Leonard Bernstein, US conductor and composer, 1990;
Keenan [Francis Xavier Aloysius] Wynn, US character actor, 1986;
Bing [Harry Lillis] Crosby, US singer, 1977;
Dame Edith Mary Evans, actress, 1976;

Errol Flynn, film actor, 1959;
Erwin Johannes Eugen Rommel, German general, committed suicide, 1944;
Dame Marie Tempest [Mary Susan Etherington], actress, 1942;
King Harold, killed in battle, 1066.

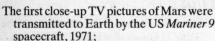

Occurred on this day:

The first close-up TV pictures of Mars were transmitted to Earth by the US *Mariner 9* spacecraft, 1971;
The first London production of the musical show *Can-Can* was presented, 1954;
Charles Yeager made the first supersonic air flight [670 mph] in California, 1947;
The musical show *Hide and Seek* was first produced, London, 1937;

Oxford degrees were first conferred on women, 1920;
The musical show *A Gaiety Girl* was first produced, London, 1893;
The Battle of Hastings was fought at Senlac Hill, Pevensey, Sussex, 1066;
William I acceded to the throne of England, 1066.

TODAY IS THE FEAST DAY OF St Angadriama, St Burchard of Würzburg, St Callixtus I, pope, St Dominic Lauricatus, St Justus of Lyons, St Manaccus and St Manechildis.

15th October

Born on this day:

HRH the Duchess of York, 1959;
Roscoe Tanner, US tennis player, 1952;
Richard Carpenter, US singer, 1946;
Perrie Mans, South African snooker player, 1940;
Keith Fordyce, radio presenter, 1928;
Mario Puzo, US novelist, 1920;
Prof. Arthur Schlesinger, US author and former presidential aide, 1917;
Charles Percy Snow [Baron Snow], scientist, civil servant and novelist, 1905;
George Sava, author and surgeon, 1903;
Mervyn Le Roy, US film director, 1900;
Melville Cooper, actor, 1896;
S.S. Van Dine [William Huntington Wright], US mystery writer, 1888;
Sir Pelham Grenville Wodehouse, novelist, 1881;

John Lawrence Sullivan, US champion heavyweight boxer, 1858;
Friedrich Wilhelm Nietzsche, German philosopher, 1844;
James-Joseph-Jacques Tissot, French painter and illustrator, 1836;
Mikhail Yuryevich Lermontov, Russian poet and novelist, 1814;
Wilhelm von Kaulbach, German painter, 1805;
Allan Ramsay, poet, 1686;
Evangelista Torricelli, Italian physicist, 1608;
Akbar the Great, Mogul emperor, 1542;
Virgil [Publius Vergilius Maro], Roman poet, 70 BC.

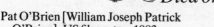
Died on this day:

Pat O'Brien [William Joseph Patrick O'Brien], US film actor, 1983;
Cole Albert Porter, US composer and lyricist, 1964;
Hermann Goering, Nazi leader, committed suicide, 1946;
Pierre Laval, Vichy Government leader, executed, 1945;
Raymond-Nicolas-Landry Poincaré, French statesman, 1934;
Mata Hari [Margaretha Geertruide Zelle], executed for espionage, 1917;

Letitia Elizabeth Landon, poet and novelist, 1838;
Tadeusz Andrzej Bonawentura Kościuszko, Polish patriot, killed, 1817;
Antoine de la Mothe Cadillac, French explorer, 1730;
Adam Frans van der Meulen, Flemish painter, 1690;
Simone Cantarini [Il Pesarese], Italian painter and etcher, 1648;
Pope Gregory XIV, 1591.

Occurred on this day:

The airship *Graf Zeppelin* completed its first transatlantic flight, 1928;
In World War I, Bulgaria joined the Central Powers, 1915;
The Comedy Theatre, London, opened, 1881;
Cologne Cathedral was solemnly opened, 1880;

The Gaiety Theatre, London, opened as the Strand Musick Hall, 1864;
Pilâtre de Rozier was the first man to make a balloon ascent, 1783;
The new calendar, as promulgated by Pope Gregory XIII, came into force in Italy and Spain, when 5th October became 15th October, 1582.

TODAY IS THE FEAST DAY OF St Euthymius the Younger, St Leonard of Vandoeuvre, St Teresa of Avila and St Thecla of Kitzingen.

16th October

Born on this day:

Michael Forsyth, MP, 1954;
Terry Griffiths, snooker champion, 1947;
Simon Ward, actor, 1940;
Peter Bowles, actor, 1936;
Günter Grass, German novelist, 1927;
Angela Lansbury, film actress, 1925;
Max Bygraves, entertainer, 1922;
Robert Urquhart, actor, 1922;
Michael Collins, Irish leader, 1890;
Eugene Gladstone O'Neill, US playwright, 1888;
David Ben Gurion, Israeli statesman, 1886;

Sir Joseph Austen Chamberlain, statesman, 1863;
Oscar Fingall O'Flahertie Wills Wilde, Irish playwright and author, 1854;
Arnold Böcklin, Swiss painter, 1827;
Robert Stephenson, civil engineer, 1803;
Noah Webster, US lexicographer, 1758;
Daniel Nikolaus Chodowiecki, Polish engraver and painter, 1726;
Victor Albrecht von Haller, Swiss biologist and poet, 1708;
James II, King of Scotland, 1430.

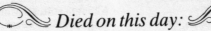

Died on this day:

Cornel Wilde [Cornelius Louis Wilde], US film actor, 1989;
George Catlett Marshall, US general and statesman, 1959;
Liaquat Ali Khan, prime minister of Pakistan, assassinated, 1951;
Sir Granville Bantock, composer, 1946;
Joseph Strutt, author, artist and antiquary, 1802;
John Hunter, surgeon and anatomist, 1793;
Marie Antoinette Austrian princess and Queen of King Louis XVI of France, executed, 1793;

Robert Fergusson, Scottish vernacular poet, 1774;
Jan Pieterszoon Sweelinck, Dutch organist and composer, 1621;
Hugh Latimer, bishop and Protestant martyr, burnt at the stake, 1555;
Nicholas Ridley, bishop and Protestant martyr, burnt at the stake, 1555;
Lucas Cranach the Elder, German painter, 1553;
Luca Signorelli, Italian painter, 1523.

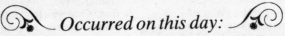

Occurred on this day:

Harold Wilson became prime minister, 1964;
German forces advanced to within 96 kilometres of Moscow, 1941;
The *Daily Graphic* newspaper was last issued, 1926;
The Simplon II railway tunnel was completed, 1922;

The first detention centre was opened at Borstal, Rochester, Kent, 1902;
The People newspaper [now the *Sunday People*] was first published, 1881;
The Eddystone Lighthouse, built by John Smeaton, was officially opened, 1759.

TODAY IS THE FEAST DAY OF St Anastasius of Cluny, St Bercharius, St Bertrand of Comminges, St Gall, St Gerard Majella, St Hedwig, St Lull, St Margaret-Mary, Saints Martinian and Maxima and St Mommolinus.

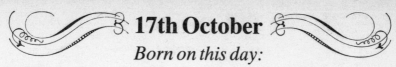

17th October

Born on this day:

Margot Kidder, Canadian actress, 1948;
Stephen Bishop-Kovacevich, concert
  pianist, 1940;
Ann Jones, tennis player, 1938;
Alan Garner, author, 1934;
Johnny Haynes, footballer, 1934;
Harry Carpenter, journalist and TV
  commentator on boxing, 1925;
George Mackay Brown, author, 1921;
Lord Kilbracken, author and journalist,
  1920;
Montgomery Clift, US film actor, 1920;
Rita Hayworth [Margarita Carmen
  Cansino], US film actress, 1918;
Arthur Miller, US playwright, 1915;
Jean Arthur [Gladys Georgianna Greene],
  US film actress, 1905;

Nathanael West [Nathan Wallenstein
  Weinstein], US novelist, 1903;
Spring Byington, US film actress, 1893;
Baroness Karen Blixen [Isak Dinesen],
  Danish author, 1885;
Elinor Glyn, novelist, 1864;
Karl Georg Büchner, German playwright,
  1813;
Claude-Henri, Comte de Saint-Simon,
  French economist and social reformer,
  1760;
John Wilkes, political reformer and
  journalist, 1727;
Nathan Field, actor and playwright,
  baptised, 1587.

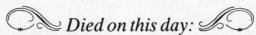

Died on this day:

Sidney Joseph Perelman, US humorist,
  1979;
Julia Ward Howe, US author of *The Battle
  Hymn of the Republic*, 1910;
Charles Wellington Furse, painter, 1904;
Marie-Edmé-Patrice-Maurice Mac-
  Mahon, Marshal of France, statesman,
  1893;
Gustav Robert Kirchhoff, German
  physicist, 1887;
Frédéric-François [Fryderyk Franciszek]
  Chopin, Polish composer, 1849;

George Colman [the Younger], playwright,
  1836;
John Brown, physician and medical
  reformer, 1788;
Edward, 1st Baron Hawke, admiral of the
  fleet, 1781;
René-Antoine-Ferchault de Réaumur,
  French scientist, 1757;
Sir Philip Sidney, poet, soldier and courtier,
  died of septicaemia after being wounded,
  Arnhem, 1586.

Occurred on this day:

The musical show *And So to Bed* was first
  produced, London, 1951;
In the United States, Al Capone,
  bootlegger, was sentenced to 11 years in
  jail for income tax evasion, 1931;
Cyrano de Bergerac was the first radio play
  broadcast in Britain from 2MT Writtle,
  1922;
Over 3,000 people died during an
  earthquake in Greece and Asia Minor,
  1914;

The Duchess of Dantzig, a comic opera by
  Henry Hamilton and Ivan Caryll, was
  first produced, London, 1903;
British troops defeated the Boers at
  Glencoe, 1899;
Napoleon was exiled and arrived on the
  island of St Helena, 1815.

TODAY IS THE FEAST DAY OF St Anstrudis or Austrude, Saints Ethelbert and
Ethelred, St Ignatius of Antioch, St John the Dwarf, St Nothelm, St Rule, St Seraphino and
The Ursuline Martyrs of Valenciennes.

18th October

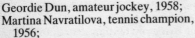

Born on this day:

Geordie Dun, amateur jockey, 1958;

Martina Navratilova, tennis champion, 1956;

Dick Taverne QC, former MP, 1928;

George C. Scott, US film actor, 1927;

Chuck Berry, rock and roll singer, 1926;

Melina Mercouri, Greek actress, 1925;

Pierre Trudeau CH, former Canadian prime minister, 1919;

Fannie Hurst, US novelist, 1889;

Emanuel, Baron Shinwell, statesman, 1884;

James Truslow Adams, US historian, 1878;

Henri Bergson, French philosopher, 1859;

Sir Samuel Luke Fildes, painter, 1844;

Frederick III, Emperor of Germany, 1831;

Christian Friedrich Schönbein, German chemist, 1799;

Thomas Love Peacock, novelist and poet, 1785;

Bernd Heinrich Wilhelm von Kleist, poet and playwright, 1777;

Canaletto [Giovanni Antonio Canale], Italian painter, 1697;

Luca Giordano ['Fa-Presto'], Italian painter, 1632;

Gianbattista Marino, Neapolitan poet, 1569;

Pope Pius II, 1405.

Died on this day:

Pierre Mendès-France, French statesman, 1982;

Elizabeth Arden [Florence Nightingale Graham], cosmetics company founder, 1966;

José Ortega y Gasset, Spanish philosopher and statesman, 1955;

Thomas Alva Edison, US inventor, 1931;

Alfred Binet, French psychologist, 1911;

Charles-François Gounod, French composer, 1893;

Charles Babbage, mathematician and computer inventor, 1871;

Jakob Jordaens, Flemish painter, 1678;

Margaret, Queen of Scotland, 1541.

 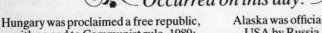

Occurred on this day:

Hungary was proclaimed a free republic, with an end to Communist rule, 1989;

The *News Chronicle* was merged with the *Daily Mail* and the *Star* was merged with the London *Evening News*, 1960;

Tripoli and Cyrenaica were ceded to Italy at the end of the Italo-Turkish War, 1912;

Alaska was officially transferred to the USA by Russia, 1866;

The Allies launched a massive attack against the French at the Battle of Leipzig, 1813;

The Edict of Nantes was revoked by King Louis XIV of France, 1685.

TODAY IS THE FEAST DAY OF St Gwen of Cornwall, St Justus of Beauvais and St Luke.

19th October

Born on this day:

Air Chief Marshal Sir Anthony Skingsley, Deputy Commander-in-Chief, Allied Forces Central Europe, 1933;
Robert Reed, US TV and film actor, 1932;
John Le Carré [David Cornwell], novelist, 1931;
Mavis Nicholson, interviewer on radio and TV, 1930;
Bernard Hepton, actor, 1925;
Rosamund John, actress, 1913;
Robert Beatty, actor, 1909;
Auguste-Marie-Louis-Nicolas Lumière, French photographic pioneer, 1862;

Alfred Dreyfus, French army officer, 1859;
Adam Lindsay Gordon, Australian poet, 1833;
Robert Pollok, poet, 1798;
Charles Robert Leslie, painter, 1794;
James Henry Leigh Hunt, poet and essayist, 1784;
Sir Thomas Browne, writer and physician, 1605 [see also Deaths];
Marsilio Ficino, Italian philosopher and classical scholar, 1433.

Died on this day:

Jacqueline du Pré, cellist, 1987;
Edna St Vincent Millay, US poet, 1950;
Ernest, 1st Baron Rutherford of Nelson, physicist, 1937;
Cesare Lombroso, Italian physician and criminologist, 1909;
George Mortimer Pullman, US sleeping-car manufacturer, 1897;
Sir Charles Wheatstone, physicist and inventor, 1875;

François-Joseph Talma, French actor-manager, 1826;
Jonathan Swift, author, 1745;
Sir Thomas Browne, writer and physician, 1682 [see also Births];
Samuel Dirksz van Hoogstraten, Dutch painter, 1678;
Jacobus Arminius [Jakob Hermansen], Dutch theologian, 1609;
King John [John Lackland], 1216.

Occurred on this day:

President Samor Machel of Mozambique and about 30 of his staff were killed in a plane crash on the South African border, 1986;
In Spain, over 200 people died in floods in the Granada, Murcia and Almeria provinces, 1973;
After her invasion of Abyssinia [Ethiopia], sanctions were imposed on Italy by the League of Nations, 1935;
The first Battle of Ypres began, 1914;

At the Battle of Cedar Creek, General Sheridan defeated the Confederate forces, 1864;
Wagner's opera *Tannhäuser* was first performed, Dresden, 1845;
With the end of the Battle of the Nations at Leipzig, the Allies defeated Napoleon, 1813;
The American War of Independence ended when Lord Cornwallis surrendered to George Washington at Yorktown, 1781.

TODAY IS THE FEAST DAY OF St Aquilinus of Evreux, St Cleopatra, St Ethbin, St Frideswide, St John de Brébeuf, St Paul of the Cross, St Peter of Alcántara, St Philip Howard, Saints Ptolemy and Lucius, St René Goupil and St Varus.

20th October

Born on this day:

Ian Rush, footballer, 1961;
Tom Petty, US guitarist and singer, 1953;
Eddie Macken, showjumper, 1949;
The Hon. Emma Tennant, writer, 1937;
Timothy West, actor, 1934;
Colin Jeavons, actor, 1929;
Lord Montagu of Beaulieu, vintage car
   enthusiast, 1926;
Frederic Dannay, US novelist [one-half of
   the 'Ellery Queen' partnership], 1905;
Anna Neagle [Marjorie Robertson],
   actress, 1904;
Charlie Chase [Charles Parrott], US film
   actor and director, 1893;
Sir James Chadwick, physicist, 1891;
Bela Lugosi [Bela Lugosi Blasko], US film
   actor, 1884;

John Dewey, US philosopher, 1859;
Jean-Nicolas-Arthur Rimbaud, French
   poet, 1854;
Odilon Redon, French painter and
   lithographer, 1840;
Thomas Hughes, author of *Tom Brown's
   Schooldays*, 1822;
Henry John Temple, 3rd Viscount
   Palmerston, statesman, 1784;
Nicolas de Largillière, French painter,
   1656;
Gerard Edelinck, Flemish engraver, 1649;
Sir Christopher Wren, mathematician and
   architect, 1632.

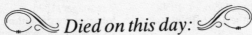

Died on this day:

Sir John Anthony Quayle, actor, 1989;
Paul Adrien Maurice Dirac, physicist, 1984;
Bud Flanagan [Robert Winthrop], 'Crazy
   Gang' comedian, 1968;
Shigeru Yoshida, Japanese statesman,
   1967;
Herbert Clark Hoover, 31st president of the
   USA, 1964;
Jack Buchanan, actor and singer, 1957;
Arthur Henderson, statesman, 1935;

James Anthony Froude, historian, 1894;
Sir Richard Francis Burton, explorer and
   Arabic scholar, 1890;
Michael William Balfe, composer, 1870;
Thomas Linacre, scholar and physician,
   1524;
Jacopo della Quercia, Italian sculptor,
   1438.

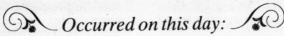

Occurred on this day:

The Sydney Opera House was opened to
   the public, 1973;
The musical show *Robert and Elizabeth* was
   first produced, London, 1964;
US troops landed at Leyte, in the Philippine
   Islands, 1944;
In Italy, Benito Mussolini, Fascist leader,
   seized power, 1922;

The British, French and Russian fleets
   annihilated the Turkish fleet at the Battle
   of Navarino, 1827;
The Sunday Times was first published, 1822;
The 49th parallel was defined as the border
   between Canada and the United States,
   1818.

TODAY IS THE FEAST DAY OF St Acca, St Andrew the Calybite of Crete, St
Artemius, St Bertilla Boscardin and St Caprasius of Agen.

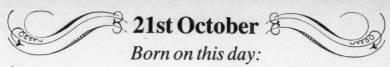

21st October

Born on this day:

Carrie Fisher, US film actress, 1956;
Geoffrey Boycott, cricketer, 1940;
Manfred Mann, rock bandleader, 1940;
Francis Warner, poet and playwright, 1937;
Simon Gray, playwright, 1936;
Maureen Duffy, novelist, 1933;
Nadia Nerina, former prima ballerina, 1927;
Malcolm Arnold, composer, 1921;
Dizzy Gillespie, jazz trumpeter, 1917;
Sir Georg Solti, conductor, 1912;
Lord Graves [Peter Graves], actor, 1911;
Egon Wellesz, composer, 1885;
Franklin Thomas Grant Richards, publisher and author, 1872;
Sir Ernest Dunlop Swinton, an inventor of the military armed vehicle, the tank, 1868;

Alfred Bernhard Nobel, Swedish industrialist and founder of the Prizes, 1833;
Alphonse-Marie-Louis de Prat de Lamartine, French poet and statesman, 1790;
Samuel Taylor Coleridge, poet and author, 1772;
George Colman [the Younger], playwright, 1762;
Katsushika Hokusai, Japanese painter, wood-engraver and printmaker, 1760;
Georg Ernst Stahl, German chemist, 1660;
Domenichino [Domenico Zampieri], Bolognese painter, 1581.

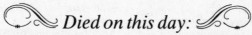

Died on this day:

Anastas Ivanovich Mikoyan, Soviet leader, 1978;
Jack [Jean-Louis] Kerouac, US poet and novelist, 1969;
Arthur Schnitzler, Austrian playwright and novelist, 1931;
George Frederick Bodley, architect, 1907;

Horatio, 1st Viscount Nelson, killed at Trafalgar, 1805;
Samuel Foote, actor and playwright, 1777;
Edmund Waller, poet, 1687;
Julius Caesar Scaliger [Bordon], French philosopher and scientist, 1558;
Pietro Aretino, Italian satirist, 1556.

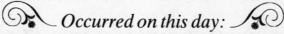

Occurred on this day:

Willy Brandt was elected as Chancellor of West Germany, 1969;
The Israeli destroyer *Eilat* was sunk by Egyptian missiles, 1967;
A slagheap at Aberfan, South Wales, collapsed, and 140 lives were lost, 1966;
The first British nuclear submarine, HMS *Dreadnought*, was launched, 1960;
Chinese forces occupied Tibet, 1950;
The present building of the Savoy Theatre, London, was opened, 1929;

Alberto Santos Dumont flew an airship around the Eiffel Tower, Paris, 1901;
The musical comedy *San Toy* was first produced, London, 1899;
Offenbach's opera *Orpheus in the Underworld* was first produced, Paris, 1858;
The Franco-Spanish fleet was defeated at the Battle of Trafalgar, 1805.

TODAY IS THE FEAST DAY OF St Condedus, St Fintan or Munnu of Taghmon, St Hilarion, St John of Bridlington, St Malchus and St Tuda.

22nd October

Born on this day:

Mike Hendrick, cricketer, 1948;
Kelvin MacKenzie, editor of the *Sun*, 1946;
Michael Stoute, racehorse trainer, 1945;
Catherine Deneuve, French film actress, 1943;
Derek Jacobi, actor, 1938;
Colonel John Blashford-Snell, adventurer, and Defence Staff officer, 1936;
Donald McIntyre, bass singer, 1934;
Doris Lessing, novelist, 1919;
Joan Fontaine, film actress, 1917;
Constance Bennett, US film actress, 1904;

Ivan Alekseyevich Bunin, Russian poet and novelist, 1870;
Lord Alfred Bruce Douglas, poet, 1870;
Sarah Bernhardt [Rosine Bernard], French actress, 1844;
Leopold Damrosch, US conductor and composer, 1832;
Franz Liszt, Hungarian composer, 1811;
James Northcote, painter, 1746;
Johann Reinhold Forster, German clergyman and naturalist, 1729;
John V, King of Portugal, 1689.

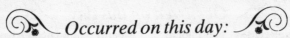

Died on this day:

Arnold Joseph Toynbee, historian, 1975;
Pablo Casals, cellist, 1973;
Sir Edward Henry, Baron Carson, lawyer and Ulster politician, 1935;
Sir John William Fortescue, military historian, 1933;
Paul Cézanne, French painter, 1906;
William Edward Hartpole Lecky, historian, 1903;
Thomas Mayne Reid, novelist, 1883;
Sir Roderick Impey Murchison, geologist, 1871;
Louis [Ludwig] Spohr, German composer, 1859;

Henry Richard Vassall Fox, 3rd Baron Holland, author and statesman, 1840;
Thomas Sheraton, cabinet-maker, 1806;
Frans van Mieris the Younger, Dutch painter, 1763;
Admiral Sir Cloudesley Shovell, wrecked and drowned off the Scilly Isles, 1707;
Gerbrand van den Eeckhout, Dutch painter, 1674;
Mathurin Regnier, French satirical poet, 1613;
Jean, Vicomte d'Aguisy Grolier, bibliophile and statesman, 1565;
Charles Martel, leader of the Franks, 741.

Occurred on this day:

Don Juan Carlos of Bourbon was proclaimed King of Spain, 1975;
The first London production of the musical show *DuBarry was a Lady* was staged, 1942;
In Haiti, over 2,000 people died after a hurricane hit the country, 1935;

In New York, the Metropolitan Opera House opened, 1883;
The magazine *Tit-Bits* was first published, 1881;
André-Jacques Garnerin made the first parachute jump from a balloon over Paris, 1797.

TODAY IS THE FEAST DAY OF St Abercius, St Donatus of Fiesole, St Mellon or Mallonus, Saints Nunilo and Alodia and St Philip of Heraclea and his Companions.

23rd October

Born on this day:

Anita Roddick, proprietor of The Body Shop, 1942;

Pelé [Edson Arantes do Nascimento], Brazilian footballer, 1940;

George Cohen, footballer, 1939;

Diana Dors [Diana Fluck], film actress, 1931;

Johnny Carson, US TV presenter, 1925;

George Rylands CH, Shakespearean scholar, 1902;

Douglas Robert Jardine, cricketer, 1900;

Jean Louis Forain, French painter and illustrator, 1852;

George Edward Bateman Saintsbury, critic and scholar, 1845;

Louis Riel, rebel leader of the Métis in Canada, 1844;

Robert Seymour Bridges, poet, 1844;

Pierre-Athanase Larousse, French lexicographer and encyclopaedist, 1817;

Adalbert Stifter, Austrian writer, 1805;

Gustav Albert Lortzing, conductor, singer and composer, 1801;

James Ward, animal painter, 1769;

Nicolas-Edme Restif de la Bretonne, French novelist, 1734.

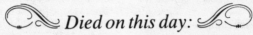 Died on this day:

Al Jolson [Asa Yoelson], US singer and actor, 1950;

Zane Grey, novelist of the American West, 1939;

John Boyd Dunlop, inventor of the pneumatic rubber tyre, 1921;

William Gilbert Grace, cricketer, 1915;

Florent Joseph Marie Willems, Belgian painter, 1905;

Michel Marie Charles Verlat, Belgian painter, 1890;

Pierre-Jules-Théophile Gautier, French author, 1872;

Edward Geoffrey Stanley, 14th Earl of Derby, statesman, 1869;

Nance [Anne] Oldfield, actress, 1730;

Thomas Pride, Cromwellian soldier, 1658;

Marcus Junius Brutus, Roman soldier, committed suicide, 42 BC.

Occurred on this day:

At Bonneville Salt Flats, Utah, Gary Gabelich in *Blue Flame* made the world land speed record of 631.367 mph, 1970;

George Blake, serving a 42-year sentence for espionage, escaped from Wormwood Scrubs prison, 1966;

The Hungarian revolt against Soviet leadership began, 1956;

The United Nations General Assembly met for the first time, New York, 1946;

Russian forces invaded East Prussia, 1944;

The Battle of Alamein started, 1942;

The Battle of Caporetto was fought, 1917;

Borodin's opera *Prince Igor* was first produced, Petrograd, 1890;

The first parliament of Great Britain met, 1707;

Both Royalists and Parliamentarians claimed victory at the Battle of Edgehill, 1642.

TODAY IS THE FEAST DAY OF St Allucio, St Elfleda or Ethelfleda, St Ignatius of Constantinople, St John of Capistrano, St Romanus of Rouen, St Severinus or Seurin of Bordeaux, St Severinus Boethius and St Theodoret.

24th October

Born on this day:

Phil Bennett, rugby player, 1948;
Frank Delaney, broadcaster, 1942;
Bill Wyman, rock musician, 1941;
Wally Herbert, Arctic explorer, 1934;
Prof. George Crumb, composer, 1929;
Clifford Rose, actor, 1929;
Luciano Berio, conductor and composer, 1925;
Sir Robin Day, TV presenter, 1923;
Sena Jurinac, Yugoslav soprano, 1921;
Tito Gobbi, Italian baritone, 1915;
Jackie [Jack Leslie] Coogan, US film actor, 1914;
Prof. Peter Gellhorn, composer, conductor and director, 1912;
Sir Fred Pontin, holiday camp founder, 1906;
Moss Hart, US playwright and director, 1904;

Jack Warner [Jack Waters], actor, 1894;
Merian C. Cooper, US author, film producer and director, 1893;
Dame Agnes Sybil Thorndike, actress, 1882;
Eugène-Samuel-Auguste Fromentin, French painter and writer, 1820;
Ferdinand von Hiller, German composer and author, 1811;
Sir Moses Haim Montefiore, philanthropist, 1784;
Jacques Laffitte, French banker and politician, 1767;
Antonie van Leeuwenhoek, Dutch microscope pioneer, 1632;
Aurangzeb, the last Mogul emperor of India, 1618.

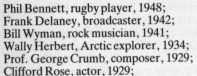

Died on this day:

George Edward Moore, philosopher, 1958;
Christian Dior, French fashion designer, 1957;
Franz Lehár, Hungarian composer, 1948;
Vidkun Quisling, Norwegian wartime traitor, executed, 1945;
Alexandre-Charles Lecocq, French composer, 1918;
Pierre-Cécile Puvis de Chavannes, French mural painter, 1898;
Francis Turner Palgrave, editor and anthologist, 1897;

Carl Ditters von Dittersdorf, Austrian composer, 1799;
Pietro Alessandro Gaspare Scarlatti, Italian composer, 1725;
Pierre Gassendi [Gassend], French scientist and philosopher, 1655;
Tycho Brahe, Danish astronomer and mathematician, 1601;
Lady Jane Seymour, 3rd wife of King Henry VIII, 1537.

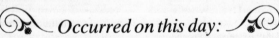

Occurred on this day:

Northern Rhodesia, renamed Zambia, became independent, 1964;
Soviet troops intervened in Hungary, 1956;
The United Nations Charter came into force, 1945;
The Battle of Alamein ended, 1942;
Strauss's operetta *Der Zigeunerbaron* was first produced in Vienna, 1885;

The Thirty Years War ended after the Treaty of Westphalia was signed, 1648;
Murderers were no longer allowed to plead Benefit of Clergy, 1513;
The cathedral of Notre Dame, Chartres, France, was consecrated, 1260.

TODAY IS THE FEAST DAY OF St Antony Claret, St Aretas, St Elesbaan, St Evergislus, St Felix of Thibiuca, St Maglorius or Maelor, St Martin or Mark, St Martin of Vertou, The Martyrs of Najran, St Proclus of Constantinople and St Senoch.

25th October

Born on this day:

Glynis Barber, actress, 1955;
Leslie Taylor, cricketer, 1953;
Helen Reddy, singer, 1942;
Juliet Fisher, dancer and teacher of
contemporary dance, 1941;
Martin Gilbert, historian, 1936;
Joe Mercer, jockey, 1934;
Tony Franciosa, US film and TV actor,
1928;
Galina Vishnevskaya, Russian operatic
soprano, 1926;
Don Banks, Australian composer, 1923;
Ex-King Michael of Romania, 1921;
Prof. Donald Wiseman, Assyriologist,
1918;
Henry Commager, US historian, 1902;
Levi Eshkol, Israeli statesman, 1895;

Abel Gance, French film director and
producer, 1889;
Richard Evelyn Byrd, US admiral, aviator
and polar explorer, 1888;
Pablo Ruiz Picasso, Spanish painter, 1881;
Georges [Alexandre-César-Léopold]
Bizet, French composer, 1838;
Johann Strauss the Younger, Austrian
composer, 1825;
Richard Parkes Bonington, painter, 1801;
Thomas Babington Macaulay, Baron
Macaulay, historian and essayist, 1800;
Dr James Beattie, Scottish poet and
philosopher, 1735;
Thomas Weelkes, composer, baptised,
1576.

Died on this day:

Edward John Moreton Drax Plunkett, 18th
Baron Dunsany, author, 1957;
King Alexander of Greece, 1920;
Frederick William Serafino Austin Lewis
Mary Rolfe ['Baron Corvo'], author,
1913;
Frank [Benjamin Franklin] Norris, US
novelist, 1902;
Sir Charles Hallé [Carl Halle], conductor
and pianist, 1895;

King George II, 1760;
Evangelista Torricelli, Italian scientist and
inventor of the barometer, 1647;
Giorgione [Giorgio da Castelfranco],
Italian painter, 1510;
Geoffrey Chaucer, poet, 1400;
King Stephen, 1154.

Occurred on this day:

US Marines and Rangers invaded Grenada,
1983;
The magazine *Private Eye* was first
published, 1961;
The first London production of the musical
show *Follow the Girls* was presented,
1945;
The Zinoviev Letter was published by the
British Foreign Office, 1924;
The Transvaal was annexed by Great
Britain, 1900;

Strauss's operetta *Wiener Blut* was first
produced in Vienna, 1899;
The Fiji Islands were annexed by Great
Britain, 1874;
The Charge of the Light Brigade took place
at Balaclava, 1854;
Bradshaw's Railway Guide was first
published, 1839;
Led by King Henry V, the English army
defeated the French at the Battle of
Agincourt, 1415.

TODAY IS THE FEAST DAY OF Saints Chrysanthus and Daria, Saints Crispin and
Crispinian, The Forty Martyrs of England and Wales, Saints Fronto and George, St
Gaudentius of Brescia and St Richard Gwyn.

26th October

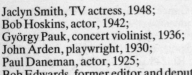

Born on this day:

Jaclyn Smith, TV actress, 1948;
Bob Hoskins, actor, 1942;
György Pauk, concert violinist, 1936;
John Arden, playwright, 1930;
Paul Daneman, actor, 1925;
Bob Edwards, former editor and deputy chairman, Mirror Group, 1925;
Shaw Taylor, TV presenter, 1924;
Mohammad Reza Pahlavi, Shah of Iran, 1919;
François Mitterand, president of France, 1916;
Lord Scanlon, former trade union leader, 1913;

Mahalia Jackson, US gospel singer, 1911;
Vassili Vassilevich Vereshchagin, Russian artist and traveller, 1842;
Henry Thomas Smart, organist and composer, 1813;
Joseph Aloysius Hansom, architect and inventor of the hansom cab, 1803;
Helmuth Karl Bernhard, Graf von Moltke, German general, 1800;
Johan Helmich Roman, Swedish composer, 1694;
Giuseppe Domenico Scarlatti, Italian composer and harpsichordist, 1685.

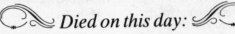

Died on this day:

Field Marshal Sir Gerald Walter Robert Templer, 1979;
Igor Ivanovich Sikorsky, helicopter pioneer, 1972;
Alma Cogan, singer, 1966;
Gerty Theresa Cori [Radnitz], US biochemist, 1957;
Sir Mark Aurel Stein, archaeologist, 1943;

Victor Schertzinger, US composer and lyricist, 1941;
Carolina Oliphant [Baroness Nairne], ballad writer, 1845;
Charles Proteus [Karl August Rudolf] Steinmetz, US electrical engineer, 1923;
William Hogarth, artist and engraver, 1764;
Gilles de Rais, Marshal of France, hanged for murder, 1440.

Occurred on this day:

After 26 years on the throne, the Shah of Iran crowned himself and his Queen in Teheran, 1967;
The International Atomic Energy Agency was formed, 1956;
In the USA, T.W. Evans of Miami, Florida, became the first mother of a child to be born in an aircraft, 1929;
The October Revolution took place in Russia [reckoned by New Style Calendar, 7th November], 1917;
The Territorial Army was founded, 1907;

The union between Sweden and Norway was ended, 1905;
The new Gaiety Theatre in the Strand, London, was opened, 1903;
The gunfight at the OK Corral took place at Tombstone, Arizona, 1881;
The English Football Association was formed, 1863;
Victor Emmanuel was proclaimed by Garibaldi as King of Italy, 1860;
The Erie Canal, North America, was opened, 1825.

TODAY IS THE FEAST DAY OF St Bean, St Cedd, St Eata, Saints Lucian and Marcian and St Rusticus of Narbonne.

 ## 27th October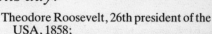

Born on this day:

Simon le Bon, rock singer, 1958;
Chris Tavaré, cricketer, 1954;
Glen Hoddle, footballer, 1947;
Peter Martins, Danish dancer and
  choreographer, 1945;
John Cleese, actor, 1939;
Jean-Pierre Cassel, French actor, 1932;
Sylvia Plath, US poet, 1932;
Ruby Dee, US film actress, 1924;
Roy Lichtenstein, US pop art painter, 1923;
Teresa Wright, US film actress, 1918;
Harry Salzman, US film-maker, 1915;
Dylan Marlais Thomas, Welsh poet, 1914;
Lord Moyne [Brian Guinness], novelist and
  poet, 1905;
Enid Bagnold [Lady Roderick Jones],
  novelist, 1889;

Theodore Roosevelt, 26th president of the
  USA, 1858;
Pierre-Eugène-Marcelin Berthelot, French
  organic chemist, 1827;
Isaac Merritt Singer, US developer of the
  sewing machine, 1811;
Dr Andrew Combe, physiologist and
  surgeon, 1797;
Niccolo Paganini, Italian violinist and
  composer, 1782;
August Wilhelm Anton Neithardt, Graf
  von Gneisenau, German soldier, 1760;
Captain James Cook, naval officer and
  explorer, 1728;
John Jenkins, composer, 1592;
Desiderius Erasmus, Dutch scholar and
  humanist, 1466.

 ### Died on this day:

James Mallahan Cain, US novelist, 1977;
Lise Meitner, nuclear physicist,
  1968;
Sydney Horler, thriller writer, 1954;
Lascelles Abercrombie, writer and critic,
  1938;

Edward Lyon Berthon, inventor of the
  screw propeller, 1899;
The Rev. John Thomson, landscape
  painter, 1840;
George Morland, painter, 1804;
Ivan III [the Great], Tsar of Russia, 1505.

 ### Occurred on this day:

The name of the Republic of the Congo was
  changed to Zaïre, 1971;
The Prince of Wales' Theatre [present
  building] was opened, 1937;
The *Pall Mall Gazette* newspaper was last
  issued, 1923;
Troops from the USA entered the war in
  France, 1917;

The New York Subway was opened, 1904;
The *Liverpool Echo* was first published,
  1879;
The French captured Berlin, 1806;
The United States Navy was established,
  1775;
The Cavaliers eluded the Roundheads in
  the Battle of Newbury, 1644.

TODAY IS THE FEAST DAY OF St Frumentius of Ethiopia and St Otteran or Odhran
of Iona.

28th October

Born on this day:

Mark James, golfer, 1953;
Wayne Fontana, rock singer, 1945;
Henry Candy, racehorse trainer, 1944;
Hank Marvin, guitarist with The Shadows, 1941;
Jane Alexander, US actress, 1939;
David Dimbleby, TV presenter and newspaper proprietor, 1938;
Carl Davis, composer and conductor, 1936;
Michael Noakes, painter, 1933;
Joan Plowright [Lady Olivier], actress, 1929;
Cleo Laine, singer, 1927;

Jonas Salk, US inventor of an anti-polio vaccine, 1914;
Francis Bacon, painter, 1909;
Evelyn Arthur St John Waugh, novelist, 1903;
Georges-Auguste Escoffier, French chef de cuisine, 1846;
Robert Liston, surgeon, 1794;
Hermann-Maurice, Comte de Saxe, French marshal, 1696;
Dr Nicholas Brady, poet, 1659;
Cornelius Jansen, Roman Catholic reformer, 1585.

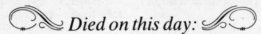

Died on this day:

Henry Robert Hall, bandleader, 1989;
Pietro Annigoni, painter, 1988;
John Braine, novelist, 1986;
David Jones, author and painter, 1974;
Grant Allen [Charles Grant Blairfindie Allen], writer and man of science, 1899;
Ottmar Mergenthaler, German/US inventor of the Linotype, 1899;

John Smeaton, engineer, 1792;
William Julius Mickle, poet, 1788;
John Locke, philosopher, 1704;
John Wallis, mathematician, 1703;
Jahangir, Mogul emperor of India, 1627;
Rudolphus Agricola [Roelof Huysmann], Dutch humanist, musician and painter, 1485;
King Alfred the Great, 901.

 Occurred on this day:

The House of Commons voted in favour of Britain joining the Common Market, with a majority of 112, 1971.
Italy invaded Greece, 1940;
The collapse of the New York Stock Exchange began a world economic crisis, 1929;
Mussolini marched on Rome, 1922;
HMS *Havelock*, the first destroyer in the Royal Navy, went on trials, 1893;

The Statue of Liberty was dedicated by President Cleveland, 1886;
Strasbourg was surrendered to the Germans, 1870;
Michael Faraday made the first dynamo, 1831;
Harvard College was founded at Newe Towne, Cambridge, Mass., 1636.

TODAY IS THE FEAST DAY OF St Abraham of Ephesus, Saints Anastasia and Cyril, St Faro, St Fidelis of Como, St Jude or Thaddeus, St Salvius or Saire and St Simon.

29th October

Born on this day:

Angela Douglas, actress, 1950;
Kate Jackson, actress, 1949;
Richard Dreyfuss, US actor, 1947;
Jack Shepherd, actor, 1940;
Michael Jayston, actor, 1935;
Douglas Cameron, radio presenter, 1933;
Frank Sedgman, tennis player, 1927;
Jon Vickers, dramatic tenor, 1926;
Robert Hardy, actor, 1925;
Neal Hefti, composer and conductor, 1922;
Edwige Feuillère, French actress, 1907;
Vivian Ellis, composer, 1904;
Susie Cooper, ceramic designer, 1902;
Paul Joseph Goebbels, Nazi propaganda chief, 1897;

Fanny Brice [Borach], actress, dancer and singer, 1891;
Edward Alexander Wadsworth, painter, 1889;
Hippolyte-Jean Giraudoux, author, 1882;
Franz von Papen, politician, 1879;
Wilfred Rhodes, cricketer, 1877;
Jean-Joseph-Charles-Louis Blanc, French socialist, 1811;
William Hayley, poet and biographer, 1745;
James Boswell, Dr Johnson's biographer, 1740;
Fernando Alvarez de Toledo, 3rd Duke of Alba, military leader, 1507.

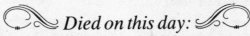 Died on this day:

Ursula Bloom [Gower Robinson], author, 1984;
Gustav V, King of Sweden, 1950;
Frances Eliza Hodgson Burnett, author of *Little Lord Fauntleroy*, 1924;
Joseph Pulitzer, US newspaper publisher, 1911;
John Leech, humorist, artist and caricaturist, 1864;

Luke Hansard, printer to the House of Commons, 1828;
Jean le Rond d'Alembert, encyclopaedist, 1783;
James Shirley, poet and playwright, 1666;
Sir Walter Raleigh, seafarer and writer, executed, 1618.

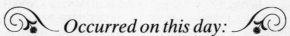 Occurred on this day:

It was announced that the union of Tanganyika and Zanzibar would be called Tanzania, 1964;
The Harwell Atomic Energy Research Establishment was set up, 1945;
The French liner *Normandie* was launched at St Nazaire, 1932;
The Russians drove back Austrian and German forces at the Battle of Warsaw, 1914;

The British South Africa Company was granted its charter, 1889;
The opera *Don Giovanni* by Mozart was first performed, Prague, 1787;
The Austrians were defeated by the Prussians under Frederick II at Freiberg, 1762.

TODAY IS THE FEAST DAY OF St Colman of Kilmacduagh, The Martyrs of Douay, St Narcissus of Jerusalem and St Theuderius or Chef.

30th October

Born on this day:

Shlomo Mintz, violinist, 1957;
Henry Winkler, US TV actor, 1945;
Bob Wilson, TV football commentator, 1941;
Michael Winner, film producer and director, 1935;
Louis Malle, French film director, 1932;
Stanley Sadie, music critic, 1929;
Ruth Hussey, US film actress, 1914;
Preston Lockwood, actor and writer, 1912;
Gerhard Domagk, German pathologist, 1895;
Peter Warlock [Philip Arnold Heseltine], composer, 1894;
Ezra Loomis Pound, US poet, 1885;
Ralph Hale Mottram, novelist, 1883;

Paul-Ambroise-Toussaint-Jules Valéry, French poet, 1871;
Gertrude Franklin Atherton, US novelist, 1857;
Alfred Sisley, painter, 1840;
John Adams, 2nd president of the USA, 1735;
Marie-André de Chenier, French poet, 1762;
Richard Brinsley Butler Sheridan, playwright, 1751;
Maria Anna Angelica Kauffmann, Swiss painter, 1741;
Christian Wilhelm Ernst Dietrich, German painter, 1712.

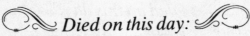

Died on this day:

Sir Barnes Neville Wallis, inventor, 1979;
James Allan Mollison, pioneer aviator, 1959;
Dame Emilie Rose Macaulay, novelist, 1958;
Pio Baroja, Spanish novelist, 1956;
Jean-Henri Dunant, Swiss founder of the Red Cross, 1910;
John Chubb, locksmith, 1872;
Nicolas-Toussaint Charlet, French designer and painter, 1845;

Allan Cunningham, poet, 1842;
Charles Robert Maturin, clergyman and author of Gothic tales, 1824;
Edmund Cartwright, power-loom inventor, 1823;
Andrew Bonar Law, statesman, 1923;
Esteban Arteaga, Spanish scholar and Jesuit priest, 1799;
Admiral Edward Vernon ['Old Grog'], naval commander, 1757.

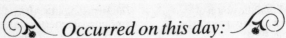

Occurred on this day:

Orson Welles' radio play, *The War of the Worlds*, caused panic in the USA, 1938;
In Turkey, a republic was proclaimed under Mustapha Kemal, 1923;
In Italy, a Fascist Ministry was formed by Benito Mussolini, 1922;
The Republic of Czechoslovakia was proclaimed in Prague, 1918;
The comic opera *Billee Taylor* was first performed, London, 1880;

The Caledonian Canal, Scotland, was opened, 1822;
Sir Francis Drake completed his circumnavigation of the world when he arrived at Plymouth in the *Golden Hind*, 1580;
The Yeomen of the Guard were established by King Henry VII, 1485.

TODAY IS THE FEAST DAY OF St Alphonsus Rodriguez, St Asterius of Amasea, St Ethelnoth, St Germanus of Capua, St Marcellus the Centurion and St Serapion of Antioch.

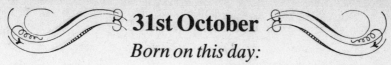

31st October

Born on this day:

Michael Kitchen, actor, 1948;
Barrie Keeffe, playwright, 1945;
Tom O'Connor, comedian, 1950;
John Gunter, theatrical designer, 1938;
Lee Grant, US film and TV actress, 1929;
H.R.F. Keating, crime novelist, 1926;
Sir Jimmy Savile, TV and radio personality, 1926;
Barbara Bel Geddes, US film actress, 1922;
John Blythe, actor, 1921;
Dick Francis, novelist, 1920;
Alastair Hetherington, former editor of the *Guardian*, 1919;
Dale Evans, US western film actress and singer, 1912;

Sir George Hubert Wilkins, Australian polar explorer and aviator, 1888;
Chiang Kai-shek, Chinese leader, 1887;
Henri Regnault, French painter, 1843;
Sir George Reid, Scottish portrait painter, 1841;
Sir Joseph Wilson Swan, chemist and inventor of the electric lamp, 1828;
Benoît Fourneyron, French engineer and inventor of the water turbine, 1802;
John Keats, poet, 1795;
Meyndert Hobbema, Dutch painter, 1638;
Jan Vermeer [Jan van der Meer van Delft], Dutch painter, 1632;
John Evelyn, diarist and founder of the Royal Society, 1620.

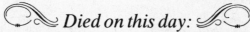

Died on this day:

Indira Gandhi, Indian prime minister, assassinated, 1984;
Augustus Edwin John, painter, 1961;
Henry Hinchliffe Ainley, actor, 1945;
Ignacio Zuloaga, Spanish painter, 1945;
Max Reinhardt [Goldmann], Austrian theatrical director, 1943;
Charles William Gordon [Ralph Connor], clergyman and novelist, 1937;
Harry Houdini [Erich Weiss], US escapologist, 1926;

Dan Leno [George Galvin], comedian, 1904;
William Parsons, 3rd Earl of Rosse, astronomer, 1867;
Thomas Cochrane, 10th Earl of Dundonald, admiral, 1860;
Richard Edwards, poet and playwright, 1566;
Fra Bartolommeo di Pagholo [Baccio della Porta], Italian painter, 1517.

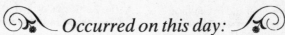

Occurred on this day:

The London *Evening News* ceased publication, 1980;
A bomb exploded at the top of the Post Office Tower, London, 1971;
The Battle of Britain ended, 1940;
The first London performance of the musical play *Wild Violets* was staged, 1932;

Offenbach's operetta *La Vie Parisienne* was first produced, Paris, 1866;
Nevada became the 36th of the United States, 1864;
Martin Luther nailed his theses to the church door in Wittenberg, 1517.

TODAY IS THE FEAST DAY OF St Bee or Bega, St Foillan of Fosses, St Quentin or Quintinus and St Wolfgang.

1st November

Born on this day:

Lee Ritenour, US jazz guitarist, 1951;
Nigel Dempster, gossip column writer, 1941;
John Pullen, rugby player, 1941;
Roger Kellaway, US popular composer and pianist, 1939;
Gary Player, South African golfer, 1935;
Prof. William Mathias, composer and conductor, 1934;
Lou Donaldson, US alto saxophonist, 1926;
Victoria de los Angeles, Spanish soprano, 1923;
Prof. Sir Hermann Bondi, mathematician, 1919;
Michael Denison, actor, 1915;
Terence Cuneo, portrait painter, 1907;
Naomi Mitchison, novelist, 1897;

Edmund Charles Blunden, scholar and poet, 1896;
Laurence Stephen Lowry, primitive painter, 1887;
Stephen Townley Crane, US author, 1871;
Madame Albani [Marie-Louise Lajeunesse], French soprano, 1852;
Jules Bastien-Lepage, French painter, 1848;
Antonio Canova, Italian sculptor, 1757;
Nicolas Boileau-Despréaux, French poet and satirist, 1636;
Pietro da Cortona, Italian painter and architect, 1596;
Benvenuto Cellini, Italian sculptor and goldsmith, 1500;
Louis II, King of France, 846.

Died on this day:

Phil Silvers, US comedian and actor, 1985;
Ezra Loomis Pound, US poet, 1972;
Christian Matthias Theodor Mommsen, German historian and archaeologist, 1903;
John Lindley, botanist and writer, 1865;
Lord George Gordon, Protestant agitator, 1793;

Alexander Cruden, compiler of the Bible *Concordance*, 1770;
John Radcliffe, physician and founder of the Radcliffe Library, Oxford, 1714;
Salomon van Ruysdael, Dutch painter, buried, 1670;
Giulio Romano [Giulio Pippi], Italian painter, 1546.

Occurred on this day:

Over 10,000 people died and five million rendered homeless after a tidal wave struck Orissa, India, 1972;
The first section of the M1 motorway was opened, 1959;
The first Premium Savings Bonds went on sale, 1956;
The first London production of the musical show *South Pacific* was staged, 1951;
The British Television service was inaugurated, 1936;
Licences for radio sets were started in Britain, 1922;

At the Battle of Coronel, the British ships *Good Hope* and *Monmouth* were sunk, 1914;
The first issue of *Woman's Weekly* was published, 1911;
Lloyd's *Register of Shipping* was first published, 1884;
The first W.H. Smith bookstall opened at Euston Station, London, 1848;
60,000 people died when Lisbon was destroyed by an earthquake, 1755;
The Bank of Scotland was founded, 1695.

TODAY IS THE FEAST DAY OF All Saints, St Austremonius or Stremoine, St Benignus of Dijon, St Cadfan, Saints Caesarius and Julian, St Marcellus of Paris, St Mary, martyr, St Mathurin or Maturinus and St Vigor.

2nd November

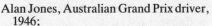

Born on this day:

Alan Jones, Australian Grand Prix driver, 1946;

Keith Emerson, rock musician, 1944;

Juliet Mills, actress, 1941;

Desmond Hamill, TV reporter, 1936;

Ken Rosewall, Australian tennis player, 1934;

Paul Johnson, author and editor, 1928;

Burt Lancaster, US film actor, 1913;

Ivor Roberts-Jones, sculptor, 1913;

Luchino Visconti, Duca di Modrone, Italian film director, 1906;

Victor Thomas Trumper, cricketer, 1877;

Warren Gamaliel Harding, 29th president of the USA, 1865;

Georges Sorel, French socialist, 1847;

James Knox Polk, 11th president of the USA, 1795;

Johan Joseph Wenzel, Count Radetzky, Austrian field marshal, 1766;

Marie Antoinette, Austrian princess and Queen of King Louis XVI of France, 1755;

Karl Ditters von Dittersdorf, Austrian violinist and composer, 1739;

Daniel Boone, US frontiersman, 1734;

Jean-Baptiste-Siméon Chardin, French painter, 1699;

King Edward V, 1470.

Died on this day:

James Grover Thurber, US humorous writer and cartoonist, 1961;

George Bernard Shaw, Irish playwright, 1950;

William Powell Frith, painter, 1909;

Jenny [Johanna Maria] Lind, Swedish soprano, 1887;

Sir Samuel Romilly, lawyer, committed suicide, 1818;

Richard Bancroft, Archbishop of Canterbury, 1610;

Richard Hooker, theologian, 1600;

Henry Stafford, 2nd Duke of Buckingham, courtier, executed, 1483.

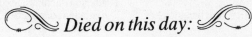

Occurred on this day:

James Earl Carter was elected as 39th president of the USA, 1976;

King Faisal ascended the throne of Saudi Arabia, 1964;

President Kennedy announced that the USSR was dismantling the missile sites in Cuba, 1962;

Penguin Books were acquitted of obscenity in the matter of publishing the book *Lady Chatterley's Lover*, 1960;

The world's first high-definition TV service began, transmitted by the BBC from Alexandra Palace, London, 1936;

Haile Selassie was crowned as Emperor of Ethiopia, 1930;

The first crossword puzzle to appear in a British newspaper was published in the *Sunday Express*, 1924;

The world's first regular broadcasting station, KDKA Pittsburgh, USA, started transmitting, 1920;

Lord Balfour made his Declaration regarding a Jewish national home in Palestine, 1917;

The *Daily Mirror* was first published as a daily newspaper for women, 1903;

North Dakota and South Dakota became the 39th and 40th of the United States, 1889;

The *Morning Post* newspaper was first published, 1772.

TODAY IS THE FEAST DAY OF All Souls, St Marcian of Cyrrhus and St Victorinus of Pettau.

3rd November

Born on this day:

Adam Ant, rock musician, 1954;
Larry Holmes, heavyweight boxing
    champion, 1949;
Lulu [Marie Lawrie], singer, 1948;
Nicholas Budgen, MP, 1937;
Roy Emerson, tennis player, 1936;
Jeremy Brett, actor, 1935;
Kenneth Baker, MP, 1934;
John Barry, popular musician and
    composer, 1933;
John Biffen, MP, 1930;
Sir Timothy Raison, MP, 1929;
Violetta Elvin, former prima ballerina,
    1925;
Charles Bronson, US film actor,
    1922;
Ludovic Kennedy, writer and broadcaster,
    1919;

Conor Cruise O'Brien, Irish editor, author
    and politician, 1917;
Leopold III, King of the Belgians, 1901;
André-Georges Malraux, French writer
    and politician, 1901;
Vilhjalmur Stefansson, US Arctic explorer,
    1879;
Karl Baedeker, German guide-book
    publisher, 1801;
Vincenzo Bellini, Italian operatic
    composer, 1801;
William Cullen Bryant, US poet and
    journalist, 1794;
Hugh, 1st Viscount Gough, field marshal,
    1779;
Francisco Pacheco, Spanish painter and
    historian, baptised, 1564;
Annibale Carracci, Italian painter, 1560.

Died on this day:

Ralph Hodgson, poet, 1962;
Harry Revel, pianist and popular
    composer, 1958;
Henri-Emile-Benoît Matisse, French
    painter, 1954;
John Gilbert Winant, US diplomat,
    1947;
Annie Oakley [Phoebe Anne Oakley], US
    entertainer and markswoman, 1926;

Sir John Leslie, Scottish physicist and
    mathematician, 1832;
Robert Lowth, Bishop of London, writer
    and poet, 1787;
Constantius II, Roman emperor of the
    East, 361.

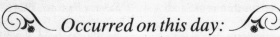

Occurred on this day:

The colony of Dominica became an
    independent republic, 1978;
Laika, the Russian space dog, was sent into
    space in *Sputnik II*, 1957;
Turkey abolished the use of the Arabic
    alphabet and adopted the Roman, 1928;
The first London production of the musical
    show *Hit the Deck* was staged, 1927;
The German fleet mutinied at Kiel, 1918;

William Howard Taft was elected as 27th
    president of the USA, 1909;
The independence of Panama from
    Colombia was proclaimed, 1903;
The Act of Supremacy was passed, making
    the king head of the English Church,
    1534;
Christopher Columbus discovered
    Dominica on his second voyage, 1493.

TODAY IS THE FEAST DAY OF St Amicus, St Hubert, St Malachy of Armagh, St
Martin de Porres, St Pirminus, St Rumwald and St Winifred or Gwenfrewi.

 ## 4th November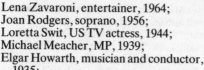

Born on this day:

Lena Zavaroni, entertainer, 1964;
Joan Rodgers, soprano, 1956;
Loretta Swit, US TV actress, 1944;
Michael Meacher, MP, 1939;
Elgar Howarth, musician and conductor, 1935;
Martin Balsam, US film and TV actor, 1919;
Art Carney, US actor, 1918;
Walter Cronkite, US radio and TV presenter, 1916;
Will [William Penn Adair] Rogers, US humorist and actor, 1879;
George Edward Moore, philosopher, 1873;
Sir Frank [Francis Robert] Benson, actor-manager, 1858;

Eden Phillpotts, novelist and playwright, 1862;
George Long, scholar and editor of the *Penny Cyclopaedia*, 1800;
James Montgomery, poet and journalist, 1771;
The Rev. Augustus Montague Toplady, writer of hymns and author of *Rock of Ages*, 1740;
King William III, 1650;
William Habington, poet, 1605;
Gerard van Honthorst, Dutch painter, 1590;
Guido Reni, Italian painter, 1575.

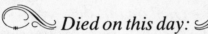 ### Died on this day:

Gilbert Frankau, novelist, 1952;
Gabriel-Urbain Fauré, French organist and composer, 1924;
Wilfred Owen, poet, killed in action, 1918;
Philip Gilbert Hamerton, artist and author, 1894;
George Peabody, US industrialist and philanthropist, 1869;

Joseph Rowntree, cocoa manufacturer and Quaker educationalist, 1859;
Hippolyte-Paul Delaroche, French painter, 1856;
Jakob Ludwig Felix Mendelssohn-Bartholdy, German composer, 1847;
Charles Churchill, poet and satirist, 1764;
Vice-Admiral John Benbow, 1702.

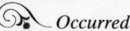 ### Occurred on this day:

Ronald Reagan was elected as 40th president of the USA, 1980;
Dwight David Eisenhower was elected as 34th president of the USA, 1952;
UNESCO was established, 1946;
The first London production of the musical show *Panama Hattie* was staged, 1943;
The tomb of Tutankhamen was discovered by Lord Carnarvon and Howard Carter, 1922;

Richard Jordan Gatling patented his machine-gun, 1862;
In Trafalgar Square, London, Nelson's Column was completed, 1843;
Guy Fawkes was arrested in the cellars of Parliament, 1605;
Antwerp was sacked by mutinous Spaniards, who killed over 8,000 citizens, 1576.

TODAY IS THE FEAST DAY OF St Birstan or Brynstan of Winchester, St Charles Borromeo, St Clarus, St Joannicus, St John Zedazneli, St Pierius and Saints Vitalis and Agricola.

5th November

Born on this day:

Tatum O'Neal, US actress, 1963;

Steve Miller, US bandleader, 1943;

Art Garfunkel, US singer and composer, 1941;

Elke Sommer, German actress, 1940;

Nicholas Maw, composer, 1935;

Lester Piggott, jockey, 1935;

John Berger, author and art critic, 1926;

Richard Annand VC, 1914;

Vivien Leigh [Vivien Hartley], actress, 1913;

Roy Rogers, US singing cowboy actor, 1912;

Paul Edward Dehn, playwright, author and poet, 1912;

General Sir John Hackett, soldier, scholar and author, 1910;

Walter Wilhelm Gieseking, German pianist, 1895;

John Burdon Sanderson Haldane, physiologist and geneticist, 1892;

James Elroy Flecker, poet and playwright, 1884;

Léon-Philippe Teisserence de Bort, French meteorologist and discoverer of the stratosphere, 1855;

Washington Allston, US landscape painter and author, 1779;

Hans Sachs, German cobbler, mastersinger, poet and playwright, 1494.

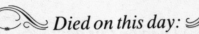

Died on this day:

Ian Robert Maxwell [Jan Ludvik Hoch], chairman of Mirror Group, at sea, 1991;

Eamonn Andrews, TV presenter, 1987;

Jacques Tati [Tatischeff], French film actor and director, 1982;

Al Capp [Alfred Gerald Caplin], US cartoonist, 1979;

King Peter of Yugoslavia, 1970;

Ward Bond, US film actor, 1960;

Maurice Utrillo, painter, 1955;

Mack Sennett [Michael Sinnott], US film producer and director of comedies, 1960;

George Michael Cohan, US actor and songwriter, 1942;

Christiaan Eijkman, Dutch physician, 1930;

August Friedrich Leopold Weismann, German biologist, 1914;

Maria Anna Angelica Kauffmann, painter, 1807;

Pierre-Ambroise-François Choderlos de Laclos, French soldier and writer, 1803.

Occurred on this day:

Richard Nixon was elected as 37th president of the USA, 1968;

US troops under General Pershing went into action for the first time on the Western Front, 1917;

On the outbreak of war with Turkey, Cyprus was annexed by Britain, 1914;

The Prince Regent of Bavaria was declared king as Ludwig III, 1913;

Italy declared war on Turkey and took Tripoli and Cyrenaica, 1911;

The musical show *The Quaker Girl* was first produced, London, 1910;

In Liverpool, the first British Woolworth's store opened, 1909;

The British and French armies defeated the Russians at the Battle of Inkerman, 1854;

The British sovereign abandoned the title 'King of France', 1800;

The Gunpowder Plot was discovered, 1605.

TODAY IS THE FEAST DAY OF St Bertilla of Chelles, Saints Elisabeth and Zachary, St Episteme and St Galation.

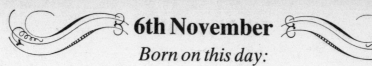

6th November

Born on this day:

Graeme Wood, Australian cricketer, 1956;
Nigel Havers, actor, 1949;
David Montgomery, editor, *Today*, 1948;
Sally Field, US actress, 1946;
P. J. Proby, rock singer, 1938;
Jacques Charrier, French actor, 1936;
Donald Churchill, actor and writer, 1930;
Frank Carson, comedian, 1926;
Ray Coniff, US songwriter and arranger, 1916;
Leonard Miall, historian, 1914;
Sir John William Alcock, pioneer aviator, 1892;
Gus Kahn, US lyricist, 1886;
Herbert, 1st Viscount Samuel, statesman, 1870;

John Philip Sousa, US conductor and composer of marches, 1854;
John Richard Jefferies, author and naturalist, 1848;
Cesare Lombroso, Italian criminologist, 1835;
Adolphe [Antoine-Joseph] Sax, Belgian inventor of the saxophone, 1814;
Alois Senefelder, Austrian inventor of lithography, 1771;
Colley Cibber, actor and playwright, 1671;
James Gregory, inventor of the reflecting telescope, 1638;
Thomas Kyd, playwright, 1558.

Died on this day:

Frank Arthur Swinnerton, novelist and critic, 1982;
Prof. Nevill Henry Kendal Aylmer Coghill, scholar and author, 1980;
Sir Johnston Forbes-Robertson, actor-manager, 1937;
R. P. [Bob] Weston, popular composer, 1936;
Kate [Catherine] Greenaway, illustrator of children's books, 1901;

Peter Ilyich Tchaikovsky, Russian composer, 1893;
Admiral Sir Charles Napier, 1860;
William Hone, satirist and editor, 1842;
Claude-Louis, Comte Berthollet, French chemist, 1822;
John Murray [McMurray], publisher, 1793;
Heinrich Schütz, German composer, 1672;
Gustavus II Adolphus, King of Sweden, killed in battle, 1632.

Occurred on this day:

The United States exploded the first hydrogen bomb at Eniwetok Atoll, in the Pacific, 1952;
In the German general election, the Nazis were the largest party, 1932;
Herbert Hoover was elected as 31st president of the USA, 1928;
The Republic of Poland was proclaimed, 1918;

The third Battle of Ypres ended after Passchendaele Ridge was captured by British and Canadian troops, 1917;
Diamonds were discovered at Kimberley, South Africa, 1869;
Abraham Lincoln was elected as 16th president of the USA, 1860;
Mexico declared herself independent, 1813.

TODAY IS THE FEAST DAY OF St Barlaam of Khutyn, St Demetrian of Khytri, St Illtud, St Leonard of Noblac, St Melaine and St Winnoc.

7th November

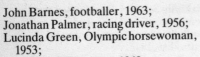

Born on this day:

John Barnes, footballer, 1963;
Jonathan Palmer, racing driver, 1956;
Lucinda Green, Olympic horsewoman, 1953;
Su Pollard, TV actress, 1949;
Joni Mitchell, Canadian singer, 1943;
Jean Shrimpton, former model, 1942;
Ian Balding, racehorse trainer, 1938;
Dame Gwyneth Jones, operatic soprano, 1936;
Dame Joan Sutherland, operatic soprano, 1926;
Wolf Mankowitz, author and playwright, 1924;
Dr Billy Graham, US evangelist, 1918;
Helen Suzman, South African politician, 1917;
Albert Camus, French novelist and playwright, 1913;
Ruth Pitter, poetess, 1897;
Herman J. Mankiewicz, US screenwriter, 1897;
Sir Chandrasekhara Venkata Raman, Indian physicist, 1888;
Leon Trotsky [Lev Davidovich Bronstein], Russian Communist leader, 1879;
Lise Meitner, Austrian physicist and a discoverer, with Otto Hahn, of nuclear fission, 1878;
Marie Curie [Manya Sklodowska], physicist, 1867;
Joseph Hocking, novelist and preacher, 1860;
Paul-Jacques-Aimé Baudry, French painter, 1828;
William Stukeley, physician and antiquarian, 1687;
Francisco de Zurbaran, Spanish painter, 1598.

Died on this day:

Terrence Steven [Steve] McQueen, US film actor, 1980;
James Joseph [Gene] Tunney, US heavyweight boxer, 1978;
John Carmel Heenan, Cardinal, RC Archbishop of Westminster, 1975;
Anna Eleanor Roosevelt, US writer and lecturer, 1962;
Victor McLaglen, film actor, 1959;
Hans Thoma, German painter, 1924;
Alfred Russel Wallace, explorer and naturalist, 1913;
Anne Grant, poet and essayist, 1838;
Jean-André Deluc, Swiss geologist, 1817;
Jean-Marc Nattier, French portrait painter, 1766;
Sir Godfrey Kneller [Gottfried Kniller], painter, 1723.

Occurred on this day:

Mary Robinson became the first woman prime minister of the Irish Republic, 1990;
The first London performance of the musical show *The Boys from Syracuse* was presented, 1963;
The first London production of the musical show *Robin Hood* was presented, 1944;
After 4½ years' work, the Canadian Pacific Railroad was completed, 1885;
The brigantine *Mary Celeste* left New York, to be found abandoned later, 1872;
The last public hanging in England took place at Tyburn, 1783;
The *London Gazette* was first published, 1665;
Pierre Gassendi made the first observation of the transit of a planet when he studied Mercury, 1631.

TODAY IS THE FEAST DAY OF St Engelbert, St Florentius of Strasbourg, St Herculanus of Perugia and St Willibrord.

8th November

Born on this day:

Elizabeth Gale, opera singer, 1948;
David Jessel, TV journalist, 1945;
Martin Peters, footballer, 1943;
Nerys Hughes, actress, 1941;
Paul Foot, journalist, 1937;
Alain Delon, French film actor, 1935;
Tamàs Vasary, conductor and pianist, 1933;
Ken Dodd, comedian, 1931;
Patti Page, US singer, 1927;
Prof. Christiaan Barnard, South African heart transplant pioneer, 1922;
June Havoc, US film actress, 1916;
Frederick Gore, painter, 1913;

Margaret Mitchell, author of *Gone with the Wind*, 1900;
Neil Miller Gunn, Scottish novelist, 1891;
Sir Arnold Edward Trevor Bax, Master of the King's Musick, 1883;
Herbert, 1st Baron Austin, motor car manufacturer, 1866;
[Abraham] Bram Stoker, author of *Dracula*, 1847;
Edward Robert, 1st Earl of Lytton ['Owen Meredith'], diplomat and poet, 1831;
Edmond Halley, astronomer and mathematician, 1656;
Teofilo Folengo [Girolamo Folengo], Italian poet and monk, 1491.

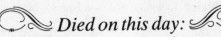
Died on this day:

Edgard Varèse [Edgar Victor Achille Charles Varèse], US composer, 1965;
Ivan Alexeyevich Bunin, poet, 1953;
Howard Pyle, US artist and writer, 1911;
Victorien Sardou, French playwright, 1908;
Francis Parkman, US historian, 1893;

César-Auguste Franck, Belgian composer, 1890;
Fred Archer, jockey, committed suicide, 1886;
Thomas Bewick, wood engraver, 1828;
John Milton, poet, 1674;
John Duns Scotus, philosopher, 1308.

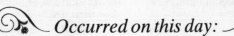
Occurred on this day:

The first local radio station in Britain, Radio Leicester, opened, 1967;
John Fitzgerald Kennedy was elected as 35th president of the USA, 1960;
The Allies landed in North Africa, 1942;
Franklin Delano Roosevelt was elected as 32nd president of the USA, 1932;
The first London performance of the musical show *Funny Face* was presented, 1928;

The Fortune Theatre, London, opened, 1924;
Adolf Hitler made his attempted putsch in Munich, 1923;
Wilhelm Röntgen discovered X-rays, 1895;
Montana became the 41st of the United States, 1889;
The Louvre, Paris, was opened to the public for the first time, 1793.

TODAY IS THE FEAST DAY OF St Cuby or Cybi, St Deusdedit, The Four Crowned Martyrs, St Godfrey of Amiens, St Tysilio or Suliau and St Willehad.

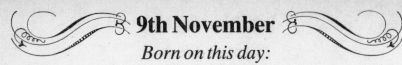

9th November

Born on this day:

Karen Dotrice, actress, 1955;
Lou Ferrigno, US film actor, 1952;
Tom Weiskopf, golfer, 1942;
Roger McGough, poet, 1937;
Donald Trelford, editor of the *Observer*, 1937;
Ronald Harwood, novelist and playwright, 1934;
Hugh Leonard, Irish playwright, 1926;
Stella Richman, TV producer, 1922;
Hedy Lamarr, US film actress, 1913;
Katharine Hepburn, US film actress, 1909;

Anthony Asquith, film director and producer, 1902;
Jean-Omer-Marie-Gabriel Monnet, French political economist, 1888;
Dr Herbert Thomas Kalmus, US inventor of Technicolor, 1881;
Sir Giles Gilbert Scott, architect, 1880;
King Edward VII, 1841;
Ivan Sergeyevich Turgenev, Russian playwright, 1818;
Walter Geikie, Scottish painter, 1795;
Mark Akenside, poet and physician, 1721.

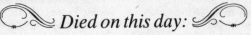

Died on this day:

Yves Montand [Ivo Livi], French singer and actor, 1991;
Egon Wellesz, composer, 1974;
General Charles de Gaulle, French statesman, 1970;
King Ibn Saud, 1953;
Dylan Marlais Thomas, Welsh poet, 1953;
Chaim Weizmann, first president of Israel, 1952;
Sigmund Romberg, US composer, 1951;
Arthur Neville Chamberlain, statesman, 1940;

James Ramsay MacDonald, statesman, 1937;
Guillaume Apollinaire [Wilhelm Apollinaris Kostrowitsky], French poet, 1918;
Paul Sandby, water-colour painter, 1809;
Thomas Girtin, painter and etcher, 1802;
Karl Stamitz, German composer, 1801;
William Camden, antiquarian and historian, 1623.

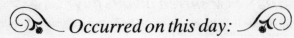

Occurred on this day:

The death penalty for murder was abolished in Britain, 1965;
The German Kaiser abdicated after a revolution in Germany, 1918;
Georges Clemenceau was elected as prime minister of France, 1917;

The first woman mayor, Elizabeth Garrett Anderson, was elected at Aldeburgh, 1908;
Flogging in the British Army was abolished, 1859;
Moses Montefiore was the first Jew to be knighted in England, 1837.

TODAY IS THE FEAST DAY OF St Benignus or Benen, St Theodore the Recruit and St Vitonus or Vanne.

314

10th November

Born on this day:

Donya Fiorentino, US fashion model, 1967;
Tim Rice, lyricist, 1944;
Don Henderson, actor, 1932;
Admiral of the Fleet Sir William Staveley, 1928;
Frank Durr, racehorse trainer, 1926;
Robert Carrier, broadcaster and writer on cookery, 1923;
Anne Shelton, singer, 1923;
Moise Tshombe, Congolese politician, 1919;
John Phillips Marquand, US novelist, 1893;
Claude Rains, film actor, 1889;
Arnold Zweig, German author, 1887;
Sir Jacob Epstein, sculptor, 1880;
Nicholas Vachel Lindsay, US poet, 1879;
Winston Churchill, US novelist, 1871;
Johann Christoph Friedrich von Schiller, German poet and playwright, 1759;
Oliver Goldsmith, playwright, 1728;
William Hogarth, painter and engraver, 1697;
King George II, 1683;
François Couperin ['Le Grand'], French composer, 1668;
Robert Devereux, 2nd Earl of Essex, soldier and courtier, 1566;
Paracelsus [Theophrastus Bombast von Hohenheim], Swiss physician, 1493;
Martin Luther, Protestant reformer, 1483.

Died on this day:

Sir Gordon Richards, jockey, 1986;
Leonid Ilyich Brezhnev, Soviet political leader, 1982;
Dennis Yates Wheatley, novelist, 1979;
Mustapha Kemal Atatürk, Turkish statesman, 1938;
Sir Archibald Geikie, geologist, 1924;
Jean-Nicolas-Arthur Rimbaud, French poet, 1891;
Isidore Geoffroy Saint-Hilaire, French geologist, 1861;
Gideon Algernon Mantell, palaeontologist, 1852;
Richard Chancellor, navigator, 1556;
Pope Leo I [the Great], 461.

 Occurred on this day:

The Greek forces drove the Italian army back into Albania, 1940;
An airmail service began between London and Paris, 1919;
Sir Henry Morton Stanley met Livingstone at Ujiji, Tanganyika, 1871;
Verdi's opera, *La Forza del Destino*, was first performed, St Petersburg, 1862;
Alois Senefelder patented the lithographic printing process, 1798;
The US Marine Corps was founded, 1775;
Christopher Columbus discovered Antigua on his second voyage, 1493.

TODAY IS THE FEAST DAY OF St Aedh MacBricc, St Andrew Avellino, St Justus of Canterbury, St Leo the Great and St Theoctista.

11th November

Born on this day:

Richard Rowe, jockey, 1959;
Rodney Marsh, Australian cricketer, 1947;
Roy Fredericks, cricketer and Guyanese politician, 1942;
Bibi Andersson, Swedish film actress, 1935;
June Whitfield, actress, 1925;
Kurt Vonnegut, US novelist, 1922;
Lord Jenkins of Hillhead, former MP, 1920;
Ivy Benson, bandleader, 1918;
Lord Carr of Hadley, former Home Secretary, 1916;
Sir Peter Shepheard, architect, 1913;
General Sir Walter Walker, former C.-in-C. Allied Forces, N. Europe, 1912;
René Clair [Chomette], French film director, 1898;
George Smith Patton, US general, 1885;
Gustav VI Adolf, King of Sweden, 1882;

Jean-Édouard Vuillard, French painter, 1868;
Antoine Meillet, French linguist, 1866;
Paul Signac, French painter, 1863;
Fyodor Mikhailovich Dostoevsky, Russian author, 1821;
Johann Kaspar Lavater, Swiss writer, pastor and founder of physiognomics, 1741;
Louis-Antoine de Bougainville, French navigator, 1729;
Johann Albert Fabricius, German classical scholar, 1688;
André-Charles Boulle [Buhl], French cabinet-maker, 1642;
Prince Ottavio Piccolomini, Italian military commander, 1599;
Frans Snyders, Flemish animal painter, 1579.

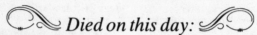

Died on this day:

Vyacheslav Mikhailovich Molotov [Skriabin], Russian leader, 1986;
James Hanley, novelist and playwright, 1985;
Dimitri Tiomkin, US composer, 1979;
Cyril Vernon Connolly, author, journalist and critic, 1974;
Sir Alan Patrick Herbert CH, author, 1971;
Victor Young, US composer and conductor, 1956;

Jerome David Kern, US composer, 1945;
Sir Edward German [Edward German Jones], composer, 1936;
Valentine Cameron Prinsep, artist, 1904;
Ned Kelly, Australian outlaw, hanged, 1880;
Sören Aabye Kierkegaard, Danish philosopher, 1855;
Johann Zoffany [Zauffely], theatrical painter, 1810.

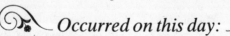

Occurred on this day:

Angola proclaimed her independence, 1975;
In London, the new Covent Garden fruit and vegetable market opened at Nine Elms in South London, 1974;
Ian Smith made a unilateral declaration of independence for Rhodesia, 1965;
The first video recorder was demonstrated in Beverly Hills, California, 1952;

An armistice was signed between the Allies and Germany in World War I, 1918;
The musical show *Floradora* was first performed, London, 1899;
Washington became the 42nd of the United States, 1889.

TODAY IS THE FEAST DAY OF St Bartholomew of Grottaferrata, St Mannas of Egypt, St Martin of Tours and St Theodore the Studite.

Born on this day:

Nadia Comaneci, Romanian gymnastic champion, 1961;

Neil Young, Canadian rock singer and guitarist, 1946;

Stephanie Powers, US TV and film actress, 1943;

Lucia Popp, operatic soprano, 1939;

Peter Lloyd, MP, 1937;

Princess Grace of Monaco [Grace Kelly], 1929;

Kim Hunter, US film actress, 1922;

Sir Ronald Millar, playwright and screenwriter, 1919;

Jo Stafford, US singer, 1918;

The Rev. Dr Chad Varah, founder of the Samaritans, 1911;

Richard A. Whiting, US popular composer, 1891;

Sun Yat-sen, first president of China, 1866;

John William Strutt, 3rd Baron Rayleigh, physicist, 1842;

François-Auguste Rodin, French sculptor, 1840;

Alexander Porfirievich Borodin, Russian composer, 1833;

Amelia Opie [Amelia Alderson], novelist, 1769;

Gerhard Johann von Scharnhorst, Prussian soldier, 1755;

Jacques-Alexandre-César Charles, French physicist and inventor, 1746;

Edward Vernon ['Old Grog'], Admiral, 1684;

Richard Baxter, Puritan minister, scholar and writer, 1615.

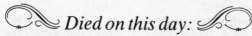

Died on this day:

Charles Rudolf Friml, US/Austrian composer, 1972;

Emma Magdalena Rosalia Marie Josepha Barbara, Baroness Orczy, novelist, 1947;

Percival Lowell, US astronomer, 1916;

Gottfried Kinkel, German poet, 1882;

Johann Friedrich Overbeck, German painter, 1869;

Elizabeth Cleghorn Gaskell, novelist, 1865;

Charles Kemble, actor, 1854;

Jean-Baptiste Regnault, French painter, 1829;

William Hayley, poet and biographer, 1820;

Jean-Sylvan Bailly, French astronomer and first mayor of Paris, guillotined, 1793;

Thomas Fairfax, 3rd Baron Fairfax of Cameron, parliamentary army C.-in-C., 1671;

Sir John Hawkins, navigator, 1595;

Stephen Gardiner, Bishop of Winchester, 1555;

Canute II [the Great], King of England and Denmark, 1035.

Occurred on this day:

The German battleship *Tirpitz* was sunk, 1944;

The Battle of Guadalcanal started, 1942;

The Emperor Karl of Austria-Hungary abdicated, and Austria became a republic, 1918;

The remains of Captain Scott and his companions were found in Antarctica, 1912;

A great eruption of Mount Vesuvius occurred, 1867;

The first flying-trapeze act was performed by Jules Léotard at the Cirque Napoléon, Paris, 1859;

Sir James Young Simpson was the first to use chloroform as an anaesthetic in Britain, 1847;

The first Jewish newspaper in Britain, the *Jewish Chronicle*, was published, 1841.

TODAY IS THE FEAST DAY OF St Astrik or Anastasius, St Benedict of Benevento, St Cadwalader, St Cumian the Tall, St Cunibert, St Emilian Cucullatus, St Josaphat of Polotsk, St Lebuin or Liafwine, St Livinus, St Machar or Mochumma and St Nilus the Elder.

13th November

Born on this day:

The Rt. Rev. Dr George Carey,
Archbishop of Canterbury, 1935;
Adrienne Corri, actress, 1931;
Joan Lestor, MP, 1931;
Eugene Ionesco, French author and
playwright, 1912;
Robert Louis Balfour Stevenson, writer
and traveller, 1850;
Edwin Thomas Booth, US actor, 1833;
Charles Frederick Worth, couturier, 1825;

Henry Brinley Richards, pianist and
composer, 1819;
Edward John Trelawny, writer and
traveller, 1792;
Esaias Tegnér, Swedish bishop, scholar and
poet, 1782;
General Sir John Moore, 1761;
Maurice of Nassau, Prince of Orange,
Dutch military leader, 1567;
King Edward III, 1312.

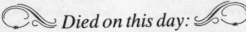

Died on this day:

Chesney Allen, comedian, 1982;
Robert Cedric Sherriff, playwright and
novelist, 1975;
Vittorio De Sica, Italian film director, 1974;
Elsa Schiaparelli, couturière, 1973;
Francis Thompson, poet, 1907;
Camille Pissarro, French painter, 1903;
Arnaud-Michel d'Abbadie, French
explorer, 1893;

Gioacchino Antonio Rossini, Italian
composer, 1868;
Arthur Hugh Clough, poet, 1861;
William Etty, painter, 1849;
George Sale, orientalist and translator of
the Koran, 1736;
Lodovico Carracci, Italian painter, 1619;
Prince Henry the Navigator, 1460;
Malcolm III, King of the Scots, killed, 1093.

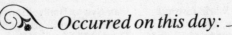

Occurred on this day:

A cyclone and tidal waves caused the death
of over 500,000 people in East Pakistan,
1970;
Sukarno became president of the Republic
of Indonesia, 1945;
A Pacific treaty was signed between the
USA, the British Empire, France and
Japan, 1921;

Serious casualties occurred among Socialist
and Irish agitators on Bloody Sunday in
Trafalgar Square, 1887;
The telegraphic service between London
and Paris started, 1851;
Texas declared its independence of Mexico,
1835.

TODAY IS THE FEAST DAY OF St Abbo of Fleury, St Arcadius, St Brice or Britius, St
Didacus or Diego of Seville, St Eugenius of Toledo, St Frances Xavia Cabrini, St
Homobonus, St Maxellendis, St Nicholas I, pope and St Stanislaus Kostka.

 # 14th November

Born on this day:

Bernard Hinault, Tour de France winner, 1954;

HRH the Prince of Wales, 1948;

Freddie Garrity, rock star, 1940;

HM King Hussein of Jordan, 1935;

Dame Elisabeth Frink CH, sculptor, 1930;

Peter Katin, concert pianist, 1930;

Quentin Crewe, writer and restaurateur, 1926;

Margaret Courtenay, actress, 1923;

Eric Crozier, author and theatrical producer, 1914;

Joseph Raymond McCarthy, US senator, 1908;

Harold Larwood, cricketer, 1904;

Dick Powell [Richard Ewing Powell], US film actor and singer, 1904;

Sir Frederick Grant Banting, Canadian physician, 1891;

Pandit Jawaharal Nehru, Indian statesman, 1889;

Leo Hendrik Baekeland, Belgian inventor of Bakelite, 1863;

Sir William Reynell Anson Bt., jurist, 1843;

Claude-Oscar Monet, French impressionistic painter, 1840;

John Curwen, musician and publisher, 1816;

Sir Charles Lyell, geologist, 1797;

William Glen, Scottish poet, 1789;

Adam Gottlob Oehlenschläger, Danish poet, 1779;

Gaspare Luigi Pacifico Spontini, Italian composer, 1774;

Robert Fulton, US steamboat pioneer, 1765;

Benjamin Hoadley, Bishop of Bangor, 1676.

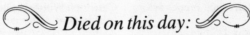 *Died on this day:*

Robert Emmet Sherwood, US playwright, 1955;

Manuel de Falla, Spanish composer, 1946;

Sir David Murray, Scottish artist, 1933;

Hector Hugh Munro ['Saki'], writer, killed in action, 1916;

Frederick Sleigh Roberts, 1st Earl, field marshal, 1914;

Dr John Abercrombie, physician, 1844;

Georg Wilhelm Friedrich Hegel, German philosopher, 1831;

Gottfried Wilhelm, Baron von Leibniz, German philosopher, 1716;

Nell [Eleanor] Gwyn, actress and mistress of Charles II, 1687.

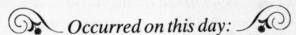 *Occurred on this day:*

Colour TV transmission was begun in Britain, 1969;

The first London performance of the musical show *The Bells Are Ringing* was presented, 1956;

The aircraft carrier *Ark Royal* was sunk, 1941;

Coventry Cathedral was destroyed by enemy bombing, 1940;

Book tokens first went on sale, 1932;

Daily broadcasting from the London radio station 2LO began, 1922.

TODAY IS THE FEAST DAY OF St Adeotus Aribert, St Dubricius or Dyfrig, St Laurence O'Toole, St Nicholas Tavelic, St Peter of Narbonne and St Stephen of Cuneo.

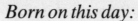

15th November

Born on this day:

Daniel Barenboim, pianist and conductor, 1942;

Sam Waterston, US actor, 1940;

Prof. Peter Dickinson, pianist and composer, 1934;

Petula Clark, singer and actress, 1934;

J.G. Ballard, science-fiction author, 1930;

Ed Asner, US TV actor, 1929;

Paul Raymond, impresario, 1925;

Andre Deutsch, publisher, 1917;

Hamish Hamilton, publisher, 1900;

Aneurin Bevan, statesman, 1897;

Sir Sacheverell Sitwell Bt., poet and author, 1897;

William Averell Harriman, US diplomat, 1891;

Erwin Johannes Eugen Rommel, German field marshal, 1891;

Schack August Steenberg Krogh, Danish physiologist, 1874;

Gerhart Hauptmann, German playwright, 1862;

Sir William [Friedrich Wilhelm] Herschel, astronomer, 1738;

William Pitt the Elder, 1st Earl of Chatham, statesman, 1708;

Madeleine de Scudéry, French novelist, 1607.

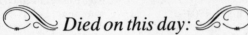

Died on this day:

John Le Mesurier, actor, 1983;

Dr Margaret Mead, US anthropologist, 1978;

Jean Gabin [Jean Moncorgé], French actor, 1976;

Tyrone Edmund Power, US film actor, 1958;

Lionel Barrymore [Blythe], US actor, 1954;

Viola Tree, actress and author, 1938;

Alfred Werner, Swiss chemist, 1919;

Henryk Adam Aleksander Pius Sienkiewicz, Polish novelist, 1916;

William Murdock, inventor of coal-gas lighting, 1839;

George Romney, portrait painter, 1802;

Christoph Willibald Gluck, German/ Bohemian composer, 1787;

Aelbert Jacobsz Cuyp, Dutch painter, 1691;

Johannes Kepler, German astronomer, 1630;

Albertus Magnus, German philosopher and theologian, 1280.

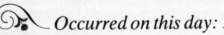

Occurred on this day:

Northern Cyprus, occupied by Turkish troops, was unilaterally declared independent, 1983;

The first London performance of the musical show *Fanny* was presented, 1956;

The Commonwealth of the Philippines was inaugurated, 1935;

Danzig was declared to be a free city, 1920;

Brazil became a republic, 1889;

Isaac Pitman published his shorthand system, 1837.

TODAY IS THE FEAST DAY OF Saints Abibus, Gurias and Samonas, St Albert the Great, St Desiderius or Didier of Cahors, St Fintan of Rheinau, St Leopold of Austria and St Malo or Machutus.

16th November

Born on this day:

Frank Bruno, boxer, 1961;

Griff Rhys Jones, actor and writer, 1953;

Joanna Pettet, film actress, 1944;

Willie Carson, jockey, 1942;

Michael Billington, author and broadcaster, 1939;

Michael Zander, professor of law, LSE, 1932;

Tony de Leeuw, Dutch composer, 1926;

Tommie Connor, songwriter, 1904;

Sir Oswald Ernald Mosley, Fascist leader, 1896;

Michael Arlen [Dikran Kouyoumdjian], novelist, 1895;

Paul Hindemith, German viola player and composer, 1895;

George Simon Kaufman, US playwright, 1889;

William John Thoms, founder and editor of *Notes and Queries*, 1885;

Aleksander Aleksandrovich Blok, Russian poet, 1880;

William Christopher Handy, US composer and cornetist, 1873;

Alphonse-Marie-Léon Daudet, French author, 1867;

William Frend de Morgan, artist and novelist, 1839;

John Bright, political reformer, 1811;

Francis Danby, Irish painter, 1793;

Tiberius, Roman emperor, 42 BC.

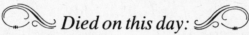

Died on this day:

Arthur Bowden Askey, comedian, 1983;

William Holden [William Franklin Beedle], US film actor, 1981;

William Clark Gable, US film actor, 1960;

Charles Maurras, French writer and philosopher, 1952;

George Alfred Henty, author of books for boys, 1902;

Louis Riel, leader of the Métis rebellion in Canada, hanged, 1885;

John Walter, founder of *The Times*, 1812;

James Ferguson, astronomer, 1776;

Jack Sheppard, highwayman, hanged, 1724;

Perkin Warbeck, pretender to the throne, executed, 1499;

King Henry III, 1272.

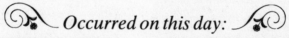

Occurred on this day:

The first London performance of the musical show *Applause* was presented, 1972;

Following a period of rampant inflation, a new currency system was introduced in Germany, 1923;

In Budapest, Hungary was proclaimed an independent republic, 1918;

Oklahoma became the 46th of the United States, 1907;

Wyndham's Theatre, London, opened, 1899;

Amadeus, Duke of Aosta, was elected King of Spain as Amadeo I, 1870;

The Suez Canal was formally opened at Port Said, 1869;

The Holborn Empire, London, opened as Weston's Music Hall, 1857;

Hamilton Hume, Australian explorer, discovered the Murray River, 1824;

Frederick Wilhelm III became King of Prussia, 1797;

Westminster Bridge was formally opened, 1750.

TODAY IS THE FEAST DAY OF St Afan, St Agnes of Assisi, St Edmund of Abingdon, St Eucherius of Lyons, St Gertrude of Helfta, St Margaret of Scotland, St Mechtildis of Helfta and St Nikon 'Metanoeite'.

17th November

Born on this day:

Jonathan Ross, broadcaster, 1960;
David Emanuel, fashion designer, 1952;
James Warwick, actor, 1947;
Jeremy Hanley, MP, 1945;
Auberon Waugh, journalist, 1939;
Gordon Lightfoot, Canadian singer and songwriter, 1938;
Peter Cook, writer and entertainer, 1937;
John Wells, writer and actor, 1936;
Fenella Fielding, actress, 1934;
Sir Charles Mackerras, conductor, 1925;
Colin Hayes, painter, 1919;
Field Marshal Sir Bernard Law Montgomery, 1st Viscount of Alamein, 1887;

Louis-Hubert-Gonzalve Lyautey, French soldier and colonial administrator, 1854;
George Grote, historian, 1794;
Sir Charles Lock Eastlake, painter, 1793;
Jacques-Étienne-Joseph-Alexandre Macdonald, Duke of Tarentum, French marshal, 1765;
Louis XVIII, King of France, 1755;
Jean le Rond d'Alembert, French scientist and mathematician, 1717;
Pierre Gaultier de Varennes, Sieur de la Vérendrye, French explorer and fur trader, 1685;
Agnolo di Cosimo di Mariano [Bronzino], Florentine painter, 1503.

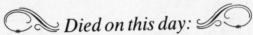 Died on this day:

Dame Gladys Cooper, actress, 1971;
Heitor Villa-Lobos, composer, 1959;
Arthur Eric Rowton Gill, stone-carver, engraver, typographer and author, 1940;
François-Auguste Rodin, French sculptor, 1917;
Richard Norman Shaw, architect, 1912;
Robert Owen, social reformer, 1858;
Thomas, 1st Baron Erskine, lawyer, 1823;

Thomas Pelham-Holles, Duke of Newcastle, politician, 1768;
Alain-René Le Sage, French novelist and playwright, 1747;
Ludolf Backhuysen, Dutch painter, 1708;
Jakob Böhme, German mystic and theosophist, 1624;
Mary I, Queen of England, 1558;
Giovanni Pico, Count of Mirandola and Concordia, Italian philosopher, 1494.

Occurred on this day:

The first London performance of the musical show *Godspell* was presented, 1971;
The Soviet *Luna 17* touched down on the moon, 1970;
Gilbert and Sullivan's opera *The Sorcerer* was first produced, London, 1877;
The opera *Mignon* by Ambroise Thomas was first performed, Paris, 1866;
Lucknow was relieved by Sir Colin Campbell, 1857;

The first meeting of the US Congress took place in Washington, 1800;
Napoleon defeated the Austrians at Arcole, 1796;
Elizabeth I acceded to the throne of England, 1558;
John Baliol acceded to the throne of Scotland, 1292.

TODAY IS THE FEAST DAY OF Saints Acisclus and Victoria, Saints Alphaeus and Zachaeus, St Anianus or Aignan of Orléans, St Dionysius of Alexandria, St Elizabeth of Hungary, St Gregory of Tours, St Gregory the Wonderworker, St Hilda, St Hugh of Lincoln and The Martyrs of Paraguay.

 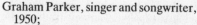

18th November

Born on this day:

Graham Parker, singer and songwriter, 1950;

David Hemmings, actor and director, 1941;

Brenda Vaccaro, US actress, 1939;

Don Cherry, US jazz trumpeter, 1936;

Alan Shepard, US astronaut, 1923;

Sir Tasker Watkins VC, a Lord Justice of Appeal, and Deputy Chief Justice of England, 1918;

John Herndon [Johnny] Mercer, US composer and singer, 1909;

Alan Pryce-Jones, author and critic, 1908;

George Horace Gallup, US public opinion pollster, 1901;

Amelita Galli-Gurci, singer, 1889;

Frank Dobson, sculptor, 1888;

Percy Wyndham Lewis, artist and writer, at sea, 1882;

Ignaz Jan Paderewski, Polish pianist, composer and statesman, 1860;

Sir William Schwenck Gilbert, playwright and librettist, 1836;

Nils Adolf Erik Nordenskjöld, Swedish Arctic explorer, 1832;

Louis-Jacques-Mandé Daguerre, French photographic pioneer, 1789;

Carl Maria Friedrich Ernst von Weber, German composer, 1786;

Sir Henry Rowley Bishop, conductor and composer, 1786;

Sir David Wilkie, painter, 1785;

Pierre Bayle, French philosopher, 1647;

Gaspard de Crayer, Flemish painter, 1582.

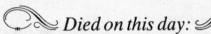 Died on this day:

Kurt von Schuschnigg, Austrian politician, 1977;

Ted Heath, bandleader, 1969;

Mervyn Laurence Peake, author and artist, 1968;

Walter Wanger [Feuchtwanger], US film producer, 1968;

Niels Henrik David Bohr, Danish physicist, 1962;

Walther Hermann Nernst, German physicist and chemist, 1941;

Thomas Power O'Connor, journalist and politician, 1929;

Marcel Proust, French author, 1922;

William Allingham, Irish poet, 1889;

Chester Alan Arthur, 21st president of the USA, 1886;

Dr Thomas Frognall Dibdin, bibliographer, 1847;

Karl von Clausewitz, Prussian strategist, 1831;

Reginald, Cardinal Pole, 1558.

Occurred on this day:

Fire broke out at King's Cross underground station, and 30 people died, 1987;

The first London production of the musical show *Little Me* was presented, 1964;

The Dartford-Purfleet tunnel under the Thames was opened, 1963;

The first Mickey Mouse cartoon – *Steamboat Willie* – was shown, 1928;

The first battle of the Somme ended, 1916;

Latvia was proclaimed an independent republic, 1918;

William Caxton issued his first dated, printed book, 1477.

TODAY IS THE FEAST DAY OF St Mawes or Maudez, St Odo of Cluny and St Romanus of Antioch.

# 19th November

Born on this day:

Jodie Foster, US actress, 1963;
Kathleen Quinlan, actress, 1954;
Dennis Taylor, snooker champion, 1949;
Mike Vernon, record-producer, 1944;
Calvin Klein, US fashion designer, 1942;
David Lloyd-Jones, opera director, 1934;
Auriol Sinclair, National Hunt trainer, 1918;
Indira Gandhi, Indian stateswoman, 1917;
Baroness Jeger, former MP, 1915;
Tommy Dorsey, US trombonist and bandleader, 1905;
Anton Walbrook [Adolf Wohlbruck], actor, 1900;

James Abram Garfield, 20th president of the USA, 1831;
Vicomte Ferdinand de Lesseps, French engineer and promoter of the Suez Canal, 1805;
René-Auguste Caillié, French explorer, 1799;
Bertel Thorwaldsen, Danish sculptor, 1770;
Jean-Antoine Nollet, French physicist, 1700;
Eustache Le Sueur, French painter, 1616;
Charles I, King of England and Scotland, 1600.

 ## Died on this day:

Elizabeth Taylor [Coles], novelist, 1975;
Edward Chace Tolman, US psychologist, 1959;
Thomas Harper Ince, US film pioneer, 1924;
Sir William [Karl Wilhelm] Siemens, metallurgist, 1883;
Franz Peter Schubert, Austrian composer, 1828;

Claude-Nicolas Ledoux, French architect, 1806;
Theobald Wolfe Tone, Irish republican, committed suicide, 1798;
Thomas Shadwell, poet and playwright, 1692;
Nicolas Poussin, French painter, 1665.

Occurred on this day:

In Paris, the Treaty on Conventional Armed Forces was signed between NATO and members of the Warsaw Pact, thus ending the 'cold war', 1990;
The lunar module from the US spacecraft *Apollo 12* touched down on the moon, 1969;
The Cunard liner *Queen Elizabeth 2* made her first voyage, 1968;
Rainier III was sworn in as 30th ruling prince of Monaco, 1949;
The first general conference of UNESCO was held in Paris, 1946;

The USSR counter-attacked at Stalingrad and surrounded the German army, 1942;
The first London performance of the musical show *Let's Face It!* was presented, 1942;
The 19,000-ton liner *Bermuda* was gutted by fire while in Belfast harbour, 1931;
President Lincoln delivered his speech at Gettysburg, 1863;
Blackfriars Bridge across the Thames was opened for carriages, 1769.

TODAY IS THE FEAST DAY OF St Barlaam of Antioch, St Ermenburga and St Nerses I.

20th November

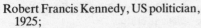

Born on this day:

Robert Francis Kennedy, US politician, 1925;

Nadine Gordimer, South African novelist and Nobel prizewinner, 1923;

Michael Alexander, explorer and writer, 1920;

Dulcie Gray, actress and author, 1920;

Gene Tierney, US film actress, 1920;

Wilfred Wooller, cricketer and Welsh rugby international, 1912;

Brigadier Bernard Cowey, Welsh rugby international, 1911;

Alistair Cooke, journalist and broadcaster, 1908;

Henri-Georges Clouzot, French film director, 1907;

Alexandra Danilova, choreographer and actress, 1906;

Edwin Powell Hubble, US astronomer, 1889;

Selma Ottiliana Lovisa Lagerlöf, Swedish novelist, 1858;

Josiah Royce, US philosopher, 1855;

William Chappell, music publisher, 1809;

Nikolai Ivanovich Lobachevsky, Russian mathematician, 1792;

Sir Samuel Cunard, shipowner, 1787;

John Wall Callcott, organist and composer, 1766;

Thomas Chatterton, poet, 1752;

Paulus Potter, Dutch animal painter, 1625;

Otto von Guericke, German physicist, 1602.

Died on this day:

General Francisco Paulino Hermengildo Teodulo Franco Bahamonde [Franco], Spanish dictator, 1975;

Francesco Cilea, Italian composer, 1950;

Francis William Aston, physicist, 1945;

Ellen Anderson Gholson Glasgow, US novelist, 1945;

Maud, Queen of Norway, 1938;

John Rushworth Jellicoe, 1st Earl, admiral of the fleet, 1935;

Queen Alexandra, consort of King Edward VII, 1925;

Count Leo Nikolayevich Tolstoy, Russian novelist, 1910;

Anton Grigoryevich Rubinstein, Russian pianist and composer, 1894;

Henry Francis Lyte, writer of hymns [Abide With Me], 1847;

Sir John Harington, translator and writer, 1612;

Sir Christopher Hatton, Lord Chancellor, 1591.

Occurred on this day:

President Sadat of Egypt visited Israel for peace talks, 1977;

After the USSR agreed to withdraw Ilyushin bombers from Cuba, the USA lifted the blockade, 1962;

Snowdonia was declared a National Park, 1951;

HM the Queen [then Princess Elizabeth] married the Duke of Edinburgh, 1947;

The War Crimes trial at Nuremberg began, 1945;

The Allied Control Commission approved the transfer of six million Germans from Austria, Hungary and Poland to West Germany, 1945;

After five years of blackout, lights were switched on in London in Piccadilly, the Strand and Fleet Street, 1944;

British tanks took part in their first major battle at Cambrai, 1917;

Charles Stewart Rolls and Frederick Henry Royce combined to form the firm of Rolls Royce, 1906;

Venezuela was declared to be independent of Spain by Simón Bolívar, 1818;

The French invasion fleet was destroyed by Admiral Hawke at Quiberon Bay, 1759.

TODAY IS THE FEAST DAY OF St Bernward, St Dasius, St Edmund the Martyr, St Felix of Valois, St Maxentia of Beauvais and St Nerses of Sahgerd.

21st November

Born on this day:

Goldie Hawn, US film actress, 1945;
Jacques Laffite, French Grand Prix driver, 1943;
Natalia Makarova, ballerina, 1940;
Beryl Bainbridge, author and actress, 1934;
Malcolm Williamson, composer and Master of the Queen's Musick, 1931;
Roy Boulting, film producer, 1913;
Georgina Battiscombe, author, 1905;
René-François-Ghislain Magritte, Belgian surrealist painter, 1898;
Adolph, or Arthur ['Harpo'] Marx, US comedian, 1888;
Sir Harold George Nicolson, diplomat and biographer, 1886;

Sir Arthur Thomas Quiller-Couch ['Q'], novelist and editor, 1863;
Sir Leslie Ward ['Spy'], caricaturist, 1851;
Arthur Goring Thomas, composer, 1850;
Walter William Skeat, philologist, 1835;
James Clarke Hook, painter, 1819;
Lewis Henry Morgan, US ethnologist and lawyer, 1818;
'Barry Cornwall' [Bryan Waller Procter], poet, 1787;
Friedrich Ernst Daniel Schleiermacher, German theologian, 1768;
Voltaire [François-Marie Arouet], French philosopher and writer, 1694.

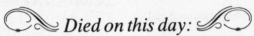

Died on this day:

Frank Martin, Swiss composer, 1974;
Sir Chandrasekhara Venkata Raman, physicist, 1970;
Franz Josef I, Emperor of Austria, 1916;
Mariano José Maria Bernardo Fortuny, Spanish painter, 1874;
James Hogg, writer, the 'Ettrick Shepherd', 1835;

Bernd Heinrich Wilhelm von Kleist, German poet and playwright, committed suicide, 1811;
Henry Purcell, composer, 1695;
Sir Thomas Gresham, founder of the Royal Exchange, 1579.

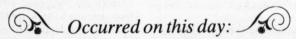

Occurred on this day:

Proceedings in parliament were televised for the first time, 1989;
Following IRA bomb explosions in Birmingham, 20 people were killed and 200 injured, 1974;
The remains of 'Piltdown Man' discovered in 1912 were proved to be forged, 1953;
The Moscow Conference ended, 1944;
A Bill making women eligible as MPs received Royal Assent, 1918;

The German battle fleet surrendered to the Allies, 1918;
Thomas Hancock patented vulcanised rubber, 1843;
The Congress of Aix-la-Chapelle ended, 1818;
North Carolina became the 12th of the United States, 1789;
The Montgolfier brothers made the first hot-air balloon flight, 1783.

TODAY IS THE FEAST DAY OF St Albert of Louvain and St Gelasius I, pope.

22nd November

Born on this day:

Boris Becker, tennis champion, 1967;

Billie Jean King, US tennis champion, 1943;

Tom Conti, actor and director, 1942;

Terry Gilliam, animator, writer and director, 1940;

John Bird, actor, 1936;

Robert Vaughn, US film and TV actor, 1932;

Sir Peter Hall, director of plays, films and operas, 1930;

Pat Koechlin-Smythe, show-jumper, 1928;

Jon Cleary, novelist, 1917;

Edward Benjamin Britten, Baron, composer, 1913;

Howard Hoagland [Hoagy] Carmichael, US songwriter, 1899;

General Charles-André-Marie-Joseph de Gaulle, French president, 1890;

André-Paul-Guillaume Gide, French author, 1869;

Wassily Kandinsky, Russian abstract painter, 1866;

Jean-Baptiste Marchand, French explorer, 1863;

George Robert Gissing, novelist, 1857;

George Eliot [Mary Ann Evans], novelist, 1819;

Thomas Cook, travel agent and temperance advocate, 1808;

Anthony Vandyke Copley Fielding, landscape painter, 1787;

Andreas Hofer, Tyrolean patriot, 1767;

Dugald Stewart, Scottish philosopher and mathematician, 1753;

René-Robert Cavelier, Sieur de la Salle, French explorer, 1643;

Richard Neville, Earl of Warwick ['The Kingmaker'], 1428.

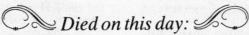

Died on this day:

Mae West, US film actress, 1980;

Clive Staples Lewis, author, 1963;

Aldous Leonard Huxley, 1963;

John Fitzgerald Kennedy, 35th president of the USA, assassinated, 1963;

Alfred Edward Woodley Mason, author, 1948;

Sir Arthur Stanley Eddington, astronomer, 1944;

Lorenz Milton [Larry] Hart, US lyricist, 1943;

John Griffith [Jack] London, US novelist, 1916;

Sir Arthur Seymour Sullivan, composer, 1900;

Robert Clive, Baron, soldier and statesman, committed suicide, 1774;

Edward Teach [Blackbeard the pirate], killed off the American coast, 1718;

Sir Martin Frobisher, navigator, 1594.

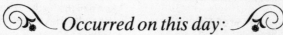

Occurred on this day:

Margaret Thatcher resigned as prime minister, 1990;

Juan Carlos of Bourbon was sworn in as King of Spain, 1975;

President Kennedy was assassinated in Dallas, 1963;

The first coelocanth 'living fossil fish' was caught off Cape Province, South Africa, 1938;

Cape Colony forbade the landing of convicts, and forced a British ship to sail on to Tasmania, 1849;

The first Battle of Ypres ended, 1914;

The Belgian Congress voted for a monarchy, 1830;

Vasco da Gama rounded the Cape of Good Hope, 1497.

TODAY IS THE FEAST DAY OF St Cecilia or Cecily and Saints Philemon and Apphia.

23rd November

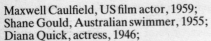

Born on this day:

Maxwell Caulfield, US film actor, 1959;
Shane Gould, Australian swimmer, 1955;
Diana Quick, actress, 1946;
Alan Mullery, footballer, 1941;
Lew Hoad, tennis champion, 1934;
Krzysztof Penderecki, Polish composer, 1933;
Jerry Bock, US composer, 1928;
John Cole, BBC TV political editor, 1927;
Christopher Logue, poet, 1926;
Michael Gough, actor, 1917;
Anne Burns, former gliding champion, 1915;
Sir Peter Saunders, theatrical producer, 1911;

Nigel Tranter, novelist and historian, 1909;
Boris Karloff [William Henry Pratt], film actor, 1887;
Manuel de Falla, Spanish composer, 1876;
Sir Gilbert Horatio George Parker, author and politician, 1862;
Marie Konstaninova Bashkirtseff, Russian author and painter, 1860;
Johannes Diderik van der Waals, Dutch physicist, 1837;
James Thomson, poet, 1834;
Franklin Pierce, 14th president of the USA, 1804;
John Wallis, mathematician, 1616;
Alfonso X, King of Castile and Leon, 1221.

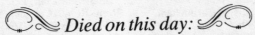

Died on this day:

Merle Oberon [Estelle Merle O'Brien Thompson], film actress, 1979;
André-Georges Malraux, French novelist, 1976;
Percival Christopher Wren, novelist, 1941;
Sir Ernest Alfred Thompson Wallis Budge, Orientalist and museum curator, 1934;
Sir Arthur Wing Pinero, playwright, 1934;
Dr Hawley Harvey Crippen, murderer, executed, 1910;

Sir Roger Newdigate, antiquary, 1806;
L'Abbé Prévost [Antoine-François Prévost D'Exiles], French author, 1763;
Richard Hakluyt, geographer, 1616;
Thomas Tallis, organist and composer, 1585;
Angelo Allori [Bronzino], Florentine painter and poet, 1572.

 ## Occurred on this day:

John Major became prime minister, 1990;
Britain's first commercial radio station was opened on the Isle of Man, 1964;
Karl I acceded to the throne of Austria, 1916;

Luxembourg was separated from the Netherlands, 1890;
Wilhelmina of Orange-Nassau became Queen of the Netherlands, 1890;
The first pillar box was erected [at St Helier, Jersey], 1852.

TODAY IS THE FEAST DAY OF St Alexander Nevsky, prince, St Amphilochius, St Clement I, pope, St Columbanus, St Felicitas, St Gregory of Girgenti and St Trudo or Trond.

24th November

Born on this day:

Ian Botham, cricketer, 1955;
Susan Gilmore, actress, 1954;
Graham Price, rugby footballer, 1951;
Vivien Saunders, golfer, 1946;
Billy Connolly, comedian, 1942;
Charles Osborne, author, 1927;
Alun Owen, playwright, 1925;
Prof. Sir Claus Moser, social statistician, 1922;
Geoffrey Cotterell, author, 1919;
David Kossoff, actor, 1919;
Lynn Chadwick, sculptor, 1914;
Geraldine Fitzgerald, film actress, 1913;
Joan Sanderson, actress, 1912;
Herbert William Sutcliffe, cricketer, 1894;
Scott Joplin, US ragtime pianist and composer, 1868;
Henri-Marie-Raymond de Toulouse-Lautrec, French painter, 1864;
Frances Eliza Hodgson Burnett, US author, 1849;
George Augustus Henry Sala, journalist, 1828;
Charles Meryon, French etcher, 1821;
Grace Horsley Darling, heroine of the wreck of the *Forfarshire*, 1815;
Zachary Taylor, 12th president of the USA, 1784;
John Bacon, sculptor, 1740;
Laurence Sterne, novelist, 1713;
Baruch [Benedict] Spinoza, Dutch philosopher, 1632.

Died on this day:

Rodney Ackland [Bernstein], playwright, 1991;
Freddie Mercury, rock singer, 1991;
Ruth Chatterton, US actress, 1961;
Edgar Algernon Robert, 1st Viscount Cecil, a founder of the League of Nations, 1958;
Lord Craigavon [James Craig], statesman, 1940;
Georges Clemenceau, French statesman, 1929;
Robert Erskine Childers, Irish nationalist and novelist, executed, 1922;
Sir Hiram Stevens Maxim, inventor of a sub-machine-gun, 1916;
Edward Robert Bulwer Lytton, 1st Earl of Lytton ['Owen Meredith'], diplomat and poet, 1891;
Sir Henry Havelock, soldier, 1857;
William Lamb, 2nd Viscount Melbourne, statesman, 1848;
John Knox, religious reformer, 1572.

Occurred on this day:

Lee Harvey Oswald was shot while in police custody by Jack Ruby, 1963;
Imperial Airways and British Airways combined to form the British Overseas Airways Corporation, 1939;
The musical play *The Shop Girl* was first produced, London, 1894;
Darwin's *Origin of Species* was published, 1859;
Van Diemen's Land [Tasmania] was discovered by Abel Tasman, 1642;
Jeremiah Horrocks and William Crabtree first observed the transit of Venus, 1639;
The English Parliament decided that clergy were permitted to marry, 1548.

TODAY IS THE FEAST DAY OF St Chrysogonus, St Colman of Cloyne and Saints Flora and Mary.

25th November

Born on this day:

Yvonne Kenny, operatic soprano, 1950;
Kerry O'Keeffe, Australian cricketer, 1949;
Kathryn Crosby, US film actress, 1933;
Dr Mauno Koivisto, president of Finland, 1923;
Ricardo Montalban, US film actor, 1920;
Lord Weatherill [Bernard Weatherill], former Speaker, 1920;
Francis Durbridge, author and playwright, 1912;
Richard Seifert, architect, 1910;
Lord Devlin, former Law Lord, 1905;
Sir John Summerson CH, architectural historian, 1904;
Arthur Schwartz, US lawyer and popular composer, 1900;

Pope John XXIII [Angelo Roncalli], 1881;
Leonard Sidney Woolf, publisher, 1880;
Harley Granville Barker, actor, playwright and critic, 1877;
Carl Friedrich Benz, German automobile pioneer, 1844;
Andrew Carnegie, industrialist and philanthropist, 1835;
Henry Mayhew, author and journalist, 1812;
Joseph Lancaster, educationist, 1778;
Charles Kemble, actor and playwright, 1775;
Lope Felix de Vega Carpio, Spanish poet and playwright, 1562.

Died on this day:

Sir Anton Dolin [Sydney Francis Patrick Chippendall Healey-Kay], ballet dancer and choreographer, 1983;
Upton Beall Sinclair, US novelist, 1968;
Dame Myra Hess, pianist, 1965;
Dame Lilian Mary Baylis, founder of the Old Vic, 1937;
Heinrich Barth, German explorer, 1865;
David Roberts, Scottish painter, 1864;
John Gibson Lockhart, editor and biographer, 1854;

Sir Augustus Wall Callcott, landscape painter, 1844;
Sir Francis Legatt Chantrey, sculptor and benefactor, 1841;
Isaac Watts, writer of hymns [*O God Our Help in Ages Past*], 1748;
Giles Farnaby, composer, buried, 1640;
Edward Alleyn, actor and founder of Dulwich College, 1626;
Andrea Doria, Genoese admiral and statesman, 1560.

Occurred on this day:

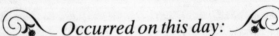

The colony of Surinam [Dutch Guiana] became an independent republic, 1975;
The play *The Mousetrap*, by Agatha Christie, opened in London, 1952;
HMS *Barham* was sunk by a U-boat off Sollum, with the loss of 868 lives, 1941;
King George II was restored to the throne of Greece after a referendum, 1935;

The battleship HMS *Bulwark* was blown to pieces in the Medway off Sheerness with the loss of 800 lives, 1914;
Gilbert and Sullivan's opera *Iolanthe* was first performed in London, 1882;
Disraeli bought 44 per cent of the Suez Canal shares from the Khedive Ismail, 1875.

TODAY IS THE FEAST DAY OF St Mercurius of Caesarea and St Moses the Martyr.

26th November

Born on this day:

Peter Wheeler, rugby footballer, 1948;
The Earl of Gowrie, chairman of Sotheby's, 1939;
John Selwyn Gummer, MP, 1939;
Tina Turner, US rock singer, 1938;
Robert Goulet, US singer and actor, 1933;
Charles Schultz, US cartoonist, creator of 'Peanuts', 1922;
Dr Cyril Cusack, actor, 1910;
Lord Forte, chairman, Trusthouse Forte, 1908;
Frances Dee, US film actress, 1907;
George Emlyn Williams, actor, playwright and author, 1905;

Nikolai Ivanovich Vavilov, Russian geneticist, 1887;
Maud, Queen of Norway, 1869;
Sir Mark Aurel Stein, archaeologist, 1862;
John Alexander Reina Newlands, chemist, 1837;
Louis Trouillon Lacombe, French pianist and composer, 1818;
William George Armstrong, 1st Baron, inventor of the hydraulic crane, 1810;
William Cowper, poet, 1731;
Sir James Ware, Irish historian, 1594.

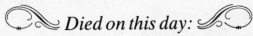

Died on this day:

Warren Stanley Tute, novelist, sailor and playwright, 1989;
Cyril Vernon Connolly, critic, 1974;
Arnold Zweig, German novelist, 1968;
Albert William Ketèlbey, composer, 1959;
Thomas Francis [Tommy] Dorsey, US bandleader, trombonist and composer, 1956;
Harold Harmsworth, 1st Viscount Rothermere, newspaper proprietor, 1940;
Sir Leander Starr Jameson, raider of the Transvaal, 1917;

Coventry Kersey Dighton Patmore, poet, 1896;
Adam Bernard Mickiewicz, Polish poet and playwright, 1855;
Nicolas-Jean de Dieu Soult, Duke of Dalmatia and Marshal of France, 1851;
John Loudon McAdam, inventor of road surfacing system, 1836;
Philippe Quinault, French playwright, 1688;
Isabella I, Queen of Castile and Aragon, 1504.

Occurred on this day:

The tidal power station at Rance, Brittany, was opened, 1966;
The USSR claimed to have exploded a hydrogen bomb of 'unprecedented force', 1955;
India became a federal republic within the Commonwealth, 1949;
The first movable bridge of aluminium alloy was opened at Sunderland, 1948;

The Great Storm raged in England, costing 8,000 lives, 1703;
The first Eddystone Lighthouse was blown down, 1703;
New College, Oxford was founded by William of Wykeham, 1379.

TODAY IS THE FEAST DAY OF St Basolus or Basle, St Conrad of Constance, St John Berchmans, St Leonard of Porto Maurizio, St Peter of Alexandria, St Silvester Gozzolini and St Siricius.

27th November

Born on this day:

Ann Mallalieu, QC, 1945;
John Alderton, actor, 1940;
Rodney Bewes, actor, 1937;
Verity Ann Lambert, film producer, 1935;
Alan Simpson, author and scriptwriter, 1929;
Ernie Wise, comedian, 1925;
Alexander Dubček, Czech statesman, 1921;
David Waller, actor, 1920;
Robert Dougall, TV presenter, 1913;
Lord Howard de Walden, racehorse owner and breeder, 1912;
James Agee, US author and screenwriter, 1910;
Sir William Newenham Montague Orpen, painter, 1878;
Chaim Weizmann, biochemist and first president of Israel, 1874;
Sir Charles Scott Sherrington, physiologist, 1857;
Fanny [Frances Anne] Kemble, actress, 1809;
Sir Julius Benedict, conductor and composer, 1804;
John Murray, publisher, 1778;
Johann Georg Forster, German travel writer, 1754;
Anders Celsius, Swedish astronomer and thermometer inventor, 1701.

Died on this day:

Arthur Honegger, French composer, 1955;
Eugene Gladstone O'Neill, US playwright, 1953;
Alexandre Dumas *fils*, French novelist and playwright, 1895;
Henry Winstanley, Eddystone lighthouse designer, drowned, 1703;
Athanasius Kircher, German Jesuit priest, scientist and inventor of the magic lantern, 1680;
Louis de Rohan-Guéménée, Chevalier de Rohan, beheaded, 1674;
Sir John Eliot, parliamentarian, 1632;
Jacopo Sansovino [Tatti], Italian sculptor, 1570;
Clovis, 1st King of France, 511;
Horace, Roman poet, 8 BC.

Occurred on this day:

Velazquez's portrait of Juan de Pareja was sold at Sotheby's, London, for £2,310,000, 1970;
The musical show *Grab Me a Gondola* was first produced, London, 1956;
In Czechoslovakia, Rudolf Slansky and ten others were sentenced to death for treason and espionage, 1952;
The French fleet was sunk at Toulon, 1942;
The Soviet forces under Marshal Timoshenko launched a counter-offensive, forcing a German retreat, 1941;
In Romania, the Iron Guard murdered 64 people, including the former prime minister, Professor Jorga, 1940;
Oscar Slater, wrongly accused and imprisoned, was released from prison and given a grant of £6,000, 1927;
The Treaty of Neuilly was signed between the Allies and Bulgaria, 1919;
Two women at Grantham, Lincs, became the first policewomen, 1914;
The Adelphi Theatre, London, opened as the 'Sans Pareil', 1806;
William Shakespeare married Anne Hathaway, 1582.

TODAY IS THE FEAST DAY OF Saints Barlaam and Josaphat, St Cungar of Somerset, St Fergus of Strathern, St James Intercisus, St Maximus of Riez, St Secundinus or Sechnall and St Virgil of Salzburg.

# 28th November

Born on this day:

Stephen Roche, cycling champion, 1959;
Lucy Gutteridge, actress, 1956;
Randy Newman, US singer and songwriter, 1943;
Frederick du Preez, rugby player, 1935;
Hope Lange, US film actress, 1931;
Dervla Murphy, author, 1931;
Geoffrey Clarke, artist and sculptor, 1924;
Cecilia Colledge, former champion skater, 1920;
Keith Miller, former Australian Test cricketer, 1919;
Alberto [Pincherle] Moravia, Italian writer, 1907;
Nancy Mitford, novelist and biographer, 1904;
José Iturbi, pianist and film actor, 1895;

Sir Leslie Stephen, biographer and editor, 1832;
Anton Grigoryevich Rubinstein, Russian pianist and composer, 1829;
Friedrich Engels, German Socialist, 1820;
William Froude, engineer and naval architect, 1810;
John Lloyd Stephens, US diplomat and archaeologist, 1805;
Victor Cousin, French moral philosopher, 1792;
Captain George William Manby, inventor of life-saving apparatus, 1765;
William Blake, poet and painter, 1757;
Jean-Baptiste Lully [Giovanni Battista Lulli], Italian/French composer, 1632.

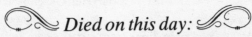## *Died on this day:*

Enid Mary Blyton, childen's book author, 1968;
Princess Wilhelmina, former Queen of the Netherlands, 1962;
Enrico Fermi, atomic scientist, 1954;
Dwight Filley Davis, US sponsor of the tennis cup, 1945;
George Henry Lewes, journalist and critic, 1878;
Karl Ernst von Baer, embryologist, 1876;

Mary Fairfax Somerville, mathematician, 1872;
Christian Karl Josias, Baron von Bunsen, Prussian statesman and writer, 1860;
Washington Irving, US author, 1859;
Cesare Bonesana Beccaria, Italian jurist and economist, 1794;
Anthony à Wood, antiquary and historian, 1695;
Giovanni Lorenzo Bernini, Italian sculptor, 1680.

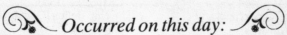## *Occurred on this day:*

Mauritania became independent, 1960;
Churchill, Roosevelt and Stalin met at Teheran, 1943;
Desiré Landru, French murderer of 10 women, was found guilty, 1921;
The first air raid on London occurred, 1916;
Albania was proclaimed independent of Turkey, 1912;

Sinn Fein was founded in Dublin by Arthur Griffith, 1905;
London University was granted its charter, 1836;
The Royal Society was founded, 1660;
Magellan reached the Pacific after sailing through the Straits, 1520.

TODAY IS THE FEAST DAY OF St Catherine Labouré, St James of the March, St Joseph Pignatelli, St Simeon Metaphrastes and St Stephen the Younger.

29th November

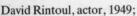

Born on this day:

David Rintoul, actor, 1949;

John Mayall, bandleader, vocalist and guitarist, 1933;

Jacques Chirac, French statesman, 1932;

Geoffrey Moorhouse, writer, 1931;

Lady Porter, leader, Westminster Council, 1930;

Derek Jameson, radio presenter and former editor, 1929;

Toby Robertson, theatrical director, 1928;

George Cansdale, former superintendent of the London Zoo, 1909;

Carlo Levi, Italian novelist, painter and journalist, 1902;

Clive Staples Lewis, scholar and writer, 1898;

Busby Berkeley [William Berkeley Enos], US film director and choreographer, 1895;

Sir John Ambrose Fleming, electrical engineer, 1849;

Sir William Blake Richmond, painter, 1842;

Louisa May Alcott, US author, 1832;

Christian Johann Doppler, Austrian physicist, 1803;

Domenico Gaetano Maria Donizetti, Italian composer, 1797;

John Ray, zoologist, 1627;

John Harvard, founder of the University, baptised, 1607;

Dr Peter Heylin, theologian and historian, 1600;

Margaret, Queen of Scotland, 1489.

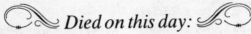

Died on this day:

Natalie Wood [Natasha Gurdin], US film actress, 1981;

Graham Hill, racing driver, killed in an air crash, 1975;

Norman Alfred William Lindsay, Australian artist and novelist, 1969;

Sir George Edward Robey [Wade], actor and comedian, 1954;

Giacomo Antonio Domenico Michele Secondo Maria Puccini, Italian composer, 1924;

Martin Farquhar Tupper, poet and inventor, 1889;

Horace Greeley, US newspaper editor, 1872;

Giambattista Bodoni, Italian type designer and printer, 1813;

Maria Theresa, Empress of Austria, 1780;

Prince Rupert, German prince and royalist commander in England, 1682;

Hans Holbein the Younger, German painter, 1543;

Thomas Wolsey, Cardinal and Lord Chancellor, 1530;

Giovanni Bellini [Giambellini], Venetian painter, 1516.

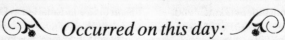

Occurred on this day:

Yugoslavia was proclaimed a Federal People's Republic, 1945;

The Eighth Army began its offensive in North Africa, 1943;

The republic of Lithuania was proclaimed at Riga, 1918;

Nicholas, King of Montenegro was deposed and the kingdom united with Serbia under King Peter, 1918;

Von Hindenburg became the German Commander-in-Chief on the Western Front, 1916;

The British under Lord Methuen defeated the Boers at the Battle of Modder River, 1899;

The first Japanese Diet opened, 1890.

TODAY IS THE FEAST DAY OF St Brendan of Birr, St Radbod, St Saturninus or Sernin of Toulouse and St Saturninus, martyr.

30th November

Born on this day:

Gary Lineker, footballer, 1960;
Marguerite Porter, ballerina, 1948;
George Duffield, jockey, 1946;
Radu Lupu, pianist, 1945;
Frank Ifield, singer, 1936;
Robert Guillaume, US singer and actor, 1930;
Graham Crowden, actor, 1922;
Virginia Mayo, US film actress, 1920;
Edgar Douglas Adrian, 1st Baron, physiologist, 1889;
Sir Winston Leonard Spencer Churchill, statesman, 1874;
Sir Jagadis Chandra Bose, Indian scientist, 1858;
Mark Twain [Samuel Langhorne Clemens], US author, 1835;
William-Adolphe Bouguereau, French painter, 1825;
Christian Matthias Theodor Mommsen, German historian, 1817;
Jonathan Swift, author, 1667;
Adriaen Vandevelde, Dutch painter, 1636;
John Bunyan, writer, baptised, 1628;
Sir Philip Sidney, poet, soldier and courtier, 1554;
Sir Henry Savile, scholar and mathematician, 1549;
Andrea Palladio [Andrea di Pietro della Gondola] Italian architect, 1508;
Andrea Doria, Genoese statesman and admiral, 1466.

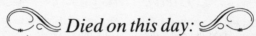

Died on this day:

Cary Grant [Alexander Archibald Leach], film actor, 1986;
Richard Llewellyn [Richard Dafydd Vivian Llewellyn Lloyd], author, 1983;
Joyce Irene Grenfell, entertainer, 1979;
Sir Terence Mervyn Rattigan, playwright, 1977;
Beniamino Gigli, Italian operatic tenor, 1957;
Wilhelm Furtwängler, German conductor and composer, 1954;
Ernst Lubitsch, US film director, 1947;
Edward John Eyre, Australian explorer, 1901;
Oscar Fingal O'Flahertie Wills Wilde, Irish playwright, 1900;
William Habington, poet, 1654;
John Selden, lawyer and antiquarian, 1654;
Michael Wolgemut [Wohlgemuth], German painter, 1519;
Edmund Ironside, King of the English, 1016.

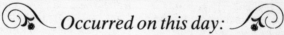

Occurred on this day:

The Trades Description Act came into force, 1968;
Barbados became independent, 1966;
Finland was invaded by the USSR, 1939;
The Crystal Palace at Sydenham, near London, was destroyed by fire, 1936;
Mexico declared war on France, 1838;
Charles XII of Sweden defeated the Russians at Narva, 1700.

TODAY IS THE FEAST DAY OF St Andrew the Apostle, St Cuthbert Mayne and St Sapor.

1st December

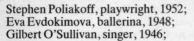

Born on this day:

Stephen Poliakoff, playwright, 1952;
Eva Evdokimova, ballerina, 1948;
Gilbert O'Sullivan, singer, 1946;
Bette Midler, US singer and comedienne, 1945;
Mike Denness, former Test cricketer, 1940;
Richard Pryor, actor, 1940;
Lee Trevino, golfer, 1939;
Gordon Crosse, composer, 1937;
Bruce Page, author, 1936;
Woody Allen, US film actor, writer and director, 1935;
Keith Michell, Australian actor and director, 1928;
Mary Martin, US actress and singer, 1913.

Dame Alicia Markova, prima ballerina assoluta, 1910;
Ray Henderson [Raymond Brost], US composer and producer, 1896;
Henry Williamson, author and novelist, 1895;
Ernst Toller, playwright and poet, 1893;
Queen Alexandra, consort of Edward VII, 1844;
Madame Marie Tussaud [Grosholz], waxwork exhibitor, 1761;
Martin Heinrich Klaproth, German chemist, 1743;
John Keill, philosopher and mathematician, 1671.

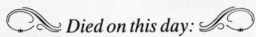

Died on this day:

David Ben Gurion, Israeli statesman, 1973;
John Burton Sanderson Haldane, scientist, 1964;
Ernest John Moeran, composer, 1950;
Paul-Marie-Théodore-Vincent d'Indy, French composer, 1931;
Alfred Rethel, German historical painter, 1859;
Ebenezer Elliott, poet and 'anti-Corn Law rhymester', 1849;

Dr George Birkbeck, founder of Birkbeck College, 1841;
Alexander I, Tsar of Russia, 1825;
Susannah Centlivre [Freeman], playwright and actress, 1723;
Pope Leo X, 1521;
Lorenzo Ghiberti, Florentine sculptor, 1455;
King Henry I, 1135.

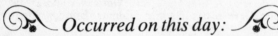

Occurred on this day:

The Isaac Newton telescope, largest in Western Europe, was inaugurated at the Royal Greenwich Observatory, 1967;
Abdullah of Transjordan was proclaimed King of Palestine by the Arab Congress at Jericho, 1948;
The Beveridge Report on social security was published, 1942;
'Points' rationing was introduced in Britain, 1941;
The Locarno Pact was signed in London, 1925;
Lady Nancy Astor became the first woman to take her seat in the House of Commons as an MP, 1919;

Iceland became a sovereign state, but with the same monarch as Denmark, 1918;
Pedro I was crowned Emperor of Brazil, 1822;
The Republic of San Domingo [Dominican Republic] was set up, independent of Spain, 1821;
The Royal Academy of Arts was founded, 1768;
Portugal became independent of Spain, 1640.

TODAY IS THE FEAST DAY OF St Agericus or Airy, St Alexander Briant, St Anasanus, St Edmund Campion, St Eligius or Eloy, St Ralph Sherwin and St Tudwal.

2nd December

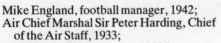

Born on this day:

Mike England, football manager, 1942;
Air Chief Marshal Sir Peter Harding, Chief of the Air Staff, 1933;
Julie Harris, US film actress, 1925;
Anthony Huxley, author and photographer, 1920;
Peter Carl Goldmark, US inventor of the long-playing record, 1906;
Sir John [Giovanni Battista] Barbirolli, conductor, 1899;

Dr George Richards Minot, US physician, 1885;
Ruth Draper, US entertainer, 1884;
Georges-Pierre Seurat, French painter, 1859;
Sir Francis Carruthers Gould, caricaturist and politician, 1844;
Pedro II, Emperor of Brazil, 1825;
Agostino Agazzari, Italian composer, 1578.

Died on this day:

Philip Arthur Larkin, poet, 1985;
Stephen Potter, author and 'gamesman', 1969;
Filippo Tommaso Emilio Marinetti, Italian novelist and poet, 1944;
E.M. Delafield [Edmée Elizabeth Monica de la Pasture], novelist, 1943;
Sir Evelyn Henry Wood, field marshal, 1919;
Edmond-Eugène-Alexis Rostand, French playwright, 1918;
John Brown, US abolitionist, executed, 1859;

Amelia Opie [Alderson], novelist, 1853;
Donatien-Alphonse-François, Marquis de Sade, French writer and philosopher, 1814;
Philippe, Duc d'Orléans, Regent of France, 1723;
Gerardus Mercator [Gerhard Kremer], cartographer, 1594;
Hernando Cortés, Spanish conqueror of Mexico, 1547.

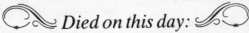

Occurred on this day:

In the reunited Germany, the Christian Democrats, under Helmut Kohl, won the first general election, 1990;
The first London performance of the musical show *Hello, Dolly!* was presented, 1965;
Senator Joseph McCarthy was condemned by the US Senate, 1954;
The first atomic pile started operating, Chicago, USA, 1942;
German and Russian delegates met at Brest-Litovsk to discuss peace proposals, 1917;
King Camp Gillette patented the first safety-razor, 1901;
Saint-Saëns's opera *Samson and Delilah* was first performed in Weimar, Germany, 1877;

The Gaiety Theatre, Strand, London, closed, 1866;
The Second French Empire was proclaimed, with Napoleon III as emperor, 1852;
Birkbeck College, London, was founded, 1823;
The Monroe Doctrine was proclaimed by President James Monroe, 1823;
Napoleon defeated the Austrians and Russians at the Battle of Austerlitz, 1805;
Napoleon was crowned Emperor in Paris by Pope Pius VII, 1804;
The new St Paul's Cathedral was opened, 1697.

TODAY IS THE FEAST DAY OF St Bibiana or Viviana, St Chromatius of Aquilea, St Nonnus and St Silvanus of Constantinople.

3rd December

Born on this day:

Franz Klammer, skier, 1953;

Mel Smith, actor and comedian, 1952;

Paul Nicholas, actor and singer, 1945;

Ralph McTell, ragtime guitarist, 1944;

Jean-Luc Godard, French film director, 1930;

Andy Williams, US singer, 1930;

Trevor Bailey, former England cricketer, 1923;

Maria Anna Cecilia Sofia Callas [Kalogeropoulos], US/Greek operatic soprano, 1923;

Charles Craig, operatic tenor, 1920;

Tanya Moiseiwitsch, designer for the theatre, 1914;

Victor Pasmore CH, artist, 1908;

Nigel Marlin Balchin, novelist, 1908;

Rajendra Prasad, first president of India, 1884;

Anton Friedrich Wilhelm von Webern, Austrian composer, 1883;

Joseph Conrad [Jósef Teodor Konrad Naleçz Korzeniowski], novelist, 1857;

Cecil Gordon Lawson, landscape painter, 1851;

George Manson, Scottish water-colour painter, 1850;

Octavia Hill, philanthropist, 1838;

Frederic Leighton, 1st Baron, painter and sculptor, 1830;

The Rev. Robert Stephen Hawker, poet and antiquary, 1803;

Sir Rowland Hill, originator of the penny post, 1795;

Robert Bloomfield, shoemaker and poet, 1766;

Samuel Crompton, inventor of the spinning mule, 1753;

Niccolo Amati, Italian violin-maker, 1596.

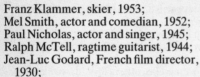

Died on this day:

Sir Oswald Ernald Mosley, Fascist leader, 1980;

Dame Mary Jean Gilmore, Australian poet, 1962;

Christian August Sinding, Norwegian composer, 1941;

Pierre-Auguste Renoir, French painter, 1919;

Mary Baker Eddy, founder of Christian Science, 1910;

Robert Louis Balfour Stevenson, novelist, 1894;

Christian Daniel Rauch, German sculptor, 1857;

Robert Montgomery, poet, 1855;

Frederick VI, King of Denmark, 1839;

Giovanni Battista Belzoni, Italian explorer and Egyptologist, 1823;

Claude Joseph Vernet, French painter, 1789;

Alessandro Farnese, 3rd Duke of Parma, military commander, 1592.

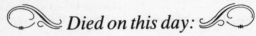

Occurred on this day:

Dr Christiaan Barnard performed the first heart transplant, South Africa, 1967;

The Home Guard 'stood down' with a parade of 7,000 in Hyde Park, London, 1944;

The Statute of Westminster was passed, under which British Dominions became sovereign states under the Crown, 1931;

The musical show *Ever Green* was first produced, London, 1930;

The present and fourth Adelphi Theatre opened in the Strand, London, 1930;

Illinois became the 21st of the United States, 1818;

Mauritius was captured from the French by the British, 1810.

TODAY IS THE FEAST DAY OF St Cassian of Tangier, Saints Claudius, Hilaria and their Companions, St Francis Xavier and St Lucius of Britain.

4th December

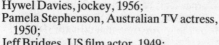

Born on this day:

Hywel Davies, jockey, 1956;
Pamela Stephenson, Australian TV actress, 1950;
Jeff Bridges, US film actor, 1949;
Ann Christopher, sculptor, 1947;
Gemma Jones, actress, 1942;
Yvonne Minton, mezzo-soprano, 1938;
Horst Buchholz, German film actor, 1932;
Ronnie Corbett, comedian, 1930;
Deanna Durbin [Mme Charles David], former film actress and singer, 1921;
Jimmy Jewel, comedian and actor, 1912;
Dr A.L. Rowse, historian, 1903;
Sir Herbert Read, poet and critic, 1893;
General Francisco Paulino Hermengildo Teodulo Franco Bahamonde [Franco], Spanish dictator, 1892;

Sir Herbert Hamilton Harty, conductor, 1879;
Rainer Maria Rilke, German poet, 1875;
Richard Horatio Edgar Wallace, thriller-writer and playwright, 1875;
Edith Louisa Cavell, nurse, 1865;
Lillian Russell [Helen Louise Leonard], US singer and actress, 1861;
Samuel Butler, author, 1835;
Dr John Kitto, author and Biblical editor, 1804;
Gen. Sir William Fenwick Williams, soldier and hero of Kars, 1800;
Thomas Carlyle, author, 1795;
John Cotton, Puritan leader in New England, 1585.

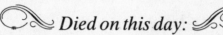

Died on this day:

Edward Benjamin Britten, Baron, composer, 1976;
Jack [John Wesley Vivian] Payne, bandleader, 1969;
John Tyndall, Irish physicist, 1893;
William Sturgeon, electrical engineer, 1850;
Robert Banks Jenkinson, 2nd Earl of Liverpool, statesman, 1828;
Luigi Galvani, Italian electrical inventor, 1798;

John Gay, poet, playwright and author, 1732;
Thomas Hobbes, political philosopher, 1679;
William Drummond of Hawthornden, Scottish poet, 1649;
Armand-Jean du Plessis, Cardinal and Duc de Richelieu, French statesman, 1642;
Nicholas Ferrar, theologian, 1637;
Pope John XXII, 1334.

Occurred on this day:

The Kingdom of Serbs, Croats and Slovenes was proclaimed, 1918;
The Chain Pier at Brighton was destroyed during heavy gales, 1896;
The Royal Courts of Justice in the Strand, London, were opened, 1882;
The colony of Queensland was established, 1859;
Suttee [the burning of a widow on her husband's funeral pyre] was abolished in India, 1829;

The Inquisition in Spain was abolished by Napoleon, 1808;
Income tax was first introduced by William Pitt the Younger, 1798;
The *Observer* was first published, 1791;
Nicholas Breakspear was elected Pope Hadrian IV, thus becoming the only Englishman to be pope, 1154.

TODAY IS THE FEAST DAY OF St Anno, St Bernard of Parma, St John of Damascus, St Maruthas, St Osmund and St Sola.

5th December

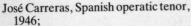

Born on this day:

José Carreras, Spanish operatic tenor, 1946;

Janet Morgan, editor and writer, 1945;

Sheridan Morley, writer, biographer and broadcaster, 1941;

Jeremy Sandford, author, 1934;

Lucie Clayton, founder of the model and secretarial agency, 1928;

Lord Chalfont, author, defence consultant and broadcasting chairman, 1919;

Otto Preminger, Austrian film director, 1906;

The Earl of Longford, writer and former minister, 1905;

Walter [Walt] Elias Disney, creator of 'Mickey Mouse' and 'Donald Duck', 1901;

Werner Karl Heisenberg, German physicist, 1901;

Fritz Lang, Austrian film director, 1890;

Vitezslav Novák, Czech composer, 1870;

Józef Clemens Piłsudski, Polish statesman, 1867;

Admiral John Rushworth Jellicoe, 1st Earl, commander of the Fleet at Jutland, 1859;

George Armstrong Custer, US cavalry commander, 1839;

Christina Georgina Rossetti, poet, 1830;

Martin van Buren, 8th president of the USA, 1782;

Robert Harley, 1st Earl of Oxford, politician, 1661.

Died on this day:

Ethel Edith Mannin, novelist and travel writer, 1984;

Joseph Erlanger, US neurophysiologist, 1965;

Jan Kubelik, Czech violinist, 1940;

Nicholas Vachel Lindsay, US poet, 1931;

Claude-Oscar Monet, French painter, 1926;

Sir Henry Tate, sugar refiner and philanthropist, 1899;

George John Whyte-Melville, novelist, 1878;

Alexandre Dumas *père* [Davy de la Pailleterie], French novelist, 1870;

Thomas Pringle, Scottish poet, 1834;

Friedrich Leopold, Count Stolberg-Stolberg, German poet and author, 1819;

Wolfgang Amadeus Mozart, composer, 1791;

Pierre Gaultier de Varennes, Sieur de La Vérendrye, French-Canadian explorer and soldier, 1749;

Sir Henry Wotton, diplomat, poet and author, 1639.

Occurred on this day:

The United Kingdom withdrew from membership of UNESCO, 1985;

The first British woman priest was ordained in New Jersey, USA, 1981;

Britain's first motorway, a bypass around Preston, opened, 1958;

Under the 21st Amendment, prohibition was repealed in the United States, 1933;

German and Russian delegates at Brest-Litovsk signed an armistice for seven days to take effect on 7th December, 1917;

The US brig *Mary Celeste* was found abandoned in the Atlantic, 1872;

James Christie, London auctioneer, held his first sale, 1766.

TODAY IS THE FEAST DAY OF St Birinus, St Christian, St Crispina, St John Almond, St Justinian or Iestin, St Nicetius of Trier, St Sabas and St Sigiramnus or Cyran.

6th December

Born on this day:

Tony Woodcock, footballer, 1956;

Wendy Ellis, ballerina, 1951;

Jill Hammersley-Parker, table-tennis player, 1951;

Peter Willey, former England cricketer, 1949;

Keke Rosberg, Finnish motor-racing champion, 1948;

Jonathan King, broadcaster and pop producer, 1944;

Tessa Kennedy, interior decorator, 1938;

Sir Nicholas Lyell, MP, 1938;

Charles Vance, actor, director and producer, 1929;

Lord Ashley of Stoke [Jack Ashley] CH, former MP, 1922;

Dave Brubeck, US jazz musician, 1920;

Cyril Washbrook, former England cricketer, 1914;

Ira Gershwin [Israel Gershvin], US lyricist, 1896;

Sir Francis Osbert Sacheverel Sitwell, writer, 1892;

Charles Martin Hall, US chemist, 1863;

August von Mackensen, German field marshal, 1849;

The Rev. Richard Harris Barham ['Thomas Ingoldsby'], humorist and author, 1788;

Louis-Joseph Gay-Lussac, French chemist and physicist, 1778;

Sir David Baird, Scottish soldier, 1757;

Warren Hastings, first Governor-General of India, 1732;

Chrétien-Guillaume de Lamoignon de Malesherbes, French statesman, 1721;

George Monck, 1st Duke of Albemarle, admiral and general, 1608;

Baldassarre Castiglione, Italian courtier, 1478;

King Henry VI, 1421.

Died on this day:

Roy Orbison [Kelton], US popular singer and composer, 1988;

Stella Benson, novelist, 1933;

Ernst Werner von Siemens, German inventor, 1892;

Jefferson Davis, former president of the Confederate States of America, 1889;

Jean-Joseph-Charles-Louis Blanc, French socialist journalist and revolutionary, 1882;

Anthony Trollope, novelist and Post Office official, 1882;

Dr Joseph Black, Scottish chemist, 1799;

Jean-Baptiste-Siméon Chardin, French painter, 1779;

Dr John Lightfoot, clergyman and scholar, 1675;

Alfonso I Henriques of Portugal, after a reign of 73 years, 220 days, 1185.

Occurred on this day:

Gerald Ford was sworn in as vice-president of the USA, 1973;

India recognised Bangladesh [East Pakistan] as an independent republic, 1971;

The Irish Free State was established, 1922;

The independence of Finland from Russia was proclaimed, 1917;

Self-government was granted to the Transvaal and Orange River colonies, 1906;

Sir Colin Campbell's men defeated the Sepoy mutineers at the Battle of Cawnpore, 1857;

Christopher Columbus discovered Hispaniola [now Haiti and the Dominican Republic], 1492.

TODAY IS THE FEAST DAY OF St Abraham of Kratia, St Asella, Saints Dionysia, Majoricus and their Companions, St Gertrude the Elder and St Nicholas of Bari.

7th December

Born on this day:

Geoff Lawson, Australian cricketer, 1958;

Ellen Burstyn, US actress, 1932;

Prof. Noam Chomsky, US linguist, 1922;

Helen Watts, concert and opera singer, 1927;

Dr Mario Soares, president of Portugal, 1924;

Eli Wallach, US film actor, 1915;

Edmundo Ros, bandleader, 1910;

Stuart Davis, US abstract painter, 1894;

Fay Bainter, US film actress, 1892;

Honoré-Gabriel Marcel, French philosopher and playwright, 1889;

Joyce [Arthur Joyce Lunel] Cary, author, 1888;

Charles Rudolf Friml, Czech composer and pianist, 1879;

Willa Sibert Cather, US novelist, 1876;

Pietro Mascagni, Italian composer, 1863;

William James Linton, wood engraver, 1812;

Theodor Ambrose Hubert Schwann, German physiologist, 1810;

Joseph Severn, painter, 1793;

Allan Cunningham, Scottish poet, 1784;

Gian Lorenzo Bernini, Italian sculptor, 1598.

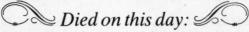

Died on this day:

Robert Ranke Graves, poet, 1985;

Thornton Niven Wilder, US novelist, 1975;

Kirsten Malfrid Flagstad, Norwegian operatic soprano, 1962;

Sir Frederick Treves, physician, 1923;

Thomas Nast, US artist and cartoonist, 1902;

Ferdinand-Marie, Vicomte de Lesseps, engineer and diplomat, 1894;

Edward Irving, religious leader, founder of the Irvingites, 1834;

John Flaxman, sculptor, 1826;

Dr John Aikin, author and physician, 1822;

William Bligh, captain of the *Bounty*, 1817;

Marshal Michel Ney, French soldier, executed for treason, 1815;

Marie-Jeanne Bécu, Comtesse du Barry, mistress of Louis XV, guillotined, 1793;

Meindert Hobbema, Dutch landscape painter, 1709;

Algernon Sidney, republican and patriot, beheaded, 1683;

Sir Peter Lely [Pieter van der Faes], portrait painter, 1680;

Robert Kett, rebel leader, hanged 1549;

Cicero, Roman orator, executed, 43 BC.

Occurred on this day:

The Ivory Coast became an independent republic, 1960;

Japanese aircraft attacked Pearl Harbor, 1941;

The first parliament of the Irish Free State met, electing William Thomas Cosgrave as president, 1922;

The parliament of Northern Ireland voted against being included in the Irish Free State, 1922;

David Lloyd George became British prime minister, 1916;

An imperial edict authorised all Chinese to cut their pigtails, 1911;

Gilbert and Sullivan's opera *The Gondoliers* was first produced, London, 1889;

Delaware became the 1st of the United States, 1787;

William Pitt the Younger became prime minister, 1783;

The Theatre Royal, Covent Garden [now the Royal Opera House], was opened, 1732;

Henry VI of England was crowned King of France, Paris, 1431.

TODAY IS THE FEAST DAY OF St Ambrose of Milan, St Buithe or Boethius, St Eutychianus, St Martin of Saujon and St Servus.

8th December

Born on this day:

Michael Unger, editor, Manchester *Evening News*, 1943;
Geoff Hurst, footballer, 1941;
Jenny Linden, actress, 1940;
James Galway, flautist, 1939;
Maximilian Schell, German actor, 1930;
Lucian Freud CH, painter, 1922;
Richard Fleischer, US film director, 1916;
Lee J. Cobb [Leo Jacoby], US film actor, 1911;
James Grover Thurber, US wit and cartoonist, 1894;
Bohuslav Martinu, Czech composer, 1890;
Padraic Colum, Irish poet, 1881;
Jean Julius Christian Sibelius, Finnish composer, 1865;
Georges-Léon-Jules-Marie Feydeau, French playwright, 1862;

Aristide Maillol, French sculptor, 1861;
Georges Méliès, French cinema pioneer, 1861;
Björnstjerne Björnson, Norwegian poet and playwright, 1832;
George Alfred Henty, author of boys' books, 1832;
Eli Whitney, US inventor of the cotton gin, 1765;
Johann Georg von Zimmermann, Swiss author, 1728;
Queen Christina of Sweden, 1626;
Mary Stuart, Queen of Scots, 1542;
Horace [Quintus Horatius Flaccus], Roman poet, 65 BC.

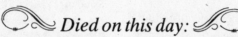 Died on this day:

John Winston Lennon, former member of the Beatles, shot in New York, 1980;
Golda Meir [Goldie Mabovitch], Israeli stateswoman, 1978;
Alphonse Legros, painter and etcher, 1911;
Herbert Spencer, writer and philosopher, 1903;

George Augustus Henry Sala, journalist, 1895;
Thomas De Quincey, author, 1859;
Richard Baxter, clergyman and writer, 1691;
John Pym, politician, 1643.

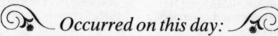 Occurred on this day:

Arthur Scargill was elected president of the National Union of Mineworkers, 1981;
Great Britain, Australia and the United States declared war on Japan, 1941;
In the Russian election for the constituent Assembly, the Bolsheviks were soundly defeated, 1917;
The German fleet was sunk in the Battle of the Falkland Islands, 1914;
In the heavyweight boxing contest in London, Georges Carpentier knocked out Bombardier Billy Wells in the first round, 1913;

The first traffic lights were erected in Westminster, London, 1868;
The Echo newspaper was first published, 1868;
Clifton Suspension Bridge, Bristol, was opened, 1864;
Pope Pius IX promulgated the dogma of the Immaculate Conception, 1854.

TODAY IS THE FEAST DAY OF The Immaculate Conception, St Eucharius, St Patapius, St Romaric and Sophronius of Cyprus.

9th December

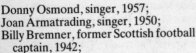

Born on this day:

Donny Osmond, singer, 1957;
Joan Armatrading, singer, 1950;
Billy Bremner, former Scottish football captain, 1942;
Beau Bridges, US film actor, 1941;
Dame Judi Dench, actress, 1934;
Ian McIntyre, writer and broadcaster, 1931;
Robert Hawke, Australian statesman, 1929;
Benny Green, musician, writer and broadcaster, 1927;
Kirk Douglas, US film actor, 1918;
Elisabeth Schwarzkopf, opera singer, 1915;
Douglas Fairbanks, Jr., US film actor, 1909;
Richard Austen Butler, Baron, statesman, 1902;
Hermione Ferdinanda Gingold, actress and entertainer, 1898;
Lancelot Thomas Hogben, scientific writer, 1895;

Clarence Birdseye, US inventor of deep-freezing process, 1886;
Joaquin Turina, Spanish composer, 1882;
Joel Chandler Harris, US author and creator of 'Uncle Remus', 1848;
Prince Peter Alexeyevich Kropotkin, Russian revolutionary and geographer, 1842;
Charles-Émile Waldteufel [Levy], French composer, 1837;
Claude-Louis, Count Berthollet, French chemist, 1749;
Carl Wilhelm Scheele, Swedish chemist, 1742;
William Whiston, theologian and translator of Josephus, 1667;
John Milton, poet, 1608;
Gustavus II Adolphus the Great, King of Sweden, 1594.

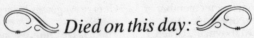

Died on this day:

Ralph Johnson Bunche, US diplomat, 1971;
Karl Barth, Swiss theologian, 1968;
Dame Edith Sitwell, author and poet, 1964;
Sir Cyril Arthur Pearson, publisher, 1921;
Joseph Bramah, locksmith and inventor of the hydraulic printing press, 1814;

Johann Reinhold Forster, German naturalist, 1798;
Edward Hyde, 1st Earl of Clarendon, statesman and historian, 1674;
Sir Anthony Van Dyck, Flemish painter, 1641.

Occurred on this day:

Lech Walesa was elected president of Poland, 1990;
Tanganyika became independent, 1961, and a republic in 1962;
The first episode of *Coronation Street* was televised, 1960;
The republic of Indonesia was established, 1949;
In Yugoslavia, Josip Tito formed his own government, 1943;
The Eighth Army began its offensive in North Africa by attacking Sidi Barrani, 1940;

During World War I, Jerusalem [held by the Turks] surrendered to General Allenby, 1917;
Richard Strauss's opera *Salome* was performed for the first time, Dresden, 1905;
Glinka's opera *Ruslan and Ludmila* was first produced, St Petersburg, 1842;
The Macquarie River in Australia was discovered by George Evans, 1813.

TODAY IS THE FEAST DAY OF St Budoc or Beuzec, St Gorgonia, St Leocadia, St Peter Fourier and The Seven Martyrs of Samosata.

10th December

Born on this day:

Jahangir Khan, squash champion, 1963;
Kenneth Branagh, actor, 1960;
Nicolas Kynaston, concert organist, 1941;
Raphael Maklouf, sculptor, 1937;
Michael Wright, writer, 1936;
Dorothy Lamour, US film actress, 1914;
Morton Gould, US composer and conductor, 1913;
Dennis Morgan, US film actor and singer, 1910;
Olivier Messiaen, French composer and organist, 1908;
Rumer Godden, playwright, poet and author, 1907;
Mary Norton, writer for children, 1903;
William Charles Franklyn Plomer, South African author, 1903;
Lew Brown [Louis Brownstein], US songwriter, 1893;

Field Marshal Harold Rupert Leofric George Alexander, 1st Earl Alexander of Tunis, 1891;
Ernest Howard Shepard, illustrator of *Winnie the Pooh*, 1879;
Emily Elizabeth Dickinson, US poet, 1830;
George MacDonald, poet and novelist, 1824;
César-Auguste Franck, Belgian composer, 1822;
Felice, Count Orsini, Italian nationalist, 1819;
Thomas Holcroft, translator and playwright, 1745;
Giovanni Battista Guarini, Italian poet, 1538.

Died on this day:

Jascha Heifetz, US violinist, 1987;
Alfred Damon Runyon, US writer, 1946;
Luigi Pirandello, Italian playwright and novelist, 1936;
Charles Rennie Mackintosh, architect, painter and art nouveau pioneer, 1928;
Sir Joseph Dalton Hooker, botanist, 1911;

Alfred Bernhard Nobel, Swedish industrialist and philanthropist, 1896;
Jules Bastien-Lepage, French painter, 1884;
Leopold I, King of the Belgians, 1865;
Edmund Gunter, mathematician, 1626;
Paolo Uccello [Paolo di Dono], Florentine painter, 1475.

Occurred on this day:

Zanzibar became independent, 1963;
The Royal Naval battleships *Prince of Wales* and *Repulse* were sunk by Japanese aircraft, 1941;
King Edward VIII abdicated, and became Duke of Windsor, 1936;
Puccini's opera *The Girl of the Golden West* was first produced, New York, 1910;

The first Nobel Prizes were awarded, 1901;
Cuba became independent of Spain, 1898;
The first pneumatic tyres were patented by Robert Thomson, 1845;
Mississippi became the 20th of the United States, 1817.

TODAY IS THE FEAST DAY OF St Edmund Gerhings, St Eulalia of Merida, St Eustace White, St Gregory III, pope, St John Roberts, Saints Mannas, Hermogenes and Eugraphus, St Melchiades or Miltiades, St Polydore Plaaden and St Swithin Wells.

11th December

Born on this day:

Sylvester Clarke, cricketer, 1955;
Jermaine Jackson, US rock singer, 1954;
Brenda Lee, US rock singer, 1944;
Anna Carteret, actress, 1942;
Tony Adams, actor, 1940;
Sir Kenneth MacMillan, choreographer, 1929;
Patrick Reyntiens, designer and artist in stained glass, 1925;
Cliff Michelmore, TV producer and broadcaster, 1919;
Alexander Solzhenitsyn, Russian author, 1918;
Carlo Ponti, Italian film director and producer, 1913;
Gilbert Roland, US film actor, 1905;
Victor McLaglen, film actor, 1883;
Heinrich Hermann Robert Koch, German bacteriologist, 1843;
Louis-Charles-Alfred de Musset, French playwright and poet, 1810;
Louis-Hector Berlioz, French composer, 1803;
Sir David Brewster, physicist, and inventor of the kaleidoscope, 1781;
Pope Leo X, 1475.

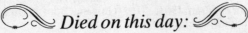

Died on this day:

Egbert Roscoe [Ed] Murrow, US journalist and broadcaster, 1965;
Emile-Charles-Marie Wauters, Belgian painter, 1933;
Olive Emilie Albertina Schreiner, South African novelist, 1920;
Ludwig Mond, chemist, 1909;
Matthias Hohner, musical instrument maker, 1902;
Richard Doyle, artist, 1883;
Jean-François-Casimir Delavigne, French playwright and poet, 1843;
Colley Cibber, playwright and actor, 1757;
Edmund Curll, bookseller and scurrilous pamphleteer, 1747;
Charles XII, King of Sweden, killed, 1718;
Sir Roger l'Estrange, journalist and translator of *Aesop's Fables*, 1704;
Bernardino Pinturicchio [Betto di Biago], Sienese painter, 1513;
Llewelyn ab Gruffydd, last native Prince of Wales, killed in battle, 1282.

Occurred on this day:

The prototype of Concorde airliner was shown for the first time at Toulouse, 1967;
The new Waterloo Bridge was opened, 1945;
The USA declared war on Germany and Italy, 1941;
The Fascist Grand Council in Rome decided to withdraw Italy from membership of the League of Nations, 1937;
King George VI acceded to the throne, 1936;
The Statute of Westminster came into effect, 1931;
The British, led by Lord Methuen, were repulsed by the Boers under Piet Cronje at the Battle of Magersfontein, Orange Free State, 1899;
The first motor show opened in Paris, 1894;
Indiana became the 19th of the United States, 1816.

TODAY IS THE FEAST DAY OF St Barsabas, St Damasus I, pope, St Daniel the Stylite and Saints Fuscianus, Victoricus and Gentianus.

12th December

Born on this day:

Tracy Austin, US tennis player, 1960;
Jasper Conran, fashion designer, 1959;
Emerson Fittipaldi, Brazilian racing driver, 1946;
Kenneth Cranham, actor, 1944;
Dionne Warwick, US singer, 1941;
Connie Francis, US singer, 1938;
Denise Coffey, actress, 1936;
Lionel Blair, dancer and entertainer, 1931;
The Hon. Gwyneth Dunwoody, MP, 1930;
John Osborne, playwright, 1929;
Frank Sinatra, US singer and actor, 1915;

Edward G. Robinson [Emanuel Goldenberg], US film actor, 1893;
Alfred Werner, Swiss chemist, 1866;
Edvard Munch, Norwegian painter, 1863;
John Richard Green, cleric and historian, 1837;
Gustave Flaubert, French novelist, 1821;
Sir William Beechey, painter, 1753;
Erasmus Darwin, physician and writer, 1731;
Admiral Samuel Hood, 1st Viscount, naval commander, 1724.

Died on this day:

Anne Baxter, US film actress, 1985;
Baroness Clementine Ogilvy Spencer-Churchill, 1977;
William [Billy] Gordon Reid, composer and pianist, 1974;
Tallulah Brockman Bankhead, US actress, 1968;
Douglas Fairbanks, Sr. [Douglas Elton Ulman], US film actor, 1939;
Sir Joseph Edgar Boehm, portrait sculptor, 1890;

Robert Browning, poet, 1889;
Sir Marc Isambard Brunel, civil engineer, 1849;
Albrecht von Haller, Swiss biologist and poet, 1777;
Henry St John, Viscount Bolingbroke, statesman, 1751;
Stephen Bathory, King of Poland, 1586;
Darius II Nothus ['The Bastard'], King of Persia, 404 BC.

Occurred on this day:

A violent earthquake in Colombia resulted in over 700 dead, 1979;
Women members were elected to the Jockey Club for the first time, 1977;
Francis Chichester arrived at Sydney after sailing 13,000 miles alone from Plymouth in 107 days, 1966;
Kenya became independent, 1963, and became a republic, 1964;
The first London production of the musical show West Side Story was staged, 1958;
Christopher Cockerell patented the first hovercraft, 1955;

In Britain, conscription was introduced for men aged between 18 and 26, 1948;
In Germany, Hugo Junkers built the first all-metal aircraft, 1915;
King George V held a great Coronation Durbar in Delhi, India, 1911;
Franz Lehar's operetta Die Lustige Witwe [The Merry Widow] was first produced, Vienna, 1905;
Pennsylvania became the 2nd of the United States, 1787.

TODAY IS THE FEAST DAY OF St Corentin or Cury, St Edburga of Minster, Saints Epimachus and Alexander, St Finnian of Clonard, St Jane Frances de Chantel and St Vicelin.

13th December

Born on this day:

Jim Davidson, comedian, 1954;
John Francombe, jockey and broadcaster, 1952;
Robert Lindsay, actor, 1949;
Paula Wilcox, actress, 1949;
Howard Brenton, playwright, 1942;
Anouska Hempel, New Zealand actress, hotelier and designer, 1941;
HH Prince Karim, the Aga Khan, 1936;
Christopher Plummer, US film actor, 1929;
Dick Van Dyke, US TV and film actor, 1925;
George Shultz, former US Secretary of State, 1920;
Lord Bullock, historian, 1914;
Sir Laurens van der Post, writer and explorer, 1906;
John Piper CH, painter and writer, 1903;
Lucien-Germain Guitry, French actor, 1860;
Franz von Lenbach, German painter, 1836;
Sir Joseph Noel Paton, painter, 1821;
Ernst Werner von Siemens, inventor, 1816;
Rev. Arthur Penrhyn Stanley, biographer, 1815;
Harry [Heinrich] Heine, German poet and journalist, 1797;
William Drummond of Hawthornden, Scottish poet, 1585;
Maximilien de Béthune, Duc de Sully, French statesman, 1560;
Pope Sixtus V, 1520.

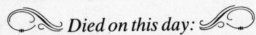

Died on this day:

Mary Renault [Mary Challans], novelist, 1983;
'Grandma Moses' [Mrs Thomas Salmon Moses (Anna Mary Robertson)], US primitive painter [aged 101], 1961;
Wassily Kandinsky, Russian abstract painter, 1944;
William Calcraft, shoemaker and hangman, 1879;
Dr Samuel Johnson, lexicographer, 1784;
Christian Fürchtegott Gellert, German poet and writer of fables, 1783;
Rev. John Strype, historian, 1737;
Anthony Collins, philosopher and writer, 1729;
François Viete de la Bigotière, French advocate and mathematician, 1603;
Konrad von Gesner, Swiss physician and naturalist, 1565;
Manoel I, King of Portugal, 1521;
Donatello [Donato de Betto Bardi], Florentine sculptor, 1466;
Frederick II, Holy Roman Emperor, 1250;
Maimonides [Moses ben Maimon], Jewish philosopher, 1204.

Occurred on this day:

The Battle of the River Plate was fought, 1939;
Dr Lee De Forest demonstrated the first sound-on-film movie in the USA, 1923;
Port Arthur was occupied by Russian forces, 1897;
The Confederate forces under Robert E. Lee were victorious at the Battle of Fredericksburg, 1862;
Basutoland became a native state under British protection, 1843;
Madrid fell to Napoleon's forces, 1808;
New Zealand was discovered by Abel Janszoon Tasman, 1642;
Sir Francis Drake left Plymouth on his voyage around the world, 1577.

TODAY IS THE FEAST DAY OF St Aubert of Cambrai, St Eustratius of Sebastea, St Judocus or Josse, St Lucy and St Othilia or Odilia.

14th December

Born on this day:

Stan Smith, US tennis champion, 1946;
Janette Scott, actress, 1938;
Barbara Leigh-Hunt, actress, 1935;
Charlie Rich, US singer, 1932;
Prof. Richard Cassily, operatic tenor, 1927;
Rosemary Sutcliff, historical novelist, 1920;
Shirley Jackson, US author, 1919;
Alberto Morrocco, painter, 1917;
Rosalyn Tureck, US conductor, lecturer and writer, 1914;
Paul I, King of the Hellenes, 1901;
Kurt von Schuschnigg, Austrian chancellor, 1897;
King George VI, 1895;
Paul Eluard [Eugene Grindal], French poet, 1895;

Joseph Jongen, Belgian composer, 1873;
Roger Eliot Fry, painter and critic, 1866;
Pierre-Cécile Puvis de Chavannes, French mural painter, 1824;
Rev. Charles Wolfe, Irish poet, 1791;
Thomas Cochrane, 10th Earl of Dundonald, admiral, 1775;
James Bruce, Scottish explorer of Africa, 1730;
Daniel Neal, cleric and historian, 1678;
Henry IV of Navarre, King of France, 1553;
Tycho Brahe, Danish astronomer and mathematician, 1546;
Nostradamus [Michel de Nostredame], French astrologer and prophet, 1503.

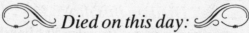

Died on this day:

Salvator de Madariaga y Rojo, Spanish author and diplomat, 1978;
William Bendix, US film actor, 1964;
Sir Stanley Spencer, painter, 1959;
Stanley, 1st Earl Baldwin of Bewdley, statesman, 1947;
Will Fyffe, Scottish comedian, 1947;
Maurice Baring, novelist, playwright and poet, 1945;
Jean-Louis Rodolphe Agassiz, Swiss/US naturalist, 1873;
Prince Albert, Consort to Queen Victoria, 1861;

George Washington, 1st president of the USA, 1799;
Carl Philipp Emanuel Bach, German composer, 1788;
Giovanni Battista Cipriani, Italian painter and engraver, 1785;
Thomas Rymer, archaeologist, 1713;
Henry Aldrich, Dean of Christ Church, Oxford, composer and architect, 1710;
James V, King of Scotland, 1542;
Sir John Oldcastle, Baron Cobham, hanged and burnt, 1417.

Occurred on this day:

Archbishop Makarios became the first president of the Republic of Cyprus, 1959;
The League of Nations condemned and expelled the USSR for aggression against Finland, 1939;
Women in Britain voted for the first time at the General Election, 1918;
Puccini's opera *Gianni Schicchi* was first performed, Milan, 1918;

Roald Amundsen reached the South Pole, 1911;
Max Planck put forward his quantum theory, 1901;
Alabama became the 22nd of the United States, 1819;
Mary acceded to the Scottish throne, 1542.

TODAY IS THE FEAST DAY OF Saints Fingar or Gwinnear and Phiala, St John of the Cross, St Nicasius of Reims, St Spiridion and St Venantius Fortunatus.

 # 15th December

Born on this day:

Joe Jordan, footballer, 1951;
Dave Clark, drummer and pop group founder, 1942;
Geoffrey Davies, actor, 1941;
Austin Savage, Welsh hockey international, 1941;
Edna O'Brien, Irish novelist, 1936;
Ida Haendel, violinist, 1928;
Bob Todd, comedy actor, 1921;
Oscar Niemeyer, architect, 1907;
Carl Ferdinand Cori, US biochemist, 1896;
Jean Paul Getty, US multi-millionaire, 1892;
Maxwell Anderson, US playwright, 1888;
Josef Hoffmann, Austrian architect, 1870;
Niels Ryberg Finsen, Danish physician, 1860;
Dr Lazarus Ludovic Zamenhof, Polish oculist and creator of Esperanto, 1859;
Antoine-Henri Becquerel, French physicist, 1852;
Sir Alfred East, painter and etcher, 1849;
Alexandre-Gustave Eiffel, French engineer, 1832;
Janos Bolyai, Hungarian mathematician, 1802;
George Romney, portrait painter, 1734;
David Teniers the Younger, Flemish painter, 1610;
Nero, Roman emperor, 37.

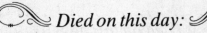 ## Died on this day:

Walter Elias Disney, cartoonist and creator of 'Mickey Mouse', 1966;
Charles Laughton, actor, 1962;
Wolfgang Pauli, US physicist, 1958;
Thomas Wright ['Fats'] Waller, US jazz pianist, 1943;
Sir George Cayley, aeronautics pioneer, 1857;
Georg Friedrich Grotefend, German classical scholar, 1853;
Isaak Walton, author of *The Compleat Angler*, 1683;
Jan Vermeer [Jan van der Meer van Delft], Dutch painter, 1675;
Haakon IV, King of Norway, 1263.

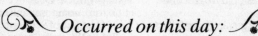 ## Occurred on this day:

The first production of the musical show *Charlie Girl* took place in London, 1965;
The General Assembly of the United Nations voted to admit the Chinese People's Republic, 1961;
In Israel, Adolf Eichmann was found guilty of crimes against the Jewish people, 1961;
The premiere of the film *Gone with the Wind* took place at Atlanta, Georgia, 1939;
The Commonwealth of the Philippines was inaugurated, 1935;
The first TV play in Britain, *Box and Cox*, was transmitted to a limited audience, 1928;
The Battle of Verdun ended, with 700,000 dead [338,000 German, 364,000 Allied soldiers], 1916;
The Piccadilly tube line in London was opened, 1906;
General Redvers Buller's troops were defeated by the Boers at the Battle of Colenso, 1899;
Napoleon and his army entered Warsaw, 1806;
The French recaptured Rome and overran the Kingdom of Naples, 1798.

TODAY IS THE FEAST DAY OF St Mary di Rosa, St Nino, St Paul of Latros and St Valerian.

 **16th December**

Born on this day:

Graham Stevenson, Yorkshire and England cricketer, 1955;
Stephanie Lawrence, singer, 1953;
Joel Garner, West Indies cricketer, 1952;
Benny Andersson, singer with Abba group, 1946;
Christopher Ellison, actor, 1946;
Liv Ullmann, Norwegian actress, 1938;
Rodion Shchedrin, Russian composer, 1932;
The Hon. Peter Dickinson, author, 1927;
Arthur C. Clarke, science fact and fiction writer, 1917;
Norman Blamey, painter, 1914;
Dr Margaret Mead, US anthropologist, 1901;
Sir Victor Pritchett, author and critic, 1900;
Sir Noël Pierce Coward, playwright, actor and composer, 1889;
Zoltán Kodály, Hungarian composer, 1882;
Sir John [Jack] Hobbs, cricketer, 1882;
Edward Emerson Barnard, US astronomer, 1857;
Isidore Geoffroy Saint-Hilaire, French geologist, 1805;
Leopold I, King of the Belgians, 1790;
Mary Russell Mitford, author, 1787;
Jane Austen, novelist, 1775;
Field Marshal Gebhard Leberecht von Blücher, Prussian military commander, 1742;
Elizabeth Carter, scholar, poet and linguist, 1717;
George Whitefield, evangelist, 1714;
John Selden, lawyer and historian, 1584;
Catherine of Aragon, 1st wife of King Henry VIII, 1485.

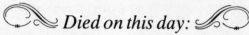 Died on this day:

William Somerset Maugham, novelist, 1965;
Alton Glenn Miller, US dance band leader, lost without trace after plane flight, 1944;
Robert William Chambers, US novelist and artist, 1933;
Charles-Camille Saint-Saëns, French composer, 1921;
Wilhelm Grimm, German philologist and folklorist, 1859;
Charles, 3rd Earl of Stanhope, reformer and inventor, 1816;
Thomas Pennant, traveller and naturalist, 1798;
Sir William Petty, economist, 1687.

Occurred on this day:

Synthetic diamonds were first produced by Prof. H.T. Hall at the G.E.C. Laboratories, USA, 1954;
The Battle of the Bulge began when the Germans under von Rundstedt launched a strong attack in the Ardennes, 1944;
The first production of the musical show *Me and My Girl* took place in London, 1937;
A landslide in the Kansu province of China resulted in 180,000 deaths, 1920;
The Manchester Ship Canal was completed, 1893;
The Transvaal Republic in South Africa was proclaimed, 1879;
Antonio López de Santa Anna was declared dictator of Mexico, 1853;
The Boston Tea Party took place, 1773;
Oliver Cromwell became Lord Protector, 1653.

TODAY IS THE FEAST DAY OF St Adelaide, St Ado, St Albina, Saints Ananiah, Azariah & Mishael [Shadrach, Meshach and Abednego] and St Irenion.

17th December

Born on this day:

Christopher Cazenove, actor, 1945;
Bernard Hill, actor, 1944;
Peter Snell, New Zealand athlete, 1938;
Brian Hayes, radio presenter, 1937;
Kerry Packer, Australian entrepreneur, 1937;
Tommy Steele, singer and actor, 1936;
Robert Robinson, broadcaster and writer, 1927;
Lord Glenamara CH, former government minister, 1912;
Erskine Preston Caldwell, US novelist, 1903;
Walter Greenwood, novelist and playwright, 1903;
Stanley Raymond [Ray] Noble, composer and conductor, 1903;
J. Robertson Hare, actor, 1891;
William Lyon MacKenzie King, Canadian statesman, 1874;

Ford Madox Ford [Ford Hermann Hueffer], novelist, 1873;
Jules-Alfred-Huot de Goncourt, French novelist and historian, 1830;
Thomas Woolner, sculptor and poet, 1825;
John Greenleaf Whittier, US poet and essayist, 1807;
Joseph Henry, US physicist, 1797;
Sir George Hayter, painter, 1792;
Sir Humphry Davy, chemist and inventor, 1778;
Ludwig van Beethoven, German composer, baptised, 1770;
Domenico Cimarosa, Neapolitan composer, 1749;
Prince Rupert of Bavaria, Royalist commander, 1619.

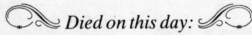

Died on this day:

Peter Warlock [Philip Arnold Heseltine], composer and editor, committed suicide, 1930;
Elizabeth Garrett Anderson, physician, 1917;
Sir William Thomson, 1st Baron Kelvin of Largs, physicist, 1907;
Bernard Quaritch, bookseller, 1899;
Louis-Marie-Alphonse Daudet, French novelist, 1897;

Lewis Henry Morgan, US anthropologist and lawyer, 1881;
Rear Admiral Sir Francis Beaufort, hydrographer, 1857;
Simón Bolívar, South American patriot, 1830;
Thomas Guy, bookseller and philanthropist, 1724;
Sir William Gascoigne, Lord Chief Justice, 1413.

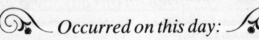

Occurred on this day:

The musical *Hans Andersen* was first produced, London, 1974;
After Arab guerrillas hijacked a West German airliner at Rome airport, 31 people were killed, 1973;
Zulficar Ali Bhutto became prime minister of Pakistan, 1971;
Alec Rose arrived at Melbourne in his ketch *Lively Lady* after a solo voyage from Portsmouth of five months, 1967;

President Roosevelt proposed 'Lease-Lend' for Britain, 1940;
The battleship *Graf Spee* was scuttled near Montevideo, after the Battle of the River Plate, 1939;
The Wright brothers made their first flight at Kitty Hawk, North Carolina, 1903;
The Lyric Theatre, Shaftesbury Avenue, London, opened, 1888.

TODAY IS THE FEAST DAY OF St Begga, St Lazarus, St Olympias, St Sturmi and St Wivina.

18th December

Born on this day:

Steven Spielberg, US film producer and director, 1947;

Keith Richards, guitarist with the Rolling Stones, 1943;

Mohammed Ali, US boxer, 1942;

Rosemary Leach, actress, 1935;

Annette Page, ballerina, 1932;

Lieut.-Comdr. Ian Fraser, VC, 1920;

Lord Merlyn-Rees [Merlyn Rees], former Home Secretary, 1920;

Betty [Elizabeth Ruth] Grable, US film actress, 1916;

Willy Brandt, former West German Chancellor, 1913;

Jules Dassin, US film director, 1912;

Christopher Fry, playwright, 1907;

Edwin Howard Armstrong, US engineer and inventor of FM radio, 1890;

Dame Gladys Cooper, actress, 1888;

Paul Klee, Swiss abstract painter, 1879;

Saki [Hector Hugh Munro], short-story writer, 1870;

Edward Alexander MacDowell, US composer and pianist, 1860;

Francis Thompson, poet, 1859;

Sir Joseph John Thomson, physicist, 1856;

Abraham Viktor Rydberg, Swedish philosopher and poet, 1828;

Joseph Grimaldi, clown, 1779;

Charles Wesley, hymn-writer ['Jesu, Lover of My Soul'], 1707;

Ludolf Backhuysen, Dutch painter, 1631.

Died on this day:

Ben Travers, writer of farces, 1980;

Dorothy Leigh Sayers, detective story writer, 1957;

Sir William Hamo Thornycroft, sculptor, 1925;

Sir John William Alcock, aviator, killed in an air crash, 1919;

Sir Richard Owen, palaeontologist, 1892;

Philipp Veit, German painter, 1877;

Samuel Rogers, poet and banker, 1855;

Jean-Baptiste-Pierre-Antoine Monnet, Chevalier de Lamarck, French zoologist, 1829;

Johann Gottfried von Herder, German theologian and philosopher, 1803;

Antonio Stradivari, Italian violin-maker, 1737.

Occurred on this day:

Stanley Barrett became the first man to break the sound barrier on land, driving in California at 739.6 mph, 1979;

After discussion in the House of Lords, the death penalty for murder was finally abolished in Britain, 1969;

The French newspaper Le Monde was issued for the first time, 1944;

The US Congress prohibited the entry of illiterate immigrants, 1912;

A treaty between the USA and Panama placed the Canal under US control for an annual rent, 1903;

Under the 13th Amendment, slavery was abolished in the United States, 1865;

New Jersey became the 3rd of the United States, 1787.

TODAY IS THE FEAST DAY OF St Flannan, St Gatian, Saints Rufus and Zosimus, St Samthan and St Winebald.

19th December

Born on this day:

Timothy Eggar, MP, 1951;
Syd Little, comedian, 1942;
Maurice White, US rock singer, 1941;
Edith Piaf [Edith Giovanna Gassion], French singer, 1915;
Jean Genet, French playwright and essayist, 1910;
Leonid Ilyich Brezhnev, Soviet leader, 1906;
Sir Ralph David Richardson, actor, 1902;

Oliver Hazard Perry La Farge, US author, 1901;
Sir Stanley Unwin, publisher, 1884;
Albert Abraham Michelson, US physicist, 1852;
Sir William Edward Parry, Arctic explorer, 1790;
Philip V, King of Spain, 1683;
Andreas Osiander [Hosemann], German religious reformer, 1498.

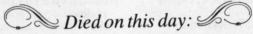

Died on this day:

Robert Andrews Millikan, US physicist, 1953;
Sir Paul Gavrilovich Vinogradoff, lawyer and historian, 1925;
Joseph Mallord William Turner, painter, 1851;
Emily Brontë ['Ellis Bell'], novelist, 1848;
Benjamin Smith Barton, US naturalist, 1815;
David Hartley the younger, statesman and inventor, 1813;

Frederick Melchior, Baron von Grimm, German statesman and wit, 1807;
Jean-Baptiste Vanloo, French painter, 1745;
Vitus Jonassen Bering, Danish navigator, 1741;
Matteo Maria Boiardo, Italian poet, 1494;
Pope Anastasius I, 401.

Occurred on this day:

Ted Hughes was appointed Poet Laureate, 1984;
Eight crew members were drowned from the Penlee lifeboat of Mousehole, Cornwall, as were eight people of the Union Star coaster, 1981;
An air service between London and Moscow was begun, 1957;
The British evacuated Penang, 1941;
The German luxury liner Columbus was scuttled by her crew after being intercepted by a British destroyer, 1939;

In the New Hebrides, over 500 people were killed following a volcanic eruption, 1913;
The United States recognised the independence of Hawaii, 1842;
During the American-British war of 1812, the Toronto parliament building was set alight, and Fort Niagara was taken by the British, 1813;
Toulon was recaptured by Napoleon Bonaparte from Alexander Hood, 1793;
Huguenots and Catholics clashed when the Battle of Dreux was fought, 1562.

TODAY IS THE FEAST DAY OF St Anastasius I of Antioch, St Gregory of Auxerre, St Nemesius of Alexandria and St Timothy.

20th December

Born on this day:

Billy Bragg, rock singer, 1958;
Bo Derek, US film actress, 1957;
Jenny Agutter, actress, 1952;
Malcolm Cooper, marksman, 1947;
Lesley Judd, actress, 1946;
Bo Diddley, US singer and guitarist, 1928;
Lord Howe of Aberavon [Sir Geoffrey Howe], QC, former MP, 1926;
James Leasor, author, 1923;
Donald Tandy, actor, 1918;
Lieut.-Gen. Sir Frederick Arthur Montague Browning, 1896;
Sir Robert Gordon Menzies, Australian statesman, 1894;
Theodore Francis Powys, novelist, 1875;

Lorenzo Perosi, Italian priest and composer, 1872;
Harvey Samuel Firestone, US industrialist, 1868;
The Rev. Edwin Abbott Abbott, headmaster and theologian, 1838;
Thomas Graham, Scottish chemist, 1805;
Nicolas-Toussaint Charlet, French designer and military painter, 1792;
William Burn, architect, 1789;
John Wilson Croker, politician and reviewer, 1780;
Pieter de Hooch, Dutch painter, 1629;
Nicholas Sanson, French cartographer, 1599.

Died on this day:

Bill Brandt, photographer, 1983;
Artur Rubinstein, US pianist, 1982;
Robert Walden Cassotto [Bobby Darin], US singer, 1973;
John Ernst Steinbeck, US novelist, 1968;
Moss Hart, US playwright, 1961;
James Hilton, novelist, 1954;
Erich Friedrich Wilhelm von Ludendorff, German general, 1937;

Émile-François Loubet, French statesman, 1929;
Thomas Hill, literary patron, prototype of 'Paul Pry', 1840;
Emmerich von Vattel, Swiss jurist, 1767;
Ambroise Paré, French surgeon, 1590;
Ignatius, Bishop of Antioch, 107.

Occurred on this day: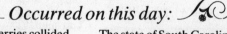

Two Townsend Thoresen ferries collided off Harwich, with the loss of six lives, 1982;
Wladyslaw Gomulka, Polish Communist leader, resigned office after riots by workers, 1970;
The first atomic ice-breaker, the Russian *Lenin*, began operating, 1959;
Karl Renner became the first president of the new Austrian republic, 1945;
The first London performance of the operetta *Madame Pompadour* was presented, 1923;

The state of South Carolina seceded from the American Union, 1860;
The State of Texas was incorporated in the United States, 1845;
The last issue of the original *Spectator* was published, 1714;
Peter the Great's reformation of the Russian calendar was announced, 1699;
The first General Assembly of the Church of Scotland was held, 1560.

TODAY IS THE FEAST DAY OF St Ammon and his Companions, St Dominic of Silos, St Philogonius and St Ursicinus.

21st December

Born on this day:

Chris Evert, US tennis champion, 1954;
Steve Perryman, footballer, 1951;
Walter Spanghero, rugby player, 1943;
Frank Zappa, US rock singer and composer, 1940;
Greville Starkey, jockey, 1939;
Jane Fonda, US actress, 1937;
Mily Alekseievich Balakirev, Russian composer, 1837;
Peter Tinniswood, playwright, 1936;
Geoff Lewis, racehorse trainer, 1935;
Jeremy Tree, racehorse trainer, 1925;
Flight Lieut. William Reid VC, 1921;
Dr Kurt Waldheim, former president of Austria, 1918;
Frank Hampson, creator of 'Dan Dare', 1918;
Heinrich Böll, German author, 1917;
Anthony Powell CH, novelist, 1905;
Harry Revel, popular composer and pianist, 1905;

Josef Vissarionovich Dzhugashvili [Joseph Stalin], Soviet leader, 1879;
Nathaniel [Nat] Gould, racing novelist, 1857;
Benjamin Disraeli, 1st Earl of Beaconsfield, statesman, 1804;
Sir Joseph Whitworth Bt., mechanical engineer, 1803;
Dr Robert Moffat, Scottish missionary and traveller, 1795;
Leopold von Ranke, German historian, 1795;
Jean Racine, French playwright, 1639;
Mathurin Regnier, French satirical poet, 1573;
Masaccio [Tommaso di Giovanni], Florentine painter, 1401;
Thomas à Becket, Archbishop of Canterbury, 1118.

Died on this day:

Sir [Jack] John Berry Hobbs, cricketer, 1963;
Lion Feuchtwanger, German novelist and playwright, 1958;
General George Smith Patton, US military leader, 1945;
Francis Scott Key Fitzgerald, US novelist, 1940;

Kurt Tucholsky, German author, 1935;
Walter Hines Page, US ambassador and editor, 1918;
Niels Wilhelm Gade, Danish composer, 1890;
James Parkinson, surgeon and palaeontologist, 1824;
Giovanni Boccaccio, Italian author, 1375.

Occurred on this day:

The first flight of Man around the moon took place when *Apollo 8* was launched, 1969;
An earthquake in Japan caused the deaths of 1,068 people, 1946;
The premiere of the first full-length full-colour animated cartoon [*Snow White and the Seven Dwarfs*] by Walt Disney, 1935;

The first newspaper to publish a crossword puzzle was the *New York World*, 1913;
Charley's Aunt, the farce by Brandon Thomas, was first performed, 1892;
Anaesthetics were used for the first time in Britain [by Robert Liston], 1846;
The Pilgrim Fathers landed at Plymouth Rock in North America, 1620.

TODAY IS THE FEAST DAY OF St Anastasius II of Antioch, St Glycerius, St John Vincent, St Peter Canisius and Saints Themistocles and Dioscorus.

356

22nd December

Born on this day:

Maurice and Robin Gibb [of the Bee Gees pop group], 1949;
Noel Edmonds, TV presenter, 1948;
Ken Whitmore, playwright, 1939;
Sir Peregrine Worsthorne, editor, 1923;
Karin Jonzen, sculptor, 1914;
Patricia Hayes, actress, 1909;
Pierre Brasseur [Pierre-Albert Espinasse], French actor, 1905;
Dr Alan Bush, composer, conductor and pianist, 1900;
Charles Stuart Calverley, poet and parodist, 1831;
Edgard [Edgar Victor Achille-Charles] Varèse, French/US composer, 1883;
Giacomo Antonio Domenico Michele Secondo Maria Puccini, Italian operatic composer, 1858;

John Nevil Maskelyne, stage magician, 1839;
William Hale White ['Mark Rutherford'], novelist, 1831;
Jean-Henri Fabre, French naturalist, 1823;
John Crome ['Old Crome'], landscape painter, 1768;
Karl Friedrich Abel, German composer, 1723;
James Edward Oglethorpe, colonist and founder of Georgia, 1696;
Hermann Samuel Reimarus, German theologian and philosopher, 1694.

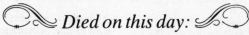

Died on this day:

Darryl Francis Zanuck, film producer, 1979;
Josef von Sternberg, German film director, 1969;
Richard Frederick Dimbleby, TV commentator, 1965;
Harry Langdon, US silent film comedian, 1944;
Helen Beatrix Potter, author and artist, 1943;
Nathanael West [Nathan Wallenstein Weinstein], US novelist, 1940;
Baron Richard von Krafft-Ebing, Austrian psychiatrist, 1902;

Dwight Lyman Moody, US evangelist, 1899;
George Eliot [Mary Ann Evans], novelist, 1880;
Sir Philip Francis, civil servant and author, 1818;
Guercino [Giovanni Francesco Barbieri], Italian painter, 1666;
Maximilien de Béthune, Duc de Sully, French soldier and statesman, 1641;
François Clouet, French miniature painter, 1572.

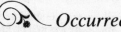

Occurred on this day:

A Pan American jumbo jet crashed on to the town of Lockerbie in Scotland, killing all 259 passengers and crew, and 11 people on the ground, 1988;
Kurt Waldheim was elected Secretary-General of the United Nations, 1971;
The musical show Balalaika opened in London, 1936;

The musical show Lilac Time was first produced in London, 1922;
Alfred Dreyfus was convicted and sentenced to imprisonment on Devil's Island, 1895;
The first pantomime in England was staged at the Lincoln's Inn Theatre, 1716.

TODAY IS THE FEAST DAY OF St Chaeremon and Others, St Flavian of Tuscany, St Ischyrion and St Zeno.

23rd December

Born on this day:

HM Queen Silvia of Sweden, 1943;
Christopher Lawrence, silversmith, 1936;
HM Akihito, Emperor of Japan, 1933;
Helmut Schmidt, former Chancellor of West Germany, 1918;
Maurice Denham, actor, 1909;
Yousuf Karsh, portrait photographer, 1908;
Joseph Arthur, 1st Baron Rank, miller and film magnate, 1888;
Arthur Reed Ropes ['Adrian Ross'], lyricist, 1859;
Samuel Smiles, author, 1812;
Karl Richard Lepsius, German Egyptologist, 1810;

Joseph Smith, founder of the Mormons [Church of Jesus Christ of Latter-Day Saints], 1805;
Charles-Augustin Sainte-Beuve, French writer and critic, 1804;
Jean-François Champollion, French Egyptologist and decipherer of the Rosetta Stone, 1790;
Alexander I, Tsar of Russia, 1777;
Sir Richard Arkwright, inventor of the spinning frame, 1732;
Frans van Mieris the Younger, Dutch painter, 1689;
James Gibbs, Scottish architect, 1682;
Robert Barclay, Scottish Quaker author, 1648.

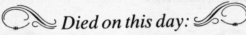

Died on this day:

Andrei Nikolayevich Tupolev, Soviet aircraft designer, 1972;
Edward Frederick Lindley Wood, 1st Earl of Halifax, Viceroy of India, 1959;
Eric Coates, composer, 1957;
Charles Dana Gibson, US artist and illustrator, 1944;
Anthony Herman Gerard Fokker, Dutch aircraft designer, 1939;
Jean-Baptiste-Édouard Detaille, French painter, 1912;
Laurence Oliphant, journalist and traveller, 1888;
George Catlin, US artist and author, 1872;

Sir Charles Lock Eastlake, painter, 1865;
Hugh Miller, Scottish geologist, 1856;
Dr James Cowles Prichard, ethnologist, 1848;
Thomas Robert Malthus, economist, 1834;
Alastair Ruadh Macdonnell, Jacobite spy ['Pickle'], 1761;
John Cotton, Puritan leader in America, 1652;
Michael Drayton, poet, 1631;
William Davison, Scottish Secretary of State to Queen Elizabeth I, 1608;
Henri I de Lorraine, 3rd Duc de Guise, assassinated, 1588.

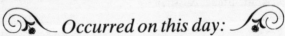

Occurred on this day:

Managua, capital of Nicaragua, was destroyed by an earthquake, with a loss of 12,000 lives, 1972;
117 people died when the cruise liner *Lakonia* burned in the Atlantic; 919 people were saved, 1963;
In the USSR, Lavrenty Beria and six others were executed for treason, 1953;
British forces took Benghazi, 1941;
In Germany, Marinus Van der Lubbe, a Dutchman, was found guilty of setting fire to the Reichstag and sentenced to death, 1933;

Wolf-Ferrari's opera *The Jewels of the Madonna* was first produced, Berlin, 1911;
The Aldwych Theatre, London, opened, 1905;
Humperdinck's opera *Hansel and Gretel* was first produced, Weimar, 1893;
Joseph Hansom patented a type of cab, 1834.

TODAY IS THE FEAST DAY OF St Dagobert II of Austria, St Frithebert, St John of Kanti, St Servulus, The Ten Martyrs of Crete, St Thorlac and Saints Victoria and Anatolia.

 # 24th December

Born on this day:

Jeremy Hindley, racehorse trainer, 1943;
Sir Nicholas Fairbairn QC, MP, 1933;
Colin Cowdrey, former cricketer, 1932;
Philip Ziegler, author and editor, 1929;
Norman Rossington, actor, 1928;
Thea Porter, fashion designer, 1927;
Ava Lavinia Gardner [Lucy Johnson], US film actress, 1922;
John Barron, actor, 1920;
Howard Robard Hughes, US millionaire and recluse, 1905;
Ruth Chatterton, US film actress, 1893;
Harry Warren [Salvatore Guaragna], US popular composer and pianist, 1893;
Michael Curtiz [Mihaly Kertesz], US film director, 1888;
Louis Jouvet, French actor and director, 1887;

Juan Ramón Jiménez, Spanish poet, 1881;
John, Viscount Morley, statesman and writer, 1838;
Matthew Arnold, poet and critic, 1822;
James Prescott Joule, physicist, 1818;
Christopher ['Kit'] Carson, US trapper, scout and Indian agent, 1809;
Adam Bernard Mickiewicz, Polish poet, 1798;
Augustin-Eugène Scribe, French playwright, 1791;
George Crabbe, poet, 1754;
William Warburton, bishop and scholar, 1698;
St Ignatius of Loyola, founder of the Jesuits, 1491;
King John [John Lackland], 1167.

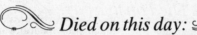 ## Died on this day:

Karl Doenitz, former German naval commander, 1980;
Frank Richards [Charles Harold St John Hamilton], author and creator of 'Billy Bunter', 1961;
Jean-Louis-Xavier-François Darlan, French admiral and politician, assassinated, 1942;
Alban Maria Johannes Berg, Austrian composer, 1935;
Leon Bakst [Lev Samoylovich Rosenberg], Russian painter and stage designer, 1924;

Charles Mackay, songwriter and journalist, 1889;
William Makepeace Thackeray, novelist, 1863;
Vasco da Gama, Portuguese explorer and navigator, 1524;
John Dunstable, astrologer and composer, 1453;
Sir Thomas Beaufort, Duke of Exeter, admiral and commander, 1426;
Jean de Joinville, French crusader and historian, 1317.

 ## Occurred on this day:

Libya became independent and King Idriss I acceded to the throne, 1951;
General Eisenhower was appointed commander-in-chief of the Allied invasion forces, 1943;
Prof. R.A. Fessendon in Canada made the first demonstration of transmitting the human voice by radio-telephone, 1906;

The Coliseum Theatre, London, opened, 1904;
Giuseppe Verdi's opera Aïda was performed for the first time, Cairo, 1871;
The War of 1812 between Britain and the USA was ended with the signing of the Treaty of Ghent, 1814;
Britain's first self-propelled vehicle was tested by Richard Trevithick, 1801.

TODAY IS THE FEAST DAY OF St Adela, St Delphinus, St Gregory of Spoleto, St Irmina, St Sharbel Makhlouf and Saints Tharsilla and Emiliana.

25th December

Born on this day:

Nick Conway, actor, 1962;
Sissy Spacek, US actress, 1949;
Kenny Everett, radio and TV comedian, 1944;
HRH Princess Alexandra, 1936;
Ismail Merchant, film producer, 1936;
Stuart Hall, radio commentator and presenter, 1934;
Anwar Sadat, Egyptian statesman, 1918;
Tony Martin, US singer and actor, 1913;
Cabell [Cab] Calloway, US jazz singer and bandleader, 1907;
Lord Grade, 1906;
HRH Princess Alice, Duchess of Gloucester, 1901;
Humphrey DeForest Bogart, US actor, 1899;

Dame Rebecca West [Cicily Isabel Fairfield], author, 1892;
Conrad Nicholson Hilton, US hotel proprietor, 1887;
Maurice Utrillo, French painter, 1883;
Charles Pathé, French film pioneer, 1863;
William Nicholson, Scottish painter, 1784;
Dorothy Wordsworth, writer and sister of the poet, 1771;
Richard Porson, classical scholar, 1759;
William Collins, poet, 1721;
Julien Offroy de La Mettrie, French army surgeon and philosopher, 1709;
Sir Isaac Newton, mathematician, physicist and astronomer, 1642;
Noel Coypel, French painter, 1628.

Died on this day:

Nicolae Ceausescu, former Romanian president and his wife, Elena, executed by firing squad, 1989;
Joan Miró, Catalan artist, 1983;
Fred Emney, comedian, 1980;
Joan Blondell, US film actress, 1979;

Sir Charles Spencer Chaplin, comedian and film producer, 1977;
W.C. Fields [William Claude Dukenfield], US film comedian, 1946;
Dr Karel Čapek, Czech playwright, 1938;
John Logan, Scottish poet, 1788.

Occurred on this day:

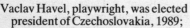

Vaclav Havel, playwright, was elected president of Czechoslovakia, 1989;
A cyclone and tidal wave devastated Southern India and Ceylon, with over 7,000 deaths, 1964;
The Stone of Scone was stolen from Westminster Abbey, 1951;
The Emperor Hirohito acceded to the Japanese throne, 1926;
The first Christmas tree in Britain was put up at Queen's Lodge, Windsor, by Queen Charlotte, 1800;

George Washington crossed the Delaware river, 1776;
The *Mayflower* arrived at Plymouth Rock, Massachusetts, 1620;
William I [the Conqueror] was crowned in Westminster Abbey, 1066;
Charlemagne was crowned by Pope Leo III as the first Holy Roman Emperor, 800.

TODAY IS CHRISTMAS DAY AND THE FEAST DAY OF St Alburga, St Anastasia of Sirmium, St Eugenia and The Martyrs of Nicomedia.

 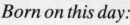 # 26th December

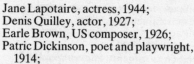
Born on this day:

Jane Lapotaire, actress, 1944;

Denis Quilley, actor, 1927;

Earle Brown, US composer, 1926;

Patric Dickinson, poet and playwright, 1914;

Richard Widmark, US film actor, 1914;

Alastair Dunnett, former editor of *The Scotsman*, 1908;

Mao Tse-tung, Chinese Communist leader, 1893;

Henry Valentine Miller, US novelist, 1891;

Sir Norman Angell [Ralph Norman Angell Lane], author and journalist, 1874;

Dion Boucicault [Dionysius Lardner Boursiquot], Irish actor and playwright, 1822;

Charles Babbage, computer pioneer, 1792;

Mary Fairfax Somerville, mathematician and writer on physics, 1780;

Lord George Gordon, anti-Catholic agitator, 1751;

Thomas Gray, poet and scholar, 1716.

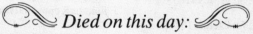
Died on this day:

Elsa Lanchester, actress, 1986;

Jack Benny [Benjamin Kubelsky], US comedian, 1974;

Harry S. Truman, 33rd president of the USA, 1972;

Charles Pathé, French film producer and director, 1957;

James Stephens, Irish poet and novelist, 1950;

Frederic Remington, US artist and illustrator, 1909;

Sir Joseph Noel Paton, painter, 1901;

Heinrich Schliemann, German archaeologist, 1890;

Stephen Girard, French/US millionaire philanthropist, 1831;

Joel Barlow, US poet and diplomat, 1812;

Mary Robinson, née Darby ['Perdita'], actress and Royal mistress, 1800;

John Wilkes, politician and journalist, 1797;

Claude-Adrien Helvetius, French philosopher and encyclopaedist, 1771.

Occurred on this day:

Fidel Castro landed in Cuba, starting a revolution against the Batista regime, 1956;

The Battle of the North Cape took place, when the German battlecruiser *Scharnhorst* was sunk in the North Sea, 1943;

The world's first feature film, *The Story of the Kelly Gang*, was shown in Melbourne, Australia, 1906;

Radium was discovered by Pierre and Marie Curie, 1898;

The Hessians, fighting for the British, were defeated by the American colonial forces at Trenton, New Jersey, 1776;

King Stephen acceded to the throne of England, 1135.

TODAY IS BOXING DAY (HANDSEL DAY IN SCOTLAND) AND THE FEAST DAY OF St Archelaus of Kashkar, St Dionysius, pope, St Stephen, St Tathai or Athaeus, St Vincentia Lopez and St Zosimus, pope.

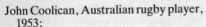

27th December

Born on this day:

John Coolican, Australian rugby player, 1953;

Janet Street-Porter, broadcaster and writer, 1946;

Christopher Benjamin, actor, 1934;

Pat Moss, former rally driver, 1934;

John Charles, footballer, 1931;

Oscar Levant, US popular composer and pianist, 1906;

Marlene Dietrich, film actress, 1901;

Louis Bromfield, US novelist, 1896;

Carl Zuckmayer, German playwright, 1896;

Sydney Greenstreet, film actor, 1878;

Sir William Henry Hadow, educationalist and musical scholar, 1859;

Louis Pasteur, French chemist and bacteriologist, 1822;

Sir John Goss, organist and composer, 1800;

Alexander Gordon Laing, Scottish explorer, 1793;

Sir George Cayley, aeronautics pioneer, 1773;

Jakob Bernoulli, Swiss mathematician, 1654;

Johannes Kepler, German astronomer, 1571.

Died on this day:

Howard Hoagland [Hoagy] Carmichael, US composer, singer and pianist, 1981;

Houari Boumedienne [Mohammed ben Brahim Boukharrouba], Algerian statesman, 1978;

Lester Bowles Pearson, Canadian statesman, 1972;

Max Beckmann, German expressionist painter, 1950;

William Archer, Scottish dramatic critic and playwright, 1924;

Charles Martin Hall, US chemist and manufacturer, 1914;

Charles Lamb, author and essayist, 1834;

Joanna Southcott, religious fanatic, 1814;

Hyacinthe Rigaud [Hyacinthe-François-Honoré-Mathias-Pierre-Martyr-André-Jean Rigau y Ros], French painter, 1743;

Pierre de Ronsard, French poet, 1585.

Occurred on this day:

Spain became a democracy after 40 years of dictatorship, 1978;

In the North Sea, the BP oil rig *Sea Gem* capsized and sank with the loss of 13 lives, 1965;

In Hungary, Archbishop Jozef Mindszenty was arrested and sentenced to life imprisonment, 1948;

The International Monetary Fund was set up in Washington, D.C., 1945;

Violent earthquakes in Anatolia, Turkey, resulted in over 10,000 deaths, 1939;

In New York, Radio City Music Hall was opened, 1932;

In the USSR, Leon Trotsky was expelled from the Communist Party, 1927;

The Globe Theatre, London opened as the Hicks Theatre, 1906;

Peter Pan, the children's play by J.M. Barrie, was first performed, London, 1904;

Charles Darwin set sail for a world voyage on HMS *Beagle*, 1831.

TODAY IS THE FEAST DAY OF St Fabiola, St John the Evangelist, St Nicarete and Saints Theodore and Theophanes Graptoi.

28th December

Born on this day:

Terry Butcher, footballer, 1958;
Nigel Kennedy, violinist, 1956;
Max Hastings, editor-in-chief, the *Daily Telegraph*, 1945;
Joan Ruddock, MP, 1943;
Dame Maggie Smith, actress, 1934;
Roy Hattersley, MP, 1932;
Simon Raven, author and playwright, 1927;
Donald Carr, former cricketer, 1926;
Hildegarde Neff, actress, 1925;
Noel Johnson, actor, 1916;
Thomas Gould VC, 1914;
Lew Ayres, US film actor, 1908;
Earl ['Fatha'] Hines, jazz pianist, 1905;

Roger Huntington Sessions, US composer, 1896;
St John Greer Ervine, playwright and dramatic critic, 1883;
Sir Arthur Stanley Eddington, astronomer, 1882;
Pio Baroja y Nessi, Spanish novelist, 1872;
Philip Wilson Steer, artist, 1860;
Sir John William Fortescue, military historian, 1859;
Thomas Woodrow Wilson, 28th president of the USA, 1856;
Sir Archibald Geikie, geologist, 1835.

Died on this day:

Sam Peckinpah, US film director, 1984;
Max [Maximilian] Raoul Steiner, Austrian/US film music composer, 1971;
Paul Hindemith, German composer, 1963;
Theodore Herman Albert Dreiser, US novelist, 1945;
Maurice-Joseph Ravel, French composer, 1937;
Alexandre-Gustave Eiffel, French engineer, 1923;
George Robert Gissing, novelist, 1903;
Thomas Creswick, painter, 1869;
Thomas Babington Macaulay, 1st Baron Macaulay, author and statesman, 1859;

Victor Emmanuel III, former King of Italy, 1947;
Emmerich de Vattel, Swiss diplomat and jurist, 1767;
Rob Roy [Robert Macgregor], Scottish clan chief, 1734;
Pierre Bayle, French philosopher and writer, 1706;
Queen Mary II [of William and Mary], 1694.

Occurred on this day:

Westminster Abbey was dedicated, 1065;
The Irish Free State became the Republic of Ireland, 1937;
The independence of Estonia was proclaimed, 1917;
Messina, Sicily was almost completely destroyed by an earthquake when over 150,000 lives were lost, 1908;

The world's first public film show took place in Paris, 1895;
The centre portion of the Tay Bridge in Scotland collapsed, taking with it a train, including 75 passengers and crew, 1879;
Iowa became the 29th of the United States, 1846.

TODAY IS THE FEAST DAY OF St Antony of Lérins, The Holy Innocents [Childermas] and St Theodore the Sanctified.

29th December

Born on this day:

Keith Crossan, rugby player, 1959;
Iain Paxton, rugby player, 1957;
Marianne Faithfull, singer and actress, 1946;
Harvey Smith, show-jumper, 1938;
Jon Voight, US film actor, 1938;
Mary Tyler Moore, US TV and film actress, 1937;
Bernard Cribbins, actor, 1928;
Viveca Lindfors, Swedish film actress, 1920;
Robert Chester Ruark, US author, 1915;
Dr Magnus Pyke, TV nutritionist, 1908;
Vera Mary Brittain, author, pacifist and feminist, 1893;
Pablo Casals, Spanish cellist, 1876;
Queen Elizabeth of Romania [Carmen Silva, author], 1843;

Karl Friedrich Wilhelm Ludwig, German physiologist, 1816;
Alexander Parkes, chemist, inventor of a second method of vulcanising rubber, 1813;
William Ewart Gladstone, statesman, 1809;
Andrew Johnson, 17th president of the USA, 1808;
Charles Goodyear, inventor of vulcanised rubber, 1800;
Sir Archibald Alison Bt., historian, 1792;
Charles Macintosh, chemist and inventor of waterproof clothing, 1766;
Jeanne-Antoinette, Marquise de Pompadour, mistress of King Louis XV, 1721.

Died on this day:

The Earl of Stockton [Harold Macmillan], statesman, 1986;
Leo Robin, US lyric-writer, 1984;
Rainer Maria Rilke, German poet, 1926;
William James Linton, wood engraver, 1897;
Christina Georgina Rossetti, poet, 1894;

Octave Feuillet, French novelist and playwright, 1890;
Jacques-Louis David, French painter, 1825;
Brook Taylor, mathematician, 1731;
Dr Thomas Sydenham, physician, 1689;
Captain John Davis, navigator, 1605;
St Thomas à Becket, Archbishop of Canterbury, murdered, 1170.

Occurred on this day:

The US magazine *Life* ceased publication, 1972;
The City of London was the subject of a fire-bomb raid, 1940;
Radio Luxembourg started operating, 1930:
The Jameson Raid took place from Bechuanaland into the Transvaal, 1895;

The massacre at Wounded Knee, South Dakota, took place, when 200 Sioux Indians were killed, 1890;
Britain's first ironclad warship, HMS *Warrior*, was launched, 1860;
Texas became the 28th of the United States, 1845;
Sarah Siddons, as Portia, made her first appearance on the London stage, 1775.

TODAY IS THE FEAST DAY OF St Ebrulf or Evroult, St Maroellus Akimetes, St Thomas of Canterbury and St Trophimus of Arles.

30th December

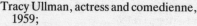

Born on this day:

Tracy Ullman, actress and comedienne, 1959;

Nick Skelton, show-jumper, 1957;

Mark Kaplan, violinist, 1953;

David Bedford, athlete, 1949;

Gordon Banks, footballer, 1937;

Sir Carol Reed, film director, 1906;

Dmitri Borisovich Kabalevsky, Russian composer, 1904;

Leslie Poles Hartley, novelist, 1895;

Hideki Tojo, Japanese prime minister, 1884;

Stephen Butler Leacock, Canadian humorous author and economist, 1869;

Simon Guggenheim, US senator and philanthropist, 1867;

Joseph Rudyard Kipling, author and poet, 1865;

André-Charles-Prosper Messager, French composer, 1853;

Theodor Fontane, German novelist, 1819;

John Philips, poet, 1676;

Sir John Holt, Lord Chief Justice, 1642.

Died on this day:

Richard Charles Rodgers, US composer, 1979;

Trygve Halvdan Lie, first secretary-general of the UN, 1968;

Charles Vincent Massey, Canadian statesman, 1967;

Ruth Draper, monologuist, 1956;

Alfred North Whitehead, US mathematician, 1947;

Romain Rolland, French author, 1944;

Rufus Daniel Isaacs, 1st Marquess of Reading, Lord Chief Justice, 1935;

Grigori Yefimovich Rasputin, Siberian peasant and mystic, murdered, 1916;

Angela Georgina Burdett-Coutts, 1st Baroness, philanthropist, 1906;

Amelia Jenks Bloomer, US social reformer, 1894;

Sir Samuel White Baker, explorer, 1893;

Marshal Juan Prim y Prats, Spanish soldier and statesman, 1870;

Robert Boyle, chemist, 1691;

Jean-Baptiste van Helmont, Belgian scientist, 1644;

Roger Ascham, scholar and writer, 1568;

Richard, Duke of York, killed, 1460.

Occurred on this day:

King Michael of Romania abdicated, 1947;

The P & O liner *Persia* was torpedoed off Crete with the loss of 200 lives, 1915;

Zululand was annexed to Natal, 1897;

Paul Kruger declared the Transvaal to be a republic, and became the first president, 1880;

Gilbert and Sullivan's opera *The Pirates of Penzance* had its first performance at Paignton, Devon, 1879;

Scindhiah, Maharajah of Gwalior, submitted to the British, 1803;

The United States took possession of Louisiana, 1803;

The Yorkists suffered a defeat at the Battle of Wakefield, 1460.

TODAY IS THE FEAST DAY OF St Anysia, St Anysius, St Egwin and St Sabinus of Spoleto.

31st December

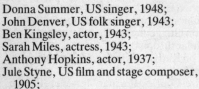
Born on this day:

Donna Summer, US singer, 1948;
John Denver, US folk singer, 1943;
Ben Kingsley, actor, 1943;
Sarah Miles, actress, 1943;
Anthony Hopkins, actor, 1937;
Jule Styne, US film and stage composer, 1905;
Nathan Milstein, US violinist, 1904;
Ernest John Moeran, composer and violinist, 1894;
George Catlett Marshall, US general, 1880;
Caradoc Evans, novelist, 1878;
Henri-Émile-Benoît Matisse, French painter, 1869;
Giovanni Pascoli, Italian poet, 1855;

Basil Hall, Scottish naval officer, traveller and writer, 1788;
Pierre-Charles-Jean-Baptiste-Silvestre Villeneuve, French admiral, 1763;
Charles, Marquess Cornwallis, statesman and soldier, 1738;
Charles Edward Stuart, the Young Pretender, 1720;
Hermann Boerhaave, Dutch physician, 1668;
Andreas Vesalius, Flemish anatomist, 1514;
Jacques Cartier, French explorer and navigator, 1494.

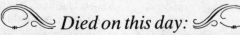
Died on this day:

Sam Spiegel, US film producer, 1985;
Sir Gerald Festus Kelly, artist, 1972;
Ray Henderson [Raymond Brost], US popular composer, 1970;
Cyril Meir Scott, composer, 1970;
Sir Malcolm Campbell, speedster on land and water, 1948;
Sir Frank Robert Benson, actor-manager, 1939;
Miguel de Unamuno y Jugo, Spanish writer, 1936;

Gustave Courbet, French painter, 1877;
Stephanie-Felicité, Comtesse de Genlis, French author, 1830;
William Gifford, editor, author and satirist, 1826;
Jean-François Marmontel, French author, 1799;
John Flamsteed, first Astronomer Royal, 1719;
Thomas Erastus, Swiss physician, 1583;
John Wycliffe, Protestant reformer, 1384.

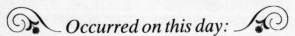
Occurred on this day:

Crown Prince Carol of Romania renounced the throne in favour of his son Michael, 1925;
The chimes of Big Ben were broadcast for the first time, 1923;
Dr Sun Yat-sen was declared the president of the Republic of China, 1911;
Ottawa was chosen by Queen Victoria as the capital of Canada, 1857;

Napoleon abolished the use of the Revolutionary Calendar, 1805;
A window tax was imposed in England, 1695;
The Honourable East India Company was chartered by Queen Elizabeth I, 1600.

TODAY IS HOGMANAY IN SCOTLAND AND THE FEAST DAY OF St Columba of Sens, St Melania the Younger and St Silvester I, pope.

INDEX OF PEOPLE

Index of People

Names shown in the following index show both birth and death dates only when these are included in the main text. It is a selective list, and not all birth dates are included, nor are all death dates. Surnames prefixed by **Mac**, **Mc**, **M'**, etc., are all indexed as if they were spelled as **Mac** in full. Those prefixed by **O'** are indexed alphabetically, ignoring the apostrophe. Foreign names, with prefixes such as **Van**, **von**, **de**, **di**, **della**, **degli**, etc., are indexed under the main surname. This does not apply to such names which have been adopted in English-speaking countries. In such cases, the prefix is regarded as part of the surname, and is indexed as such.

Aalto, Alvar, b. 3 Feb.
Abbadie, Antoine d', d. 19 Mar.
Abbadie, Arnaud d', b. 15 Jul., d. 13 Nov.
Abbado, Claudio, b. 26 Jun.
Abbe, Ernst, b. 23 Jan.
Abbey, Edwin A., d. 1 Aug.
Abbot, Budd, b. 2 Oct.
Abbott, Anthony, b. 21 Aug.
Abbott, Edwin, b. 20 Dec.
Abbott, George, b. 25 Jun.
Abbott, Russ, b. 16 Sept.
Abe, Komei, b. 1 Sept.
à Becket, Thomas, b. 21 Dec., d. 29 Dec.
A Beckett, Gilbert, b. 9 Jan., d. 30 Aug.
Abel, Karl, b. 22 Dec., d. 20 Jun.
Abel, Niels, b. 5 Aug.
Abel, Walter, b. 6 Jun., d. 26 Mar.
Abelard, Peter, d. 21 Apr.
Aberconway, 1st Baron, b. 12 May
Abercrombie, John, d. 14 Nov.
Abercrombie, Lascelles, d. 27 Oct.
Abercromby, Ralph, b. 7 Oct.
Abernethy, John, d. 28 Apr.
Abildgaard, Nicolai, d. 4 Jun.
Abse, Dannie, b. 22 Sept.
Acheson, Dean, b. 11 Apr.
Acheson, Ernest G., b. 9 Mar.
Ackermann, Rudolph, d. 30 Mar.
Ackland, Joss, b. 29 Feb.
Ackland, Rodney, b. 18 May, d. 24 Nov.
Acton, 1st Baron, b. 10 Jan., d. 19 Jun.
Acton, Harold, b. 5 Jul.
Adam, Adolphe, b. 24 Jul.
Adam, Benno, b. 15 Jul.
Adam, Eugen, d. 4 Jun.
Adam, Madge, b. 6 Mar.
Adam, Robert, b. 3 Jul., d. 3 Mar.

Adams, Henry Brooks, d. 27 Mar.
Adams, James Truslow, b. 18 Oct., d. 18 May
Adams, John (president) b. 30 Oct., d. 4 Jul.
Adams, John Couch, b. 5 Jun.,
Adams, John Quincy, b. 11 Jul., d. 23 Feb.
Adams, Richard, b. 9 May
Adams, Samuel, b. 27 Sept., d. 2 Oct.
Adams, Tony, b. 11 Dec.
Adams, William, b. 30 Apr.
Adamson, Joy, b. 20 Jan., d. 4 Jan.
Addams, Dawn, b. 21 Sept., d. 7 May
Addams, Jane, b. 6 Sept., d. 21 May
Addison, Joseph, b. 1 May, d. 17 Jun.
Adelaide, Queen, b. 13 Aug.
Adenauer, Konrad, b. 5 Jan., d. 19 Apr.
Adie, Kate, b. 19 Sept.
Adler, Alfred, b. 7 Feb., d. 28 May
Adler, Larry, b. 10 Feb.
Adler, Richard, b. 3 Aug.
Adrian, 1st Baron, b. 30 Nov., d. 4 Aug.
Adrian IV, *see* Hadrian IV
Adshead, Mary, b. 15 Feb.
Alfonso I, of Portugal, d. 6 Dec.
Aga Khan, b. 13 Dec.
Aga Khan, Sadruddin, b. 17 Jan.
Agassiz, Jean-Louis, b. 28 May, d. 14 Dec.
Agate, James, b. 9 Sept., d. 6 Jun.
Agazzari, Agostino, b. 2 Dec., d. 10 Apr.
Agee, James, b. 27 Nov., d. 16 May
Ager, Milton, b. 6 Oct., d. 6 Apr.
Agnelli, Giovanni, b. 12 Mar.
Agricola, Georg, b. 24 Mar.
Agricola, Johannes, b. 20 Apr.
Agricola, Rudolphus, d. 28 Oct.
Aguilar, Grace, b. 2 Jun., d. 16 Sept.

Agutter, Jenny, b. 20 Dec.
Aherne, Brian, b. 2 May, d. 10 Feb.
Aiken, Conrad, b. 5 Aug., d. 17 Aug.
Aiken, Joan, b. 4 Sept
Aikin, John, d. 7 Dec.
Aimée, Anouk, b. 27 Apr.
Ainley, Henry, b. 21 Aug., d. 31 Oct.
Ainsworth, W. Harrison, b. 4 Feb., d. 3
  Jan.
Airy, George, b. 27 Jul., d. 2 Jan.
Aitchison, Craigie, b. 13 Jan.
Aitken, Maria, b. 12 Sept.
Akbar the Great, b. 15 Oct.
Akenside, Mark, b. 9 Nov., d. 23 Jun.
Akhmatova, Anna, b. 23 Jun.
Akihito, of Japan, b. 23 Dec.
Akins, Claude, b. 25 May
Alain, b. 3 Mar., d. 2 Jun.
Alain-Fournier, b. 3 Oct., d. 22 Sept.
Alan, Ray, b. 18 Sept.
Alanbrooke, 1st Viscount, b. 23 Jul.
Alarcón, Pedro de, d. 10 Jul.
Alard, Jean, b. 8 Mar.
Alaric I, d. 24 Aug.
Alba, 3rd Duke, b. 29 Oct., d. 12 Jan.
Albani, Francesco, b. 17 Mar., d. 4 Oct.
Albani, Madame, b. 1 Nov., d. 3 Apr.
Albee, Edward, b. 12 Mar.
Albers, Joseph, b. 19 Mar.
Albert, Eddie, b. 22 Apr.
Albert, Prince, b. 26 Aug., d. 14 Dec.
Albert I, of the Belgians, b. 8 Apr.,
  d. 17 Feb.
Alberti, Leon Bat., d. 25 Apr.
Albertus Magnus, d. 15 Nov.
Albery, Bronson, b. 6 Mar.
Albery, Ian, b. 21 Sept.
Albery, John, b. 5 Apr.
Albéniz, Isaac, b. 29 May, d. 18 May
Albinoni, Tomaso, b. 14 Jun., d. 17 Jan.
Alcock, John, b. 6 Nov., d. 18 Dec.
Alcott, Louisa May, b. 29 Nov., d. 6
  Mar.
Alcuin, d. 19 May
Alda, Alan, b. 28 Jan.
Alderton, John, b. 27 Nov.
Aldington, Richard, b. 8 Jul., d. 27 Jul.
Aldiss, Brian, b. 18 Aug.
Aldous, Lucette, b. 26 Sept.
Aldrich, Henry, d. 14 Dec.

Aldrich, Robert, b. 9 Aug.
Aldridge, James, b. 10 Jul.
Aldridge, Michael, b. 9 Sept.
Aldrin, Buzz, b. 20 Jan.
Aldus Manutius, d. 6 Feb.
Aleichem, Sholem, b. 18 Feb., d. 13 May
Alembert, Jean d', b. 17 Nov., d. 29 Oct.
Alexander, 1st Earl, d. 16 Jun.
Alexander, George, b. 19 Jun.
Alexander, Jane, b. 28 Oct.
Alexander, John W., d. 31 May
Alexander, Maev, b. 3 Feb.
Alexander, Michael, b. 20 Nov.
Alexander, Terence, b. 11 Mar.
Alexander, of Greece, d. 25 Oct.
Alexander I, of Russia, b. 23 Dec., d. 1
  Dec.
Alexander, of Serbia, d. 11 Jun.
Alexander of Tunis, Earl, b. 10 Dec.
Alexander the Great, b. 20 Sept., d. 13
  Jun.
Alexander VIII, Pope, d. 1 Feb.
Alexander-Sinclair, Maj.-Gen. David, b. 2
  May
Alexandra, of Yugoslavia, b. 25th Mar.
Alexandra, Princess, b. 25 Dec.
Alexandra, Queen, b. 1 Dec., d. 20 Nov.
Alfieri, Vittorio, d. 8 Oct.
Alfonso III, of Portugal, d. 16 Feb.
Alfonso X, of Castile, b. 23 Nov., d. 4
  Apr.
Alfonso XIII, of Spain, d. 28 Feb.
Alfred the Great, of England, d. 28 Oct.
Alger, Horatio, b. 13 Jan., d. 18 Jul.
Ali Khan, Liaquat, d. 16 Oct.
Alice, Countess of Athlone, d. 2 Jan.
Alison, Archibald, b. 29 Dec.
Allan, David, b. 13 Feb., d. 6 Aug.
Allan, Mabel, b. 11 Feb.
Alldis, John, b. 10 Aug.
Allen, Chesney, d. 13 Nov.
Allen, Dave, b. 6 Jul.
Allen, Grant, b. 24 Feb., d. 28 Oct.
Allen, Patrick, b. 17 Mar.
Allen, Woody, b. 1 Dec.
Allenby, 1st Viscount, d. 14 May
Allende, Salvador, d. 11 Sept.
Alleyn, Edward, b. 1 Sept., d. 25 Nov.
Allingham, Margery, b. 20 May, d. 30
  Jun.

Allingham, William, b. 19 Mar., d. 18 Nov.

Allison, Malcolm, b. 5 Sept.

Alliss, Peter, b. 28 Feb.

Allori, Alessandro, b. 3 May, d. 22 Sept.

Allott, Paul, b. 14 Sept.

Allston, Washington, b. 5 Nov.

Allyson, June, b. 7 Oct.

Alma-Tadema, Laurence, d. 25 Jun.

Almeida, Dom Francisco d', d. 1 Mar.

Alment, Anthony, b. 3 Feb.

Alpert, Herb, b. 31 Mar.

Altman, Robert, b. 20 Feb.

Altwegg, Jeannette, b. 8 Sept.

Amati, Niccolo, b. 3 Dec., d. 12 Apr.

Ambler, Eric, b. 28 Jun.

Ameche, Don, b. 31 May

Amery, L.S., d. 16 Sept.

Amici, Giovanni, b. 25th Mar.

Amicis, Edmondo De, d. 11 Mar.

Amiel, Henri, b. 27 Sept.

Amies, Hardy, b. 17 Jul.

Amis, Kingsley, b. 16 Apr.

Amis, Martin, b. 25 Aug.

Amiss, Dennis, b. 7 Apr.

Amory, 1st Viscount, d. 20 Jan.

Ampère, André, b. 20 Jan., d. 10 Jun.

Amundsen, Roald, b. 16 Jul., d. 18 Jun.

Amyot, Jacques, d. 6 Feb.

Anastasius I, Pope, d. 19 Dec.

Andersen, Hans C., b. 2 Apr., d. 4 Aug.

Andersen, Lale, b. 23 Mar.

Anderson, Elizabeth Garrett, b. 9 Jun., d. 17 Dec.

Anderson, Lindsay, b. 17 Apr.

Anderson, Marian, b. 17 Feb.

Anderson, Maxwell, b. 15 Dec., d. 28 Feb.

Anderson, Moira, b. 5 Jun.

Anderson, Richard, b. 8 Aug.

Anderson, Robert, d. 26 Sept.

Anderson, Sherwood, b. 13 Sept., d. 8 Mar.

Andersson, Benny, b. 16 Dec.

Andersson, Bibi, b. 11 Nov.

Anderton, James, b. 24 May

Andress, Ursula, b. 19 Mar.

Andretti, Mario, b. 29 Feb.

Andrewes, Lancelot, d. 26 Sept.

Andrews, Anthony, b. 12 Jan.

Andrews, Dana, b. 1 Jan.

Andrews, Eamonn, d. 5 Nov.

Andrews, Julie, b. 1 Oct.

Andrews, Maxene, b. 3 Jan.

Andrews, Patti, b. 16 Feb.

Andreyev, Leonid, b. 9 Aug.

André, John, d. 2 Oct.

Andros, Edmund, d. 24 Feb.

Angelico, Fra, d. 18 Feb.

Angell, Norman, b. 26 Dec., d. 7 Oct.

Angers, Avril, b. 18 Apr.

Angoulême, Marguerite d', b. 11 Apr., d. 21 Sept.

Anka, Paul, b. 30 Jul.

Annand, Richard, b. 5 Nov.

Anne, Queen, b. 6 Feb., d. 1 Aug.

Anne of Cleves, d. 16 Jul.

Annenberg, Walter, b. 13 Mar.

Annigoni, Pietro, d. 28 Oct.

Anning, Mary, d. 19 Mar.

Annis, Francesca, b. 14 May

Annunzio, Gabriele D', b. 12 Mar., d. 1 Mar.

Ann-Margret, b. 28 Apr.

Anouilh, Jean, d. 3 Oct.

Anselm, St., d. 21 Apr.

Anson, Admiral, b. 23 Apr., d. 6 Jun.

Anson, William, b. 14 Nov.

Anstey, F., b. 8 Aug., d. 10 Mar.

Ant, Adam, b. 3 Nov.

Antheil, George, d. 12 Feb.

Anthony, Evelyn, b. 3 Jul.

Antonescu, Ion, d. 1 Jun.

Antoninus, Marcus Aurelius, d. 8 Apr.

Antoninus Pius, d. 7 Mar.

Antonioni, Michelangelo, b. 29 Sept.

Apollinaire, Guillaume, b. 26 Aug., d. 9 Nov.

Appia, Adolphe, d. 29 Feb.

Appleton, Edward, b. 6 Sept., d. 21 Apr.

Appleton, George, b. 20 Feb.

Aquinas, St Thomas, d. 7 Mar.

Aquino, Benigno, d. 21 Aug.

Arafat, Yasser, b. 17 Feb.

Aragon, Catherine of, b. 16 Dec., d. 7 Jan.

Aragon, Louis, b. 3 Oct.

Aram, Eugene, d. 6 Aug.

Arbuthnot, John, d. 27 Feb.

Archer, Fred, b. 11 Jan., d. 8 Nov.

Archer, Jeffrey, b. 15 Apr.

Archer, William, b. 23 Sept., d. 27 Dec.

Archipenko, Alexander, b. 30 May, d. 25 Feb.

Arden, Elizabeth, d. 18 Oct.

Arden, John, b. 26 Oct.

Ardiles, Osvaldo, b. 3 Aug.

Arditi, Luigi, b. 16 Jul.

Aretino, Pietro, b. 20 Apr., d. 21 Oct.

Arif, Abdul Salam, d. 13 Apr.

Ariosto, Ludovico, b. 8 Sept., d. 6 Jul.

Arkin, Alan, b. 26 Mar.

Arkwright, Richard, b. 23 Dec., d. 3 Aug.

Arlen, Harold, b. 15 Feb., d. 23 Apr.

Arlen, Michael, b. 16 Nov., d. 23 Jun.

Arliss, George, b. 10 Apr., d. 5 Feb.

Armatrading, Joan, b. 9 Dec.

Arminius, Jacobus, b. 10 Oct., d. 19 Oct.

Armitage, Kenneth, b. 18 Jul.

Armour, Philip D., b. 16 May, d. 6 Jan.

Armstrong, 1st Baron, b. 26 Nov.

Armstrong, Edmund, d. 24 Feb.

Armstrong, Edwin H., b. 18 Dec.

Armstrong, Louis, b. 4 Jul., d. 6 Jul.

Armstrong, Neil, b. 5 Aug.

Armstrong, Pamela, b. 25 Aug.

Armstrong-Jones, Lady Sarah, b. 1 May

Arnatt, John, b. 9 May

Arne, Thomas, b. 12 Mar., d. 5 Mar.

Arnell, Richard, b. 15 Sept.

Arness, James, b. 26 May

Arnold, Benedict, b. 14 Jan., d. 14 Jun.

Arnold, Edward, b. 18 Feb., d. 26 Apr.

Arnold, Edwin, b. 10 Jun.

Arnold, Geoff, b. 3 Sept.

Arnold, Malcolm, b. 21 Oct.

Arnold, Matthew, b. 24 Dec., d. 15 Apr.

Arnold, Samuel, b. 10 Aug.

Arnold, Thomas, b. 13 Jun., d. 12 Jun.

Arp, Hans, b. 15 Sept., d. 7 Jun.

Arrhenius, Svante, d. 2 Oct.

Arriaga, Juan, d. 17 Jan.

Arrowsmith, Pat, b. 2 Mar.

Artaud, Antonin, b. 4 Sept., d. 4 Mar.

Arteaga, Esteban, d. 30 Oct.

Artevelde, Jacob van, d. 24 Jul.

Arthur, Beatrice, b. 13 May

Arthur, Chester, b. 5 Oct., d. 18 Nov.

Arthur, Jean, b. 17 Oct., d. 19 Jun.

Asch, Sholem, d. 10 Jul.

Ascham, Roger, d. 30 Dec.

Ashdown, Paddy, b. 27 Feb. '

Ashe, Arthur, b. 10 Jul.

Asher, Jane, b. 5 Apr.

Ashford, Daisy, b. 7 Apr., d. 15 Jan.

Ashkenazy, Vladimir, b. 6 Jul.

Ashley, Elizabeth, b. 30 Aug.

Ashley, Jack, b. 6 Dec.

Ashmole, Elias, b. 23 May, d. 18 May

Ashton, Frederick, b. 17 Sept., d. 19 Aug.

Asimov, Isaac, b. 2 Jan.

Askey, Arthur, d. 16 Nov.

Askwith, Betty, b. 26 Jun.

Asner, Ed, b. 15 Nov.

Asola, Giovanni, b. 1 Oct.

Aspel, Michael, b. 12 Jan.

Asper, Hans, d. 21 Mar.

Aspinall, Nigel, b. 29 Jul.

Asquith, Anthony, b. 9 Nov.

Asquith, Herbert, b. 12 Sept., d. 15 Feb.

Asquith, Margot, d. 28 Jul.

Astaire, Fred, b. 10 May, d. 22 Jun.

Astin, John, b. 30 Mar.

Aston, Francis, b. 1 Sept., d. 20 Nov.

Astor, 2nd Viscount, b. 19 May

Astor, John Jacob, b. 17 Jul., d. 29 Mar.

Astor, Mary, b. 3 May

Astor, Nancy, b. 19 May, d. 2 May

Atatürk, Kemal, b. 12 Mar., d. 10 Nov.

Atherton, Gertrude, b. 30 Oct.

Atkins, Eileen, b. 16 Jun.

Atkinson, Rowan, b. 6 Jan.

Attenborough, David, b. 8 May

Attenborough, Michael, b. 13 Feb.

Attenborough, Richard, b. 29 Aug.

Attlee, Clement, b. 3 Jan., d. 8 Oct.

Atwell, Winifred, d. 31 Jan.

Aubrey, John, b. 12 Mar.

Auchinleck, Claude, b. 21 Jun., d. 23 Mar.

Auden, W.H., b. 21 Feb., d. 28 Sept.

Audran, Edmond, b. 12 Apr.

Audran, Gérard, b. 2 Aug., d. 26 Jul.

Audran, Jean, b. 28 Apr., d. 17 Jun.

Audubon, J.J., b. 26 Apr., d. 27 Jan.

Augustine, St., d. 26 May

Augustus, emperor, b. 23 Sept., d. 19 Aug.

Aumont, Jean-Pierre, b. 5 Jan.

Aurangzeb, emperor, b. 24 Oct., d. 20 Feb.

Austen, Jane, b. 16 Dec., d. 18 Jul.

Austin, Alfred, b. 30 May
Austin, Bunny, b. 20 Aug.
Austin, Herbert, b. 8 Nov., d. 23 May
Austin, Tracy, b. 12 Dec.
Autry, Gene, b. 29 Sept.
Avalon, Frankie, b. 8 Sept.
Avebury, Lord, d. 28 May
Avercamp, Hendrik van, b. 25 Jan.
Ayckbourn, Alan, b. 12 Apr.
Aylmer, Felix, d. 2 Sept.
Aylmer, Gerald, b. 30 Apr.
Ayres, Gillian, b. 3 Feb.
Ayres, Lew, b. 28 Dec.
Ayres, Pam, b. 14 Mar.
Ayres, Ruby M., b. 28 Jan.
Ayrton, Norman, b. 25 Sept.
Aytoun, William, b. 21 Jun.
Aznavour, Charles, b. 22 May
Azorín, b. 11 Jun.

Babbage, Charles, b. 26 Dec., d. 18 Oct.
Babel, Isaak, b. 1 Jul., d. 17 Mar.
Bacall, Lauren, b. 16 Sept.
Bach, Carl Philipp Emanuel, b. 8 Mar., d.
   14 Dec.
Bach, Johann Christian, b. 5 Sept., d. 1
   Jan.
Bach, Johann Sebastian, b. 21 Mar., d. 28
   Jul.
Bacharach, Burt, b. 12 May
Backhaus, Wilhelm, d. 5 Jul.
Backhuysen, Ludolf, b. 18 Dec., d. 17
   Nov.
Bacon, Francis (painter), b. 28 Oct., d. 28
   Apr.
Bacon, Francis (philosopher), b. 22 Jan.,
   d. 9 Apr.
Bacon, John, b. 24 Nov.
Bacon, Nathaniel, b. 2 Jan.
Baddeley, Hermione, d. 19 Aug.
Badel, Alan, d. 19 Mar.
Badel, Sarah, b. 30 Mar.
Baden-Powell, Lady Olave, b. 22 Feb.
Baden-Powell, Robert, b. 22 Feb., d. 8
   Jan.
Bader, Douglas, b. 21 Feb., d. 5 Sept.
Baedeker, Karl, b. 3 Nov.
Baekeland, Leo, b. 14 Nov., d. 23 Feb.
Baer, Karl von, b. 29 Feb., d. 28 Nov.
Baez, Joan, b. 9 Jan.

Baffin, William, d. 23 Jan.
Bagehot, Walter, b. 3 Feb.
Bagley, Desmond, d. 12 Apr.
Bagnall, Nigel, b. 10 Feb.
Bagnold, Enid, b. 27 Oct., d. 31 Mar.
Bailey, David, b. 2 Jan.
Bailey, Donald, d. 5 May
Bailey, James A., d. 11 Apr.
Bailey, Norman, b. 23 Mar.
Bailey, Paul, b. 16 Feb.
Bailey, Robin, b. 5 Oct.
Bailey, Trevor, b. 3 Dec.
Baillie, Isobel, 24 Sept.
Baillie, William, b. 20 Apr.
Bailly, Jean, d. 12 Nov.
Baily, Francis, d. 30 Aug.
Bainbridge, Beryl, b. 21 Nov.
Bainter, Fay, b. 7 Dec., d. 16 Apr.
Baird, David, b. 6 Dec.
Baird, John L., b. 13 Aug., d. 14 Jun.
Bairnsfather, Bruce, b. 9 Jul., d. 29 Sept.
Bairstow, David, b. 1 Sept.
Baker, Carroll, b. 28 May
Baker, Colin, b. 8 Jun.
Baker, George, b. 1 Apr.
Baker, Janet, b. 21 Aug.
Baker, Josephine, b. 3 Jun., d. 12 Apr.
Baker, Kenneth, b. 3 Nov.
Baker, Richard, b. 15 Jun.
Baker, Samuel White, b. 8 Jun., d. 30 Dec.
Baker, Tom, b. 20 Jan.
Bakewell, Joan, b. 16 Apr.
Bakst, Leon, d. 24 Dec.
Bakunin, Mikhail, b. 30 May, d. 13 Jun.
Balakirev, Mily, b. 21 Dec.
Balanchine, George, b. 9 Jan., d. 30 Apr.
Balchin, Nigel, b. 3 Dec., d. 17 May
Balding, Ian, b. 7 Nov.
Balding, Toby, b. 23 Sept.
Baldovinetti, Alessio, b. 14 Oct., d. 29
   Aug.
Baldwin, Faith, d. 19 Mar.
Baldwin, Stanley, b. 3 Aug., d. 14 Dec.
Balfe, Michael, b. 15 May, d. 20 Oct.
Balfour, Arthur, b. 25 Jul., d. 19 Mar.
Ball, Alan, b. 12 May
Ball, Kenny, b. 22 May
Ball, Robert, b. 1 Jul.
Ballantyne, R.M., d. 8 Feb.
Ballard, J.G., b. 15 Nov.

Ballesteros, Severiano, b. 9 Apr.
Balmain, Pierre, d. 29 Jun.
Balsam, Martin, b. 4 Nov.
Baltard, Louis-Pierre, d. 13 Jan.
Balzac, Honoré de, b. 20 May, d. 17 Aug.
Bancroft, Anne, b. 17 Sept.
Bancroft, George, b. 3 Oct., d. 17 Jan.
Bancroft, Richard, d. 2 Nov.
Bancroft, Squire, b. 14 May, d. 19 Apr.
Banda, Hastings, b. 14 May
Bandaranaike, Sirimavo, b. 17 Apr.
Bandaranaike, Solomon, b. 8 Jan.
Banham, John, b. 22 Aug.
Bankhead, Tallulah, b. 31 Jan., d. 12 Dec.
Banks, Don, b. 25 Oct.
Banks, Gordon, b. 30 Dec.
Banks, Joseph,, d. 19 Jun.
Banks, Lynne Reid, b. 31 Jul.
Bannen, Ian, b. 29 Jun.
Bannister, Sir Roger, b. 23 Mar.
Banting, Frederick, b. 14 Nov., d. 21 Feb.
Banting, William, d. 16 Mar.
Bantock, Granville, b. 7 Aug., d. 16 Oct.
Bara, Theda, b. 20 Jul., d. 7 Apr.
Barbarossa, d. 10 Jun.
Barbauld, Anna, b. 20 Jun., d. 9 Mar.
Barber, Chris, b. 17 Apr.
Barber, Glynis, b. 25 Oct.
Barber, Samuel, b. 9 Mar., d. 23 Jan.
Barbieri, Giovanni, b. 8 Feb., d. 22 Dec.
Barbieri, Margaret, b. 2 Mar.
Barbirolli, John, b. 2 Dec., d. 29 Jul.
Barbour, John, d. 13 Mar.
Barbusse, Henri, b. 17 May, d. 30 Aug.
Barclay, Robert, b. 23 Dec.
Bardot, Brigitte, b. 28 Sept.
Barenboim, Daniel, b. 15 Nov.
Barents, Willem, d. 20 Jun.
Barham, Richard, b. 6 Dec., d. 17 Jun.
Baring, Maurice, b. 27 Apr., d. 14 Dec.
Baring, Francis, b. 18 Apr.
Baring-Gould, Sabine, b. 28 Jan., d. 2 Jan.
Barker, Harley Granville, b. 25 Nov., d.
   31 Aug.
Barker, Paul, b. 24 Aug.
Barker, Ronnie, b. 25 Sept.
Barker, Herbert, b. 21 Apr.
Barker, Sue, b. 19 Apr.
Barkworth, Peter, b. 14 Jan.
Barlow, Joel, d. 26 Dec.

Barnard, Christiaan, b. 8 Nov.
Barnard, Edward E., b. 16 Dec.
Barnardo, Thomas, b. 4 Jul., d. 19 Sept.
Barnby, Joseph, b. 12 Aug.
Barnes, Carol, b. 13 Sept.
Barnes, Clive, b. 13 May
Barnes, John, b. 7 Nov.
Barnes, Thomas, b. 11 Sept.
Barnes, William, b. 20 Mar., d. 7 Oct.
Barnett, Correlli, b. 28 Jun.
Barnett, John (composer), b. 15 Jul.
Barnum, Phineas T., b. 5 Jul., d. 7 Apr.
Baroja, Pio, b. 28 Dec., d. 30 Oct.
Barraclough, John, b. 2 May
Barras, Paul de, b. 30 Jun.
Barratt, Michael, b. 3 Jan.
Barrault, Jean-Louis, b. 8 Sept.
Barre, Raymond, b. 12 Apr.
Barrett, Wilson, d. 22 Jul.
Barrie, Amanda, b. 14 Sept.
Barrie, James, b. 9 May, d. 19 Jun.
Barron, John, b. 24 Dec.
Barron, Keith, b. 8 Aug.
Barrow, Clyde, d. 23 May
Barry, Charles, b. 23 May, d. 12 May
Barry, Comtesse du, d. 7 Dec.
Barry, Gene, b. 4 Jun.
Barry, James, b. 11 Oct., d. 22 Feb.
Barry, John, b. 3 Nov.
Barrymore, Ethel, b. 15 Aug., d. 18 Jun.
Barrymore, John, b. 15 Feb., d. 29 May
Barrymore, Lionel, b. 28 Apr., d. 15 Nov.
Barstow, Josephine, b. 27 Sept.
Barstow, Stan, b. 28 Jun.
Bart, Lionel, b. 1 Aug.
Bartels, Hans von, d. 5 Oct.
Barth, Heinrich, b. 16 Feb., d. 25 Nov.
Barth, Karl, b. 10 May, d. 9 Dec.
Barthélemy, Jean-Jacques, b. 20 Jan.
Bartholomew, Freddie, b. 28 Mar., d. 23
   Jan.
Bartók, Béla, b. 25th Mar., d. 26 Sept.
Bartok, Eva, b. 18 Jun.
Bartolommeo di Pagholo, Fra, b. 28 Mar.,
   d. 31 Oct.
Bartolozzi, Francesco, b. 21 Sept., d. 7
   Mar.
Barton, Benjamin S., d. 19 Dec.
Barton, Bernard,d. 19 Feb.
Barton, Eliza, d. 20 Apr.

374

Baruch, Bernard, d. 20 Jun.
Barye, Antoine, b. 24 Sept.
Baryshnikov, Mikhail, b. 28 Jan.
Basehart, Richard, b. 31 Aug., d. 17 Sept.
Bashkirtseff, Marie, b. 23 Nov.
Basie, 'Count', b. 21 Aug., d. 26 Apr.
Baskerville, John, b. 28 Jan., d. 8 Jan.
Bassano, Jacopo, d. 13 Feb.
Bassey, Shirley, b. 8 Jan.
Bastien-Lepage, Jules, b. 1 Nov., d. 10 Dec.
Bateman, H.M., b. 15 Feb., d. 11 Feb.
Bates, Alan, b. 17 Feb.
Bates, H.E., b. 16 May, d. 28 Jan.
Bates, Henry Walter, b. 8 Feb., d. 16 Feb.
Bates, Thomas, d. 30 Jan.
Bateson, Timothy, b. 3 Apr.
Bateson, William, d. 8 Feb.
Bath, Marquess of, b. 26 Jan.
Bathurst, Benjamin, b. 27 May
Batista, Fulgencio, b. 16 Jan., d. 6 Aug.
Batoni, Pompeo, b. 25 Jan., d. 4 Feb.
Batten, Jean, b. 15 Sept.
Battiscombe, Georgina, b. 21 Nov.
Baudelaire, Charles, d. 31 Aug., b. 9 Apr.
Baudouin, of the Belgians, b. 7 Sept.
Baudry, Paul, b. 7 Nov.
Baum, L. Frank, b. 15 May, d. 6 May
Baum, Vicki, d. 29 Aug.
Bawden, Nina, b. 19 Jan.
Bax, Arnold, b. 8 Nov., d. 3 Oct.
Bax, Clifford, b. 13 Jun.
Baxter, Anne, b. 7 May, d. 12 Dec.
Baxter, Geoff, b. 18 Sept.
Baxter, Raymond, b. 25 Jan.
Baxter, Richard, b. 12 Nov., d. 8 Dec.
Baxter, Stanley, b. 24 May
Bayldon, Geoffrey, b. 7 Jan.
Bayle, Pierre, b. 18 Nov., d. 28 Dec.
Baylis, Lilian, b. 9 May, d. 25 Nov.
Baynes, Pauline, b. 9 Sept.
Bazalgette, Sir Joseph, b. 28 Mar., d. 15 Mar.
Beach, Ann, b. 7 Jun.
Beach, Hugh, b. 20 May
Beach, Rex, b. 1 Sept.
Beacham, Stephanie, b. 28 Feb.
Beal, John, b. 13 Aug.
Beale, Dorothea, b. 21 Mar.

Beardsley, Aubrey, b. 21 Aug., d. 16 Mar.
Beaton, Cecil, b. 14 Jan., d. 18 Jan.
Beatrice d'Este, Duchess of Milan, d. 3 Jan.
Beatrix, Queen, b. 31 Jan.
Beattie, David, b. 29 Feb.
Beattie, James, b. 25 Oct., d. 18 Aug.
Beatty, Earl, d. 10 Mar.
Beatty, Robert, b. 19 Oct.
Beatty, Warren, b. 30 Mar.
Beaufort, Francis, b. 27 May, d. 17 Dec.
Beaufort, Thomas, d. 24 Dec.
Beauharnais, Joséphine de, b. 23 Jun.
Beaumarchais, Pierre de, b. 24 Jan., d. 18 May
Beaumont, Bill, b. 9 Mar.
Beaumont, Francis, d. 6 Mar.
Beauvoir, Simone de, b. 9 Jan., d. 14 Apr.
Beaverbrook, 1st Baron, b. 25 May, d. 9 Jun.
Beccaria, Cesare, d. 28 Nov.
Beck, Jeff, b. 24 Jun.
Becker, Boris, b. 22 Nov.
Becker, Jacques, d. 21 Feb.
Beckford, William, b. 1 Oct.
Beckmann, Max, d. 27 Dec.
Becquerel, Antoine, b. 15 Dec., d. 25 Aug.
Bede, Ven., d. 25 May
Bedford, David (athlete), b. 30 Dec.
Bedford, David (composer), b. 4 Aug.
Bedford, Duke of, b. 24 May
Bedford, Steuart, b. 31 Jul.
Bedford, Sybille, b. 16 Mar.
Bedser, Alec, b. 4 Jul.
Bedser, Eric, b. 4 Jul.
Beecham, Thomas, b. 29 Apr., d. 8 Mar.
Beecher, Henry Ward, b. 24 Jun.
Beechey, William, b. 12 Dec.
Beeching, Lord, d. 23 Mar.
Beerbohm, Max, b. 24 Aug., d. 20 May
Beery, Noah, b. 10 Aug.
Beery, Wallace, b. 1 Apr., d. 15 Apr.
Beetham, Michael, b. 17 May
Beethoven, Ludwig van, b. 17 Dec., d. 26 Mar.
Beeton, Isabella, b. 14 Mar., d. 6 Feb.
Begas, Karl, b. 30 Sept.
Begas, Oskar, b. 31 Jul.
Begas, Reinhold, b. 15 Jul., d. 3 Aug.

Begin, Menachem, b. 16 Aug.

Begley, Ed, d. 28 Apr.

Behan, Brendan, b. 9 Feb., d. 20 Mar.

Behn, Aphra, b. 10 Jul., d. 16 Apr.

Behrens, Peter, b. 14 Apr., d. 27 Feb.

Behring, Emil von, b. 15 Mar.

Beiderbecke, Bix, b. 10 Mar., d. 7 Aug.

Békésy, Georg von, d. 13 Jun.

Belafonte, Harry, b. 1 Mar.

Belasco, David, b. 25 Jul., d. 14 May

Bell, Alexander Graham, b. 3 Mar., d. 2 Aug.

Bell, Ann, b. 29 Apr.

Bell, Charles, d. 28 Apr., d. 29 Apr.

Bell, Gertrude, b. 14 Jul., d. 12 Jul.

Bell, Mary Hayley, b. 22 Jan.

Bellamy, David, b. 18 Jan.

Bellamy, Ralph, b. 17 Jun.

Bellingham, Lynda, b. 31 May

Bellingshausen, Fabian, b. 9 Aug.

Bellini, Gentile, d. 20 Feb.

Bellini, Giovanni, d. 29 Nov.

Bellini, Vincenzo, b. 3 Nov.

Bellman, Karl, b. 4 Feb.

Belloc, Hilaire, b. 27 Jul., d. 16 Jul.

Bellow, Saul, b. 10 Jun.

Belmondo, Jean-Paul, b. 9 Apr.

Beloff, Lord, b. 2 Jul.

Beloff, Nora, b. 24 Jan.

Belsky, Franta, b. 6 Apr.

Bely, Andrei, d. 7 Jan.

Belzoni, Giovanni, d. 3 Dec.

Bembo, Pietro, b. 20 May

Bemelmans, Ludwig, b. 27 Apr., d. 1 Oct.

Benaud, Richie, b. 6 Oct.

Benavente, Jacinto, b. 12 Aug., d. 14 Jul.

Benbow, John, d. 4 Nov.

Benchley, Peter, b. 8 May

Benchley, Robert, b. 15 Sept.

Bencivieni di Pepo, d. 4 Jul.

Bendix, William, b. 4 Jan., d. 14 Dec.

Benedict, Julius, b. 27 Nov.

Benedict XV, Pope, d. 22 Jan.

Beneš, Eduard, b. 28 May, d. 3 Sept.

Benét, Stephen Vincent, b. 22 Jul., d. 13 Mar.

Benét, William Rose, d. 4 May

Ben Gurion, David, b. 16 Oct., d. 1 Dec.

Benham, Gurney, b. 16 Feb., d. 13 May

Benjamin, Arthur, b. 18 Sept., d. 10 Apr.

Benjamin, Christopher, b. 27 Dec.

Benjamin, Richard, b. 22 May

Benn, Anthony Wedgwood, b. 3 Apr.

Bennett, 1st Viscount, b. 3 Jul.

Bennett, Alan, b. 9 May

Bennett, Arnold, b. 27 May, d. 27 Mar.

Bennett, Bruce, b. 19 May

Bennett, Constance, b. 22 Oct., d. 24 Jul.

Bennett, Hywel, b. 8 Apr.

Bennett, James Gordon, d. 14 May

Bennett, Lennie, b. 26 Sept.

Bennett, Phil, b. 24 Oct.

Bennett, Richard, b. 29 Mar.

Bennett, Tony, b. 3 Aug.

Bennett, W. Sterndale, b. 13 Apr.

Benney, Gerald, b. 21 Apr.

Benny, Jack, b. 14 Feb., d. 26 Dec.

Benois, Alexandre, b. 4 May, d. 9 Feb.

Benoît, Pierre, b. 17 Aug.

Benson, A.C., b. 24 Apr., d. 17 Jun.

Benson, E.F., b. 24 Jul., d. 29 Feb.

Benson, Frank, b. 4 Nov., d. 31 Dec.

Benson, Frank Weston, b. 24 Mar.

Benson, George, b. 22 Mar.

Benson, Ivy, b. 11 Nov.

Benson, Stella, d. 6 Dec.

Bentham, George, b. 22 Sept., d. 10 Sept.

Bentham, Jeremy, b. 15 Feb., d. 6 Jun.

Bentinck, William, d. 21 Sept.

Bentine, Michael, b. 26 Jan.

Bentley, Harry, b. 13 Oct.

Benz, Karl, b. 25 Nov., d. 4 Apr.

Béranger, Pierre de, d. 16 Jul.

Bérard, Christian, b. 20 Aug.

Berchem, Nicolaes, d. 22 Feb.

Beresford, Patrick, b. 16 Jun.

Berg, Alban, b. 9 Feb., d. 24 Dec.

Berganza, Teresa, b. 16 Mar.

Bergen, Candice, b. 9 May

Bergen, Polly, b. 14 Jul.

Berger, Gerhard, b. 27 Aug.

Berger, John, b. 5 Nov.

Berger, Peter, b. 11 Feb.

Bergerac, Jacques, b. 26 May

Bergerac, *see* Cyrano de Bergerac

Bergius, Friedrich, b. 11 Oct., d. 30 Mar.

Bergman, Ingmar, b. 14 Jul.

Bergman, Ingrid, b. and d. 29 Aug.

Bergner, Elisabeth, d. 12 May

Bergson, Henri, b. 18 Oct., d. 4 Jan.

Beria, Lavrenti, b. 18 Mar.
Bering, Vitus, d. 19 Dec.
Berio, Luciano, b. 24 Oct.
Bériot, Charles de, b. 20 Feb.
Beriozova, Svetlana, b. 24 Sept.
Berk, Lottie, b. 17 Jan.
Berkeley, Busby, b. 29 Nov., d. 14 Mar.
Berkeley, Michael, b. 29 May
Berkeley, William, d. 9 Jul.
Berkoff, Steven, b. 3 Aug.
Berle, Milton, b. 12 Jul.
Berlin, Irving, b. 11 May, d. 22 Sept.
Berlin, Isaiah, b. 6 Jun.
Berlioz, Hector, b. 11 Dec., d. 8 Mar.
Berman, Shelley, b. 3 Feb.
Bernadette, St., b. 7 Jan.
Bernadotte, Folke, d. 17 Sept.
Bernanos, Georges, b. 20 Feb., d. 5 Jul.
Bernard, Jean-Jacques, b. 30 Jul.
Bernard, Jeffrey, b. 27 May
Bernardin de Saint-Pierre, J.-H., b. 19 Jan.
Berners, 14th Baron, b. 18 Sept.
Bernhard, Prince, b. 29 Jun.
Bernhardt, Sarah, b. 22 Oct., d. 26 Mar.
Bernini, Giovanni, b. 7 Dec., d. 28 Nov.
Bernoulli, Daniel, b. 9 Feb., d. 17 Mar.
Bernoulli, Jacques, d. 16 Aug.
Bernoulli, Jakob, b. 27 Dec.
Bernoulli, Jean (Johann), b. 27 Jul., d. 1 Jan.
Bernstein, Leonard, b. 25 Aug., d. 14 Oct.
Berry, Chuck, b. 18 Oct.
Berthelot, Marcelin, b. 27 Oct.
Berthelot, Pierre, d. 18 Mar.
Berthollet, Claude, b. 9 Dec., d. 6 Nov.
Berthon, Edward, d. 27 Oct.
Bertillon, Alphonse, d. 13 Feb.
Bertini, Gary, b. 1 May
Bertolucci, Bernardo, b. 16 Mar.
Berwald, Franz, b. 23 Jul.
Berzelius, Jöns, b. 20 Aug.
Besant, Annie, b. 1 Oct., d. 20 Sept.
Besant, Walter, b. 14 Aug., d. 9 Jun.
Bessel, Friedrich, b. 22 Jul.
Bessemer, Sir Henry, b. 19 Jan., d. 15 Mar.
Best, Charles, b. 27 Feb.
Best, George, b. 22 May
Betjeman, Sir John, b. 6 Apr., d. 19 May
Betterton, Thomas, d. 28 Apr.

Betti, Ugo, b. 4 Feb., d. 9 Jun.
Betty, William, b. 13 Sept.
Bevan, Aneurin, b. 15 Nov., d. 6 Jul.
Beveridge, William, b. 5 Mar., d. 16 Mar.
Bevin, Ernest, b. 9 Mar., d. 14 Apr.
Bewes, Rodney, b. 27 Nov.
Bewick, Thomas, b. 12 Aug., d. 8 Nov.
Bhutto, Zulfikar Ali, d. 4 Apr.
Bichat, Marie-François, d. 22 Jul.
Bickford, Charles, b. 1 Jan.
Bidault, Georges, d. 26 Jan.
Bierce, Ambrose, b. 24 Jun.
Biffen, John, b. 3 Nov.
Bikel, Theodore, b. 2 May
Bilk, Acker, b. 28 Jan.
Billington, Michael, b. 16 Nov.
Billington, Rachel, b. 11 May
Binet, Alfred, d. 18 Oct.
Bing, Rudolf, b. 9 Jan.
Bingham, Caroline, b. 7 Feb.
Bingham, Charlotte, b. 29 Jun.
Bingham, John, b. 29 Feb.
Binyon, Laurence, b. 10 Aug.
Binyon, Robert, d. 10 Mar.
Bird, Edward, b. 12 Apr.
Bird, John, b. 22 Nov.
Birdseye, Clarence, b. 9 Dec., d. 7 Oct.
Birkbeck, George, b. 10 Jan., d. 1 Dec.
Birkenhead, Earl, b. 12 Jul., d. 30 Sept.
Birley, Derek, b. 31 May
Birmingham George A., b. 16 Jul.
Birtwistle, Harrison, b. 15 Jul.
Bishop, Henry, b. 18 Nov., d. 30 Apr.
Bishop-Kovacevich, Stephen, b. 17 Oct.
Bismarck, Otto von, b. 1 Apr., d. 30 Jul.
Bissett, Jacqueline, b. 13 Sept.
Bizet, Georges, b. 25 Oct., d. 3 Jun.
Bjelke-Petersen, Johannes, b. 13 Jan.
Björling, Jussi, b. 2 Feb.
Björnson, B., b. 8 Dec., d. 26 Apr.
Black, Adam, b. 20 Feb., d. 24 Jan.
Black, Cilla, b. 27 May
Black, Conrad, b. 25 Aug.
Black, Joseph, d. 6 Dec.
Blackbeard, d. 22 Nov.
Blacker, Philip, b. 27 Sept.
Blacklock, Thomas, d. 7 Jul.
Blackmer, Sidney, b. 13 Jun.
Blackmore, R.D., b. 7 Jun., d. 20 Jan.
Blackstone, William, b. 10 Jul., d. 14 Feb.

Blackwell, Basil, d. 9 Apr.
Blackwell, Elizabeth, b. 3 Feb., d. 31 May
Blair, Linda, b. 22 Jan.
Blair, Lionel, b. 12 Dec.
Blair, Robert, d. 4 Feb.
Blake, Christopher, b. 23 Aug.
Blake, Robert (actor), b. 18 Sept.
Blake, Robert (adm.), b. 15 Aug., d. 7 Aug.
Blake, William, b. 28 Nov., d. 12 Aug.
Blakemore, Michael, b. 18 Jun.
Blakiston, Caroline, b. 13 Feb.
Blamey, Norman, b. 16 Dec.
Blamey, Thomas, b. 24 Jan., d. 27 May
Blanc, Louis, b. 29 Oct., d. 6 Dec.
Blanchard, Jean, b. 4 Jul., d. 7 Mar.
Blanchflower, Danny, b. 10 Feb.
Blasco Ibañez, Vicente, b. 29 Jan., d. 28 Jan.
Blashford-Snell, John, b. 22 Oct.
Blavatsky, Helena, d. 9 May
Blech, Harry, b. 2 Mar.
Blériot, Louis, b. 1 Jul., d. 2 Aug.
Blessed, Brian, b. 9 Oct.
Blessington, Marguerite, d. 4 Jun.
Bligh, William, b. 9 Sept., d. 7 Dec.
Bliss, Arthur, b. 2 Aug.
Blixen, Karen, b. 17 Oct.
Bloch, Ernst, b. 24 Jul.
Blok, Aleksander, b. 16 Nov., d. 7 Aug.
Blom-Cooper, Louis, b. 27 Mar.
Blond, Anthony, b. 20 Mar.
Blondell, Joan, b. 30 Aug., d. 25 Dec.
Blondin, Charles, b. 28 Feb., d. 19 Feb.
Blood, Thomas, d. 24 Aug.
Bloom, Claire, b. 15 Feb.
Bloom, Ursula, d. 29 Oct.
Bloomer, Amelia, b. 27 May, d. 30 Dec.
Bloomfield, Leonard, b. 1 Apr., d. 18 Apr.
Bloomfield, Robert, b. 3 Dec.
Blow, John, d. 1 Oct.
Blow, Sandra, b. 14 Sept.
Blücher, Gebhard von, b. 16 Dec., d. 12 Sept.
Blum, Léon, b. 9 Apr., d. 30 Mar.
Blum, Robert F., b. 9 Jul.
Blunden, Edmund, b. 1 Nov., d. 20 Jan.
Blunt, Wilfrid, b. 17 Aug., d. 10 Sept.
Blyth, Ann, b. 16 Aug.
Blyth, Chay, b. 14 May

Blythe, John, b. 31 Oct.
Blyton, Enid, b. 11 Aug., d. 28 Nov.
Boas, Franz, b. 9 Jul.
Boccaccio, Giovanni, d. 21 Dec.
Boccherini, Luigi, b. 19 Feb.
Boccioni, Umberto, d. 16 Aug.
Bochsa, Robert, b. 9 Aug.
Bock, Jerry, b. 23 Nov.
Böcklin, Arnold, b. 16 Oct., d. 16 Jan.
Bodenheim, Maxwell, d. 7 Feb.
Bodley, George, d. 21 Oct.
Bodley, Thomas, b. 2 Mar., d. 28 Jan.
Bodoni, Giambattista, b. 16 Feb., d. 29 Nov.
Boehm, Joseph, d. 12 Dec.
Boëllmann, Léon, b. 25 Sept., d. 11 Oct.
Boerhaave, Hermann, b. 31 Dec., d. 23 Sept.
Bogarde, Dirk, b. 28 Mar.
Bogart, Humphrey, b. 25 Dec., d. 14 Jan.
Bogdanovich, Peter, b. 30 Jul.
Bohan, Marc, b. 22 Aug.
Böhme, Jakob, d. 17 Nov.
Bohn, Henry, b. 4 Jan., d. 22 Aug.
Bohr, Niels, b. 7 Oct., d. 18 Nov.
Boht, Jean, b. 6 Mar.
Boiardo, Matteo, d. 19 Dec.
Boileau-Despréaux, Nicolas, b. 1 Nov., d. 13 Mar.
Bolam, James, b. 16 Jun.
Boldrewood, Rolf, b. 6 Aug., d. 11 Mar.
Boleyn, Ann, d. 19 May
Bolingbroke, Viscount, d. 12 Dec.
Bolívar, Simón, d. 17 Dec., b. 24 Jul.
Böll, Heinrich, b. 21 Dec.
Bolt, Robert, b. 15 Aug.
Bolyai, Janos, b. 15 Dec.
Bonallack, Angela, b. 7 Apr.
Bonaparte, Joseph, b. 7 Jan.
Bonaparte, see also Napoleon
Bond, Edward, b. 18 Jul.
Bond, Michael, b. 13 Jan.
Bond, Ward, b. 9 Apr., d. 5 Nov.
Bondfield, Margaret, b. 17 Mar., d. 16 Jun.
Bondi, Hermann, b. 1 Nov.
Bonds, Billy, b. 17 Sept.
Bone, Charles, b. 15 Sept.
Bonham-Carter, Helena, b. 26 May
Bonheur, Auguste, d. 23 Feb.

Bonheur, Rosa, b. 16 Mar., d. 25 May
Bonhoeffer, Dietrich, b. 4 Feb., d. 9 Apr.
Bonington, Chris, b. 6 Aug.
Bonington, Richard, b. 25 Oct., d. 23 Sept.
Bonnard, Pierre, b. 3 Oct., d. 23 Jan.
Bonnat, Léon, d. 8 Sept.
Bonomi, Giuseppi (the Younger), b. 9 Oct., d. 3 Mar.
Bonynge, Richard, b. 29 Sept.
Booker, Christopher, b. 7 Oct.
Boone, Daniel, b. 2 Nov., d. 26 Sept.
Boone, Pat, b. 1 Jun.
Boone, Richard, b. 18 Jun.
Boorman, John, b. 18 Jan.
Booth, Charles, b. 30 Mar.
Booth, Edwin, b. 13 Nov.
Booth, John Wilkes, b. 10 May, d. 26 Apr.
Booth, Shirley, b. 30 Aug.
Booth, William, b. 10 Apr., d. 20 Aug.
Boothroyd, Betty, b. 8 Oct.
Borden, Lizzie, b. 19 Jul., d. 1 Jun.
Borden, Robert, b. 26 Jun.
Bordet, Jules, b. 13 Jun., d. 6 Apr.
Bordone, Paris, d. 19 Jan.
Borg, Alan, b. 21 Jan.
Borg, Björn, b. 6 Jun.
Borge, Victor, b. 3 Jan.
Borges, Jorge, b. 24 Aug., d. 14 Jun.
Borgia, Cesare, d. 12 Mar.
Borgia, Lucrezia, b. 18 Apr., d. 24 Jun.
Borgnine, Ernest, b. 24 Jan.
Borodin, Alexander, b. 12 Nov., d. 27 Feb.
Borotra, Jean, b. 13 Aug.
Borrow, George, b. 5 Jul., d. 26 Jul.
Borwick, Leonard, b. 26 Feb.
Borzage, Frank, b. 23 Apr.
Bosanquet, Bernard, b. 14 Jun.
Bosch, Karl, d. 26 Apr.
Bosco, Philip, b. 26 Sept.
Bose, Jagadis Chandra, b. 30 Nov.
Bose, Subhas Chandra, b. 23 Jan.
Bossom, Sir Clive, b. 4 Feb.
Bossuet, Jacques, b. 25 Sept.
Bostock, James, b. 11 Jun.
Boswell, James, b. 29 Oct., d. 19 May
Bosworth, Joseph, d. 27 May
Botha, Louis, d. 27 Aug.
Botha, Piet, b. 12 Jan.
Botha, Pik, b. 27 Apr.

Botham, Ian, b. 24 Nov.
Bothwell, Earl of, d. 14 Apr.
Bott, Jean Joseph, b. 9 Mar.
Botticelli, Sandro, d. 17 May
Bottomley, Horatio, b. 23 Mar.
Bottomley, Lord, b. 7 Feb.
Boucher, François, b. 29 Sept., d. 30 May
Bouchier, Chili, b. 12 Sept.
Boucicault, Dion, b. 26 Dec., d. 18 Sept.
Boudin, Eugène, b. 12 Jul., d. 8 Aug.
Bougainville, Louis de, b. 11 Nov.
Bough, Frank, b. 15 Jan.
Boughton, George, d. 19 Jan.
Boughton, Rutland, b. 23 Jan., d. 25 Jan.
Bouguereau, William, b. 30 Nov., d. 20 Aug.
Boulanger, Georges, d. 30 Sept.
Boulanger, Louis, b. 11 Mar., d. 7 Mar.
Boulez, Pierre, b. 26 Mar.
Boulle, André, b. 11 Nov.
Boult, Adrian, b. 8 Apr., d. 23 Feb.
Boulting, Roy, b. 21 Nov.
Boulton, Matthew, b. 3 Sept., d. 18 Aug.
Boumedienne, Houari, d. 27 Dec.
Bow, Clara, b. 25 Aug., d. 27 Sept.
Bowdler, Thomas, b. 11 Jul., d. 24 Feb.
Bowen, Elizabeth, b. 7 Jun., d. 22 Feb.
Bowie, David, b. 8 Jan.
Bowlby, Ronald, b. 16 Aug.
Bowles, Peter, b. 16 Oct.
Bowlly, Al, b. 7 Jan., d. 16 Apr.
Box, Sydney, d. 25 May
Boyce, William, d. 7 Feb.
Boycott, Capt., b. 12 Mar.
Boycott, Geoffrey, b. 21 Oct.
Boyd, Bill, b. 5 Jun., d. 12 Sept.
Boyd, James, d. 25 Feb.
Boyd, William (author), b. 7 Mar.
Boyer, Charles, b. 28 Aug., d. 26 Aug.
Boyland, Prof. Eric, b. 24 Feb.
Boyle, Robert, b. 25 Jan., d. 30 Dec.
Boyson, Rhodes, b. 11 May
Brabham, Jack, b. 2 Apr.
Bracken, Eddie, b. 7 Feb.
Bracquemond, Félix, b. 22 May
Bradbury, Malcolm, b. 7 Sept.
Bradbury, Ray, b. 22 Aug.
Braddon, Russell, b. 25 Jan.
Braden, Bernard, b. 16 May
Bradford, John, d. 1 Jul.

Bradford, William, d. 9 May
Bradlaugh, Charles, b. 26 Sept.
Bradley, Francis, b. 30 Jan., d. 18 Sept.
Bradley, James, d. 13 Jun.
Bradley, Omar, d. 8 Apr.
Bradley, Will, b. 10 Jul.
Bradman, Donald, b. 27 Aug.
Bradshaw, George, b. 29 Jul., d. 8 Sept.
Brady, Jim, d. 13 Apr.
Brady, Liam, b. 13 Feb.
Brady, Mathew B., d. 15 Jan.
Brady, Nicholas, b. 28 Oct.
Brady, Scott, d. 17 Apr.
Brady, Terence, b. 13 Mar.
Braekeleer, Ferdinand de, b. 12 Feb.
Bragg, Billy, b. 20 Dec.
Bragg, Melvyn, b. 6 Oct.
Bragg, William, b. 2 Jul., d. 12 Mar.
Brahe, Tycho, b. 14 Dec., d. 24 Oct.
Brahms, Johannes, b. 7 May, d. 3 Apr.
Braille, Louis, b. 4 Jan., d. 6 Jan.
Braine, John, b. 13 Apr., d. 28 Oct.
Brainin, Norbert, b. 12 Mar.
Braithwaite, Lilian, d. 17 Sept.
Bramah, Joseph, b. 13 Apr., d. 9 Dec.
Bramante, Donato, d. 11 Apr.
Branagh, Kenneth, b. 10 Dec.
Branco, Luís de, b. 12 Oct.
Brancusi, Constantin, b. 21 Feb.
Brand, John, d. 11 Sept.
Brand, Max, b. 20 Mar., d. 16 May
Brand, Neville, b. 13 Aug.
Brando, Marlon, b. 3 Apr.
Brandreth, Gyles, b. 8 Mar.
Brandt, Bill, d. 20 Dec.
Brandt, Willy, b. 18 Dec.
Brangwyn, Frank, b. 13 May, d. 11 Jun.
Branson, Richard, b. 18 Jul.
Braque, Georges, b. 13 May, d. 31 Aug.
Brascassat, Jacques, d. 28 Feb.
Brasher, Christopher, b. 21 Aug.
Brasseur, Pierre, b. 22 Dec.
Bratby, John, b. 19 Jul.
Braun, Eva, b. 6 Feb., d. 30 Apr.
Braun, Wernher von, b. 23 Mar., d. 16 Jun.
Brazil, Angela, d. 13 Mar.
Brazzi, Rossano, b. 18 Sept.
Bream, Julian, b. 15 Jul.
Breasley, Scobie, b. 7 May

Brecht, Bertolt, b. 10 Feb., d. 14 Aug.
Bremner, Billy, b. 9 Dec.
Brendel, Alfred, b. 5 Jan.
Brennan, Walter, b. 25 Jul., d. 21 Sept.
Brenner, Sydney, b. 13 Jan.
Brent, George, b. 15 Mar., d. 26 May
Brentano, Franz, b. 16 Jan.
Brenton, Howard, b. 13 Dec.
Bresslaw, Bernard, b. 25 Feb.
Bresson, Robert, b. 25 Sept.
Breton, André, d. 28 Sept.
Brett, Jeremy, b. 3 Nov.
Breuil, Henri, d. 14 Aug.
Brewer, E. Cobham, b. 2 May, d. 6 Feb.
Brewer, Teresa, b. 7 May
Brewster, David, b. 11 Dec.
Brezhnev, Leonid, b. 19 Dec., d. 10 Nov.
Brian, Havergal, b. 29 Jan.
Briand, Aristide, b. 28 Mar., d. 7 Mar.
Brice, Fanny, b. 29 Oct., d. 29 May
Bricusse, Leslie, b. 29 Jan.
Bridge, Frank, b. 26 Feb., d. 10 Jan.
Bridges, Beau, b. 9 Dec.
Bridges, Jeff, b. 4 Dec.
Bridges, Lloyd, b. 15 Jan.
Bridges, Robert, b. 23 Oct., d. 21 Apr.
Bridgewater, 3rd Duke, b. 21 May, d. 3 Mar.
Bridie, James, b. 3 Jan., d. 29 Jan.
Briers, Richard, b. 14 Jan.
Briggs, Johnny, b. 5 Sept.
Briggs, Lord, b. 7 May
Briggs, Raymond, b. 18 Jan.
Bright, John, b. 16 Nov., d. 27 Mar.
Brightman, Sarah, b. 14 Aug.
Bril, Paul, d. 7 Oct.
Brilliant, Fredda, b. 7 Apr.
Brindley, James, d. 30 Sept.
Bristow, Eric, b. 25 Apr.
Brittain, Vera, b. 29 Dec., d. 29 Mar.
Brittan, Leon, b. 25 Sept.
Britten, Benjamin, b. 22 Nov., d. 4 Dec.
Britton, Tony, b. 9 Jun.
Brix, Herman, b. 19 May
Broch, Hermann, d. 30 May
Broderick, Helen, b. 11 Aug., d. 25 Sept.
Brolin, James, b. 18 Jul.
Brome, Alexander, d. 30 Jun.
Bromfield, Louis, b. 27 Dec., d. 18 Mar.
Bronson, Charles, b. 3 Nov.

Brontë, Anne, b. 25th Mar., d. 28 May
Brontë, Charlotte, b. 21 Apr., d. 31 Mar.
Brontë, Emily, b. 30 Jul., d. 19 Dec.
Bronzino, d. 23 Nov.
Brook, Lyndon, b. 10 Apr.
Brook, Peter, b. 21 Mar.
Brooke, James, b. 29 Apr., d. 11 Jun.
Brooke, Rupert, b. 3 Aug., d. 23 Apr.
Brooke-Taylor, Tim, b. 17 Jul.
Brooking, Trevor, b. 2 Oct.
Brookner, Anita, b. 16 Jul.
Brooks, Elkie, b. 25 Feb.
Brooks, Louise, d. 8 Aug.
Brooks, Mel, b. 28 Jun.
Brooks, Ray, b. 20 Apr.
Brooks, Richard, b. 18 May
Broom, Ivor, b. 2 Jun.
Broome, David, b. 1 Mar.
Brophy, Brigid, b. 12 Jun.
Brosnan, Pierce, b. 16 May
Brough, Louise, b. 11 Mar.
Brouncker, William, d. 5 Apr.
Brown, Arthur W., b. 23 Jul., d. 4 Oct.
Brown, 'Capability', d. 6 Feb.
Brown, Earle, b. 26 Dec.
Brown, Ford Madox, b. 16 Apr., d. 6 Oct.
Brown, George Mackay, b. 17 Oct.
Brown, Helen Gurley, b. 18 Feb.
Brown, James, b. 3 May
Brown, Jim, b. 17 Feb.
Brown, Joe, b. 13 May
Brown, John (abolitionist), b. 9 May, d. 2 Dec.
Brown, John (physician), d. 17 Oct.
Brown, John (theologian), d. 19 Jun.
Brown, Lew, b. 10 Dec.
Brown, Nacio Herb, b. 22 Feb.
Brown, Ralph, b. 24 Apr.
Brown, Robert Hanbury, b. 31 Aug.
Brown, Susan, b. 6 May
Browne, Hablot K., b. 11 Jun., d. 8 Jul.
Browne, J. Collis, d. 30 Aug.
Browne, Thomas (physician), b. 19 Oct., d. 19 Oct.
Browning, Elizabeth Barrett, b. 6 Mar., d. 29 Jun.
Browning, Frederick, b. 20 Dec.
Browning, Michael, b. 15 May
Browning, Robert, b. 7 May, d. 12 Dec.
Brubeck, Dave, b. 6 Dec.

Bruce, Brenda, b. 7 Jul.
Bruce, Christopher, b. 3 Oct.
Bruce, James, b. 14 Dec., d. 27 Apr.
Bruch, Max, b. 6 Jan., d. 2 Oct.
Bruckner, Anton, b. 4 Sept., d. 11 Oct.
Brueghel, Jan, the Elder, d. 12 Jan.
Brueghel, Pieter, the Elder, d. 5 Sept.
Brugmann, Karl, d. 29 Jun.
Brummel, 'Beau', b. 7 Jun., d. 30 Mar.
Brunel, Isambard Kingdom, b. 9 Apr., d. 15 Sept.
Brunel, Marc Isambard, b. 25 Apr., d. 12 Dec.
Bruno, Frank, b. 16 Nov.
Bruno, Giordano, d. 17 Feb.
Brunson, Michael, b. 12 Aug.
Brush, George, d. 24 Apr.
Brutus, Marcus Junius, d. 23 Oct.
Bryan, Dora, b. 7 Feb.
Bryan, William Jennings, b. 19 Mar.
Bryant, Arthur, d. 22 Jan.
Bryant, Michael, b. 5 Apr.
Bryant, William C., b. 3 Nov.
Bryce, 1st Viscount, b. 10 May, d. 22 Jan.
Brynner, Yul, b. 12 Jul., d. 10 Oct.
Buache, Jean-Nicolas, b. 15 Feb.
Buache, Philippe, b. 7 Feb.
Buber, Martin, b. 8 Feb., d. 13 Jun.
Buchan, Alexander, d. 13 May
Buchan, John, b. 26 Aug., d. 11 Feb.
Buchanan, Jack, b. 2 Apr., d. 20 Oct.
Buchanan, James, b. 23 Apr., d. 1 Jun.
Buchholz, Horst, b. 4 Dec.
Büchner, Georg, d. 19 Feb.
Büchner, Karl, b. 17 Oct.
Buck, Pearl, b. 26 Jun., d. 6 Mar.
Buckingham, 2nd Duke, d. 2 Nov.
Buckland, William, d. 14 Aug.
Budd, Zola, b. 26 May
Budé, Guillaume, d. 23 Aug.
Budge, E.A. Wallis, b. 27 Jul., d. 23 Nov.
Budgen, Nicholas, b. 3 Nov.
Bueno, Maria, b. 11 Oct.
Buffon, Comte de, b. 7 Sept., d. 16 Apr.
Bugner, Joe, b. 13 Mar.
Bujold, Genevieve, b. 1 Jul.
Bukharin, Nikolai, b. 9 Oct., d. 14 Mar.
Bulgakov, Mikhail, b. 15 May, d. 10 Mar.
Buller, Redvers, d. 2 Jun.
Bullock, Jeremy, b. 16 Feb.

Bullock, Lord, b. 13 Dec.

Bülow, Bernhard von, b. 3 May

Bülow, Hans von, b. 8 Jan., d. 12 Feb.

Bumbry, Grace, b. 4 Jan.

Bunche, Ralph, b. 7 Aug., d. 9 Dec.

Bunin, Ivan, b. 22 Oct., d. 8 Nov.

Bunn, Douglas, b. 1 Mar.

Bunsen, Christian von, d. 28 Nov.

Bunsen, Robert, b. 31 Mar., d. 16 Aug.

Buntline, Ned, b. 20 Mar., d. 16 Jul.

Buñuel, Luis, b. 22 Feb., d. 29 Jul.

Bunyan, John, b. 30 Nov., d. 31 Aug.

Burbage, Richard, d. 13 Mar.

Burbank, Luther, d. 11 Apr.

Burchfield, Robert, b. 27 Jan.

Burden, Hugh, b. 3 Apr.

Burdett-Coutts, Baroness, d. 30 Dec.

Burdon, Eric, b. 11 May

Burgess, Anthony, b. 25 Feb.

Burgess, Mark, b. 17 Jul.

Burghley, 1st Baron, b. 13 Sept., d. 4
Aug.

Burgos, Rafael de, b. 15 Sept.

Burgoyne, John, d. 4 Aug.

Burke, Billie, b. 7 Aug., d. 14 May

Burke, Edmund, b. 12 Jan., d. 9 Jul.

Burke, John, b. 5 Jan.

Burke, Robert, d. 28 Jun.

Burke, Thomas (novelist), d. 22 Sept.

Burke, William, d. 28 Jan.

Burkitt, William, b. 25 Jul.

Burn, William, b. 20 Dec.

Burne-Jones, Edward, b. 28 Aug., d. 17
Jun.

Burnet, Alastair, b. 12 Jul.

Burnet, Frank, b. 3 Sept.

Burnet, Gilbert, b. 18 Sept.

Burnett, Brian, b. 10 Mar.

Burnett, Carol, b. 26 Apr.

Burnett, Chester, d. 10 Jan.

Burnett, Frances Hodgson, b. 24 Nov., d.
29 Oct.

Burnett, John, b. 21 Jan.

Burney, Charles, d. 12 Apr.

Burney, Fanny, b. 13 Jun., d. 6 Jan.

Burns, Anne, b. 23 Nov.

Burns, George, b. 20 Jan.

Burns, Sir George, b. 29 Jan.

Burns, Robert, b. 25 Jan., d. 21 Jul.

Burr, Raymond, b. 21 May

Burrell, Sheila, b. 9 May

Burroughs, Edgar Rice, b. 1 Sept., d. 19
Mar.

Burroughs, William S. (novelist), 5 Feb.

Burroughs, William Seward (inventor),
b. 28 Jan., d. 15 Sept.

Burstyn, Ellen, b. 7 Dec.

Burt, Cyril, d. 10 Oct.

Burton, John Hill, b. 22 Aug.

Burton, Richard (actor), b. 11 Oct., d. 5
Aug.

Burton, Richard (explorer), b. 19 Mar., d.
20 Oct.

Burton, Robert, b. 8 Feb., d. 25 Jan.

Bury, John, b. 27 Jan.

Busby, Matt, b. 26 May

Busch, Wilhelm, b. 15 Apr., d. 9 Jan.

Bush, Alan, b. 22 Dec.

Bush, Charles, d. 15 Jun.

Bush, Geoffrey, b. 23 Mar.

Bush, George, b. 12 Jun.

Bush, Kate, b. 30 Jul.

Bushman, Francis X., b. 10 Jan.

Busoni, Ferruccio, d. 27 Jul.

Butcher, Roland, b. 14 Oct.

Butcher, Terry, b. 28 Dec.

Butler, James, b. 25 Jul.

Butler, Josephine, b. 13 May

Butler, Marilyn, b. 11 Feb.

Butler, R.A., b. 9 Dec., d. 8 Mar.

Butler, Robin, b. 3 Jan.

Butler, Rohan, b. 21 Jan.

Butler, Samuel (novelist), b. 4 Dec., d. 18
Jun.

Butler, Samuel (satirist), b. 8 Feb., d. 25
Sept.

Butler-Sloss, Elizabeth, b. 10 Aug.

Butlin, Billy, b. 29 Sept.

Butt, Clara, b. 1 Feb.,b., d. 23 Jan.

Butterfield, William, b. 7 Sept., d. 23
Feb.

Butterworth, Charles, b. 26 Jul., d. 13
Jun.

Butterworth, George, d. 5 Aug.

Buttons, Red, b. 5 Feb.

Byatt, Antonia, b. 24 Aug.

Bygraves, Max, b. 16 Oct.

Byington, Spring, b. 17 Oct., d. 7 Sept.

Byng, John, d. 14 Mar.

Byrd, Richard, b. 25 Oct., d. 11 Mar.

Byrne, Peter, b. 29 Jan.
Byrom, John, b. 29 Feb.
Byron, Kathleen, b. 11 Jan.
Byron, Lord, b. 22 Jan., d. 19 Apr.

Caan, James, b. 26 Mar.
Caballé, Montserrat, b. 12 Apr.
Cabell, James, b. 14 Apr., d. 5 May
Cabot, Bruce, b. 20 Apr., d. 3 May
Cacoyannis, Michael, b. 11 Jun.
Cadbury, George, b. 19 Sept.
Cadbury-Brown, Henry, b. 20 May
Cade, Jack, d. 12 Jul.
Cadell, Simon, b. 19 Jul.
Cadillac, Antoine de, b. 5 Mar., d. 15 Oct.
Caesar, Julius, b. 12 Jul., d. 15 Mar.
Cage, John, b. 5 Sept.
Cagliostro, Alessandro de, d. 26 Aug.
Cagney, James, b. 17 Jul., d. 30 Mar.
Cahill, Teresa, b. 30 Jul.
Cahn, Sammy, b. 18 Jun.
Caillié, René, b. 19 Nov.
Cain, James M., b. 28 Jun., d. 27 Oct.
Caine, Hall, b. 14 May, d. 31 Aug.
Caine, Marti, b. 26 Jan.
Caine, Michael, b. 14 Mar.
Caird, John, b. 22 Sept.
Cairncross, Alexander, b. 11 Feb.
Caius, John, d. 19 Jul.
Calcavecchia, Mark, b. 12 Jun.
Calcraft, William, d. 13 Dec.
Caldecott, Randolph, b. 22 Mar., d. 12
  Feb.
Calder, Alexander, b. 22 Jul.
Calder-Marshall, Anna, b. 11 Jan.
Calder-Marshall, Arthur, b. 19 Aug.
Calderón de la Barca, Pedro, b. 17 Jun.,
  d. 25 May
Caldicot, Richard, b. 7 Oct.
Caldwell, Erskine, b. 17 Dec., d. 11 Apr.
Calhern, Louis, b. 16 Feb., d. 12 May
Calhoun, Rory, b. 8 Aug.
Caligula, b. 31 Aug., d. 24 Jan.
Callaghan, Lord, b. 27 Mar.
Callas, Maria, b. 3 Dec., d. 16 Sept.
Callcott, Augustus, d. 25 Nov.
Callcott, John, b. 20 Nov.
Callil, Carmen, b. 15 Jul.
Callot, Jacques, d. 24 Mar.
Callow, Simon, b. 15 Jun.

Calloway, Cab, b. 25 Dec.
Calman, Mel, b. 19 May
Calvaert, Denys, d. 17 Mar.
Calverley, Charles, b. 22 Dec.
Calvert, Phyllis, b. 18 Feb.
Calvin, John, b. 10 Jul., d. 27 May
Camden, William, b. 2 May, d. 9 Nov.
Cameron, Averil, b. 8 Feb.
Cameron, Douglas, b. 29 Oct.
Cameron, James, d. 26 Jan.
Cameron, Lord, b. 11 Jun.
Cammaerts, Émile, b. 16 Mar.
Camões, Luis de, d. 10 Jun.
Campbell, Cheryl, b. 22 May
Campbell, Christopher, b. 2 Jan.
Campbell, Donald, b. 23 Mar., d. 4 Jan.
Campbell, Glen, b. 22 Apr.
Campbell, John, d. 27 Jun.
Campbell, Malcolm, b. 11 Mar., d. 31 Dec.
Campbell, Mrs Patrick, b. 9 Feb., d. 9
  Apr.
Campbell, Patrick, d. 7 Sept.
Campbell, Roy, b. 2 Oct., d. 22 Apr.
Campbell, Thomas, b. 27 Jul., d. 15 Jun.
Campbell-Bannerman, Henry, b. 7 Sept.,
  d. 22 Apr.
Campi, Vincenzo, d. 3 Oct.
Campion, Edmund, b. 25 Jan.
Campion, Thomas, b. 12 Feb., d. 1 Mar.
Camrose, 1st Viscount, b. 23 Jun.
Camrose, 2nd Viscount, b. 12 Jul.
Camus, Albert, b. 7 Nov., d. 4 Jan.
Canaletto, b. 18 Oct., d. 20 Apr.
Candeille, Amelie, b. 31 Jul.
Candy, Henry, b. 28 Oct.
Canizares, José-Maria, b. 18 Feb.
Cannan, Denis, b. 14 May
Canning, Victor, d. 21 Feb.
Cannon, Dyan, b. 4 Jan.
Cannon, Tommy, b. 27 Jun.
Cano, Alonso, b. 19 Mar., d. 4 Oct.
Canova, Antonio, b. 1 Nov., d. 13 Oct.
Cansdale, George, b. 29 Nov.
Cantarini, Simone, d. 15 Oct.
Canton, John, b. 31 Jul., d. 22 Mar.
Cantor, Eddie, b. 31 Jan., d. 10 Oct.
Canute II, of England, d. 12 Nov.
Capa, Robert, d. 25 May
Čapek, Karel, b. 9 Jan., d. 25 Dec.
Capone, Al, b. 17 Jan., d. 25 Jan.

Capote, Truman, b. 30 Sept., d. 25 Aug

Capp, Al, d. 5 Nov.

Capra, Frank, b. 18 May, d. 3 Sept.

Caran d'Ache, d. 26 Feb.

Caravaggio, Michelangelo da, b. 28 Sept.,
   d. 18 Jul.

Carberry, Tommy, b. 16 Sept.

Cardano, Geronimo, b. 24 Sept.

Cardin, Pierre, b. 7 Jul.

Cardinale, Claudia, b. 15 Apr.

Carducci, Giosuè, b. 27 Jul., d. 16 Feb.

Cardus, Neville, b. 2 Apr.

Carew, Nicholas, d. 3 Mar.

Carew, Thomas, d. 22 Mar.

Carey, George, Archbishop, b. 13 Nov.

Carey, Henry, d. 4 Oct.

Carey, Joyce, b. 30 Mar.

Carey, Macdonald, b. 15 Mar.

Carey, Peter, b. 7 May

Carey, William, b. 17 Aug.

Cargill, Patrick, b. 3 Jun.

Caritat, Marie-Jean, d. 8 Apr.

Carl XVI Gustav, of Sweden, b. 30 Apr.

Carlos I, of Portugal, d. 1 Feb.

Carlson, Chester, b. 8 Feb.

Carlyle, Joan, b. 6 Apr.

Carlyle, Thomas, b. 4 Dec., d. 5 Feb.

Carman, William Bliss, b. 15 Apr.

Carmichael, Hoagy, b. 22 Nov., d. 27 Dec.

Carmichael, Ian, b. 18 Jun.

Carmody, Tommy, b. 10 Jul.

Carnarvon, 5th Earl, d. 5 Apr.

Carnegie, Andrew, b. 25 Nov., d. 11 Aug.

Carney, Art, b. 4 Nov.

Carné, Marcel, b. 18 Aug.

Carnot, Nicolas, d. 24 Aug.

Carnot, Sadi, b. 1 Jun.

Caro, Anthony, b. 8 Mar.

Carol, Martine, b. 16 May

Carol I, of Romania, d. 10 Oct.

Carol II, of Romania, d. 4 Apr.

Caroline, of Monaco, b. 23 Jan.

Caroline, Queen, d. 7 Aug.

Carolus-Duran, d. 18 Feb.

Caron, Leslie, b. 1 Jul.

Carothers, Wallace, b. 27 Apr., d. 29 Apr.

Carpenter, Harry, b. 17 Oct.

Carpenter, Karen, d. 4 Feb.

Carpenter, Richard, b. 15 Oct.

Carpenter, Sue, b. 17 May

Carr, Carole, b. 26 Mar.

Carr, Donald, b. 28 Dec.

Carr, John Dickson, d. 27 Feb.

Carr, Lord, b. 11 Nov.

Carr, Michael, d. 16 Sept.

Carracci, Agostino, b. 15 Aug., d. 23 Feb.

Carracci, Annibale, b. 3 Nov., d. 15 Jul.

Carracci, Lodovico, b. 21 Apr., d. 13 Nov.

Carradine, David, b. 8 Oct.

Carradine, Keith, b. 8 Aug.

Carreras, José, b. 5 Dec.

Carrier, Robert, b. 10 Nov.

Carrillo, Leo, b. 6 Aug.

Carrington, Desmond, b. 23 May

Carrington, Lord, b. 6 Jun.

Carroll, Diahann, b. 17 Jul.

Carroll, Lewis, b. 27 Jan., d. 14 Jan.

Carroll, Nancy, d. 6 Aug.

Carrott, Jasper, b. 14 Mar.

Carson, 1st Baron, b. 9 Feb., d. 22 Oct.

Carson, Elisabeth, b. 10 Feb.

Carson, Frank, b. 6 Nov.

Carson, John, b. 28 Feb.

Carson, Johnny, b. 23 Oct.

Carson, Kit, b. 24 Dec., d. 23 May

Carson, Willie, b. 16 Nov.

Carte, Rupert D'Oyly, d. 12 Sept.

Carter, Bernard, b. 6 Apr.

Carter, Elizabeth, b. 16 Dec., d. 19 Feb.

Carter, Howard, b. 9 May, d. 2 Mar.

Carter, Jimmy, b. 1 Oct.

Carter, Lynda, b. 24 Jul.

Carteret, Anna, b. 11 Dec.

Cartier, Jacques, b. 31 Dec., d. 1 Sept.

Cartier-Bresson, Henri, b. 22 Aug.

Cartland, Barbara, b. 9 Jul.

Cartwright, Edmund, b. 24 Apr.,
   d. 30 Oct.

Caruso, Enrico, b. 27 Feb., d. 2 Aug.

Carvalho, Alexandre de, d. 13 Sept.

Carver, George W., d. 5 Jan.

Carver, Lord, b. 24 Apr.

Cary, Joyce, b. 7 Dec., d. 29 Mar.

Casals, Pablo, b. 29 Dec., d. 22 Oct.

Casals, Rosemary, b. 19 Sept.

Casanova, Giovanni, b. 5 Apr., d. 4 Jun.

Casella, Alfredo, b. 25 Jul.

Casement, Roger, b. 1 Sept., d. 3 Aug.

Cash, Johnny, b. 26 Feb.

Cash, Pat, b. 27 May

Casimir III, of Poland, b. 30 Apr.
Caslon, William, d. 23 Jan.
Cassavetes, John, d. 3 Feb.
Cassel, Jean-Pierre, b. 27 Oct.
Cassels, James, b. 28 Feb.
Cassidi, Desmond, b. 26 Jan.
Cassidy, David, b. 12 Apr.
Cassily, Richard, b. 14 Dec.
Cassini, Giovanni, b. 8 Jun., d. 11 Sept.
Casson, Hugh, b. 23 May
Castelnuovo-Tedesco, Mario, d. 15 Mar.
Castiglione, Baldassarre, b. 6 Dec., d. 2 Feb.
Castle, Barbara, b. 6 Oct.
Castle, Enid, b. 28 Jan.
Castle, Roy, b. 31 Aug.
Castro, Fidel, b. 13 Aug.
Catelani, Angelo, b. 30 Mar.
Cather, Willa, b. 7 Dec., d. 24 Apr.
Catherine of Aragon, d. 7 Jan.
Catherine, of France, d. 5 Jan.
Catherine I, of Russia, d. 17 May
Catherine the Great, b. 2 May
Catlett, Walter, b. 4 Feb.
Catley, Gwen, b. 9 Feb.
Catlin, George, b. 23 Jul., d. 23 Dec.
Catrufo, Giuseppe, b. 19 Apr.
Catt, Carrie Chapman, b. 9 Jan.
Cattermole, George, b. 8 Aug.
Caulfield, Joan, b. 1 Jun., d. 18 Jun.
Caulfield, Maxwell, b. 23 Nov.
Causley, Charles, b. 24 Aug.
Cavafy, Constantine, b. 17 Apr., d. 29 Apr.
Cavalcanti, Alberto, b. 6 Feb.
Cavalli, Pietro, b. 14 Feb., d. 14 Jan.
Cave, Edward, d. 10 Jan.
Cavell, Edith, b. 4 Dec., d. 12 Oct.
Cavendish, Henry, b. 10 Oct., d. 24 Feb.
Cavour, Camillo de, b. 10 Aug., d. 6 Jun.
Cawley, Evonne, b. 31 Jul.
Cayley, Arthur, b. 16 Aug.
Cayley, George, b. 27 Dec., d. 15 Dec.
Cayzer, Lord, b. 21 Jan.
Cazenove, Christopher, b. 17 Dec.
Ceausescu, Nicolae, d. 25 Dec.
Cecil, 1st Viscount, d. 24 Nov.
Cecil, David, b. 11 Jan.
Cecil, Henry, b. 11 Jan.
Cecil, Lord David, d. 1 Jan.

Celestine III, Pope, d. 8 Jan.
Cellini, Benvenuto, b. 1 Nov., d. 13 Feb.
Celsius, Anders, b. 27 Nov., d. 25 Apr.
Centlivre, Susannah, d. 1 Dec.
Cervantes, b. 29 Sept., d. 23 Apr.
Cesari, Giuseppe, d. 3 Jul.
Cespedes, Pablo de, d. 26 Jul.
Cézanne, Paul, b. 19 Jan., d. 22 Oct.
Chabrier, Alexis, b. 18 Jan., d. 13 Sept.
Chabrol, Claude, b. 24 Jun.
Chacksfield, Frank, b. 9 May
Chadbon, Tom, b. 27 Feb.
Chadwick, Edwin, b. 24 Jan.
Chadwick, James, b. 20 Oct., d. 24 Jul.
Chadwick, Lynn, b. 24 Nov.
Chadwick, Owen, b. 20 May
Chagall, Marc, b. 7 Jul., d. 28 Mar.
Chain, Ernst, b. 19 Jun.
Chakiris, George, b. 16 Sept.
Chalfont, Lord, b. 5 Dec.
Chaliapin, Feodor, b. 13 Feb., d. 12 Apr.
Chalker, Lynda, b. 29 Apr.
Challis, Jean, b. 22 May
Chalmers, George, d. 20 Feb.
Chamberlain, Austen, b. 16 Oct., d. 16 Mar.
Chamberlain, Houston Stewart, b. 9 Sept.
Chamberlain, Joseph, b. 8 Jul., d. 2 Jul.
Chamberlain, Neville, b. 18 Mar., d. 9 Nov.
Chamberlain, Richard, b. 31 Mar.
Chamberlayne, William, d. 31 Jan.
Chambers, Ephraim, d. 15 May
Chambers, Robert, b. 10 Jul., d. 17 Mar.
Chambers, Robert W., d. 16 Dec.
Chambers, William, b. 16 Apr., d. 20 May
Chaminade, Cécile, b. 8 Aug., d. 18 Apr.
Champaigne, Philippe de, d. 12 Aug.
Champion, Bob, b. 4 Jun.
Champollion, Jean-François, b. 23 Dec., d. 4 Mar.
Chancellor, Richard, d. 10 Nov.
Chandler, Raymond, b. 23 Jul., d. 26 Mar.
Chandrasekhar, Bhagwat, b. 17 May
Chanel, Coco, b. 19 Aug., d. 10 Jan.
Chaney, Lon, b. 1 Apr., d. 26 Aug.
Chaney, Lon, Jr., b. 10 Feb.
Channing, Carol, b. 31 Jan.
Channon, Paul, b. 9 Oct.
Chantrey, Francis, d. 25 Nov.

Chaplin, Charles, b. 16 Apr., d. 25 Dec.

Chaplin, Geraldine, b. 31 Jul.

Chaplin, Sydney, b. 17 Mar.

Chaplin, Sydney, b. 31 Mar.

Chappell, Greg, b. 7 Aug.

Chappell, Ian, b. 26 Sept.

Chappell, William, b. 20 Nov.

Chapple, Gen. Sir John, b. 27 May

Chapple, Lord, b. 8 Aug.

Chardin, Jean, b. 2 Nov., d. 6 Dec.

Chardonnet, Hilaire de, d. 12 Mar.

Charisse, Cyd, b. 8 Mar.

Charlemagne, b. 2 Apr., d. 28 Jan.

Charles, Jacques, b. 12 Nov.

Charles, John, b. 27 Dec.

Charles, Maria, b. 22 Sept.

Charles, Miriam, b. 18 May

Charles, Ray, b. 23 Sept.

Charles I, of Great Britain, b. 19 Nov., d. 30 Jan.

Charles II, Holy Roman Emperor, d. 6 Oct.

Charles II, of Great Britain, b. 29 May, d. 6 Feb.

Charles IV, Holy Roman Emperor, b. 14 May

Charles V, Holy Roman Emperor, b. 24 Feb.

Charles VII, Holy Roman Emperor, d. 20 Jan.

Charles VII of France, d. 22 Jul.

Charles IX, of France, b. 27 Jun.

Charles X, of France, b. 9 Oct.

Charles XII, of Sweden, b. 17 Jun., d. 11 Dec.

Charles XIV, of Sweden, b. 26 Jan., d. 8 Mar.

Charlet, Nicolas, b. 20 Dec., d. 30 Oct.

Charlot, André, b. 26 Jul., d. 20 May

Charlton, Bobby, b. 11 Oct.

Charlton, Jack, b. 8 May

Charpentier, Gustave, d. 18 Feb.

Charpentier, Marc-Antoine, d. 24 Feb.

Charrier, Jacques, b. 6 Nov.

Charteris, Leslie, b. 12 May

Chase, Charlie, b. 20 Oct.

Chase, Ilka, b. 8 Apr.

Chase, James Hadley, d. 6 Feb.

Chataway, Christopher, b. 31 Jan.

Chateaubriand, François de, b. 4 Sept., d. 4 Jul.

Chatterton, Ruth, b. 24 Dec., d. 24 Nov.

Chatterton, Thomas, b. 20 Nov., d. 24 Aug.

Chaucer, Geoffrey, d. 25 Oct.

Chausson, Amédée-Ernest, b. 21 Jan.

Chauviré, Yvette, b. 22 Apr.

Chávez, Carlos, b. 13 Jun., d. 2 Aug.

Chayefsky, Paddy, b. 29 Jan.

Checker, Chubby, b. 3 Oct.

Checkland, Michael, b. 13 Mar.

Cheke, John, b. 16 Jun., d. 13 Sept.

Chekhov, Anton, d. 15 Jul.

Chenier, André de, b. 30 Oct., d. 25 Jul.

Cherkassky, Shura, b. 7 Oct.

Cherry, Don, b. 18 Nov.

Cherubini, Luigi, b. 14 Sept., d. 15 Mar.

Cheshire, Lord, b. 7 Sept., d. 31 Jul.

Chesterfield, 4th Earl, b. 22 Sept., d. 24 Mar.

Chesterton, G.K., b. 29 May, d. 14 Jun.

Chevalier, Albert, b. 21 Mar., d. 10 Jul.

Chevalier, Maurice, b. 12 Sept., d. 1 Jan.

Chevrolet, Louis, d. 6 Jun.

Chiang Kai-shek, b. 31 Oct., d. 5 Apr.

Chichester, Francis, b. 17 Sept, d. 26 Aug.

Chichester-Clark, Robin, b. 10 Jan.

Child, Jeremy, b. 20 Sept.

Childe, Vere Gordon, b. 14 Apr.

Childers, Erskine, b. 25 Jun., d. 24 Nov.

Chirac, Jacques, b. 29 Nov.

Chirico, Giorgio de, d. 10 Jul.

Chisholm, George, b. 29 Mar.

Chodowiecki, Daniel, b. 16 Oct.

Cholmondeley, Mary, b. 8 Jun.

Chomsky, Noam, b. 7 Dec.

Chopin, Frédéric, b. 1 Mar., d. 17 Oct.

Christiaan, Huygens, b. 14 Apr.

Christian IV, of Denmark, d. 28 Feb.

Christian X, of Denmark, d. 20 Apr.

Christie, Agatha, b. 15 Sept., d. 12 Jan.

Christie, Julie, b. 14 Apr.

Christie, Linford, b. 2 Apr.

Christina, of Sweden, b. 8 Dec., d. 19 Apr.

Christoff, Boris, b. 18 May

Christopher, Ann, b. 4 Dec.

Christopher, Ernest, d. 23 Feb.

Christopher, Gretchen, b. 29 Feb.

Chubb, John, d. 30 Oct.

Church, Richard, b. 26 Mar., d. 4 Mar.
Churchill, Chalres, d. 4 Nov.
Churchill, Clementine, b. 1 Apr., d. 12 Dec.
Churchill, Diana, b. 21 Aug.
Churchill, Donald, b. 6 Nov.
Churchill, Lady Randolph, b. 9 Jan., d. 29 Jun.
Churchill, Lord Randolph, b. 13 Feb., d. 24 Jan.
Churchill, Sir Winston, b. 30 Nov., d. 24 Jan.
Churchill, Winston S. (grandson), b. 10 Oct.
Churchill, Winston (US novelist), b. 10 Nov., d. 13 Mar.
Churchyard, Thomas, d. 4 Apr.
Ciano, Galeazzo, d. 11 Jan.
Cibber, Colley, b. 6 Nov., d. 11 Dec.
Cicero, b. 3 Jan., d. 7 Dec.
Cicognara, Leopoldo, d. 5 Mar.
Cignani, Carlo, b. 15 May, d. 6 Sept.
Cigoli, Lodovico Cardi da, b. 12 Sept.
Cilea, Francesco, b. 26 Jul., d. 20 Nov.
Cilento, Diane, b. 5 Oct.
Cimarosa, Domenico, b. 17 Dec., d. 11 Jan.
Cipriani, Giovanni, d. 14 Dec.
Clair, René, b. 11 Nov.
Clapperton, Hugh, d. 13 Apr.
Clapton, Eric, b. 30 Mar.
Clare, John, b. 13 Jun., d. 20 May
Clare, Mary, b. 17 Jul.
Clarendon, 1st Earl, d. 9 Dec.
Clark, 1st Baron, b. 13 Jun.
Clark, Dane, b. 18 Feb.
Clark, Dave, b. 15 Dec.
Clark, Jim, d. 7 Apr.
Clark, Kenneth, Baron, d. 21 May
Clark, Mark, d. 17 Apr.
Clark, Petula, b. 15 Nov.
Clark, Walter, b. 3 Aug.
Clark, William, b. 1 Aug., d. 1 Sept.
Clarke, Arthur C., b. 16 Dec.
Clarke, Geoffrey, b. 28 Nov.
Clarke, Jacqueline, b. 13 Feb.
Clarke, Kenneth, b. 2 Jul.
Clarke, Marcus, b. 24 Apr., d. 2 Aug.
Clarke, Sylvester, b. 11 Dec.
Clarkson, Thomas, b. 28 Mar.

Clarkson, Willie, d. 13 Oct.
Clatworthy, Robert, b. 31 Jan.
Claude, Georges, b. 24 Sept.
Claudel, Paul, b. 6 Aug., d. 23 Feb.
Claudius, emperor, b. 1 Aug., d. 13 Oct.
Clausen, George, b. 18 Apr.
Clausewitz, Karl von, d. 18 Nov.
Clavell, James, b. 10 Oct.
Clay, Frederic, b. 3 Aug.
Clay, Henry, b. 12 Apr.
Clayburgh, Jill, b. 30 Apr.
Clayton, Lucie, b. 5 Dec.
Clayton, Peter, b. 25 Jun.
Cleary, Jon, b. 22 Nov.
Cledwyn, Lord, b. 14 Sept.
Cleese, John, b. 27 Oct.
Cleland, John, d. 23 Jan.
Clemence, Ray, b. 5 Aug.
Clemenceau, Georges, b. 28 Sept., d. 24 Nov.
Clement, Dick, b. 5 Sept.
Clément, Jacques, b. 13 Jan.
Clement, René, b. 18 Mar.
Clement XIII, Pope, d. 2 Feb.
Clementi, Muzio, b. 23 Jan.
Cleopatra, d. 30 Aug.
Cleveland, Grover, b. 18 Mar., d. 24 Jun.
Cleveland, John, d. 29 Apr.
Cleves, Anne of, b. 22 Sept.
Clift, Montgomery, b. 17 Oct., d. 23 Jul.
Clive, Colin, d. 25 Jun.
Clive, Robert, b. 29 Sept., d. 22 Nov.
Clooney, Rosemary, b. 23 May
Close, Brian, b. 24 Feb.
Close, Glenn, b. 19 Mar.
Clouet, François, d. 22 Dec.
Clough, Arthur, b. 1 Jan., d. 13 Nov.
Clough, Brian, b. 21 Mar.
Clough, Gordon, b. 26 Aug.
Clouzot, Henri, b. 20 Nov.
Clovis, of France, d. 27 Nov.
Clyde, Andy, b. 25th Mar.
Coates, Eric, b. 27 Aug., d. 23 Dec.
Cobb, Irvin S., b. 23 Jun., d. 10 Mar.
Cobb, Lee J., b. 8 Dec., d. 11 Feb.
Cobb, Richard, b. 20 May
Cobbett, William, b. 9 Mar., d. 18 Jun.
Cobden, Richard, b. 3 Jun., d. 2 Apr.
Coburn, Charles, b. 19 Jun.
Coburn, James, b. 31 Aug.

Cochran, C.B., b. 25 Sept., d. 31 Jan.
Cochrane, Thomas, d. 31 Oct.
Cockburn, Alison, b. 8 Oct.
Cockburn, Catharine, b. 16 Aug., d. 11 May
Cockcroft, John, b. 27 May, d. 18 Sept.
Cockerell, Christopher, b. 4 Jun.
Cockerell, Michael, b. 26 Aug.
Cocteau, Jean, b. 5 Jul., d. 11 Oct.
Cocx, Gonzales, d. 18 Apr.
Cody, Lew, b. 22 Feb.
Cody, William F., b. 26 Feb., d. 10 Jan.
Coe, Sebastian, b. 29 Sept.
Coello, Alonso, d. 8 Aug.
Coello, Claudio, d. 20 Apr.
Coffey, Denise, b. 12 Dec.
Cogan, Alma, d. 26 Oct.
Coggan, Lord, b. 9 Oct.
Coghill, Nevill, d. 6 Nov.
Cohan, George M., b. 3 Jul., d. 5 Nov.
Cohen, George, b. 23 Oct.
Cohl, Emile, d. 27 Jan.
Coke, Edward, b. 1 Feb., d. 3 Sept.
Coker, Peter, b. 27 Jul.
Colbert, Claudette, b. 13 Sept.
Colbert, Jean, b. 29 Aug., d. 6 Sept.
Cole, George, b. 22 Apr.
Cole, John, b. 23 Nov.
Cole, Monica, b. 5 May
Cole, Nat 'King', b. 17 Mar., d. 15 Feb.
Cole, Paul, b. 11 Sept.
Cole, Vicat, b. 17 Apr.
Coleman, David, b. 26 Apr.
Coleridge, Hartley, d. 6 Jan.
Coleridge, Mary, b. 23 Sept.
Coleridge, Samuel Taylor, b. 21 Oct., d. 25 Jul.
Coleridge-Taylor, Samuel, b. 15 Aug., d. 1 Sept.
Coles, Neil, b. 26 Sept.
Colet, John, d. 16 Sept.
Colette, b. 28 Jan., d. 3 Aug.
Coligny, Gaspard de, d. 24 Aug.
Colledge, Cecilia, b. 28 Nov.
Collier, Constance, d. 25 Apr.
Collier, Jeremy, b. 23 Sept., d. 26 Apr.
Collier, Lesley, b. 13 Mar.
Collingwood, Admiral, b. 26 Sept., d. 7 Mar.
Collins, Anthony, d. 13 Dec.

Collins, Dale, b. 7 Apr., d. 4 Mar.
Collins, Jackie, b. 4 Oct.
Collins, Joan, b. 23 May
Collins, Michael, b. 16 Oct., d. 22 Aug.
Collins, Pauline, b. 3 Sept.
Collins, Phil, b. 30 Jan.
Collins, Wilkie, b. 8 Jan., d. 23 Sept.
Collins, William (painter), b. 8 Sept., d. 17 Feb.
Collins, William (poet), b. 25 Dec., d. 12 Jun.
Collot d'Herbois, Jean-Marie, d. 8 Jan.
Colman, George, the elder, b. 18 Apr., d. 14 Aug.
Colman, George, the younger, b. 21 Oct., d. 17 Oct.
Colman, Ronald, b. 9 Feb., d. 19 May
Colt, Samuel, b. 19 Jul., d. 10 Jan.
Colum, Padraic, b. 8 Dec., d. 11 Jan.
Columbo, Russ, d. 2 Sept.
Columbus, Christopher, d. 20 May
Comaneci, Nadia, b. 12 Nov.
Combe, Andrew, b. 27 Oct.
Combe, George, d. 14 Aug.
Combe, William, d. 18 Jun.
Comden, Betty, b. 3 May
Comenius, Johann, b. 28 Mar.
Comfort, Dr Alexander, b. 10 Feb.
Commager, Henry, b. 25 Oct.
Como, Perry, b. 18 May
Compson, Betty, b. 18 Mar.
Compton, Arthur, d. 15 Mar.
Compton, Denis, b. 23 May
Compton, Fay, b. 18 Sept.
Compton-Burnett, Ivy, b. 5 Jun., d. 27 Aug.
Comte, Auguste, b. 19 Jan., d. 5 Sept.
Conder, Charles, b. 10 Oct., d. 9 Apr.
Condillac, Étienne de, b. 30 Sept.
Condorcet, Marquis de, b. 17 Sept., d. 8 Apr.
Coney, Jeremy, b. 21 Jun.
Confucius, b. 27 Aug.
Congdon, Bevan, b. 11 Feb.
Congreve, William, b. 24 Jan., d. 19 Jan.
Coniff, Ray, b. 6 Nov.
Coninck, Joseph, b. 10 Mar.
Conlon, James, b. 18 Mar.
Connaught, Prince Arthur of, b. 13 Jan.
Connery, Jason, b. 11 Jan.

Connery, Sean, b. 25 Aug.
Connolly, Billy, b. 24 Nov.
Connolly, Cyril, d. 11 Nov., d. 26 Nov.
Connolly, Walter, b. 8 Apr.
Connor, Ralph, b. 13 Sept., d. 31 Oct.
Connor, Tommie, b. 16 Nov.
Connors, Chuck, b. 10 Apr.
Connors, Jimmy, b. 2 Sept.
Conquest, Robert, b. 15 Jul.
Conrad, Joseph, b. 3 Dec., d. 3 Aug.
Conran, Jasper, b. 12 Dec.
Conran, Shirley, b. 21 Sept.
Constable, John, b. 11 Jun., d. 31 Mar.
Constant, Jean, d. 26 May
Constantine, Hugh, b. 23 May
Constantine, Learie, b. 21 Sept.
Constantine, of the Hellenes, b. 2 Jun.
Constantine the Great, b. 27 Feb., d. 22
   May
Constantius, Flavius Valerius, d. 25
   Jul.
Constantius II, emperor, 3 Nov.
Conte, Richard, b. 24 Mar., d. 15 Apr.
Conteh, John, b. 27 May
Conti, Francesco, b. 20 Jan.
Conti, Tom, b. 22 Nov.
Conway, Nick, b. 25 Dec.
Conway, Russ, b. 2 Sept.
Conway, Tom, b. 15 Sept.
Conybeare, William, d. 12 Aug.
Cooder, Ry, b. 15 Mar.
Coogan, Jackie, b. 24 Oct., d. 1 Mar.
Cook, Beryl, b. 10 Sept.
Cook, Eliza, d. 23 Sept.
Cook, Geoff, b. 9 Oct.
Cook, James, b. 27 Oct., d. 14 Feb.
Cook, Kathy, b. 3 May
Cook, Paul, b. 12 Apr.
Cook, Peter, b. 17 Nov.
Cook, Thomas, b. 22 Nov., d. 19 Jul.
Cooke, Alistair, b. 20 Nov.
Cookson, Catherine, b. 20 Jun.
Coolican, John, b. 27 Dec.
Coolidge, Calvin, b. 4 Jul., d. 5 Jan.
Cooney, Ray, b. 30 May
Cooper, Astley, b. 23 Aug.
Cooper, Gary, b. 7 May, d. 13 May
Cooper, George, b. 10 Aug.
Cooper, Giles, b. 9 Aug.
Cooper, Gladys, b. 18 Dec., d. 17 Nov.

Cooper, Henry, b. 3 May
Cooper, Imogen, b. 28 Aug.
Cooper, Jackie, b. 15 Sept.
Cooper, James Fenimore, b. 15 Sept.,
   d. 14 Sept.
Cooper, Jilly, b. 21 Feb.
Cooper, Joseph, b. 7 Oct.
Cooper, Malcolm, b. 20 Dec.
Cooper, Melville, b. 15 Oct.
Cooper, Merian C., b. 24 Oct.
Cooper, Samuel, d. 5 May
Cooper, Susie, b. 29 Oct.
Cooper, Thomas, b. 26 Sept.
Cooper, Tommy, d. 15 Apr.
Cooper, William, b. 4 Aug.
Copernicus, Nicolaus, b. 19 Feb., d. 24
   May
Copley, John, b. 3 Jul., d. 9 Sept.
Copley, Peter, b. 20 May
Coppard, A.E., b. 4 Jan., d. 13 Jan.
Coppell, Steve, b. 9 Jul.
Coppola, Francis, b. 7 Apr.
Coquelin, Benoît-Constant, b. 23 Jan.
Corbett, Harry H., d. 21 Mar.
Corbett, Jim, b. 1 Sept., d. 18 Feb.
Corbett, Ronnie, b. 4 Dec.
Corbusier, Le, b. 6 Oct., d. 27 Aug.
Corday, Charlotte, d. 17 Jul.
Cordella, Giacomo, b. 25 Jul.
Corder, Frederick, b. 26 Jan.
Corelli, Arcangelo, b. 17 Feb., d. 8 Jan.
Corelli, Marie, b. 1 May, d. 21 Apr.
Coren, Alan, b. 27 Jun.
Corey, Wendell, b. 20 Mar.
Cori, Carl, b. 15 Dec.
Cori, Gerty, d. 26 Oct.
Cork, 1st Earl, d. 15 Sept.
Corman, Roger, b. 5 Apr.
Corneille, Pierre, d. 1 Oct.
Corneille, Thomas, b. 20 Aug.
Cornelius Agrippa, b. 14 Sept.
Cornelius, Henry, d. 3 May
Cornelius, Peter von, b. 23 Sept., d. 6 Mar.
Cornell, Ezra, b. 11 Jan.
Cornell, Katharine, b. 16 Feb., d. 8 Jun.
Cornwall, Barry, b. 21 Nov., d. 5 Oct.
Cornwallis, Marquess, b. 31 Dec., d. 5
   Oct.
Cornwell, Judy, b. 22 Feb.
Corot, Camille, b. 16 Jul., d. 22 Feb.

Correggio, Antonio, d. 5 Mar.
Corri, Adrienne, b. 13 Nov.
Cortés, Hernando, d. 2 Dec.
Cortese, Valentina, b. 1 Jan.
Cortez, Ricardo, b. 19 Sept.
Cortona, Pietro da, b. 1 Nov., d. 16 May
Corvo, *see* Rolfe
Cosby, Bill, b. 12 Jul.
Cossons, Neil, b. 15 Jan.
Costa, Lorenzo, d. 3 May
Costello, Dolores, b. 17 Sept.
Costello, Lou, b. 6 Mar., d. 3 Mar.
Costello, Louisa, d. 24 Apr.
Cotman, John Sell, b. 16 May, d. 24 Jul.
Cotten, Joseph, b. 15 May
Cotterell, Geoffrey, b. 24 Nov.
Cottet, Charles, b. 12 Jul.
Cotton, Bill, b. 23 Apr.
Cotton, Fran, b. 3 Jan.
Cotton, John, b. 4 Dec., d. 23 Dec.
Coty, François, b. 3 May
Coubertin, Pierre de, b. 1 Jan., d. 2 Sept.
Coué, Émile, b. 26 Feb., d. 2 Jul.
Coulomb, Charles de, b. 14 Jun., d. 23 Aug.
Counsell, Elizabeth, b. 7 Jun.
Couper, Heather, b. 2 Jun.
Couperin, François, b. 10 Nov., d. 12 Sept.
Couperin, Louis, d. 29 Aug.
Courbet, Gustave, b. 10 Jun., d. 31 Dec.
Cournand, André, b. 24 Sept.
Courrèges, André, b. 9 Mar.
Court, Margaret, b. 16 Jul.
Courtenay, Margaret, b. 14 Nov.
Courtenay, Tom, b. 25 Feb.
Courtneidge, Cicely, b. 1 Apr., d. 26 Apr.
Courtneidge, Robert, d. 6 Apr.
Courtois, Guillaume, d. 15 Jun.
Courtois, Jacques, b. 12 Feb.
Cousin, Victor, b. 28 Nov.
Cousins, Robin, b. 17 Aug.
Coussemaker, Charles, b. 19 Apr.
Cousteau, Jacques, b. 11 Jun.
Coutts, Thomas, b. 7 Sept., d. 24 Feb.
Couture, Thomas, d. 30 Mar.
Coward, Noël, b. 16 Dec., d. 26 Mar.
Cowdray, Viscount, b. 27 Feb.
Cowdrey, Colin, b. 24 Dec.
Cowey, Bernard, b. 20 Nov.
Cowie, Edward, b. 17 Aug.

Cowley, Abraham, d. 28 Jul.
Cowley, Hannah, d. 11 Mar.
Cowper, David, b. 1 Mar.
Cowper, William, b. 26 Nov., d. 25 Apr.
Cox, Anthony, b. 18 Jul.
Cox, David, d. 7 Jun.
Cox, Mark, b. 5 Jul.
Coxcie, Michael, d. 5 Mar.
Coypel, Antoine, d. 11 Apr.
Coypel, Charles, b. 11 Jul.
Coypel, Noel, b. 25 Dec.
Cozzens, James G., d. 8 Aug.
Crabbe, Buster, d. 23 Apr.
Crabbe, George, b. 24 Dec., d. 3 Feb.
Craig, Charles, b. 3 Dec.
Craig, Edward Gordon, b. 16 Jan., d. 29 Jul.
Craig, Elizabeth, d. 7 Jun.
Craig, James, d. 24 Nov.
Craig, Michael, b. 27 Jan.
Craig, Wendy, b. 20 Jun.
Craigavon, Viscount, b. 8 Jan.
Craigie, William, b. 13 Aug., d. 2 Sept.
Craik, Mrs, b. 20 Apr.
Crain, Jeanne, b. 25 May
Cram, Steve, b. 14 Oct.
Cramp, Rosemary, b. 6 May
Cranach, Lucas, the Elder, b. 4 Oct., d. 16 Oct.
Cranach, Lucas, the Younger, b. 4 Oct., d. 25 Jan.
Crane, Harold Hart, b. 21 Jul., d. 27 Apr.
Crane, Stephen, b. 1 Nov., d. 5 Jun.
Crane, Walter, b. 15 Aug., d. 14 Mar.
Cranham, Kenneth, b. 12 Dec.
Cranmer, Thomas, b. 2 Jul., d. 21 Mar.
Crashaw, Richard, d. 21 Aug.
Craven, Gemma, b. 1 Jun.
Crawford, Broderick, d. 26 Apr.
Crawford, Francis Marion, b. 2 Aug.
Crawford, Joan, b. 23 Mar., d. 10 May
Crawford, Michael, b. 19 Jan.
Crawley, Aidan, b. 10 Apr.
Crayer, Gaspard de, b. 18 Nov.
Creasy, Edward, b. 12 Sept., d. 27 Jan.
Credi, Lorenzo di, d. 12 Jan.
Crenshaw, Ben, b. 11 Jan.
Crescentini, Girolamo, b. 2 Feb.
Crespi, Giuseppe, b. 16 Mar., d. 16 Jul.
Creswick, Thomas, b. 5 Feb., d. 28 Dec.

Crevecoeur, Michel de, b. 31 Jan.
Crewe, Quentin, b. 14 Nov.
Cribb, Tom, b. 8 Jul., d. 11 May
Cribbins, Bernard, b. 29 Dec.
Crichton, James, b. 19 Aug.
Crippen, Harvey, d. 23 Nov.
Cripps, Stafford, b. 24 Apr., d. 21 Apr.
Cristofori, Bartolommeo, b. 4 May
Croce, Benedetto, b. 25 Feb.
Crockett, Davy, b. 17 Aug., d. 6 Mar.
Crockett, Samuel, b. 24 Sept.
Crofts, Freeman Wills, d. 11 Apr.
Croker, John, b. 20 Dec.
Crome, John, b. 22 Dec., d. 22 Apr.
Cromer, 1st Earl, b. 26 Feb., d. 29 Jan.
Crompton, Richmal, d. 11 Jan.
Crompton, Samuel, b. 3 Dec., d. 26 Jun.
Cromwell, Oliver, b. 25 Apr., d. 3 Sept.
Cromwell, Richard, b. 4 Oct., d. 13 Jun.
Cromwell, Thomas, d. 28 Jul.
Cronin, A.J., b. 19 Jul., d. 6 Jan.
Cronkite, Walter, b. 4 Nov.
Crookes, William, b. 17 Jun., d. 4 Apr.
Crosbie, Annette, b. 12 Feb.
Crosbie, William, b. 31 Jan.
Crosby, Bing, b. 2 May, d. 14 Oct.
Crosby, Bob, b. 25 Aug.
Crosby, Kathryn, b. 25 Nov.
Cross, Beverley, b. 13 Apr.
Cross, Joan, b. 7 Sept.
Crossan, Keith, b. 29 Dec.
Crosse, Gordon, b. 1 Dec.
Crotch, William, b. 5 Jul.
Crouch, Frederick, d. 18 Aug.
Crowden, Graham, b. 30 Nov.
Crowe, Sylvia, b. 15 Sept.
Crowley, Aleister, b. 12 Oct.
Crowley-Milling, A.M. Sir Denis, b. 22
    Mar.
Crowther, Leslie, b. 6 Feb.
Crozier, Bill, b. 11 Jul.
Crozier, Eric, b. 14 Nov.
Cruden, Alexander, b. 31 May, d. 1 Nov.
Cruft, Charles, d. 10 Sept.
Cruickshank, John, b. 20 May
Cruikshank, George, b. 27 Sept., d. 1 Feb.
Crumb, George, b. 24 Oct.
Crutchley, Rosalie, b. 4 Jan.
Cruze, James, d. 4 Aug.
Cryer, Barry, b. 23 Mar.

Cudlipp, Lord, b. 28 Aug.
Cukor, George, b. 7 Jul., d. 24 Jan.
Culver, Michael, b. 16 Jun.
Culver, Roland, b. 31 Aug.
Cumberland, Richard, b. 19 Feb.
Cuming, Frederick, b. 16 Feb.
Cummings, Constance, b. 15 May
cummings, e.e., b. 14 Oct., d. 3 Sept.
Cummings, Robert, b. 9 Jun.
Cunard, Samuel, b. 20 Nov.
Cuneo, Terence, b. 1 Nov.
Cunningham, Allan, b. 7 Dec., d. 30 Oct.
Cunningham, John, b. 27 Jul.
Curie, Marie, b. 7 Nov., d. 4 Jul.
Curie, Pierre, b. 15 May, d. 19 Apr.
Curley, Carlo, b. 24 Aug.
Curll, Edmund, d. 11 Dec.
Currie, Edwina, b. 13 Oct.
Curry, David, b. 13 Jun.
Curry, John, b. 9 Sept.
Curteis, Ian, b. 1 May
Curtin, John, b. 8 Jan.
Curtis, Cyrus H., b. 18 Jun.
Curtis, Tony, b. 3 Jun.
Curtiss, Glenn, b. 21 May, d. 23 Jul.
Curtiz, Michael, b. 24 Dec., d. 10 Apr.
Curwen, John, b. 14 Nov., d. 26 May
Curzon, George, b. 11 Jan., d. 20 Mar.
Cusack, Cyril, b. 26 Nov.
Cusack, Sinead, b. 18 Feb.
Cushing, Peter, b. 26 May
Custer, George, b. 5 Dec., d. 25 Jun.
Cutforth, René, d. 1 Apr.
Cuthbertson, Iain, b. 4 Jan.
Cutler, Roden, b. 24 May
Cuvier, Baron, b. 23 Aug., d. 13 May
Cuyp, Aelbert, d. 15 Nov.
Cyrano de Bergerac, b. 6 Mar., d. 28 Jul.
Czerny, Carl, d. 15 Jul.

d'Ache, Caran, see Caran d'Ache
Dacre of Glanton, Lord, b. 15 Jan.
Daguerre, Louis, b. 18 Nov., d. 10 Jul.
Dahl, Arlene, b. 11 Aug.
Dahl, Johan, b. 16 Aug.
Dahlberg, Edward, d. 27 Feb.
Dahrendorf, Ralf, b. 1 May
Daimler, Gottlieb, b. 17 Mar., d. 6 Mar.
Daladier, Édouard, b. 18 Jun., d. 10 Oct.
Dalayrac, Nicolas, b. 13 Jun.

Dalberg, Johann von, b. 17 May
Dale, Jim, b. 15 Aug.
Dalglish, Kenny, b. 4 Mar.
Dallapiccola, Luigi, d. 19 Feb.
Dalrymple, Sir John, d. 8 Jan.
Dalton, Geoffrey, b. 14 Apr.
Dalton, John, b. 6 Sept., d. 22 Jul.
Dalton, Timothy, b. 21 Mar.
Daltrey, Roger, b. 1 Mar.
Daly, Barbara, b. 24 Mar.
Daly, John A., b. 20 Jul.
Damien, Father, b. 3 Jan., d. 15 Apr.
Damone, Vic, b. 12 Jun.
Dampier, William, b. 8 Jun.
Damrosch, Leopold, b. 22 Oct.
Dana, Richard Henry, b. 1 Aug., d. 6 Jan.
Danby, Francis, b. 16 Nov.
Danby, Nicholas, b. 19 Jul.
Dance, Charles, b. 10 Oct.
Daneman, Paul, b. 26 Oct.
Daniell, Thomas, d. 19 Mar.
Daniels, Paul, b. 6 Apr.
Danilova, Alexandra, b. 20 Nov.
Dankworth, John, b. 20 Sept.
Dannay, Frederic, b. 20 Oct., d. 3 Sept.
Dante Alighieri, b. 13 May, d. 14 Sept.
d'Arblay, Madame, *see* Fanny Burney
Darby, Abraham, d. 8 Mar.
Dare, Virginia, b. 18 Aug.
Darewski, Hermann, d. 2 Jun.
Darin, Bobby, d. 20 Dec.
Darío, Rubén, b. 18 Jan.
Darius II, of Persia, d. 12 Dec.
Darlan, Jean, d. 24 Dec.
Darling, Grace, b. 24 Nov.
Darling, William, d. 4 Feb.
Darnley, Lord, d. 10 Feb.
Darrow, Clarence, d. 13 Mar.
Darwin, Charles, b. 12 Feb., d. 19 Apr.
Darwin, Erasmus, b. 12 Dec., d. 18 Apr.
Dassin, Jules, b. 18 Dec.
Daubigny, Charles, d. 19 Feb.
Daudet, Alphonse, b. 13 May, d. 17 Dec.
Daudet, Léon, b. 16 Nov., d. 1 Jul.
Daumier, Honoré, b. 20 Feb., d. 11 Feb.
D'Avenant, Sir William, baptised 3 Mar., d. 7 Apr.
Davenport, Nigel, b. 23 May
David, Félicien, b. 13 Apr., d. 29 Aug.
David, Gerard, d. 13 Aug.

David, Jacques, b. 30 Aug., d. 29 Dec.
David I, of Scots, d. 24 May
Davidson, Alan, b. 30 Mar.
Davidson, Emily, d. 4 Jun.
Davidson, Jim, b. 13 Dec.
Davidson, Jo, b. 30 Mar.
Davidson, Ross, b. 25 Aug.
Davies, Anna, b. 21 Jun.
Davies, Denzil, b. 9 Oct.
Davies, Gareth, b. 29 Sept.
Davies, Geoffrey, b. 15 Dec.
Davies, Gerald, b. 7 Feb.
Davies, Hunter, b. 7 Jan.
Davies, Huw, b. 18 Feb.
Davies, Hywel, b. 4 Dec.
Davies, Laura, b. 10 Oct.
Davies, Lynn, b. 20 May
Davies, Meredith, b. 30 Jul.
Davies, Peter, b. 8 Sept.
Davies, Ryland, b. 9 Feb.
Davies, Walford, b. 6 Sept., d. 11 Mar.
Davies, W.H., b. 3 Jul., d. 26 Sept.
Davies, Windsor, b. 28 Aug.
Davis, Allan, b. 30 Aug.
Davis, Andrew, b. 2 Feb.
Davis, Bette, b. 5 Apr.
Davis, Carl, b. 28 Oct.
Davis, Colin, b. 25 Sept.
Davis, Dwight, b. 5 Jul., d. 28 Nov.
Davis, Fred, b. 14 Aug.
Davis, Jefferson, b. 3 Jun., d. 6 Dec.
Davis, John, d. 29 Dec.
Davis, Miles, b. 25 May
Davis, Richard Harding, b. 18 Apr.
Davis, Rodger, b. 18 May
Davis, Steve, b. 22 Aug.
Davis, Stuart, b. 7 Dec., d. 24 Jun.
Davis, William (editor), b. 6 Mar.
Davis, William M., d. 5 Feb.
Davison, Peter, b. 13 Apr.
Davison, William, d. 23 Dec.
Davy, Humphry, b. 17 Dec., d. 29 May
Dawes, John, b. 29 Sept.
Dawson, Anna, b. 27 Jul.
Dawson, A.R., b. 5 Jun.
Dawson, Walter, b. 6 May
Dawson, Les, b. 2 Feb.
Dawson, Peter, b. 31 Jan., d. 26 Sept.
Dawson, Viscount, b. 9 Mar., d. 7 Mar.
Day, Doris, b. 3 Apr.

Day, Laraine, b. 13 Oct.
Day, Robin, b. 24 Oct.
Day, Thomas, b. 22 Jun., d. 28 Sept.
Day Lewis, Cecil, b. 27 Apr., d. 22 May
Dayan, Moshe, b. 20 May
Dean, Basil, d. 22 Apr.
Dean, Christopher, b. 27 Jul.
Dean, James, b. 8 Feb., d. 30 Sept.
Dean, Percy, d. 20 Mar.
Deane, Henry, Archbishop, d. 16 Feb.
de Bono, Edward, b. 19 May
Debussy, Claude, b. 22 Aug., d. 25 Mar.
Decaë, Henri, b. 31 Jul.
Decamps, Alexandre, b. 3 Mar., d. 22 Aug.
de Cardi, Beatrice, b. 5 Jun.
de Carlo, Yvonne, b. 1 Sept.
Dee, Frances, b. 26 Nov.
Dee, John, b. 13 Jun.
Dee, Ruby, b. 27 Oct.
Deedes, Lord, b. 1 Jun.
Deeley, Michael, b. 6 Aug.
Defoe, Daniel, d. 24 Apr.
DeForest, Lee, b. 26 Aug., d. 30 Jun.
Degas, Edgar, b. 19 Jul., d. 27 Sept.
de Grey, Roger, b. 18 Apr.
de Guingand, Maj.-Gen. Francis, d. 29 Jun.
DeHaven, Gloria, b. 23 Jul.
de Havilland, Olivia, b. 1 Jul.
Dehn, Paul, b. 5 Nov.
Deighton, Len, b. 18 Feb.
de la Billière, Lt.-Gen. Sir Peter, b. 29 Apr.
Delacroix, Eugène, b. 26 Apr., d. 13 Aug.
Delafield, E.M., b. 9 Jun., d. 2 Dec.
de la Mare, Walter, b. 25 Apr., d. 22 Jun.
Delaney, Frank, b. 24 Oct.
Delaroche, Hippolyte, b. 17 Jul., d. 4 Nov.
de la Roche, Mazo, b. 15 Jan., d. 12 Jul.
de la Tour, Frances, b. 30 Jul.
Delaunay, Jules, d. 5 Sept.
Delavigne, Jean, d. 11 Dec.
Delfont, Lord, b. 5 Sept.
Delibes, Léo, b. 21 Feb., d. 16 Jan.
Delius, Frederick, b. 29 Jan., d. 10 Jun.
Dell, Ethel M., b. 2 Aug., d. 17 Sept.
Del Mar, Norman, b. 31 Jul.
Delon, Alain, b. 8 Nov.
Delors, Jacques, b. 20 Jul.

Delraux, Paul, b. 23 Sept.
Deluc, Jean, d. 7 Nov.
Demarco, Richard, b. 9 Jul.
De Mille, Cecil B., b. 12 Aug., d. 21 Jan.
De Mille, William, b. 25 Jun., d. 18 Mar.
de Montfort, Simon, d. 4 Aug.
De Morgan, William, b. 16 Nov., d. 13 Jan.
Dempsey, Jack, b. 24 Jun., d. 31 May
Dempster, Nigel, b. 1 Nov.
Dench, Judi, b. 9 Dec.
Deneuve, Catherine, b. 22 Oct.
Denham, John, d. 10 Mar.
Denham, Maurice, b. 23 Dec.
Denikin, Anton, d. 8 Aug.
De Niro, Robert, b. 17 Aug.
Denison, Michael, b. 1 Nov.
Denness, Mike, b. 1 Dec.
Denning, Lord, b. 23 Jan.
Denning, Richard, b. 27 Mar.
Dennis, C.J., d. 22 Jun.
Dent, J.M., b. 30 Aug., d. 9 May
Denver, John, b. 31 Dec.
de Paul, Lindsey, b. 11 Jun.
de Peyer, Gervase, b. 11 Apr.
De Quincey, Thomas, b. 15 Aug., d. 8 Dec.
Derain, André, d. 8 Sept.
Derby, 14th Earl, b. 29 Mar., d. 23 Oct.
Derek, Bo, b. 20 Dec.
Desai, Shri Morarji, b. 29 Feb.
de Savary, Peter, b. 11 Jul.
Descartes, René, b. 31 Mar., d. 1 Feb.
Desmond, Florence, b. 31 May
de Soto, *see* Hernando de Soto
Desprez, Josquin, d. 27 Aug.
DeSylva, Buddy, b. 27 Jan., d. 11 Jul.
Detaille, Jean, b. 5 Oct., d. 23 Dec.
Deutsch, Andre, b. 15 Nov.
Dev, Kapil, b. 6 Jan.
de Valera, Éamon, b. 14 Oct., d. 29 Aug.
de Valois, Ninette, b. 6 Jun.
Devant, David, d. 13 Oct.
Devlin, Lord, b. 25 Nov.
Devonshire, Alan, b. 13 Apr.
Devonshire, Duke of, b. 2 Jan.
Dewar, James, b. 20 Sept., d. 27 Mar.
Dewey, John, b. 20 Oct.
Dewey, Thomas E., b. 24 Mar.
De Wint, Peter, b. 21 Jan.

Dews, Peter, b. 26 Sept.

Dexter, Ted, b. 15 May

Dhenin, A.M., Sir Geoffrey, b. 2 Apr.

Diabelli, Anton, b. 6 Sept., d. 7 Apr.

Diaghilev, Sergei, b. 19 Mar., d. 19 Aug.

Diamond, Anne, b. 8 Sept.

Diamond, Neil, b. 24 Jan.

Diaz, Narcisse, b. 25 Aug.

Dibdin, Charles, b. 4 Mar., d. 25 Jul.

Dibdin, Thomas, b. 21 Mar., d. 18 Nov.

Dicey, Albert, d. 7 Apr.

Dick, Kay, b. 29 Jul.

Dickens, Charles, b. 7 Feb., d. 9 Jun.

Dickens, Monica, b. 10 May

Dickinson, Angie, b. 30 Sept.

Dickinson, Emily, b. 10 Dec., d. 15 May

Dickinson, Michael, b. 3 Feb.

Dickinson, Patric, b. 26 Dec.

Dickinson, Peter (author), b. 16 Dec.

Dickinson, Peter (composer), b. 15 Nov.

Dickson, Barbara, b. 27 Sept.

Dickson, Carter, *see* John Dickson Carr

Dickson, Jennifer, b. 17 Sept.

Diddley, Bo, b. 20 Dec.

Diderot, Denis, b. 5 Oct., d. 30 Jul.

Diefenbaker, John, b. 18 Sept.

Diemen, Anton van, d. 19 Apr.

Diepenbeeck, Abraham van, b. 9 May

Diesel, Rudolf, b. 18 Mar., d. 29 Sept.

Dietrich, Christian, b. 30 Oct.

Dietrich, Marlene, b. 27 Dec., d. 6 May

Dietz, Howard, b. 8 Sept., d. 30 Jul.

Digby, Everard, d. 30 Jan.

Digby, Kenelm, b. 11 Jul.

Dilke, Charles, d. 10 Aug.

Diller, Phyllis, b. 17 Jul.

Dillinger, John, d. 22 Jul.

Dillman, Bradford, b. 14 Apr.

Dilthey, Wilhelm, d. 1 Oct.

Dimbleby, David, b. 28 Oct.

Dimbleby, Jonathan, b. 31 Jul.

Dimbleby, Richard, d. 22 Dec.

Dindorf, Karl Wilhelm, b. 2 Jan.

Dionne quintuplets, b. 28 May

Dior, Christian, b. 21 Jan., d. 24 Oct.

Dirac, Paul, b. 8 Aug., d. 20 Oct.

Disney, Walt, b. 5 Dec., d. 15 Dec.

Disraeli, Benjamin, b. 21 Dec., d. 19 Apr.

Diss, Eileen, b. 13 May

Distel, Sacha, b. 6 Jan.

Dittersdorf, Karl von, b. 2 Nov., d. 24 Oct.

Diver, Jenny, d. 18 Mar.

Dixon, Adèle, b. 3 Jun.

Díaz, José, d. 2 Jul.

Dobell, Sydney, d. 22 Aug.

Dobell, William, d. 14 May

Dobson, Frank, b. 18 Nov.

Dodd, Ken, b. 8 Nov.

Dodsley, Robert, b. 13 Feb., d. 23 Sept.

Doenitz, Karl, b. 16 Sept., d. 24 Dec.

Dohnányi, Ernö von, b. 27 Jul., d. 11 Feb.

Dolby, Thomas, b. 14 Oct.

Dolci, Carlo, b. 25 May, d. 17 Jan.

Dolin, Anton, b. 27 Jul., d. 25 Nov.

D'Oliveira, Basil, b. 4 Oct.

Dollfuss, Engelbert, b. 4 Oct., d. 25 Jul.

Dolmetsch, Arnold, b. 24 Feb., d. 28 Feb.

Dolmetsch, Carl, b. 23 Aug.

Domagk, Gerhard, b. 30 Oct., d. 24 Apr.

Domenichino, b. 21 Oct., d. 15 Apr.

Domingo, Placido, b. 21 Jan.

Domino, Fats, b. 26 Feb.

Don, George, d. 25 Feb.

Donaldson, David, b. 29 Jun.

Donaldson, Lou, b. 1 Nov.

Donaldson, Mary, b. 29 Aug.

Donaldson, Walter, b. 15 Feb., d. 13 Jun.

Donat, Robert, b. 18 Mar.

Donatello, d. 13 Dec.

Donati, Giovanni, d. 19 Sept.

Donegan, Lonnie, b. 29 Apr.

Donen, Stanley, b. 13 Apr.

Donizetti, Domenico, b. 29 Nov., d. 8 Apr.

Donleavy, James, b. 23 Apr.

Donne, John, d. 31 Mar.

Donovan, Terence, b. 14 Sept.

Doonican, Val, b. 3 Feb.

Doppler, Christian, b. 29 Nov., d. 17 Mar.

Doré, Gustave-Paul, b. 6 Jan., d. 23 Jan.

Doria, Andrea, b. 30 Nov., d. 25 Nov.

Dors, Diana, b. 23 Oct., d. 4 May

Dorsey, Jimmy, b. 29 Feb.

Dorsey, Tommy, b. 19 Nov., d. 26 Nov.

Dos Passos, John, b. 14 Jan., d. 28 Sept.

Dostoevsky, Fyodor, b. 11 Nov., d. 9 Feb.

Dotrice, Karen, b. 9 Nov.

Dotrice, Michele, b. 27 Sept.

Dotrice, Roy, b. 26 May

Doubleday, Frank Nelson, b. 8 Jan., d. 30 Jan.

Dougall, Robert, b. 27 Nov.

Douglas, Angela, b. 29 Oct.

Douglas, Desmond, b. 20 Jul.

Douglas, Henry, d. 14 Feb.

Douglas, Kirk, b. 9 Dec.

Douglas, Lloyd, b. 27 Aug., d. 13 Feb.

Douglas, Lord Alfred, b. 22 Oct., d. 20 Mar.

Douglas, Mary, b. 25 Mar.

Douglas, Michael, b. 25 Sept.

Douglas, Norman, d. 9 Feb.

Douglas-Home, William, b. 3 Jun.

Doumer, Paul, d. 7 May

Douw, Gerhard, b. 7 Apr.

Dowdeswell, Colin, b. 12 May

Dowding, Lord, b. 24 Apr.

Dowell, Anthony, b. 16 Feb.

Dowling, Graham, b. 4 Mar.

Down, Lesley-Anne, b. 17 Mar.

Downes, Terry, b. 9 May

Dowson, Ernest, b. 2 Aug.

Doyle, Arthur Conan, b. 22 May, d. 7 Jul.

Doyle, Richard, d. 11 Dec.

D'Oyly Carte, Richard, b. 3 May, d. 3 Apr.

Drabble, Margaret, b. 5 Jun.

Drabble, Phil, b. 14 May

Draga, of Serbia, d. 11 Jun.

Drake, Charlie, b. 19 Jun.

Drake, Francis, d. 28 Jan.

Drake, Ted, b. 16 Aug.

Draper, Henry, b. 7 Mar.

Draper, Ruth, b. 2 Dec., d. 30 Dec.

Draud, Georg, b. 9 Jan.

Drayton, Michael, d. 23 Dec.

Dreiser, Theodore, b. 27 Aug., d. 28 Dec.

Drew, Jane, b. 24 Mar.

Dreyer, Desmond, b. 6 Apr.

Dreyfus, Alfred, b. 19 Oct., d. 11 Jul.

Dreyfuss, Richard, b. 29 Oct.

Driberg, Tom, b. 22 May

Drinkwater, Carole, b. 22 Apr.

Drinkwater, John, b. 1 Jun., d. 25 Mar.

Drobisch, Moritz, b. 16 Aug.

Drobny, Jaroslav, b. 12 Oct.

Drogheda, Earl of, b. 14 Jan.

Dru, Joanne, b. 31 Jan.

Drummond, William, b. 13 Dec., d. 4 Dec.

Dryden, John, b. 19 Aug., d. 1 May

Dubček, Alexander, b. 27 Nov.

Dubin, Al, b. 10 Jun., d. 11 Feb.

Du Bois, William, b. 23 Feb.

du Cann, Sir Edward, b. 28 May

Duchamp, Marcel, b. 28 Jul., d. 2 Oct.

Duckham, David, b. 28 Jun.

Duffield, George, b. 30 Nov.

Duffy, Maureen, b. 21 Oct.

Duffy, Patrick, b. 17 Mar.

Dufy, Raoul, b. 3 Jun., d. 23 Mar.

Dugdale, William, b. 12 Sept.

Duggan, Willie, b. 12 Mar.

Dukas, Paul, b. 1 Oct., d. 17 May

Duke, Neville, b. 11 Jan.

Dulles, John Foster, b. 25 Feb., d. 24 May

Dulon, Friedrich, b. 14 Aug.

Dumas, Alexandre, *fils*, b. 27 Jul., d. 27 Nov.

Dumas, Alexandre, *père*, b. 24 Jul., d. 5 Dec.

du Maurier, Daphne, b. 13 May

du Maurier, George, b. 6 Mar., d. 6 Oct.

du Maurier, Gerald, b. 26 Mar., d. 11 Apr.

Dummett, Ann, b. 4 Sept.

Dummett, Michael, b. 27 Jun.

Dun, Geordie, b. 18 Oct.

Dunant, Jean-Henri, b. 8 May, d. 30 Oct.

Dunaway, Faye, b. 14 Jan.

Dunbar, Paul, b. 27 Jun.

Duncan, Isadora, b. 27 May, d. 14 Sept.

Duncan, Thomas, d. 25 May

Dundonald, 10th Earl, b. 14 Dec.

Dunham, Joanna, b. 6 May

Dunham, Katherine, b. 22 Jun.

Dunlop, Frank, b. 15 Feb.

Dunlop, John Boyd, b. 5 Feb., d. 23 Oct.

Dunlop, John (trainer), b. 10 Jul.

Dunluce, Viscount, b. 3 Feb.

Dunn, Baroness, b. 29 Feb.

Dunn, Clive, b. 9 Jan.

Dunne, John, d. 24 Aug.

Dunnett, Alastair, b. 26 Dec.

Dunsany, Lord, b. 24 Jul., d. 25 Oct.

Dunstable, John, d. 24 Dec.

Dunstan, Bernard, b. 19 Jan.

Dunwoody, Gwyneth, b. 12 Dec.

Dunwoody, Richard, b. 18 Jan.

Duparc, Marie, d. 12 Feb.

Dupont, Margaret, b. 4 Apr.

du Preez, Frederick, b. 28 Nov.
du Pré, Jacqueline, d. 19 Oct.
Dupré, Jules, d. 6 Oct.
Dupré, Marcel, d. 30 May
Durante, Jimmy, b. 10 Feb., d. 29 Jan.
Duras, Marguerite, b. 4 Apr.
Durbin, Deanna, b. 4 Dec.
Durbridge, Francis, b. 25 Nov.
Dürer, Albrecht, b. 21 May, d. 6 Apr.
D'Urfey, Thomas, d. 26 Feb.
Durham, Judith, b. 3 Jul.
Durie, Jo, b. 27 Jul.
Durr, Frank, b. 10 Nov.
Durrell, Gerald, b. 7 Jan.
Duruflé, Maurice, b. 11 Jan.
Duse, Eleanora, b. 3 Oct., d. 21 Apr.
Duttine, John, b. 15 Mar.
Dutton, Clarence, b. 15 May
Duvalier, François, b. 14 Apr., d. 21 Apr.
Duvall, Robert, b. 5 Jan.
Duveen, 1st Baron, d. 25 May
Dvořák, Antonín, b. 8 Sept., d. 1 May
Dwan, Allan, b. 3 Apr.
Dwight, Timothy, b. 14 May
Dyall, Valentine, d. 24 Jun.
Dyce, William, b. 19 Sept., d. 14 Feb.
Dyck, Anthony van, b. 22 Mar., d. 9 Dec.
Dyer, Charles, b. 7 Jul.
Dyer, Edward, d. 11 May
Dyer, John, d. 24 Jul.
Dylan, Bob, b. 24 May
Dyson, John, b. 11 Jun.
Dyson, Will, d. 21 Jan.

Eakins, Thomas, b. 25 Jul.
Earhart, Amelia, b. 24 Jul., d. 2 Jul.
Earlom, Richard, d. 8 Oct.
East, Alfred, b. 15 Dec., d. 28 Sept.
Easterby, Peter, b. 3 Aug.
Eastlake, Charles, b. 17 Nov., d. 23 Dec.
Eastman, George, b. 12 Jul., d. 14 Mar.
Easton, Sheena, b. 27 Apr.
Eastwood, Clint, b. 31 May
Eban, Abba, b. 2 Feb.
Eberl, Anton, b. 13 Jun.
Ebert, Friedrich, d. 28 Feb.
Ebsen, Buddy, b. 2 Apr.
Eccles, Sir John, b. 27 Jan.
Eccles, Viscount, b. 18 Sept.
Echegaray, José, b. 4 Apr., d. 15 Sept.

Eckener, Hugo, b. 10 Aug.
Eckstine, Billy, b. 8 Jul.
Edberg, Stefan, b. 19 Jan.
Eddington, Arthur, b. 28 Dec., d. 22 Nov.
Eddington, Paul, b. 18 Jun.
Eddison, Robert, b. 10 Jun.
Eddy, Mary Baker, b. 16 Jul., d. 3 Dec.
Eddy, Nelson, b. 29 Jun.
Edelinck, Gerard, b. 20 Oct., d. 2 Apr.
Eden, Anthony, b. 12 Jun., d. 14 Jan.
Edgar, David, b. 26 Feb.
Edgar, Liz, b. 28 May
Edgar, Ted, b. 10 Oct.
Edgeworth, Maria, b. 1 Jan., d. 22 May
Edison, Thomas, b. 11 Feb., d. 18 Oct.
Edmonds, Noel, b. 22 Dec.
Edmund Ironside, of the English, d. 30 Nov.
Edrich, Bill, d. 24 Apr.
Edrich, John, b. 21 Jun.
Edward, St, of the English, d. 18 Mar.
Edward, Prince, b. 10 Mar.
Edward, the Black Prince, b. 15 Jun., d. 8 Jun.
Edward the Confessor, d. 5 Jan.
Edward I, of England, b. 17 Jun., d. 7 Jul.
Edward II, of England, b. 25 Apr., d. 21 Sept.
Edward III, of England, b. 13 Nov., d. 21 Jun.
Edward IV, of England, b. 28 Apr., d. 9 Apr.
Edward V, of England, b. 2 Nov.
Edward VI, of England, b. 12 Oct., d. 6 Jul.
Edward VII, of Great Britain, b. 9 Nov., d. 6 May
Edwards, Bob, b. 26 Oct.
Edwards, Gareth, b. 12 Jul.
Edwards, George, b. 9 Jul.
Edwards, Glynn, b. 2 Feb.
Edwards, John Passmore, b. 24 Mar., d. 22 Apr.
Edwards, Richard, d. 31 Oct.
Edwards, Sam, b. 1 Feb.
Edwards, Tracy, b. 5 Sept.
Eeckhout, Gerbrand van den, b. 19 Aug., d. 22 Oct.
Egan, Peter, b. 28 Sept.
Eggar, Samantha, b. 5 Mar.

Eggar, Timothy, b. 19 Dec.
Ehrenburg, Christian, b. 19 Apr.
Ehrenburg, Ilya, b. 27 Jan., d. 1 Sept.
Ehrlich, Paul, b. 14 Mar., d. 20 Aug.
Eichmann, Adolf, d. 31 May
Eiffel, Gustave, b. 15 Dec., d. 28 Dec.
Eijkman, Christiaan, b. 11 Aug., d. 5 Nov.
Einstein, Albert, b. 14 Mar., d. 18 Apr.
Einthoven, Willem, d. 29 Sept.
Eisenhower, Dwight, b. 14 Oct., d. 28
  Mar.
Eisenhower, Milton, d. 2 May
Eisenstein, Sergei, b. 23 Jan., d. 11 Feb.
Ekberg, Anita, b. 29 Sept.
Ekland, Britt, b. 6 Sept.
El Cid, d. 10 Jul.
Eldon, 1st Earl of, b. 4 Jun.
Eleanor of Aquitaine, d. 1 Apr.
Elen, Gus, b. 22 Jul., d. 17 Feb.
Elgar, Edward, b. 2 Jun., d. 23 Feb.
Eliot, George, b. 22 Nov., d. 22 Dec.
Eliot, John (parliamentarian), b. 11 Apr.,
  d. 27 Nov.
Eliot, T.S., b. 26 Sept., d. 4 Jan.
Elizabeth I, of England, b. 7 Sept., d. 24
  Mar.
Elizabeth II, b. 21 Apr.
Elizabeth, of Romania, b. 29 Dec., d. 2
  Mar.
Elizabeth, of the Belgians, b. 25 Jul.
Elizabeth, Queen Mother, b. 4 Aug.
Elizabeth Petrovna, of Russia, d. 5 Jan.
Ellesmere, Earl of, 1 Jan.
Ellington, Duke, b. 29 Apr., d. 24 May
Elliott, Denholm, b. 31 May
Elliott, Ebenezer, d. 1 Dec.
Ellis, Havelock, b. 2 Feb., d. 8 Jul.
Ellis, Mary, b. 15 Jun.
Ellis, Osian, b. 8 Feb.
Ellis, Peter, b. 30 May
Ellis, Vivian, b. 29 Oct.
Ellis, Wendy, b. 6 Dec.
Ellison, Christopher, b. 16 Dec.
Ellison, Richard, b. 21 Sept.
Ellsworth, Lincoln, b. 12 May
Ellwood, Thomas, d. 1 Mar.
Elphick, Michael, b. 19 Sept.
Eluard, Paul, b. 14 Dec.
Elvin, Violetta, b. 3 Nov.
Elworthy, Lord, b. 23 Mar.

Elyot, Thomas, d. 20 Mar.
Elzevier, Louis, d. 4 Feb.
Emanuel, David, b. 17 Nov.
Emanuel, Elizabeth, b. 5 Jul.
Emburey, John, b. 20 Aug.
Emerson, Keith, b. 2 Nov.
Emerson, Ralph Waldo, b. 25 May, d. 27
  Apr.
Emerson, Roy, b. 3 Nov.
Emery, Dick, d. 2 Jan.
Eminescu, Mihail, d. 15 Jun.
Emmet, Robert, d. 20 Sept.
Emney, Fred, d. 25 Dec.
Empson, William, b. 27 Sept.
Emson, Reginald, b. 11 Jan.
Encke, Johann, d. 2 Sept.
Enderby, John, b. 16 Jan.
Enesco, Georges, b. 19 Aug., d. 4 May
Engel, Karl, b. 6 Jul.
Engels, Friedrich, b. 28 Nov., d. 5 Aug.
Engineer, Farokh, b. 25 Feb.
England, Mike, b. 2 Dec.
Engleheart, George, d. 21 Mar.
English, Arthur, b. 9 May
English, David, b. 26 May
Eno, Brian, b. 15 May
Éon, Chevalier d', b. 5 Oct.
Epstein, Jacob, b. 10 Nov., d. 21 Aug.
Epstein, Jean, d. 2 Apr.
Érard, Sébastien, b. 5 Apr.
Erasmus, Desiderius, b. 27 Oct., d. 12 Jul.
Erastus, Thomas, d. 31 Dec.
Erhard, Ludwig, d. 5 May
Ericsson, John, b. 31 Jul., d. 8 Mar.
Erlanger, Joseph, d. 5 Dec.
Ernst, Max, b. 2 Apr., d. 1 Apr.
Erskine, 1st Baron, d. 17 Nov.
Ervine, St John, b. 28 Dec., d. 24 Jan.
Ervine-Andrews, Harold, b. 29 Jul.
Escoffier, Auguste, b. 28 Oct.
Eshkol, Levi, b. 25 Oct., d. 26 Feb.
Eshley, Norman, b. 30 May
Esser, Heinrich, b. 15 Jul.
Essex, 2nd Earl, b. 10 Nov., d. 25 Feb.
Essex, 3rd Earl, d. 14 Sept.
Essex, David, b. 23 Jul.
Esterhazy, Prince Paul, b. 11 Mar., d. 21
  May
Ettedgui, Joseph, b. 22 Feb.
Etty, William, b. 10 Mar., d. 13 Nov.

Eugene IV, Pope, d. 23 Feb.
Eugénie, Empress, b. 5 May
Euler, Leonhard, d. 18 Sept.
Eurich, Richard, b. 14 Mar.
Euripides, b. 23 Sept.
Eusden, Laurence, d. 27 Sept.
Eusebio, Ferreira da Silva, b. 5 Jan.
Evans, Arthur, b. 8 Jul., d. 11 Jul.
Evans, Barry, b. 18 Jun.
Evans, Caradoc, b. 31 Dec., d. 11 Jan.
Evans, Dale, b. 31 Oct.
Evans, David, b. 14 Jul.
Evans, Edgar, b. 9 Jun.
Evans, Edith, b. 8 Feb., d. 14 Oct.
Evans, Eric, b. 1 Feb.
Evans, Geraint, b. 16 Feb.
Evans, Godfrey, b. 18 Aug.
Evans, Gwynfor, b. 1 Sept.
Evans, Harold, b. 28 Jun.
Evans, Haydn Tudor, b. 20 Jun.
Evans, Oliver, b. 13 Sept., d. 15 Apr.
Evans, Rod, b. 19 Jan.
Evans, Tolchard, d. 12 Mar.
Evdokimova, Eva, b. 1 Dec.
Eve, Trevor, b. 1 Jul.
Evelyn, John, b. 31 Oct., d. 27 Feb.
Everett, Kenny, b. 25 Dec.
Everett, Rupert, b. 29 May
Everly, Don, b. 1 Feb.
Everly, Phil, b. 19 Jan.
Evert, Chris, b. 21 Dec.
Ewing, Juliana Horatia, b. 3 Aug., d. 13 May
Ewing, Maria, b. 27 Mar.
Exton, Clive, b. 11 Apr.
Eyck, Hubert van, d. 18 Sept.
Eyck, Jan van, d. 9 Jul.
Eyre, Edward John, b. 5 Aug., d. 30 Nov.
Eysenck, Hans, b. 4 Mar.
Ezra, Lord, b. 23 Feb.

Fabergé, Peter, b. 30 May
Fabre, Jean-Henri, b. 22 Dec., d. 11 Oct.
Fabricius, Hieronymus, d. 21 May
Fabricius, Johann, b. 11 Nov.
Fabritius, Carel, d. 12 Oct.
Fabyan, Robert, d. 28 Feb.
Faccio, Franco, b. 8 Mar.
Faed, Thomas, d. 17 Aug.
Faglioni, Maria, d. 24 Apr.

Fahrenheit, Gabriel, b. 24 May, d. 16 Sept.
Fairbairn, Nicholas, b. 24 Dec.
Fairbairn, Stephen, d. 16 May
Fairbairn, William, d. 18 Aug.
Fairbanks, Douglas, Jr., b. 9 Dec.
Fairbanks, Douglas, Sr., b. 23 May. d. 12 Dec.
Fairfax, Thomas, b. 17 Jan., d. 12 Nov.
Fairless, Michael, d. 24 Aug.
Faisal, of Saudi Arabia, d. 25 Mar.
Faith, Adam, b. 23 Jun.
Faithfull, Marianne, b. 29 Dec.
Faldo, Nick, b. 18 Jul.
Falk, Peter, b. 16 Sept.
Falkender, Lady, b. 10 Mar.
Falkner, John Meade, b. 8 May, d. 22 Jul.
Falkner, Keith, b. 1 Mar.
Falla, Manuel de, b. 23 Nov., d. 14 Nov.
Fallopius, Gabriel, d. 9 Oct.
Fältskog, Agnetha, b. 5 Apr.
Fame, Georgie, b. 26 Jun.
Fangio, Juan, b. 24 Jun.
Fanshawe, Catherine, b. 6 Jul., d. 17 Apr.
Fantin-Latour, Henri, b. 14 Jan., d. 25 Aug.
Fantoni, Barry, b. 28 Feb.
Faraday, Michael, b. 22 Sept., d. 25 Aug.
Farentino, James, b. 24 Feb.
Fargo, William G., b. 20 May
Farinelli, b. 24 Jan.
Farjeon, Eleanor, b. 13 Feb.
Farjeon, Herbert, b. 5 Mar., d. 3 May
Farman, Henry, b. 26 May
Farnaby, Giles, d. 25 Nov.
Farnese, Alessandro, b. 27 Aug., d. 3 Dec.
Farnol, Jeffrey, d. 9 Aug.
Farnon, Robert, b. 24 Jul.
Farouk I, b. 11 Feb., d. 18 Mar.
Farquhar, George, d. 29 Apr.
Farquharson, Sir Donald, b. 26 Feb.
Farr, Tommy, d. 1 Mar.
Farragut, David, d. 14 Aug.
Farrar, Dean, b. 7 Aug., d. 22 Mar.
Farrar-Hockley, Anthony, b. 8 Apr.
Farrell, Eileen, b. 13 Feb.
Farrow, Mia, b. 9 Feb.
Faulds, Andrew, b. 1 Mar.
Faulkner, Max, b. 29 Jul.
Faulkner, William, b. 25 Sept., d. 6 Jul.
Fauré, Gabriel, b. 12 May, d. 4 Nov.

Faure, Jean-Baptiste, b. 15 Jan.
Fawcett, Farrah, b. 2 Feb.
Fawkes, Guy, d. 31 Jan.
Fawkes, Wally, b. 21 Jun.
Faye, Alice, b. 5 May
Feibusch, Hans, b. 15 Aug.
Feiffer, Jules, b. 26 Jan.
Feilden, Bernard, b. 11 Sept.
Feliciano, José, b. 10 Sept.
Fellini, Federico, b. 20 Jan.
Fénelon, François de, b. 6 Aug., d. 7 Jan.
Fenn, G. Manville, d. 26 Aug.
Fennessy, Edward, b. 17 Jan.
Ferber, Edna, b. 15 Aug., d. 16 Apr.
Ferdinand I, Holy Roman Emperor, b. 10
    Mar.
Ferdinand I, of Castile, d. 24 Jun.
Ferdinand IV, of Castile, d. 7 Sept.
Ferdinand VI, of Spain, b. 23 Sept., d. 10
    Aug.
Ferdinand VII, of Spain, b. 14 Oct.
Ferguson, James, b. 25 Apr., d. 16 Nov.
Ferguson, Samuel, b. 10 Mar., d. 9 Aug.
Fergusson, Robert, b. 5 Sept., d. 16 Oct.
Fermat, Pierre de, b. 17 Aug., d. 12 Jan.
Fermi, Enrico, b. 29 Sept., d. 28 Nov.
Fermor, Patrick Leigh, b. 11 Feb.
Fernandel, d. 26 Feb.
Ferranti, Sebastian de, d. 13 Jan.
Ferrar, Nicholas, d. 4 Dec.
Ferrari, Gaudenzio, d. 31 Jan.
Ferrari, Lodovico, b. 2 Feb., d. 5 Oct.
Ferrer, José, b. 8 Jan., d. 26 Jan.
Ferrer, Mel, b. 25 Aug.
Ferri, Alessandra, b. 6 May
Ferrier, Kathleen, b. 22 Apr., d. 8 Oct.
Ferrigno, Lou, b. 9 Nov.
Ferry, Jules, b. 5 Apr., d. 17 Mar.
Feuchtwanger, Lion, b. 7 Jul., d. 21 Dec.
Feuerbach, Anselm, b. 12 Sept.
Feuerbach, Ludwig, d. 13 Sept.
Feuillère, Edwige, b. 29 Oct.
Feuillet, Octave, d. 29 Dec.
Féval, Paul, b. 27 Sept.
Feydeau, Georges, b. 8 Dec., d. 5 Jun.
Feyder, Jacques, b. 21 Jul., d. 25 May
Ffrangcon-Davies, Gwen, b. 25 Jan., d. 27
    Jan.
Ficino, Marsilio, b. 19 Oct., d. 1 Oct.
Field, John, b. 26 Jul.

Field, Marshall, d. 16 Jan.
Field, Nathan, b. 17 Oct.
Field, Sally, b. 6 Nov.
Field, Shirley Ann, b. 27 Jun.
Fielding, Anthony, b. 22 Nov.
Fielding, Fenella, b. 17 Nov.
Fielding, Henry, b. 22 Apr., d. 8 Oct.
Fielding, Keith, b. 8 Jul.
Fields, Dorothy, b. 15 Jul., d. 28 Mar.
Fields, Gracie, b. 9 Jan., d. 27 Sept.
Fields, W.C., b. 29 Jan., d. 25 Dec.
Fiennes, Ranulph, b. 7 Mar.
Fildes, Luke, b. 18 Oct., d. 27 Feb.
Fillmore, Millard, b. 7 Jan., d. 8 Mar.
Finch, Jon, b. 2 Mar.
Finch, Peter, b. 28 Sept., d. 14 Jan.
Finlay, Frank, b. 6 Aug.
Finnegan, Chris, b. 5 Jun.
Finney, Albert, b. 9 May
Finney, Tom, b. 5 Apr.
Finnissy, Michael, b. 7 Mar.
Finsen, Niels, b. 15 Dec., d. 24 Sept.
Finzi, Gerald, b. 14 Jul., d. 27 Sept.
Fiorentino, Donya, b. 10 Nov.
Firbank, Ann, b. 11 Jan.
Firbank, Ronald, b. 17 Jan., d. 21 May
Firestone, Harvey S., b. 20 Dec.
Firth, Raymond, b. 25th Mar.
Fischer, Bobby, b. 9 Mar.
Fischer-Dieskau, Dietrich, b. 28 May
Fish, Michael. b. 27 Apr.
Fisher, 1st Baron, b. 25 Jan.
Fisher, Carrie, b. 21 Oct.
Fisher, Eddie, b. 10 Aug.
Fisher, Geoffrey, Archbishop, d. 15
    Sept.
Fisher, H.A.L., b. 21 Mar., d. 18 Apr.
Fisher, Juliet, b. 25 Oct.
Fisher, Sylvia, b. 18 Apr.
Fistoulari, Anatole, b. 20 Aug.
Fitch, Richard, b. 2 Jun.
Fittipaldi, Emerson, b. 12 Dec.
FitzGerald, Edward, b. 31 Mar., d. 14 Jun.
Fitzgerald, Ella, b. 25 Apr.
FitzGerald, Garret, b. 9 Feb.
Fitzgerald, Geraldine, b. 24 Nov.
Fitzgerald, Scott, b. 24 Sept., d. 21 Dec.
FitzGibbon, Constantine, d. 23 Mar.
Fitzherbert, Maria, d. 29 Mar.
Fitzroy, Robert, d. 30 Apr.

Fizeau, Armand, b. 23 Sept., d. 18 Sept.

Flack, Roberta, b. 10 Feb.

Flagstad, Kirsten, b. 12 Jul., d. 7 Dec.

Flaherty, Robert, b. 16 Feb., d. 23 Jul.

Flamsteed, John, b. 19 Aug., d. 31 Dec.

Flanagan, Barry, b. 11 Jan.

Flanagan, Bud, d. 20 Oct.

Flanders, Dennis, b. 2 Jul.

Flandin, Gaston, d. 13 Jun.

Flandrin, Hippolyte, b. 23 Mar., d. 21 Mar.

Flaubert, Gustave, b. 12 Dec., d. 8 May

Flavin, Tim, b. 13 Jan.

Flaxman, John, b. 6 Jul., d. 7 Dec.

Flecker, James Elroy, b. 5 Nov., d. 3 Jan.

Fleetwood, Mick, b. 24 Jun.

Fleetwood, Susan, b. 21 Sept.

Fleischer, Richard, b. 8 Dec.

Fleming, Alexander, b. 6 Aug., d. 11 Mar.

Fleming, Ambrose, b. 29 Nov., d. 18 Apr.

Fleming, Ian, b. 28 May, d. 12 Aug.

Fleming, Rhonda, b. 10 Aug.

Fleming, Victor, b. 23 Feb., d. 6 Jan.

Fletcher, Brian, b. 18 May

Fletcher, Cyril, b. 25 Jun.

Fletcher, Graham, b. 9 Jan.

Fletcher, John, d. 29 Aug.

Fletcher, Keith, b. 20 May

Fletcher, Ken, b. 15 Jun.

Flinck, Govaert, b. 25 Jan., d. 22 Feb.

Flinders, Matthew, b. 16 Mar., d. 19 Jul.

Flint, Rachael Heyhoe, b. 11 Jun.

Florey, Howard, b. 24 Sept., d. 21 Feb.

Flotow, Friedrich von, b. 27 Apr., d. 24 Jan.

Flower, Desmond, b. 25 Aug.

Flynn, Errol, b. 20 Jun., d. 14 Oct.

Foch, Ferdinand, b. 2 Oct., d. 20 Mar.

Foch, Nina, b. 20 Apr.

Fogazzaro, Antonio, d. 7 Mar.

Fokine, Michel, b. 26 Apr., d. 22 Aug.

Fokker, Anthony, b. 6 Apr., d. 23 Dec.

Folengo, Teofilo, b. 8 Nov.

Foley, John, d. 27 Aug.

Fonda, Henry, b. 16 May, d. 12 Aug.

Fonda, Jane, b. 21 Dec.

Fonda, Peter, b. 23 Feb.

Fontaine, Joan, b. 22 Oct.

Fontana, Wayne, b. 28 Oct.

Fontane, Theodor, b. 30 Dec., d. 20 Sept.

Fontanne, Lynn, d. 30 Jul.

Fontenelle, Sieur de, d. 9 Jan.

Foot, Lord, b. 17 Feb.

Foot, Michael, b. 23 Jul.

Foot, Paul, b. 8 Nov.

Foote, Samuel, b. 27 Jan., d. 21 Oct.

Forain, Jean, b. 23 Oct.

Forbes, Alastair, b. 2 May

Forbes, Bryan, b. 22 Jul.

Forbes, Edward, b. 12 Feb.

Forbes, Lord, b. 19 Feb.

Forbes, Rosita, b. 16 Jan., d. 30 Jun.

Forbes-Robertson, Johnston, b. 16 Jan., d. 6 Nov.

Ford, Anna, b. 2 Oct.

Ford, Ford Madox, b. 17 Dec., d. 26 Jun.

Ford, Glenn, b. 1 May

Ford, Harrison, b. 13 Jun.

Ford, Henry, b. 30 Jul., d. 7 Apr.

Ford, John (director), b. 1 Feb., d. 31 Aug.

Ford, John (playwright), b. 17 Apr.

Forde, Florrie, d. 18 Apr.

Fordyce, Keith, b. 15 Oct.

Foreman, Carl, d. 26 Jun.

Foreman, George, b. 22 Jan.

Foreman, Michael, b. 21 Mar.

Forester, C.S., b. 27 Aug., d. 2 Apr.

Forman, Milos, b. 18 Feb.

Formby, George, b. 24 May, d. 6 Mar.

Forrest, Patrick, b. 25 Mar.

Forster, E.M., b. 1 Jan., d. 7 Jun.

Forster, Johann Georg, b. 27 Nov., d. 10 Jan.

Forster, Johann Reinhard, b. 22 Oct., d. 9 Dec.

Forster, Margaret, b. 25 May

Forsyth, Bruce, b. 22 Feb.

Forsyth, Frederick, b. 25 Aug.

Forsyth, Michael, b. 16 Oct.

Forsythe, John, b. 29 Jan.

Forte, Lord, b. 26 Nov.

Forte, Rocco, b. 18 Jan.

Fortescue, John, b. 28 Dec., d. 22 Oct.

Förtsch, Johann, b. 14 May

Fortuny, Mariano, d. 21 Nov.

Foscolo, Ugo, b. 26 Jan., d. 10 Sept.

Foss, Lukas, b. 15 Aug.

Foster, Brendan, b. 12 Jan.

Foster, Jodie, b. 19 Nov.

Foster, Peter, b. 2 May
Foster, Stephen, b. 4 Jul., d. 13 Jan.
Fothergill, John, b. 8 Mar.
Foucault, Jean, b. 18 Sept.
Foulis, Andrew, d. 18 Sept.
Fourier, François, d. 10 Oct.
Fourneyron, Benoît, b. 31 Oct., d. 31 Jul.
Fournier, Pierre, d. 8 Oct.
Fouroux, Jacques, b. 24 Jul.
Fou Ts'ong, b. 10 Mar.
Fowlds, Derek, b. 2 Sept.
Fowler, Henry W., b. 10 Mar.
Fowler, Norman, b. 2 Feb.
Fowles, John, b. 31 Mar.
Fox, Charles James, b. 24 Jan., d. 13 Sept.
Fox, Edward, b. 13 Apr.
Fox, George, d. 13 Jan.
Fox, James, b. 19 May
Fox, Jim, b. 19 Sept.
Fox, Robert, b. 24 Mar.
Fox, Samantha, b. 15 Apr.
Fox, William, b. 1 Jan., d. 1 May
Foxe, John, d. 18 Apr.
Foxley-Norris, Christopher, b. 16 Mar.
Foyle, Christina, b. 30 Jan.
Fracastoro, Girolamo, d. 8 Aug.
Fragonard, Jean, b. 5 Apr., d. 22 Aug.
Frame, Janet, b. 28 Aug.
Frampton, Peter, b. 22 Apr.
Françaix, Jean, b. 23 May
France, Anatole, b. 16 Apr., d. 12 Oct.
Francesca, Piero della, d. 12 Oct.
Franciabigio, d. 24 Jan.
Franciosa, Tony, b. 25 Oct.
Francis, Anne, b. 16 Sept.
Francis, Clare, b. 17 Apr.
Francis, Connie, b. 12 Dec.
Francis, Dick, b. 31 Oct.
Francis, John, b. 3 Sept.
Francis, Philip, d. 22 Dec.
Francis, Trevor, b. 19 Apr.
Francis I, of France, d. 31 Mar.
Francis II, Holy Roman Emperor, b. 12 Feb., d. 2 Mar.
Francis II, of Austria, b. 12 Feb.
Francis II, of France, b. 19 Jan.
Francis Xavier, St., b. 7 Apr.
Franck, César, b. 10 Dec., d. 8 Nov.

Francken, Frans, the Younger, b. 6 May, d. 6 May
Franco, Gen., b. 4 Dec., d. 20 Nov.
Francombe, John, b. 13 Dec.
Frank, Anne, b. 12 Jun.
Frank, Ernst, b. 7 Feb.
Frank, Waldo David, d. 9 Jan.
Frankau, Gilbert, b. 21 Apr., d. 4 Nov.
Frankau, Pamela, b. 3 Jan., d. 8 Jun.
Frankel, Benjamin, d. 12 Feb.
Frankl, Peter, b. 2 Oct.
Frankland, Edward, b. 18 Jan., d. 9 Aug.
Franklin, Aretha, b. 25 Mar.
Franklin, Benjamin, b. 17 Jan., d. 17 Apr.
Franklin, Gretchen, b. 7 Jul.
Franklin, John, b. 16 Apr., d. 11 Jun.
Franklyn, William, b. 22 Sept.
Franks, Lord, b. 16 Feb.
Franz Josef I, of Austria, b. 18 Aug., d. 21 Nov.
Fraser, Antonia, b. 27 Aug.
Fraser, Donald, b. 30 Jul.
Fraser, George MacDonald, b. 2 Apr.
Fraser, Ian, b. 18 Dec.
Fraser, John, b. 18 Mar.
Fraser, Malcolm, b. 21 May
Fraser, Neale, b. 3 Oct.
Fraser, Ronald, b. 11 Apr.
Fratini, Gina, b. 22 Sept.
Frayn, Michael, b. 8 Sept.
Frazer, James, b. 1 Jan., d. 7 May
Frazier, Joe, b. 12 Jan.
Frears, Stephen, b. 20 Jun.
Freberg, Stan, b. 7 Aug.
Frederick, Lynne, b. 25 Jul.
Frederick, Pauline, d. 19 Sept.
Frederick I, of Prussia, b. 11 Jul., d. 25 Feb.
Frederick II, Holy Roman Emperor, d. 13 Dec.
Frederick II, of Denmark, d. 4 Apr.
Frederick II, of Prussia, b. 24 Jan., d. 17 Aug.
Frederick III, of Germany, b. 18 Oct., d. 15 Jun.
Frederick VI, of Denmark, d. 3 Dec.
Frederick IX, of Denmark, d. 14 Jan.
Frederick William I, of Prussia, b. 15 Aug.
Fredericks, Roy, b. 11 Nov.

Freed, Arthur, b. 9 Sept.
Freeman, Edward, b. 2 Aug., d. 16 May
Freeman, John, b. 19 Feb.
Freeman, Paul, b. 18 Jan.
Freeman, R. Austin, d. 30 Sept.
Frémont, John C., b. 21 Jan., d. 13 Jun.
French, Dawn, b. 11 Oct.
French, F.M. John, b. 28 Sept., d. 22
   May
French, Harold, b. 23 Apr.
French, Leslie, b. 23 Apr.
Freneau, Philip Morin, b. 2 Jan.
Frere, John Hookham, d. 7 Jan.
Frescobaldi, Girolamo, d. 1 Mar.
Fresnay, Pierre, d. 9 Jan.
Fresnel, Augustin-Jean, b. 10 May
Fretwell, Sir George, b. 21 Mar.
Freud, Clement, b. 24 Apr.
Freud, Lucian, b. 8 Dec.
Freud, Sigmund, b. 6 May, d. 23 Sept.
Freund, Karl, b. 16 Jan., d. 3 May
Friedman, Milton, b. 31 Jul.
Friedrich Wilhelm IV, d. 2 Jan.
Friese-Greene, William, b. 7 Sept., d. 5
   May
Friml, Rudolf, b. 7 Dec., d. 12 Nov.
Frink, Elisabeth, b. 14 Nov.
Frith, William, b. 9 Jan., d. 2 Nov.
Frobisher, Martin, d. 22 Nov.
Fröding, Gustaf, b. 22 Aug., d. 8 Feb.
Froebel, Friedrich, b. 21 Apr.
Fromentin, Eugène, b. 24 Oct., d. 27 Aug.
Frost, David, b. 7 Apr.
Frost, Robert, b. 26 Mar., d. 29 Jan.
Frost, William, d. 4 Jun.
Froude, James Anthony, b. 23 Apr., d. 20
   Oct.
Froude, William, b. 28 Nov., d. 4 May
Fry, C.B., b. 25 Apr., d. 7 Sept.
Fry, Christopher, b. 18 Dec.
Fry, Elizabeth, b. 21 May, d. 12 Oct.
Fry, Margery, d. 21 Apr.
Fry, Roger Eliot, b. 14 Dec., d. 9 Sept.
Fry, Stephen, b. 24 Aug.
Fuad I, of Egypt, d. 28 Apr.
Fuchs, Leonhard, d. 10 May
Fuchs, Vivian, b. 11 Feb.
Fugard, Athol, b. 11 Jun.
Fullerton, Fiona, b. 10 Oct.
Fulton, Robert, b. 14 Nov., d. 24 Feb.

Furlong, Monica, b. 17 Jan.
Furniss, Harry, b. 26 Mar., d. 14 Jan.
Furse, Charles, d. 17 Oct.
Furtwängler, Wilhelm, b. 25 Jan., d. 30
   Nov.
Fuseli, Henry, b. 7 Feb.
Fyffe, Will, d. 14 Dec.

Gabin, Jean, d. 15 Nov.
Gable, Christopher, b. 13 Mar.
Gable, Clark, b. 1 Feb., d. 16 Nov.
Gabor, Zsa Zsa, b. 6 Feb.
Gaboriau, Émile, d. 28 Sept.
Gabriel, Peter, b. 13 Feb.
Gabrieli, Giovanni, d. 12 Aug.
Gade, Niels, d. 21 Dec.
Gagarin, Yuri, b. 9 Mar., d. 27 Mar.
Gainsborough, Thomas, b. 14 May, d. 2
   Aug.
Gaitskell, Hugh, b. 9 Apr., d. 18 Jan.
Galba, Servius Sulpicius, d. 15 Jan.
Gale, Elizabeth, b. 8 Nov.
Galileo, b. 15 Feb., d. 8 Jan.
Gall, Franz Joseph, d. 22 Aug.
Gall, Sandy, b. 1 Oct.
Gallacher, Bernard, b. 9 Feb.
Galland, Antoine, d. 17 Feb.
Gallico, Paul, b. 26 Jul., d. 15 Jul.
Galli-Gurci, Amelita, b. 18 Nov.
Gallup, George, b. 18 Nov., d. 26 Jun.
Galsworthy, John, b. 14 Aug., d. 31 Jan.
Galton, Francis, b. 16 Feb., d. 17 Jan.
Galton, Ray, b. 17 Jul.
Galvani, Luigi, b. 9 Sept., d. 4 Dec.
Galway, James, b. 8 Dec.
Gambetta, Léon, b. 2 Apr., d. 26 Jan.
Gance, Abel, b. 25 Oct.
Gandhi, Indira, b. 19 Nov., d. 31 Oct.
Gandhi, Mohandas, b. 2 Oct., d. 30 Jan.
Gandhi, Rajiv, d. 22 May
Garbo, Greta, b. 18 Sept.
Garden, Graeme, b. 18 Feb.
Gardiner, John Eliot, b. 20 Apr.
Gardiner, Samuel, d. 23 Feb.
Gardiner, Stephen, d. 12 Nov.
Gardner, Andrew, b. 25 Sept.
Gardner, Ava, b. 24 Dec.
Gardner, Edward, b. 10 May
Gardner, Erle Stanley, b. 17 Jul., d. 11
   Mar.

Gardner, John, b. 2 Mar.
Garfield, James, b. 19 Nov., d. 19 Sept.
Garfield, Leon, b. 14 Jul.
Garfunkel, Art, b. 5 Nov.
Garibaldi, Giuseppe, b. 4 Jul., d. 2 Jun.
Garland, Judy, b. 10 Jun., d. 22 Jun.
Garland, Patrick, b. 10 Apr.
Garner, Alan, b. 17 Oct.
Garner, James, b. 7 Apr.
Garner, Joel, b. 16 Dec.
Garnerin, André, b. 31 Jan., d. 18 Aug.
Garnett, David, b. 9 Mar., d. 11 Feb.
Garnett, Richard, d. 13 Apr.
Garnham, Mike, b. 20 Aug.
Garnier, Jean, d. 3 Aug.
Garrett, Betty, b. 23 May
Garrick, David, b. 19 Feb., d. 20 Jan.
Garrity, Freddie, b. 14 Nov.
Garson, Greer, b. 29 Sept.
Garvin, J.L., b. 12 Apr.
Gascoigne, Bamber, b. 24 Jan.
Gascoigne, George, d. 7 Oct.
Gascoigne, William, d. 17 Dec.
Gascoine, Jill, b. 11 Apr.
Gaskell, Elizabeth, b. 29 Sept., d. 12 Nov.
Gaskin, Catherine, b. 2 Apr.
Gassendi, Pierre, d. 24 Oct.
Gatehouse, Sir Robert, b. 30 Jan.
Gatling, Richard, b. 12 Sept., d. 26 Feb.
Gatting, Mike, b. 6 Jun.
Gaudier-Brzeska, Henri, b. 4 Oct., d. 5
   Jun.
Gauermann, Friedrich, b. 20 Sept.
Gauguin, Paul, b. 7 Jun., d. 8 May
Gaulle, Charles de, b. 22 Nov., d. 9 Nov.
Gaunt, John of, d. 3 Feb.
Gauss, Karl, d. 23 Feb.
Gautier, Théophile, b. 31 Aug., d. 23 Oct.
Gaveston, Piers, d. 19 Jun.
Gay, John, b. 30 Jun., d. 4 Dec.
Gay, Noel, b. 15 Jul., d. 3 Mar.
Gay-Lussac, Louis, b. 6 Dec., d. 9 May
Gaynor, Janet, d. 14 Sept.
Gaynor, Mitzi, b. 4 Sept.
Gazzara, Ben, b. 28 Aug.
Geddes, Alexander, d. 26 Feb.
Geddes, Barbara Bel, b. 31 Oct.
Gee, Prunella, b. 17 Feb.
Geeson, Judy, b. 10 Sept.
Geikie, Archibald, b. 28 Dec., d. 10 Nov.

Geikie, Walter, b. 9 Nov., d. 1 Aug.
Geldof, Bob, b. 5 Oct.
Gellert, Christian, d. 13 Dec.
Gellhorn, Peter, b. 24 Oct.
Gemmill, Archie, b. 24 Mar.
Genet, Jean, b. 19 Dec.
Genga, Girolamo, d. 11 Jul.
Genghis Khan, d. 18 Aug.
Genlis, Comtesse de, b. 25 Jan., d. 31 Dec.
Gentleman, David, b. 11 Mar.
Gentry, Bobbie, b. 27 Jul.
Geoffroy Saint-Hilaire, Étienne, b. 15
   Apr., d. 19 Jun.
Geoffrey Saint-Hilaire, Isidore, b. 16
   Dec., d. 10 Nov.
George, Susan, b. 26 Jul.
George I, of Great Britain, b. 28 Mar., d.
   10 Jun.
George I, of the Hellenes, d. 18 Mar.
George II, of Great Britain, b. 10 Nov., d.
   25 Oct.
George III, of Great Britain, b. 4 Jun., d.
   29 Jan.
George IV, of Great Britain, b. 12 Aug.,
   d. 26 Jun.
George V, of Great Britain, b. 3 Jun., d.
   20 Jan.
George VI, of Great Britain, b. 14 Dec., d.
   6 Feb.
George-Brown, Lord, b. 2 Sept., d. 2 Jun.
Gérard, Jean, d. 17 Mar.
Gere, Richard, b. 29 Aug.
Gerhardt, Charles, b. 21 Aug.
Géricault, Théodore, b. 26 Sept., d. 26
   Jan.
German, Edward, b. 17 Feb., d. 11 Nov.
Germany, Jean, b. 25 Feb.
Gérôme, Jean-Léon, d. 12 Jan.
Geronimo, d. 17 Feb.
Gershwin, George, b. 26 Sept., d. 11 Jul.
Gershwin, Ira, b. 6 Dec., d. 17 Aug.
Gerstenberg, Frank, b. 23 Feb.
Gertler, Mark, d. 23 Jun.
Gesner, Konrad von, b. 26 Mar., d. 13
   Dec.
Getty, Jean Paul, b. 15 Dec., d. 6 Jun.
Getty, J. Paul II, b. 7 Sept.
Gevaert, François, b. 31 Jul.
Ghazi, of Iraq, d. 4 Apr.
Ghiberti, Lorenzo, d. 1 Dec.

Ghirlandaio, Domenico, d. 11 Jan.
Giacometti, Alberto, b. 10 Oct., d. 11 Jan.
Gibb, Barry, b. 1 Sept.
Gibb, Maurice and Robin, b. 22 Dec.
Gibberd, Frederick, d. 9 Jan.
Gibbings, Robert, b. 23 Mar.
Gibbon, Edward, b. 27 Apr., d. 16 Jan.
Gibbon, Lewis Grassic, d. 21 Feb.
Gibbons, Grinling, b. 4 Apr., d. 3 Aug.
Gibbons, Orlando, d. 5 Jun.
Gibbons, Stella, b. 5 Jan.
Gibbs, James, b. 23 Dec.
Gibbs, Lance, b. 29 Sept.
Gibbs, Philip, b. 1 May, d. 10 Mar.
Gibbs, Roland, b. 22 Jun.
Gibran, Khalil, b. 6 Jan.
Gibson, Alexander, b. 11 Feb.
Gibson, Charles, b. 14 Sept., d. 23 Dec.
Gibson, John, b. 19 Jun., d. 27 Jan.
Gibson, Richard, d. 23 Jul.
Gibson, William H., d. 16 Jul.
Gide, André, b. 22 Nov., d. 19 Feb.
Gielgud, John, b. 14 Apr.
Gielgud, Maina, b. 14 Jan.
Gieseking, Walter, b. 5 Nov.
Gifford, Josh, b. 3 Aug.
Gifford, William, d. 31 Dec.
Gigli, Beniamino, b. 20 Mar., d. 30 Nov.
Gilbert, Alfred, b. 12 Aug.
Gilbert, Humphrey, d. 9 Sept.
Gilbert, John, d. 6 Oct.
Gilbert, Joseph, b. 15 Jun.
Gilbert, Martin, b. 25 Oct.
Gilbert, W.S., b. 18 Nov., d. 29 May
Giles, Carl, b. 29 Sept.
Gill, Eric, b. 22 Feb., d. 17 Nov.
Gillespie, Dizzy, b. 21 Oct.
Gillette, King C., b. 5 Jan., d. 9 Jul.
Gilliam, Terry, b. 22 Nov.
Gilliatt, Penelope, b. 25th Mar.
Gillott, Joseph, b. 11 Oct., d. 5 Jan.
Gillray, James, b. 13 Aug., d. 1 Jun.
Gilmore, Mary, b. 16 Aug., d. 3 Dec.
Gilmore, Susan, b. 24 Nov.
Gilpin, Bernard, d. 4 Mar.
Gilpin, Sawrey, d. 8 Mar.
Gingell, John, b. 3 Feb.
Gingold, Hermione, b. 9 Dec., d. 24 May
Ginsberg, Allen, b. 3 Jun.
Giordano, Luca, b. 18 Oct.

Giorgione, d. 25 Oct.
Giotto di Bondone, d. 8 Jan.
Gipps, Ruth, b. 20 Feb.
Girard, Stephen, d. 26 Dec.
Giraudoux, Jean, b. 29 Oct., d. 31 Jan.
Girouard, Mark, b. 7 Oct.
Girtin, Thomas, d. 9 Nov.
Giscard d'Estaing, Valéry, b. 2 Feb.
Gish, Dorothy, b. 11 Mar., d. 4 Jun.
Gish, Lillian, b. 14 Oct.
Gissing, George, b. 22 Nov., d. 28 Dec.
Gittings, Robert, b. 1 Feb.
Giuliani, Mauro, b. 27 Jul.
Giulini, Carlo Maria, b. 9 May
Givenchy, Hubert de, b. 21 Feb.
Gladstone, William Ewart, b. 29 Dec., d. 19 May
Gladwyn, Lord, b. 25 Apr.
Glanville, Brian, b. 24 Sept.
Glaser, Paul Michael, b. 25th Mar.
Glasgow, Ellen, d. 20 Nov.
Glazunov, Alexander, b. 21 Mar., d. 21 Mar.
Glen, William, b. 14 Nov.
Glendinning, Victoria, b. 23 Apr.
Glenn, John, b. 18 Jul.
Glidewell, Sir Iain, b. 8 Jun.
Glinka, Mikhail, b. 1 Jun., d. 15 Feb.
Glitter, Gary, b. 8 May
Glock, William, b. 3 May
Gloria von Thurn and Taxis, b. 23 Feb.
Glossop, Peter, b. 6 Jul.
Gloucester, Alice, Duchess of, b. 25 Dec.
Gloucester, Duchess of, b. 20 Jun.
Gloucester, Henry, Duke of, d. 10 Jun.
Gloucester, Prince William of, d. 28 Aug.
Gloucester, Richard, Duke of, b. 26 Aug.
Glover, Brian, b. 2 Apr.
Glover, Jane, b. 13 May
Glover, Julian, b. 27 Mar.
Glubb, John, d. 17 Mar.
Glück, Christoph, d. 15 Nov., b. 2 Jul.
Glyn, Elinor, b. 17 Oct., d. 23 Sept.
Gneisenau, August von, b. 27 Oct.
Gobbi, Tito, b. 24 Oct., d. 5 Mar.
Gobineau, Comte de, b. 14 Jul.
Godard, Benjamin, b. 18 Aug.
Godard, Jean-Luc, b. 3 Dec.
Goddard, Liza, b. 20 Jan.
Goddard, Paulette, b. 3 Jun.

Godden, Rumer, b. 10 Dec.
Godfree, Kitty, b. 7 May
Godfrey, Daniel, b. 4 Sept.
Godunov, Boris, d. 13 Apr.
Godwin, Earl, d. 14 Apr.
Godwin, Mary, b. 27 Apr., d. 10 Sept.
Godwin, William, b. 3 Mar.
Goebbels, Joseph, b. 29 Oct., d. 1 May
Goehr, Alexander, b. 10 Aug.
Goering, Hermann, b. 12 Jan., d. 15 Oct.
Goethals, George W., b. 29 Jun.
Goethe, Johann von, b. 28 Aug., d. 22 Mar.
Gogh, Vincent Van, b. 30 Mar., d. 29 Jul.
Gogol, Nikolai, b. 31 Mar., d. 4 Mar.
Gold, Jack, b. 28 Jun.
Golding, William, b. 19 Sept.
Goldmark, Peter, b. 2 Dec.
Goldoni, Carlo, b. 25 Feb., d. 6 Feb.
Goldsmith, Harvey, b. 4 Mar.
Goldsmith, James, b. 26 Feb.
Goldsmith, Oliver, b. 10 Nov., d. 4 Apr.
Goldsmith, Robert, b. 21 Jun.
Goldwyn, Samuel, b. 27 Aug., d. 31 Jan.
Gollancz, Livia, b. 25 May
Gollancz, Victor, d. 8 Feb.
Gombrich, Ernst, b. 30 Mar.
Gomes, Larry, b. 13 Jun.
Goncharov, Ivan, d. 27 Sept.
Goncourt, Edmond de, b. 26 May, d. 16 Jul.
Goncourt, Jules de, b. 17 Dec., d. 20 Jun.
Góngora, Luis de, b. 11 Jul.
Gonzales, Pancho, b. 9 May
Gooch, Graham, b. 23 Jul.
Goodhew, Duncan, b. 27 May
Goodlad, Alastair, b. 4 Jul.
Goodman, Benny, b. 30 May, d. 13 Jun.
Goodman, Lord, b. 21 Aug.
Goodyear, Charles, b. 29 Dec., d. 1 Jul.
Goolden, Barbara, b. 5 Jun., d. 29 Apr.
Goossens, Eugene, b. 26 May, d. 13 Jun.
Goossens, Marie, b. 11 Aug.
Goossens, Sidonie, b. 19 Sept.
Gorbachev, Mikhail, b. 2 Mar.
Gorchakov, Prince Alexander, d. 1 Mar.
Gordimer, Nadine, b. 20 Nov.
Gordon, Adam Lindsay, b. 19 Oct., d. 24 Jun.

Gordon, Charles George, b. 28 Jan., d. 26 Jan.
Gordon, Hannah, b. 9 Apr.
Gordon, Lord George, b. 26 Dec., d. 1 Nov.
Gordon, Mack, b. 21 Jun., d. 1 Mar.
Gordon, Richard, b. 15 Sept.
Gore, Frederick, b. 8 Nov.
Goring, Marius, b. 23 May
Gorki, Maxim, b. 28 Mar., d. 14 Jun.
Gormé, Eydie, b. 16 Aug.
Gormley, Lord, b. 5 Jul.
Gort, 6th Viscount, b. 10 Jul.
Gorton, John, b. 9 Sept.
Goss, John, b. 27 Dec.
Gosse, Edmund, b. 21 Sept., d. 16 May
Gosse, Philip, d. 23 Aug.
Gossec, François-Joseph, d. 16 Feb.
Gottlieb, Fabian, d. 2 Jan.
Gottwald, Klement, d. 14 Mar.
Goudge, Elizabeth, d. 1 Apr.
Goudy, Frederic, b. 8 Mar., d. 11 May
Gough, 1st Viscount, b. 3 Nov., d. 2 Mar.
Gough, Michael, b. 23 Nov.
Gould, Chester, d. 11 May
Gould, Elliott, b. 29 Aug.
Gould, Francis, b. 2 Dec.
Gould, Ian, b. 19 Aug.
Gould, John, b. 1 Jul.
Gould, Morton, b. 10 Dec.
Gould, Nat, b. 21 Dec., d. 25 Jul.
Gould, Shane, b. 23 Nov.
Gould, Thomas, b. 28 Dec.
Goulet, Robert, b. 26 Nov.
Gounod, Charles, b. 17 Jun., d. 18 Oct.
Gourmont, Rémy de, b. 4 Apr., d. 27 Sept.
Gowrie, Earl of, b. 26 Nov.
Goya, Francisco, b. 30 Mar.
Goyen, Jan van, b. 13 Jan., d. 27 Apr.
Gozzoli, Benozzo, d. 4 Oct.
Grable, Betty, b. 18 Dec., d. 2 Jul.
Grace, Princess, b. 12 Nov., d. 14 Sept.
Grace, W.G., b. 18 Jul., d. 23 Oct.
Grade, Lord, b. 25 Dec.
Graebner, Fritz, b. 4 Mar.
Graf, Steffi, b. 14 Jun.
Graham, Billy, b. 7 Nov.
Graham, Colin, b. 22 Sept.

Graham, Robert Cunninghame, b. 24 May, d. 20 Mar.

Graham, Stephen, d. 19 Mar.

Graham, Thomas, b. 20 Dec., d. 11 Sept.

Graham, Virginia, b. 4 Jul.

Grahame, Kenneth, b. 8 Mar., d. 6 Jul.

Graham-Smith, Francis, b. 25 Apr.

Grainger, Percy, b. 8 Jul., d. 20 Feb.

Granados, Enrique, b. 27 Jul., d. 24 Mar.

Grandi, Dino, d. 21 May

Grandjany, Marcel, b. 3 Sept., d. 24 Feb.

Grandville, d. 17 Mar.

Grandy, John, b. 8 Feb.

Granger, Farley, b. 1 Jul.

Granger, Stewart, b. 6 May

Grant, Anne, b. 21 Feb., d. 7 Nov.

Grant, Cary, b. 18 Jan., d. 30 Nov.

Grant, Francis, d. 5 Oct.

Grant, James, d. 11 Feb.

Grant, John, d. 30 Jan.

Grant, Lee, b. 31 Oct.

Grant, Ulysses S., b. 27 Apr., d. 23 Jul.

Grantham, Leslie, b. 30 Apr.

Grappelli, Stephane, b. 26 Jan.

Grass, Günter, b. 16 Oct.

Grattan, Henry, b. 3 Jul.

Graveney, Tom, b. 16 Jun.

Graves, Lord (Peter Graves), b. 21 Oct.

Graves, Robert, b. 26 Jul., d. 7 Dec.

Gray, Cardinal Gordon, b. 10 Aug.

Gray, Dulcie, b. 20 Nov.

Gray, Elisha, b. 2 Aug., d. 21 Jan.

Gray, Linda Esther (singer), b. 29 May

Gray, Linda (actress), b. 12 Sept.

Gray, Milner, b. 8 Oct.

Gray, Simon, b. 21 Oct.

Gray, Thomas, b. 26 Dec., d. 30 Jul.

Grayson, Kathryn, b. 9 Feb.

Grayson, Larry, b. 31 Aug.

Greaves, Jimmy, b. 20 Feb.

Greco, Buddy, b. 14 Aug.

Greco, El, d. 7 Apr.

Greeley, Horace, b. 3 Feb., d. 29 Nov.

Green, Anthony, b. 30 Sept.

Green, Benny, b. 9 Dec.

Green, Dave 'Boy', b. 2 Jun.

Green, George, d. 31 May

Green, Hughie, b. 2 Feb.

Green, John Richard, b. 12 Dec., d. 7 Mar.

Green, Lucinda, b. 7 Nov.

Greenaway, Kate, b. 17 Mar., d. 6 Nov.

Greenaway, Roger, b. 23 Aug.

Greene, Graham (novelist), b. 2 Oct., d. 3 Apr.

Greene, Graham C., b. 10 Jun.

Greene, Richard, b. 25 Aug., d. 1 Jun.

Greene, Robert, d. 3 Sept.

Greene, Victor, b. 24 Sept.

Greenhill, Basil, b. 26 Feb.

Greenidge, Gordon, b. 1 May

Greenstreet, Sydney, b. 27 Dec., d. 18 Jan.

Greenwood, Joan, d. 2 Mar.

Greenwood, Walter, b. 17 Dec., d. 16 Sept.

Greer, Germaine, b. 29 Jan.

Greeves, Maj.-Gen. Sir Stuart, b. 2 Apr.

Gregory, Edward, b. 19 Apr.

Gregory, James, b. 6 Nov.

Gregory, Lady, b. 15 Mar., d. 22 May

Gregory, Maundy, b. 1 Jul.

Gregory I, St., d. 12 Mar.

Gregory VII, Pope, d. 25 May

Gregory IX, Pope, d. 22 Aug.

Gregory X, Pope, d. 10 Jan.

Gregory XI, Pope, d. 27 Mar.

Gregory XII, Pope, d. 13 Oct.

Gregory XIII, Pope, b. 7 Jan.

Gregory XIV, Pope, b. 11 Feb., d. 15 Oct.

Gregory XV, Pope, b. 9 Jan., d. 8 Jul.

Gregory XVI, Pope, b. 18 Sept., d. 9 Jun.

Greig, Tony, b. 6 Oct.

Grenfell, Joyce, b. 10 Feb., d. 30 Nov.

Gresham, Thomas, d. 21 Nov.

Grétry, André, d. 29 Sept.

Greuze, Jean, b. 21 Aug., d. 21 Mar.

Greville, Fulke, d. 30 Sept.

Grey, Beryl, b. 11 Jun.

Grey, Clifford, b. 5 Jan.

Grey, 2nd Earl, b. 13 Mar., d. 17 Jul.

Grey, Joel, b. 11 Apr.

Grey, Lady Jane, d. 12 Feb.

Grey, Zane, b. 31 Jan., d. 23 Oct.

Grieg, Edvard, b. 15 Jun., d. 4 Sept.

Grierson, John, b. 26 Apr., d. 19 Feb.

Griffith, D.W., b. 22 Jan., d. 23 Jul.

Griffith, Kenneth, b. 12 Oct.

Griffiths, Terry, b. 16 Oct.

Griffiths, Trevor, b. 4 Apr.

Grigson, Geoffrey, b. 2 Mar.

Griller, Sidney, b. 10 Jan.
Grillparzer, Franz, b. 15 Jan., d. 21 Jan.
Grimaldi, Joseph, b. 18 Dec., d. 31 May
Grimm, Frederick von, d. 19 Dec.
Grimm, Jakob, b. 4 Jan., d. 20 Sept.
Grimm, Wilhelm, b. 24 Feb., d. 16 Dec.
Grimond, Lord, b. 29 Jul.
Grindea, Miron, b. 31 Jan.
Gris, Juan, b. 23 Mar.
Grock, b. 10 Jan., d. 14 Jul.
Grofé, Ferde, b. 27 Mar., d. 3 Apr.
Grolier, Jean, d. 22 Oct.
Groom, Simon, b. 12 Aug.
Gropius, Walter, b. 18 May, d. 5 Jul.
Grosseteste, Robert, d. 9 Oct.
Grossmith, George, d. 1 Mar.
Grossmith, George, the Younger, b. 11 May, d. 6 Jun.
Grosz, Georg, b. 26 Jul.
Grote, George, b. 17 Nov., d. 18 Jun.
Grotefend, Georg, b. 9 Jun., d. 15 Dec.
Grotius, Hugo, d. 28 Aug.
Grove, George, b. 13 Aug., d. 28 May
Grove, William, d. 1 Aug.
Groves, Charles, b. 10 Mar.
Gruenberg, Louis, b. 3 Aug.
Gruffydd, Geraint, b. 9 Jun.
Guardi, Francesco, b. 5 Oct.
Guarini, Giovanni, b. 10 Dec., d. 7 Oct.
Guedalla, Philip, b. 12 Mar.
Guercino, b. 8 Jan., d. 22 Dec.
Guericke, Otto von, b. 20 Nov., d. 11 May
Guérin, Maurice de, b. 4 Aug., d. 19 Jul.
Guérin, Pierre, d. 6 Jul.
Guesclin, Bertrand du, d. 13 Jun.
Guest, Douglas, b. 9 May
Guest, George, b. 9 Feb.
Guettard, Jean, b. 22 Sept., d. 6 Jan.
Guevara, Che, b. 14 Jun., d. 9 Oct.
Gugelmin, Mauricio, b. 20 Apr.
Guggenheim, Simon, b. 30 Dec.
Guicciardini, Francesco, b. 6 Mar., d. 22 May
Guillaume, Robert, b. 30 Nov.
Guillem, Sylvie, b. 23 Feb.
Guillotin, Joseph, b. 28 May
Guinness, Alec, b. 2 Apr.
Guinness, Brian, b. 27 Oct.
Guise, 3rd Duc de, d. 23 Dec.
Guise, Francis, Duc de, d. 24 Feb.

Guitry, Lucien, b. 13 Dec., d. 1 Jun.
Guitry, Sacha, b. 21 Feb., d. 24 Jul.
Guizot, François, b. 4 Oct., d. 12 Oct.
Gulbenkian, Nubar, b. 2 Jun., d. 10 Jan.
Gully, John, d. 9 Mar.
Gummer, John Selwyn, b. 26 Nov.
Gunn, Neil, b. 8 Nov., d. 17 Jan.
Gunn, Thom, b. 29 Aug.
Gunter, Edmund, d. 10 Dec.
Gunter, John, b. 31 Oct.
Gunther, John, b. 30 Aug., d. 1 Jun.
Gustav II, of Sweden, b. 9 Dec., d. 6 Nov.
Gustav III, of Sweden, b. 24 Jan.
Gustav IV, of Sweden, d. 7 Feb.
Gustav V, of Sweden, b. 16 Jun., d. 29 Oct.
Gustav VI, of Sweden, b. 11 Nov., d. 15 Sept.
Guthrie, James, d. 6 Sept.
Guthrie, Woody, b. 14 Jul., d. 3 Oct.
Gutteridge, Lucy, b. 28 Nov.
Guy, Thomas, d. 17 Dec.
Guyler, Deryck, b. 29 Apr.
Gwyn, Nell, b. 2 Feb., d. 14 Nov.
Gwynn, Stephen, d. 11 Jun.
Gyngell, Bruce, b. 8 Jul.

Haakon IV, of Norway, d. 15 Dec.
Haakon VII, of Norway, b. 3 Aug., d. 21 Sept.
Habakkuk, John, b. 13 May
Habgood, John, b. 23 Jun.
Habington, William, b. 4 Nov., d. 30 Nov.
Hachette, Louis, b. 5 May, d. 31 Jul.
Hacker, Alan, b. 30 Sept.
Hackett, Buddy, b. 31 Aug.
Hackett, John, b. 5 Nov.
Hackman, Gene, b. 30 Jan.
Hackney, Rod, b. 3 Mar.
Hadfield, John, b. 16 Jun.
Hadfield, Robert, d. 30 Sept.
Hadlee, Richard, b. 3 Jul.
Hadley, John, d. 14 Feb.
Hadow, William, b. 27 Dec., d. 8 Apr.
Hadrian, b. 24 Jan., d. 10 Jul.
Hadrian IV, Pope, d. 1 Sept.
Haeckel, Ernst, b. 16 Feb., d. 9 Aug.
Haendel, Ida, b. 15 Dec.
Haggard, H. Rider, b. 22 Jun., d. 14 May
Hagman, Larry, b. 21 Sept.

Hahn, Otto, b. 8 Mar., d. 28 Jul.

Hahn, Reynaldo, b. 9 Aug.

Hahnemann, Samuel, b. 10 Apr., d. 2 Jul.

Haig, 1st Earl, b. 19 Jun., d. 29 Jan.

Haig, 2nd Earl, b. 15 Mar.

Haigh, John George, d. 6 Aug.

Hailey, Arthur, b. 5 Apr.

Hailsham, 1st Viscount, b. 28 Feb.

Hailsham, Lord, b. 9 Oct.

Hailwood, Mike, d. 23 Mar.

Haitink, Bernard, b. 4 Mar.

Hake, Thomas, b. 10 Mar.

Hakluyt, Richard, d. 23 Nov.

Haldane, 1st Viscount, b. 30 Jul., d. 19
    Aug.

Haldane, J.B.S., b. 5 Nov., d. 1 Dec.

Hale, Barbara, b. 18 Apr.

Hale, Binnie, d. 10 Jan.

Hale, Edward Everett, b. 3 Apr.

Hale, George E., b. 29 Jun., d. 21 Feb.

Hale, Georgina, b. 4 Aug.

Hale, Kathleen, b. 24 May

Hale, Nathan, d. 22 Sept.

Hales, Stephen, b. 7 Sept.

Halévy, Fromental, b. 27 May

Haley, Bill, d. 9 Feb.

Halifax, 1st Earl, d. 23 Dec.

Hall, Basil, b. 31 Dec.

Hall, Charles, b. 6 Dec., d. 27 Dec.

Hall, Edward Marshall, d. 24 Feb.

Hall, Henry, d. 28 Oct.

Hall, James, b. 12 Sept., d. 7 Aug.

Hall, Margaret, b. 22 Jan.

Hall, Marguerite, b. 12 Aug., d. 7 Oct.

Hall, Marshall, b. 16 Sept., d. 11 Aug.

Hall, Peter, b. 22 Nov.

Hall, Stuart, b. 25 Dec.

Hall, Wesley, b. 12 Sept.

Hall, Willis, b. 6 Apr.

Hallam, Arthur Henry, d. 15 Sept.

Hallam, Henry, b. 9 Jul., d. 21 Jan.

Hallé, Charles, b. 11 Apr., d. 25 Oct.

Hallé, Lady, b. 29 Mar.

Haller, Albrecht von, d. 12 Dec.

Haller, Victor von, b. 16 Oct.

Halley, Edmond, b. 8 Nov., d. 14 Jan.

Halliburton, Richard, d. 23 Mar.

Hallowes, Odette, b. 28 Apr.

Hals, Dirck, b. 17 Mar.

Hals, Frans, d. 26 Aug.

Halsbury, Earl of, b. 4 Jun.

Hamer, Robert, b. 31 Mar.

Hamerton, Philip, b. 10 Sept., d. 4 Nov.

Hamill, Desmond, b. 2 Nov.

Hamilton, Alexander, b. 11 Jan., d. 12 Jul.

Hamilton, David, b. 10 Sept.

Hamilton, Elizabeth, b. 21 Jul., d. 23 Jul.

Hamilton, George (actor), b. 12 Aug.

Hamilton, George (singer), b. 19 Jul.

Hamilton, Hamish, b. 15 Nov., d. 24 May

Hamilton, Iain, b. 6 Jun.

Hamilton, Lady, b. 12 May, d. 15 Jan.

Hamilton, Margaret, d. 17 May

Hamilton, Mary, b. 8 Jul.

Hamilton, Patrick, d. 29 Feb.

Hamilton, Richard, b. 24 Feb.

Hamilton, William (astronomer), d. 2
    Sept.

Hamilton, William (former MP), b. 26 Jun.

Hamilton, William (poet), d. 25 Mar.

Hamlisch, Marvin, b. 2 Jun.

Hamlyn, Paul, b. 12 Feb.

Hammarskjöld, Dag, d. 18 Sept.

Hammarskjöld, Hjalmar, b. 29 Jul.

Hammersley-Parker, Jill, b. 6 Dec.

Hammerstein, Oscar, II, b. 12 Jul., d. 23
    Aug.

Hammerton, John, d. 12 May

Hammett, Dashiell, b. 27 May, d. 10 Jan.

Hammond, Joan, b. 24 May

Hammond, Walter, b. 19 Jun.

Hammond-Stroud, Derek, b. 10 Jan.

Hamnett, Katharine, b. 16 Aug.

Hampden, John, d. 24 Jun.

Hampshire, Susan, b. 12 May

Hampson, Frank, b. 21 Dec., d. 8 Jul.

Hampton, Christopher, b. 26 Jan.

Hampton, Lionel, b. 12 Apr.

Hamsun, Knut, b. 4 Aug., d. 19 Feb.

Han Suyin, b. 12 Sept.

Hanbury-Tennison, Robin, b. 7 May

Hancock, Sheila, b. 22 Feb.

Hancock, Valston, b. 31 May

Handel, George Frederick, b. 23 Feb., d.
    14 Apr.

Händl, Jakob, d. 31 Jul.

Hands, Terry, b. 9 Jan.

Handy, W.C., b. 16 Nov., d. 28 Mar.

Hanley, James, b. 3 Sept., d. 11 Nov.

Hanley, Jenny, b. 15 Aug.

Hanley, Jeremy, b. 17 Nov.
Hannington, James, b. 3 Sept.
Hanrahan, Brian, b. 22 Mar.
Hansard, Luke, b. 5 Jul., d. 29 Oct.
Hanslick, Eduard, b. 11 Sept.
Hansom, Joseph, b. 26 Oct., d. 29 Jun.
Hanson, Lord, b. 20 Jan.
Harald V, of Norway, b. 21 Feb.
Harbach, Otto, b. 18 Aug., d. 24 Jan.
Harburg, E.Y., b. 8 Apr., d. 5 Mar.
Hardie, Keir, b. 15 Aug., d. 26 Sept.
Hardin, Charles, b. 7 Sept.
Harding, Gilbert, b. 5 Jun.
Harding, Peter, b. 2 Dec.
Harding, Roy, b. 3 Jan.
Harding, Warren, b. 2 Nov., d. 2 Aug.
Hardinge, 1st Viscount, 24 Sept.
Hardy, Françoise, b. 17 Jan.
Hardy, Oliver, b. 18 Jan., d. 7 Aug.
Hardy, Robert, b. 29 Oct.
Hardy, Thomas (adm.), d. 20 Sept.
Hardy, Thomas (author), b. 2 Jun., d. 11
  Jan.
Hare, David, b. 5 Jun.
Hare, Robertson, b. 17 Dec., d. 25 Jan.
Harewood, Earl of, b. 7 Feb.
Hargreaves, James, d. 22 Apr.
Harington, Charles, b. 5 May
Harington, John, d. 20 Nov.
Harley, Robert, b. 5 Dec.
Harlow, Jean, b. 3 Mar., d. 7 Jun.
Harman, Harriet, b. 30 Jul.
Harman, Jeremiah, b. 13 Apr.
Harold, of the English, d. 14 Oct.
Harold Harefoot, King, d. 17 Mar.
Haroun-al-Raschid, d. 24 Mar.
Harper, Gerald, b. 15 Feb.
Harper, Heather, b. 8 May
Harper, Roy, b. 12 Jun.
Harpignies, Henri, b. 28 Jul., d. 25 Aug.
Harpley, Sydney, b. 19 Apr.
Harraden, Beatrice, b. 24 Jan., d. 5 May
Harries, Richard, b. 2 Jun.
Harriman, Averell, b. 15 Nov.
Harrington, James, b. 7 Jan., d. 11 Sept.
Harris, Anita, b. 3 Jun.
Harris, Arthur, b. 13 Apr., d. 5 Apr.
Harris, Frank, b. 14 Feb., d. 26 Aug.
Harris, Ian, b. 7 Jul.
Harris, Joel Chandler, b. 9 Dec., d. 3 Jul.

Harris, John, b. 13 Feb.
Harris, Julie, b. 2 Dec.
Harris, Phil, b. 24 Jun.
Harris, Richard, b. 1 Oct.
Harris, Robert, b. 28 Mar.
Harris, Rolf, b. 30 Mar.
Harris, Rosemary, b. 19 Sept.
Harris, Roy, d. 1 Oct.
Harris, Wilson, b. 24 Mar.
Harrison, Benjamin, b. 20 Aug., d. 13
  Mar.
Harrison, George, b. 25 Feb.
Harrison, Jane, b. 9 Sept., d. 5 Apr.
Harrison, John, d. 24 Mar.
Harrison, Kathleen, b. 23 Feb.
Harrison, Rex, b. 5 Mar., d. 2 Jun.
Harrison, William, d. 4 Apr.
Hart, Baroness, b. 18 Sept.
Hart, Lorenz, b. 2 May, d. 22 Nov.
Hart, Moss, b. 24 Oct., d. 20 Dec.
Hart, William, d. 17 Jun.
Hart-Davis, Rupert, b. 28 Aug.
Harte, Bret, b. 25 Aug., d. 5 May
Hartley, David, d. 19 Dec.
Hartley, L.P., b. 30 Dec.
Hartmann, Johann, b. 14 May
Hartnell, Norman, d. 8 Jun.
Hartog, Edouard de, b. 15 Aug.
Harty, Hamilton, b. 4 Dec., d. 19 Feb.
Harvard, John, b. 29 Nov.
Harvey, George, d. 22 Jan.
Harvey, Laurence, b. 1 Oct.
Harvey, Neil, b. 8 Oct.
Harvey, William, b. 1 Apr., d. 3 Jun.
Harvey-Jones, John, b. 16 Apr.
Harwood, Guy, b. 10 Jun.
Harwood, Gwen, b. 8 Jun.
Harwood, Ronald, b. 9 Nov.
Hašek, Jaroslav, b. 30 Apr., d. 3 Jan.
Hassall, Christopher, b. 24 Mar.
Hassett, Lindsay, b. 28 Aug.
Hastings, Charles, d. 30 Jul.
Hastings, Max, b. 28 Dec.
Hastings, Michael, b. 2 Sept.
Hastings, Patrick, b. 17 Mar., d. 26
  Feb.
Hastings, Warren, b. 6 Dec., d. 22 Aug.
Hatch, Tony, b. 30 Jun.
Hatchard, John, d. 21 Jun.
Hathaway, Anne, d. 6 Aug.

Hathaway, Henry, b. 13 Mar., d. 12 Feb.
Hattersley, Roy, b. 28 Dec.
Hatton, Christopher, d. 20 Nov.
Hatton, John, b. 12 Oct.
Haughey, Charles, b. 16 Sept.
Hauptmann, Bruno, d. 3 Apr.
Hauptmann, Gerhart, b. 15 Nov.
Hauser, Frank, b. 1 Aug.
Haussmann, Georges, b. 27 Mar., d. 11 Jan.
Havelock, Henry, d. 24 Nov.
Havelock-Allan, Anthony, b. 28 Feb.
Haver, June, b. 10 Jun.
Havers, Nigel, b. 6 Nov.
Havoc, June, b. 8 Nov.
Hawke, 1st Baron, d. 17 Oct.
Hawke, Robert, b. 9 Dec.
Hawker, Robert, b. 3 Dec.
Hawkes, Christopher, b. 5 Jun.
Hawkes, Jacquetta, b. 5 Aug.
Hawking, Stephen, b. 8 Jan.
Hawkins, Jack, b. 14 Sept., d. 18 Jul.
Hawkins, John (magistrate), b. 30 Mar.
Hawkins, John (seaman), d. 12 Nov.
Hawks, Howard, b. 30 May
Hawksmoor, Nicholas, d. 25th Mar.
Hawn, Goldie, b. 21 Nov.
Hawthorne, Nathaniel, b. 4 Jul., d. 19 May
Hawthorne, Nigel, b. 5 Apr.
Haw-Haw, Lord, d. 3 Jan.
Hay, Ian, b. 17 Apr.
Hayden, William, b. 23 Jan.
Haydn, Franz Joseph, b. 31 Mar., d. 31 May
Haydn, Joseph (lexicographer), d. 18 Jan.
Hayek, Friedrich, b. 8 May, d. 23 Mar.
Hayes, Brian, b. 17 Dec.
Hayes, Colin, b. 17 Nov.
Hayes, Helen, b. 10 Oct.
Hayes, John, b. 21 Jan.
Hayes, Patricia, b. 22 Dec.
Hayes, Rutherford, b. 4 Oct.
Hayley, William, b. 29 Oct., d. 12 Nov.
Hayman, Francis, d. 2 Feb.
Haynes, Johnny, b. 17 Oct.
Hayter, George, b. 17 Dec., d. 18 Jan.
Hayter, William, b. 1 Aug.
Hayward, Eliza, novelist, d. 25 Feb.
Hayward, Louis, d. 21 Feb.
Hayward, Susan, b. 30 Jun.

Hayward, Tom, d. 19 Jul.
Hayworth, Rita, b. 17 Oct., d. 15 May
Hazlitt, William, b. 10 Apr., d. 18 Sept.
Healey, Denis, b. 30 Aug.
Heaney, Seamus, b. 13 Apr.
Hearn, Lafcadio, d. 26 Sept.
Hearst, William Randolph, b. 29 Apr., d. 14 Aug.
Hearst, William Randolph, Jr., b. 27 Jan.
Heath, Edward, b. 9 Jul.
Heath, Ted (musician), d. 18 Nov.
Heath-Stubbs, John, b. 9 Jul.
Heaviside, Oliver, b. 18 May, d. 3 Feb.
Heber, Reginald, b. 21 Apr.
Hedges, Anthony, b. 5 Mar.
Hedin, Sven, b. 19 Feb.
Heem, Cornelis de, b. 8 Apr., d. 17 May
Heenan, Cardinal, d. 7 Nov.
Hefti, Neal, b. 29 Oct.
Hegel, Georg, b. 27 Aug., d. 14 Nov.
Heidegger, Martin, b. 26 Sept.
Heifetz, Jascha, d. 10 Dec.
Heilbron, Rose, b. 19 Aug.
Heine, Heinrich, b. 13 Dec., d. 17 Feb.
Heinemann, William, b. 18 May, d. 5 Oct.
Heiney, Paul, b. 20 Apr.
Heinz, H.J., b. 11 Oct., d. 14 May
Heinze, Sir Bernard, b. 1 Jul.
Heisenberg, Werner, b. 5 Dec.
Heller, Joseph, b. 1 May
Hellman, Lillian, d. 30 Jun.
Helmont, Jean van, b. 12 Jan., d. 30 Dec.
Helpmann, Robert, b. 9 Apr., d. 28 Sept.
Helvetius, Claude, b. 26 Jan., d. 26 Dec.
Hely-Hutchinson, Victor, d. 11 Mar.
Hemans, Felicia, b. 25 Sept., d. 16 May
Hemery, David, b. 18 Jul.
Hemingway, Ernest, b. 21 Jul., d. 2 Jul.
Hemmings, David, b. 18 Nov.
Hemmings, Eddie, b. 20 Feb.
Hempel, Anouska, b. 13 Dec.
Henderson, Arthur, b. 13 Sept., d. 20 Oct.
Henderson, Don, b. 10 Nov.
Henderson, Ray, b. 1 Dec., d. 31 Dec.
Hendren, 'Patsy', b. 5 Feb.
Hendrick, Mike, b. 22 Oct.
Hendry, Stephen, b. 13 Jan.
Henie, Sonja, b. 8 Apr., d. 12 Oct.
Henley, W.E., b. 23 Aug., d. 11 Jul.
Henreid, Paul, b. 10 Jan., d. 29 Mar.

Henry, Joseph, b. 17 Dec.
Henry, Lenny, b. 29 Aug.
Henry, O., b. 11 Sept., d. 5 Jun.
Henry, Patrick, b. 29 May, d. 6 Jun.
Henry I, of England, d. 1 Dec.
Henry I, of France, d. 4 Aug.
Henry II, of England, b. 25 Mar., d. 6 Jul.
Henry II, of France, d. 10 Jul.
Henry III, of England, b. 1 Oct., d. 16 Nov.
Henry III, of France, d. 22 Jul.
Henry IV, of England, b. 3 Apr., d. 20 Mar.
Henry IV, of France, b. 14 Dec., d. 14 May
Henry V, of England, b. 16 Sept., d. 31 Aug.
Henry VI, of England, d. 21 May
Henry VII, of England, b. 28 Jan., d. 21 Apr.
Henry VIII, of England, b. 28 Jun., d. 28 Jan.
Henry the Fowler, of Germany, d. 2 Jul.
Henry the Navigator, b. 4 Mar., d. 13 Nov.
Henson, Leslie, b. 2 Aug.
Henson, Nicky, b. 12 May
Henty, G.A., b. 8 Dec., d. 16 Nov.
Henze, Hans Werner, b. 1 Jul.
Hepburn, Audrey, b. 4 May
Hepburn, Katharine, b. 9 Nov.
Hepple, Norman, b. 18 May
Hepton, Bernard, b. 19 Oct.
Hepworth, Barbara, b. 10 Jan., d. 20 May
Herbert, 1st Baron, b. 3 Mar., d. 20 Aug.
Herbert, A.P., b. 24 Sept., d. 11 Nov.
Herbert, George, d. 1 Mar.
Herbert, Victor, b. 1 Feb., d. 26 May
Herbert, Wally, b. 24 Oct.
Herbison, Margaret, b. 11 Mar.
Herder, Johann von, b. 25 Aug., d. 18 Dec.
Hergesheimer, Joseph, d. 25 Apr.
Hering, Karl, b. 2 Sept.
Heriot, George, b. 15 Jun., d. 12 Feb.
Herkomer, Hubert von, d. 31 Mar.
Herlie, Eileen, b. 8 Mar.
Herman, Woody, b. 16 May
Hern, Dick, b. 20 Jan.
Hérold, Louis, d. 19 Jan.
Heron, Patrick, b. 30 Jan.

Herrick, Robert, b. 24 Aug.
Herries, Lady, b. 12 Jun.
Herriot, Édouard, b. 5 Jul., d. 26 Mar.
Herriot, James, b. 3 Oct.
Herschel, Caroline, b. 16 Mar., d. 9 Jan.
Herschel, John, b. 7 Mar., d. 11 May
Herschel, William, b. 15 Nov., d. 25 Aug.
Hersey, John, b. 17 Jun.
Hershey, Milton, b. 13 Sept.
Hertz, Heinrich, d. 1 Jan.
Hertzog, James, b. 3 Apr.
Hervé, b. 30 Jun.
Herzl, Theodor, b. 2 May, d. 3 Jul.
Herzog, Chaim, b. 17 Sept.
Heseltine, Michael, b. 21 Mar.
Hess, Heinrich von, b. 19 Apr.
Hess, Karl, d. 3 Jul.
Hess, Myra, b. 25 Feb., d. 25 Nov.
Hess, Peter von, b. 29 Jul.
Hess, Rudolf, b. 26 Apr., d. 17 Aug.
Hessayon, David, b. 13 Feb.
Hesse, Hermann, b. 2 Jul., d. 9 Aug.
Heston, Charlton, b. 4 Oct.
Hetherington, Alastair, b. 31 Oct.
Hewish, Antony, b. 11 May
Hewlett, Maurice, b. 22 Jan., d. 15 Jun.
Heydrich, Reinhard, d. 31 May
Heyer, Georgette, b. 16 Aug., d. 5 Jul.
Heyerdahl, Thor, b. 6 Oct.
Heylin, Peter, b. 29 Nov.
Heymans, Corneille, b. 28 Mar.
Heyward, DuBose, b. 31 Aug., d. 16 Jun.
Hibbert, Jack, b. 14 Feb.
Hickok, 'Wild Bill', b. 27 May, d. 2 Aug.
Hickox, Richard, b. 5 Mar.
Hicks, David, b. 25th Mar.
Hicks, Seymour, b. 30 Jan.
Hickson, Joan, b. 5 Aug.
Hide, Edward, b. 12 Apr.
Higden, Ranulf, d. 12 Mar.
Higgins, Alex, b. 18 Mar.
Higgins, Jack, b. 27 Jul.
Higgins, Terence, b. 18 Jan.
Highsmith, Patricia, b. 19 Jan.
Hildebrand, Theodor, b. 2 Jul.
Hildegarde, b. 1 Feb.
Hilder, Rowland, b. 28 Jun.
Hill, Benny, b. 21 Jan., d. 18 Apr.
Hill, Bernard, b. 17 Dec.

411

Hill, Graham, b. 15 Feb., d. 29 Nov.
Hill, Jimmy, b. 22 Jul.
Hill, Octavia, b. 3 Dec.
Hill, Polly, b. 10 Jun.
Hill, Rose, b. 5 Jun.
Hill, Rowland, Viscount, b. 11 Aug.
Hill, Rowland (post pioneer), b. 3 Dec., d. 27 Aug.
Hill, Susan, b. 5 Feb.
Hill, Thomas, d. 20 Dec.
Hill, Vince, b. 16 Apr.
Hillary, Edmund, b. 20 Jul.
Hiller, Ferdinand von, b. 24 Oct.
Hiller, Wendy, b. 15 Aug.
Hill-Norton, Lord, b. 8 Feb.
Hillyarde, Nicholas, d. 7 Jan.
Hilton, Conrad, b. 25 Dec., d. 2 Jan.
Hilton, James, b. 9 Sept., d. 20 Dec.
Hilton, John, b. 25 Jun.
Himmler, Heinrich, b. 7 Oct., d. 23 May
Hinault, Bernard, b. 14 Nov.
Hindemith, Paul, b. 16 Nov., d. 28 Dec.
Hindenburg, Paul von, b. 2 Oct., d. 2 Aug.
Hindley, Jeremy, b. 24 Dec.
Hines, Earl, b. 28 Dec.
Hines, Ronald, b. 20 Jun.
Hipwood, Julian, b. 23 Jun.
Hird, Thora, b. 28 May
Hiroshige, Ando, d. 12 Oct.
Hirsch, Peter, b. 16 Jan.
Hirschbach, Hermann, b. 29 Feb.
Hitchcock, Alfred, b. 13 Aug., d. 29 Apr.
Hitler, Adolf, b. 20 Apr., d. 30 Apr.
Hoad, Lew, b. 23 Nov.
Hoadley, Benjamin, b. 14 Nov.
Hoadly, John, d. 16 Mar.
Hoban, Russell, b. 4 Feb.
Hobbema, Meyndert, b. 31 Oct., d. 7 Dec.
Hobbes, Thomas, b. 5 Apr., d. 4 Dec.
Hobbs, Anne, b. 21 Aug.
Hobbs, Jack, b. 16 Dec., d. 21 Dec.
Hobbs, Michael, b. 28 Feb.
Hobday, Peter, b. 16 Feb.
Hobson, Harold, b. 4 Aug.
Hobson, John, d. 1 Apr.
Hobson, Valerie, b. 14 Apr.
Hochhauser, Victor, b. 27 Mar.
Ho Chi Minh, b. 19 May, d. 3 Sept.
Hocking, Joseph, b. 7 Nov.
Hocking, Silas K., b. 24 Mar.

Hockney, David, b. 9 Jul.
Hoddinott, Alun, b. 11 Aug.
Hoddle, Glen, b. 27 Oct.
Hodge, Patricia, b. 29 Sept.
Hodgkin, Alan, b. 5 Feb.
Hodgkin, Dorothy, b. 12 May
Hodgkin, Howard, b. 6 Aug.
Hodgkins, Frances, b. 28 Apr., d. 13 May
Hodgson, Alfreda, b. 7 Jun., d. 16 Apr.
Hodgson, Ralph, b. 9 Sept., d. 3 Nov.
Hoe, Richard, b. 12 Sept., d. 7 Jun.
Hofer, Andreas, b. 22 Nov., d. 20 Feb.
Hoffman, Dustin, b. 8 Aug.
Hoffmann, Ernst, d. 5 Jul.
Hoffmann, Josef, b. 15 Dec.
Hofmannsthal, Hugo von, b. 1 Feb., d. 15 Jul.
Hogan, Ben, b. 13 Aug.
Hogarth, William, b. 10 Nov., d. 26 Oct.
Hogben, Lancelot, b. 9 Dec., d. 23 Aug.
Hogg, James, d. 21 Nov.
Hogg, Quintin, b. 14 Feb., d. 17 Jan.
Hoggart, Richard, b. 24 Sept.
Hohner, Matthias, d. 11 Dec.
Hokusai, Katsushika, b. 21 Oct., d. 10 May
Holbein, Hans, the Younger, d. 29 Nov.
Holbrook, David, b. 9 Jan.
Holbrooke, Joseph, d. 5 Aug.
Holcroft, Thomas, b. 10 Dec., d. 23 Mar.
Holden, Anthony, b. 22 May
Holden, William, d. 16 Nov.
Holderness, Sue, b. 28 May
Holiday, Billie, b. 7 Apr., d. 17 Jul.
Holl, Frank, d. 31 Jul.
Holland, 3rd Baron, d. 22 Oct.
Holland, John Philip, b. 29 Feb., d. 12 Aug.
Holländer, Alexis, b. 26 Feb.
Hollar, Wenzel, b. 13 Jun.
Hollings, Sir Kenneth, b. 12 Jun.
Holloway, Stanley, b. 1 Oct., d. 30 Jan.
Holloway, Sterling, b. 4 Jan.
Holm, Celeste, b. 29 Apr.
Holm, Ian, b. 12 Sept.
Holmes, Larry, b. 3 Nov.
Holmes, Oliver Wendell, b. 29 Aug., d. 7 Oct.
Holmes, Terry, b. 10 Mar.
Holroyd, Frank, b. 30 Aug.

Holroyd, Michael, b. 27 Aug.

Holst, Gustav, b. 21 Sept., d. 25 May

Holst, Imogen, d. 9 Mar.

Holt, James, b. 26 Apr .

Holt, John, b. 30 Dec.

Holtby, Winifred, b. 23 Jun., d. 29 Sept.

Home, John, b. 21 Sept., d. 5 Sept.

Home, Lord, b. 2 Jul.

Homer, Winslow, b. 24 Feb., d. 29 Sept.

Hondecoeter, Melchior D', d. 3 Apr.

Hone, William, b. 3 Jun., d. 6 Nov.

Honegger, Arthur, b. 10 Mar., d. 27 Nov.

Honeycombe, Gordon, b. 27 Sept.

Honeyghan, Lloyd, b. 22 Apr.

Honthorst, Gerard van, b. 4 Nov., d. 27 Apr.

Hooch, Pieter de, b. 20 Dec.

Hood, 1st Viscount, b. 12 Dec., d. 27 Jan.

Hood, Thomas, b. 23 May, d. 3 May

Hooft, Pieter, b. 16 Mar.

Hoogstraten, Samuel van, b. 2 Aug., d. 19 Oct.

Hook, James Clarke, b. 21 Nov.

Hook, Theodore, b. 22 Sept., d. 24 Aug.

Hooke, Robert, b. 18 Jul., d. 3 Mar.

Hooker, Joseph, b. 30 Jun., d. 10 Dec.

Hooker, Richard, d. 2 Nov.

Hooker, Thomas, b. 7 Jul., d. 7 Jul.

Hooker, William, b. 6 Jul., d. 12 Aug.

Hooper, Baroness, b. 25 May

Hoover, Herbert, b. 10 Aug., d. 20 Oct.

Hoover, J. Edgar, b. 1 Jan., d. 2 May

Hope, Adrian, b. 21 Jan.

Hope, Anthony, b. 9 Feb., d. 8 Jul.

Hope, Bob, b. 29 May

Hope, Lord, b. 27 Jun.

Hopkins, Anthony (actor), b. 31 Dec.

Hopkins, Antony (composer), b. 21 Mar.

Hopkins, Gerard Manley, b. 28 Jul., d. 8 Jun.

Hopkins, John, b. 27 Jan.

Hoppner, John, b. 4 Apr., d. 23 Jan.

Horace, b. 8 Dec., d. 27 Nov.

Hordern, Michael, b. 3 Oct.

Hore-Belisha, Leslie, d. 16 Feb.

Horler, Sydney, b. 18 Jul., d. 27 Oct.

Horn, Trevor, b. 15 Jul.

Horne, Lena, b. 30 Jun.

Hornung, E.W., b. 7 Jun., d. 22 Mar.

Horrocks, Brian, d. 4 Jan.

Horsley, Peter, b. 26 Mar.

Horthy, Miklós, b. 18 Jun., d. 9 Feb.

Hoskins, Bob, b. 26 Oct.

Hotspur, Harry, b. 20 May

Hotter, Hans, b. 19 Jan.

Houdini, Harry, b. 6 Apr., d. 31 Oct.

Houdon, Jean, b. 20 Mar., d. 15 Jul.

Hough, Richard, b. 15 May

Houghton, Gaie Johnson, b. 1 Apr.

Hounsfield, Godfrey, b. 28 Aug.

Housman, A.E., b. 26 Mar., d. 30 Apr.

Housman, Laurence, b. 18 Jul., d. 20 Feb.

Houston, Samuel, b. 2 Mar., d. 26 Jul.

Hovick, Rose, b. 9 Jan.

Howard, Alan, b. 5 Aug.

Howard, Anthony, b. 12 Feb.

Howard, Catherine, d. 13 Feb.

Howard, Elizabeth Jane, b. 26 Mar.

Howard, Henry, Earl of Surrey, d. 19 Jan.

Howard, John, b. 2 Sept., d. 20 Jan.

Howard, Michael, b. 7 Jul.

Howard, Sidney (playwright), d. 23 Aug.

Howard, Sydney (comedian), b. 7 Aug.

Howard, Trevor, d. 7 Jan.

Howard de Walden, Lord, b. 27 Nov.

Howarth, Elgar, b. 4 Nov.

Howe, 1st Earl, b. 8 Mar., d. 5 Aug.

Howe, Elias, b. 9 Jul., d. 3 Oct.

Howe, Geoffrey, b. 20 Dec.

Howe, Julia Ward, d. 17 Oct.

Howell, Denis, b. 4 Sept.

Howell, Gwynne, b. 13 Jun.

Howells, Anne, b. 12 Jan.

Howerd, Frankie, b. 6 Mar., d. 19 Apr.

Howes, Sally Ann, b. 20 Jul.

Hoyle, Edmond, d. 29 Aug.

Hoyle, Fred, b. 24 Jun.

Hubbard, L. Ron, d. 1 Jan.

Hubble, Edwin P., b. 20 Nov.

Hudd, Roy, b. 16 May

Huddleston, Trevor, b. 15 Jun.

Hudson, Rock, d. 2 Oct.

Hudson, W.H., b. 4 Aug., d. 18 Aug.

Huggins, Sir William, b. 7 Feb.

Hughes, David Edward, b. 16 May, d. 22 Jan.

Hughes, David (cricketer), b. 13 May

Hughes, Emlyn, b. 28 Aug.

Hughes, Howard, b. 24 Dec., d. 5 Apr.

Hughes, Nerys, b. 8 Nov.
Hughes, Richard, b. 19 Apr., d. 28 Apr.
Hughes, Shirley, b. 16 Jul.
Hughes, Ted, b. 16 Aug.
Hughes, Thomas, b. 20 Oct., d. 22 Mar.
Hugo, Victor, b. 26 Feb., d. 22 May
Hull, Cordell, b. 2 Oct., d. 23 Jul.
Humboldt, Alexander von, b. 14 Sept., d. 6 May
Humboldt, Karl Wilhelm von, b. 22 Jun., d. 8 Apr.
Hume, Basil, b. 2 Mar.
Hume, David, b. 7 May, d. 25 Aug.
Hume, Fergus, b. 8 Jul., d. 12 Jul.
Humfrey, Pelham, d. 14 Jul.
Humperdinck, Engelbert (composer), b. 1 Sept., d. 27 Sept.
Humperdinck, Engelbert (singer), b. 2 May
Humphrey, Hubert, d. 13 Jan.
Humphreys, Christmas, d. 13 Apr.
Humphreys, Robert, b. 6 Jun.
Humphries, Barry, b. 17 Feb.
Humphry, Ozias, d. 9 Mar.
Hunnicutt, Gayle, b. 6 Feb.
Hunniford, Gloria, b. 10 Apr.
Hunt, Alfred, d. 3 May
Hunt, David, b. 21 May
Hunt, Gareth, b. 7 Feb.
Hunt, James, b. 29 Aug.
Hunt, Leigh, b. 19 Oct., d. 28 Aug.
Hunt, Lord, b. 22 Jun.
Hunt, Roger, b. 20 Jul.
Hunt, William Holman, b. 2 Apr., d. 7 Sept.
Hunter, Archibald, b. 16 Jan.
Hunter, Ian, b. 2 Apr.
Hunter, John, b. 13 Feb., d. 16 Oct.
Hunter, Kim, b. 12 Nov.
Hunter, William, b. 23 May, d. 30 Mar.
Hunyadi, János, d. 11 Aug.
Hurd, Douglas, b. 8 Mar.
Hurok, Sol, b. 9 Apr.
Hurst, Fannie, b. 18 Oct., d. 23 Feb.
Hurst, Geoff, b. 8 Dec.
Hurt, John, b. 22 Jan.
Huss, Jan, d. 6 Jul.
Hussein of Jordan, b. 14 Nov.
Hussein, Saddam, b. 29 Apr.
Hussey, Marmaduke, b. 29 Aug.

Hussey, Olivia, b. 17 Apr.
Hussey, Ruth, b. 30 Oct.
Hutchinson, A.S.M., b. 2 Jun.
Hutton, Barbara, d. 11 May
Hutton, Betty, b. 26 Feb.
Hutton, Brian, b. 29 Jun.
Huxley, Aldous, b. 26 Jul., d. 22 Nov.
Huxley, Anthony, b. 2 Dec.
Huxley, Elspeth, b. 23 Jul.
Huxley, Julian, b. 22 Jun., d. 14 Feb.
Huxley, Leonard, d. 8 Sept.
Huxley, T.H., b. 4 May, d. 29 Jun.
Huygens, Christiaan, d. 8 Jul.
Huysmans, Cornelius, d. 1 Jun.
Huysmans, Joris, b. 5 Feb., d. 12 May
Huysum, Jan van, b. 15 Apr., d. 7 Feb.
Hyde, Douglas, b. 17 Jan., d. 12 Jul.
Hyde, Robin, b. 19 Jan.
Hylton, Jack, b. 2 Jul.
Hyne, Cutcliffe, b. 11 May, d. 10 Mar.

Ibbotson, Derek, b. 17 Jun.
Ibert, Jacques, b. 15 Aug., d. 5 Feb.
Ibn Saud, King, d. 9 Nov.
Ibsen, Henrik, b. 20 Mar., d. 23 May
Ifield, Frank, b. 30 Nov.
Iglesias, Julio, b. 23 Sept.
Ignatius, d. 20 Dec.
Iles, John, b. 17 May
Illingworth, Ray, b. 8 Jun.
Ilyushin, Sergei, d. 9 Feb.
Imbert, Peter, b. 27 Apr.
Ince, Thomas H., d. 19 Nov.
Inchbald, Elizabeth, d. 1 Aug.
Indy, Vincent d', b. 27 Mar., d. 1 Dec.
Ingelow, Jean, b. 17 Mar., d. 20 Jul.
Ingersoll, Ralph, d. 8 Mar.
Ingham, Sir Bernard, b. 21 Jun.
Inglis, Brian, b. 31 Jul.
Inglis, Henry, d. 20 Mar.
Ingoldsby, Thomas, b. 6 Dec.
Ingram, Rex, d. 21 Jun.
Ingrams, Richard, b. 19 Aug.
Ingres, Jean, b. 29 Aug., d. 14 Jan.
Ingrid, Queen of Denmark, b. 28 Mar.
Inman, John, b. 28 Jun.
Innes, Brian, b. 4 May
Innes, Hammond, b. 15 Jul.
Innes, Michael, b. 30 Sept.

Innocent II, Pope, 24 Sept.
Innocent III, Pope, d. 16 Jul.
Innocent V, Pope, d. 22 Jun.
Innocent VIII, Pope, d. 25 Jul.
Innocent X, Pope, d. 1 Jan.
Innocent XIII, Pope, d. 7 Mar.
Ionesco, Eugene, b. 13 Nov.
Iqbal, Asif, b. 6 Jun.
Iran, Shah of, d. 27 Jun.
Ireland, John (actor), b. 30 Jan.
Ireland, John (composer), b. 13 Aug., d.
   12 Jun.
Ireland, William, d. 17 Apr.
Irons, Jeremy, b. 19 Sept.
Ironside, 1st Baron, b. 6 May
Irving, Edward, b. 4 Aug., d. 7 Dec.
Irving, Henry, b. 6 Feb., d. 13 Oct.
Irving, Washington, b. 3 Apr., d. 28 Nov.
Irwin, Hale, b. 3 Jun.
Irwin, Margaret, b. 27 Mar.
Isaacs, Jeremy, b. 28 Sept.
Isabella I, of Castile, b. 22 Apr., d. 26
   Nov.
Isabella II, of Spain, b. 10 Oct., d. 9 Apr.
Isabey, Eugène, b. 22 Jul., d. 25 Apr.
Isabey, Jean-Baptiste, b. 11 Apr.
Isherwood, Christopher, b. 26 Aug., d. 4
   Jan.
Ismail Pasha, d. 2 Mar.
Israëls, Jozef, b. 27 Jan.
Iturbi, José, b. 28 Nov.
Ivan III, of Russia, d. 27 Oct.
Ivan IV, the Terrible, of Russia, b. 25
   Aug., d. 18 Mar.
Ives, Burl, b. 14 Jun.
Ives, Charles, d. 19 May
Ives, Frederick, b. 17 Feb.
Ivory, James, b. 7 Jun.
Iwerks, U.B., b. 24 Mar.
Izumi, Shigechiyo, d. 21 Feb.

Jacklin, Tony, b. 7 Jul.
Jackman, Robin, b. 13 Aug.
Jackson, Andrew, b. 15 Mar., d. 8 Jun.
Jackson, Glenda, b. 9 May
Jackson, Jermaine, b. 11 Dec.
Jackson, Kate, b. 29 Oct.
Jackson, Mahalia, b. 26 Oct., d. 27 Jan.
Jackson, Michael, b. 29 Aug.
Jackson, Nicholas, b. 4 Sept.

Jackson, Shirley, b. 14 Dec., d. 8 Aug.
Jackson, Stanley, b. 28 Sept.
Jackson, 'Stonewall', b. 21 Jan., d. 10 May
Jacob, Alaric, b. 8 Jun.
Jacob, Gordon, b. 5 Jul.
Jacob, Naomi, d. 26 Aug.
Jacobi, Derek, b. 22 Oct.
Jacobs, David, b. 19 May
Jacobs, W.W., b. 8 Sept., d. 1 Sept.
Jacobson, Dan, b. 7 Mar.
Jacquard, Joseph, b. 7 Jul., d. 7 Aug.
Jaeger, Andrea, b. 4 Jun.
Jaffrey, Madhur, b. 13 Aug.
Jagger, Mick, b. 26 Jul.
Jahangir, emperor, b. 31 Aug., d. 28 Oct.
Jahn, Otto, b. 16 Jun.
Jak (Raymond Jackson), b. 11 Mar.
Jakobovits, Lord, b. 8 Feb.
James, Clive, b. 7 Oct.
James, George, b. 9 Aug., d. 9 Jun.
James, Geraldine, b. 6 Jul.
James, Harry, d. 5 Jun.
James, Henry, b. 15 Apr., d. 28 Feb.
James, Jesse, b. 5 Sept., d. 3 Apr.
James, Mark, b. 28 Oct.
James, M.R., b. 1 Aug., d. 12 Jun.
James, P.D., b. 3 Aug.
James, Robert Rhodes, b. 10 Apr.
James, William, d. 26 Aug.
James I, of Great Britain, b. 19 Jun., d. 27
   Mar.
James I, of Scotland, d. 20 Feb.
James II, of Great Britain, b. 14 Oct.
James II, of Scotland, b. 16 Oct., d. 3 Aug.
James III, of Scotland, d. 11 Jun.
James IV, of Scotland, b. 17 Mar., d. 9
   Sept.
James V, of Scotland, b. 10 Apr., d. 14
   Dec.
Jameson, Andrew, b. 19 Feb.
Jameson, Anna, b. 17 May
Jameson, Derek, b. 29 Nov.
Jameson, Leander, d. 26 Nov.
Jameson, Susan, b. 13 Aug.
Jamieson, David, b. 1 Oct.
Janáček, Leoš, b. 3 Jul., d. 12 Aug.
Janet, Pierre, b. 30 May, d. 24 Feb.
Janner, Greville, b. 11 Jul.
Jansen, Cornelius, b. 28 Oct., d. 6 May
Janssen, Cornelis, b. 14 Oct.

Jardine, Douglas, b. 23 Oct.
Jarvis, Martin, b. 4 Aug.
Jarvis, William, b. 14 Oct.
Jason, David, b. 2 Feb.
Jaspers, Karl, b. 23 Feb., d. 26 Feb.
Jauncey, Lord, b. 8 May
Jaurès, Jean, b. 3 Sept.
Jay, Antony, b. 20 Apr.
Jay, Lord, b. 23 Mar.
Jay, Peter, b. 7 Feb.
Jayston, Michael, b. 29 Oct.
Jean, Grand Duke, b. 5 Jan.
Jeans, James, b. 11 Sept., d. 16 Sept.
Jeavons, Colin, b. 20 Oct.
Jebb, Samuel, d. 9 Mar.
Jeffers, John, b. 10 Jan.
Jefferies, Richard, b. 6 Nov., d. 14 Aug.
Jefferson, Thomas, b. 13 Apr., d. 4 Jul.
Jefford, Barbara, b. 26 Jul.
Jeffrey, Peter, b. 18 Apr.
Jeffreys, Judge, d. 18 Apr.
Jeffries, Lionel, b. 10 Jun.
Jeger, Baroness, b. 19 Nov.
Jelf, Richard, b. 16 Jun.
Jellicoe, 1st Earl, b. 5 Dec., d. 20 Nov.
Jellicoe, Ann, b. 15 Jul.
Jenkin, Lord, b. 7 Sept.
Jenkins, Clive, b. 2 May
Jenkins, David (athlete), b. 25 May
Jenkins, David, Bishop, b. 26 Jan.
Jenkins, Jennifer, b. 18 Jan.
Jenkins, John, b. 27 Oct.
Jenkins, Lord, b. 11 Nov.
Jenkins, Simon, b. 10 Jun.
Jenner, Ann, b. 8 Mar.
Jenner, Edward, b. 17 May, d. 26 Jan.
Jennings, Pat, b. 12 Jun.
Jensen, Johannes, b. 20 Jan.
Jepson, Edgar, d. 11 Apr.
Jerome, Jerome K., b. 2 May, d. 14 Jun.
Jerrold, Douglas, b. 3 Jan., d. 8 Jun.
Jervis, John, 9 Jan.
Jespersen, Otto, b. 16 Jul., d. 30 Apr.
Jessel, David, b. 8 Nov.
Jewel, Jimmy, b. 4 Dec.
Jewison, Norman, b. 21 Jul.
Jex-Blake, Sophia, b. 21 Jan., d. 7 Jan.
Jiménez, Juan, b. 24 Dec., d. 29 May
Jinnah, Mohammed Ali, d. 11 Sept.
Joachim, Joseph, d. 15 Aug.

Joan of Arc, b. 6 Jan., d. 30 May
Joel, Billy, b. 9 May
Joel, Harry, b. 4 Sept.
Joffre, Joseph, b. 12 Jan., d. 3 Jan.
Johansson, Stefan, b. 8 Sept.
John, Augustus, b. 4 Jan., d. 31 Oct.
John, Barry, b. 6 Jan.
John, Don, of Austria, b. 24 Feb., d. 1
  Oct.
John, Elton, b. 25th Mar.
John, of England, b. 24 Dec., d. 19 Oct.
John I, of Portugal, d. 11 Aug.
John V, of Portugal, b. 22 Oct.
John XXII, Pope, d. 4 Dec.
John XXIII, Pope, b. 25 Nov., d. 3 Jun.
John Paul I, Pope, d. 29 Sept.
John Paul II, Pope, b. 18 May
John, Rosamund, b. 19 Oct.
John III Sobieski, d. 17 Jun.
Johns, Glynis, b. 5 Oct.
Johnson, Amy, b. 1 Jul., d. 5 Jan.
Johnson, Andrew, b. 29 Dec., d. 31 Jul.
Johnson, Celia, d. 25 Apr.
Johnson, Hugh, b. 10 Mar.
Johnson, Joe, b. 29 Jul.
Johnson, Lyndon B., b. 27 Aug., d. 22 Jan.
Johnson, Manuel John, d. 28 Feb.
Johnson, Noel, b. 28 Dec.
Johnson, Paul, b. 2 Nov.
Johnson, Richard, b. 30 Jul.
Johnson, Samuel, b. 18 Sept., d. 13 Dec.
Johnson, Van, b. 25 Aug.
Johnston, A.K., the Elder, d. 9 Jul.
Johnston, Brian, b. 24 Jun.
Johnston, Harry, d. 31 Jul.
Johnston, Russell, b. 28 Jul.
Joinville, Jean de, d. 24 Dec.
Joliet, Louis, b. 21 Sept.
Jolson, Al, b. 26 May, d. 23 Oct.
Jommelli, Niccoló, b. 10 Sept.
Jones, Adrian, b. 9 Feb.
Jones, Alan (racing driver), b. 2 Nov.
Jones, Allan (singer), b. 14 Oct., d. 27
  Jun.
Jones, Allen (artist), b. 1 Sept.
Jones, Ann, b. 17 Oct.
Jones, Bobby, b. 17 Mar.
Jones, David, d. 28 Oct.
Jones, Diana, b. 15 Feb.
Jones, Freddie, b. 12 Sept.

Jones, Gemma, b. 4 Dec.
Jones, Geraint, b. 16 May
Jones, Griff Rhys, b. 16 Nov.
Jones, Gwyneth, b. 7 Nov.
Jones, Henry Arthur, b. 20 Sept., d. 7 Jan.
Jones, Henry (lexicographer), d. 29 Jun.
Jones, Inigo, b. 15 Jul., d. 21 Jun.
Jones, Jack (singer), b. 14 Jan.
Jones, Jack (trade unionist), b. 29 Mar.
Jones, James, d. 9 May
Jones, Jennifer, b. 2 Mar.
Jones, John Paul (US hero) b. 6 Jul., d. 18 Jul.
Jones, John Paul (singer) b. 3 Jan.
Jones, Mervyn, b. 27 Feb.
Jones, Owen, d. 19 Apr.
Jones, Paul, b. 24 Feb.
Jones, Peter, b. 12 Jun.
Jones, Quincy, b. 14 Mar.
Jones, Shirley, b. 31 Mar.
Jones, Tom, b. 7 Jun.
Jones, William, d. 27 Apr.
Jongen, Joseph, b. 14 Dec., d. 12 Jul.
Jonson, Ben, b. 11 Jun., d. 6 Aug.
Jonzen, Karin, b. 22 Dec.
Joplin, Scott, b. 24 Nov.
Jordaens, Jacob, b. 19 May, d. 18 Oct.
Jordan, Dorothea, d. 3 Jul.
Jordan, Joe, b. 15 Dec.
Joseph, Lord, b. 17 Jan.
Joseph I, Holy Roman Emperor, d. 17 Apr.
Joseph II, Holy Roman Emperor, b. 13 Mar.
Josephs, Wilfred, b. 24 Jul.
Josephson, Brian, b. 4 Jan.
Joubert, John, b. 20 Mar.
Joule, James, b. 24 Dec., d. 11 Oct.
Jourdan, Louis, b. 19 Jun.
Jouvet, Louis, b. 24 Dec.
Jowett, Benjamin, d. 1 Oct.
Joyce, James, b. 2 Feb., d. 13 Jan.
Joyce, William, b. 24 Apr., d. 3 Jan.
Juan Carlos, of Spain, b. 5 Jan.
Jeffers, John, b. 10 Jan.
Judd, Lesley, b. 20 Dec.
Juliana, of the Netherlands, b. 30 Apr.
Julius II, Pope, d. 21 Feb.
Jullien, Louis-Antoine, d. 14 Mar.
Jung, Carl, b. 26 Jul., d. 6 Jun.

Junkin, John, b. 29 Jan.
Junor, John, b. 15 Jan.
Jurinac, Sena, b. 24 Oct.
Justin I, emperor, d. 1 Aug.

Kabalevsky, Dmitri, b. 30 Dec.
Kafka, Franz, b. 3 Jul., d. 3 Jun.
Kahn, Gus, b. 6 Nov., d. 8 Oct.
Kaiser, Georg, d. 4 Jun.
Kallicharran, Alvin, b. 21 Mar.
Kalmus, Herbert T., b. 9 Nov.
Kammerlander, Karl, b. 30 Apr.
Kandinsky, Wassily, b. 22 Nov., d. 13 Dec.
Kane, Elisha, d. 16 Feb.
Kant, Immanuel, b. 22 Apr., d. 12 Feb.
Kaplan, Mark, b. 30 Dec.
Karas, Anton, d. 10 Jan.
Karl, of Austria, d. 1 Apr.
Karlfeldt, Eric, d. 8 Apr.
Karlin, Miriam, b. 23 Jun.
Karloff, Boris, b. 23 Nov., d. 3 Feb.
Karpov, Anatoly, b. 23 May
Karsavina, Tamara, b. 10 Mar.
Karsh, Yousuf, b. 23 Dec.
Karume, Sheik Abeid, d. 7 Apr.
Kasparov, Gary, b. 13 Apr.
Kastler, Alfred, d. 7 Jan.
Kästner, Erich, b. 23 Feb., d. 29 Jul.
Katin, Peter, b. 14 Nov.
Kauffmann, Angelica, b. 30 Oct., d. 5 Nov.
Kaufman, George S., b. 16 Nov., d. 2 Jun.
Kaufman, Gerald, b. 21 Jun.
Kaulbach, Wilhelm von, b. 15 Oct.
Kaunda, Kenneth, b. 28 Apr.
Kavanagh, P.J., b. 6 Jan.
Kay, Charles, b. 31 Aug.
Kaye, Danny, d. 3 Mar.
Kaye, Gorden, b. 7 Apr.
Kazan, Elia, b. 7 Sept.
Keach, Stacy, b. 2 Jun.
Kean, Mrs Charles, d. 20 Aug.
Kean, Charles John, b. 18 Jan., d. 22 Jan.
Kean, Edmund, b. 17 Mar., d. 15 May
Keane, Molly, b. 20 Jul.
Kearton, Lord, b. 17 Feb.
Keating, H.R.F., b. 31 Oct.
Keating, Tom, d. 12 Feb.
Keaton, Buster, b. 4 Oct., d. 1 Feb.

Keaton, Diane, b. 5 Jan.
Keats, John, b. 31 Oct., d. 23 Feb.
Keble, John, b. 25 Apr., d. 29 Mar.
Kee, Robert, b. 5 Oct.
Keeffe, Barrie, b. 31 Oct.
Keegan, Kevin, b. 14 Feb.
Keel, Howard, b. 13 Apr.
Keeler, Ruby, b. 25 Aug.
Keen, Diane, b. 29 Jul.
Keene, Charles, b. 10 Aug., d. 4 Jan.
Keene, Raymond, b. 29 Jan.
Keightley, Thomas, b. 6 Oct.
Keill, John, b. 1 Dec.
Keith, Arthur, b. 5 Feb.
Keith, Penelope, b. 2 Apr.
Keith, Sheila, b. 9 Jun.
Kekkonen, Urho, b. 3 Sept.
Kellaway, Roger, b. 1 Nov.
Keller, Gottfried, b. 19 Jul., d. 16 Jul.
Keller, Helen, b. 27 Jun., d. 1 Jun.
Kellerman, Sally, b. 2 Jun.
Kelly, Barbara, b. 5 Oct.
Kelly, Gene, b. 23 Aug.
Kelly, Gerald, b. 9 Apr., d. 31 Dec.
Kelly, Jack, b. 16 Sept.
Kelly, Matthew, b. 9 May
Kelly, Ned, d. 11 Nov.
Kelvin, 1st Baron, b. 26 Jun., d. 17 Dec.
Kemble, Charles, b. 25 Nov., d. 12 Nov.
Kemble, Fanny, b. 27 Nov., d. 15 Jan.
Kemble, John Philip, b. 1 Feb., d. 26 Feb.
Kemp, Jeremy, b. 3 Feb.
Kempis, Thomas à, d. 8 Aug.
Kempson, Rachel, b. 28 May
Kendal, Felicity, b. 25 Sept.
Kendall, Henry, b. 18 Apr., d. 1 Aug.
Kendall, Kenneth, b. 7 Aug.
Kendall, Madge, b. 15 Mar., d. 14 Sept.
Keneally, Thomas, b. 7 Oct.
Kennedy, Cheryl, b. 29 Apr.
Kennedy, Edward, b. 22 Feb.
Kennedy, Jimmy, b. 20 Jul., d. 6 Apr.
Kennedy, John F., b. 29 May, d. 22 Nov.
Kennedy, Joseph, b. 6 Sept.
Kennedy, Ludovic, b. 3 Nov.
Kennedy, Margaret, b. 23 Apr., d. 31 Jul.
Kennedy, Nigel, b. 28 Dec.
Kennedy, Paul, b. 12 Jun.
Kennedy, Robert, b. 20 Nov., d. 6 Jun.
Kennedy, Rose, b. 22 Jul.

Kennedy, Tessa, b. 6 Dec.
Kennedy, Thomas, b. 19 May
Kenny, Brian, b. 18 Jun.
Kenny, Yvonne, b. 25 Nov.
Kent, Bruce, b. 22 Jun.
Kent, Duchess of, b. 22 Feb.
Kent, Duke of, b. 9 Oct.
Kent, Holy Maid of, d. 20 Apr.
Kent, James, b. 13 Mar.
Kent, Princess Michael of, b. 15 Jan.
Kent, William, d. 12 Apr.
Kenton, Godfrey, b. 13 Apr.
Kenton, Stan, b. 19 Feb.
Kenwright, Bill, b. 4 Sept.
Kenyatta, Jomo, d. 22 Aug.
Kepler, Johannes, b. 27 Dec., d. 15 Nov.
Kerensky, Alexander, d. 11 Jun.
Kern, Jerome, b. 27 Jan., d. 11 Nov.
Kerouac, Jack, b. 12 Mar., d. 21 Oct.
Kerr, Deborah, b. 30 Sept.
Ketèlbey, Albert, b. 9 Aug., d. 26 Nov.
Kett, Robert, d. 7 Dec.
Key, Francis Scott, b. 1 Aug., d. 11 Jan.
Keyes, Frances Parkinson, b. 21 Jul.
Keyes, Roger, b. 4 Oct.
Keynes, John Maynard, b. 5 Jun., d. 21
   Apr.
Keys, Nelson, d. 26 Apr.
Khama, Seretse, d. 13 Jun.
Khan, Jahangir, b. 10 Dec.
Khatchaturian, Aram, b. 6 Jun.
Khrushchev, Nikita, b. 17 Apr., d. 11 Sept.
Kidd, Capt. William, d. 23 May
Kidder, Margot, b. 17 Oct.
Kierkegaard, Sören, b. 5 May, d. 11 Nov.
Kiernan, Tom, b. 7 Jan.
Kilbracken, Lord, b. 17 Oct.
Killanin, Lord, b. 30 Jul.
Killigrew, Thomas, b. 7 Feb., d. 19 Mar.
Kilmartin, Terence, b. 10 Jan.
Kilroy-Silk, Robert, b. 19 May
King, B.B., b. 16 Sept.
King, Billie Jean, b. 22 Nov.
King, Francis, b. 4 Mar.
King, Jeff, b. 6 Jul.
King, Jonathan, b. 6 Dec.
King, MacKenzie, b. 17 Dec., d. 22 Jul.
King, Martin Luther, b. 15 Jan., d. 4 Apr.
King, Philip, b. 1 May
King, Stephen, b. 21 Sept.

King, Truby, b. 1 Apr.
Kinglake, Alexander, b. 5 Aug., d. 2 Jan.
Kingsley, Ben, b. 31 Dec.
Kingsley, Charles, b. 12 Jun., d. 23 Jan.
Kingsley, Mary, b. 13 Oct.
Kingston, W.H.G., b. 28 Feb., d. 5 Aug.
Kinkel, Gottfried, d. 12 Nov.
Kinnear, Roy, d. 19 Sept.
Kinnock, Neil, b. 28 Mar.
Kinsey, Alfred, b. 23 Jun.
Kinski, Nastassya, b. 24 Jan.
Kipling, Rudyard, b. 30 Dec., d. 18 Jan.
Kirby, William, b. 19 Sept.
Kircher, Athanasius, d. 27 Nov.
Kirchhoff, Gustav, d. 17 Oct.
Kirkby, Emma, b. 26 Feb.
Kirkup, James, b. 23 Apr.
Kirshbaum, Ralph, b. 4 Mar.
Kirsten, Peter, b. 14 May
Kirwan, Laurence, b. 13 May
Kisch, Royalton, b. 20 Jan.
Kissinger, Henry, b. 27 May
Kitagawa, Utamaro, d. 20 Sept.
Kitchen, Michael, b. 31 Oct.
Kitchener, Earl, b. 24 Jun., d. 5 Jun.
Kitt, Eartha, b. 26 Jan.
Kitto, John, b. 4 Dec.
Klammer, Franz, b. 3 Dec.
Klaproth, Martin, b. 1 Dec.
Klee, Paul, b. 18 Dec., d. 29 Jun.
Kleiber, Carlos, b. 3 Jul.
Klein, Calvin, b. 19 Nov.
Klein, Melanie, b. 30 Mar.
Kleist, Bernd von, b. 18 Oct., d. 21 Nov.
Klemperer, Otto, b. 14 May, d. 6 Jul.
Klemperer, Werner, b. 22 Mar.
Klimt, Gustav, b. 14 Jul., d. 6 Feb.
Klopstock, Friedrich, b. 2 Jul., d. 14 Mar.
Klug, Aaron, b. 11 Aug.
Klugman, Jack, b. 27 Apr.
Kneale, Bryan, b. 19 Jun.
Kneller, Godfrey, b. 8 Aug., d. 7 Nov.
Knight, Charles, d. 9 Mar.
Knoblock, Edward, b. 7 Apr., d. 19 Jul.
Knopfler, Mark, b. 12 Aug.
Knowles, James, b. 13 Oct.
Knox, Alexander, b. 16 Jan.
Knox, John (judge), b. 6 Apr.
Knox, John (reformer), d. 24 Nov.
Knox, Robert, b. 29 May

Knox, Ronald, b. 17 Feb.
Knox-Johnston, Robin, b. 17 Mar.
Knox-Mawer, June, b. 10 May
Knussen, Oliver, b. 12 Jun.
Koch, Robert, b. 11 Dec., d. 27 May
Kochanowski, Jan, d. 22 Aug.
Kodály, Zoltán, b. 16 Dec., d. 6 Mar.
Koestler, Arthur, b. 5 Sept., d. 3 Mar.
Koffka, Kurt, b. 18 Mar.
Kohl, Helmut, b. 3 Apr.
Koivisto, Mauno, b. 25 Nov.
Kokoschka, Oskar, b. 1 Mar., d. 22 Feb.
Koldewey, Robert, b. 10 Sept.
Kollar, Jan, b. 29 Jul.
Koltai, Ralph, b. 31 Jul.
Koltchak, Alexander, d. 2 Feb.
Komisarjevsky, Theodore, d. 17 Apr.
Konstant, David, b. 16 Jun.
Korchnoi, Viktor, b. 23 Jul.
Korda, Alexander, b. 16 Sept., d. 23 Jan.
Kornberg, Hans, b. 14 Jan.
Körner, Theodor, b. 23 Sept., d. 28 Aug.
Korte, Karl, b. 25 Aug.
Kortright, Charles, b. 9 Jan.
Kościuszko, Tadeusz, b. 4 Feb., d. 15 Oct.
Kossoff, David, b. 24 Nov.
Kossuth, Lajos, b. 19 Sept., d. 20 Mar.
Kotzebue, August von, b. 3 May, d. 23 Mar.
Koussevitsky, Serge, d. 4 Jun.
Krafft-Ebing, Richard von, b. 14 Aug., d. 22 Dec.
Kramer, Billy J., b. 19 Aug.
Kramer, Jack, b. 1 Aug.
Kramer, Stanley, b. 29 Sept.
Kreisler, Fritz, b. 2 Feb., d. 29 Jan.
Kretschmer, Ernst, b. 8 Oct.
Kretzmer, Herbert, b. 5 Oct.
Kreuger, Ivar, b. 2 Mar., d. 12 Mar.
Kristal, Sylvia, b. 28 Sept.
Kristofferson, Kris, b. 22 Jun.
Krogh, August, b. 15 Nov., d. 13 Sept.
Kropotkin, Peter, b. 9 Dec., d. 8 Feb.
Kruger, Hardy, b. 12 Apr.
Kruger, Paul, b. 10 Oct., d. 14 Jul.
Krupp, Alfred, b. 26 Apr., d. 14 Jul.
Kubelik, Jan, b. 5 Jul., d. 5 Dec.
Kubelik, Rafael, b. 29 Jun.
Kubrick, Stanley, b. 26 Jul.
Kuchatov, Igor, d. 7 Feb.

Kühnert, Wilhelm, b. 28 Sept.
Kulukundis, Eddie, b. 20 Apr.
Kun, Béla, b. 20 Feb.
Kurosawa, Akira, b. 23 Mar.
Kutuzov, Mikhail, b. 16 Sept.
Kyd, Thomas, b. 6 Nov.
Kynaston, Nicolas, b. 10 Dec.
Kyosai, Kawanabe, b. 18 May, d. 25 Apr.
Kyser, Kay, d. 23 Jun.
Kyung-wha Chung, b. 26 Mar.

Labiche, Eugene, b. 5 May
Laclos, Pierre de, d. 5 Nov.
Lacombe, Louis, b. 26 Nov.
Lacoste, René, b. 2 Jul.
Ladd, Alan, b. 3 Sept.
Laemmle, Carl, b. 7 Jan., d. 24 Sept.
Laënnec, René, b. 17 Feb., d. 13 Aug.
Laer, Pieter van, d. 30 Jun.
La Farge, John, b. 31 Mar.
La Farge, Oliver, b. 19 Dec., d. 2 Aug.
La Fayette, Marie de, bap. 18 Mar., d. 25 May
Lafayette, Marquis de, b. 6 Sept., d. 20 May
Laffite, Jacques (driver), b. 21 Nov.
Laffitte, Jacques (banker), b. 24 Oct.
La Follette, Robert, b. 14 Jun., d. 18 Jun.
la Fontaine, Jean de, b. 8 Jul., d. 13 Apr.
Laforgue, Jules, b. 16 Aug.
Lafosse, Charles de, b. 15 Jun.
La Frenais, Ian, b. 7 Jan.
Lagerkvist, Pär, b. 23 May
Lagerlöf, Selma, b. 20 Nov., d. 16 Mar.
Lagrange, Joseph-Louis, b. 25 Jan., d. 10 Apr.
La Guardia, Fiorello, d. 20 Sept.
Laine, Cleo, b. 28 Oct.
Laine, Frankie, b. 30 Mar.
Laing, Alexander, b. 27 Dec.
Laker, Freddie, b. 6 Aug.
Lal, Madan, b. 20 Mar.
Lalande, Joseph de, b. 11 Jul., d. 4 Apr.
Lalique, René, b. 6 Apr.
Lalo, Édouard, b. 27 Jan., d. 22 Apr.
Lamarck, Jean de, b. 1 Aug., d. 18 Dec.
Lamarr, Hedy, b. 9 Nov.
Lamartine, Alphonse de, b. 21 Oct., d. 28 Feb.
Lamb, Alan, b. 20 Jun.

Lamb, Charles, b. 10 Feb., d. 27 Dec.
Lamb, Mary, d. 20 May
Lambert, Constant, b. 23 Aug., d. 21 Aug.
Lambert, Daniel, b. 13 Mar.
Lambert, Johann, b. 26 Aug., d. 25 Sept.
Lambert, Michael, b. 11 Sept.
Lambert, Verity, b. 27 Nov.
Lambton, Ann, b. 8 Feb.
Lamennais, Hugues de, d. 27 Feb.
La Mettrie, Julien de, b. 25 Dec.
Lamont, Norman, b. 8 May
Lamorisse, Albert, b. 13 Jan.
Lamour, Dorothy, b. 10 Dec.
Lancaster, Burt, b. 2 Nov.
Lancaster, Joseph, b. 25 Nov.
Lancaster, Osbert, b. 4 Aug.
Lanchester, Elsa, d. 26 Dec.
Lancret, Nicolas, d. 14 Sept.
Landau, Lev, d. 1 Apr.
Landen, Dinsdale, b. 4 Sept.
Landon, Letitia, b. 14 Aug., d. 15 Oct.
Landor, Walter Savage, b. 30 Jan., d. 17 Sept.
Landowska, Wanda, d. 16 Aug.
Landru, Henri, d. 25 Feb.
Landseer, Edwin, b. 7 Mar., d. 1 Oct.
Landseer, John, d. 29 Feb.
Landsteiner, Karl, b. 14 Jun.
Lane, Allen, b. 21 Sept., d. 7 Jul.
Lane, Edward, b. 17 Sept., d. 10 Aug.
Lane, John, b. 14 Mar., d. 3 Feb.
Lane, Lord, b. 17 Jul.
Lane, Lupino, b. 16 Jun.
Lane, Margaret, b. 23 Jun.
Lane, Priscilla, b. 12 Jun.
Lanfranc, d. 28 May
Lang, Andrew, b. 31 Mar., d. 20 Jul.
Lang, Fritz, b. 5 Dec., d. 2 Aug.
Lang, Ian, b. 27 Jun.
Lang, Robert, b. 24 Sept.
Langdon, David, b. 24 Feb.
Langdon, Harry, b. 15 Jun., d. 22 Dec.
Lange, Hope, b. 28 Nov.
Langer, Bernhard, b. 27 Aug.
Langford, Bonnie, b. 22 Jul.
Langford, Frances, b. 4 Apr.
Langham, Simon, d. 22 Jul.
Langley, Desmond, b. 16 May
Langley, Samuel, d. 27 Feb.
Langston, James, d. 22 May

Langton, Stephen, d. 9 Jul.
Langtry, Lillie, b. 13 Oct., d. 12 Feb.
Lanier, Sidney, d. 7 Sept.
Lansbury, Angela, b. 16 Oct.
Lansbury, George, b. 21 Feb., d. 7 May
Laplace, Pierre, b. 23 Mar.
Lapotaire, Jane, b. 26 Dec.
Lardner, Ring, b. 6 Mar.
Laredo, Jaime, b. 7 Jun.
Large, Eddie, b. 25 Jun.
Largillière, Nicolas de, b. 20 Oct.
Larkin, Philip, b. 9 Aug., d. 2 Dec.
La Rochefoucauld, b. 15 Sept., d. 17 Mar.
Larousse, Pierre, b. 23 Oct., d. 3 Jan.
La Rue, Danny, b. 26 Jul.
Larwood, Harold, b. 14 Nov.
La Salle, Jean-Baptiste de, d. 7 Apr.
la Salle, René de, b. 22 Nov., d. 19 Mar.
Laski, Harold, b. 30 Jun.
Laski, Marghanita, d. 6 Feb.
Lasky, Melvin, b. 15 Jan.
Last, James, b. 17 Apr.
Latimer, Hugh, d. 16 Oct.
La Tour, Georges de, b. 19 Mar.
La Tour, Maurice de, b. 5 Sept., d. 18 Feb.
Lattre de Tassigny, Gen., d. 11 Jan.
Laud, William, b. 7 Oct., d. 10 Jan.
Lauda, Niki, b. 22 Feb.
Lauder, Harry, b. 4 Aug., d. 26 Feb.
Laue, Max von, b. 9 Oct.
Laughton, Anthony, b. 29 Apr.
Laughton, Charles, b. 1 Jul., d. 15 Dec.
Laurel, Stan, b. 16 Jun., d. 23 Feb.
Laurie, Piper, b. 22 Jan.
Laval, Pierre, b. 28 Jun., d. 15 Oct.
Lavater, Johann, b. 11 Nov.
Lavender, Ian, b. 16 Feb.
Laver, James, b. 14 Mar., d. 3 Jun.
Laver, Rod, b. 9 Aug.
Lavery, John, b. 16 Mar., d. 10 Jan.
Lavoisier, Antoine, b. 26 Aug., d. 8 May
Law, Bonar, b. 16 Sept., d. 30 Oct.
Law, Denis, b. 24 Feb.
Law, Horace, b. 23 Jun.
Law, Roger, b. 6 Sept.
Lawford, Peter, d. 7 Sept.
Lawley, Sue, b. 14 Jul.
Lawrence, Christopher, b. 23 Dec.
Lawrence, D.H., b. 11 Sept., d. 2 Mar.
Lawrence, Ernest O., d. 28 Aug.

Lawrence, Gertrude, b. 4 Jul.
Lawrence, Leigh, b. 21 Jul.
Lawrence, Stephanie, b. 16 Dec.
Lawrence, Syd, b. 26 Jun.
Lawrence, Thomas, b. 4 May, d. 7 Jan.
Lawrence, T.E., b. 15 Aug., d. 19 May
Lawson, Cecil, b. 3 Dec.
Lawson, Denis, b. 27 Sept.
Lawson, Geoff, b. 7 Dec.
Lawson, Henry, b. 17 Jun., d. 2 Sept.
Lawson, Neil, b. 8 Apr.
Lawson, Nigel, b. 11 Mar.
Lawton, Tommy, b. 6 Oct.
Layard, Austen, b. 5 Mar., d. 5 Jul.
Laye, Evelyn, b. 10 Jul.
Layton, Turner, b. 6 Feb.
Leach, David, b. 7 May
Leach, Graham, b. 1 Oct.
Leach, Rosemary, b. 18 Dec.
Leachman, Cloris, b. 30 Apr.
Leacock, Stephen, b. 30 Dec., d. 28 Mar.
Leader, Benjamin, d. 22 Mar.
Leakey, Louis, b. 7 Aug., d. 1 Oct.
Lean, David, b. 25th Mar., d. 16 Apr.
Lear, Edward, b. 12 May, d. 29 Jan.
Learoyd, Roderick, b. 5 Feb.
Leask, Henry, b. 30 Jun.
Leasor, James, b. 20 Dec.
Leather, Edwin, b. 22 May
Leathers, Viscount, b. 4 Apr.
le Bon, Simon, b. 27 Oct.
Le Brun, Charles, b. 24 Feb., d. 12 Feb.
Le Carré, John, b. 19 Oct.
Le Châtelier, Henri, b. 8 Oct.
Le Cheminant, Peter, b. 17 Jun.
Lecky, William, b. 26 Mar., d. 22 Oct.
Leclair, Jean-Marie, b. 10 May
Leclanché, Georges, d. 14 Sept.
Lecocq, Alexandre, d. 24 Oct.
Leconte de Lisle, Charles, d. 17 Jan.
Le Corbusier, b. 6 Oct.
Ledbetter, Huddie, b. 20 Jan.
Ledoux, Claude, b. 21 Mar., d. 19 Nov.
Ledward, Gilbert, b. 23 Jan.
Lee, Ann, b. 29 Feb.
Lee, Bert, b. 11 Jun., d. 27 Jan.
Lee, Brenda, b. 11 Dec.
Lee, Christopher, b. 27 May
Lee, Gypsy Rose, b. 9 Jan.
Lee, Laurie, b. 26 Jun.

Lee, Manfred B., b. 11 Jan.
Lee, Peggy, b. 26 May
Lee, Robert E., b. 19 Jan., d. 12 Oct.
Lee, Sammy, b. 7 Feb.
Lee, Sidney, d. 3 Mar.
Lee, Sophia, d. 13 Mar.
Lee Kuan Yew, b. 16 Sept.
Leech, John, b. 29 Aug., d. 29 Oct.
Lees, Michael, b. 5 Sept.
Leeuw, Tony de, b. 16 Nov.
Leeuwenhoek, Antonie van, b. 24 Oct., d. 26 Aug.
Le Fanu, Joseph, d. 7 Feb.
Le Fanu, Nicola, b. 28 Apr.
Le Fanu, Sheridan, b. 28 Aug.
Le Gallienne, Richard, b. 20 Jan., d. 14 Sept.
Legendre, Adrien, d. 10 Jan.
Léger, Fernand, b. 4 Feb., d. 17 Aug.
Legrand, Michel, b. 24 Feb.
Legros, Alphonse, d. 8 Dec.
Lehár, Franz, b. 30 Apr., d. 24 Oct.
Lehmann, Lilli, d. 16 May
Lehrer, Tom, b. 9 Apr.
Leibniz, Gottfried, b. 1 Jul., d. 14 Nov.
Leicester, Earl of, d. 4 Sept.
Leigh, Janet, b. 6 Jul.
Leigh, Mike, b. 20 Feb.
Leigh, Vivien, b. 5 Nov., d. 8 Jul.
Leigh-Hunt, Barbara, b. 14 Dec.
Leigh-Pemberton, Robin, b. 5 Jan.
Leighton, Frederic, b. 3 Dec., d. 25 Jan.
Leighton, Margaret, b. 26 Feb.
Leighton of St Mellons, Lord, b. 11 Jan.
Leinsdorf, Erich, b. 4 Feb.
Leith, Prue, b. 18 Feb.
Leland, John, d. 18 Apr.
Lely, Peter, b. 14 Sept., d. 7 Dec.
Lémery, Nicholas, d. 19 Jun.
Le Mesurier, John, d. 15 Nov.
Lemmon, Jack, b. 8 Feb.
Lemprière, John, d. 1 Feb.
Lenbach, Franz von, b. 13 Dec., d. 6 May
Lendl, Ivan, b. 7 Mar.
Lenglen, Suzanne, b. 24 May, d. 4 Jul.
Lenin, b. 22 Apr., d. 21 Jan.
Lennon, John, b. 9 Oct., d. 8 Dec.
Lennon, Julian, b. 8 Apr.
Lennon, Yoko Ono, b. 18 Feb.
Lennox, Charlotte, d. 4 Jan.

Leno, Dan, d. 31 Oct.
Lenôtre, André de, b. 12 Mar.
Lenska, Rula, b. 30 Sept.
Leo I, Pope, d. 10 Nov.
Leo IX, Pope, b. 21 Jun., d. 19 Apr.
Leo X, Pope, b. 11 Dec., d. 1 Dec.
Leo XII, Pope, b. 22 Aug., d. 10 Feb.
Leo XIII, Pope, b. 2 Mar., d. 20 Jul.
Leonard, Graham, b. 8 May
Leonard, Hugh, b. 9 Nov.
Leonard, Sugar Ray, b. 17 May
Leonardo da Vinci, b. 26 Apr., d. 2 May
Leoncavallo, Ruggiero, b. 8 Mar., d. 9 Aug.
Leopardi, Giacomo, b. 29 Jun.
Leopold I, Holy Roman Emperor, b. 9 Jun.
Leopold I, of the Belgians, b. 16 Dec., d. 10 Dec.
Leopold II, Holy Roman Emperor, b. 5 May, d. 1 Mar.
Leopold II, of the Belgians, b. 9 Apr.
Leopold III, of the Belgians, b. 3 Nov., d. 25 Sept.
Leppard, Raymond, b. 11 Aug.
Lepsius, Karl, b. 23 Dec., d. 10 Jul.
Lermontov, Mikhail, b. 15 Oct., d. 27 Jul.
Lerner, Alan Jay, b. 31 Aug., d. 14 Jun.
LeRoy, Mervyn, b. 15 Oct.
Le Sage, Alain, d. 17 Nov.
Leslie, Charles, b. 19 Oct.
Leslie, Joan, b. 26 Jan.
Leslie, John, d. 3 Nov.
Lesseps, Ferdinand de, b. 19 Nov., d. 7 Dec.
Lessing, Doris, b. 22 Oct.
Lessing, Gotthold, d. 15 Feb.
Lester, Richard, b. 19 Jan.
Lestor, Joan, b. 13 Nov.
l'Estrange, Roger, d. 11 Dec.
Le Sueur, Eustache, b. 19 Nov.
Leszczynska, Marie, d. 24 Jun.
Le Tellier, François, d. 16 Jul.
Leuchars, Anne, b. 2 Aug.
Levant, Oscar, b. 27 Dec., d. 14 Aug.
Lever, Charles, b. 31 Aug., d. 1 Jun.
Leverhulme, 1st Viscount, b. 19 Sept., d. 7 May
Leverrier, Urbain, d. 23 Sept.
Levett, Howard, b. 25 Jan.

Levi, Carlo, b. 29 Nov.
Levi, Peter, b. 16 May
Levin, Bernard, b. 19 Aug.
Lévy-Bruhl, Lucien, b. 19 Apr., d. 13 Mar.
Lewes, George, b. 18 Apr., d. 28 Nov.
Lewis, C.S., b. 29 Nov., d. 22 Nov.
Lewis, Fiona, b. 28 Sept.
Lewis, Geoff, b. 21 Dec.
Lewis, Jerry Lee, b. 29 Sept.
Lewis, John L., d. 11 Jun.
Lewis, Kenneth, b. 29 Jan.
Lewis, Martyn, b. 7 Apr.
Lewis, Meriwether, b. 18 Aug., d. 11 Oct.
Lewis, Monk, d. 14 May
Lewis, Sinclair, b. 7 Feb., d. 10 Jan.
Lewis, Wyndham, b. 18 Nov., d. 7 Mar.
Leyden, John, d. 28 Aug.
Liadov, Anatol, d. 28 Aug.
Liberace, b. 16 May
Lichfield, Earl of, b. 25 Apr.
Lichtenstein, Roy, b. 27 Oct.
Liddell, Alice, b. 4 May
Lidell, Alvar, d. 7 Jan.
Lie, Trygve, b. 16 Jul., d. 30 Dec.
Lieb, Michael, d. 1 May
Liebermann, Max, b. 20 Jul., d. 8 Feb.
Liebig, Justus von, b. 12 May
Liebig, Karl, b. 25 Jul.
Liebknecht, Wilhelm, d. 6 Aug.
Liechtenstein, Prince Hans Adam, b. 14 Feb.
Lifar, Serge, b. 2 Apr.
Ligeti, György, b. 28 May
Lightfoot, Gordon, b. 17 Nov.
Lightfoot, John, d. 6 Dec.
Lightfoot, Terry, b. 21 May
Lilienthal, Otto, b. 23 May, d. 10 Aug.
Lill, John, b. 17 Mar.
Lillee, Dennis, b. 18 Jul.
Lilley, Peter, b. 23 Aug.
Lillicrap, Christopher, b. 14 Feb.
Lillo, George, b. 4 Feb., d. 3 Sept.
Lilly, William, b. 30 Apr., d. 9 Jun.
Linacre, Thomas, d. 20 Oct.
Lincoln, Abraham, b. 12 Feb., d. 15 Apr.
Lincoln, Anthony, b. 7 Apr.
Lind, Jenny, b. 6 Oct., d. 2 Nov.
Lindbergh, Charles, b. 4 Feb., d. 26 Aug.
Linden, Jenny, b. 8 Dec.
Lindfors, Viveca, b. 29 Dec.

Lindley, John, d. 1 Nov.
Lindley, Robert, b. 4 Mar.
Lindsay, Norman, b. 22 Feb., d. 29 Nov.
Lindsay, Robert, b. 13 Dec.
Lindsay, Vachel, b. 10 Nov., d. 5 Dec.
Lindwall, Ray, b. 3 Oct.
Lineker, Gary, b. 30 Nov.
Lingard, Anthony, b. 29 Feb.
Lingard, John, b. 5 Feb., d. 17 Jul.
Linley, Richard, b. 11 Sept.
Linnaeus, Carolus, b. 23 May, d. 10 Jan.
Linton, William, b. 7 Dec., d. 29 Dec.
Liotard, Jean, d. 12 Jun.
Lipchitz, Jacques, b. 22 Aug., d. 26 May
Lipkin, Malcolm, b. 2 May
Lipman, Maureen, b. 10 May
Lippi, Filippino, d. 18 Apr.
Lippi, Lorenzo, b. 6 May, d. 15 Apr.
Lippman, Walter, b. 23 Sept.
Lipton, Thomas, b. 10 May, d. 2 Oct.
Lisle, Charles de, d. 18 Jul.
Lister, 1st Baron, b. 5 Apr., d. 10 Feb.
Lister, Moira, b. 6 Aug.
Lister, Raymond, b. 28 Mar.
Liston, Robert, b. 28 Oct.
Liszt, Franz, b. 22 Oct., d. 31 Jul.
Litolff, Henry, b. 7 Aug., d. 5 Aug.
Little, Syd, b. 19 Dec.
Littler, Emile, d. 23 Jan.
Littleton, Thomas, d. 23 Aug.
Littré, Maximilien, b. 1 Feb., d. 2 Jun.
Litvinov, Maxim, b. 17 Jul.
Lively, Penelope, b. 17 Mar.
Liverpool, 2nd Earl, d. 4 Dec.
Livingston, Jerry, b. 25 Mar.
Livingstone, David, b. 19 Mar., d. 1 May
Livingstone, Ken, b. 17 Jun.
Llewellyn, Richard, d. 30 Nov.
Llewelyn ab Gruffydd, d. 11 Dec.
Lloyd, Clive, b. 31 Aug.
Lloyd, Edward, b. 7 Mar.
Lloyd, Guy, b. 7 Aug.
Lloyd, Harold, b. 20 Apr.
Lloyd, John, b. 27 Aug.
Lloyd, Marie, b. 12 Feb., d. 7 Oct.
Lloyd, Nicholas, b. 9 Jun.
Lloyd, Peter, b. 12 Nov.
Lloyd, Robert, b. 2 Mar.
Lloyd, Seton, b. 30 May
Lloyd, Sue, b. 7 Aug.

Lloyd George, David, b. 17 Jan., d. 26 Mar.

Lloyd-Jones, David, b. 19 Nov.

Lloyd Webber, Andrew, b. 22 Mar.

Lloyd Webber, Julian, b. 14 Apr.

Llywelyn ap Iorwerth, d. 11 Apr.

Lo, Kenneth, b. 12 Sept.

Loach, Kenneth, b. 17 Jun.

Lobachevsky, Nikolai, b. 20 Nov.

Lochore, Brian, b. 3 Sept.

Lock, Tony, b. 5 Jul.

Locke, John, b. 29 Aug., d. 28 Oct.

Locke, W.J., d. 15 May

Lockhart, John, d. 25 Nov.

Lockhart, Robert Bruce, b. 2 Sept.

Lockridge, Ross, b. 25 Apr.

Lockwood, Baroness, b. 22 Jan.

Lockwood, Margaret, b. 15 Sept., d. 15 Jul.

Lockwood, Preston, b. 30 Oct.

Lockyer, Joseph, b. 17 May

Lodge, David, b. 28 Jan.

Lodge, Henry Cabot, d. 16 Feb.

Lodge, Oliver, b. 12 Jun., d. 22 Aug.

Loesser, Frank, b. 29 Jun.

Loewe, Frederick, b. 10 Jun., d. 14 Feb.

Lofting, Hugh, b. 14 Jan., d. 26 Sept.

Logan, John, d. 25 Dec.

Logan, Joshua, b. 5 Oct.

Logue, Christopher, b. 23 Nov.

Löhr, Marie, b. 28 Jul., d. 21 Jan.

Lollobrigida, Gina, b. 4 Jul.

Lom, Herbert, b. 9 Jan.

Lombard, Carole, d. 16 Jan.

Lombardo, Guy, b. 19 Jun.

Lombroso, Cesare, b. 6 Nov., d. 19 Oct.

Lomonosov, Mikhail, d. 15 Apr.

London, Jack, b. 12 Jan., d. 22 Nov.

Lonen, Ray, b. 18 May

Long, George, b. 4 Nov., d. 10 Aug.

Long, Huey, d. 10 Sept.

Longair, Malcolm, b. 18 May

Longfellow, Henry, b. 27 Feb., d. 24 Mar.

Longford, Countess of, b. 30 Aug.

Longford, Earl, b. 5 Dec.

Lonsdale, 5th Earl, d. 13 Apr.

Loos, Anita, b. 26 Apr.

Lopez-Melton, Nancy, b. 6 Jan.

Lorca, Federico, b. 5 Jun., d. 19 Aug.

Loren, Sophia, b. 20 Sept.

Lorenzo, Fiorenzo di, d. 14 Feb.

Lorimer, Hew, b. 22 May

Lorre, Peter, b. 26 Jun., d. 23 Mar.

Lortzing, Gustav, b. 23 Oct.

los Angeles, Victoria de, b. 1 Nov.

Losey, Joseph, b. 14 Jan., d. 22 Jun.

Loti, Pierre, b. 14 Jan., d. 10 Jun.

Lott, Barbara, b. 15 May

Lott, Felicity, b. 8 May

Loubet, Émile, d. 20 Dec.

Loudon, John, b. 8 Apr.

Loughran, James, b. 30 Jun.

Louis, Joe, b. 13 May, d. 12 Apr.

Louis II, of France, b. 1 Nov.

Louis II, of Monaco, d. 9 May

Louis III, of France, d. 5 Aug.

Louis IV, of France, d. 10 Sept.

Louis VI, of France, d. 1 Aug.

Louis VIII, of France, b. 5 Sept.

Louis IX, of France, d. 25 Aug.

Louis X, of France, d. 5 Jun.

Louis XI, of France, b. 3 Jul., d. 30 Aug.

Louis XII, of France, b. 27 Jun., d. 1 Jan.

Louis XIII, of France, d. 14 May

Louis XIV, of France, b. 5 Sept., d. 1 Sept.

Louis XV, of France, b. 15 Feb., d. 10 May

Louis XVI, of France, b. 23 Aug., d. 21 Jan.

Louis XVII, of France, b. 27 Mar.

Louis XVIII, of France, b. 17 Nov., d. 16 Sept.

Louis-Philippe, b. 6 Oct., d. 26 Aug.

Loutherbourg, Philip de, d. 11 Mar.

Lovat, Simon Fraser, Baron, d. 9 Mar.

Love, Bessie, b. 10 Sept.

Lovecraft, Howard, b. 20 Aug., d. 15 Mar.

Loveday, Alan, b. 29 Feb.

Lovell, Bernard, b. 31 Aug.

Low, David, b. 7 Apr., d. 19 Sept.

Lowe, Arthur, d. 15 Apr.

Lowe, Douglas, b. 14 Mar.

Lowe, Nick, b. 25 Mar.

Lowell, Amy, b. 9 Feb., d. 12 May

Lowell, James R., d. 12 Aug.

Lowell, Percival, b. 13 Mar., d. 12 Nov.

Lowell, Robert, b. 1 Mar., d. 12 Sept.

Lowry, Lord, b. 30 Jan.

Lowry, L.S., b. 1 Nov., d. 23 Feb.

Lowry, Malcolm, b. 28 Jul., d. 27 Jun.

Lowth, Robert, 3 Nov.

Lowther, Hugh Cecil, b. 25 Jan.
Loy, Myrna, b. 2 Aug.
Loyola, Ignatius of, b. 24 Dec., d. 31 Jul.
Lubbock, Sir John, b. 30 Apr.
Lüber, Thomas, b. 7 Sept.
Lubitsch, Ernst, b. 28 Jan., d. 30 Nov.
Lucas, E.V., d. 26 Jun.
Luce, Claire Booth, b. 10 Apr.
Luce, Henry, b. 3 Apr., d. 28 Feb.
Ludendorff, Erich von, b. 9 Apr., d. 20 Dec.
Luder, Owen, b. 7 Aug.
Ludwig, Karl, b. 29 Dec.
Ludwig I, of Bavaria, b. 25 Aug.
Ludwig II, of Bavaria, b. 25 Aug., d. 13 Jun.
Lugosi, Bela, b. 20 Oct., d. 16 Aug.
Lukacs, György, d. 4 Jun.
Lukin, Lionel, d. 16 Feb.
Lully, Jean, b. 28 Nov., d. 22 Mar.
Lulu, b. 3 Nov.
Lumet, Sidney, b. 25 Jun.
Lumière, Auguste, b. 19 Oct., d. 10 Apr.
Lumley, Joanna, b. 1 May
Lunn, Arnold, b. 18 Apr.
Lunn, Henry, d. 18 Mar.
Lupino, Ida, b. 4 Feb.
Lupu, Radu, b. 30 Nov.
Lusty, Sir Robert, b. 7 Jun.
Luther, Martin, b. 10 Nov., d. 18 Feb.
Luthuli, Albert, d. 21 Jul.
Lutoslawski, Witold, b. 25 Jan.
Lutyens, Edwin, b. 29 Mar., d. 1 Jan.
Lutyens, Elisabeth, b. 6 Jul.
Luxembourg, Marie-Astrid of, b. 17 Feb.
Luxemburg, Rosa, b. 5 Mar., d. 15 Jan.
Luxon, Benjamin, b. 24 Mar.
Lyall, Gavin, b. 9 May
Lyautey, Louis, b. 17 Nov., d. 21 Jul.
Lyell, Charles, b. 14 Nov., d. 22 Feb.
Lyell, Nicholas, b. 6 Dec.
Lygo, Raymond, b. 15 Mar.
Lyle, Sandy, b. 9 Feb.
Lympany, Moura, b. 18 Aug.
Lynam, Desmond, b. 17 Sept.
Lynch, Kenny, b. 18 Mar.
Lynden-Bell, Donald, b. 5 Apr.
Lyndhurst, Nicholas, b. 20 Apr.
Lynn, Jeffrey, b. 16 Feb.
Lynn, Jonathan, b. 3 Apr.

Lynn, Loretta, b. 14 Apr.
Lynn, Vera, b. 20 Mar.
Lyon, Ben, d. 22 Mar.
Lyons, Joseph, d. 7 Apr.
Lyte, Henry, b. 1 Jun., d. 20 Nov.
Lyttelton, George, 17 Jan.
Lyttelton, Humphrey, b. 23 May
Lytton, 1st Baron, b. 25 May, d. 18 Jan.
Lytton, 1st Earl, b. 8 Nov., d. 24 Nov.

Maby, Tim, b. 26 Aug.
McAdam, John, b. 21 Sept., d. 26 Nov.
MacArthur, Douglas, d. 5 Apr.
Macaulay, Lord, b. 25 Oct., d. 28 Dec.
Macaulay, Rose, b. 1 Aug., d. 30 Oct.
Macbeth, of Scotland, d. 15 Aug.
McBride, Willie-John, b. 6 Jun.
McCabe, John, b. 21 Apr.
McCain, Donald, b. 21 Sept.
McCallum, David, b. 19 Sept.
McCarey, Leo, b. 3 Oct.
McCarthy, Joseph, b. 14 Nov., d. 2 May
M'Carthy, Justin, d. 24 Apr.
McCartney, Linda, b. 24 Sept.
McCartney, Paul, b. 18 Jun.
McClure, Doug, b. 11 May
McCormack, John, b. 14 Jun., d. 16 Sept.
McCormick, Cyrus, d. 13 May
MacCormick, Donald, b. 16 Apr.
McCowen, Alec, b. 26 May
McCullers, Carson, b. 19 Feb.
McCullin, Don, b. 9 Oct.
MacDiarmid, Hugh, b. 11 Aug., d. 9 Sept.
McDonald, Arthur, b. 14 Jun.
MacDonald, George, b. 10 Dec., d. 18 Sept.
Macdonald, Jacques, b. 17 Nov., d. 25 Sept.
MacDonald, Ramsay, b. 12 Oct., d. 9 Nov.
McDonald, Trevor, b. 16 Aug.
Macdonald-Smith, Iain, b. 3 Jul.
Macdonald-Wright, Stanton, b. 8 Jul.
Macdonnell, Alastair, d. 23 Dec.
MacDowell, Edward A., b. 18 Dec.
McDowell, Malcolm, b. 13 Jun.
McDowell, Roddy, b. 17 Sept.
McEwan, Geraldine, b. 9 May
McGough, Roger, b. 9 Nov.
MacGraw, Ali, b. 1 Apr.
MacGregor, Sue, b. 30 Aug.

McGuire, Dorothy, b. 14 Jun.

Mach, Ernst, b. 18 Feb.

Machiavelli, Niccolò dei, b. 3 May, d. 21 Jun.

McHugh, Jimmy, b. 10 Jul., d. 23 May

McIlroy, Sammy, b. 2 Aug.

McIndoe, Archibald, b. 4 May, d. 12 Apr.

MacInnes, Hamish, b. 7 Jul.

Macintosh, Charles, b. 29 Dec., d. 25 Jul.

McIntyre, Donald, b. 22 Oct.

McIntyre, Ian, b. 9 Dec.

McIntyre, Michael, b. 29 Jun.

McKaig, Rae, b. 24 Apr.

Mackay, Charles, d. 24 Dec.

Mackay, Lord, b. 2 Jul.

McKellen, Ian, b. 25 May

Macken, Eddie, b. 20 Oct.

McKenna, Virginia, b. 7 Jun.

Mackensen, August von, b. 6 Dec.

Mackenzie, Alexander, b. 22 Aug., d. 11 Mar.

MacKenzie, Kelvin, b. 22 Oct.

Mackerras, Charles, b. 17 Nov.

McKinley, William, d. 14 Sept.

Mackintosh, Charles, d. 10 Dec.

Macklin, Charles, d. 11 Jul.

Macknight, Ella, b. 7 Aug.

McKuen, Rod, b. 29 Apr.

McLaglen, Victor, b. 11 Dec., d. 7 Nov.

Maclaine, Shirley, b. 24 Apr.

McLaren, Anne, b. 26 Apr.

McLaren, Malcolm, b. 20 Jan.

McLaren, Norman, b. 11 Apr.

MacLaurin, Ian, b. 30 Mar.

McLean, Don (singer), b. 2 Oct.

Maclean, Donald, d. 6 Mar.

Maclean, Fitzroy, b. 11 Mar.

Macleod, Iain, d. 20 Jul.

Macleod, J.J.R., b. 6 Sept.

Maclise, Daniel, b. 25 Jan., d. 25 Apr.

MacMahon, Marshal, b. 13 Jul., d. 17 Oct.

Macmillan, Harold, d. 29 Dec.

MacMillan, Kenneth, b. 11 Dec.

MacMurray, Fred, b. 30 Aug.

MacNee, Patrick, b. 6 Feb.

MacNeice, Louis, b. 12 Sept., d. 3 Sept.

Maconchy, Elizabeth, b. 19 Mar.

Macpherson, William, b. 1 Apr.

McQueen, Gordon, b. 26 Jun.

McQueen, Steve, b. 24 Mar., d. 7 Nov.

Macqueen-Pope, W.J., b. 11 Apr.

McRae, Carmen, b. 8 Apr.

Macready, William, b. 3 Mar., d. 27 Apr.

McTell, Ralph, b. 3 Dec.

McWhirter, Norris, b. 12 Aug.

McWilliam, Edward, b. 30 Apr.

Madariaga, Salvador de, b. 23 Jul., d. 14 Dec.

Madden, Charles, b. 15 Jun.

Madero, Francisco, d. 22 Feb.

Madison, James, d. 28 Jun.

Madoc, Philip, b. 5 Jul.

Madoc, Ruth, b. 16 Apr.

Madonna, b. 16 Aug.

Madrazo y Kuntz, José de, d. 8 May

Maeterlinck, Maurice, b. 29 Aug., d. 6 May

Magellan, Ferdinand, d. 27 Apr.

Magill, Ronald, b. 21 Apr.

Maginn, William, d. 21 Aug.

Magnusson, Magnus, b. 12 Oct.

Magritte, René, b. 21 Nov., d. 15 Aug.

Mahler, Gustav, b. 7 Jul., d. 18 May

Maillol, Aristide, b. 8 Dec., d. 27 Sept.

Maiman, Theodore, b. 11 Jul.

Maimonides, b. 30 Mar., d. 13 Dec.

Major, John, b. 29 Mar.

Major, Kathleen, b. 10 Apr.

Majors, Lee, b. 23 Apr.

Makarios III, b. 13 Aug., d. 3 Aug.

Makarova, Natalia, b. 21 Nov.

Makart, Hans, d. 3 Oct.

Maklouf, Raphael, b. 10 Dec.

Malan, Daniel, b. 22 May

Malcolm, Ellen, b. 28 Sept.

Malcolm III, of Scotland, d. 13 Nov.

Malebranche, Nicolas de, d. 13 Oct.

Malesherbes, Chrétien de, b. 6 Dec.

Malinowski, Bronislaw, d. 16 May

Malipiero, Gian, d. 31 Jul.

Mallalieu, Ann, b. 27 Nov.

Mallarmé, Stéphane, d. 9 Sept.

Malle, Louis, b. 30 Oct.

Malleson, Miles, b. 25 May

Malone, Dorothy, b. 10 Jan.

Malone, Edmund, b. 4 Oct.

Malraux, André, b. 3 Nov., d. 23 Nov.

Malthus, Thomas, d. 23 Dec.

Mamoulian, Rouben, b. 8 Oct.

Manasseh, Leonard, b. 21 May

Manby, George, b. 28 Nov.
Manchester, William, b. 1 Apr.
Mancini, Henry, b. 16 Apr.
Mandela, Nelson, b. 18 Jul.
Mander, Karel van, d. 2 Sept.
Mander, Noel, b. 19 May
Manet, Édouard, b. 23 Jan., d. 30 Apr.
Manilow, Barry, b. 17 Jun.
Mankiewicz, Herman J., b. 7 Nov.
Mankowitz, Wolf, b. 7 Nov.
Mann, Anthony, b. 30 Jun.
Mann, George, b. 6 Sept.
Mann, Manfred, b. 21 Oct.
Mann, Thomas, b. 6 Jun., d. 12 Aug.
Mannerheim, Carl, b. 4 Jun., d. 27 Jan.
Mannheim, Karl, b. 27 Mar.
Mannin, Ethel, b. 11 Oct., d. 5 Dec.
Manning, Cardinal, b. 15 Jul.
Manning, Jane, b. 20 Sept.
Manning, Olivia, d. 23 Jun.
Manoel I, of Portugal, d. 13 Dec.
Manoel II, of Portugal, d. 2 Jul.
Mans, Perrie, b. 15 Oct.
Mansart, Nicholas, d. 23 Sept.
Mansell, Nigel, b. 8 Aug.
Mansfield, Jayne, b. 19 Apr., d. 29
  Jun.
Mansfield, Katherine, b. 14 Oct.
Manson, George, b. 3 Dec.
Manson, Patrick, b. 3 Oct.
Mantegna, Andrea, d. 13 Sept.
Mantell, Gideon, d. 10 Nov.
Mantovani, Annunzio, d. 29 Mar.
Manwaring, Randle, b. 3 May
Manzoni, Alessandro, d. 22 May
Mao Tse-tung, b. 26 Dec., d. 9 Sept.
Marat, Jean-Paul, d. 13 Jun.
Marcel, Gabriel, b. 7 Dec.
Marcello, Benedetto, b. 1 Aug., d. 24 Jul.
March, Fredric, b. 31 Aug., d. 14 Apr.
Marchand, Jean, b. 22 Nov.
Marciano, Rocky, b. 1 Sept., d. 31 Aug.
Marconi, Guglielmo, b. 25 Apr., d. 20 Jul.
Marcus Aurelius, b. 26 Apr.
Marcuse, Herbert, b. 19 Jul., d. 29 Jul.
Marenzio, Luca, d. 22 Aug.
Marey, Étienne-Jules, d. 15 May
Margaret, of Scotland, b. 29 Nov., d. 18
  Oct.
Margaret, Princess, b. 21 Aug.

Margolyes, Miriam, b. 18 May
Margrethe, of Denmark, b. 16 Apr.
Maria Theresa, of Austria, b. 13 May, d.
  29 Nov.
Marie Antoinette, b. 2 Nov., d. 16 Oct.
Mariner, Paul, b. 22 May
Marinetti, Filippo, d. 2 Dec.
Marini, Marino, b. 27 Feb.
Marino, Gianbattista, b. 18 Oct.
Marion, Francis, d. 27 Feb.
Maris, Jacob, b. 25 Aug., d. 7 Aug.
Markova, Alicia, b. 1 Dec.
Marks, Simon, b. 9 Jul.
Marks, Victor, b. 25 Jun.
Markus, Rika, b. 27 Jun., d. 4 Apr.
Marlborough, 1st Duke, b. 26 May, d. 16
  Jun.
Marlowe, Christopher, d. 30 May
Marmontel, Jean, d. 31 Dec.
Marquand, John P., b. 10 Nov., d. 16 Jul.
Marquis, Don, b. 29 Jul.
Marriner, Neville, b. 15 Apr.
Marryat, Frederick, b. 10 Jul., d. 9 Aug.
Marschner, Heinrich, b. 16 Aug.
Marsden, Betty, b. 24 Feb.
Marsden, Charles, b. 15 Apr.
Marsden, Gerry, b. 24 Sept.
Marsden, Roy, b. 25 Jun.
Marsh, Jean, b. 1 Jul.
Marsh, Ngaio, b. 23 Apr.
Marsh, Reginald, b. 17 Sept.
Marsh, Rodney, b. 11 Nov.
Marshall, Bruce, d. 18 Jun.
Marshall, George, b. 31 Dec., d. 16 Oct.
Marshall, Herbert, b. 23 May
Marshall, John, b. 24 Sept.
Marston, John, d. 25 Jun.
Martel, Charles, d. 22 Oct.
Martell, Hugh, b. 6 May
Martens, Conrad, d. 21 Aug.
Martin, Dean, b. 17 Jun.
Martin, Frank, b. 15 Sept., d. 21 Nov.
Martin, John, b. 19 Jul.
Martin, Mary, b. 1 Dec.
Martin, Millicent, b. 8 Jun.
Martin, Tony, b. 25 Dec.
Martin du Gard, Roger, d. 22 Aug.
Martineau, Harriet, b. 12 Jun., d. 27 Jun.
Martínez Sierra, Gregorio, d. 1 Oct.
Martini, Giambattista, b. 24 Apr.

Martins, Peter, b. 27 Oct.
Martinu, Bohuslav, b. 8 Dec., d. 28 Aug.
Martí y Pérez, José, d. 19 May
Marvell, Andrew, b. 31 Mar., d. 16 Aug.
Marvin, Hank, b. 28 Oct.
Marvin, Lee, d. 29 Aug.
Marx, Chico, b. 26 Mar., d. 11 Oct.
Marx, Groucho, b. 2 Oct., d. 19 Aug.
Marx, Harpo, b. 21 Nov., d. 28 Sept.
Marx, Karl, b. 5 May, d. 14 Mar.
Marx, Zeppo, b. 25 Feb.
Mary I, of England, d. 17 Nov.
Mary II, of Great Britain, b. 30 Apr., d. 28 Dec.
Mary of Teck, Princess, b. 26 May
Mary Stuart, of Scots, b. 8 Dec.
Masaccio, b. 21 Dec.
Masaryk, Jan, b. 14 Sept.
Masaryk, Tomás, d. 14 Sept.
Mascagni, Pietro, b. 7 Dec., d. 2 Aug.
Masefield, John, b. 1 Jun., d. 12 May
Maskelyne, John Nevil, b. 22 Dec., d. 18 May
Maskelyne, Nevil, b. 6 Oct.
Mason, A.E.W., b. 7 May, d. 22 Nov.
Mason, James, b. 15 May, d. 27 Jul.
Mason, Monica, b. 6 Sept.
Mason, Richard, b. 16 May
Mason of Barnsley, Lord, b. 18 Apr.
Massena, André, b. 6 May
Massenet, Jules, b. 12 May, d. 13 Aug.
Massey, Anna, b. 11 Aug.
Massey, Daniel, b. 10 Oct.
Massey, Raymond, b. 30 Aug., d. 29 Jul.
Massey, Vincent, d. 30 Dec.
Massine, Léonide, b. 9 Aug., d. 16 Mar.
Massys, Jan, d. 8 Oct.
Massys, Quentin, b. 10 Sept.
Masters, Edgar Lee, b. 23 Aug.
Masters, John, d. 7 May
Mastroianni, Marcello, b. 28 Sept.
Mata, Eduardo, b. 5 Sept.
Mata Hari, b. 7 Aug., d. 15 Oct.
Mates, Michael, b. 9 Jun.
Mather, Cotton, b. 12 Feb.
Mather, Increase, b. 21 Jun.
Mathias, Peter, b. 10 Jan.
Mathias, William, b. 1 Nov.
Mathis, Johnny, b. 30 Sept.
Matisse, Henri, b. 31 Dec., d. 3 Nov.

Mattei, Tito, d. 30 Mar.
Matteotti, Giacomo, b. 22 May, d. 10 Jun.
Matthau, Walter, b. 1 Oct.
Mattheson, Johann, b. 28 Sept.
Matthew, Brian, b. 17 Sept.
Matthews, Francis, b. 2 Sept.
Matthews, Jessie, b. 11 Mar., d. 20 Aug.
Matthews, Michael Gough, b. 12 Jul.
Matthias Corvinus, of Hungary, d. 6 Apr.
Maturin, Charles, d. 30 Oct.
Maud, of Norway, b. 26 Nov., d. 20 Nov.
Maudslay, Henry, d. 14 Feb.
Maugham, Somerset, d. 16 Dec.
Maupassant, Guy de, b. 5 Aug., d. 6 Jul.
Maupertius, Pierre de, b. 28 Sept.
Mauriac, François, b. 11 Oct., d. 1 Sept.
Maurice of Nassau, b. 13 Nov.
Maurois, André, b. 26 Jul., d. 9 Oct.
Maurras, Charles, b. 20 Apr., d. 16 Nov.
Mauve, Anton, b. 18 Sept.
Maw, Janet, b. 16 May
Maw, Nicholas, b. 5 Nov.
Mawson, Douglas, b. 5 May
Maxim, Hiram, d. 24 Nov.
Maximilian, of Mexico, b. 6 Jul., d. 19 Jun.
Maximilian I, of Bavaria, d. 13 Oct.
Maximilian II, Holy Roman Emperor, b. 31 Jul.
Maximinus the Thracian, d. 10 May
Maxwell, James Clerk, b. 13 Jun.
Maxwell, Robert, b. 10 Jun., d. 5 Nov.
Maxwell, William B., d. 4 Aug.
May, Karl, d. 31 Mar.
May, Phil, b. 22 Apr., d. 5 Aug.
Mayakovsky, Vladimir, b. 19 Jul.
Mayall, John, b. 29 Nov.
Mayer, Louis B., b. 4 Jul.
Mayer, Robert, b. 5 Jun.
Mayhew, Henry, b. 25 Nov., d. 25 Jul.
Mayhew, Lord, b. 12 Jun.
Mayhew, Patrick, b. 11 Sept.
Maynard, Bill, b. 8 Oct.
Mayo, Charles H., b. 19 Jul., d. 26 May
Mayo, Virginia, b. 30 Nov.
Mayo, William J., b. 29 Jun., d. 28 Jul.
Mayo, William W., b. 31 May
Mazarin, Cardinal, b. 14 Jul., d. 9 Mar.
Mazzini, Giuseppe, b. 22 Jun.
Mboya, Thomas, d. 5 Jul.
Meacher, Michael, b. 4 Nov.

Mead, Margaret, b. 16 Dec., d. 15 Nov.
Mead, Richard, b. 11 Aug.
Meads, Colin, b. 3 Jun.
Meale, Richard, b. 24 Aug.
Medawar, Peter, b. 28 Feb.
Medici, Lorenzo de', b. 1 Jan., d. 9 Apr.
Medici, Marie de', d. 3 Jul.
Medwin, Michael, b. 18 Jul.
Mehta, Zubin, b. 29 Apr.
Meighen, Arthur, b. 16 Jun.
Meillet, Antoine, b. 11 Nov.
Meir, Golda, b. 3 May, d. 8 Dec.
Meissonier, Juste, d. 31 Jul.
Meitner, Lise, b. 7 Nov., d. 27 Oct.
Melanchthon, Philip, b. 15 Feb.
Melba, Nellie, b. 19 May, d. 23 Feb.
Melbourne, 2nd Viscount, d. 24 Nov.
Méliès, Georges, b. 8 Dec.
Mellers, Wilfrid, b. 26 Apr.
Mellor, David, b. 5 Oct.
Mellor, Elain, b. 28 Aug.
Melly, George, b. 17 Aug.
Melville, 1st Viscount, b. 29 May
Melville, Herman, b. 1 Aug., d. 28
    Sept.
Memling, Hans, d. 11 Aug.
Mencken, H.L., b. 12 Sept.
Mendel, Gregor, b. 22 Jul.
Mendelssohn, Felix, d. 4 Nov.
Mendès-France, Pierre, d. 18 Oct.
Mendoza, Pedro de, d. 23 Jun.
Menendez de Avilés, b. 15 Feb., d. 17
    Sept.
Mennin, Peter, b. 17 May
Menotti, Gian Carlo, b. 7 Jul.
Menpes, Mortimer, d. 1 Apr.
Menuhin, Yaltah, b. 7 Oct.
Menuhin, Yehudi, b. 22 Apr.
Menzies, Robert, b. 20 Dec., d. 15 May
Menzies, William C., b. 29 Jul.
Meo, Tony, b. 4 Oct.
Mercator, Gerardus, b. 5 Mar., d. 2 Dec.
Mercer, Joe, b. 25 Oct.
Mercer, Johnny, b. 18 Nov., d. 25 Jun.
Merchant, Ismail, b. 25 Dec.
Mercouri, Melina, b. 18 Oct.
Mercury, Freddie, b. 15 Sept., d. 24
    Nov.
Meredith, George, d. 18 May
Meredith, Owen, b. 8 Nov., d. 24 Nov.

Mergenthaler, Ottmar, b. 11 May, d. 28
    Oct.
Merian, Kaspar, d. 12 Apr.
Merian, Matthew, the Elder, b. 25 Sept.,
    d. 19 Jun.
Merimée, Prosper, b. 28 Sept., d. 23 Sept.
Merulo, Claudio, b. 8 Apr.
Meryon, Charles, b. 24 Nov.
Mesmer, Franz, b. 23 May
Messager, André, b. 30 Dec.
Messel, Oliver, d. 13 Jun.
Messerschmitt, Willy, b. 26 Jun.
Messiaen, Olivier, b. 10 Dec.
Messier, Charles-Joseph, b. 26 Jun., d. 12
    Apr.
Mestrovic, Ivan, b. 1 Aug.
Metastasio, Pietro, d. 12 Apr.
Metternich, Prince, b. 15 May
Meulen, Adam van der, d. 15 Oct.
Meyerbeer, Giacomo, b. 5 Sept., d. 2 May
Meynell, Francis, b. 12 May, d. 9 Jul.
Miall, Leonard, b. 6 Nov.
Miaskovsky, Nikolai, d. 9 Aug.
Michael of Kent, Prince, b. 4 Jul.
Michael, of Romania, b. 25 Oct.
Michelangelo, b. 6 Mar., d. 18 Feb.
Michelet, Jules, b. 21 Aug.
Michelin, André, d. 4 Apr.
Michell, Keith, b. 1 Dec.
Michelmore, Cliff, b. 11 Dec.
Michelson, Albert A., b. 19 Dec.
Michener, Roland, b. 19 Apr.
Mickiewicz, Adam, b. 24 Dec., d. 26 Nov.
Mickle, William, b. 28 Sept., d. 28 Oct.
Middlemass, Frank, b. 28 May
Middleton, Edgar, d. 10 Apr.
Middleton, Stanley, b. 1 Aug.
Midler, Bette, b. 1 Dec.
Mierevelt, Michiel van, b. 1 May, d. 27
    Jun.
Mieris, Frans van, the Younger, b. 23
    Dec., d. 22 Oct.
Mieris, Jan van, b. 17 Jun.
Mieris, Willem van, b. 3 Jun.
Mies van der Rohe, Ludwig, b. 27 Mar., d.
    17 Aug.
Mignard, Pierre, d. 30 May
Mignon, Abraham, b. 21 Jun.
Mihajlovic, Draza, d. 17 Jul.
Mikoyan, Anastas, d. 21 Oct.

Miles, Dillwyn, b. 25 May
Miles, Sarah, b. 31 Dec.
Milestone, Lewis, b. 30 Sept.
Milhaud, Darius, b. 4 Sept., d. 22 Jun.
Mill, John Stuart, b. 20 May, d. 8 May
Millais, John, b. 8 Jun., d. 13 Aug.
Millar, Gertie, d. 25 Apr.
Millar, Ronald, b. 12 Nov.
Millay, Edna, d. 19 Oct.
Miller, Ann, b. 12 Apr.
Miller, Arthur, b. 17 Oct.
Miller, Geoff, b. 8 Sept.
Miller, George, d. 18 Aug.
Miller, Glenn, d. 16 Dec.
Miller, Henry, b. 26 Dec., d. 7 Jun.
Miller, Hugh, b. 10 Oct., d. 23 Dec.
Miller, Joe, d. 16 Aug.
Miller, Jonathan, b. 21 Jul.
Miller, Keith, b. 28 Nov.
Miller, Roger, b. 2 Jan.
Miller, Steve, b. 5 Nov.
Miller, William, d. 20 Aug.
Millet, Jean, b. 4 Oct.
Millet, Jean-François, b. 27 Apr., d. 3 Jun.
Millett, Peter, b. 23 Jun.
Milligan, Spike, b. 16 Apr.
Millikan, Robert A., d. 19 Dec.
Mills, Barbara, b. 10 Aug.
Mills, Bertram, d. 16 Apr.
Mills, Hayley, b. 18 Apr.
Mills, John, b. 22 Feb.
Mills, Juliet, b. 2 Nov.
Milman, Henry, 24 Sept.
Milner, 1st Viscount, d. 13 May
Milnes, 1st Baron, b. 19 Jun.
Milnes, Richard, d. 11 Aug.
Milstein, Nathan, b. 31 Dec.
Milton, John, b. 9 Dec., d. 8 Nov.
Minot, George, b. 2 Dec.
Minter, Alan, b. 17 Aug.
Minton, Yvonne, b. 4 Dec.
Mintz, Shlomo, b. 30 Oct.
Mirabeau, Comte de, b. 9 Mar., d. 2 Apr.
Miró, Joan, b. 20 Apr., d. 25 Dec.
Mirren, Helen, b. 26 Jul.
Mirvish, Edwin, b. 24 Jul.
Mishcon, Lord, b. 14 Aug.
Mistral, Frédéric, b. 8 Sept., d. 25 Mar.
Mitchell, Joni, b. 7 Nov.
Mitchell, Julian, b. 1 May

Mitchell, Margaret, b. 8 Nov.
Mitchison, Naomi, b. 1 Nov.
Mitchum, Robert, b. 6 Aug.
Mitford, Jessica, b. 11 Sept.
Mitford, Mary, b. 16 Dec.
Mitford, Nancy, b. 28 Nov., d. 30 Jun.
Mittelholzer, Edgar, d. 6 May
Mitterand, François, b. 26 Oct.
Mix, Tom, d. 12 Oct.
Mize, Larry, b. 23 Sept.
Modigliani, Amedeo, b. 12 Jul.
Modjeska, Helen, b. 12 Oct.
Moeran, Ernest, b. 31 Dec., d. 1 Dec.
Moffat, Robert, b. 21 Dec.
Mohammed, the Prophet, d. 8 Jun.
Mohammed Ali (boxer), b. 18 Dec.
Moiseiwitsch, Tanya, b. 3 Dec.
Molay, Jacques de, d. 18 Mar.
Molière, baptised, 15 Jan., d. 17 Feb.
Molitor, Ludwig, b. 12 Jul.
Mollison, James, d. 30 Oct.
Molnár, Ferenc, d. 1 Apr.
Molotov, Vyacheslav, b. 9 Mar., d. 11
   Nov.
Moltke, Helmuth von, b. 26 Oct.
Mommsen, Theodor, b. 30 Nov., d. 1 Nov.
Monash, John, b. 27 Jun., d. 8 Oct.
Monck, George, b. 6 Dec.
Mond, Ludwig, d. 11 Dec.
Mondrian, Piet, b. 7 Mar.
Monet, Claude, b. 14 Nov., d. 5 Dec.
Monk, Thelonius, b. 10 Oct.
Monkhouse, Bob, b. 1 Jun.
Monmouth, Duke of, b. 9 Apr., d. 15 Jul.
Monnet, Jean, b. 9 Nov., d. 16 Mar.
Monroe, James, b. 28 Apr., d. 4 Jul.
Monroe, Marilyn, b. 1 Jun., d. 5 Aug.
Montagu, Lady Mary, d. 21 Aug.
Montagu, Lord, b. 20 Oct.
Montaigne, Michel de, d. 13 Sept.
Montalban, Ricardo, b. 25 Nov.
Montand, Yves, b. 13 Oct., d. 9 Nov.
Montcalm, Marquis de, b. 28 Feb., d. 14
   Sept.
Montefiore, Hugh, b. 12 May
Montefiore, Moses, b. 24 Oct., d. 28 Jul.
Montesquieu, Baron, b. 18 Jan., d. 10 Feb.
Montessori, Maria, b. 31 Aug., d. 6 May
Montezuma II, d. 30 Jun.
Montgolfier, Jacques, d. 2 Aug.

Montgolfier, Joseph, b. 26 Aug., d. 26 Jun.
Montgomery, Bernard, b. 17 Nov.
Montgomery, David, b. 6 Nov.
Montgomery, Elizabeth, b. 15 Apr.
Montgomery, James, b. 4 Nov.
Montgomery, Robert, d. 3 Dec.
Montherlant, Henri de, b. 21 Apr., d. 21 Sept.
Monticelli, Adolphe, b. 14 Oct., d. 29 Jun.
Montsarrat, Nicholas, d. 8 Aug.
Moody, Dwight L., d. 22 Dec.
Moody, Helen Wills, b. 6 Oct.
Moorcroft, David, b. 10 Apr.
Moore, Albert, b. 4 Sept.
Moore, Bobby, b. 12 Apr.
Moore, Brian, b. 25 Aug.
Moore, Douglas, b. 10 Aug., d. 25 Jul.
Moore, Dudley, b. 19 Apr.
Moore, George Edward, b. 4 Nov., d. 24 Oct.
Moore, Grace, d. 26 Jan.
Moore, Henry, b. 30 Jul., d. 31 Aug.
Moore, Jeremy, b. 5 Jul.
Moore, John (general), b. 13 Nov.
Moore, Mary Tyler, b. 29 Dec.
Moore, Roger, b. 14 Oct.
Moore, Thomas, b. 28 May, d. 18 Jul.
Moorhouse, Geoffrey, b. 29 Nov.
Moran, 1st Baron, d. 12 Apr.
Moran, Edward, d. 9 Jun.
Moravia, Alberto, b. 28 Nov.
More, Hannah, d. 7 Sept.
More, Kenneth, b. 20 Sept., d. 12 Jul.
More, Thomas, d. 6 Jul.
Moreau, Gustave, b. 6 Apr.
Moreau, Jean, b. 11 Aug., d. 2 Sept.
Morecambe, Eric, d. 28 May
Morgan, Charles Langbridge, b. 21 Jan.
Morgan, Cliff, b. 7 Apr.
Morgan, Dennis, b. 10 Dec.
Morgan, Garfield, b. 19 Apr.
Morgan, Henry (buccaneer), d. 25 Aug.
Morgan, Henry (comedian), b. 31 Mar.
Morgan, Janet, b. 5 Dec.
Morgan, John Pierpont, b. 17 Apr., d. 31 Mar.
Morgan, Lewis H., b. 21 Nov., d. 17 Dec.
Moriarty, Paul, b. 19 May
Mörike, Eduard, b. 8 Sept.
Morison, Stanley Arthur, b. 6 May

Morland, George, b. 26 Jun., d. 27 Oct.
Morley, Christopher, b. 5 May, d. 28 Mar.
Morley, John, d. 23 Sept.
Morley, Robert, b. 26 May, d. 3 Jun.
Morley, Sheridan, b. 5 Dec.
Morley, Viscount, b. 24 Dec.
Morpurgo, Jack, b. 26 Apr.
Morris, Alec, b. 11 Mar.
Morris, Jan, b. 2 Oct.
Morris, Johnny, b. 20 Jun.
Morris, Jonathon, b. 20 Jul.
Morris, William, d. 3 Oct.
Morrison, Van, b. 31 Aug.
Morrocco, Alberto, b. 14 Dec.
Morse, Samuel, b. 27 Apr., d. 2 Apr.
Mortensen, Stan, b. 26 May
Mortimer, Angela, b. 21 Apr.
Mortimer, Harry, b. 10 Apr.
Mortimer, John, b. 21 Apr.
Mortimer, Penelope, b. 19 Sept.
Morton, J.B., d. 10 May
Morton, Jelly Roll, d. 10 Jul.
Moser, Claus, b. 24 Nov.
Moses, Edwin, b. 31 Aug.
Moses, Grandma, b. 7 Sept., d. 13 Dec.
Mosley, Oswald, b. 16 Nov., d. 3 Dec.
Moss, Pat, b. 27 Dec.
Moss, Stirling, b. 17 Sept.
Moszkowski, Moritz, b. 23 Aug.
Motley, John, b. 15 Apr., d. 29 May
Mottram, Ralph, b. 30 Oct.
Mottram, Tony, b. 8 Jun.
Mould, Marion, b. 6 Jun.
Mount, Peggy, b. 2 May
Mountbatten, Earl, b. 25 Jun., d. 27 Aug.
Mountbatten, Louis, b. 24 May, d. 11 Sept.
Mountjoy, Doug, b. 8 Jun.
Mower, Patrick, b. 12 Sept.
Moyet, Alison, b. 18 Jun.
Moyne, Lord, b. 27 Oct.
Mozart, Wolfgang Amadeus, d. 5 Dec.
Mubarak, Muhammad, b. 4 May
Muir, Edwin, b. 15 May
Muldowney, Dominic, b. 19 Jul.
Müller, William, d. 8 Sept.
Mullery, Alan, b. 23 Nov.
Mulligan, Gerry, b. 6 Apr.
Mulready, William, b. 30 Apr.
Munch, Edvard, b. 12 Dec.

Muni, Paul, b. 22 Sept., d. 25 Aug.
Munnings, Alfred, b. 8 Oct.
Murat, Joachim, d. 13 Oct.
Murchison, Roderick, b. 19 Feb., d. 22 Oct.
Murdoch, Iris, b. 15 Jul.
Murdoch, Rupert, b. 11 Mar.
Murdock, William, b. 21 Aug., d. 15 Nov.
Murillo, Bartolomé, d. 3 Apr.
Murphy, Dervla, b. 28 Nov.
Murphy, George, b. 4 Jul., d. 3 May
Murray, Barbara, b. 27 Sept.
Murray, Bryan, b. 13 Jun.
Murray, David, d. 14 Nov.
Murray, Deryck, b. 20 May
Murray, James, d. 26 Jul.
Murray, John, b. 27 Nov., d. 6 Nov.
Murray, Pete, b. 19 Sept.
Murray, Ruby, b. 29 Mar.
Murray, Stephen, b. 6 Sept.
Murray, Yvonne, b. 4 Oct.
Murrow, Ed, b. 25 Apr., d. 11 Dec.
Murry, John Middleton, b. 6 Aug.
Musgrave, Thea, b. 27 May
Musset, Alfred de, b. 11 Dec., d. 2 May
Mussolini, Benito, b. 29 Jul., d. 28 Apr.
Mussorgsky, Modest, b. 21 Mar., d. 28 Mar.
Mustill, Michael, b. 10 May
Muti, Riccardo, b. 28 Jul.
Muybridge, Eadweard, b. 9 Apr., d. 8 May

Nabokov, Vladimir, b. 22 Apr., d. 2 Jul.
Nader, Ralph, b. 27 Feb.
Nagy, Imre, d. 16 Jun.
Naipaul, Vidiadhar, b. 17 Aug.
Namier, Lewis, b. 27 Jun.
Nanak, b. 15 Apr.
Nannini, Alessandro, b. 7 Jul.
Nansen, Fridtjof, b. 10 Oct., d. 13 May
Nanteuil, Celestin, b. 11 Jul., d. 4 Sept.
Naoroji, Dadabhai, b. 4 Sept.
Napier, Charles (adm.), d. 6 Nov.
Napier, Charles (soldier), b. 10 Aug., d. 29 Aug.
Napier, John, d. 4 Apr.
Napier, Lord, d. 14 Jan.
Napley, David, b. 25 Jul.
Napoleon I, b. 15 Aug., d. 5 May
Napoleon III, b. 20 Apr., d. 9 Jan.

Nares, Owen, d. 31 Jul.
Nash, John, d. 13 May
Nash, Ogden, b. 19 Aug., d. 19 May
Nash, Paul, b. 11 May, d. 11 Jul.
Nash, Richard 'Beau', d. 3 Feb.
Nasmyth, Alexander, b. 9 Sept.
Nasmyth, James, b. 19 Aug., d. 7 May
Nasser, Gamal Abdel, b. 15 Jan.
Nast, Thomas, b. 27 Sept., d. 7 Dec.
Nastase, Ilie, b. 19 Jul.
Nattier, Jean, d. 7 Nov.
Naumann, Johann, b. 17 Apr.
Naundorff, Karl, d. 10 Aug.
Navarrete, Juan Fernández de, d. 28 Mar.
Navratilova, Martina, b. 18 Oct.
Neagle, Anna, b. 20 Oct., d. 3 Jun.
Neal, Daniel, b. 14 Dec.
Neal, Patricia, b. 20 Jan.
Neal, Phil, b. 20 Feb.
Neame, Ronald, b. 23 Apr.
Neave, Airey, d. 30 Mar.
Necker, Jacques, b. 30 Sept.
Nedwell, Robin, b. 27 Sept.
Neer, Eglon van der, d. 3 May
Neff, Hildegarde, b. 28 Dec.
Nehru, Pandit, b. 14 Nov., d. 27 May
Neil, Andrew, b. 21 May
Neilson, Lilian, b. 3 Mar., d. 15 Aug.
Nelligan, Kate, b. 16 Mar.
Nelson, Gene, b. 24 Mar.
Nelson, Horatio, b. 29 Sept., d. 21 Oct.
Nelson, John, b. 15 Jun.
Nelson of Stafford, Lord, b. 2 Jan.
Nerina, Nadia, b. 21 Oct.
Nernst, Walther, d. 18 Nov.
Nero, emperor, b. 15 Dec.
Neruda, Pablo, d. 23 Sept.
Nerval, Gérard de, b. 22 May
Nervi, Pier Luigi, b. 21 Jun.
Nervo, Jimmy, b. 2 Jan.
Nettleton, John, b. 5 Feb.
Neuberger, Julia, b. 27 Feb.
Neville, John, b. 2 May
Neville, Oliver, b. 14 Aug.
Nevinson, Christopher, b. 13 Aug., d. 7 Oct.
Newbolt, Henry, b. 6 Jun., d. 19 Apr.
Newby, Howard, b. 25 Jun.
Newcomen, Thomas, d. 5 Aug.
Newdigate, Roger, d. 23 Nov.

Newhart, Bob, b. 5 Sept.
Newlands, John, b. 26 Nov.
Newley, Anthony, b. 24 Sept.
Newman, John Henry, b. 21 Feb., d. 11 Aug.
Newman, Nanette, b. 29 May
Newman, Paul, b. 26 Jan.
Newman, Randy, b. 28 Nov.
Newton, Antony, b. 29 Aug.
Newton, Isaac, b. 25 Dec., d. 20 Mar.
Newton-John, Olivia, b. 26 Sept.
Ney, Marie, d. 11 Apr.
Ney, Marshal, d. 7 Dec.
Ney, Michel, b. 10 Jan.
Niarchos, Stavros, b. 3 Jul.
Niblo, Fred, b. 6 Jan.
Nicholas, David, b. 25 Jan.
Nicholas, of Greece, d. 8 Feb.
Nicholas, Paul, b. 3 Dec.
Nicholas I, of Russia, b. 6 Jul., d. 2 Mar.
Nicholas II, of Russia, b. 18 May, d. 16 Jul.
Nicholls, Horatio, b. 15 Feb., d. 19 May
Nichols, Peter, b. 31 Jul.
Nicholson, Jack, b. 22 Apr.
Nicholson, James, b. 4 Feb.
Nicholson, Mavis, b. 19 Oct.
Nicholson, Sir William, b. 5 Feb.
Nicholson, William, b. 25 Dec.
Nicklaus, Jack, b. 21 Jan.
Nicolson, Harold, b. 21 Nov., d. 1 May
Nicolson, Nigel, b. 19 Jan.
Nielsen, Carl, d. 3 Oct.
Nielsen, Leslie, b. 11 Feb.
Niemeyer, Oscar, b. 15 Dec.
Niemöller, Martin, b. 1 Jan.
Niepce, Joseph, b. 7 Mar., d. 5 Jul.
Nietzsche, Friedrich, b. 15 Oct., d. 25 Aug.
Nieuwentijt, Bernhard, b. 10 Aug.
Nightingale, Florence, b. 12 May, d. 13 Aug.
Nijinsky, Vaslav, b. 12 Mar., d. 8 Apr.
Nilsson, Birgit, b. 17 May
Nilsson, Bo, b. 1 May
Nilsson, Kristina, b. 20 Aug.
Nimitz, Chester, b. 24 Feb., d. 20 Feb.
Nimmo, Derek, b. 19 Sept.
Nimoy, Leonard, b. 26 Mar.
Nin, Anaïs, b. 21 Feb., d. 14 Jan.
Niven, David, b. 1 Mar., d. 29 Jul.

Nixon, Richard, b. 9 Jan.
Nkrumah, Kwame, b. 18 Sept., d. 27 Apr.
Noakes, George, b. 13 Sept.
Noakes, Michael, b. 28 Oct.
Nobel, Alfred, b. 21 Oct., d. 10 Dec.
Noble, Adrian, b. 19 Jul.
Noble, Ray, b. 17 Dec., d. 3 Apr.
Nolan, Eileen, b. 19 Jun.
Nolan, Lloyd, d. 27 Sept.
Nolan, Sidney, b. 22 Apr.
Nollekens, Joseph, b. 11 Aug.
Nollet, Jean, b. 19 Nov.
Norden, Denis, b. 6 Feb.
Nordenskjöld, Nils, b. 18 Nov., d. 12 Aug.
Norman, Barry, b. 21 Aug.
Norman, Greg, b. 10 Feb.
Norman, Jessye, b. 15 Sept.
Norman, Montagu, d. 4 Feb.
Norrington, Roger, b. 16 Mar.
Norris, Frank, d. 25 Oct.
North, Lord, d. 5 Aug.
Northcliffe, Viscount, b. 15 Jul., d. 14 Aug.
Northcote, James, b. 22 Oct., d. 13 Jun.
Northcote, Stafford, d. 12 Jan.
Northcott, Richard, b. 24 Sept.
Norton, Mary, b. 10 Dec.
Nostradamus, b. 14 Dec., d. 2 Jul.
Nott, John, b. 1 Feb.
Nourse, Martin, b. 3 Apr.
Novak, Kim, b. 13 Feb.
Novák, Vitezslav, b. 5 Dec., d. 18 Jul.
Novalis, d. 25 Mar.
Novarro, Ramon, b. 6 Feb.
Novello, Ivor, b. 15 Jan., d. 6 Mar.
Novello, Vincent, b. 6 Sept.
Noyes, Alfred, b. 16 Sept., d. 28 Jun.
Nuffield, Viscount, b. 10 Oct., d. 22 Aug.
Nugent, Robert, d. 13 Oct.
Numan, Gary, b. 8 Mar.
Nunn, John, b. 25 Apr.
Nunn, Trevor, b. 14 Jan.
Nureyev, Rudolf, b. 17 Mar.
Nurmi, Paavo, d. 2 Oct.
Nye, Robert, b. 15 Mar.

Oakeley, Herbert, b. 22 Jul.
Oakley, Annie, 3 Nov.
Oaksey, Lord, b. 21 Mar.
Oates, Titus, b. 15 Sept., d. 12 Jul.

Oberon, Merle, b. 19 Feb., d. 23 Nov.
Oberth, Hermann, b. 25 Jun.
Oberthür, Charles, b. 4 Mar.
Obolensky, Dimitri, b. 1 Apr.
O'Brian, Hugh, b. 19 Apr.
O'Brien, Conor Cruise, b. 3 Nov.
O'Brien, David, b. 6 Aug.
O'Brien, Edmond, d. 9 May
O'Brien, Edna, b. 15 Dec.
O'Brien, Margaret, b. 15 Jan.
O'Brien, Pat, d. 15 Oct.
O'Brien, Virginia, b. 8 Apr.
O'Brien of Lothbury, Lord, b. 8 Feb.
O'Casey, Sean, b. 30 Mar., d. 18 Sept.
Ochs, Adolph, b. 12 Mar., d. 8 Apr.
O'Connell, Daniel, b. 6 Aug., d. 15 May
O'Connor, Des, b. 12 Jan.
O'Connor, Donald, b. 28 Aug.
O'Connor, Feargus, d. 30 Aug.
O'Connor, Frank, d. 10 Mar.
O'Connor, Tom, b. 31 Oct.
O'Connor, T.P., d. 18 Nov.
Oddie, Bill, b. 7 Jul.
Odets, Clifford, b. 18 Jul., d. 14 Aug.
Odoric of Pordenone, d. 14 Jan.
Oehlenschläger, Adam, b. 14 Nov.
Offenbach, Jacques, b. 20 Jun., d. 5 Oct.
O'Flaherty, Liam, b. 28 Aug., d. 7 Sept.
Ogden, C.K., b. 1 Jun.
Ogilvy, Angus, b. 14 Sept.
Ogilvy, Ian, b. 30 Sept.
Ogilvy, James, b. 29 Feb.
Oglethorpe, James, b. 22 Dec.
O'Hara, John, b. 31 Jan., d. 11 Apr.
O'Hara, Maureen, b. 17 Aug.
O'Herlihy, Dan, b. 1 May
O'Higgins, Bernardo, b. 20 Aug.
Ohm, Georg, b. 16 Mar., d. 7 Jul.
Oistrakh, David, b. 30 Sept.
Oistrakh, Igor, b. 27 Apr.
O'Keeffe, Kerry, b. 25 Nov.
Olbers, Heinrich, b. 11 Oct., d. 2 Mar.
Olcott, Henry S., b. 2 Aug., d. 17 Feb.
Oldcastle, John, d. 14 Dec.
Oldenburg, Claes, b. 28 Jan.
Oldfield, Bruce, b. 14 Jul.
Oldfield, Mike, b. 15 May
Oldfield, Nance, d. 23 Oct.
Oldham, Steve, b. 26 Jul.
Oliphant, Carolina, d. 26 Oct.

Oliphant, Laurence, d. 23 Dec.
Oliphant, Margaret, b. 4 Apr., d. 25 Jun.
Oliver, Alan, b. 8 Sept.
Oliver, Isaac, d. 2 Oct.
Oliver, Tom, b. 30 Jun.
Olivier, Laurence, b. 22 May. d. 11 Jul.
Oman, Julia, b. 11 Jul.
O'Mara, Kate, b. 10 Aug.
Onassis, Aristotle, b. 15 Jan., d. 15 Mar.
Onassis, Jacqueline, b. 28 Jul.
O'Neal, Ryan, b. 20 Apr.
O'Neal, Tatum, b. 5 Nov.
O'Neill, Eugene, b. 16 Oct., d. 27 Nov.
O'Neill, Hugh, d. 20 Jul.
O'Neill, Norman, b. 14 Mar.
Onslow, Georges, b. 27 Jul.
Oosterhuis, Peter, b. 3 May
Ophüls, Max, b. 6 May, d. 26 Mar.
Opie, Amelia, b. 12 Nov., d. 2 Dec.
Opie, John, b. 16 May, d. 9 Apr.
Opitz, Martin, d. 20 Aug.
Oppenheim, E. Phillips, d. 3 Feb.
Oppenheimer, Ernest, b. 22 May, d. 18 Feb.
Orantes, Manuel, b. 6 Feb.
Orbison, Roy, d. 6 Dec.
Orchardson, Sir William, d. 13 Apr.
Orczy, Baroness, b. 23 Sept., d. 12 Nov.
O'Reilly, Tony, b. 7 May
Orff, Carl, b. 10 Jul.
Organ, Bryan, b. 31 Aug.
Orléans, Charles, Duc d', b. 26 May
Orléans, Philippe, Duc d', d. 2 Dec.
Orme, Stanley, b. 5 Apr.
Orpen, William, b. 27 Nov., d. 29 Sept.
Orr, Robin, b. 2 Jun.
Orsini, Felice, b. 10 Dec., d. 13 Mar.
Ortega, José, d. 18 Oct.
Ortelius, Abraham, b. 14 Apr., d. 4 Jul.
Orton, Joe, b. 1 Jan.
Orwell, George, b. 25 Jun., d. 21 Jan.
Ory, 'Kid', d. 23 Jan.
Osborne, Charles, b. 24 Nov.
Osborne, John, b. 12 Dec.
Oscar II, of Sweden, b. 21 Jan.
O'Shea, Tessie, b. 13 Mar.
Osiander, Andreas, b. 19 Dec.
Osman, Louis, b. 30 Jan.
Osmond, Alan, b. 22 Jun.
Osmond, Donny, b. 9 Dec.

Osmond, Marie, b. 13 Oct.
Ossietzky, Carl von, d. 4 May
Ostrovsky, Alexander, d. 2 Jun.
Ostwald, Friedrich, b. 2 Sept.
Ostwald, Wilhelm, d. 4 Apr.
O'Sullevan, Peter, b. 3 Mar.
O'Sullivan, Gilbert, b. 1 Dec.
O'Sullivan, Richard, b. 7 May
Oswald, Julian, b. 11 Aug.
Oswald, St., d. 29 Feb.
Otis, Elisha, b. 3 Aug., d. 8 Apr.
O'Toole, Peter, b. 2 Aug.
Ottakar II, of Bohemia, d. 26 Aug.
Otto, Nikolaus, b. 10 Jun., d. 26 Jan.
Otto I, of Greece, b. 1 Jun.
Otway, Thomas, b. 3 Mar., d. 14 Apr.
Oughtred, William, d. 30 Jun.
Ouida, b. 1 Jan., d. 25 Jan.
Ouseley, Frederick, b. 12 Aug.
Outram, James, d. 11 Mar.
Overbeck, Johann, d. 12 Nov.
Overbury, Thomas, b. 18 Jun., d. 15 Sept.
Ovett, Steve, b. 9 Oct.
Ovid, b. 20 Mar., d. 2 Jan.
Owen, Alun, b. 24 Nov.
Owen, Bill, b. 14 Mar.
Owen, David, b. 2 Jul.
Owen, Frank, d. 23 Jan.
Owen, Richard, b. 20 Jul., d. 18 Dec.
Owen, Robert, b. 14 May, d. 17 Nov.
Owen, Wilfred, b. 18 Mar., d. 4 Nov.
Owens, Jesse, b. 12 Sept., d. 31 Mar.
Oxenberg, Catherine, b. 22 Sept.
Oxford, 1st Earl, d. 21 May
Oxford and Asquith, Earl of, d. 15 Feb.
Oxfuird, Viscount of, b. 7 Jan.
Oxley, John, d. 25 May

Pacheco, Francisco, b. 3 Nov.
Pacino, Al, b. 25 Apr.
Packard, Douglas, b. 17 May
Packer, Kerry, b. 17 Dec.
Paderewski, Jan, b. 18 Nov., d. 29 Jun.
Paganini, Niccolò, b. 18 Feb., d. 27 May
Page, Annette, b. 18 Dec.
Page, Bruce, b. 1 Dec.
Page, Patti, b. 8 Nov.
Page, Walter H., d. 21 Dec.
Pagett, Nicola, b. 15 Jun.
Paige, Janis, b. 16 Sept.

Paine, Thomas, b. 29 Jan., d. 8 Jun.
Paisley, Bob, b. 23 Jan.
Paisley, Ian, b. 6 Apr.
Pal, George, b. 1 Feb.
Palance, Jack, b. 18 Feb.
Palestrina, Giovanni da, d. 2 Feb.
Palgrave, Francis, b. 28 Sept., d. 24 Oct.
Palin, Michael, b. 5 May
Palladio, Andrea, b. 30 Nov.
Pallo, Jackie, b. 12 Jun.
Palma, Jacopo, d. 30 Jul.
Palme, Olof, b. 30 Jan.
Palmer, Arnold, b. 10 Sept.
Palmer, Felicity, b. 6 Apr.
Palmer, Geoffrey, b. 4 Jun.
Palmer, Jonathan, b. 7 Nov.
Palmer, Patrick, b. 29 Apr.
Palmer, Robert, b. 19 Jan.
Palmer, Samuel, b. 27 Jan.
Palmerston, 3rd Viscount, b. 20 Oct.
Palomino de Castro, Antonio, d. 13 Aug.
Panizzi, Anthony, b. 16 Sept.
Pankhurst, Christabel, b. 22 Sept., d. 13 Feb.
Pankhurst, Emmeline, b. 14 Jul., d. 14 Jun.
Pankhurst, Sylvia, b. 4 May, d. 28 Sept.
Pannett, Juliet, b. 15 Jul.
Panofka, Heinrich, b. 3 Oct.
Panufnik, Andrzej, b. 24 Sept.
Paolozzi, Eduardo, b. 7 Mar.
Papen, Franz von, b. 29 Oct.
Papin, Denis, b. 22 Aug.
Paracelsus, b. 10 Nov., d. 24 Sept.
Pardoe, John, b. 27 Jul.
Paré, Ambroise, d. 20 Dec.
Pareto, Vilfredo, d. 20 Aug.
Park, Merle, b. 8 Oct.
Park, Mungo, b. 10 Sept.
Parker, Bonnie, d. 23 May
Parker, Cecil, b. 3 Sept.
Parker, Dorothy, b. 22 Aug., d. 7 Jun.
Parker, Eleanor, b. 26 Jun.
Parker, Gilbert, b. 23 Nov., d. 6 Sept.
Parker, Graham, b. 18 Nov.
Parker, Jean, b. 11 Aug.
Parker, Matthew, b. 6 Aug., d. 17 May
Parker, Peter, b. 30 Aug.
Parkes, Alexander, b. 29 Dec.
Parkin, Leonard, b. 2 Jun.

Parkinson, Cecil, b. 1 Sept.
Parkinson, C. Northcote, b. 30 Jul.
Parkinson, James, b. 11 Apr., d. 21 Dec.
Parkinson, Michael, b. 28 Mar.
Parkman, Francis, b. 16 Sept., d. 8 Nov.
Parmigianino, Francesco, b. 11 Jan., d. 24 Aug.
Parnell, Charles, b. 27 Jun., d. 6 Oct.
Parr, Catherine, d. 7 Sept.
Parrish, Matthew, b. 7 Aug.
Parry, Hubert, b. 27 Feb., d. 7 Oct.
Parry, William, b. 19 Dec., d. 8 Jul.
Parsons, Charles, b. 13 Jun., d. 11 Feb.
Parsons, Nicholas, b. 10 Oct.
Parton, Dolly, b. 19 Jan.
Partridge, Bernard, b. 11 Oct., d. 9 Aug.
Partridge, Eric, d. 1 Jun.
Pascal, Blaise, b. 19 Jun., d. 19 Aug.
Pascal, Françoise, b. 14 Oct.
Paschal II, Pope, d. 21 Jan.
Pasco, Richard, b. 18 Jul.
Pascoe, Alan, b. 11 Oct.
Pascoe, Leonard, b. 13 Feb.
Pascoli, Giovanni, b. 31 Dec.
Pasmore, Victor, b. 3 Dec.
Pasque, Ernst, b. 3 Sept.
Pasternak, Boris, b. 10 Feb., d. 30 May
Pasternak, Joe, b. 19 Sept.
Pasteur, Louis, b. 27 Dec., d. 28 Sept.
Patenier, Joachim de, d. 5 Oct.
Pater, Walter, b. 4 Aug., d. 30 Jul.
Paterson, A.B. 'Banjo', b. 17 Feb., d. 5 Feb.
Paterson, William, d. 22 Jan.
Pathé, Charles, b. 25 Dec., d. 26 Dec.
Patmore, Coventry, b. 23 Jul., d. 26 Nov.
Paton, Alan, d. 12 Apr.
Paton, Joseph, b. 13 Dec., d. 26 Dec.
Patrick, James, b. 4 Feb.
Patten, Chris, b. 12 May
Patten, John, b. 17 Jul.
Patterson, Floyd, b. 4 Jan.
Patti, Adelina, b. 19 Feb., d. 26 Sept.
Pattison, Rodney, b. 5 Aug.
Patton, George, b. 11 Nov., d. 21 Dec.
Pauk, György, b. 26 Oct.
Paul I, of Russia, b. 1 Oct., d. 23 Mar.
Paul I, of the Hellenes, b. 14 Dec., d. 6 Mar.

Paul I, Pope, d. 28 Jun.
Paul II, Pope, d. 26 Jul.
Paul III, Pope, b. 29 Feb.
Paul IV, Pope, b. 28 Jun., d. 18 Aug.
Paul V, Pope, b. 17 Sept.
Paul VI, Pope, b. 26 Sept., d. 6 Aug.
Pauli, Wolfgang, b. 25 Apr., d. 15 Dec.
Paulin, Jean-Baptiste, d. 19 Jan.
Pauling, Linus, b. 28 Feb.
Pavarotti, Luciano, b. 12 Oct.
Pavlov, Ivan, b. 26 Sept., d. 27 Feb.
Pavlova, Anna, b. 31 Jan., d. 23 Jan.
Paxman, Jeremy, b. 11 May
Paxton, Iain, b. 29 Dec.
Paxton, Joseph, b. 3 Aug., d. 8 Jun.
Payn, James, d. 25 Mar.
Payne, Jack, d. 4 Dec.
Peabody, Elizabeth, b. 16 May
Peabody, George, d. 4 Nov.
Peacock, Thomas, b. 18 Oct., d. 23 Jan.
Peake, Felicity, b. 1 May
Peake, Mervyn, d. 18 Nov.
Pears, Peter, b. 22 Jun.
Pearson, C. Arthur, b. 24 Feb., d. 9 Dec.
Pearson, Lester, d. 27 Dec.
Pearson, Neville, b. 13 Feb.
Peary, Robert, b. 6 May, d. 20 Feb.
Peck, Gregory, b. 5 Apr.
Peckinpah, Sam, d. 28 Dec.
Pedder, Ian, b. 2 May
Pedro I, of Brazil, b. 12 Oct.
Pedro II, of Brazil, b. 2 Dec.
Pedro the Cruel, of Castile, b. 30 Aug., d. 23 Mar.
Peel, Robert, b. 5 Feb., d. 2 Jul.
Péguy, Charles, b. 7 Jan., d. 5 Sept.
Pelé, b. 23 Oct.
Pelham-Holles, Thomas, d. 17 Nov.
Pemberton, Max, b. 19 Jun., d. 22 Feb.
Penderecki, Krzysztof, b. 23 Nov.
Penhaligon, Susan, b. 3 Jul.
Penn, William, b. 14 Oct., d. 30 Jul.
Pennant, Thomas, d. 16 Dec.
Pennell, Joseph, b. 4 Jul., d. 23 Apr.
Pennethorne, James, b. 4 Jun.
Penney, Jennifer, b. 5 Apr.
Pennington, Michael, b. 7 Jun.
Pépin III, of the Franks, 24 Sept.
Pepys, Samuel, b. 23 Feb., d. 26 May
Perahia, Murray, b. 19 Apr.

Perceval, Spencer, d. 11 May
Percival, Lance, b. 26 Jul.
Percy, Henry, b. 20 May, d. 23 Jul.
Perdita, d. 26 Dec.
Perelman, S.J., b. 1 Feb., d. 17 Oct.
Pérez Galdós, Benito, b. 10 May, d. 4 Jan.
Pergolesi, Giovanni, b. 4 Jan., d. 16 Mar.
Perkin, William, b. 12 Mar., d. 14 Jul.
Perkins, Anthony, b. 4 Apr.
Perkins, Carl, b. 9 Apr.
Perlman, Itzhak, b. 31 Aug.
Perón, Eva, b. 7 May
Perón, Juan, b. 8 Oct., d. 1 Jul.
Perosi, Lorenzo, b. 20 Dec.
Perrault, Charles, b. 13 Jan., d. 16 May
Perry, Frances, b. 19 Feb.
Perry, Fred, b. 18 May
Perry, Matthew, b. 10 Apr.
Perry, Stephen, b. 26 Aug.
Perryman, Steve, b. 21 Dec.
Pershing, John, b. 13 Sept., d. 15 Jul.
Pertinax, Publius Helvius, d. 28 Mar.
Pertwee, Bill, b. 21 Jul.
Pertwee, Jon, b. 7 Jul.
Perutz, Max, b. 19 May
Peruzzi, Baldassare, d. 6 Jan.
Pestalozzi, Johann, b. 12 Jan., d. 17 Feb.
Pétain, Henri-Philippe, b. 24 Apr., d. 23 Jul.
Peter, of Yugoslavia, b. 6 Sept., d. 5 Nov.
Peter I, the Great, b. 9 Jun., d. 8 Feb.
Peter II, of Russia, d. 30 Jan.
Peter III, of Russia, d. 18 Jul.
Peters, Martin, b. 8 Nov.
Peters, Mary, b. 6 Jul.
Petersen, Peter, b. 2 Sept.
Peterson, Oscar, b. 15 Aug.
Petipa, Marius, b. 11 Mar.
Petit, Jean-Louis, d. 20 Apr.
Petitot, Jean, b. 12 Jul.
Petöfi, Sándor, b. 1 Jan., d. 31 Jul.
Petrarch, b. 20 Jul., d. 19 Jul.
Petrie, Flinders, b. 3 Jun., d. 27 Jul.
Petterssen, Gustaf, d. 20 Jun.
Pettet, Joanna, b. 16 Nov.
Pettifer, Julian, b. 21 Jul.
Petty, Tom, b. 20 Oct.
Petty, William, d. 16 Dec.
Pevsner, Antoine, b. 18 Jan., d. 12 Apr.
Pevsner, Nikolaus, d. 18 Aug.

Philby, Kim, b. 1 Jan., d. 11 May
Philip, Prince, b. 10 Jun.
Philip I, of France, d. 29 Jul.
Philip I, of Spain, b. 22 Jul., d. 25 Sept.
Philip II, of France, b. 21 Aug., d. 14 Jul.
Philip II, of Spain, b. 21 May, d. 13 Sept.
Philip III, of France, b. 3 Apr., d. 5 Oct.
Philip III, of Spain, b. 14 Apr., d. 31 Mar.
Philip IV, of Spain, b. 8 Apr., d. 17 Sept.
Philip V, of France, d. 2 Jan.
Philip V, of Spain, b. 19 Dec., d. 9 Jul.
Philip VI, of France, d. 22 Aug.
Philip the Good, of Burgundy, d. 15 Jun.
Philips, John, b. 30 Dec.
Philips, Katherine, d. 22 Jun.
Phillip, Arthur, b. 11 Oct., d. 31 Aug.
Phillip, John, b. 19 Apr.
Phillips, Leslie, b. 20 Apr.
Phillips, Mark, b. 22 Sept.
Phillips, Nicholas, b. 21 Jan.
Phillips, Robin, b. 28 Feb.
Phillips, Siân, b. 14 May
Phillpotts, Eden, b. 4 Nov.
Piaf, Edith, b. 19 Dec., d. 10 Oct.
Piaget, Jean, b. 9 Aug.
Picard, Jean, b. 21 Jul., d. 12 Jul.
Picasso, Pablo, b. 25 Oct., d. 8 Apr.
Piccard, Auguste, b. 28 Jan., d. 24 Mar.
Piccinni, Niccolò, b. 16 Jan.
Piccolomini, Prince, b. 11 Nov.
Pickering, Edward, d. 3 Feb.
Pickett, Wilson, b. 18 Mar.
Pickford, Mary, b. 8 Apr., d. 29 May
Pickup, Ronald, b. 7 Jun.
Pico, Giovanni, d. 17 Nov.
Picon, Molly, b. 1 Jun., d. 5 Apr.
Pidal, Ramón, b. 13 Mar.
Pidgeon, Walter, d. 25 Sept.
Pierce, Charles, d. 19 Apr.
Pierce, Franklin, b. 23 Nov., d. 8 Oct.
Pierson, Henry, b. 12 Apr.
Piestre, Fernand, d. 21 Mar.
Piggott, Lester, b. 5 Nov.
Piggott, Stuart, b. 28 May
Pigott, Tony, b. 4 Jun.
Pigott-Smith, Tim, b. 13 May
Pike, William, b. 24 Jun.
Pilkington, Alastair, b. 7 Jan.
Pilon, Germain, d. 3 Feb.
Piloty, Karl von, b. 1 Oct.

Piłsudski, Józef, b. 5 Dec., d. 12 May
Pincher, Chapman, b. 29 Mar.
Pinero, Arthur, b. 24 May, d. 23 Nov.
Pinero, Manuel, b. 1 Sept.
Pinkerton, Allan, d. 1 Jul.
Pinkerton, John, b. 17 Feb.
Pinkham, Lydia, d. 17 May
Pinter, Harold, b. 10 Oct.
Pinturicchio, Bernardino, d. 11 Dec.
Piper, John, b. 13 Dec.
Piquet, Nelson, b. 17 Aug.
Pirandello, Luigi, b. 28 Jun., d. 10 Dec.
Piranesi, Giambattista, b. 4 Oct., d. 9
    Sept.
Pissarro, Camille, b. 10 Jul., d. 13 Nov.
Pissarro, Lucien, d. 11 Jul.
Pitman, Isaac, b. 4 Jan., d. 12 Jan.
Pitman, Jenny, b. 11 Jun.
Pitney, Gene, b. 17 Feb.
Pitt, William, the Elder, b. 15 Nov., d. 11
    May
Pitt, William, the Younger, b. 28 May, d.
    23 Jan.
Pitter, Ruth, b. 7 Nov.
Pius II, Pope, b. 18 Oct., d. 15 Aug.
Pius IV, Pope, b. 31 Mar.
Pius VII, Pope, d. 20 Aug.
Pius IX, Pope, d. 7 Feb.
Pius X, Pope, b. 2 Jun.
Pius XI, Pope, b. 31 May, d. 10 Feb.
Pius XII, Pope, b. 2 Mar., d. 9 Oct.
Piutti, Karl, b. 30 Apr.
Pizarro, Francisco, d. 26 Jun.
Pizzetti, Ildebrando, b. 20 Sept.
Pizzey, Erin, b. 19 Feb.
Place, Godfrey, b. 19 Jul.
Planck, Max, b. 23 Apr., d. 4 Oct.
Plant, Robert, b. 20 Aug.
Plantin, Christophe, d. 1 Jul.
Plath, Sylvia, b. 27 Oct.
Player, Gary, b. 1 Nov.
Playfair, Giles, b. 27 Sept.
Playfair, John, b. 10 Mar., d. 20 Jul.
Playfair, Nigel, b. 1 Jul.
Playfair, William, d. 19 Mar.
Pleasance, Donald, b. 5 Oct.
Plimsoll, Samuel, b. 10 Feb., d. 3 Jun.
Pliny the Elder, d. 24 Aug.
Plomer, William, b. 10 Dec., d. 21 Sept.
Plowden, Lady, b. 5 May

Plowright, Joan, b. 28 Oct.
Plowright, Rosalind, b. 21 May
Plummer, Christopher, b. 13 Dec.
Pococke, Edward, d. 10 Sept.
Poe, Edgar Allan, b. 19 Jan., d. 7 Oct.
Poel, William, b. 22 Jul.
Poincaré, Raymond, b. 20 Aug., d. 15 Oct.
Poitier, Sidney, b. 20 Feb.
Polanski, Roman, b. 18 Aug.
Pole, Cardinal, b. 11 May, d. 18 Nov.
Poliakoff, Stephen, b. 1 Dec.
Polk, James, b. 2 Nov., d. 15 Jun.
Pollack, Sydney, b. 1 Jul.
Pollaiuolo, Antonio, d. 4 Feb.
Pollard, Su, b. 7 Nov.
Pollock, Ellen, b. 29 Jun.
Pollock, Jackson, b. 28 Jan., d. 11 Aug.
Pollok, Robert, b. 19 Oct., d. 18 Sept.
Pommier, Jean, b. 17 Aug.
Pompadour, Marquise de, b. 29 Dec., d.
    15 Apr.
Pompidou, Georges, b. 5 Jul., d. 2 Apr.
Ponce, Manuel, d. 24 Apr.
Poncet, André-François, d. 8 Jan.
Ponchielli, Amilcare, b. 1 Sept., d. 16 Jan.
Pons, Lily, d. 13 Feb.
Ponti, Carlo, b. 11 Dec.
Pontiac, d. 20 Apr.
Pontin, Fred, b. 24 Oct.
Pope, Alexander, b. 21 May, d. 30 May
Popp, Lucia, b. 12 Nov.
Popper, Karl, b. 28 Jul.
Porpora, Niccola, b. 17 Aug., d. 3 Mar.
Porritt, Jonathon, b. 6 Jul.
Porson, Richard, b. 25 Dec., d. 25 Sept.
Porta, Giambattista della, d. 4 Feb.
Portaels, Jean-François, d. 8 Feb.
Porteous, Patrick, b. 1 Jan.
Porter, Anita, b. 10 Aug.
Porter, Cole, b. 9 Jun., d. 15 Oct.
Porter, Eric, b. 8 Apr.
Porter, Katherine, b. 15 May, d. 17 Sept.
Porter, Lady, b. 29 Nov.
Porter, Marguerite, b. 30 Nov.
Porter, Nyree Dawn, b. 22 Jan.
Porter, Peter, b. 16 Feb.
Porter, Thea, b. 24 Dec.
Portillo, Michael, b. 26 May
Portland, 3rd Duke, b. 14 Apr.
Post, Emily, d. 25 Sept.

Post, Wiley, d. 15 Aug.
Postgate, Raymond, d. 29 Mar.
Potter, Beatrix, b. 28 Jul., d. 22 Dec.
Potter, Dennis, b. 17 May
Potter, Paulus, b. 20 Nov.
Potter, Stephen, b. 1 Feb., d. 2 Dec.
Poulenc, Francis, b. 7 Jan., d. 30 Jan.
Pound, Ezra, b. 30 Oct., d. 1 Nov.
Poussin, Gaspard, d. 25 May
Poussin, Nicolas, b. 15 Jun., d. 19 Nov.
Powell, Anthony, b. 21 Dec.
Powell, Dick, b. 14 Nov., d. 3 Jan.
Powell, Dilys, b. 20 Jul.
Powell, Enoch, b. 16 Jun.
Powell, Jane, b. 1 Apr.
Powell, Peter, b. 24 Mar.
Powell, Philip, b. 15 Mar.
Powell, Robert, b. 1 Jun.
Powell, Sandy, d. 26 Jun.
Powell, William, d. 5 Mar.
Power, Tyrone, d. 15 Nov.
Powers, Stephanie, b. 12 Nov.
Powys, John Cowper, b. 8 Oct., d. 17 Jun.
Powys, T.F., b. 20 Dec.
Praetorius, Michael, d. 15 Feb.
Prasad, Rajendra, b. 3 Dec., d. 28 Feb.
Pratt, E.J., b. 4 Feb., d. 26 Apr.
Prawer Jhabvala, Ruth, b. 7 May
Prebble, John, b. 23 Jun.
Preminger, Otto, b. 5 Dec., d. 23 Apr.
Prentiss, Paula, b. 4 Mar.
Prescott, John, b. 31 May
Prescott, William H., b. 4 May, d. 28 Jan.
Presley, Elvis, b. 8 Jan., d. 16 Aug.
Pressburger, Emeric, d. 5 Feb.
Preston, Peter, b. 23 May
Preston, Robert, b. 8 Jun., d. 21 Mar.
Preston, Simon, b. 4 Aug.
Prestt, Ian, b. 26 Jun.
Prévert, Jacques, b. 4 Feb.
Previn, André, b. 6 Apr.
Prévost d'Exiles, Abbé, b. 1 Apr., d. 23 Nov.
Prévost, Marcel, d. 8 Apr.
Prey, Hermann, b. 11 Jul.
Price, Alan, b. 19 Apr.
Price, Graham, b. 24 Nov.
Price, Leontyne, b. 10 Feb.
Price, Margaret, b. 13 Apr.
Price, Vincent, b. 27 May

Prichard, James, d. 23 Dec.
Pride, Thomas, d. 23 Oct.
Priestley, J.B., b. 13 Sept., d. 14 Aug.
Priestley, Joseph, b. 13 Mar., d. 6 Feb.
Prim, Juan, d. 30 Dec.
Primo de Rivera, Miguel, d. 16 Mar.
Prince, Hal, b. 30 Jan.
Princess Royal, b. 15 Aug.
Princip, Gavrilo, d. 28 Apr.
Principal, Victoria, b. 30 Jan.
Pringle, Charles, 6 Jun.
Pringle, John, d. 18 Jan.
Pringle, Thomas, d. 5 Dec.
Prinsep, Valentine, d. 11 Nov.
Prior, Matthew, b. 21 Jul., d. 18 Sept.
Pritchard-Gordon, Gavin, b. 4 Oct.
Pritchett, Victor, b. 16 Dec.
Proby, P.J., b. 6 Nov.
Procter, Mike, b. 15 Sept.
Profumo, John, b. 30 Jan.
Prokofiev, Sergei, b. 22 Apr., d. 5 Mar.
Prost, Alain, b. 24 Feb.
Proudhon, Pierre-Joseph, b. 15 Jan., d. 19 Jan.
Proust, Marcel, b. 10 Jul., d. 18 Nov.
Prout, Ebenezer, b. 1 Mar.
Prout, Samuel, b. 17 Sept.
Prout, William, d. 9 Apr.
Prowse, Juliet, b. 25 Sept.
Prud'hon, Pierre, b. 4 Apr., d. 16 Feb.
Pryce, Jonathan, b. 1 Jun.
Pryce-Jones, Alan, b. 18 Nov.
Pryor, Richard, b. 1 Dec.
Puccini, Giacomo, b. 22 Dec., d. 29 Nov.
Pugin, Augustus, b. 1 Mar., d. 14 Sept.
Pulaski, Casimir, b. 4 Mar.
Pulci, Luigi, b. 15 Aug.
Pulitzer, Joseph, b. 10 Apr., d. 29 Oct.
Pullen, John, b. 1 Nov.
Pullman, George, b. 3 Mar., d. 19 Oct.
Purcell, Henry, d. 21 Nov.
Purchas, Francis, b. 19 Jun.
Purdy, James Otis, b. 14 Jul.
Purves, Libby, b. 2 Feb.
Pusey, Edward, d. 16 Sept.
Pushkin, Alexander, b. 6 Jun., d. 10 Feb.
Puttnam, David, b. 25 Feb.
Puvis de Chavannes, Pièrre, b. 14 Dec., d. 24 Oct.
Puzo, Mario, b. 15 Oct.

Pye, Henry, d. 11 Aug.
Pyke, Magnus, b. 29 Dec.
Pyle, Howard, b. 5 Mar., d. 8 Nov.
Pym, Barbara, d. 11 Jan.
Pym, John, d. 8 Dec.
Pym, Lord, b. 13 Feb.
Pyrah, Malcolm, b. 26 Aug.

Quant, Mary, b. 11 Feb.
Quaritch, Bernard, d. 17 Dec.
Quarles, Francis, d. 8 Sept.
Quartermaine, Leon, d. 25 Jun.
Quatro, Suzi, b. 3 Jun.
Quayle, Anna, b. 6 Oct.
Quayle, Anthony, b. 7 Sept., d. 20 Oct.
Queen, Ellery, *see* 11 Jan. and 20 Oct.
Quennell, Peter, b. 9 Mar.
Quental, Antero de, b. 18 Apr., d. 11
   Sept.
Quercia, Jacopo della, d. 20 Oct.
Quevado, Francisco de, b. 17 Sept., d. 8
   Sept.
Quick, Diana, b. 23 Nov.
Quiller-Couch, Arthur, b. 21 Nov.
Quilley, Denis, b. 26 Dec.
Quilter, Harry, b. 24 Jan.
Quilter, Roger, d. 21 Sept.
Quinault, Philippe, d. 26 Nov.
Quinlan, Kathleen, b. 19 Nov.
Quinn, Anthony, b. 21 Apr.
Quinn, Elizabeth, b. 17 Jul.
Quinn, James, b. 23 Aug.
Quinn, Michael, b. 20 Jul.
Quirk, Randolph, b. 12 Jul.
Quisling, Vidkun, b. 18 Jul., d. 24 Oct.

Raban, Jonathan, b. 14 Jun.
Rabelais, François, d. 9 Apr.
Rabinowitz, Harry, b. 26 Mar.
Race, Steve, b. 1 Apr.
Rachel, d. 3 Jan.
Rachmaninov, Sergei, b. 1 Apr., d. 28
   Mar.
Racine, Jean, b. 21 Dec., d. 21 Apr.
Rackham, Arthur, b. 19 Sept., d. 6 Sept.
Radcliffe, Ann, b. 9 Jul., d. 7 Feb.
Radcliffe, James, d. 24 Feb.
Radcliffe, John, d. 1 Nov.
Radetzky, Count, b. 2 Nov., d. 5 Jan.
Raeburn, Henry, b. 4 Mar., d. 8 Jul.

Raemaekers, Louis, b. 6 Apr.
Raffles, Stamford, b. 6 Jul., d. 5 Jul.
Raft, George, b. 27 Sept.
Raglan, 1st Baron, b. 30 Sept., d. 28 Jun.
Raiffeisen, Friedrich, b. 30 Mar.
Raikes, Robert, b. 4 Sept., d. 5 Apr.
Railton, Mary, b. 28 May
Raimondi, Ruggero, b. 3 Oct.
Raimu, d. 19 Sept.
Rainer, Luise, b. 12 Jan.
Rainier III, b. 31 May
Rains, Claude, b. 10 Nov., d. 30 May
Rais, Gilles de, d. 26 Oct.
Raison, Timothy, b. 3 Nov.
Raleigh, Walter, d. 29 Oct.
Ramadhin, Sonny, b. 1 May
Ramakrishna, d. 16 Aug.
Raman, Chandrasekhara, b. 7 Nov., d. 21
   Nov.
Rambert, Marie, b. 20 Feb., d. 12 Jun.
Rameau, Jean, b. 25 Sept., d. 12 Sept.
Ramirez, Paul, b. 20 Jun.
Rampling, Charlotte, b. 5 Feb.
Ramsay, Allan (painter), b. 13 Oct., d. 10
   Aug.
Ramsay, Allan (poet), b. 15 Oct., d. 7
   Jan.
Ramsay, Andrew, b. 9 Jun.
Ramsay, William, b. 2 Oct., d. 23 Jul.
Ramsey, Alf, b. 22 Jan.
Ramsey, Lord, d. 23 Apr.
Randall, Freddy, b. 6 May
Randolph, Thomas, b. 15 Jun.
Ranjitsinghi, Vibhaji, b. 10 Sept., d. 2
   Apr.
Rank, J. Arthur, b. 23 Dec., d. 29 Mar.
Ranke, Leopold von, b. 21 Dec., d. 23
   May
Ransome, Arthur, b. 18 Jan., d. 3 Jun.
Rantzen, Esther, b. 22 Jun.
Raphael, Frederic, b. 14 Aug.
Rasputin, Grigori, d. 30 Dec.
Rathbone, Basil, b. 13 Jun., d. 21 Jul.
Rathbone, Eleanor, d. 2 Jan.
Rathenau, Walter, d. 24 Jun.
Rattee, Donald, b. 9 Mar.
Rattigan, Terence, b. 10 Jun., d. 30 Nov.
Rattle, Simon, b. 19 Jan.
Rauch, Christian, d. 3 Dec.
Ravel, Maurice, b. 7 Mar., d. 28 Dec.

Raven, Simon, b. 28 Dec.
Raven-Hill, Leonard, b. 10 Mar., d. 31 Mar.
Ravensdale, Lord, b. 25 Jun.
Rawlings, Margaret, b. 5 Jun.
Rawlings, Marjorie, b. 8 Aug.
Rawsthorne, Alan, d. 24 Jul.
Ray, John, b. 29 Nov., d. 17 Jan.
Ray, Satyajit, b. 2 May, d. 23 Apr.
Raye, Martha, b. 27 Aug.
Rayleigh, 3rd Baron, b. 12 Nov., d. 30 Jun.
Raymond, Gene, b. 13 Aug.
Raymond, Paul, b. 15 Nov.
Rayner, Claire, b. 22 Jan.
Rayner, Lord, b. 30 Mar.
Read, Herbert, b. 4 Dec., d. 12 Jun.
Read, Mike, b. 1 Mar.
Read, Piers Paul, b. 7 Mar.
Reade, Charles, b. 8 Jun., d. 11 Apr.
Reading, 1st Earl, d. 29 Dec.
Reading, 1st Marquess, b. 10 Oct., d. 30 Dec.
Reagan, Ronald, b. 6 Feb.
Reardon, Ray, b. 8 Oct.
Réaumur, René de, b. 28 Feb.
Reddaway, Brian, b. 8 Jan.
Reddy, Helen, b. 25 Oct.
Redford, Robert, b. 18 Aug.
Redgrave, Lynn, b. 8 Mar.
Redgrave, Michael, b. 20 Mar., d. 21 Mar.
Redgrave, Richard, b. 30 Apr.
Redgrave, Vanessa, b. 30 Jan.
Redon, Odilon, b. 20 Oct., d. 6 Jul.
Redpath, Ian, b. 11 May
Redwood, John, b. 15 Jun.
Reece, Charles, b. 2 Jan.
Reed, Carol, b. 30 Dec., d. 25 Apr.
Reed, Les, b. 24 Jul.
Reed, Oliver, b. 13 Feb.
Reed, Robert, b. 19 Oct.
Reed, Walter, b. 13 Sept.
Rees, Clive, b. 6 Oct.
Rees, Llewellyn, b. 18 Jun.
Rees, Martin, b. 23 Jun.
Rees, Merlyn, b. 18 Dec.
Rees, Nigel, b. 5 Jun.
Rees, Roger, b. 5 May
Rees-Mogg, Lord, b. 14 Jul.
Reeve, Christopher, b. 25 Sept.
Reeves, Jim, b. 20 Aug., d. 31 Jul.

Reeves, John, b. 26 Sept.
Regan, Joan, b. 19 Jan.
Regnard, Jean, d. 5 Sept.
Regnault, Henri, b. 31 Oct., d. 19 Jan.
Regnault, Jean, d. 12 Nov.
Regnier, Mathurin, b. 21 Dec., d. 22 Oct.
Reich, Steve, b. 3 Oct.
Reicha, Antonin, b. 26 Feb.
Reid, Beryl, b. 17 Jun.
Reid, Billy, b. 19 Sept., d. 12 Dec.
Reid, Chris, b. 4 Mar.
Reid, George, b. 31 Oct.
Reid, John, b. 6 Aug.
Reid, Sir Bob, b. 1 May
Reid, Thomas Mayne, d. 22 Oct.
Reid, William, b. 21 Dec.
Reimarus, Hermann, b. 22 Dec.
Reinhardt, Max, b. 9 Sept., d. 31 Oct.
Reisz, Karel, b. 21 Jul.
Reith, John, b. 20 Jul., d. 16 Jun.
Remarque, Erich Maria, b. 22 Jun., d. 25 Sept.
Rembrandt, b. 15 Jul., d. 4 Oct.
Remedios, Alberto, b. 27 Feb.
Remington, Frederic, b. 4 Oct., d. 26 Dec.
Renan, Ernest, b. 28 Feb., d. 2 Oct.
Renaud, Madeleine, b. 21 Feb.
Renault, Mary, b. 4 Sept., d. 13 Dec.
Rendall, David, b. 11 Oct.
Rendell, Ruth, b. 17 Feb.
Renfrew, Colin, b. 25 Jul.
Reni, Guido, b. 4 Nov., d. 18 Aug.
Rennie, John, b. 7 Jun., d. 4 Oct.
Renoir, Jean, b. 15 Sept., d. 13 Feb.
Renoir, Pierre-Auguste, b. 25 Feb., d. 3 Dec.
Renwick, James, d. 17 Feb.
Repp, Dr Richard, b. 1 Apr.
Resnais, Alain, b. 3 Jun.
Respighi, Ottorino, b. 9 Jul., d. 18 Apr.
Restif de la Bretonne, Nicolas, b. 23 Oct., d. 3 Feb.
Reszke, Jean de, b. 14 Jan., d. 3 Apr.
Rethel, Alfred, d. 1 Dec.
Retz, Cardinal de, d. 24 Aug.
Reuter, Paul von, b. 21 Jul., d. 25 Feb.
Revel, Harry, b. 21 Dec., d. 3 Nov.
Revere, Paul, b. 1 Jan., d. 10 May
Reynolds, Alan, b. 27 Apr.
Reynolds, Barbara, b. 13 Jun.

Reynolds, Burt, b. 11 Feb.
Reynolds, Debbie, b. 1 Apr.
Reynolds, Joshua, b. 16 Jul., d. 23 Feb.
Reyntiens, Patrick, b. 11 Dec.
Réaumur, René, b. 28 Feb., d. 17 Oct.
Rhodes, Cecil, b. 5 Jul., d. 26 Mar.
Rhodes, Wilfred, b. 29 Oct.
Rhodes, Zandra, b. 19 Sept.
Rhondda, 1st Viscount, d. 3 Jul.
Rhys, Jean, b. 24 Aug., d. 14 May
Ribbentrop, Joachim von, b. 30 Apr.
Ribera, José, b. 12 Jan., d. 2 Sept.
Ribot, Theodule, b. 8 Aug., d. 11 Sept.
Ricardo, David, b. 19 Apr., d. 11 Sept.
Ricci, Curbastro, d. 7 Aug.
Ricci, Matteo, b. 6 Oct., d. 11 May
Ricci, Ruggiero, b. 24 Jul.
Rice, Anneka, b. 4 Oct.
Rice, Tim, b. 10 Nov.
Rich, Charlie, b. 14 Dec.
Richard, Cliff, b. 14 Oct.
Richard, Duke of York, d. 30 Dec.
Richard, Eric, b. 27 Jun.
Richard I, of England, b. 8 Sept., d. 6 Apr.
Richard II, of England, b. 6 Jan., d. 14
   Feb.
Richard III, of England, b. 2 Oct., d. 22
   Aug.
Richards, Barry, b. 21 Jul.
Richards, Frank, b. 8 Aug., d. 24 Dec.
Richards, Gordon, b. 5 May, d. 10 Nov.
Richards, Grant, b. 21 Oct., d. 24 Feb.
Richards, Henry, b. 13 Nov.
Richards, Keith, b. 18 Dec.
Richards, Viv, b. 7 Mar.
Richardson, Dorothy M., b. 17 May, d. 17
   Jun.
Richardson, Henry Handel, b. 3 Jan., d. 20
   Mar.
Richardson, Henry Hobson, d. 27 Apr.
Richardson, Ian, b. 7 Apr.
Richardson, Miranda, b. 3 Mar.
Richardson, Natasha, b. 11 May
Richardson, Ralph, b. 19 Dec., d. 10 Oct.
Richardson, Samuel, b. 19 Aug., d. 4 Jul.
Richardson, Tony, b. 5 Jun.
Richardson, William, b. 10 Feb.
Richelieu, Cardinal, b. 9 Sept., d. 4 Dec.
Richemont, Comte de, d. 10 Aug.
Richie, Lionel, b. 20 Jun.

Richler, Mordecai, b. 27 Jan.
Richman, Stella, b. 9 Nov.
Richmond, George, d. 19 Mar.
Richmond, William, b. 29 Nov.
Richter, Conrad, b. 13 Oct.
Richter, Hans, b. 4 Apr., d. 18 Feb.
Richter, Johann Paul, b. 21 Mar.
Richter, Sviatoslav, b. 20 Mar.
Richthofen, Manfred von, b. 2 May, d. 21
   Apr.
Rickenbacker, Eddie, b. 8 Oct., d. 23 Jul.
Ricketts, Charles, d. 7 Oct.
Ricketts, Derek, b. 30 Jan.
Rickover, Hyman, b. 27 Jan.
Riddle, Nelson, d. 5 Oct.
Ridler, Anne, b. 30 Jul.
Ridley, Arnold, d. 12 Mar.
Ridley, Nicholas (martyr), d. 16 Oct.
Ridley, Nicholas (politician), b. 17 Feb.
Rie, Dame Lucie, b. 16 Mar.
Riebeeck, Jan van, b. 21 Apr., d. 18 Jan.
Riefenstahl, Leni, b. 22 Aug.
Riegger, Wallingford, d. 2 Apr.
Riel, Louis, b. 23 Oct., d. 16 Nov.
Rienzi, Cola di, d. 8 Oct.
Rifkind, Malcolm, b. 21 Jun.
Rigaud, Hyacinthe, b. 20 Jul., d. 27 Dec.
Rigg, Diana, b. 20 Jul.
Riley, Bridget, b. 24 Apr.
Riley, James, b. 7 Oct., d. 22 Jul.
Rilke, Rainer Maria, b. 4 Dec., d. 29 Dec.
Rimbaud, Arthur, b. 20 Oct., d. 10 Nov.
Rimsky-Korsakov, Nikolai, b. 18 Mar., d.
   21 Jun.
Rinehart, Mary R., b. 12 Aug., d. 22 Sept.
Rintoul, David, b. 29 Nov.
Rippon, Angela, b. 12 Oct.
Rippon, Lord, b. 28 May
Rita, d. 1 Jan.
Ritchie, Lady Anne, d. 26 Feb.
Ritenour, Lee, b. 1 Nov.
Ritter, Tex, b. 12 Jan.
Rivero, José, b. 20 Sept.
Rivers, 2nd Earl, d. 25 Jun.
Rivers, William, d. 4 Jun.
Riviere, Briton, b. 14 Aug., d. 20 Apr.
Rix, Brian, b. 27 Jan.
Rizzello, Michael, b. 2 Apr.
Rizzio, David, d. 9 Mar.
Roach, Hal, b. 14 Jan.

Roache, William, b. 25 Apr.

Robards, Jason, b. 26 Jul.

Robb, David, b. 23 Aug.

Robbe-Grillet, Alain, b. 18 Aug.

Robbia, Luca della, d. 20 Feb.

Robbins, Harold, b. 21 May

Robbins, Jerome, b. 11 Oct.

Robert, Hubert, b. 22 May, d. 15 Apr.

Robert, Louis-Léopold, d. 20 Mar.

Robert I, of the Franks, d. 15 Jun.

Robert II, of France, d. 20 Jul.

Robert II, of Scotland, d. 19 Apr.

Robert III, of Scotland, d. 1 Apr.

Robert the Bruce, b. 11 Jul., d. 7 Jun.

Robert-Fleury, Joseph-Nicolas, d. 5 May

Roberts, 1st Earl, d. 14 Nov.

Roberts, David, d. 25 Nov.

Roberts, Frederick, b. 30 Sept.

Roberts, Ivor, b. 19 Jul.

Roberts, John, b. 14 Apr.

Roberts, Kenneth, d. 21 Jul.

Roberts, Wyn, b. 10 Jul.

Roberts-Jones, Ivor, b. 2 Nov.

Robertson, Anne, b. 3 May

Robertson, Cliff, b. 9 Sept.

Robertson, Liz, b. 4 May

Robertson, Max, b. 28 Aug.

Robertson, Toby, b. 29 Nov.

Robertson, Walford, d. 4 Sept.

Robertson, William, d. 11 Jul.

Robertson-Justice, James, b. 15 Jun.

Robeson, Paul, b. 9 Apr., d. 23 Jan.

Robespierre, Maximilien de, b. 6 May, d. 28 Jul.

Robey, George, b. 20 Sept., d. 29 Nov.

Robin, Leo, b. 6 Apr., d. 29 Dec.

Robinson, Edward A., d. 6 Apr.

Robinson, Edward G., b. 12 Dec., d. 26 Jan.

Robinson, Henry C., d. 5 Feb.

Robinson, James H., b. 29 Jun., d. 16 Feb.

Robinson, Mary, d. 26 Dec.

Robinson, Robert, b. 17 Dec.

Robinson, W. Heath, b. 31 May, d. 13 Sept.

Robles, Marisa, b. 4 May

Rob Roy, d. 28 Dec.

Robson, Bobby, b. 18 Feb.

Robson, Bryan, b. 11 Jan.

Robson, Flora, b. 28 Mar., d. 7 Jul.

Roche, Stephen, b. 28 Nov.

Rochemont, Louis de, b. 13 Jan.

Rockefeller, John D., b. 8 Jul., d. 23 May

Rockefeller, Nelson, b. 8 Jul., d. 26 Jan.

Roddick, Anita, b. 23 Oct.

Rodgers, Anton, b. 10 Jan.

Rodgers, Joan, b. 4 Nov.

Rodgers, Richard, b. 28 Jun., d. 30 Dec.

Rodin, Auguste, b. 12 Nov., d. 17 Nov.

Rodney, 1st Baron, b. 19 Feb.

Roethke, Theodore, d. 1 Aug.

Roëves, Maurice, b. 19 Mar.

Roger I, of Sicily, d. 22 Jun.

Roger II, of Sicily, d. 26 Feb.

Rogers, Bernard, d. 24 May

Rogers, Bill, b. 10 Sept.

Rogers, Budge, b. 20 Jun.

Rogers, Ginger, b. 16 Jul.

Rogers, John, b. 11 Jan.

Rogers, Kenny, b. 21 Aug.

Rogers, Paul, b. 22 Mar.

Rogers, Richard, b. 23 Jul.

Rogers, Roy, b. 5 Nov.

Rogers, Samuel, b. 30 Jul., d. 18 Dec.

Rogers, Ted, b. 20 Jul.

Rogers, Will, b. 4 Nov., d. 15 Aug.

Roget, Peter Mark, b. 18 Jan., d. 12 Sept.

Rohan-Guéménée, Louis de, d. 27 Nov.

Roland, Gilbert, b. 11 Dec.

Rolfe, Frederick, b. 22 Jul., d. 25 Oct.

Rolland, Romain, d. 30 Dec.

Rolls, Charles, b. 27 Aug., d. 12 Jul.

Rolph, C.H., b. 23 Aug.

Romains, Jules, b. 26 Aug., d. 14 Aug.

Roman, Johan, b. 26 Oct.

Romano, Giulio, d. 1 Nov.

Romberg, Sigmund, b. 29 Jul., d. 9 Nov.

Romero, Cesar, b. 15 Feb.

Romilly, Samuel, b. 1 Mar., d. 2 Nov.

Rommel, Erwin, b. 15 Nov., d. 14 Oct.

Romney, George, b. 15 Dec., d. 15 Nov.

Ronald, Landon, b. 7 Jun., d. 14 Aug.

Ronsard, Pierre de, b. 11 Sept., d. 27 Dec.

Ronstadt, Linda, b. 15 Jul.

Röntgen, Wilhelm von, b. 27 Mar., d. 10 Feb.

Rooney, Mickey, b. 23 Sept.

Roosevelt, Eleanor, b. 11 Oct., d. 7 Nov.

Roosevelt, Franklin D., b. 30 Jan., d. 12 Apr.

Roosevelt, Theodore, b. 27 Oct., d. 6 Jan.

Root, Elihu, b. 15 Feb., d. 6 Feb.

Rootes, Lord, b. 14 Jun.

Ropes, Arthur, b. 23 Dec., d. 10 Sept.

Rops, Félicien, b. 7 Jul., d. 23 Aug.

Ros, Edmundo, b. 7 Dec.

Rosa, Carl, b. 22 Mar., d. 30 Apr.

Rosa, Salvatore, b. 20 Jun., d. 15 Mar.

Rosberg, Keke, b. 6 Dec.

Rose, Bernard, b. 9 May

Rose, Billy, b. 6 Sept., d. 10 Feb.

Rose, Christopher, b. 10 Feb.

Rose, Clifford, b. 24 Oct.

Rosenberg, Ethel, d. 19 Jun.

Rosenberg, Julius, d. 19 Jun.

Rosenthal, Jack, b. 8 Sept.

Rosenthal, Toby, b. 15 Mar.

Rosenthal, Tom, b. 16 Jul.

Rosewall, Ken, b. 2 Nov.

Roskill, Lord, b. 6 Feb.

Ross, Adrian, b. 23 Dec., d. 10 Sept.

Ross, Alan, b. 6 May

Ross, Annie, b. 25 Jul.

Ross, Diana, b. 26 Mar.

Ross, James Clark, b. 15 Apr., d. 3 Apr.

Ross, John, b. 24 Jun., d. 30 Aug.

Ross, Jonathan, b. 17 Nov.

Ross, Katharine, b. 29 Jan.

Ross, Nick, b. 7 Aug.

Ross, Ronald, b. 13 May

Rosse, 3rd Earl, d. 31 Oct.

Rossen, Robert, b. 16 Mar.

Rossetti, Christina, b. 5 Dec., d. 29 Dec.

Rossetti, Dante Gabriel, b. 12 May, d. 9 Apr.

Rossington, Norman, b. 24 Dec.

Rossini, Gioacchino, b. 29 Feb., d. 13 Nov.

Rosso, Medardo, b. 20 Jun.

Rostand, Edmond, b. 1 Apr., d. 2 Dec.

Rosten, Leo C., b. 11 Apr.

Rostropovich, Mstislav, b. 27 Mar.

Roth, Philip, b. 19 Mar.

Rotha, Paul, b. 3 Jun.

Rothenstein, John, b. 11 Jul.

Rothenstein, Michael, b. 19 Mar.

Rothenstein, William, b. 29 Jan., d. 14 Feb.

Rothermere, 1st Viscount, b. 26 Apr., d. 26 Nov.

Rothermere, 3rd Viscount, b. 27 Aug.

Rothko, Mark, b. 25 Sept., d. 25 Feb.

Rothschild, Edmund de, b. 2 Jan.

Rothschild, Lionel de, d. 3 Jun.

Rothschild, Meyer, b. 23 Feb., d. 19 Sept.

Rothschild, Nathan, b. 16 Sept., d. 28 Jul.

Rouault, Georges-Henri, d. 13 Feb.

Roubillac, Louis-François, d. 11 Jan.

Rouget de Lisle, Claude, b. 10 May, d. 26 Jun.

Rousseau, Henri, b. 21 May, d. 2 Sept.

Rousseau, Jean-Baptiste, b. 6 Apr., d. 17 Mar.

Rousseau, Jean-Jacques, b. 28 Jun., d. 2 Jul.

Rousseau, Théodore, b. 15 Apr.

Roussel, Albert, d. 23 Aug.

Routledge, Patricia, b. 17 Feb.

Rouvroy, Louis de, b. 15 Jan.

Roux, Albert, b. 8 Oct.

Roux, Michel, b. 19 Apr.

Rowe, Richard, b. 11 Nov.

Rowlands, Patsy, b. 19 Jan.

Rowlandson, Thomas, d. 22 Apr.

Rowntree, Joseph, d. 4 Nov.

Rowse, A.L., b. 4 Dec.

Rowton, 1st Baron, b. 8 Oct.

Roxburgh, Andy, b. 1 Aug.

Royce, Henry, b. 27 Mar., d. 22 Apr.

Royce, Josiah, b. 20 Nov.

Rozhdestvensky, Gennadi, b. 4 May

Rozsa, Miklos, b. 18 Apr.

Ruark, Robert, b. 29 Dec., d. 30 Jun.

Rubbra, Edmund, b. 23 May

Rubens, Peter, b. 28 Jun., d. 30 May

Rubinstein, Anton, b. 28 Nov., d. 20 Nov.

Rubinstein, Artur, b. 28 Jan., d. 20 Dec.

Ruddock, Joan, b. 28 Dec.

Rudman, Michael, b. 14 Feb.

Rudolf I, of Germany, d. 15 Jul.

Rudolf II, Holy Roman Emperor, d. 20 Jan.

Rumbold, Angela, b. 11 Aug.

Rumbold, Jack, b. 5 Mar.

Rumford, Count von, d. 21 Aug.

Runcie, Lord, b. 2 Oct.

Runciman, Steven, b. 7 Jul.

Runciman, Walter, b. 6 Jul., d. 13 Aug.

Runyon, Damon, b. 4 Oct., d. 10 Dec.

Rupert, of Bavaria, b. 17 Dec.

Rupert, of Germany, b. 5 May, d. 18 May
Rupert, Prince, d. 29 Nov.
Rush, Barbara, b. 4 Jan.
Rush, Benjamin, b. 5 Jan.
Rush, Ian, b. 20 Oct.
Rushdie, Salman, b. 19 Jun.
Rushton, Willie, b. 18 Aug.
Rusk, Dean, b. 9 Feb.
Ruskin, John, b. 8 Feb., d. 20 Jan.
Russell, 1st Earl, b. 18 Aug., d. 28 May
Russell, Bertrand, b. 18 May, d. 2 Feb.
Russell, Edwin, b. 4 May
Russell, George, d. 17 Jul.
Russell, Jane, b. 21 Jun.
Russell, Ken, b. 3 Jul.
Russell, Lillian, b. 4 Dec.
Russell, Willy, b. 23 Aug.
Ruth, Babe, b. 6 Feb., d. 16 Aug.
Rutherford, Ernest, b. 30 Aug., d. 19 Oct.
Rutherford, John, b. 4 Oct.
Rutherford, Margaret, b. 11 May
Rutherford, Mark, b. 22 Dec., d. 14 Mar.
Ruysdael, Jakob van, d. 14 Mar.
Ruysdael, Salomon van, d. 1 Nov.
Ruyter, Michiel de, b. 24 Mar., d. 29 Apr.
Ryan, Helen, b. 16 Jun.
Rydberg, Abraham, b. 18 Dec.
Ryder, Baroness, b. 3 Jul.
Ryecart, Patrick, b. 9 May
Rylands, George, b. 23 Oct.
Ryle, Martin, b. 27 Sept.
Rymer, Thomas, d. 14 Dec.

Saatchi, Charles, b. 9 Jun.
Saatchi, Maurice, b. 21 Jun.
Sabatini, Gabriella, b. 16 Apr.
Sabatini, Rafael, b. 29 Apr., d. 13 Feb.
Sabine, Edward, b. 14 Oct.
Sacchini, Antonio, b. 23 Jul.
Sachs, Andrew, b. 7 Apr.
Sachs, Hans, b. 5 Nov., d. 19 Jan.
Sachs, Julius von, b. 2 Oct.
Sackville, Charles, Earl of Dorset, b. 24 Jan.
Sackville, Lord George, b. 26 Jan.
Sackville-West, Vita, b. 9 Mar., d. 2 Jun.
Sadat, Anwar, b. 25 Dec., d. 6 Oct.
Sade, Marquis de, b. 2 Jun., d. 2 Dec.
Sadie, Stanley, b. 30 Oct.
Sagan, Françoise, b. 21 Jun.

Sahl, Mort, b. 11 May
Sainsbury, Lord, b. 13 Aug.
Sainsbury, Timothy, b. 11 Jun.
St Aldwyn, Earl, b. 9 Oct.
St Andrews, Earl of, b. 26 Jun.
Saint-Exupéry, Antoine de, b. 29 Jun.
Saint-Gaudens, Augustus, d. 3 Aug.
Saint-Hilaire, Auguste de, b. 4 Oct., d. 30 Sept.
St John, Jill, b. 19 Aug.
St John, Lord, b. 18 May
St John of the Cross, b. 24 Jun.
St Just, Louis de, b. 25 Aug., d. 28 Jul.
St Laurent, Louis, b. 1 Feb., d. 25 Jul.
Saint Laurent, Yves, b. 1 Aug.
St Martin, Yves, b. 8 Sept.
Saint-Saëns, Camille, b. 9 Oct., d. 16 Dec.
Saint-Simon, Claude de, b. 17 Oct.
St Vincent, Earl of, d. 14 Mar.
Sainte-Beuve, Charles, b. 23 Dec.
Sainton-Dolby, Charlotte, b. 17 May
Saintsbury, George, b. 23 Oct.
Saki, b. 18 Dec., d. 14 Nov.
Sala, George, b. 24 Nov., d. 8 Dec.
Saladin, d. 4 Mar.
Salazar, Adolfo, b. 6 Mar.
Salazar, Antonio, b. 28 Apr., d. 27 Jul.
Sale, George, d. 13 Nov.
Sales, St Francis de, b. 21 Aug.
Salieri, Antonio, b. 18 Aug.
Salinger, J.D., b. 1 Jan.
Salinger, Pierre, b. 14 Jun.
Salisbury, 1st Earl, b. 1 Jun., d. 24 May
Salisbury, 3rd Marquess, b. 3 Feb., d. 22 Aug.
Salk, Jonas, b. 28 Oct.
Sallis, Peter, b. 1 Feb.
Salt, Titus, b. 20 Sept., d. 20 Sept.
Salthouse, John, b. 16 Jun.
Salzman, Harry, b. 27 Oct.
Sammartini, Giuseppe, b. 6 Jan.
Sampson, Anthony, b. 3 Aug.
Samsova, Galina, b. 17 Mar.
Samuel, Herbert, b. 6 Nov.
Sand, George, b. 1 Jul., d. 8 Jun.
Sandburg, Carl, b. 6 Jan., d. 22 Jul.
Sandby, Paul, d. 9 Nov.
Sanderson, Joan, b. 24 Nov.
Sanderson, Tessa, b. 14 Mar.

Sandford, Jeremy, b. 5 Dec.
Sands, Leslie, b. 19 May
Sanger, Frederick, b. 13 Aug.
Sankey, Ira, b. 28 Aug.
San Martín, José de, b. 25 Feb., d. 17 Aug.
Sannazaro, Jacopo, b. 28 Jul., d. 24 Apr.
Sansom, Kenny, b. 26 Sept.
Sansom, William, b. 18 Jan., d. 20 Apr.
Sanson, Nicholas, b. 20 Dec.
Sansovino, Jacopo, b. 2 Jul., d. 27 Nov.
Santa Anna, Antonio de, b. 21 Feb.
Santley, Charles, d. 22 Sept.
Santos-Dumont, Alberto, b. 20 Jul.
Sanzio, Raphael, b. 28 Mar., d. 6 Apr.
Sapir, Edward, b. 26 Jan., d. 4 Feb.
Sapper, b. 28 Sept.
Sarasate, Pablo, b. 10 Mar., d. 20 Sept.
Sarazen, Gene, b. 27 Feb.
Sardou, Victorien, b. 5 Sept., d. 8 Nov.
Sargent, John Singer, b. 12 Jan., d. 15 Apr.
Sargent, Malcolm, b. 29 Apr., d. 3 Oct.
Saroyan, William, b. 31 Aug., d. 18 May
Sarpi, Fra Paolo, b. 14 Aug.
Sarti, Giuseppe, d. 28 Jul.
Sarto, Andrea del, b. 16 Jul., d. 28 Sept.
Sartre, Jean-Paul, b. 21 Jun., d. 15 Apr.
Sassoon, Siegfried, b. 8 Sept., d. 1 Sept.
Sassoon, Vidal, b. 17 Jan.
Satie, Erik, b. 17 May, d. 1 Jul.
Saunders, Jennifer, b. 12 Jul.
Saunders, Peter, b. 23 Nov.
Saunders, Vivien, b. 24 Nov.
Sava, George, b. 15 Oct.
Savage, Austin, b. 15 Dec.
Savage, Richard, b. 16 Jan., d. 1 Aug.
Savalas, Telly, b. 21 Jan.
Savile, Henry, b. 30 Nov., d. 19 Feb.
Savile, Jimmy, b. 31 Oct.
Saville, Mark, b. 20 Mar.
Savonarola, Girolamo, b. 21 Sept., d. 23 May
Sax, Adolphe, b. 6 Nov., d. 7 Feb.
Saxe, Maurice, Comte de, b. 28 Oct.
Saxon, John, b. 5 Aug.
Say, Jean-Baptiste, b. 5 Jan., d. 21 Apr.
Sayer, Leo, b. 21 May
Sayers, Dorothy L., b. 13 Jun., d. 18 Dec.
Sayers, Tom, b. 25 May
Sayle, Alexei, b. 7 Aug.

Scacchi, Greta, b. 18 Feb.
Scales, Prunella, b. 22 Jun.
Scaliger, Julius Caesar, d. 21 Oct.
Scanlon, Lord, b. 26 Oct.
Scannell, Tony, b. 14 Aug.
Scarfe, Gerald, b. 1 Jun.
Scargill, Arthur, b. 11 Jan.
Scarlatti, Alessandro, b. 2 May, d. 24 Oct.
Scarlatti, Domenico, d. 23 Jul.
Scarlatti, Giuseppe, b. 26 Oct.
Scarman, Lord, b. 29 Jul.
Schacht, Hjalmar, b. 22 Jan., d. 4 Jun.
Schadow, Rudolf, b. 9 Jul.
Schadow-Godenhaus, Friedrich, b. 6 Sept., d. 19 Mar.
Schapera, Isaac, b. 23 Jun.
Scharnhorst, Gerhard von, b. 12 Nov., d. 28 Jun.
Schaufuss, Peter, b. 26 Apr.
Scheele, Carl, b. 9 Dec., d. 19 May
Scheffer, Ary, d. 15 Jun.
Scheffer, Henri, b. 25 Sept., d. 15 Mar.
Schell, Maria, b. 15 Jan.
Schell, Maximilian, b. 8 Dec.
Schelling, Friedrich von, d. 20 Aug.
Schertzinger, Victor, b. 8 Apr., d. 26 Oct.
Schetky, John, b. 11 Aug., d. 5 Sept.
Schiaparelli, Elsa, d. 13 Nov.
Schiaparelli, Giovanni, b. 14 Mar.
Schiller, Friedrich von, b. 10 Nov., d. 9 May
Schinkel, Karl, b. 13 Mar., d. 9 Oct.
Schlegel, August von, b. 8 Sept.
Schlegel, Friedrich von, b. 10 Mar.
Schleiermacher, Friedrich, b. 21 Nov.
Schlesinger, Arthur, b. 15 Oct.
Schlesinger, John, b. 16 Feb.
Schliemann, Heinrich, 6 Jan., d. 26 Dec.
Schmidt, Franz, d. 11 Feb.
Schmidt, Helmut, b. 23 Dec.
Schneiderhan, Wolfgang, b. 28 May
Schnitzler, Arthur, b. 15 May, d. 21 Oct.
Schockemöhle, Alwin, b. 29 May
Schockemöhle, Paul, b. 22 Mar.
Schoenberg, Arnold, b. 13 Sept., d. 13 Jul.
Schönbein, Christian, b. 18 Oct., d. 29 Aug.
Schongauer, Martin, d. 2 Feb.

Schopenhauer, Arthur, b. 22 Feb., d. 21 Sept.

Schreiner, Olive, b. 24 Mar., d. 11 Dec.

Schreker, Franz, d. 21 Mar.

Schrödinger, Erwin, b. 12 Aug.

Schubert, Franz, b. 31 Jan., d. 19 Nov.

Schultz, Charles, b. 26 Nov.

Schuman, Robert (statesman) b. 29 Jun., d. 4 Sept.

Schumann, Clara, b. 13 Sept., d. 20 May

Schumann, Elisabeth, b. 13 Jun., d. 23 Apr.

Schumann, Maurice, b. 10 Apr.

Schumann, Robert (composer), b. 8 Jun., d. 29 Jul.

Schuschnigg, Kurt von, b. 14 Dec., d. 18 Nov.

Schütz, Heinrich, b. 8 Oct., d. 6 Nov.

Schwann, Theodor, b. 7 Dec.

Schwartz, Arthur, b. 25 Nov., d. 3 Sept.

Schwarz, Rudolf, b. 29 Apr.

Schwarzkopf, Elisabeth, b. 9 Dec.

Schweitzer, Albert, b. 14 Jan., d. 4 Sept.

Schwind, Moritz von, b. 21 Jan.

Schwitters, Kurt, b. 20 Jun.

Scofield, Paul, b. 21 Jan.

Scoresby, William, b. 5 Oct.

Scott, Cyril, b. 27 Sept., d. 31 Dec.

Scott, Douglas, b. 29 May

Scott, George C., b. 18 Oct.

Scott, George Gilbert, b. 13 Jun., d. 27 Mar.

Scott, Giles Gilbert, b. 9 Nov.

Scott, Janette, b. 14 Dec.

Scott, Lizabeth, b. 29 Sept.

Scott, Margaretta, b. 13 Feb.

Scott, Nicholas, b. 5 Aug.

Scott, Randolph, d. 2 Mar.

Scott, Robert F., b. 6 Jun., d. 29 Mar.

Scott, Ronnie, b. 28 Jan.

Scott, Selina, b. 13 May

Scott, Terry, b. 4 May

Scott, Walter, b. 15 Aug., d. 21 Sept.

Scotus, John Duns, d. 8 Nov.

Scriabin, Alexander, b. 6 Jan., d. 27 Apr.

Scribe, Augustin, b. 24 Dec., d. 20 Feb.

Scripps, Edward W., b. 18 Jun.

Scudamore, Peter, b. 13 Jun.

Scudéry, Madeleine de, b. 15 Nov., d. 2 Jun.

Seaman, Owen, d. 2 Feb.

Searle, Ronald, b. 3 Mar.

Sebastian, of Portugal, d. 4 Aug.

Secombe, Harry, b. 8 Sept.

Secondat, Charles de, b. 18 Jan.

Sedaka, Neil, b. 13 Mar.

Seddon, Richard, d. 10 Jun.

Sedgman, Frank, b. 29 Oct.

Sedgwick, Adam, b. 22 Mar., d. 27 Feb.

Sedley, Charles, b. 31 Mar., d. 20 Aug.

Seear, Baroness, b. 7 Aug.

Seefried, Irmgard, b. 9 Oct.

Seeger, Pete, b. 3 May

Seeley, John, b. 10 Sept.

Seeling, Hans, b. 14 Feb.

Seferis, George, b. 13 Mar., d. 20 Sept.

Segal, George, b. 13 Feb.

Segal, Jeffrey, b. 1 Aug.

Segovia, Andrés, b. 18 Feb., d. 2 Jun.

Segrave, Henry, d. 13 Jun.

Seiber, Mátyás, b. 4 May, d. 24 Sept.

Seifert, Richard, b. 25 Nov.

Selby, Tony, b. 26 Feb.

Selden, John, b. 16 Dec., d. 30 Nov.

Selfridge, Gordon, b. 11 Jan., d. 8 May

Selleck, Tom, b. 29 Jan.

Sellers, Peter, b. 8 Sept., d. 24 Jul.

Selwyn, George Augustus, d. 25 Jan.

Selwyn-Lloyd, Baron, d. 17 May

Selznick, David O., b. 10 May

Sendak, Maurice, b. 10 Jun.

Senefelder, Alois, b. 6 Nov., d. 26 Feb.

Senior, Nassau, b. 4 Jun.

Senna, Ayrton, b. 21 Mar.

Sennett, Mack, b. 17 Jan., d. 5 Nov.

Sergius III, Pope, d. 14 Apr.

Serle, Chris, b. 13 Jun.

Serling, Rod, d. 28 Jun.

Serlio, Sebastiano, b. 6 Sept.

Servan-Schreiber, Jean, b. 13 Feb.

Service, Robert, b. 16 Jan., d. 11 Sept.

Sessions, John, b. 11 Jan.

Sessions, Roger H., b. 28 Dec.

Seurat, Georges, b. 2 Dec., d. 29 Mar.

Severac, Joseph de, b. 20 Jul.

Severin, Timothy, b. 25 Sept.

Severn, Joseph, b. 7 Dec.

Severus, Lucius Septimius, d. 4 Feb.

Sévigné, Marie de, b. 5 Feb., d. 17 Apr.

Seward, Anna, d. 25 Mar.

Seymour, Jane, b. 15 Feb., d. 24 Oct.
Seymour, Lynn, b. 8 Mar.
Seymour, Thomas, d. 20 Mar.
Seymour-Smith, Martin, b. 24 Apr.
Seyss-Inquart, Artur von, b. 22 Jul.
Sforza, Francesco, b. 23 Jul.
Shackleton, Ernest, b. 15 Feb., d. 5 Jan.
Shackleton, Keith, b. 16 Jan.
Shacklock, Constance, b. 16 Apr.
Shadwell, Thomas, d. 19 Nov.
Shaffer, Anthony, b. 15 May
Shaffer, Peter, b. 15 May
Shaftesbury, 1st Earl, b. 22 Jul., d. 21 Jan.
Shaftesbury, 3rd Earl, b. 26 Feb.
Shaftesbury, 7th Earl, b. 28 Apr., d. 1 Oct.
Shah of Iran, 1919, b. 26 Oct.
Shakespeare, William, b. 23 Apr., d. 23
  Apr.
Shankar, Ravi, b. 7 Apr.
Shapey, Ralph, b. 12 Mar.
Shapiro, Helen, b. 28 Sept.
Sharif, Omar, b. 10 Apr.
Sharp, Cecil, d. 23 Jun.
Sharpe, Richard, b. 9 Sept.
Sharpe, Tom, b. 30 Mar.
Shatner, William, b. 22 Mar.
Shaw, Artie, b. 23 May
Shaw, George Bernard, b. 26 Jul., d. 2
  Nov.
Shaw, Irwin, d. 16 May
Shaw, John, b. 13 Oct.
Shaw, Martin, b. 21 Jan.
Shaw, Richard, d. 17 Nov.
Shaw, Roy, b. 8 Jul.
Shaw, Sandie, b. 26 Feb.
Shaw, Sebastian, b. 29 May
Shaw, Thurstan, b. 27 Jun.
Shawcross, Lord, b. 4 Feb.
Shcharansky, Natan, b. 20 Jan.
Shchedrin, Rodion, b. 16 Dec.
Shearer, Moira, b. 17 Jan.
Shearing, George, b. 13 Aug.
Shee, Martin Archer, d. 19 Aug.
Sheen, Martin, b. 3 Aug.
Sheene, Barry, b. 11 Sept.
Sheil, Richard, b. 17 Aug.
Shelley, Mary, b. 30 Aug., d. 1 Feb.
Shelley, Norman, d. 21 Aug.
Shelley, Percy Bysshe, b. 4 Aug., d. 8 Jul.
Shelton, Anne, b. 10 Nov.

Shenstone, William, d. 11 Feb.
Shepard, Alan, b. 18 Nov.
Shepard, E.H., b. 10 Dec., d. 24 Mar.
Shephard, Gillian, b. 22 Jan.
Shepheard, Peter, b. 11 Nov.
Shepherd, David (artist), b. 25 Apr.
Shepherd, Jack, b. 29 Oct., d. 16 Nov.
Sheppard, David (bishop), b. 6 Mar.
Sheraton, Thomas, d. 22 Oct.
Sherfield, Lord, b. 3 Feb.
Sheridan, Dinah, b. 17 Sept.
Sheridan, Richard, b. 30 Oct., d. 7 Jul.
Sherman, William, b. 8 Feb., d. 14 Feb.
Sherriff, R.C., b. 6 Jun., d. 13 Nov.
Sherrin, Ned, b. 18 Feb.
Sherrington, Charles, b. 27 Nov.
Sherwood, Mary, d. 22 Sept.
Sherwood, Robert, b. 4 Apr., d. 14 Nov.
Shiki, Masaoka, b. 14 Oct.
Shillibeer, George, d. 22 Aug.
Shinwell, Emanuel, b. 18 Oct., d. 8 May
Shirley, Ann, b. 17 Apr.
Shirley, James, d. 29 Oct.
Shirley-Quirk, John, b. 28 Aug.
Shoemaker, Willie, b. 19 Aug.
Sholes, Christopher, b. 14 Feb., d. 17 Feb.
Sholokhov, Mikhail, b. 11 May, d. 20 Feb.
Shore, Dinah, b. 1 Mar.
Shore, Peter, b. 20 May
Short, Nigel, b. 14 Jun.
Shostakovich, Dmitri, b. 25 Sept., d. 9
  Aug.
Shovell, Cloudesley, d. 22 Oct.
Shrimpton, Jean, b. 7 Nov.
Shuftan, Eugene, b. 21 Jul.
Shulman, Milton, b. 1 Sept.
Shultz, George, b. 13 Dec.
Shute, Nevil, b. 17 Jan., d. 12 Jan.
Siamese twins, b. 11 May
Sibelius, Jean, b. 8 Dec., d. 20 Sept.
Sibley, Antoinette, b. 27 Feb.
Sibson, Tony, b. 9 Apr.
Sica, Vittorio de, b. 7 Jul., d. 13 Nov.
Sickert, Walter, b. 31 May, d. 22 Jan.
Siddons, Sarah, b. 5 Jul., d. 8 Jun.
Sidey, Ernest, b. 2 Jan.
Sidgwick, Nevil, b. 8 May, d. 15 Mar.
Sidney, Algernon, d. 7 Dec.
Sidney, Philip, b. 30 Nov., d. 17 Oct.
Sidney, Sylvia, b. 8 Aug.

Sieff, Lord, b. 4 May
Siemens, Charles, b. 4 Apr.
Siemens, Ernst von, b. 13 Dec., d. 6 Dec.
Siemens, William, d. 19 Nov.
Sienkiewicz, Henryk, b. 5 May, d. 15 Nov.
Sieyès, Emmanuel, d. 20 Jun.
Sigismund I, of Poland, d. 1 Apr.
Sigismund II, of Poland, b. 1 Aug., d. 6 Jul.
Signac, Paul, b. 11 Nov., d. 15 Aug.
Signorelli, Luca, d. 16 Oct.
Signoret, Simone, d. 30 Sept.
Sikorski, Wladyslaw, b. 20 May
Sikorsky, Igor, b. 25 May, d. 26 Oct.
Sillitoe, Alan, b. 4 Mar.
Sills, Beverley, b. 25 May
Silvers, Phil, d. 1 Nov.
Silvester II, Pope, d. 12 May
Silvia, of Sweden, b. 23 Dec.
Sim, Alastair, b. 9 Oct., d. 19 Aug.
Simenon, Georges, b. 13 Feb.
Simmons, Jean, b. 31 Jan.
Simmons, Michael, b. 8 May
Simon, Carly, b. 25 Jun.
Simon, Neil, b. 4 Jul.
Simon, Paul, b. 13 Oct.
Simone, Nina, b. 21 Feb.
Simpson, Alan, b. 27 Nov.
Simpson, John A., b. 7 Jun.
Simpson, Robert (composer), b. 2 Mar.
Simpson, Robert (cricketer), b. 3 Feb.
Simpson, Wallis, *see* Duchess of Windsor
Sims, Joan, b. 9 May
Sinatra, Frank, b. 12 Dec.
Sinatra, Nancy, b. 8 Jun.
Sinclair, Auriol, b. 19 Nov.
Sinclair, Upton, b. 20 Sept., d. 25 Nov.
Sinden, Donald, b. 9 Oct.
Sinden, Jeremy, b. 14 Jun.
Sinding, Christian, d. 3 Dec.
Singer, Isaac (author), b. 14 Jul.
Singer, Isaac (inventor), b. 27 Oct., d. 23 Jul.
Sisley, Alfred, b. 30 Oct., d. 29 Jan.
Sismondi, Jean de, d. 25 Jul.
Sisson, Charles, b. 22 Apr.
Sisson, Rosemary Anne, b. 13 Oct.
Sissons, Peter, b. 17 Jul.
Sitwell, Edith, b. 7 Sept., d. 9 Dec.
Sitwell, Osbert, b. 6 Dec.

Sitwell, Sacheverell, b. 15 Nov., d. 4 May
Sixtus V, Pope, b. 13 Dec.
Skalkottas, Nikolaos, b. 21 Mar.
Skeat, Walter, b. 21 Nov.
Skellern, Peter, b. 4 Mar.
Skelton, John, d. 21 Jun.
Skelton, Nick, b. 30 Dec.
Skingsley, Anthony, b. 19 Oct.
Skinner, Dennis, b. 11 Feb.
Slade, Christopher, b. 2 Jun.
Slade, Julian, b. 28 May
Slatkin, Leonard, b. 1 Sept.
Sleep, Wayne, b. 17 Jul.
Sleman, Mike, b. 11 May
Slim, 1st Viscount, b. 6 Aug.
Sloane, Hans, b. 16 Apr., d. 11 Jan.
Sloman, Albert, b. 14 Feb.
Smart, Henry, b. 26 Oct.
Smeaton, John, b. 8 Jun., d. 28 Oct.
Smellie, William, d. 25 Jun.
Smetana, Bedřich, b. 2 Mar., d. 12 May
Smiles, Samuel, b. 23 Dec., 16 Apr.
Smirke, Robert, b. 1 Oct., d. 19 Apr.
Smith, Adam, b. 5 Jun., d. 17 Jul.
Smith, Alexis, b. 8 Jun.
Smith, Bessie, b. 15 Apr.
Smith, Colvin, d. 21 Jul.
Smith, Cyril, b. 28 Jun.
Smith, David, b. 9 Mar.
Smith, Delia, b. 18 Jun.
Smith, George, b. 26 Mar., d. 19 Aug.
Smith, Harvey, b. 29 Dec.
Smith, Jaclyn, b. 26 Oct.
Smith, John (colonist), d. 21 Jun.
Smith, John (MP), b. 13 Sept.
Smith, Joseph, b. 23 Dec., d. 27 Jun.
Smith, Kent, d. 23 Apr.
Smith, Lloyd Pearsall, d. 2 Mar.
Smith, Maggie, b. 28 Dec.
Smith, Mel, b. 3 Dec.
Smith, Mike J.K., b. 30 Jun.
Smith, Robert, b. 12 Jun.
Smith, Stan, b. 14 Dec.
Smith, Stevie, d. 7 Mar.
Smith, Sydney, d. 22 Feb.
Smith, Theobald, b. 31 Jul.
Smith, W.H., b. 24 Jun., d. 6 Oct.
Smith, William (abolitionist), d. 31 May
Smith, William (geologist), d. 28 Aug.
Smithson, James, d. 27 Jun.

Smollett, Tobias, b. 19 Mar., d. 17 Sept.
Smuts, Jan, b. 24 May, d. 11 Sept.
Smyth, Ethel, b. 23 Apr., d. 8 May
Smythe, Pat, b. 22 Nov.
Smythe, Reg, b. 10 Jul.
Snagge, John, b. 8 May
Snead, Sam, b. 27 May
Snell, Peter, b. 17 Dec.
Snorri, Sturluson, d. 22 Sept.
Snow, C.P., b. 15 Oct.
Snow, Peter, b. 20 Apr.
Snow, Philip, b. 7 Aug.
Snowden, Philip, d. 15 May
Snowdon, Earl of, b. 7 Mar.
Snyders, Frans, b. 11 Nov.
Soane, John, b. 10 Sept., d. 20 Jan.
Soares, Mario, b. 7 Dec.
Sobers, Garfield, b. 28 Jul.
Soddy, Frederick, b. 2 Sept., d. 22 Sept.
Södermann, August, b. 17 Jul.
Söderström, Elizabeth, b. 7 May
Sodoma, Il, d. 15 Feb.
Solander, Daniel, d. 16 May
Solti, Georg, b. 21 Oct.
Solvay, Ernest, d. 26 May
Solzhenitsyn, Alexander, b. 11 Dec.
Somerville, Mary, b. 26 Dec., d. 28 Nov.
Somerville, William, d. 17 Jul.
Somes, Michael, b. 28 Sept.
Sommer, Elke, b. 5 Nov.
Sondheim, Stephen, b. 22 Mar.
Soper, Lord, b. 31 Jan.
Sorbon, Robert de, b. 9 Oct.
Sorel, Agnes, d. 9 Feb.
Sorel, Georges, b. 2 Nov., d. 30 Aug.
Sorolla, Joaquin, d. 11 Aug.
Soskice, Frank, d. 1 Jan.
Sothern, Ann, b. 22 Jan.
Soubirous, Bernadette, d. 16 Apr.
Soul, David, b. 28 Aug.
Soult, Nicolas, b. 29 Mar., d. 26 Nov.
Sousa, John Philip, b. 6 Nov., d. 6 Mar.
Southcott, Joanna, d. 27 Dec.
Southey, Robert, b. 12 Aug., d. 21 Mar.
Southwell, Robert, d. 21 Feb.
Sowerby, Leo, d. 7 Jul.
Soyer, Alexis-Benoît, d. 5 Aug.
Spaak, Paul-Henri, b. 25 Jan.
Spacek, Sissy, b. 25 Dec.
Spallanzani, Lazzaro, b. 12 Jan.

Spanghero, Walter, b. 21 Dec.
Spark, Muriel, b. 1 Feb.
Spassky, Boris, b. 30 Jan.
Speed, Doris, b. 3 Feb.
Speed, John, d. 28 Jul.
Speight, Johnny, b. 2 Jun.
Speke, John, b. 4 May, d. 15 Sept.
Spelman, Cardinal, b. 4 May
Spence, Basil, b. 13 Aug.
Spencer, Countess, b. 9 Sept.
Spencer, Gilbert, d. 14 Jan.
Spencer, Herbert, b. 27 Apr., d. 8 Dec.
Spencer, John, b. 18 Sept.
Spencer, Stanley, b. 30 Jun., d. 14 Dec.
Spender, Stephen, b. 28 Feb.
Spener, Philipp Jakob, b. 23 Jan., d. 5 Feb.
Spengler, Oswald, b. 29 May, d. 8 May
Spenser, Edmund, d. 16 Jan.
Sperry, Elmer, b. 12 Oct.
Spiegel, Sam, d. 31 Dec.
Spielberg, Steven, b. 18 Dec.
Spillane, Mickey, b. 9 Mar.
Spinetti, Victor, b. 2 Sept.
Spinoza, Baruch, b. 24 Nov., d. 21 Feb.
Spitz, Mark, b. 10 Feb.
Spock, Dr Benjamin, b. 2 May
Spode, Josiah, d. 16 Jul.
Spofforth, Frederick, d. 4 Jun.
Spohr, Louis, d. 22 Oct.
Spontini, Gaspare, b. 14 Nov., d. 24 Jan.
Spooner, William, b. 22 Jul., d. 29 Aug.
Spring, Howard, b. 10 Feb.
Springer, Axel, d. 22 Sept.
Springfield, Dusty, b. 16 Apr.
Springsteen, Bruce, b. 23 Sept.
Spurgeon, Charles, b. 19 Jun., d. 31 Jan.
Spy (caricaturist), b. 21 Nov.
Squire, Jeff, b. 23 Sept.
Squires, Dorothy, b. 25th Mar.
Squires, Peter, b. 4 Aug.
Stacey, Neil, b. 15 May
Stack, Prunella, b. 28 Jul.
Stack, Robert, b. 13 Jan.
Stackpole, Keith, b. 10 Jul.
Stadler, Maximilian, b. 7 Aug.
Staël, Madame de, b. 22 Apr., d. 14 Jul.
Stafford, Jo, b. 12 Nov.
Stafford-Clark, David, b. 17 Mar.
Stahl, Georg, b. 21 Oct.
Stainer, Jakob, b. 14 Jul.

Stainer, John, d. 31 Mar.
Stalin, Joseph, b. 21 Dec., d. 5 Mar.
Stallone, Sylvester, b. 6 Jul.
Stamitz, Karl, d. 9 Nov.
Stamp, 1st Baron, d. 16 Apr.
Stamp, Terence, b. 22 Jul.
Standing, John, b. 16 Aug.
Standish, Myles, d. 3 Oct.
Stanford, Charles, b. 30 Sept., d. 29 Mar.
Stanhope, 3rd Earl, d. 16 Dec.
Stanhope, Lady Hester, d. 23 Jun.
Stanislavsky, Konstantin, b. 17 Jan., d. 7 Aug.
Stanley, Arthur, b. 13 Dec.
Stanley, Henry M., b. 28 Jan., d. 10 May
Stanley, Kim, b. 11 Feb.
Stardust, Alvin, b. 27 Sept.
Stark, Freya, b. 31 Jan.
Stark, Ian, b. 22 Feb.
Starkey, Greville, b. 21 Dec.
Starr, Freddie, b. 10 Jan.
Starr, Kay, b. 21 Jul.
Starr, Ringo, b. 7 Jul.
Statham, Brian, b. 17 Jun.
Staughton, Christopher, b. 24 May
Staveley, William, b. 10 Nov.
Stead, Christina, b. 17 Jul.
Stead, W.T., b. 5 Jul., d. 15 Apr.
Steadman, Alison, b. 26 Aug.
Steadman, Ralph, b. 15 May
Steegmuller, Francis, b. 3 Jul.
Steel, Flora Annie, d. 12 Apr.
Steel, Sir David (politician), b. 31 Mar.
Steele, David (cricketer), b. 29 Sept.
Steele, Richard, d. 1 Sept.
Steele, Tommy, b. 17 Dec.
Steele-Perkins, Derek, b. 19 Jun.
Steer, Philip Wilson, b. 28 Dec., d. 21 Mar.
Stefansson, Vilhjalmur, b. 3 Nov.
Steiger, Rod, b. 14 Apr.
Stein, Aurel, b. 26 Nov., d. 26 Oct.
Stein, Gertrude, b. 3 Feb., d. 27 Jul.
Steinbeck, John, b. 27 Feb., d. 20 Dec.
Steiner, George, b. 23 Apr.
Steiner, Max, b. 10 May, d. 28 Dec.
Steiner, Rudolf, b. 27 Feb., d. 30 Mar.
Steinmetz, Charles, d. 26 Oct.
Stendhal, b. 23 Jan., d. 23 Mar.
Stenmark, Ingemar, b. 18 Mar.

Stennett, Stan, b. 30 Jul.
Stensen, Niels, b. 10 Jan.
Stephan, Heinrich von, b. 7 Jan., d. 8 Apr.
Stephanie, of Monaco, b. 1 Feb.
Stephen, James, d. 14 Sept.
Stephen, Leslie, b. 28 Nov., d. 22 Feb.
Stephen, of England, d. 25 Oct.
Stephen Bathory, of Poland, d. 12 Dec.
Stephens, James, b. 2 Feb., d. 26 Dec.
Stephens, John L., b. 28 Nov.
Stephens, Robert, b. 14 Jul.
Stephenson, George, b. 9 Jun., d. 12 Aug.
Stephenson, Pamela, b. 4 Dec.
Stephenson, Robert, b. 16 Oct., d. 12 Oct.
Sterling, Antoinette, b. 23 Jan.
Sterling, Jan, b. 3 Apr.
Stern, Isaac, b. 21 Jul.
Sternberg, Josef von, b. 29 May, d. 22 Dec.
Sterne, Laurence, b. 24 Nov., d. 18 Mar.
Steven, Stewart, b. 30 Sept.
Stevens, Cat, b. 21 Jul.
Stevens, Connie, b. 8 Aug.
Stevens, George A., d. 6 Sept.
Stevens, Jocelyn, b. 14 Feb.
Stevens, Ronnie, b. 2 Sept.
Stevens, Shakin', b. 4 Mar.
Stevens, Wallace, b. 2 Oct., d. 2 Aug.
Stevenson, Adlai, b. 5 Feb., d. 14 Jul.
Stevenson, Graham, b. 16 Dec.
Stevenson, Robert, b. 8 Jun., d. 12 Jul.
Stevenson, Robert Louis, b. 13 Nov., d. 3 Dec.
Stewart, Al, b. 5 Sept.
Stewart, Alastair, b. 22 Jun.
Stewart, Dugald, b. 22 Nov.
Stewart, Duncan, b. 14 Feb.
Stewart, Eric, b. 20 Jan.
Stewart, Frederick, b. 16 Jan.
Stewart, Jackie, b. 11 Jun.
Stewart, James, Earl of Moray, d. 7 Feb.
Stewart, James (actor), b. 20 May
Stewart, Mary, b. 17 Sept.
Stewart, Mickey, b. 16 Sept.
Stewart, Patrick, b. 13 Jun.
Stewart, Rod, b. 10 Jan.
Stifter, Adalbert, b. 23 Oct., d. 28 Jan.
Stiles, Nobby, b. 18 May
Stilgoe, Richard, b. 28 Mar.
Still, Robert, b. 10 Jun., d. 13 Jan.

Stillman, William J., b. 1 Jun.
Sting, b. 2 Oct.
Stock, Nigel, b. 21 Sept.
Stockhausen, Karlheinz, b. 22 Aug.
Stockwell, Dean, b. 5 Mar.
Stockwood, Mervyn, b. 27 May
Stoker, Bram, b. 8 Nov., d. 20 Apr.
Stokes, George, d. 1 Feb.
Stokowski, Leopold, b. 18 Apr., d. 13 Sept.
Stolberg, Friedrich, d. 5 Dec.
Stone, Marcus, d. 24 Mar.
Stone, Norman, b. 8 Mar.
Stonor, Thomas, b. 5 Mar.
Stopes, Marie, d. 2 Oct.
Stoppard, Miriam, b. 12 May
Stoppard, Tom, b. 3 Jul.
Storey, David, b. 13 Jun.
Storm, Theodor, b. 14 Sept.
Stothard, Thomas, b. 17 Aug.
Stott, Richard, b. 17 Aug.
Stoute, Michael, b. 22 Oct.
Stove, Betty, b. 24 Jun.
Stow, John, d. 6 Apr.
Stowe, Harriet Beecher, b. 14 Jun., d. 1 Jul.
Strachey, John, b. 9 Feb.
Strachey, Lytton, b. 1 Mar., d. 21 Jan.
Stradella, Alessandro, b. 1 Oct.
Stradivari, Antonio, d. 18 Dec.
Strafford, 1st Earl, d. 12 May
Strang, William, b. 13 Feb., d. 12 Apr.
Strasberg, Lee, d. 17 Feb.
Strathcarron, Lord, b. 23 Jan.
Strauli, Christopher, b. 13 Apr.
Straus, Oscar, d. 11 Jan., b. 6 Mar.
Strauss, Johann, the Elder, b. 14 Mar., d. 25 Sept.
Strauss, Johann, the Younger, b. 25 Oct., d. 3 Jun.
Strauss, Richard, b. 11 Jun., d. 8 Sept.
Stravinsky, Igor, b. 17 Jun., d. 6 Apr.
Streep, Meryl, b. 22 Jun.
Street-Porter, Janet, b. 27 Dec.
Streisand, Barbra, b. 24 Apr.
Stresemann, Gustav, d. 3 Oct.
Stride, John, b. 11 Jul.
Strindberg, August, b. 22 Jan., d. 14 May
Stritch, Elaine, b. 2 Feb.

Stroheim, Erich von, b. 22 Sept., d. 12 May
Strong, L.A.G., b. 8 Mar., d. 17 Aug.
Strong, Roy, b. 23 Aug.
Strouse, Norman, b. 7 Jun.
Struensee, Johann von, b. 5 Aug.
Strutt, Joseph, d. 16 Oct.
Strype, John, d. 11 Dec.
Stuart, Charles Edward, b. 31 Dec., d. 31 Jan.
Stuart, Gilbert, d. 27 Jul.
Stuart, James Francis Edward, b. 10 Jun., d. 1 Jan.
Stuart, John (explorer), b. 7 Sept., d. 5 Jun.
Stuart, Leslie, b. 15 Mar., d. 27 Mar.
Stubblefield, James, b. 6 Sept.
Stubbs, George, b. 24 Aug., d. 10 Jul.
Stubbs, Una, b. 1 May
Stubbs, William, d. 22 Apr.
Stuck, Franz von, b. 23 Feb.
Stukeley, William, b. 7 Nov., d. 3 Mar.
Sturgeon, William, b. 22 May, d. 4 Dec.
Sturges, Preston, d. 6 Aug.
Sturt, Charles, b. 28 Apr., d. 16 Jun.
Styne, Jule, b. 31 Dec.
Suchet, David, b. 2 May
Suchet, John, b. 29 Mar.
Sudermann, Hermann, b. 30 Sept.
Sugar, Alan, b. 24 Mar.
Suggia, Guilhermina, d. 31 Jul.
Sukarno, d. 21 Jun.
Suleiman I, of Turkey, d. 6 Sept.
Sullivan, Arthur, b. 13 May, d. 22 Nov.
Sullivan, John L., b. 15 Oct., d. 2 Feb.
Sullivan, Louis, b. 3 Sept., d. 14 Apr.
Sullivan, Thomas, d. 3 May
Sully, Maximilien de, b. 13 Dec., d. 22 Dec.
Sully Prudhomme, René, b. 16 Mar., d. 7 Sept.
Sulzberger, Arthur, b. 5 Feb.
Summer, Donna, b. 31 Dec.
Summerskill, Shirley, b. 9 Sept.
Summerson, John, b. 25 Nov.
Sun Yat-sen, b. 12 Nov., d. 12 Mar.
Suppé, Franz von, b. 18 Apr., d. 21 May
Surtees, John, b. 11 Feb.
Surtees, Robert, b. 17 May, d. 16 Mar.
Susskind, Walter, d. 25 Mar.

Sutcliff, Rosemary, b. 14 Dec.
Sutcliffe, Herbert, b. 24 Nov., d. 22 Jan.
Sutherland, Donald, b. 17 Jul.
Sutherland, Graham, b. 24 Aug., d. 17 Feb.
Sutherland, Joan, b. 7 Nov.
Sutherland, Stewart, b. 25 Feb.
Suthern, John, b. 3 Oct.
Sutton, Dudley, b. 6 Apr.
Suzman, Helen, b. 7 Nov.
Suzman, Janet, b. 9 Feb.
Svendsen, Johan, b. 30 Sept.
Swan, Joseph, b. 31 Oct., d. 27 May
Swann, Donald, b. 30 Sept.
Swanson, Gloria, b. 27 Mar., d. 4 Apr.
Swanton, E.W., b. 11 Feb.
Swedenborg, Emanuel, b. 29 Jan., d. 29 Mar.
Sweelinck, Jan, d. 16 Oct.
Sweet, Henry, b. 15 Sept.
Swift, Clive, b. 9 Feb.
Swift, Jonathan, b. 30 Nov., d. 19 Oct.
Swinburn, Walter, b. 7 Aug.
Swinburne, Algernon, b. 5 Apr., d. 10 Apr.
Swinburne, Nora, b. 24 Jul.
Swinnerton, Frank, b. 12 Aug., d. 6 Nov.
Swinton, Ernest, b. 21 Oct.
Swit, Loretta, b. 4 Nov.
Sydenham, Thomas, b. 10 Sept., d. 29 Dec.
Sydow, Max von, b. 10 Apr.
Sykes, Eric, b. 4 May
Sykes, John, b. 26 Jan.
Sykes, Keble, b. 7 Jan.
Sykes, Richard, d. 22 Mar.
Sylvester, James, b. 3 Sept., d. 15 Mar.
Symonds, John, b. 5 Oct., d. 19 Apr.
Symons, Julian, b. 30 May
Symons, Patrick, b. 9 Jun.
Syms, Sylvia, b. 6 Jan.
Synge, J.M., b. 16 Apr., d. 24 Mar.
Szymanowski, Karol, b. 6 Oct.

Taft, William, b. 15 Sept., d. 8 Mar.
Taglioni, Maria, b. 23 Apr., d. 23 Apr.
Tagore, Rabindranath, b. 7 May, d. 7 Aug.
Taine, Hippolyte, b. 21 Apr.
Tait, Arthur F., d. 28 Apr.
Takada, Kenzo, b. 27 Feb.

Takemitsu, Toru, b. 8 Oct.
Talbot, Godfrey, b. 8 Oct.
Talbot, William Fox, b. 11 Feb., d. 17 Sept.
Talleyrand, b. 2 Feb., d. 17 May
Tallis, Thomas, d. 23 Nov.
Talma, François, b. 16 Jan., d. 19 Oct.
Tambay, Patrick, b. 25 Jun.
Tamerlane the Great, d. 17 Feb.
Tamm, Mary, b. 22 Mar.
Tandy, Donald, b. 20 Dec.
Tandy, Jessica, b. 7 Jun.
Tanner, Roscoe, b. 15 Oct.
Tarbuck, Jimmy, b. 6 Feb.
Tarkington, Booth, b. 29 Jul., d. 19 May
Tarlton, Richard, d. 5 Sept.
Tartini, Giuseppe, b. 8 Apr.
Tasso, Torquato, b. 11 Mar., d. 25 Apr.
Tate, Dr Jeffrey, b. 28 Apr.
Tate, Henry, b. 11 Mar., d. 5 Dec.
Tate, Nahum, d. 12 Aug.
Tati, Jacques, b. 9 Oct., d. 5 Nov.
Tauber, Richard, b. 16 May, d. 8 Jan.
Tavaré, Chris, b. 27 Oct.
Tavener, John, b. 28 Jan.
Taverne, Dick, b. 18 Oct.
Tavistock, Marquess of, b. 21 Jan.
Taylor, A.J.P., d. 25 Mar.
Taylor, Brook, d. 29 Dec.
Taylor, Deems, d. 3 Jul.
Taylor, Dennis, b. 19 Nov.
Taylor, Elizabeth (actress), b. 27 Feb.
Taylor, Elizabeth (novelist), b. 3 Jul., d. 19 Nov.
Taylor, George, 15 Feb.
Taylor, Graham, b. 15 Sept.
Taylor, Gwen, b. 19 Feb.
Taylor, Laurie, b. 1 Aug.
Taylor, Leslie, b. 25 Oct.
Taylor, Peter, b. 1 May
Taylor, Robert, b. 5 Aug.
Taylor, Rod, b. 11 Jan.
Taylor, Roger, b. 14 Oct.
Taylor, Rowland, d. 9 Feb.
Taylor, Shaw, b. 26 Oct.
Taylor, Wendy, b. 29 Jul.
Taylor, Zachary, b. 24 Nov., d. 9 Jul.
Taylor of Hadfield, Lord, b. 7 Jan.
Taylor-Young, Leigh, b. 25 Jan.
Tchaikovsky, Peter, b. 7 May, d. 6 Nov.

Tchaikowsky, André, d. 26 Jun.

Tchernichowski, Shaul, b. 20 Aug., d. 13 Oct.

Teach, Edward, d. 22 Nov.

Teagarden, Jack, b. 29 Aug., d. 15 Jan.

Tear, Robert, b. 8 Mar.

Tearle, Conway, d. 1 Oct.

Tearle, Godfrey, b. 12 Oct., d. 8 Jun.

Tebaldi, Renata, b. 1 Feb.

Tebbit, Norman, b. 29 Mar.

Tedder, Lord, b. 11 Jul.

Tegnér, Esaias, b. 13 Nov.

Teisserence de Bort, Léon, b. 5 Nov., d. 2 Jan.

Te Kanawa, Dame Kiri, b. 6 Mar.

Telford, Thomas, b. 9 Aug., d. 2 Sept.

Tempest, Marie, b. 15 Jul., d. 14 Oct.

Temple, Shirley, b. 23 Apr.

Temple, William, d. 27 Jan.

Templer, Gerald, d. 26 Oct.

Teniers, David, the Elder, d. 29 Jul.

Teniers, David, the Younger, b. 15 Dec., d. 25 Apr.

Tennant, Emma, b. 20 Oct.

Tennant, Kylie, b. 12 Mar.

Tenniel, John, b. 28 Feb., d. 25 Feb.

Tennstedt, Klaus, b. 6 Jun.

Tennyson, Alfred, Lord, b. 6 Aug., d. 6 Oct.

Tennyson, Frederick, d. 26 Feb.

Teresa, Mother, b. 27 Aug.

Teresa of Avila, St., b. 28 Mar.

Tereshkova, Valentina, b. 6 Mar.

Terkel, Studs, b. 16 May

Terraine, John, b. 15 Jan.

Terriss, William, b. 20 Feb.

Terry, Edward, d. 2 Apr.

Terry, Ellen, b. 27 Feb., d. 21 Jul.

Terry, Richard, d. 18 Apr.

Tesla, Nikola, b. 9 Jul., d. 7 Jan.

Tetley, Glen, b. 3 Feb.

Tetrazzini, Luisa, b. 28 Jun., d. 28 Apr.

Te Wiata, Inia, d. 26 Jun.

Teyte, Margaret, b. 17 Apr.

Thackeray, William, b. 18 Jul., d. 24 Dec.

Thatcher, Denis, b. 10 May

Thatcher, Margaret, b. 13 Oct.

Thaw, John, b. 3 Jan.

Theed, William, the Younger, d. 9 Sept.

Thelwell, Norman, b. 3 May

Theodorakis, Mikis, b. 29 Jul.

Theroux, Paul, b. 10 Apr.

Thesiger, Wilfred, b. 3 Jun.

Thierry, Augustin, d. 22 May

Thiers, Louis, b. 18 Apr., d. 3 Sept.

Thirkell, Angela, b. 30 Jan., d. 29 Jan.

Thom, James, b. 17 Apr., d. 17 Apr.

Thoma, Hans, b. 2 Oct., d. 7 Nov.

Thomas, Ambroise, b. 5 Aug.

Thomas, Arthur, b. 21 Nov.

Thomas, Dylan, b. 27 Oct., d. 9 Nov.

Thomas, Edward, d. 9 Apr.

Thomas, Keith, b. 2 Jan.

Thomas, Leslie, b. 22 Mar.

Thomas, Margaret, b. 26 Sept.

Thomas, Philip Edward, b. 3 Mar.

Thompson, Daley, b. 30 Jul.

Thompson, David, b. 30 Apr.

Thompson, Emma, b. 15 Apr.

Thompson, Francis, b. 18 Dec., d. 13 Nov.

Thompson, Henry, d. 18 Aug.

Thompson, Randall, b. 21 Apr., d. 9 Jul.

Thompson, Richard, b. 3 Apr.

Thoms, William, b. 16 Nov.

Thomson, Elihu, b. 29 Mar.

Thomson, James (18th-cent. poet), b. 11 Sept., d. 27 Aug.

Thomson, James (19th-cent. poet), b. 23 Nov.

Thomson, Jeff, b. 16 Aug.

Thomson, J.J., b. 18 Dec., d. 30 Aug.

Thomson, John, b. 1 Sept., d. 27 Oct.

Thomson, Peter, b. 23 Aug.

Thomson, Roy, d. 4 Aug.

Thorburn, Cliff, b. 16 Jan.

Thoreau, Henry D., b. 12 Jul., d. 6 May

Thorndike, Sybil, b. 24 Oct., d. 9 Jun.

Thorne, Angela, b. 25 Jan.

Thorneycroft, Lord, b. 26 Jul.

Thornhill, James, d. 4 May

Thornton, Frank, b. 15 Jan.

Thornycroft, Thomas, d. 30 Aug.

Thornycroft, William, b. 9 Mar., d. 18 Dec.

Thorpe, Jeremy, b. 29 Apr.

Thorsen, Linda, b. 18 Jun.

Thorwaldsen, Bertel, b. 19 Nov.

Threlfall, David, b. 12 Oct.

Thumb, General Tom, d. 2 Jan.

Thurber, James, b. 8 Dec., d. 2 Nov.
Thwaite, Anthony, b. 23 Jun.
Tiberius, emperor, b. 16 Nov., d. 16 Mar.
Tickner, Martin, b. 7 Mar.
Tidy, Bill, b. 9 Oct.
Tiepolo, Giovanni Battista, b. 5 Mar.,
    d. 27 Mar.
Tiepolo, Giovanni Domenico, b. 10 Sept.,
    d. 3 Mar.
Tierney, Gene, b. 20 Nov.
Tilden, Bill, b. 10 Feb.
Tillotson, Kathleen, b. 3 Apr.
Timothy, Christopher, b. 14 Oct.
Timpson, John, b. 2 Jul.
Tindale, Patricia, b. 11 Mar.
Tinniswood, Peter, b. 21 Dec.
Tintoretto, b. 29 Sept., d. 31 May
Tiomkin, Dimitri, b. 10 May, d. 11 Nov.
Tippett, Michael, b. 2 Jan.
Tirpitz, Alfred von, d. 6 Mar.
Tisio, Benvenuto, d. 6 Sept.
Tissot, James, b. 15 Oct., d. 8 Aug.
Titian, d. 27 Aug.
Tito, Josip, b. 7 May, d. 4 May
Tizard, Henry, b. 23 Aug.
Tizard, Thomas, b. 13 Mar.
Todd, Ann, b. 24 Jan.
Todd, Bob, b. 15 Dec.
Todd, Lord, b. 2 Oct.
Todd, Michael, b. 22 Jun., d. 22 Mar.
Todd, Richard, b. 11 Jun.
Todd, Ron, b. 11 Mar.
Tojo, Hideki, b. 30 Dec.
Tolkien, J.R.R., b. 3 Jan., d. 2 Sept.
Toller, Ernst, b. 1 Dec.
Tolman, Edward C., d. 19 Nov.
Tolstoy, Alexei, b. 10 Jan.
Tolstoy, Leo, b. 9 Sept., d. 20 Nov.
Tomalin, Claire, b. 20 Jun.
Tomasek, Vaclav, b. 17 Apr.
Tomlin, Lily, b. 1 Sept.
Tomlinson, Charles, b. 8 Jan.
Tomlinson, David, b. 7 May
Tomlinson, H.M., b. 21 Jun., d. 5 Feb.
Toms, Carl, b. 29 May
Tone, Franchot, d. 18 Sept.
Tone, Theobald Wolfe, b. 20 Jan., d. 19
    Nov.
Tong, Jacqueline, b. 21 Feb.
Tonypandy, Viscount, b. 29 Jan.

Tooke, John Horne, b. 25 Jun.
Toole, John L., d. 30 Jul.
Toplady, Augustus, b. 4 Nov., d. 14 Aug.
Topol, Chaim, b. 9 Sept.
Topolski, Daniel, b. 4 Jun.
Torelli, Giacomo, b. 1 Sept., d. 17 Jun.
Torelli, Giuseppe, b. 22 Apr., d. 8 Feb.
Tormé, Mel, b. 13 Sept.
Torn, Rip, b. 6 Feb.
Torquemada, Tomás de, d. 16 Sept.
Torrance, Sam, b. 24 Aug.
Torricelli, Evangelista, b. 15 Oct., d. 25
    Oct.
Torvill, Jayne, b. 7 Oct.
Toscanini, Arturo, b. 25th Mar., d. 16 Jan.
Tosti, Paolo, b. 9 Apr.
Toulouse-Lautrec, b. 24 Nov., d. 9 Sept.
Tovey, Donald, b. 17 Jul.
Townsend, Peter, b. 16 Sept.
Townshend, Charles, d. 4 Sept.
Townshend, Pete, b. 19 May
Toye, Wendy, b. 1 May
Toynbee, Arnold, b. 14 Apr., d. 22 Oct.
Tracy, Arthur, b. 25 Jun.
Tracy, Spencer, b. 5 Apr., d. 10 Jun.
Tradescant, John the Younger, b. 4 Aug.,
    d. 22 Apr.
Trajan, emperor, b. 15 Sept., d. 9 Aug.
Tranter, Nigel, b. 23 Nov.
Travers, Ben, d. 18 Dec.
Travolta, John, b. 18 Feb.
Tree, Herbert, d. 2 Jul.
Tree, Jeremy, b. 21 Dec.
Tree, Viola, d. 15 Nov.
Trelawny, Edward, b. 13 Nov., d. 13 Aug.
Trelford, Donald, b. 9 Nov.
Tremain, Rose, b. 2 Aug.
Tremlett, George, b. 5 Sept.
Trenchard, 1st Viscount, d. 10 Feb.
Trent, Jackie, b. 6 Sept.
Trevelyan, G.M., b. 16 Feb., d. 21 Jul.
Treves, Frederick, b. 29 Mar., d. 7 Dec.
Trevino, Lee, b. 1 Dec.
Trevithick, Richard, b. 13 Apr., d. 22 Apr.
Trevor, Claire, b. 8 Mar.
Trevor, Elleston, b. 17 Feb.
Trevor, Meriol, b. 15 Apr.
Trevor, William, b. 24 May
Trollope, Anthony, b. 24 Apr., d. 6 Dec.
Tromp, Maarten, b. 23 Apr., d. 9 Aug.

Trotsky, Leon, b. 7 Nov., d. 20 Aug.
Troughton, David, b. 9 Jun.
Troughton, Edward, d. 12 Jun.
Trowbridge, Richard, b. 21 Jan.
Troy, Jean-François de, b. 27 Jan., d. 1 May
Troyon, Constant, b. 28 Aug.
Trubshaw, Brian, b. 29 Jan.
Trudeau, Pierre, b. 18 Oct.
Trueman, Fred, b. 6 Feb.
Truffaut, François, b. 6 Feb.
Truman, Christine, b. 16 Jan.
Truman, Harry S., b. 8 May, d. 26 Dec.
Trumper, Victor, b. 2 Nov., d. 28 Jun.
Tshombe, Moise, b. 10 Nov.
Tucholsky, Kurt, d. 21 Dec.
Tucker, Sophie, d. 10 Feb.
Tuckwell, Barry, b. 5 Mar.
Tull, Jethro, d. 21 Feb.
Tunney, Gene, d. 7 Nov.
Tupolev, Andrei, d. 23 Dec.
Tupper, Martin, d. 29 Nov.
Tureck, Rosalyn, b. 14 Dec.
Turenne, Vicomte de, b. 11 Sept.
Turgenev, Ivan, b. 9 Nov., d. 3 Sept.
Turina, Joaquin, b. 9 Dec.
Turnell, Andy, b. 27 Aug.
Turner, Francis, b. 23 Jun.
Turner, Margot, b. 10 May
Turner, Charles, d. 1 Aug.
Turner, J.M.W., b. 23 Apr., d. 19 Dec.
Turner, Lana, b. 8 Feb.
Turner, Michael, b. 31 May
Turner, Patricia, b. 14 May
Turner, Tina, b. 26 Nov.
Turner, Walter, b. 13 Oct.
Turner-Warwick, Richard, b. 21 Feb.
Turpin, Dick, d. 7 Apr.
Turpin, Randolph, d. 16 May
Tushingham, Rita, b. 14 Mar.
Tussaud, Madame, b. 1 Dec., d. 16 Apr.
Tute, Warren, b. 22 Feb., d. 26 Nov.
Tutin, Dorothy, b. 8 Apr.
Tutu, Desmond, b. 7 Oct.
Twain, Mark, b. 30 Nov., d. 21 Apr.
Twiggy, b. 19 Sept.
Twiss, Peter, b. 23 Jul.
Tyler, John, b. 29 Mar., d. 18 Jan.
Tyler, Leslie, b. 26 Apr.
Tyler, Wat, d. 15 Jun.

Tylor, Edward, b. 2 Oct.
Tyndale, William, d. 6 Oct.
Tyndall, John, d. 4 Dec.
Tyson, Frank, b. 6 Jun.
Tyson, Mike, b. 30 Jun.
Tyzack, Margaret, b. 9 Sept.

Uccello, Paolo, d. 10 Dec.
Ulanova, Galina, b. 8 Jan.
Ulbricht, Walter, b. 30 Jun.
Ullendorff, Edward, b. 25 Jan.
Ullman, Tracy, b. 30 Dec.
Ullmann, Liv, b. 16 Dec.
Umberto I, of Italy, d. 29 Jul.
Umlauf, Michael, b. 9 Aug.
Unamuno, Miguel de, d. 31 Dec.
Underhill, Evelyn, d. 15 Jun.
Underwood, Derek, b. 8 Jun.
Undset, Sigrid, b. 20 May
Unger, Michael, b. 8 Dec.
Unwin, Stanley, b. 19 Dec.
Updike, John, b. 18 Mar.
Ure, Gudrun, b. 12 Mar.
Urfe, Honoré d', d. 1 Jun.
Urquhart, Robert, b. 16 Oct.
Ussher, James, d. 21 Mar.
Ustinov, Peter, b. 16 Apr.
U Thant, b. 22 Jan.
Utrillo, Maurice, b. 25 Dec., d. 5 Nov.
Uttley, Roger, b. 11 Sept.

Vaccai, Nicola, b. 15 Mar.
Vaccaro, Brenda, b. 18 Nov.
Vaizey, Lady Marina, b. 16 Jan.
Valente, Caterina, b. 14 Jan.
Valentine, Anthony, b. 17 Aug.
Valentino, Rudolph, b. 6 May, d. 23 Aug.
Valéry, Paul, b. 30 Oct., d. 20 Jul.
Vallee, Rudy, b. 28 Jul.
Valois, Marguerite de, b. 14 May, d. 27 Mar.
Vanbrugh, John, b. 24 Jan., d. 26 Mar.
van Buren, Martin, b. 5 Dec., d. 24 Jul.
Vance, Charles, b. 6 Dec.
Vance, Cyrus, b. 27 Mar.
Vancouver, George, b. 22 Jun., d. 10 May
Van de Graaff, Robert, d. 16 Jan.
van der Post, Laurens, b. 13 Dec.
Vandevelde, Adriaen, b. 30 Nov., d. 21 Jan.

Van Dine, S.S., b. 15 Oct.
Van Dyke, Dick, b. 13 Dec.
Vane, Henry, d. 14 Jun.
Van Heusen, Jimmy, b. 26 Jan.
Vanloo, Charles, b. 15 Feb.
Vanloo, Jean, b. 14 Jan., d. 19 Dec.
Vanneck, Peter, b. 7 Jan.
Varah, Chad, b. 12 Nov.
Varèse, Edgard, b. 22 Dec., d. 8 Nov.
Vargas, Getulio, b. 19 Apr., d. 24 Aug.
Varley, John, b. 17 Aug.
Vasari, Giorgio, b. 30 Jul., d. 27 Jun.
Vasary, Tamàs, b. 8 Nov.
Vasco da Gama, d. 24 Dec.
Vattel, Emerich de, b. 25 Apr., d. 28 Dec.
Vauban, Sébastien, d. 30 Mar.
Vaughan, Elizabeth, b. 12 Mar.
Vaughan, Frankie, b. 3 Feb.
Vaughan Williams, Ralph, b. 12 Oct., d. 4
  Jan.
Vaughn, Robert, b. 22 Nov.
Vavilov, Nikolai, b. 26 Nov.
Veasey, Josephine, b. 10 Jul.
Veblen, Oswald, d. 10 Aug.
Vedder, Elihu, b. 26 Feb.
Vega Carpio, Lope de, b. 25 Nov., d. 27
  Aug.
Veidt, Conrad, d. 3 Apr.
Veit, Philipp, d. 18 Dec.
Velázquez, Diego, b. 6 Jun., d. 6 Aug.
Venables, Terry, b. 6 Jan.
Venizelos, Eleutherios, b. 23 Aug., d. 18
  Mar.
Venkataraghavan, Srinivas, b. 21 Apr.
Veracini, Francesco, b. 1 Feb.
Verdi, Giuseppe, b. 10 Oct., d. 27 Jan.
Vereen, Ben, b. 10 Oct.
Vereshchagin, Vasili, b. 26 Oct., d. 13
  Apr.
Verga, Giovanni, b. 2 Sept., d. 27 Jan.
Verhaeren, Émile, b. 21 May
Verity, Hedley, d. 31 Jul.
Verlaine, Paul, b. 30 Mar., d. 8 Jan.
Verlat, Michel, d. 23 Oct.
Vermeer, Jan (van Delft), b. 31 Oct., d. 15
  Dec.
Vermeer, Jan (van Haarlem), d. 25 Aug.
Vermeer, Jan, the Younger (van
  Haarlem), d. 28 May
Verne, Jules, b. 8 Feb., d. 24 Mar.

Vernet, Claude, b. 14 Aug., d. 3 Dec.
Vernet, Horace, b. 30 Jun., d. 17 Jan.
Vernon, Edward, Adm., b. 12 Nov., d. 30
  Oct.
Vernon, Mike, b. 19 Nov.
Vernon, Richard, b. 7 Mar.
Veronese, Paolo, d. 19 Apr.
Verwoerd, Hendrik, b. 8 Sept., d. 6 Sept.
Vesalius, Andreas, b. 31 Dec.
Vespasian, d. 23 Jun.
Vespucci, Amerigo, b. 9 Mar., d. 22 Feb.
Vérendrye, Pierre de la, b. 17 Nov., d. 5
  Dec.
Vickers, Jon, b. 29 Oct.
Victor Emmanuel II, King, b. 14 Mar.
Victor Emmanuel III, d. 28 Dec.
Victoria, Queen, b. 24 May, d. 22 Jan.
Victoria, Tomás de, d. 27 Aug.
Vida, Marco, d. 27 Sept.
Vidal, Gore, b. 3 Oct.
Vidocq, Eugène, b. 24 Aug.
Vidocq, François, b. 23 Jul., d. 11 May
Vidor, King, b. 8 Feb.
Viete, François, d. 13 Dec.
Vigée-Lebrun, Marie-Louise, d. 30 Mar.
Vignola, Giacomo da, b. 1 Oct., d. 7 Jul.
Vigny, Comte de, d. 17 Sept.
Vigo, Jean, d. 5 Oct.
Vilas, Guillermo, b. 17 Aug.
Villa, Pancho, b. 5 Jun., d. 20 Jun.
Villa-Lobos, Heitor, b. 5 Mar., d. 17
  Nov.
Villeneuve, Pierre de, b. 31 Dec.
Villiers, Barbara, d. 9 Oct.
Villiers, George, b. 20 Aug.
Villiers, James, b. 29 Sept.
Villiers, William, b. 12 Jan.
Vincent, Richard, b. 23 Aug.
Vinci, *see* Leonardo
Vine, David, b. 3 Jan.
Vinogradoff, Paul, d. 19 Dec.
Vinson, Helen, b. 17 Sept.
Viollet-le-Duc, Eugène, b. 27 Jan., d. 17
  Sept.
Viotta, Henri, b. 16 Jul.
Virchow, Rudolf, b. 13 Oct.
Virgil, b. 15 Oct., d. 21 Sept.
Virgo, John, b. 3 Apr.
Visconti, Luchino, b. 2 Nov.
Vishnevskaya, Galina, b. 25 Oct.

457

Visvanath, Gundappa, b. 12 Feb.
Vito, Gioconda De, b. 26 Jul.
Vivaldi, Antonio, b. 4 Mar., d. 28 Jul.
Vlaminck, Maurice de, b. 4 Apr., d. 11
  Oct.
Voce, Bill, d. 6 Jun.
Voight, Jon, b. 29 Dec.
Volta, Alessandro, b. 18 Feb., d. 5 Mar.
Voltaire, b. 21 Nov., d. 30 May
Von Tilzer, Albert, d. 1 Oct.
Von Tilzer, Harry, b. 8 Jul., d. 10 Jan.
Vondel, Joost van den, d. 5 Feb.
Vonnegut, Kurt, b. 11 Nov.
Vorster, Balthazar, d. 10 Sept.
Voss, Charles, b. 20 Sept.
Vouet, Simon, b. 9 Jan., d. 30 Jun.
Voysey, Charles, d. 12 Feb.
Vries, Hugo de, b. 16 Feb., d. 21 May
Vuillard, Jean, b. 11 Nov., d. 21 Jun.

Waals, Johannes van der, b. 23 Nov.
Waddell, Helen, b. 31 May
Waddington, Bill, b. 10 Jun.
Wade, George, d. 14 Mar.
Wade, Virginia, b. 10 Jul.
Wadsworth, Edward, b. 29 Oct.
Wagner, Richard, b. 22 May, d. 13 Feb.
Wagner, Robert, b. 10 Feb.
Wahlström, Jarl, b. 9 Jul.
Wain, John, b. 14 Mar.
Wain, Louis, d. 4 Jul.
Wainwright, Richard, b. 11 Apr.
Waite, Terry, b. 31 May
Waites, Brian, b. 1 Mar.
Wakeham, John, b. 22 Jun.
Wakeman, Rick, b. 18 May
Waksman, Selman, b. 22 Jul., d. 16 Aug.
Walbrook, Anton, b. 19 Nov.
Walcott, Clyde, b. 17 Jan.
Waldegrave, William, b. 15 Aug.
Walden, Brian, b. 8 Jul.
Waldheim, Kurt, b. 21 Dec.
Waldteufel, Émile, b. 9 Dec.
Wales, Prince of, b. 14 Nov.
Wales, Princess of, b. 1 Jul.
Walesa, Lech, b. 29 Sept.
Waley, Arthur, b. 19 Aug., d. 27 Jun.
Waley-Cohen, Bernard, b. 29 May
Walker, Clint, b. 30 May
Walker, Dr John, d. 1 May

Walker, Max, b. 12 Sept.
Walker, Peter, b. 25 Mar.
Walker, Walter, b. 11 Nov.
Walker, Zena, b. 7 Mar.
Wallace, Alfred Russel, b. 8 Jan.,
  d. 7 Nov.
Wallace, Edgar, b. 1 Apr., d. 10 Feb.
Wallace, Ian, b. 10 Jul.
Wallace, Lew, b. 10 Apr., d. 15 Feb.
Wallace, Richard, b. 26 Jul., d. 20 Jul.
Wallace, William, d. 23 Aug.
Wallach, Eli, b. 7 Dec.
Wallenstein, Albrecht von, b. 15 Sept.,
  d. 25 Feb.
Waller, David, b. 27 Nov.
Waller, Edmund, b. 3 Mar., d. 21 Oct.
Waller, Fats, b. 21 May, d. 15 Dec.
Wallis, Barnes, b. 26 Sept., d. 30 Oct.
Wallis, John, b. 23 Nov., d. 28 Oct.
Walpole, Horace, b. 24 Sept., d. 2 Mar.
Walpole, Hugh, b. 13 Mar., d. 1 Jun.
Walpole, Robert, b. 26 Aug., d. 18 Mar.
Walsh, Raoul, b. 11 Mar.
Walsingham, Francis, d. 6 Apr.
Walter, Bruno, b. 15 Sept.
Walter, John, d. 16 Nov.
Walters, Julie, b. 22 Feb.
Walters, Thorley, b. 12 May
Walton, Isaak, d. 15 Dec., b. 9 Aug.
Walton, William, b. 29 Mar., d. 8 Mar.
Walwyn, Peter, b. 1 Jul.
Wanamaker, Sam, b. 14 Jun.
Wanamaker, Zoë, b. 13 May
Wanger, Walter, d. 18 Nov.
Wankel, Felix, b. 13 Aug.
Warbeck, Perkin, d. 16 Nov.
Warburton, William, b. 24 Dec.
Ward, Artemus, d. 6 Mar.
Ward, Mrs Humphry, b. 11 Jun.
Ward, James, b. 23 Oct.
Ward, Leslie, b. 21 Nov.
Ward, Rachel, b. 12 Sept.
Ward, Seth, d. 6 Jan.
Ward, Simon, b. 16 Oct.
Warden, Jack, b. 18 Sept.
Ware, James, b. 26 Nov.
Waring, Derek, b. 26 Apr.
Waring, George, b. 20 Feb.
Warlock, Peter, b. 30 Oct., d. 17 Dec.
Warner, Francis, b. 21 Oct.

Warner, Jack (actor), b. 24 Oct., d. 24 May
Warner, Rex, b. 9 Mar., d. 24 Jun.
Warner, Sylvia T., d. 1 May
Warnock, Baroness, b. 14 Apr.
Warren, Harry, b. 24 Dec., d. 22 Sept.
Warren-Green, Christopher, b. 30 Jul.
Warwick, Dionne, b. 12 Dec.
Warwick, Earl of, b. 22 Nov., d. 14 Apr.
Warwick, James, b. 17 Nov.
Warwick, Richard, b. 29 Apr.
Washbrook, Cyril, b. 6 Dec.
Washington, George, b. 22 Feb., d. 14 Dec.
Wasserman, August von, b. 21 Feb.
Wasserman, Jakob, d. 1 Jan.
Waterhouse, Dame Rachel, b. 2 Jan.
Waterhouse, Keith, b. 6 Feb.
Waterlow, Ernest, b. 24 May
Waterman, Dennis, b. 24 Feb.
Waters, Muddy, b. 4 Apr.
Waterston, Sam, b. 15 Nov.
Watford, Gwen, b. 10 Sept.
Watkin, Dom Aelred, b. 23 Feb.
Watkins, Tasker, b. 18 Nov.
Watling, Dilys, b. 5 May
Watson, Dave, b. 5 Oct.
Watson, Moray, b. 25 Jun.
Watson, Tom, b. 4 Sept.
Watt, Donald Cameron, b. 17 May
Watt, James, b. 19 Jan., d. 25 Aug.
Watteau, Antoine, b. 10 Oct., d. 18 Jul.
Watts, G.F., b. 23 Feb., d. 1 Jul.
Watts, Helen, b. 7 Dec.
Watts, Isaac, b. 17 Jul., d. 25 Nov.
Watts-Dunton, Theodore, b. 12 Oct., d. 7 Jun.
Waugh, Alec, b. 8 Jul.
owaugh, Auberon, b. 17 Nov.
Waugh, Evelyn, b. 28 Oct., d. 10 Apr.
Wauters, Emile, d. 11 Dec.
Wavell, 1st Earl, b. 5 May
Wayne, John, b. 26 May, d. 11 Jun.
Weatherall, David, b. 9 Mar.
Weatherill, Bernard, b. 25 Nov.
Weaver, Dennis, b. 4 Jun.
Webb, Aston, d. 21 Aug.
Webb, Beatrice, b. 22 Jan., d. 30 Apr.
Webb, Jimmy, b. 15 Aug.
Webb, Kaye, b. 26 Jan.

Webb, Matthew, d. 24 Jul.
Webb, Sidney, b. 13 Jun., d. 13 Oct.
Weber, Bernhard, b. 18 Apr.
Weber, Carl von, b. 18 Nov.
Weber, Gottfried, b. 1 Mar.
Webern, Anton von, b. 3 Dec., d. 15 Sept.
Webster, Daniel, b. 18 Jan.
Webster, Noah, b. 16 Oct., d. 28 May
Webster, Thomas, b. 20 Mar.
Weddell, James, b. 24 Aug.
Wedekind, Frank, b. 24 Jul., d. 9 Mar.
Wedgwood, C.V., b. 20 Jul.
Wedgwood, Josiah, b. 12 Jul., d. 3 Jan.
Weekes, Everton, b. 26 Feb.
Weelkes, Thomas, b. 25 Oct.
Weidenfeld, Lord, b. 13 Sept.
Weill, Kurt, b. 2 Mar., d. 3 Apr.
Weinberger, Caspar, b. 18 Aug.
Weinberger, Jaromir, b. 8 Jan., d. 8 Aug.
Weingartner, Felix, d. 7 May
Weir, Gillian, b. 17 Jan.
Weiskopf, Tom, b. 9 Nov.
Weismann, August, d. 5 Nov.
Weissmuller, Johnny, b. 2 Jun., d. 20 Jan.
Weizmann, Chaim, b. 27 Nov., d. 9 Nov.
Weizsäcker, Richard von, b. 15 Apr.
Welch, Raquel, b. 5 Sept.
Weldon, Fay, b. 22 Sept.
Welland, Colin, b. 4 Jul.
Welles, Orson, b. 6 May, d. 10 Oct.
Wellesz, Egon, b. 21 Oct., d. 9 Nov.
Welling, Albert, b. 29 Feb.
Wellington, 1st Duke, b. 1 May, d. 14 Sept.
Wellman, William, b. 29 Feb.
Wells, Alan, b. 3 May
Wells, Doreen, b. 25 Jun.
Wells, H.G., b. 21 Sept., d. 13 Aug.
Wells, John, b. 17 Nov.
Wells, Stanley, b. 21 May
Welsbach, Carl von, b. 1 Sept., d. 4 Aug.
Werberniuk, Bill, b. 14 Jan.
Werfel, Franz, b. 10 Sept.
Werner, Abraham, b. 25 Sept., d. 30 Jun.
Werner, Alfred, b. 12 Dec., d. 15 Nov.
Wescott, Glenway, b. 11 Apr.
Wesker, Arnold, b. 24 May
Wesley, Charles, b. 18 Dec., d. 29 Mar.
Wesley, John, b. 17 Jun., d. 2 Mar.
Wesley, Samuel, b. 14 Aug., d. 11 Oct.

Wessels, Kepler, b. 14 Sept.
West, Benjamin, b. 10 Oct., d. 11 Mar.
West, Mae, b. 17 Aug., d. 22 Nov.
West, Morris, b. 26 Apr.
West, Nathanael, b. 17 Oct., d. 22 Dec.
West, Peter, b. 12 Aug.
West, Rebecca, b. 25 Dec., d. 15 Mar.
West, Timothy, b. 20 Oct.
Westinghouse, George, b. 6 Oct., d. 12
   Mar.
Westmacott, Richard, d. 1 Sept.
Weston, Garfield, b. 28 Apr.
Weston, R.P., d. 6 Nov.
Weyden, Rogier van der, d. 18 Jun.
Weyman, Stanley John, d. 10 Apr.
Whale, James, b. 22 Jul.
Wharton, Edith, b. 24 Jan., d. 11 Aug.
Wheatley, Dennis, b. 8 Jan., d. 10 Nov.
Wheatstone, Charles, b. 6 Feb., d. 19 Oct.
Wheeler, Mortimer, d. 22 Jul.
Wheeler, Peter, b. 26 Nov.
Wheldon, Huw, d. 14 Mar.
Whicker, Alan, b. 2 Aug.
Whistler, James, b. 14 Jul., d. 17 Jul.
Whistler, Laurence, b. 21 Jan.
Whiston, William, b. 9 Dec., d. 22 Aug.
Whitaker, John, b. 5 Aug.
Whitaker, Joseph, d. 15 May
White, Antonia, d. 10 Apr.
White, Gilbert, b. 18 Jul., d. 26 Jun.
White, Joseph Blanco, d. 20 May
White, Josh, d. 5 Sept.
White, Maurice, b. 19 Dec.
White, Michael, b. 16 Jan.
White, Pearl, d. 4 Aug.
White, T.H., b. 29 May, d. 17 Jan.
White, Wilfrid Hyde, b. 12 May
White, William H., b. 22 Dec., d. 14 Mar.
Whitefield, George, b. 16 Dec., d. 30 Sept.
Whitehead, Alfred, b. 15 Feb., d. 30 Dec.
Whitehead, Geoffrey, b. 1 Oct.
Whitelaw, Billie, b. 6 Jun.
Whitelaw, Viscount, b. 28 Jun.
Whiteley, William, d. 23 Jan.
Whiteman, Paul, b. 28 Mar.
Whitfield, June, b. 11 Nov.
Whitgift, John, d. 29 Feb.
Whiting, Richard A., b. 12 Nov.
Whitlam, Gough, b. 11 Jul.
Whitman, Walt, b. 31 May, d. 26 Mar.

Whitmore, James, b. 1 Oct.
Whitmore, Ken, b. 22 Dec.
Whitney, Eli, b. 8 Dec., d. 8 Jan.
Whittaker, Roger, b. 21 Mar.
Whittam Smith, Andreas, b. 13 Jun.
Whittier, John G., b. 17 Dec., d. 7 Sept.
Whittington, Harry, b. 24 Mar.
Whittle, Frank, b. 1 Jun.
Whitworth, Joseph, b. 21 Dec., d. 22 Jan.
Whymper, Edward, b. 27 Apr.
Whyte-Melville, George, d. 5 Dec.
Wickramasinghe, Nalin, b. 20 Jan.
Widdecombe, Ann, b. 4 Oct.
Widmark, Richard, b. 26 Dec.
Widor, Charles, d. 12 Mar.
Wien, Wilhelm, d. 30 Aug.
Wigglesworth, Vincent, b. 17 Apr.
Wigoder, Lord, b. 12 Feb.
Wilander, Mats, b. 22 Aug.
Wilberforce, William, b. 24 Aug., d. 29
   Jul.
Wilcox, Desmond, b. 21 May
Wilcox, Herbert, d. 15 May
Wilcox, Paula, b. 13 Dec.
Wilcoxon, Henry, d. 6 Mar.
Wilde, Cornel, d. 16 Oct.
Wilde, Marty, b. 15 Apr.
Wilde, Oscar, b. 16 Oct., d. 30 Nov.
Wilder, Billy, b. 22 Jun.
Wilder, Gene, b. 11 Jun.
Wilder, Thornton, b. 17 Apr., d. 7 Dec.
Wilding, Michael, b. 23 Jul., d. 8 Jul.
Wilhelm I, of Germany, b. 22 Mar., d. 9
   Mar.
Wilhelm II, of Germany, b. 27 Jan., d. 4
   Jun.
Wilhelmina, Princess, b. 31 Aug., d. 28
   Nov.
Wilkes, John, b. 17 Oct., d. 26 Dec.
Wilkes, Michael, b. 11 Jun.
Wilkie, David, b. 18 Nov.
Wilkie, Wendell, b. 18 Feb.
Wilkins, Hubert, b. 31 Oct., d. 17 Mar.
Wilkins, Ray, b. 14 Sept.
Willcox, Toyah, b. 18 May
Willems, Florent, d. 23 Oct.
Willett, William, b. 30 Sept., d. 4 Mar.
Willette, Leon, b. 31 Jul.
Willey, Peter, b. 6 Dec.
William, Prince, b. 21 Jun.

William I, the Conqueror, d. 9 Sept.
William I, the Silent, b. 24 Apr., d. 10 Jul.
William II, of England, d. 2 Aug.
William III, of Great Britain, b. 4 Nov., d. 8 Mar.
William IV, of Great Britain, b. 21 Aug., d. 20 Jun.
Williams, Andy, b. 3 Dec.
Williams, Charles, b. 20 Sept.
Williams, Emlyn, b. 26 Nov.
Williams, Esther, b. 8 Aug.
Williams, George, b. 11 Oct.
Williams, Glanmor, b. 5 May
Williams, John (composer), b. 8 Feb.
Williams, John (guitarist), b. 24 Apr.
Williams, J.P.R., b. 2 Mar.
Williams, Michael, b. 9 Jul.
Williams, Paul, b. 19 Sept.
Williams, Shirley, b. 27 Jul.
Williams, Simon, b. 16 Jun.
Williams, Tennessee, b. 26 Mar., d. 25 Feb.
Williams, William Carlos, d. 4 Mar.
Williams, William Fenwick, b. 4 Dec.
Williamson, Henry, b. 1 Dec., d. 13 Aug.
Williamson, Keith, b. 25 Feb.
Williamson, Malcolm, b. 21 Nov.
Williamson, Nicol, b. 14 Sept.
Willis, Bob, b. 30 May
Willis, Lord, b. 13 Jan.
Willis, Norman, b. 21 Jan.
Wills, Arthur, b. 19 Sept.
Wilmot, Gary, b. 8 May
Wilsey, John, b. 18 Feb.
Wilson, Alexander, d. 23 Aug.
Wilson, Bob, b. 30 Oct.
Wilson, Colin, b. 26 Jun.
Wilson, Dooley, b. 3 Apr.
Wilson, Edmund, b. 8 May, d. 12 Jun.
Wilson, Enid, b. 15 Mar.
Wilson, Eric, b. 2 Oct.
Wilson, Harold, b. 11 Mar.
Wilson, Henry, b. 5 Mar., d. 22 Jun.
Wilson, James, d. 11 Aug.
Wilson, Lord (of Hong Kong), b. 14 Feb.
Wilson, Lord (of Langside), b. 21 Mar.
Wilson, Mary, b. 6 Mar.
Wilson, Richard (actor), b. 9 Jul.
Wilson, Richard (painter), b. 1 Aug.
Wilson, Sandy, b. 19 May

Wilson, Sir Sandy, b. 27 Feb.
Wilson, Woodrow, b. 28 Dec., d. 23 Feb.
Wilton, Joseph, b. 16 Jul.
Wilton, Penelope, b. 3 Jun.
Winant, John, b. 23 Feb. d., 3 Nov.
Winckler, Hugo, b. 4 Jul.
Windlesham, Lord, b. 28 Jan.
Windsor, Barbara, b. 6 Aug.
Windsor, Duchess of, b. 19 Jun., d. 24 Apr.
Windsor, Duke of, b. 23 Jun., d. 28 May
Windsor, Frank, b. 12 Jul.
Windsor, Lady Rose, b. 1 Mar.
Wingate, Orde, d. 24 Mar.
Winkler, Henry, b. 30 Oct.
Winner, Michael, b. 30 Oct.
Winstanley, Henry, d. 27 Nov.
Winstanley, Lord, b. 27 Aug.
Winter, Fred, b. 20 Sept.
Winter, Thomas, d. 30 Jan.
Winters, Shelley, b. 18 Aug.
Winthrop, John, b. 12 Feb., d. 26 Mar.
Winwood, Steve, b. 12 May
Wisden, John, b. 5 Sept.
Wisdom, Norman, b. 4 Feb.
Wise, Ernie, b. 27 Nov.
Wise, Robert, b. 10 Sept.
Wiseman, Cardinal, b. 2 Aug.
Wiseman, Donald, b. 25 Oct.
Wister, Owen, b. 14 Jul.
Witchell, Nicholas, b. 23 Sept.
Withers, Googie, b. 12 Mar.
Withers, Jane, b. 12 Apr.
Witt, Johan de, b. 24 Sept.
Wittgenstein, Ludwig, b. 26 Apr.
Wodehouse, P.G., b. 15 Oct., d. 14 Feb.
Woffington, Peg, d. 28 Mar.
Wogan, Terry, b. 3 Aug.
Wöhler, Friedrich, b. 31 Jul.
Woledge, Brian, b. 16 Aug.
Wolf, Hugo, b. 13 Mar.
Wolf, Josef, d. 20 Apr.
Wolfe, Charles, b. 14 Dec.
Wolfe, Humbert, b. 5 Jan., d. 5 Jan.
Wolfe, James, b. 2 Jan.
Wolff, Heinz, b. 29 Apr.
Wolf-Ferrari, Ermanno, d. 21 Jan.
Wolfit, Donald, b. 20 Apr., d. 17 Feb.
Wolgemut, Michael, d. 30 Nov.
Wollaston, William, b. 6 Aug.

Wolseley, Garnet, b. 4 Jun., d. 25 Mar.
Wolsey, Thomas, d. 29 Nov.
Wonder, Stevie, b. 13 May
Wood, Anthony à, d. 28 Nov.
Wood, Charles, b. 6 Aug.
Wood, David, b. 21 Feb.
Wood, Evelyn, b. 9 Feb., d. 2 Dec.
Wood, Graeme, b. 6 Nov.
Wood, Henry, b. 3 Mar., d. 19 Aug.
Wood, Hugh, b. 27 Jun.
Wood, Natalie, d. 29 Nov.
Wood, Peter, b. 8 Oct.
Wood, Rev. J.G., b. 21 Jul., d. 3 Mar.
Wood, Victoria, b. 19 May
Woodcock, Tony, b. 6 Dec.
Wooderson, Sydney, b. 14 Aug.
Woodhouse, Montague, b. 11 May
Woods, Henry, b. 7 May
Woodward, Edward, b. 1 Jun.
Woodward, Joanne, b. 27 Feb.
Woolf, Leonard, b. 25 Nov., d. 14 Aug.
Woolf, Virginia, b. 25 Jan., d. 28 Mar.
Wooller, Wilfred, b. 20 Nov.
Woolley, Geoffrey, b. 29 Jun.
Woolley, Leonard, b. 17 Apr., d. 20 Feb.
Woolmer, Bob, b. 14 May
Woolner, Thomas, b. 17 Dec., d. 7 Oct.
Woolworth, F.W., b. 13 Apr., d. 8 Aug.
Woosnam, Ian, b. 2 Mar.
Wordsworth, Dorothy, b. 25 Dec., d. 25 Jan.
Wordsworth, William, b. 7 Apr., d. 23 Apr.
Worlock, Derek, b. 4 Feb.
Worsthorne, Peregrine, b. 22 Dec.
Worth, Charles, b. 13 Nov., d. 10 Mar.
Worth, Helen, b. 7 Jan.
Worth, Irene, b. 23 Jun.
Wotton, Henry, d. 5 Dec.
Wouk, Herman, b. 27 May
Wouwerman, Philip, b. 24 May
Wragg, Geoffrey, b. 9 Jan.
Wray, Fay, b. 10 Sept.
Wren, Christopher, b. 20 Oct., d. 25 Feb.
Wren, P.C., d. 23 Nov.
Wright, Almroth, d. 30 Apr.
Wright, Billy, b. 6 Feb.
Wright, Fanny, d. 6 Jan.
Wright, Frank Lloyd, b. 8 Jun., d. 9 Apr.
Wright, John, b. 5 Jul.

Wright, Joseph, b. 3 Sept., d. 29 Aug.
Wright, Judith, b. 31 May
Wright, Michael, b. 10 Dec.
Wright, Orville, b. 19 Aug., d. 30 Jan.
Wright, Richard, b. 4 Sept.
Wright, Teresa, b. 27 Oct.
Wright, Wilbur, b. 16 Apr., d. 30 May
Wyatt, James, d. 4 Sept.
Wyatt, Jane, b. 10 Aug.
Wyatt, Robert, b. 28 Jan.
Wyatt, Tessa, b. 23 Apr.
Wyatt, Thomas, the Younger, d. 11 Apr.
Wyatt, Woodrow, b. 4 Jul.
Wycherley, William, d. 1 Jan.
Wycliffe, John, d. 31 Dec.
Wykeham, William of, d. 27 Sept.
Wyler, William, b. 1 Jul., d. 28 Jun.
Wyman, Bill, b. 24 Oct.
Wyman, Jane, b. 4 Jan.
Wynette, Tammy, b. 5 May
Wynn, Keenan, d. 14 Oct.
Wynne, David, b. 25 May

X, Malcolm, d. 21 Feb.
Xenakis, Iannis, b. 29 May

Yale, Elihu, b. 5 Apr.
Yallop, Graham, b. 7 Oct.
Yamagata, Prince Aritomo, d. 1 Feb.
Yardley, Bruce, b. 7 Sept.
Yarwood, Mike, b. 14 Jun.
Yasunari, Kawabata, d. 17 Apr.
Yates, Marjorie, b. 13 Apr.
Yates, Peter, b. 24 Jul.
Yeats, W.B., b. 13 Jun., d. 28 Jan.
Yerby, Frank, b. 5 Sept.
Yevtushenko, Yevgeny, b. 18 Jul.
Yonge, Charlotte M., b. 11 Aug., d. 24 Mar.
York, Duchess of, b. 15 Oct.
York, Duke of, b. 19 Feb.
York, Michael, b. 27 Mar.
York, Susannah, b. 9 Jan.
Yorke, Charles, d. 20 Jan.
Yoshida, Shigeru, b. 22 Sept., d. 20 Oct.
Youmans, Vincent, b. 27 Sept., d. 5 Apr.
Young, Brigham, b. 1 Jun., d. 29 Aug.
Young, Diana, b. 22 Jun.
Young, Edward, d. 5 Apr.
Young, Jimmy, b. 21 Sept.

Young, John (actor), b. 18 Jun.
Young, John (zoologist), b. 18 Mar.
Young, Loretta, b. 6 Jan.
Young, Neil, b. 12 Nov.
Young, Paul (actor), b. 3 Jul.
Young, Paul (singer), b. 17 Jan.
Young, Robert, b. 22 Feb.
Young, Thomas, b. 13 Jun., d. 10 May
Young, Victor, b. 8 Aug., d. 11 Nov.
Younghusband, Francis, d. 31 Jul., b. 31 May
Yo Yo Ma, b. 7 Oct.
Ysaye, Eugène, b. 16 Jul.
Yudkin, John, b. 8 Aug.

Zamenhof, Dr Ludovik, b. 15 Dec., d. 14 Apr.
Zander, Michael, b. 16 Nov.
Zangwill, Israel, b. 14 Feb.
Zanuck, Darryl, b. 5 Sept., d. 22 Dec.
Zappa, Frank, b. 21 Dec.
Zaragoza, Federico, b. 27 Jan.
Zavaroni, Lena, b. 4 Nov.

Zeffirelli, Franco, b. 12 Feb.
Zeppelin, Count von, b. 8 Jul., d. 8 Mar.
Zetterling, Mai, b. 24 May
Zhou Enlai, d. 8 Jan.
Ziegfeld, Florenz, b. 21 Mar., d. 22 Jul.
Ziegler, Philip, b. 24 Dec.
Zimbalist, Efrem, b. 9 Apr.
Zimmermann, Johann von, b. 8 Dec.
Zingarelli, Nicolo, b. 4 Apr.
Zinnemann, Fred, b. 29 Apr.
Zoffany, Johann, d. 11 Nov.
Zola, Émile, b. 2 Apr., d. 28 Sept.
Zuccaro, Taddeo, b. 1 Sept., d. 2 Sept.
Zuckerman, Lord, b. 30 May
Zuckmayer, Carl, b. 27 Dec.
Zukerman, Pinchas, b. 16 Jul.
Zukor, Adolph, b. 7 Jan.
Zuloaga, Ignacio, d. 31 Oct.
Zurbaran, Francisco de, b. 7 Nov., d. 28 Feb.
Zweig, Arnold, b. 10 Nov., d. 26 Nov.
Zweig, Stefan, d. 22 Feb.
Zwingli, Huldrych, d. 11 Oct.

INDEX OF EVENTS

Index of Events

In the following index, when 'first perf.' is shown, it refers to theatrical, musical or operatic performances; although the first performance will be usually the *first performance in the London theatre*. Other first performances are given, but in all cases it is necessary to consult the actual entries on individual pages.

Amoco Cadiz, tanker, runs aground,
17 Mar.

Amundsen, crosses North Pole in airship,
12 May, reaches South Pole, 14 Dec.

Anaesthetics, used for first time, 21 Dec.

And So to Bed, first perf., 17 Oct.

Anderson, Elizabeth Garrett, first woman
doctor, 28 Sept.

Angola, independence, 11 Nov.,
mercenaries executed, 8 Feb.

Angora, name changes to Ankara, 28 Mar.

Anguilla, troops take over, 19 Mar.

Ankara, new capital of Turkey, 13 Oct.

Anne, Princess, becomes Princess Royal,
13 Jun.

Annie, first perf., 3 May

Annie Get Your Gun, first perf., 7 Jun.

Annunzio, D', seizes Fiume, 12 Sept.

Anschluss, the, 13 Mar.

Antarctic, coast discovered, 19 Jan.,
French territories, 5 Aug., new
mountains, 3 May

Anti-Semitic League, founded, 13 Apr.

Antwerp, liberated, 4 Sept., sacked by
Spaniards, 4 Nov.

Anything Goes, first perf., 14 Jun.

Anzio, landings, 22 May

Apartheid, repealed, 17 Jun.

Apollo, tests, lives lost, 27 Jan.

Apollo 7, launched, 11 Oct.

Apollo 9, launch, 3 Mar.

Apollo 14, launched, 31 Jan.

Apollo and *Soyuz*, spacecraft dock, 17 Jul.

Apollo Theatre, opened, 21 Feb.

Appendicitis, first operation, 4 Jan.

Applause, first perf., 16 Nov.

Arab League, founded, 22 Mar.

Arab revolt, against Turks, 5 Jun.

Arandora Star, sinks, 2 Jul.

Arbitration, Court of, set up, 29 Jul.

Arcadians, The, first produced, 28 Apr.

Argentines, surrender, 15 Jun.

Ariel, satellite, launched, 26 Apr.

Arizona, statehood, 14 Feb.

Ark Royal, sinks, 14 Nov.

Arkansas, statehood, 15 Jun.

Armada, sets sail, 12 Jul.

Armistice, France and Germany, 22 Jun.

Armstrong, Neil, walks on moon, 21 Jul.

Arnhem, Br. Airborne Div. lands, 17 Sept.

Ascension Is., discovered, 20 May

Ascot, first race meeting, 7 Aug.

Ashanti War, ends, 4 Feb.

Ashes, The, in cricket, first mention,
29 Aug.

Ashmolean Museum, founded, 15 May,
opens, 6 Jun.

Asquith, Herbert, becomes prime
minister, 8 Apr.

Astor, Lady, first woman in House of
Commons, 1 Dec.

Astronaut, first to walk in space, 3 Jun.,
see also Cosmonaut

Aswan High Dam, opened, 15 Jan.

Athenaeum Club, founded, 16 Feb.

Athenia, torpedoed, 4 Sept.

Athens, Germans occupy, 27 Apr.,
liberated, 13 Oct.

Atlantic, telegraph cable, laid, 27 Jul.

Atlantic Charter, signed, 11 Aug.

Atlantique, fire, 4 Jan.

Atomic Energy Agency, formed, 26 Oct.,
test, first, 16 Jul.

Atom bomb, British, 26 Feb., 3 Oct.,
USSR, 8 Mar.

Atom test, first, 16 Jul.

Atomic pile, first, 2 Dec.

Auchinleck, commands Eighth Army,
25 Jun.

Auckland, NZ, founded, 19 Sept.

Auriol, Vincent, elected French president,
16 Jan.

Australia, aborigines, cricket, 13 May,
gold discovered, 21 May, national
anthem, 4 May, proclaimed federal
union, 17 Sept.

Austria, and Prussia, alliance, 7 Feb.,
becomes republic, 12 Nov., parliament
suspended, 7 Mar., declared bankrupt,
20 Feb., Germans march into, 11 Mar.,
incorporated into Germany, 13 Mar.,
new republic, president, 20 Dec.,
regains independence, 27 Jul.,
avalanche, 12 Jan.

Austria-Hungary, France declares war,
10 Aug.

Autobahn, first, 10 Sept.

Autogiro, demonstrated, 10 Jan.

Automobile Association, founded, 16 Jun.

Azores, earthquakes, 11 Aug.

468

Baby, test-tube, first, 25 Jul.
Bacon rationing, 8 Jan.
Baghdad, captured by Mongols, 17 Jan.
Bahamas, independence, 9 Jul.
Bahrain, independence, 15 Aug.
Baird, J.L., demonstrates television,
27 Jan., transmits, 3 Jul.
Bakerloo Line, opens, 10 Mar.
Balalaika, first perf., 22 Dec.
Balfour Declaration, 2 Nov.
Baliol, John, accedes to Scottish throne, 17
Nov.
Balkan Entente, Conference, 15 Feb.
Balloon, ascent, first, 15 Oct., in Britain,
27 Aug., in USA, 9 Jan., Channel
crossing, 7 Jan., St George's Channel,
22 Jun., hot-air, demonstrated, 5 Jun.,
hot-air, flight, 21 Nov.
Baltic Exchange, founded, 22 Apr.
Bananas, first seen in shop, 10 Apr.
Bandoeng Conference, ends, 24 Apr.
Bangladesh, admitted to Commonwealth,
19 Apr., independence, 23 Mar.,
recognised by Pakistan, 22 Feb., India
recognises, 6 Dec.
Bank of England, charter, 27 Jul.,
foundation stone, 1 Aug., nationalised,
14 Feb.
Bank of Scotland, founded, 1 Nov.
Banknotes, first, 16 Jul., £20 issued, 9 Jul.
Barbados, independence, 30 Nov.
Barber of Seville, The, first performed,
5 Feb.
Barham, warship, sinks, 25 Nov.
Bari harbour, USS *Liberty* explodes in, 9
Apr.
Barnard, Christiaan, performs first heart
transplant, 3 Dec.
Barnum, first perf., 11 Jun.
Baronet, title created, 22 May
Bartered Bride, The, first perf., 30 May
Bartholomew Fair, last, 3 Sept.
Barthou, Louis, assassinated, 9 Oct.
Basketball, first game, 20 Jan.
Basle, University, founded, 4 Apr.
Bastille, stormed, 14 Jul.
Basutoland, Britain annexes, 12 Mar.,
native state, 13 Dec.
Bataan, surrenders, 9 Apr., US forces
take, 16 Feb.

Bath, Order of, constituted, 11 Oct.,
revived, 18 Feb.
Battenberg families, peerages, 19 Jun.
Battersea Bridge, opens, 21 Jul.
Battles:
Aboukir, 21 Mar., 25 Jul.
Actium, 2 Sept.
Adrianople, 9 Aug.
Agincourt, 25 Oct.
Aisne I, starts, 13 Sept.
Aisne II, 16 Apr., ends, 20 Apr.
Aisne River, III, 27 May
Alamein, 23 Oct., ends 4 Nov.
Alamo, the, 24 Feb., ends, 6 Mar.
Albuera, 16 May
Alcazarquivir, 4 Aug.
Alexandria, 21 Mar.
Aljubarotta, 14 Aug.
Alma, 20 Sept.
Amiens, 8 Aug.
Anjou, 22 Mar.
Anzio, 22 May, ends, 25 May
Arcis-sur-Aube, 20 Mar.
Arcole, 17 Nov.
Arras, 9 Apr.
Arsouf, 6 Sept.
Ashdown, 6 Jan.
Aspern-Essling, 21 May
Assaye, 23 Sept.
Atherton Moor, 30 Jun.
Aughrim, 12 Jul.
Austerlitz, 2 Dec.
Bannockburn, 24 Jun.
Bapaume-Péronne, 21 Aug.
Barnet, 14 Apr.
Bautzen, 20 May
Beachy Head, 30 Jun.
Belleau Wood, 10 Jun.
Benevento, 26 Feb.
Berlin, 15 Apr., ends, 2 May
Bismarck Sea, the, 2 Mar., ends, 5 Mar.
Blenheim, 13 Aug., 2 Aug.
Bloreheath, 23 Sept.
Borodino, 7 Sept.
Bosworth Field, 22 Aug.
Boyne, the, 1 Jul.
Brandywine Creek, 11 Sept.
Britain, 10 Jul., 8 Aug., ends, 31 Oct.
Buena Vista, 22 Feb.
Bulge, 16 Dec., ends, 6 Jan.

Bull Run, 21 Jul.
Bunker Hill, 17 Jun.
Caen, 25 Jun.
Calatafimi, 15 May
Cambrai, 20 Nov.
Camperdown, 11 Oct.
Cannae, 3 Aug.
Cape Finisterre, 22 Jul.
Caporetto, 23 Oct.
Cassino, 8 May
Castillon, 17 Jul.
Cawnpore, 6 Dec.
Cedar Creek, 19 Oct.
Cerignola, 28 Apr.
Châlons-sur-Marne, 20 Sept.
Chancellorsville, 2-6 May
Charleston, 28 Jun.
Château Thierry, 27 Jun.
Chesapeake Capes, 30 Aug.
Chotusitz, 17 May
Colenso, 15 Dec.
Copenhagen, 2 Apr.
Coral Sea, the, 4 May, ends, 8 May
Coronel, 1 Nov.
Corunna, 16 Jan.
Craonne, 7 Mar.
Crécy, 26 Aug.
Culloden, 16 Apr.
Custoza, 24 Jun.
Czaslau, 17 May
Dettingen, 16 Jun.
Devizes, 13 Jun.
Dien Bien Phu, 13 Mar.
Dogger Bank, the, 24 Jan.
Dover Strait, 11 Jun.
Dresden, 27 Aug.
Dreux, 19 Dec.
Dunbar, 27 Apr., 3 Sept.
Edgehill, 23 Oct.
Evesham, 4 Aug.
Falkirk, 22 Jul.
Falkland Is., 8 Dec.
Finisterre, 3 May
Flamborough Head, 23 Sept.
Flanders, 10 May
Flodden Field, 9 Sept.
Flores, 31 Aug.
Fontenoy, 11 May
Fort Sumter, 14 Apr.
Fort Ticonderoga, 8 Jul.

Fredericksburg, 13 Dec.
Freiberg, 29 Oct.
Fuentes de Oñoro, 5 May
Gainsborough, 27 Jul.
Germanstown, 4 Oct.
Gettysburg, 1 Jul., ends, 3 Jul.
Gisors, 20 Sept.
Givenchy, 15 Jun.
Glencoe (S. Africa), 17 Oct.
Gravelines, 13 Jun.
Gravelotte, 18 Aug.
Grossbeeren, 23 Aug.
Guadalcanal, 12 Nov.
Guilford Courthouse, 15 Mar.
Halidon Hill, 19 Jul.
Hampton Roads, 8–9 Mar.
Harfleur, 15 Aug.
Hastings, 14 Oct.
Heligoland Bight, 28 Aug.
Herrings, 12 Feb.
Hohenfriedberg, 4 Jun.
Homildon-hill, 14 Sept.
Inkerman, 5 Nov.
Isandhlwana, 22 Jan.
Ivry-la-Bataille, 14 Mar.
Iwo Jima, 17 Mar., ends, 26 Mar.
Jarnac, 13 Mar.
Johannisberg, 30 Aug.
Jutland, 31 May, ends, 1 Jun.
Katzbach, 26 Aug.
Key, 24 Aug.
Kumasi, 4 Feb.
Kunersdorf, 12 Aug.
Lagos, 18 Aug.
Lake Champlain, 11 Sept., 13 Oct.
Landen, 19 Jul.
Landshut, 21 Apr.
Langside, 13 May
Laon, 10 Mar.
Leipzig, 18 Oct.
Lepanto, 7 Oct.
Lewes, 14 May
Liegnitz, 9 Apr.
Lincoln, 2 Feb., 20 May
Little Big Horn, 25 Jun.
Loos, 25 Sept., ends, 8 Oct.
Lowestoft, 3 Jun.
Lützen, 2 May
Magenta, 4 Jun.
Magersfontein, 11 Dec.

Majuba Hill, 27 Feb.
Malaga, 24 Aug.
Malplaquet, 11 Sept.
Marathon, 28 Sept.
Marengo, 14 Jun.
Marignano, 13 Sept.
Marne, first, 5 Sep., 12 Sept., second,
   18 Jul.
Marston Moor, 2 Jul.
Megiddo, 18 Sept.
Messines, 7 Jun.
Meuse-Argonne, 26 Sept.
Midway Is., 3 Jun., ends, 6 Jun.
Millesimo, 13-14 Apr.
Minden, 1 Aug.
Modder River, 29 Nov.
Mohacs, 12 Aug., 29 Aug.
Monmouth, N.J., 28 Jun.
Mons, 14 Aug., 23 Aug.
Montaperti, 4 Sept.
Montebello Casteggio, 9 Jun.
Montenotte, 12 Apr.
Mortimer's Cross, 2 Feb.
Mühlberg, 24 Apr.
Mukden, 9 Mar.
Narva, 30 Nov.
Narvik, 28 May, ends 10 Jun.
Naseby, 14 Jun.
Nations, 19 Oct.
Navarino, 20 Oct.
Neerwindwen, 18 Mar.
Neuve-Chapelle, 10 Mar.
Newburn, 28 Aug.
Newbury, 27 Oct.
New Orleans, 8 Jan., 25 Apr.
Newton Butler, 30 Jul.
Nile, 1 Aug.
Northampton, 10 Jul.
North Cape, 26 Dec.
North Foreland, 25 Jul.
Novara, 23 Mar.
Okinawa, 1 Apr., ends, 22 Jun.
Omdurman, 2 Sept.
Oporto, 12 May
Otterburn, 10 Aug.
Oudenarde, 11 Jul.
Ourique, 25 Jul.
Paardeberg, 18 Feb.
Palo Alto, 8 May
Panipat, 20 Apr.

Passero Cape, 11 Aug.
Patay, 18 Jun.
Pavia, 24 Feb.
Philiphaugh, 13 Sept.
Philippine Sea, 19–20 Jun.
Pinkie, 10 Sept.
Plassey, 23 Jun.
Poitiers, 19 Sept.
Poltava, 8 Jul.
Prague, 6 May
Preston, 17 Aug.
Prestonpans, 21 Sept.
Pyramids, 21 Jul.
Quebec, 13 Sept., 27 Jun.
Queenston Heights, 13 Oct.
Ramillies, 23 May
Ravenna, 11 Apr.
Rieti, 7 Mar.
River Plate, 13 Dec.
Rocroi, 19 May
Sadowa, 3 Jul.
St Albans, 17 Feb., 22 May
St Quentin, 10 Aug.
St Vincent, 16 Jun.
Saintes, 22 Jul.
Saints, the, 12 Apr.
Sakkaria River, 24 Aug.
Salamanca, 22 Jul.
Salamis, 23 Sept.
San Jacinto, 21 Apr.
Santa Cruz, 20 Apr.
Saragossa, 1710, 20 Aug., 1809, 20
   Feb.
Sedan, 1 Sept.
Sedgemoor, 6 Jul.
Selby, 11 Apr.
Shrewsbury, 23 Jul.
Simancas, 6 Aug.
Sluys, 24 Jun.
Smolensk, 16 Aug., ends 18 Aug.
Solferino, 24 Jun.
Somme, first, 1 Jul., ends, 18 Nov.;
   second, 21 Mar., ends, 4 Apr.
Spion Kop, 23 Jan.
Spotsylvania, 7–21 May
Spurs, 16 Aug.
Stalingrad, 23 Aug.
Stamford, 13 Mar.
Stamford Bridge, 25 Sept.
Standard, 22 Aug.

Steinkirk, 24 Jul.
Stirling Bridge, 11 Sept.
Talavera, 28 Jul.
Tannenberg, 15 Jul., starts, 1914,
   26 Aug., ends, 30 Aug.
Tara, 26 May
Tel el Kebir, 13 Sept.
Tewkesbury, 4 May
Thames, 5 Oct.
Tiberias, 4 Jul.
Tolosa, 16 Jul.
Toulouse, 10 Apr.
Tours, 10 Oct.
Towton, 29 Mar.
Trafalgar, 21 Oct.
Trenton, 26 Dec.
Tugela, 12 Apr.
Turin, 7 Sept.
Valmy, 20 Sept.
Verdun, 21 Feb., ends, 15 Dec.
Verneuil, 17 Aug.
Vicksburg, 7 May, ends, 4 Jul.
Vigo, 12 Oct.
Vimiero, 21 Aug.
Vitoria, 21 Jun.
Waitzen, 14 Jul.
Wakefield, 30 Dec.
Warsaw, 1656, 28 Jul., ends, 30 Jul.,
   1914, 29 Oct.
Waterloo, 18 Jun.
Wilderness, the, 5-6 May
Williamsburg, 5 May
Winchelsea, 29 Aug.
Worcester, 1615, 3 Sept., 1642, 23 Sept.
Yellow Sea, 10 Aug.
Yorktown, 4 Apr.
Ypres, first, 19 Oct., ends, 22 Nov.,
   second, 22 Apr., ends, 25 May, third,
   31 Jul., ends, 6 Nov.
Zeebrugge, ends, 23 Apr.
Bavaria, king of, elected, 5 Nov.
BBC, first gramophone programme, 7 Jul.,
   BBC TV, begins, 22 Aug., first
   broadcast, 30 Sept., first play, 14 Jul.
Beatrix of the Netherlands, marries von
   Amsberg, 10 Mar.
Bechuanaland, proclaimed British, 8 Oct.
Beebe, William, explores ocean, 16 Aug.
Beggar's Opera, The, first performed, 29
   Jan.

Beirut, fighting between Moslems and
   Christians, 13 Apr.
Belgium, becomes part of France, 1 Oct.,
   independence, 4 Oct., votes for
   monarchy, 22 Nov., first king, 4 Jun.,
   army surrenders, 28 May
Belgrade, besieged, 22 Jul.
Bell, Alexander Graham, makes first
   phone call, 11 Mar., patents telephone,
   7 Mar.
Bell Rock, lighthouse, operates, 1 Feb.
Belle of New York, The, first London perf.,
   12 Apr.
Bells Are Ringing, The, first perf., 14 Nov.
Benedict XV, elected Pope, 3 Sept.
Benefit of Clergy, plea no long allowed,
   24 Oct.
Benghazi, British take, 23 Dec., captured,
   7 Feb., by Germans, 3 Apr.
Beria, and others, executed, 23 Dec.
Berlin, Olympic Games, 20 Jul., RAF first
   raid on, 25 Aug., RAF bombs, 20 Jan.,
   US bombs, 6 Mar., bombed by Allies,
   3 Feb., Soviet troops enter, 20 Apr.,
   occupation, 3 Jul., blockade by USSR,
   1 Apr., 24 Jun., airlift, ends, 30 Sept.,
   blockade lifted, 12 May
Bermuda, English colony, 12 Mar.
Bermuda, liner burns, 19 Nov.
Bernadette, St., vision, 11 Feb.
Bernadotte, Marshal, as Swedish crown
   prince, 21 Aug.
Bernhard, Prince, marries, 7 Jan.
Betjeman, John, Poet Laureate, 10 Oct.
Beveridge report, 1 Dec.
Bhutto, Ali, Pakistani prime minister,
   17 Dec.
Biafran army, surrenders, 12 Jan.
Bible, Authorised Version, published,
   2 May, New English [NT], 14 Mar.,
   [OT], 16 Mar.
Big Ben, chimes first broadcast, 31 Dec.
Big Bertha, shells Paris, 23 Mar.
Bikini Atoll, atom tests, 1 Jul.
Billee Taylor, first perf., 30 Oct.
Billy, first produced, 1 May
Bing Boys Are Here, The, first London
   perf., 19 Apr.
Birkbeck College, founded, 2 Dec.
Birkenhead, sinks, 26 Feb.

Birth of a Nation, first shown, 8 Feb.

Births, Marriages and Deaths, registration starts, 17 Aug.

Bismarck, battleship, launched, 14 Feb., sinks Br. ship, 24 May, sinks, 27 May

Bitter Sweet, first perf., 12 Jul.

Blackfriars Bridge, opens for carriages, 19 Nov.

Black Letter type, in Germany, abandoned, 31 May

Blackout in Britain, ends, 20 Nov.

Black Sea, fleet mutiny, 24 Jun.

Blackwall Tunnel, opens, 22 May

Blake, Admiral, defeats Dutch off Portsmouth, 20 Feb.

Blake, George, spy, escapes, 23 Oct.

Bless the Bride, first produced, 26 Apr.

Blériot, crosses Channel, 25 Jul.

Bloemfontein, captured, 13 Mar.

Blood Brothers, first London perf., 11 Apr.

Bloody Sunday, St Petersburg, 22 Jan.

Blue Danube, The, waltz, first played, 13 Feb.

Bly, Nelly, US journalist, 25 Jan.

BOAC, formed from Imperial and British Airways, 24 Nov.

Boat Race, first, 10 Jun., first broadcast, 2 Apr.

Boeing 747, first transatlantic flight, 12 Jan.

Boer War, 11 Oct., ends 31 May

Bolívar, Simón, dictator of Peru, 10 Sept.

Bolivia, independence, 6 Aug., republic, 16 Aug., floods, 10 Feb.

Bolshoi Ballet, Covent Garden, 3 Oct.

Bonaparte, Joseph, as king of Naples, 30 Mar.

Bonaparte, Louis, king of Holland, 5 Jun.

Bonaparte, *see also* Napoleon

Book tokens, first, 14 Nov.

Booth, William, founds Salvation Army, 23 Jul.

Borazon, made in US, 12 Feb.

Boris Godunov, first performed, 24 Jan.

Borley Rectory, burns, 27 Feb.

Bormann, Martin, skeleton, 11 Apr.

Borstal, first, opens, 16 Oct.

Bosnia and Herzegovina, annexed by Austria, 6 Oct., become Austrian, 13 Jul.

Boston, British troops withdraw, 17 Mar., Massacre, 5 Mar., Tea Party, 16 Dec.

Boston News-Letter, first issued, 24 Apr.

Botany Bay, discovered, 9 Apr., first fleet, 20 Jan., penal colony, 28 Jan.

Bottomley, publishes *John Bull*, 12 May

Bounty, mutiny, 28 Apr., mutineers land on Pitcairn, 23 Jan.

Box and Cox, first perf., 11 May

Boxer Rebellion, starts, 13 Jun., ends 14 Aug.

Boy Friend, The, musical, opens, 14 Jan.

Boy Scouts, first troop formed, 24 Jan., inaugurated, 31 Jul., of America, chartered, 6 Feb., incorporated, 15 Jun., first world rally, 4 Sept.

Boys Brigade, founded, 4 Oct.

Boys from Syracuse, The, first perf., 7 Nov.

Bradfield reservoir, bursts banks, 11 Mar.

Bradshaw, first issue, 25 Oct.

Bramham Moor, rebels defeated, 19 Feb.

Brandt, Willi, becomes W. German chancellor, 21 Oct., meets head of East Germany, 19 Mar.

Brazil, discovered, 26 Jan., reached by Cabral, 22 Apr., Cabral lands, 3 May, independence, 7 Sept., Pedro I as emperor, 1 Dec., becomes republic, 15 Nov.

Bread, price of, 3 Jan., riots, 19 Feb.

Bremen, 1,000 bomber raid, 25 Jun.

Brest-Litovsk, armistice, 5 Dec., Germans and Russians meet, 2 Dec.

Bridge, aluminium alloy, first movable, 26 Nov.

Brigadoon, first London perf., 14 Apr.

Brighton, Chain Pier, destroyed, 4 Dec.

Britain, monarchy restored, 8 May, last invasion, 22 Feb., at war with US, 18 Jun., declares war on Germany, 3 Sept.

British Academy, charter, 8 Aug.

British Columbia, Crown Colony, 2 Aug.

British Council, established, 20 Mar., charter, 2 Oct.

British Empire Exhibition, opens, 23 Apr.

British Expeditionary Force, evacuated, 17 Jun.

British Guiana, 1-cent stamp, sold, 24 Mar.

British Museum, opens, 15 Jan.
British South Africa Company, chartered,
    29 Oct.
Broadcast, football match, 22 Jan.
Broadcasting station, first, 2 Nov.
Brooklands, motor circuit, opens, 6 Jul.,
    first Grand Prix, 7 Aug.
Brooklyn Bridge, 3 Jan., work begins,
    opens, 24 May
Brussels, Germans occupy, 1914, 20 Aug.,
    liberated, 5 Sept.
Buckingham Palace, Queen Victoria lives
    in, 13 Jun.
Buenos Aires, founded, 2 Feb.
Bulganin, succeeds Malenkov, 8 Feb.
Bulgaria, tsar accedes, 5 Oct., joins
    Central Powers, 15 Oct.
Bulwark, warship, blown to pieces,
    25 Nov.
Burgess, Guy, flees, 23 Jun.
Burlington Arcade, opened, 20 Mar.
Burma, invaded by Japan, 19 Jan.,
    independence, 4 Jan.
Bus, petrol, first in London, 9 Oct.
Bus service, London, starts, 7 Jan.
Butter rationing, 8 Jan.
Bye Bye Birdie, first perf., 15 Jun.

Cabaret, first London production, 28 Feb.
Cable, transatlantic, 9 Aug.
Cabot, John, reaches America, 24 Jun.
Cade, Jack, defeats Henry VI, 27 Jun.
Cadiz, Francis Drake sails into harbour,
    19 Apr.
Caen, captured, 9 Jul.
Caesar, Julius, lands in Britain, 26 Aug.
Cage Me a Peacock, first perf., 18 Jun.
Cairo, British enter, 27 Jun.
Calais, recaptured, 7 Jan.
Calcutta, Black Hole, 20 Jun.
Calder Hall, operates, 20 Aug.
Caledonian Canal, opens, 30 Oct.
Calendar, *see* Gregorian, *and*
    Revolutionary Calendar
California [New Albion], Drake claims,
    17 Jun., gold discovered, 24 Jan.,
    statehood, 9 Sept.
Calley, Lieut., guilty, 29 Mar.
Cambodia, civil war ends, 17 Apr.
Cambridge Theatre, opens, 4 Sept.

Camelot, first perf., 19 Aug.
Campbell, Donald, speed record, 17 Jul.
Campbell, Malcolm, speed record, 3 Sept.,
    24 Feb.
Canada, Cartier lands, 24 Jul., and US,
    border, 9 Aug., border defined, 20 Oct.,
    dominion established, 1 Jul., Grand
    Trunk Rly., completed, 7 Apr.,
    Mounted Police, established, 21 Apr.
Canadian Pacific railroad, completed,
    7 Nov.
Canberra, foundation stone, 12 Mar.
Can-Can, first perf., 14 Oct.
Candida, first perf., 1 Jul.
Candide, first perf., 30 Apr.
Cannon, lady fired from, 2 Apr.
Canterbury, Archbishop, meets the Pope,
    23 Mar.
Cape Colony, forbids convicts, 22 Nov.
Cape Horn, rounded, 24 Jan.
Cape of Good Hope, Diaz lands, 3 Feb.,
    occupied, 8 Jan., to Britain, 13 Aug.
Cape St Vincent, Spanish defeated, 16 Jan.
Capone, Al, sentenced, 17 Oct.
Carlton Theatre, opens, 27 Apr.
Carmen, first performed, 3 Mar.
Carnegie Institute, established, 28 Jan.
Carol II, of Romania, renounces throne,
    31 Dec., resumes throne, 8 Jun.,
    abdicates, 6 Sept.
Caroline, Queen, and coronation,
    19 Jul.
Carousel, first perf., 7 Jun.
Carpentier, beats Billy Wells, 8 Dec.
Carpet-sweeper, first, 19 Sept.
Carter, Howard, discovers Tutankhamun's
    tomb, 3 Jan.
Carter, Jimmy, elected president, 2 Nov.
Cartier, Jacques, reaches Labrador,
    20 Apr.
Casablanca, Conference, 14 Jan., ends,
    24 Jan.
Casement, Roger, condemned, 29 Jun.
Castro, Fidel, starts revolution, 26 Dec.,
    prime minister of Cuba, 16 Feb.
Cat and the Fiddle, The, first London perf.,
    4 Mar.
Catherine I, succeeds Peter the Great,
    8 Feb.
Catholic Emancipation Act, 13 Apr.

Cato Street Conspiracy, 23 Feb.

Cats, first perf., 11 May

Cavalleria Rusticana, first perf., 17 May

Caxton, first printed book, 18 Nov.

Census, first British, 10 Mar.

Central Africa Republic, independence, 13 Aug.

Central London Railway, opens, 27 Jun.

Cetewayo, captured, 28 Aug., received by Queen Victoria, 14 Aug.

Ceylon, becomes Sri Lanka, 22 May, independence, 4 Feb., cyclone and tidal wave, 25 Dec., *see also* Sri Lanka

Chad, independence, 11 Aug.

Challenger, space shuttle, explodes, 28 Jan.

Chamberlain, Neville, as prime minister, 28 May

Channel, first swum, 24 Aug., by a woman, 6 Aug., crossing by balloon, 7 Jan., Channel Tunnel, agreement, 6 Feb.

Charge of the Light Brigade, 25 Oct.

Charing Cross station, London, opened, 11 Jan.

Charlemagne, crowned, 25 Dec.

Charles, becomes Prince of Wales, 26 Jul.

Charles I, trial, 20 Jan.

Charles the Bold, killed, 5 Jan.

Charles V, Holy Roman Emperor, 16 Jan.

Charles XIV, proclaimed King of Sweden, 5 Feb.

Charleston, falls to British, 12 May, taken by Union, 18 Feb.

Charley's Aunt, first perf., 21 Dec.

Charlie Girl, first perf., 15 Dec.

Chartist riots, 27 Jul., Chartists meet, London, 10 Apr.

Chelsea Hospital, founded, 11 Mar.

Cherbourg, taken by Allies, 27 Jun.

Chernobyl, accident, 26 Apr.

Chess, first perf., 14 May

Chiang Kai-shek, Chinese president, 6 Oct., 13 Sept.

Chicago, first London perf., 10 Apr.

Chicago, great fire starts, 7 Oct., ends 11 Oct.

Chichester, Francis, arrives at Sydney, 12 Dec.

Childers, Erskine, Irish president, 25 Jun.

Chile, independence, 1810, 18 Sept., 1818, 12 Feb., military coup, 11 Sept.

Chimney-sweeps, boys, ends, 7 Aug.

China, ambassador to, 13 Jan., trade with Britain forbidden, 30 Jan., edict allows cut pigtails, 7 Dec., republic, first president, 14 Feb., Communist regime, 6 Jan., People's Republic, 1 Oct., first TV station, 2 Sept., Kansu province, landslide, 16 Dec., Tangsham earthquake, 28 Jul.

Chinese Honeymoon, A, first perf., 5 Oct.

Chloroform, first used, 12 Nov.

Chocolate Soldier, The, first perf., 10 Sept.

Cholera, in Belfast, 14 Mar., in London, 13 Feb.

Chorus Line, A, first perf., 22 Jul.

Christ Church, Oxford, founded, 13 Jun.

Christians, recognised in Roman Empire, 30 Apr.

Christie, James, first auction, 5 Dec.

Christmas Island, nuclear bomb, 15 May

Christmas tree, first, 25 Dec.

Christ's Hospital, chartered, 26 Jun.

Chu Chin Chow, first perf., 31 Aug.

Church of Scotland, first General Assembly, 20 Dec.

Churchill, Winston, resigns, 5 Apr., 'Iron Curtain' speech, 5 Mar., state funeral, 30 Jan.

Cinemascope, first film, 24 Sept., British, 14 May

Cinerama, first shown, 30 Sept.

Civil Defence, starts, 21 Aug.

Civil rights, black Americans meet, 28 Aug., Bill, USA, 10 Apr.

Civil War, England, begins, 22 Aug.

Clemenceau, Georges, elected French prime minister, 9 Nov.

Cleopatra's Needle, erected, 12 Sept.

Clergy, in England, permitted to marry, 24 Nov.

Cleveland, Grover, marries, 2 Jun.

Clifton Suspension Bridge, opens, 8 Dec.

Cloth of Gold, Field of the, 7 Jun.

Coal and Steel Community, meets, 10 Jan., set up, 18 Apr., came into being, 25 Jul.

Coal strike, begins, 1944, 8 Mar.

Coelocanth, caught off South Africa,
22 Nov.
Coliseum Theatre, opens, 24 Dec.
Cologne, cathedral completed, 14 Aug.,
opens, 15 Oct.
Colombia, earthquake, 1979, 12 Dec.
Colorado, statehood, 1 Aug.
Colour TV, CBS demonstrates, 4 Sept.
Columbia, District of, established, 16 Jul.
Columbia, space shuttle, into space,
12 Apr.
Columbia Broadcasting, inaugurated,
18 Sept.
Columbus, Ger. liner, scuttled, 19 Dec.
Columbus, grant signed, 17 Apr., leaves
on first voyage, 3 Aug., returns to Spain,
15 Mar., returns from America, 4 Jan.,
third voyage, 30 May, begins 4th voyage,
9 May, discovers Dominica, 3 Nov.,
Antigua, 10 Nov., Hispaniola, 6 Dec.
Comedy Theatre, opens, 15 Oct.
Comic Cuts, first weekly comic, 17 May
Cominform, dissolved, 7 Apr.
Comintern, formed, 4 Mar.
Commissionaires, Corps, founded, 13 Feb.
Common Market, Parliament votes for,
28 Oct.
Common Prayer, Book of, to all dioceses,
9 Jun.
Commons, proceedings broadcast, 9 Jun.
Commonwealth, England declared to be a,
17 Mar., established, 30 Jan.
Commonwealth, of Australia, title, 1 Apr.
Commonwealth Office, amalgamation,
1 Jan.
Communications satellite, first, 12 Aug.
Communist Manifesto, published, 4 Jul.
Company, musical, first production, 8 Jan.
Concorde, prototype, 11 Dec., first trial,
9 Jan., test flight, 2 Mar., inaugural
flight, 21 Jan.
Confederate States, formation, 8 Feb.,
first congress, 18 Feb., submarine
Hunley, sinks ship, 17 Feb., surrender,
16 Feb.
Conference, Bimetallist, meets, 20 Apr.
Conference, Moscow, ends, 21 Nov.
Conference, San Francisco, opens, 25 Apr.
Congo, French, independence, 15 Aug.
Congo Republic, becomes Zaïre, 27 Oct.

Congress, first American Continental,
5 Sept.
Congress, Library of, established, 24 Apr.
Congress, US, first meets, 4 Mar.
Congress of Aix-la-Chapelle, 29 Sept.,
ends, 21 Nov.
Congress of Tucuman, 9 Jul.
Connecticut, as English colony,
23 Apr.
Conscription, British, 1916, 24 Jan., call-
up, 24 May, 1939, 2 Sept., 1948, 12 Dec.
Constantine, of Greece, abdicates, 12 Jun.
Constantine II, accedes, 6 Mar.
Constantinople, as capital, Roman
Empire, 11 May, captured, 12 Apr.,
falls, 29 May, name changes to Istanbul,
28 Mar., earthquake, 1912, 9 Aug.
Convention of Bartenstein, 26 Apr.
Conversation Piece, first produced, 16 Feb.
Cook, Capt., crosses Antarctic Circle, 17
Jan., lands at Botany Bay, 28 Apr., sails
on first voyage, 25 May, sails on last
voyage, 11 Jul.
Cook, Thomas, founded, 5 Jul.
Copenhagen, bombardment, 2 Sept.
Corday, Charlotte, murders Marat, 13 Jun.
Corfu, Greeks occupy, 2 Jun.
Corinth Canal, begun, 5 May, opens,
6 Aug.
Corn Laws, repealed, 31 Jan.
Cornwall, Duchy created, 17 Mar.
Coronation Street, first episode, 9 Dec.
Corporative State in Italy, 5 Feb.
Corregidor, surrenders, 6 May
Cortés, takes Tenochtitlán, 13 Aug.
Cosí Fan Tutte, first performed, 26 Jan.
Cosmonaut, complete orbit, 16 Mar., first
woman, 16 Jun.
Cotton Library, presented, 12 Jun.
County Hall, London, foundation stone,
9 Mar.
Covent Garden, opera house, opens,
7 Dec., burns, 5 Mar., second theatre,
18 Sept., third building, opens, 15 May,
market, at Nine Elms, 11 Nov.
Coventry, air raid, 11 Apr., Cathedral,
bombed, 14 Nov., consecrated, 25
May
Coverdale, Bible translation, 4 Oct.
Co-Optimists, The, first perf., 27 Jun.

Crematorium, first, 2 Jan., cremation, first, 26 Mar.

Crete, invasion of, 20 May

Cricket, first test match, Eng., 6 Sept., rules formulated, 25 Feb., test match, first, Aust., 15 Mar.

Crimean War, declared, 28 Mar.

Crippen, Dr., arrested, 31 Jul.

Croatia, declares independence, 6 Jun.

Cromwell, Oliver, as Lord Protector, 16 Dec., Richard, Lord Protector, 3 Sept.

Cronje, Piet, surrenders, 18 Feb.

Crossword puzzle, first newspaper to publish, 21 Dec., first in Britain, 2 Nov.

Crown Jewels, robbery attempt, 9 May

Cruisers, torpedoed, WW1, 22 Sept.

Crystal Palace, opens. 10 Jun., destroyed by fire, 30 Nov.

Cuba, independence, 10 Dec., republic, 21 Feb., attempted invasion, 17 Apr. US lifts blockade, 20 Nov.

Cullinan Diamond, found, 26 Jan.

Cunard line, founded, 4 May

Cup Final, first, 16 Mar.

Cupro-nickel coins, 2 Jan.

Custer, Last Stand, 25 Jun.

Cyprus, annexed by Britain, 5 Nov., Britain takes possession, 12 Jul., becomes Crown Colony, 1 May, independence, 16 Aug., Makarios becomes president, 14 Dec., Turkey invades, 20 Jul., North, occupied by Turkey, 15 Nov., agreement, 19 Feb., UN peace force, 27 Mar.,

Cyrenaica, taken by Italy, 5 Nov., ceded to Italy, 18 Oct.

Czechoslovakia, independence, republic proclaimed, 30 Oct., constitution, 29 Feb., Germans invade, 15 Mar., accepts ceding of Sudeten, 21 Sept., Communist coup, 25 Feb., treason trial, 1952, 27 Nov., Russians invade, 20 Aug.

Dachau, first concentration camp, 20 Mar.

Daguerre, Louis, 2 Jan.

Dahomey, independence, 1 Aug.

Daily Chronicle, ceases, 31 May

Daily Express, first issue, 24 Apr.

Daily Graphic, last issue, 16 Oct.

Daily Herald, first issue, 15 Apr.

Daily Mail, first issue, 4 May

Daily Mirror, The, first issue, 2 Nov.

Daily News, first issue, 21 Jan., ceases, 31 May

Daily Sketch, last issue, 11 May

Daily Telegraph, first published, 29 Jun.

Dakota, North, and Dakota, South, statehood, 2 Nov.

Dales, The, radio serial ends, 25 Apr.

Dallas, airport opens, 13 Jan.

Daly's Theatre, opens, 25 Apr.

Damascus, captured by Tamerlane, 24 Mar.

Dancing Years, The, first produced, 23 Mar.

Danish West Indies, US purchase, 25 Jan., takeover, 31 Mar.

Danzig, free city, 15 Nov., seized by Germany, 1 Sept.

Dardanelles, closed to ships, 2 Mar.

Darling, Grace, rescues crew, 7 Sept.

Dartford-Purfleet Tunnel, opens, 18 Nov.

Dartmoor Prison, foundation, 20 Mar., opens, 24 May

Darwin, bombed by Japan, 19 Feb.

Darwin, Charles, sails in HMS *Beagle*, 27 Dec.

David II, becomes King of Scotland, 7 Jun.

Davis, Jefferson, as president of Confederacy, 22 Feb.

Daylight Saving, begun, 21 May, permanently established, 7 Aug.

De Forest, Lee, radio broadcast, 5 Mar., first sound-on-film movie, 13 Dec.

de Valera, Éamon, Irish president, 9 Mar.

Dead Sea Scrolls, discovered, 7 Feb.

Death duties, introduced, 2 Aug.

Death penalty, abolished, 9 Nov., 18 Dec.

Decimal currency, Britain, 15 Feb., report, 24 Mar., coins issued, 23 Apr.

Defence of the Realm Act, 9 Mar.

Defender of the Faith, title, 11 Oct.

Degrees for women, Oxford, first, 14 Oct.

Delaware, statehood, 7 Dec.

Del Cano, completes first circumnavigation, 6 Sept.

Delhi, Coronation Durbar, 12 Dec.

Dempsey, Jack, beaten by Tunney, 22 Sept.

Denmark, joins Common Market, 22 Jan.,
and Norway, Germany invades, 9 Apr.

Der Freischütz, first perf., 18 Jun.

Der Rosenkavalier, first performed, 26 Jan.

Der Zigeunerbaron, first perf., 24 Oct.

Derby, first run, 4 May

'Desert Island Discs', first broadcast, 29
Jan.

Desert Song, The, first London perf.,
7 Apr.

Dessalines, Jean, in Haiti, 29 Mar.

Destroyer, first in Navy, 28 Oct.

Detroit, founded, 24 Jul.

Deutsche Luft-Reederei airline
established, 6 Feb.

Deutschland, Zeppelin, 19 Jun., wrecked,
16 May

Diamond, 388-carat, 13 Jan., synthetic,
produced, 16 Dec.

Die Dreigroschenoper, first perf., 31
Aug.

Die Fledermaus, first performed, 5 Apr.

Die Lustige Witwe, first perf., 12 Dec.

Die Meistersinger, first perf., 21 Jun.

Dien Bien Phu, captured by Vietminh,
7 May

Dieppe, commando raid, 19 Aug.

Diet of Worms, 28 Jan.

Dillinger, John, captured, 25 Jan.

Dirigible balloon, first, 24 Sept.

Disneyland, opens, 17 Jul.

Djemnah, torpedoed, 14 Jul.

Doctor, first woman, 28 Sept.

Dog, into space in *Sputnik II*, 3 Nov.,
9 Mar.

Doggett's Coat and Badge, first, 1 Aug.

Dollar Princess, The, first perf., 25 Sept.

Dollfuss, dissolves parties, 1 Feb.

Dolmetsch, Arnold, foundation, 24 Feb.

Dominica, independence, 3 Nov.

Dominican Republic, set up, 1 Dec.,
hurricane destruction, 3 Sept., US forces
in, 28 Apr.

Don Carlos, of Spain, abdicates, 18 May

Don Giovanni, first perf., 29 Oct.

Don Juan, first feature sound film, 6 Aug.

Don Pasquale, first perf., 4 Jan.

Dordrecht, sea breaks dykes, 17 Apr.

Dorothy, first perf., 25 Sept.

Draisine, early bicycle, 17 Feb.

Drake, Francis, leaves for world voyage,
13 Dec., circumnavigates, 30 Oct., ends
circumnavigation, 4 Apr.

Dreadnought, battleship, 10 Feb.

Dresden, Allies bomb, 4 Mar.

Dresden, cruiser, sinks, 14 Mar.

Dreyfus, Alfred, sentenced to Devil's
Island, 22 Dec., pardoned, 12 Jul.

Driving tests, started, 26 Mar.

Drug Convention, signed, 19 Feb.

Drury Lane Theatre, first, 7 May, second,
26 Mar., third, 12 Mar., fourth, 10 Oct.

Dubarry, The, first London perf., 14 Apr.

DuBarry was a Lady, first perf., 22 Oct.

Dublin, British Embassy burns, 2 Feb.,
Nelson Column, destroyed, 8 Mar., post
office, burnt, 29 Apr.

Duchess of Dantzig, The, first perf.,
17 Oct.

Duke of York's Theatre, opens, 10 Sept.

Dulwich College, founded, 21 Jun.

Dumbarton Oaks, conference, 21 Aug.

Dunbar Castle liner, hits mine, 9 Jan.

Dunkirk, evacuation, 29 May, 3 Jun.

Dunlop, patents tyre, 23 Jul.

Dutch East India Company, founded,
20 Mar.

Dynamite, demonstrated, 14 Jul.

Dynamo, first, 28 Oct.

Earhart, Amelia, flies Atlantic, 18 Jun.,
solo flight, 20 May

Early Bird, first TV relay satellite,
launched, 6 Apr., began operating,
2 May

East India Company, chartered, 31 Dec.

East Pakistan, cyclone, 13 Nov.

East Prussia, Russians invade, 23 Oct.

Ebert, Friedrich, president of Germany,
11 Feb.

Echo, The, first issue, 8 Dec., last issue,
31 Jul.

Ecuador, earthquakes, 13 Aug.

Eddystone lighthouse, opens, 18 May,
16 Oct., blown down, 26 Nov.

Eden, Anthony, resigns as foreign sec.,
20 Feb., becomes prime minister,
6 Apr., resigns, 9 Jan.

Edict of Nantes, 13 Apr., revoked,
18 Oct.

Edison, electric patent, 27 Jan., invents
phonograph, 19 Feb.
Education Act, Elementary, 9 Aug.
Edward III, accedes, 25 Jan.
Edward VI, accedes, 28 Jan.
Edward VII, marries, 10 Mar., accedes,
22 Jan.
Edward VIII, accedes, 21 Jan., abdicates,
10 Dec.
Egypt, British protectorate ends, 28 Feb.,
republic, 18 Jun., diplomatic relations
with Israel, 26 Feb.
Egypt, liner, sinks, 20 May
Eichmann, found guilty in Israel, 15 Dec.
Eiffel Tower, inaugurated, 31 Mar., Santos
Dumont flies over, 21 Oct.
Eighth Army, retreats to El Alamein,
28 Jan., offensive, 9 Dec. (1940),
29 Nov. (1943)
Eire, becomes republic, 18 Apr.
Eisenhower, commander-in-chief,
24 Dec., supreme commander, 21 Feb.,
elected president, 4 Nov.
Election, USA, first, 7 Jan.
Electric chair, adopted, 1 Jan., first time
used, 6 Aug.
Electric lamp, patent, 27 Jan.
Electricity, nationalised, 1 Apr.
Elijah, oratorio, first perf., 26 Aug.
Elizabeth I, accedes, 17 Nov.,
excommunicated, 25 Feb.
Elizabeth II, marries Prince Philip,
20 Nov., succeeds, 6 Feb., coronation,
2 Jun.
Elizabeth of York, marries, 18 Jan.
Emley Moor, TV mast, crashes, 19 Mar.
Empire Day, first celebrated, 24 May
Empire State Building, opens, 1 May, fire,
8 Jan.
Empire Theatre, opens, 17 Apr.
Empress of Britain, launched, 11 Jun.,
sinks, 2 Oct.
Engels, publishes *Manifesto*, 4 Jul.
England, first naval victory, 24 Aug., great
storm, 1703, 26 Nov., 1861, 20 Feb.,
great storms, 9 Mar., last battle, 6 Jul.
English Channel, flown by a woman,
16 Apr., telephone line, 14 Mar.
Entebbe, raid on, 3 Jul.
Entente Cordiale signed, 8 Apr.

Equatorial Guinea, independence, 12
Oct.
Erie Canal, opens, 26 Oct.
Erskine Bridge, opens, 2 Jul.
Escalator, public, first, 4 Oct.
Esterhazy, Major, acquitted, 11 Jan.
Estonia, independence, 1917, 28 Dec.,
votes to secede, 3 Mar., declared
independent, 2 Feb., admitted to UN,
17 Sept.
Ethiopia, Italians invade, 1895, 25th Mar.,
1935, 2 Oct., British invade, 7 Mar.
Etna, Mount, erupts, 11 Mar., 5 Apr.,
26 May
Eton, receives charter, 12 Sept.
Eugène Onegin, first performed, 29 Mar.
Europe, Council of, set up, 5 May,
inaugurated, 3 Aug.
European Broadcasting Union, formed,
12 Feb.
European Community, set up, 16 Apr.,
starts, 1 Jan., Britain, Denmark,
Ireland join, 1 Jan.
European Defence Community, 27 May
Eurovision, begins, 6 Jun.
Eurydice, submarine, sinks, 4 Mar.
Euston Station, opens, 20 Jul.
Evening News, London, last issue, 31 Oct.
Evening newspaper, first, 3 May
Evening Standard, first published, 11 Jun.
Everest, reconnaissance, 18 May
Ever Green, first perf., 3 Dec.
Evita, first perf., 21 Jun.
Explorer I, launched, 31 Jan.
Expresso Bongo, first perf., 23 Apr.
Eyre, E.J., explores Australia, 25 Feb.

Fabian Society, formation, 4 Jan.
Fairbanks, Douglas, marries, 28 Mar.
Faisal, ascends Saudi throne, 2 Nov.
Faisal II, accedes, Iraq, 4 Apr.
Falklands, ceded to Britain, 22 Jan.,
sovereignty, 1 Jan., Argentine invasion,
2 Apr., cease-fire, 14 Jun.
Falstaff, first performed, 9 Feb.
Fanny, first perf., 15 Nov.
Faraday, discovers induction of electric
currents, 29 Aug.
Farouk, becomes king, 28 Apr., deposed,
23 Jul.

Fascists, founded, 23 Feb., in Italian election, 14 Jan., elected, 14 May, government, first, 30 Sept.

Faust, first performance, 19 Mar.

Fawkes, Guy, arrested, 4 Nov.

FBI, inaugurated, 26 Jul.

February Revolution, 8 Mar. (23 Feb.)

Ferdinand, Archduke, shot, 28 Jun.

Ferdinand, of Bulgaria, as tsar, 5 Oct., abdicates, 3 Oct.

Festival of Britain, opens, 3 May

Fianna Fáil, wins Irish election, 16 Feb.

Fiddler on the Roof, first London production, 16 Feb.

Fiji Is., annexed by Britain, 25 Oct., independence, 10 Oct.

Film, celluloid, motion pictures demonstration, 22 Mar., show, first public, 28 Dec., first feature, 26 Dec., sound-on, first, 15 Apr.

Fings Ain't Wot They Used t'Be, first produced, 11 Feb.

Finland, independence, 6 Dec., invaded by USSR, 30 Nov., declares war on USSR, 6 Jun., peace treaty, 12 Mar.

Fire Service, National, established, 18 Aug.

Fishing limits, 200 miles, 1 Jan.

Fitzsimmons, beats heavyweight Corbett, 17 Mar., loses, 9 Jun.

Fiume, Italy annexes, 9 Mar.

Five-pound note, first, 15 Apr.

Flappers' Vote, 7 May

Flight, transatlantic, first non-stop, 15 Jun., round the world, first woman, 15 Jul.

Flogging, in Army, abolished, 9 Nov.

Floradora, first perf., 11 Nov.

Florida, discovered, 8 Apr., ceded to US, 22 Feb., statehood, 3 Mar.

Flying Dutchman, The, 2 Jan.

Flying Scotsman, in service, 24 Feb.

Flying-trapeze act, first, 12 Nov.

FM radio, demonstrated, 5 Jan.

Foch, Marshal, commander-in-chief, 26 Mar.

Follow the Girls, first perf., 25 Oct.

Follow Through, 3 Oct.

Football Association, English, formed, 26 Oct., League, English, founded,

22 Mar., match, 1st broadcast, 22 Jan., World Cup, England wins, 30 Jul.

Ford, Gerald, nominated US vice-president, 12 Oct., as vice-president, 6 Dec., US president, 9 Aug., grants pardon to Nixon, 8 Sept.

Ford, Model T, 1 Oct.

Foreign Office, amalgamation, 1 Jan.

Formosa, Japan takes, 2 Jun.

Forsyte Saga, The, TV serialisation, 7 Jan.

Fort Duquesne, attacked, 9 Jul.

Fort Niagara, taken by British, 19 Dec.

Forth and Clyde Canal, opens, 28 Jul.

Forth Bridge, official opening, 4 Mar., first train, 24 Jan., Road bridge, opens, 4 Sept.

42nd Street, first perf., 8 Aug.

La Forza del Destino, first performed, 10 Nov.

Four-minute mile, 6 May

France, republic, 1792, 22 Sept., republic, second, 26 Feb., Second Empire, 2 Dec., invades England, 1216, 22 May, 1797, 22 Feb., King of, British sovereign ends title, 5 Nov., first woman prime minister, 15 May, Foreign Legion, founded, 9 Mar., troops capture Berlin, 1806, 27 Oct., declares war on Germany, 3 Sept., British arrive, 10 Sept., Br. Expeditionary Force, 1939, 30 Sept., Vichy govt., 2 Jul., fleet sunk at Toulon, 27 Nov., Oran, fleets sunk, 3 Jul., army, revolt, 26 Apr.

France, liner, launched, 11 May

France II, wrecked, 13 Jun.

Franco government, recognised, 27 Feb.

Franco-German war, begins, 19 Jul.

Frasquita, first London perf., 23 Apr.

Frederica, first perf., 9 Sept.

Frederick William III, becomes king of Prussia, 16 Nov.

Freemasonry, condemned by Pope, 28 Apr.

Frobisher, enters bay, 11 Aug.

Frozen food, on sale, 6 Mar.

Fuchs, Vivian, leader of expedition, 20 Jan.

Fulton, Robert, operates steamboat, 17 Aug.

Funny Face, first perf., 8 Nov.
Funny Girl, first London perf., 13 Apr.
Funny Thing Happened on the Way to the Forum, A, first perf., 3 Oct.

Gaddafi, seizes power in Libya, 1 Sept., becomes prime minister of Libya, 16 Jan.
Gagarin, Yuri, orbits Earth, 5 May
Gaiety Girl, A, first perf., 14 Oct.
Gaiety Theatre, opens, 15 Oct., closes, 1866, 2 Dec., 1939, 25 Feb.
Gallipoli, Allies land, Suvla Bay, 6 Aug., 25 Apr., evacuation, 6-8 Jan.
Gama, Vasco da, sails from Lisbon, 8 Jul., round the Cape, 22 Nov., in India, 20 May
Gambia, independence, 18 Feb., proclaimed republic, 24 Apr.
Gandhi, civil disobedience, 8 Mar.
Gandhi, Indira, becomes Indian prime minister, 19 Jan.
Garfield, president, shot, 2 Jul.
Garrick Theatre, opens, 24 Apr.
Garter, Order of the, established, 19 Jan.
Gatling, patents machine-gun, 4 Nov.
Gaulle, Charles de, forms govt., 29 May, prime minister, 1 Jun., president, 8 Jan., resigns, 28 Apr.
Gaumont-British Film Corporation, founded, 26 Mar.
Geisha, The, first perf., 25 Apr.
General Election, 1974, 28 Feb.
General Strike, begins, 4 May, collapses, 12 May
Gentlemen Prefer Blondes, first perf., 20 Aug.
George Cross, inaugurated, 23 May, and George Medal, instituted, 23 Sept.
George I, of England, proclaimed, 1 Aug.
George II, proclaimed king, 11 Jun.
George II, restored to Greek throne, 25 Nov.
George IV, accedes, 29 Jan.
George V, marries, 6 Jul., accedes, 6 May
George VI, marriage, 26 Apr., accedes, 11 Dec., coronation, 12 May
Georgia, USA, statehood, 2 Jan., University, founded, 27 Jan.

Georgia, votes to secede from USSR, 9 Apr.
Georgia Gazette, first issued, 17 Apr.
Germany, Emperor, first, 18 Jan., Reich, proclaimed, 18 Jan., declàres war on France, 1914, 3 Aug., invades USSR, 22 Jun., Britain declares war, 1914, 4 Aug., retreat, 1918, 4 Sept., battle fleet surrenders, 1918, 21 Nov., fleet scuttled, 21 Jun., fleet mutinies, 3 Nov., in League of Nations, 8 Sept., inflation, 11 Oct., new currency, 1923, 16 Nov., Nazis win many seats, 24 Apr., Nazis largest party, 6 Nov., invades France, 17 May, all parties but Nazis banned, 13 Jun., naval blockade by Britain, 4 Feb., submarine warfare, 4 Feb., blockades Britain, 18 Feb., German Navy ordered to sink merchantmen, 29 Feb., breaks diplomatic relations with United States, 3 Feb., US bombing raid, 27 Jan., Germans in Tunisia, surrender, 12 May, battleships *Blücher* and *Karlsruhe*, sink, 10 Apr., Army in Italy, surrenders, 29 Apr., Germany surrenders, 7 May, Germans outside Germany transfer, 20 Nov., Allied Military control abolished, 31 Jan., Fed. Republic, founded, 5 May, inaugurated, 21 Sept., East frontier closed, 13 Aug., Germany united, 3 Oct., Helmut Kohl wins, 2 Dec.
Geronimo, surrenders, 4 Sept.
Gettysburg, Lincoln speaks, 19 Nov.
Ghana, independence, 6 Mar.
Gianni Schicchi, first perf., 14 Dec.
Gibraltar, won from Spain, 24 Jul., votes to stay British, 10 Sept.
Gillette, patents safety-razor, 2 Dec.
Gilmore, Gary, executed, 17 Jan.
Gipsy Love, first perf., 1 Jun.
Gipsy Princess, The, first perf., 20 May
Girl Guides, in US, 12 Mar.
Girl in the Taxi, The, first perf., 5 Sept.
Girl of the Golden West, The, first perf., 10 Dec.
Glasgow, Kelvin Hall, burns, 7 Jul., University, founded, 7 Jan.
Glencoe Massacre, 13 Feb.

Glenn, John, US astronaut, 20 Feb.

Globe, The, last issued, 5 Feb.

Globe Theatre, burns, 29 Jun.

Gloster-Whittle turbojet, first flight, 15 May

Goddard, Robert H., demonstrates rockets, 16 Mar.

Godspell, first perf., 17 Nov., first London production, 26 Jan.

Godwin-Austin, Mt., climbed, 31 Jul.

Going Up, first perf., 22 May

Gold Coast, *see* Ghana

Gold discovered, California, 24 Jan.

Gold Standard, Britain ends, 21 Sept.

Golda Meir, received by the Pope, 15 Jan.

Golden Gate Bridge, opens, 27 May

Gomulka, Polish leader, resigns, 20 Dec.

Gondoliers, The, first perf., 7 Dec.

Gone with the Wind, published, 30 Jun., film premiere, 15 Dec.

Good Companions, The, novel, published, 29 Jul.

Good-Natured Man, The, first performed, 29 Jan.

Good News, first perf., 15 Aug.

Gorbachev, coup fails, 21 Aug., Nobel Peace Prize, 5 Jun.

Gordobuc, first perf., 18 Jan.

Gordon, Lord George, leads riots, 2 Jun.

Governor, US, first woman elected, 5 Jan.

Götterdämmerung, first perf., 17 Aug.

Grab Me a Gondola, first perf., 27 Nov.

Graf Spee, battleship, scuttled, 17 Dec.

Graf Zeppelin, first transatlantic flight, 15 Oct.

Gramophone, patented, 26 Sept.

Granada, recaptured, 2 Jan.

Grand National, first run, 26 Feb.

Grease, first perf., 26 Jun.

Great Comet, seen, 29 Jun.

Great Eastern, launched, 31 Jan., first voyage, 17 Jun.

Great Exhibition, opens, 1 May

Great Western, launched, 19 Jul., maiden voyage, 8 Apr.

Greater London Council, bill to abolish, 16 Jul.

Greece, proclaims independence, 27 Jan., independent kingdom, 7 May, declares war on Turkey, 2 Feb., drives Italians

out, 10 Nov., Germans call for surrender, 6 Apr., King George deposed, 25 Mar., declares republic, 25 Mar., martial law, 22 Apr., and Asia Minor, earthquake, 17 Oct.

Greenwich, Observatory, founded, 10 Aug., universal meridian, 13 Oct.

Gregorian Calendar, announced, 24 Feb., comes into force, 15 Oct., Switzerland, 12 Jan., introduced in Britain, 3 Sept., adopted in Britain, 14 Sept.

Grenada, independence, 7 Feb., US marines invade, 25 Oct.

Grenadier Guards, formed, 30 May

Grey, Lady Jane, queen, 10 Jul.

Guadalcanal, evacuated by Japanese, 9 Feb., US lands, 7 Aug.

Guatemala, founded, 17 Apr., independence, 15 Sept., German ambassador murdered, 5 Apr.

Guernica, bombed, 26 Apr.

Guernsey, occupied by Germany, 30 Jun.

Guillotine, first erected, 25 Apr.

Guinea, independence, 2 Oct.

Gulf War, begins, 16 Jan., ends, 27 Feb.

Gulflight, sunk by U-boat, 1 May

Gunfight at the OK Corral, 26 Oct.

Gunpowder Plot, discovered, 5 Nov.

Gustavus III of Sweden, shot, 16 Mar.

Guyana, independence, 26 May, becomes republic, 23 Feb.

Guys and Dolls first perf., 28 May

Gwalior, Maharajah of, submits to British, 30 Dec.

Gypsy, first perf., 29 May

Habeas Corpus Act, 27 May

Hadrian IV, first English Pope, 4 Dec.

Haile Selassie, as Emperor, 3 Apr., crowned, 2 Nov.

Hair, first perf., 27 Sept.

Haiti, and Dessalines, 29 Mar., hurricane, 22 Oct.

Half a Sixpence, first performed, 21 Mar.

Hallé Orchestra, first concert, 30 Jan.

Halley's Comet, perihelion, 13 Mar.

Hammarskjöld, Dag, Sec.-Gen., UN, 7 Apr.

Hampshire, cruiser, sinks, 5 Jun.

Hanging, public, last at Tyburn, 7 Nov.,
  last public, 26 May, last, 13 Aug
Hanoi, bombed by US, 29 Jun.
Hans Andersen, first perf., 17 Dec.
Hansel and Gretel, first perf., 23 Dec.
Hansom, patents cab, 23 Dec.
Hardie, Keir, forms ILP, 13 Jan.
Harold, crowned king, 6 Jan.
Harrow and Wealdstone, train disaster,
  8 Oct.
Harrow School, founded, 15 Jun.
Harvard College, founded, 28 Oct.
Harwell, atom research, 29 Oct.
Harwich, ferries collide, 20 Dec.
Hastings, Warren, governor of Bengal,
  13 Apr., impeached, 10 May, trial,
  13 Feb., acquitted of treason, 23 Apr.
Hatry, Clarence, guilty of fraud, 24 Jan.
Haunted house, most, 27 Feb.
Havel, Vaclav, elected Czechoslovak
  president, 25 Dec.
Hawaii, discovered, 18 Jan., becomes
  republic, 17 Jan., US recognises
  independence, 19 Dec., annexed to US,
  (first), 14 Feb., becomes US territory,
  30 Apr., statehood, 21 Aug.
Haymarket, Theatre Royal, 2 Jan.
Health Service, White Paper, 17 Feb.
Heath, resigns, Wilson becomes prime
  minister, 4 Mar.
Heathrow, diamonds and currency
  robbery, 7 Mar.
Heidelberg Catechism, published, 19 Jan.
Heilbron, Rose, sits at Old Bailey, 4 Jan.
Heinemann, Gustav, German president,
  5 Mar.
Helicopter, first flight, 4 Jul.
Heligoland, seized by British, 5 Sept., to
  Germany, 9 Aug.
Hello, Dolly!, first perf., 2 Dec.
Helvetic Republic, formed, 29 Mar.
Henley Regatta, first held, 14 Jun.
Henry II, marries, 18 May
Henry III, marries Eleanor of Provence,
  24 Jan.
Henry VI, of England, accedes,
  31 Aug., crowned king of France,
  7 Dec.
Henry VII, bid for crown, 7 Aug., married,
  18 Jan.

Henry VIII, marries Catherine of Aragon,
  11 Jun., divorces Catherine, 23 May,
  marries Anne Boleyn, 25 Jan., marries
  Jane Seymour, 30 May, marries Anne of
  Cleves, 6 Jan., divorces Anne of Cleves,
  9 Jul., marries Catherine Parr, 12 Jul.
Her Majesty's Theatre (second), opens,
  26 Mar., (fourth), opens, 28 Apr.
Hernando de Soto, in Florida, 28 May
Hess, Rudolf, flies to Scotland, 10 May
Heyerdahl, Thor, on Kon-Tiki exp., 28
  Apr., crosses Atlantic, 12 Jul.
Hide and Seek, first perf., 14 Oct.
Hillary, Edmund, Everest, 29 May, South
  Pole, 3 Jan.
Hindenburg, becomes chief of staff, 30
  Aug., German C.-in-C., 29 Nov.,
  becomes president, 25 Apr.
Hindenburg, Zeppelin, crashes, 6 May
Hindenburg Line, Allies break, 1918,
  29 Sept., Germans retreat to, 14 Mar.
Hindi, becomes official language in India,
  26 Jan.
Hirohito, accedes, 25 Dec.
Hiroshima, atom bomb, 6 Aug.
Hit the Deck, first perf., 3 Nov.
Hitler, attempts putsch, 8 Nov., appointed
  Chancellor, 30 Jan., gets sole power,
  19 Aug., becomes dictator, 23 Mar.,
  renounces Versailles Treaty, 16 Mar.,
  seizes Memel, 21 Mar., invades Low
  Countries, 10 May
Hobart, Tasmania, founded, 9 Oct.
Holborn Empire, opens, 16 Nov.
Hold Everything!, first perf., 12 Jun.
Holland, joined to France, 9 Jul.
Holy Roman Empire, ends, 6 Aug.
Home Guard, begins, 10 May, stands
  down, 3 Dec.
Honduras, floods, 21 Sept., US forces land,
  28 Feb.
Hong Kong, ceded to Britain, 20 Jan.,
  26 Jan., becomes British territory, taken
  by British, 23 Aug.
Hood, battleship, sunk, 24 May
Hoover, Herbert, elected president, 6 Nov.
Horthy, Admiral, regent, 1 Mar., dictator,
  28 Mar.
Housatonic, US ship, sunk by submarine,
  17 Feb.

House of Commons, destroyed, 10 May
Hovercraft, patented, 12 Dec., largest,
    4 Feb., first flight, 30 May, first Channel
    crossing, 25 Jul., cross-channel service,
    31 Jul.
Huascaran, Peru, landslide, 11 Jan.
Hudson, Henry, sails from Amsterdam,
    25th Mar., cast adrift, 23 Jun.
Hudson river, discovered, 12 Sept.
Hudson's Bay, discovered, 3 Aug.
Hudson's Bay Co., chartered, 2 May
Hughes, Ted, as Poet Laureate, 19 Dec.
Huguenots, massacred, 1 Mar.
Human Rights, Convention in force,
    18 May
Hume, discovers Murray River,
    16 Nov.
Hungary, becomes republic, 16 Nov.,
    Soviets enter, 24 Oct., revolt against
    Soviets, 23 Oct., free republic, 18 Oct.
Huskisson, William, MP, killed by *Rocket*,
    15 Sept.
Hussein, of Jordan, accedes, 11 Aug.
Hyde, Douglas, elected as Irish president,
    4 May, inaugurated, 25 Jun.
Hydrogen bomb, first, 1 Nov., dropped
    20 May, first exploded, 6 Nov.
HMS Pinafore, first produced, 25 May

Ibn Saud, king, 8 Jan.
Ibrox Park, collapse, 2 Jan.
Ice-breaker, atomic, operates, 20 Dec.
Iceland, sovereign state, 1 Dec., gunboat
    holes ship, 26 May
Idaho, statehood, 3 Jul.
Identity cards, issued, 30 Sept., abolished,
    21 Feb.
Idi Amin, deposes Milton Obote, 25 Jan.,
    becomes absolute ruler, 2 Feb., expels
    Asians from Uganda, 4 Aug.
Iena, French battleship, 12 Mar.
Ignatius of Loyola, Superior-General of
    Jesuits, 4 Apr.
IJsselmeer, lake, 28 May
Il Seraglio, first perf., 16 Jul.
Il Trovatore, first performed, 19 Jan.
Illinois, organised as territory, 3 Feb.,
    statehood, 3 Dec.
Illustrated London News, first issued, 14
    May

Illustrious, HMS, crippled by bombers, 10
    Jan.
Immaculate Conception, dogma, 8 Dec.
Income tax, first introduced, 4 Dec., 9 Jan.
Independent, first issue, 7 Oct., the
    Independent on Sunday, first published,
    28 Jan.
Independent Labour Party, formed, 13 Jan.
India, Mogul Empire founded, 21 Apr.,
    Mutiny, 10 May, transferred to the
    Crown, 2 Aug., Empress of, 1 Jan.,
    Indian Navy, mutiny, 21 Feb.,
    independence, 15 Aug., British troops
    leave, 28 Feb., becomes republic, 26
    Jan., invades Pakistan, 6 Sept., Southern
    India, cyclone and tidal wave, 25 Dec.
Indian, first to be a peer, 13 Jan.
Indiana, statehood, 11 Dec.
Indonesia, independence, 17 Aug.,
    republic, established, 9 Dec.
Infallibility, Papal, dogma, 18 Jul.
Inquisition, abolished, 4 Dec.
Insulin, discovery, 15 Apr., isolated,
    27 Jul.
International Labour Organisation,
    founded, 11 Apr.
International Monetary Fund, set up,
    27 Dec.
Invasion of Britain, last, 22 Feb.
Iolanthe, first perf., 25 Nov.
Iowa, statehood, 28 Dec.
I Pagliacci, first perf., 21 May
IRA, Birmingham bomb explosions,
    21 Nov., bomb attack at Aldershot,
    22 Feb.
Iran, severe earthquakes, 10 Apr., Shah,
    abdicates, 16 Sept.
Iraq, Feisal I crowned, 23 Aug., invades
    Kuwait, 2 Aug.
Ireland, Act of Union, 28 Mar., Easter
    Rising, 24 Apr., Irish Home Rule Act,
    25 May, Irish Free State, established,
    6 Dec., first parliament, 7 Dec.,
    Republic, formed, 28 Dec., joins
    Common Market, 22 Jan., first woman
    prime minister, 7 Nov.
Irene, first London perf., 7 Apr.
Irma La Douce, first perf., 17 Jul.
Iron lung, first used, 12 Oct.
Ironclad warship, first British, 29 Dec.

Irving, Henry, becomes knight, 24 May
Islamic Era, begins, 16 Jul.
Israel, independence, 14 May, Britain
    recognises, 27 Apr., Arab nations
    armistice, 3 Apr., diplomatic relations
    with Egypt, 26 Feb., Israeli destroyer,
    sunk by Egyptians, 21 Oct.
Istanbul, great fire, 3 Jun., *see also*
    Constantinople
Italy, first parliament, 2 Apr., declares war
    on Turkey, 29 Sept., takes Tripoli and
    Cyrenaica, 5 Nov., withdraws from
    League of Nations, 11 Dec., Fascist
    ministry, 30 Oct., invades Greece,
    28 Oct., declares war on Germany, 1943,
    13 Oct., central, earthquake, 13 Jan., *see
    also* Fascists
ITV, begins, 22 Sept.
Ivan the Terrible, crowned, 16 Jan.
Ivory Coast, independence, 7 Aug.,
    republic, 7 Dec.
Iwo Jima, US troops land, 19 Feb.

Jack the Ripper, first victim, 31 Aug.
Jamaica, discovered by Columbus, 3 May,
    earthquake, 14 Jan., independence,
    6 Aug.
James II, accedes, 6 Feb.
James IV, becomes King of Scotland,
    11 Jun.
James I/James VI, ascends throne, 24 Mar.
Jameson Raid, into the Transvaal, 29 Dec.
Jamestown, Virginia, settlement, 13 May
Japan, Capt. Perry arrives, 7 Jul., Diet
    opens, 29 Nov., declares war on
    Germany, 23 Aug., attacks Pearl
    Harbor, 7 Dec., Britain, Australia and
    US declare war, 8 Dec., surrenders,
    14 Aug., US forces land, 28 Aug., regains
    sovereignty, 28 Apr., earthquake, 1946,
    21 Dec., earthquake, 1968, 16 May
Jarrow, unemployed march, 5 Oct.
Java, Japanese attack, 27 Feb.
Jazz record, first, 7 Mar.
Jazz Singer, The, first feature-length talkie,
    6 Oct.
Jeffreys, Judge, as Lord Chancellor,
    28 Sept.
Jeffries, James J., boxer, wins, 9 Jun.
Jersey, occupied, 1 Jul.

Jerusalem, captured by Crusaders, 15 Jul.,
    surrenders to Allenby, 9 Dec.
Jesus, Society of, 27 Sept., founded,
    15 Aug., Ignatius of Loyola, Superior-
    General, 4 Apr., dissolved, 21 Jul.
Jesus Christ, Superstar, first perf., 9 Aug.
Jet aircraft, first, 27 Aug.
Jet-liner service, world's first, 21 Apr.,
    transatlantic, 4 Oct., London to
    Johannesburg, 2 May
Jewels of the Madonna, The, first perf.,
    23 Dec.
Jewish Disabilities Bill, 23 Jul.
Jewish MP, first, 26 Jul.
Jewish newspaper, first, 12 Nov.
Jews, persecution of, 1 Apr.
Joan of Arc, taken prisoner, 23 May
Jockey Club, women members, 12 Dec.
Johannesburg, founded, 8 Sept.
John Bull, first issue, 12 May
Johnson, Amy, lands at Port Darwin,
    24 May
Johnson, Andrew, as president, 15 Apr.
Johnson, Samuel, *Dictionary*, 15 Apr.
Joliet and Marquette, explore Mississippi,
    17 May
Jordan, independence, 22 Mar., 25 May
Joyce, William, sentenced to death,
    19 Sept.
Juan Carlos, Don, proclaimed King of
    Spain, 22 Oct.
Juárez, Benito, returns, 11 Jan.
Juliana, Princess, marries, 7 Jan., becomes
    Queen of the Netherlands, 6 Sept.
Junius, Letters of, 21 Jan.
Junkers, builds metal aircraft, 12 Dec.
Jupiter, discovery of satellites, 7 Jan.
Jurors, first women, 11 Jan.
Justice, International Court of, opens,
    18 Apr.

Kaiser, of Germany, abdicates, 9 Nov.
Kansas, statehood, 29 Jan.
Karl I, accedes to Austrian throne, 23 Nov.
Katanga, independence, 11 Jul.
Keble College, Oxford, opens, 23 Jun.
Kelly, Grace, marries Rainier, 19 Apr.
Kelly's Theatre, opens, 25 May
Kemal, Mustapha, Turkish president,
    13 Aug.

Kennedy, John, elected president, 8 Nov., inaugurated, 20 Jan., assassinated, 22 Nov.

Kennedy, Robert, shot, 5 Jun.

Kentucky, statehood, 1 Jun.

Kentucky Derby, first, 16 May

Kenya, Britain takes over, 8 Jul., independence, 12 Dec., invaded by Italy, 4 Aug.

Kenyatta, Jomo, convicted, 8 Apr.

Kerensky, Alexander, Russian prime minister, 22 Jul.

Khama, Seretse, president of Botswana, 10 Sept.

Khartoum, captured by the Mahdi, 26 Jan., relief force, 28 Jan.

Khrushchev, chairman, USSR, 27 Mar., denounces Stalin, 14 Feb.

Kiel Canal, opens, 20 Jun.

Kiev, captured by Bolsheviks, 3 Feb., Germans take, 19 Sept.

Kimberley, relieved, 15 Feb., diamonds discovered, 6 Nov.

Kinetoscope, demonstrated, 15 Apr.

King, Martin Luther, leads civil rights march, 21 Mar.

King and I, The, first perf., 8 Oct.

King of England, position abolished, 17 Mar.

Kingsford-Smith, flies Pacific, 9 Jun.

Kingsway Theatre, closes, 11 May

King's College, London, opens, 8 Oct.

King's Cross Station, fire, 18 Nov.

King's Rhapsody, first perf., 15 Sept.

Kismet, first London perf., 20 Apr.

Kiss Me Kate, first London perf., 8 Mar.

KLM, founded, 7 Oct.

Klondyke, gold discovered, 17 Aug.

Knox-Johnston, Robin, completes voyage, 22 Apr.

Kon-Tiki expedition, 28 Apr.

Korea, annexed by Japan, 22 Aug., Truman orders forces to, 27 Jun., Boeing 727 hijack, 3 Apr.

Krakatoa, erupts, 26 Aug.

Kronstadt, sailors mutiny, 2 Mar., mutineers surrender, 17 Mar.

Kruger, Paul, president of South African Republic, 16 Apr.

Krupps factory, destroyed, 11 Mar.

K2, climbed, 31 Jul.

Kuwait, independence, 19 Jun., Iraq invades, 2 Aug.

La Belle Hélène, first performed, 31 Jan.

La Bohème, first performed, 1 Feb.

La Cage aux Folles, first perf., 7 May

La Cenerentola, first performed, 25 Jan.

La Gioconda, first performed, 8 Apr.

La Scala, Milan, opens, 3 Aug.

La Traviata, first performed, 6 Mar.

La Vie Parisienne, first perf., 31 Oct.

Labour Party, founded, 27 Feb., government, first, 23 Jan., second, 8 Jun., comes to power, 1945, 26 Jul., first absolute majority, 5 Jul.

Ladies' Mercury, The, 27 Jun.

Lady Be Good, first London perf., 14 Apr.

Ladysmith, relieved, 28 Feb.

Laker Airways, collapse, 5 Feb.

Lakonia, liner, burns, 23 Dec.

Lancastria, troopship, sinks, 17 Jun.

Land speed record, 1970, 23 Oct., 1979, 18 Dec.

Landru, Desiré, found guilty, 28 Nov.

Laos, independence, 19 Jul.

Lascaux Caves, discovered, 12 Sept.

Latvia, independence, 1917, 21 Sept., 1918, 18 Nov., occupied, 17 Jun., becomes part of USSR, 3 Aug., votes to secede, 3 Mar., proclaims independence, 9 Apr., admitted to UN, 17 Sept.

Launderette, first, 9 May

Lawn Tennis, patented, 23 Feb.

LBC, radio station, starts, 8 Oct.

Le Monde, first issue, 18 Dec.

Le Morte D'Arthur, published, 31 Jul.

Le Surcouf, submarine, rammed, 18 Feb.

Leaflets, aerial propaganda, first, 15 Jan.

League of Nations, founded, 28 Apr., inaugurated, 10 Jan., meets, 16 Jan., 3 Feb., 16 Jun., US Senate refuses, 19 Mar., US votes against joining, 16 Jan., final assembly, 8 Apr., dissolved, 18 Apr.

Lease-Lend, Roosevelt proposes, 17 Dec.

Lee, Robert E., becomes commander-in-chief of Confederate Army, 6 Feb., surrenders, 9 Apr.

Légion d'Honneur, instituted, 19 May
Leningrad, siege of, 30 Aug., relieved,
  18 Jan.
Leopold I, becomes king of Belgians,
  21 Jul.
Leopold III, of Belgium, abdicates, 16 Jul.
Les Cloches de Corneville, first produced,
  19 Apr.
Let's Face It, first perf., 19 Nov.
Leyte, US troops land, 20 Oct.
Lhasa, troops enter, 3 Aug.
Liberal landslide, 12 Jan.
Liberia, independence, 26 Jul.
Liberté, Fr. battleship, explodes, 25 Sept.
Liberty, Statue of, presented, 4 Jul.
Libya, independence, 24 Dec.
Lidice, burns, 6 Jun.
Liebknecht, Karl, assassinated, 15 Jan.
Liechtenstein, constituted, 23 Jan.
Life, magazine, last issue, 29 Dec.
Lifeboat Institution, Royal, founded, 4 Mar.
Lights of New York, The, first all-talking
  film, 6 Jul.
Lilac Time, first perf., 22 Dec.
Lima, Peru, founded, 18 Jan.
Lincoln, Abraham, elected president,
  6 Nov., shot, 14 Apr.
Lincoln Cathedral, consecrated, 9 May
Lind, Jenny, debut, 7 Mar.
Lindbergh, reaches Paris, 21 May, baby
  kidnapped, 1 Mar., baby, found dead,
  12 May
Lisbon, earthquake, 26 Feb., destroyed in
  earthquake, 1 Nov.
Listener, The, published, 16 Jan.
Lithographic process, patented, 10 Nov.
Lithuania, proclaimed republic, 1918,
  29 Nov., votes to secede, 9 Feb.,
  independence, 23 Mar., admitted to UN,
  17 Sept.
Little Me, first perf., 18 Nov.
Little Night Music, A, first London perf.,
  15 Apr.
Little Theatre, Strand, closes, 16 Apr.
Liverpool, bread riots, 19 Feb., Cathedral
  consecrated, 19 Jul., port radar station,
  30 Jul.
Liverpool Echo, first issue, 27 Oct.
Lloyd George, becomes prime minister,
  7 Dec.

Lloyd's, Royal Charter, 25 May, *Register*,
  first issued, 1 Nov.
Loaf, national, in Britain, 24 Mar.
Local Defence Volunteers, 10 May
Locarno Pact, signed, 1 Dec.
Lock Up Your Daughters, first perf.,
  28 May
Lockerbie, Pan Am jet crashes, 22 Dec.
Loetschberg Tunnel, opens, 28 Jun.
Lofoten Is., commando raid, 4 Mar.
Lohengrin, first perf., 28 Aug.
London, Great Frost, ends, 8 Feb., Great
  Fire, 2 Sept., ends, 6 Sept., first bus,
  4 Jul., munitions factory explosion,
  19 Jan., air raid, 1915, 13 Oct., daylight
  air raid, 1917, 13 Jun., 'blitz' begins,
  23 Aug., on docks, 1940, 29 Dec., last
  tram, 6 Jul., and Moscow, air service,
  19 Dec.
London, Chatham and Dover, railway,
  7 Feb.
London Bridge, opened, 1 Aug., old, stone
  laid, 15 Jun., sold to oil company,
  18 Apr., new, opens, 16 Mar.
London County Council, formed, 12 Feb.
London Docks, opened, 20 Jan.
London *Evening News*, first issue, 26 Jul.
London Gazette, first issue, 7 Nov.
London Hippodrome, opened, 15 Jan.
London Library, opens, 1 May
London Pavilion, opens as theatre, 3 Aug.
London Philharmonic Orchestra, first
  perf., 7 Oct.
London Symphony Orchestra, first concert,
  9 Jun.
London University, charter, 28 Nov., deed
  of settlement, 10 Feb., women's degrees,
  15 Jan.
Londonderry, Siege of, 20 Apr., civilians
  shot by troops, 30 Jan.
Long Parliament, dissolved, 16 Mar.
Long-play records, demonstrated, 17 Sept.
Look Back in Anger, first perf.,
  8 May
Lords, House of, reduced power, 10 Aug.,
  televised, 23 Jan.
Lord's, first cricket match, 22 Jun.
Lorenz, Peter, kidnapped, 28 Feb.
Los Angeles, earthquake, 9 Feb., St Francis
  Dam bursts, 13 Mar.

Mandela, Nelson, released, 11 Feb.
Manhattan Island, bought, 6 May
Manila, troops under MacArthur, enter, 5 Feb.
Manoel, of Portugal, deposed, 5 Oct.
Manon, first performed, 19 Jan.
Manon Lescaut, first performed, 1 Feb.
Manson, Charles, guilty of murder, 25 Jan.
Marble Arch, unveiled, 20 Mar.
Marconi, patents wireless, 2 Jun., first transmissions, 14 Feb.
Margaret, Princess, marries, 6 May
Margarine, patented, 15 Jul.
Margrethe II, Queen, Danish throne, 15 Jan.
Marienwerder, plebiscite, 11 Jul.
Marks and Spencer, first shop, 28 Sept.
Marriage Market, The, first perf., 17 May
Marriage of Figaro, The, first perf., 1 May
Married Women's Property Act, 9 Aug.
Mars, close-up pictures, 15 Jul., moons discovered, 11 Aug., soft landing by Viking 1, 20 Jul., TV pictures, 14 Oct., 30 Jul.
Marseillaise, adopted as national anthem, 15 Jul.
Marshall Is., admitted to UN, 17 Sept.
Martinique, Mount Pelée erupts, 8 May
Marx, publishes *Manifesto*, 4 Jul.
Mary, Queen of Scots, marries Dauphin, 24 Apr., marries Lord Darnley, 29 Jul., accedes to Scottish throne, 14 Dec.
Mary I, marries Philip of Spain, 25 Jul.
Mary Celeste, leaves New York, 7 Nov., found, 5 Dec.
Mary Rose, sinks, 19 Jul.
Massachusetts, statehood, 6 Feb.
Massey, Vincent, appointed governor-general of Canada, 25 Jan.
Matrimonial Causes Bill, 18 Jul.
Matterhorn, first ascent, 14 Jul.
Mauretania, launched, 1906, 20 Sept., 1938, 28 Jul.
Mauritania, independence, 28 Nov.
Mauritius, capture from French, 3 Dec., independence, 12 Mar.
Maximilian, emperor of Mexico, 10 Apr.
Maxwell, Robert, Mirror Group sold to, 12 Jul.
May Fair Theatre, opens, 17 Jun.

Maybrick, Florence, guilty of murder, 7 Aug.
Mayerling, suicides, 30 Jan.
Mayflower, arrives in New World, 25 Dec.
Mayor, first woman, 9 Nov.
Me and My Girl, first perf., 16 Dec.
Mecklenburg declaration of independence, 20 May
Mehemet Ali, obtains total power in Egypt, 1 Mar.
Mein Kampf, published, 18 Jul.
Melbourne, founded, 29 Aug.
Memel, seized by Hitler, 21 Mar., seized by Lithuania, 10 Jan.
Menai Bridge, opened, 1826, 30 Jan., 1980, 11 Jul.
Mercury, close-up pictures, 29 Mar.
Merrie England, first performed, 2 Apr.
Merry Widow, The, first perf., 8 Jun.
Mersey Tunnel, opened, 1886, 20 Jan., 1934, 18 Jul., 1971, 24 Jun.
Messiah, The, first performed, 13 Apr.
Messina, Italy, destroyed in earthquake, 28 Dec.
Methodist Church of Gt. Britain, established, 20 Sept.
Metre, France adopts, 7 Apr.
Metropolitan Opera House, opens, 22 Oct., burns, 27 Aug.
Metropolitan Police, founded, 19 Jun.
Metropolitan Railway, started, 10 Jan.
Mexico, independence, 1821, 23 Aug., 1813, 6 Nov., declares war on France, 30 Nov., and US, war, 4 Jun., Mexico City, captured, 14 Sept., French occupy, 7 Jun., US war, ends, 2 Feb., Santa Anna is dictator, 16 Dec.
Michael, of Romania, abdicates, 30 Dec.
Michigan, statehood, 26 Jan.
Mickey Mouse film, first, 18 Nov.
Micronesia, admitted to UN, 17 Sept.
Microscope, electron, demonstrated, 20 Apr.
Mignon, first perf., 17 Nov.
Mikado, The, first production, 14 Mar.
Milan, revolts against Austrians, 18 Mar.
Mindszenty, Josef, arrested in Hungary, 27 Dec.
Mines Act, 1842, 10 Aug.

Minnesota, statehood, 11 May

Minorca, captured by Spanish, 5 Feb.

Mississippi, statehood, 10 Dec.

Missouri, statehood, 10 Aug.

Möhne Dam, bombed, 16 May

Mollison, 1st westward transatlantic flight,
19 Aug.

'Mona Lisa', stolen, 21 Aug.

Money orders, first issued, 1 Oct.

Mongolia, independence, 10 Jul.

Monroe Doctrine, proclaimed, 2 Dec.

Mons, retreat from, 24 Aug.

Monsieur Beaucaire, first produced,
19 Apr.

Montana, statehood, 8 Nov.

Mont Blanc, road tunnel, 16 Jul.

Mont Cenis tunnel, opens, 17 Sept.

Monte Cassino, bombed, 15 Feb.,
captured, 18 May, Fifth Army, 4 Jan.

Montefiore, Moses, first Jewish knight,
9 Nov.

Montenegro, independence, 28 Aug.,
united with Serbia, 29 Nov.

Montevideo, taken by British, 3 Feb.

Montgolfiers, hot-air balloon flight,
21 Nov.

Montgomery, Gen., commands Eighth
Army, 19 Aug.

Montini, elected Pope Paul VI, 30 Jun.

Montreal, founded, 18 May

Moon, reached, 3 Feb., close-up pictures,
4 Oct., far side, pictures, 7 Oct., first
flight around, 21 Dec., Soviet *Luna 17*,
touches down, 17 Nov., US lunar module
touches down, 19 Nov.

Moorgate, underground train crash,
28 Feb.

Morgan, J.P., founds US Steel, 23 Feb.

Mormon, Book of, 22 Sept.

Mormon Church, organised, 6 Apr.,
renounces bigamy, 6 Oct.

Morning Chronicle, first version published,
28 Jun., second, 2 Mar.

Morning Post, The, first issue, 2 Nov., last
issue, 30 Sept.

Morocco, independence, 2 Mar., Spain
relinquishes, 7 Apr.

Morris Minor car, first, 12 Oct.

Morse, Samuel, demonstrates telegraph,
6 Jan.

Moscow, on fire to halt French, 15 Sept.,
becomes capital, 9 Mar., Germans
advance on, 16 Oct.

Mosley, Sir Osward, expelled from Labour
Party, 10 Mar.

Most Happy Fella, The, first London perf.,
21 Apr.

Mother's Day, first, 10 May

Motor Show, first, 11 Dec.

Motorway, first, 10 Sept., first British,
5 Dec., M1, first section opens, 1 Nov.

Mousetrap, The, first perf., 25 Nov.

Movie, sound-on-film, demonstrated,
13 Dec.

Mozambique, discovered, 1 Mar.

MPs, first salaries, 10 Aug.

Mr Cinders, first produced, 11 Feb.

Munich agreement, signed, 29 Sept.

Murat, Joachim, deserts Napoleon,
11 Jan.

Music Box Revue, first perf., 15 May

Music in the Air, first perf., 19 May

Mussolini, founds Fascists, 23 Feb.,
marches on Rome, 28 Oct., seizes power,
20 Oct., resigns, 25 Jul., rescued by
Germans, 12 Sept.

Mutiny, first perf., 7 Jul.

My Fair Lady, first perf., 30 Apr.

Nagasaki, atom bomb, 9 Aug.

Namibia, independence, 21 Mar.

Napier and Hastings, New Zealand,
earthquake, 3 Feb.

Naples, earthquake, 1805, 26 Jul., king of,
30 Mar.

Napoleon, arrives at Fontainebleau, 20
Mar., becomes First Consul, 19 Feb.,
Consul for life, 2 Aug., becomes
emperor, 18 May, crowned emperor,
2 Dec., marries Josephine, 9 Mar., as
King of Italy, 26 May, invades Russia,
24 Jun., enters Moscow, 14 Sept.,
abdicates, 11 Apr., escapes from Elba,
26 Feb., at St Helena, 17 Oct.

Napoleon III, marriage, 29 Jan., deposed,
4 Sept., attempt on life, 14 Jan.

Nasser, president of Egypt, 23 Jun.

National Gallery, London, founded,
22 Mar., opens, 9 Apr.

National Health Insurance, begins, 15 Jan.

National Health Service, begins, 5 Jul.
National Socialist party formed, 5 Jan.
NATO, Treaty, signed, 4 Apr., Allied
  Command, 2 Apr., USSR offers to join,
  31 Mar.
Natural History Museum, opens, 18 Apr.
Nautch Girl, The, first perf., 30 Jun.
Nautilus, submarine, 21 Jan.
Nazis, gains in election, 5 Mar., large vote,
  29 Mar., purged by Hitler, 30 Jun.
Nebraska, statehood, 1 Mar.
Neguib, president of Egypt, 18 Jun.
Nelson, defeats Spanish, 14 Feb.
Nelson's Column, completed, 4 Nov.
Nepal, constitutional monarchy, 18 Feb.
Neptune, discovered, 23 Sept.
Nessler, Chas., hair-waving machine,
  8 Oct.
Netherlands, independence, 25 Jul.
Nevada, statehood, 31 Oct.
New Amsterdam, becomes New York,
  8 Sept.
New Caledonia, annexed by France,
  24 Sept.
New College, Oxford, foundation, 5 Mar.,
  26 Nov.
New Delhi, as capital of India, 10 Feb.
New England, Company, formed, 19 Mar.
New England, Restriction Act, 30 Mar.,
  Weekly Journal, first published, 20 Mar.
New England Courant, first issue, 7 Aug.
New Faces, first produced, 11 Apr.
Newfoundland, declared English, 5 Aug.,
  joins Canada, 1 Apr.
New Guinea, Allied forces land, 22 Apr.,
  US forces land, 29 Jun.
New Hampshire, statehood, 21 Jun.
New Hebrides, volanic eruption, 19 Dec.
New Jersey, statehood, 18 Dec.
New London Theatre, opens, 10 Jan.
New Mexico, annexed by US, 22 Aug.,
  statehood, 6 Jan.
New Moon, The, first London perf., 4 Apr.
New River, London, opens, 29 Sept.
News Chronicle, first issue, 31 May, merges
  with *Daily Mail*, 18 Oct.
News of the World, first issue, 1 Oct.
New South Wales, discovered, 20 Apr.
Newspaper, first colour pictures, 22 Mar.,
  first evening, 3 May, first illustrated daily,

4 Mar., first provincial, 24 Sept., first
  successful English daily, 11 Mar., advert.
  duty repealed, 4 Aug., stamp duty
  abolished, 15 Jun.
New Statesman, founded, 21 Feb.
New Testament, Revised Standard, 17 May
New York, becomes US capital, 13 Sept.,
  subway opens, 27 Oct., Stock Exchange
  collapses, 28 Oct., statehood, 26 Jul.
New York *Daily Sun*, first issue, 23 Sept.
New York Times, first issue, 18 Sept.
New York World's Fair, opens, 1964,
  22 Apr., 1939, 30 Apr., 1940, 11 May
New Zealand, discovered, 13 Dec., Capt.
  Cook lands, 6 Oct., proclaimed British,
  21 May, as colony, 3 May, first cargo of
  meat, 15 Feb., as dominion, 26 Sept.,
  parliament, Queen Elizabeth opens,
  12 Jan.
Niagara Falls, explorer reaches, 8 Jan.
Nicaragua, Sandinistas enter Managua,
  19 Jul.
Nicholas II, Tsar, abdicates, 15 Mar.
Nigeria, independence, 1 Oct., civil war,
  6 Jul., Northern, conquest, 15 Mar.,
  military coup, 29 Jul.
Nile, source discovered, 3 Aug.
Nîmes, Grand Council ends, 14 Jul.
Nixon, Richard, elected president, 5 Nov.,
  impeachment, 9 May, resigns, 8 Aug.
Nkrumah, Kwame, first African prime
  minister, 21 Mar., overthrown, 24 Feb.
Nobel Prize, first, 10 Dec.
No, No, Nanette, first London perf.,
  11 Mar.
Nonuplets, born, 13 Jun.
No Popery Riots, 2 Jun.
Nore, mutiny, begins, 2 May, suppressed,
  30 Jun.
Normandie, liner, launched, 29 Oct.,
  maiden voyage, 29 May, burns at pier,
  9 Feb.
Normandy, Allied invasion, 6 Jun.
North Africa, Allies land, 8 Nov., British/
  US link up, 6 Apr., Germans counter-
  attack, 31 Mar.
North Carolina, statehood, 21 Nov.
Northern Ireland, votes against inclusion in
  Irish Free State, 7 Dec.
Northern Line, opens, 22 Jun.

Northern Rhodesia, independence,
24 Oct.
North Korea, independence, 9 Sept.,
admitted to UN, 17 Sept.
North Pole, flight over, 9 May
North Sea gas, first piped ashore, 4 Mar.
North West Mounted Police, starts, 23 May
Norway, ceded to Sweden, 14 Jan., union
ends, 26 Oct., and Denmark, Germany
invades, 9 Apr., Quisling govt., 25 Sept.,
votes against Common Market, 25 Sept.
Notes, treasury, £1 and 10s., 7 Aug.
Notre Dame, Chartres, consecrated, 24 Oct.
Nova Scotia, French settlement, 25 Jun.
Nuclear submarine, *Triton*, 16 Feb.
Nuclear tests, ban, 5 Aug.
Nuffield Foundation, set up, 13 Feb.
Nuremburg, War Crimes trial, 20 Nov.
Nuremburg Laws, passed, 15 Sept.
Nyasa, Lake, discovered, 16 Sept.
Nyasaland, independence, 6 Jul.
Nylon, first product, 24 Feb.
Nymph Errant, first perf., 6 Oct.

Oates, Lawrence, in Antarctica, 17 Mar.
Obote, Milton, deposed, 25 Jan.
Observer, first issue, 4 Dec., acquired by
Astor, 5 Apr.
October Revolution, 26 Oct.
Ohio, statehood, 1 Mar.
Oh, Kay!, first perf., 21 Sept.
Oil, North Sea, first, 11 Jun.
Oil rig, *Sea Gem* capsizes, 27 Dec.
Oklahoma, statehood, 16 Nov.
Oklahoma!, first perf., 29 Apr.
Oliver, first perf., 30 Jun.
Olympic Games, modern, inaugurated,
6 Apr., first gold medal, 25th Mar., 1972,
terrorists kill Israelis, 5 Sept.
Once Upon a Mattress, first perf., 20 Sept.
On the Town, first perf., 30 May
On Your Toes, first London performance,
5 Feb.
Open University, first degrees, 11 Jan.
Opera, broadcast in New York, 13 Jan.,
first British broadcast, 6 Jan.
Opera House, London, burns, 17 Jun.
Oporto, French defeated, 12 May
Orange River Colony, self-government, 6
Dec.

Order of Merit, instituted, 26 Jun.
Order of the British Empire, begins, 4 Jun.
Order of the Garter, founded, 23 Apr.
Oregon, statehood, 14 Feb.
Origin of Species, by Darwin, published,
24 Nov.
Orissa, India, tidal wave, 1 Nov.
Orpheus, HMS, wrecked, 7 Feb.
Orpheus in the Underworld, first perf.,
21 Oct.
Ostend, naval raid, 1 May
Oswald, Lee Harvey, shot by Jack Ruby,
24 Nov.
Otello, first performed, 5 Feb.
Ottawa, chosen by Queen Victoria, 7 Aug.,
chosen as Canadian capital, 31 Dec.,
parliament buildings, destroyed by fire,
3 Feb.
Our Miss Gibbs, first performed, 23 Jan.
Owens, Jesse, five world records, 25 May
Oxford, women admitted to exams, 29 Apr.
Oxford-Cambridge boat race, dead heat,
24 Mar.
Oxford English Dictionary, first volume
published, 1 Feb.
Oxford Movement, launched, 14 Jul.
Oxygen, discovered, 1 Aug.

Pacelli, Eugenio, becomes Pope,
2 Mar.
Pacific Is., bought by Germany, 12 Feb.,
Japanese, UN trustees, 2 Apr.
Pacific Ocean, discovered, 25 Sept.
Pact of London, 26 Apr.
Paint Your Wagon, first London
production, 11 Feb.
Pajama Game, The, first perf., 13 Oct.
Pakistan, independence, 15 Aug., becomes
Islamic republic, 29 Feb., leaves
Commonwealth, 30 Jan., earthquake,
1 Feb.
Palace Theatre, opens, 31 Jan.
Palestine, British mandate, 11 Sept.
Pal Joey, first London perf., 31 Mar.
Pall Mall Gazette, first published, 7 Feb.,
last issue, 27 Oct.
Palmer, William, guilty of murder,
27 May
Palomar, Mount, telescope, 3 Jun.
Panama, independence, 3 Nov.

Panama Canal, begun, 4 Jul., work starts, 4 May, opens officially, 15 Aug., first ship, 3 Aug., US acquires, 22 Jan., Canal Zone, agreement, 8 Apr.
Panama Hattie, first perf., 4 Nov.
Pan American Airways, bankruptcy, 8 Jan., USA/Europe, 20 May
Pan American Union, established, d. 14 Apr.
Pangalos, General, 3 Jan.
Pankhurst, Emily, penal servitude, 3 Apr.
Pantomime, first, 22 Dec.
Papal See, removed from Avignon, 17 Jan.
Paper currency, US, 25 Feb.
Papua New Guinea, independence, 16 Sept.
Parachute jump, first, 22 Oct.
Paraguay, independence, 14 May
Paris, Allies against Napoleon in, 30 Mar., Commune, 9 Aug., established, 26 Mar., Metro opens, 19 Jul., bombed by Zeppelins, 29 Jan., surrenders to Germans, 28 Jan., Germans enter, 14 Jun., liberated, 25 Aug., Paris/London, daily scheduled flights, 25 Aug.
Paris, Declaration of, 16 Apr.
Parking meters, first, 16 Jul., London, 10 Jul.
Parliament, first English, 20 Jan., Addled, 5 Apr., Great Britain, first, 2 Feb., electric lighting installed, 28 Mar., televised, 21 Nov.
Parsifal, first perf., 26 Jul.
Parthenon, destroyed, 26 Sept.
Passchendaele Ridge, captured, 6 Nov.
Passion According to St Matthew, first perf., 15 Apr.
Pasteur, anti-rabies vaccine, 6 Jul.
Patience, first produced, 23 Apr.
Paulus, General, captured, 30 Jan.
Pay As You Earn, income tax, introduced, 10 Feb.
Peace, Charles, guilty of murder, 4 Feb.
Peace Conference, Paris, 20 Jul.
Peace of: Pekin, 7 Sept., Vereeniging, 31 May, Westminster, 19 Feb.
Pearl Fishers, The, first perf., 30 Sept.
Pearl Harbor, Japan attacks, 7 Dec.
Pedro I, of Brazil, 1 Dec.
Peenemünde, RAF raid, 17 Aug.

Peers, life, first, 24 Jul.
Pembrokeshire, French attempt to invade, 12 Feb.
Penang, British evacuate, 19 Dec.
Penguin Books, first, 30 Jul., acquitted of obscenity, 2 Nov.
Penicillin, discovery, 30 Sept.
Penlee lifeboat, crew is drowned, 19 Dec.
Pennsylvania, granted to Penn, 4 Mar., statehood, 12 Dec.
Penny Black, stamp, issued, 6 May
Penny post, begins, 10 Jan.
Pentagon, completed, 25 Jan.
People, The, first issue, 16 Oct.
Perchance to Dream, first perf., 21 Apr.
Perón, Isabel, deposed as president, 24 Mar., jailed, 20 Mar.
Perón, Juan, president of Argentina, 24 Feb., deposed, 22 Sept.
Perry, Capt. Matthew, arrives in Japan, 7 Jul.
Persia, liner, torpedoed, 30 Dec.
Peru, earthquakes, 13 Aug., independence, 28 Jul.
Pétain, appointed Chief of Staff, 29 Apr., becomes C.-in-C., 15 May, takes over French govt., 16 Jun.
Peter the Great, accedes, 11 Oct.
Peter Grimes, first perf., 7 Jun.
Peterloo, massacre, 16 Aug.
Peter Pan, first perf., 27 Dec.
Petrograd, ceases as capital, 9 Mar.
Petrushka, ballet, first perf., 13 Jun.
Philippines, Commonwealth, 15 Nov.
Phoenix Theatre, opens, 24 Sept.
Phonograph, invented, 19 Feb.
Photographic negative, invented, 25 Jan.
Piccadilly Circus, lit electrically, 9 May
Piccadilly Theatre, opens, 27 Apr.
Piccadilly tubeline, opens, 15 Dec.
Piccard, Auguste, first ascent, 1 May
Pickford, Mary, marries, 28 Mar.
Pickwick Papers, first instalment, 31 Mar.
Picture-by-wire service, 7 Jan.
Pilgrim Fathers, land in N. America, 21 Dec.
Pilgrim's Progress, published, 18 Feb.
Pillar box, first, 23 Nov.
Pillory, abolished, 30 Jun.
Piltdown Man, proves to be forged, 21 Nov.

Pioneer spacecraft is launched, 25 Feb.
Pirates of Penzance, The, first perf., 30 Dec.
Pisa, Council of, 25th Mar.
Pitcairn Island, *Bounty* mutineers, 23 Jan.
Pitman, Isaac, publishes shorthand,
15 Nov.
Pitt, William, the Younger, becomes prime
minister, 7 Dec.
Pius XII, as Pope, 2 Mar.
Planet, transit of, first observed, 7 Nov.
Planetarium, London, opens, 21 Mar.
Players' Theatre, London, opened, 14 Jan.
Playhouse Theatre, opens as Royal
Avenue, 11 Mar.
Pluto, planet discovered, 18 Mar.
PLUTO (pipeline), 12 Aug.
Poland, annexed by Russia, 26 Feb.,
republic proclaimed, 6 Nov., invaded by
Germany, 1 Sept., German-USSR
partition, 30 Sept., Britain & France
agree to support, 31 Mar., invaded by
USSR, 17 Sept., Western, part of
German Reich, 8 Oct.
Polaris submarine, first British, 16 Sept.
Police force, London, begins, 29 Sept.
Polygamy, abolished in Turkey, 5 Aug.
Pony Express, begins, 3 Apr.
Pope Paul VI, elected, 30 Jun., first to visit
Africa, 31 Jul., tour of Holy Land, 4 Jan.,
meets Orthodox Patriarch, 5 Jan.
Popular Front, wins in Spain, 16 Feb.
Porgy and Bess, first New York perf.,
10 Oct., first London perf., 30 Sept.
Portland Vase, smashed, 7 Feb.
Portugal, independence from Spain,
1 Dec., republic, 19 Jun., Salazar, head
of state, 5 Jul., free elections, 25 Apr.
Post, Wiley, solo flight, 22 Jul.
Postal orders, first, 1 Jan.
Postal Union, Universal, founded, 9 Oct.
Postcards, first, 1 Oct.
Post Office, pneumatic conveyors, 21 Feb.,
and telephones, 1 Jan., Tower, London,
opens, 8 Oct., bomb explosion, 31 Oct.
Potatoes, first to England, 28 Jul.
Potemkin, mutiny, 28 Jun.
Potsdam, Conference, 17 Jul., 2 Aug.
Pound note, first, 26 Feb.
Power station, tidal, at Rance, opens,
26 Nov.

Premium Bonds, introduced, 17 Apr., first
sale, 1 Nov., first draw, 1 Jun.
Press Association, founded, 29 Jun.
Priest, first British woman, 5 Dec.
Prince Igor, first perf., 23 Oct.
Prince of Pilsen, The, first perf., 14 May
Prince of Wales, battleship, sinks, 10 Dec.
Prince of Wales, created, 7 Feb.
Prince of Wales' Theatre, London,
opened, 18 Jan., 27 Oct.
Prince Regent, declared, 5 Feb.
Princess Caprice first perf., 11 May
Princess Ida first performed, 5 Jan.
Principe de Asturias, steamer, sinks,
5 Mar.
Private Eye, first issue, 25 Oct.
Prohibition starts, USA, 16 Jan., repealed,
5 Dec.
Promenade Concert, first, 10 Aug.
Provence II, sinks, 26 Feb.
Providence, Rhode Is., founded, 4 Jul.
Prussia, and Austria, alliance, 7 Feb.
Pueblo, USS, seized by N. Koreans,
23 Jan.
Pullman train, Britain, first, 1 Jun.
Pulsar, discovery of first, 29 Feb.
Punch, first issue, 17 Jul.
Purchase Tax, abolished, 1 Apr.

Quadruple Alliance, 2 Aug.
Quaker Girl, The, first perf., 5 Nov.
Quantum Theory, put forward, 14 Dec.
Queen, HM, coronation, 2 Jun., pistol
fired at, 13 Jun.
Queen Elizabeth, liner, launched, 27 Sept.,
sold, 5 Apr., on fire, 9 Jan.
Queen Elizabeth II, launched, 20 Sept.,
maiden voyage, 2 May, first voyage,
19 Nov.
Queen Mary, liner, launched, 26 Sept.,
maiden voyage, 27 May, sold, 18 Aug.
Queensland, as colony, 6 Jul., established,
4 Dec.
Quiberon Bay, invasion fleet destroyed,
20 Nov.
Quisling, becomes Norwegian prime
minister, 1 Feb., sentenced to death,
10 Sept.
Quito, Presidency of, becomes Ecuador,
13 May

R100, airship, Atlantic trip, 29 Jul.
R101 airship, crashes, 5 Oct.
R34 airship, returns from USA, 13 Jun.
Rabies, anti-, vaccine, 6 Jul.
RAC, founded, 10 Aug.
Radek, Karl, trial of, 23 Jan.
Radio, licences, 1 Nov., broadcast,
    experimental, 5 Mar., transatlantic,
    14 Mar., play, first in Britain, 17 Oct.,
    station, 2LO, starts, 14 Nov.,
    commercial, first British, 23 Nov., first
    local, 8 Nov., *see also* Wireless
Radio Caroline, pirate radio, 28 Mar.
Radio City Music Hall, opens, 27 Dec.
Radio Times, first issue, 28 Sept.
Radio-telephone, first demonstration,
    24 Dec., transatlantic, 7 Mar.
Radium, discovered, 26 Dec.
RAF, begins, 1 Apr.
Railway, trials, Rainhill, begin, 6 Oct., first
    passenger, 27 Sept., 3rd-class abolished,
    3 Jun.
Rainier III, of Monaco, 9 May, 19 Nov.,
    marries Grace Kelly, 19 Apr.
Raleigh, Walter, and Virginia, 25 Mar.
Rangoon, British withdraw, 7 Mar., falls to
    Japan, 10 Mar.
Rationing, bacon, 8 Jan., bread, 2 Feb.,
    22 Jul., bread, ends, 25 Jul., clothes,
    2 Jun., clothes, ends, 1 Feb., food, 8 Jan.,
    food, ends, 3 Jul., meat, 11 Mar., meat
    and butter, 25 Feb., sugar, 8 Jan., sugar,
    ends, 26 Sept., tea, ends, 5 Oct., 'points',
    1 Dec.
Ratti, Achille, elected Pope, 6 Feb.
Ray, James Earl, arrested, 8 Jun.
Rayon, first patent, 30 Sept.
Reagan, Ronald, elected president,
    4 Nov., shot, 30 Mar., visits China,
    26 Apr.
Record, long-play, first, 21 Jun.,
    7 Sept.
Red Cross, founded, 8 Aug., International,
    founded, 22 Aug., British, founded,
    4 Aug.
Referendum, first British, 5 Jun.
Reichstag, opens, 21 Mar., burns,
    27 Feb.
Repulse, battleship, sinks, 10 Dec.
Revere, Paul, ride, 18 Apr.

Revolutionary Calendar, adopted in
    France, 22 Sept., abolished, 31 Dec.,
Rhapsody in Blue, first performed,
    12 Feb.
Rhine, British troops, reach, 15 Feb.
Rhode Island, statehood, 29 May
Rhodesia, declaration of independence,
    11 Nov., proclaimed a republic, 2 Mar.
Richard II, ascends throne, 22 Jun.,
    abdicates, 29 Sept.
Richelieu, Cardinal, 2 Jan.
Richmond Park, opens, 29 Mar.
Riebeeck, Jan van, lands at the Cape,
    6 Apr.
Rights of Man, adopted by French
    Assembly, 27 Aug.
Rigoletto, first performance, 11 Mar.
Rio Rita, first London perf., 3 Apr.
Robert and Elizabeth, first perf., 20 Oct.
Robert Bruce, king of Scots, 25 Mar.
Robert II, accedes, 22 Feb.
Robin Hood, first perf., 7 Nov.
Rolls and Royce combine, 20 Nov.
Roman Catholic, Hierarchy, England,
    24 Sept., priests, married,
    excommunicated, 9 Mar.
Romania, independence, 13 Jun., Iron
    Guard murders, 27 Nov.
Rome, city, founded, 21 Apr., captured by
    Visigoths, 24 Aug., becomes Italian
    capital, 2 Oct., French recapture,
    15 Dec., liberated, 4 Jun.
Romeo and Juliet, opera, first perf., 27 Apr.
Roosevelt, F.D., elected president, 8 Nov.
Rose, Alec, arrives at Melbourne, 17 Dec.
Rose-Marie, first London perf., 20 Mar.
Rotherhithe Tunnel, opened, 1842, 1 Aug.,
    1843, 25 Mar.
Rotterdam, destroyed, 14 May
Round-the-world flight, completed, 2 Mar.
Rouse, Arthur Alfred, guilty of murder,
    31 Jan.
Royal Academy, founded, 1 Dec.
Royal Aeronautical Society, founded,
    12 Jan.
Royal Albert Hall, founded, 20 May,
    opens, 29 Mar.
Royal Court Theatre, opens, 25 Sept.
Royal Courts of Justice, open, 4 Dec.
Royal Edward, sinks, 14 Aug.

Royal Exchange, opens, 23 Jan., London, burns, 10 Jan.

Royal Family, renounces German titles, 19 Jun.

Royal Flying Corps, constituted, 13 Apr.

Royal George, sinks, 29 Aug.

Royal Military Academy, Woolwich, 13 Apr.

Royal Society, founded, 28 Nov., charter, 15 Jul., incorporated, 22 Apr.

Royalty Theatre, opens, 23 Jun.

Rubber, vulcanised, patent, 21 Nov.

Ruddigore, first performed, 22 Jan.

Rugby League, formed, 29 Aug.

Rugby Union, formed, 26 Jan., first played at Twickenham, 2 Oct.

Ruhr, occupied, 1921, 8 Mar., 1923, 11 Jan.

Runcorn Bridge, opens, 21 Jul.

Ruslan and Ludmila, first perf., 9 Dec.

Russia, calendar reformed, 1699, 20 Dec., abolishes serfdom, 3 Mar., occupies Port Arthur, 13 Dec., Tsar and Tsarina, arrested, 21 Mar., Royal family, murdered, 16 Jul., proclaimed a republic, 15 Sept., provisional government, 14 Mar., Bolsheviks beaten in election, 1917, 8 Dec., trade mission to London, 27 Feb.

Russo-Japanese war, begins, 4 Feb.

Ruthenia, Hungary annexes, 16 Mar.

Saar, plebiscite, 13 Jan., becomes German, 6 Jul.

Sadat, Anwar, as president of Egypt, 28 Apr., visits Israel, 20 Nov.

Sadler's Wells, opens, 6 Jan.

Safety lamp, Davy's, 9 Jan.

Sahara, Spain withdraws, 28 Feb.

Saigon, US Embassy captured, 30 Jan., USAF crash, orphans aboard, 4 Apr.

St Bartholomew, Massacre, 24 Aug.

St Dunstan's, opened as blind hostel, 1 Mar.

St Gothard Tunnel, completed, 29 Feb.

St Helena, discovered, 21 May, occupied, 5 May, crown colony, 22 Apr.

St Helens, Mount, erupts, 18 May

St James's Theatre, closes, 27 Jul.

St Lawrence Seaway, opens, 26 Jun.

St Leger, race, first run, 24 Sept.

St Michael and St George, Order, founded, 27 Apr.

St Nazaire, raid, 28 Mar.

St Pancras Station, opens, 1 Oct.

St Paul's, damaged in earthquake, 6 Apr., new cathedral, 21 Jun., new, opens, 2 Dec.

St Petersburg, founded, 27 May, Bloody Sunday, 22 Jan., becomes Petrograd, 1 Sept.

Salad Days, first perf., 5 Aug.

Salazar, Oliveira, Portugal, head of state, 5 Jul.

Salem, first witch hanged, 10 Jun.

Salerno, Allies land, 3 Sept.

Salisbury Cathedral, founded, 28 Apr., consecrated, 20 Sept.

Sally, first perf., 10 Sept.

Salome, first perf., 9 Dec.

Salonika, Allies land, 5 Oct.

Salt Lake City, Mormons reach, 22 Jul.

Salvation Army, founded, 5 Jul.

Samson and Delilah, first perf., 2 Dec.

Sandhurst, combines with Woolwich, 2 Apr.

Sandwich Islands, discovered, 18 Jan.

San Francisco, earthquake, 18 Apr., ends, 19 Apr., Exposition, 18 Feb., 20 Feb.

San Sebastian, surrenders, 9 Sept.

Santa Fé, US captures, 18 Aug.

San Toy, first perf., 21 Oct.

Sarajevo, shooting, 28 Jun.

Sarawak, Brooke becomes rajah, 24 Sept., ceded to Great Britain, 6 Feb.

Satellite, artificial, first, 4 Oct.

Savannah, crosses Atlantic, 22 May, 20 Jun.

Saville Theatre, opens, 8 Oct.

Savoy Hill, last programme, 14 May

Savoy Hotel, London, opens, 6 Aug.

Savoy Theatre, opens, 1812, 10 Oct., 1929, 21 Oct.

Scargill, Arthur, elected president of NUM, 8 Dec.

Schuschnigg, Austrian chancellor, 30 Jul.

Scotland, Mary accedes to throne, 14 Dec., and England, union, 1 May

Scott, Robert Falcon, reaches South Pole, 18 Jan., remains found, 12 Nov.

Scott, Sheila, solo flight, 20 Jun.

Scottish National Gallery, opens, 21 Mar.

Scottish Reform Act, 13 Jun.

Sebastopol, Allies take, 11 Sept.

Selassie, Haile, deposed, 12 Sept.

Selfridges, opens, 15 Mar.

Selkirk, Alexander, discovered, 1 Feb., rescued, 12 Feb.

Senegal, independence, 20 Aug.

Serbia, becomes kingdom, 6 Mar., Austria-Hungary declares war, 28 Jul.

Serbs, Croats and Slovenes, Kingdom of, proclaimed, 4 Dec.

Serpentine, mixed bathing, 16 Jun.

Serrano, Francisco, 3 Jan.

1776, first perf., 16 Jun.

Severn Road Bridge, opens, 8 Sept.

Severn Tunnel, opens, 8 Jan.

Sewing machine, patented, 17 Jul.

Seychelles, republic, 28 Jun.

Shah of Iran, crowns himself, 1967, 26 Oct.

Shakespeare, marries, 27 Nov.

Shakespeare, Theatre, burns, 6 Mar., Memorial Theatre, opens, 23 Apr.

Shanghai, occupied by Japanese, 28 Jan.

Sharpeville, shootings, 21 Mar.

She Loves Me, first perf., 29 Apr.

Sherlock Holmes story, first, 25 Jun.

Ship, merchant, first nuclear, 21 Jul.

Shop Girl, The, first perf., 24 Nov.

Show Boat, first perf., 3 May

Siam, changes name to Thailand, 11 May

Sicily, Allies invade, 10 Jul.

Siddons, Sarah, first appearance, 29 Dec.

Sidney, Philip, mortally wounded at Zutphen, 22 Sept.

Sidney Street, Siege, 3 Jan.

Siege of Limerick, 9 Aug.

Siege of Orleans, relieved, 29 Apr.

Sierra Leone, independence, 27 Apr., army seizes power, 24 Feb.

Sikorsky, tests airliner, 13 May

Simplon Tunnel, completed, 24 Feb., opened, 19 May, tunnel II, completed, 16 Oct.

Simpson, Mrs Wallis, marries, 3 Jun.

Singapore, surrenders, 15 Feb., independence, 9 Aug.

Singin' in the Rain, first perf., 30 Jun.

Sinn Fein, founded, 28 Nov., burns post office, 29 Apr., elected, 5 Apr.

Sioux Indians, revolt, 17 Aug.

Six-Day War, 5 Jun.

Slater, Oscar, imprisoned, 25 May, conviction quashed, 20 Jul., freed, 27 Nov.

Slave trade, abolished, 25th Mar.

Slavery, abolished in Br. Empire, 1 Aug., abolished in Pennsylvania, 1 Mar.

Slocum, Joshua, sets sail, 24 Apr.

Slovakia, German 'protection', 16 Mar.

Slovenia, declares independence, 6 Jun.

Smiles, Land of, The, first perf., 8 May

Smith, Madeleine, acquitted, 9 Jul.

Smith, W.H., first bookstall, 1 Nov.

Smithsonian, established, 10 Aug.

Snowdonia, a national park, 20 Nov.

Snow White and the Seven Dwarfs, premiere, 21 Dec.

Soap rationing begins, 9 Feb.

Social insurance, begins, 15 Jul.

Soldiers, may wear spectacles, 6 Mar.

Solomon Is., US raids, 29 Jun.

Solzhenitsyn, Alexander, expelled from USSR, 13 Feb.

Somaliland, Br., invaded by Italy, 4 Aug., British driven out, 19 Aug., British invade, 19 Feb., falls, 3 Mar.

Song of Norway, first London perf., 7 Mar.

Sorcerer, The, first perf., 17 Nov.

Sound barrier on land, broken, 18 Dec.

Sound of Music, The, first perf., 18 May

South Africa, British settlers, 10 Apr., dominion formed, 1 Jul., Nationalist win, 26 May, republic, 31 May

Southampton, HMS, crippled by bombers, 10 Jan.

South Carolina, secedes from US, 20 Dec.

Southend-on-Sea, Zeppelin bombs, 10 May

South Korea, republic, 15 Aug., admitted to UN, 17 Sept.

South Pacific, first perf., 1 Nov.

South Pole, Scott reaches, 18 Jan.

South Sea Bubble, speculation, 22 Jan.

South-West Africa, surrenders, 9 Jul.

Sovereign, first coin, 5 Jul.

Space, flight, first manned, 12 Apr.,

Mercury, 5 May, walk in, first, 18 Mar., craft, first on moon, 14 Sept.

Spain, Armada, sets sail, 19 May, sighted, 19 Jul., defeated, 29 Jul., fleet, defeated, 14 Feb., invaded by France, 16 Feb., declares war on Britain, 5 Oct., declares war on US, 24 Apr., revolutionary govt., 14 Apr., Civil War, begins, 18 Jul., ends, 28 Mar., diplomatic relations with USSR, 9 Feb., Juan Carlos becomes king, 22 Nov., many die in floods, 1973, 19 Oct., election after 40 years, 15 Jun., becomes democracy, 27 Dec.

Spartacus party, formed, 27 Jan.

Spectator, The, first published, 1 Mar., original, last issue, 20 Dec.

Speed limit, Britain, 12 Mar.

Speke, J.H., discovers Nile source, 23 Feb.

Spithead, naval mutiny, 15 Apr.

Sputnik 3, launched, 27 Aug.

Sputnik 9, 9 Mar.

Squirrel, frigate, sinks, 9 Sept.

Sri Lanka, independence, 4 Feb., *see also* Ceylon

Stalin, becomes Marshal, 6 Mar.

Stalingrad, Germans attack, 13 Sept., Germans surrounded, 19 Nov., Germans surrender, 2 Feb.

Stamp Act, in American colonies, 22 Mar., passed by Parliament, 23 Mar.

Stamps, first triangular, 1 Sept.

Standard, first published, 21 May

Stanley, H.M., meets Livingstone, 10 Nov.

Star, The, first published, 17 Jan., merges with *Evening News*, 18 Oct.

Star Chamber, abolished, 5 Jul.

Stars and Stripes, adopted as US flag, 14 Jun.

Star-Spangled Banner, The, written, 14 Sept., as US anthem, 3 Mar.

Statistical Office, Central, founded, 24 Jan.

Statue of Liberty, dedicated, 28 Oct.

Statute of Westminster, passed, 3 Dec., comes into effect, 11 Dec.

Stauffenburg, attempts to kill Hitler, 20 Jul.

Steamer, first transatlantic, 20 Jun.

Stephen, accedes to English throne, 26 Dec., defeated, 2 Feb.

Stern Gang, mines train, 29 Feb.

Stock Exchange, London, women allowed, 26 Mar.

Stockton–Darlington railway, opens, 27 Sept.

Stone of Scone, stolen, 25 Dec.

Stonehenge, sold by auction, 21 Sept.

Stop the World - I Want to Get Off, first perf., 20 Jul.

Strand Theatre, opens, 22 May

Streptomycin, discovery, 22 Feb.

Stuart, Charles, lands in Hebrides, 23 Jul.

Student Prince, The, first London perf., 3 Feb.

Sturt, Charles, reaches Murray River, 9 Feb., enters Simpson's Desert, 20 Jul.

Submarine, first in R.N., 2 Oct., British nuclear, first, 21 Oct., first ballistic-missile, 9 Jun., nuclear, under North Pole, 3 Aug.

Sudan, Anglo-Egyptian Condominium, 19 Jan., independence, 21 Mar., invaded by Italy, 4 Aug.

Sudetenland, Hitler to annex, 27 Sept., Germans enter, 1 Oct.

Suez, British troops leave, 13 Jun.

Suez Canal, construction begins, 25 Apr., opens, 16 Nov., Disraeli buys shares, 25 Nov., cleared of shipping, 9 Apr.

Sukarno, president of Indonesia, 13 Nov.

Summer Time, *see* Daylight Saving

Sun, newspaper, first issue, 15 Sept.

Sun Yat-sen, declared president of China, 31 Dec.

Sunday Citizen, last issue, 18 Jun.

Sunday newspaper, first, 26 Mar.

Sunday Telegraph, first published, 5 Feb.

Sunday Times, The, first issue, 20 Oct., colour supplement, 4 Feb.

Surgeons, Royal College, founded, 21 Jun.

Surinam, independence, 25 Nov.

Suttee, abolished, 4 Dec.

Swan and Edgar, closes, 9 Jan.

Swaziland, independence, 6 Sept.

Sweden and Norway, union ends, 26 Oct.

Sydney, Australia, founded, 26 Jan., Harbour Bridge, opened, 19 Mar., Opera House opens, 20 Oct.

Taft, elected US president, 3 Nov.
Tahiti, annexed to France, 29 Jun.
Taiwan, Japan takes, 2 Jun.
Talal, of Jordan, deposed, 11 Aug.
Talbot, W. Fox, photographic negative, 25 Jan.
Tales of Hoffman, The, first performed, 10 Feb.
Talking picture, first feature-length, 6 Oct.
Tanganyika, independence, 9 Dec., as part of Tanzania, 26 Apr.
Tanks, first used in battle, 15 Sept., in major battle, 20 Nov.
Tannhäuser, first perf., 19 Oct.
Tanzania, new name for union, 29 Oct.
Tasmania, proved to be an island, 11 Jan., *see also* Van Diemen's Land
Tate Gallery, opens, 21 Jul.
Tatler, first published, 12 Apr.
Taxi-cabs, recognised, 21 Jan.
Tay Bridge, collapses, 1879, 28 Dec., railway bridge, new, 20 Jun., road bridge, opens, 18 Aug.
Teck families, peerages, 19 Jun.
Teheran, conference, 28 Nov.
Telegraph, electric, patented, 12 Jun., cable, transatlantic, snaps, 2 Aug., service, London-Paris, starts, 13 Nov.
Telephone, patented, 7 Mar., exchange, first, 6 Sept., first call, 11 Mar., and Post Office, 1 Jan., concert relayed by, 14 Jan., link, London/Paris, opened, 18 Mar.
Telescope, largest in Europe, 1 Dec.
Television, demonstrated by J.L. Baird, 27 Jan., *see also* TV service
Telstar, launched, 10 Jul., transmissions, 11 Jul.
Templars, arrested, 13 Oct., abolished, 22 Mar.
Tenerife, air collision, 27 Mar.
Tennessee, statehood, 1 Jun., Act forbids teaching of evolution, 23 Mar.
Ten-pound notes, new design, 20 Feb.
Tenzing, Sherpa, climbs Everest, 29 May
Territorial Army, founded, 1 Apr., formed, 26 Oct.
Texas, proclaimed republic, 2 Mar., independence, 13 Nov., annexed by the

US, 1 Mar., incorporated in US, 20 Dec., statehood, 29 Dec.
Thames, Frost Fairs, 14 Jan., steamboat service, 17 Jun., Tunnel, begins, 2 Mar., opens, 25 Mar., Rotherhithe, opens, 12 Jun.
Thatcher, Margaret, first woman leader, 11 Feb., first woman prime minister, 4 May, resigns as prime minister, 22 Nov.
Thetis, sinks, 1 Jun.
Thieving Magpie, The, first perf., 31 May
This Year of Grace!, first produced, 22 Mar.
Thompson and Bywaters, hanged, 9 Jan.
Thorndike, Sybil, London debut, 9 Feb.
Threepenny Opera, The, first London performance, 9 Feb.
Thresher, US submarine, lost, 10 Apr.
Tibet, expedition to, 7 Sept., occupied by Chinese, 21 Oct., Chinese republic proclaimed, 4 Apr.
Tichborne claimant, found guilty, 28 Feb.
Times, The, first issue, 1 Jan., attempt to blow up office, 15 Mar.
Tip-Toes, first perf., 31 Aug.
Tiros 1, launched, 1 Apr.
Tirpitz, battleship, sunk, 12 Nov.
Titanic, launched, 31 May, sinks, 15 Apr.
Tit-Bits, first issue, 22 Oct.
Tito, Josip, forms Yugoslav government, 9 Dec., 1st president of Yugoslavia, 14 Jan.
Tivoli Theatre, London, closed, 7 Feb.
Togo, independence, 27 Apr.
Togoland, *see* Ghana
Tokyo, earthquakes, 1 Sept.
Tolpuddle, labourers sentenced, 18 Mar.
Tom Jones, first produced, 17 Apr.
Tonga, annexed by Britain, 19 May, British protectorate, 18 May, independence, 4 Jun.
Toronto, founded, 30 Jul.
Torrey Canyon, tanker, grounds, 18 Mar.
Tosca, first performed, 14 Jan.
Toulon, recaptured by Napoleon, 19 Dec.
Trades Description Act, 30 Nov.
Trafalgar Square, casualties, 1887, 13 Nov., looting and riots, 8 Feb.

Traffic lights, first, in Westminster, 8 Dec.,
    first electric, 5 Aug.
Train, electric, first UK, 12 Mar.
Train robbery, first US, 5 May, Great,
    8 Aug.
Tram service, first British, 30 Aug.
Trams, electric, first, 16 May
Transvaal Republic, proclaimed, 16 Dec.,
    Kruger becomes first president, 30 Dec.,
    annexed by Britain, 25 Oct., self-
    government, 6 Dec.
Treaties:
    Alliance, 18 Aug.
    Amiens, 27 Mar.
    Badajoz, 6 Jun.
    Behring Sea, 29 Feb.
    Berlin, 13 Jun.
    Brest-Litovsk, 3 Mar.
    Brussels, 25 Jul.
    Fontainebleau, 11 Apr.
    Ghent, 24 Dec.
    Guadalupe, 2 Feb.
    Hampton Court, 20 Sept.
    Kanagawa, 31 Mar.
    Lausanne, 24 Jul.
    London, 30 May
    Nanking, 29 Aug.
    NATO, 4 Apr.
    NATO/Warsaw Pact, 19 Nov.
    Neuilly, 27 Nov.
    Pacific, 13 Nov.
    Panama Canal, 18 Dec.
    Paris, 1856, 30 Mar., 1947, 10 Feb.
    Peace, with Japan, 8 Sept.
    Peace of Cateau-Cambresis, 3 Apr.
    Peking, 20 Jan.
    Portsmouth, 5 Sept.
    Rawalpindi, 8 Aug.
    Rome, 25 Mar.
    Ryswick, 20 Sept.
    South East Asia Defence, 8 Sept.
    Utrecht, 11 Apr.
    Versailles, 28 Jun.
    Vienna, 15 May
    Waitangi, 6 Feb.
    Westphalia, 24 Oct.
Trevithick, demonstrates locomotive,
    21 Feb., tests self-propelled vehicle,
    24 Dec.
Trial by Jury, first produced, 25 Mar.

Trident, maiden flight, 9 Jan.
Trieste, bathyscaphe, 23 Jan.
Trincomalee, surrendered, 11 Jan.
Trinidad, discovered, 31 Jul., and Tobago,
    independence, 31 Aug.
Trip to Chinatown, A, first perf., 29 Sept.
Tripoli, taken by Italy, 5 Nov., ceded to
    Italy, 18 Oct., occupied by Italians,
    5 Oct., captured by British, 23 Jan.
Tristan da Cunha, annexed to Britain,
    14 Aug.
Tristan und Isolde, first perf., 10 Jun.
Trolley-bus, first, 20 Jun.
Trotsky, Leon, expelled from Communist
    Party, 27 Dec., from USSR, 31 Jan.
Tunney, Gene, beats Dempsey, 22 Sept.
Tupolev-144, crashes, 3 Jun.
Turandot, first perf., 25 Apr.
Turkey, Italy declares war on, 29 Sept.,
    abolishes Caliphate, 3 Mar., republic
    proclaimed, 30 Oct., abolishes Arabic
    alphabet, 3 Nov., earthquake, 22 May,
    earthquake at Lice, 6 Sept., Anatolia,
    violent earthquakes, 27 Dec.
Turkish airline, crash at Paris, 3 Mar.
Turks, repulsed at Vienna, 21 Sept.
Turner, watercolour, auctioned, 18 Jun.
Tuscany, Napoleon annexes, 30 May
Tutankhamun, tomb, found, 4 Nov.,
    sarcophagus found, 3 Jan., opened,
    17 Feb.
TV service, first high-definition, 22 Mar.,
    from Alexandra Palace, 2 Nov., British,
    inaugurated, 1 Nov., first play, in
    Britain, 15 Dec., colour, in Britain,
    starts, 14 Nov., *see also* Television
Twiss, Peter, flies at over 1,000 mph,
    10 Mar.
Two Gentlemen of Verona, first produced,
    26 Apr.
2,000 Guineas horse-race, first run,
    18 Apr.
Tyres, pneumatic, patented, 10 Dec.
Uganda, British protectorate, 11 Apr.,
    independence, 9 Oct., Idi Amin
    becomes ruler, 2 Feb., Asians expelled,
    4 Aug.
Ukraine, Germans enter, 27 Jul.
Ulm, Charles, flies Pacific, 9 Jun.
Ulster, parliament opens, 15 Apr.

Umberto I, of Italy, becomes king, 9 Jan.
Un Ballo in Maschera, first produced, 17 Feb.
Uncle Sam, first reference, 7 Sept.
Uncle Tom's Cabin, first published as book, 20 Mar.
Underground, Victoria Line, opens, 7 Mar., driverless trains, 5 Apr.
UNESCO, established, 4 Nov., first conference, 19 Nov., UK withdraws from, 5 Dec.
Union, Act of, 1 Jan.
Union Flag, first adopted, 12 Apr.
United Kingdom, joins Common Market, 22 Jan.
United Nations, first held, 10 Jan., first meeting, 23 Oct., Charter signed, 26 Jun., comes into force, 24 Oct., votes to admit China (People's Rep.), 15 Dec.
United States: 14th Amendment, 28 Jul., Canada, border, 9 Aug., defined, 20 Oct., blizzards, 1 Feb., breaks diplomatic relations with Germany, 3 Feb., Britain, ambassador to, first, 30 Mar., British ambassador, first, 5 Jul., Civil Rights Act, 2 Jul., Civil War begins, 12 Apr., concludes armistice with Spain, 12 Aug., Congress, first meeting, 17 Nov., the Queen addresses, 16 May, continental rail link-up, 10 May, Cuba, lifts blockade on, 20 Nov., declares war on Mexico, 13 May, on Germany, 6 Apr., on German and Italy, 1941, 11 Dec., election, first, 7 Jan., Emancipation Declaration, 22 Sept., France, enters WWI in, 27 Oct., illiterate immigrants banned, 18 Dec., Independence Declaration, 4 Jul., Indians as citizens, 2 Jun., Lease Lend destroyers, 3 Sept., Louisiana, takes possession of, 30 Dec., Marine Corps founded, 10 Nov., Mexico, war, 4 Jun., Mint established, 2 Apr., Navy established, 27 Oct., formed, 27 Mar., neutral in WWI, 4 Aug., Pacific coast, earthquakes, 27 Mar., Panama Canal treaty, 18 Dec., slavery abolished, 18 Dec., standard time established, 13 Mar., Supreme Court created, 24 Sept., first meeting, 1 Feb., troops in

WWI, 5 Nov., U-2 aircraft, shot down, 1 May, war with Britain, 18 Jun., women granted right to vote, 26 Aug.
United States liner, Blue Riband, 7 Jul.
Upper Volta, independence, 5 Aug.
Uranus, discovered, 13 Mar.
Uruguay, independence, 25 Aug., British ambassador, kidnapped, 8 Jan.
USSR, joins League of Nations, 18 Sept., expelled, 14 Dec., forces counterattack and Germans retreat, 27 Nov., diplomatic relations with Spain, 9 Feb., explodes hydrogen bomb, 26 Nov., 29 Aug., shoots down Korean airliner, 31 Aug., agrees to withdraw from Cuba, 19 Feb., dismantles missiles in Cuba, 2 Nov., votes to end Communist monopoly, 13 Mar.
Utah, statehood, 4 Jan.

V1, first bomb, 13 Jun.
V2 flying bombs, first, land on London, 8 Sept.
V2 rocket, last, 28 Mar.
Vaccination, first, 14 May
Vacuum cleaner, patented, 30 Aug.
Vagabond King, The, first London perf., 19 Apr.
Valentine's Day massacre, 14 Feb.
Valkyries, The, first perf., 26 Jun.
Valmouth, first perf., 2 Oct.
Vancouver, founded, 6 Apr., Vancouver Island, acquired by Hudson's Bay Co., 13 Jan.
Van Diemen's Land, discovered, 24 Nov.
Vanguard I spacecraft, launched, 17 Mar.
Van Tromp, defeated by Blake, 28 Sept.
VAT, introduced, 1 Apr.
Vatican City, set up, 7 Jun., established, 11 Feb., sovereign state, 7 Jul.
Vaudeville Theatre, first, opens, 16 Apr., second, opens, 13 Jan., third, opens, 23 Feb.
Vauxhall Bridge, opens, 26 May
Velazquez, painting sold for £2 million, 27 Nov., 'Venus' damaged, 10 Mar.
Venezuela, independence, 20 Nov.
Venus, Russian spacecraft lands, 22 Jul., transit of, observed, 24 Nov.

Venus spacecraft, touches down on Venus,
1 Mar., 16 May
Vermont, statehood, 4 Mar.
Versailles, Peace Conference, 18 Jan.,
Treaty, ratified, 9 Jul., US Senate
refuses, 19 Mar., Hitler renounces,
16 Mar.
Vesuvius, erupts, AD 79, 24 Aug., 1867,
12 Nov.
VHF broadcasting, 2 May
Vicar of Wakefield, The, published,
27 Mar.
Victor Emmanuel I, proclaimed King of
Italy, by Italian parliament, 18 Feb.,
by Garibaldi, 26 Oct.
Victor Emmanuel III, abdicates, 9 May
Victoria, ascends throne, 20 Jun.,
crowned, 28 Jun., marries Prince Albert,
10 Feb., Empress of India, 1 May,
shooting attempt, 19 May, diamond
jubilee, 22 Jun.
Victoria Cross, founded, 29 Jan., awarded
for Alma, 20 Sept.
Victoria Embankment, opens, 12 Jul.
Victoria and Albert Museum, foundation,
17 May, opens, 26 Jun.
Victory, launched, 7 May
Video recorder, first, 11 Nov.
Vienna, Turks repulsed, 21 Sept.,
bombed, 17 Mar.
Vietnam, joins UN, 18 Jul., divided,
20 Jul., US Embassy blown up, 30 Mar.,
cease-fire, 27 Jan., US lands marines,
8 Mar., US troops leave, 29 Mar., last
US troops leave, 13 Aug.
Viktoria and Her Hussar, first perf.,
17 Sept.
Vimy Ridge, stormed, 9 Apr., taken,
10 Apr.
Virgin Islands, US sovereignty, 31 Mar.
Virginia, sinks USS *Cumberland*, 8 Mar.
Virginia, statehood, 25 Jun.
Virginia Gazette, The, first issued, 6 Aug.
Volga-Don Canal, opens, 31 May
Votes, for women, 11 Jan., granted, 6 Feb.
VTOL, 'Flying Bedstead', 3 Aug.

Waldheim, Kurt, as UN secretary-general,
22 Dec.
Walesa, Lach, president of Poland, 9 Dec.

Wallace, William, captured, 5 Aug.
Wallace Collection, opens, 22 Jun.
Walpole, Robert, first prime minister in
Downing St., 22 Sept.
Waltzes from Vienna, first perf., 17 Aug.
War: of 1812, 18 Jun., of Independence,
starts, 19 Apr., ends, 3 Sept., of
Oranges, starts, 2 Mar.
Warsaw, Napoleon enters, 15 Dec.,
Germans enter, 1915, 5 Aug., occupied
by Germany, 27 Sept.
Warsaw Pact, signed, 14 May,
disbandment, 1 Apr., abolished, 1 Jul.
Warships, Japanese, sunk, 6 Apr.
Washington, George, crosses Delaware,
25 Dec. defeats British, 3 Jan., elected
president, 6 Apr., 1st US president,
30 Apr.
Washington, D.C., captured by British,
24 Aug.
Washington, statehood, 11 Nov.
Watch Your Step, first perf., 4 May
Watergate, burglary, 16 Jun., trial, starts,
1 Oct.
Waterloo Bridge, opens, 1817, 18 Jun.,
1942, 11 Aug.
Waterloo Station, opens, 11 Jul., rebuilt,
21 Mar.
Weather report, weekly, first, 11 Feb.
Webster, Noah, dictionary, 14 Apr.
Welles, Orson, radio play panic, 30 Oct.
Welsh Guards, founded, 11 Feb.
Wesley, John, signs 'deed of declaration',
28 Feb.
West, Mae, makes London debut, 24 Jan.
Western European Union, opens, 5 Jul.
Western Union, begins, 25 Jul.
West Indies, federation, 3 Jan.,
Netherlands, bought by US, 20 Feb.
Westminster Abbey, dedicated, 28 Dec.
Westminster Bridge, opens, 1750, 16 Nov.,
1862, 24 May
Westminster Cathedral, consecrated,
28 Jun.
Westminster Gazette, last issued, 31 Jan.
Westminster Theatre, opens, 7 Oct.
West Point, established, 16 Mar., opens,
4 Jul.
West Side Story, first perf., 12 Dec.
West Virginia, statehood, 23 Jun.

Whipsnade Zoo, opens, 23 May
Whitehall Theatre, opens, 29 Sept.
White Horse Inn, first London perf., 8 Apr.
White House, Washington, foundation,
  13 Oct.
White Russians, surrender, 9 Jan.
Wiener Blut, first perf., 25 Oct.
Wild Violets, first perf., 31 Oct.
Wilhelm II, telegram to Kruger, 3 Jan.
Wilhelmina, becomes Queen of
  Netherlands, 23 Nov., abdicates,
  4 Sept.
Wilkes, John, guilty of 'impious libel',
  21 Feb.
William and Mary, ascend throne, 13 Feb.,
  crowned, 11 Apr.
William I, accedes, 14 Oct., crowned,
  25 Dec.
William III, lands in Ireland, 14 Jun.
William IV, ascends throne, 26 Jun.,
  crowned, 8 Sept.
Wilson, Harold, leads Labour Party,
  14 Feb., becomes prime minister, 1974,
  4 Mar., 1964, 16 Oct., resigns, 5 Apr.
Wilson, Woodrow, becomes US president,
  4 Mar.
Wimbledon, Men's Singles, first, 19 Jul.
Window tax, imposed, 31 Dec.,
  abolished, 24 Jul.
Windsor, Duke, marries, 3 Jun.
Wireless, Roosevelt sends message to
  King, 19 Jan.
Wisconsin, statehood, 29 May
Woman's magazine, first, 27 Jun.
Woman's Weekly, first issue, 1 Nov.
Women, vote for first time, 14 Dec., as
  MPs, eligibility, 21 Nov., police, first,
  27 Nov., ordination of, approved,
  16 Sept.
Woolworth, opens first store, 22 Feb., first
  in Britain, 5 Nov.
World Health Organization, formed,
  7 Apr.
World War I, British in France, 8 Aug.,
  US troops go into action, 5 Nov.,
  armistice, 11 Nov.
Wounded Knee, massacre, 29 Dec.

Wright Bros., first flight, 17 Dec.
Wyndham's Theatre, opens, 16 Nov.
Wyoming, statehood, 10 Jul.

X-rays, discovered, 8 Nov., demonstrated,
  5 Jan.

Yale College, chartered, 9 Oct.
Yalta, conference, 4 Feb.
Yarmouth, bombarded by warships,
  14 Jan.
Yeltsin, president of Russia, 12 Jun.
Yeomen of the Guard, established,
  30 Oct.
Yeomen of the Guard, first perf.,
  3 Oct.
Yokohama, earthquakes, 1 Sept.
York Minster, fire, 20 May
Yorkists, defeated by Lancastrians,
  17 Feb.
Yugoslavia, established, 5 Jan., name
  begins, 3 Oct., proclaimed a republic,
  29 Nov., Germans call for surrender,
  6 Apr., surrenders, 17 Apr., Soviets
  invade, 29 Sept.

Zaïre, independence, 30 Jun., volcano
  eruption, 10 Jan.
Zanzibar, Sultan banished, 12 Jan.,
  independence, 10 Dec., as part of
  Tanzania, 26 Apr.
Zeebrugge, British raid, 22 Apr.
Zeppelins, raid, first, 1 Jun., raid England,
  19 Jan., *L15*, 31 Mar., raid London,
  24 Aug., shot down, 3 Sept., *Z3*, flies to
  New Jersey, 12 Oct.
Ziegfeld Follies, opens, 8 Jul.
Zinoviev, Grigori, convicted, 15 Jan.
Zinoviev Letter, published, 25 Oct.
Zip fastener, patented, 31 Mar.
Zog, King, abdicates, 8 Apr.
Zola, Émile, writes open letter, 13 Jan.,
  imprisoned, 23 Feb.
Zoo, London, opens, 27 Apr.
Zuider Zee, becomes lake, 28 May
Zululand, annexed to Natal, 30 Dec.
Zulu War, begins, 12 Jan.